Candie for the Foundling

Candie for the Foundling

Anne Gordon

THE PENTLAND PRESS LTD.
EDINBURGH · CAMBRIDGE · DURHAM

© Anne Gordon 1992
First published in 1992 by
The Pentland Press Ltd.
1 Hutton Close
South Church
Bishop Auckland
Durham

ISBN 1 872795 75 7

Typeset by Spire Origination Ltd., Norwich
Printed and bound by Antony Rowe Ltd., Chippenham,
Wiltshire SN14 6LH

Acknowledgements

I am very indebted to Rev. G. F. M. Thomson for his great kindness in readin
text for me and giving helpful advice.

I am also very grateful to Professor A. Fenton for kindly writing a foreword to
book, and to Rev. G. R. Taverner for giving up time to supply me with infort
tion. I also appreciate the assistance given by staff in Hawick Library, the Bord
Regional Library Headquarters, the National Library, Edinburgh, the Mitch
Library, Glasgow, H. M. Register House, Stirling Archives and Moray Archive
Mrs J. Smith and Mr I. Horn have kindly helped with proof-reading and m
daughter, Venetia Thomson, has, as always, given invaluable help in many ways.

Contents

Foreword

I first came to know of Anne Gordon when, together with Barbara Scott, she compiled a book for a Village History Competition, run by the Scottish Women's Rural Institutes in 1967. I happened to be one of the judges. The book, on *The Parish of Nigg*, came top in a tough competition. She then went on to collaborate with Jessie Macdonald in a book on three Easter Ross fishing villages, *Down to the Sea*. Since then she has gone from strength to strength. In her *Death is for the Living*, 1984, she identified an area that had been little written about in Scotland. The same was true of *To Move with the Times: the Story of Transport and Travel in Scotland*, 1988. Now, having established a highly productive four-year routine, she has completed a major work in *Candie for the Foundling*.

This new book is the outcome of intensive reading and research, and the sorting of masses of information into seventeen very full chapters. It is of special value because it deals thoroughly with the forms of organisation that have controlled and directed everyday existence in town and country parishes alike over several centuries. Each chapter is in a sense an actor on the stage of human life, each interacting with and complementing the other. The outcome is a performance played against the historical backdrop of the life-cycle of individuals and of their family and community roles.

What Anne Gordon gives the reader is a picture of the period that led up to the eventual take-over by the State of a host of functions formerly carried out by the Kirk. The Welfare State may control almost every aspect of our present-day existence, but it does not seem that Kirk Sessions were far behind. In his book, *Discipline and Punish*, 1982, the French thinker Michel Foucault refers to the way in which human beings were increasingly logged and documented and allocated to spaces, at first, for example, in hospitals, monasteries or in the army, and then more generally within their communities. His point was that the more central authority knew about the individual, the more it could exert power and control the individual. The justness of his thinking is fully reflected in what Anne Gordon tells us in each and every one of her chapters, even though she does not spell out the way in which social controls have gone spiralling up, computer assisted, from parish to national levels since Victorian days.

There is here a tremendous mass of detail, much of it never having had such systematic treatment. The role of bell-ringing at funerals, about which whole books have been written in, for example, Sweden, is one such example. It is to be found in the Kirk Session and in the Burial chapters. Even where topics, such as Witchcraft and Superstition, have been well aired before, much fresh detail has been recovered from the sources. Anne Gordon has a sharp, precise sense of observation.

Some areas of current concern are conspicuous by their absence: child abuse, for instance, receives no mention in the sources consulted, though adultery, abortion and even homosexuality are there. Does this mean that there was a different ethic in earlier days? What is certain, however, is that in this volume there is a rich mine of material for the study of past attitudes and perceptions, and their changes over time. This could well be set alongside other kinds of sources such as literary works, whether of the quality of John Galt's *Annals of a Parish* or like the chapbooks that were meant to satisfy the most popular tastes. And in turn, present day creative writers could well find in a volume such as this not only a fertile source of inspiration, but also a ready made background of historically accurate detail.

Alexander Fenton.

A Note on the Text

This book is concerned with the social impact made by the Kirk on the lives of the ordinary people of Scotland and for that reason it omits church politics entirely.

So as to avoid having over-many reference numbers in the text, references and notes have often been grouped together under one number but the details are given in the Notes at the end of the book.

Scots money went out of use officially in 1707 but in spite of that it continued to be used for long afterwards with accounts appearing, in some cases, in both Scots money and sterling. The following information may be useful:

Scots money: (often abbreviated to 'Sc') = one-twelfth of sterling, often abbreviated to 'stg.'.
doit — coin worth about ¹/₂ farthing.
bodle — coin worth about one-sixth of an English penny.
merk — coin worth 13*s*. 4*d*. Scots or 13¹/₂*d*. sterling.
1 boll — 6 imperial bushels.
1 firlot – ¹/₄ boll.
1 bushel — 8 gallons dry measure.
1 peck — 2 gallons dry measure.
stent — assessment, valuation, tax.
bere, bear — 4- or 6-rowed barley.
@rent — annual rent or interest.
delate — to inform against, to charge with a crime.

1

Kirk Sessions

It is impossible to consider the social history of Scotland after the Reformation without considering also the role of Kirk Sessions in the lives of the people and so the first question must be, what are Kirk Sessions and what are or were their functions?

A Kirk Session consists of the elders of a congregation with the minister as moderator or chairman. In the days with which this book is mainly concerned, all of these were men and Sessions came to be responsible for much of the life of a parish, especially so in rural areas. The eldership became one of the special features of the Presbyterian church but it had begun just before the Reformation of 1560. By 1558 there were such groups in both Dundee and Edinburgh and the first register of the Kirk Session of St. Andrews, Fife, begins on 27 October 1559.[1] According to John Knox these groups began with Protestants meeting for prayer and Scripture reading but they soon 'sought to have the face of the Church amang us and open crymes to be punished without respect of persone. And for that purpose, by common electioun, war elderis appointed, to whom the hole brethren promissed obedience: for at that tyme we had na publick ministeris of the Worde.' This small beginning tied in well with Knox's own ideas and he and the other authors of the First Book of Discipline of 1560 proposed that elders should be nominated and voted for by the congregation and should have general oversight of the discipline of parishes. To start with it was thought that they should hold office for only one year at a time lest by remaining longer in the position they might 'presume upon the liberty of the Kirk', although it was provided that they might hold office for longer if there was a popular election annually. With the idea that appointments should be for just one year, no salary was suggested and there does not seem at that early date to have been any form of ordination.

The Second Book of Discipline which was drawn up by a Committee of the General Assembly, the governing body of the Church of Scotland, and accepted by the Assembly in 1578, changed this system of annual appointment of elders to life-appointment and their position was enhanced by the decision that once lawfully called to be elders, they might not demit office, although if there were sufficient of them in any particular parish, they might serve in rotation. Nevertheless, yearly election of elders lasted in St. Andrews until 1600 and continued in some other parts of the country till 1705. This desire for continuance of annual elections may be what lay behind the decision in 1653 of all the elders of Fenwick, Ayrshire, to resign *en bloc* and then submit to the vote of the 'remanent eldership' which presumably means that in spite of resigning they still considered themselves eligible to vote. The result was that some were elected and others were asked 'to surcease and be eased of that burden for a while, according to their own desire.'[2] An alternative to either annual or life-time appointment, which was practised in the parish of Whitekirk, East Lothian, in the later seventeenth century, was to appoint elders for a fixed term of years at the most. Even where the life-appointment of elders had come to be accepted, they might still be ousted; in 1688 the reason for appointing new ones in Inverness was given as 'others being put off' but although the reason behind this is not given, at that date it might well have been political. It was not long before the system changed to what it is now, with Kirk Sessions putting forward the names of possible new elders (nowadays including women), and these being intimated to the congregation and time given for objections to be made to their lives or doctrine, failing which they are duly admitted. Objections were undoubtedly made but if not substantiated were rejected. This happened, for instance, in Ancrum, Roxburghshire, but it appears that the objector, having made his point, was thereafter perfectly happy to withdraw his objection. One objection which sounds very odd to modern ears was made in January 1843 when three out of six names proposed in a parish were turned down because they were unmarried and in May 1776 an Act of the General Assembly stated that no one should be ordained an elder until twenty-one years of age. The Second Book of Discipline introduced ordination by fasting, prayer and the imposition of the hands of the eldership, something which in the latter half of the seventeenth century could also be achieved by taking an oath to be faithful 'with uplifted hands in precence of the people' but in 1690 the General Assembly required that the Confession of Faith should be signed as well, extending this in 1700 to a requirement that all ministers and elders sign what is now called the Formula.[3] A number of Kirk Session minute books have inside the back cover or elsewhere, the list of questions to be put to elders at their ordination and the Formula with their signatures below.

It is sometimes thought that the term 'ruling elder' is a specially important person in the Kirk Session but the office of all elders is to rule and therefore they are all ruling elders as opposed to preaching elders who are ministers. At one time, however, the elder appointed to represent the Session in Presbytery or Synod was designated 'ruling elder' as when in 1658 Rothesay Kirk Session, on the island of Bute, chose one of their number to be 'ruling elder for the next Presbytery' and when in 1692 Mauchline Kirk Session, Ayrshire, voted another man 'to be ruling elder until the next Synod'. The Second Book of Discipline which raised the position of elders also added to their duties — they were to carry out any instructions of the General Assembly, to help to examine Communicants and to visit the sick; and in 1592 when Presbyterian government was established in the church by Act of Parliament, the eldership was legally defined with elders required to see that the Word of God was purely preached, the sacraments rightly administered, discipline imposed and ecclesiastical goods incorruptly distributed. A glance down the index of the Acts of the Scottish Parliament under various headings shows a variety of matters thereafter committed to Kirk Sessions and it came to be that before there was a local authority of any sort, Kirk Sessions were prepared to tackle virtually any problem that came their way, officially or otherwise — administration of discipline, dealing with drunkenness, caring for the aged, the infirm and the mentally ill, coping with orphans and foundlings, dealing with education, famine relief, marriage problems, handling national charitable collections at local level and very much more.[4]

That being so, it is not surprising that some elders were chosen not so much for their spiritual qualities as for any position and influence which could be used to bring people to discipline and in making authoritative decisions. Resident heritors or at least their factors were often elders but there was still a genuine desire to see that Sessions were as representative as possible and a list of those in Kinross in 1699 shows that there were four men whose status is unspecified, as well as a merchant, four portioners, a baker, a fisherman, a meal maker and a weaver. According to the Book of Common Order (Knox's Liturgy) elders were to be men of good life and godly conversation, without blame or suspicion, careful for their flock, wise and, above all things, fearing God. Unfortunately such a standard was impossible to achieve and it was inevitable that Sessions consisted of men 'just as the grund could produce' and there is an indication that the members of one Session were not entirely confident about those they proposed to add to their number when they recommended that each existing elder should 'make further inquiry into their behaviour and how the rest of the parish are pleased with such persons.' The lowest labouring class never seem to have become elders; their need to toil incessantly and their poverty both militated against their doing so and many were, or would undoubtedly become, the very paupers whom the Session would find themselves supporting. The illiteracy of that group did not help either although, in fact, in the early days of the Reformed church, when education was scarce, few elders could have been able to read and even their religious knowledge must have been scanty, so much so that the General Assembly felt it necessary in 1648 to decree that all ignorant and scandalous persons should be put off Kirk Sessions and kept off. It was probably a follow-up from this Act that caused the Presbytery of Fordyce, Banffshire, two years later to require all elders to be 'cairfullie catechised that so thes that are grossly ignorant may be examined.'[5] Even as late as 1796 when parish schools were fairly general although education was still not compulsory, the minutes of the Kirk Session of Tongue, Sutherland, record that just the minister and a committee would deal with the treasurer's accounts, partly because it was a busy time of the year but also because 'some of the Elders are incapable to examine written accounts from want of education.'

Between 1606–37 and 1661–90 the church in Scotland was under Episcopalian and not Presbyterian rule but that made little difference to Kirk Sessions. Apart from the fact that there were in the church such positions as bishop, archdeacon, chancellor, vicar and sub-dean, there is little in church records to show that any real change took place in church courts during these times. Kirk Sessions continued to meet and proceedings were conducted as before because although these subordinate courts were initially forbidden after the Restoration of Charles II along with Episcopacy in 1661, they were nevertheless permitted by the Privy Council. The continuation of the eldership during Episcopacy has been explained on the ground that it was necessary that suitable people should help clergymen with church repairs, providing Communion elements and collecting for the poor, but the real truth is that it was a matter of sheer necessity rather than church policy. Civil and burgh laws had not become the complex machinery they later did and much fell to the church, and the work of elders was so wide-ranging that they covered the whole social scene. Episcopacy could not do without them: 'They were far too important to be done away with and therefore we find them just as powerful under Episcopacy as under the strictest Presbyterianism.' So much was this so that in 1690 after the re-establishment of Presbyterianism, the Kirk Session of Inverness continued to use the same minute book that Episcopalians had used but, as if to mark the epoch, contrary to custom one page about the centre of the book was only half filled and the following two pages torn or cut out and the next page was numbered '1' to show that a new ecclesiastical era had begun.[6]

The First Book of Discipline also referred to another group of laymen — deacons, who were closely associated with many but by no means all Kirk Sessions in control of kirk finance and who have been described as the first Inspectors of the Poor. The qualities expected of them as given in the Book of Common Order were as impossibly high as those for elders — that they should be of good esteem and report, discreet, of good conscience, charitable, wise and endowed with such virtues as St. Paul required in them. They were to gather alms diligently and faithfully distribute them with the consent of the minister and elders, to provide for the sick and impotent and at the same time to take care that the charity of godly men should not be wasted on loiterers and vagabonds. The office of deacon, although one which was initially also elected by the congregation, was of less importance than that of elder and deacons were not officially members of Kirk Sessions; in many parishes they were deacons and no more. Nevertheless, they might be regarded as serving an apprenticeship to the higher office of elder; a Glasgow Kirk Session decided in 1700 'to advance some who are Deacons, to the office of elders' and another 'thought fit to advance the Deacons' and in this particular case, as they had recently appeared publicly to be admitted to the deaconship, the Session decided that they did not need to appear again and that it would be sufficient to read out their names to the congregation, after allowing a day for objections. In some places, however, deacons were more closely identified with Kirk Sessions. Both elders and deacons were ordered to attend the Kirk Session at Montrose in the mid–1600s and Arbuthnott, Kincardineshire, was a parish where the deacons were included in the sederunt of the Session and, like the elders, had districts allotted to them, shared in the administration of discipline and assisted at Communion, although this assistance was limited to drawing the wine but not serving in any way. This made them a kind of assistant elder and possibly even more than that as in 1772 three men there were ordained as 'elders and deacons' and it is suggested that it was the custom in some places to appoint men to this dual office.[7]

The requirement imposed by Act of Parliament that elders should see that the Word of God was purely preached, was taken very literally by some Sessions in early post-Reformation days, to the extent that they might take it upon themselves to decide upon the minister's 'ordinary' as his text was called. The Canongate Kirk Session, Edinburgh, asked their minister to take up the Book of Acts; St. Andrews elders prescribed II Samuel; Aberdeen Kirk Session ordered the minister to preach from Romans. Some went further: about 1620 Elgin Kirk Session recommended that sermons should be shorter and at much the same date actually minuted that no member of Session could find fault with the minister's doctrine the previous Sunday.[8] Such excessive supervision of preaching is unlikely to have happened in rural parishes unless some of the elders were adequately educated and even where it did occur, it appears to have died out fairly soon although many Session minute books record, Sunday by Sunday, the texts for the day. A minister, nowadays, is responsible to the Presbytery for the conduct of worship.

There was other ministerial supervision for elders to do. It was because the Reformed church desperately wanted to avoid the bad features which had crept into the old Roman Catholic clergy that the First Book of Discipline provided that not only should elders assist with discipline of the people but that they should also watch over the conduct of the minster and his family. If he did not do his duty or was 'light in his conversation', then they could reprove him and if that did not work, they could bring their complaints to the ministers of two adjacent parishes; once a year, they were expected to report on his 'life, manners, study and diligence' to the Clergy of the Superintendent's kirk. In theory this gave the people, through elected elders, a voice in the running of the church which itself more or less ran them. The Kirk Session — minister and elders — was and is subject to the oversight of the Presbytery which is the next highest church court and consists of the ministers and one ruling elder from each church within a given district. It has to give a full account of everything to do with themselves and their church during Presbyterial Visitations, and this used to include elders giving their opinions about the minister. On one such occasion, in Falkirk about 1650, all but one of the elders spoke well of their minister — and the exception was conveniently 'found ignorant'. There was also a practice of holding what were called 'privy censures', both in Sessions and in Presbyteries. How these were gone about appears in the minutes of Sorbie Kirk Session, Wigtownshire, in 1702: 'The Session having through's [sic] their business they went about their privie censures, and several of their members having prayed, the elders were removed one by one' (or it could occasionally be two by two, as happened in Melrose Kirk Session in 1703) 'and their carriage and behaviour strictly inquired into . . .' In other words, each elder in turn had to leave while the others were asked if they knew anything against him and if there were no bad reports, then he was recalled to be 'exhorted and encouraged'. Should reports not be favourable, then any problems had to be sorted out by inquiry and if possible by reconciliation. This was a practice that was considered desirable. As the minutes of Sorbie had put it the year before, 'The Session considering the necessity and expediency of keeping up privie censures in the Session, they appointed that from this time and henceforth there be a day set apart for privie censures the week immediately preceding the Synod, and that the same be gone about by humiliation and prayer.'[9]

In large burghs, there were for a time General Sessions. In Edinburgh these consisted of the ministers, elders and deacons of the city, the latter two categories being changed annually. In Glasgow the General Session was composed of ministers and elders of the different parishes and had the allocating of their total income amongst them. Although the establishment of Presbyteries in 1578 reduced the authority of General Sessions, some of them continued long after that, even into the nineteenth century, and they are developing once more. In many multiple parishes today a joint Kirk Session, composed of all Kirk Sessions in the linking, is specifically provided for in the Basis of Linking, but only to deal with matters common to the linkage. There is now, for instance, a General Session of Upper Tweeddale which includes the four Kirk Sessions of the four parishes served by the one minister.[10]

All the local duties of elders emanated from attendance at Kirk Session meetings which might be held in the church, the manse or, where there was one, the Session house. In rural areas these meetings might be held only once a year and that just to distribute the poor's money, as happened at Laggan, Inverness-shire, or even less often. The Kirk Session of Tongue, a wild and scattered parish, met in July 1788, December 1789, April 1790 with the next recorded meeting not until March 1795. A country parish in southern Scotland, such as Ancrum, regularly met two or three times a year although there was a gap there between July 1847 and November 1849 which is unexplained. That was however the time when railway construction was going on in the vicinity and there was an outbreak of cholera too. In more populous areas and in burghs, however, things were different. South Leith Kirk Session's index in the General Register House shows a long catalogue of minutes and registers, indicating many meetings; Banff seems to have had meetings at least once a week in the early 1700s, as did Dornoch, Sutherland. At about the same date, Mr Dysart, the minister of Coldingham, Berwickshire, held 1169 meetings in sixteen years, an average of about $1^1/_2$ per week, while in the first half of the seventeenth century an East Lothian Session met every Sunday and as a rule, on Tuesdays and Fridays too, which were both preaching days, and more frequently if necessary. The statement that a 'diet', a word meaning in this sense a meeting, 'was wholly spent in prayer to God' appears frequently in the records of one Session about the 1730s and may mean that there was no business to transact but that a meeting was held nevertheless for devotions, although in some parishes elders were expected to meet fortnightly for a fellowship meeting 'on such day as arranged for the four quarters': not a formal Session meeting, in other words, but still a meeting. At Session meetings, Acts of Session could be passed on all sorts of matters, giving great power to Kirk Sessions. Sometimes they drew up their own Acts in accordance with Acts of Parliament on such subjects as fornication, adultery and so on, so that their Acts became a local version of national ones, although many of them were passed without any official instigation.[11]

How any elder with a living to earn could be expected to find time for such frequent meetings is astonishing and it is hardly surprising that one minister reported at a Presbyterial Visitation about 1650 that his elders did 'keip not the Session well' and an entry in the minutes of Kinghorn Kirk Session, Fife, in 1631 shows that although the bell of the Session house was rung for a meeting of the Session, neither minister nor anyone else met that day. The only remedy was to impose a penalty, something adopted in Aberdeen in 1568 when it was decided that absentees should be fined 2s. Scots, equivalent to 2d. stg., which was raised in 1620 to 6s. 8d. Scots. The same thing happened in other parishes which held frequent Session meetings, such as Montrose, Angus, where in 1634 the Session ordained that 'the haill Elders and Deacons shall frequently convene every Tuesday precisely, which failing every one of them being absent shall pay to the poor two shillings without they have a reasonable excuse' but this decree had to be 'ordered of new' in 1658. Even therefore with threats and penalties, absenteeism continued to be a problem, so much so that in one parish when something important came up, the 'haill sessioun' had to be specially warned to be sure that they would be present.[12]

Attendance at the higher courts of the church — Presbytery, Synod and Assembly — was a great burden to those elders appointed to attend, especially where distances were great and travelling was difficult. It meant being away from work, with resultant financial loss, and it could mean missing something special going on at home, and that could be a great disappointment. An example of this was the annual 'land-setting' at Hawick when the Commissioners to the Duke of Buccleuch came to the burgh to let his lands. This was always a great day, with a fattened ox killed for the occasion in a very ceremonial manner and old people still alive in 1900 could remember what used to happen: the ox was adorned with a chaplet of flowers and led in procession to the music of the town piper into the burgh, a procession which people eagerly awaited and joined as it passed, all the way to the butcher's door where the unfortunate beast was killed. This was such a special day in Hawick that it was not one to be missed for any meetings. In addition, any elder wanting to rent land needed to be present and so the records show that at one time the minister found that none of the elders could or would accompany him to the Synod of Kelso because of the land-setting. This sort of thing could mean that elders might have to be ordered to attend such meetings and in 1717, when none had attended the Synod with the minister 'these several times', the Session decreed that an elder *must* go to the next one with him, something achieved surely only under great pressure. Although elders might not want to attend the General Assembly, noblemen and others with private interests to serve were often glad to do so as they had to depend on what they could achieve in and through that body. Furthermore, burghs often wanted to be represented at the General Assembly and put forward names to Kirk Sessions: in 1801 a Commission from the Town Council of Lauder, Berwickshire, gave a Commission to the Kirk Session of the parish in favour of the Earl of Lauderdale who was also an elder, to represent them — the burgh — at the forthcoming General Assembly, 'desiring that the Session would attest the same, which they agreed to do.' That this practice was accepted by the Assembly is clear from the fact that a Commission from the burgh of Dumfries in favour of Archibald Hamilton, a lawyer in the town, resulted in a certificate being signed by the minister and Session Clerk, certifying in terms of an Act of General Assembly, that he was a bona fide acting elder. As time went on and church activities developed, elders found that apart from the type of meetings already mentioned, there were other meetings or gatherings to attend as well. An idea of this may be judged from what was happening in Banff in 1838 as described by G.D. Henderson: there was the Sabbath school held in the church for two hours each week; a Bible class on Sunday and on week days taught by the minister and an elder; a weekly prayer meeting presided over by an elder; a monthly meeting in the church 'for prayer and religious exercise', a parochial and Sabbath school library to oversee; young Communicants' classes; the annual catechising throughout the parish; and making arrangements to see the minister on business; or it might be representing the Session in other ways, such as serving as governor of a charity or a school.[13]

So far as Session meetings went, they were always recorded. In 1565 the elders in Aberdeen were sworn to secrecy concerning what happened during their meetings and it would be interesting to know what happened at Boleskine, Inverness-shire, about 1809 when a large part of a minute is heavily scored out although it had already been signed by the minister, and a lesser part is also scored out. Among the records of the Kirk Session of Cambuslang, Lanarkshire, in the early 1750s, there is a small booklet containing reports of the 'Visitors of the Books belonging to the Kirk Session of Cambuslang'. Such 'visitors' were authorised by the Presbytery to inspect the books for the purposes of supervision and this was something which was clearly needed. These visitors found cases where people had been cited to appear before the Session but no mention of the citations appeared in the minutes and that meetings to 'compt with' the treasurer were recorded as meetings for prayer although there were no Sessional meetings for prayer at other times. Nevertheless, the impression given generally by Session minutes is that their meetings were recorded carefully and accurately, sometimes indeed in extreme detail, although very often the outcome of cases is not given, possibly because if everyone knew what had happened, then there was no need to mention it again.[14] It is only occasionally that a really entertaining error appears such as a 'fragrant scandal' in Chirnside, Berwickshire, in 1700.

In 1648 the General Assembly decreed that each elder should be allocated a district or 'quarter' as it came to be known, within the parish, to be his own special charge. Elders were expected to have family worship in their own homes and to visit the houses in their quarters to see that they too remembered about this — 'to try who uses to sit down upon their knees and pray to God; and they are likewise ordained to hear the form of their prayers.' Extreme though this was, it is the origin of modern elders' visits to those in their districts. A large part of the elders' work in their quarters used, of course, to be seeking out sinners to be reported to the Session for discipline.15

Very often it was an elder who was chosen to act as treasurer of the kirk funds — only occasionally did this fall to the minister or Session Clerk — and elders usually had to take turns of standing at the collection plates at church services which, as will be seen, was not a popular duty. They might have to go round collecting from house to house should there be a particular need for funds or even to go collecting in neighbouring parishes too. Although they were not paid, in one case at least, those who had collected in other parishes were given 'a firlot [of meal] for their pains' which was more a way of paying expenses than anything else.16

In the event of a minister's absence for any reason, it was to his elders that he committed the care of the parish: the minister of Arbuthnott had to be away in 1691 for several Sundays on a Visitation of northern churches but before he left he exhorted the people to behave soberly and Christianly in his absence and re-minded the elders and deacons to 'suppress vice and sin so far as they could and other public sins, especially swearing, and be frequent in visiting the sick and praying over them.' That same year the minister of Ashkirk, Selkirkshire, had to attend the General Assembly and before going suggested that several of the elders be appointed as a 'comotoe' (committee) to make any necessary distribution of aid to the poor, to see to the repair of bridges giving access to the church and to report what they had done to the next full Session meeting. In 1695 a new minister, Mr Charles Gordon, was inducted to Ashkirk before the arrival of his family and shortly afterwards he told the Session of 'his intention to go to Dalmeny for Transporting his family and therefore recommended to them the care of the poor or any thing which concerns the parioch till he returns.'17

Legal matters could also fall on Kirk Sessions. Some came directly from Parliament, such as the requirement in 1695 that some elders should be present at the coffining of bodies to ensure that Scots linen was used for the shroud; or it might be the instruction that elders should collect excise in country parishes, something also imposed by Act of Parliament in 1645 but very probably imper-fectly observed. Sessions could find themselves as a body appointed trustees of charitable funds bequeathed to the parish or even administering much lesser testamentary bequests and it is not unknown for a complete Will to be written into a minute book for this reason. In one case a man left nothing for his widow's maintenance apart from a little house worth about £8–10 stg. but in his Will he appointed his Kirk Session as his trustees, giving them power, should she be reduced to straitened circumstances, to sell the house and give her an allowance for her life as they saw fit and at her death to give anything that remained to his heirs. In time the Session were informed that she was in a weak and sickly condition and needed support in some way and so they did as her husband had instructed and allowed her 15*d.* per week during her distressed state. There never seems to have been any reluctance to undertake these responsibilities. When a man named Francis Ruecastle appointed the Kirk Session of Hawick trustees for a minor to whom he left his whole estate, the elders replied, when asked if they would accept the trust, 'with one voice' that they would and a committee of four was chosen to look into everything and report back. They were obviously chosen for their abilities — two were ex-bailies, another the master of the grammar school and one was a member of the Ruecastle family. Another case concerning a minor arose not as a result of trusteeship but from a sheer sense of responsibility for the child. A man named Rodger Bennet, living in Falkirk, had been entrusted by his late stepfather as executor of his estate, with a condition attached that he would see to the care and maintenance of his six-year-old stepbrother. Far from carrying this out, Bennet refused the child maintenance, frequently beat him and finally turned him out of his house. At this point the Session stepped in and applied to a bailie to force him to fulfil his obligations to the boy but the bailie got no satisfaction from Bennet and as a result sequestrated his effects, which were later sold by order of the Session and the money used for the boy until it was exhausted, after which he was supplied from the kirk's poor's funds until he could look after himself. In a totally different type of legal case a Session 'agreed to certify the loss incurred at Balvraid by the burning of the house with a view to obtaining some relief from the Proprietor' and some years earlier that same Session had to make inquiries about a man supposed to be living under an assumed name and were able to establish his innocence.[18]

Some Sessions would even interfere in labour practices. Although it was normal for people to seek harvest work in other parts of the country, in 1645 the Kirk Session of Ashkirk ordered that no one should leave the parish to do this work elsewhere under threat of not being received by the church again and equally, anyone who took them to work would be under sentence of the church. Admittedly that was a time of political trouble and the order may have been to do with that but it seems just as likely that it was given to ensure an adequate number of harvest workers in the parish. If that is so, what influence was brought to bear upon the Session and by whom, to make them issue such an order? Just two years later the same thing happened in Elgin and there is a little more evidence there of what lay behind the decision: the Session and Town Council decided 'because of servants insolencies in this troubled time, with some rejecting service so that they may live loosely and others leave their masters without their knowledge or consent' that no workers, men or women, might leave their jobs at the coming term without their employers' consent, under pain of losing half a year's wages; that none should leave under pretext of setting up house themselves under pain of imprisonment; and that none should take harvest work outside the burgh without the bailies' consent — in other words, the townsfolk were to have a monopoly of available workers. Only a few years later a case comes from South Ronaldshay and Burray, Orkney, which has a ring of slavery about it. 'A fugitive and misbehaving servant' was ordered by the Sheriff Court to be put in the jougs, an iron collar, throughout the time of divine worship one Sunday as an example to 'all such fugitive and undutiful servants in time coming, who are appointed to be punished in like manner.' This was a clear case of the kirk co-operating with civil authorities and in sympathy with employers, each helping and using the other. At one point a Session ordered that all women who kept their daughters at home and did not put them into service, should be put out of the parish along with their daughters; and was the real reason for imprisoning an unemployed woman of no fixed abode for wandering about on Sundays a concern for good conduct or because she was 'without a master in the middle of the year'? It does seem, however, that an order in 1611 that an Aberdeen tailor should enter service or remove himself may have been based on the idea that the devil finds work for idle hands to do.[19]

Kirk Sessions always stuck up bravely for the rights of the church, something which landed them in court proceedings more often than one might think and it must have been particularly unnerving for individual elders when actions were raised by the Session as a body but each of them was held liable as an individual to pay his proportional share of the action, as could happen.[20]

Because Kirk Sessions were the only national body with intimate local knowledge, duties which may seem surprising fell on them in earlier times. The minutes of Kinghorn Kirk Session have the following entry for June 1627: 'Which day there was presented to the Session his M. Letteris [His Majesty's Letters] ordaining the minister and one of the Justices of Peace to nominate two of the elders to try the parochin qr ydill [idle] men yr be in it quha are not bound to service.' Although this may have meant no more than that such people should be put to work, there is an implication that they were expected to serve the king in the army or at sea and certainly in 1650 the Scottish Parliament ordered elders to supply lists of fencible men in their parishes, that is men who could be enlisted in time of crisis. An example of this aspect of Session work appeared in 1746 when in Sutherland the Kirk Sessions of the various parishes were assigned the task of raising men for the Earl of Loudon's army, then based in Dornoch, and if the 373 men raised in the parish of Dornoch alone are anything to go by, they must have been very successful. A minute in the records of the parish of Auchterhouse, Angus, in 1648 shows that £96 Scots which came from the army was distributed in the parish to soldiers who were wounded and to the families of those killed in Lord Dudhope's regiment. This indicated that a number of men had been recruited there and it would be interesting to know whether the Session, who must have been involved in the distribution as it appears in kirk records, had been involved in raising the men in the first place — yet in 1711 a Session accepted the reason given by a man for not appearing before the Presbytery: he said he was afraid that he might be caught *en route* as a recruit but that when recruiting was over he would attend.[21]

The press-gang, however, was something entirely different. It was a body of sailors, under an officer, empowered to seize men and force them into the navy. People were terrified of being kidnapped themselves or having any of their families kidnapped, because that is what it amounted to, and it is difficult to believe that any Kirk Session would have helped in the forcible removal, in the event of there being no volunteers, of a fixed number of able-bodied men from their community. The following case seems surprising therefore and one wonders to what extent the minister involved his elders. When one day in 1777 the people of Dunrossness, Shetland, were told that the government had sent a tender with a demand for a hundred men, their immediate reaction was to flee inland to safety. The following Sunday the minister, Mr John Mill, spoke of their flight 'saying they made great haste in running away for fear of the Press Gang who did not want to hang them or put them in prison, but only to serve their King and Countrey in the suppression of Rebells in America . . . and might be better employed for a year or two than at home; for when the rebellion was over they might return again with their pockets full of money; and O! that they were as eager in fleeing from the wrath of a Sin avenging God, to the blood of sprinkling for pardon and cleansing . . .' At that time the government needed a large navy and soon Mr Mill received a letter from Sir John Sinclair asking him to offer ten guineas, along with other advantages, to any man who would agree to serve, adding that if he could persuade anyone to raise thirty or forty men, Sir John would, on Mr Mill's recommendation, obtain a commission for him. When this carrot failed, a stick was used and when further demands for men were made a month or two later, there were threats that if the stipulated number were not forthcoming a cess or tax would be laid on the island of £25 for each man short of the specified number, a frightening prospect for minister, elders or people.[22]

The troubled times which gave rise to what has just been said, were part of the general trouble and turmoil, both internal and external, which affected Scotland in the sixteenth, seventeenth and eighteenth centuries and caused problems of all sorts to many people and bodies, including the kirk. There could be troubles too from purely local sources and it is said that about 1649 a band of caterans — reivers or freebooters — led by a man named MacAllister, kept much of Caithness in terror. When the people of Thurso somehow offended him, he decided to revenge himself by burning them in church one Sunday, but word of this plan got out and on arrival at the church he met with resistance. In the end MacAllister, who had gone up a stairway to attack Sir James Sinclair of Murkle, was shot through the ear and mortally wounded. In a remarkably mild manner, he is reported to have declared in Gaelic, 'Hoot-toot, the bodach has deafened me!' before tumbling dying down the stairs. Without going into the church politics of Covenanting times which is a subject not dealt with in this book, nevertheless a great impact was made on the work of the kirk by the civil wars of 1642–6 and 1648–9 and the battles fought then on Scottish soil as well as English after the signing of the Solemn League and Covenant in 1643, as well as the establishment of the Commonwealth under Cromwell in 1649. Many Scotsmen were involved in the fighting at those times so that a problem for Kirk Sessions might not only be a 'paucity of elders, many being slain and others otherwise dead', but also a great increase in the number of widows and orphans to provide for. A serious epidemic broke out during this time and this also reduced the ranks of elders and in 1646 St. Cuthbert's Church, Edinburgh, had to have a fresh election of elders because so many had died of this plague.[23]

During these times of strife and also during the Stuart risings of 1715 and 1745 travelling became so dangerous that it was difficult to hold Presbytery meetings or to have Presbyterial Visitations of parishes and, in addition, troops of whatever persuasion could make church life very difficult for any district in which they were quartered. In 1678 the parish of Muirkirk, Ayrshire, was one that was troubled with what they called 'hielanders lying amongst us'. This was much worse than it sounds as these 'hielanders' were what was known as the Highland Host, a body of men including lowland militia as well as highlanders, quartered and let loose upon the ecclesiastical dissidents of Renfrewshire and Ayrshire in 1678. Churches were converted into armouries and churchyards used as enclosures for horses seized by these troops, but it was not only at that time that churches were used in this way; it seems surprising that a godly man like Cromwell had so little respect for Scottish kirks that his men, horses and equipment were also sometimes quartered in or at them. There were soldiers in the church of Whitekirk in 1650; a mound in Inveresk kirkyard, Midlothian, was used as a gun battery; the kirkyard of St. Mary's, Leith, held stores; and in 1658 there could be no worship in Elgin, 'English horses being in the kirk quartered.' In 1745 Jacobite soldiers stored gunpowder in St. Ninian's Church, Stirling, which accidentally exploded and damaged the church very badly; and a much later use of a kirkyard building for storing ammunition was when the Round House in Aberdeenshire, an anti-body-snatching device at Udny, was used by volunteers in the mid-nineteenth century for this purpose.[24]

It was not unknown for ministers to ride out armed which may have had a bearing on another exceptional reason for there being no preaching in a parish, as happened at Alyth, Perthshire, in 1651 when there was a meeting there of the Committee of Estates. This was a body which included lairds and burgesses who were not Members of Parliament but who had wide powers to act on its behalf, yet did not need to report to it. From 1640–51 this committee was in effect the government of the country and in that last year, when the town of Dundee was besieged by General Monck, they met, along with other peers, gentlemen and churchmen to try to find a way of raising the siege. The meeting was broken up, however, by the surprise attack of a detachment of English soldiers and some of them were taken prisoner, among them Mr John Rattray, minister of Alyth. The Kirk Session's report of this says, 'August, the last day 1651: This day no preaching, because our minister was taken on Thursday last by the Englishes being the 28 of August 1651.' Not only did they take him but they also kept him in England until the following summer. The parish of Speymouth was another which went without public worship owing to troubles. The unfortunate minister had a number of Bonnie Prince Charlie's officers arrive unexpectedly and stay at the manse prior to the Battle of Culloden in 1746. A week or two later, the Duke of Cumberland crossed the River Spey there and while his men camped in the area, he 'sleeped' at the manse and so for several weeks there was no public worship. Even when church services were held, there could still be interruptions or fear of them and when Montrose's army was stationed in the neighbourhood of Alyth in the mid-seventeenth century, the Session minutes show that there was 'Given to Hendrie Cargill x sh[ll] for to go to the camp to trie to search some news from the malignants' (a term applied by Covenanters to Royalist opponents) 'and that he may be for warnisse of their coming upon us.' It is not clear whether the following kindly action by an English soldier occurred in the parish of Alyth or not (but it may well have done as it occurred during the minister's enforced absence in England), or whether it is just given in that parish's New Statistical Account as an illustration of what happened elsewhere: 'March the 28, 1652. No preaching, except only ane Englishe trouper went to the pulpit, and made ane forme of ane preaching, but hade no warrant to preach, whose text was upon the 45 Ps, 13, 14 vs.' Unfortunately when troops were stationed in an area, they were not above trying to lay their hands on kirk money; one Session had taken the precaution of having the funds in charge of two men, one with the box and the other with the key but about 1650 both box and key were 'taken away by force be the English soldiers' as these two men testified before the Session. The minutes of another Session show that in 1651 Cromwell's men broke their kirk box and 'plunderit' it, and the Stuart rising of 1745 brought the same problem in places, with church money 'taken away by the Rebels'.[25]

As the church could be used to help with recruitment, so it could also be used to make intimations forbidding people to join rebellions: this happened in Auchterhouse in 1650, with the threat of excommunication for anyone who did so. In addition, although leaders of rebellions were taken before higher authorities and suffered severe punishment or death for their part, what might be termed small rebels were left to be dealt with at local level by the church. This was done by their humbly acknowledging their offence on their knees, first of all before the Presbytery and then before their own congregation on a Sunday and, during Covenanting times, the kirk might also be required to see that they subscribed the Covenant. Similarly, in February 1746 after the second Stuart rising, the Duke of Cumberland signed an order at Montrose requiring all

> ordinary Common people concerned in the Wicked and Unnaturall Rebellion who may be Lurking in the Country to deliver up their arms and give ane account of their names and place of Abode to a Magistrate or Minister of the Church of Scotland and Submit entirely to His Majesties Mercy. And that all such as have knowledge of Arms or Effects belonging to any Concerned in the said Rebellion to make known and deliver up the same to a Magistrate or Minister under pain of being prosecuted with the utmost severity as Rebells and Traitours.

This had to be read from pulpits by ministers after worship and it is obvious that with them so closely involved, they would undoubtedly have invoked the help of their elders. The consequence was that these rebels might have to appear in church on the stool of repentance for the offence.[26]

It was inevitable that elders were directly involved in many of these troubles as participants because they, as much as anyone else, held their own views one way or another on matters of national or religious importance. During the 1745 rising John Brown, an elder in Kinnell, Angus, was one of those who took up arms and took part in it to such an extent that his Session found that 'none in this Corner could be ignorant of his Irregular and Detestable Conduct while Associate with the Rebells' but they were unable to do anything about him as they did not know whether he was alive or dead. The Presbytery, however, had no such qualms and deposed him from the eldership at once, although later on it came to be thought that he had indeed been killed at Culloden. Where elders were suspected of having acted in a subversive manner, investigations were always made: in November 1649 the minister of Petty, Inverness-shire, 'made intimation to the elders to be prepared again the next day to give their oaths whether ilk ane of them did know of others anent the engagement and insurrection at Inverness.' What had gone on there is uncertain but they all swore that they knew nothing about it and had done nothing more than go to both Morayshire and Inverness with Lord Moray, their master, but they still had to appear before the Presbytery whose records, unfortunately, do not exist prior to 1702. It was on the Presbytery's orders that after the first Stuart rising of 1715, the minister of Scone, Perthshire, 'interrogated the Session who among them carried favourable to the Rebels' and it emerged that three had committed the sin of attending a sermon in their company.[27]

Intimidation of church staff was another problem of troubled times. In 1746 Charles Air, the kirk officer at Kinnell, had openly, after public worship was over, called upon all able-bodied men to go to Montrose to join the John Brown who has already been mentioned, and for doing this he was immediately dismissed by the minister. It was not until early the following year that the Session summoned him to account for this and he had the opportunity to say that he had been forced into it owing to 'mear fear of the Mischief of the Rebells threatened him with on all occasions and particularly on Saturday immediately before if he disobeyed their Order.' The Session referred this to the Presbytery, saying that they believed his story, which the Presbytery must have accepted as they ordered nothing worse for him than a rebuke. In 1716 the schoolmaster in the parish of Craig, Angus, found himself in trouble for reading and publishing pro-rebellion papers and was suspended by the Presbytery but the Kirk Session re-engaged him believing, it is said, that he was not truly in sympathy with the rebels — but did they do this because they suspected intimidation or was the real reason that they did not want to lose a good teacher? Not so, however, in the case of Thomas Young who taught the parish school of Kinnettles, Angus, who was dismissed from this post and from being Session Clerk and precentor there or anywhere else within the bounds of the Presbytery. The minister of Kinnettles at that time was very pro-Stuart and had preached and prayed for the Stuart cause, with Thomas precenting the while, but Thomas compounded his sin not only by drinking the Pretender's health long and liberally but also by going to the Inverarity manse during the rebellion of 1745, carrying off the minister's servant and imprisoning him in the tolbooth of Forfar to try to force him into the Pretender's service. Not surprisingly troubles also caused the loss of Kirk Session records, such as those of Scone from 25 November 1713 to 5 February 1716. Those that survive start on the latter date and refer to the dispersing of the rebels, saying that they had 'banished many of the Mem[rs] of this corner from their flocks, and that Confusion and Disturbance occ[d] the loss of the Session Minutes' prior to that date; and parochial libraries, as well as Presbyterial ones, suffered in the same way.[28]

In spite of all this, the kirk supported those soldiers they considered were serving or suffering in a righteous cause and so it was through Kirk Sessions that collections in cash or kind were gathered for soldiers in need in 1650. That year the Church Commissioners asked for donations for 'captive sojors' in England who were said to be famished with cold and hunger and there was also a request for help for the army itself. The donations for the captives were meant to be collected by ministers as they went visiting round their parishes but in practice such collections required the help of elders too. St. Andrews Kirk Session was one that considered 'the present straits of our armies for want of victual' and agreed upon a voluntary contribution throughout the parish, of money and cheese. The money was to be brought in to the ministers — there were two of them — and the magistrates, who were to be present at the Session house to receive it, and it was to be spent on 'readie baken bread' which, with the cheese, was to be sent to the army with 'all convenient diligence'. In addition, the General Assembly was concerned that wherever regular troops were stationed throughout the country, they should be provided with seats in church and that they should come under the care of the local kirk — 'be inspected and noticed' is the phrase used, by the minister who should, if need be, apply to commanding officers to do so but nevertheless the wisdom of 'walking inoffensively' in this connection was recommended to them. Distributing money given by the army for crippled soldiers and bereaved service families has already been mentioned, something which would have been gladly done by all Sessions but, in later years, they were closely involved with collections for servicemen and their dependents in the aftermath of wars. A fairly typical instance of this appears in the minutes of a Session in 1806: 'This day's collection amounting to £10 7s. 11d. is appropriated for the relief of the relations of those brave men who fell in the glorious victory obtained over the combined Fleets of France and Spain on the 21st October 1805 off Cape Trafalgar by the British Fleet under the command of Admiral Lord Nelson and in which the brave Admiral fell.' After the Battle of Waterloo collections were again organised and referred to in minutes in a similar vein: a 'collection made this day at the church door for the relief of the wounded and relatives of those who died in the late glorious battle of Waterloo' was one of them; and in the same way money was raised for those who had suffered in the Indian Mutiny and other cases too.[29] There were other ways in which times of strife affected the work of Kirk Sessions but they appear in different chapters. However, not all Kirk life was as difficult as that and elders had many other concerns.

For one thing, Kirk Sessions were responsible for a considerable amount of movable church property. While more details of such items are given later on, the following inventory of property in the parish of Cruden, Aberdeenshire, in 1720 gives an idea of what might be held by a comparable Session, with less or more — possibly much more — depending on the type of parish:

> 4 large silver cups for Communion.
> 2 lesser ones.
> 2 bound books of church registers.
> One of Doctrine and discipline, collections and distributions, commencing 30 August 1713, the other of Baptisms and marriages beginning October 1707.
> A pewter basin for Baptisms.
> A baptising cloath laced about.
> A large velvet mortcloath.
> A lesser velvet mortcloath for children.
> A large cloath mortcloath, all lined and fringed.
> 3 long linning [linen] Communion table cloaths and a little one for a square table.
> A pock for carrying the mortcloaths and a chest without a lock for holding the mortcloaths and Communion cloaths.
> A little box with foreign copper coin and another box empty.
> A box with two locks and keys.
> 7 Communion tables of a dale length.
> The old church Bible in quarto.[30]

A great deal of Session time was taken up with matters to do with the fabric of church buildings, some of which were actually dangerous. In 1742 the roof of Fearn Abbey, Ross-shire, came down one Sunday killing thirty-six of the congregation then and there, while eight died soon afterwards. In 1813 as people were gathering in Rosskeen Church, also in Ross-shire, part of the crowded loft fell, many people were trampled and seriously bruised, two women died soon after and others were reported in the press as being in a hopeless condition. Part of the roof of Kintail Church, in Ross-shire too, gave way in 1855, also during a service, but fortunately rested on the sarking and plaster and fell no further. The minister managed to keep the congregation calm and averted a panic so that no one was hurt although the danger had been greater than anyone had realised at the time. All three of these disasters happened in the same county but it was by no means the only one to suffer like this. Some churches, however, did not even have roofs to fall. In 1698 that of Deskford, Banffshire, was open to the skies, as was that of Rathven in the same county some twenty or so years later with the result that on a particularly stormy February day 'the uncovered kirk was so very cold' that the minister had to preach elsewhere, while in the late 1830s the church in the parish of Strath, Skye, an old Roman Catholic place of worship, had been unusable for two years. In his *Reminiscences of a Highland Parish* Norman Macleod tells of a 130–square mile parish with a seaboard of a hundred miles which only had what he called two 'so-called churches', more like sheds or barns, each no more than 40' x

16′ and without seating. In the years 1699–1707 Rev. Thomas Boston used a large barn at Simprim, Berwickshire, not as a parish church, it is true, but regularly nevertheless for sacramental and other special occasions. Mr Archibald Bowie, minister of Dornoch, complained to the Presbytery in 1707 that he had no church but just 'some thing of a meeting house' which could not accommodate one half of the parish and was such a confused place that a third of the congregation could not see him nor he them and to make it worse, the roof leaked. It was inevitable that in the Western Isles things would be even more difficult and on South Uist, as late as 1820, the walls of an old house were roofed and it was thatched to serve as a church, there being no other; only in 1837 when it was finally ruinous was it decided to build a proper church at last. On the island of Eigg a school-house was being used in 1836 for worship and on various of the other islands services had to be held in open fields while in the parish of Strath where, as has been said, there was an unsuitable old church, the size of the parish made it necessary for the minister to preach in another district also and for fifty-two years in the late eighteenth and early nineteenth century he did so, every third Sunday, sheltering in a small cave.[31]

All this was in spite of the fact that it was the duty of heritors in rural areas to provide and maintain parish churches but what has been said shows how reluctant they must have been to carry out these responsibilities which were a form of tax; and no one, then or now, likes paying taxes. No heritor or factor who was an elder was willingly going to run himself or his employer into additional expenses; many elders were tenants and naturally they were unwilling to annoy or offend their landlords with tiresome demands; in towns there was friction between Kirk Sessions and Burgh Councils as to their respective responsibilities concerning provision of buildings and upkeep but solutions could be found: in 1597 the records of Elgin show that there was a general taxation of the whole town for repairing the church floor and some other items, which may have been imposed by the magistrates. Certainly in 1705 when the church of Kilmaurs, Ayrshire, required repair, it was the magistrates who ordered each heritor and feuar to pay 17s. Scots towards it; and when Craig Kirk Session felt it necessary in 1849 to have worship in the Ferryden area of the parish, they used money from collections made there to fit up a new infant school to make it suitable for this dual role.[32]

Even when heritors did agree to do something about church building or maintenance, there could still be delays if a decree of Presbytery was required for an assessment to be uplifted and, in any event, part of the cost of many heritors' obligations could legally be passed on to tenants, and that could include elders, something which also discouraged them from pressing unduly for expensive works to be done. In fact, much of the effort of repairing churches fell on tenants anyway. When the heritors and elders of Ashkirk decided in the mid-seventeenth century to re-thatch the church, they worked out how much turf each landowner should provide and this is minuted but what is not said is that it would be the tenants who would have had to cut and carry this turf. Similarly, when the Kirk Session and Burgh Council of Tain, Ross-shire, decided to rebuild the common loft in the church, the expense was to be divided among the heritors but it was the people of the town who had to bring the necessary timber up from where it was landed on the shore. Although heritors were entitled for many years to so many 'carriages' a year from their tenants — carrying of fuel, farm produce and so on — it seems very likely that carriages for church work of this sort would have been in addition to, rather than part of, those laid down with their rents. Sometimes it was Kirk Sessions who ordered people to bring materials, presumably when they either by-passed the heritors or could not get help from them: late in 1706 one Session not only ordered their treasurer to pay for lath for the church and something towards thatching, arranged to pay a man in victual (meal) 'for mending the holes on the roof with heather', spent 8s. Scots on nails but also instructed the kirk officer 'to acquaint the parroch to carrie their proportion of heath to the kirk.' It was late in the year and a bad time to expect people to gather and carry heather and it was not surprising that in the following February it was reported that 'the affair of thatching the Kirk' had been delayed and it was only in July that year that the Session again raised it, recommending to every oxgate — approximately thirteen acres of land and, in this sense, the occupiers of that land — to fetch twelve sheaves of heather to repair the kirk roof from a place which was some six or so miles away 'and that instantly'. Although called a recommendation, this was an order and one which it was sensible to issue in summer rather than in winter, especially at a time before harvest work began, but unfortunately that was the time of the year when country people were busy trying to secure their supply of winter fuel which, in that particular parish, was particularly difficult to get as peat could only be obtained in another parish which required the crossing of a long ford across a bay when the tide was out. Additional work was something that people did not need and such demands for kirk repairs were very hard on ordinary folk. Provision of a pulpit was also the heritors' responsibility but even that could be difficult; in the early seventeenth century Mr John Lauder, minister of Tynninghame, East Lothian, felt so strongly that a new one was needed that he paid for it 'out of his ain purse'. Windows were part of the church fabric which also fell to heritors to maintain but they were very vulnerable to damage and repairs and replacements were often borne by Sessions, either out of Sunday offerings or by holding special collections. This happened in one parish in 1722 when £1 4s. was raised by an extraordinary collection and again in 1776 when £1 2s. 6d. was raised for repairing the window of the eastern gable of the church which had been blown in by a storm but as the repair turned out to cost only 18s., the kirk funds were in hand as a result of it. When Swinton and Simprim Kirk Session paid 3s. 6d. in 1806 for a pane of glass for the church the minutes state that 'the above pane of glass had either been blown out by the wind or taken out and carried off by some person.' Building materials of any sort, even those intended for a church, were always in demand and at risk of being stolen; Hawick Town Council dealt with a young weaver 'for abstracting and resetting of lime from the church while building' in 1696, an offence which was easily proved as one of the bailies had seen him doing it.[33]

The authors of the First Book of Discipline considered that a church bell was essential for every parish so that the people could be called to worship and this too heritors were meant to provide and, while some individual ones might gift a bell — the Earl of Lauderdale was one of those who did so, presenting a fine bell bearing his arms to Lauder Church in 1687 — few parishes had either bell or belfry until the seventeenth century and some not until even later. An enterprising parish could manage without one however. In Tynninghame, until a church bell was provided in 1625, the beadle went through the village three times each Sunday morning, just like a town crier, ringing a hand-bell, the one usually used to announce deaths but given this additional use. In many places it was a bell alone that the heritors provided, not a belfry, and so the bell had to be rung from any convenient spot. In Kilmaurs this was done on rising ground in the kirkyard, which came to be known as the Bell Knowe, until the 1870s when it was ultimately housed. Very often the bell was tied to some convenient tree and rung from there with the aid of a dangling rope, something still to be seen at Ewes Church, Dumfries-shire. To have a belfry seems to have been a matter of pride to a parish and when considerable improvements were being done to the church in Nigg, Ross-shire, many of the tenants signified 'their inclination to contribute towards the building of a bell house' and later agreed 'to stint themselves in a voluntary contribution' for it. They must meanwhile have been casting admiring and envious eyes at the belfry of Cromarty, in the same county and a mere ferry ride away and, imitation being the sincerest form of flattery, commissioned a mason named David Denoon to build one for them 'after the form and dimension of the bell house at Cromarty' which he completed in eight months for the sum of £88 0s. 4d. Scots which was paid in victual at the rate of £5 Scots per boll. The cost of 'hinging the bell' at Tynninghame in 1625 was, rather improperly, paid out of an assessment laid on the heritors some time before for Communion cups and baptismal basins but which had been lying unused for some seven years while a lawsuit went on. In towns, where burgh councils had some control over church matters and where, at certain dates, it was not uncommon for the church bell to be tolled for funerals, an element of blackmail could slip into fund-raising for bell provision, with the rule being that only those who contributed should benefit. In Hawick, for instance, it was decided in 1694 that the names of all those who gave towards the founding and cost of a new church bell should be listed, along with a note of the sum that they gave, and that neither the church bell nor the hand-bell should be rung on the death of anyone in the parish apart from them, their heirs, successors or representatives; and when the kirk steeple was rebuilt there in 1723 the Town Council ordered that non-contributors should not be allowed the use of the bell for funerals. In Glasgow at the end of the eighteenth century a donation of £10 from a bereaved family on the occasion of a funeral qualified for the tolling of the city bells.[34]

A social benefit of having a bell-house was that it could provide a night's lodging for poor travellers, something which was almost certainly unofficial in most places but which in the mid-seventeenth century appears to have been

accepted in both Whitekirk and Tynninghame, although how safe the accommodation was seems doubtful as a gap between belfry and church was big enough to
allow birds to find their way into the church and a man had to be paid to shoot
them. The church bell itself provided a social service in places where it was rung
regularly on weekdays to let people know the time. It was rung possibly at 8.00
p.m. or 10.00 p.m. and at 5.00 a.m. in summer or 6.00 a.m. in winter although in
Montrose in 1659 the first bell, even in January, was rung at 4.00 a.m. Ringing
bells in towns on weekdays seems to have been a secular service for the community, provided in many cases by the church rather than the burgh, perhaps
because, in spite of any extra expense, many town Kirk Sessions must have felt
that it was better to use the church bell to let people know the time than to have it
notified by the town drummer or piper whose music tended to lead to the sin of
dancing in the streets. Just how the bell-man knew the time himself is uncertain
but Sessions insisted on punctuality of ringing — in 1655 Montrose Kirk Session
reprimanded William Low for ringing the bell too late on week days and he was
told that it must be rung at precisely the right time 'with Certification if he fail he
shall be censured.' Having and ringing a bell, of course, increased the basic
running costs of any church and Session records show fairly frequent minor
expenses to do with bells such as 'mending the bell 1s.' or the cost of a new 'tow'
(rope) for it, something which could come in the mid-eighteenth century to about
7s. stg. In some cases, butter or soap was used to reduce friction on the rope. These
expenses were small and irregular but whoever rang the bell had to be paid. In
1773 Tweedsmuir Kirk Session, Peebles-shire, paid the kirk officer his salary and
also 'in regard that the church is now provided with a bell, they appoint for his
additional trouble 2 shs to be added to his former salary, making 10 shs in all',
which was good news for him. In winter there could be the cost of candles to
provide light for the ringer after dark and one Session ordered their treasurer in
1703 to give their kirk officer a pound of candles monthly for this.[35]

Public time-keeping of this sort was a great help to communities and the next
stage was to have not just a belfry or steeple with a bell but with a clock. As with
bells, clocks might be presented by kindly heritors but, as with many other church
needs, it was often public subscription that produced a clock which was why in
1718 a Session appointed two men to go through the town to see whether people
would be willing to give something towards provision of one for the church. A
church clock or a town clock was of such advantage that both Burgh Council and
Kirk Session often shared the costs, as indeed they might do for a bell too — in
1831 the Provost of Arbroath, Angus, asked for financial help for a new bell for the
steeple there and the Session of the nearby parish of St. Vigeans, also in Angus,
agreed to help as it would be useful for their congregation as well as that of
Arbroath. Unfortunately there could be disputes over who should pay what of
shared expenses and common sense was needed to put things right, in the manner
achieved by Kirkwall Kirk Session, Orkney, in 1764: 'The Session appoints their
two ministers and the Treasurer to meet with the Council for a committee of them
to settle the proportion due by the Session as their third share of the town clock,

and how the clock is to be kept going in the future, and agree to sustain whatever settlement is made.' The outcome was that the Town Council paid two-thirds and the Session one-third of all expenses of maintaining the clock.[36]

Many country churches, especially in southern Scotland, have a sundial somewhere on the outside walls — a few have free-standing ones — and their Kirk Sessions must have considered themselves lucky even if telling the time was dependent on the sun shining, because the expenses of having a clock were considerable. While clockmakers were more common in earlier days than now, it does seem nevertheless from some records that they thought oil was a sure cure for all troubles. The records of Melrose Kirk Session, Roxburghshire, for 1754 show so many entries for 'oyl for the clock' at about 5d. a time that one can only feel that overmuch oil may have been the cause of its problems. Session minutes show such entries as 'To Mr Kirkwood for mending the clock £3' or that the man in charge of it 'had been at a good deal of pains about the kirk clock in bringing her to work regularly' or the costs of winding, of a new chain or other repairs. What a relief it must have been when a good all-round workman could be found who could do kirk maintenance and who included care of clocks in his accomplishments. In 1744 Kirkwall Kirk Session considered 'the great loss they have of late been at for want of sufficient men to slate and glaze the kirk, and being informed that there is one David Gills presently in this town, a slater and glazier, who is willing to agree with the Session for the work of the kirk as slater, glazier and bellman, together with keeping the clock right', they decided that even although he insisted on a wage of £88 Scots yearly, over £7 sterling, 'there is none to be got in this country at present (to) whom they could trust the slating and glazing of the kirk' and understanding that he was skilful and diligent, they agreed to engage him.

The primary purpose, of course, for either bell or clock was to get people to worship and Sessions also did what they could to see that access to church was as convenient as possible. The gate had to be kept right, which explains such an item as 12s. Scots paid in 1724 to James Young, a smith in Shotts, 'for ane crook to the kirk-yett.' Stiles were regularly provided in churchyard walls so that those coming by country paths could get over at the nearest handy spot but they also often appear beside gates and this is probably a relic of the days when animals were grazed in the churchyard and the gate was for them, while human beings were expected to get over the wall. Work on stiles often features in accounts but it seems that the word 'stile' was sometimes used to mean access; in 1856 St. Monance Kirk Session, Fife, considered that the proximity of the church stile to the sea and its rough and unprotected condition unfitted it as a proper entrance to any church. Elderly people were complaining that it was the reason for their unwilling absence from services because the tide came over about twelve yards of it and left such a mass of seaweed as to make it dangerous about high water.[37] Mounting blocks were another necessity. Anyone who could do so rode to church and many of the blocks which are still standing at churchyard gates were designed as much for women as for men because it was the custom for women to 'ride double' on a pillion behind their husbands, some other male relative or a groom, and a mounting block was necessary for them to get up behind the rider. These had therefore to be kept in good condition and accounts include costs to do with them, including the following very descriptive one: 'Given Walter Gibson for making up the louping-on stone at the wester kirkyard yeat 14*s*.'

When the Reformers took over Roman Catholic churches, they found them unseated because previously there was little preaching and seating was unnecessary. All that was needed was space to stand or kneel for prayers or to receive the blessed Sacrament; in many churches it was only when an itinerant preacher with a gift of oratory appeared that there would be a sermon. So convenient was the open space thus provided, that courts had been held in churches, something forbidden by the General Assembly in 1571 and, even more surprisingly, fairs were held in them, with pedlars and others given permission by the church to set up their stalls and sell their wares within them. The result was that for many years after the Reformation, lack of seating in churches was a great problem and its ultimate provision, distribution, and the resultant negotiations and arrangements to do with it, take up many pages of Kirk Session minutes. Even although there might be no fixed seats or 'daskies' (desks) as they were called, in the body of a church, heritors who had the duty of providing and maintaining rural churches, had the right to erect galleries or lofts for their own families, their staff and their tenants. Seating a church was very expensive and initially much of it was done by heritors, some other individuals and by bodies such as trade guilds, rather than by Sessions, although some Sessions, in a subtle move, required such bodies to maintain the windows adjacent to their seats. If such bodies wished, they could let any spare seats to members of the congregation, with the rents going to church funds for the poor, but such seats were jealously guarded: the masters of Ships and Seamen, for instance, who had their own loft in the Old West Kirk, Greenock, Renfrewshire, sat there in order of rank with an old sailor standing sentry at the door to keep others out, especially women. Such seating was fitted up and cared for by the group erecting it, with craft guilds very often affixing the motto of their craft and other tablets, which explains why in 1702 James Vaus asked permission on behalf of the Skinners of Inverness to put boards above their seat to protect it and its embellishments from filth that was coming down upon it from above. A very early instance of a Session providing seating was in 1588 when some ash trees in the High Churchyard in Glasgow were cut to make forms for people to sit on, or at least for men to sit on, as was made clear the following year when it was decreed that 'no women sit upon or occupy the forms men should sit on but either sit laigh' — low, so presumably on the floor — 'or else bring stools with them', and in 1604 Glasgow Session went further and ordered that all women should sit together in church.[38] For some reason, although women were expected to go to church, they were for a long time not considered deserving of fixed seating, so that in 1598 Elgin Session ordered that any women's fixed stools should be removed from the church within fifteen days. Low and sometimes folding stools were known as 'creepies' and many women carried their own to church but in some parishes these could be hired from the beadle for a small fee, all or part of which he was allowed to keep for himself. In 1634 one Session decreed that John Low should have half the 'stool silver', with the other half presumably going to the poor, while in 1662 the mother of the kirk officer in an Ayrshire parish must have been in some need and felt that she should be allowed some benefit from all that her son gained from his lucrative appointment, comparatively speaking, and the Session ordered him to give her the baptism fees and also 'what advantage she could make of the church chairs and stools'. An attempt to make stools compulsory for women occurred in 1604 in Aberdeen when the Session ordered all women of honest reputation to sit on them during prayer and preaching and any seats for women which were already 'before the desks' to be removed but whether this was to maintain decorum or to increase revenue is not clear. In practice, of course, this meant that until there was sufficient seating, many men had to stand while women at least had stools. A Kirk Session might on occasion show sympathy to women, as for instance when Inverness Session ordered that Elspet Cuthbert, wife of William Keiloch, and another woman, both of whom seem to have been poor relations, might sit 'wt'out any molesan upon the footgang before the seat, sometime belonging to Provost Alexander Cuthbert, ay and untill they give further order.' This was kindly meant even if the 'footgang before the seat' sounds neither comfortable nor particularly dignified. Heritors' staff and tenants benefited from seating provided by their employers or landlords and paid no annual rent for this although in some cases anyway the tenants might have contributed to its original provision, as happened in one Ross-shire parish where into the mid-nineteenth century between 14s. and 16s. was still being paid by incoming tenants to outgoing ones 'which sum for each was originally paid by the tenants to the heritors in order to cover the expenses of seating the church.'[39]

There were, of course, many ordinary people who were neither employees nor tenants and they too came to want seating. In time it was the heritor who gave permission for this but to start with it was to Kirk Sessions that applications for it had to be made; a man came before Montrose Kirk Session in 1634 and 'craved licence of the Session to set ane seat for his goodmother right against the reader's door' — but more than mere asking had to be done. Money had to be paid one way or another for the privilege. This might be 2s. to 2s. 6d. per seat, 'pay'd before the seats be set up', or permission might be given for the seating and a rent charged in place of the initial payment, or it could be space for a chair, not the chair itself, which was let. In 1722 at West Linton, Peebles-shire, 2s. 6d. was charged in this way and anyone not paying had his chair put out 'and the room let to another', but however the charge was made the money went to the poor. All things considered, it seems surprising that people might go ahead and erect seats for themselves without permission. How on earth was it not noticed that '. . . sundries has built some seats for themselves neglecting the Session's orders' in Montrose in 1658, with the result that it was ordered that 'all and several persons who builds any desks or seats shall come before the Session and crave their liberty and tolerance thereanent' and presumably pay for this liberty and tolerance. That same year that

Session decreed that the seats of anyone who had been given permission to erect them but who later left the town, would be disposed of by the Session for what they could get, for the benefit of the poor's funds. As might be expected there was altercation about the right to seats. When two women disputed ownership of one beside that of the magistrates in Montrose in 1642 it was the Session who had to decide the matter, as indeed they always had to do in such cases. In 1700 the Kirk Session of the parish of Holm, Orkney, had heard so many complaints and grievances about seating that all of the heritors and heads of families were ordered to appear and produce evidence of their right to the seats they occupied and at the same time, those wishing seats were told to apply for them. In 1715 there had to be a special meeting in one burgh to sort out a particular squabble over trades' seats and when the ownership of a 'desk' in another town church resulted, during worship, in what was described as a tumult, with one man fighting to get into this seat and two others struggling to keep him out, the Session ordered it to be moved to a different position near the church door, and only the poor to use it until the rights of the case were investigated and the whole thing sorted out.[40]

A logical development of this, especially once earth gave way to proper flooring, was for a Session itself to instal seating for sale or hire to members of the congregation to raise money for the poor's funds and to avoid squabbling; this practice had in general begun by the early eighteenth century. This meant that not only had the Session to engage a craftsman to do the work but it almost certainly fell to them also to get the materials and that could involve considerable inquiry and effort. When Cromarty Kirk Session, Ross-shire, required 'dales' (wood) to build seating in 1738 and learnt that at Nairn there were 'noroway dales sold at four pounds Scots per dozen they ordered John Keith wright to go with a yoal (yawl) to Nairn to take eight dozen' and shortly afterwards they also 'sent to Redcastle Mercat to buy more dales.' So valuable were such seats to the kirk that they may appear under the heading of 'Property' in lists of Sessions' belongings. A few seats of the type erected in those days survive in at least parts of some churches and if the nine-inch deep seats of one are anything to go by, they were far from comfortable, but people were only too glad of them. Some Sessions made a fixed charge for rent of their seats. In 1657 Montrose Kirk Session charged 6s. 8d. per year for a seat in the 'foarseatt of the Quire loft' but that was before seating was general in the body of churches; once this had become common, letting or sale was usually done by an annual roup, possibly held at Michaelmas and with whoever was acting as auctioneer standing on a seat and extolling the particular virtues of any pews up for bids. It is little wonder that the gift of seating in a church to a Session was more than welcome. In 1802 the principal heritor in the parish of Tongue, in a most generous manner, seated the church at his own expense, then called a meeting of Session and parishioners and distributed the seats by tickets but stipulated that none of these seats might be sold privately. What he suggested was that if anyone left the parish then the Session, whom he appointed superintendents of the seats, should allocate those of the outgoing person to the incoming one, without any charge apparently being made. Even so, wrangling did break out among the parishioners over them and a brisk reminder from the minister about these conditions was needed to settle things. Lesser gifts of seats were very welcome too, such as the following one — in 1747 'James Bailie, tenant in Carfrae, having a claim to the desk behind the door, assigned his right to the poor of the parish by a letter to the Kirk Session, which was read. The Session appointed the letter to be kept in retentis and Thomas Logan, weaver, engaging to pay rent for the seat, accordingly paid 12 shs Sc for the first year.'[41]

While some Sessions provided seating for their ministers' wives fairly early on — at Stirling in 1627 and at Montrose by 1634, where it was specifically stated that no one else might enter the manse seat without permission from the Session — manse wives were in general given no special consideration until long afterwards. It was only when provision of seating greatly increased that there came to be a regular manse pew and usually pews for the elders too, often under the pulpit and sometimes with a lock and key on the door. People with a specially valuable role in the parish, such as the schoolmaster or the midwife, might be rewarded with a special seat, and there was often special seating for the school children. According to George Hay in *Architecture of Scottish post-Reformation Churches* the development of the choir movement in the late eighteenth century required special seats to be set aside for these singers or 'band' as they were called, either in a box pew or a loft, sometimes in fact ousting the elders from their usual places; and in addition special seats were also provided for the participants in marriages and baptisms.[42]

When major improvements were made to one church in 1729, the heritors who had built the north and east lofts for themselves, were authorised to let any seats that they did not need, apparently for their own financial advantage, which may have been a way for them to raise their share of the money for the poor. It was the fact of such letting that threw up doubts about the validity of ownership of a seat in Kirkwall. In 1731 Beatrix Sinclair, widow of John Boynd, claimed possession of Sinclair's loft, as it was called, 'and tis said she draws rent therefor.' The Session ordered that she should be spoken to about this and the minutes say that she pretended to be 'lineally descended from the Sinclairs who had a right to the seat and had repaired it and had been in possession of it for forty years and by no means would she cede the possession thereof.' She was ordered to produce evidence of her claim but when her son appeared on her behalf, he said that it would take her six months to establish her rights. It became a legal obligation for heritors and Town Councils to provide seating for two-thirds of the 'examinable persons', which in this case meant those over twelve years old, as well as a Communion table and pews for it, a pulpit, a reader's desk, elders' and manse pews, as well as a place of public repentance, but from what has been said, clearly this was by no means always done. However, when churches ultimately became fully seated a proper division of seating obviously had to be made, in a similar way to that which the principal heritor of Tongue had done, although his decisions on the matter could be entirely arbitrary. Much seating was allotted to heritors in proportion to the valued rents of their property within the parish, something which was regarded as of such importance that the principles to be applied to it were laid down thus in 1776 in an action by Lord Home against the Earl of Marchmont and others in the parish of Eccles, Berwickshire:

1. The process must be conducted before a Sheriff.
2. Division to be conform to the valuation of each heritor.
3. Where there are galleries, they should be set aside as family seats for the larger heritors, the patron to have first choice and others in accordance with their valuation.
4. Back seats in the gallery and in the area to be allocated to tenants, the tenants of each heritor to be in one place if at all possible, but not necessarily contiguous to the landlords' seats.[43]

Divisions of seating were not achieved without great deliberation and complicated calculations. Nigg Kirk Session got the Master of Tain Academy, some ten miles away, to work it all out for them in 1821 and were not alone in calling for similar expert help; and the minutes of Fetlar Kirk Session, Shetland, are particularly detailed about the division of seating there in 1793.

The impression which emerges is that there was seating in churches for all, or at least for everyone over twelve years old; for heritors it was by right and for their tenants and staff by favour, while craftsmen and villagers bought or leased it if they could, with any income from it going to church funds for the poor. But there was seldom any seating for the poor themselves although those on the poor's roll were expected to attend worship regularly. However, some old churches had a long passage, perhaps two yards wide, running from end to end of the church, the whole length of which was taken up by the Communion table, which had a seat along each side, and in some churches the poor were allowed to sit there except on Communion Sundays. It could be argued that this was a seat of honour but in the circumstances it was nothing more than paupers' seating. By the early twentieth century such an arrangement might still be found, but only in remote country districts. Elsewhere the seats at the Communion table might well be let for the financial benefit of the poor and it was often only if seats at the Communion table could not be let that they were made available to paupers, who got little consideration in this regard. Even when a new church was built at Tranent, East Lothian, in 1800 there were only twenty free sittings out of 888 and when a new one was opened in Dunbar, in the same county, in 1821 for 1800 people the position was only a little better with sixty-one sittings for the poor. The best solution to the problem of accommodating the poor in church was that used at Kilmalie, Inverness-shire, where by the mid-eighteenth century all the seats were free which was said to be 'an immense advantage to a poor population. It removes a common excuse for absence' — but the real reason for free seats in such an area may well have been the very fact that a poor population could not pay for seating anyway. Even when a Kirk Session had the kindliest intentions towards the poor, things might go against them. In 1729 when considerable alterations and improvements were done to the church in Nigg, Ross-shire, the Session decided to build a common loft over the west aisle for the use of the poor, not for income, using not only some of the poor's funds to construct it but also ordering a voluntary collection to be made for it by the elders throughout the parish. In the end the cost of the loft came to £115 Scots (£9 11s. 8d. stg.) and the need to square their accounts made the Session decide to let the seats rather than allow the poor to use them free of charge.[44]

It was only because the church needed money for all the work it had to do that the following case occurred which seems harsh but in the circumstances is understandable. In 1829 the elders of St. John's Church, Glasgow, reported that a considerable number of parishioners wanted sittings in the church but could not get them because 'of the seats being occupied by the charity children attending the church, and that in other respects the attendance of these children was very inconvenient to the congregation, Messrs. Paul and Falconer were requested to bring the matter under the notice of the proper authorities in the view of getting the children transferred to some one or other of the city churches which might be less crowded.' These examples are given to show the difficulties there could be in providing church seating but in very many cases everything went smoothly and it proved a useful source of revenue, even indirectly when fighting over the right to seats brought fines to the kirk coffers. Although seat rents ceased to be charged as early as 1817 in Kilmaurs, with no reason for this being given, the practice went on elsewhere for many years, even into the 1960s. This was so, perhaps, particularly in towns where pews bore seat holders' names and any unwitting visitor sitting in such a seat might be asked to move.[45]

In burghs where Burgh Councils had, as has been said, some control of church matters, there could be friction between them and Kirk Sessions over seating, especially in later years. In 1822 a new method was adopted by the Burgh of Dunbar for letting seats in the church opened there the previous year — the one with sixty-one sittings for the poor out of a total of 1800. A price was marked on certain pews belonging to the burgh and the Provost went so far as to nail them shut so that no one could use them until they were let. This caused the Session to complain to the Sheriff who ordered them to be opened up, saying that although the heritors of the parish might be entitled to stipulate for and receive rents from parishioners for church seats, yet in default of obtaining tenants, they were not entitled to shut them up in this way and forbade it to happen again. He also found the Provost liable for the costs of this action but this he resisted, saying that closing the seats was an act of the magistrates and not his alone, to which the Session answered that they had no way of knowing by what authority he had acted as he did. The Sheriff then forbade the magistrates and council to shut up seats, upon which they appealed to the Court of Session but were defeated there and the case was remitted to the Sheriff and ultimately the magistrates did have to pay the costs. A similar controversy over church seating arose in Inverness between the Town Council and the High Church Kirk Session when the Council recalled permission given to the minister and Session to allocate seats and appointed the Town Chamberlain and magistrates to do this instead.[46]

In the days when lack of education meant that the general public were unable to read, an ill-lit church did not inconvenience them; all that mattered was that the minister, the reader who read the Bible before the service began, and the precentor who led the singing, could see adequately. This explains why in the early seventeenth century a 'gryt hears', which sounds odd but which was an early form of candelabra, hung before a pulpit while the rest of that church was apparently unlit. Many parishes did not have afternoon worship in the winter months because of both the lack of lighting and the difficulty of travelling in the darkening but, where it was continued, lighting was provided by candles supplied by the Kirk Session or else people might carry a lantern to church and transfer its candle into a candleholder at their pew — examples of these can still be seen at Holy Trinity Church, St. Andrews. The introduction of oil lighting was a great improvement and some churches, even small rural ones, acquired beautiful lamp-holders. As public lighting became general, churches introduced it where they could, earlier in the south, later in the north. It was in 1905 that 'incandescent gas lighting' was installed in the parish of Dingwall, Ross-shire, and 1920 when it was supplied with electricity from the Strathpeffer Electric Company, replacing the earlier gas. It was only in the early 1950s that hydro-electricity became available in the highlands and so it was only after that date that rural churches there could be lighted by it. By the mid-nineteenth century, a desire for greater comfort had made people less willing to put up with the dreadful cold of churches and the invention of heating devices encouraged their use. The church of Clackmannan was built on clay and held the moisture so that it was damp as well as cold but in 1839, after the heritors and congregation subscribed for 'one of the heating and ventilation apparatus of the Messrs. Haden, Wiltshire' the church was said to be 'perfectly comfortable'. Heating required coal and that was expensive but it could be bought by holding special collections although it might still be necessary for church funds to have to contribute towards it, and a little local spin-off was that lighting church stoves brought a small income to someone living near the church. Rising standards also led to church cleaning appearing in kirk accounts, with items such as brooms having to be bought, but it is clear from the following minute of 1849 that cleaning was not regarded as something to be done regularly but only when really necessary: 'The allowance for sweeping and cleaning the church was fixed to be one shilling for every time the Moderator (minister) should direct this to be done — and half a crown for washing the seats and floor and for sweeping and cleaning the church.' A rather touching appeal is recorded in 1844 in another Session's minutes: 'The Clerk was desired to prepare a notice to be put on the church door expressing all the desire of the Session to keep the church in a clean and comfortable condition and requesting the congregation to refrain from scattering down any nuisance on the floor.' Improvements continued to be made, including such refinements as umbrella-holders at the ends of pews, still to be seen in churches and a relic of the not-so-distant days when most people walked to church; and churches are now bright, well lit, well heated places, often with hearing aids for those needing them and toilet facilities as well. It was in 1925 that a Church of

Scotland Properties and Endowments Bill was passed, in advance of hoped-for reunion with the United Free Church, which transferred all church property from the heritors into the care of the General Trustees of the Church of Scotland, relieving the heritors of their burdens in this connection and requiring each parish kirk to start a fabric fund for repairs.[47] It would have broken the hearts of the members of erstwhile Kirk Sessions, who strove so hard to look after their churches, to know that some of them have been demolished to make way for housing or have been converted into houses, others have become stores for various businesses or have been made into museums or put to a variety of secular uses; in Ayr alone old church buildings are said by Dane Love in his book *Scottish Kirkyards* to have been used as theatre, auction rooms, dancing school and pensioners' day centre. But that is jumping ahead.

Various members of kirk staffs have already been mentioned, and without the work of such people, the kirk could not possibly have achieved all that it did. It is difficult to decide whether the Session Clerk or the beadle held the key position so far as general usefulness went but as the former was the superior position, it must come first. The need for having a clerk was summed up in 1758 by one session as 'the usefulness and necessity of keeping a regular Session register' and in order to achieve that end, 'the expediency of having a proper Session Clerk'. It was decided that he should be paid £1 sterling annually 'for his trouble' and so that he might have something in which to record their transactions they asked the minister to order from Glasgow 'a proper paper book for keeping the minutes and proceedings.' Kirk Session minutes, which have already been briefly mentioned, were often called just that but other names occur too, such as 'The Present state of the Pariochin of Banchory Devenick with reference to the churches the concernes thereof' in 1708, a title which had given way there in the 1780s to a 'Register of Discipline containing the Acts and Proceedings of the Church Session' because in that parish, and in many others, maintaining discipline was such an important part of Session work that the minutes recorded little else. However, because many Kirk Sessions passed Acts, the minute book might be called something like 'The Particular Acts of the Parish of Tweedsmuir'. Well written minutes were obviously desirable and while it is not clear what was the normal occupation of one Session Clerk in 1707, the prospect of a Presbyterial inspection of their records unnerved the Session sufficiently for them to appoint someone else in his place, purely because of his writing: 'considering that their session minutes will shortly be revised by the presbytery, and that by Acts of Assembly . . . every session are obliged to have their minutes written in a fair hand, and have a register of births and baptisms, and in regard our present Clerk does not write so fair a hand as we would require, the Session went on to choose a clerk.' They did not choose very well, in fact, as the writing thereafter got worse, not better. It was almost certainly the lack of a sufficiently educated man to take the post that caused some ministers to double up as Session Clerks but that was not really satisfactory. The best solution was to employ the schoolmaster as Session Clerk and this was what happened wherever possible, although not invariably, because by definition he could read and write at a time when most people could not do so.[48]

One of the problems about a schoolmaster being Session Clerk was that he might well only teach during the summer months and then spend the winter ones at university in the hopes of qualifying for the ministry, something which used to be the goal of many of these men. This problem was mentioned in the records of Tongue where, about 1781, nothing was written in the minutes 'because the clerk was frequently absent attending college' but, as several important transactions had taken place during that time, the problem was overcome by writing them into the records later on although this meant that they lost the immediacy of contemporary reporting. Another parish which found itself with blanks in the minutes, although there was no explanation for them, was Ashkirk. When the Session Clerk there died in 1710, it was discovered that nothing had been written up from 1706 until then. A new minister and some of the elders tried to investigate as best they might and ordered the new Session Clerk to insert as much as he could but this was often without a date or a year. Nevertheless, in general schoolmasters made excellent Session Clerks and naturally Kirk Sessions had a very strong interest in who was appointed to parish schools, something discussed, as there is an inevitable overlap, in a later chapter. Unfortunately, relationships between burgh and kirk were not always harmonious over such matters. It was alleged by the Kirk Session of Selkirk that during a vacancy from 1691–94 the Town Council had usurped several of their rights. With no minister in charge, the Council probably meant well when they appointed a man to ring the bell to summon people to funerals and also took to do with appointment and dismissal of both precentor and Session Clerk. In January 1692 they appointed someone other than John Binnie, the parish schoolmaster, as Clerk at which he petitioned the Presbytery, claiming his right to officiate in this capacity, and as precentor, either himself or by a substitute. He did not in fact have any such right unless promised the post but the Presbytery set aside the Town Council's appointee and ordered him to return the parish registers, which he refused to do, but after several private interviews with some of the Council, all that the Presbytery did was decide 'not to meddle further with the matter till a minister was appointed.' An instance of a Kirk Session's wish to avoid trouble with a Town Council happened in 1736 when the Session of St. Michael's Church, Linlithgow, West Lothian, chose a precentor and appointed a committee of their members 'to deal with the magistrates of Council for their consent' and 'earnestly entreated the Town Council to agree or at least declare that they are willing to go to an accommodation, to avoid a process at law', all of which had a happy outcome and the precentor was given the post. Such problems did not occur in rural parishes, nor indeed in all burghs, but they show the background against which Sessions might have to operate in certain matters.[49]

When Kirk Sessions made up their accounts, their first concern was always to pay their staff and it was always the Session Clerk's salary which topped the list. Their salaries varied considerably around the country and it is often difficult to work out just what any particular Session paid as the length of time covered by a payment may not be given and arrears may be included. For instance, Montrose's Clerk received £46 13s. Scots in 1707 which was equivalent to £3 17s. 9d. stg., whereas nearly ninety years later Orphir Kirk Session, in the Orkneys, raised their Clerk's salary to 15s. stg. and that was only because there had been a decrease in the value of money about then. In the first case, the payment may have been for more than a year because it was a very high figure for that date and the second one may have been for less than a year but fortunately the length of time which applies to a payment is sometimes made perfectly clear: Kilconquhar Kirk Session, Fife, paid £3 for their Clerk's half year's salary of meal and house in 1689 and £7 2s. for his fee, all in Scots money. In 1758 the Kirk Session of Kilninver and Kilmelford, Argyllshire, fixed their Clerk's annual salary at £1 stg., but without any mention of certain extras which normally came his way such as fees for proclamation of marriages, for giving certificates and for extracts of minutes and for registration of marriages, baptisms and burials — one Session Clerk's average annual income in the late eighteenth century for registrations alone came to £1 10s. Scots. There could be payments for extra work when Communion was celebrated, as well as for various other tasks which are mentioned in other chapters. Sometimes a proportion of the fines which came to Sessions from delinquents were allowed to the Clerk: Nigg Kirk Session, Ross-shire, decided in 1707 that their Clerk should have, in addition to various other perquisites, £10 from fines but 'if there be no fines the Clerk is not to get the forsaid ten pounds.' On the island of Lismore, Argyllshire, the Session decided in 1758 that the Clerk's salary should be a quarter of whatever fines came into their hands, as well as half the fees for marriages and baptisms, with no mention of the normal basic annual salary. This system of perquisites and additions allowed a small basic salary to be made up into something worth having, which could in turn help to attract a good schoolmaster to the parish. Even so, basing it on uncertain and fluctuating monies cannot have been satisfactory and was one which could encourage abuse in regard to fines. There is more on this subject elsewhere but it is appropriate to mention here that many Sessions seem to have been happy to leave fines outstanding so that they could be called in when needed and, although this was usually done for the benefit of the poor, on occasion they could be used to make up the Clerk's salary: when Rathven Kirk Session found in 1717 that they had insufficient funds to pay him, they remembered that there were available to them unpaid fines of 'several scandalous persons of the popish persuasion' but it was left to the Clerk 'to pursue them before the judges competent' which seems a very cavalier way of paying a salary. Session Clerks had neither the time, the money nor the authority to pursue legal actions of this sort.[50]

Lack of money afflicted many Kirk Sessions and the Session Clerk of Rathven was by no means the only one who had to wait for his salary. In 1786 Tongue Kirk Session found that they still owed their former Clerk 1½ years' salary — 50s. stg. — 'which they authorised the Moderator to pay as soon as the Sessional funds will enable him' but it was only much later that this promise was even remembered. Less than ten years afterwards that same Session, finding that their funds were very low indeed, decided to reduce the Clerk's money from £1 13s. 4d. stg. to 1 guinea but he was having none of that and appealed successfully to the Presbytery. Kirkwall Session did a similar thing in 1749, although not to the Session Clerk. For some years they had employed one of the town officers to do some church work for which he was paid £5 12s. Scots but that year the Session 'thinking this too much resolved to give him no more than a crown in the year', a five-shilling piece, to which reduction 'the said Hutchinson, being called, agreed.' Kirks employed other staff besides Session Clerks and they too shared in the perquisites that were going, according to whatever was arranged on their engagement — but they were double-edged. Giving them was a benefit but withholding them could be used as a punishment, as happened to a beadle in Kilconquhar who was denied his share of £1 15s. Scots of baptism and marriage money for not doing his work properly. Sharing perquisites with other church staff was always a potential source of disagreement and a wise Session made the position clear at the outset — that if they 'should violate or break or defraud one another, they would be deprived of their office' as one put it, but even when it was clearly laid down what each member of staff was to be allowed, unsatisfactory clauses could be included. This happened at Wick in 1701 when it was left to the Clerk and the kirk officer to divide certain dues between them according to which side of the river each of them lived. In 1863 one Session solved the problem by arranging with the heritors that the kirk officer should be paid a fixed salary of £2 stg. per annum on condition that he waived all claims to a third of the proclamation fees he had been in the habit of receiving and resolved that in future all fees, along with ordinary church collections, up to a joint sum of not over £5 should be the annual salary of the newly appointed parish schoolmaster for acting as Clerk and for precenting in both English and Gaelic.[51] This was, of course, after the passing of the 1845 Poor Law, prior to which these collections would largely have gone to the poor.

So far as fees for marriages and baptisms went, for many years people registered neither. 'They ought to consider that therefore they deprive the session clerk of a very considerable perquisite' was a comment made at the end of the eighteenth century about this but the official fee of 3d. stg. levied at that time by Act of Parliament for such registration, although it was not apparently compulsory, was a lot for ordinary people to find and especially as it inevitably fell at a time of extra expense anyway. When registrations of births, deaths and marriages were put on a regular and compulsory footing by Act of Parliament in 1855, a Registrar was appointed for each parish or district but where church records were already being kept by the Session Clerk — not all parishes were doing so — the Act wisely provided that any Clerk in office at the date of the passing of the Act should become registrar of the parish unless he was unfit or his other duties were not compatible with the office. From all this, it is obvious that the Session Clerk used to be a paid official of Kirk Sessions and not necessarily a member of Session, although he could be one. This has now changed and the present position is that while Session Clerks can be paid officials, they are usually elders undertaking this special task voluntarily. The payments made to various officials for a variety of functions throughout the years appear in appropriate chapters.[52]

From a Kirk Session's point of view, if a man who was already schoolmaster and Session Clerk had a musical talent to put at their disposal, they were only too glad to employ him as precentor to lead the singing in church and, as his teaching salary was usually very low, he was only too thankful to have the opportunity to enhance it in any way he could. Although combining several offices in one man meant that if he left the parish, he was that much more difficult to replace, nevertheless Sessions always tried to ensure that any schoolmaster appointed could also precent. However, much as they wanted to have one man fill several roles, not all good teachers could sing and so precentors often had to be found among non-schoolmasters, although one way round the problem was for the schoolmaster to be appointed precentor and for him to pay someone to precent for him, a form of sub-contracting which, while not common, was not unusual either. An instance of this was when in the mid–1760s a schoolmaster was appointed Session Clerk and precentor in a parish, with a salary of £20 Scots but it was noted in the Session minutes that he had assigned 20 merks of that to Alexander Stronach 'in regard he officiates for him as Precentor'. Something of the sort must have been happening in the parish of Falkirk prior to 1806 as in that year the Session decided to appoint the precentor themselves and to keep £5 stg. per annum off the Clerk's fees 'to support singing in church', a payment which was soon raised to £10 to encourage the church music. By that date it may have been generally more usual for the precentor to be a separate person from the Clerk, perhaps receiving all or part of the marriage and baptism dues as well as a salary which by the beginning of the nineteenth century could be about £2 stg. per annum. In 1874 the precentor in a Borders parish received £15 per year but this was not only for leading congregational singing but also for training the church choir and making public proclamations of marriage, while in a highland parish in 1889 his salary was £10 a year.[53] The modern church organist is a lineal descendant of the precentors of former days. Other church staff for whom the ability to read was an essential qualification were catechists, readers and exhorters who are discussed in other chapters.

A very important person in kirk life was the beadle, a word defined as the church officer attending on the minister. In populated parishes there might be a beadle and one or more kirk officers but as the one person fulfilled both functions in many places, under one or the other name, they are dealt with jointly here. In rural parishes especially, the beadle was very much the minister's man, acting as his handyman, tending his glebe land, critical if he wished to be but loyal and trustworthy, a person with a definite position in the parish and very often a 'character'. While he had no need for literacy, he had to be prepared to turn his hand to anything. Much of his work was in and about the church — when the floor was earthen it had to be watered and once it was floored, it had to be brushed although church cleaning was not then a major task. He had to keep order in church — 'guide the Kirk in right ordour . . . and hold out bairns out of the Kirk, and other things which may hinder God's service', and that included keeping out 'vagabondis' too. He rang the church bell, announced funerals by ringing a hand-bell, and dug graves; he might have to remove crippled strangers from the parish and in the days when kirk discipline was very severe it was often he who kept such things as sackcloth gowns, jougs or branks for the punishment of offenders and, should the church steeple be used as a prison, then he might have charge of it too. The minutes of St. Mary's Church, Dumfries, have a long, long list of rules for beadles which were laid down in 1849. On a happier note, he attended baptisms and weddings and in general carried out any tasks allotted to him, but much of his time was taken up with summoning delinquents or witnesses to appear before the Session. It does seem rather hard on those summoned that they should have to pay for the privilege as was decreed in Montrose in 1642: 'that the Church Officer should have of every person that he shall warn to the Session either scandelers or witnesses, the persons shall pay to the said Kirk Officer 2 shs for every person that he shall happen to warn.'[54]

Because the beadle often lived in a house at the stile leading into the church-yard, he was sometimes referred to as the 'kirkstile', even to the extent that this name may appear in Session records such as those of Greenlaw, Berwickshire, where in the 1730s there were payments 'to kirk stile, his Martinmas [or Whitsunday] shoes, £1 10s. Sc.' The beadle had to do so much work on foot that this was recognised by Sessions who, besides giving him a small fee for each long journey, which might be included in his salary, also allowed him a pair of shoes, summer and winter, as a necessary extra. Even in the 1830s Kilbride Kirk Session, on the island of Arran, provided shoes for their beadle at a cost of 8s. stg. Sometimes a cloak was added to the shoes. This was done at Kilconquhar where 'the gentlemen and elders did give him three dollars to buy him a cloak, because he is an obedient servant to them' but not wanting him to think that a precedent was being established they added, 'but not that he should mak ane use of it, to look for as much at ane uther tyme.' In 1621 a minister and his elders decided that their beadle who, until then, had served the kirk wearing his own clothes, should be given some money to buy a 'clok or juip' (cloak or flannel shirt) in which to do his work. In this particular case it may have been because he was lacking clothing to such an extent that the Session gave him £4 Scots to buy clothes on his promising to take no wages until Lammas the following year, which was fifteen months ahead. In fact, it soon became an annual arrangement to provide his gown and indeed this became common all round the country, though whether as a perquisite or to achieve some sort of uniform is not clear. In 1697 for instance the kirk officers in Inverness were given £8 Scots to buy coats and there too, in 1703, 'Donald Gillmore got a white plaid at the price of 8 merks in part payment of his dues', and the records of city churches such as St. Cuthbert's, Edinburgh, also show clothing provided for their staff.[55] There was also, of course, an annual salary which might be something like £10 Scots in 1645 in Kilconquhar but only 2s. 6d. per quarter in Borgue, Stewartry of Kirkcudbright, about forty years later; by the early eighteenth century it might be £12 Scots or even £20, and in addition he received small fees for keeping mortcloths and the like.[56]

Money was often just as short for paying the beadle as for paying the Session Clerk and in 1802 when one beadle asked to be paid, there was only a little money meant for the poor — 'scanty funds peculiarly and solely the property of the poor', as it was put, and the elders felt that it was up to the heritors and parishioners to find a way of paying him regularly and that this matter should be put before the gentlemen of the parish. Meanwhile the beadle agreed to carry on as he was. What happened in the end was that the Session gave him 15s. stg. per annum themselves but recommended the heritors and tenants to give him, when the spring came and before seed-time, 'the common gift' bestowed on Church of Scotland officers in neighbouring parishes. What the 'common gift' was is not stated but many Sessions expected parishioners to give some victual — grain or meal — to the schoolmaster or the catechist and sometimes to the kirk officer also. In Angus it appears to have been the general practice to give the kirk officer 'as much corn as each person may think fit' and about 1713 Auchterhouse Kirk Session expressed the hope that 'all to whom he might apply would contribute' which meant that if he wanted it, he had to go out and ask for it. The Session minutes of the island parish of Coll, Argyllshire, have the following entry in 1733: 'The Session appoints the ancient custom of giving a cheese to the Bedle together with' (there is a hole in the page here) . . . 'Sheafs should be renewed and observed by all in this country who have any labouring and orders that this be intimated on the next Lord's Day.'[57]

An idea of a beadle's position in kirk and parish life is shown by the fact that when Donald Macleod, one of two beadles in Dornoch in 1721, became 'superannuated' the man engaged to replace him was required to pay Donald 'half the sett salarie and emoluments of the said station.' That a workman should be willing to hand over half his income to his predecessor seems strange to modern ears but it is an indication of how highly that Session regarded their former employee and how valuable the job, even at half-pay, must have been to his successor. In fact, Donald died the following year but the Session continued their special consideration for him by paying 4 merks for his coffin. His immediate successor must have been elderly too as in 1724 the Session appointed the catechist to take over his work and allowed the old man a small sum for his lifetime; and when the catechist died in 1737 they paid for his burial — £6 9s. Scots for 'Coffin, Linnen and Aquavitae etc. for the Interment of John Ross, Kirk Officer.'[58] Another instance of kindness, though on a much lesser scale, to a beadle was shown by Cullen Kirk Session, Banffshire, when they lent him a groat in 1725. Admittedly this was a coin worth only 4d. sterling but Sessions did not normally lend money like that.

The beadle who summoned the people of Tynninghame to church by ringing a hand-bell through the village has already been mentioned and for doing this special service he was given a special payment. On the first page of the minute book was written, 'Nota, that in all the gatherings and collects to the poor, there is the price of ane pint of ale, given to the bellman every Sunday, because of the pains qlk . . . maun take in going thrice about the toon before noon, and once after noon; this custom in giving sae meikle to the bellman has been usit of auld in this parish.' Even once the church bell was hung in 1625 and ringing of the hand-bell through the village stopped, there is no record of this fee being withdrawn and it continued to be paid although the beadle, who was poor, took it in cash rather than in kind.[59]

That man was poor but so long as their salaries and perquisites were paid on time, which most probably were, beadles of those days were generally well paid for the times in which they lived, with a fixed wage and a variety of extras and one Session, whose beadle was often drunk, looked on his failing as 'the effects of too large an income of money from his office.' A minute of Montrose Kirk Session in 1635 which recorded the appointment of a beadle, provided for summary dismissal 'if he be found drunk or misbehaves himself in any point' although in 1782 the beadle in Mauchline was let off with nothing worse than a rebuke after being drunk at a funeral, and there is sometimes an impression that beadles were allowed more rope than other individuals would have been given. In 1716 a Session decided before paying their beadle's fees to inquire about his drinking as he had previously been suspended for this but re-engaged on the understanding that if it happened again he would definitely lose his job, 'be laid aside', as the minutes phrased it, and when he appeared drunk at a funeral this simply could not be overlooked. However, as this episode had occurred some time before the Session meeting when his conduct was being discussed, the Session wondered whether it would not be better to rebuke him themselves rather than to revive the scandal by bringing him before the congregation. It was finally decided that he should be paid for work he had already done but that some of his fee might be witheld meantime to see how he went on and it was made clear to him that although he was being allowed to remain as beadle he was being closely watched. Although not so stated, it seems very probable that alcohol played some part in things when a Hawick beadle, John Scott, went to a fair in Selkirk on Saturday and did not return until the following Monday, leaving the minister to find someone else to perform his Sunday duties. His excuse was that he had fallen sick on the way home, which was probably only too true although the reason for the sickness was not given. In 1724 he was in trouble again, this time for undoubted drunkenness and was ordered to be disciplined, something to which he initially refused to submit but ultimately gave in and appeared before the congregation. Even so, he was allowed to continue in office but with a threat of dismissal hanging over him; and when a Thurso beadle was dismissed in 1804 it was only after a catalogue of offences: he had repeatedly been drunk before breakfast and was considerably in debt to various retailers of spirits and ale who had no prospect of being paid and in addition he had also swindled many poor credulous people of little belongings they had earned by their own hard work. The puzzle is how a church officer had been allowed to carry on in this way for some time.[60] Having said all that, the fact remains that beadles as a whole were a remarkable lot of men but their great days in parish life ended as the church ceased to administer discipline and, with no more need to summon delinquents, three-quarters of their work was gone and it is said that many of them thereafter hung about Justice Courts and others joined the rural police.[61]

Although in many parishes it was the beadle or kirk officer who rang the church bell, in some places there was a separate bell-man, some of whose duties have been mentioned already. He too was normally paid although in 1772 one Session realised that their bell-man had served them well for four years but had been unpaid all that time, apart from a fine which he had received, and it was only then that they decided that he should be given 10s. stg. yearly, to 'conform to the practice of other sessions who generally allow their servants some small salary for their trouble.' A casual attitude towards their bell-man was shown by a Session when they distributed money to the poor but kept back 'a few pence of bad copper' and gave it to him, but he was probably only too grateful to have this paltry addition to his wage. Even when fees were not shared, they might just not be given and when a bell-man complained in 1758 that he got 'no justice for his dues from the parish', in other words, the special fees to which he was entitled, his Session fell back on the system already referred to: 'It was enacted by the Session in presence of so many of the tenants that he and his successors in office is to have half a peck oatmeal payable by every merkland' (a piece of land, originally valued at one merk) 'of this parish yearly.' Oatmeal, even if he had to go and get it himself, must have been far more acceptable than bad copper.[62]

While these various members of church staff were subject to the supervision of their Sessions and to their censure in the event of bad conduct, to be an elder was sufficient to lay oneself open to ready criticism, even when it might not be justified. When an elder named Donald Robson had a violent quarrel with another man, in no time at all a 'scandalous report was passing through the town regarding the unsuitable carriage of the two men.' One can just imagine the tittle-tattle that would fly around about such a matter and it was soon reported to the Session, whose investigations showed that there had indeed been a quarrel but that the other man was the chief offender and he was ordered to ask the pardon of God, the Session and Donald Robson, and both he and Donald were ordered to be on their guard against such behaviour in future and to be friends with one another. An elder's public conduct obviously mattered very much and one was suspended in 1697 for playing football on Fastern's E'en and then deposed altogether for playing at the wheel of fortune in the public market. Because of the standards expected of an elder, when any of them got into financial trouble they could be very hardly treated by the general public and in 1710 there was a particularly sad case at Inchinnan, Renfrewshire. Robert Hall, although a most estimable man, got into debt with his landlord and lost all he had. He left the parish in such disgrace that he felt he could only return in secret and, being a man who could not live happily without attending worship, he disguised himself in women's clothes to do so. He normally went to a different church from the one he had formerly attended but one day he felt a great desire to go to his old kirk at Inchinnan; but as he crossed a ferry, the boatman and a beadle were suspicious that this 'woman' might really be a man and he was traced to the church and the minister told. The minister proposed to speak privately to Robert but a Justice of the Peace arrived at that point and had to be told what was going on and called for an examination of the woman/man. Robert admitted the truth but asked to be taken to his former minister whom he said would know him. The minister did know him and protected him for the rest of the day to spare him the rudeness of the mob and the following day he was taken to Renfrew and allowed to go in peace; but for an ex-elder to be reduced to such shifts just for falling on hard times, makes pathetic reading. And it was the same for deacons; they too could be struck off, although one in St. Andrews, rather like the Thurso beadle, was only removed after many offences — non-attendance at church, disobedience to the magistrates and not paying his debts.[63]

Some parishes allowed their elders special privileges such as free use of the parish mortcloth for their burials, something which happened widely, and some allowed free ringing of the church bell at their funerals also. In these instances it could be said that it was the elders' relatives who benefited by not having to pay the charges on an elder's death but there were other cases where living elders were given special consideration. Whereas anyone applying for regular help from a Session because of poverty would have their circumstances thoroughly investigated and would be expected to bequeath their effects to the Session, the following case shows a completely different attitude. In 1775 the Kirk Session of Banff considered the position of James Todd who had been an elder for about twenty years but who had been unable to work for several years because of disease. He was regarded as a truly respectable man and indeed this must have been so for, rather than be a burden on others, he had managed to live so far on what he had, even to the extent of selling his looms and other working equipment, and even his furniture too. The Session felt it incumbent upon them 'to make the remainder of his life as comfortable as possible and therefore appoint the minister to take care that his wants be duly supplied.' This was kind and Christian of the Session but normally any poor person receiving such help had to go on to the paupers' roll with all the invidiousness that that involved. An entry in the records of St. Vigeans Kirk Session in 1733 seems to indicate something similar:

> To Jannet Monny's monthly pension £2
> To William Arnott, an old man once an elder, £3.

Jannet was receiving a regular allowance and was therefore on the poor roll while the ex-elder appears to have received a straight donation. For some unspecified reason, Robert Wishart, a Kirkcaldy elder, was the subject of a recommendation for charity from the Presbytery of Kinross in 1706 and one parish, Portmoak, alone gave 40s. Scots for his benefit. In 1712 the whole of one Sunday's church collection in a parish was given to hire a horse for a Mr Davidson who was preaching there during a vacancy, because it was the 'busie time of the sowing of the seid'. Considering that, and as Sessions would buy horses to set up poor people as carriers, it seems reasonable enough that a horse could be bought for an elder in need and this certainly happened, although in a case in Kilconquhar in 1741 it was made clear that the animal which had cost three guineas was to remain the property of the Session. Kirk Sessions often made a contract with a wright to supply coffins for the poor at a fixed price but one does suspect that a bit of favouritism may have crept in when that of Selkirk made an agreement in the late 1720s with one of the elders that he should have a monopoly of coffin-making for the poor.[64]

Elders were not paid but an occasional one expected perquisites which were more commonly those of church staff, and James Russell in his *Reminiscences of Yarrow* says that when his father first went as minister to the parish of Ettrick, Selkirkshire, in 1790, his one and only elder, Robert Hogg, father of the Ettrick Shepherd, came to him at the first Martinmas to say that Mr Potts, the previous minister, had always allowed him 5*s.* at that time of year for 'gathering the bawbees' so that he might buy a pair of shoes. Whether this was true or merely a try-on upon a new minister is not known but in any case his attempt to get this particular benefit was refused. Good though elders were, there were inevitably some bad ones who had to be deposed for worse things than playing football or enjoying the wheel of fortune — for such things as intemperance or 'bad conversation heretofore and now found customary swearers', both of which were common enough vices; but one who showed violence to the minister, even at Session meetings, must have been unique. However, John Ross in the parish of Kincardine, Ross-shire, was one such, repeatedly and openly insulting the minister at these meetings and on one occasion aiming a blow at him which finally got the rest of the elders to order him to appear before the Presbytery to confess his sin, as a result of which he had to appear before the congregation in sackcloth. Two elders in Portmoak, Kinross-shire, found themselves in trouble with their Session in 1788 for not attending Session meetings nor taking up Sunday collections as they should have done, upon which they 'replied that they could not be edified by the minister's preaching and that, therefore, their consciences would not allow them to discharge their duties as elders in this society.' This reason appears to have been given in all sincerity and humility but the other elders did not consider it adequate and suspended them. These few examples are given, of course, not to show a poor standard in the eldership but, through the fact that they were exceptions, to prove the rule of a high standard.[65]

Gradually, however, the authority of Kirk Sessions diminished, a process started in 1733 by the first secession from the established church and continued by a second one in 1761. Each of these loosened the control of the kirk over those who seceded and as kirk discipline began to relax in any case, there was much less work for Sessions to do. G.D. Henderson says in *The Scottish Ruling Elder* that by 1826 the General Assembly found many parishes with practically no elders and holding no Session meetings. The parish of Dalserf, Lanarkshire, had no regular Session for nearly fifty years before 1812 and Ballingry, Fife, appears to have had practically no Session during the first half of the nineteenth century. This gave ministers a free hand but it was not Presbyterian. During the early nineteenth century, too, representatives were often not appointed to attend Presbytery or Synod, or else did not bother to go, but the controversies which led to the Disruption in 1843 and the formation of the Free Church, the biggest secession of them all, succeeded in rousing the country to fresh interest in church matters. In 1845 a legal blow was struck at the duties of the church in the form of the Poor Law passed that year, although it was not intended as such; it was simply meant to be a measure to relieve the established church of the care of the poor, a burden which had become too great for it although some Kirk Sessions continued to do this work until 1894. The Poor Law greatly reduced the caring role of elders and their need to raise money, with a consequent effect on their former active purpose. In 1872 the Education Act removed elementary education from kirk supervision and there was then little left for Sessions to do in comparison with what they had formerly done. They still cared for the fabric of both church and manse and dealt with church expenses, something with which congregational boards now assist. They supervised graveyards but even these slipped out of their hands with the Burial Grounds Act of 1855 and amending Acts from 1857 onwards and major changes in 1929 and 1947; now graveyards are controlled by District Councils while churches have become the property of the General Trustees of the Church of Scotland, something which happened in 1925. The Church of Scotland as a whole still plays a part in education and runs the largest voluntary social work programme in the country but that is operated from Edinburgh and not by local Kirk Sessions.

But that is moving far ahead and for many years after the Reformation, Sessions not only cared for church buildings, engaged kirk staff and undertook the responsibilities already mentioned but also coped with a very wide range of social work, or work with social effects, which is often forgotten or overlooked.

2

The Poor's Money

As far back as 1424, well before the Reformation, vagrants and beggars were such a problem that the Scottish Parliament passed an Act that year restricting begging to those unable to work, although it was only in 1503 that those 'unable to work' were defined as people who were 'crooked', blind, impotent or weak[1] but unfortunately this did not include other genuine cases of need such as widows with young families, orphans, foundlings, the insane and those whose circumstances suddenly changed owing to some disaster or other. The care of the poor became such a major matter that it had to be faced and of all the many social duties taken on by the kirk, the first statutory one imposed on it by law was this one.

It was in 1574, just fourteen years after the Reformation, that an Act of Parliament was passed which directly involved the church in this work.[2] Its main provisions were that elders and deacons of towns and the head men of landward parishes were required to prepare a yearly roll of all old, poor and unfit people who had been born or who had lived in the parish for seven years; any others were to be sent back to their own parishes; a weekly contribution or collection was to be apportioned for the poor from among the parishioners and if neither money nor victual — food — could be collected in this way, then the poor should be given licences to beg round the houses. Those of the poor who refused to remain where they were told to be, or to work if they were able to do so, were to be punished as vagrants; and beggars' children between 5 and 14 years of age were to be taken into service, males until they were 24 years old and females until they were 18. This last condition was really an early form of the boarding-out system, although extended to such an age that it could be regarded as forced labour or even as slavery. In 1579, however, another Act of Parliament which referred primarily to beggars, also provided for the poor but withdrew their supervision in towns from elders and deacons and transferred it to the provost and bailies, and in landward parishes to justices appointed by the king. The emphasis on *landward* parishes is important as, in burghs, Town Councils and trade guilds undertook much of the care of the poor. That Act was ratified in 1581 but in 1592 Judges Ordinary were ordered to appoint deputies and, failing them, ministers, elders and deacons in each parish were to elect persons as justices and commissioners to enforce the Act and so Kirk Sessions were once again involved, albeit only indirectly, through appointing those who were to carry out the Act. There was another change in 1597 when a wide-ranging Act was passed, the execution of which was given entirely to Kirk Sessions, to such an extent that three years later a further Act ordered a penalty of £20 Scots to be exacted from them in the event of their neglecting these matters, with Presbyteries required 'to take trial' of them concerning it.[3]

Yet another Act was passed in 1617 but it was in 1649 that one of more importance to Sessions came into being. 'In consideration of the number of indigent persons exposed to great misery through the want of a general and orderly way of entertainment' — that being the word used to describe what would now be called maintenance — it was 'ordained that each Presbytery and parish entertain their own native poor', with lists of them to be made up twice a year. How this was to be financed was laid down and it was decreed that when alms were distributed, distinction should be made between 'the pious and the vicious', vicious in this sense meaning those addicted to bad habits rather than its more violent modern interpretation, and elders were to see that beggars who were well able to work were apprehended and made to do so. Begging from house to house, which had been allowed before, was forbidden by this Act although begging with permission later on became, as will be seen, an accepted way of enabling the poor to help themselves. In 1672 an Act which sought to establish Correction Houses reduced the residential qualification of the poor from the seven years stated in 1574 to three, but all these Acts, while laying a foundation for future action, were more or less unworkable at the time that they were passed and at the end of the seventeenth century the country was over-run with vagrants and beggars, largely owing to civil wars and Covenanting troubles. In 1698 Parliament ratified all these former Acts and in 1701 ordered the heritors of each parish to confer with their Kirk Sessions regarding care of the poor, making clear that there was a joint responsibility.[4] As Rev. J. Headrick, writer of the *General View of the Agriculture of Angus* put it, the heritors were responsible for maintaining paupers but it was Kirk Sessions who were their factors. In parishes where heritors lived locally, they did meet with Sessions and the poor's records were duly submitted to them but this certainly did not apply in all areas and the everyday work of poor relief fell to Sessions, except in burghs where, as has been said, other bodies shared in it. It was on this basis that the Kirk Sessions of the Church of Scotland cared for the poor of the country until this duty was removed from them by the passing of the Poor Law Amendment Act in 1845 although, in some cases, they were still concerned with it until 1894.

Although Fletcher of Saltoun declared in 1698 that the poor were 'very meanly provided by the church boxes'[5] this was said during a time not only of very severe famine but just as the Church of Scotland was getting onto its feet. More fairly, it was said of the kirk's management of the poor's money that 'No funds in this island are more frugally or conscientiously managed than the poor's funds in Scotland'[6], although it is a pity that the word 'conscientiously' does not come before 'frugally' as that would be fairer to the Sessions who worked so hard to care for the poor, because it was also said of them that 'Never perhaps, will Scotland find a more proper jury to determine the objects of public charity, nor the quantum necessary to supply it.'[7]

The poor were maintained out of the parish poor's funds which were raised in a whole variety of ways which are described in another chapter. Although the church's general income was loosely referred to as the poor's money and kept in the poor's box, and was meant by law to be used for the poor, a good proportion of it had to be used for other expenses such as payment of kirk officials, expenses to do with the kirk, various Presbytery dues and sometimes the parish school. Although Communion elements were not meant to be paid for out of the poor's money, they might be charged to it or the money meant for the poor might be used to pay for such items as Communion tables which could be expensive enough to oblige a Session to stop distributing the poor's money for the time being[8] and as the kirk's activities became wider, so money was sent further afield. In 1828, for example, the following sums were sent by an Angus Session for the Schemes of the General Assembly:

Church extension at home	£1	– 8
Education in the Highlands	1	4 8
Colonial churches	–	17 8
Mission in India	1	2 3
	£4	5 3[9]

By that date, kirk income in general had risen sufficiently for there to be something to spare for work outside the parish but in earlier days when funds were always short, what Sessions achieved with the little they had was remarkable, although admittedly standards and expectations were low. How otherwise could parishes like Rerrick, in the Stewartry of Kirkcudbright, and Edzell in Angus, have always found their funds adequate for the poor, as stated in their Old Statistical Accounts? That of Edzell says that interest on a sum of money and church-door collections managed to 'maintain the poor in such a way as not only to be free of complaint, but to give full satisfaction to themselves, and to those who live around them.'[10] In fact, the poor found that they were treated much more severely under the Poor Law of 1845 than by the all-embracing and often imaginative ways in which their Sessions had formerly coped with them, although that is not to say that Sessions did not have to be strict. With limited funds they had to be.

A break-down of 64 names on the list of the poor in the Argyllshire parish of Kilninian and Kilmore in 1768 shows that 37 of those named had very specific needs. With the spelling given as in the minutes, these were:

A mother with three orphans	1 old and bedridden
1 epileptical	1 bedridden and poor
1 lunatick	1 old and arthritick
A natural	1 old and blind
A child ideotical and an orphan	3 old and infirm
1 paralytick	1 very old and poor
A woman with a lame child	1 old and poor
3 cripples	8 infirm
4 bedridden	1 deserving object,

the word 'object' or 'object of charity' being a common term for the very poor. Shocking though this list is, it was not out of the way for the times and although nowadays all sorts of bodies would be called upon to help with such varied cases, at that date there was only the church to whom to turn and the local kirk did what it could for them, which was to allow them sums varying from 1s. to 3s. 6d. sterling per year which was the least and the most they could do to try to make life tolerable.

With the cause of the poverty of 37 out of these 64 stated, that means that there were still 27 other paupers in that parish with no reason given for their condition, but there could be many grounds for it. Writing in 1825 of his own parish of Kirriemuir, Angus, Rev. Thomas Easton said in his *Statements relative to the Pauperism of Kirriemuir*, that drunkenness was by far and away the main cause and this is confirmed by comments made about Prestonpans, East Lothian, in the mid-nineteenth century: 'To a very great extent, it [pauperism] may be traced to the sale of ardent spirits on the Sabbath, and the many evil habits that ensue from that vicious practice.' In the month just before that was written, the third lunatic in two years had been 'cast upon the poors funds, and in each of these lamentable cases the origin was excessive drinking on the Lord's Day — because of the cessation of toil, enjoyment of wages [too generally paid on the Saturday night] and the open sale of alcohol at all hours on the Sabbath day.'[11] Yet to give a different view of alcohol and poverty, some fifty years earlier in the parish of Straiton, Ayrshire, it was said that the decline of smuggling, in this context meaning illegal distilling, had brought several families who had formerly lived well to great poverty so that the number of paupers was expected to increase;[12] and there seems to be a note of regret for the days when distilling itself, or growing the grain to supply it, could support people and thereby save the poor's money.

According to Mr Easton, the next most common cause for pauperism was providence, by which he meant physical or mental handicap, and then old age and infirmity. This he followed with widows and orphans. Mortality was high and the death of a father, particularly common in seafaring communities, let alone that of a mother, could leave very great hardship if a very young family remained and when both parents died, leaving children 'doubly orphaned', then things were even worse. War obviously added to this problem and in addition left a legacy of maimed or disabled men. Illegitimate children were also listed as a reason; they presented a particular problem because Kirk Sessions never wished it to be thought that any aid they gave to the mother might be construed as countenancing vice. Every effort was always made to find the father so that he could be made to take responsibility but if he could not be located, then a sensible Session would get round the problem by giving 'a little temporary supply to mothers to prevent starvation or further crime.' To put flesh on the bones of that statement, the minutes of one Session show what happened when a girl with an illegitimate baby got into a state of great destitution, with her condition becoming daily more and more deplorable. The Session did not wish to call a special meeting of heritors about her case — making special arrangements about her could be considered to be giving tacit approval — but they arranged that food and lodging for her and the child should be found, albeit at the lowest possible rate, until the next regular meeting of heritors was due and the whole matter could be properly discussed. They realised that if help was to be given in certain cases, it must be given at once if it was to be of any use, and given in a spirit of compassion and common-sense.[13]

Yet another fairly common reason for pauperism was runaway husbands — married men who joined the army and did not return — and bigamous marriages, where girls had married soldiers quartered for a time in the area without knowing enough about them. Early marriage produced problems too. Although many apprenticeships were long and weddings delayed until they were completed, a comparatively easily-learnt skill, such as the weaving of brown linen, meant that a young man could be expert by the age of fifteen or sixteen and could marry early and, in the way of the times, soon have a large family. All was well unless one or other parent died young, which was only too common, or if the man's particular trade went into decline or if there was a famine which, also, was all too common and which pushed up the cost of food, something which of course affected all classes when it happened. Accidents from falls, injury caused by animals, from machinery and tools and 'general calamities' such as epidemics and 'personal calamities' such as outbreaks of fire were all additional reasons for people to fall into poverty or to turn existing poverty into destitution.[14] All of these were genuine causes of poverty but there were others which Mr Easton did not mention, perhaps because his report was addressed to a principal heritor of the parish who, as a landowner, might have been touchy about them. By the time he wrote his *Statements*, small farms were being amalgamated into large ones, with a consequent reduction in the number of sub-tenants. Fewer farms to let meant higher rents to pay and what had formerly been common land was by then largely enclosed and divided up among the heritors, something which caused great hardship to those who had relied on it for grazing their few beasts and for getting fuel. The lime trade which had formerly fitted in well with the small farm system and had given a lot of work in certain areas, was not compatible with large farms and so this work could be lost locally, although lime was still prepared in many places.[15] Coastal parishes had the problems caused by boom-and-bust fishing years and all round the country additional local problems could contribute to pauperism.

Making up a yearly list of the poor, provided for in some of the Acts of Parliament already mentioned, was preparing a paupers' or poor's roll and anyone needing regular assistance from the kirk had to be admitted to this roll although temporary help could be given without the necessity to become a formal pauper or, as they were called in some parishes, a pensioner. During much of the time that the kirk undertook the care of the poor, a large part of the population was living at subsistence level and to be officially classed as a pauper meant being below that level — desperately, grindingly poor, quite different from the modern definition of poverty. It was normally however only when sickness, handicap or old age were added to poverty that people were admitted to the roll, an attitude which, although understandable when funds were small, did not allow for the fact that poverty begets ill-health which, in turn, begets further poverty. People in need, and it had to be real need, applied to their Kirk Sessions either for temporary relief or for admission to the roll. Once on the roll, maintenance of paupers was an obligation on the Kirk Session and they qualified for a share in the distribution of the poor's money but, on the other hand, if they were refused admission there was no way they could appeal against such a decision. In the first half of the nineteenth century, a woman in the Black Isle, Ross-shire, who had been deserted by her husband, appealed to her Session for help and a committee of elders was sent to see what her circumstances were and 'after a minute scrutiny' all that they found in the house was enough grain for one meal and a very few potatoes. This convinced them that she really was in great poverty and they allowed her to be admitted to the roll at 3s. stg. per week. Such a detailed scrutiny was perhaps exceptional but the idea of having the elders of the kirk poking through one's pathetic empty larder gives an idea of the humiliation that a poor person might have to endure rather than starve. At that particular time that parish had a total income of some £25 per year and some 32 paupers to care for, which explains why it was necessary to check people's circumstances very carefully so as to conserve their funds for those in real need. It was certainly better than what happened in St. Andrews back in 1597. That year the Session decreed that should anyone in the town ask for alms, they should be apprehended and put in the thieves' hole until 'tryell be takin of thair esteat.'16

It was usual for each Session, with any heritors who chose to attend, to meet after due public intimation on one day in the year for what was really a business meeting. In some counties the Justices of the Peace passed an Act requiring such meetings.17 The accounts were gone over and the poor's roll made up and checked, with names added or deleted as appropriate and finances worked out. The principle on which parish aid was given is variously summed up: 'Care is taken not to encourage idleness and no more is given to the necessitous than what, with the exertion of their own industry, will support them'; 'There is no encouragement given to idleness whilst none are allowed to starve'; or the statement that the object is 'not to encourage idleness but to enable those barely to live who cannot live without an addition to what they can gain by their labour.'[18] The able-bodied poor were expected to work for their living, something for which there was considered to be good Scriptural warrant: 'For even during our stay with you we laid down the rule: the man who will not work shall not eat', which St. Paul said in his Second Letter to the Thessalonians. This 'work or want' attitude explains the unfortunate phrase in the minutes of one Kirk Session that two women were 'to be scraped out of the Poor's Roll in regard they can fend for themselves.'[19] In the same way, lists of the poor can have comments alongside their names, such as the following ones written in pencil and presumably added by the minister or Session Clerk after the roll was made up: 'Able to work'; 'Offered 6d. a day for work'; 'Have an able family'; 'Stout [fit] person living with her'; 'Should not receive — has an able family'.[20] Another poor's list has the comment 'All these can work' written alongside six names which meant that those people must expect nothing from the poor's funds and a very unusual entry, therefore, is the one where money was given to 'Susan Wilson being out of employment and so in want of support'[21] but there was probably more to it than the minute says and possibly she was off work owing to illness or injury. This blanket attitude of not supporting anyone able to work perhaps caused some qualms; why otherwise would a Session have felt it necessary to minute in 1781 that they were satisfied 'with the propriety of giving so much money to the greatest objects in the parish, while sturdy vigorous beggars or the poor that were able to work received none'?[22] It is worth noting however that some Sessions tried to see that people took up such benefit as they were entitled to: the deacons who took turns at collecting at the church doors on Sundays in Montrose in the 1650s were also ordered to 'use diligence to search through the parish who are neidful persons that they may be supplied.'[23]

At this time there were no national funds to support the poor; anything raised for them was found within the parish and it was understandably felt that funds should only be used for the native parish poor entitled to them, as this minute shows: 'The Session observing that several poor families have of late come from other parishes and settled in this, resolve that they would give none of the poor's money towards their maintenance as it was an injustice done to those born in the place or who had spent a considerable part of their time in it.'[24] The residential qualification already referred to — originally seven years but reduced in 1672 to three, which it remained for as long as the kirk was in charge of poor relief — was designed as both protection and compulsion to Sessions in this work. The compulsion element of the ruling was designed to cover those who moved from place to place, by obliging any parish to give them relief so long as they had established a legal residence of three years although the three years did not require to have been immediately preceding the application for assistance. What could happen was that someone lived in a parish for that length of time, then moved on but never thereafter stayed anywhere long enough to establish a new legal settlement, so that when they needed help in the parish where they by then were, they did not qualify for it. In such a case, if help was given it was reclaimed from the legal parish. A case of this sort befell the Kirk Session of Dingwall in 1843 when a letter arrived from the office of Edinburgh Charity Workhouse to the Session Clerk concerning a 'very interesting, well behaved young woman' who was 'almost quite blind and has to be led.' For the previous few months she had been receiving help from the parish of the City of Edinburgh but, said the letter, 'it is evident that she has never required a Parish claim since she left Dingwall and therefore we charge that parish for her aliment' — and that was ten years after she had left there. The letter made it clear that great efforts had been made to establish her legal parish, from which it emerged that she had lived with her father, a pensioner of the 78th Regiment, in Dingwall for about sixteen years until 1833, then went to work in Glasgow for eighteen months, to Edinburgh for two or three months, to Dumfries for a further three, to Portobello for a short while, to Duddingston for six months and to Aberdeenshire for a further six, by which time she was in bad health. She was in Edinburgh Infirmary for some time before November 1840, then moved back north to Ross-shire, but came south again to Edinburgh in 1841 and then moved out of the capital to service for a while. From July to September 1842 she was again in the Infirmary and it was then that she applied for relief because of her health and blindness and £3 8s. was spent on her care which, once it was established that Dingwall was her only legal residence, was demanded from that Kirk Session along with an undertaking to support her in Edinburgh.[25] The effect of a totally unexpected demand of this sort coming out of the blue to any Session may be imagined but, while Dingwall had to pay up, the many other parishes where this young woman had stayed briefly were protected from a claim.

The distinction which the Act of Parliament of 1649 required to be made between the pious and the vicious when distributing alms has already been mentioned but it was a practice well in existence before the passing of that Act and well used after it too. The most obvious form of piety that could be ordered and shown was attendance at worship and although one writer says that elders made the poor attend church out of concern for their spiritual welfare and that attendance was not a condition for receiving relief,[26] that was not so. A variety of early Sessional decrees from all round the country show that there was a form of religious test for the poor: in St. Andrews in 1570 it was ordained that those who received relief should attend sermons, prayers, examination and Communion unless they could produce an adequate reason for absence and also that they should either be able to repeat the Lord's Prayer, the Creed and the Commandments or agree to learn them within a month. In Elgin in 1596 paupers were ordered to appear one day so that they could be ordered to 'haunt and remane' within the church on Sundays and not go begging on the roads 'under pain of being put off the roll' but there must have been doubts about how effective this was as, the following year, it was decided that the deacons, along with a bailie and another man, should meet in the church after every Wednesday weekday sermon and call the poor before them to 'try them' about their attendance at worship and morning and evening prayers and about their general behaviour the previous week. The same thing was happening in Perth around that date. Those who distributed the poor's money were told to order paupers to come to church on Sundays and on weekdays and to sit in St.

Catherine's Aisle where they could be easily seen and any absentees noted and excluded from receiving alms, although this did not apply to the sick or infirm. It was the same in Aberdeen where in 1620 the deacons who gave relief to the poor had to tell them to attend catechising but, rather as had happened earlier in Elgin, this had to be followed up the next year by clear instructions to those on the poor's roll that, among other things, they had to attend worship daily, come to catechising every Monday and be 'tried' to ensure that they were doing so; and in addition any of them found swearing would lose their pensions for the week.[27] Montrose Kirk Session records have a rather ambiguous entry for 1642, that the poor should stand outside the church stile on Sundays before sermon and not come near those taking up the collection. It seems likely that what this meant was that they should wait there without demanding alms from the collectors until the service began, rather than that they were to remain outside throughout it. Although later Session minutes hardly ever mention that church attendance was required of paupers, they do use wording like 'Godly poor people', 'the pious poor', or 'the poor fearing the Lord', and it seems very possible that church attendance was still a condition of receiving assistance and was perhaps so normal that it went without saying. For instance, entries in Kirkwall's Kirk Session minutes in the 1720s about the admission of people to the poor's roll, say nothing about any necessity to go to church, yet in July 1731 there is this entry:

> This day there was a petition given in by Anna Moir lately one of the pensioners whose pension was abstracted because of her not attending the ordinances, craves that she may again be enrolled. The Session allows her this Lambmass quarter as formerly wt certification that if she does not attend ordinances for the future, when she is ease to walk abroad, that it will again be abstracted.

In 1734 a Presbytery recommended to a Kirk Session that a couple who would not submit to discipline should be regarded as contumacious and scandalous persons and 'not capable of receiving any church benefit' until they gave in. While this decree certainly referred to church privileges such as baptism and attending the Lord's Supper, the wording may imply that this covered kirk relief also.[28] Unsuitable behaviour of any sort could also cause a pauper's name to be removed from the roll and one would love to know the nature of 'a number of shameful, obscene and libellous songs or poems' which were the downfall of a Lauder man, John Halliday, in 1832.[29]

Because of the legal residence ruling, every effort was made to see that poor short-term residents whom it was thought might in time apply for admission to the poor's roll, did not settle in the parish for long enough to be able to do so, which was in accordance with the Acts of both 1574 and 1649. Very much later a Session became worried about a woman who 'had already been about two years here and would soon by her residence become a burden on the parish as she had no visible [means of support] for the sustenance of herself and her children.'[30] The problem could be solved in various ways, the first of which was by trying to prevent them coming in in the first place, as happened in St. Andrews in 1640 where a man was paid 'viij s weekly and a new stand of grey clothes zeirlie' for keeping strangers out. Another was to make things difficult for them if they did get in: Falkirk Kirk Session forbade all parishioners to give help of any kind to vagrant strangers even when they offered to pay for it. Yet another answer was to put them out or otherwise ensure that they would not become a burden on the local kirk: in 1649 the magistrates, minister and some of the elders of Montrose arranged a general visitation of the town, firstly to find out which of the native poor needed help but also to see to it that any poor people who had neither been born nor brought up in the town and who had no way of supporting themselves, either left or else found surety that they would not become a charge on the poor's funds.[31] An order to leave could be very hard on such people, as a 'decrepit' Irish woman found, who begged to be allowed to remain where she was 'during the dead of the year' but was nevertheless made to go. In 1773 Hawick Kirk Session and some of the heritors ordered several people in a similar position to remove themselves and their families at the following Whitsunday unless they could produce an undertaking from their parish of legal residence to support them in case of need, and the parish officers were told to inform these people's landlords about this and to make it clear to them that if houses were let to such persons without their producing the required obligation, then the landlords would be held liable for all such expenses as might be incurred by having or keeping them in the parish. Just how legal this particular action was is doubtful but it was probably effective in a small parish. As late as 1823 the Session and heritors of Greenlaw met 'to take steps to prevent strangers acquiring residence in the parish and becoming burdensome to it' and in 1841 a committee of heritors and Session was appointed to examine the roll of people who had come into that parish, with powers to do anything necessary to prevent them becoming a drain on the parish. In neither case, however, is what they did about the problem known.[32] That church and burghs co-operated in this matter is clear from the poor's accounts to be found at the end of the minute book of Blackfriars, the College Parish, Kirk Session in Glasgow, for 1797–1807. One section is entitled a 'List of Poor Persons, who have been examined, and warned away by the Magistrates in the Police Office, as not being three years in the town, also such as did not appear to be examined in 1802.' This list covers several years and gives the parish from which each person came and where they were then living. One can see the kirk's side of this: it was the law and funds had to be saved for those most entitled to receive them; but the pauper's view of things must have been quite different. In 1827 Widow McAlister, who was not a native of the parish of West Kilbride, Ayrshire, applied to the Session there for charity only to have the heritors recommend them to tell her that she would not be relieved in any way out of their funds, adding that they 'expressed their complete satisfaction with the conduct of the Kirk Session generally and, in particular, returned them their best thanks for their prudent management of the poor's funds.' That was all very well for the heritors but it did not help poor Widow McAlister. When she came before a later meeting of the Session she said that she did not want to leave the parish but neither did she wish to become chargeable on the poor's funds, whereupon she was told to write to the minister of Skipness where she had previously lived, asking him to let the West Kilbride minister know if his Session would support her, otherwise West Kilbride would have to remove her to her own parish or take measures to secure themselves against all liability for her support.[33] That seems particularly severe and an altogether kindlier attitude was shown to Widow O'Leary who asked a different Session for aliment for herself and her infant and, although this had to be refused on the grounds that she had no legal residence she was still given a generous gift of 10s. stg. Two or three months later, that same Session was asked by a widow for travelling expenses so that her two children could go to the care of her brother-in-law in Ireland, saying that if this were done she would not be a burden on the Parochial Board, newly-formed under the 1845 Poor Law. The Board would not have paid such costs but the Kirk Session did and kindly added £1 for clothing.[34]

An easy way out for an unmarried mother was to dump her child on its grandparents but this made things very difficult for them if they lived in a different parish from her and needed assistance to care for it. In 1789 a man had to ask his Session for help for a child which his daughter 'had left upon him' while she took a post as a wet nurse. They considered that it was up to her to care for it herself or at least pay for its care out of the wages she received but also pointed out that although she was born in that parish, she now lived in an adjoining one where the child had been begotten. Even so, they tempered justice with mercy and gave the old man 2s. stg. for the child's support although they hoped that this money would be repaid by the other parish.[35] A case which seems very distressing for the applicant happened in 1826. The wife of a labourer from Saltcoats in the parish of Ardrossan, Ayrshire who, by the very nature of her husband's job, would have been living on a minimum income, came to West Kilbride Kirk Session to say that about six months before, her stepdaughter had smuggled an illegitimate child into her house and had immediately left the parish of Ardrossan and no one knew for certain where she was, nor the name of the child's father. Nevertheless, as the child had been born in the parish of West Kilbride, she asked the Session to undertake its maintenance but this was refused on the grounds that the child's mother, before coming to West Kilbride

> had by a three years' residence become legally entitled to a Parochial settlement with all the advantages arising therefrom in the parish of Ardrossan and had not subsequently resided long enough in this parish to entitle her to the same privileges here . . . It was moreover pointedly stated to Deponent that there could not exist a plausible pretext for settling this parish with the burden of maintaining the child, as the law fixes the maintenance of an illegitimate child on the parish in which the mother had previously obtained a legal settlement by a residence of three years, in all cases where the father of the child is unknown.'[36]

The to-ing and fro-ing which cases could involve, and the anxiety to recoup sums which seem pitifully small to modern ideas, show how vitally important this matter of legal residence was to poor's funds. When a young woman, Jean Girvan, applied to West Kilbride Session in 1832 saying that she was pregnant, destitute of every necessity and had recently been put out of her lodgings, the Session agreed to pay her board and lodging for one night so as to provide for her immediate needs but decided that she should then be returned to her own parish of Kilmarnock, which was done. However, the next month a letter came from Rev. George Smith of Kilmarnock to say that this action had been illegal as the alleged father of the child belonged to West Kilbride, and as her inability to support herself arose solely from pregnancy, it was West Kilbride which was bound to maintain her and the child, making a claim against the father if he could be found. West Kilbride Kirk Session decided to resist all efforts to make them support either mother or child until they could discover whether they were bound to do so as she was definitely not one of their parishioners and because it was uncertain whether or not the man she named as father would accept responsibility. Mr Smith wanted West Kilbride to pay the expense of keeping Jean in Kilmarnock for a few days and returning her to West Kilbride but that parish countered this with a claim for 4s. 6d. sterling which had been the cost of keeping her for the original one night, and sending her to Kilmarnock. Several months later, after Jean's child was born, she was in West Kilbride and again asking for help, accusing a young man there of being the father, but the Session refused her request, on the grounds that if the parents could not support the child, then it was the mother's parish which was legally bound to do so.[37]

In cases where repayment of money spent was absolutely resisted, it was sometimes necessary to go to law. This happened in 1752 in Coldingham where the Session minutes show that the Session Clerk was appointed to go to Greenlaw to hear the Interlocution 'anent getting our parish relieved of the burden of Grissel Orock's bastard child', but it must have been very disconcerting, to say the least, for a Session to be on the receiving end of such a legal enforcement and when in 1772 Heriot Kirk Session refused the application of that of Stow to relieve them of the support of a widow and her family, that Session, in accordance with a recommendation of the heritors, decided to prosecute the minister and Session of Heriot before the Sheriff.[38]

While some of those ordered to leave a parish were physically able to go when told to do so, they would have to pass through one or more parishes *en route* for home and that could be expensive for those parishes. Nevertheless, the policy had to be, Speed them on their way, and entries like 'By forwarding travellers 2s.' or 'Assisting a vagrant to get to Aberdeen 6s. 8d.' or money spent on 'two cart load of women in great distress going to Fala'[39] do not indicate lifts kindly provided by Sessions but were all part of pushing them out of the parish and on to the next. Even so, wording often shows compassion, with phrases like 'a poor traveller', 'a poor distrest travelling woman', or a 'poor distempered stranger', all of which appear in the Session Book of Bunkle and Preston, in the late seventeenth century. However, many of those sent out of parishes were so unfit that the Session sending them away realised that it was up to them to do something about it. 'Cart and pontage for conveying a poor woman of silly mind to Montrose on her way to Aberdeen 2s. 3d.', 'Conveying a pauper woman and three children 2s. 6d.',

'Conveying Janet McKenzie and two children in a cart to Lunan Toll 3s. 6d.' are all cases of helping people out of a parish, a task which was sometimes done in a more official way as shown by an entry 'to constable conveying a pauper 2s.'. A longer journey or a more incapacitated pauper might involve an overnight stay, hence a payment 'To two men for carrying a poor woman to the Mairns and a day's boarding in the public house 1s. 8d. stg.' In some cases Sessions probably found it practical just to pay these removal costs themselves but they could be charged to the parish of legal residence or even to several such parishes: the accounts of Craig Kirk Session, Angus, show that in 1843 8s. 4d. stg. was spent sending a pauper to Arbroath, of which Craig, Marytown, Lunan, St. Vigeans and another parish were all due to pay equal shares of 1s. 8d., from which it appears that a legal residence must have been established in each of them[40] and, in fact, the weekly allowance of paupers might in similar cases be shared by several parishes.

Although these instances have been given of Kirk Sessions resisting claims for maintenance and of paupers being more or less forcibly returned to their legal parishes, there were far more cases where matters were amicably arranged, with poor people allowed to stay where they wanted to be and given assistance there, in the knowledge that what was spent on them would be repaid by their legal parishes. Furthermore, if the following extracts from the minutes of Banchory-Devenick Kirk Session, Kincardineshire, are anything to go by, a kindly Session could show spontaneous, unsolicited generosity to former parishioners who had moved elsewhere. In 1808, hearing that two men who had gone away were in need, 10s. was sent to each of them and 20s. to another man, who had spent most of his life in the parish but who had by then moved to the parish of Fetteresso, also in Kincardineshire, and had for several years been 'in a state of Dotage or Mental Derangement and was now bedridden.' The following year 10s. was sent to an ex-parishioner who was also living in Fetteresso 'on account of his having a foolish daughter' and the same amount was sent as a temporary supply to a man in Old Machar, Aberdeenshire, 'because of the great age of himself and his wife and because of his known poverty before he left here.' Kindness could also be shown to needy people in other parishes who had no claim apart from their dire circumstances: in 1682 when Cromarty Kirk Session were distributing meal to twenty-nine of their own paupers they also gave some 'to a supplicant from Rosemarkie' and in the same way, at a time when the Kirk Session of Tarbat, Ross-shire, had 106 of their own people in poverty or sickness, they still found 2s. stg. for people from elsewhere who asked for charity.[41]

There was a limit to how much any parish could raise for the poor and during famines or epidemics their numbers increased at the same time as income inevitably fell, which was why, during a terrible famine at the end of the seventeenth century, the magistrates and Kirk Session of Aberdeen decided to close the poor's roll and to give help only where anyone's condition was 'very extraordinary'. Even then an elder and a deacon had 'to attest the condition of the petitioner', which probably involved something along the lines of the 'minute scrutiny' endured by the poor woman in the Black Isle. Thus it was that from about the

1720s–1730s, but in some places much later, it became common although not universal for Sessions to require anyone coming on to the poor's roll to bequeath their effects to them for behoof of the poor, making the Session their heirs. Even before a Session began to require this, where a poor person had been maintained for a long time, they might still feel entitled to retain his goods and chattels after death. In 1708 a Session learnt that a man had removed a plaid off the coffin of 'an object of charity who had lived some time upon the [poor's] box' and decided that it, and all her effects, belonged to the poor, although it was not until 1717 that they introduced the formal bequest of effects. The kirk officer was ordered to get the plaid back, under threat of further action, and this proved successful.[42]

It was said of the bequeathing of effects that because people 'generally wish to retain these effects as long as possible, few make application till forced to by dire necessity',[43] but this was not as brutal as it sounds. It was necessary and sensible, for reasons given in one Session minute:

> The meeting taking under their serious consideration the numbers of those in indigent circumstances and finding that by reason of the lowness of their funds, they are scarce able to support that number, finding that others apply who cannot be reckoned among the number of real poor, unanimously agreed that for the future none shall be admitted into the Roll except those who by Petition make their condition known to the Session to dispose of the effects they may have at their decease to the use of the surviving poor. This they judge the most effectual method to discover that none but real objects of charity partake of the funds appropriate for that use.[44]

'Going on the [poor's] box' was thought by some as being lost to all shame but there were plenty of people perfectly ready to batten on kirk funds — the Old Statistical Account for Langholm, Dumfries-shire, written by the minister, states this clearly — and one Session minuted that 'many who do not greatly need, yet pretend to be indigent . . . press for Supply' and because of this they decreed that 'none whatsomever shall have any privilege of the poor's meal or money save they that give a dispensation and obligation of all they have remaining after death to the Session.'[45] When Mr Robert Arthur became minister of Resolis, Ross-shire, in 1774 he found that owing to what he called 'the undue influence' of a dozen elders there were ninety people on the poor's roll, many of them by no means in want. Tactfully, he left things as they were for several years but at last obtained an Act of Session ordaining that in future no one would share in the poor's money who did not bequeath their belongings to the poor, unless they had 'near relations who could be proved to have been liberal and kind to the deceased in their distress.'[46] Requiring would-be paupers to bequeath their effects undoubtedly encouraged their relatives to pay them more attention than they might otherwise have done, even if from all the wrong motives: 'The relations of people who are supposed to have stocks of linen or other valuable articles about them, are led to pay attention to them in their distress and this acts as a check on pauperism', was how Mr Easton put it in his *Statements*. Mr Arthur's efforts in Resolis, unpopular though they were, had the desired effect, reducing the number on the roll from 90 to 34, so that the money available could be targeted to the right people. While bequest of effects might be introduced in a parish for a particular reason, such as an excessive number of paupers on the roll when the true figure was much less, or due to shortage of funds or increased demand for some reason, the practice could fall into disuse if not necessary but it could always be reactivated if required. This happened in Resolis where it died out, only to be re-enacted in 1840 but without formality, just a decision that when anyone on the roll died leaving effects, these should be sold to pay for burial expenses, the Session only paying any outstanding balance.[47]

Some Sessions regarded their paupers' bequests as a form of insurance. In return, they undertook to care for them in any illness and to pay their funeral charges — no more than £1 stg. was allowed for this — but permitted the relatives to redeem any effects by repaying these costs and anything spent on the pauper for the year immediately preceding death. Others expected families to repay 'at least as much as will compensate' what had been spent by the Session, while Resolis's Mr Arthur indicated that those who had been good to pauper relatives might share in their effects even if these had been bequeathed to the poor. In the parish of Kirriemuir the Session's right to effects was not insisted upon if there were children or poor relations and the same thing obviously applied in St. Monance where the minutes show that it was only because 'Bina Fial had no near relatives' that they 'directed the balance to be placed to the charge side of the Session's accounts', while in the parish of Knockbain, Ross-shire, the Session retained all effects left to them unless the pauper left children or grandchildren under the age of fourteen years or, surprisingly, if they paid a rent of £10 sterling or more.[48] Bequeathing effects was therefore both a preventive measure and a way of making relatives repay money spent if they were able to do so, and was at the same time a way of raising money for other poor people. Although the practice of requiring paupers to bequeath their property was widespread and effective, it appears that for much of the time it was used it did not have the authority of Parliament. In 1737 it was by an Act of the Sheriff and Justices of Roxburghshire that certain of the Sessions in that county introduced it — in other words, it was ordered at county level, with the encouragement of the heritors who had a strong financial interest in the matter. When Mr Arthur started it in Resolis, he achieved it by an Act of Session, a purely parish decision, but it seems that by 1832 Parliament had legalised the procedure,[49] but whatever type of Act was passed to that effect, the details were notified in such a manner as 'ane Intimation hereof from the pulpit . . . desiring all that would expect any supply to come and attend the next week day Session which shall be intimated to them in order to give their assent to this Act.' Every effort seems to have been made to explain to people just what was involved: 'Henry Arbuthnott was called in, he was interrogate if he was satisfied with the Act, viz. that after the expense of his funeral his remaining effects should be furthcoming to the Session for the use of the poor else he could get no supply from the Session, he declared he acquiesced.' So did several others in this particular case 'but John Lyon absolutely declined to goe in with the proposal' and was therefore ordered 'to be scored out of the poor's roll.'[50] Those who agreed were always required to sign a bond to this effect and some Sessions kept special books for the purpose like the Testamentary Book of the Parish of Knockando, Morayshire, which contains sixty separate bonds signed between February 1775 and August 1794, each given a page to itself, and all more or less exactly like the first one which says:

> I Janet Cameron, spouse to Colin Fraser in Balvennie of Wester Elchies, Whereas I am admitted on the Poors roll of the Parish of Knockando, therefore, in order to reimburse the Parish box of such sums as shall appear by the Session books to have been given by the Kirk Session of Knockando to me, I hereby legate and bequeath to the same Kirk Session all and sundry goods, gear, Debts and sums of money as shall pertain or belong to me at the time of my death, and nominate and appoint the Kirk Treasurer of the said Parish of Knockando for the time being, executor of my last will and Testament with power to him immediately after my death, to inventary, appretiate, roup and dispose of my goods, gear and moveables . . . and after payment of my funeral charges to reimburse the Kirk Session of such money as shall be so advanced to me and to account to my nearest kin for the balance if any be; Consenting to the registration hereof in any judges' books competent and thereto nominate. My Prors [Procurators] In Witness whereof these presents written by Mr. Daniel Cruickshank, Schoolmaster, Archiestown, are subscribed at Manse of Knockando this fourth day of February seventeen hundred and seventy five years in presence of the Kirk Session and before these witnesses, William Grant and Alexander Nicholson, both students at school of Knockando.

> IC.

> as commanded by the said Janet Cameron who cannot write as she affirmeth but by two initial letters of her name by the adhibited Mr. John Dunbar Minr of Knockando have subscribed these presents for her in the presence of the witnesses aforesaid John Dunbar Minr.
> William Grant Witness
> Alexander Nicholson Witness.

These Knockando bonds were for new paupers being admitted to the poor's roll but where a Session decided on the bequeathing of effects, but already had paupers on its books, it seems that a mass bond could be signed instead, like the one prepared on a folio sheet by Dingwall Kirk Session in 1824 in the following terms:

> We whose names are hereunto subscribed having been for some time partly supported by the aid afforded to us by the Kirk Session of Dingwall and it being just and reasonable that we should henceforth derive no aid from the Funds under their management unless we should grant to them a general Disposition in the terms underwritten, do hereby give, grant, assign and dispone from us, our heirs and representatives, all goods, gear and effects whereof we severally may be possessed at the time of our respective deaths and in favour of the said session for behoof of the poor of Dingwall, with liberty to the said Session immediately on the death of any of us to take possession, without the necessity of any form of law, of any moveable subject belonging to us to dispose thereof at their pleasure. In witness whereof these presents written on this Sheet by William Glass, schoolmaster of Dingwall are subscribed by us at Dingwall the twenty-ninth day of November eighteen hundred

and twenty four before these witnesses —

There follow sixty-four names, all signing with a 'X' but without the signatures of any witnesses.

In order to enforce this system, it is said that it was usual for an inventory to be made of a pauper's possessions on admission to the poor's roll but how general this was is uncertain. Certainly it must have been tempting for members of the family or for relatives to appropriate what they could on the pauper's death but some Sessions prevented this with the threat that any such 'meddling' would result in the offender being held responsible for all the funeral costs.[51] On the death of any pauper who had bequeathed effects there was a roup or auction of these goods, which involved the cost of 'crying the roup' in addition to intimation in the churchyard on Sunday and both an auctioneer and a clerk were needed, the latter usually the Session Clerk who got a fee — about £3 Scots in the early eighteenth century — which was a welcome addition to his income; and some-times there was 'a judge of the roup' who might be the minister. The cost of such roups seems to have been rather high: between 1833–37 inclusively several sales of paupers' goods in one parish brought in £11 14s. 1d. sterling while the expenses came to £4 16s. 3½d., leaving only £6 17s. 9½d. for the poor; but, even so, this income was a useful addition to the poor's funds.[52]

The first thing for a Session to do with such money was to pay for the care given to the dead pauper. A roup in 1837 brought in £7 18s. 5d. sterling out of which 18s. 6d. was paid to three women for washing the corpse, while the coffin cost 16s. and soap and other funeral necessaries came to £1 4s. 3d. Less the auctioneer's fee of 3s. 6d. this left a useful balance for kirk funds[53] but it was not unusual for the proceeds of the roup and the cost of the funeral to manage somehow to be the same. Inevitably a Session might sometimes be out of pocket. When a pauper funeral cost £1 6s. 6d. and the effects only brought in 19s. 9d., 'the Session sanctioned payment of the deficiency' of 6s. 9d. but even with this deficit, they were less out of pocket than they would have been had they not had the effects to sell. In other cases an initial loss on a roup might be recouped later as in a case where effects were sold for just 7s. 4d. sterling but an unsold silver ring, a brooch and a chain were to be re-rouped and would more than offset the sum of 11s. 6d. spent on the woman's care for four weeks and her burial.[54]

In exceptional cases, where something like special medical care was needed, a person might be asked to relinquish not their goods but their house. This might be when care in an asylum was required and had to be paid for, which is described in another chapter, and there is also more information on burial of the poor in the appropriate chapter.

When Janet Cameron in Knockando bequeathed her goods and gear to the Kirk Session, she also bequeathed her debts and as there could be creditors wanting their money, Kirk Sessions might have to act as any executor would do. One considered 'the roup of Agnes Matthison's furniture and the several claims against it which had been lodged in the hands of the Clerk and determined that all the expenses attending the deathbed, funeral and roup should be discharged in the first instance, and that the remainder be divided among the Creditors according to their respective claims.' An elder was appointed to help the clerk decide what claims should be sustained and at the end of the day, there was sufficient to pay all those that had been lodged.[55] This is how another Session wound up the affairs of one of their paupers. Firstly they paid the expenses of her care:

	£	s	d
Paid a man due his deceased sister for waiting on Jean Moffat during part of her illness	-	6	-
To a woman for caring for her during part of her illness and washing her clothes after death. (Was this so that they could be rouped?)	-	2	-

Then they paid for her burial:

	£	s	d
For her coffin	-	13	-
To a merchant, for expenses for her funeral	-	10	-

Then they paid the costs of the roup:

	£	s	d
Postage of a letter from Stonehaven enclosing the Sheriff's warrant for rouping Jean Moffat's effects, including l*d.* to Fordoun Post Office for bringing the said letter from Bervie	-	-	7
Paid the officer at Kinneff for intimating the roup	-	-	2
Paid a man for going to Stonehaven to do with the roup and acting as auctioneer	-	6	-
To Session Clerk for his trouble for attending the roup	-	2	6

And finally they paid some little debts:

	£	s	d
To a shoemaker for a pair of shoes, due to him by Jean Moffat	-	2	-
To a woman, as the price of an empty bottle lent to Jean Moffat and not returned	-	-	2

The roup brought in £3 10*s.* 6*d.* and when all was paid, a balance of £1 4*s.* 8*d.* went into the poor's box.[56]

There should have been no problems with relatives once paupers bequeathed their belongings but it is not really surprising that they did arise. In 1844 a pauper named James Birnie, who lived in Baldernock, Stirlingshire, died leaving about £16 in the hands of one of his sisters who lived in Paisley. With so much money, it seems odd that he had ever needed to apply for admission to the poor's roll but nevertheless he was on it and when he died his Session appointed two men to visit his sister 'to ascertain whether she is willing to give up her late brother's effects' but this she refused to do, also refusing to return the £2 10*s.* he had received from the Session in aliment on the grounds that she had paid his funeral costs herself.

James had, however, on his deathbed left the care of his youngest child to her and as she was willing to accept this charge which relieved his Kirk Session of it, this was accepted in lieu of the money but the two-man deputation took the precaution of having her sign a 'form of obligation' about what had been agreed. Trying to claw back what had been spent on a pauper was fairly normal, should money appear to be available (although that was not the same thing as allowing families to redeem their relatives' effects in the way already mentioned) and just the year before the case of James Birnie, that Kirk Session had refused to admit a man to the poor's roll as his family were 'legally bound and able to support him' and they demanded the return of £2 9s. stg. of temporary aid already given to him which the family showed no enthusiasm to repay and which they certainly had not done six months later.[57] Many parishes did not expect those who required only temporary aid, and were therefore not on the poor's roll, to bequeath their goods but they might insist on being given a claim on these goods to the full amount of any help given.[58]

After the passing of the Poor Law of 1845 there was no further need for paupers to bequeath their goods but it was still possible for roups of effects to be held after that date and one can only assume in such cases that the effects had been left to the Session before the introduction of the new law.[59] As it was possible to have possessions but no income, the poor on occasion gave these voluntarily to the Kirk Session for sale ahead of death. Whether this was done because the Session needed the money immediately or whether it resulted in a better level of assistance is not made clear in the following minutes: '27th May 1761. Received from Elspit Crow, one of the poor, as the price of some household plenishing sold by roup by her order and delivered to the Kirk Session to be laid out by them for maintenance and funeral charges £4 Sc' and on '25th November 1761, Received more of Elspit Crow's effects which before her death she ordered to be delivered to the Session, £5.'[60] In much the same way, David Allan, an Elie, Fife, fisherman who was supported by his Session, transferred to them a house he owned, estimated to be worth £19 sterling, to repay what had already been spent on him and what might yet be needed.[61] A slightly different slant appeared in the case of Agnes Baine, who was obviously not a pauper. When she died her brother and other friends asked the Session to maintain her children and to take her effects for this purpose; in other words they were asking for the children to be admitted to the poor's roll rather than have to look after them themselves. This was accepted and the roup intimated in the kirkyard the following Sunday and so as to encourage good bidding, it was also announced that the Session would give 'three months credit to those that purchases above the value of 5s. at the roup upon giving a Bill of Caution' but ready money would be expected from all those buying below 5s. worth.[62]

Whether or not any parish had instituted the bequest of effects, the basic form of help given by Kirk Sessions to paupers was a share in the distribution or division of the poor's money or 'charities to be distributed to the poor' as one minute put it. After the Revolution of 1689 and re-establishment of Presbyteria-nism in 1690 many Kirk Sessions needed time to pull themselves together and the famine which struck the country in the 1690s and went on till 1701 did nothing to help them to get down to regular poor relief. In one parish these troubles were followed by a four-year vacancy so that in 1705 it was hardly surprising that the Session minutes said that 'the poor's money was not distributed for a long time'. Such difficulties could however be overcome with goodwill and effort and during a vacancy in Fife, at more or less the same date, when it so happened that there were not even any elders to help to organise things, the church collections were still 'distribut by som of the well affected in the parish.'[63] Even after things might be thought to have had time to settle down sufficiently for there to be regular distributions, the frequency of these and how much was given to paupers de-pended entirely on the circumstances of each parish; there was no national stan-dard. From the records of Kirk Sessions and from both Old and New Statistical Accounts the factors which mainly affected distributions were the physical characteristics and size of the parish, the number of the poor and the well-being or otherwise of the parish at any given time which directly affected church door collections. Some Kirk Sessions distributed weekly, some fortnightly, while for others it was monthly or quarterly, or even six-monthly in, for example, the large outlying Aberdeenshire parish of Strathdon, while others, even more isolated, paid only once a year and, indeed, that might be the only reason for holding a Kirk Session meeting at all.[64] There was certainly at least one parish in Skye, Kilmuir, which even as late as 1840 could only manage to give anything to paupers once every two years. In some parishes in the Outer Hebrides things were even worse. In Harris church collections were so small that a distribution could rarely be made because such money as the Session received had to be kept back to bury paupers, while in South Uist the people were so poverty-stricken that there were no church collections, let alone distributions.[65]

Where the distribution day was not over-frequent, it was such a high point in the parish year that, rather like market days, events could be dated from it, such as 'the first day after the Divide'.[66] Where distribution was only made once a year it usually fell in summer but knowing that a year is a long time and that winters could be hard, some Sessions who paid only yearly still helped their most needy poor with a little interim aid throughout the year as required. In the days before com-munications and transport improved, sometimes just whereabouts particular poor people lived in a parish affected the number of times they received their al-lowances, and should a parish have both a town and landward district within its bounds, then those in or near the burgh were often paid weekly with the result, it is said, that they might receive more than those in outlying areas who were only receiving monthly or quarterly, but this may not be so. A breakdown of what was given out in the parish of Hawick in June 1712 shows that the landward poor received an average of 11s. 8d. Scots and the town poor about 11s. 4d. which, were it not for individual larger sums given to two of the town poor, would come to even less.[67]

Sessions gave different paupers different amounts, according to their needs. Some did this by breaking them down into categories such as first or second class; highest, middle or lowest; or ordinary poor, extraordinary poor — those receiving help for a special or 'extraordinary' reason — and widows. Others were classified in a more particular way: blind and bedridden; widows with families to support, with the qualification that they should be industrious; and old strolling beggars. Classification was considered to be 'attended with much benefit to the greatest objects'[68] but many Sessions managed perfectly well without specific categories by using their knowledge of their paupers' needs to assist them as best as they could within their means. What was given out to both landward and town poor in Hawick in 1712 shows the variations of necessity recognised there, with one man named as 'Uncle John' receiving £2, and another man getting £1, after which the sums given ranged downwards with one at 18s., four at 16s., four at 15s., nine at 12s., fourteen at 10s., fourteen at 8s. and finally three at 6s., all Scots money.

These were fairly generous allowances for that date. In 1730 the poor of Rathven received between 6s. and 12s. Scots once or twice a year although distributions were increased to quarterly in the 1790s; nearly forty years later the parish of Kilninian and Kilmore, with 64 on its roll, was giving between 1s. to 3s. 6d. stg. per year. In the 1790s Strathdon could only give its forty paupers what was described as 'a trifling supply' twice a year and even a low ground parish in the Highlands could just manage what they called a 'scanty pittance' of between 3s. and 10s. stg. per annum to each of their 28 poor.[69] At that date allowances varied around the country from 25 people in Alvie, Inverness-shire, sharing £15, an average of 2s. 5d. per annum each; 36 sharing £15, an average of 9s. 4d. per year, in Glassary, Argyllshire; and approximately 18 people receiving an average of £1 13s. 4d. per annum in Borthwick, Midlothian, by sharing £30 between them.[70] To relate that to living costs, at that date a ploughman's wage was about £5 to £8 stg. per annum plus food, women servants were paid about £2 10s. per year, while daily workers such as labourers received 1s. per day, masons 1s. 8d., joiners 1s. 1d., and a tailor, the most lowly paid of all, got about 8d. per day but with food added. Although daily workers seem by that to be reasonably well paid, they were not necessarily employed all year. By the early nineteenth century, allowances for the poor might be 1s. 6d. to 2s. stg. per week but were often below that. Even widows with up to three or four children, supposedly a special category, might be given just 15s. to 16s. per quarter, 1s. or so per week, and as soon as any of the children was old enough to support itself, the mother's money was proportionately cut till all of them reached that age and then, if she could provide for herself, she was struck off the roll.[71] Harsh though this may seem, St. Paul said in his First Letter to Timothy that a widow should not be put on the roll under sixty years of age, adding that she should have been faithful in marriage and a doer of good.

Towards the middle of the nineteenth century costs and wages had increased, with farm workers receiving £10 to £20 stg. with full board and lodging, and women servants £6 to £8 per year but, even so, paupers' allowances do not seem to have risen significantly. New Statistical Accounts for East Lothian, for instance, show that these were an average of 1s. 3d. per week in Gladsmuir, 1s. to 1s. 8d. in Bara and Garvald, and 2s. 1d. per week, with 8s. 6d. per quarter for children in Whittingham, and that was a prosperous agricultural county. At the same date, in an agricultural parish in Ross-shire, some 80–100 paupers shared an annual total of £39 which worked out at below 10s. each per year.[72] It must be remembered, of course, that private charity often subsidised what the church could afford and in any event what the church gave was 'granted only as an help to their industry, not as an encouragement to sloth and idleness.'[73]

A valuable feature of the Kirk Sessions' care of their poor was the direct contact it gave them with their paupers as all those capable of attending distributions were expected to come to receive their allowance in person. But there were always some who could not do this because of ill-health — the list already given of 37 severely afflicted people in one parish alone makes that very clear — and in that case they were visited by an elder or the minister, the catechist or the beadle and, in burghs, perhaps by a bailie.[74] This enabled a close eye to be kept on them and was how cases of extra-special need were spotted. There was nothing haphazard about the arrangements: if it was known that certain people could not be present, then the names of those whose task it was to deliver their allowances were listed in a column opposite their names in the Session minutes, but it made heavy work for those doing it and it is very understandable that in the parish with the 37 particularly sad cases, the minutes say in 1768, 'The Session having been the whole day employed in this distribution and about other church matters, judged it reasonable to take a moderate refreshment out of the common fund and to reserve what remains thereof to be applied hereafter as shall be thought requisited.' In that parish, at any rate, this became the custom and the following year the Session 'resolved that for the future, a sum not exceeding 5s. shall be allotted for giving a refreshment to such of the elders as attend on occasions of this kind in respect of the trouble and loss of time they thereby sustain and the minister is appointed to give this day for that purpose 2s. . . .' Two years later the elders who were present considered 'that several of them have come from afar and are like to be late' and therefore agreed that it would not be improper to use a little of the balance remaining 'for a refreshment to themselves at parting and therefore allot to this purpose 4s. 6d.' By 1774 what had come to be regarded as the 'necessary expense' of the day came to 3s. 6d., all this at a time when the poor of the parish were receiving 5s. a year or even less but this is quoted, not to find fault with the elders but to indicate the amount of time, trouble and the distances they covered in serving their communities.[75] As has been said earlier, elders were not paid and it is unusual to find Sessions charging anything for expenses although they would often have been justified in doing so; however, a few instances do occur: 'Spent by the minister and Kirk Treasurer attending several different times when Imployed in the Sessions affairs, 19s. 10d.' or 7s. spent when visiting a house belonging to the poor along with tradesmen to see about work needing to be done to it, both of these sums probably being Scots money. Similarly, when materials for a new mortcloth were bought by another Session, the accounts included 'the expense of buying'.[76]

The poor's money — always called money whether given as cash or as meal or a combination of the two — helped with feeding and not much more and Sessions, if they could afford it, often gave additional help in a variety of thoroughly practical ways. Poorly-clad, cold, ill-shod and badly housed people were liable to become sick people and so these ways could include assistance with clothing, heating and accommodation, with such items as the following appearing in the accounts of one Session:

1697.	'Given to a poor lad to buy a pair of shoes 10s. Sc.'
1698.	'Shoes to poor children . . . 14s. Sc.'
''	'Shoes for a poor Las 6s. Sc.'
1699.	'Shoes for the poor of the parish £2 3s. Sc.'
1730.	Paid a tailor 'for making clothes to a poor boy £1. 8s. Sc.'[77]

Other Sessions' accounts show items like 'Bot to Donald Cilm cloth 5 shillings' or a payment of 1s. sterling for mending clothing; 2s. sterling given 'to Pat. McLeod to help buy a blanket' while full details of the cost of the materials bought to clothe 'Alexander Finlay's yst child' are given in Cathcart Kirk Session's accounts in 1788: '3 ells of blue plyding @ 15$\frac{1}{2}$d. per ell, 3 ells of harn @ 12d. per ell $\frac{1}{4}$ and a half at 5 pence which comes to in whole 7s. 3$\frac{1}{4}$d.' (sic)[78] Just who made these purchases is seldom stated but certainly on occasion it was elders who were deputed to get clothing for the poor and even if a Session did not actually supply the necessary money or clothing themselves, they might act as intermediary as happened when it was decided in 1832 to get two blankets on loan from the stock of the Board of Health for a poor woman who very probably, at that date, had cholera.[79] When special donations were given, it was often on clothing that they were spent and the use made of £10 given to West Kilbride Kirk Session in August 1826 shows good local knowledge of what was needed: they gave Archibald Stewart 2 pairs of 'course stockings', 9s. to Oran Stewart to buy a pair of shoes, money for some small articles was allocated 'to the girl kept by Janet Motion', who must have been an orphan or a foundling, and the balance of the money was shared out among eight other people. In addition to normal distributions to the poor, Elie Kirk Session gave out every December, from the mid-seventeenth century onwards for a good many years, what might be regarded as a winter bonus. This might be in money or in cloth, cloth of two kinds, grays or pleathen. Grays was a coarse, homespun undyed woollen fabric, gray in colour because it was woven from black and white wool, and pleathen was almost certainly plaiden material. With one exception, men were given grays and women pleathen. The Session sent an elder to negotiate a price with the supplier every October and with an order of over 20 ells of each, was able to secure a reasonable deal.[80] In the mid-nineteenth century an institution existed in Haddington, East Lothian, for supplying flannel clothing to the poor and the Earl and Countess of Hopetoun who were subscribers, gave permission to the minister of nearby Ormiston to draw from it upon their joint names such clothing as the poor of his parish needed in winter. Although this early version of the WRVS Clothing Store did not directly concern the Kirk Session, without doubt the minister would have depended on the advice of his elders as to what was needed and for whom.[81]

Heating is now a very topical subject, with a much higher level of warmth expected for everyday life than in former times, but even then Sessions realised the necessity of providing fuel. Giving 12s. Scots to a woman 'to cast her peats' must have been because she was either ill or too old or unfit to do this for herself and was practical and timely help so that she would have a supply for the bad weather. When another Session learnt that a woman was in distress they gave 16s. Scots to send her a cart-load of coal, again a really useful thing to do, and there is nothing new about the modern idea of giving bad weather heating allowances. That is what Langholm Kirk Session were providing two hundred years ago, when bad weather in January 1789 made them decide to spend £1 1s. sterling so that a cart-load of peats could be given to each person on a specially made out list. By the late eighteenth century, places which had previously relied on peat for fuel found that improvements in transport — roads, bridges, better carts and shipping — enabled them to obtain coal, and thereafter it became fairly common for this to be supplied, not to all but to particularly needy paupers.[82] At that date, for instance, Inchinnan Kirk Session, Renfrewshire, were not only giving 5s. stg. per month and their rent to four old people but coal also. As time went on, many parishes provided coal for a wider range of their poor, usually by organising church door collections, which in burghs had the encouragement and support of the bailies. A Poor's Coal Fund which had begun in Inverness by 1806 had raised some £680 stg. by 1822; in Dollar, Clackmannanshire, a collection was made as well as a subscription paper sent round the parish, while in Aberdeen the coal fund of the Kirk Session had become such that by 1827 it required managers. In rural parishes collections for coal might fall far short of what was needed but at least they helped towards it and it could be supplemented from the poor's money and, even in parishes where the heritors ultimately took over the care of the poor from the Kirk Session, the latter might still use any money that came their way to supply coal to the needy.[83]

A practical way of helping with housing was for Sessions to pay house rents for the poor and so items such as 'Rent for George Rorie's house 15s. stg.' or 'Half year's rent of Alexander Ross's house 12s. 6d.' appear in accounts. Some Sessions did this more than others, possibly owing to the fact that some parishes had more accommodation for let than others. Sometimes people who were not on the poor's roll were given this useful form of support which probably made all the difference in keeping them off it altogether. One Session certainly hoped that by paying a man's rent he would make no more demands: 'For James Glasgow's house rent, he promised he would trouble us no more' say the minutes, but these hopes were not fulfilled and his name continued to appear in the records until there was a final contribution for 'a coffin to James Glasgow £2 8s. 0d.' after which he really did trouble them no more.[84] Even when rent might have to be refused some help could still be given. When a woman in West Kilbride was refused it in 1825 'because she and her family were in good health and able to labour for their subsistence' she was given 5s. stg. when she explained that she was 'in narrow circumstances' due to the illness of her son. Sometimes it was lodging or board and lodging that were paid for rather than rent. 'To David Wyllie for lodging 15s. ' and 'For lodging and victualling a poor man for a short time' are examples of this.[85]

Where paupers had houses, they were often in bad condition and their occupants could not afford to repair them and this also was an area in which Sessions gave assistance. 'It being reported to the Session that the little house in which Margaret Fettes, one of the poor lives, is so ruinous that it is like to fall altogether — therefore ordered workmen to be employed to repair it' say the minutes of Arbuthnott Kirk Session in 1757. In 1829 it was a couple of elders who brought the plight of two people to the attention of the Session, asking help for them because their houses were 'in such a state as to render them unsafe to live in . . . the Session appointed that the sum of 9s. [stg.] each should be given them out of the poors funds in consideration of their poverty, the said sums to be laid out in purchasing wood for repairing their dwellings', while in 1694 the accounts of another Session show the following payments for repairs, all in Scots money:

> To Alexander Bennet for straw to thook [thatch] Janet Mylnes house, £2 8s. 0d.
> To Will Myln for thieking (thatching) Jennet Mylne's house, £1.
> To David Cockburn for works at Janet Mylne's house, £1.[86]

Perhaps more surprising was the 5s. given to Nicholas or Nicky M'Candlish by his Session to help him to build himself a house but if this was going to keep him off the poor's roll it made good sense. The amount given seems pathetically small for a house but at that date, 1751, almost anyone could build a basic house which was quite adequate to live in at an extremely modest cost.[87]

Inadequate fuel probably saved many a house fire but 12s. given 'to a man that had his house burnt' or 1s. stg. given to a poor man 'who had his house consumed by fire'[88] are further examples of how Sessions stepped in with timely aid because in the days before there was any fire insurance, such a disaster could turn someone into a pauper overnight and make them homeless too. A sad case occurred in 1708 when a St. Monance house caught fire and three children died in the blaze and the father of the family died as a result two days later. Only the mother and a baby survived and while the bereavement aspect of the tragedy could not be helped with money, life still had to go on for the homeless mother and child and a voluntary collection ordered by the Presbytery must have been a great practical help, with one parish alone raising £20 18s. Scots.[89]

In addition to helping people with their own houses in this way, Sessions showed good thinking by themselves providing housing for their poor. Occasionally a parish found itself with a poor house, or poor's house as it was often called, which was left over from Roman Catholic days, when there was a church tradition of accommodating the old and the sick. In the thirteenth century there was a considerable number of leper hospitals around the country and one of these, designed to house 'seven leprous souls' was established about 1226 by John Bisset in the parish of Rathven. By 1445 the inmates appear to have been no longer lepers but simply bedemen — poor men who in return for accommodation and a yearly pension had to attend church morning and afternoon to pray for the soul of the founder of their establishment. For all practical purposes this turned the place into a poor house and by 1724 anyway, the Kirk Session there were in some position of authority in relation to it as it was they who threatened one of the occupants, James Reed, that if he ever again came into the bedehouse drunk, cursing and swearing, they would see to it that he lost his entitlement to stay there. By 1842 the Session were recommending people to fill vacancies although the final decision rested with Lord Seafield, but by 1886 the house had been demolished and three acres which really belonged to the bedemen, of whom there were still six, were re-let to a neighbouring farmer.[90] Although such convenient ready-made accommodation did not often come the way of parishes, in fact it was not long after the Reformation that certain Sessions realised that something of the sort was required and as early as 1596 Perth Kirk Session decided that a 'hospital-house' for the 'entertainment' or maintenance of the poor of the parish should be built.[91] Realisation of this need spread so much that when a scheme to erect a poor house was put forward in 1745 by the Justices of the Peace in East Lothian (and later abandoned) the Kirk Session of Tynninghame refused to go along with it on the grounds that they already had sufficient poor's houses of their own. These were eleven houses with gardens, built by the Session on land gifted by the Earl of Haddington, houses which came to be collectively known as the Widows' Row and which in the mid-nineteenth century were still occupied by widows who were also given a small coal allowance.[92] The standard of these Tynninghame houses appears to have been good but not all were so, nor could they be. One of a series of lantern slides of the Hebridean Islands taken by the photographer George Washington Wilson in the late nineteenth century shows an individual poor house there, described as a wretched hut, a mere apology for a poor house and partly burrowed into the earth but, in fact, the hut shown does not seem much worse than other 'black houses' appearing in the slide, which were normal accommodation in these islands and, however simple these poor's houses might be, at least a pauper could have the dignity of living in the privacy of her — it seems to have been women who lived in them — own home.[93]

The idea of individual houses for the poor had been put forward by Parliament in 1661 when it was decreed that overseers of the poor should have a convenient house for them, either apart or together [94] but it says much for any Session which actually provided individual accommodation. It was not always possible for this to be done but at least something was done and by the end of the eighteenth century, even in far-flung parts of the Shetland Islands, a Session with the agreement of the heritors 'appointed a certain place in the parish where paupers were maintained and clothed' which sounds as if it were some kind of multiple-occupancy centre, which was in keeping with an Act of Parliament which referred to heritors, ministers and elders appointing those unable to work to go to 'places wherein to

abide'.[95] If any house which came to a Session through legacy or purchase —
there is more about this in another chapter — was big enough, it was sometimes
practical to use it as accommodation for paupers rather than letting it, as the saving
on their rents offset any loss of income and for this reason when the tenants of one
such house gave it up in 1843 the Session decided 'that the best way of disposing
of it would be to fill it up with individuals selected from those who require their
house rent to be paid from the Session's funds'. This was agreed and when shortly
afterwards a woman asked for money for her rent, the Session paid what was due
but arranged that in future she should live 'in an apartment in the house at the
Burnside belonging to the Session.' When another woman was asked to move
there, she replied that she had no objection to doing so provided that she could be
given some bedding, and so a Mrs Simpson was appointed 'to examine her bed
and report what will be necessary to make it comfortable', with the result that she
moved in and lived there perfectly happily until her death in 1857. Others lived
there too, also apparently contentedly, and the impression that comes through
these minutes[96] is one of care and consideration, something which is reinforced by
another Session's minute about a 'nurse for the poor house'.

In 1845 the Kirk Session of Creich, Sutherland, had considerable trouble with
people who had joined the Free Church at the Disruption in 1843 but still expected
aid from the parish church, alleging that if they did not receive it, it would show
that it was dependent on the religious views of those seeking it, a religious means
test. The prime mover in all this was Mary or May Macleod who organised some
sixty petitions and took matters to the Sheriff-Substitute and later to the Lords of
Council and Session. The Kirk Session felt that the answer to this 'vexatious
matter' would be to accommodate her in a poor house, obviously thinking in terms
of an institutional establishment as might be provided under the new Poor Law. In
the meantime, however, they learnt that a Mrs Fraser, 'a highly respectable
parishioner', planned to move into a roomy house and would be prepared to take in
as many boarders 'as she may be contracted to expect' and as her accommodation
would allow. Terms for Mary Macleod to live in what was really a private poor
house were arranged between the Session and Mrs Fraser, in just the same way
that board and lodging were sometimes provided in lesser establishments. In
towns public institutions developed for the accommodation of old or unfit
paupers, and indeed for pauper children too, where the person or body responsible
for sending them there was also responsible for their costs. A Kirk Session in the
vicinity of one such institution has a book of 'King James Hospital Accounts
1647–1725' showing such entries as 'Mrs Lamb's pension from Candlemas 1709–
Candlemas 1710, £24 Sc' while a man's for just six months came to £15 14s. Scots,
although in some cases only a proportion was paid by that Session which indicates
that the person concerned must have been a shared expense with another parish.[97]
Gradually public poor houses or charity workhouses, where the poor were given
both shelter and work, were established more widely in towns, usually through co-
operation between various bodies, often including local Kirk Sessions. For example, a charity workhouse which opened in Dalkeith, Midlothian, in 1750 was

provided by contributions from heritors, townspeople and the church, and was managed by heritors and what was termed 'a certain class of the inhabitants' and the Session. In many towns, it was the Town Council, the trade guilds and the Session who served equally on workhouse committees and meetings to choose management committees were frequently intimated from pulpits, while a further indication of the extent to which the kirk might support these public ventures comes from the Canongate parish of Edinburgh. There, the church door collections, the dues of the kirk's mortcloth and of private baptisms, as well as what was paid for the privilege of lodging corpses in an aisle of the church when they were *en route* for burial elsewhere, all helped, along with income from other sources, to support a workhouse built by subscription in 1761. A rather touching entry in the minutes of Inveresk Session in 1752 shows the attitude of that Session to 'a tender child' and an awareness of public poor house conditions, when they decided that the infant was unfit to be put into the poor house and should continue to be maintained as it had been until then, half by the Session and half by the relevant craft guild, as it was the child of a shoemaker.[98]

Even although Kirk Sessions were represented on their boards, official poor's houses always had a stigma attached to them, something which does not seem to have applied to the poor houses provided in parishes by Sessions for their own poor. For example, whenever one of the widows' houses at Tynninghame fell vacant, there was always more than person waiting for it and there even seemed to be 'too great a willingness even on the part of healthy, young and vigorous persons, to obtain an establishment in the Widows' Row'[99] and it seems likely that the standard set by Church of Scotland Eventide Homes after the Second World War and the kirk's pioneering of sheltered housing were a continuation of earlier kirk ideas on provision for the poor which contributed to the great improvement of local authority homes for the elderly.

The best way of all, of course, was to keep people out of institutions if at all possible, and so Sessions often gave people a small amount of help which was just as much as they needed to keep their heads above water. As one minister said, occasional supplies given to needy families might be small but 'added to what they can earn by any kind of labour, enables them to live more comfortably in their own houses, than they could possibly do in the best endowed hospitals.'[100]

Where any Session had poor's money to spare, it became common to treat it as capital and to lend it out at interest, using only the income for the poor, and some Sessions were willing to lend money to people who, though temporarily in need, appeared likely to be able to repay it; but it could be tempting to some poor people to try to borrow their way out of trouble from these funds and it was a wise Session which prevented them getting into debt this way by *giving* them part or even all of what they asked: a one-off payment of 1s. 9d. to James Kennedy 'for relief of the linnen work' when he got into difficulties at a waulk mill, is just one small instance of this.[101]

Mr Easton referred to runaway husbands as a source of poverty and a sad entry in this context appeared in 1790: 'Given to Mary M'Lean, being very poor, deserted by her husband and having lately had two of her children to bury, 3s. 1d. stg.' In a much later case, in 1872, a woman came before her Session saying that her husband had left her some nineteen years before and that until recently she had not known whether he was alive or dead but she had now been credibly informed that he was alive and in a not-too-distant parish. The Session ordered the collector, the man who had charge of their funds, to advance her 3s. 6d. per week 'and to take steps for securing repayment of what may be advanced for her relief, she being unable to provide for herself', steps which presumably involved pursuing the husband for her maintenance. Very often wives with husbands in the army or navy endured many years of not knowing whether their men were alive or dead, which was the reason that one such, Jean Ellice, begged her Session for some help, undertaking 'in the event of her husband's return to repay what money shall be given her.'[102] In 1828 a pensioner of the 3rd Veterans, who lived with his wife and four children in Aberdeen, got into financial straits through unemployment and illness but once he was better, he asked the Session to allow him 6s. stg. per week for his family as he planned to go into the country to seek work. This was agreed, with the treasurer told to take steps to secure repayment of what was given. This was doubly constructive on the part of the Session: it could not only help him to find work but could possibly result in him and his family establishing a legal settlement in another parish; and it was for similar reasons that 10s. Scots was given to a man 'who was now going to leave the place and stood much in need of something to carry him to some part till he fall into business', and 1s. stg. 'to Thomas Clark going in search of work.'[103]

Because the kirk strongly believed in people supporting themselves if they possibly could rather than declining into poverty and onto the poor's roll, they developed an early version of the present-day Enterprise Scheme to set poor people up in business. A recognised way for a young man to seek his fortune used to be 'shouldering a pack' but a poor lad needed a helping hand for this which could really only come from the Session: 'Given to a poor boy within the parioch, John Scott, for beginning a pack to him, 10s. Sc' and 'To John Wilson to buy a pack £1 10s. Sc' are examples of this but what would a modern Kirk Session think about giving a youth 9s. to buy a pound of tobacco to start trading with? On the same principle, goods could be bought to help poor widows set up as shop-keepers — according to their auditors' report in 1849, St. Monance Kirk Session spent no less than £19 14s. 3d. stg. in this way — or raw materials could be bought. Janet Stewart was given ½ stone of wool which cost 3s. 6d., for her to spin and weave, although it is not clear in this case how the output was to be used.[104] Often it was just something quite small but very practical that made all the difference to the recipient: 14s. Scots spent on mending Isa Helm's wheel enabled her to keep spinning for her living; a loom which cost 10s. stg. let Colin Bayne go on weaving; David Wales's new pick-axe helped him to get or to keep work and 12s. Scots for a wallet for 'Old Dand' must have been given for some good reason. A more puzzling donation was money given to a boy to buy a comb but it, too, must have had to do with work, perhaps for use on wool or flax. Provision of a little seed grain to prevent future hunger was the wise thinking that lay behind 'ane firlot and ane half of oats . . . given to Robert Hyslop to sow his lands, £1 10s.' and £5 8s. Scots given to Matthew Thornton in 1724 'to buy seed to sow his lands.'[105] Before railways developed, there was always a demand for carriers and a particular need for delivery of fuel and so provision of a horse or a donkey could be sufficient to enable someone to earn an adequate living. After Hawick Kirk Session had had many appeals for help from James Hardie who was in a very poor way and unable to support his wife and considerable number of small children, they finally decided to give him 5s. to buy a beast — it must have been a donkey at that price — so that he could carry fuel, heather or such things for 'any who would employ him for his present necessity'. Another Session's minute stated quite baldly their reason for setting up a man as a carrier: 'To John Low to buy a horse to prevent him coming on the poor's fund, 10s. stg.' If someone was already making a living as a carrier, loss of his beast could throw him on to the poor's roll and it made good sense to buy another whether the earlier one had died of old age, 'by misfortune' or had been stolen and so it was that a coal cadger (carrier) was given 7s. 6d. stg. in 1756 so that he could keep his cart going to and from the coal pit, and two men were given the money 'to buy horses to call [carry] coales with, their beasts being dead'. The reason why the Session gave a man £1 10s. Scots 'for helping to buy ane horse for carrying his motherless child in the country in the summer' is not known but it could have been so that if he worked in outlying places, or went begging there, he could take the child with him and so save the cost of having someone to care for it in his absence. Because beasts were valuable, some at least of those given to the poor remained the property of Sessions. This is clear from a case in 1751. A minister reported that a man who had such a horse was apparently on his deathbed and the animal, their property, was idle and the expense of keeping it considerable. He suggested that John Ruecastle, who was looking after it meantime, should be asked to sell it as best he could and a roup was agreed upon, along with a decision that the said John should be 'Skaithless [blameless] on all events'.[106]

So too with a cow. When a Session paid £3 5s. Scots to replace George Coupar's one which had been accidentally killed, it was made clear that it remained the Session's property. A milking cow was a tremendous asset to a poor family, providing milk and butter for themselves and for sale and so one finds this sort of Session minute: 'Given by the unanimous consent of the Session to James Christie in Kirktoun, having a poor, small family, to help him buy a cow 5s. stg.' Loss of a cow could more or less break such a family and so, as with carriers' horses, Sessions might help with replacements should something befall the original one: 'Andrew Donald, being old and impoverished by the death of a cow in bringing forth a monstrous calf with two heads . . . was ordered to receive 6 lib to help buy another cow.' Clearly the birth of such a calf had been a sensation in the parish to have been recorded thus in the minutes. If a Session could not pay for a cow, they might still institute steps to see that it was provided; when a poor man asked for help to replace one that he had lost, his Session decided to hold a voluntary collection for it and the minister earnestly exhorted the people to give towards it and presumably, in such a case, the animal would become the man's property rather than the Session's.[107]

People who had plenty of livestock and were considered well-off could still lose them through disasters of various sorts. In 1729 a man in the Orkney Islands begged Kirkwall Kirk Session's help because he had lost his cattle and his horses in some unspecified happening which he called the providence of God. They gave him some money and agreed to his request for a recommendation to the Presbytery for charity. Also in Orkney, but this time in the parish of Holm, another man 'suffered a great loss of horses and craved a recommendation to the Presbytery' which was also granted. These recommendations were asking the Presbytery to authorise a public collection throughout their bounds, the equivalent of a modern disaster fund.[108]

The poor had little to steal but even that little could attract a thief and Sessions would take pity on these people, either by organising a collection on their behalf or by a direct donation:

1651. 'Collected for William Bell, a robbed man.'
1734. 'Given to a poor widow woman of Seathland rob'd 4s.'
1755. 'Given to a poor man who was robbed near the causey moss £1 4s.'
1767. 'To a poor man that had his house rob'd 4s.'

It could also be calamitous for the well-off to be robbed. In one year, the Session of Fordyce gave 8s. 1d. to a woman whose husband had been murdered and robbed of the large sum of £250 stg., leaving her destitute with six young children, and they also gave 6s. to a man and his daughter-in-law and her three children when they were ruined by a flood which destroyed property to the value of £900 stg.[109] which, although not a robbery, had the same effect.

A long and detailed apprentice's indenture appears in the records of Falkirk parish, Stirlingshire, for 1779 and although it is not clear in this case if it directly concerned the Session (although it probably did) or whether it was inserted as an official registration of the contract, apprenticeships were certainly something with which many Kirk Sessions became involved because they were another constructive way of helping poor people to support themselves. In 1598 David Craig, a poor boy in Perth, begged the Kirk Session to give him some help to learn a trade and his plea fell on sympathetic ears, with the Master of the Hospital ordered to apprentice him to a tailor who was to be paid £10 Scots by the Session 'to learn him the tailor-craft' in accordance with a proper indenture which was prepared. A particularly kind Session saw to it that a foundling whom they had cared for all his life was not only apprenticed but adequately clothed for his new life; the minutes show that they paid £4 'to John Anderson, tailor, upon the accompt of making the ffoundlin's cloathes the time of his apprenticeship and other necessaries to him' and in fact they gave him £3 a couple of years later to buy shirts, shoes and stockings. Naturally enough, when a Session supported an apprentice, they expected him to work hard and become as proficient as possible and for that reason when Arbuthnott Kirk Session gave James Edie 4 merks to help with his apprentice fee as a weaver, they also appointed someone to 'make enquiry thereanent'. It is not clear whether apprentice fees were always meant to be repaid once training was completed but this was certainly so in some cases. In 1705 the Kirk Session of Aberdeen St. Nicholas decided that eight of 'the Session's apprentices' as they were called — one wright, four weavers, one tailor and two masons — were by then in such circumstances that they could pay back the apprentice fees which had been advanced for them but nevertheless the matter was approached with delicacy, with the collector appointed to speak to each of them privately about it 'before any legal Diligence be used against them upon their obligations to this Session . . .' A slightly puzzling minute of Morebattle Kirk Session, Roxburghshire, refers to £3 given in 1735 to Mr George Hall by appointment of the Presbytery 'for assisting him to provide necessaries for his son James, when he was to be sent away to an apprenticeship.'[110] The fact that James's father is styled 'Mr' implies that he was not one of the poor and, in fact, it seems possible that he may have been the George Hall who was minister of nearby Linton from 1728–40 which, if so, raises some interesting speculations. (Fasti, however, does not attribute a son James to George Hall).

Although the following instances of what would now be called job-sharing and job-creation occurred during a time of famine, they are included here as examples of the wide-ranging efforts of Kirk Sessions to prevent or alleviate poverty. In January 1741 the Kirk Session of Kilconquhar suggested that the office of beadle might be shared between two men which they felt 'might be a means to subsist two families, and particularly in these straitening years.' This well-meant proposal came to nothing because the existing beadle would not accept the appointment of a man called David Wallace with whom it was thought he would share the work, insisting that he would stick to this 'even if they dispossessed him'. And that is just what they did and offered the post to another man who said he would only accept it with a partner who knew about grave-digging, of which he thought David Wallace knew nothing. At that the Session offered the partnership back again to the original beadle who refused and the outcome was that David Wallace, although spurned by those with whom he had been meant to work, was given the beadleship all to himself and a good idea on the part of the Session came to nothing owing to what appears to have been human intransigence.[111] That same year, the Kirk Session of Culross had an idea which did work. It was to create jobs through the Session buying lint — flax — and distributing it to those of the poor who could spin, paying them for their work and selling the finished product, for which there was a good demand. The transactions are fully described in the minutes:

> 6th October 1741. The Session has agreed to cause purchase an Hundredweight of lint in order to be distributed to such of the poor as are able to spin and appoint the poor to return the yarn to such as the Session shall name. The Session appoints John Robertson and James B —, kirk treasurers, to buy the lint out of the poor's money

and to cause to be prepared and given out in parcels, to pay for the spinning and allow the treasurers a penny sterling for every spindle of yarn that shall be spun and returned to them.

17th November 1741. The Session sold the yarn of the first Hundredweight of lint to John Law and John Rotson amounting to [blank] spindles to be equally divided between them at sixteen pence . . . the spindle and appointed the yarn to be delivered to them upon their accepting of bills to the value and appointed them to provide cautioners for the payment of the same . . .

On 15th December 1741, the treasurers reported that they had

bought Two Hundredweight of lint, mentioned in the former minutes, amounting to Five and Fifty pounds Scots, being Seven and twenty pound ten shillings the Hundredweight, and that according to the last appointment they had bought four Stone twelve pound conform to the foresaid prices, the merchant not having any more at the foresaid prices at the time. The Session had agreed that my Lady Preston shall buy twenty spindles of yarn of the Two Hundredweight at seventeen pence stg the spindle, and that John Law shall buy the remainder at the same price and appoints William Drysdale and John Rotson to divide and deliver it at their conveniency

they both being elders. In January 1742 yet more lint was bought and spun and sold and so successful was the scheme that it was decided to buy another hundredweight in February at as reasonable a rate as possible, to be given out for spinning 'to such as the Session shall name'. Meanwhile, the same idea of job-creation was being practised elsewhere too in an attempt to counteract the problems of famine: Auchterhouse Kirk Session was one that decided to allow any women who could spin to have 1lb. of lint on credit, plus a 6d. for their maintenance while spinning it. Once it was spun and sold, the women paid for it and were allowed credit for a further pound weight and so on, during the famine.[112]

Direct supplications for help constantly came to Sessions and were seldom refused, sometimes indeed even more help being given than what was initially asked: when one poor man asked for help to feed his family, not only was he given a boll of meal but they generously undertook to maintain one of his children for a year. The kirk was always concerned when cases involved children and therefore entries such as 'Given to a very poor man with young motherless children 10s. stg' are far from unusual. Supplicants from near or far constantly appeared at the church door on Sundays and it would have been a hard heart that could have refused the pleas of 'five poor children at the door' who were in fact given 5s. and there is evident compassion in the wording of minutes which refer to help given to 'a puir decent-looking auld man', to two 'hirpling women, sairly needing something out of the box', 'a lass with a cruikit backbone' and even a man 'sairly fashed with a long-tongued wife'. True kindness was shown by the Session which, in addition to other assistance, allowed $1^1/_2d$. stg. weekly to Jean Watson and Widow Young so that they could buy a little tobacco but it seems astonishingly generous of any Session to have given 4s. 'to a broken Excise officer' as excise officers were nobody's favourite people. One way and another, what was given in temporary and casual assistance could come to almost as much as was given to those on the poor's roll.[113]

Without legal aid, poor people who felt that injustice had been done to them found it difficult to get redress and this was another matter with which Sessions could give help. Even where such people were not actual paupers, they could become technical ones by grant of a certificate of poverty to enable them to raise a court action *in forma pauperis* which meant that they did not have to pay the expenses of the case although this did not apparently admit them to the poor's roll. The legal requirements for the granting of such a certificate were that the applicant should be poor, of good character and a not a litigious person. In some cases certificates were given readily, possibly because the background to the case was already known to the Session: 'Euphen Rutherford applied for a certificate of poverty to carry on a law suit which was agreed' says one minute but in other cases considerable inquiry was made. When in 1832 James Findlay asked for a certificate to pursue a case between him and his apprentice, John Bell, and David Clark who was John's surety, the Session held a special meeting to establish whether or not James Findlay was of good character and to this end required him to produce certificates from his neighbours and from other people too, of his qualification to teach an apprentice and his ability to maintain him sufficiently comfortably. They called James, John and David before them but after hearing what they had to say decided in the end that it was not something in which they should interfere — but at least that had investigated it all. The following case, however, seems rather surprising. Alexander McKenzie, a vintner or wine-seller, appeared before his Session bringing with him a writer or lawyer as his Counsel and asking for a certificate of poverty to pursue a law suit against a man named Alexander Taylor. One might have thought that the ability to employ a writer implied anything but poverty and Mr Taylor also considered that Mr McKenzie was anything but impoverished and wrote to the Session objecting to the grant of a certificate to him, pointing out that he had a farm, houses, kept an inn and, through his wife, had money too. Even so, after hearing the applicants' declarations, the Session decided to give the certificate which seems such an odd decision in the circumstances that one wonders whether they knew more than the minutes tell or else were biased in some way. Another case in which there certainly seems to have been bias was that of Mrs Bank, a St. Monance woman, who asked for a certificate to raise an action against the owners of Duddingston colliery to support her children, claiming that her husband's death in one of their pits was due to 'insufficiency of the machinery and the unskilfulness of the men employed about the pit where he worked'. The Session gave her the certificate but they also wrote to the colliery manager to warn him of her intentions. He replied to them, saying that the colliery had paid the funeral costs and the man's outstanding lodging costs although they were not required to do so and pointing out that 35*s.* had been collected from Bank's fellow workers and sent to his widow, plus an additional sum from Mr Ellis, who appears to have been the pit owner. At this point the Session were told that Mrs Bank's friends would like it if the Session would become the pursuers in the action but this they refused to do, saying that if any of her friends wished to do so on her behalf, then they would grant the necessary certificate. There is a possibility that there was also bias when a Resolis man asked for a certificate in order to raise an action in the Supreme Court against a heritor, Donald McKenzie of Newhall, and his factor. These gentlemen were called to the next Session meeting and brought witnesses who gave evidence of the applicant's bad character, saying that he attacked people and was given to fighting. Not surprisingly his application was refused but it cannot have been often that a request for a certificate to sue a heritor and a factor could ever have succeeded. It took a brave Session to stand up to a factor, let alone a heritor, but it could happen and one such case occurred in Nigg, Ross-shire, as a direct result of an application for a certificate of poverty, a story told in the chapter on 'Good and Christian Works'.[114]

In one parish's list of allowances for the poor, which were all for 4s. stg. or less, there appears a charmingly-phrased and perfectly public entry, 'Given to Agnes Guffag in a Compliment 10s.' — and there followed immediately four more 10s. 'compliments'. No reason is given why these people should be so signally honoured so why, one wonders, did it happen? The truth is that in certain cases people were given what they required anonymously — although names were given in the case just quoted — so as to conceal the shame, as some saw it, of being funded from the poor's money and in the belief that this would preserve their self-respect and industrious habits which would have been lost were it known that they had received help from the Session. The fact of giving anonymously was not concealed but the recipients' names were not made public, something which was sometimes done through a 'private list'. Such a list appears in Banff Kirk Session's records in November 1774 when £2 11s. went to a 'private list' as against £3 18s. spent on the poor of the town and landward area. Some records show money given to unnamed people in need 'by the minister's order' and entries in the records of Kinconquhar show that recipients' names might be known only to the minister and heritors. Other instances of this sort of thing are money given 'to a private family', 'to a supplicant recommended by a person of honour' who in spite of being unnamed got £3 10s. Scots, or even, when giving out monthly allowances to the poor which varied from 1s. to 5s., a donation of 10s. given to an unspecified person 'by order of the committee'. Another Session stated that 12s. was given 'to a man whose name the session thought right to conceal' and it is clear from the context that these anonymous donations were not given to stranger poor but to parishioners. Perhaps rather suitably, Traquair Kirk Session, Peebles-shire, decided that money for private giving should come from the penalties of 1s. stg. imposed for private baptism and could be given out by the minister alone.[115] While it is unlikely that there was any malpractice to any extent, the giving of the poor's money to unnamed people privately was improper, however good the motives were, because it was possible for it to be directed to dependents and old servants of those who should have looked after them themselves and it could also lead to embezzlement which happened, as will be seen later, in the case of a minister of Channelkirk, Berwickshire.

The effects of war and Kirk Session involvement in raising and distributing national collections for victims have already been mentioned but, at purely local level, the resultant drain on poor's funds could be considerable. In 1645 Kinghorn Kirk Session allowed 6s. 8d. per week to three women for as long as they should need it after they lost their husbands at the Battle of Tippermuir the previous year and in 1646 they gave relief to the many widows and orphans left after the defeat at Kilsyth. War left many disabled men or men in need of some sort, like the one for whom a Session held a special collection because he had been 'herried by James Graham of Clavers followers'. The activities of the press gang could also leave families unprovided for at home and heavy pressure on kirk funds could come from ex-soldiers travelling home, should a parish lie on a main routeway. These people were not entitled to financial help but the logical thing to do, as with other strangers, was to assist them on their way to their own parishes and during and just after the Stuart rising of 1745 the parish of Channelkirk, on the line of the modern A68 road, was one of those that came under considerable pressure from such people:

Feb. 1745	'To two ighlanders travelling home, 4s.'
Sept 1745	'To several wounded soldiers, and wifes with children, 3s. 2d.'
Jan, Feb. 1746	'To wounded soldiers and their wifes travelling on the road, £3 4s.'
Aug. 1746	'To several soldiers, lame, with wifes etc.' (The 'etc' presumably refers to children.)

In 1748 there are about a dozen references to wounded soldiers and their families being helped in Channelkirk but for some it was too late and the records in November 1745 show £1 1s. spent for 'rebel Highlanders graves'. Other Session minutes refer about this date to 'Highland women lurking' in parishes, the wives and camp followers of these men, but while the wording does not sound kindly, such people were assisted so far as possible. They were after all fellow Scots but in 1589 the Kirk Session Register of Perth shows that orders were given to the keepers of the city gates to allow no Spaniards or other vagrants to come within the town. These were the unfortunate sailors and soldiers of the Spanish Armada who had survived defeat in the English Channel the previous summer only to have their ships destroyed by a storm in the Hebrides and who were trying to make their way home through Scotland as best they might.[116]

Poor travellers were a great problem to Kirk Sessions. Many of them came from Ireland owing to its economic, religious and political problems and in 1689 one Session alone gave relief at various times to 'honest men', 'poor strangers', 'old men' and 'old people', all of them from Ireland, and also to 'four poore people, pretending they had fled from Ireland'. Charity in the last case seems surprising but what mattered was not so much fraud as moving them on. These stranger poor were travelling on their own account; they were different from those being moved on to home parishes but Kirk Sessions whose parishes they passed through took the same attitude to them as to the others. One minutes shows that 6s. was given 'to a stranger that had his horse hurt' but whether this was to help him while the horse recovered or to help the horse is not stated. In addition, transport might be provided, as opposed to just paid for, to move sick strangers: Shotts Kirk Sessions paid Thomas Paitcairn 18s. Scots 'for taking ane sick travelling woman to Livingstone Kirk' in 1725 and that is just one of the many instances. In exceptional cases horses themselves might be provided. This is mentioned in another minute of Shotts Kirk Session that year. Five poor travellers were given 12s. by that Session but the minute gives a bit more information about them than that. They had been taken prisoner by the Spaniards and were going to Edinburgh to petition the Government and four of them who were sick had been given 'horses from Hamilton Session to carry them to blaikburn'.[117]

Some strangers travelled with what was really a form of passport, usually termed a 'pass' which gave their place of origin as well as the object and destination of their journey and acted as a recommendation for charity. 'Two sailors with a pass' or the words 'on pass' added to the names of those given help, or the description 'passengers' which may appear in accounts all refer to this. Sometimes the pass was in the form of a 'testimonial' or 'testificate' — 'To stranger poor with testimonials, 12s.' or 'to a sick travelling woman with her child but nine days old, cloathed with a sufficient testificate, requiring charity, 5s.' are just two examples of help given to these sad travellers. (The word testificate also applies to certificates of character in a different context which is described later.) A few travellers came with more specific recommendations than mere passes: 'This day there were given 6s. Scots to John Anderson, a poor lame stranger recommended by the Archbishop and Synod of Glasgow' says one Kirk Session minute in 1688 while another said in 1703, 'The whilk day there came other two distressed families seeking supply, having a recommendation from the mayor and ministers of Oxford to whom the Session allows 20s. Sc.' Why these people were given these recommendations is not known but certainly there are a good many references to gentlefolk who were commended for help, for instance, 'There was . . . given 8s. Sc to Jean Guthrie a poor creeple gentlewoman recommended by the Ministers of Edinburgh, and likewise 4s. Sc was given to James Montgomery to transport her on his horse to St. Bothans' and similarly 14s. Scots given to 'an honest gentleman come from Ireland being recommended by the Moderator of the Presbytery.' Even without special recommendations, Sessions appear to have had considerable sympathy for gentlefolk down on their luck and even if such a person had been reduced to beggary, the fact of their real social status might be indicated along with the sum given, 'To a gentle beggar . . .', for instance.[118] Many strangers were sick and one can only feel pity for 'a poor stranger in a dropsy with four children' who was given 6s. as she passed through a parish, but inevitably many of the women were pregnant and had their babies somewhere or other on their journeys and this was a very great worry and expense to Kirk Sessions.

Entries from Melrose Kirk Session's records show that 3*s*. was given 'to a travelling woman who has brought forth a child in Newstead', and the same year money was paid 'to William Williamson, for a coffin and winding sheet to a child brought forth in his house by a travelling woman and ten days attendance of his wife on the said woman'. Should mother and child survive childbirth, then there would be transport costs to pay to set them on their way, which could come to an expensive total, like the £6 Scots also paid by Melrose, for such a case.[119] The circumstances of some of these pregnant travelling women were very sad. In 1751 a woman whose husband was a sailor in the East India Company's ship *Prince George*, lost her husband's bond for wages in London and decided to set off home to her father in Scotland. She had only got to Coldingham, not so very far over the Border, when her baby was born but the Session there saw to it that she had a woman to look after her for three weeks and they also paid the baby's burial costs, a total of £6 4*s*. Scots. While needed help was given, it was always hoped that the money spent might be repaid. This particular woman had a husband so all was probably well but where there was doubt about a woman's married status a Session would institute inquiries about her home parish and her husband, partly to see whether information should be sent to her own Session about her morals but also to try to ensure that the husband would be made to pay if at all possible. In 1752 another pregnant woman arrived in the parish of Coldingham and for eight days found accommodation in a house there and was employed spinning but when she went into labour the householders gave her 6*d*. for her work and put her out, telling her to go to the Session 'but by no means tell that she had been in their house'. While she was still in labour, three elders and the Session Clerk visited her to try to find out what was what. She said that she was married but could not say where the marriage had taken place and neither did she have any marriage certificate. Her husband had joined the army and gone to Newcastle, where she had followed him, only to learn that he had moved elsewhere in the north of England at which point she had decided to return home. It was an all too familiar story of a silly girl taken in by an unscrupulous man. She promised the deputation that she would leave the parish with her baby as soon as she had recovered her health and could walk and in the meantime the Session paid her expenses of £4 2*s*. Scots which included a woman to care for her and the child. They felt however that the people whom they discovered had employed and housed her and thereby kept her in the parish, should contribute to her costs: 'It is the mind of the Session that Patrick Cowan should immediately pay 3*s*. stg in part of the above expenses, and in case of refusing be pursued before the Sheriff for the whole.'[120] Where a stranger's condition was particularly bad it might be brought to the notice of the Presbytery. David Mowat was a 'poor strange seaman' who arrived in Portsoy, Banffshire, in 1719 with one leg broken and the other 'miserably crushed' which happened while trying to save his ship, only to find that 'the ship to which he belonged has gone and left him' but fortunately the Session's initiative resulted in the Presbytery authorising collections to be made on his behalf throughout the bounds.[121]

But there were other sorts of travellers too. The Session records of island parishes often refer to tempestuous weather affecting the movement of ministers on Sundays and this affected other people too so that it was no unusual thing for travellers to be storm-stayed and find themselves in financial difficulties and, just as modern travellers in foreign parts nowadays go to their Consul for help, so these people went to the local Session who did what they could for them. In one case, a poor man with his wife and children, were delayed in Orkney on their way to Shetland 'after a great tempest of storm and rain' and the help they were given was provided out of a collection organised by the Session for their benefit.[122] All of these instances refer to living strangers entering parishes in need of help but when they came in and died, or were found dead, that was yet another expense, one which is dealt with in the chapter on burial. Dead or alive, strangers were a great burden and every penny of help given to them meant that much less for the native poor of a parish.

The requirement that those on the poor's roll should be pious has already been mentioned, which implied attendance at the established church, so what happened to those who did not belong to it? The following entries in the accounts of Morham Kirk Session, East Lothian, show kindness to at least one clergyman of another denomination: in 1722, 'Given by the minister's order to an Episcopal minister £1 10s. Sc.,' and in 1723, 'to an old distressed Episcopal minister 12s.' Roman Catholics had to survive as best they might but once they were allowed to worship in freedom, they had their own collections and received nothing from what was taken up in parish churches. They got their share, however, of any money bequeathed for the parish poor in general and when a sum of £10 was given to one parish's poor, the Session ordered that £3 10s. of it should be given to the most needy of the Roman Catholic poor.[123] These were people who had never belonged to the Church of Scotland. A much tougher attitude was taken to those who defected, taking not only themselves but their collections to seceding establishments which were regarded as 'very hostile to the interest of the poor; because what is collected there is generally laid out in defraying the expense of building and repairing their church, or in maintaining their minister.' Little wonder that ministers of the kirk and their elders often complained about people who gave their Sunday contributions to these chapels and then expected help from the parish kirk funds when they fell on hard times.[124] In some cases, it appears that poor people remained in the established church only because of its poor relief: 'from certain motives [they] remain but too firmly attached to the church', was how one minister put it, a statement which seems to imply some regret that these burdensome people had not obliged by seceding. In fact, some dissenters maintained their own poor or else contributed to the general poor's funds but in many cases seceders had to beg for their living. It was 1830 before any seceders appeared in the poor's list of a parish where a major secession had taken place in 1756 but four of them were then admitted to the roll at the lowest rate of 3s. stg. each.[125]

It may seem terrible that the church could leave people to beg for their living but for years this had been a recognised way for people to help themselves and was one which ultimately the kirk sought to regularise and indeed encourage. Initially, however, that was not so. The vast numbers of beggars and vagrants roaming Scotland at the end of the seventeenth century has already been mentioned and many of them were far from the pathetic creatures which the word 'beggar' conjures up. Many were described as being 'sturdy' which meant that they were well able to work for their livings had they wished to do so and others were called 'masterful' which meant that they intimidated those on whom they preyed. Worst of all were 'sorners' who took up lodgings in barns or outhouses forcibly, which was very frightening for their involuntary hosts, especially when they travelled in large groups. In addition, people going to church were harried by groups of beggars who sat outside waiting for them and while giving alms to the poor at the kirk door has already been mentioned, these beggars were not ones to sit quietly; instead, they made a fearful nuisance of themselves by clutching at people's clothing to draw attention to their plight. Early Session records have references therefore to forceful dealing with this type of beggar but this was quite different to the removal of stranger poor simply because they were poor and likely to seek to join the paupers' roll. In 1587 Elgin Kirk Session ordered that stranger beggars should be warned to remove by sound of the bell; about the mid-seventeenth century another Session paid 15s. Scots for five weeks' work by 'Robert Guthrie, for keeping out vagrant and sturdy beggars' and about the same time Montrose Kirk Session paid 6s. a week to John Anderson, the scourger, 'to hold out all sturdie beggars out of the town'. In Aberdeen in 1608 all sturdy beggars who would not come into the church for services but stayed in the churchyard being a nuisance were threatened with imprisonment and in Stirling in 1665, where the church was 'troubled with sturdy beggars every Sabbath', a constable was instructed 'to wait at the style next Sabbath to put them away and if refractorie, to put them in the stocks or steeple'. When in the early seventeenth century Perth found itself in the unfortunate position of being the home of Patrick Crombie, said to be king of the beggars, whom many of his kind came to see and then remained, the Session asked the Laird of Muirtown, on whose land Patrick was living, to remove him altogether.[126]

Not only did beggars sit at church doors or at the churchyard gate but they sometimes settled down at the door of wherever a Session meeting was being held, something sufficiently common for one Session to decree in 1687 that 'no beggar or pensioner sitt at the session house door in tyme of their meeting, otherwise they are to have no benefit from them,' adding that if they persisted in this they would be censured by the magistrates who would 'take course with them'. This was in keeping with several Acts of Parliament passed against beggars, one of which ordered in 1579 that all idle, strong beggars, loafers and ruffians who would not work for their bread should be scourged, burnt through the ear with a hot iron and forced to work and if this did not reform them, then they were to be hanged as thieves. An Act of 1592 which required irons and stocks to be provided at kirks for punishment of idle beggars and vagabonds sounds mild in comparison. This drastic treatment was imposed because of a sincere belief that able-bodied begging vagrants should be punished for not working but legal provision for the arrest of sturdy beggars could produce its own problems: in 1730 a special collection among nearby parishes was called for by the Town Clerk of Banff to maintain sturdy beggars in prison and although this can hardly have been a very popular cause to support, one parish alone produced £1 4s. Scots. Neither can an Act of Parliament in 1655 have encouraged parishes to arrest vagabonds because it provided that any who were waiting to be transported to the West Indies must be maintained by the parishes where they had been apprehended until they were finally shipped abroad. Throughout the later sixteenth century Acts of Parliament aimed at restraining beggars, which overlapped with care of the poor, continued to be passed, including the one of 1592 already mentioned, which concerned the ordinary poor but was largely directed at beggars and empowered Kirk Sessions to appoint two or three people to enforce earlier Acts to do with both categories; and just as the later Act of 1597 directly involved Sessions with the poor in their parishes, so it involved them with beggars.[127]

In spite of this repressive attitude towards beggars, the necessity for others who could not work to be allowed to beg had been recognised for a long time. In 1424 Parliament, as said at the beginning of this chapter, passed an Act, albeit in negative phraseology, which forbade those between the ages of fourteen and seventy to beg unless they had a 'token' from the Sheriff or bailies stating that they could not work, without which they were to be branded and banished. Another Act, both forbidding and permitting, was passed in 1535 and repeated in 1551 and 1555, decreeing that no one should beg except in their parish of birth and then only with a token from the headsman of the parish. In 1574 permission was given for licensed begging if it was considered necessary, and tokens must have been given out reasonably freely as in Elgin prior to 1601 'signs for marking the poor' were being obtained by the Session, as well as a stamp for making more but there was a condition attached: those issued with these 'taikins and tounes signe', as they were called, had to wear them or else have them taken from them and themselves be banished from the town.[128] During the first half of the seventeenth century, however, attempts were made to stop all begging. In 1625 a missive from the king required beggars with no parish of their own to be distributed throughout the country, though there is no evidence that this was carried out, and also required the poor to remain indoors and not go begging, and the Act of 1649 which has been mentioned already and which was of major importance in the care of the poor, also forbade begging. Unfortunately the political and ecclesiastical troubles of the seventeenth century were such that there was a great increase in poverty and in the number of beggars and vagrants, so much so that at the end of the century, it is said that there were 200,000 of them, nearly a fifth of the population. As a result, by 1672 Parliament had to face up to the position and by an Act that year decreed that where collections at parish churches were insufficient to support the poor of any parish, then they should be given badges or tickets by their Kirk Sessions to license them to beg for their living. This took a great burden off poor's funds and freed what money there was for the really needy. Thereafter licensed begging was introduced as and when Sessions felt it necessary for those poor they felt should do so and for those wishing to beg.[129] Kilconquhar, for instance, began in 1699 but it was only in 1722 that a man named Davie Hoom reported to Inverness Kirk Session that he had had 'Meddals' made for the poor and all the beggars in the parish were ordered to meet in the churchyard where a committee of elders saw 'the said Meddals or Bages delivered to them'. Even so, it was considerably later that licensed begging really came into its own and it was probably due to the aftermath of the Stuart Rising of 1745 that there are so many Session minutes about the introduction of beggars' badges from about 1750 to the 1770s. It was in 1757 that one Ross-shire Session minuted: 'The Synod having passed an Act appointing the several Sessions to distribute badges to the poor of their respective parishes that vagrant beggars may be discouraged . . .' and then went on to consider this; and it was in 1775 that beggars had increased so much in the town of Montrose, and had become so bold in their demands, that the Town Council consulted the magistrates of Aberdeen who were already regulating beggars with the issue of badges. Following this there was a lengthy meeting between the magistrates and the Session which came down in favour of issuing badges but while it was stated clearly that these beggars in Montrose should at no time try to enforce their pleas for alms but simply exist on their 'chance of charity of passers-by' they were nevertheless permitted to go through the town in a body on the first day of the week to beg *en masse*, which seems a surprising decision in view of the complaints about their boldness.[130]

Beggars' badges were made of pewter or lead and although there must have been wide variation in them around the country, one which survives in an interesting collection at Holy Trinity Church, St. Andrews, is fairly heavy, 2" wide, 2½" long and about ⅛" thick. They were stamped with a letter or letters to indicate the name of the parish and had to be worn prominently, like a bus driver's badge, so that parishioners could easily recognise their own parish's authorised beggars. They were fairly expensive. Having decided in 1775 to issue badges, an entry in the treasurer's book of Montrose Kirk Session that year shows 'To 72 badges for the begging poor at 4d. apiece £1 4s.; to a brass mould for casting them in, 10s. 6d.' Sometimes the beggar's name was written on the back of the badge which must have made it difficult to transfer it to anyone else but that may only have been when the authorisation was on parchment with 'an attestation thereupon showing the persons to receive them to be the poor of this parish', something which had to be prepared by the Session Clerk. It was apparently not uncommon for begging certificates to be signed just by the minister or in other cases by the minister with two or more elders, as well as a Justice of the Peace, although how a largely illiterate population could read these is not explained.[131]

The reason for giving out these badges was to distinguish a parish's own beggars from vagrant strangers and to give them the right to beg within, and only within, their own parish because to go beyond its bounds would have been to infringe the begging rights of other parishes. Once any parish introduced this system their parishioners were not meant to give alms to any but beggars with their parish badge — people could be prosecuted if they gave to others — and additionally the badges acted as an implied, although not explicit, recommendation for charity although, just occasionally, this recommendation could be turned into a threat: 'Tenants unwilling to give the begging poor such supply as they can reasonably afford, [are] to be stented', in other words taxed, said the minutes of one Session, which was a clear case of coercion. To be fair to the parishioners there, at that date there were twenty-eight begging poor continually making their rounds and while for many people it was easier to give a little something to a beggar than to put money in the church collection plate, it is very understandable that people living none too well themselves could have got remarkably fed up with so many people constantly knocking on their doors asking for something. What is interesting in this case, however, is that the stricture applied only to tenants, not to cottars. One way and another, beggars could usually live fairly well in a prosperous district, receiving in addition to food and meal, perhaps wool, clothing and grain, but in a very poor area, such as much of Skye, while they might receive such little food as could be spared, they got nothing more and were always miserably off for clothing. The term 'strolling beggars' was sometimes used for these people which has a misleadingly happy-go-lucky sound to it, because there was little that was jolly about a genuine beggar's life.[132]

The division of the poor into classes according to their needs has already been mentioned and once any parish began licensing beggars, then they became an additional class and at the annual meeting to check the poor's roll the names of those who 'can neither work nor beg' and those who were physically able to beg were decided. Intimation from the pulpit let people know when their badges would be issued and this was minuted: 'The badges for the poor having come home it was this day advertised that the objects on the list may have one for each, and the parish warned against encouraging vagrants.' Some ministers made assurance doubly sure by reading out to the congregation the names of those who were to receive badges, as well as those too infirm to beg who would have to be supported at home by the Session, but a beggar's badge did not necessarily exclude a person from some share in the distribution of the poor's money as some parishes gave these people a small allowance. By giving the begging poor their special status the kirk turned them into professional beggars although this was not as bad as it sounds now because to be a licensed beggar was a privilege at a time when the country was overrun with vagrants of all sorts. Even so, there was a restriction, in some places at any rate, which disqualified beggars from being witnesses.[133]

Badges were normally only issued or re-issued for a year at a time but one minister, writing in the early nineteenth century, considered that even a year might be too long. In twenty-one years he could only remember there being four or five beggars in his parish but

> Upon very pressing emergencies . . . such as long and severe distress in a poor man's family, or his stock being lost by fire, or by other unforeseen accidents, the

Kirk Session of this parish have granted a written certificate (besides all that our own funds could afford of assistance at the time) to such objects, when honest and of good character, recommending them to the more extensive charity of the country and neighbourhood [not just the parish, in this case] but we have generally appointed these recommendations to be used for only three, four or six months from their respective dates, more or less according to the pressure of the case, and then to be returned to the Session, conceiving that we had no right except in very urgent cases, to send out such petitioners to the country at large. We have refused nearly one half of such applications; nor do I remember to have signed above ten or twelve of even these limited certificates . . . Were this mode of granting only temporary recommendation more generally adopted by Kirk Sessions, strolling beggars would become less frequent and troublesome.[134]

One parish where there must have been similar views was Oldhamstocks, East Lothian, where in 1812 some people whose house had been burnt were permitted to beg for the space of four weeks throughout the parish. Nevertheless the yearly system was the usual one but as soon as a badge was no longer required, because of death or because the particular circumstances which had caused its issue had ended, then it had to be returned to the Session. Some Sessions licensed beggars during years of famine, as Kirkcaldy did in 1836, but not in others, restarting only if circumstances warranted it. The licensing of beggars must have worked well as otherwise its use would not have been as popular with Sessions as it was but the intention that such beggars should confine their activities only to their own parishes certainly did not always work out. Just one of the General Views of the Agriculture of a county — Ross and Cromarty, by Sir George Steuart Mackenzie in 1813 — frequently comments on strolling beggars. The minister of Rosemarkie said that no beggars from there went to other parishes 'but there are numbers who frequent it (Rosemarkie) from other parishes.' In the parish of Contin few of the parish poor went begging but while the number of beggars from elsewhere was uncertain, during the summer of 1812 there might have been ten or twelve a day, not only from elsewhere in the county but from neighbouring counties also and the minister felt it necessary to say, 'It would be a proper thing that every parish should maintain its own poor', meaning in this sense their own, and only their own beggars, which was what licensing was meant to achieve.[135]

One of the reasons why beggars went where they should not have gone was given by a writer in 1799 and sheds a kind light on the ordinary people of Scotland, so often said to be mean. While efforts were being made to control begging by licensing, 'the country people of Scotland are so charitable from principle and habit, that they will not be restrained from serving the poor at their houses. So long as they esteem it a Christian duty . . . to give alms, they will persevere in this practice; and so long as beggars are served, beggars will go, in the face of every regulation to suppress begging.' On this subject of charity, many poor people used to leave bags at mills so that people having grain ground could put a little into them if they wished,[136] similar to the modern idea of placing collecting tins in strategic places.

In parishes which included burghs, Town Councils and Kirk Sessions worked closely with one another over the problems of beggars as, for example, the case already given when Montrose Town Council consulted Aberdeen magistrates, then met with its own Session which was followed up by the Session obtaining and paying for beggars' badges. In Dunbar in 1725, however, the Burgh Council and Session found that because of a 'want of a proper concert' between them, beggars were receiving aid from one and then the other, and because of that the magistrates got in touch with the Session about the matter and the Session replied with a memorial or record of facts. It is not clear which side had produced the decisions in the memorial but if it was not the Session, what was said was certainly agreed and minuted by them:

1) that a common allowance between Town Council and Kirk Session in equal proportions be given to stranger beggars and distressed persons that pass through the burgh, to be distributed by the Treasurer of each body turn about, with accounts kept and countersigned by the Magistrates and the minister.

2) A ration of coarse wheat bread worth 1*d.* stg. with $^1/_2d.$ in money to be given to such as arrived in the town two hours or more before sunset and therefore had time to walk out of the burgh; but 1*d.* more to be given to those arriving later who would have to stay in the town all night, to be given by the Treasurer himself or with a token or tally from him to the baker who supplied the bread.

3) This was to be the same for everyone unless in the opinion of the Magistrates and minister that there was some special extra need.[137]

Licensed begging was designed for the able-bodied poor but in practice it could be extended to the handicapped also. In 1742 one list of paupers had two classes: there were twelve bedridden poor and twenty-eight 'travellers with badges of lead numbered' which indicates that anyone not actually bedfast was expected to get out and beg. Even someone who was blind might have to do so provided they had someone sighted to lead them — there was a case of this in the parish of Banchory-Devenick in 1716 when a young lad led his old blind mother about the parish. There was a case elsewhere of a woman who was not only blind and an epileptic but was also disabled down one side whom the Session, after supporting for two years, recommended should be led from house to house to beg, although her problems were solved by death the following year.[138] Strictly speaking, crippled beggars came under the direction of the heritors but it was mainly Kirk Sessions who coped with them by using the kirk's fore-runner of the wheelchair — a hand barrow. The handicapped person had to find someone to wheel him or her along the streets or to somewhere like a farm where there would be food and lodging for the night and next day someone would be ordered to push the barrow and its load on to another place as soon as possible. It sounds a dreadful practice but it was often the best a Session could do and so various kirk records have entries like the following; '1756. The Kirk Session ordered a barrow to be made for Jean Guthry that she can be carried from door to door in the parish as her friends are so unnatural as to have abandoned her.' The mentally ill were sent out in barrows as well. In 1759 a letter from the physician and managers of the Infirmary of Aberdeen came to a Session saying that Margaret Steinson, who was in the hospital, was likely to lose her reason entirely and as there was no hope of recovery they asked for suitable people to be sent to take her home. Two men were paid £6 7s. Scots to do so but once home, all that the Session could due for her was to provide her with a barrow — it cost 26s. Scots — so that she could beg for a living. During the next five years, her barrow was twice repaired and 8s. 4d. was spent on a plaid to keep her warm and when she died in 1764 her funeral costs came to 3s. 9¹/₂d. Even the bedridden might be got out of bed and into a barrow: a bedridden orphan was supported for a while by his Session but in 1702, possibly because of a shortage of funds after a long famine, they decided to get him a barrow, 'he now having losed the use of his legs'. Just as other licensed beggars might receive a little assistance from the poor's funds, so those carried in barrows were also given some help, like the money given 'to one Wallace, carried on a barrow, 3 shs Scots.'[139]

Beggars gravitated to where alms were most likely to be forthcoming, which was where there were plenty of people, in busy streets, and in the case of those carried in barrows they could become a public nuisance. In 1804 a bailie in Lauder reported on the number of beggars being taken about the streets in barrows and it was decided to authorise the Sheriff officer to remove them from the parish at the expense of the heritors. While this appears to have been a decision of the burgh council rather than the Kirk Session, it shows how numerous such people were. But barrows were not the only form of transport for the crippled begging poor and Session minutes refer to such items as 4s. Scots given in 1666 'to a poor woman carried in a creel', 4s. Scots given in 1749 'to a singular object of charity, John Hamilton, carried upon an ass', 6d. given 'to a poor object on crutches' and what sounds an extraordinary form of aid to a cripple, 'To Alexander Stewart, wricht, for ane pair of stilts to Henry Cary, Crippell, 4s.' but in fact, stilts in this context were almost certainly crutches. In 1726 a Session gave 6s. Scots 'to the cripple that goes on the clogs', which may have been just what it says, a long-lasting type of wooden footwear, but it has been suggested that these clogs might have been blocks of wood or patterns for the hands so that the body and legs could be dragged along behind.[140]

When crippled strangers arrived in a parish they were inevitably beggars and were a terrible burden because not only did humanity demand that they be given a little financial help but, because of their disabilities, any Session was more than anxious to move them on and removing cripples was more expensive than sending ordinary strangers on their way. One minister reported that 'the [poor's] box was much prejudiced by hiring horses for taking away creeples', and in the first half of the seventeenth century the removal of cripples from another parish was a constant worry to the minister and Session, especially as it was not always easy to find someone free to do it: 'We could get naen in the toun to carry away this crepill the morn because of their business' said the minutes at one point and the only solution was to divide the 'toun' into four quarters, each of which was required to remove cripples 'their week about'. Very many Session minutes refer to the carrying of cripples and a payment of 4s. 'given to two women for carrying away a cripple in a barrow' indicates that not only barrows, but also women, were considered suitable for this work.[141]

But however they were carried, there are stories of these physically handicapped beggars, local or strangers, being very high-handed, perhaps a relic of the old masterful beggar. It was said of one old woman that as she was being barrowed from house to house by each household's servant, she would not hesitate to give that unlucky person a good whack with her crutch if she did not think she was being pushed steadily enough. Another example of this sort of behaviour was when a farmer proposed to send a beggar on to another farm in a barrow — he must have arrived by some other means — but the beggar would have none of this and insisted, even although it was in the middle of turnip sowing, that the farmer must stop his work and send him in a cart. Where it was necessary, licensed begging continued until the passing of the Poor Law in 1845 and the custom of sending cripple beggars from house to house in a parish was, even in the 1870s, still a living memory in some places.[142]

Bedemen have been mentioned as residents in bedehouses but there was a type of beggar known as a King's Bedesman or King's Beggar, which was something different. Often known as Bluegowns from the colour of their cloaks, these beggars were not licensed by the church but their position originated from an ancient custom of giving a blue gown, a purse, and as many Scots shillings as the king's age to selected old men, in return for which they had to attend prayers and preaching in the parish church, wearing their gowns, and to pray daily for the king. At the time these conditions were laid down, these men must have been confined to their parish if they were to attend its church regularly but certainly later on, the King's Bedesmen were allowed to travel the whole country, which they often did in pairs, wearing a pewter badge to show their authority from the king to seek alms as they went and the kirk was always good to them. Money 'given to a beadman' in 1727 and 'to an old blewgown' in 1734 are examples of generosity to these old men, who were still roaming Scotland well into the nineteenth century.[143] There were, however, still more categories of the poor and other special circumstances which involved the kirk in yet more poor relief.

3

The Fatherless, the Foundlings and the Famished

In 1734 the Kirk Session of Coll 'moved with the miserable condition of a fatherless and motherless boy . . . that is much distressed by sickness and exposure to the severity of the weather through want of Cloath, did bestow 3s. stg. upon him out of the poor's box, in order that he may provide himself with some cloaths'. The previous year a minute of that Session shows that 'Donald Mcian mhoir's child being left destitute of all the necessaries of life is become ane object very deserving of compassion the Session therefore in consideration of this child's care and also in commiseration of his sister's condition appoint . . . four merks to support them in their extremity.'[1] These touching entries give a very good idea of the attitude of Kirk Sessions to orphans and in the days when mortality was high, it was inevitable that there were orphans. The term was also used, however, for the children of a widow, i.e., 'a poor woman with two orphans'[2] but it also applied in the modern sense of totally parentless children although some Sessions referred to these as being 'doubly orphaned'.

It was the heritors who were really responsible for orphans and foundlings but as the practical administrators of poor relief on their behalf, it was the Kirk Sessions of the country who dealt with the needs of these children who, under Scots law, were entitled to relief until they were fourteen years old[3] although, as will be seen, they were often expected to do what they could to help themselves well before that. Swift remarriage of a widow could solve the problem of maintaining orphans. This was not common, of course, but it certainly happened in Stornoway in the Island of Lewis where in the late eighteenth century it was usual for a woman to marry again very soon after her husband's death, so that sometimes the new marriage contract was drawn up before the burial of her husband.[4] This implies church approval, but that is understandable if kirk funds were tight. The most obvious thing to do normally was to see whether any relations would take the orphans in although if they had not done so at the outset, there was an implicit indication of unwillingness. In 1832 a Session decided that the grandparents of two orphans should each take one of them and that the Session would give some help towards their maintenance if this was necessary. Two elders, who were authorised to offer a small clothing allowance, were deputed to visit the grandparents to see if they would agree but while one did, the other refused, saying he was utterly unable to care for any more than his own immediate family. The Session discussed whether they should seek legal advice about compelling him to care for the child but were advised that this would not be possible and in the end arranged with the willing grandfather that he would care for both children and that they would give him as much help as possible. This sounds a much more satisfactory solution from the children's point of view but it all took time to arrange, including getting the approval of the resident heritors.[5] A Session who had supported an orphan for two years then found themselves with a second one to care for and decided at that point to speak to the uncle of the first child 'to see if he would ease them of the burden of him' and although it is not clear if they succeeded in this aim, it seems surprising that they took so long to approach this relative. Sessions were naturally thankful if relatives or friends would take orphans off their hands and were perhaps too ready to leave it at that. When a widow died in 1773 leaving several children, the Session rouped what little she had — it only came to 11s. 7d. stg. — and arranged for the youngest child to be put out to a wet nurse and seemed quite happy that friends 'carried away the rest of the family'. Yet another Session found that no one would take in an orphan family but the children's half-sister and her husband, who lived in another parish. This couple were prepared to free the children's home Session and parish of all further expense and trouble about them if the Session would give them £20 Scots outright. The minister suggested offering £18 Scots but the elders thought it better to give what was asked rather than have the trouble of maintaining the children which would soon amount to much more. It was left to the minister to make what arrangements he could and the sum agreed upon was £18 12s. Scots. This was an admirable solution for the Session but one does wonder whether it was the best thing for the children. When the money ran out, what protection did they have? Would they be neglected, half starved or exploited workwise? Nevertheless, the Session were doing what they truly believed was the best they could.[6]

Another alternative was to send orphans to an orphanage or Orphan Hospital as such institutions were usually called. These only began to be established about the early eighteenth century but were always few on the ground and, although they had the support of the kirk, with parishes holding collections for their benefit, they were grim places. The Edinburgh Orphan Hospital took up to 160 children from seven to thirteen or fourteen years of age, from any part of Scotland, and taught them various trades but an idea of the conditions is evident from the fact that they had to make all their own clothing and shoes and also bind their own books. Any Session sending a child to such a place had to pay for it to be kept there: one paid £20 15s. Scots for a child there in 1743 although the length of time this payment covered is not given.[7] In many cases, however, orphans were cared for in their own home parish but nothing could ever be decided until the Session knew what their financial position was and therefore the first step was always to discover whether the dead parents had left any goods or property which could be used for the children's care. To this end, a couple or so of elders were often instructed to visit the home to see what was what. In one such case, the elders were appointed to find out what was in a house and 'make sale of it', only to find little of any value, not even enough to pay any debts, which left the Session to maintain the children entirely. In another case where there were six children left, instructions were given to 'appryse the goods and gear' of the family and a week or two later it was reported that these had been 'sighted' and that after all debts were allowed for, there was £34 15s. Scots worth left from which the Session gave the children 10 firlots of oats — 2½ bolls — 'for their present necessity'. More maintenance would have been given to them, of course, once these goods were sold, the most usual way of doing this being to hold a roup, as was done with the effects of paupers.[8]

Orphans kept in their home parish were usually boarded out but in the case of these six children, it may be that the older ones could look after the younger ones and that the first 10 firlots of oats were to feed them rather than to pay a foster-parent. Session minutes do not always make it clear whether money or victual shown as going to an orphan actually went to the child or to the person caring for it: for instance, Coldingham Kirk Session paid 8s. roughly every two weeks to an orphan named Katharin and Ashkirk Kirk Session has entries showing money given to an 'orfan' named James Scott and to various others too, but who got it?[9] The term foster-parent is seldom used in minutes and was perhaps too kindly a one for the circumstances of the times but boarding-out was usually the only practical solution and was very common although finding suitable people who were pre-pared to undertake the task involved Sessions in considerable effort: 'This day the Session considering that James —, orphan, was in great distress by reason he had none to take care of him and to keep him clean, therefor they thought fit to agree with any that would undertake to give him bodroom a quarter a year and keep him clean . . .'. As no one could or would take in an orphan without payment, entries like the following often appear in minutes: '30th June 1763, Margaret Paterson, a poor child, deprived of father and mother, who belonged to the parish, was burded in a herd's house and stude in need of supply, the session ordered fifteen shieling sterlin to be given to Allexander Welsh in Stenhope on her account', or 'Given to James Alme for maintaining a fatherless and motherless child the space of a year 2 lib.'[10]

What was paid for orphans' board or 'wages' as it was often called, could vary considerably even in the same parish. In 1702 a woman in Ashkirk offered to take in William Scott for £4 Scots per quarter, which seems to have risen to £15 Scots for six months by the following year but in 1703 another woman in that parish agreed to keep an orphan for £8 Scots the quarter, yet that same year, when a home was being sought for still another orphan, a boy, the kirk officer readily agreed to take him for just £1 10s. Scots in hand, which was paid at once. These variations are so great that there must have been a reason for them which probably had to do with the ages and needs of the children and it seems very possible that the kirk officer took a boy so willingly because he was of an age to be useful and the work he could do would offset the cost of his keep. An Ashkirk woman who a few years earlier accepted £8 Scots a quarter to keep an orphan was taking over from another who had refused to keep the child any longer without an increase in her fee, and disputes about the amounts of boarding-out payments appear constantly in minutes. Those who took orphans in at an agreed rate were very soon asking for more for doing so, saying they could or would not keep the child unless they got it, and they usually did get it. In 1697 a man named Adam Scott was caring for an orphan — in reality it would have been his wife who was doing so — for a payment of £6 per quarter but by the following August he refused to keep him any longer without a larger allowance and the Session decided to pay him what was due, as he was apparently out of pocket at the time, and two pecks of meal in addition. However, by that November he finally refused to have the child any longer and the elders had to search the parish until they found a woman willing to look after him for £6 a quarter plus half a firlot of meal. Such little extras, or at least the promise of them, could be the clinching factor even when the promise was rather doubtful, like one which offered a payment for two orphans plus 'a Blanket to the woman who has them' as and when any delinquents' penalties came in.[11]

Those taking in orphans obviously hoped that the care element of their maintenance allowance would contribute to their own family budget but unfortunately, as Adam Scott found, the payments agreed upon were not always made promptly, and so it was quite common for there to be complaints about this. A Wick man, for instance, was promised something like 20 merks a year but after six months said he could not continue to keep the child as in fact he had so far got nothing for it, whereupon he was immediately given some money — but what sort of food and care could this unpaid-for child have been receiving in the meantime? No Session meant to defraud those looking after orphans but trying to make scanty poor's money go a long way was always difficult.

The maintenance of orphans, as with paupers, fell on the parish of residence and could in certain cases involve considerable correspondence and work. In 1842 a widow arrived in the parish of Speymouth, Morayshire, only to die there the next day, leaving three children who were initially cared for by the kindness of local people until proper arrangements could be made. The minister wrote to the Kirk Session of Resolis, from where the woman had come, asking whether the children should be returned there or whether that Session would pay for their support in Speymouth. Copies of everything to do with the case were sent to the Resolis heritors — the children's ages, the circumstances of the parents at the time of their deaths, whether there were any relatives able or bound to support them. Several meetings were needed to get all the answers, one of the most important being the question of whether Resolis was bound to support the children or not. The factor for Newhall consulted Newhall's Counsel and it was decided that as the parents had their last legal settlement in Resolis, although they had not been born there, that the parish was bound to care for the orphans. While all this was going on in Resolis, however, the Kirk Session of Speymouth had not been idle and the minister then wrote to say that a merchant in nearby Garmouth had taken charge of one child, a fisherman in Lossiemouth in the same county had taken another and would see to her education and in both these cases, the Session vouched for the respectability of these people. The youngest child was boarded out at about £6 or a little more per year, which the sale of the mother's belongings would cover until the following year. The matter was therefore adjourned in Resolis *sine die* although their poor's accounts in 1844 show a payment to 'Pauper McIntyre in the parish of Speymouth' which may refer to one of the orphans.[12]

If there was insufficient money in the poor's box to maintain orphans until they were fourteen years old, then other means had to be devised for their support and begging could be the answer. This was done without the usual beggars' badges but with the approval and encouragement of their Sessions, encouragement which extended in the case of one Session to the appointment of a man to instruct a poor orphan boy how to beg and 'quhair to goe' because his boarding out was over-great a burden on the funds. In another parish two orphans were boarded out separately, one at a place called Boghall, but after frequent payments for them the Session decided 'by a majority of votes that the youngest of the orphans be sometimes set out to beg in or near to Boghall as far as his strength can allow.' This child was only seven years old and while begging was an accepted way of helping the poor to help themselves, if this was expected of a seven-year-old child, what was being required of the older one? Orphan children had to grow up fast: in 1773 a Session decided that one who was 'full nine years old . . . may shift for himself with the help of his friends in time coming.' Famines always placed great burdens on poor's funds and in 1699, during a famine, a Session which had looked after an orphan for some time decided that he would have to fend for himself and as it was by then May, with the summer coming on, 'they thought fit to let him go begging through the parish desiring the elders to recommend his case to their several bounds.'[13]

Apart from basic board and lodging, there were other forms of help which orphans might need. If ill there might be medical expenses like the £1 10s. 6d. stg. paid in 1782 'to the Surgeon for attendance upon and drugs to the orphan boy' or the 7s. Scots paid in 1701 'for cureing a poor orphan's face dangerously wounded by a horse's foot.' Footwear for orphans was a common expense and so was clothing: 'For harn to be three shirts to the orphan and a coat and breeches, 8s.' is a fairly typical entry but while, in this case, allowance was being made for a change of shirts, basically all that could be provided was enough to stand up in and no more, like the 'Coarse Suit and two Skirts' allowed to an Inverness orphan in the 1780s. In 1702 it was reported to a Session that an orphan named William Scott was 'very naked' and the man making the report was authorised to buy as much plaiding as would be necessary for him which showed considerable generosity. It cost 16s. Scots and the records show that 9s. Scots was 'payd to a tailour for making William Scott orphans cloaths and furnishing thread to them.' Later that year £3 Scots was given 'for to buy cloths and other things needful' for the child and the following year it was again found that his clothes were very bad and so 4 ells of 'shirten' were bought to be made into two shirts for him at the price of 16 s. Scots. As fortunately for the Session as for William, he was then befriended by Mrs Archibald of Meggetland whose husband, a writer from Edinburgh, sent £20 Scots to the Session for him and with this money behind them, they were able to order sufficient material to make more clothes for him which cost £5 10s. Scots so, although he began 'very naked' he ended up better clad than most.[14]

William Scott was described in the Session minutes as 'never taught to read' which was hardly surprising considering the original state he was in, and so the Session agreed that he should go to school for three months and be boarded during that time with some suitable woman. When the three months were up, it was decided to continue the arrangement for 'another quarter that he might tarry at school'. By this time, of course, there was Mr and Mrs Archibald's £20 to help with the school fees and boarding but even without such help, Session minutes often show concern for orphans' education so long as the particular children they sent to school showed natural ability and so long as there was money to pay for it, because elementary education did not become free until 1872. The kirk also made efforts to get orphans into suitable employment rather than let them drift into permanent begging and poverty. For this reason, one Session decided to continue a payment of 1s. 6d. stg. per week for an orphan for the time being but also asked an elder to try 'to procure employment at Draning for said boy, that as soon as possible he may support himself.' An expectation that orphans would stay in any jobs found for them are implicit in a case which came before that same Session a few years earlier. A girl who had been in their care left the employment to which she had been sent and her employer asked the Session to take her back into their care but as she was by then over fifteen years old, they told her that she must either return to her former work 'and quietly submit to her master and mistress or seek out a situation for herself' but they kindly offered to pay her board and lodging for three nights.[15]

In spite of all that the kirk might do for orphans, sad outcomes were fairly frequent which is not surprising as any destitute child of parents who had been poor was vulnerable right from the start. A series of entries about a child whose surname was Joly in the minutes of Hawick Kirk Session in the early eighteenth century tells its own story:

> Given to Margaret Turnbull for little Joly's half year keeping £3.
> Given for a pair of shoes for Little Joly 5s.
> Given for seven ells of Harn for Little Joly's sarks 18s.
> Given for seven ells of Stuff for Joly's cloes £2.
> Given for making Little Joly's cloathes 12s.
> Given for Joly bairn's cofine £1 4. 0.,

all of which is Scots money.

The bedridden orphan mentioned earlier as being got out of his bed and into a barrow to beg had already been given money payments and shortly after he got his barrow he was given 6s. for shoes but within a month or so the story of his sad life ends with the entry 'John Botch orphans coffin £2' plus 8s. for making his grave.

In the early seventeenth century a pedlar named Ogilvie travelled about East Lothian selling the type of ale-measures known as chopins, from which he got his nickname. As was often the case with pedlars his wife wandered with him and on one expedition they got to Tynninghame where, after almost three weeks without making any sales, his wife died leaving him with an infant son. He cared for the child as best he could but one cold November night he died in a byre where his body was found next morning along with the baby which had somehow managed to survive although it was only 'ane quarter old'. Immediately the minister arranged for a woman in the village to 'nurisch' it and made other arrangements 'seeing it was most necessary to have ane care of the bairn, and not to suffer it to perish.' While use of words like the 'burden' or the 'heavy load' of orphans and foundlings tends to make people think that the kirk was hard on these children this statement about Chopin's child sums up their concern for such children in their midst. They were as responsible in their care for them as circumstances permitted them to be and such words merely express the truth which was that they *were* a financial burden and a heavy load in worry and care. Sadly the efforts made for the pedlar's baby were of no avail and soon afterwards the minutes report that 'This day, Chopins his bairn, was buried'.[16]

Should a Session be particularly hard-pressed to support orphans a collection was sometimes organised on their behalf. This was the solution found in 1811 by Banchory-Devenick Kirk Session for the children of a shoemaker. Following his death two years previously, his widow and the children lived for some time in the parish of New Machar until she also died. At that point the Session of Banchory-Devenick accepted that the children had a natural claim on that parish as their father had been a parishioner, because there were relations living there and because the children were in need. They were only receiving very little assistance in New Machar and were thrown on the care of their grandmother and other relations who were unable to support them. Aware of these problems and in true concern for the children, the Session resolved to collect for them, both at the parish church and at the Chapel of Portlethen, raising the good sum of £8 14s. 4½d. stg. for them. In another parish a collection was arranged on the death of a man not only for his children but also for his widow.[17] In the event of a big disaster, it became usual for a fund to be started for the benefit of both widows and orphans. This was usually asked for by a Kirk Session and ordered by Presbytery or Synod with each parish within their bounds holding its own collection and sending what was raised in to a central point. On 9 March 1780 a fishing boat from Stotfield, Morayshire, was lost with all nine of its crew drowned. A minute book of Drainie Kirk Session, Morayshire, opens that year with the list of what had been gathered 'for behoof of the widows children and others rendered destitute by the loss of a Stotfield boat . . .' and names the parishes which had held collections for them: Drainie, Duffus, Kinloss, Alves, Urquhart, New Spynie, Elgin, St. Andrews, Edinkillie, Speymouth, Dallas, Dyke, Rafford, Forres, Birnie, and also refers to donations given. By 27 March 1780 the first distribution was made at Stotfield 'in presence and with the advice of two honest men of the place' just two and a half weeks after the disaster, to eight widows. Of these, two had no children and one had a grown-up daughter. Of the rest, one had a child and four older youngsters, one had four children 'all unfit to gain their bread', one had a sucking child, another had four very young children and yet another had two children and a baby on the way. There was also a widow who did not require assistance but the list included William Edward, an old man who lost his sons, his brother and his son-in-law, who had been supporting him; and there was also another elderly male member of the Edward family in need. With some money in hand, the Session also gave something to a woman whose husband had been taken by the press gang and two months later there was a further distribution, the accounts of which show 6d. paid to 'a poor woman for carrying the bagg w^t the money to Stotfield' and the final distribution from this fund was in July 1784, all of it having been handled by the local Kirk Session. In the same way a collection was made in 1807 for the relatives of thirty-seven fishermen lost when six boats were sunk in a storm in the Moray Firth on Christmas Day 1806 but this was on a far wider scale and was generously supported with one Kincardineshire Kirk Session collecting no less than £8 5s. stg. for it.[18]

A sad case occurred in 1738 when Kirkwall Kirk Session had to deal with the case of a child who was not just an orphan but also illegitimate, with no one at all to care for it. A Mr Burn, who was obviously worried about this poor child, applied to the provost and a bailie asking that they would stent the people for its maintenance seeing that it was 'no better than a foundling'; their reply was that they thought that the Kirk Session should send some of the elders through the town to collect what they could but they did at least offer to send one of the town officers along with them. This was duly done and £8 13s. Scots was raised which was given to the woman nursing the child, so that yet another collection was put to good use.[19]

As for foundlings, the cruel phrase about being no better than one was Mr Burn's, not that of the Kirk Session. Sessions showed particular care and concern for these especially unfortunate children whose hapless mothers so feared the punishment of the church that they concealed pregnancy and abandoned their children rather than face up to censure for the sin of fornication. So much did foundlings become their Sessions' adopted children that they often acquired the parish name. While not for a moment suggesting that all place-name surnames originate with foundlings, it was fairly common for a parish to designate such children by the parish name or that of a local town or the place where the child was living. This was not necessarily done consciously but could develop gradually as happened in the case of a child in the parish of Urr. In 1808 and 1810 there are payments for 'the child at Dalbeattie', a town in the parish, which then became 'the child Dalbeattie'. Similarly Andrew Shotts acquired his surname over several years in the parish of Shotts, Lanarkshire; Greenlaw gave its name to Alexander Greenlaw[20] and Tain had a child not only called but baptised Tam Tain.

There was one great difference between orphans and foundlings. The latter were almost certainly illegitimate and also unbaptised and because of this an Act of the General Assembly in 1712 said 'In the case of children exposed' — found-lings were often called exposed children because of being abandoned in the open — 'whose baptism after inquiry cannot be known, the Kirk Session is to order the presenting of the child for baptism and to see to the education of the child.' This put the Session *in loco parentis* and it was because of this baptismal responsibility that a Register of Births and Baptisms has an entry for 17 July 1788 stating that a male child was found early one morning on the front doorstep of a house, that certain steps were taken for his welfare and that as the mother could not be found 'the Session ordered him to be baptized on the 21st and gave him to name Nicholas.' A recent Minister of that parish has suggested that the name Nicholas may have been given because it was not common there and thus avoided any unfair suspicion of paternity. Because the privilege of baptism was withheld from an illegitimate child until the parents had served the appropriate punishment for their sin, this could in itself cause a child to be abandoned; when Janet Smith was accused of 'deserting and casting away her child' the poor girl said she had been moved to do so because it had not been baptised. The need for baptism was held in almost superstitious regard and Janet probably thought that this was a way of having her child safely baptised and that she was therefore doing her best for it.[21]

Exposing children was very wrong and every effort was always made to find who had done such a thing. When a baby was found 'in a ditch besouth Castle-barns' in Edinburgh, a city Kirk Session recommended that the minister should intimate to the congregation the next Sunday that this 'barbarous wickedness' must be brought to light, and the usual way of bringing such matters to light was for elders 'to inquire in their several quarters after suspected persons in order to find out the mother.' These searches could involve not just inquiries by these worthy men but physical examinations by midwives of any suspected women, as could happen in moral cases too, and where child murder was suspected. In the Grange area of Banffshire, for example, no fewer than 248 women were examined in this way in an effort in 1803 to discover the mother of a foundling.[22] The details of the steps taken to find a foundling's mother are fully given in the minutes of Inverness Kirk Session in January 1764:

> It was reported to the Session that about 2 o'clock this morning a Male Child was laid down at the door of Baillie Pheneas McIntosh's house, which was discovered by the Infant's cries and he having ordered his servants to take up the child and bring it in lest it should perish with Cold, he thereafter sent it to a proper person, to be taken care of, till the Session should Consert what was to be done in the affair.

As a result, the Session met later that day and divided the elders into districts to 'perambulate the whole Parish with a constable and a Burrow officer, to find, if possible, the mother, and at the same time that proper Care be taken of the Child.' People were appointed to search areas as follows:

> Kirk Street — 4 men, 1 constable, 1 midwife, 1 woman.
> Bewest the Water — 2 men, 1 midwife.
> East Street and Barronry — 2 men, 1 constable and 1 woman.

New Street and Vennels — 3 men, 1 midwife.
Bridge Street and Castle Wynd — 2 men, 1 constable.
Castle Street — 3 men, 1 constable and 1 midwife.
Clachnaharry, Muirtown and Kinmylies and Bught — 3 men who were to 'bring some honest women along with them.'
Dunean and Lochend — 2 men who were 'to bring a Discreet woman along with them'.
Essick, Torbreck, Knocknagial — 4 men and a discreet woman.
Culduthel, Londuach, Altnaskiach — 2 men and a discreet woman.
Bogbain, Inches, Castlehill, Kingsmills, Little Drakies, Cradlehall etc. — 3 men and a discreet woman.
Easter Drakies and Culloden, with the Moor — 3 men and a discreet woman.

Their instructions were that they must pass no house whatever without searching; that they take a strict account of any woman who had left the family or of any stranger who had lately come into any family, and midwives were told that their reports must be made on oath. Even with so many people searching, the mother was not discovered although it was reported that a pregnant girl had left the house where she had been living and no one knew where she was, and suspicion inevitably rested on her. Five months later, however, the real mother was discovered (who was not the disappearing girl), and the outcome was that the child's grandfather came to the town and agreed to repay the money spent on it and to take it off the Session's hands.[23] This must have been a very costly search but anything of the kind involved expense. Just one example is the £1 17s. stg. spent seeking the mother of an abandoned child, one that could hardly be called exposed concealed would be a better word, as it was only found by chance when a man felt the child move as he thrust a fork into a load of hay which had stood overnight. Although this seems more like attempted murder than exposure, the practical result was that the Session had a foundling on their hands. Some foundlings, of course, did not survive long enough to need the care of any Session. One Sunday, for instance, a man reported that a child which seemed to be about 8–10 days old had been left at his door before sunrise and that while it did not seem to be hurt in any way, it had shortly died. The Session ordered three men to bring its body to the church at the close of afternoon worship and ordered it to be seen by a doctor and some women, who all confirmed that it was unhurt, in other words that it had not been murdered. All neighbouring parishes were notified and the elders ordered to search the parish but as there is nothing more about the case in the minutes, it appears that these efforts met with no success. The remarkable thing is how many foundlings did survive and it says much for the prompt action taken by Kirk Sessions to save them that they feature as largely in Session minutes as they do.[24]

The most pressing need for a foundling was to find a wet nurse for it at once. In fact, foundlings apart, when illness or death of a mother followed childbirth as it often did, Kirk Sessions were frequently asked to pay for these women's services. £6 10s. Scots was given in 1748 to a poor man 'to help in paying for the nursing of his child, in respect of the great distress of the mother' and another man was given 10s. stg. 'for providing a nurse to one of his bairns' but in other cases the nurse was paid directly by the Session as in the case of a payment 'to a woman for nursing Thomas Denoon's child'. Not only paying wet nurses but actually finding them fell to Sessions: in 1717 one considered the indigent condition of Robert Scott whose wife had died leaving him 'with a child on the breasts' and they managed to find a woman to care for it, although it was her husband, John Garland, who was paid £5 Scots for this plus £1 6s. 8d. more for the nursing. In the case of foundlings, cold, hungry and wet, a temporary arrangement had to be made immediately if they were not to die, leaving a longer-term solution to be sorted out later once the mother had been found or her disappearance from the area confirmed. It was for this reason that one kirk treasurer was ordered to pay the woman who kept a foundling 'until inquiries be made anent the parents thereof.'[25] In 1832 when a woman in the parish of Resolis had a baby and then disappeared at the same time that a baby was found abandoned, everyone put two and two together and made four, especially as she had been seen carrying something beneath her cloak but although the Session instituted an immediate search for her, she managed to make a clean getaway. The Session at once arranged for a nurse to be found for the child at the rate of £1 stg. per month for eight months and thereafter at 2s. 6¹/₂d. per week, the same sum which they paid to the foster mother they found after the nursing was over.[26] They also arranged about clothing and other requirements for the baby because as with orphans, there was no one else to provide them. Also as with orphans, when weaned, foundlings had to be boarded out, clothed and cared for in sickness. A little foundling girl turns up for several years in the parish accounts of Kinnell, starting with £1 14s. Scots paid for 'Cloaths to the Exposed child' and 18s. 'for a creadle blanket' and going on with payments for frocks, bonnets and even mutches which though usually associated with married women can also be caps for infants. When she was ill the child got 'drogs' (drugs) and at one point was given 'sugar when she had the Pox'. This was one example of how kindly Kirk Sessions often treated their foundling children and another was when Greenlaw Kirk Session spent 4s. Scots in 1723 to give Alexander Greenlaw not only a Proverbs, which was a school book, but also 'an ounce of candie and a loaf when he was sick'. This was a most touching gesture, going far beyond what was required and showing, one feels, real love for the child. Little wonder that a book about the parish says that foundlings could be better off than if brought up by their own parents.[27] Entries from the minutes of two more Kirk Sessions give more examples of the basic care given to these children, starting with Andrew Shotts, one of those given the parish name. In 1721 James Lennox was paid £15 10s. Scots for boarding him from 4 February to 4 May; in 1724, 10s. was spent on mending his clothes and in 1726 James Lennox was again paid 'for boarding and maintaining Andrew Shotts in the pox and other sicknesse six weeks', something which came to £4 4s. Scots. In 1778 another Session paid £2 stg. for the board of a foundling for half a year and 1s. 7¹/₂d. for an ell of blue plaiding to be made into a garment called a 'hanging down coat' and also a 'pair of Bodies' which was body-clothing of some sort. Two years later the child was given a body coat, another hanging down coat, two shirts and a pair of stockings, all at a total cost of 10s. 1d.

Scots. Unfortunately, boarding agreements were not always adhered to, as happened with orphans also, and in 1720 for instance, Inverness Kirk Session received a petition from a man who was keeping a 'found child' saying that he had 2½ years board outstanding but that if this was paid up, he would not ask for any more for the child or alternatively, that he would waive this payment if they removed it. He seems to have been remarkably generous in his request and in this case, the Session paid him promptly but there were many other instances of outstanding payments.[28]

As the population of cities increased with the Industrial Revolution there grew up a large number of charity children in towns which involved Kirk Sessions in regular supervision of them and, in certain cases, obvious concern about their accommodation. This was why in 1833 the Kirk Session of St. John's, Glasgow, asked a Mr Buchanan 'to visit the foundling children for the current month as from the last report it seemed advisable to make some changes in the residence of the children . . . The Moderator and one elder were authorised in conjunction with Mr Buchanan to examine into the different cases and to do in them as they think proper.'[29] It is very clear from all this that in the case of foundlings the kirk put first things first and at once saw to the children's immediate care, but that did not prevent them trying to see that if costs were due from another parish, they should be paid by it, hence the following minute from Banff in 1700: 'The Session finding that the foundling with whom they are burdened, does originally belong to Elgine, It's thought fit the Minister write to Mr. Johnstone at Elgine to make inquiry thereanent.' The kirk was also more concerned with the financial implications than the criminal ones if the mother of a foundling was found elsewhere. In 1808 a child was found abandoned in the parish of King-Edward, Aberdeenshire, and the mother found later in the parish of Boyndie, Banffshire, whereupon the Kirk Session of Boyndie petitioned the Sheriff to apprehend her, not for the offence but to ensure that she could find caution that the child would not be burdensome to that parish.[30] Ultimately it was the heritors who were responsible for both foundlings and orphans should no-one else be found to bear the costs but payments had frequently to come out of the poor's box rather than from the heritors. Even when a Session might feel confident that expenses would be met by them, things might still not work out. In the case of the absconding Resolis mother, the Session called the heritors to a meeting at the manse to get funds for its care but no heritors came that day and only two attended a second meeting which explains why the following year the Session decided that the sum of £8 due by them to the wet nurse should be raised by a church door collection and that if this did not bring in sufficient, that it should be made up by the heritors. In the event the Session paid the nurse £3 of the £8 owing, and a further £1 when she handed the child over to the foster mother, leaving £4 to be repaid by the heritors but it is not clear if the money they paid was the proceeds of the collection or came out of the poor's box. Twelve years later, the question of this foundling, as well as an orphan, was still unsettled because of some question about one heritor's valuation and therefore about the proportion he was due to pay which in turn affected what the others were due to pay. On the subject of collections, a Session which had borne the 'heavy load' of a foundling for a year decided to hold one, minuting that it was 'customary in such cases to Solicit the Charity of Individuals for Support and Maintenance, knowing that the Humane and benevolent will be ready to Bestowe Libraly Something upon an Object of Sympathy and Compassion.'[31]

Naturally enough, foundlings were expected to maintain themselves as soon as they possibly could which was why, although one Session agreed in 1741 to maintain one of these children, it was with the stipulation that this would be 'till it was capable to do for itself by begging' and five years later it was indeed 'dismissed to beg its bread'. Another Session decided to give an 'orphan foundling' 10s. or 12s. for clothing but at the same time did not think that 'she should be a burden any longer on the Session, seeing she is eight years of age, and can travel about for her bread.' The Session which gave 'sugar when she had the Pox' to a foundling girl ultimately had to decide 'that the Fundlin is past ten years and may now work for her meat' but they gave her enough to buy half a boll of meal as she had no immediate provision.[32]

Possibly these particular foundlings showed little scholastic potential as Sessions often educated these children as they did orphans, and they might also help with apprenticeships as they did with poor children belonging to the parish. In later years anyway, care was taken to see that such children had a religious upbringing and it seems that when it was proposed by St. John's Kirk Session, Glasgow, in 1831 that the foundlings in their charge should be submitted once a year to the Moderator for examination — later changed to twice a year — that this referred to catechising them. The minutes of this Session, however, throw an intriguing little sidelight on this aspect of things. In March 1829 several of the elders reported that a number of parishioners were unable to have seats in the church because they were 'occupied by the charity children attending the church, and that in other respects the attendance of these children was very inconvenient to the congregation, Messrs. Paul and Falconer were requested to bring the matter under the notice of the proper authorities in the view of getting the children transferred to some one or other of the city churches which might be less crowded.' Unkind as this may seem, when seats could be let for the benefit of the poor, then it was essential that they should be, for without the income from such lettings, as well as other forms of money-raising, there would have been little to give to charity.[33]

Certain foundling cases deserve a special mention. Sometimes the circumstances behind the abandonment of a child had nothing particularly to do with fear of church censure for immorality, as when in April 1709 a child was found in Edinburgh and shortly afterwards the mother was discovered. It turned out that she had married a meal maker in Dirleton, East Lothian, but only a fortnight after their marriage he lost all his goods because of debt and they had to part. However, they met again and the child was conceived but almost immediately her husband was seized by the press gang and sent to Flanders, since when she heard that he had found himself another wife. Her child was born but as she had nothing with which to support it, she had left it at a particular spot but took care to wait at a little distance to be sure that it was safely found. However, when she returned without it to the house where it had been born the people there naturally suspected that she had murdered it as she would give no proper explanation of its whereabouts and so they sent for the elder of the bounds who had her imprisoned in the Canongate Tolbooth and ordered her to produce proper evidence of her marriage. When a Kirk Session committee was called to see her, all this sad story came out but when, four days later, it was reported that she had escaped from prison, it was intimated from the pulpit that anyone who knew where she was should report it to the minister or an elder and the Presbytery were also asked to intimate this within their bounds, so she was not going to be allowed to escape kirk vigilance.[34] A rather surprising case happened in 1802. It was reported that a baby boy, thought to be three or four weeks old, was left about 2.00 a.m. in the window of a house. The Session appointed an elder to try to find a woman to nurse the child, took all the normal steps they could to find the mother and also advertised in the *Aberdeen Journal*, offering a reward of £10 for her discovery but all without success. However, three weeks later a woman appeared and claimed the child but the Session, much as they must have hoped that she was the mother, hesitated to hand over the child at once, preferring first of all to have her examined by a Justice of the Peace, who decided that she was indeed the mother. Understanding that she was the daughter of a shoemaker in Cullen, the minister wrote to the minister there as she and the child were that parish's responsibility but, even so, the Session of the parish where the child had been found had to pay all the expenses of what they called this 'very troublesome affair'.[35]

In another case of an abandoned child, everyone knew perfectly well who the mother was. When it was laid down at the door of David Glen in the parish of Craig in 1735, there was no doubt that this had been done by Elizabeth Brown who had named him as its father. When told of this, the minister wasted no time in instructing the beadle to tell the couple with whom Elizabeth lived to go at once to see if the child had been taken in by David and if not, to take it home with them. His immediate concern was the child's welfare but in this case the Session were not responsible for the child's maintenance and applied to the Justices of the Peace for aliment. But the story did not end there. The following month there were scenes in the parish that must have set tongues wagging for days. A young child was found beside the church 'exposed and ready to perish' and it was reported that a woman named Jean Smart had been seen leaving it there and so she was duly summoned to appear before the Kirk Session. The minister then said that this woman's servant had taken the child to the manse the previous night, abandoned it and made a quick retreat, but he had managed to find her and when she admitted leaving it, he had ordered her to take it away. Later on, Jean Smart was found laying a child down at the manse door and said it was Elizabeth Brown's child, fathered by David Glen, but when David heard about all this, he arrived at the manse between 1.00 and 2.00 a.m., threatening to break the place up. For his own safety, the minister felt obliged to recommend that he should be pursued before the civil authorities — adding that this had also been a breach of the Sabbath![36] An unusual case of child abandonment occurred in the parish of Bellie, Morayshire, in 1829. A girl whose child had been begotten and born in another parish was told that Bellie was not responsible for it but she declared that she was ready to throw it down at the church door and leave it to be taken care of by the Session. In spite of being warned by the minister that if she did so, she would be immediately sent to gaol, she did just that but was caught by the beadle and handed over to the Sheriff's officer to be sent to the Procurator Fiscal. She cannot have been imprisoned, or at any rate not for long, as the minister shortly reported that she had left the unfortunate child in his back court and run off but as a result of an application to the Procurator Fiscal, she was arrested and imprisoned overnight and ultimately sentenced to forty days in Bridewell, the house of correction. Meantime the child was a burden on the parish although this was something which the Kirk Session of Bellie contested.[37] Kirk care of both orphans and foundlings continued in its varied ways until the Poor Law of 1845 lifted this burden from them, but it was one with which they had coped manfully.

What Kirk Sessions did to care for the fatherless and foundlings was most creditable but even more impressive was what they faced up to and achieved in times of famine, both local and national, and Session records are a fine testimony to the work that they did. Famines are now so associated in the public mind with Third World countries that it is easy to forget how common and how disastrous they used to be in Scotland. 'Times of dearth and scarcity', as Session minutes often refer to them, were only too prevalent in the sixteenth, seventeenth and eighteenth centuries and even into the first half of the nineteenth. They were largely due to the Little Ice Age between roughly 1580–1850/60, with its falling temperatures — although John Knox managed to blame Queen Mary for a year of dearth in 1563 which happened to be particularly severe in areas she had visited the previous autumn.[38]

Professor Smout's *History of the Scottish People 1560–1830* and J.A. Symon's *Scottish Farming* both describe frequent famine years. Many of the seasons between 1570–90 were bad and 1595 saw a very serious famine. In 1614–15 frost was so severe that most of the livestock in the country died; 1622–23 produced yet another very severe famine when many starving people came to Edinburgh in the hope of getting help, only for some of them to die in the streets. 1634–35 was such an ill season that meal cost £10–£12 Scots per boll and, according to J.A. Symon, even the clergy, to their shame, were perfectly ready to sell some of their teind oatmeal at this price. In 1640 famine yet again caused oatmeal to rise in price, from about £2 Scots to £10 per boll and in 1649–51 the scarcity was such that bere, a type of barley, cost £20 Scots and people were reduced to eating dogs, those on the coast were thankful to eat seaweed and suicide became common. In 1674 there were what was called the 'thirteen drifty days', thirteen days of non-stop snow, especially in southern Scotland where nearly all the sheep were lost and desperate long-term hardship followed. 1680 was another ill season and the winter of 1683–84 was so cold that part of the River Tay froze over at Dundee. From 1694 — some say 1696 — until 1701 there was the prolonged and terrible famine which came later, perhaps inaccurately, to be known as the Seven Years' Famine, and it too left serious long-term effects. In 1733 and 1745 crops, in some areas at least, suffered seriously owing to hail damage; 1740–41 was a time of great shortage, due in some places to frost and in others to a fog which scathed crops as if by fire. There were crop failures in 1756 and 1762 and, with frost for 94 days, 1763's harvest also failed. There was a shortage again in 1771 and 1782–83 produced a particularly serious famine, known as the Black Year. In 1795 there was yet another serious famine followed by shortages in 1796 and the years 1799–1800 were so bad that they were remembered as 'the dear years'. 1808 was bad, 1811–12 very bad and 1816, 1817 and 1819 were all years of crop failure and shortages. 1835–36 was a particularly bad time and 1845–46 saw the failure of the potato crop which was especially disastrous in the highlands.[39]

The reasons for famines are well described in the New Statistical Account for Kirkintilloch, Dunbartonshire,[40] which shows how desperately vulnerable people were to weather conditions when they existed at subsistence level. There were many double years of famine, partly because in the first year people were reduced to eating their seed corn, leaving little to sow, and also because if a crop failed or was scanty one autumn, then it was in the late summer of the following year, while awaiting the new harvest, that the shortage was most greatly felt. Although the worst famines were national ones, there were also many local ones. Thunderstorms, gales, floods or other disasters might strike one area and devastate its crops while neighbouring ones went unscathed but because of lack of roads and transport, it was difficult to send food from one district to another, even had there been any to spare which there seldom was, when agriculture was only practised on a scale sufficient to support immediate needs with nothing available for hungry people elsewhere.

In the early days of the Reformed church there was little that a parish could do on its own about famines although help came from the kirk in an indirect way during one in 1680 which was very bad in some highland areas; the earliest spring growth was to be found in the churchyard and this the people pulled, often fighting over it, to eat it boiled without either salt or meal.[41] Of the few practical things that could be done to alleviate famine, one was to help with a public collection for another area: for example, in 1647 the Kirk Session of St. Cuthbert's, Edinburgh, organised a collection which raised 525 merks to help the people of Orkney when there was a severe shortage there; or it could be something like putting a temporary limit on the cost of bridal meals. One Session, because of what they called 'the charseness of victuals', meaning the scarcity of food, ordered that no more than 5s. Scots for dinner or 3s. for supper should be paid and that if this was exceeded, the young couple would find themselves in trouble, an idea very similar to the cost limit placed on restaurant meals during the 1939–45 war. In general, however, the least and the most that could be done was to hold a fast day for humiliation and prayer; after all, Deuteronomy 11: 13–17, included famine as one of the punishments for ungodliness and the first reaction to any disaster, actual or expected, was to regard it as divine retribution for the wickedness of the people. In the famine of 1623 when starving people died in the streets of Edinburgh, the kirks there held a fast for some days, with sermons beginning at 7.00 a.m. daily during the week, but it all ended with a climax for which they had not bargained — so tremendous a thunderstorm that the people thought the day of judgment had come. Fasts might be ordered by Kirk Sessions or by Presbytery, Synod or by the government and, in the same spirit, when things got back to normal, it was usual for there to be a service of thanksgiving.[42]

The first major famine to begin after the establishment of the Church of Scotland in 1690 was the Seven Years' Famine, sometimes known as the Ill Years or King William's Ill Years, an unfair slur on the new monarch. At that time some parishes still had Episcopal incumbents while others might have vacancies while they waited for new ministers, there was a lack of elders and to a large extent the kirk could not cope with such a disaster at such a time, especially as at its outset large areas of Scotland were still reeling from an outbreak of plague in 1694 and it was into a situation of utter misery and ill health that this famine arrived. The trouble began in August 1694 with a very cold east wind and a dense fog which mildewed the ripening grain so that it withered and shrank and the harvest was ruined and, because potatoes did not come into general use in Scotland until the mid-eighteenth century, they were not available as an alternative food for the people. In *Scenes and Legends of the North of Scotland* Hugh Miller wrote of this famine:

> From this unfortunate year [1694] till the year 1701, the land seemed as if struck with barrenness and such was the change in the climate, that the seasons of summer and winter were cold and gloomy in nearly the same degree. The wonted heat of the sun was witholden, the very cattle became stunted and meagre . . . November, December and in some places January and February became the months of harvest; and labouring people contracted diseases which terminated in death, when employed in cutting down the corn among ice and snow.

So great was the impact of this famine that 140 years after it a Statistical Account particularly mentioned this 'awful period' when so many died of want, the rich became poor, land changed hands, the whole face of society altered and, all in all, it was regarded as one of the events which notably affected the character and identity of the people. It also explains why in 1703 Inverness Kirk Session still had moral cases involving married people, outstanding after ten, twelve or even fourteen years when these would normally have been vigilantly pursued; and other Sessions would have been in the same position too.[43]

It is hardly surprising, all things considered, that some Kirk Session minutes do not mention this famine at all. If nothing could be done about it, then there was nothing to record. One of these is North Berwick, East Lothian, another the Barony Kirk in Glasgow. Other Sessions were concerned that efforts to obtain food should not profane the Sabbath. In 1697 four Langholm men went one Saturday to get food in Carlisle, over the border in England, but found on their return that the River Esk was impassable, settled down by it for the night and crossed on Sunday morning, only to be rebuked for not leaving their loads by the river, crossing without them and going back for them on Monday. In August 1697 another Session forbade anyone to go to Newcastle on Sundays for food and it says much for the strength of these Sessions' Sabbatarianism that they were so strict at that time of the year because, as has been said, late summer was the worst time for the people in famine years.[44] Even with the logistical difficulties of the period, however, the remarkable thing about this famine is the number of positive things, rather than negative ones, that Kirk Sessions did. In 1696 that of Ashkirk began to take practical steps to deal with the situation, starting of course with a day of fasting and humiliation. In January 1697 they bought two bolls of meal at a cost of £41 15s. Scots to distribute to the poor and in June 1698, when they met to distribute the collections taken at the last two fast days, and realised that there was not enough money to 'pairt amongst so many persons as they know to be in great necessity' they made it up to £20 Scots. In June 1699 the Commissioners of Supply of Selkirkshire made an order concerning care of the poor, as happened in other counties also, as a result of which the heritors and Kirk Session of Ashkirk met and decided to stent the heritors according to their valuations for those in need. In anticipation of this, the elders gave out a week's provisions in July, doing the work themselves, and it must have been hard work too as by then there were 98 on the list of poor and as these would have been heads of households rather than individuals, the true figure would have been much higher. Unfortunately the heritors did not all pay their share of the stent and without it there was little or nothing more to give out. There was only one thing for the Session to do and that was to 'allow them beging abroad as formerly', and, indeed, allowing begging during famines was a common solution where no other help was available. Where possible, however, meal was obtained somehow or other: in May 1699 the elders of the parish of Holm, Orkney, were ordered to be present at the storehouse of a landowner to 'sie the bear bought from Grahamshall distributed among the poor of the parish according to their necessities.' In 1700 Arbuthnott Kirk Session ordered the treasurer to spend £20 Sc. on two bolls of bear and to 'make meal thereof for relief of the poor who were in great straits.'[45] Chirnside Kirk Session, Berwickshire, found another way of giving relief. In July 1699 they allocated each poor person to someone better off who was required to give them either 10s. Sc. or a peck of beans or 'three-four parts' of meal as was most convenient, and the minister set a good example by undertaking to maintain one poor person himself. In practice, it was found that the quotas decreed were not given punctually. That this Session were not alone in ordering what they called this 'home supply' is clear in their minutes for March 1700 which state that strangers were arriving in the parish because 'home supply' was 'broke up' in other areas. A particular problem during famines was that there were more deaths than usual just at the same time that church collections obviously fell and in Ashkirk the Kirk Session had to make another decision: 'Considered the box is now burdened with paying coffins for the poor in a time when there is such difficulty to provide them with bread by reason of the present dearth, theirfor they thought fit and ordered the mending of the common Coffine for the parioch for burying the poor.' This was a re-usable coffin — more of this elsewhere — something which may sound unpleasant but which was the only practical solution when food for the living was of greater importance than an individual coffin for those who died.[46] At that date, the very end of the seventeenth century, supplying a little food or ordering others to do so, permitting begging and seeing to the burial of the dead was as far as Kirk Sessions could go.

Bad weather in the autumn of 1740–41 had a disastrous effect on crops but by that date Kirk Sessions were better able to handle such situations and it was during and after this famine that the Kirk Session of Culross introduced the job-creation scheme of lint-processing and Kilconquhar Kirk Session suggested that the beadle's job might be shared to support two families, both of which have been mentioned in an earlier chapter. Also showing the extent to which the kirk by then felt more on top of the job, on 30 November 1740 the Kirk Session of Currie, Midlothian, made a remarkable declaration of intent to care for their needy people in this famine:

> The Session taking into their serious consideration and being doubly affected by the straitening circumstances of many families, especially those of the ordinary sort, through the threatening scarcity and dearth that now prevails in the country, and is probable will do so for a considerable time, do unanimously resolve that they to the utmost of their power will provide for all indigent persons, not only in the ordinary way of giving pensions and extraordinary allowances, but also by providing Housekeepers [i.e. householders] with meal at a moderate price, and the Session considering that by the good hand of God upon them, they are now provided with a considerable stock, and resolved not to spare the same while any one family or a single person in the parish are in want and they, understanding that the Magistrates of Edinburgh in consert with the gentlemen of this shire, have imported from England and elsewhere a great quantity of Corns which they are to give to the several parishes at a moderate price

and so they appointed their treasurer and another man as a committee to see to this. In December these two men reported that the magistrates were to provide the parish with what was needed, although it had to be paid for, and that they had bought 12 bolls of oats @ 12s. 6d. each and to make these oats more immediately useful to the people the Session ordered the treasurer to 'make the same into meal'. The elders made up a list of those who should receive it at the special price of 1s. per peck — almost 9 lbs. — arranging with a meal maker in Currie to handle its sale and to take the money for it.[47] Those on the poor's roll were, of course, supplied free but it was a great help in times of famine when the kirk bought grain wholesale in this way and then sold it in small amounts, even if the recipients had to pay something for it, because without these little supplies many would have had to do without entirely. Moreover, Sessions often subsidised the price of meal during famines in the manner proposed by the minister of Traquair in late 1740; he suggested:

1) that each Thursday there should be a market for meal at the kirk;

2)   that the Kirk Session should buy a quantity of meal and sell it to the people, who have need, at prime cost and if the prime cost be as dear or as near the market price, then it is to be sold a penny or two cheaper;

3)   for this, the Kirk Session is to raise some money on their credit, in case their money cannot be commanded. If the Kirk Session should lose on one boll one penny a peck, and the prime cost be 2 pennies below the market price, this will make the price 3 pence below the market. And if the Kirk Session lose, on the whole £100 Sc. per annum, this will provide 125 bolls of meal, which at 2¹/₂ bolls per week would serve for twelve months;

4)   and to this, all that we give to the value of £50 Sc. to the poor who cannot buy, which at 10*d*. per week would be 100 pecks or 6 bolls and 1 firlot, this in all should amount to £150 which would be no great charge considering the afflicting season;

5)   that the Kirk Session draw up a roll of persons who may, or may not, according to their circumstances, be entitled to buy at the Kirk Session's market;

6)   that the elders attend day about to see the poor served;

7)   that no more than 2 stones at once be given to one family.

To these suggestions the Kirk Session unanimously agreed, resolving with the help of God to put them into practice and to borrow £20 stg. at £1 interest per annum to carry them out. Having set about all this so efficiently and enterprisingly, one wonders what they must have made of a letter received two months later from the Commission of the General Assembly recommending Presbyteries and Kirk Sessions to be exemplary in acts of charity.[48]

When a Session was trying to provide famine relief, it did not help if the heritors made difficulties and although it was unusual for them to do so, the provision of subsidised meal could cause them to complain. Between 1730 and 1740 there were several years of severe frosts which affected crops and caused high prices and in order to help the people of the parish, the Kirk Session of Falkirk was one that gave meal out in this way, distributing 8 bolls of meal at £6 Scots per boll when the real price was £7 4*s*. Scots. This did not please the heritors as it could mean that larger contributions would be demanded from them and thinking that the Session had sufficient means at their disposal to provide further assistance themselves, without seeking their aid, they demanded to see the Session books. The minister consulted the Presbytery about this and was told that they could certainly see the books which should be in good order for this inspection, and the Presbytery also recommended the Session to 'beware of quitting any part of their administration of the said money'. The heritors did not want a casual inspection of the books but demanded that all of them should be produced to a committee of their number, saying that in the event of refusal the committee might summon the Session before a Justice of the Peace 'in order to oblige them'. The heritors must soon have regretted their action because the Presbytery decided to visit the parish themselves and, having appointed a committee to go over the Session's books, realised that 6,000 merks Scots had been lent out in bonds to two heritors and that several hundreds of pounds of the poor's money had from time to time been spent on things for which the heritors should have paid and they proposed that the heritors should repay these sums. The result was that when the time came for the heritors to inspect the books there was not even a quorum[49] and a lot of time was wasted when there were more important things to be done.

For a Kirk Session to borrow money in time of famine, as that of Traquair did in 1740, showed considerable financial courage and it says much for Sessions that they were prepared to enter into such transactions. The mid–1750s were bad years and in 1754–55 all the money that Falkirk Kirk Session received had to be distributed at once and still more was needed. The interest on poor's money out on loan was not due until Martinmas and to tide them over this interval, it was decided to borrow £8 stg. from the Merchant Company, only for it to be soon found that this should be increased to £10 stg. 1756 was a better year locally although not nationally but by 1757 there was again famine, especially during the spring and summer and the Session had to work very hard to cope with everything. To add to their troubles, the minister fell ill and died in March that year and the elders had to meet frequently on their own during his illness to decide what to do about the needy. Immediately after his death an application was made to the Presbytery to call in some of the poor's money out on loan, which they agreed might be done on condition that the heritors approved which, in view of their last clash with the Presbytery, they did and 1,000 merks were called in. With this, and the various dues and collections at their disposal the elders set to work in a systematic way with each of them allotted a district in which he had to find out the condition of the people and who needed help. Besides the ordinary poor, there were 196 households in need, some with four to six dependents, who were given from 6s. to 24s. Scots per month, usually in 6s. steps. For the next four months the expenditure was:

May	£176 13s. Scots
June	£158 8
July	£153 8
August	£152 2
	£640 11s. Scots or £53 7s. 7d. stg.

This was in addition to the £6 14s. Scots already being spent weekly on the regular poor. The Session also bought flour and meal to sell below current rates to those who did not necessarily require help in cash but who could not afford the high prices of food. Fortunately, after a bad start to 1757, the harvest that year was good, the Session received a legacy of 100 merks for the poor, collections improved and by the end of the year they were able to repay the Merchant Company and have a small balance left over, an excellent example of good management and efficiency.[50] Even a fairly small highland parish could spend a lot on meal for the needy and in this same famine the Session of Cromarty instructed two elders to buy meal for them. They got 20 bolls @ 9s. per stone which cost £18 stg. plus 7s. for transport which was paid out of the poor's box. But still more was required and the two elders were told to buy as much again, and more if they could. They got 54 bolls in two lots, the getting of which involved 12s. 10$^{1}/_{2}$d. stg. in expenses and 10s.

to one of them 'for all his trouble and care'. This was sold in small amounts with the Session making a very small loss but this they were happy to accept 'considering the great advantage accruing to the poor of the place by such seasonable supplies in a time of such Scarcity.'[51]

Following the famine of 1771 there were some years of hardship and once again, as minutes show, Kirk Sessions arranged for the supply of meal in small quantities. The following extract is from Tweedsmuir Kirk Session in 1773:

> The Session having formerly deposited two pounds stg of the poor's money into the hands of Jo Walker schoolmaster here for buying up and selling out meal to the poor of the parish in small quantities, they did and hereby do enact the following regulation to be observed, viz. that the schoolmaster shall be allowed the two shillings and sixpence for carriage, Toll and Custom upon each load to be laid on the meal in selling it out and that, upon his receiving a fresh load he shall report the same to the minister that the price thereof may be fixed and settled.[52]

Bearing in mind the degree of hardship required for ordinary poverty, the state of the following people, all assisted by one Session in that time of scarcity, must have been very terrible:

> May 1772, 1s. given to a woman 'in a starving condition.'
> July 1772. 'To Angus McIntaylor's wife distriessed for want of victuals, 1s. 6d.'
> July 1773. 'To the smith's wife in a starving condition with three children,' 1s. [53]

Within ten years there came the Black Year, with a catastrophic failure of grain crops throughout Scotland in 1782, caused by very large hail stones in May and June and frost during the harvesting of what survived. Things would have been blacker still had the potato not come into general use by then so that the people had something to fall back on to make up for their grain crops but inevitably in such circumstances their price rose to 8d. stg. the small peck. This famine lasted well into the summer of 1783 while waiting for the harvesting of the next crop and because the need for relief on a national scale was not immediately appreciated, nor could it be at once provided when the seriousness of the famine became apparent, yet again Kirk Sessions had to get on with things themselves. The minutes of one Session, written a little after the event, say that 'Before any supply was received from any other quarters, the Session met several times to consider what was to be done to prevent the poor from Starving.' They met with local gentlemen to discuss the position and appointed elders to districts 'to solicit the charitable aid of those who had some victual to spare and some bolls of meal were collected' and were distributed along with money they had gathered. It is obvious that this Session worked very hard but there is no full record of what they did because the Session Clerk was away at college for much of the time and it was only later that a brief summary of their efforts was written into the minute book. In many cases, landowners provided relief for those on their own estates and the gift of 20 bolls of meal to those on the Reay estate in Sutherland led the absent Session Clerk to write later that 'providentially the hearts of the great and opulent were touched with pity for the distress of the poor insomuch that not only individuals but societies and, at last, Government itself, were roused to grant such supplies of Victual imported from abroad, as effectually prevented the famine dreaded.'[54] In this famine landowners around the country were very good about assessing themselves or giving money to Kirk Sessions so that oatmeal could be provided at generous discounts, but the handling of the distributions was still entrusted to Sessions. Whether or not landowners provided for their own people or gave to the poor in general, it was normal for relief needs to be worked out estate by estate although not all were as neatly set out as at Knockando:

Person in each Family	Distribution of 28th July	Distribution of 26th August	Distribution of 11th October	Sum Total of the Different Quantities
I	II	III	IV	V

Below these columns names were listed, some occurring in very heavy black capitals, usually a single person getting a bigger allowance than one person normally received, but no reason is given for this.[55]

The same sort of steps were taken in this famine as those already described in earlier ones, apart from the use of common coffins. For example, Arbuthnott Kirk Session asked the minister to write to a meal merchant in Brechin who was known to have supplies, asking for 30 bolls (although they only got 20) and then the following regulations about its sale and distribution in small amounts were made:

> 1) that the Treasurer be authorised to give a bill or other security to Mr. Gillies for it, to be paid in six months, or earlier if Mr. Gillies insisted;
> 2) that Mr. John Skea, Mill of Arbuthnott, be appointed to sell it, for doing which he is allowed to demand from the buyers, as recompense for his trouble $1/4d$. for each half firlot sold to them;
> 3) that the price of the meal is neither over nor under what the Session is to pay Mr. Gillies for it, unless the Kirk Session decide to vary this at some time;
> 4) that the persons to whom it may be sold are only those named in a list made out by the Kirk Session;
> 5) that the meal is to be sold weekly on Saturdays in amounts not more than 2 pecks to each person and the price to be paid in ready money constantly;
> 6) that the money paid for the meal is to be deposited by the Treasurer in the kirk box in order to be applied to payment of the bill to Mr. Gillies.[56]

In January 1783 Banff Kirk Session formed a committee of the minister, treasurer and a Mr Garden, to discover whether any meal could be bought and if so 'to procure such a quantity as shall be judged necessary for the relief of the poor.' They realised that if help did not come from some other sources, much if not all of their funds would be used up 'in procuring provisions that the necessity of the poor may be supplied.' It is not clear whether or not they asked people for financial help but in a couple of months some money had come in, either by collection or by donation. One man gave £20 and the 'Brewrie' and Fishing companies each gave three guineas, making £26 6s. stg., which was brought up to £29 3s. by money given by Lord Fyfe and the gentry of the town of Banff, and this was immediately distributed by the elders.[57] Some Sessions helped people by lending money for food: £2 2s. 8d. 'lent out to sundry persons in distress for want of bread with this year of famine' was one instance of this and in the same way, when several tenants in another parish were 'in such straits both for want of victual and money to support their families till the new crop come on, the meeting . . . resolved to lend the said sum (£18 16s. 4¹/₂d. stg.) to the most necessitous of them, no person getting more than the price of 2 bolls, which is supposed will cost about fifty shillings. The money to be repaid at farthest at or before the next Rarichie market', which would fall in November that year. This lending was of course quite different from the lending at interest which was a recognised way for the kirk to raise money.[58]

Some needy families were provided with fuel at the best of times but in the case of famine more help of this sort was necessary. Many people were hungry and needing support and they were cold as well and it seems very probable that that was why Melrose Kirk Session minutes for 2 December 1783 say, 'This day the minister intimated a collection from house to house for encouraging the search for coal at Redpath.' Unfortunately no further reference is made in these minutes to this enterprising venture, the methods to be used nor the amount of the collection raised. In general, however, Kirk Sessions did not think of mining investigations and simply bought coal. In January 1783 Banff Session ordered their treasurer to buy 60 barrels of coal and to find a suitable place to store it. It cost 2s. 2d. per barrel, but with 5s. stg. for carriage added, it came to 2s. 3d. per barrel but Bailie McGilligan, who supplied it, gave back 10s. of the cost price which brought it down to 2s. 1d. The needy poor received their share of this free but the rest was sold at 1s. 8d. to those who wanted it and a further 100 barrels were bought the following month when a ship brought more in.[59]

What has been said of the efforts of Banff Kirk Session in the early months of 1783 all sounds straightforward and practical but at the same time as buying meal and coal to help the people, the Session were also dealing with other associated problems. Banff is a parish with a burgh and a landward area and to save overlapping between Town Council and Kirk Session, the Session decided that all relief efforts should be co-ordinated, an eminently sensible plan but one which met with virtually no co-operation. The Session arranged a meeting of heritors, magistrates and anyone else legally entitled to attend, to see how best Session funds might be used, saying that if those called to the meeting did not come, the Session would simply use the funds they had as they thought best. Neither heritors nor magistrates came, only the Provost and Lord Fyfe's factor, 'neither of whom presented commissions from their constituents' but they, along with the minister, were appointed as a committee to use the Session's funds 'and likewise for inquiring if there are any other funds belonging to any other societies and Corporations in Banff and forming a plan for the management of their funds along with the funds of the Session.' It was a long meeting and 'the weather being cold, the Session adjourned till after dinner' and thereafter completed their business. This meeting produced little result and when a further meeting was called for 24 April, none of the town representatives nor heritors came and the minister reported that he had reason to believe that the magistrates had formed their own committee for relieving the poor but that he knew nothing of their plans. Considering the Session's attempts to co-operate with others, this could only be regarded as going behind their backs and so they withdrew the powers given to the Provost and factor and instead appointed the minister, along with the treasurer and Mr Garden, to inquire about the magistrates' plan and to find out how several sums collected for the poor at several times had been spent. They were also anxious that the money in the poor's box, just over £42, should be put in a safer place considering 'the danger of leaving such a sum in the box in the present licentious times' and as it was not easy to lend it at interest in the circumstances, it was placed in the minister's hands for safe keeping. He gave a receipt for it, promising that he would try to get some interest for it from the bank in Aberdeen, a safer measure than lending it to an individual and he managed to do so, at 5% interest. All in all, this Kirk Session showed great responsibility in the face of considerable odds.[60]

It was not until June 1783 that Government help was at last offered in this famine. In the north of Scotland this began with a letter to parish ministers from the Deputy King's Remembrancer saying that the Lords of the Treasury had been directed by the Barons of the Exchequer to draw £10,000 for relief of the poor in the highlands and the north of Scotland[61] which were particularly in need of help. The letter told them that it was hoped to import grain from the Baltic but in the meantime, owing to the urgency in many parishes, the government had bought a quantity of bread meal, barley and white pease — a considerable amount of pease meal was distributed by the government in this famine which explains why it was sometimes referred to as the pease-meal year[62] — and this was to be sent to various ports in the following quantities:

County	Port	Bolls of meal	Bolls of Barley	Bolls of pease
Caithness	Thurso	200	200	100
Sutherland	Dornoch	300	200	200
Ross-shire	Dingwall	300	300	200
Inverness	Inverness	500	? (blot here)	200
Nairn	Nairn	200	—	100
Aberdeen	Aberdeen	500	—	200
Banff	Portsoy	300	—	—
Elgin (Moray)	Lossiemouth	300	—	—
Orkney	Kirkwall	500	—	—[63]

Distribution of this grain was initially under the direction of the Sheriffs of counties but local distribution largely fell on Kirk Sessions which was why the official letter asked ministers to call their Kirk Sessions and heritors together and to list the number of poor on the poor's roll to whom charity was already being given, the funds in hand or expected to be raised for their support, the additional number of poor to whom assistance would be given if Session funds were larger and the approximate number of bolls of meal that it was thought would be needed over and above what any Session could themselves provide, in order 'to afford a reasonable support to those who cannot contribute to their own maintenance by their labour, and to those who can only contribute in part, till they can be relieved by the crop of this year.'[64] In spite of what Sessions had done themselves, these government supplies were so welcome that the minutes of Nigg Kirk Session, in Ross-shire, have this entry, 'The meeting applaud the conduct of the Barons of His M's Exchequer in sending the immediate relief forward to the several ports . . . as it was very much wanted to preserve the lives of many poor people in the meantime.' Even so, after receiving their share, this Session still felt that a further 36 to 40 bolls would be needed 'to support or rather keep alive the persons mentioned . . . until they can have any relief from the crop of this year, that is reckoning a firlot or thereby to each at an average.'[65]

Fortunately for everyone, further distributions of government aid were forthcoming in July, August and December 1783, but it must have involved a lot of work and organisation at local level. In July some of Ross-shire's grain came to Cromarty and was allocated from there to various parishes. To take just one example, 15 bolls for the parish of Tarbat were taken by boat from Cromarty to a small local harbour 'and thereafter distributed in small quantities to poor housekeepers through the parish according to a list made out.' The August distribution took place in the manse barn where the Session met 'in consequence of an Intimation made yesterday to the poor and others in the parish in straitened circumstances thro' the prevailing famine to attend here this day to have a supply of pease and oat meal ordered by Government for the relief of the different parishes distributed amongst them.' In December an allocation of some 46 bolls was distributed by the Session to well over 116 people. Even so, as was found elsewhere, the government meal, though very welcome, was not enough and in the parish of Cromarty, which had seen the arrival and despatch of some of the county's meal allocation, there were 213 needy people in July 1783, a figure which rose later to 227.[66] Although this meal was supplied, it was not free. Kirk Sessions had to pay for their allotment and then recoup the money as best they might from those able to pay for it. This meant that Sessions had to raise or gather in as much money as they could and this was where the accepted practice of lending out any surplus poor's money could run them into difficulties because it might have to be called in at a time when the borrowers were least able to return it. Nevertheless, that might have to be done: 'It was also agreed that such of the tenants as had borrowed on their bills any part of the poors funds should be advertised immediately to pay it in to Mr. Morrison and retire their bills' ordered one Session, adding that 'this is to be pushed as there are immediately expected to Cromarty twenty eight bolls and one firlot of meal, sent by the Barons of H.M. Exchequer for the use of the poor of this parish, to be sold to them at eight shillings and eight pence the eight stone, and without that money be paid there is no other fund to pay immediately for the meal.' Local delivery costs of this grain also had to be paid for and a rather pathetic entry in one Argyllshire minute in January 1784 refers to payment of 1s. stg., 'arrears of expense to the hands that brought the Government meal from Oban last year.'[67]

Some of the government supplies arrived as meal but often it came as unmilled grain, not ready for immediate consumption. In one parish the minister immediately dealt with this problem by having the grain taken to the kiln, providing the peats to dry it and then 'drew it upon his Horses from the Kiln to the Milns of Farness, got it ground and carried back to his own House where he divided it according to the list.' With great kindness he refused the payment which his Kirk Session wanted him to have for his efforts saying that 'he made a present of his Trouble and expenses to the Session and the poor.'[68]

People's generosity to others worse off than themselves during famines was remarkable. There were the people who gave to collections of food or money, such as a 'part of the Inhabitants of this place' in Cromarty who raised £30 stg. during 1782 for the poor. In 1783 when neither heritors nor magistrates attended meetings called by the Kirk Session of Banff it must have been a great consolation that a man came to tell the Session that a group which he represented had used their own money to buy peasemeal and planned to distribute ten bolls weekly for three months to the labouring poor of the town. Mercifully Nature could give a helping hand as well and one instance of this is that during the spring and summer of 1783 there were more and better cockles than ever before on the seashore near Tain, which greatly helped the poor to survive and indirectly helped the Kirk Session by reducing demand and distress.[69]

A great deal of Kirk Session famine relief fell on particular people, something which was recognised by Banff Kirk Session at the end of 1783 when 'on account of the extraordinary trouble which the Treasurer had during the bygone year, in distributing money, meal, and coals to the poor' he was given £5 stg. Similar payments must have been made elsewhere too but church staff who had not been involved in this work were less fortunate and in July 1784 one west highland Session found their finances so bad in the aftermath of this famine that 'they reserved to themselves the power to pay the Question-man' (a form of catechist) 'in proportion to the smallness of their funds'.[70]

In 1796 there was yet another famine and once again Sessions provided meal for the people at subsidised prices, if necessary borrowing to do so. Another way of doing things was that suggested by the principal heritor of the parish of Arbuthnott, that subscription papers could be used to raise money, something with which the Session agreed and the Session Clerk was given the task of preparing these papers for the elders to take round their districts. This must have worked well as in 'the dear years' of 1799–1800 they once again sent round subscription papers and managed to buy 60 bolls of grain with what these brought in but, unfortunately, this time they ran into terrible difficulties. In 1800 they arranged that meal would be available at a mill at the cost of 22d. per peck and that an elder should be present to sell it and those unable to pay for it were to be given assistance from the poor's funds. In June that year more meal was obtained and in July the treasurer was ordered to go to a nearby town 'to buy 30 bolls of Bear from any person from whom he can get it.' Not only was this done but a further 24 bolls were bought in August with the result that by early September the Session owed £85 10s. to the supplier. Payment for the original thirty bolls was due in September but by that time the grain harvest had been successfully cut, causing a sudden fall in the price and the Session found themselves having to sell part of what they had bought at just 15d. per peck. It must have been daunting for them to be in this position as a result of foresight for their people's welfare and all they could think of doing was to borrow up to £62 from a bank to be repaid in three months — but none of the local banks would lend this to them. The treasurer went to see the supplier, taking with him a bill he had prepared which had been authorised by the minister and an elder, payable three months later, but in December they were still trying to borrow £40 from anyone who would lend it to them — at which point the minister said he would lend them the money. What a pity he did not make his offer earlier and save the Session so much worry.[71]

While the Kirk Session of Arbuthnott was struggling to cope with the debt they had run into due to the famine, that of Lauder found a very different solution to famine fund-raising. Owing to the high price of food in 1800 the Session had supplied oatmeal and bread meal to a number of the poor at reduced prices, but by the turn of the year it was obvious that more money was needed and early in January 1801 the Session and magistrates met

> in order to take into their consideration the state of the laborious poor not enrolled [not on the poor's roll] and considering the very high price of every article of consumption, find that it is absolutely necessary that something should be immediately done for their relief, and being informed that subscription Charity balls have been attended with success in other places, they mean to have a subscription ball here at Lauder on Friday 30th instant and the amount of this subscription after the necessary expenses are deducted to be applied for their relief. It is proposed that each gentleman shall pay for his ticket of admittance 5 shillings and each lady half a crown.

Subscription papers were lodged with the magistrates and with the Kirk Session, with one copy to a Mr Bowmaker. The ball was a great success, making a profit of £36 15s. 6d. stg. and a week later £16 13s. 6d. was given out to those seeking help. In March over £16 was again distributed and in mid-May the remainder was given out. No wonder that the initial suggestion for the venture had stated that Charity balls were successful fund-raisers.[72]

The early years of the 19th century produced several seasons of great want but according to one writer, they were trifling in comparison with what happened in 1836–37. The trouble began in the spring of 1835 which was very cold and not only was sowing late but, because of the wet, much of the seed never germinated. Potatoes that were planted rotted in the ground owing to the cold soil and to some unaccountable disease. Such grain as grew was deluged with rain before ripening so that the heads never filled and straw was poor. This made a bad start for 1836, a year when the land was difficult to prepare and even when cultivated often remained unsown and what was sown was largely destroyed before harvest by piercing frost and snow in October. So bad were things that one parish decided not to hold the Sacrament of the Lord's Supper in 1836 owing to 'the lateness of the harvest and the alarmingly unfavourable state of the weather'. Government help was forthcoming in this famine also and Sessions did not forget to record their appreciation for it but they, as always, more than did their bit.[73]

That was the last major famine before the disastrous Potato Famine of 1845–46 but by then the Poor Law had been passed and care of the poor no longer fell on the kirk. However, there were famines at sea as well as on land. Fish had a way of being plentiful around the coasts for years and then disappearing for no apparent reason, causing great hardship in fishing communities. While people living near the coast always fared better than those inland during normal famines, thanks to shellfish and seaweed being available, fisherfolk suffered dreadfully when both their living and their food disappeared simultaneously but, as far back as 1660 the kirk would help them if it could as the Kirk Session minutes of Montrose show:

> 3rd January 1660. The indigent persons of the fishers of Montrose gave in a supplication to the Session desiring that they would be pleased to consider their poor state and condition . . . that they were not able to live nor subsist any longer by reason that it hath pleased God that the sea did not yield anything for their sustenance, therefore the Session taking to consideration their great necessity for the time, ordered a Collection to be gathered the next Lord's Day at the church door afternoon of 8 January.

In all the many famines that occurred, it was inevitable that some ministers would fall ill or die or be absent for some reasons during them and it says much for the elders of those days, such as those at Falkirk in 1757, that they could cope in such times without the guiding hand of the minister on whom they normally relied. An instance of this was when the minister of Ashkirk had to go away for a considerable time in 1699 during the Seven Years' Famine, just after the decision had been made to start reusing the common coffin. This was a critical time but the minister must have felt confidence in his elders, leaving them to be 'careful of the poor, that if they were in any great necessitie for shoes or any other thing before his return, they should be supplied out of the box and lykways to visit the sick every one in his own bounds.' Very practically, he also left a boll of bear for the poor and this the elders distributed three days after his departure.[74] Elders also showed an extraordinary degree of goodwill during famines. In spite of the fact that they were suffering from the effects of shortages along with everyone else, they threw themselves into very varied forms of relief work and it is clear from what has already been said that this meant doing much of it themselves or at least being present at particular times to see that what was done was done correctly and fairly, as well as bearing the burden of great anxieties about the financial aspects of what was needed.

4
Poor Bodies and Sick Folk

Long before there was any form of health service, it was to the church that the sick poor looked for such help as they might get. In pre-Reformation days they might receive care in hospices or infirmaries but as these were few on the ground, the number of people able to use them was small. People were more likely to pray to saints, touch holy relics or go to holy wells in the hope of cures but although such popish practices as these were forbidden after the Reformation, the kirk thereafter found many practical ways to look after the sick.

As with famines, so with sickness: initially prayer and fasting were the least and frequently the most that the church could think of doing in an effort to gain divine help by repenting of the sins to which such trials were attributed. In an outbreak of what was called 'pest' in 1574 the Kirk Session of Edinburgh ordered an eight-day fast, with daily sermons and prayers and the people eating only 'breid and drink with all kind of sobriety'. In another outbreak in much the same area in 1587 yet another eight-day fast was ordered, also with daily services, in an endeavour to end it but as sickness often went hand in hand with famine or other disasters, very often these fasts were held to try to remove the combined afflictions.[1] In 1606 Aberdeen Kirk Session ordered a fast because of an outbreak of plague only twelve miles away in the parish of Strachan and also because of the damage being done to the grain crop by a great inundation of 'wettis', and in 1610 when a 'plague of the pocks' was causing illness and death among children at the same time that very wet weather was once again affecting grain crops, it was a fast and public humiliation that was ordered. Sometimes specific sins were thought to be the cause of God's wrath which manifested itself in these misfortunes and when Aberdeen Kirk Session was greatly worried in 1608 about plague breaking out in Torrie, which was much closer than Strachan, along with the unusual occurrence of an earthquake, it was suspected that fishing on Sundays was what had angered God and so the fishermen were summoned to see if they would give up this practice. The minutes show the names of those who agreed to this, as well as those who refused.[2] In cases of individual sickness prayer was also the first resort and in

1596 St. Andrews Kirk Session ordained that whenever there was illness in a family, the elder of the district should be told within twenty-four hours so that the minister might be 'advertised to go and comfort them with holy admonition'. The importance of this was felt so strongly that it was also decreed that failure to pass on the necessary information would result in a penalty of 10s. Scots for the elder, and if both he and the householder where the sick person was, failed to notify the minister, then both of them would have to appear before the congregation.[3] This type of pastoral care occurred elsewhere too — during the pestilence which broke out in 1699 during the Seven Years' Famine, one group of elders were told 'because of the great wickedness which rageth in the country, wherewith many of the parish are visited' that it was their duty 'frequently to visit the sick, to pray with them, and to converse and discourse about matters tending to eternal welfare of their souls.'[4] Public prayer for specific people came to be offered too, as it still is, and when a malady described as 'fever and cold' was spreading all over the country in 1743 the city churches of Edinburgh prayed for fifty people ill with it.

The impression one gets from Kirk Session minutes is that it was into the eighteenth century before the church could give actual medical help to parishioners, although there are occasional instances before that of assistance being given, as well as cash donations. The most needed form of relief was nursing care for the dying, the bedridden and the injured: 'For . . . weeks attendance as nurse on Mary McDonald terribly burned, 7s. st.' say the accounts of one Session in 1779. In 1741 another paid a woman 10d. monthly 'for taking care of Helen Glendinning who is confined to bed with none to look after her' and when it was reported to yet another Session in 1845 that a pauper seemed to be 'in a dying condition' they decided that someone should be 'appointed to watch her bed' and also that a doctor should be asked to visit her. More surprisingly it was a man to whom a parish paid £3 10s. stg. for 'waiting on' Margaret Kerr for the first three months of 1766 but it was almost certainly his wife who did the caring although payment was made to him, just as the husband of a wet nurse might be the one who received the money for her efforts. Sometimes the near relations of 'wholly helpless' people were paid their boarding costs to help them to look after them, which was a good way of caring for them among people they knew. In 1736 a Session became very worried about the condition of James Strachan who had come there from elsewhere and then lost the use of his legs owing to a fever, after which his body became so covered with sores that he was neither fit enough to go begging 'to seek his meat' nor to be carried on a barrow, and in this sad case the Session offered 20s. Scots to anyone who would take him in and look after him while he was bedridden. The names of a possible couple were suggested and they agreed to accept him for this sum, which seems to have been per week, on condition that they also got half a boll of coal for the winter.[5] In 1764 however, one Session decided on what seemed to them a thoroughly practical way of providing home nursing which would make fewer demands on the poor's funds than it usually did. They resolved that those paupers on the roll who were fit enough, should care for the bedridden who had no one else to do this for them. They were prepared to pay them something for this work — 'to allow them what they thought fit for their trouble' was the phrase used — but they also made it compulsory, decreeing that should any of them refuse to help in this way when told to, they would be struck off the poor's roll and lose their pensions.[6] Financially this was sensible although what kind of care could have been given by unwilling paupers is open to question but fortunately this seems to have been an exceptional decision. In 1842 a woman was paid for fetching and washing the clothing and bedding of a man who was able, the following year, to go in search of work. From this it is not clear whether he had been ill and the washing was part of nursing him or whether it was an early form of home help for a man on his own which it may well have been, as that same Session had paid the previous year for a woman to clean the house and do the washing for a pensioner. In addition washing of clothing was almost always needed after a death, often so that it could be rouped, and payments for this frequently occur in accounts.[7]

Nursing care was normally paid for out of the poor's funds but a collection could be asked for from other parishes or locally, or the normal Sunday collections could be given over to a specially needy case. In 1743 the minister of the parish of Drainie, Morayshire, intimated that the following Sunday's takings at church were to be used to help

> a poor distressed object called Isobel Grant, at present in Elgin, who had by trouble been deprived of the use of her hands for several years bygone, and had some time ago by an accidental fall broken one of her arms, which putrified to such a degree that it behoved to be cut off last summer, so that now she was not able to put off or on her own clothes or to take her own food, but behoved to be obliged to another to do it for her, so that now she was a very great object of Christian compassion.[8]

In many cases it was not nursing care that was paid for but, as in that case, straight cash that was given. This may have been because money was what was specifically needed in certain cases or because nursing care could not be found and at least a little money could help with other aspects of the situation. It was given for a wide variety of reasons to do with ill health: it might be a donation to a poor man 'whose wife died of a mad-dog bite', or 8s. Scots 'to a poor man without arms', something for 'a poor lad that had a rupture', 5s. to a woman 'for support in her illness', £1 2s. to a woman 'in sickness and straits', 12s. to 'John Fairfoul when his child was dying', or 10s. stg. to a man because 'his wife and children have been for several weeks confined by sickness' — in fact, money was often given to a household where the mother and children were ill. The Session minutes of Dornoch record that 'Alex. Robson a poor object in this town represented his miserable condition by being obliged to beg his daily bread for himself and his wife, who now by Six or Seven Years close confinement to her bed is both Deaf and Dumb and Senseless the Session considering this pitiful case, ordered the Thesaurer to give him twelve pence directly' and the minister was asked to commend their 'clamant case' to the congregation the following Sunday.[9]

King's Evil, scrofula or the 'cruels' were names for a form of tuberculosis which mainly affected the lymph glands and which very commonly appears in Kirk Session minutes. A 'charitable supply' or collection was ordered in all the kirks within the Presbytery of Fordyce in 1685 for a boy with this disease and 2*s*. stg. was given by a Session in 1775 to a woman whose daughter had the 'cruels in her leg'. Other wide-ranging collections for people in need include one ordered by the Presbytery of Inverness for a man in Keith, Banffshire, 'newly cutt of the gravel', and another for 'a paralytick schoolmaster in Buchan' to which a Kincardineshire parish gave 20*s*. Scots. 1763 saw an outbreak of bloody flux in Kirkwall, as a result of which the Session collected £3 stg. for the victims' relief and authorised their treasurer to add as much to this as was necessary, while in 1791 a mainland Session ordered a collection 'for sundry persons in the parish confined to bed by long sickness.'[10] In one parish a boy who led his old blind mother about begging, tumbled off a dyke on which he was resting and a sharp knife which he had in his pocket stuck into his stomach. He was found by some men who took him to surgeons in the nearest large town but it was obvious that even if he lived he would need something for his support for the rest of his life. The minister explained this to the congregation the next Sunday and urged them to extend their charity on his behalf the following week. Sadly, within the week he was dead but, at least, the intention to collect for him was there.[11] Sometimes what was collected for the sick or bedridden was food rather than money. An early instance of this was a collection of provisions made in the parish of Tynninghame in the seventeenth century for 'Alisone skugall bedfast and extremely poor' and another example was an appeal for food from the pulpit of Drainie church for

> Janet Morrice, one of the enrolled poor, who is a cripple and all overrun with the King's Evil, and thereby rendered altogether incapable to make the least shift for her livelihood. The Session, finding the small allowance they could give her out of the collections quarterly was not sufficient for supporting her, did therefore agree that the elders should quam primum collect meal or victual, as much as they could thorrow the parish.

A very little thing could, of course, make all the difference to somebody, like permission for a seat in church for a woman who could not stand throughout the service or the gift of a Bible 'in large characters' given to a Melrose woman whose desire not to be named was also respected when the gift was recorded in the minutes.[12]

Alcohol fell into the category of a little something that could help. Although the kirk was violently opposed to excessive, degrading drinking, it was aware of the benefits that a little alcohol could give in sickness. In 1718 the Kirk Session of Selkirk paid for 12 pints of ale so that a woman could infuse them with herbs, under the direction of her doctor, for her health. This might have been regarded as truly medicinal but alcohol also seems to have been provided simply as a pick-me-up or to cheer up those were ill, such as Janet Greig who 'had long been in trouble, was now brought very low and needed drink and other things to support her spirits.' In 1723 a Session provided a mutchkin of sack for a man who was very weak, while the Kirk Session of Tynninghame often paid small bills at Sandie Davidson's ale house for providing cordials to 'poor bodies' and 'sick folk'. Other records also show similar entries: 'To Alexander Spinks, for ail since his sickness, £3 5s. Sc', 'wine to a widow on two occasions 5s. stg.', 'ale and brandy to umquhll Arthur Bruce 9s. 6d. Sc' and a bottle of whisky costing 2s. stg. given to Thomas Craford and his daughter were all instances of this.[13]

For many years there were few doctors and those there were, were still too expensive for poor people to call upon but when necessary, Sessions would arrange for parishioners to be given treatment, paying for it out of the poor's funds or by special collections. In 1652 the elders of Govan were ordered to collect for Margaret Lochhead who was under Glasgow physicians for 'a sair disease yt has come to hir' while in 1727 a woman who had lost her sight owing to cataract in both eyes told the Kirk Session that a doctor in a nearby town said he could operate and restore her sight but that it would cost a guinea. The Session contributed to 'this charitable work' but also asked for support from the Presbytery and it was later reported that £1 12s. was paid for the treatment which to some extent succeeded in improving the woman's vision. Another Session collected £11 15s. Scots for 'couching' a woman's eyes which was almost certainly also to do with a cataract. Selkirk Kirk Session paid 30s. Scots about 1702 for 'purging and blooding a poor man . . . who was in great danger of sickness', treatment which was considered appropriate at the time but which to modern ears sounds neither pleasant nor curative. Craig Kirk Session paid a Dr Bruce 15s. stg. in 1841 for attending a man who was ill and Greenlaw paid £18 Scots for William Wood's treatment 'under physicians' in 1722. When a little financial assistance was sought for a sick woman in another parish in 1844, not only was the request granted but it was decided 'to call Mr Constable, surgeon, to visit her'. A poor man in the parish of Arbuthnott was subject to stoppages of urine and when he suddenly became seriously ill because of this, the minister told the Session that an immediate operation was thought essential if he were not to die and suggested that they should obtain the services of a surgeon named Mr Fordyce and 'engage in the name of the Kirk Session for Mr. Fordyce's payment', all of which was agreed and swiftly implemented. As far back as 1682 a collection was ordered in the parish of Traquair to help a poor man to pay for an operation on his child, in 1725 Craig Kirk Session ordered a collection which raised £17 14s. Scots for the expense of 'cutting David Laird of the stone' and the same thing happened three years later in Fordyce when enough was raised to more than pay the necessary £30 Scots 'for cutting George Minty of the stone', an operation which was not successful as he died soon after. However, the balance of the money raised did not go into the poor's fund as it might well have done but was given out in small amounts to his widow and children and it would be nice to think that the collection proposed for the beggar boy who fell off a dyke perhaps went ahead for the benefit of his old mother although this seems unlikely to have happened.[14]

Leg and foot injuries were very common and there were payments such as £12 12s. Scots 'for taking care of . . . Merrilies foot', 10d. paid to 'a woman with a broken leg', £7 Scots given to 'Isobel Denning to help pay her broken leg', or £1 'to a woman who had her leg cut by Act of Presbytery' — that is what the minute says. One parish held a special collection 'for a poor man in the parish who had gott his leg dangerously hurt with a mill-stone and had nothing to pay the chirurgion.' About 1694 Coldingham Kirk Session gave 3s. 10d. Scots to a poor woman whose legs had been 'shorn off' and £2 1s. Scots to another poor woman whose leg was to be cut off. Amputations seem to have been fairly common, examples being £4 stg. paid in 1782 'to the Doctors for cutting off Robert Weir's leg and healing it' and a collection held elsewhere that year for a man's benefit, 'to defray the expense incurred by his long illness and the amputation of one of his legs.'[15]

The records of a parish in Angus in 1713 give a detailed list of expenses for an amputation which came to a total of £142 10s. Scots and was paid for by a collection throughout the Presbytery bounds. These expenses included:

	£	s	d	
To the surgeon for amputating a man's leg	37	16	—	
The mixtures to him	1	16	—	
The powders to him	—	12	—	
The cordial mixture to him	—	10	—	
The ointment to him	—	15	—	
The ditto to him	1	—	—	
The cerat to him [wax or wax-dipped cloth]	1	—	—	
A timber leg to him	1	4	—	
To leathers and buckles to the leg	—	15	—	[16]

This man's wooden leg came to 2s. in sterling money but when Jean Lobban needed one in 1785 the cost had risen four times and it was not 2s. but 8s. stg. that the Session gave her for it. Other medical supplies than wooden legs were provided too, such as a rupture bandage which cost 5s. stg. in 1851, 'drogis [drugs] and cures' for a 'vehemently diseaset' child or a 'batter' for a woman, 'her arm being strayned'. This was probably a medicinal paste or plaster of some sort. In certain cases orders for provision of medicines came from higher up: in the famine year of 1740 an Act of Synod in Orkney was read in all churches there appointing a collection for medicines for the poor, the money to be given to Dr Sutherland, Kirkwall, 'he offering his advice and applications of the said medicines gratis.' Three years later the records of an Orkney parish show that this must still have been going on, with £3 7s. 6d. collected 'for buying some medicines for the poor' which was also handed over to the doctor.[17]

In general, the kirk frowned on medical cures offered by any other than proper medical men but when these were scarce the people were thankful to consult 'wise women' or anyone who had some native skill and a knowledge of herbal lore. It was because these people were thought to dip into white, if not black, witchcraft, that the records of a Session said in 1661: 'Considering the said Janet goes under the name of a witch or a deceiver by undertaking to heal desperate diseases by herbs and suchlike, the Session do discharge the said Janet, in time coming, to use the giving of any physic or herbs to any body under the certification that she shall be esteemed a witch if she do so.' For the same reasons a woman herbalist who reinforced her potions with spells, was called before an Orkney Session 'to answer to the scandalous reportes which ar of hir in curing of sick persones and beasts by charming or witchcraft'. In spite of this, however, the kirk in time accepted the help of certain quacks who were believed to be skilful. One Session gave 6s. to 'Main's daughter, to take her to a seventh sone to be cured of the cruels', which seems to imply superstition on their part about the powers of seventh sons. Another Session gave a woman money 'to pay a man for a Drink curing her child of a convultion' while Tynninghame Kirk Session paid a considerable sum to a man 'who promised a cure' for a boy 'likely to be a cripple', although as it turned out his treatment was unsuccessful. Although this man was probably a local bone-setter, clearly neither he nor the seventh son nor the maker of anti-convulsion drinks were proper doctors and the use of quacks may be what lay behind one Session's proviso that while a man was to be paid an initial part-payment of 40s. Scots to heal a lad's leg that had been hurt in an accident with a plough, he was only to receive the other 40s. 'when it is heall'.[18]

One Session paid £3 12s. Scots 'to the minister for mending Elizabeth Inglis' leg' and although such a payment would have been uncommon, any Session took pride in a minister with medical skill and approved his use of it. To such an extent was this so that some people, even in the mid-nineteenth century would ask for the minister's sanction before taking any medicines prescribed by doctors, against whom they sometimes had a strong prejudice. It was in the early nineteenth century especially — although earlier than that too — that a number of ministers let it be known that they would treat sick parishioners, which may have had something to do with the burst of medical learning which was going on in Scotland then, particularly in Edinburgh which, of course, was simultaneously leading to the nasty custom of body-snatching. In his *Reminiscences of a Highland Parish*, Norman Macleod says that it was to the manse of Morven that everyone went for help, and to receive medicines which were kept in a chest which was annually replenished from Glasgow by the minister. Thomas Guthrie in the parish of Arbirlot, Angus, in the 1830s, also kept a medicine chest and acted as parish dispenser, and even as late as the 1850s there were places such as Garrabost in the parish of Stornoway, on the Island of Lewis, which still depended on the manse for medical supplies.[19] Even when a minister was himself unwelcome in a parish, his medical skill would not be scorned and although the opposition to the induction of Rev. Patrick Grant to the parish of Nigg, Ross-shire, in 1756 was so violent that the bulk of the congregation seceded, he was still found 'greatly useful to the people by his medical skill'. (Even this however did not bring them into his church and after thirty years there his congregation never exceeded sixty people.) Rev. James Gordon, minister of Fetlar and North Yell, Shetland, in the late eighteenth century, was another of those with medical skill and wrote in his parish's Statistical Account that buttermilk was a 'powerful remedy' with which he put an end to a condition that he called an anafarca that had gone on for four years and was far advanced. The manse womenfolk also took a hand in all this and one cure which was as effective as it must have been popular was used by the minister's sister when a putrid fever broke out in Kinnellar, Aberdeenshire, in 1771. Many people who had used bark and other medicines did not recover but she gave a bottle of warmed strong beer at the outset which 'produced a great perspiration and carried off the fever from all that took it.'[20]

There used to be a general belief in the virtue of blood-letting, with many people having it done regularly every spring, and often done by ministers too, and so acceptable was it that Yarrow Kirk Session allowed a man to come to church an hour early on Sundays to let the blood of anyone wishing this. There were kirk objections in Falkirk, however, when it was noticed that people had a habit of falling ill on Sunday mornings and going in crowds to the house of John Wilson, a skilled blood-letter. It turned out that that was not the only remedy offered and an alcoholic cure was as often prescribed as blood-letting with the result that Wilson was rebuked before the Session and warned that in future he must only let blood in cases of emergency.[21]

In the same way that the church gradually accepted the medical help of non-medical people, so it gradually accepted the health-giving value of certain wells. Before the Reformation people had regularly gone to such wells, having realised that drinking their water really did do them good, but because they were often given saints' names, the Reformers regarded them as idolatrous and forbade anyone to go near them. However, as time went on, the genuine curative qualities of mineral wells were sufficiently obvious to make them acceptable and even a minister might visit them, although in the case of Mr John Robertson, minister of Lairg, Sutherland, who went to Peterhead Well, Aberdeenshire, in 1712 the outcome was not successful as he was dead within two months. In 1764 a Session in the county of Kincardine paid a man £1 16s. Scots for bringing water from a mineral well all the way from Aboyne in Aberdeenshire for the use of a woman with the cruels, but it became more usual for a sick person to be given the money to go themselves for treatment at wells. This was why, three years later, that Session gave half a crown to 'William Anderson, a poor lad, ill of the cruels, to help him bear his charges going to Pitkethly Wells.' In the 1790s Hawick Kirk Session gave Margaret Turnbull 5s. stg. for going 'to the well' and with what seems to have been very advanced medical thinking, several times allowed John Ekron £1 to go sea-bathing. There were other places too, where Sessions were prepared to send or help to send people for treatment. Inverness Kirk Session agreed to help a man who asked for assistance to go to London to try to recover his sight, a formidable journey to undertake in 1708, let alone doing so with impaired vision. Tarbat Kirk Session, Ross-shire, organised a collection in 1776 'for the relief of Isobel Millar, confined to her bed by a Cancer in her head' and four years later organised another one which raised £3 18s. stg. 'to support the expense of her going to Aberdeen to be cutt of a cancer in her breast.' For this journey she would almost certainly have sailed from the local harbour of Portmahomack to Aberdeen, which made it a direct journey, just as a Session in Angus considered that it would be easier for a man to go by ship to Leith *en route* to the Infirmary at Edinburgh, rather than overland at a time when there were very few roads. People living inland had little option but to ride to hospital and in 1731 a Roxburghshire Session paid £2 to hire a horse to take a man to Edinburgh for treatment and £2 10s. for one to bring him home again, as well as £5 8s. to maintain him there until he was admitted to the Infirmary.[22]

Although Sessions allowed the severely disabled poor to beg from hand-barrows, they often acted differently in the case of physically handicapped youngsters by trying to make them as independent as possible with a consequently better lifestyle. How far-seeing it was for one to help a blind boy learn to be a musician by paying for both his board in Dundee and instruction from a teacher there, and for another to give 8d. weekly to a poor cripple boy so that he could 'get an education to make his bread by teaching a country school which he was otherwise incapable of making.' A country school would be small and so not too arduous for him; and when the bone-setter was unable to cure the boy 'likely to be a cripple' the Session finally put him to learn the trade of tailoring, one requiring little physical exertion, another instance of helping with an apprenticeship but in this case for a health reason.[23]

Wet-nursing, although a health measure, has already been mentioned in relation to orphans and foundlings but other help associated with childbirth does not feature largely to do with parishioners; it was much more often given to pregnant travelling women but nevertheless there were occasions when local people were given assistance. It might be something like the £1 Scots given in 1707 by Ashkirk Kirk Session to 'a poor woman in this parish travailing in childbirth in sore labour' or two cases from Abernethy where, in 1757, £1 14s. Scots was given 'to John Ferrier's wife during her lying in' and the following year £1 4s. Scots to 'Will Smith's wife when dying in childbed', with the added expense in the latter case of a nurse for the child when the mother finally died. It was worse still when it was not one but two motherless infants that were left and Abernethy Kirk Session, which seems to have been particularly good about childbirth expenses, agreed in 1751 'to pay the expense of nursing one of Will Davidson's twins, lately born to him, in respect of his great poverty and the death of his wife.' The birth of twins would have been a cause for great excitement and delight in a family able to care for them but it was a tragedy in a poor one and money was often needed for extra nursing, for clothing and because the mother was ill after the birth. An absent husband leaving a wife with twins meant yet more expense for any Session unfortunate enough to have such a problem, as Abernethy did in 1775, when the accounts show several payments of about £1 10s. stg. a time to the mother in such a case. The birth of triplets was even more of a disaster and when this happened in the parish of Fetteresso a collection was held through several parishes for them, and when an Inverness salmon fisher begged the Session for charity to maintain his triplets, they ordered one Sunday's collection to be given to them until they could think of another way of helping him, 'whyll they fall upon some oyr fund', as the minutes put it.[24]

Much of the sickness and death which followed childbirth was due to ignorant unskilled 'howdies' as the unqualified women who practised midwifery were called. Writing an official report in 1841, a surgeon said:

> The want of a provision toward women lying-in is much to be deplored, this important duty being in general intrusted to a set of inexperienced old quacks who call themselves midwives. Death is a frequent consequence of their mode of treatment; and the wives of the district have to thank their constitution and hardy habits that it is not more frequent. It is seldom indeed that medical skill is called in till the manifest symptoms of death have frightened them to try the last resource.

It says a great deal for the Kirk Session of Forgandenny, Perthshire, that almost seventy years before that was written they were aware of the need for better midwifery and prepared to help to obtain it:

> Session met after sermon because Helen Stobie, wife of Robert Beveridge in the Eastfield had offered herself to go to Edinburgh to be taught the art of midwifery, that Lady Ruthven had given her 5 gns to enable her to pay the expense of her education, but that more would still be wanting and the minister was of opinion that the Session should give something to so necessary a purpose. The Session considering the great need there was of a skilled woman of that kind in this place, as of late there had been many reflections, and even bad consequences by unskilled practioners, and being well pleased with both the character and fitness of the person named, agreed to give her 3 gns and unanimously voted their thanks to Lady Ruthven for contributing so liberally for a good so much needed in the parish, and appointed the minister to intimate the same to her Ladyship.[25]

What sounds like an acute case of post-natal depression came before a Morayshire Kirk Session in 1740. John Cumming, a fisherman, had married a Caithness girl but after he brought her home to Lossiemouth she was extremely homesick and, following the birth of her baby, became so emotionally disturbed that she threatened to abandon it and return home. Various sums of money were given to the family to try to tide them over these difficulties but she fell ill of a fever, during which the Session paid a woman to care for the child and when she ultimately got better they sent both mother and child to Caithness, paying for their transport. Whether her husband followed her or whether the marriage broke up is not known but the Session must have considered her case to be very extreme to have separated man and wife in this way.[26] Conditions such as that were not understood but nevertheless Sessions were often concerned with mental illness and although the words 'idiot', 'lunatic' and 'imbecile' are no longer acceptable terms, their use is unavoidable when quoting Session minutes. Sadly, many people regarded as imbeciles in earlier days had little more wrong with them than depression or epilepsy, complaints which would now be cured or controlled but which formerly received no treatment and might even receive punishment. In 1592, for instance, an Elgin woman found guilty of committing cruelty on her own person with a knife, was ordered to stand publicly in the town with her neck fastened in the jougs, an iron collar chained to a fixed point, and to have 'the said knife . . . infixit in the tree beside her.' Another case, almost thirty years later, also indicates misunderstanding of the problem but shows kindly concern. A man reported to the Session in Perth that he was afraid that Margaret Alexander, who was 'deprived of her right wits', might drown herself in the Tay as she had several times tried to do and, being sometime one of the congregation and well thought of, he felt that it would be a great sin and shame to the town 'if they took not order with her to disappoint Satan's working in her'. The Session and as many members of the Town Council as were present decided that she should be put in Halkerston's Tower, and closely kept there, on bread and small drink, at the Session's expense 'till God in his mercy restore her to her right wits.'[27]

All that could be done for some of the mentally ill was to give them money from time to time. Examples of this are 2s. 'given to Mary McNeil, a natural', £1 10s. Scots 'to Janet Hay in distraction', 5s. to a man and his 'distressed clamorous wife', 1s. stg. 'to a young damsel that wanted the exercise of her reason', 4s. Scots to 'Alexander Gairdn a madman' and payments to 'Ann McCulloch Epileptic and Imbecile' and to 'William Macleod . . . hypondriac'.[28] A young woman who lived in a Borders parish in the 1760s suffered from some mental disorder and the Session were so concerned about her case that they approached the principal heritor and also wrote to an Edinburgh lawyer about 'Jean Gray's affair depending before the Lords'. It was ultimately decided that 'poor Jean Gray' should be taken in and maintained in a heritor's house but if that were not possible, that she should be given an allowance of 1s. stg. per week. One feels that she was indeed 'poor Jean Gray' as at that point both a portioner and a weaver-portioner offered to take her in 'and maintain her for her work' which probably meant that she would have to work very hard and moreover, not being in a heritor's house, her 1s. stg. presumably found its way into the pocket of whichever of these two took her in. Such a solution to care of the mentally handicapped was wide open to abuse.[29] A question which arises is whether the mentally afflicted, when supplied by the kirk, were required to attend worship as paupers were expected to do. The fact that money was paid to two men 'for keeping a distracted man in time of sermon' does not make it plain whether they kept control of him in church or whether this was done at home to let his family attend worship.[30]

Simple-minded girls were easily led into immorality and could get short shrift from their Sessions in consequence. In 1667 when a man gave his oath before the congregation that he had not been guilty with one such young woman, his word was accepted but she 'being ideot' was banished. Similar treatment was meted out in 1702 by her Session to a girl named Elizabeth Stewart: after she had been rebuked for immorality it was found that she was 'almost an idiot . . . and of a very bad fame' and so the Session recommended the magistrates to banish her from the town, which was duly done. Some eighty years later, however, this same Session showed real compassion to a mentally handicapped girl who lived either in the landward part of the parish or at any rate not far away, when she arrived, pregnant, in the town:

> This day the Session were informed that a poor idiot called Jean Carr had come into the town and was delivered of a child. The Session being informed that she was utterly incapable of taking any care of the child — or of nursing it even if she had milk — they appointed a nurse to be found and the Kirk Treasurer to make as reasonable a bargain with her as he could. They appointed 1*d.* pence half penny to be paid to Peter Alaster for necessaries which had been bought for the mother during her labour.

This girl was perhaps regarded as a special case. According to Walter Jack, writing in *The Scots Magazine* in 1988 she had been in her youth the victim of a cruel demented father who kept her chained up so that she became afraid of the confinement of four walls and, after his death, took to the open roads between Banff and Fochabers. After the birth of her illegitimate baby son, whom the Session cared for because she was mentally and physically unable to do so herself, she still desperately wanted him back, even tearing some of the thatch off the wet-nurse's cottage in her efforts to get to him and she is said thereafter to have become a baby-snatcher or at least was feared as one, until she died alone in the open in the lee of a rock on Ordequish Hill, Morayshire, which bears her name to this day. Her son who, rather like a foundling, was known as John Banff, only lived for fifteen months in spite of the Session's efforts on his behalf: a thoroughly tragic story.[31]

The birth of illegitimate babies to idiot girls was a particular problem. In his book *The Kirk of St. Ternan, Arbuthnott*, George Henderson describes the consequences of one such birth in that parish in 1774. Poor feeble-minded Isobel Roger had a baby but was quite unable to say who the father was. She lived with her aunt and the aunt's husband, Robert Clark, and it was he who asked the Session's advice about maintenance of the child, saying he felt that it was their responsibility and that neither he nor the child's uncles would accept its care unless they were given something towards its support 'and that he would soon shake himself loose of the maintenance or care of the Idiot.' Thereafter things moved away from the matter of the mother's idiocy to the vexed question of which parish was responsible for the child, and there was a scene reminiscent of the one mentioned in the previous chapter concerning Elizabeth Brown in the parish of Craig in 1735. Isobel's aunt and another woman came and dumped the child in the manse kitchen, 'left the said child weltering in the floor and went off', doing so when all the servants except a boy were out. It took a threat of bringing the Sheriff into the affair to bring Clark to his senses and he and his wife agreed to look after the child. Certainly its maintenance never fell on the church thereafter — but did he somehow or other shake himself loose of their care?[32]

As has been said in an earlier chapter, certain cases of what were called lunacy were due to very heavy drinking and must really have been alcoholism but, whatever the cause, remarkable kindness could be shown to lunatics who were poor, for example, John Spark, a mental defective in the parish of Arbuthnott. During the last seven years of his life, not only was he given 2*s.* stg. per week but the accounts also show the additional care he received:

	£	s	d
To a woman for cleaning his shirts per quarter	£ -	2	-
For meal for John Spark	-	3	-
To buy a neck napkin	-	2	-
Thatching his house	-	5	-
To John Hall's servant for carrying victuals to John Spark during the winter	-	-	2
To John Spark, as a supply	-	3	-
To James Hall for attending and giving victuals to John Spark during the winter	-	10	-
A coat to John Spark	-	12	6
6½ yards linen cloth for shirts to John Spark	-	10	-
For making them	-	2	6
½ boll meal and other articles for John Spark	-	14	6
For thatching and thatch for his house	-	3	6
2 pecks of oatmeal	-	2	6
To a woman for cleaning his bedclothes	-	3	-
For getting his bed mended	-	1	-
'For sap to John's meat'	-	3	2
Coffin	-	15	-
Cleaning his clothes previous to their being rouped	-	5	-
To a woman for waiting upon him and making his victuals for fourteen days before he died	-	6	-
To a merchant for his funeral expenses	-	15	8½d.[33]

John Spark was obviously cared for in his own home but in some cases Sessions paid for the mentally ill to be boarded out with suitable people. Cromarty Kirk Session's accounts in 1841 show payments of 26 weeks' board @ 2s. 6d. stg. per week 'for Christian Smith, a foolish person' and for 'McGrigor, the Idiot's child' while in addition they were paying 2s. 6d. a week for 'a maniac at Davidstoun' and 2s. weekly 'for Sinclair's idiots at Navity', the same for another idiot, as well as 3s. 6d. for 'an Imbecile in Cromarty' and although it is not stated that these last people were boarded out, it seems from the sums paid that this was the case. An imbecile named Ann McCulloch was only receiving 1s. per week so it may be that she lived at home and was able to be reasonably useful there. It is possible that some of the others may also have been with their own families, technically boarded out at home, a practice which went on long after the kirk had ceased to care for the mentally afflicted: for instance some Parish Council minutes refer in 1925 to two sisters, aged 17 and 19, who were boarded out with their mother.[34]

Naturally some unfortunate people could not be cared for within the parish and before there was a health service, it fell to their Sessions to make necessary decisions, even to diagnosing whether or not a person was mentally ill and if so organising suitable care for them. A great deal was expected of Sessions in this respect. In 1841, not only did Cromarty Kirk Session look after all the mentally afflicted people mentioned already but they also paid 'the expense of sending Angus Hutton to Edinburgh and a quarter's board (£3 14s. stg.) in the Royal

Lunatic Asylum' which came in all to £8 2s. 3¹/₂d. Nine years before, they had had to send Christy Smith, a pauper who became so deranged as to be a nuisance to other people, to the Infirmary in Inverness, thereby incurring a weekly charge of 5s. which was more than the poor's funds could provide. All that could be done was have the minister write to ask the heritors to pay this sum, but although how Christy fared in the Infirmary is not known, these examples from just one parish and not a very populous one at that, show the extent to which a Kirk Session could be involved with mental health matters.[35]

Infirmaries were not suitable for the treatment of mental patients and it was unusual for such people to be sent to them; rather, once lunatic asylums began to open in the late eighteenth and early nineteenth centuries, it was normal to make use of them but this usually meant contributing to their establishment and maintenance. These institutions received generous help from the kirk, with Presbyteries frequently taking an organising role in fund-raising and some having annual collections for their Presbyterial Lunatic Funds. Montrose Kirk Session was one that gave the collection at the Spring Sacrament, after deducting expenses, to Montrose Asylum in 1781. Every effort was made to raise as much as possible: when the Synod of Angus and Mearns ordered a collection for the Lunatic Hospital at Montrose in 1787 one minister suggested that this should be done on a house-to-house basis because, being December, this method would bring in more money at that time of year than a church door one. The urgency for a good result was because, unlike modern hospitals, the right of presenting patients, should the need arise, depended on sufficient financial contributions in the first place. A pamphlet produced by the managers of the Royal Lunatic Asylum in Edinburgh gives an idea of how this worked. The asylum had opened in 1813 and the pamphlet was produced to describe its extension in the mid-nineteenth century at a cost of £25,000 and the expanded services then being made available. New extensions were intended for patients of 'the poorer sort' and, although mainly meant to serve Edinburgh and its environs, it was also intended to be regarded as a national institution for areas not provided with a suitable establishment because the managers believed that the more such people were congregated in one place, 'the more perfect may be their classification and the lower the average expense of their maintenance.' Patients of this poorer type could be admitted at a charge of £20 per annum but it was planned to accept some at a special charge of £15 per year, to include bedding and clothing (which was not always provided), the right of presenting patients at this special rate being conferred on people, parishes or other collective bodies who had already contributed £10 or more to the asylum or who would do so forthwith — in other words, one patient could be sent at the £15 rate for every £10 given. A limited number of perpetual rights of presentation were also allowed — £40 for a perpetual right to present patients from within the Parliamentary bounds of Edinburgh and Leith, and £50 for each right for patients from elsewhere. While this may sound as if those who could pay extra were being unduly favoured, the pamphlet clearly stated that the managers felt they must keep in view the sources whence the institution's cost had been defrayed and as they opened the extensions with a debt of £2,500 their financial reasoning was under-standable. With a glorious unawareness of the possibility of rising costs, however, 'perpetual' meant what it said and one of the Asylum's printed certificates, with blanks to be filled in as appropriate, showed that because of £50 contributed in June 1844 a parish had become entitled to recommend one patient for admission at the lowest rate 'for ever'. Such a donation must have been regarded as a very good investment and it is hardly surprising that Cromarty Kirk Session, with so many mentally afflicted people in 1841, sent £60 the following year to this Asylum 'whereof £50 for one perpetual right of Presentation and ten pounds for one Life Presentation', and within six months a patient had to be sent there who happened to be the catechist.36

It was in 1832 that St. Monance Kirk Session heard a 'complaint alleged against Thomas Allan, still under mental derangement' and decided that he should be returned to the asylum in Dundee if he continued to be what they termed 'out-rageous'. As further complaints came in during the following month they asked their Clerk to make the necessary arrangements to return him to Dundee and to inform the heritors of their intention, and there he apparently stayed for a number of years. In 1841, however, presumably hoping that he would be fit to return home and thereby save the Session a good deal of money, the minister wrote to the asylum managers about him but received a reply saying that he was quite unfit to be anywhere but in some such institution and so the Session decided that he should be left where he was. In spite of that, he was allowed to come home a year later and lived peacefully with his mother and sister; but as he had no work the Session allowed him 2s. stg. per week 'till they see how he is to be disposed of'. He must have found some light job as late the following year they were able to reduce this, but still allowed him 1s. 6d. per week because of the 'scanty wages' which were all that he could earn. When the original complaint was made about him in 1832, the Session also had another mental health problem to deal with. John Irvine appeared before them on behalf of his son William against whom various accusations had been levelled, as a result of which several elders were sent to visit the family and report back. In the end it was found that there were so many difficulties in getting the parents to agree to anything proposed for their son that all the Session could do was to recommend them to do their best to keep him 'whole and within the bounds of the parish'.37

No Session wanted to spend their own or the heritors' money on mentally ill patients if their families could pay for them and when in 1841 a Mrs Duncan asked St. Monance Kirk Session if her husband could be sent to an asylum, they ques-tioned her carefully about her financial position and whether she could support him should he be sent there and the questions and answers which were written into the minutes make interesting reading:

> Q. What money have you in your possession or convenient which could be applied to the purpose of sending your husband to the Asylum?
> A. I have nothing which I could apply to that purpose.

Q. What money have you received since your husband's illness commenced?

A. Fifty-six pounds.

Q. Are you willing to relinquish your house to the session if they shall take him on the Fund and send him to the Asylum?

A. No.

Q. Could you produce any receipts for sums which you have paid away since you received the fifty-six pounds?

A. No, I did not receive receipts.

Q. What income have you at present for the support of your family?

A. Nothing but 3s. per week from two boxes. [These were the Brotherly and Sea-box Societies, i.e. friendly societies.]

Q. Does your husband commit acts of violence against you or other members of the family?

A. He has struck me times innumerable and also the boy William.

Q. Can you name any person who has seen your husband in an outrageous state?

A. Jean Duncan once saw him also Thoma Hutt.

The minutes show that a week after this her husband William's friends suggested that he should be boarded apart from his family so as to keep the peace between them and asked that the Session would give him a little financial support which was agreed although it was left to be decided later how much would be necessary. This living-apart solution may not have taken place after all because, three months later, Mrs Duncan applied to Sir Ralph Anstruther, a heritor, saying that her husband had repeatedly been very violent towards her which she said one of the bailies could confirm (although he in fact refused to do so) and the Session 'resolved to make further inquiries in order to ascertain the real state of the case and what steps may be taken in order to put William Duncan into a more satisfactory state.' These inquiries took the form of summoning his friends to meet the Session, after which two elders and the Session Clerk went to his house 'and getting him to confront with his wife examined them in the presence of each other concerning their repeated complaints made to the Session of his insolence and severity to his family.' Each of them accused the other but 'William Duncan did not betray any tendency to lunacy or aberration of mind but, on the contrary, appeared to the Session to make his replies with as much pertinency as his wife.' This unusual method of examination by confrontation was followed by a statement from William's sisters that he suffered very aggravated conduct from his wife and children and as the Session could not decide the truth of it all, they just admonished the couple and exhorted them to conduct themselves with propriety and not to lay violent hands on each other. But that was not the end of the story. That was in August and three months later Mrs Duncan again applied very earnestly to the minister to have her husband put into the asylum 'he being still in a state of lunacy' which made her frightened to live with him. This time the Session asked their Clerk to have her prepare a written statement of the circumstances, particularly giving her husband's financial position, after which they would be in a position to say how far they could assist her. The outcome was that they offered to pay 'half of his flitting out and removal to the Asylum in Dundee and maintain him there' providing that his wife could come forward with the remaining half of the costs and make over to them what she was receiving from the funds of the two 'boxes'. By May the following year she had to apply to the Session for aid but they decided that before she could be given this she must make her house over to them; this seems a very severe demand and much more than the movable effects paupers were asked to bequeath to Sessions. The following month a letter came from the asylum asking Mrs Duncan to visit her husband as he was much better and might be allowed to go home with her and although she could not have been very enthusiastic about this suggestion, the Session decided that she must do as requested. This case makes it clear how much the decision to send him to the asylum had been influenced by the ability to pay and had Mrs Duncan been prepared to give her house to the Session at the outset, he would have been sent to the asylum then in spite of the fact that the elders, wrongly as it appears, later found no evidence of lunacy, and even when he was ultimately sent away, it was only on condition that his wife contributed to his maintenance. This all seems very hard but it must be remembered that funds were limited and had to be shared among many other people.[38]

Only a year or two later St. Monance Kirk Session had to deal yet again with another serious mental health case. They had known for some time that Helen Currie had shown 'evident symptoms of being disordered in her mind and that many complaints have been made by the town and neighbourhood that she is become outrageous and troublesome . . .' and decided therefore to ask Dundee Asylum about terms there and whether she could be admitted. The superintendent replied sending 'a list of questions regarding the patient, to be answered and returned, which was done, on the receipt of which he again sent us Forms and Certificates etc. to be filled up and returned to him within three days, and then allowing him one day more to get the Sheriff's order, we were to send her in on Tuesday the 13th May curt, paying upon her entry the sum of £2 2s. Board till the 1st of July, the first Quarter Day.' These certificates were returned the same day, she was admitted the following month and in just one more month the asylum was able to report that she was improved and that it was expected that she would soon be well. For some time before being sent to the asylum, Helen had been supplied with foodstuffs by Isabella Reikie and the Session kindly agreed 'to pay Isabella Reikie her account . . . although they do not find themselves compelled to do so, yet in consideration that the said Isabella Reikie is a poor woman and finds difficulty in wanting her money . . .', an attitude probably as wise as it was generous.[39]

From all this it may seem as if the parishes of St. Monance and Cromarty had more than their fair share of mentally ill people but their numbers were in keeping with those elsewhere. For instance, between 1814–25 the parish of Kirriemuir had three lunatics in Dundee Asylum, and several being cared for by relatives with financial help from the Session; there were always a number of 'imbeciles more or less gifted with reason' as well as one man who was unmanageable and dangerous and who should undoubtedly have been in an asylum although for some reason it had never been possible to obtain a certificate from a doctor which could be sustained, with the result that the unfortunate man often found himself confined in the county gaol. Just how serious the problem of a violent lunatic was in the days before there were suitable institutions for them is clear from the fact that in 1693 one Session gave assistance to a man to make 'fetters and shakles to his demented son'. Burgh records in Hawick show that in 1811 £3 stg. was paid to keep a man named Gillis in Bridewell, the gaol or house of correction, just because he was insane and this seems to have been a normal practice when there was no other place of confinement for a violent person. Furthermore, when someone appeared to be deranged when away from home, it was very understandable that the civil authorities would pick them up and incarcerate them, at least until inquiries and other arrangements could be made and this apparently happened in the following case. In 1838 Catherine Chisholm, a seventeen-year old girl, originally from Dingwall, was put in Bridewell in Edinburgh but her mental condition was such that, with a medical certificate and warrant from the Sheriff, she was transferred to the bedlam or asylum of the Charity Workhouse. It took eight months for the workhouse authorities to trace her history back to Dingwall and to write to the minister there, saying that the charge made to their home parishes of boarders in bedlam was £5 per quarter, paid in advance, plus an initial fee of £1 1s. to the surgeon on admittance. The total already spent on this girl had come to £16 1s. stg. and this the workhouse authorities wished Dingwall Kirk Session to repay and it seems likely that they would have had to do so.[40]

Although Kirriemuir Kirk Session could not send a dangerous patient to an institution because they could not obtain a doctor's certificate, and although transfer of Catherine Chisholm from one institution to another required a new warrant and doctor's certificate, yet in the cases quoted from St. Monance it seems that no doctor was called in and that it was left to the members of the Session, even although they were not medically qualified, to decide whether or not someone was mentally ill. In addition, they appear to have cheerfully filled in forms sent by the asylum about a patient's condition, again with no qualifications to do so. This was a great responsibility to impose on such people and a great one to accept. It is hardly surprising therefore that a Presbytery's observations in 1829 on the proposed Poor Law Bill regarding the removal of 'persons furiously insane to Asylums and maintaining them there' stated that there was no good reason why it should be made imperative on unpaid functionaries such as heritors and Sessions to take charge of lunatics and unless authorised to do so by relatives, it was considered that this should be a matter for the civil magistrate, with the asylum's board and other costs paid by the parish to which the patient belonged, with recourse against that person's property, parents or children by an action, if necessary, before any appropriate court.[41]

Infirmaries have been briefly referred to already but before mental institutions were established, ordinary infirmaries had already been founded, largely thanks to the contributions of congregations throughout the country. The Infirmary in Edinburgh, like the later Royal Lunatic Asylum there, was open to people from the whole of Scotland thanks to a nationwide collection appointed by Act of Assembly in the 1720s following a petition by the College of Physicians for this, so that a hospital for the sick poor could be established to which they were prepared to give their services free. When this Assembly-ordered fund-raising is mentioned in Session minutes, it is sometimes described as being for the diseased poor and sometimes 'for the benefit of such poor as are afflicted with curable disease', two rather different interpretations of its purpose. From that initial collection, such contributions became an important part of the church's charitable work and Session minutes from all round Scotland mention collections or donations for this and other infirmaries and dispensaries.[42] In 1738 Ashkirk Kirk Session 'collected at the doors £6 which collection was sent to Ed[r] for the Cherugon Hospital' and in 1787 far-flung Dunrossness Kirk Session, in the Shetland Islands, also collected for Edinburgh Infirmary by another appointment of the General Assembly. In 1732 St. Vigeans collected £4 9s. for the Infirmary at Dundee; in 1841 Kinnell gathered in £3 17s. 6d. for Montrose Infirmary; while in 1777 Sprouston Kirk Session had raised £2 2s. for the Dispensary in Kelso, both of these in Roxburghshire; and in 1805 Tarbat, Ross-shire, sent £12 7s. 1d. to the Northern Infirmary in Inverness, which also received £9 from Kintail Kirk Session, Ross-shire, in 1873. These are only a very few instances of the great contribution made to provision of hospital services by the kirk and many collections or donations were made so regularly that entries in accounts showing annual subscriptions are far from unusual. An idea of the importance of these collections comes from the Session records of Inverness. In 1781 the managers of Aberdeen Infirmary realised that that Session had not held a collection for the hospital in twenty years although patients from Inverness had been accepted during all that time and, thinking that no money was likely to be forthcoming in the future, they began sending patients back untreated, with the result that a door-to-door collection was promptly ordered.[43] It is surprising that this situation had been allowed to go on for so long as normally it was regular contributions that gave a right of presentation, in the way already described for asylums. Knowing who presented patients was very important to any hospital as that person or body was responsible for payment and the records of Kelso Dispensary for 1780–81 include this in the details of their patients. Although the following people were all recommended by ministers, on behalf of Kirk Sessions, there were others, not mentioned here, who were presented by individuals:

	Name	Parish	Recommended by	Age	Disease	Result	
1780	Jane Fox	Roxburgh	Rev. Mr. Hogg	—	Ague	Cured	
1780	Nany Fox	Roxburgh	Rev. Mr. Hogg	—	Ague	Cured	
1780	Robert Fox	Roxburgh	Rev. Mr. Hogg	—	Fever	Cured	
1781	Isobell Ross	Eccles	Rev. Mr. Murray	—	Tumour on face	Cured	44

Although this sample is small, the 100% rate of cures is exceptionally creditable but if these institutions were only for those with curable disease, as some records said, then it is understandable. The accounts of Abernethy Kirk Session show that in 1757 12s. was given 'to an incurable from the Royal Infirmary' so it may be that incurables were simply sent home to die in their own beds, freeing hospital space for those who could be helped.

Where Kirk Sessions presented people to hospitals and therefore became liable for their costs there, they still made every effort to pass these costs to another parish if they could legally do so, or even to an individual. Thus when Alexander Leadingham asked his Session for a recommendation to the Infirmary of Aberdeen in 1783 they agreed but ensured financial assistance by having the Session Clerk 'take the ordinary security from his master, James Brown, weaver in Banff', something comparable, it would seem, to an employer's share of national insurance schemes nowadays. Sometimes money entrusted to a Session for a patient's support ultimately ran out which caused great worry and meant that efforts had to be made to find funds elsewhere, and of course expenses to Sessions could also include the burial of patients who died in hospital.[45] Sessions kept a watchful eye on the condition of any parishioners in hospital. By definition, those they were interested in were the poor but it was essential to see that only the really needy received help. In 1825 a Glasgow Session, along with the Deacons' Court, examined their list of patients and found that six of them could have their allowances stopped immediately, three should have theirs reduced, one should be increased and the rest left as they were for the time being; at the same time, an indirect suggestion from the hospital committee that the Session might pay for medicines and attendance was rejected.[46] There were very heavy demands on city kirks at that time as populations within them increased and financial vigilance was very necessary.

Sessions also had to watch the professional conduct of some doctors and an instance of the need for this appeared in Glasgow in 1832. An elder reported that he had recently recommended that a poor person in his area should receive medical advice from Dr Bryce, the district surgeon, but the doctor had refused to attend him on the grounds that he did not appear to be a pauper and that he had been clearly told on his appointment by the managers of the Town Hospital that elders could be imposed upon by people seeking free medical aid and that doctors were therefore at liberty to use their judgment as to whether or not to give their services. The Session considered Dr Bryce's refusal to be 'in direct opposition to the printed instructions issued to the District Surgeons by the Directors of the Town Hospital, that this was calculated to affect the usefulness of the elders among the poor and that at all times, and especially at such an alarming time as the present' (a cholera outbreak was feared just then) 'it was indispensably necessary that the parish should be supplied with effective District Surgeons willing, without questioning the order, to attend to the recommendation of the elders.' The Session recommended the directors to take steps to prevent such a thing happening again and appointed a committee of three to meet them, taking with them an extract of that minute. At the meeting Dr Bryce, who was present, climbed down from his earlier position, expressed his sorrow at what had taken place and promised that no case of the kind would occur in future.[47] From this it is plain that even with recommendations, had the Session not been prepared to champion the people, medical aid in some cases would not have been given.

In the nineteenth century benefit societies of various sorts developed and were of very great help to people in need and some city churches became involved with ones for the sick poor, such as South Leith's Destitute Sick Society, the accounts of which are in H.M. Register House. These show that the parish was divided into up to eight districts, each in charge of one man, presumably an elder, with each claimant receiving 1s. to 1s. 6d. per week. An unusual feature of these accounts is that the sums were added up in totals of shillings, e.g. 1125 shillings.[48]

The kirk also played a very considerable part in public health matters. John Ekron, the man who was given money to go sea-bathing, was also paid to put away his 'skathly' or diseased dog, while in many places free-ranging pigs were a real problem. All sorts of people kept a pig, regardless of whether or not they had adequate keep or housing for them and they roamed where they pleased. In the following example of concern about them, it is not clear whether the minister acted on his own or on behalf of his Session — Register House does not have the appropriate minutes. In 1761 Rev. John Sutherland, minister of Dornoch, Sutherland, wrote to the Town Council pointing out 'that there are daily such Number of Swine kept within this Burgh and have access to the Churchyard, which is unfenced and digg up the Graves and Bones of the Defuncts, which of itself is Shocking to Nature and Disconsonant to Good Policy.' The Council took his point and ordered the common crier to intimate that no one should allow pigs into the graveyard at any time and that the owners of any found there would be punished by the magistrates and their pigs would be shot — they even appointed a man to do the shooting — and their carcases given to the poor of the parish gratis. In spite of these penalties, the various nuisances caused by the roaming Dornoch swine continued into the early nineteenth century and indeed were a problem in many other places too. It was in Dornoch also that, on a human level, the Session became concerned about the conditions in which offenders were being kept in prison. In 1828 eighteen prisoners were confined in two small rooms, with a woman in the same room as five men, and it was this which caused them to lodge a complaint with the magistrates although it was probably as much to do with morals as with health. Awareness of the need for accessible and clean water lay behind the willingness of Falkirk Kirk Session to help the burgh out with a loan of £20 stg. for two months, a lot of money at the time, because a bill for pipes for laying a water supply was due to be paid at once and the bailies found the town short of money and were 'unwilling to be hard upon the residents of the town until harvest be over.'[49]

Preventive medicine also came within the scope of the kirk. Inoculation was used in some parts in the 1730s but did not become at all common for another thirty years, while vaccination did not start until the very end of the eighteenth century and until these measures were generally accepted, the ravages of smallpox, which first occurred in Scotland in 1610, were terrible. One small highland parish lost 75 children because of it in 1757, 46 in 1768 and 38 in 1791 while another, not far away, lost 50 in 1792. In spite of such terrible mortality there was initially a great suspicion about inoculation and vaccination and many actually believed them to be sinful. This prejudice may really have had something to do with expense; certainly one writer suggested that its sparse use in the late eighteenth century among the lower classes was 'not so much owing to invincible aversions as to their having little access to medical practioners who would inoculate children either gratis or for a small fee.' This statement is reinforced by the fact that about the same time that it was made, it was rare to hear of anyone dying of smallpox in the parish of Eccles because the gentlemen there paid for poor children to be inoculated which did 'more to promote it than either reason or eloquence could do.' Something else which must have encouraged its use was that in the eighteenth century vaccination was often performed by ministers, albeit unqualified to do so — one such was Rev. Patrick Forbes of Boharm, Banffshire, who acted as the district vaccinator from 1800–16. Rev. James Nichol, minister of Traquair from 1802–19 went further and used Communion visits to the parish of Yarrow to perform this service for children there, arriving several hours early on the Communion Saturday, bringing the necessary lymph with him and getting on with the job. This probably benefited far more youngsters than just those of Yarrow as Communion weeks were great gatherings and it is likely that anyone who could, made use of his skill and willingness, but it was something so different to normal Communion activities that it could only have been allowed with the active cooperation of the Kirk Session. Any Kirk Session however would have been as proud of a minister able to vaccinate as they were of one with any other medical skills.[50]

In 1583 Perth Kirk Session ordered their officer 'to despatch off the town all lepers, commanding none to receive them under pain of £20' and gave him and his helper extra payment for doing this work. Brutal though this sounds, it was really a public health measure as isolation was essential so that lepers did not spread infection and although it is not so stated, it is virtually certain that, in keeping with a pre-Reformation tradition, there would have been some special place appointed for these people's accommodation. The kirk had control over some of these places: in 1578, for instance, Aberdeen Kirk Session were in a position to elect and appoint the master of the leper hospital and in 1604 when a poor woman contracted the disease it was they who ordered her to be put in the leper hospital which was described as being 'betwixt towns,' obviously for better isolation. The fact that they keys of it were given directly to her implies that the hospital was more of a house or refuge and also that she was the only leper there at the time. In 1610 another leper woman was put in the 'lipper house' by the Session and given two merks for her support but, of course, a number of these establishments came under the supervision of Burgh Councils. A late case of leprosy occurred in the parish of

Fetlar and North Yell, Shetland, somewhere between 1754–94 and the victim was 'totally removed at the expense of the parish' but he later went back to his former lifestyle and did not stick to the course of treatment prescribed by the doctor with the result, according to the minister, Rev. James Gordon, that they 'were reduced to the disagreeable necessity of setting him apart, where he very soon died.' Although it has not been possible to pick this case up in the Session minutes, it seems from the minister's wording that the decision to isolate the leper must have been a Kirk Session one.[51] A number of churches which date from pre-Reformation times still have lepers' squints to enable them to see into the church and watch Mass from outside — but were post-Reformation lepers allowed to look in as well, or victims of other diseases too?

Although as has been said, the immediate reaction to outbreaks of disease was a fast and a day of public humiliation, it did not take long for the kirk, and burgh authorities also, to realise that there were practical health measures which could and should be taken in epidemics. One of the first of these to strike them was that where people gathered together infection was liable to spread and it was for this reason that in 1604 the Kirk Session of Elgin voted that a wapinshaw should be delayed, and indeed it was agreed that wapinshawing should cease altogether until such time as the Session decided that it might continue. Wapinshaws were quite literally weapon-shows, when all the men of a district would muster to show that they were armed in accordance with certain rules but they usually turned into times of general sporting and showing-off of prowess — they were referred to in Elgin as a 'profane pastime' — and it is very possible that the Session were quite glad of any excuse to stop them. As far back as 1585 Perth Kirk Session, after enduring several bad months of plague, decreed that so long as it continued there should be neither banquets nor guests at weddings although a small concession permitted up to four guests a side to attend the ceremony and any ensuing meal; and for the same reasons, with the advice of the magistrates, Aberdeen Kirk Session limited the number allowed to attend the watch over the dead — the lykewake — to just five or six, during an outbreak of plague in 1606. In an epidemic in 1645 St. Cuthbert's Kirk Session, Edinburgh, limited the number of wedding guests to twelve and those at baptisms to six, a ban lifted, to some extent anyway, at the end of the outbreak, but in 1648 they felt obliged to forbid lykewakes entirely because of what they termed a 'dangerous time of infectioune'. In the 1606 epidemic the parish of Strachan, Aberdeenshire, took direct action to end it, engaging two Dundee men to cleanse the parish of plague, something which they apparently did very well but which cost 'gryt sowmes' so that help from outwith the parish was needed; the Kirk Session of Aberdeen, which was only twelve miles away, contributed 50 merks to help to pay them and probably thought it was cheap at the price.[52]

Early epidemics are variously called plague, pest or pestilence. It seems likely that those of the sixteenth century were bubonic plague which is often called the Black Death although a contemporary description of an epidemic in Edinburgh in 1568 has, along with other descriptions, led Graham Twigg, a biologist at London

University, to suggest that anthrax was the killer in that instance. In 1649 typhus was prevalent in much of Scotland and one way in which a parish might try to contain it was to isolate all or part of itself. Montrose was a parish with a burgh and a landward area and its Session decreed that year that it was 'dangerous for these of the landward people to come in amongst us in respect of our conditions for the present, that all these our neighbours round about us shall not come to our town . . .' Throwing a *cordon sanitaire* around greater or lesser areas in this way was a measure used not only in this case but elsewhere too (though not necessarily always at the instance of a Kirk Session), as during the 1832 cholera outbreak when the parish of Tain, Ross-shire, protected itself in this way, and also in Nigg in the same county, where watchmen were posted at three landing places on the coast to prevent people from entering by sea once the parish had been cleared of infection. During 1645 an epidemic of either bubonic plague or typhus broke out in Edinburgh during which different parts of the parish of St. Cuthbert's were 'enclosed' but just what that meant is not clear although it seems to have been quarantine. Many infected people were accommodated in huts in the King's Park although some were kept at home and it may be that the 'enclosed' areas were the houses where infection was known to exist. Such people could not get out to earn their livelihood and an allowance had to be given to them through the aid of charity invoked from the pulpit. There was also concern that water could carry infection and while people on the south side of the Water of Leith were allowed to move about freely, this was only on condition that they took in no clothes to wash — much of the washing was done in the river — and when a miller whose mill was 'enclosed' asked permission to restart working, the Session decided that he should wait until the change of the moon.[53] Going to church was recognised as an opportunity for passing on infection and during a seventeenth century epidemic in the Borders one Session arranged that preaching should take place outside in the churchyard rather than in the church, with the collection taken up in a 'brazen laidel' which must have been considered less likely to be contagious than the normal way of receiving it. During the outbreak of 1645 worship was cancelled altogether in some places, quite different from the earlier reaction of church services for prayer and humiliation.[54]

Burial of the dead was a vital matter during any epidemic. It was during epidemics in the seventeenth century and just into the early eighteenth that the common coffin, already mentioned in relation to times of famine, came into its own. Although all parishes had been meant for some time to have a bier, which could be little more than rails to carry the body or which could be a re-usable coffin, there were many that had nothing of the sort and in some areas it took a really bad epidemic to introduce a common coffin, not so much to give decent burial as to enclose bodies which might otherwise spread infection on the way to burial. A common coffin is reputed to have been specially made in Anstruther, Fife, in 1645 and to have made no fewer than fifteen trips to the churchyard in one day but in other areas where use of such a coffin might have begun and then been given up, it was restarted if the outbreak was sufficiently bad.[55] Epidemics could also mean that victims might not be buried in family graves. Swift disposal of corpses was what mattered and in many cases they were tipped into common graves as happened in Edinburgh when those dying in a sixteenth century out-break were buried at Greyfriars churchyard in a grave described as 'large and wide, of deipness seven feet'. There were always some people who could afford individual coffins but when space in a common grave was limited this could prove a problem and for this reason the order was given by Edinburgh Burgh Council in 1597 that no pest victims might be buried in a coffin. Where individual coffins *were* supplied in an epidemic, as happened in later years, it was a heavy drain on Session funds as the parish of Kirriemuir found in 1819 when they had the double burden of paying for 38 coffins for typhus victims as well as giving temporary financial help to an additional 71 families, over and above the ordinary poor. In view of the fears associated with disease, the necessity for the following minute of St Cuthbert's Kirk Session, Edinburgh, in 1648 seems astonishing. It was decreed that an ordinance should 'be sent to the bailzie of the Westport to caus enclose Donald Brabane and his wyf for being fund houking up foul graves in St. Leonard's Hill', which they had apparently done to get at the clothing which had been buried too, probably to sell it, an appalling thing to have done in view not only of the risk to themselves but to those who might have bought the clothes.[56]

Many parish graveyards accepted the corpses of people who died in epidemics but sometimes special conditions were imposed. At St. Vigeans, in 1832, anyone certified as having died of cholera had to be buried at least six feet deep, whether in their own burying plot or in a special area 'eastward of the west entry of the burial ground' and a supply of several bolls of quicklime was obtained but whether this was for graves or for cleaning houses is not stated. Some graveyards still have areas of bare grass with no memorials which are 'cholera ground' where the dead were disposed of in 'cholera holes' in outbreaks in both 1832 and 1849. Even when victims had individual graves, there may still have been discrimination because it is said that sometimes these corpses were laid north and south, rather than the usual east and west. Not all epidemic victims were buried in parish graveyards, however. This was partly because it was feared that the re-opening of graves for future burials might let disease escape and break out again but mainly because if bodies were to be disposed of as quickly as possible then it was easier and undoubtedly wiser to bury them in some place near to where they died or else in open fields. To some extent this was forced on people. In the Black Isle area of Ross-shire, during the famine and pestilence of the 1690s, it is said that 'whole villages were depopulated and the living so much wearied with burying the dead that they ceased at last to do so' and if this means, as it appears to, that bodies lay unburied, then there was another serious public health problem in addition to the original plague. The situation there was such that people who realised that they were infected soon decided that they had to do something about their own burial — 'aware that they would not be buried if they did not themselves take some previous measures, so long as they had any strength remaining, [they] dug their own graves and laid themselves down in them until they died.' This was perhaps an extreme case but it was bound to be difficult at such a time to find sufficient people to carry a corpse all the way to a kirkyard and in any case there was a feeling that such burials in a churchyard posed a risk of infection to those going to worship, where worship continued. When Sunday worship was resumed in 1646 at St. Cuthbert's, Edinburgh, after being suspended owing to the 1645 epidemic, burials were forbidden between 6.00 a.m. and 7.00 p.m. because of the risk of infection which, as it was January, meant they would have had to take place in darkness. It was the same concern which lay behind the following extract from the Kirk Session minutes of Nigg, Ross-shire, in August 1832:

> In consequence of its being ascertained that a man named Andrew Ross a fisherman in Shandwick died suddenly yesterday and that his death is strongly suspected to have been by cholera . . . The Kirk Session are not aware of there being any regularly constituted Board of Health in the Parish. They therefore think it the more incumbent on them to take such measures as are within their reach for preventing the spread of the disease; and for this purpose resolve to petition one or more of HM Justices of the Peace for the County of Ross to grant warrant to prevent the interment in the burying ground of Nigg of any person who may have died of cholera, as the carrying of bodies from Shandwick and the contiguous villages of Ballintore and Hilltown . . . may be very injurious to the Parish and country.[57]

To most people the prospect of burial anywhere other than in the parish kirkyard with deceased members of their family was a terrible thing but during epidemics such fineness of feeling had to be forsaken and the authorities, whether Kirk Sessions, burgh councils or temporary health boards, had to find alternative places for interment of the dead. In 1645 plague victims in Falkirk, Stirlingshire, were buried outside the town at Graham's Muir with each grave — they appear to have been individual ones — covered with a flat stone and the whole area enclosed with a stone wall which was some time later removed. In 1649 it was in the links at Montrose that the Session decreed that typhus victims should be buried with the graves 'all levelled and dyked about with feall', at the same time organising a collection which brought in £67 Scots to pay those who did this work. The Nigg minute just referred to went on to say that it was appreciated how people would feel about being forbidden to bury their dead in the churchyard and so their solution was to re-open former traditional places of burial: 'The apparent severity of such a measure is justified by necessity. But it must be much modified by the consideration that there are in the immediate neighbourhood of the fishing villages already mentioned several old burying grounds in which (tho' they have been disused for a considerable time back) such as die of Cholera may be interred.' What is intriguing is that although they closed the kirkyard to victims of cholera, they did not do so to cholera itself as it was there that the kirk officer buried cholera after he saw it floating about the parish as a yellow cloud and courageously caught it in a linen bag. This story is not so odd as it sounds; there is a long tradition of various diseases being seen in the form of yellow or blue clouds and whatever it was that he saw and buried in the churchyard, the stone with which he covered it is still there to this day and no one would think of removing it lest infection should be released and start an outbreak all over again.[58]

Use of the mortcloth or funeral pall, at one time an essential adjunct to funerals, was frequently forbidden during any pestilence. With hurried interment and virtually no one present to appreciate the air of respectability that it gave, there was no need for one and there was always the risk that it could carry disease. When one was inadvertently used in 1832 for a cholera victim, the Kirk Session acted swiftly, regretting 'that the Mortcloth was sent to his house without their knowledge. They however now instruct the Kirk Officer to place the Mortcloth (when he gets it back) in a detached place and not to give it to any one for fourteen days from this date.'[59]

The best documented public health role of Kirk Sessions during epidemics was this cholera outbreak of 1832. Its arrival had been anticipated for at least a year as it was known to be marching steadily westwards from India where it had broken out in 1831, arriving on the east coast of Britain in the summer of 1832. What has already been quoted from the minutes of Nigg Kirk Session shows how swiftly they dealt with the situation when a death from cholera was suspected and did so on their own because they did not regard an unofficial Parochial Board of Health formed at the beginning of the year as regularly constituted. Ultimately an official Health Board was established in that parish and in others too, and undoubtedly elders served on these boards or co-operated with them as well as taking part in anti-cholera measures purely as Kirk Session members. An idea of their involvement comes from Resolis. In March 1832 the Session received a letter from Cromarty's Board of Health telling them that the parishes of Cromarty and Resolis had been united in regard to provision of food and clothing for the poor, which was looked upon as a preventive measure, and £10 15s. 2d. stg. was at their disposal for that purpose. The Session appointed each elder to find out who in his district most needed food, clothing and bedding as it had by then been widely recognised that nourishing food, warmth and also cleanliness were conducive to good health and helped people to withstand infection. A list of names was made up and two elders were told to go to Cromarty to buy what they felt was necessary. It presents a touching picture of service, these two men setting off to buy supplies for 46 of their parishioners and what they got was 2 bolls and 2 firkins — a firkin is a quarter of a barrel — of meal, 72 yards of plaiding for bedding and 58½ yards of flannel but the Session apparently did not think that this was enough and later recommended buying 80 yards more of plaiding and 60 of flannel and that these, along with the meal, should be distributed at the schoolhouse on a particular day.[60]

During this particular epidemic some Sessions were appointed *en bloc* as part of a Parochial Board of Health. The minutes of Kilconquhar Kirk Session in late 1831 show that a Board was formed consisting of all the heritors, the doctors, the minister who was appointed convener, the whole Session and also the members of district committees which it was intended should be formed. These committees were given wide powers by the meeting held to form the board, including:

that the committees shall go through every house within their districts and see that all kinds of filth, such as dung hills, dead animal substances, decaying vegetables and offals, be removed without delay to a convenient spot distant at least 100 yards from any dwelling house, that a few handfuls of newly slacked lime be thrown into each privy after the removal of its contents, and the future accumulation of these noxious matters be guarded against;

that the roofs and walls of the houses of the poorer inhabitants be thoroughly cleaned with hot lime and water, and the floors and furniture well scrubbed, that free air be admitted daily by the windows and doors when the weather permits, and that well-prepared peat be used as fuel where it can be conveniently had;

that great attention be paid to personal cleanliness by frequent changes of bedding and body clothes, that blankets be scoured and mattresses exposed to the open air for a couple of hours every third or fourth day when the weather is favourable, and that the whole surface of the body be spunged with cold water daily or as often as may be practicable and afterwards carefully rubbed dry;

that unnecessary exposure to cold, rain and excessive bodily fatigue be avoided, and above all that every person shall avoid the use of ardent spirits, as it appears from the general reports on this subject that persons given to habits of drinking are sure to fall the first victims to this disease;

that all unnecessary communication with houses infected with Typhus fever or other contagious diseases be refrained from;

that no encouragement be given to beggars, sorners or vagabonds of any description, and that these when belonging to another parish be given in charge to a Constable to be by him conveyed to the nearest town in progress to their proper parish, and further, that a vigilant eye be kept on such persons as are in the habit of harbouring or lodging such individuals and a report made of them that they may be dealt with according to law;

that the committees appointed for enforcing and superintending the execution of these preventive measures shall report the names of all people who may refuse or neglect to comply with these instructions to the Secretary of the District at Largo for the information and orders of the head Board at St. Andrews;

that the medical practioners in the parish shall be requested to report officially in a signed abstract every Monday morning to the Rev. Dr. Ferrie, the prevailing diseases of the preceding week, especially such as may partake of a doubtful, suspicious or epidemic character, along with any observations which may suggest themselves;

that a subscription be immediately raised, to the amount of £20 for the expenses of the committees.'[61]

A man was appointed treasurer and the names of committee members are listed, any three of them to be a quorum. Very similar steps were taken in St. Vigeans where, although the Kirk Session were not named as participants in a meeting of heritors, factors and tenants in March 1832, nevertheless they were sufficiently involved for the meeting to be minuted in their records, which show that districts were allocated to the care of specific people and inspectors appointed to check on cleanliness, to see that people had what they needed and to discover whether there were any urgent cases. By August, however, when cholera was working its way up the east coast of Scotland with the herring fleet, there was a further meeting, this time including the Session, in order to make an assessment to raise money for prevention and cure of the disease. When assessments were laid on heritors in such cases, a share was passed on to their tenants so it was right and proper for them to be present at such meetings too. The minister read out a letter from the chairman of the Board of Health which asked that the meeting, in addition to laying on an assessment, would invest the Board with powers specified in an Order of Council of 24 July 1831 and of 10 March 1832 and that the Board should be 'invested with funds' for the following purposes, for which an estimate was given:

> 1) for furnishing medicines and medical assistance, nurses and necessary attendance to the sick poor at their own habitations in all those cases where persons afflicted with cholera cannot be conveniently removed to the hospital;
> 2) the necessary incidental expenses of the Board of Health, namely rent of the hospital, rent of a Quarantine station, wages to hospital surgeon and nurses, expense of Soup kitchen and other incidental expenses; and
> 3) their expense of cleaning and whitewashing any house or habitation in which there exist dangerous impurities and of removing, taking and carrying away any corrupt, offensive and dangerous matter within or contiguous to any house or habitation and burning and destroying beds, bedding or body clothes or other articles which it may be necessary to burn or destroy;
> 4) to effect the removal of any offal or filth from any slaughter house in the suburbs of Arbroath and parish of St. Vigeans;
> 5) to engage Medical Inspectors to visit and report upon the sanitary state of Health of all lodging houses kept for the reception of vagrants;
> 6) to pay the funeral expenses of persons dying of cholera.

To this was added the statement that 'At present the Board do not ask power to open and scour drains or water courses and of closing and covering open drains, ditches and cess pools — these, they trust, the proper authorities will attend to without the Board being obliged to interfere.'[62]

These are only a few examples of the ways in which the kirk became involved in the control of epidemics. After the passing of the Poor Law in 1845 epidemics, along with other health care for the poor ceased to be a kirk duty and thereafter, should any Sessions take health measures on their own, it was purely out of social responsibility. During a second outbreak of cholera, in 1849, for instance, Craig Kirk Session showed practical concern which began with the purchase of lime and other requirements for cleaning houses in Ferryden in 1848 as a precautionary pre-outbreak measure, and then moved on to a variety of small but helpful actions which appear in the accounts as a record of how they coped. Both Widow Mather and Susan Wear were paid for making up beds for families in Ferryden during the outbreak and Miss Nicholson and Miss Gow were paid for 'vinegar to patients in Ferryden during the cholera.' 4s. 6d. was spent on 1½ bolls of lime, as well as 1s. 6d. for its carriage and pontage, and repairing a temporary schoolroom for some unspecified reason due to the epidemic cost 3s.[63]

Although a great deal of additional work fell on Sessions in epidemics, there could be a spin-off benefit to church life as well. The Presbytery of Tain was one of those which in 1832 recommended the holding of meetings in the various parishes as often as possible 'for prayer and humiliation because of the visitation of the Lord by pestilence' and after cholera died out these meetings continued, with many people who had previously shown little interest in kirk life, going both to them and to church. Even when people were afraid to attend their own church because of the risk of infection, this could benefit another parish to which they might go instead; the collections in the parish of Petty, not far from Inverness, were increased in 1832, 'the appearance of cholera at Inverness having led the inhabitants of that parish, on the east, to attend at Petty.' And as has been said already, parishes did not forget to say thank you when epidemics ended: a Day of Thanksgiving in November 1832 was held in one parish because of 'the goodness of Almighty God in that it has pleased Him not only during the prevalence of the Cholera to deal so mercifully with the parish that only one case appeared, and that not a fatal one, but that He has now removed the pestilence entirely from this part of the country and almost from the United Kingdom as well as having also abundantly blessed the fruits of the earth so that there is food enough and to spare for man and beast.'[64]

There are still very useful things for the kirk to do in relation to health matters but while an individual minister or Kirk Session may on occasion take steps which they deem to be necessary in this regard, work with the physically or mentally handicapped, drug addicts and the like is in the main done through the committees and boards of the Church of Scotland offices in Edinburgh.

5

The Poor's Box

But how was all this care for the poor, the sick and other needy people to be paid for?

At the time of the Reformation, John Knox had expected that money for church expenses — ministers' stipends, salaries, maintenance of church fabric, the poor, school costs and so on — would come from the teinds, the tenth part of their produce which parishioners were expected to give for the support of the local clergyman and church. Unfortunately, at that time a great deal of church property was taken into secular hands and according to the *Dictionary of Scottish History*, most of the teinds had already been appropriated to larger church institutions, leaving little for parishes, but fortunately the efforts of Charles I enabled provision to be made for payment of stipends to ministers, a system which lasted with little change until 1925. That, however, still meant that other ways had to be found to fill the poor's box for behoof of the kirk and the people — although called by that name, it held the money for a whole variety of expenses. There was considerable variety in the methods used to raise money but the most general were collections, assessments and the income from penalties.

To start with collections — some have been mentioned already, those extra ones for specific needs which were really topping-up funds, but collections at church services were the normal ones. They are the earliest form of fund-raising known to man: II Chronicles 24: 8–11 tells of a collection ordered by King Joash nearly 3,000 years ago in order to repair the temple of Jerusalem and I Corinthians 16: 1–2 refers to a collection ordered by Paul. In Professor Barclay's *Commentary on the Acts of the Apostles*, he describes a routine custom of the synagogue in the days of the early church whereby two collectors visited the market and houses every Friday morning to collect for the needy, partly in cash and partly in kind, distributing what was received later that day, although there was also a daily house-to-house collection for those in particularly pressing need.[1]

In Scotland too, collections were made for poor relief and when an Act of Parliament of 1574, which was Scotland's first proper poor law, spoke of what was to be done in parishes where money or food could *not* be collected for the poor, it implies that such collections were already taking place. In 1649 the use of voluntary contributions, a phrase for collections, was specifically referred to in another Act of Parliament and, in fact, Sabbath collections came to be a very important way of bringing in money. In 1573 the General Assembly ruled that collections on Sundays should be taken 'only at the kirk doores' although later on, in some places, collections were taken up during services, something which must have become fairly common because in 1648 the General Assembly felt it necessary to forbid it. In practice they were taken up as was handiest, 'in the most convenient place for it', inside or outside the church door and sometimes at the kirkyard gate which was why the Kirk Session of Banff felt it necessary to have 'boxes' erected in 1765 so that the elders on duty might be 'screened from the inclemency of the weather'. Pencaitland kirkyard in East Lothian still has two offertory houses at each entrance, formerly used for taking up collections and Torphichen too has a gatehouse where offerings were still taken in 1957 but not now.[2]

Taking up Sabbath collections was one of the elders' or deacons' duties, taken in turns perhaps on a monthly rota, or for three months at a time, or from one distribution of the poor's money to the next as happened when the collecting elders in the parish of Tongue at one point 'desired to be relieved from that trouble, and successors to be appointed', and it was 'until the next distribution' that three others were nominated 'to officiate in said stations'. That collectors were often neither enthusiastic nor punctilious about this task is clear from the following mid-seventeenth century Kirk Session minutes:

> 22nd January 1642. It is ordained that whatsoever person, either Elder or Deacon being lawfully advertized by the Church Officer, that shall happen to refuse to stand at the church door and collect the offering, shall pay every one of them twell shs Sc. precisely so oft as they shall be found transgressing.

> 28th April 1655. Collectors of the church door are ordered to come tymously when they are called by course with Certification that if they fail they shall be obliged to pay to the poor the whole collection that is collected before either Sabbath or weekday, providing always they have not a reasonable excuse, this done with consent of the whole members of the Session.

This meant that they would themselves have to give a sum similar to the last collection; the records of Elgin make this plain by saying that should any collectors fail to carry out this duty 'their time and day about as it falls to them' they must 'pay themselves the alms that would have been collected'. Reasonable excuses such as 'sickness or other lawful cause' were allowed for but even in those circumstances they were expected to find a neighbour to take their place.[3]

Collections were taken up in a variety of receptacles. The words 'bred' or 'brod' both meaning board, refer to these collecting vessels and indicates that they were made of wood. Certainly some of them were, wooden platters or the long-handled ladles for passing along the pews from person to person, which may still be seen in certain churches and are in use in a few, such as Channelkirk. They might be metal plates or even alms basins with decorated work, which smacks of Roman Catholic days, which could be held by the elders or laid on the ground outside the church but more often they were simply placed on something handy and appropriate or possibly on something rather impressive. At St. Andrews what was given to a special church door collection in 1642 was placed 'in basons set there upon little Casles or stooles' at the kirk doors. Such a stool was probably an offertory stool, a small rectangular long-legged table specifically made to hold the collection plate. In time, a wooden bowl, fringed and felt-lined, might be fixed to the wall of the church by a bracket just inside the entrance — and so on to the velvet bags so common today — but whatever kind of receptacle was used, it produced its own initial expense as it had to be paid for at the outset.[4]

The main role of the collectors was to ensure that people did not slip into church without putting something into the plate, 'to keep the people from raming past without putting anything in the box', as one Session put it. Another way of achieving 'furtherance of contributions for the poor on Sundays' was to have not only elders but also bailies, members of the Burgh Council and 'others of the most honourable rank' taking turns to stand at the church doors to watch over the givers and, it would seem, to intimidate them into as much generosity as possible. In parishes where collections were taken at the churchyard gate, an obvious way of ensuring givings was for the Session to insist 'that there shall be none but one entry into the churchyard, at which two elders may attend to receive the contributions of the congregation every Sabbath morning' because 'the disadvantages of having two or three entries into the churchyard must be obvious to every person as occasioning loss to the poor.' Just how closely people could be watched and indeed threatened appears from a decision of St. Andrews in each of the three years from 1597–9 that no one who had not paid their contributions to the poor would receive tickets for Communion.[5]

Acts of Parliament in 1574 and 1579 which concerned the poor, referred to landward parishes separately from town ones; Town Councils and to some extent, trade guilds too, were involved in caring for the poor in towns and Sessions were not so totally concerned there as they were in rural districts. But many parishes included both burgh and landward areas which meant that matters had to be clarified and to this end, following Parliament's ratification in 1698 of previous Acts about church funds for the poor, the magistrates and Council of Forfar, for instance, met several times the following year with the landward heritors when it was agreed that town and landward should each maintain their own poor, a division and classification which continued until the passing of the 1845 Poor Law. This was done by using separate collecting plates on Sundays which, in Forfar, continued till the late 1830s and the same solution was found elsewhere too. In Montrose in the mid-seventeenth century it was ordered that four deacons should take turns of collecting for the landward poor at the quire door from all those from that area who entered the church that way, and even in a small place like Kilrenny, Fife, there were two plates at the kirkyard gate, one watched over by the town elders and the other by rural ones so that the poor of each area could be supported from the appropriate fund, with separate accounts carefully kept.[6]

Parliament decreed in 1672 that heritors and 'possessors of land' should be responsible for maintaining the poor — the landward poor is meant here, of course — but also confirmed in 1701 that half of the collections for the poor should be at the disposal of Kirk Sessions. What this actually meant was that the heritors who were responsible for the poor, were entitled to receive the other half of the collections and although to what extent they claimed this is uncertain, those of Melrose, for example, did so until the late eighteenth century. They must have been entitled to a share of other kirk funds too because Ashkirk Kirk Session's records for 1751 refer to a heritors' bag into which a proportion of any interest received went, in this case 2s. 10d. to the bag and 7s. 10d. to the poor. Session records often show the amount of each Sunday's collection which must either have been their share of the total, or all of it if the heritors allowed them to have that. Efforts were made to see that everything was done in as businesslike a manner as possible as at Sorbie where in 1701 one of the elders was ordered 'to get what is collected' while another was instructed 'to record the same in a book, and every Lord's Day to mark exactly what is collected.' Accurate records were, of course, dependent on money being handed in promptly, something which the following extract implies was not always done: in 1670 it was enacted by a Session 'that whatever Collector hereafter fail to convene in the Session house each Tuesday after sermon for giving in their collection to the Kirk Treasurer there to pay 2 shs t.q.' (*toties quoties.*) After the money was received, counted and entered up, it was transferred to the kirk box. Every now and then a new box might have to be bought and its costs then appear in the records as 'To a new timber box for collecting the poors money in the church 12s.' There are frequent references in Session minutes to 'the box' which is sometimes called just that or sometimes 'the poor's box'. Some parishes had a 'big box' or 'larger box' as well as a 'little box', intended to hold different categories of church funds and, possibly, as a safe repository for such things as Communion cups, while in some places the money was kept in a poor's bag. In addition to these boxes for church door collections and other income, Sessions might have other boxes, such as a 'mid-box' for marriage contract money and other incidentals and they might also have some responsibility for something like a friendly society's 'sea-box' although these were largely in lay hands.[7]

Kirk Session records show that Sunday collections often came to no more than a pound or two and often less. In 1617 a Presbytery Visitation considered that what was being given in one parish was 'mean' and in another 'verie small' and ordered the people to be enjoined to be more liberal in future. Just how small takings could be in the early post-Reformation years may be judged from what was gathered in the parish of Monifieth, Angus, about then: in 1578 the usual collection was eight-twelfths of a penny; on 29 June that year, the whole fund for the poor came to just over 6d. but in some eighty years or so times had improved sufficiently for the collections to come to about 4d. which, in about another thirty years had risen to

8*d*. Scots, a twelve-fold increase in a century, with another large increase by the 1790s which brought the average to about 7*s*. 3*d*. stg. In 1755 the accounts of Torphichen Kirk, West Lothian, show Sunday collections of about 1*s*. 3*d*. or 2*s*.; in 1773 at Stow in 1773 they were about 1*s*. 8*d*. to 3*s*. 11*d*., yet in 1790 collections in Ashkirk were in the range of 4¹/₂*d*., 6¹/₂*d*., 10¹/₄*d*. to 1*s*. 6*d*., admittedly in the late summer, always a time of shortage even if not of famine. All sorts of factors came into how much was given to church collections, such as the prosperity or otherwise of the people, local or national shortages, perhaps the intrusion of an Episcopalian clergyman into a church and, of course, weather conditions which affected attendance. If the weather was bad enough, collections could be so trifling that it was not worth putting them into the poor's box at all and what little there might be was just given to the beadle. In particularly remote and poor areas, such as South Uist in the Hebrides, collections were not even taken up, 'the people being so poor that nothing can be collected in that way for religious and charitable objects' — and that statement was made in the mid-nineteenth century. In spite of many good reasons for small collections, one late eighteenth century minister knew where he laid the blame for them. It was, he said, because many parishes had no resident heritors which had an adverse effect on church income but then, rather contradicting what he had just said, he added that when heritors were resident they gave themselves not the smallest trouble about the poor. 'The tenants naturally imitate their superiors in relaxing their attendance at public worship and the trifling sums collected at church may be said to be half extorted from the very poorest of the community.' Having made this statement in the Old Statistical Account, this particular minister took care to keep on good terms with his own heritors by saying that this did not happen in *his* parish.[8] Fortunately things were not always so bleak and the records of Greenlaw show that on a Sunday in 1832 £1 9*s*. 6³/₄*d*. was collected, 'the Speaker of the House of Commons being in the church', so either he was particularly generous or else his presence attracted an extra-large congregation; and one day in 1756 the collection at Golspie included five guineas given by Lord Sutherland 'being the first day his Lordp. came to church after entering on his estate.' The parish of Barry, Angus, was singularly fortunate in the course of 1774 during which year two Portuguese pieces of gold, each worth 36*s*. stg. were found in the collections, as well as 23 guineas. These contributions were intentional and gratefully received but it is nice to know that should someone accidentally put into the plate more than they had meant or could afford, then a Session could be understanding about it and return it if it had been 'thrown in by mistake to the poor'.[9]

Collections were often taken up at weddings and might go straight to the beadle as a perk although this was not always so, and when the beadle in Ceres, Fife, tried to claim one such collection in 1657 he was told that he would get nothing apart from what he could collect for himself. A collection at a laird's marriage in 1679 was distributed thereafter to the poor by Inverary Kirk Session, Argyllshire, and by 1830 the accounts of Kilbride Kirk Session, on the island of Arran, have frequent entries showing collections at weddings bringing in anything from 5*d*. to

3*s*. to kirk funds. In the days when private marriages were officially forbidden but could still take place if money changed hands, the couple might be given the choice of paying a fine or allowing a collection to be held. They were also taken at baptisms, whether in church or at private ceremonies or as the minister went on his preaching and catechising rounds, and at private Communions as well.[10]

So far as church door collections were concerned, there was obviously a great loss if for any reason there were no Sunday services, what were called Silent Sundays. A common reason for this was protracted vacancies; during one which began in January 1836 and lasted until April the following year, there were thirty-two Sundays with no service, pulpit supply apparently being difficult to obtain. Lack of services could be due to a minister's illness, or his being away for his health, going to fetch his family or away on business. This last was not a very common reason for absence but it did happen — one incumbent was absent for a total of 24 months out of nine years, spending that time in Edinburgh pursuing various private lawsuits of his own. Going to Presbytery or Synod meetings could also cause empty pulpits. One Kirk Session minute reported that the minister was away from 2 to 30 August 1772 'partly attending the Synod at Campbellton and partly in the Island of Tirie and detained by contrary winds.' Where a parish included islands or was so situated that sea travel was often required, it was not unusual for the minister to be storm-stayed or be delayed on his travels by adverse weather. Bad weather could also mean that although he was not away, he might still not be able to preach in church and would just 'keep exercises in his own family'. In one parish such manse meetings were called 'storm prayers' and it is said that the small congregation who managed to attend were 'regalet after the service' with a plate of hot broth. None of that, however, helped church funds and even when church services were held in bad weather only a very few people might be able to get to them: 'The weather most tempestuous by windes and rains. Ane raire [sparse] meeting of the people' said one minute in 1658. When ministers were absent at other parishes' Communion services, that was technically a Silent Sunday in their own churches but not regarded as such because many of their own people would also be away at these Communion services. The large collections taken at them helped the poor of the particular parish and also stranger poor and it is very likely that Communion collections in different parishes evened out over all.[11]

Silent Sundays could mean no collections but the giving of bad coin could mean that what was taken in could be of little value and this was a great problem for the church for a long time. It was for this reason that one Session 'desired the minister to exhort the people next Lord's Day to forbear to mock God and the poor by casting into the offerings dytes or any other money that is not current' and similar exhortations occurred all round the country. One of the commonest of almost worthless coins was the doit (dyte, Harper's dyte) which was equal to one-twelfth of a penny. There appears to have been a regular system of coining base money abroad, especially in the Low Countries, for introduction by merchants into Scotland, and doits from Holland and also from France were among it. There were also Scottish bodles, the smallest Scots copper coin, worth about one-sixth of a penny stg.; and there was a variety of halfpennies which were widely used. There were Edinburgh and Inverness ones and Irish ones, as well as Woods halfpennies and Maggie Robs, the latter being counterfeit. There were also raps which might be either counterfeit Irish halfpennies or Swiss copper coins. Halfpennies were sometimes described as 'bad ' or 'ill' but that did not necessarily prevent them and other coins from being sanded or clipped. There could also be bad brass, copper and silver. Continued use of non-current money and bad coin well into the eighteenth and even nineteenth centuries seems to have been due to the scarcity of legal copper.[12] Although it has been said that country people in Aberdeenshire were in the habit of putting bad coin into the collecting plate and taking out good, and even that people in general bought doits specially for church collections, this was not necessarily so and the truth was that many people had nothing else to give but bad coin. It was not really surprising that a thief was quickly caught after he broke into the poor's box at New Machar, Aberdeenshire, and then staked bodles, doits and bad halfpennies at cards; everyone knew that such money could only have come from kirk funds.[13]

When collections were counted at the end of Sunday services, bad coin and non-current money had to be kept separately and that in itself could require a small outlay from funds: in 1800 6d. stg. had to be paid 'for two shot bags to hold the bad money' and just how much of it could be collected is evident from the fact that in 1708 a small highland parish had acquired 1152 doits; about fifty years later a lowland one reported having a 'vast amount of doits and other bad copper' but fortunately there were ways in which this bad coin could be turned to good account. A Kirk Session could arrange to have it melted down to make into a bell or jougs and at least one had bad copper made into cups for collecting for the poor. It seems surprising that bad coin never seems to have been made into beggars' badges or Communion tokens which would seem to have been a good use for it but this was probably because the lead or pewter used for them was softer to work and to stamp. Some Synods took a hand in all this by ordering the melting down of bad copper but this was to prevent its return to circulation and the government, which had made efforts to standardise money between England and Scotland at the union of the Parliaments in 1707 (an unsuccessful effort as it turned out), passed an Act regulating bad copper in the latter part of the eighteenth century which was to some extent effective.[14]

A better way of dealing with the problem than melting down bad coin after it was received was to try to prevent it being given in the first place. Exhortations from the pulpit were all very well but a better way was for the elders at the plate to watch even more closely than usual what was put into it. After the treasurer at Dornoch Cathedral complained in 1731 of the number of raps he got in collections, the elders were charged 'to have an eye upon such as shall give any Raps that their sinful and graceless behaviour may be duly rebuked,' while at Peterculter, Aberdeenshire, bad coin was returned to anyone who gave it, but what was really needed was an alternative to bad coin for people to give. It was for this reason that the Synod of Aberdeen decided in 1749 to discourage the use of doits by obtaining farthings from the London Mint. Kirk Sessions within the bounds had to advance money to get these — one gave £3 stg. for this purpose — and the plan worked so well that in 1753 the Synod was able to report on the good effect the farthings had had, so good that a further £50 stg. was advanced to get more of them for the use of the several Kirk Sessions in the Synod and a 'proper person' was employed to go to fetch them. Finding a 'proper person' may have proved difficult or else the practice may just have lapsed for some years as by 1763 it was reported that the poor's funds were again suffering for lack of farthings and the Synod recommended the ministers to try to find someone in town to help them to find a proper way of getting £100 stg. worth from London. When travel was neither safe nor easy, to ask anyone to carry some 96,000 coins, albeit small ones, was no trifling request. Other Synods appear to have had the same idea and perhaps the demand for farthings became too great for the Mint as in 1764 the Synod of Aberdeen received a letter from London saying that there were no farthings to be had nor were any to be coined for several years. What is not explained is how the farthings which were obtained were put into circulation so as to be put in the collection plate. During all this time, however, a practical measure used by the Synod of Aberdeen to control bad coin, much of which came from the continent, was to ask the Officers of Customs to do what they could to prevent its importation 'by which the poor are so greatly injured'. All in all these measures must have proved effective as the use of doits, in particular, stopped in some places by the mid–1750s and in others about the late 1760s, but unfortunately other bad coin took their place. Bad silver was first mentioned in Greenlaw, for instance, in 1814 although the last mention of bad money there is in 1819 and it would have been much the same elsewhere.[15]

In parishes where heritors either attended church and gave to the collections there or else sent contributions for the poor in cash or victual, things were reasonably good for the poor but if they did not do this, then church door collections alone might be inadequate to meet the demands made on them. As early as 1595 the General Kirk Session of Glasgow appointed a committee to make up a roll of people who could be stented to help the poor but such a course was never popular and when the Privy Council, fearing a famine as a result of a crop failure in 1623, ordered Justices of the Peace to raise a temporary poor's rate there was never any thought that such a thing should be permanent. Even so, as Professor Smout says, they received a remarkably brisk answer from several counties, especially East Lothian, where the Justices threatened to go on strike if they were forced to do as the Privy Council asked. In 1625 a missive from the king required each parish to tax itself for the maintenance of the poor and said that non-resident heritors should contribute too but it was in 1649 that Parliament provided for the levying of an assessment where necessary, to be fixed by the elders and deacons of the parish and to be paid by the heritors. Assessments were therefore not compulsory in Scotland although by the second half of the seventeenth century they were almost universal in England. While there were certainly some people who believed that those whose land was made productive through the work of the poorer classes should share its produce with them when they were in need, there was in general a far stronger feeling that poor's rates, which is what assessments were, were a bad thing. They were believed to encourage idleness and to create the very poverty they were meant to relieve; that much of what was raised went in administration costs; that although people were heavily taxed the poor were not relieved; and the example of England was not a happy one as it was said that 'the direful effects of poor's rates in England . . . uniformly follow their progress in every country where they have been established.' 'Whenever poor's rates have been introduced the amount of them has rapidly increased and debauchery flourished,' said another writer, while yet another declared that they were in some places 'a fertile source of corruption, and even of poverty itself.' While much of the opposition to them was based on a natural aversion to paying taxes, there was a genuine belief in the evil consequences of assessments.[16]

In general, legal assessments were not used until the introduction of the 1845 Poor Law. The writer of the General View of the Agriculture of Perth stated in 1799 that 'There are no such things as poor rates as these are understood on the south side of the Tweed,' and another writer referred in 1813 to what he termed 'ancient laws for imposing something like a poor rate' but said that many people considered these laws to be obsolete, adding 'It is certain that no such laws have ever been enforced in this country.' What in fact happened was that assessments were used to provide support for the poor in cash or in kind or a combination of the two but every effort was made to avoid them becoming 'legal assessments', in other words compulsory — better by far to make them voluntary 'so that the poor may not be led to rely upon a legal assessment' as one person put it. Should there be some special emergency such as a famine or a decline in trade which reduced the normal funds for the poor, then a special meeting of heritors was called and the minister and Kirk Session laid the facts of the poor's funds before them and explained what was needed. The law allowed for ministers or Justices of the Peace to call such meetings, with intimation normally made from the pulpit on the two preceding Sundays. As the purpose was to work out what was needed and then assess half of this on the heritors and the other half on the tenants or parishioners according to their circumstances, it is nice to know that householders and inhabitants were sometimes bidden to attend these special meetings and to vote in the distribution of what was raised. Not that this necessarily came in as expected; in 1732 the collector of the parish stent in one part of East Lothian found that not only several heritors but almost all the tenants 'were deficient in paying their respective shares'.[17]

Where heritors were non-resident — owning land in a parish but not living there — they did not usually attend such meetings; even when they did live locally they often did not appear either, perhaps being represented by a factor but often not and Session minutes may well say 'No heritors present' or have margin notes saying 'Heritors did not attend'. Nevertheless, Statistical Accounts of the 1790s and 1830–40s make it clear that in certain places heritors, ministers and elders did meet, sometimes every half year, usually in the church, to check the number and condition of the poor, to decide what their allowances should be and to calculate whether an assessment was needed and if so how much it should be — but it was all voluntary. This meant that the heritors did not leave the matter of assessing to elders and deacons as decreed in 1649; they assessed themselves according to what was 'absolutely needful' and whatever that sum might be was kept secret from the poor so that none but the really needy would apply. People who were neither heritors nor tenants might in certain circumstances, as has been said, have to pay too: in Kilmaurs in November 1699, during the Seven Years' Famine, a meeting of heritors, elders and heads of families ordered all tradesmen and others to pay a share for maintaining the poor which, in that particular case, made it more of a poll-tax than an assessment. The minute of one meeting of heritors and Session gives a good idea of how such things went and the attitude of the heritors. It was found that the number of the poor never averaged below fifty, 'some of them bedridden and many in a state of the most abject poverty', while the average income from collections and other sources never exceeded £25 per annum, 'a sum wholly inadequate to meet the exigencies of the case . . . The meeting, consisting of Heritors, minister and elders knew that as such they are a meeting constituted by statute for laying on a legal assessment for the support of the poor, but even though they had the power to do so they were reluctant to do so if the necessitie could at all be met and provided for any other way . . .' A voluntary assessment would seem to have been the obvious answer but even when there were such desperate needs to be met that was not what happened — it was decided instead to seek help from non-resident heritors.[18]

Even when voluntary assessments were introduced in a parish, they were only levied when required. In Ormiston, East Lothian, for example, one was laid on in 1757 but thereafter they were only occasionally called for until the beginning of the nineteenth century, when they were imposed half yearly but they were still voluntary and the amounts were fixed locally. While Scotland used voluntary assessments, a main difference from what was happening in England was that there the people who fixed and levied them were not the same as those paying them and their influence lay in the amount they could manage to raise. It was quite different in Scotland but at least what was raised was distributed free of charge although someone usually had to be paid for doing the collecting. In 1692 a kirk officer was paid £20 Scots for this while in some parishes this could be yet another task for the Session Clerk: one was paid £36 Scots in 1730 for doing so. In time, other parishes had a special collector paid, by the late eighteenth century, between £1 5s. and £1 10s. The beadle in North Berwick received £1 4s. in 1701 for gathering in poor's money but it is not clear if this was an assessment or not.[19]

Nowadays when there is a disaster or an international emergency, people give very generously to special appeals for help, with adverse effects on other charities which are possibly just as deserving and so it was with assessments of which it was said, quite plainly, that 'what is given in one form is apt to be witheld in another.' When assessments finally became compulsory in 1845 some Kirk Sessions found that Sunday collections were 'almost annihilated among the tenantry and well nigh extinct among all but the highest classes.' (The same thing happened in Denny, Stirlingshire, after a new church came into use in 1814. There was a five-year dispute about seating, during which no seat rents were paid and people gave generously to the collection plate but when they finally had to pay for seats, they said they would withhold collections. For a while the heritors, who took over all financial responsibilities, stood at the collection plates themselves but soon paid the grave-digger 1s. per Sunday, or so it was said, to do so.) This attitude of paying once but not twice was sufficiently common for the minister of Dirleton to decide in 1823, well before the 1845 Poor Law, to give up assessments and to rely instead on voluntary contributions, in other words, the church collections. This worked well although it was not truly voluntary as it was understood that proprietors and tenants would give a certain sum weekly at the church door and in fact most of the burden fell on the most regular and generous of the church-goers.[20]

Assessments ran into particular difficulties when a parish had both a landward area and a burgh within its bounds and the New Statistical Account for Dunbar has a long account of the difficulties which arose there in the 1820s when the heritors and tenants of the landward district were paying five-sixths of the money for the poor while the burgh paid only one-sixth which resulted in a law suit which went to and fro between various courts and ultimately to the House of Lords.[21]

In the event of heritors proving obstinate, ministers had the power to enforce payment by an action before the Judge Ordinary or the Sheriff of the bounds but this does not seem to have often happened and, in fact, the minister of Callender, writing the General View of the Agriculture of Perthshire in 1799, said that he had 'never heard of an instance when the minister and elders had had to sue before the Sheriff for rates.' Obviously such a course was one which no Kirk Session would wish to embark upon but it could happen that the advice of the Sheriff might be sought without any action being raised. This happened in Kilconquhar in 1692 when, in spite of all the heritors having had letters delivered to them by the Session Clerk notifying them of a meeting, only two came to it. The Sheriff's opinion is not given in the minutes but at a meeting some two months later, it was decided that an assessment for the whole parish of 50 bolls of meal and £50 Scots should be imposed, which was 1 firlot of meal and 5s. Scots on every £100 of yearly rent. This was a parish in which collections had fallen off very much at the time of the Revolution, with many heritors giving up coming to church as they felt disaffected with the government of William and Mary, which made the need for assessments inevitable. By 1697 the assessment was 2½ lippies (a lippie = ½ gallon of dry measure) of meal on each £100 Scots of rent, paid half and half by heritors and tenants; in 1731 it became 2s. stg. on every £100 Scots of rent, with tenants paying 2s. stg. for each plough, of which there were 35, and other heads of families paying according to their ability.[22]

Even when money raised by assessments was put into the hands of 'the over-seers of the poor' this was likely to be a pseudonym for the Kirk Session or its representatives because in the main, the heritors left it to Sessions to handle poor relief, although they could call them to account for their spending whenever they pleased or could take over the complete maintenance of the poor themselves. This last was unusual and only happened when they squabbled with the Kirk Session or thought that costs were too high but it usually resulted in the ordinary people resenting the action they had taken and refusing to give to collections so that the heritors ended up with enforced assessments. A place where this happened was Balfron, Stirlingshire, where until 1832 kirk income came from collections and voluntary assessments, the funds were managed by the Session and the heritors met with them twice a year to go over their accounts. The assessments were based on the nominal valuation of the parish and only came to about $^1/_2$% of the real rent so what the poor of the parish were being kept by was Sunday collections and this small extra amount. Yet the heritors regarded these payments as a grievance and when the Session met the assembled poor to pay them their monthly allowances, one heritor let it be known that he refused to pay anything unless compelled by law to do so. The Session therefore had nothing more to give out 'and had no alternative but to resign their charge into the hands of the heritors.' This they did in a most respectful manner, expressing their great reluctance and regret at having to do so; the heritors accepted their resignation from this particular duty but found that costs rose and there had to be an assessment on their real rental, paid half by them and half by householders and other people according to what was called their 'supposed wealth and substance'; which meant that everyone in the parish whose earnings were thought to come to 10s. per week was taxed for the poor, with the result that church door collections dropped to around 1s. per day. There was displeasure all round and the poor felt that they were being neglected. 'All the evils of the compulsory assessment are felt' it was said on this occasion but the problem only arose because the heritors had been difficult in the first place. Baldernock, in the same county, was another parish where the heritors largely took the care of the poor into their own hands, only to find themselves wriggling like fish on a hook trying to avoid the imposition of a legal assessment. In 1841 the number of poor in the parish was increasing and it was estimated that the poor's money would be £27 short of what was needed. The minutes show however that for the next couple of years the Session met and distributed what they had, presumably with the deficit growing all the time although that is not said. In May 1843 finances became still more stretched because a man named James Mitchell was admitted to the Glasgow Lunatic Asylum where his board, lodging and care cost some £20 per year; this was probably the straw that broke the heritors' backs and caused them in August that year to appoint a committee of themselves to act with the Session in management of the poor's funds. This committee consisted of seven men, including the church treasurer and two elders but not the minister and so the heritors had a majority. They began by making a distribution to the poor and then set about establishing whether or not James Mitchell had a legal residence in the parish — and found that he did and was therefore entitled to his asylum costs. In 1844 with income about £42 and expenses around £86 two of the committee began to complain about the expense of holding a winter Communion as it would not bring in the large collections that summer ones did. The minister and Session were also asked to consider whether a legacy left for the poor and to be distributed as the minister and Session thought fit, might be used to pay off the deficit, a suggestion which was refused; the Session had already spent interest from this sum on coal for the poor. Quite apart from the ethics of it all, having left the minister off the committee and then coming to him with this proposal seems, at the very least, impertinent. A bond of £500 of kirk money was out at interest and the committee also considered using some of this but the minister made it clear to them that this money had been entrusted to a former minister and his successors and that it was a trust for the minister alone, nothing to do with the heritors or Session. The committee decided to investigate the source of this money and if necessary to take the opinion of counsel and also decided to write to non-resident heritors asking them to contribute liberally 'in order to avoid the imposition of a legal assessment', which was what all these efforts and rather dubious proposals were designed to avert. By this time however it was 1845 and the problem was overtaken by the Poor Law when compulsory assessments were enforced.[23]

In 1766 the minister of Falkirk spent £10, later repaid to him by the Session, 'in defending the poor's fund' which was almost certainly resisting an attempt by heritors to gain control of Session funds, although at the very beginning of the nineteenth century care of the poor in that parish was ceded, apparently harmoniously, to the heritors with the Session, helping them to raise money by increasing the charge for proclamations of marriage. Not all ministers were as meticulous as those of Baldernock and Falkirk. In June 1844, following the Disruption, a Ross-shire parish found its income so decreased that the heritors had to assess themselves, and to make matters easier for themselves, authorised the minister to use up to £10 stg. of a legacy for the poor which he did, although this was not in terms of the bequest. In 1850 he allowed more of this bequest to be used to pay the Parochial Board's proportion of the cost of the Easter Ross Poor House but in 1856, eleven years after the passing of the Poor Law, he became nervous about the legality of this use of the legacy and the Parochial Board thought it advisable to give him an indemnity against any charges he might have to face.[24]

Sometimes circumstances forced heritors to step in and take control of financial matters. The minister of Torphichen was enfeebled for the last years of his ministry and the parishioners resisted the settlement of James Watson, his successor. Matters went back and forth between Presbytery, Synod and Assembly and finally to the Supreme Court which ordered the Presbytery to induct him, something achieved with military assistance, the last settlement made in a church by what was called a 'riding committee'. It was during this difficult time that a general meeting of heritors appointed a committee to manage the poor's funds but all these disagreements cast long shadows and seven years on, in 1758, it was stated that a proper account of the funds was absolutely necessary as the committee had never got one from the surviving members of the old Kirk Session during the previous minister's time: 'Although frequently asked, besides repeated applications to said members [Kirk Session] to deliver up the Session books . . .

gave for answer that John Davie, their late precentor and Session Clerk had carried them off with him when he left the parish' and he, in spite of often being 'wrote to' had only recently produced an 'incompleat sort of minute book' in which the committee could not find any proper account of the poor's funds. All the heritors could do to prevent the funds 'from running into confusion' was to work out what was what themselves.[25]

The system of using voluntary assessments when there was special need worked, in general, well enough so that in many places it became almost routine and by the nineteenth century a movement in their favour developed and even the church began to look kindly on the idea, especially in rapidly developing towns where Sessions could not begin to cope with the queues of people requiring assistance and after the Disruption which decimated the finances of the established church.[26]

The third early form of fund-raising permitted to the church by Parliament was penalties or fines for moral offences, drunkenness and, from 1641 until repealed in 1690, for any sin that resulted in excommunication. Under Scots laws of the time fines for certain offences went in their entirety to pious uses within the parish concerned, such as those for excommunication, fornication and, more surprisingly, for salmon fishing on Sundays, as did civil fines for such crimes as poaching and those for certain breaches of licensing laws but in many cases it was only half of any fines that came to Kirk Sessions. In time Kirk Sessions began to impose fines by Acts of Session, without any legal authority, and these became a very important source of revenue as the whole amount always came to the poor's box. There is more on this subject in a later chapter — but fines were never fully exacted; had they been, the poor's boxes of the country would never have been short.[27]

The problems of providing seating have been mentioned in an earlier chapter but income from church seats was an important form of money raising and a minute book of Banchory-Devenick Kirk Session which begins in 1773 lists all the kirk's belongings such as Registers, Communion cups, hand-bell and so on but also has a heading of 'Property', which includes the north and west galleries of the church and seven pews below the west one. Unfortunately, providing seating as a means of raising money for the poor did not always work out as planned, as has already been said, with some odd effects on the poor's funds. In 1767 Tarbat Kirk Session, Ross-shire, discovered that 'a considerable number of people are greatly incommoded in attending Divine Worship being obliged to stand without [outside] and many to stay at home', and so they decided to instal seating to get over this problem and to help the poor's funds. What they did was to use some of the poor's money which was in their hands to build pews in the gallery 'and when finished to sett [let] them to such as wanted seats for a rent that might indemnify the outlay and afterwards yield an annual fund to the poor.' In order to pay for this fairly long-term investment, the Session restricted the number of people receiving help from the poor's money to those they knew to be the most needy. They paid for the necessary materials and paid James Ross, a wright, £2 'for his trouble' but it does not appear to have been a speedily completed job as it was only in 1771 that it was reported that the seats had cost £7 3s. 2d. stg. and a meeting was announced to let them. This was duly done, including five seats which went to a skipper and two fishermen for themselves and as cautioners for the rest of their crews for one year at a rent of 10s. In all, the rent for the year came to £1 5s. stg., approximately 17%, a remarkably high return on capital — at least it would have been had it been received. Five years later the position was the same; the gallery was given up to the heritors and the £7 stg. given by them to the Session for the poor, which had been spent on the gallery seats, was applied towards building what they called 'a convenient parochial school' for which the necessary money had apparently fallen short. Thus the heritors came out of all this rather well as the duty of providing a school was theirs, not the Session's; the poor came out of it worst, money for all but the most necessitous having been withheld in 1767 and the hoped-for benefits having not materialised. Golspie was another parish where the Session hoped to obtain an income from seat rents provided in much the same way as Tarbat did but in the event they also found that they could not gather in the rents and ultimately decided to sell the pews outright 'for money or victual'. This was a good solution had the money or victual been forthcoming but three years later the seats were still 'not yet near paid up' and the minister was instructed, by the Presbytery, it seems, to 'use all proper diligence at executing Summonses and other Diligences against Deficients in payment, that the whole may be recovered by Martinmas next.' How this was arranged is not known but at the end of the day there was a loss of £30 on the whole transaction. The mistake in these instances was giving people time to pay instead of insisting on payment at the outset because seating *was* a good form of money-raising; for instance in Cromarty in 1755 the listed public funds of the poor included 'The Ile of the church above and below, being built out of the Poors money and contributions of the people and the rents of the seats are appointed to the use of the poor, and for supporting the Fabrick', both aims which were apparently achieved.[28]

The great occasions of human life — birth, marriage and death — all brought income to the kirk, with half of the fees for baptism and burial being devoted to the poor. Every prohibition on such things as private baptisms or marriages could also be turned to good account as they could usually be overcome by paying money either as a direct fine or by allowing, as has been said, a collection to be taken up at them, although where heritors took over the management of the poor, as happened in Falkirk, they were entitled to and did claim a portion of baptism and marriage dues, as well as collections. Marriage is mentioned more fully in the appropriate chapter but with payment for proclamation of banns, wedding fees, collections, fines for breach of contract and for irregular and clandestine marriages, it became an expensive business for the couples concerned and a money-spinner for the kirk. There was also forfeited consignation money which began as a pledge in cash or kind, undertaking that the marriage contract would be carried out and that there would be no ante-nuptial fornication between contract and marriage. The money was held by the Session for up to nine months but whether or not it was used during that time as an interest-free loan is not clear although it seems more likely that it just lay in the poor's box, serving no useful purpose other than as a threat to the prospective bride and groom to watch their step, until it was either returned to them or forfeited, in which latter case it did go to the poor. With all its formalities and procedures, death was a wonderful source of income for the church. There was the hire of the little bell (mort-bell) to announce funerals and perhaps payment for ringing the church bell, both of which may appear in accounts as 'bell-penny'. There was hire of the mortcloth to cover the coffin; hire of the litter, spokes, hearse and horse-clothes once roads had developed sufficiently for corpses to be carried to burial by other means than on the shoulders of men; there were special charges for burial inside the church even when this was not meant to take place or else 'donations' to get permission to do so. There was payment for non-parishioners' burial in a parish graveyard and, more rarely, hire of the common or re-usable coffin at perhaps 1s. a time. There was a charge for permission to erect headstones and, should a corpse be laid in the church or Session house before burial or in transit to it, this also brought in money. (There was no income, of course, when the church was used as a mortuary for drowned bodies or corpses rescued from body-snatchers while they awaited identification.) More than corpses could be accommodated in kirk premises in return for a fee, however: during Jacobite troubles, the Kirk Session of Inverness stored the bread for the King's army in the kirk officer's house and some two years later, received rent due for this.[29] In many of these cases, church staff received a proportion of the income but there was always money for kirk funds. When a member of a well-off family died, it was customary for the family to distribute alms to the poor, either immediately after the funeral or by putting a donation into the collection plate on a Sunday, in which case some would be distributed immediately and some retained in the poor's funds. There is more detail about this in the chapter on burial.

Donations were particularly generous when given during famines but they came in fairly frequently at other times too and not just in cases of bereavement. For instance, Andrew Gibson, a member of an old Govan family and a seafarer constantly going on long voyages, was in the habit of giving donations to the church as he was about to sail and also when he returned safely. If kirk funds were very low, it was not unknown for a Session to ask, or more probably to request the minister to ask specific people for a donation, but land-owners repeatedly sent 'their compliment' voluntarily to the poor's funds and the ladies of any parish were always generous with gifts in cash or kind. These might go directly into the poor's box for future use or the donor might specify how the gift was to be used: when Mr Macleod of Geanies, Ross-shire, gave three guineas in 1806 to the Kirk Session of Tarbat, it was his wish that it be given to three families where there had been sickness for several weeks, to a blind man and to eight indigent widows. In 1833 Major Munro of Poyntzfield wrote to the Kirk Session of Resolis to say that he was about to leave the parish for some time and feared that the winter would be a hard one and so he wanted to give a barrel of coals to ten needy people and a firlot of meal to each needy person on his estate, leaving it to the Kirk Session to decide who should benefit. He added that although he felt that he could rely on the other proprietors to look after their own people, yet there might be needs outside his own estate — 'yet let me not in any singular case cramp your humanity when ever it may be within the parish', was how he indicated that his generosity was not necessarily to be confined to his own people. That parish seemed to be blessed with kindly proprietors at that moment as, that year, when there were 76 on the poor's roll, the Session received a donation of £2 stg. for the poor's box from Thomas Urquhart of Kinbeachy to make up for the loss of some land from which the poor had formerly got their firing. This land had been apportioned to his estate in a division of commonty or common land and he felt it only right that heritors who got land in this way should make up to the poor for its loss to them, and this he planned to do annually. Although directed towards specific needy people, such donations helped them not to be a burden on the poor's box as they would otherwise have been and thus indirectly helped kirk funds.[30]

In former times, proceedings at Parliamentary elections were less strictly controlled than they are nowadays and it was possible for donations to be handed to every Kirk Session in a county by a successful candidate as happened in the early 1820s in Ross-shire. The Reform Act of 1832 increased the number of those eligible to vote and made elections altogether more worrying for candidates and Colonel Grant, who had already been an MP for twenty-five years before 1832, gratefully gave £15 stg. to the poor of the parish of Drainie when he was safely returned and he would certainly not have been the only MP to do this sort of thing. The question is, were such donations thank-offerings or bribes?[31]

Among the records of St. Ninian's Kirk Session, Stirlingshire, is a book entitled the 'Accounts of Extra Money called the Extra Book with money received and disbursed . . . from various sources — executry, mortifications, legacies, marriage money etc.' The book covers the years 1814–36 and that a special one was required to record this income shows how important it was and indeed legacies and mortifications were particularly valuable. A way of encouraging such gifts was to publicise them on a benefactions board, placed on an inside wall of the church where Sunday by Sunday all might see the generosity of particular people. A board was provided at Kirkmahoe, Dumfries, headed 'Legacies given for the behoof of the poor & School of the Parish of Kirkmahoe'; St. Cuthbert's Church in Edinburgh was another where the Session ordered the treasurer to erect a board with the names and designations of those who left money for the poor, inscribed in letters of gold, as a good example to others; and the Old West Kirk at Greenock had nine such boards, painted in yellow and red, the largest of them 4'6" x 2'7" and mounted in a frame painted to imitate red marble, which seems a costly way to encourage donations. Legacies could come in cash or kind and one of those listed at Kirkmahoe was a mortcloth, to be hired out to bring in money for the poor. Brechin Cathedral Kirk still has painted boards listing seventeenth-century gifts of money and church equipment and examples may be found elsewhere too. An unusual form of legacy was the £120 Scots left for the poor of Drainie by Alexander Gordon of Dykeside, the Session receiving not money but a debt to add to their bonds and bills, in the hope that they would recoup it. In a quite different case, £500 stg. was left by Dr James Oswald in 1809 to be equally divided among the ten parishes in the county of Caithness and this had a further £500 added to it by his executors. In this case, it was stated that the money was to be invested and the income used for the poor, with the Moderator of the Presbytery of Caithness to accept the money and see to its investment. When news of any legacy came to a Session, they tried to take care to secure it as soon as possible. That of Holm, Orkney, paid 24s. Scots in 1691 to send the kirk officer over the Pentland Firth to Caithness carrying a letter concerning money left to them by a woman named Barbara Smyth, which was lying in the hands of the minister at Bower. In much the same way the box masters of Stirling were appointed in 1701 'to take the best method to secure that monny left by the deceased Umphery Menloch, being ane hundred merks.'[32]

Although strictly speaking a mortification is a bequest, some of these were given during the donor's lifetime: Lord Cromartie mortified 12 bolls and 2 firlots of bear annually for the poor on his property in a particular parish in the mid-eighteenth century and some time early that century in a nearby parish John Forrester mortified 5 bolls of bear to the poor. Much of the charity received by Sessions was in the form of grain, so much so that many Sessions kept a chest for holding the poor's meal. A mortification handed over during the donor's lifetime could well have conditions attached. In 1682 one parish minister was given one to hold until it might be required, with details of the transaction written into the Session book thus, 'for security of the money which the minister acknowledge to being in his hands to be paid when need is . . . ', a useful safety net for any Session to have. Although money was not often handed over during a person's lifetime in this way, the arrangements for payment of it after death might be inserted in Session records, a form of making one's will but one which must have made it difficult if not impossible to change one's mind at a later date. One such appears in the minutes of Cambuslang Kirk Session. Written into the book on 10 August 1700 is the statement that Gabriel Hamilton of Westburn gave 600 merks during his lifetime, 'which sum I pledge me, my airs, exers [executors] and successors to pay to the minister and Kirk Session for the use and behoof of the parish . . . upon the first terme to Whitsunday or Martinmas next after my decease under the pain of 50 merks money foresaid of liquidebt expense in case of failzie [failure] with the ordinary @rent [annual interest] of the principal sum after the said term of pay-ment.' He instructed the minister and Session to use the interest for buying shoes and hose yearly for the poor and they were empowered to uplift and use the principal on sufficient security but might not diminish the capital nor use the @rent in any other way than what was prescribed and to make assurance doubly sure he inserted the clause, 'the airs of me, Gabriel Hamilton, to have a vote in distribution thereof.'[33]

When the Rev. Mr Innes and his brother Dr Innes mortified £200 to the Kirk Session of Yester, East Lothian, it was so that the interest of the money should be used to help pay house rents for the poor. Banff Kirk Session received a legacy of

100 merks from John Watson, an Edinburgh merchant, for keeping a boy at school in Banff, as well as £50 to pay the schoolmaster, while that of Durris, Aberdeenshire, received £500 in old 4% bank annuities from Alexander Hogg, a parishioner who died in 1787. How it was to be used is interesting: firstly some was to be used to pay the schoolmaster to teach some poor children, 10s. was to go for 'their mid-summer fee' to those herding stock around Cairn-Shee, and the rest to 'poor housekeepers [householders] on the poor's roll,' except for — and this must have been very welcome to the Session — enough to pay for 'a dinner to the members of the Kirk Session when they distribute the interest of the mortification.'[34] A small croft mortified about the beginning of the eighteenth century to one Session brought in a yearly rent of 3 bolls, and lands mortified for the poor about the mid-seventeenth century brought in 6 bolls and 6$^1/_2$ pecks of bear or meal to another; in both cases it appears that the property remained in private hands and that it was just the rent which was bequeathed. This also seems to have been the position in another case when it was not rent but the feu-duty on some land that went to the church.[35]

'Vacant stipend', the minister's salary which went unpaid during a vacancy, did not accrue to kirk funds but was meant to be used for various pious purposes. In 1733, for instance, the Presbytery of Deer, Aberdeenshire, allowed one-third of the vacant stipend of Rathven Church to be used for the transport of the incoming minister all the way from Kirkwall, and two-thirds for buying church utensils, repairing the bell house and building a bridge over the Rathven which ran between the manse and the kirk and was 'many times in time of speat and in winter impassable.' As with donations and legacies directed to specific causes, this freed kirk funds for the poor.[36]

In 1731 a Session bought a chest to hold the poor's meal — a big one too, as it could take 8$^1/_2$ bolls — paying for it in kind with 3 firlots and 2 pecks of meal. The previous year they had sold 2 bolls of bear which had been collected for the poor, which may have been because at that time they had nothing in which to store it and so it was better to convert it into money rather than risk it deteriorating or it may have been because it was surplus to requirements at that time and the money it made could be invested for the benefit of the poor. Although Sessions were in general short of money, it could happen that they found themselves with money or victual on hand and, if there was no great pressure on their funds, then it was customary to invest it so as to have an assured income for the poor but whether this encouraged them sometimes to economise on the poor rather than use capital seems uncertain. Until banks were established, or were accessible, there was no way that money could be invested other than by lending it on heritable security or by buying property; nor were there many people or bodies prepared to lend money and so it was that Sessions became, for all practical purposes, bankers to their parishes and further afield. It became an accepted and perfectly respectable thing to borrow from kirk funds, to borrow the poor's money, but this was normally never done without clear acknowledgement of the loan being given and its conditions written out, a kind of IOU usually referred to as a bond or bill, which was kept in a secure place which was the larger poor's box in parishes which had more than one and if not, in the ordinary box. Money was lent to individuals and to public bodies. Sessions tried to ensure that their investment was secure — when the box masters of one parish lent £40 Scots to a soldier they were ordered by the Kirk Session to 'restore it' because a soldier was a bad risk, not so much because of the chance of his being killed in action but because troops constantly moved about the country and it was very difficult to keep track of where individual men got to. Sessions therefore liked what they called 'good hands' — as one minute put it, a Session 'hearing of Good hands to put out the poors money to has unanimously consented to let five hundred merks to . . . eldest lawful son to . . .' but as has been said in an earlier chapter, should someone ask to borrow money who was obviously not a good risk, a Session might put that person on the poor's roll and help them that way rather than lend them what they might not be able to repay, burdening them with debt and themselves with a debtor. Town Councils depended greatly on the kirk as a source of funding. For nearly the whole of the eighteenth century, for example, that of Inverness borrowed from the Kirk Session for all sorts of purposes, including putting the finishing touches to the new Court House and jail and, if the following extract is anything to go by, some burghs may have agreed a general permission to borrow: '25th May 1775. According to the appointment of the Session it wàs transacted with the Magistrates of Banff a contract (which was put in the books of Session) of an Act of Council authorizing the Treasurer of Banff to borrow money from the Kirk Session.' About 1828 the Kirk Session of St. Nicholas Church, Aberdeen, had £400 out on loan to the Town treasurer but burghs did not necessarily confine their requests for finance to their own Kirk Sessions. They approached others too, although these were usually reasonably close by. Arbroath Town Council, called Aberbrothock in the minutes, borrowed £137 15s. 6d. Scots from Craig Kirk Session in 1719 and in 1754 was paying interest of over £33 to St. Vigean's Kirk Session, only to borrow £300 from them the following year although this sum was only required for six months. These public bodies, of course, paid interest in cash whereas individuals might well pay in victual.[37]

Interest rates were a matter of agreement between lender and borrower but usually worked out at around $3^1/2$% up to perhaps 5%. In general, this was properly paid but it could happen that once money had left their hands a Session could be at the mercy of the borrower, even one whose hands might have been expected to be good. An example of this was when a Session lent 3,000 merks to Lord Seafield who in 1823 and 1833 unilaterally reduced and further reduced the amount of interest he was willing to pay; and Scone Kirk Session must have felt perfectly confident when it was the Sheriff who borrowed from them but his behaviour was even worse. For four years he paid no interest at all on 500 merks. After 1716, when the Session sought legal advice, some was paid now and then but there was still money owing in 1724. At that point, fortunately for the Session, his affairs appear to have been put into other hands owing to either illness or death, and it was other people who arranged for payment to be made. Legal action was sometimes taken more quickly; one Session used part of a fine which had been assigned to them by the Synod to pay for the expense of 'horning Ankerville's tenants' which was part of a legal process to recover money which this heritor had borrowed. He had assigned the rents of some of his property to the Session for three years as repayment and it was for this that the Session had to pursue his tenants. Such unethical behaviour on the part of people in such positions cannot have been viewed kindly by any Kirk Session, yet they might take a compassionate and certainly a practical view when a borrower genuinely got into difficulties. Realising that Patrick Nisbet could never repay money lent to him, but being told that his brother-in-law offered 100 merks provided it was accepted as a full discharge, Yester Kirk Session unanimously agreed 'that they had better take the hundred merks than to distress the poor man and perhaps not get payment in the end.'[38]

There were, of course, some Sessions which did lend the poor's money without adequate or proper security and a further problem was that if capital was not required for the poor, then it could be left lying out at interest and be more or less forgotten about for such a long time that it might never be applied to the purpose for which it was originally given or collected. To let things run on in this way, especially if the bonds had been somewhat informally written in the first place, was asking for trouble. During a secession, various items of church property belonging to Abernethy Kirk Session were taken into safe keeping by the Presbytery and returned once things had settled down sufficiently, at which point the Session went through all their bonds and bills and decided to renew them with the borrowers or their heirs as soon as this could be done. Because some of them were 'very old as to date' and not very well drawn up, they wisely empowered the minister to allow a reasonable reduction of interest to those who would renew their securities because they realised that the outcome of any legal action could well be uncertain.[39] With money lying out at interest for years, people could die owing the Session and then some sensible course of action had to be found. It was in fact the death of his father owing a bond to the kirk, a debt transferred to him, that got poor Patrick Nisbet into difficulties. In another such case a man named James Boynd 'declared his willingness to pay and be discharged of the debt which was owing to the Session by his father but craved that in consideration [as he says he succeeded to nothing by his father] that therefore the Session would grant him some ease with @rents [interest] due on his father's bond.' They agreed to discharge the bond of £78 Scots along with the @rents due on it for an immediate payment of 200 merks Scots (£133 6s. 0d. Scots) which showed that a considerable amount of interest had been allowed to accrue. James accepted this 'and promised to pay immediately upon their rising from the Sederunt.'[40]

While public bodies usually borrowed for a specific length of time, it is obvious that many other loans were open-ended with no time limit, as opposed to just being left lying out, which was all very well unless there was an emergency, such as a famine, when the capital had to be clawed back as quickly as possible as happened in the Black Year when loans had to be swiftly called in to pay for government meal. At such times the borrower was likely to be as hard-pressed as anyone else and could find it particularly difficult to repay any loan. It was not always an emergency that caused the calling in of money — it could be something like church improvements, but at least they were unlikely to be made during hard times, so that those who had borrowed were in a better position to return what they had of the poor's money. Lending the poor's money went on until the Poor Law of 1845 although by then, owing to the various reasons already given, funds were becoming much tighter and such money as was available was needed for immediate relief and was not likely to be lent. In spite of the fact that the kirk lent money in this way, or perhaps because of it, there was great disapproval by the kirk of money-lending by ordinary people. Issobell Clark was described as a 'usurar and lennar of money for proffeit', which was clearly regarded as being very sinful; and over 200 years later, in the 1790s, the Old Statistical Account for Kincardine, Ross-shire, described money-lending there. Young men and women went south every year for summer work and by 'hard work and low living' were able to return each autumn with plenty of money, much of which they lent at exorbitant interest, and in addition they 'lived with and are a burden on their friends and acquaintance, especially those whom necessity has obliged to borrow from them and who are not punctual in repaying.' This was a great abuse of money-lending and one which the parish minister, who was writing about it, considered could only be remedied by finding proper employment for young people at home — what a modern ring that has![41]

An alternative to lending money at interest or investing it in church seating was to put it into property. The kirk belongings listed in the Banchory-Devenick minute book, already quoted, include 'A park at Gilcolmtown rented at £4 8s. per annum'. Many Sessions considered that it was better to invest any spare poor's money in land or buildings which were sound, tangible, realisable assets rather than risk lending it to borrowers. When the Kirk Session of Yester received the handsome sum of £1,519 3s. Scots for the poor from the Laird of Newtonhall in 1710 they used it to buy thirteen acres of land from the Marquis of Tweeddale, subject to a feu-duty of 1s. per acre, and by the 1830s the rent of this land amounted to £29 stg. per year which was a very useful sum. This kirk land in Yester was known as the 'precious land' but property bought with the poor's money was usually referred to as 'poor's lands', 'kirklands' or, in the case of buildings, as 'poor's houses' although these were not the same as the later poor's houses for the destitute. The occupiers of kirk property of this sort might be called the poor's tenants and technically this meant that the poor became landlords although they were not regarded as such; it was the Kirk Session who held that position. Inverness Kirk Session was one that became considerably involved in property ownership, both bought and bequeathed to them, so that in time they controlled and let two stretches of fishing on the River Ness @ £40 stg. for each coble that went fishing but they still kindly reserved for the townspeople a supply of salmon for family use during the whole fishing season at the equivalent of a penny stg. per lb. They let farms and mills, sold houses well and reinvested to better purpose and managed their operations to the extent of being almost prosperous. Whether in cash or in kind, rents of kirk property were invaluable to Session and sometimes provided little benefits for staff too: a property owned by Elie Kirk Session paid 8¹/₂ bolls of oats and 4 bolls of bear which could be distributed to the poor or sold for their benefit, but 12 poultry which were also part of the rent went as an additional and welcome fee to the Session Clerk.[42]

Some property came to a Session neither by purchase nor bequest but because it was demanded from someone in return for special expenditure on their behalf, such as maintenance in a lunatic asylum, as was suggested for Mrs Duncan's husband but refused by her; or it might come because it had been offered as security for a loan and the borrower failed to repay or died without doing so. This happened in St. Monance in 1836 when the Session had to decide what to do about a house held by them 'on a Deposition in security for money advanced thereon to the late And. Mathieson.' Owning property always involves expense and this house was one on which the Session had to spend a considerable amount. They found that repairs were needed at once to make it habitable for the winter in the hope that they could let it as well as possible but whatever was done then, a surprising amount of work was required the following year. The Session Clerk had to make out specifications and call for estimates for raising the walls to the same height as those of an adjoining house; for raising the couples and garret floor and covering them with new lath and tiles; for the roof to be lathed and plastered between the couples; the window to be raised to correspond with the floor; for the main floor to be overhauled and relaid as necessary, with any new flooring to be estimated for by the square yard; for a passage 3¹/₂' wide to be made through the ground flat to the garden behind, with a partition to divide it from the rest of the house; and lastly, for the stone stair in front of the house to be removed to the back of the house along with the door of the upper flat, and the walls and roof of the back 'jam' to be repaired. Three years later the heritors and Session decided to sell the house by private bargain but they gave notice of their intention to Andrew Mathieson's heirs, which was a courteous gesture, and an offer of £100 was soon accepted, on condition that the buyers paid the cost of the conveyance and that the minister should sign the disposition and receive the money, to all of which the heirs agreed.[43] That particular case went smoothly but a few years previously, in 1834, St. Monance Kirk Session had had difficulties when a man named Andrew Wallace tried to get back a property which had formerly belonged to his great-grandfather and been 'resigned' by him to the Session from which it appears that it had been security for a loan which could not be repaid or something of the sort. Andrew Wallace's demands became such that the Session felt it necessary to get advice as 'to the validity of the tenure by which they now hold the property' and 'after mature deliberation' decided the following month to hold on to it and therefore instructed their clerk to write to tell Andrew of this decision. A difference of opinion continued about it all, however, as some fifteen months later the Session decided to get a legal opinion as to how prudent or possible it would be for them to defend any attempt to 'wrest the property in St. Monance from them'. They received this advice in April 1836 and although what it was is not stated in the minutes, it may be inferred from the fact that a committee was appointed to confer with Andrew, with full power to make whatever arrangements they thought fit, but these are not recorded either.[44]

Even without doing such extensive works as St. Monance Kirk Session did to their house, any property-owning Session was involved with basic maintenance, such as £5 16s. Scots spent by St. Vigeans Kirk Session in 1732 on its property, while in Hawick in the early years of the same century a good deal had to be spent repairing a property belonging to the Session and sometimes called the Session House, which was let to Lady Chesters, expenses which included 18s. for refreshments at Mrs Ruecastle's for the masons and wrights. Ownership of land also brought problems of a different sort. In 1834 St. Monance Kirk Session had difficulties with their neighbouring Session, Easter Anstruther, both of them holding adjoining pieces of land but when St. Monance claimed a road along the top of theirs, this was refused unless they either paid for the privilege or bought it. St. Monance Session considered the road to be 'absolutely necessary' and in spite of the rebuffing answer they got initially, they went about trying to get what they wanted in a most conciliatory manner, appointing an elder and the Session Clerk to 'hold a friendly communing' with the other Session to discover whether they were 'entitled to a road free from all expenses'. The two men were given a free hand to conclude the matter and as there is no further report, one must assume that the outcome was satisfactory. A regrettable feature of Kirk Session records is that there seemed to be no need to record things when the solution was known to everyone anyway, but that does not help posterity. Another problem that cropped up about St. Monance's land at the same time was when someone began digging a drain through it without the Session's knowledge and the Clerk was instructed to find out what was going on and to 'request the parties concerned to explain upon what authority they have proceeded without consulting the Session.'[45]

Letting property had the great advantage over lending money that if a borrower did not pay interest regularly or failed to repay capital, it was difficult to get the money back but in the case of rented property the kirk had no qualms about eviction. One Session, deciding in 1748 to remove a tenant from land they owned, empowered the minister 'to sign the precept of warning in the name of the Kirk Session and cause execute the same in due form and to raise and execute a removing against the said Andrew Buist to the effect the said Kirk Session or others in their name may enter into and possess these lands in time coming.' About the same time a treasurer reported that a couple of tenants were 'very slow and defective' in paying their rents to the Session, whereupon no time was wasted in ordering him 'to prosecute the said Tennants for their arrears etc and to set [let] their possessions to more responsible tennants.' Such evictions did not indicate that kirk rents were over-high; they appear to have been very reasonable. In 1844 two lots of kirk land were let for £5 18s. 11½d. and £5 17s. 8½d. per acre, said to be 'on the whole a reasonable rent', with the leases to run for thirteen years. So far as tenants were concerned fair rents and fairly long leases were a very good thing and so, in spite of the work involved, not only did owning property benefit kirk funds but it benefited good tenants too.[46]

If the object was worthwhile, Kirk Sessions tried never to refuse a plea for help and would cheerfully tell their treasurer to 'think on a fund for paying of the samen' or to 'fall upon a methode' or to give temporary assistance 'whyll they fall upon some oyr fund' and the methods fallen upon were very varied. Some had the authority of law behind them, others were achieved by Acts of Session, perhaps in conjunction with a Town Council. One of the former was that, by law, a Session could cut any trees which they had planted round a churchyard and use the money for the poor but if it was the heritors who had planted them, then the trees were their property and could not be cut and sold — although in fact they frequently gave them to the poor's funds anyway. Sales of such wood were therefore some-times carried out by Sessions, with intimation made beforehand by the beadle and with strict regulations like those made at Auchterhouse in 1713:

1) Highest bidder always to be accepted.
2) Credit to be given on such security as shall satisfy the offerers.
3) Each bode (sic) must exceed the former by one pennie.
4) All below a croon must be ready money.
5) C — J — is appointed baillie of the said roup.
6) The Cryer must have the ordinary dues.

Alternatively straight barter could be used instead of a roup. In 1776 Muirkirk Kirk Session allowed a tradesman have trees to the value of £2 19s. in return for work done for the kirk and two years later the kirkyard was replanted.[47]

There were other ways in which a graveyard could be made profitable. Making public announcements in them was a very old custom but in many places this was turned to good use by forbidding them unless they were made by the kirk officer, approved by the Kirk Session and, most importantly, paid for. Kirkyards could also bring in a rent for grazing beasts although in some parishes it was the minister who had the right of kirkyard grass 'according to use and wont' but even so, a kindly one might roup it for the benefit of the poor. Animals which were not even inside the graveyard could also bring money to the church as unmarked stray sheep and other stock were sometimes sold for behoof of the poor; or they might be poinded until the owner paid a fine to reclaim them, and then it was the fine which went to the church.[48]

If church equipment of any sort was no longer needed or had become damaged, every effort was made to put it to some make-do-and-mend purpose such as turning an old Communion table and cloth into a coffin and a winding sheet but if something of this sort was not practical, then it was sold if possible. Thus it was that a minister reported to his Session that he had 'disposed to Hugh Ross, Goldsmith in Tain, a silver cup which had become useless' and as a result the kirk funds were better off to the tune of £2 3s. 6d. stg. When Mauchline Kirk Session's Communion tent or preaching booth fell to pieces a decision was taken for the 'remains to be rouped', and when, much earlier, in 1574 Aberdeen Kirk Session decided to remove an organ from the church on the grounds that it was a super-stitious object, it was still done so as to bring profit to the poor's funds. Kirk equipment in good condition could be hired out: rather surprisingly Communion tables might be let as huxters' stalls for fairs while, more suitably, Communion utensils could be let to neighbouring parishes which did not have enough of their own. Lowlier things such as ladders could be hired too although the charge made for them was possibly as much to prevent damage as to make money: 'The Session finding that the kirk ladders are abused by lending out, therefore appoint that every day any one of them is out, the borrower pay 12*d*. Sc. and that he send them in as whole as he took them out, and that none be lent out by the beadle without orders from Alexander Roben and that the money be paid in to him.' So said the Kirk Session of Clackmannan in 1702 while that of Banchory-Devenick decreed in 1736 that because the church ladders were 'being very much abused by being lent and kept a long time away' they would charge a penny stg. a day for them 'to prevent this abuse and to gather the money laid out upon them.' Cows could also be hired out, so it is said, but just how this was arranged is not clear.[49]

Any building materials which a Session might have but which were surplus to requirements or for some reason unsuitable were if possible also sold. When one minister wanted some limestone belonging to the Session for his own use it was left to him to 'charge himself with a reasonable price' and this he did. Another Session had lime which workmen considered unfit for the kirk roof but which could perfectly well be used for other building work and when someone offered to buy it the workmen 'viewed it' in presence of the kirk treasurer and a bailie, valued it at 6*d*. per barrel and at that price it was sold. Twenty years later that Session thought of going in for slate-quarrying but there is only the one entry about this proposal in the minutes: '5th March 1764. As the Session are informed that slate might be found on the hill head above — dale, appoint Mr. Hugh Mowat to converse with the Magistrates and inform himself how far they would concur in endeavouring to put it in the Session's power to sell the slate found there to reimburse the money laid out in the breaking it up or if they could think of any other better method for the purpose.'[50] The possibility that the purchase of school books for resale by one Kirk Session was intended as a money-raiser as well as to help with education is mentioned in a later chapter, as the income from be-queathed effects has already been mentioned. An early form of fund-raising in coastal districts was something totally different: levying a little something from incoming ships, and an Act of Montrose Kirk Session in June 1658 shows that they decided to revive this practice which had obviously fallen into disuse: 'William Reid and George Erskine should have a care to wait upon any ship that comes from Norraway that they should pay ane trie according to the old custom for the use of the poor, either the . . . trie that is put in the ship or the price of it being rouped either by skipper or meat [mate].'

Although the relevant part of the Kirk Session minutes of Eday and Harray Kirk Session, Orkney, does not show up on microfilm, it appears that when there was a vacancy in a mission station there, the mission land was partly let out in grass and partly cropped. For this a quarter of oats and half a bushel of rye grass were sown and two barrels of potatoes planted which cost £1 7s. stg. plus £1 5s. 8d. stg. for labour, apparently a case of waste not want not, with the hope of some profit to the funds.[51]

Some sources of money were surprising but it must be remembered that they were not regular methods of fund-raising. In 1826, 5 guineas came jointly to two Sessions as a result of an unusual case. In January that year the minister of West Kilbride laid before his Session a copy of a Decreet Arbitral concerning a woman servant who had been owed 10 guineas of wages by her employer at the time of his death, after which she had removed some of his property. Arbiters who were called in about this decided that one of the heirs should pay her half the money she was owed — 5 guineas — and pay the other half to the Kirk Sessions of Ardrossan and West Kilbride, for which the ministers were required to give a stamped receipt. Another unexpected windfall occurred in Edinburgh in the first half of the eighteenth century when a bailie, who was also an elder of St. Cuthbert's Church, reported that a man who had been arrested for being drunk and disorderly was found to have £54 on him which was taken from him and the next day he was asked by the bailie 'to bring documents of his civil deportment' and evidence that this money was his. This sounds very high-handed but there were probably good reasons for suspicion and as the man could provide no answer to the request, the bailie gave the money to the Session's treasurer for the kirk funds.[52]

A law of 1621 decreed that winnings of over 100 merks Scots on horse racing or on play at cards or dice in less than 24 hours should be forfeit to the poor. Had this been enforced the kirk would never have lacked for money but it does not seem that it was in spite of at least one valiant attempt. About 1707 Sir Andrew Ramsay of Abbotshall lost 28,000 merks gaming with Sir Scipio Hill and granted a bond for that amount on his estate, at which point the kirk treasurer claimed the excess over 100 merks in terms of the 1621 Act. The outcome is not known but it can hardly have been successful as otherwise it would be well remembered as a famous victory for the kirk. What seems a curious source of income for the poor was a boxing-match: in 1790 the *British Chronicle* advertised such a match, the fight being for £20-a-side, with £50 promised to the poor of the parish in which the fight should take place, this to come from the drawings at the door. This event appears to have been held in Scotland, not England, as the paper also advertised a performance at Kelso, Roxburghshire, of the play *Inkle and Yarico* for the benefit of the Sunday Charity School. This last case was not strictly raising money for the poor's funds of the kirk although it was designed to benefit the poor but it shows that even although the early reformed kirk had a horror of play-acting and amusements generally, including dancing, attitudes did change so that innocent pleasures could be put to constructive use. This was how a charity workhouse in the Canongate parish of Edinburgh, built by public subscriptions in 1761, was maintained by various church funds and also by a benefit play granted annually by the manager of the Edinburgh Theatre; and, by 1763, the profit from a dancing assembly room, where the decorum was said to be very strict, also went to support the workhouse. Soon, it appears, charity balls, like the one held in Lauder in 1801, were proving useful sources of funds and kirk ingenuity probably produced many other ways of bringing in money than those already mentioned.[53]

The care of kirk money fell to the treasurer, usually appointed from amongst the elders and sometimes known as the box-master because he was responsible for the poor's box, perhaps even to the extent of taking it home with him for safety. The parish of Baldernock was one where in addition to the elders on collecting duty in the church on Sundays there was another who was called the 'collector for the poor of Baldernock', a duty undertaken for terms of six months at a time and sometimes longer, from which it appears that there could be a form of revolving treasurership in places. In others there was a special official who had the duty of handling finance: at St. Michael's Church, Linlithgow, this was done by the Eleemosynar from before 1728 until at least 1852. This splendidly-titled functionary was really an almoner and much involved with distributing the poor's money. Deacons, of course, had a very important role in financial matters but they did not exist in many parishes, while in very outlying ones, lack of education could mean that there was no one in the Session able to fill the post of treasurer and the Session Clerk could find himself appointed to it. For the same reason, a good many ministers had to take charge of kirk funds. When one treasurer 'resigned his office, refusing to continue in it any longer' there was no one else suitable to take over the task and the Session had to deposit their money with the minister. This seems as if it were the last resort, yet the minister of Kilninian and Kilmore was a regular treasurer as in 1776 he was 'appointed to act as Treasurer for another year and be at all due pains as formerly to keep the Session's accounts, uplift fines and give out moneys where he knows the case to be of such a nature that the Session will sustain what he may do in their name.' This Session continued for a further four years to expect their minister to act as treasurer at which point he finally asked to be relieved of the task, promising to give all the help he could to make things easy for anyone the Session appointed. The outcome was that an elder undertook to keep the money and to present a list of it to the Session but the minister still kept the book and continued to enter all financial transactions. In Fetlar, Shetland, a minister also acted as treasurer until he asked to be relieved and one minister of Tongue had to point out to the Session the inconvenience of his keeping the poor's money, not because of the effort this put him to but because he found himself distributing it without the benefit of advice from the elders about applicants' circumstances. He insisted that 'a place should be fitted up under the pulpit, with a lock and key where the money should lie in a box, with a cash book, pen and ink, that the weekly collection may be marked by the clerk, in presence of a quorum of the elders', with three of them remaining behind every Sunday until the collection was 'entered in the cash book and the press for it locked, and the keys given to the Moderator.' One can see how easily a minister could slip into holding kirk money and how convenient it was for him to act as treasurer, not only because of his superior education but because when weekday services were held in outlying areas and baptisms performed in different localities at which collections were taken up, it was eminently practical for the minister to receive the money and bring it back with him. As the minutes of an Argyllshire parish said, 'the several collections made in distant parts of the parish' could not be lodged immediately in any hands but the minister's and, so as to prevent confusion in their accounts, the Session appointed him to keep such money in his own hands until the next distribution of the poor's money;[54] but confusion is just what it sounds as if this would produce.

It was the treasurer, whatever other positions he might hold, who had to account for the money at Kirk Session meetings. The post was no sinecure and at the end of each year, if not at lesser intervals too, a reckoning of 'charge and discharge' was formally made between him and the Session and a note of the monies on hand inserted in the minute book. Entries in the minutes about these special meetings may appear thus: 'The box being sighted thair was found in it 18 lb 2s. 4d. ' or in more detail: 'The whilk day the minister with the Elders met according to appointment and received John Jameson Treasurer his accounts of the poors money and after comparing all charge with Disbursements found Resting in his hands four hundred thirty three pounds, seven shillings, four pennies Scots, And this besides what is contained in Bill or Bond lying in the Kirk Box,' all of which was witnessed by those present. Yet another minute says that 'The Minister and elders counted the box and found therein fourty two shillings and six pence, besides bad money, as also by bonds and bills four hundred and twenty six pounds 17 shillings and 7 pennies Scots, after which they distributed to the poor £20, which pays for month of January instant.'[55]

What could make accurate account-keeping very difficult was when needy people persuaded elders to give them something out of Sunday collections before these were entered up 'which partial distribution insensibly diminished the amount of the clerk's account in the cash book,' as one Session complained. Equally money could be handed out on the orders of the minister or elders to help to bury poor people, without this being recorded, and money for hire of the mortcloth might be unpaid — and so it could go on, and something that cannot have helped was when a Session ordered their treasurer 'to pay Alexander Brodie £12 Sc and appoint him to take no receipt for it.' Whyever not? Bad arithmetic was a problem too. The accounts of one parish show that in 1838 the poors funds came to £10 7s. 4³/₄d. of which £4 18s. 6d. was distributed. According to the treasurer's sums this left £6 2s. 6d. for contingencies but his subtraction was poor and he got his answer wrong. The following year it was his addition which was at fault when he added £6 16s. 8d. paid as salaries to £14 16s. 8d. which was for the poor and contingencies, and came up with a total of £21 4s. 4d. which should have been £21 13s. 4d. A minute of 1838 said that there was a deficit in the accounts of 10s. 0¹/₂d. which does not seem at all surprising in the circumstances. Another treasurer recorded 12d. spent on 'the making up of William Lookup's coat' but put the 12d. in the shilling column, and in both these parishes the mistakes went unnoticed. Sometimes a payment is referred to in the minutes as well as in the accounts, in sterling in one and Scots money in the other, which when worked out may not tally; but, having said all that, most accounts were adequately kept.[56]

It was inevitable that the poor's box was a target for theft, quite apart from that perpetrated by soldiers during troubled times. In 1734 the minutes of one Session say; 'The Session box with the whole money therein was stolen 13th June, therefore no ballance arising from this date.' Another poor's box was kept in a school, presumably in the charge of the school-master-cum-Session Clerk, but it was stolen after a break-in. The Session Clerk was ordered to get a warrant from the Justices of the Peace to try to recover it and a reward of £24 Scots was offered; a week later it was found with £2 8s. of farthings in it and fortunately all the bonds and similar papers were still there too. The parish of Kilconquhar seems to have been singularly unfortunate: the box was stolen from the Session house one Sunday in 1706 and all the money taken; in 1710 it was stolen from the house of the elder who had charge of it and over £22 Scots was lost; and there must have been other problems too because when the Presbytery visited in 1716 they told the Session that if any of the poor's money should again be lost, they should answer for it which implies that they thought that there had been, at the very least, carelessness.[57]

Carelessness there certainly was in some cases. Elders on duty were always meant to hand church collections to the treasurer or whoever had been appointed to take charge of them but this cannot always have been done or there could not be such an entry as 'Lost by William Dickson dying Bankrupt, a collection in his hand, £5 5s. ' There were other risks in leaving collections lying out in that way and around the same date that Session lost £9 16s. 'by James Watson's Elopement of collection in his hand'. Another Session found it necessary to ask the elder in charge of the box, along with the beadle, to answer a charge that 'the contents of the box did not tally with the monie statements', at the same time as the smith had to mend the lock of the box which had evidently been tampered with, and in 1808 a Session summarily dismissed an elder who was also the catechist who embezzled from the poor's funds. Some time prior to 1746 Dornoch Kirk Session suffered a serious loss by the embezzlement of a large part of their funds by Alexander Sutherland, their Clerk and treasurer; and in March 1797 another Session met to go over the poor's funds but the kirk officer reported that the treasurer was away from home and so nothing could be done. The next meeting was fixed for 3 July that year, called by an intimation from the pulpit as before.

> Notwithstanding of this second public notice given at the request of some of the Elders of a meeting of Session . . . their Treasurer made his Elopement again, leaving the Parish this morning on some pretended business . . . This second Desertion, without sending an apology, so provoked the Session that they resolved to discontinue him Treasurer, and to get the Session box into its old quarters, viz. under the pulpit in the press made for it, the Moderator to have the keys: one of the Elders, viz. Don. MacPherson to have the outer key — or that of the press, that the box so deposited may, by the elder, be produced every Sunday, and by the Clerk, in

presence of two elders, the collection dropt in by the slit made for the purpose of conveying in the cash.[58]

Alarm bells had obviously rung about the possibility of the treasurer's misconduct and this Session wisely took immediate steps to secure their funds.

Even a minister could fall victim to the temptation of using the poor's money improperly. In 1730 a libel drawn up by a committee against the minister of Traquair, Mr Livingston, included the accusation that he owned the Session £330 Scots 'surreptitiously taken out of the box and not accounted for and 159 lib interest and a 160 lib bill.' He had managed to get into debt in a variety of ways, including the expenses of courting during eight years of widowerhood in his efforts to find a second wife. Archibald Allan in his *History of Channelkirk Church* described how in 1746 the minister there, Rev. Henry Home, was accused of what can only be called cooking the books for over forty years, which came to light as a result of local complaints but which in the dignified terms of the indictment appears as a charge of having laid aside all due sense of his character and the duties of his office in perpetrating crimes and offences intolerable in one of his calling. He had been treasurer of the collections and had managed his embezzlements by falsifying accounts, showing session meetings which never took place, elders approving proceedings which had never happened, mortcloths bought for large sums when they had not been bought at all and money given to travelling poor who had never existed, let alone passed through the parish. In this case, the problem was conveniently solved by his death in 1751 when he was over seventy-six. Thurso Kirk Session received a legacy for the poor and left it to their minister, Mr Patrick Nicholson, to invest but there must have been mismanagement of some sort, to put it no higher, as after his death the Session had to take action against his son to retrieve the legacy and also other money owed them by their former minister. That was a case of a son being left to sort out the problems of a father but things happened the other way in Fearn in 1746. The minister, Mr Hugh Duff, had a son who became a professor but also became financially embarrassed; to save his reputation his father assigned him part of the Fearn stipend, which was generous of him, but he also lent him 500 merks Scots which belonged to the poor's money. Knowing his son's financial position, this was clearly wrong and although the professor was meant to pay interest and repay the principal by a specified date he was unable to do so and so as to make up the loss to the poor, his old father had to allocate to the poor 50 bolls of victual from his already-reduced stipend.[59]

Although these cases of theft, embezzlement or misuse of funds have been mentioned, the point that really matters is not how frequently they happened but how seldom, especially bearing in mind the extreme poverty of those days, and so far as ministers were concerned, Kirk Session records show that when there was nothing with which to pay essential expenses, such as a pauper's needs or for a new Communion table, it was often the minister who would step into the breach. This is usually only recorded when he was ultimately repaid but in some cases what he advanced was never paid back in his lifetime and it was left to his pension-less widow to have to ask for it. One such woman told the Session that her late husband had paid 12s. for a boll of meal for 'an object in Sorn' and 3s. for the burial of a poor child who had died in their house, obviously taken into the manse as an act of true Christian charity, but neither sum had been repaid out of the box and so the Session agreed to give her what was due. His successor soon found that he was advancing money too, to pay church officials and for the expense of beggars' badges, on the basis that he would be repaid 'out of the first and readiest funds to be got in.'[60]

In spite of all these ways of raising money for the poor — collections, assess-ments, re-use of bad copper, fines, marriage, baptism and funeral expenses, seat-ing, legacies and donations, investment and lending of money, hire of equipment, charity balls and a whole variety of expedients — in time they became insuffi-cient. In the eighteenth century secessions from the Church of Scotland drained away its collections, the fines from which the kirk had benefited were stopped by the General Assembly in 1837 and income from other sources began to fall. The introduction of hearses meant that large numbers of people were no longer needed to carry coffins to burial and so people gave up hiring the mort-bell to summon all and sundry to attend and, as coffins borne in hearses did not require a mortcloth to give them dignity, so its hire fell off too. At the same time, the population throughout the country was beginning to rise, thanks to the introduction of the potato which could feed people for nine months of the year, to vaccination and to improving standards of health and cleanliness. The Napoleonic Wars resulted in an increase in the numbers of widows and orphans and disabled ex-servicemen, and famines still occurred. While there were still plenty of people and problems in rural parishes for their Kirk Sessions to cope with, the Industrial Revolution of the late eighteenth and nineteenth centuries began drawing country people into towns and cities, causing a great growth in numbers there and equally great problems for town Sessions. Caring for the poor under the old system was becoming a great strain for the kirk but one minister who firmly believed in it was Dr Thomas Chalmers. The population of Glasgow had increased vastly after 1810, the General Session there no longer knew what the circumstances of the poor were and church collections, even with burgh help, were inadequate for the needy but nevertheless Dr Chalmers was sure that he could still care for the poor of his parish well and cheaply and managed to persuade the town council in 1819 to erect and endow a new parish, St. John's, in which he could prove his point. The work done by him and his elders did prove his point but the church in general was not convinced that ways which had worked in the past could continue to do so and especially if he were not at the helm.[61]

The Disruption and consequent formation of the Free Church in 1843 has already been mentioned but what it did to church collections may be gathered from the fact that the takings in one parish for the ten months before it, came to £23 7s. but in the twelve months following they fell to £2 7s. It was against this background that the Poor Law Amendment Act was passed in 1845 under which a

Central Board of Supervision was formed to deal with all major matters relating to poor relief while the practical care of the poor was transferred to Parochial Boards in parishes where assessments were already customary. There these boards, with Kirk Session representatives, assumed responsibilities and in burghs, where the work had been shared between Kirk Sessions and Town Councils, the boards took over completely. In parishes where no assessments had been made before 1845, it was assumed that they were unnecessary and that church door collections were sufficient and so in such parishes as Ballingry and Balmerino, both in Fife, and Airlie in Angus, the heritors and Kirk Sessions continued to administer poor relief until 1894 when Parish Councils were instituted to handle poor relief in all parishes and formal Kirk Session representation ceased.[62] The new system of caring for the poor was to consider what each applicant required and to assess the parish according to what was considered necessary. Anyone refused relief had a right of appeal to the Sheriff and Board of Supervision but in the early years of the Act there were no other safeguards and the strict economy with which the law was at first administered deprived the poor of their last shreds of dignity. In 1851 one Session referred to the 'stringent and unyielding provisions' of the new law. Under the old system people knew that Sessions gave the poor all they could, were wide-ranging and imaginative in what they did and that it was done in a spirit of genuine interest combined with spiritual supervision. Many ministers regretted the loss of this truly pastoral work although there must have been some who were loath to lose the authority and power which it had given them.[63]

Church door collections had never been meant to be used for anything other than the poor and after the 1845 Act was passed they should have ceased in parishes where compulsory assessments replaced them. In practice, of course, part of any collections had always been needed for running expenses and so kirks had to decide what to do for the future; while they had no wish to give up collections, they still had to make the position clear. In 1845 one Session minuted that 'All collections made at the church doors since the Parochial Board was formed be reserved in the hands of the Kirk Session', something which was repeated in 1868 so there may have been some local puzzlement about the matter. Two years later another intimated 'that the collections which may be made within the walls of this church, or at the church doors, are not from this date for behoof of the poor of the parish because they are alimented by the assessment ordered by the Parochial Board' and so it became usual, and is still the case, that Sunday collections are made for congregational purposes, church schemes and the like, with Sessions deciding how to use any balance. Some Sessions realised that even with the new Act, there could still be poor people needing help and let it be known that although the usual church door collections would be given up, anyone wishing to give to the poor could still do so at the church door. At Keith, Banffshire, the Session ordered plates to be set at the church door for taking money for the poor not covered by the Act, which included the unemployed and the able-bodied poor, and Parochial Boards might give permission to Kirk Sessions to distribute to the poor, as happened at Daviot, Inverness-shire, in 1846.[64]

Kirk Session minutes make it clear that they were well represented on Parochial Boards, possibly by as many as five elders as well as the minister, and another way in which a Session might maintain a strong although indirect hand in care of the poor was where the parish schoolmaster was appointed to an official post with the Parochial Board. Whether or not he was also Session Clerk, a schoolmaster's close link with the kirk through education was bound to give them influence with him and it was undoubtedly for that reason that in 1845 one Session moved 'that the parish schoolmaster, John Maim, should be appointed Inspector of the Poor.'[65]

Kirk Session funds which had been intended for the poor or were regarded as belonging to them, were meant to be handed over to the new Parochial Boards, which made all possible efforts to lay hands on everything to which they thought that they, as the new guardians of the poor, had a right. Funds in their hands meant smaller assessments which was why, in September 1845, the Parochial Board of Baldernock deferred laying on an assessment until they knew the state of kirk funds and asked the minister to prepare a statement of the position. The Session Clerk was instructed by the Session to supply all the information in former minutes 'regarding how the right to the present parish funds was originally acquired and any other particulars he may find requisite', the idea being to discover whether any funds or property held by the Session belonged to that body or to the poor. Such careful checking involved a lot of work and in one particularly difficult case, the minister felt constrained to inform the elders that the Clerk 'had been at great pains going through old Kirk Session minutes' and they agreed to give him £12 12s. stg. as payment for his extra efforts. When Sessions considered that the poor had a right to any funds in their keeping, then they transferred them willingly: 'The Treasurer was appointed to pay to the Inspector of the Poor £12 stg. from Session funds' was minuted by a Session in 1849. In another parish a meeting 'for the purpose of making arrangements with the Kirk Session . . . relative to the funds in their hands and now belonging to the Parochial Board' was held at the inn in Jemimaville, Ross-shire, a somewhat unusual venue for a Kirk Session, and as a result, they handed over the money in their hands, including a legacy of £100 stg. but kept back another £100 given by a Mr Barclay from London so as to keep its management in their own hands in accordance with his wishes. Sessions were also required to provide abstracts of their accounts which was, in general, willingly done too as is shown by this minute: 'The Clerk was appointed to fill up the printed form and transmit the same to the Board of Supervision in terms of their requisition.' Difficulties undoubtedly arose because kirk funds had so often been indiscriminately known as the poor's money, poor's stock, Session's money or even the 'common guid of the Session', whether it was intended for the poor or not and Parochial Boards could hardly be blamed for trying to lay claim to it.[66]

In 1851 a property case arose in the parish of Linlithgow when the Parochial Board, having taken Counsel's opinion, claimed land which belonged to the Kirk Session and had always been known as the 'Session's lands', and which appeared to have been bought mainly, if not entirely, with the interest of money lent by the

Session to the town of Linlithgow. About the same time, the Kirk Sessions of both Falkirk and Arbroath were having problems with similar claims and both were consulted by the minister of Linlithgow. They made it clear that by the new law the funds for the poor of the parish came under the charge of the Parochial Board but if money or property had been expressly bequeathed to a Session rather than to the 'heritors and Kirk Session' then the Session was not bound to hand them over. The Kirk Session was a different body from the 'heritors and Kirk Session', a distinction which was recognised in the Poor Law and, said the Kirk Session of Falkirk, 'as a Parochial Board came in place of the heritors and Kirk Session, they could only claim funds under their administration. They cannot claim funds bequeathed to the Kirk Session which is a distinct and independent body.' The Linlithgow Kirk Session readily allowed the agent for the Parochial Board to have access to their records although requiring them to be read in the presence of the Session Clerk, only to have the Board issue a summons against them to have it found that lands called Magdalens, held by the Session for their own behoof and that of the poor, should be handed over to the Board. The Session had thus far relied on the advice that had been obtained elsewhere because they felt that 'it would be unwarrantable to subject the funds entrusted to them to the expense that would be incurred by taking the opinion of any other counsel' but at this point they decided that they must appoint an Edinburgh lawyer and obtain Counsel's opinion themselves. The result of this was 'protracted litigation' won initially by the Parochial Board in the Outer House but appealed by the Kirk Session who ultimately won their case.[67] In April 1853, while this action was still pending in the Court of Session, there was a proposal by a number of Parochial Boards near Linlithgow to build a Poor House in the area. Any parish with a population of over 5,000 was now authorised to build such premises for those who were aged, unable to care for themselves and with no one to do so for them, for those incapable of managing their own affairs, and also for vagrants. The Parochial Boards near Linlithgow appointed delegates to form a Union Board to carry out their idea and after visiting a number of sites, including the Linlithgow Kirk Session land which was the one they particularly favoured, they let it be known that they would recommend it provided that the Session would grant them a feu of the land required and that the feu duty would be moderate. The Session replied that they would certainly make the land available but as it would then be held by the Union Board as feuars, for the benefit of other parishes than theirs, it would not be consistent with their duty to accept anything less than the full feuable value, which shows the responsible and exact attitude taken by this Session to property entrusted to it for specific purposes.[68]

Another case to do with property occurred in St. Monance in 1857. When a pauper named Margaret Dowie died there that year, the room which she had occupied for some thirteen years fell vacant. It was in a building known as the Session's house which belonged to the Session and was used by them as a local poor house. Until then, occupancy of the room had been a matter decided by the Session alone but at this point, three elders who were members of the new

Parochial Board, claimed their right to allocate the room. The minister had different views, however; he claimed that the room and the whole building was the Session's and theirs alone, adding that he would take such steps as were required in law to secure it to the Session and warned the three elders that if further proceedings required it, a legal protest would in due time be served on them, holding them collectively and individually liable for any loss of property that might result to the Session from their vote on the matter. In this case it appears that it was the minister rather than the Kirk Session who was the moving force in this strong opposition to Parochial Board encroachment but he would certainly have had the consent of the rest of his Session.[69] Even lesser Kirk Session property than money or land might be claimed by Parochial Boards: in 1857 one asked for the mortcloths and spokes (burial litter) for the use of the Board, 'seeing that the churchyard is now closed up and these articles can be of no use to the Kirk Session but will be of great use to the Parochial Board for interment of paupers.' This somewhat high-handed appeal cut no ice with the Session who decided to keep what belonged to them but agreed to allow free use of these items for the burial of paupers connected with their own parish.[70]

Thanks to Kirk Sessions' insistence on retaining certain mortifications and property left specifically to them for behoof of the poor, many of these remained under Sessional administration and such Sessions were able to use these monies for the care of those poor who were ineligible for, or unwilling to accept, Parochial Board relief; and there were many who, before the institution of modern pension, health and unemployment schemes, were almost totally dependent on what voluntary assistance the kirk could provide.[71] Not only did the kirk work very hard to raise funds when they were largely responsible for the poor, they held on to all they could, as long as they could, in order to serve the poor.

6

A School in every Parish

Long before the Reformation, it was the church which pioneered education, beginning with early Celtic missionaries and on to the chapels and monasteries, schools and colleges of Roman Catholic days but only a limited number of people could ever benefit from such teaching. Even when an Act of Parliament of 1496 decreed that parents should send their sons to grammar schools at eight or nine years old and keep them there until they had learnt 'perfect Latin' and then send them for three further years to schools of art and law, it was clear that such an Act was not meant for the masses.[1]

Prior to the Reformation, a knowledge of music was regarded as an essential part of the education of any man entering the service of the church so that he could lead and participate in services and after the Reformation as well, one of the earliest forms of direct education continued to be basically musical, with Parliament in 1579 ordering that 'sang-schools' should be established in burghs, as indeed they were. In that of Old Aberdeen instruction in the psalms was a particular feature although some elementary education was included too. From the records of Elgin, it appears that both Town Council and Kirk Session were involved in control of these schools which existed in many quite small towns and were sometimes later transformed into grammar or parish schools. In general, however, rural parish schools were a different matter and the efforts of the kirk to obtain education nationwide are most creditable, especially as there were so many difficulties in their way.[2]

Although John Knox is mainly remembered as a religious reformer, he was a social one too and believed that education would be a good influence on young people, would ensure that everyone could read the Word of God themselves and was the best way of achieving what he called a 'Godly Commonwealth' which would reflect the Kingdom of Heaven on earth, and so universal education was his aim. At the time of the Reformation he and five other men, all of them with the Christian name John, put forward in the First Book of Discipline sound and far-reaching proposals which have lasted, in their main points, until the present day.

They wanted to see a school provided in every parish and a compulsory system of elementary education introduced, based on a child's aptitude and independent of social class which, although it could not be free, would nevertheless be subsidised for those who could not afford it. When children were old enough to leave school, it was proposed they should learn either a craft or a trade while the brighter ones continued their studies and the very best went to university. To Knox education was the same as religion and morality and his educational scheme laid great stress on these subjects. He felt therefore that it was essential that control of education should be in church hands, although he expected the heritors to pay for it, and so within five years of the Reformation, the Reformers petitioned Queen Mary to allow the kirk to have superintendence of schools in order that they could ensure that teachers were able and sound in doctrine. In fact, the kirk was already exercising this power for which it was asking but it must have been glad neverthe-less when in 1567 the first Parliament after her abdication provided that teachers, whether public or private, should be approved by superintendents of the kirk.[3]

Following upon the suggestions of the First Book of Discipline, one Kirk Session ordered as early as 1595 that all the young of the town should go to school and 'sic as are puir sall be furnished upon the common expenses . . . and the manner of their help sall be they sall haif thrie hours granted to them everie day throu the toun to seek their meit', which was time off to go begging for their subsistence. But such early efforts to provide education and make it compulsory were exceptional and in spite of the proposals of the First Book of Discipline and Parliament's support, getting education off the ground was a slow business. Much of the church's property and funds had passed into secular hands at the Reforma-tion so that the wherewithal for many things was lacking and there were so many years of turmoil thereafter that it took over a hundred years for things to settle down sufficiently for Knox's educational ideas to come into practice. Indeed, the provision for kirk superintendence of schools, originally enacted by Parliament in 1567, had to be repeated in 1662. It was not until 1696, after the Revolution and the final establishment of Presbyterian church government, that the Scottish Parlia-ment passed the Act for Settling of Schools which was the real basis of Scottish education but between the days of John Knox and 1696, various other Acts were passed which also laid foundations, even if these were not built upon for a considerable time. A look at pre–1696 legislation concerning education shows therefore a patchy picture but it must always be remembered that passing Acts of Parliament in Scotland was quite a different matter from enforcing them and it must also be remembered that for many years, Bible reading and family worship were equated with education.[4]

In 1616 the Privy Council co-operated with the wishes of the kirk and ordered that a school should be established in every parish 'where convenient means may be had', a phrase which gave a useful loophole to any parish where enthusiasm was lacking on the part of the heritors because, in accordance with Knox's ideas, it was they who were to pay. This Act was ratified by the Privy Council in 1633 but with a provision that the bishop — in practice, that meant the church — might impose a tax for a school on every plough of land, subject to the consent of the heritors and parishioners and that too was a loophole. 1641 saw the kirk making an overture to Parliament asking yet again that every parish should have a school where reading, writing and the basics of religion might be taught; that grammar schools should be established in burghs and 'other considerable places'; that ministers and elders should report on these schools to Presbyteries which in turn would report to Synods and so to the General Assembly; and Parliament was urged to provide some means of education for the poor and that committees should be formed to report to the next General Assembly about the time and manner of visiting schools and the best way of teaching grammar. The overture also asked for something which was more achievable: that there should be a reader in every parish, because an early form of education was that provided by readers and exhorters, both of whom read the Scriptures aloud in church before the service proper began and in this way an illiterate population could at least hear the Word of God even if they themselves could not read. In this context one may mention the painted Scripture texts and especially the words of the Lord's Prayer and the Ten Commandments which began to be painted on church walls, close to pulpits in the late sixteenth or early seventeenth centuries. A few late examples may still be found in some churches; their original purpose was educational although they were also decorative. It would be interesting to know whether illustrations of the story of Adam and Eve and of Abraham and Isaac, as well as emblems of mortality and of immortality, carved on gravestones were done at the behest of Kirk Sessions or of the ministers of parishes as another form of visual aid.[5] In spite of these efforts, another Act of Parliament in 1646 makes it plain that schools were still not being established at that date in landward areas as had been hoped: 'The kirk desires that the Act of 1633' (the one that provided for a tax for schools) 'be extended for the foundation of schools in every congregation: the want of them being the main obstruction of piety and virtue in the kingdom.' This was followed almost immediately by a differently worded Act by which it was no longer a matter just of what the kirk wanted but a decree that a school should be founded in every parish which did not already have one, with the advice of the Presbytery, that the heritors should provide a schoolhouse and agree a salary, paying for these in proportion to their valued rents. If they failed to agree about this, then Presbyteries were entitled to nominate twelve men to settle matters and any appeals against unequal imposition of the salary were to be brought before the Privy Council or the Session within a year and a day.[6]

Heritors were seldom enthusiastic about education for all. Many began their own children's education within the family circle, through a secretary, a chaplain or a factor, and a major reason for delay in provision of school buildings for the parish children was a genuine belief that universal education was neither a good idea nor necessary and there was even the occasional minister who agreed with this. A seventeenth century one said that it was 'not needful for the common people to learn to read . . . it was never good for the land since there were so many scholars in it,' but as that was contrary to official kirk policy he soon found himself up before the Presbytery for what he had said. Rev. Nathaniel Paterson, minister of Galashiels, Selkirkshire, in the early nineteenth century, has been castigated for saying that 'there can be no training of the volatile minds of youth equal to that which is maintained at the factories', but this is not the complete quotation. What he said was that parents were in the habit of having their children alternate with each other in work and school and, as they looked perfectly healthy, he felt that it was far better for them to do that and bring in about 3*s*. a week and have some education than be a total financial burden on their parents. He was only taking a practical view of things.[7]

Whether or not there was progress in educational provision in the seventeenth century depended very much on individual Kirk Sessions and Presbyteries and, where they were keen, a considerable amount could be done, even if it was just encouraging learning at home. In the Berwickshire parish of Channelkirk, for instance, it is clear that by the 1650s the local kirk was promoting the idea of education even although there does not appear to have been a school, because the minutes for April 1653 show that the elders 'had visited families, and that in every family, there was prayer as they were informed, but that there was no reading in the most part of families because none in the family could read. Recommended to the elders they would be careful to stir up such masters' (employers) 'that could not read themselves to provide a servant against the next term' (when new staff were engaged) 'that might read the Scripture to the family and the Lesser Catechism.' This was in keeping with an Act of the General Assembly passed in 1649 which stated that every minister with the help of his elders, should 'take course' that in every house where there was anyone able to read, there should be at least one copy of the Shorter and Larger Catechisms, the Confession of Faith and the Directory of Family Worship, although to think that this could be fully carried out was too much to expect. In spite of the urgings of Channelkirk's Kirk Session that parishioners should engage people able to read, when a man and his mother living in the adjoining parish of Lauder did just that some thirty years later, their Session accused them of having 'reset a disorderly person for teaching of children' although they knew nothing to the man's discredit. To be fair to that Session this was after certificates of character began to be required of incomers to a parish, of which more later, and this family's teacher was required to produce such a certificate or to leave the parish. Going back to Channelkirk, the minister there must have been very diligent as by the end of 1653 he was able to report that he had visited every family in the parish and 'set the masters of families upon their duty of praying and reading of the Scriptures, saying of psalms, and catechising their children and servants according to the laudable acts of the general assembly.' Although the writing in the minutes of Channelkirk Kirk Session is difficult to read, it appears that in 1661 this Session had managed to provide a school for the parish although it is not now known where it was, and were thinking about a school-house too, hoping all the while that they would be repaid by the heritors for what they had spent.[8]

Educational initiative was shown by some other Kirk Sessions even earlier than this. A note in the parish registers of Dunino, Fife, in 1643 stated that a declaration by the Presbytery of St. Andrews, based on instructions from the Synod of Fife in 1641 and later confirmed by the General Assembly, was published in every parish within their bounds, stating that 'the woful ignorance, rudeness, stubbornness, incapacity seen among the common people' proceeded from lack of schools in landward areas and the habit of not putting children to school even where these existed and it urged the establishment of schools in any places where they were lacking 'and that where there is one already, every one that hath children put them to school, if past seven years old . . . if the parents be able, then let them be obliged both to send their bairns when the session gives order, and not to remove them till the session be acquainted.' The position of parents who were poor was also covered in this declaration which, in Dunino at least, was followed up by action as the heritors, minister and Session met in June that year and ordered that a school should start the following Monday. This was not such a sudden decision as it sounds as by then they had already engaged a schoolmaster. A later instance of getting on with the job happened in 1695 when the Kirk Session of Abernethy, Perthshire, considered the 'necessity of building a school before winter' and saw to it themselves. It was admittedly not very big, only eighteen feet long, but the minutes give the Session's very exact specifications and provide a very good idea of such a building at that date.[9]

The Act for Settling of Schools, passed in 1696, was gradually able to achieve results because it included a much stronger element of compulsion, providing that a school must be established and a master appointed in every parish, with the advice of the heritors and minister, with the heritors providing a 'commodious' schoolhouse and a salary of not less than 100 merks ($£5$ $11s.$ $1^1/_3d.$ stg.) and not over 200 merks ($£11$ $2s.$ $2^2/_3d.$ stg.). This heritors regarded as a heavy load but half of it was passed on to their tenants. The house and salary decreed in 1696 were exactly the same as had been ordered in 1646, fifty years before, and in this latest Act provision was once again made for redress should any heritors be neglectful or unable to agree on what each should pay, although this time it had to be by application of a Presbytery to five Commissioners of Supply of the relevant county. This Act was passed at a time when church politics were settling down and there was a fresh impetus for education but it also came during the Seven Years' Famine when parishes had sufficient other difficulties with which to contend without tackling any more. This largely explains why, in spite of the compulsory nature of the Act, the General Assembly still found it necessary, almost ten years later, to advise ministers to take care to see that schools were provided in their parishes in accordance with the 1696 Act.[10]

Apart from the rather vague description of a 'commodious' schoolhouse, the type of school accommodation to be supplied was not specified in the various Acts of Parliament already mentioned and so a school, in the sense of education, might be provided but not necessarily in a regular school building. Even when proper schoolhouses were erected, 'commodious' usually meant just two rooms, including the kitchen, and many teachers therefore did their work in any available building. This might be a barn, byre or stable but could also be the church, which had the added advantage of a ready-made playground around it. In 1624, for instance, the schoolmaster at Fordyce was given permission to hold the school in the kirk; the school at Whitekirk was kept in the church well after the 1660s, with considerable damage done by the children to the seating. At Auchterderran, the school was also taught in the church until 1688 when it was not the heritors who provided a building but the minister who gave stones and lime, the Kirk Session who gave some money which came from forfeited pledges and the schoolmaster who was allowed to cut what wood was needed for building and roofing the house. The aisle of the Laigh Kirk at Kilmarnock was used for teaching children until at least 1695; the parish school at Hawick appears to have been held in the church until 1718; and at Blackford, Perthshire, the school was in the upper floor of the church until the day in 1738 when, in the absence of the minister, the boys began to throw hot peats about with the result that fire broke out and the church was burnt. The east end of the church at Mauchline was the school until 1789 and it too was suffering damage as a result: in 1782 the Kirk Session had to warn people by tuck of drum that in future anyone found guilty of breaking the kirk windows would be prosecuted for three times the amount of damage done and the schoolmaster was authorised to prosecute children or parents as he thought proper. As late as the 1790s children in the parish of Kilchoman on the island of Islay were taught in the church, about forty of them, although by then there were also several other schools in the parish.[11] So closely was the church as a building associated with education that even when it and the school were separate, they were often still very close together, both within the kirkyard. In 1821 the school at Ashkirk was still being held in an old aisle adjoining the church and the old school of Moneydie, Perthshire, still adjoins the church. In other cases they might be attached to the kirkyard wall, as at Dirleton, at Hobkirk, Roxburghshire, and at Gladsmuir, East Lothian, where the school was described in the mid-nineteenth century as being 'close by the church and manse and very much shut up by the schoolmaster's garden.' In the old graveyard at Marnoch, Banffshire, there is a mort-house where coffined bodies lay safely out of the way of body-snatchers while they awaited burial; at some point this building was also used as a school, possibly after an addition was made to it in 1877 rather than in the days when coffins lay below. Although there may now be no record of buildings in or near churchyards being schools, some still exist which look suspiciously like them. One adjoining the churchyard wall at Moulin, Perthshire, is a case in point. Not surprisingly, the manse too was sometimes pressed into service as a school; this happened at Forbes and Kearn, Aberdeenshire, into the 1790s and the parish school 'at the manse' at Farr, Sutherland, about the same date, was presumably held *in* the manse.[12]

An alternative to using a church or building a school was to rent accommodation. In 1715 the Town Council and Kirk Session of Hawick joined together to pay the 'mail' or rent of the English school there while in Falkirk it appears that into the 1760s and later, buildings were leased from year to year. This had the advantage that if they were found inadequate, then a change could be made to other rented property, although it was not always easy to find somewhere of a suitable size which was why in 1761 the heritors turned their eyes towards the church itself and suggested that the west end of it might be turned into a school, something about which the Session showed no preference one way or the other. It is not known what was the outcome of the proposal, although it was not until 1775 that it was decided to put up a proper building.[13]

Delays in building schools were also due to something mentioned in earlier chapters, the reluctance of ministers and Kirk Sessions to offend heritors because of their dependence upon them, whether as providers of ministers' stipends or as the landlords of elders. This must have been especially so when there was a perfectly good alternative building available, whether secular or ecclesiastical, which could be used as a school. In any event, should a Presbytery apply to the Commissioners of Supply for redress, that body was composed of the kind of people who were likely to be heritors or their friends and it appears that, for a long time, it was easier for a Kirk Session to get hold of the tenants' half share of the school money, often in kind — building materials, thatching, carting work and so on — than it was to obtain anything from the heritors. There were, however, some ministers brave enough, and presumably backed by their Sessions, who took on recalcitrant heritors. In 1721 Thomas Boston snr., minister of Ettrick, reported to the Presbytery that no heritors had attended a meeting he had called to see about providing a school and he was advised to give them a second chance to stent themselves for this purpose and if that did not succeed, to apply to the Commissioners of Supply. Mr John Sutherland, minister of Golspie, Sutherland, had to resort to the legal procedure of a 'horning' in 1731 to make the heritors pay for the schoolmaster's salary, and four years later the parishioners of Dalgain, Riccarton, Kirkoswald, Craigie, New Cumnock, Dailly, Bar, Muirkirk, Auchinleck, Symington, Stair and Monckton were all induced, probably by their ministers, to take legal action against their heritors for non-provision of schools and masters' salaries. The hand of the Presbytery was possibly behind this concerted move as all of these parishes belong to the Presbytery of Ayr. In 1766 the Kirk Session of Tweedsmuir went further and took a case for establishing a school in the parish to the Lords, which involved holding a collection to pay for the action; and in 1773 Mr Alexander Pope, minister of Reay, sued the heritors for a school in the Court of Session and won. It says much for the kirk's desire for education for youngsters that they took such steps.[14]

Even after the passing of the 1696 Act with its compulsive measures, kirk records show that Kirk Sessions often paid for building schools themselves without help from heritors or even tenants, although they may have hoped for it. The accounts of Kilninian and Kilmore Kirk Session, Argyllshire, in 1774 show the costs of 'attempting to build a schoolhouse at the desire of the minister and several of the elders', not apparently at the desire of the heritors, nor with their authority. Not surprisingly therefore, it was found impossible to get any support from them and the minister who had advanced money for the project four years previously, had to be repaid out of kirk funds. Another instance appears in the records of the parish of St. Vigeans in 1732 where the Session paid

> For trees and dales furnished to the school house, £71 6s. 0d. Sc.
> For leading [bringing] stones to the school house, £8 10s. 0d. Sc.
> Given to the carrier for carrying up the money and bringing the Discharge [receipt] 4s. Sc.

Another way in which a Session might help towards provision of a school was to lend money towards its erection or maintenance, like the £4 4s. Scots 'lent for the schoolhouse' which was done in the usual hope of repayment from the heritors or from a parish stent. One minute refers to 'friendly borrowing for building and completing of the school house.'[15] When heritors did decide to provide a school most of the groundwork was usually left to the Kirk Session. In the autumn of 1758 rumours that a school was going to be built were flying round an Argyllshire parish and there was obvious excitement in the Session minute which said: 'Its talked in Session that there will be a school settled here soon' but it was not until the following April that the minister told the Session that he had been instructed by a heritor to call a meeting of the Session to stent the parish for putting up a schoolhouse on a particular farm. From then on the Session got matters moving. Four days later, they called for tradesmen to estimate the cost of the building and found that it could not be provided for less than £2 15s. stg. which they accepted. They then visited the farm and 'condescended upon' a suitable site and in November ordered their officer to tell people at the church door to send in their money for the building. From this it appears that it could be through the church that the law requiring tenants to pay half the costs was implemented, but as has already been said, it could be easier to get what was owed from them than from anyone else. In such circumstances, the money raised went to the builders via the Session, not via the heritors, and where the stent was insufficient a Session might well make up the amount needed, even although that was not their responsibility. One Session lent a workman 17s. stg. 'till he obtains payment of what he expended on the schoolhouse' which was a considerate action as, although they obviously knew that he would be paid in the end, they still did not wish him to suffer because of any delay in payment.[16]

Schools in outlying areas could be of a very low standard but then, so was the housing of the common people. In his *History of Inverness* Dr Cameron Lees describes an early school of a type common at one time in that county, which had walls and roof of turf, a fire in the centre of the room without any chimney and only one desk where just three of the twenty pupils could write at a time. Abernethy's little eighteen feet long school was probably very similar. It may be assumed that schools in burghs and in populous parishes were better but some doubt creeps in when one reads that Cathcart Kirk Session glazed the windows of the school in 1734 at a cost of £5 — did that mean reglazing or that there had been unglazed openings previously? Certainly the following extract from the minutes of Scone

Kirk Session gives the impression that although it was very close to the burgh of Perth, what had been provided by way of a school must have been very inadequate: '23rd October 1720. The Session orders a chimney and a glass window to be put into the School in regard of the Cold the Children endure in the winter time.' Glass windows were vulnerable things and so items like 'For the school windows £1 4s. Sc.' or 'For mending the school windows 18s. stg.' appear in accounts although they were not an expense which should have fallen on the kirk because maintenance of school buildings also fell on heritors. Some of them did meet with Kirk Sessions to see what needed to be done but the outcome of one such meeting in 1764 is revealing: it was decided that it was 'absolutely necessary to keep the schoolhouse roof in repair and conform to the custom in other places, that the parishioners should provide straw and simmonds' (ropes of straw, heather or rushes, used with stones to hold down thatch) 'annually for that purpose and the parish be divided into quarters to furnish the same, one year after another.' Although this was a meeting of heritors and Session, the 'custom in other places' amounted to the tenants doing their bit, with no mention of the heritors doing anything about it and the tenants would have viewed the burden of maintaining schools with as little enthusiasm as the heritors did. In this case the heritors had at least come to the meeting but a not uncommon attitude appeared when those of the parish of Golspie were summoned in 1743 by the Presbytery to meet them at the school to see what repairs were needed and not one of them turned up. This availed them nothing as the Presbytery simply used their legal rights to have the work done, under the supervision of the minister, the same one who in 1731 had got a horning to make the heritors pay the master's salary. In 1727 a highland parish school was in such a state that rain came in the roof, flowed about it and over-ran the whole building, which was also bitterly cold, a state of affairs which caused the Session to petition the Justices of the Peace to order the heritors to put things right.[17]

Sessions often got on with repairs themselves or took their own steps to have them done; repair of thatch was one thing that was constantly required. It has a limited life and was often allowed to become so rotten that not only did rain come in but it swarmed with rats. Some Sessions ordered children to bring straw for thatching but it was too scarce for them to be able to bring enough and it was far better to engage a thatcher to get the straw and do the work. This whole problem and its solution is summed up in a minute which says: 'The Kirk Session considering the bad state of the schoolmaster's house and that the children cannot learn in it, it rains so much, appoints Archibald Tweedie to buy straw and thatch it, £5 Sc.' In the same way another session paid £1 2s. 8d. stg. in 1788 'for repairs of the schoolhouse, thatching it with straw and clay, materials, workmanship and leading the materials included' and two years later paid Alexander Corbett 3s. 4d. stg. 'for Divots [turfs] cut at Inver to thatch the schoolhouse.' In 1742 a Session employed a man to thatch the schoolhouse which cost £4 16s. Scots but he either made a poor job of it or else the weather damaged it because it had to be rethatched the following year and this time ropes were included to hold the thatch down, so that the cost came to £10 2s. Scots, more than double the original charge. Yet another's Session's accounts show money spent on 'thack' (thatch) to the school house and chamber', for 'thacking and service' and for 'rigging Divots to the schoolhouse and chamber', and all these costs were somehow met by the church although it could mean having to hold an extraordinary collection for them.[18] The various Acts to do with provision of schools did not mention provision of equipment and so such entries as the following appear in Session records: 'To a table to the school £1 Sc.' or £12 Scots spent on 'seats in the form of pews' while the Kirk Session of Ordiquhill, Banffshire, went even further in 1713 in efforts to 'encourage' their schoolmaster and 'did dedicat an bed and table, at 13 merks of price, for his and his successor's use.'[19]

The most important requirement for any school was to have a teacher rather than special buildings or equipment. In the days of kirk involvement, it was always men who were in charge of parish schools or legal schools, as they were originally called, but as exceptions prove rules, it must be said that at Inverkeithing, Fife, in the early eighteenth century the schoolmaster's widow was allowed to carry on his school after he had been murdered. One of the many early problems of staffing schools was that after the Reformation, when there was a great shortage of qualified men for the ministry, there was an equal shortage of men suitable to be schoolmasters. Inevitably it was easier to find teachers for burgh schools than for rural ones but even so, in some towns, such as Dunbar, Haddington, Inverkeithing and others also, it was the reader who for a while had to act as teacher in return for the school fees. From about 1560–1600 it was the minister in some country areas who had to double up as schoolmaster and some made a remarkable job of it too: William Gray, 'a guid learned kynd of man', kept a school or academy in Logie-Montrose with a curriculum which would be no disgrace nowadays: catechism, prayers, Scripture, Latin grammar and French language, something of Horace, Virgil, Cicero and even of Erasmus and, as if that were not enough, there was archery, fencing, swimming, wrestling, running, jumping and golf too. Presumably he taught the 3 Rs as well. It is not clear whether ministers who undertook this dual role did it for the love of it or for the money but one who was certainly paid was Mr James Carmichael, minister of Haddington from 1570–84. In 1570 he was appointed schoolmaster as well at £40 per annum but gave this up in 1576 when the Town Council decided 'that in no time coming should the minister of the kirk be admitted schoolmaster of the burgh', because it appeared that such a role reduced the dignity and position of the ministerial office. However, when he was succeeded in 1585 it was by the burgh school master who held the offices of minister and teacher until his translation to Aberlady in 1587 where he also acted as schoolmaster until 1591. As late as the end of the eighteenth century the only education available in the Aberdeenshire parish of Forbes and Kearn was by the minister either running a school himself or employing a youth to teach his own children and allowing others to 'partake of the benefit'.[20]

It was possible to find non-clerical teachers but by no means easy to start with. There was little accommodation in universities, there were no colleges to train them and no means of advertising vacant posts. All that could be done was to ask around to find someone as capable as possible and willing to accept the job. That being so, it is surprising just how quickly a teacher could sometimes be found. A Selkirkshire parish, where a school had already been established, found itself in 1653 without a master and the Session 'fervently recommended' the minister to go and find one. This request was made on 22 May and just a fortnight later, on 5 June, a man named Thomas Whyt was engaged to take over the school. Such good fortune was not usual and in 1701 the Synod of Aberdeen felt it necessary to urge Presbyteries to try to find some suitable men and only a little while later the Presbytery of Tain went so far as to write to the Synods of Argyll and of Moray to find out if they knew of any adequate young men. In this latter case, on hearing that there were two in Elgin, they recommended their ministers 'to lay forth themselves' in encouraging them to come to the Tain area. In the parish of Kiltearn the Session decided, after looking locally for a teacher and asking the help of the schoolmaster of Inverness, both without success, to have 'a placard set up . . . in order to invite young men to compeat for the same' but this brought no results either. Getting a master could, of course, be achieved by the expedient of poaching. This happened at Clackmannan in 1685: the Session minutes show that in March that year 'the minister having called Mr. Walter Anderson, the schoolmaster at Dollar to officiate in the foresaid office as schoolmaster and precentor at the church of Clackmannan, the said Mr. Walter was admitted.' In 1711 while the Town Council of Tain was seeking a teacher, the neighbouring parish of Fearn secured the services of Mr Alexander Falconer, only to find that when several months had passed and Tain still had no teacher, the Town Council turned envious eyes towards this man, with no thought about coveting a neighbour's manservant nor the ethics of a burgh poaching from a rural school. The Council decided to call him but first of all to get the approval of the Presbytery, which they received, the Presbytery stating that they were aware of 'a due sense of the care the Magistrates and Town Council evidenced in this matter' but as they appear never to have looked beyond Fearn, this may have been sarcasm. Although it was the magistrates and Council who usually chose schoolmasters in towns, normally this was done with the approval of the minister, and the appointment made was almost certainly inserted in the Kirk Session minutes to show that the Session approved what had been decided even if not themselves involved in it. In the case of Mr Falconer, he did not go to Tain which saved the local Kirk Session from taking any part in the proceedings and also saved the Kirk Session of Fearn having to find a replacement for him.[21]

As time went on and more potential teachers became available, it was Presbyteries which had the task of checking their qualifications, which arose from the Act of Parliament of 1662, already mentioned, as providing for kirk superintendence of schools. This was something which continued until 1861 when the responsibility was transferred to universities. A Kirk Session minute of 1821 shows that when Adam Gibson, described as a student at the local Academy, was chosen to be schoolmaster of a highland country parish, his engagement was provisional until his literary qualifications, which included Latin and Greek, could be examined by the Presbytery. Such subjects may seem quite unnecessary for elementary schools but although there was provision for secondary education in burghs, there was nothing of the kind in rural areas and many schoolmasters therefore had to prepare boys to go straight from the parochial school to university. Once appointed, schoolmasters' tenure was normally fairly secure unless there was some fault but the minutes of a Glasgow Kirk Session in the nineteenth century show that there the teacher of the parish school was elected yearly and could be removed at the end of any year. This man was also expected to teach a Sunday Evening School, four elders were appointed as a committee to superintend the affairs of the school and more surprisingly, as minimum and maximum teachers' salaries were laid down by law, this important matter was left entirely to the discretion of the Kirk Session. In rural areas it was the heritors and ministers who were meant to choose parish schoolmasters but as tenants contributed so much to parish education, it is nice to know that sometimes at least they were involved in decision-making, with the heritors and 'fewars' of Tillycoultry, Clackmannanshire, meeting in the kirk in 1745 to elect a teacher for the parish. In 1720 a meeting of the landowners of St. Boswells and the minister together considered the need for a schoolmaster 'and being fully satisfied with the Dexterity and skill of Zaccheus Laurie for teaching of children to Read and write And also to instruct them in Arithmetic, they did and hereby do unanimously make choice of him the said Zaccheus Laurie to be schoolmaster of the said toun and parish.' As there is no mention of any Presbytery examination of Zaccheus, it seems that he must already have been regarded as a competent teacher. Neither the Tillycoultry nor St. Boswells meetings involved the Kirk Session, yet they are both minuted in Session records and in 1829 at a meeting of heritors to fix a schoolmaster's salary in another parish, those present specifically asked that a minute should be inserted in the Session record book. Where the heritors did not keep minutes of their meetings, this was one way of recording decisions taken but it also shows how closely they linked the school to the Session and, in fact, in very many instances Sessions shared the responsibility for making appointments or even made them entirely themselves and so it is that minutes such as the following appear: 'The Session orders a call to be drawn up for Mr. John Row to be Schoolmaster in Kinross' or 'Patrick Mclaus, schoolmaster, being [sic] to demit at Martinmas next, the Session agreed to provide another schoolmaster and Session Clerk with their first conveniency.' Heritors who lived elsewhere were only too glad to delegate this task to men on the spot who were willing to do it and in close touch with parish affairs but they were still entitled to receive a report from the Session about any arrangements made so as to give their 'consent and concurrence' although some did not insist on such reports.[22]

All this made extra work for Sessions but it suited them very well as it gave them direct involvement with the parish school and increased their control beyond the merely supervisory role which Acts of Parliament had allowed them. To a large extent unwillingness and indifference on the part of heritors had a positive side for Kirk Sessions by preventing interference. Furthermore they had a very particular interest in who was appointed parish schoolmaster as the 1696 Act of Parliament had made it clear that the salary he received was additional to what he might be paid as Session Clerk or reader, because these were offices which he almost always undertook as well, often becoming precentor and sometimes treasurer too. Even when a man was suitably qualified academically, so important were these other abilities that a Session might ask him to come on trial to see whether his reading and his precenting were good enough. In 1697 a young man named James Murray who was 'fit and willing' to be schoolmaster and precentor of Ashkirk was nevertheless invited to come to 'make tryall of precenting a day or two before the parioch.' This he did, but the Session 'considered his gift of precenting to be but small' and asked him 'to continue a day or two till there be a meeting of heritors.' About a fortnight later, however, they had their minds made up for them when he wrote asking to be excused from accepting the post because the parish was not satisfied with his precenting. The Session then decided to ask a man who was teaching privately nearby to come temporarily to the parish school until a new teacher could be found and in no time he had 'a full school and the children beginning to profite remarkably under him more than hath been seen in the parish for several years begone.' So good was he that it was decided to engage him permanently and also to engage permanently the temporary precentor because the new schoolmaster could not precent; it was left to the schoolmaster to arrange what part of his salary, which included precenting, he would give to the precentor. When all was said and done, the Session might just as well have engaged James Murray at the outset but it is obvious that it was only the new master's exceptional teaching qualities that made splitting of the post acceptable. This is a case which shows how ability for church duties could influence the engagement of a parish schoolmaster.[23]

Many schoolmasters were aiming for the ministry and so the dual role of schoolmaster and Session Clerk, whether also precentor or not, and the close association with the minister that it involved, was an excellent training. In time a considerable number of those teaching were divinity students or had already reached the stage of being licensed to preach and were simply awaiting a charge; in 1677 only one teacher in the Presbytery of Turriff was not a licenciate of the church and, of course, there were always some 'stickit ministers' who, though educated, had failed to make the grade.[24]

The schoolmaster's legal salary, as it was termed, was low but it was a basic one on top of which came school fees, income from any other offices held, and in rural areas he was also meant to have a garden of at least a quarter acre or else money in lieu. Although there were legal limits for top and bottom salaries, there was considerable variation around the country with the parish schoolmaster of Duffus, Morayshire, receiving as late as the 1790s, nothing other than seven bolls of bear called the Reader's Bear. The following figures, all from Volume III of the

Old Statistical Account of the 1790s, show the wide range of salaries possible across the country:

Parish	School salary	Session Clerk's fee	Extras
Dingwall	£16	£3 10s. 0d.	
Petty	12 bolls oatmeal	– 13s. 4d.	6d. for each marriage and baptism etc. making total c.£20.
Kingussie,	£11 6s. 8d.	£2. 0s. 0d.	Small allowance for marriage, baptisms.
Fordyce	Total incl. every-thing £26		
Anstruther Wr	£8 6s. 8d. stg.		
Marnoch	100 merks	2 gns	3½d. for each certificate of character, 6½d. each baptism, 1s. 7d. each marriage.
Loudon	Total not over £30 stg.		
Luggan	500 merks		
Maybole	200 merks Scots.		
Stobo	£5 11s. 1⅓d. stg.		
Larbert and Dunipace	£100 Scots	£1 stg.	c.£8 10s. stg. for marriages, baptisms, certificates.
Applecross	200 merks Scots		Cockfighting dues equal to a quarter's fees for each child.
Durness	100 merks Scots		Board and lodging; 1s. for each marriage, 3d. for each baptism.

The salary was paid in meal or money or a combination of the two and, as with provision of school buildings, the duty of paying it was laid on heritors in proportion to their valued rents but, as with similar costs, they shared it with their tenants. A reference in 1718 to the 'school meal' which was 1 'furlet' or firlot (¼ boll) for each plough of land, was the tenants' contribution to the master's salary and the 12 bolls which were the salary at Petty in the 1790s were all provided by the tenants.[25] The heritors' proportions must often have been calculated by the schoolmaster in his role as Session Clerk: in 1827 one such man was probably showing off his arithmetic when he worked out the shares as far as he possibly could, even going to the length of establishing that one heritor should pay 5s. 2¼d. and 75241/84111 of a farthing. Not only might the schoolmaster have to do this paperwork concerning his salary but in some cases at any rate, he was expected to go and get his meal himself. One in a Speyside parish found great difficulty in collecting the meal which formed the main part of his income. Some of it he never got at all and what he did receive was of very poor quality because it was hardly to be expected that anyone would part with good meal for what was an unwelcome tax. The Kirk Session to whom he complained, finding that what he said was perfectly true, decided to give him instead an addition to the £1 stg. he was receiving as Session Clerk, subsidising his salary in fact, although this increase was unguaranteed: 'if eight pounds Scots of penalties be got in yearly above his present salary and the officer's fee, he shall have it.' The schoolmaster was sometimes expected to collect the minister's stipend meal too. The master in Fordyce put forward as an excuse for poor school results the fact that, among other things, he had to go to 'extraordinary pains' every year to get the minister's victual in small amounts from various tenants and it proved such a hindrance to the school that he suggested that the heritors should have chamberlains or millers to gather in the meal and deliver it all at once.[26]

In addition to his basic salary, the schoolmaster was paid school fees for each pupil which, in the case of poor children, were paid by the Kirk Session. By the late eighteenth century these fees were something like 2s. per quarter for reading; writing and arithmetic together might be 2s. 6d.; Latin or Greek 5s.; while book-keeping, the most expensive of all, was about 7s. 6d. Although it was not their responsibility to do so, Kirk Sessions sometimes helped out with the school salary. One year, that of Kinnell ordered that the schoolmaster should be given £3 seeing that there were few or no children at school. This sounds a most extraordinary thing to do but no pupils meant no fees and even with the legal salary, such a drop in income could mean losing a Session Clerk and no Session wanted a man who was filling that role well to leave; but what the heritors thought about this payment in the circumstances is not recorded. This Session also gave their schoolmaster summer and winter shoes, sometimes in his role as teacher and sometimes as Session Clerk. On occasion Sessional help towards the salary was more direct. When a new master was appointed to Jedburgh Grammar School, Roxburghshire, at a salary of £100 Scots, £20 of this was paid by the Kirk Session; in 1716 the Town Council and the Kirk Session of Crail, Fife, were combining to pay the school salary; and in Nigg, Ross-shire, in 1822–23 the accounts show a 'part payment to David Ross, Schoolmaster', of 18s. 6d. In 1850 the Kirk Session of Edderton, Ross-shire, 'considered the state of the Parish School of Edderton and agreed to employ Mr. John Mackay as Teacher from then till Whitsunday 1851, promising to pay him the sum of Ten pounds stg. for precenting in the parish Church and teaching the parochial School' and in addition he was given the opportunity to take up the 1851 Census which brought him in a further £7 10s. stg. During this time he was 'teaching as substitute' for another man and for three years received £20 a year and at least once this sum, in half-yearly instalments of £10, was drawn from kirk funds with no apparent contributions from anyone else nor any reasons given as to why the Kirk Session should have helped out in this way.[27]

More detail appears in other chapters about the work and incidental fees that could come the way of church officials, including the Session Clerk but there was often an overlap about perquisites paid for one post or the other: for instance, some Session Clerks might be entitled to a share of delinquents' penalties but they might go to the schoolmaster in other parishes, although either way the same person probably got them. It was so common for the schoolmaster to be the Session Clerk that it is worth summarising some of the work that fell on him in this dual role. The Kirk Session and the heritors expected a great deal of him. He had to write up the Kirk Session minutes, which was no light task as even trifling matters might require the calling of witnesses and the detailed recording of their evidence and this alone must have taken a long time. He had to write letters on behalf of the Session and to give extracts of minutes if they were called for, to issue certificates of character and to write out such beggars' badges as were made of parchment. He might be clerk of the roup when the effects of any pauper were sold and had to make the arrangements should anyone have to be sent to hospital or asylum. It was he who would have to make the inquiries regarding background information should a stranger woman give birth in the parish and, should the Session own property, this too could involve him in work such as making out specifications for improvements and calling for estimates. Should there be no one else to keep and give out the funeral pall or mortcloth, then that too might fall to him. He might have to collect any special stent for the poor and in some parishes the heritors employed him to collect not only the poor's rates where these were levied but statute road money as well. When a kirk boat in one parish needed repair, it was the schoolmaster and the kirk officer who had to 'go to the towns on the North side of the water and gather up twenty shillings from each plough' and before the postal service was put on a proper footing, he might find himself acting as postmaster. There was the collecting of his own and the minister's meal which has just been mentioned and he also had to deal with baptism and marriage matters — one Session decreed in 1783 that the schoolmaster should be at home every Saturday to enter up baptismal registrations and marriage proclamations. The Reform Bill of 1832 kept schoolmasters at home all summer accepting new voters' registrations and objections to them. For virtually all these services he was paid but in addition to them, if anyone needed advice but hesitated to trouble the minister, it was to the schoolmaster that they went instead, as Norman Macleod records in his *Reminiscences of a Highland Parish*. Should he be licensed to preach, then taking services could be expected of him too if need arose: 'The minister being from home, Mr. Milne schoolmaster at Alva lectured forenoon from the 1st psalm afternoon preached from Romans 2, v. 6', say the minutes of Banff Kirk Session in the summer of 1744 and the Fordyce schoolmaster who partly blamed poor school results on the time spent getting his and the minister's meal, also attributed them to the fact that he had been kept very busy preaching, catechising and visiting the sick during the minister's illness. The schoolmaster of Cullen, Banffshire, had to say prayers in 1694 morning and evening in the church but that may have been in the role of reader.[28] With all these many extra tasks to perform, it is a wonder that any schoolmaster ever found time to teach at all but because these extra-curricular activities were either to do with the church or of benefit to the minister or to the heritors — some even did land-surveying for them — they were regarded as acceptable by them and profitable to him.[29]

All in all, it may sound as if schoolmasters were well paid but they were not, which probably explains why for some hundred years they were allowed to augment their income with once-a-year cockfighting in the school. According to F. Marion McNeill, cockfighting was introduced into Scotland in 1685 by the Duke of York and by 1702 had become a permitted and popular sport among schoolboys particularly on Fastern's E'en (Shrove Tuesday) in the lowlands and on either that day or Candlemas (1/2 February) in the highlands, with schoolrooms turned into cockpits and every boy trying to produce a bird to compete. The schoolmaster presided at the fight, getting not only entry money from those with birds but also admission money from those who came to watch. On top of that he received the carcases of the birds which were killed, as well as any which ran away and were known as 'fugies' or fugitives. Alexander Simpson who was schoolmaster, Session Clerk and precentor of the parish of Dingwall, described how there, if not everywhere, the boy who owned the king of the cocks, went to church in state the Sunday after the cockfight with crown and sceptre, attended by his equerries. His reign lasted for six weeks and during it he had the power of saving schoolfellows from the tawse. There is no way in which Kirk Sessions could have been ignorant of this practice and the very fact that the schoolmaster associated with St. Cuthbert's parish, Edinburgh, in the first half of the eighteenth century received 'cock money' and that of Applecross, Ross-shire, received cockfight dues as one of his perquisites at the end of that century, indicates that this abhorrent sport was probably regarded by everyone, kirk included, as a welcome and entertaining way of raising money for the parish schoolmaster. By the very end of the eighteenth century, ideas began to change however and cockfighting generally became unpopular with the public. By 1782 Mauchline Kirk Session forbade it to be held in the parish school, describing it as a 'cruel and inhuman custom' and particularly ordered the schoolmaster to ensure that none of his pupils 'do provide or bring cocks for that purpose, and that there is no vacancy in the school that day.' Nevertheless in the highlands the practice lasted for some time longer. Hugh Miller described it going on in Cromarty School in 1812 which was the year of the last fight in Dingwall.[30] There was an overlap in this with Fastern's E'en and Candlemas which could fall very close together should Easter be very early and, although cockfighting was not involved, a partially similar thing to what Alexander Simpson described at Dingwall happened at Candlemas in such places as St. Andrews. It was a custom which though not cruel was certainly open to abuse: the children competed for a Candlemas Crown according to who could give the biggest cash donation to the master, which at St. Andrews in the 1790s might be anything from 5s. to 5 guineas and the Candlemas King, and Queen if it were a mixed school, reigned for six weeks, could demand an afternoon's play for the children once a week and could remit all punishment. Unfortunately for school-masters, not all of them got such additional extras and one writer said in the 1790s that a parish schoolmaster's income 'though by no means one of the worst livings of the kind, never can be an object to a man who has got anything like a liberal education. To one who is . . . at all qualified to be useful, and who must dress, and is supposed to live a little above the common rate, it is only a sort of genteel starving', going on to point out that although the wages of ordinary working people had been doubled and in many instances trebled before the end of the eighteenth century, those of schoolmasters had remained within the same legal limits for a hundred years. At the same date another writer said that the minimum legal salary of £8 6s. 8d. stg. was 'a paltry consideration to induce any young man who has been at the expense of a liberal education to undertake an office of all others the most slavish', yet both these comments were written by ministers who, by piling work on to schoolmasters, contributed to the descriptions given of their conditions. It was because of inadequate pay that some schoolmasters found still other ways of augmenting their earnings but it was only when these outside activities had an adverse effect on the school that official displeasure manifested itself. The master of the Charity School at Rathven became a meal-dealer as well, which was apparently quite in order; it was only when he abandoned the school one day in order to take meal by sea to Inverness that the Session summoned and rebuked him, upon which he promised not to repeat this particular offence. His meal-dealing apparently continued, however, and it seems that he must have stored it at or near the school because two years later, in 1734, he was admonished by the Session for having his register badly torn by rats. A couple of years later, the master there, by then a different man, was summoned before the Session because he was not attending to his school duties as he had taken on a public house. This was not such a strange thing to do as it may sound as, at one point, the General Assembly allowed ministers to do so too. In this instance, the master made out that it was his wife who had taken it but when the Presbytery was consulted, they decided that this was not something to be tolerated and he was told that August to give it up or be dismissed from his official post. Even although he was both Session Clerk and precentor, he defied this order and still had his inn in October. At this point the Presbytery decreed that if he persisted, he would be suspended as Clerk and precentor which was a sufficiently dire threat to make him give in. Another instance of unacceptable conduct was at Inverary where in 1659 the master was discovered to be letting boys out of school to run errands for people.[31]

In spite of the fact that a Glasgow Kirk Session elected their schoolmaster annually in the 1820s, as has been said, it is sometimes maintained that a parish schoolmaster could only be dismissed for heresy or immorality but the fact is that Sessions supervised their schoolmasters very closely although, strictly speaking, this was the minister's duty. If they found that he was either inefficient or very unsatisfactory or so disliked that no children were sent to him — education not being compulsory until 1872 — then they took immediate steps to replace him, without any fuss about the giving of notice or unfair dismissal. When one master complained that he had been illegally deposed by the minister — 'thrust out of his place' was the descriptive phrase used by another teacher when the same thing happened to him — it transpired that the school had been 'brought to naught' by, among other things, his absences, and the heritors and Session agreed with the minister's action. The minutes of New Abbey Kirk Session, Kirkcudbrightshire, show a similarly brisk attitude to an inadequate master:

> 13th August 1698. This day, the Session taking to their consideration that the people are unwilling to put their children to the present schoolmaster for their education, they desire the minister to inquire for another . . .
> 28th August 1698. The minister makes report that he hath engaged a schoolmaster; and the Session appoints the former schoolmaster to be acquainted with it, and desired to desist from exercising that office here any more.

The reason is not given why at one point in the seventeenth century an East Lothian school had so few pupils that it was 'totally dissolvit' but in the following case the reasons were very clear. Within a year of Mr James Williamson's appointment as teacher in Dornoch, a libel against him was brought before the Session — that he was a dismal failure; the children were so poorly taught that parents had to send them elsewhere; that he beat and kicked them, or at least such as were left. Where there had previously been a flourishing school only three pupils remained and they were to be sent elsewhere as soon as other schooling could be found for them. In view of the alleged beating and kicking it seems surprising that the libel stated that through familiarity with the pupils he had lost his authority; and lastly there was a complaint that because of his 'pitiful low voice' he could be heard neither reading nor singing in church. The result was inevitable; the Session simply dispensed with his services on the grounds of incapacity. Ashkirk was another parish which found that its school was 'quite deserted' at one point. Georg Redpath, the schoolmaster, informed the Session about this and they ordered 'that publick intimation be given the next Lord's Day that parents send their children to School for being instructed.' That was in late October 1695 but at the beginning of December when it was 'again represented and complained of the school that it was disfrequented and laid desolate and notwithstanding of the public intimation that was given, parents did not bring in their children, it was thought fit and ordered that the minister should speak and deal with them att going through the parioch for taking up the examing [sic] Roll.' Ordering the children's attendance indicates that the Session had thought the master was satisfactory but this anxiety in December to get to the root of things shows that they kept open minds and the minister found, through talking with the parents, that the cause of the trouble was dissatisfaction with Mr Redpath. 'The Session, taking this into consideration, after they had dealt with him to carry differently towards children in times to come, ordered that yet intimation should be made out of the pulpit for bringing them in and their parents should be earnestly exhorted to do it or otherwise to come and give in their reasons to wherefore they kept them back.' This must have been effective to some extent but in 1697 the schoolmaster, presumably the same man, was summarily dismissed although not for anything to do with his school work. The offence that was his undoing was spoiling a new Session minute book by tearing out a lot of the clean paper, something which only came to light when the minister planned to transcribe some minutes into a new book himself.[32]

Although there was no incompetence on the part of the schoolmaster in the parish of Craig in 1715, yet the minister found so much ignorance as he went visiting that he urged the elders to encourage people to send youngsters to school and it does seem possible that complaints about schoolmasters may have partly been a cover for unwilling parents. While beating and kicking had been a cause for complaint in Dornoch, corporal punishment was an accepted fact both of the educational system and of family life then and for many years thereafter. In 1675, for example, directions were given by the Synod of Aberdeen to the Presbyteries within its bounds regarding visitation of parishes, which included the following questions to be put regarding education: 'if he [the schoolmaster] chastises them [the children] for cursing, swearing, lying, speaking profanity, for disobedience to parents and other vices that appear in them.' In Dundonald school, Ayrshire, it was laid down in 1640 that the master could strike his pupils with a belt, tawse or birch wand on the palm of the hand or on 'the hips' but never under any circumstances on the face or head, but because schoolmasters were in general remarkably good and because corporal punishment was such an integral part of the system, it was possible for some complaints about overmuch of it to be disregarded by Kirk Sessions. In spite of many expressions of dissatisfaction in one parish in 1806, the Session dismissed them as 'informal'; the same attitude was taken towards a second lot of complaints and it took a petition from a group which included two of the elders, to produce action which resulted in the Presbytery censuring the master 'for improper treatment of the scholars'. Sometimes the evidence of excessive punishment was such that it could not possibly be thought anything other than it was, as in 1638 when the schoolmaster at Kirkcaldy was 'sharply and gravely admonished' for striking a boy 'till he is become sick' and there too it was brought to the Session's notice that the 'doctor', as the schoolmaster was sometimes called, should be advised 'to be more calm to the scholars and not so outrageous in his speeches to them'. Probably the worst case of all was when John Douglas, a pupil in Moffat, Dumfries-shire, was whipped to death by the master in 1699. The Kirk Session minutes for this date no longer exist so it cannot be discovered whether it was the Session or the burgh authorities who dealt with the matter but certainly the schoolmaster was tried in Edinburgh, found guilty, lashed and banished from Scotland.[33]

The work that a schoolmaster did for the Session was so important that it is astonishing that one Session endured seven years of negligence on the part of their schoolmaster-cum-Session Clerk during which he often lost the Session minutes and on one occasion destroyed them. He tried to get his own back when they offered him only half of the two years' salary owed to him by removing the Session records altogether and it took the Sheriff Officer to recover them. It must have been particularly difficult for any Kirk Session when a schoolmaster was accused of immorality, especially when he was Session Clerk as well. If anything, a man's word was always taken in preference to that of a woman in such cases but when the schoolmaster of Mauchline was found not guilty by the Session of an accusation of adultery, the presumption of guilt was nevertheless sufficient for three of the elders to threaten to resign if he continued as Session Clerk. Although charity schools were different from parish schools, they still came under the eye of the local Kirk Session and when the teacher of one was found guilty of fornication with a widow with whom he lodged, the matter came to the Session whose minutes give the daughter's evidence — that she had demanded of her mother 'what could she mean by lying with that beast of a Schoolmaster', adding that her suspicion and disgust were such that she refused to attend his school any longer.[34]

Drink was the common vice of the people in earlier times and a schoolmaster could fall victim to it just as much as anyone else. About 1698 it was reported that one had been so drunk that he was found quite unable to walk, sleeping by the wayside. At much the same date, another was delated to his Session as a graceless, prayerless person, frequently guilty of drunkenness, tippling, swearing and imprecations even in the presence of his pupils who, not unnaturally, copied him and when rebuked for profaning the Lord's Day replied that the master did it as well as them. This case was fully investigated and the master admitted his faults, although pleading that he was no worse than his predecessors. The very first case in the Session minutes of the parish of Kilmaurs in 1698 was a complaint by the minister about the former schoolmaster concerning 'a great many things very scandalous in the said Mr. Robert's practice, particularly that he did steal a new peiry-wig [periwig] from him.' By altering its appearance by 'clipping it about with sizzars' he had managed to wear it for a good few weeks before being found out and, after initial denials, admitting the theft. Poor man, he had neither 'salary, house nor convenient school' and in the circumstances one feels that there might have been more useful things to appropriate than a wig, but only a very foolish schoolmaster would have got on the wrong side of the minister anyway. Having said all that, the fact remains that parish schoolmasters were a remarkable body of men who, with very few resources, produced amazingly good school results.[35]

Although education was officially supervised by Presbyteries through periodic inspections, Sessions kept a close eye on schools to ensure that religious instruction had pride of place and that what was taught was doctrinally correct. The stress laid on this is made clear in a list of the master's duties prepared by the Kirk Session of Tynninghame in 1703 which emphasises the need for morning and evening prayers, catechisms, churchgoing on Sundays and having the children summarise sermons on Mondays. This last must have made children dread the start of each new week when they were expected to show what they had understood of the sermon the day before. Godliness and good manners were always stressed and unnecessary holidays were not encouraged as the following minute from Dumbarton Kirk Session makes clear:

> The Session considering the great loss the scholars are at by reason of their frequent getting of Play, do lay it upon the schoolmaster that it be not given at marriages, though sought by the parties; likeas that if it happen to be granted to a stranger to whom it cannot be denied, or for a new scholar's entry, then it is not to be given thereafter that week, and further the Session enjoins that it be given as seldom as possible.[36]

The efforts of Ashkirk Kirk Session to have children sent to school although the master was not liked have been mentioned, as have the efforts at compulsion recorded in Dunino's registers and, although education was not compulsory until 1872, there were a number of other Sessions too which behaved as if it were. In 1650 that of Aberdour, Fife, fined a man for not sending his boys to school and in 1651 tried to have every child between five and fifteen years old sent there, going even further in 1653 by attempting to debar from church privileges all parents who failed in this respect. In 1717 they were at it again, with elders visiting their quarters to see that the children were at school and bringing in the names of those who were not. Although this was going far beyond anything the Kirk Session had the right to do, it was well meant and such actions on the part of a Session were an indication of their belief in the value of learning. In Torryburn the elders in 1642 went round the parish taking note of all children between the ages of seven and ten 'that they may be put to school' and ordered that parents who were irresponsible about this should be fined and make public repentance 'for perjury in breaking the oath made at the baptism of their children.' That same year the elders of Yester, East Lothian, were required to delate to the Session the parents of any children 'fit to put to school' who were not being sent there, whereas the Kirk Session of Inverary were milder in their approach, just asking the minister in 1677 to speak to certain people who were not sending their children to school.[37]

Because Kirk Sessions were composed of practical people they tried to overcome any difficulties which lay in the way of school attendance owing to the lack of roads and bridges in the days when these were thin on the ground. That of Fala, Midlothian, for instance, decided in 1721 to provide 'tua trees for a bridge of Soutray water fur the scholars use at 15s. Scots.' In 1722 another Session provided school transport, paying 20s. to have the children ferried 'over water' to school during the winter months. Logie Buchan Kirk Session, Aberdeenshire, found a different way round the problem of water dividing the parish and had two schoolmasters, one on either side of the River Ythan with the legal salary divided between them. Good though this intention was the legal salary was only £5 9s. and once divided in two was so small that no suitably qualified man would remain in such a post and the idea had to be given up. Tynninghame Kirk Session also had the problem of a river in the parish and solved it by erecting a school on the far side of it; sensibly they did not divide the legal salary but fixed a special one for the additional teacher: 'The Session, considering how necessar it is that a school be erected in the Knows ground because of the difficulties of children coming over the Watter, they allow a schoole to be erected there. And allows 10 lib. Scots yearlie as a salarie for a sufficient school master whom the Session shall be pleased with, which is to continue during their pleasure.' Parishes in large burghs often needed more than one legal school and the salary in such cases had to be divided: no fewer than four schoolmasters shared the one income in the Barony parish of Glasgow in 1703, 'divided among them by the minister and elders as they think fit', but this was probably a maximum rather than a minimum salary which could withstand such division.[38]

The distance and inaccessibility of some parts of a parish to the parochial school were another reason for Sessions to see to the establishment of additional schools and in 1702 the following entry was made in the minutes of Dumbarton Kirk Session: 'Anent a school in the countrey. Considered the necessity of a school in the country part of the parish for such as cannot come to the town, and appoint Margaret McAdam to the service of that cure and appointed the Treasurer to pay her 2 merks quarterly.' To be sure that all went well with this venture, a total of four deacons and elders were ordered 'to take notice how the children in the country repair to the said school and how they profit therein, and report accordingly.' In 1755 Inverchaolain, Argyllshire, had no legal school because it would have been of little use in a mountainous parish with twenty miles of coastline and instead of the normal parish school, the legal provision was divided so that five little schools could be established in suitable places, operating for six months a year. These could hardly be regarded as parish schools as the standards expected of them were bound to be lower than normal. Should any reasonable request come in for help to establish such additional schools, then the kirk authorities — Presbytery and Kirk Session — were only too willing to co-operate one way or another. For example, when Lord Deskford along with the people of Portsoy, Banffshire, asked for a collection to be held throughout the Presbytery bounds to enable a school to be built there, this was agreed by the Presbytery and the local Kirk Sessions. A lesser but still practical form of help was given by the Kirk Session of Kilmory, Arran, when they ordered that timber should be given to the people in Donriddeor to build a school. Just as Sessions helped out with normal parochial schools, so too was help given for repairs, materials and other expenses for these additional schools — glass for the windows, repairs to desks, payment of feu-duty or the cost of what was called chalkboard. Similarly, they might help with the salaries of teachers in these schools; when more than one was set up in the east end of the parish of St. Andrews, the salaries of £3 stg. each were chiefly paid by the Kirk Session. When some people in Cromarty petitioned the Session in 1758 'anent a school to be set up at Davidstoun for teaching the young ones to read English' the initial reply they were given was to go and get subscriptions towards it from heads of families. This they did but soon returned to the Session to say that a considerable number of these were willing to contribute and could raise a salary of £1 7s. 9d. stg. but they asked that the Session would add something to this. The Session agreed to give £1 and nominated a man as teacher and 'for his further encouragement ordered half of the £1 to be paid to him instantly (he being obliged to set up school presently) and the other half at Whitsunday 1759' and they also recommended those sending their children to him 'to pay him quarterly for their children over and above their Subscription,' in other words, not to think that their subscription exempted them from paying the normal fees. The Session were exerting a lot of control in return for their £1.[39]

It was not uncommon for a group of parents to club together to engage a temporary teacher for their children, often a needy student who would be glad of board and lodging during the summer months to help him through his winter studies at university and, although this was private teaching, a Session would sometimes give financial help towards it. This may have had something to do with the fact that the young man probably hoped to qualify for either teaching or the ministry. These little private schools, however, were totally different from what were called 'adventure schools' which were not nearly as exciting as they sound and were in fact just 'private venture' schools, established for profit. The church never wanted anyone outside its control to educate children and as far back as 1623 one Presbytery decreed that no one should 'presume to teach any bairnes without the approbatione of the Presbytery'; in 1662 Parliament also forbade anyone to teach in any school without church permission. It seems probable that the teacher taken on temporarily in Ashkirk in 1697 who, in no time, had a full school and the children getting on splendidly, must have been teaching in an adventure school of some sort and in that particular case it was certainly not held against him although in general Sessions initially viewed adventure schools with the greatest suspicion, fearful that the teachers might not be competent, nor their religious views sound, and immediate inquiries were made about the teacher should any such school be set up in a parish. In 1833 the Session Clerk of Edderton was ordered to write to the Kirk Session of Lairg to inquire about a young man from there who 'had set up as a teacher' in Edderton, asking particularly about his principles, character, conduct and acquirements and whether they could recommend him or employ him as a teacher.[40] If the answer to such an inquiry about a private school was unsatisfactory, then the Session could have it closed, perhaps using the services of the magistrate to implement this, but if the answer was favourable then it could be allowed to continue so long as it did not have any adverse effect on the parochial school. One way of achieving this was to limit the range of subjects that might be taught in these schools: in 1703, for the 'encouragement' of the parish schoolmaster the Kirk Session of Falkirk forbade any private schools teaching reading and Latin to exist either in the town or within a mile around it. In Hawick no one not licensed by the heritors and Session was allowed to teach in the town and even when licensed was not allowed to teach anything other than the Psalm Book. In 1697 the Kirk Session of Greenock, with the agreement of the heritors, ordered that there should be no other school in the parish apart from the parochial one on the grounds that private schools were prejudicial to it, although they stipulated that the parish school should be established in a 'commodious place' in the parish. This condition was a wise one because many schools were not large enough to accommodate all their pupils properly and there could be serious overcrowding but some Sessions, in spite of this, still closed alternative schools.[41] All this was nothing less than the kirk giving the parish schoolmaster a monopoly and denying choice to the people, but it was soon realised that if all children were to be educated, then it was essential to come to terms with private schools and harness them to good use rather than keep them at arm's length. In any event, according to Professor Smout, by the mid-eighteenth century Sessions were virtually powerless to close these schools and when some parish schoolmasters made complaints about private schools affecting their interests in Aberdeenshire about 1748, in Stirlingshire in 1757 and about 1766 in Ayrshire, it does not seem that any action was taken as a result. This means that Edderton's inquiries of Lairg Kirk Session about a teacher must at the date they were made have been largely irrelevant and certainly by the end of the Napoleonic wars, twice as many children in Scotland were being taught in private schools as in parish ones.[42]

Until elementary education became both compulsory and free in 1872, fees had to be paid, as has already been said. Because such payments would obviously be a problem for poor parents the First Book of Discipline had recommended that their children's fees should be paid for them and in 1641 the overtures made by the church to Parliament regarding schools included a reference to poor children. It appears that the church was already taking its own steps in the matter and that year the Synod of Fife, for one, required Sessions to pay for the teaching of poor youngsters, either out of the poor's box or by a quarterly collection. Payment of fees gave Sessions a particularly close interest in their parish schools and Kirk Session accounts have many entries about them. These fees appear under a variety of terms: 'school wages'; 'poor scholars' school-maile'; 'poor scholars' quarters' referring to the custom of paying quarterly; 'schoolage'; and the phrase 'scholars' college fee' appears to refer to school fees also.[43] Poor children's fees were paid to parish schoolmasters and, once private teachers were accepted, to them too, including women: the minutes of North Berwick Kirk Session say on 14 July 1699 that 'This day Mistress Hepburne craving payment for eight poor scholars and Mr. Clephane craving payment for eleven poor scholars, the Session appoints the Treasurer to pay them both.' In Dornoch, in addition to a grammar school, there was also what was called an English school, taught by a mistress who received 6s. Scots for each pupil, while the Session accounts for 1738 show £1 4s. stg. paid 'for ½ year's dues for two poor schollars at the Woman's School.' The Session which in 1595 had wanted all the youngsters of the town to go to school with time off, if necessary, to go begging, later on agreed to pay the fees of all poor children in the parish according to how they got on at school. While any Kirk Session was entitled to expect to see results for their money, not many put it as bluntly as that. All this changed in 1803 when an Act of Parliament increased the salaries of parish schoolmasters but also made it a condition that they should teach poor children gratis. In theory this lifted the burden of educating the poor from the kirk but in practice there could still be a need for their help. In one parish some poor children lived four miles from the parish school and had therefore either to be uneducated or to go to some other school nearer their homes 'and in that case, it was contended, the school wages must, according to use and wont, be paid out of the poor's fund. This was resisted but for Peace's sake, the session acquiesced.'[44] Payments of perhaps 5s. 'to a poor Las to buy a Byble' or for a 'psalm book to a poor scholar' were made because these books were in the main the only English reading matter in schools and Sessions paid for them to help poor children with their lessons. An Argyllshire Session showed an enterprising attitude to school-books, albeit not for the poor, but allowing for a wider range of titles. In 1781 the minister and treasurer recommended that the Session should buy 'for the parish school such books from time to time as may be necessary, to be sold by the master to his scholars for ready money, and to return to the box for behoof of the poor.' It seems that there was a profit to be made on these sales which would have made the whole transaction doubly beneficial, helping the school and a good use of the poor's funds.[45]

The parochial educational system did not make as much progress in the high-lands as it did in lowland Scotland. Parishes were often too large and scattered for a legal school, even if supplemented with additional small ones, to be adequate and the people were Gaelic-speaking, in addition to which the political troubles of the times lasted longer there than elsewhere. Even where schools had been started in the seventeenth century, many of them closed down, a Roman Catholic influence began to creep in and superstition and ignorance continued. It was to combat all this that a group of gentlefolk decided to form a Scottish Society for the Propagation of Christian Knowledge, based on an English group which had been formed in 1699. In 1709 the Scottish Society, which was Presbyterian in creed, was granted a royal charter to establish schools where by means of instruction in the Scriptures and the 3 Rs 'religion and virtue might be taught to young and old.' Most of these schools were, says Professor Smout, set up in the highlands proper but there were also some in Orkney, lowland Caithness, Banffshire, eastern Aberdeenshire, and for a time even in Fife, the Borders and Edinburgh. A useful development came with the grant of a second patent in 1738, providing for the setting up of spinning schools for girls where reading was also taught. The idea behind these Society schools was initially not just philanthropic but was also intended to promote Hanoverian sympathies and with this rather political bias it is not surprising that to start with, the Society forbade the use of Gaelic — often called Irish — which meant that the unfortunate pupils were taught in a language they did not understand. This anti-Gaelic attitude was not new. The Act of Privy Council of 1616 which has been mentioned earlier, also described Gaelic as one 'of the chieff and principale causes of the continuance of barbaritie and incivilitie among the inhabitants of the Isles and the Heylandis' and intended it to be 'abolished and removit' and the English tongue 'universallie planted' in its place. The efforts to eliminate Gaelic did not succeed even although after the Stuart risings of 1715 and 1745 stronger measures were taken and the reading and even speaking of it were forbidden. This ban was lifted in 1766 and it is greatly to the credit of the SPCK, as the Society for the Propagation of Christian Knowledge was widely known, that it printed a Gaelic translation of the New Testament the following year. Nevertheless, learning of English was a primary concern in highland charity schools and although people might not like the language they were sufficiently outward-looking to realise that it was virtually essential for children to speak it if they ever hoped to work and live in non-Gaelic-speaking areas.[46]

The educational standards in SPCK schools were lower than those of parochial schools. In the early days of the Society's existence, any aspiring teacher was examined by about three local ministers and if found satisfactory by them, then application was made to the SPCK for a commission for him, but later on would-be teachers were examined by two clerical directors of the Society in Edinburgh. Great emphasis was placed on religion and the need for the teacher to be able to impart the principles of the Reformed church and in addition, the children had to be catechised at least twice a week and prayed with publicly twice a day. English reading and spelling, arithmetic and church music were required subjects which is borne out by the type of books supplied at one point by the Society for the use of poor children at the school at Hall-Morton in the parish of Langholm: Bibles, New Testaments, Catechisms and some copies of *Vincent on the Catechism*, Psalm books, the Confession of Faith, *Proverbs, Guthrie's Saving Interests*, as well as some arithmetic books, music and copperplate books, with two quires of clean paper, for all of which the parish minister returned thanks.[47] SPCK schools were sometimes called 'Free Schools' and their teachers were often called missionaries because for a time any rate, they were *ex officio* catechists of the districts to which they were attached.[48]

The SPCK never had much money, just enough to pay salaries and the cost of some books. While the state gave moral support funds had to come from the General Assembly which meant in fact from Kirk Sessions by means of special collections held on the orders of the Assembly, which often appear in Session minutes: '13th August 1716. Act of General Assembly for a collection to be made next Lord's Day for books and paper for the boys in the Charity Schools in the highlands, likewise the minister intimated that the collection for erecting the said schools, which should have been made six years ago, has not yet been gathered through the parish, but only in the town of Scone.' He thought it would be best to hold the collection after the harvest, which was done and £9 4s. 2d. Scots was raised. In Elie it was the minister himself who went out collecting, announcing one Sunday in 1713 from the pulpit that he would go through the parish from house to house 'to receive the people's liberality for propagating Christian knowledge' and his efforts raised £60 Scots. All in all, Kirk Sessions supported the SPCK manfully with collections and by providing school buildings and other practical help towards the teachers' domestic economy such as 2s. 3d. stg. given to 'Donald Ross, Teacher of the Charity School of Inver, for grass to his Cow.' Other useful help could be given such as 7s. stg. paid by the Kirk Session of the island of Coll in 1800 for carriage of a box of books, without which they could never have got there.[49]

The Society did not aim to replace but to supplement parochial schools. They began their work by approaching Presbyteries to find out what schools already existed and where any additional ones might be needed. The answers to their queries were supplied by Kirk Sessions and often provide the basic educational history of any parish. Some parishes however failed to carry out their legal obligations for school provision and simply relied on the SPCK to make up the deficiency so that in 1758 the Society had to tell the General Assembly that they would withdraw schools from parishes where this was happening. Their schools were only established or allowed to continue where they were of real use and what happened in the parish of Lairg in the early years of the Society's work is a good example of how the system operated. In 1712 the Society asked the Presbytery of Dornoch and Lord Strathnaver, the principal heritor, to decide on two parishes within the bounds which would benefit from having such schools and Lairg and Kildonan, also in Sutherland, were recommended. In Lairg a suitable teacher was found locally and the school began but two years later the Society felt that it was not being sufficiently used and asked the Presbytery to discuss with Lord Strathnaver the possibility of moving it to the parish of Creich which meant, of course, moving the teacher, not the building. However, the Presbytery considered that the school should stay where it was as it answered 'the design of the Society more by being in Lairg than being in the paroch of Creich' and so it remained in Lairg for another year. In 1715 however the Society again wrote to say that it was sorry to find that its schools in the Presbytery bounds 'seem to do so little service, and to find that parents value so little the Christian education of their children that they prefer their pettie services about their houses to so great a blessing'; in other words, the children were kept at home to work instead of going to school. The Presbytery seriously recommended the ministers of the parishes with Society schools to do their utmost to remove the grounds for such complaints and appointed the Society's letter to be read from the pulpits of Lairg and Kildonan, which did some good. Fortunately not all parents were so unappreciative.[50]

The suggestion that the school could be moved from one parish to another was because many, though not all, of the Society's teachers were 'ambulatory' which meant that they could move from place to place as the Society decreed. They could also move within a parish, staying long enough in any one area to give children a basic educational grounding before moving on to start teaching a different group. Any decision about when a teacher should move within a parish and which part of it he should visit next was normally left to the Kirk Session to decide in the light of local requests. In 1728 the people in the eastern end of the parish of Orphir, Orkney, asked that the 'Honourable Society's school' should come at Martinmas to their part of the parish and the Session agreed that this might be done for two years, or longer if necessary. This of course gave rise to accommodation problems and as there was no schoolhouse in that part of the parish, the Session agreed to give the teacher half a crown stg. out of kirk funds for a year's rent of a house to use as a school. In 1731 the Swanbister people thought that it was time that their children had some schooling and petitioned the Session to allow the Society schoolmaster to come to them seeing that there were over thirty children of school age there, and they offered to provide a house and peats without any cost to the

Session and, as the school had been in the east of the parish for 2¹/₂ years, the Session agreed that it should move.[51] In this way the SPCK did great work in providing education in many places which would otherwise have lacked it altogether but their practice of only keeping schools where they seemed most useful, while eminently sensible, could cause considerable problems to Sessions and this parish of Orphir is a case in point. In 1717 the Society allocated 50 merks to pay a teacher there but it was left to the Session to see to the building of a schoolhouse, in agreement with the magistrate of the parish. The stonework was put up by local men who were paid 6*d*. Scots each per day out of kirk funds, as was the cost of timber, iron and other materials. The elders supervised the work, each of them bringing with him 'out of every house' someone to carry stones or mortar. This great community effort was begun in June 1717 and completed, apart from two door jambs, three windows and five deals, by November that year and all expenses were paid. Having done all that work with high hopes and enthusiasm, it must have been heartbreaking for the Session to be informed by the Society in February 1723 that they were removing their 'bounty' from Orphir to the island of Stroma but, practical as always, they kept their heads and ordered the kirk officer to go to the schoolmaster and get from him any books in his hands which it seems must have been paid for by the Session as it was decided that the minister should dispose of them as he saw fit; and later on they ordered that some deals in the schoolmaster's hands should also be collected and made into a table for a charity school of some sort which either existed already or which came into being by the end of the year. This Society school was obviously re-established in time to move from the west of the parish to the east and from there to the Swanbister district in the late 1720s–early 1730s, but the salary was again withdrawn in 1743 and restored the following year. Not surprisingly, this time the Session said that they would repair an available existing house as a school but declared that they would not build a new one after their earlier experience.[52]

In another instance, the SPCK paid the salary of a teacher in the Drumcudden area of the parish of Resolis but in 1823 'after some difference' it was withdrawn and half of it was paid instead to a woman to run a sewing school for girls under the patronage of a local lady, but this too was discontinued, leaving the Session with a group of dissatisfied parents and trouble over the house which the male teacher had occupied. The people said it had been built by public subscription but he maintained that he had some claims because while it was begun by subscription, he had had to finish it at his own expense. The Session decided to fill the gap left by the removal of the SPCK school by providing another one, with costs met by yet another public subscription. In order to encourage local generosity, Mr Paterson, the owner of land at Drumcudden, gave 'a piece of ground in perpetual feu of sufficient extent for the site of the Houses to be erected, for a garden for the schoolmaster and a plot of play ground to the scholars,' the feu to be 1*s*. stg. a year on condition that the land was only used for the purpose stated. 'The Session appointed further that the people should be aided in clearing the expenses of the school house etc by collections at the church doors and that application should be made without delay to the Secretary of the Inverness Education Society for a salary and the appointment of a teacher.' By the following year, the schoolhouse and master's house were largely finished, with windows and glass paid for out of collections but 'writing tables' and forms were still needed. The Session decided that there should be another subscription to pay for these but that the tradesmen should all be paid out of the money already raised. By January 1826 it was reported that all was complete, the mason work having come to £29 14s. 5¹/₂d., and carpenter work, including 'thatching school house £1 16s. and making table desks and forms £1 2s.' came to £18 15s. 4d. stg.[53] Although the actual result of the Society's withdrawal of a school was in this case to spur the parish into a mood of self-help, these sudden retractions were, to say the least, disconcerting for the communities concerned. However, the fact remains that the SPCK gave great service to Scotland and these problems are only mentioned to show how involved Kirk Sessions could be even though other bodies than the heritors were providing educational facilities.

Some other forms of charity schools were started up in the eighteenth century and where appropriate Kirk Sessions co-operated with them also. An example of these was the Forfeited Estate Schools. After the Stuart rising of 1715 the estates of a large number of Jacobite supporters were forfeited to the crown and sold, although after a variety of expenses were paid, only some £1,100 was left. Following the 1745 rising, however, when further estates were forfeited, the Crown retained them to be administered by commissioners for the benefit of the highlands and to a limited extent they provided additional schools where they were seen to be needed. This turned the government into landlords and technical heritors and therefore this was a right and proper use of this money. Another educational development in the eighteenth century was the Royal Bounty Committee appointed by the General Assembly to administer an annual royal gift of £1,000. Such schools as were provided through this aid were known as Royal Schools although the real aim was to provide itinerant preachers for the highlands. This committee co-operated with the SPCK between 1729–50 but the Society found it inconvenient to have their teachers working as catechists on Saturdays, Sunday afternoons and on Mondays as this left only four days in the week for teaching in school. In 1758 the Royal Bounty Committee reduced its financial support and the SPCK ended the contract, saying that all men jointly employed must be purely schoolmasters, apart from fifteen who were to be catechists. Their joint work had increased the number of schools but the end of their co-operation meant that some of them closed. A description of the effects of such a closure says that the people 'suffered greatly for want of the schoolmaster that the Society was wont to employ in their bounds' but not just the local people suffered. So did the unfortunate teachers who found themselves out of a job. When the school in Kildonan closed, the Society teacher, whose only aptitude was for teaching, kept on a little school himself, in spite of the fact that all the people could manage to give him was grass for a cow or two and a few sheep and on this he, and his old mother who lived with him, had to exist; and there were others in the same position. This was all of great concern to Sessions in the parishes affected but fortunately there were other bodies willing to establish schools: between 1811–92 various Gaelic Societies provided schools in suitable areas but, while they would have been welcomed where they opened, they were usually ambulatory with the benefits and disadvantages that that system produced. Assistance also came from the Ladies' Auxiliary in Support of Gaelic Schools formed in 1846 but what it could achieve was limited by the nature of the organisation. Local voluntary efforts, such as the Kelso Friendly School Society, instituted in 1816, also provided teaching for certain classes of children. In this case it was for orphans and poor children and was supported by payments of 1*d*. per week by members and donations from interested people, as well as occasional collections in the different places of worship in the town which, at the time, amounted to seven — the parish church, Episcopal, Relief, Burgher, Anti-Burgher, Cameronian and Quaker.[54]

Although the kirk was involved to varying degrees with education for many years, James Scotland says in his *History of Scottish Education* that it was only in 1824 that it became directly concerned with provision of schools, with the establishment that year of an Education Committee of the General Assembly, the oldest committee of that body. Although the committee's main concern was with the 143 parishes in the Synods of Argyll, Glenelg, Ross, Sutherland and Caithness, questionnaires were sent out to every Church of Scotland minister in the country. A collection was ordered and in 1826 the provision of 'Assembly Schools' began, primarily intended as Bible schools, providing teaching in Gaelic where necessary and providing elementary books in that language. As with the SPCK, these schools were intended to complement and not to replace parochial ones. The standard of education was said to be middling, described as 'none so good as the best parish schools, nor so poor as the worst,' but their most remarkable feature was that they were non-sectarian.[55] There is considerable variety in the terms applied to different types of school. There was a reference to a 'Church school' in the early eighteenth century at Lairg but this cannot have been an Assembly one and may just have referred to the parochial one with its close church connections. One which was supported by the General Assembly in the parish of Kilmuir Wester and Suddy, Ross-shire, was generally called Principal Baird's School and a 'Society School' might well refer to something other than the SPCK.[56]

In 1837 a Parliamentary grant enabled Assembly schools to be established in the lowlands and one of these was in Yetholm, Roxburghshire, a parish marching with the English border. Its log book makes interesting reading, showing how work at home — potato planting and lifting, weeding, gathering wool, lambing and so on affected attendance, the same problem that had afflicted the parish of Lairg in 1715. The long summer 'harvest holiday' on top of so much absence meant that 'the children having forgot, during the vacation, much of what they had learned before', special attention had to be paid when the school re-started to the writing and arithmetic of the younger ones. This gives an impression of strict earnestness, which is something always connected with school life in former days so it is nice to find that in this Assembly school there was a considerable degree of enjoyment: on 2 May 1864 the children were all treated to tea and cake in the schoolroom although the reason for this is not given, and there was always an understanding of their anxiety to enjoy certain extra-mural excitements. On a Fair Day that October, when the children were meant to be at school and not at the fair, those who did not play truant were rewarded with a little longer playtime, and in February 1865 there was no school one day because of 'the Border Festival of Fastern's E'en' when, although cockfighting had died out, inter-community football matches were a special feature. In the following month 'Proceedings terminated rather abruptly in the afternoon by the ''Tally-ho'' of the foxhunters' and the entry for 26 March 1869 says 'As Foxhunters hunting this district today for the last time this season, the children asked and got the afternoon to enjoy the fun.' It may be that this particular schoolmaster had some sporting leanings himself but the wording gives an impression of kindliness. What the Kirk Session thought of such happenings is not known although they cannot have been unaware of them. But there was strictness too and something that was not popular with the dominie was another custom: 'December 1872. Owing to a stupid custom of barring out the master, there was no schooling today. This is always done on the shortest day and the children are encouraged by their parents to do all in their power to keep the School-door shut and obtain a Holiday.'[57]

This Assembly school in Yetholm has sometimes been called the first Ragged School in Scotland but it was nothing of the sort. It was a perfectly normal school of its kind but one which became involved in a small but remarkable educational and social experiment initiated by the parish minister, without Sessional support at the outset although this was very soon gained. The minister was John Baird, a son of the manse, born in 1799, who grew up at a time when considerable interest in gypsies was developing in both Scotland and England through the writings of John Hoyland, Sir Walter Scott and others. In 1829 John Baird came to Yetholm, the principal base of the gypsies of south-east Scotland. There were 125 of them there at the time, in twenty-five families, who spent the winter months in the village before going off on their roaming way during the spring, summer and autumn of each year. Mr Baird found that a number of adult gypsies could read and that one or two could write and, when asked, they all said that they wanted their children to be educated but that they could not afford school fees. Mr Baird felt that the only way the children would really benefit from any education would be if they stayed at home all year, boarded in the village while their parents went travelling which would give them a chance to consolidate what they learnt; he hoped that this would break their ingrained wandering habits and induce them to take up a settled mode of life. The villagers did not object to the idea in itself but no one wanted to take in gypsy children as boarders and the first two had to be accommodated in the manse, a ministerial example of true charity which had its effect as in no time lodgings were easily found for these children in the village. From this it is clear that the Kirk Session came round to the plan in the end, a plan which for a considerable time did good work for a deprived class.[58]

True Ragged Schools were aimed at saving vagrant children from being transported. The church took an interest in these schools but they were begun by individuals rather than by Kirk Sessions or the kirk in general. The first of them was begun by a Sheriff Substitute of Aberdeen in 1841 when he set up the Aberdeen Ragged or Industrial Feeding School which met in a loft above a smithy. His idea was to take in neglected boys and give them food and elementary education in return for work — picking oakum (untwisting and teasing out old tarred ropes so that they could be used for caulking ships' seams), mending salmon nets and so on — which was meant to instil in them the habits of industry. This was not a church school, but six years later Dr Guthrie, a famous Edinburgh minister and a friend of the Sheriff Substitute, took up the idea and established the Edinburgh Ragged School and these were the first steps towards the development of reformatories and approved schools.

Although burgh schools came to be regarded as grammar or 'great' schools, they were legally parish schools because Parliament had decreed that every parish, whether in town or in the countryside, should have a school. However, as Professor Smout says, burgh schools were supported by the funds of Burgh Councils and came under their control and the church could often find it hard to have any say in their running. This partly arose because many of the best of these schools, such as those in Edinburgh and Aberdeen, were pre-Reformation foundations which fell into secular control, although at an early period a school endowed with funds came into the possession of the Kirk Session of South Leith but such a thing was unusual. Other burghs wanted to control education in their own areas as happened in Edinburgh and Aberdeen but there must still have been a limited amount of co-operation with the kirk, particularly in smaller towns. At Kelso, for instance, early in the seventeenth century the Session Clerk was 'ordeined to ring the six hour bell for the convenency of the bairnes to the school' which appears to have been a service performed by a kirk official for the benefit of a burgh school. The Parochial and Burgh Schoolmasters Act of 1861 slightly altered the position of burgh schools. Nevertheless, in small places Sessions tried to keep a foot in the door and nothing was so effective as a financial one. In 1665 when a new schoolmaster was appointed by the Town Council of Forfar, part of his salary was paid by the heritors and Kirk Session of the parish. Part-payment of salaries has already been mentioned in other places, although not necessarily to do with burgh schools, but one clear case ensuring involvement was in the early eighteenth century when the Kirk Session of Falkirk made themselves responsible for the upkeep of the school, not asking the help of the heritors or anyone else to defray costs or help in its management.[59]

Sessional schools, which were town schools run and paid for by the Kirk Session of a town parish, appeared from 1813 onwards. James Scotland says that they took two forms, one of which originated in an unusual way. Following riots in Edinburgh on New Year's Day 1812 the clergy of the city decided to establish Sabbath schools in every parish but, knowing that pupils' ability to read would be of great help to anyone seeking to give religious instruction, they also decided to set up a central day school in the city to which each Sunday school might send five pupils for free teaching and ten more at a fee of 6*d*. per month, and later on an evening school, open from 8.00–10.00 p.m., was also established. The system was a good one which did much valuable work as it also spread to other cities, but Sessional schools could also take a more usual form: about 1843 the Kirk Session of St. Michael's, Linlithgow, decided that the Grammar School fees were beyond the reach of the more humble in the community. They leased premises for a school, engaged a teacher, paid his salary, arranged that he must charge fees which could be afforded by the less well-to-do and themselves paid the fees of $2^1/_2d$. per week for several poor children. This was a generous and practical action but as it meant competition with an established school, its kirk connection may have helped it to overcome any difficulties. Although this school was an ill-lit, ill-ventilated, one-apartment building in a back lane of the town, it was very good educationally and when by 1863 the Grammar School had lost its teacher and had to be closed, there were 230 boys attending it and it was felt that even if the Grammar School reopened, it would not attract more than 40–50 of these young-sters because of its higher fees. Obviously therefore the premises were too small and as the Kirk Session could not find anywhere else suitable to lease, they bought a site at a cost of £180 and considered spending about £400 on a building, proposing to borrow the whole amount on the security of the property and other lands they held and to repay this sum by saving on expenditure. This shows how strongly they felt about the need for education for all classes and how they were prepared to go out on a limb to achieve it. They were however advised to obtain Counsel's opinion as to whether or not what they proposed was within their powers as administrators of Kirk Session funds. They were told that if they wanted to devote such a large part of their funds to such a project, they should do so through a private Act of Parliament which would have been a major and rather daunting proceeding to undertake but within two days of this opinion being received, two members of the Session handsomely offered to relieve the Session of the purchase of the land already bought, take over the disposition in their own names, build the school there and allow the Session to rent it at a fair figure in the same way as they were doing with the existing school. Such an offer was even more fortunate for the Session than they realised at the time because, after the passing of the Education Act in 1872, the newly formed School Board asked the Session if they would transfer the school and land to the Board. As it did not belong to them, any potential conflict about the matter was avoided and the Session simply gave up the lease but did not forget at the same time to thank the men who had shown such generosity and helpfulness in the matter.[60]

Many poor children were far too busy working at home or, after the start of the Industrial Revolution, in factories to be able to go to school on weekdays and a solution was for them to go to Sabbath schools on Sunday evenings for both religious instruction and reading lessons. The earliest such school in Scotland is believed to have been established by the schoolmaster at Banchory-Devenick in 1782 and the idea quickly spread so that by 1790 there was one in Inveresk,

Midlothian, and only eight years thereafter, four in Inverness and one in Tain, Ross-shire. The General Assembly had some initial misgivings about these schools and in 1799 issued a report 'Concerning Vagrant Teachers and Sunday Schools' which stated that the Sunday School movement was hostile to the Established Church. If this was indeed ever so, it was quickly overcome and soon after 1800 the church was actively encouraging these schools. As already said, Edinburgh ministers were promoting the idea in 1813 as a form of Sessional School, New Statistical Accounts in the mid-nineteenth century refer to such schools existing under the patronage of Kirk Sessions, and Session accounts show practical help given too: 'Allowance for kindling fire for the Sabbath School' is just one example. Those teaching Sunday schools might be parish schoolmasters, and a willingness to undertake this extra task was a recommendation for any schoolmaster seeking a post; or it might be the minister, or local people 'bred up' to the work by his taking them for classes on weekdays. At Tain the Sunday School met from 6.00–8.00 p.m. and began with singing, prayers and reading, after which

> such as have made good progress . . . are to be employed for the improvement of themselves and others in reading audibly . . . and learning the Church tunes . . . In distributing books, regard is to be had to the scholars that behave well, and those that attend not with decency and in submission to the rules of the school are to be dismissed. The scholars are to attend upon public worship and through the whole of the Sabbath Day behave regularly and also during the week abstain from lying, cursing, quarrels, and other naughty practices. Complaints either of masters or of scholars are to be referred to the minister and he, if thought necessary, to call for the assistance of the magistrates . . .'

And that would have been by no means untypical. This particular school was financed by 'a charitable lady', Lady Ross Baillie, who paid the master a salary of £5 stg., provided free books and gave an allowance for coal and candles in the winter which was a great help to the Kirk Session. Some Sunday Schools, and this was one of them, were called Ragged Schools although this was not an accurate description of them.[61]

After the passing of the Education Act in 1872 which made elementary education compulsory, there was no further need for Sunday Schools to teach reading; thereafter they concentrated on religious instruction but managed at the same time to bring considerable enjoyment into drab lives. The minute book of Cambuslang Church Sabbath School begins in 1878 and records meetings, a soirée, a concert, and a New Year's Day treat in 1887 when it was planned 'to meet in the area of the church, to have some bright hymn singing, a song or reading if possible, and a few words from friends', and 'in retiring to get a card, an orange and some bun.' They must have expected a very high turn-out as not only was an appeal for the buns to be made from the pulpit but also through *Life and Work*. It is from such schools that the Sunday Schools of the present day have developed.[62]

Thanks to donations or legacies, Kirk Sessions sometimes found themselves administering educational funds. In 1753 when Viscount Stormont donated £200 of vacant stipend to augment the salary of the schoolmaster at Abernethy, Perth-shire, the Kirk Session when asked to do so unanimously agreed to accept the Trust and took upon themselves the handling of the fund and must have been only too delighted to have such financial strength to enable them to attract good teachers. A much larger and more demanding role fell to the Kirk Session of Dollar. In the early nineteenth century the minister was notified that Captain John MacNab had died leaving half the residue of his estate to the minister and church of the parish, the money to be invested to provide an income for a charity or for a school for the poor of the town. After consultation, this was accepted and the minister and Session found themselves governors and patrons of MacNab's School or Dollar Academy as it was called, which became an excellent school, attracting a large number of pupils who do not, however, seem necessarily to have been poor, although there were reduced fees for children of artisans and labourers who had been in the parish for three years. In one case a legacy came not to a Session, but to the minister and two lairds in the parish of Salton, East Lothian. It was left to them by Gilbert Burnett, Bishop of Salisbury, who became minister of Salton in 1665 but left in 1669 to occupy the chair of Theology at Glasgow, before moving south. He left 20,000 merks to the parish in gratitude for the kindness and encouragement he had received there but the legacy had interesting conditions. It was to be used for the education and clothing of thirty children 'of the poorer sort', for the erection of a new schoolhouse and a perpetual augmentation of the master's salary, for the increase of a library 'for the minister's house and use' and for the nec-essitous poor, the library having already been begun. For children to qualify for ad-mission to the fund, their parents had to have lived in the parish for not less than two years and to be nominated by the two lairds and the minister and each child could benefit from it for four years. Although the legacy placed all this in the hands of just three people, the Session must have been closely involved too as a list of the chil-dren's attendance at both school and church had to be accurately kept and if any great irregularity of either occurred without sufficient cause, the defaulter was either struck off the list or, as a reduced punishment, deprived of the clothing al-lowance given. In fact, only one or two instances of even the lesser penalty were ever imposed. So church-related was this legacy that even in the mid-nineteenth century the children benefiting from it were termed 'bishops' and the church gallery which they used was still at that time called the 'bishops' laft'. A considerable number of other Sessions found themselves handling a variety of school funding.[63]

An advanced level of education for which Kirk Sessions found themselves paying, even at an early stage, was that of the Presbytery Bursar. In 1641 an Act of the General Assembly ordered that every Presbytery with twelve ministers should maintain a bursar of Divinity, in other words provide a divinity student's scholar-ship. Where a Presbytery consisted of fewer than twelve ministers, then it was expected to join up with another larger one to make two. This Act was repeated in 1644 and 1645 when it was decreed that every bursar should receive £100 Scots yearly, over £8 stg., which was more or less what many qualified schoolmasters were being paid many years later. The money to support the bursar came from each parish, out of kirk penalties in proportion to the number of communicants, and entries about sending in this money to the Presbytery appear in Kirk Session records from all round the country. Things could however work both ways and the Kirk Session of North Berwick in 1695 received back from the Presbytery collector the sum of £11 collected for poor students as they had not found a use for it that year. The bursary system was particularly directed towards the Highlands and Islands because of the backward state of those Gaelic-speaking areas. The elimination of Gaelic was, as has been said, one of the early although unsuccessful objects of education in the highlands and presumably it was a desire that at least the gentry should learn English that had prompted the Assembly to pass an Act in 1646 which required all gentlemen living in these parts who could manage it, to send at least their eldest sons to be 'bred in the inland'. In spite of that, the Assembly that year also ordered a ministry of men able to speak Gaelic to be planted in the Highlands and Islands which was in keeping with an Act of Parliament of 1644 ordering vacant stipends in the highlands to be used to educate Gaelic-speaking youths, which was extended to Argyllshire in 1661. It was obvious that no one could profit from listening to preaching in an unintelligible tongue and the hope was that these young men would ultimately enter the ministry in Gaelic-speaking areas. Although Gaelic was forbidden to be used for some years after the Stuart risings, the kirk took a practical view and when it legally could it helped not only bursars, who were young men of promise, but also other Gaelic speakers, as when 10s. Scots was given by one Session 'to a poor scholar to buy him ane Irish Psalm Book'.[64] Synods were allowed to make variations in arrangements to do with bursary money and in 1730 that of Lothian and Tweeddale ordered the Presbytery of Dunbar to pay their 'burse' to a lowland bursar and the Presbytery of Haddington to pay theirs, which had formerly been divided between highland and lowland students, to Lithuanian ones instead.[65]

Provision of Bibles and Psalm books by Kirk Sessions to needy people has already been mentioned, provision which was in keeping with the Presbyterian belief in the value not only of being able to read but having suitable reading matter. In 1704 the General Assembly passed an Act for providing libraries in the highlands, following a move by various well-disposed people in both Scotland and England towards this end. The books that were provided were divided by decision of the Assembly into two types of library, Presbyterial and parochial. Inverness, for instance, received one of the first category and three of the second. Unfortunately the plan was too ambitious and by 1709 it was found impossible to supply sufficient books for all the highland Presbyteries and the Assembly recommended that those which received none should raise money for libraries themselves. Between 1739–47 an Orkney parish was sending £1 10s. annually 'to the use of the Library in Kirkwall', payments always made in conjunction with their contribution to the salary of the Presbytery Clerk and so almost certainly their donations to a Presbyterial library, in accordance with the recommendation of the Assembly. The Presbytery of Tain reacted to the Assembly's suggestion by requesting all its ministers to ask the gentlemen in their parishes to help to provide libraries and they did achieve a Presbyterial one but unfortunately the minister of Tain, who acted as librarian, was so inefficient that he kept losing the books. He must have been thankful for the 1715 uprising which provided him with the excuse that in moving books about from place to place for safety, some had got lost, an excuse which was accepted. Certainly these troubles undoubtedly harmed some libraries: in 1718 the General Assembly's advice and agreement had to be sought in connection with a process instituted by the Presbytery of Dingwall for recovering payment for the Presbyterial Library and two parochial ones, destroyed in what was termed 'the late unnatural rebellion'.[66] Parochial libraries came under the direction of individual Kirk Sessions. At the outset, in the highlands anyway, they appear to have been no more than a box of books — but what books! The first minute in the oldest records of the parish of Lairg, before 6 May 1707, gave an idea of just what such an early parochial library consisted — 11 folio volumes, seven of them in Latin, and 7 quarto volumes of which three were in Latin, leaving only 8 books available to those who only understood English or Gaelic. The titles of only a few show that the content of this literature was of a most improving nature:

The Book of Psalms	Jewell's Apology against Papists
Braye's Cathechetical Lectures	Hammond's Practical Catechisme
Allan and Kettlewell's Select Discourses	Riveli Cathol: Orthodoxus
Calvini Institue: Religionis Christianae	Johannis Rossini: Antiquitat

Lloyd's *Chronology*, on the science of computing time, was also included and at a time when technical information on this type of thing was not readily available, it must have been of great interest to those capable of absorbing it. In 1713 this box of books was sent to the parish of Kildonan, the minister there having 'represented the need that the paroch of Kildonan hade of a box of books, being one of the longest and most remote in the country, and therefore craved that the Presbytery might bestow the box which was at Larg on the sd paroch of Kildonan.' A very much later minister of Lairg commented, 'The Lairg people had either finished with the books or failed to appreciate them, so they were allowed to be sent to enlighten the regions about Kildonan. Whether the Kildonan people greatly advanced their learning by means of the Lairg books I do not know but — always excepting the Psalm book — Lairg did not seem to suffer much by their removal.'[67]

In the nineteenth century, parish libraries of a different calibre appear in many Kirk Session records. These references may appear as nothing more than a donation of 10s. or so to the library or paying a similar amount for its books or they may show considerable Sessional involvement. The minute book of St. Monance Kirk Session for October 1849 includes the report of the auditors on, among much else, the parish library begun there in June 1843. There were 221 books, not all of them those originally acquired as some had had to be replaced, and the following extract shows that there was a small charge made for use of the books, which must have varied from year to year or according to what was borrowed:

Year	No of readers	Money
1843	63	£1 0s. 8d.
1844	55	£1 13s. 0d.
1845	45	£1 3s. 8d.
1846	43	£1 2s. 5d.
1847	49	£1 3s. 9d.
1848	55	£1 5s. 1d.[68]

At Evie and Rendall, Orkney, the Kirk Session paid allowances in the 1840s to the two librarians and also provided two copies of the *Scottish Christian Herald* for the Parochial Library and in January 1843 were able to show a credit balance of £3 18s. after paying these expenses. A very different picture appears, however, in the minutes of the College Church Kirk Session, Glasgow, which show that the treasurer reported receiving £27 from the General Session to help in the establishment of a Parochial Library and a committee was appointed to see to things — but a year later the committee had still not reported. Were there more urgent things to see to or was there little demand there for library services or were the members of that Kirk Session less interested than others were in different areas?[69]

It cannot have been easy to deliver books to libraries in outlying areas and childishness on the part of a minister did not help: in 1730 the minutes of the Presbytery of Mull show that when a minister had gone from Coll to Harris eighteen years previously, he had taken the library with him because he had not been paid for his expenses in bringing the books to Coll. To pay carriage all over again because he had not been paid for it in the first instance, seems an odd piece of reasoning but it may be that he found the books of great interest himself. This particular library was one of a number provided by the SPCK and luckily the minister's action was almost certainly unique.[70]

Thus, as time went on, education in the form of schools and Sunday schools, bursaries and libraries kept on improving but the Disruption of 1843 had a dramatic effect on the church's influence upon it. Not only did ministers leave the Church of Scotland to join the Free Church but schoolmasters did too and as a result were deposed from their offices. This did not greatly affect the children of Free Church households as that church, seeking to provide employment for ousted schoolmasters and aware of children's needs, established many schools. Furthermore, Free Church parents in the enthusiasm of the moment were more than usually anxious for their young to be educated. Children of families which remained within the Church of Scotland were more likely to be adversely affected, as parish schools were left without teachers just as pulpits were left with no ministers, and depleted and demoralised Kirk Sessions had to start all over again to find schoolmasters for empty schools. In cases where a Free Church schoolmaster retained possession of a school after dismissal and civil force had to be used to evict him — Contin, Ross-shire, was one parish where this happened — this must have caused very bad feeling as well as a lot of speculation and unfortunate talk.[71]

But still more changes for Scottish education were in the air and by 1851 the church was taking steps to oppose the Education Bill of Viscount Melgund, MP for Greenock, and a petition which was prepared shows why the church was so concerned. It stated that the church regarded parish schools as part of the ecclesiastical establishment of Scotland and that the trial of schoolmaster's qualifications, their admission and the superintendence of schools had been in kirk hands since the system had been established. Furthermore, it was felt that the proposed reform of parish schools would abolish the cheap and efficient system of education which had done so much to elevate the intellectual, religious and moral condition of the people. This petition was sent round the country for approval by Kirk Sessions and signed by all males over fourteen years of age who were connected with a congregation. In 1855 Kirk Sessions were again dealing with draft petitions against the proposed Bill but in 1861 when something different, the Parochial and Burgh Schoolmasters Act, was passed it did not make any drastic alterations so far as the work of Kirk Sessions was concerned although it abolished Presbytery supervision and the examination of schoolmasters was transferred to the university of the bounds.[72]

What really did affect the kirk's role in education was the Education (Scotland) Act, 1872, which took elementary education out of the care of the kirk and placed it in the hands of Parochial School Boards, at the same time making it free and compulsory. Like the Parochial Boards which took over the care of the poor in 1845, the new School Boards expected to have existing school property transferred to them. How the Session at Linlithgow were saved trouble and disputes about this in 1872 because their school was leased and not owned, has already been mentioned. They were very lucky because many Kirk Sessions, as had happened with poor's funds in 1845, had to go to great trouble to get things right, sometimes having to seek expert advice as to the legality of what was asked of them and what they might or might not do. An example of what happened was when the Kirk Session of Cromarty met with the School Board in June 1873 'anent the disposal of the Sessional School Funds which the Session hold as Trustees', as a result of which the following queries were sent to the Lord Advocate:

> 1. Can the School Board under the Education (Scotland) Act 1872 legally claim the Heritable property and the funds . . . from the Kirk Session of Cromarty, who are the Trustees of said funds . . .?
> 2. Have the Kirk Session the power to hand over to the School Board the Fund and Heritable property in their hands for educational purposes and, if so, from whom should they receive a legal discharge?
> 3. [If so] . . . have the Kirk Session the power to attach conditions on their handing over to the School Board?

Both Session and Board agreed to abide by the Lord Advocate's opinion. Unfortunately that opinion does not appear in the records but things must have gone smoothly as some four months later the minister proposed that two members of the new School Board, who had formerly 'complied with the rules of membership, as contained in the Deed of Constitution of the Sessional School Society' should be appointed managers of the school, along with members of the Session, which was agreed. The property and funds were handed over 'on the understanding that a valid Discharge be granted to the Managers of the Session School by said School Board freeing and relieving said School Managers from liability of every kind, in respect to and in consequence of said transference.'[73]

For three hundred years Kirk Sessions had struggled beyond the call of duty or legal requirement to achieve elementary education for all but when at last it came, through this Act of Parliament, they both won and lost as it effectively stripped them of direct supervision of schools and greatly reduced their impact on the lives of the people. The Act did, however, guarantee religious instruction to children unless their parents objected and, in rural areas especially, ministers and elders, as at Cromarty, continued to exert an influence as school managers and members of School Boards although even this was much diminished by further Acts of Parliament to do with local government in 1918 and 1929. During this time, however, church influence had helped the establishment of teacher training colleges which remained under church control until 1906. Nowadays, while ministers may help with religious instruction in schools, Kirk Sessions themselves are no longer officially involved with state education at parish level. Nevertheless, an article in *Life and Work* in November 1989 makes the kirk position clear; its Committee on Education keeps watch on state education on the Church's behalf: 'Its interest encompasses but is not limited to religious education, and it is in frequent contact with the Government. Representatives are appointed to Regional and Islands Education Authorities, to college of education governing bodies and to the General Teaching Council. The committee works closely with other Scottish churches.' That is a wide-ranging remit.

7

Such Good and Christian Works

'So good a work and Christian a purpose' was the wording used when the kirk was being asked to help nationally with building a bridge over the River Clyde at Lanark in the late seventeenth century. This phrase truly represented the church's feeling towards the need for water crossings and was a main cause for Kirk Sessions getting involved with public works at both local and national level. Access to church, as well as to schools, was a major reason for local bridge building because for some reason many parish churches are sited close to rivers or sizeable streams and how to get people over them to attend worship or to serve discipline was of great concern to many Sessions. When some Coldingham elders were told in 1701 to find out why so many people from one part of the parish were not coming to church, it was discovered that the reason was lack of a bridge, but the people of Applecross must have been much hardier because, even as late as 1836, while some did not attend worship because the church was near a river with no bridge, a good number waded across and then sat in church wet through, 'which no doubt,' said the minister, 'occasions many serious complaints amongst them.' The problem could work both ways and in the spring of 1721 when there were two successive Sundays when one parish had no services it was because the minister was 'barred by the water'. The fact that a delinquent couple's excuse that 'the water was not passable' was readily accepted as a valid reason for not appearing before their Session shows how greatly water was regarded as a restraint.[1]

To take local bridges first — an obvious form of early water crossing was a ferry but until the late eighteenth century ferries did not normally operate on Sundays although, where there was no alternative, the kirk in some places provided boats or gave financial assistance towards their repair and maintenance, specifically so that they could bring people to church and children to school. A case of this happening was on the River Tyne in East Lothian where a ferry boat was established in 1637, its upkeep thereafter largely depending on Kirk Session support, with Magnus Clark the ferryman frequently coming to the Session to get money for 'beiting [supplying] the boat' or for such items as '3 pints tarr to lay on the boat'. The reasons for the Session's support of the boat and the conditions imposed on the ferryman were given in a minute which said that they had allowed him '3 lib Sc during the winter season for setting through . . . the poor of the parish on the Sabbath day, coming to sermon, and have strictly discharged the boatman that he set no bodie through the water on the Sabbath day in time of sermon or any other time of the day, as he will be answerable to them.' On Sundays, therefore, he was to take people across the water to and from church and nowhere else, but part of his work was helping to move poor strangers on and taking children to school. The parish of Banchory-Devenick was another where the Session paid for school children to be taken across a river in the early eighteenth century, very probably in what was referred to in 1728 as the 'kirk boat' which implies that it either belonged to the church or was primarily used for church purposes. This was the Session which decided, when the boat needed repairs in 1728, that the schoolmaster and the kirk officer should 'go to the towns on the North side of the water and gather up twenty shillings from each plough. And what should be wanting to be made up out of the box till the workman be satisfied.' Two years later more repairs were required and the Session minutes said,

> This day the Session finding that the kirk boat was ruinous and the people on the north side very much endangered in their passage to church and discouraged from attending public worship, finding also that Arthur Gibbon in Torry was content to repair the said boat and provide materials for twenty seven pounds ten shillings Sc, as appeared by his acco[t] after visiting the said boat, also finding that it had been usual for the Session upon such occasions to direct the reparation of the said boat, and to undertake for the payment till such time as it could be collected from the parishioners in the North side of the water, who are liable for the same, they did therefore agree to employ the said Gibbon for that effect foresaid, and recommend to the minister in his course of visitation to collect 2 shs and six pennies Sc from each principal tenant and 2 shs from each other person within the respective families on the North side of the water, it being found that this will very near amount to the sum demanded and the Session resolved to make up any small balance that should remain, also that due intimation be made of this Act, that so recusants, if any should be, may be prosecute before the judge competent.

The very next year, 1731, the boat fell victim to vandalism when 'an evil disposed person' pierced the bottom with a gimlet in several places but although the Session offered a reward of two guineas for information 'so as to convict the delinquent' this does not seem to have borne fruit and some three months later £9 10s. stg. was spent on a new boat. Even at the beginning of the nineteenth century, this Session was still concerned with provision of a boat: in 1806 the minister gave in receipted accounts from James Massie, a boat-builder, for the new one got the previous summer and for 'beating' her. A subscription towards the costs raised £8 6s. 10d. which left a balance of £2 14s. 8d. due by the treasurer to the minister. When one of Banchory-Devenick's various boats was 'carried away by a violent swaling water' in 1710 the Session gave £4 10s. for its salvage and twelve years later contributed £3 to rescue it from where it had been carried by 'the violence of spait water', but whether this was or became the 'kirk boat' of 1728 is not known. The Kirk Session of Fettercairn, Kincardine, gave £3 in 1730 towards replacement of a boat on the Northwater, and Coldingham Kirk Session contributed towards the 'making of a new boat on the New Water' because the old one had been 'broken' the previous winter and these donations, which would have been repeated in other parishes, eased people's lives greatly although the kirk had a strong vested interest.[2]

But boats were expensive, both in initial outlay and in running costs and it was far better, where practical, to provide a permanent water crossing. The most basic form of this was stepping stones. When one Session found in 1704 that 'the want of a bridge over the water proved a great hindrance to frequenting the church' they told two of the elders 'to cause stones to be layed in the water and them that layed them to be payed out of the box', an expense which came to 18s. Scots. Prior to 1766 Greenlaw Kirk Session's minutes show frequent entries 'for laying steps' through the River Blackadder 'in front of the manse', which gave access to the church as well, and the records of Roberton, Roxburghshire, also show that money was spent there 'for laying and keeping passable the steps of the water'. Unfortunately the spates which swept boats away could make stepping stones temporarily unusable too and a simple alternative was to throw a tree trunk over the water so that people could hop across on it, as Fala Kirk Session did to help children get to school. That such basic bridges were found satisfactory is evident from a request made to Morebattle Kirk Session in 1726 by some people in the parish for 'a tree to be laid over the water for convenient passage as they had been in use to do formerly' so as to cross the River Bowmont to get to church. A plank could do as well and in the parish of Edenkillie, Morayshire, that was what was put over a seven foot gap between two rocks on the River Findhorn; this was sufficient to enable the considerable number of people who lived on the west side of the parish, to attend worship.[3]

From the simplicity of a mere tree trunk or plank, Kirk Sessions gradually began to provide proper wooden bridges. The timber might have to be bought as whole trees and, if these were not available locally, then there was transport to be paid for in addition. In January 1731 Morebattle Kirk Session spent £7 16s. in this way, of which £3 was 'for the hire of a wain from Berwick with four trees for a bridge at Clifton and Attonburn.' It was a fortunate Session that had suitable trees in its own kirkyard which could be used but one wonders about the safety of the following bridge: '. . . the minister and Session resolved to cut down a tree in the kirk yard which was decaying for putting up a bridge upon the — gaing of Kinnell mill, and likewise that there should be a new tree planted in the kirkyard.' A few instances taken from just one Borders parish give a good idea of the work involved in seeing to water crossings and the care taken by Kirk Sessions:

1697. 7th November. 'Report that bridges over the burns in the parish was decayed . . . which was a great hindrance to people in repairing to the Kirk, and that it was the custom for the Session to uphold them, therefore appointed two ruling elders to agree with a workman for mending them.'

1698. 'This day payed to Patrick Lockie, wright, for making a new bridge on Langhope burn with mending the blindhaugh brig and for repairing that on the other Headshawburn £6 18s. Scots.'

1701. January. 'Reported that the bridge over Headshaw Miln Burne was now quite useless, ordered arrangements for a workman to repair it again.'

1704. November. 'Report that the bridge over Langhopeburn was greatly wasted and was a great hindrance to coming to church so ordered two elders to agree with a workman to by timber for repairing it, £7 16s. Scots.'[4]

Should a Session see a need for a bridge, one way to get it built was to put by a little money for it as and when they could afford to do so until they had enough to pay the cost. This is what happened at St. Vigeans in 1732. In April that year it was felt that £39 14s. Scots could be set aside and then in December a further £27 17s. 4d. was put by for a bridge. Whatever the primary reasons for kirk bridge-building, the spin-off social benefits to the community were very great, even if not to the poor specifically although it was from the poor's funds, in such cases, that the money was coming. But Session funds had so many claims upon them that an alternative and better course was for a special collection to be organised by the Session throughout the parish and it was a wise one that made do with whatever was raised: at Fettercairn, for instance, a collection for a bridge raised £6 and £6 was its cost. But things could not always work out so tidily and there might not be enough raised to pay for the work and then the extra might be borrowed from the poor's money and used for the bridge 'until it be gotten in other ways.' In Coldingham where, as has been said, lack of a bridge was preventing people from attending worship, it was stated that it was 'the earnest desire of many that a collection through the parish may be made for that effort, and that the Session would appoint the intimation' which they willingly did but very sensibly also told two of the elders to get the agreement of the landowner on whose property it was thought that the bridge should be built. Similar parish house-to-house collections were held elsewhere but very often special collections for bridges were made at church on Sundays, the equivalent of a modern retiring offering, as happened at Hownam, Roxburghshire, in 1738, about which the minutes say: 'Considering the ruinous condition of the bridge above the kirk, which is now rendered unfite for passengers, especially such as attend the ordinances, therefore, to remove the said inconveniency, the Session think it proper that intimation be made this day from the Desk that people according to their Several Abilities may give in their collections against next Lord's Day which shall be gathered att the Kirk door for rebuilding the said bridge that those that attend the Ordinances may both come to and go from the same at all possible Conveniency.' Unfortunately that is all the minutes say about this particular collection.[5]

Any narrow, hump-backed bridge close to a church is almost certainly one built in the seventeenth or early eighteenth centuries with money raised by public collections. A good and particularly noticeable example is at Stow, clearly visible from the A7 road, erected with collection money between 1654–55, and there are many others still to be seen. One at Keith seems to fulfil all these qualifications; according to legend, however, it was built in 1609 by Thomas Murray and his wife because, it is said, that they could not sleep either for the cries of people in trouble crossing the ford or because their son had been drowned there.[6]

Some parishes were fortunate enough to have bridges paid for out of vacant stipend. The Old or Cuddy Bridge at Innerleithen, Peebles-shire, is one of these. A rather intriguing case involving heritors and a bridge, but not a church one, occurred in Dollar in 1794. The Session received a minute from them asking for £10 or £12 of the poor's funds to pay part of the cost of building a wooden bridge at the Rack Miln 'as a prudent measure.' The Session agreed to give a total of £10 of which £8 was paid at once with the balance to be given when more funds came in. The reasons they gave for giving this money was that the sums subscribed for the bridge had proved insufficient and that 'by the conveniency of this bridge, the people on the south side of the Dovan will have more ready access to church whereby the collections at the church doors will be considerably augmented and a probability that in a very few years, that sum to be advanced by the Kirk Session will be reimbursed to the funds' and therefore it must be considered a 'proper and prudent measure.' There was not a word about the people getting to *worship*, just collections, and with the best will in the world, it is difficult not to feel that they were trying very hard to justify doing something the heritors wanted — access to a mill, after all, was very desirable — even although their funds were obviously fairly short.[7]

In some cases Sessions found themselves administering a bequest or donation to do with a bridge. Alexander Christie, a tenant in Cantley in the parish of Grange, Banffshire, built a bridge 'for the Glory of God and the good of the people of Grange' with the intention of making the church accessible to the people of Cantley, and lodged 100 merks Scots in the hands of a heritor, to be used at the direction of the Session for maintenance and repair of the bridge, a practical action although the sum appears from the records to have run out by 1740. In 1732 a tenant farmer in the parish of Edzell, James Black, built the Gannachie bridge over the River North Esk on the west side of the parish of Fettercairn, providing the materials and paying a mason 300 merks to do the main work although, being a handy kind of man, he built the parapets himself. In addition, he left 50 merks for upkeep of the bridge, this to be managed by the Session.[8]

Should the cost of a badly needed bridge be beyond the resources of a parish on its own, it became fairly common for help to be sought from neighbouring ones. About 1729 the minister of one wrote to the incumbent of nearby Fettercairn, 'craveing some supply' towards the construction of a bridge which obviously gave access to a church. The Session of Fettercairn 'taking the same into consideration and understanding the necessity thereof, and that it was already built, and being so pious a work' decided to give £4 Scots towards it. Where a bridge would be of general community benefit, even if not leading to a church, a Session might still be sympathetic and when James Guthrie who lived in the parish of Fettercairn petitioned the Session for help in 1773 to build a bridge 'anent the saw mill' he was given £1 Scots towards it. While the case of the Rack Miln in Dollar seems to have been bridge-building for the heritors' benefit, mills were very important in the rural economy, much frequented by the people and often useful as a distribution point for the poor's meal and it is little wonder that Sessions looked favourably on bridges leading to them. The Kirk Session of Rathven gave 7s. in 1728 for a bridge tree to put on a mill dam and it was at a mill that the decaying kirkyard tree, already mentioned, was to be put. In 1735 the minister of Stracathro and one of his parishioners, John Preshok 'of the market ford' together asked the Kirk Session of Fettercairn for a donation towards a wooden bridge at the ford because it was 'on the public road between Fettercairn and Brechin, very useful for such as travel on foot that way.' It so happened that Fettercairn Kirk Session were already short of money just then because there were many poor on the roll but they considered the project so worthwhile that they arranged to have a collection jointly for the bridge and for a particularly necessitous family and when some £12 Scots was raised, about a fifth was allocated to the bridge and the rest given to the needy family.[9]

That was local bridge building but it was not just neighbouring parishes which sought help to erect bridges to give access to churches. Instructions for special collections for these often came from the General Assembly. One of these occurs in the records of Craig Kirk Session in 1723 when by Act of Assembly a collection was intimated for 'building a brig for making a convenient passage to and from the churches of Lethnot and Navar', but when a bridge was thought to be of very great importance nationally, then the church found itself co-operating in nationwide fund-raising. This was because the church was the only national organisation which could be called upon for this and therefore Parliament often ordered, with the encouragement of the General Assembly, special Sunday collections, usually throughout Scotland but occasionally confined to a specific area such as 'south of the Forth'. Parishes were expected to comply even though the object of the collection might have nothing to do with church life and the bridge, or indeed any other public works, might be at a great distance from them and of no interest to them either. It was through such collections that bridges were built at such places as Linton and Leith in 1668, at Coldstream in 1671, at Inverness in the 1680s, at Dumbarton in 1683, the Bridge of Dye in 1688, over the Clyde at Lanark in the 1690s, over the Teviot at Ancrum, Roxburghshire, in 1798, and many more. These were at least on the mainland but how sympathetic could mainland parishes have been to a General Assembly edict for a national collection for the Bridge of Strong in Shetland in 1715 and how did island parishes feel when the boot was on the other foot? Undoubtedly the parish of Kirkwall in Orkney did very well to raise £10 8s. Scots by a church door collection in 1724 for a bridge at Berriedale, Caithness. Once a bridge was built, national collections might still have to be sought for its upkeep — one example is the bridge built at Leith in 1668 which needed repair in 1717, something for which the parish of Banff, many miles away, raised £6 10s. Scots. The degree of co-operation on the part of local kirks and of generosity on the part of the people was truly remarkable.[10]

There was another way in which the church in Scotland contributed towards bridge building and that was through the accepted custom of lending the poor's money at interest to individuals or to public bodies such as bridge trustees. Those, for example, of Kelso Bridge borrowed in 1756 from the Kirk Session of Bowden, Roxburghshire, with repayment to be made thirteen years later.[11]

As the church was willing to organise collections to help to build bridges, especially those giving access to worship, it follows that support was also given to erect church buildings. In 1697 there was a collection for putting up a church at Queensberry, Dumfries-shire; in 1717 for one in the parish of St. Ninian's, Stirlingshire; for one at Livingstone in the Presbytery of Linlithgow in 1720; and for a church in the large parish of Lairg in 1723 while, the previous year, contributions had been sought for an additional church in the parish of Durness which was fifty by thirteen miles in area. A practical little slant appears in the minutes of a Session which in 1730 contributed to the construction of an aisle for the kirk of Slammanan, Stirlingshire, but did so with a reservation, requiring a receipt stating that the money was to be refunded 'if the erection go not on in three years space.'[12] Furthermore, while the kirk did not like those who dissented from its own practices, it nevertheless gave encouragement and help to those who dissented outwith Scotland, usually by raising money for building meeting houses in England and Ireland. Protestant congregations abroad received a lot of support from the Church of Scotland, mainly for building of churches. Many records refer to collections made for the church in Konisberg in Prussia, a reformed church where, owing to the trade existing between Scotland and the Baltic ports in the sixteenth and seventeenth centuries, Scots formed a large part of the worshippers. Among others to receive assistance were the Protestant church in Lavonia and a church and school at Breslau.[13]

Not only church buildings but also people from other countries received a great deal of support from Scotland if they were of the right denomination. In 1718 the General Assembly ordered a collection to be held for the 'distressed and persecuted Protestants in Lithuania' at a time when that country was ravaged by famine and disease. The following year money was being collected for 'our distressed Protestant brethren in Franconia, in Germany' and in 1721 it was the turn of French Protestants in Saxony; four years later the General Assembly recommended a collection for a colony of French refugees there while in 1729 and 1730 there was yet another collection, this time for the 'distressed French and German church in Copenhagen'. Nor was it just to Europe that the kirk looked. In 1724 there was a contribution for building a church 'for our brethren' in New York and the following year another 'for relief of the Presbyterians in New York' while in 1752 there was still another 'for the foreign Protestants in our plantations in North America'. Occasionally money might be sent to an individual foreign Protestant, such as Anastasius Camnenus, 'a distressed Waldensian minister', for whom a collection was made in 1656.[14]

Coming back to Scottish public works, road-making also benefited from special collections made through churches and although these were not so common as for bridge-building, several south-of-Scotland Kirk Session minutes refer to 'an Act of Council ordering a Voluntar contribution towards making an Highway through Looher-moss' — Lochar moss in Dumfries-shire — 'to be collected the next Lord's Day.' Another collection which seems to have been similar but within a smaller area was one in the seventeenth century for the repair of Kirk Street in Dingwall. Where there was already access of whatever sort it was important to maintain it if not to construct it and a threat to close a right of way to St. Cuthbert's Church, Edinburgh, made the Session take the matter in 1722 to the Court of Session where they won and when, later, access was again threatened in a way which would have affected a substantial number of the congregation, the Session again took it to the Court of Session with the result that the person wanting to close the access had to open a gate for specified hours daily. It cost the kirk £50 stg. to fight this case but the sum was made up by voluntary contributions. In 1831 Mr Murray, a heritor in the parish of Nigg, Ross-shire, closed an old and much used right of way to the church and elsewhere and allowed a certain amount of intimidation to be used on anyone attempting to use it — one of his employees threatened to shoot three men he found on it. After this, several fishermen came to the Session, asking for certificates of poverty so that they could sue over the road closure and as the Session regarded this 'shutting up, ploughing, ditching and rendering impassable in the most oppressive and unwarrantable manner the Church, Funeral, market, School, Ferry and Public road leading through the lands of Pitcalzean from the church of Nigg to the Ferry of Cromarty' as a very serious matter, they granted the certificates and took action themselves. This caused a very difficult situation in the parish, far beyond what the fishermen had initiated, so difficult in fact that the Session 'judged it expedient to put off the administration of the Lord's Supper' because of the 'present state of the parish in consequence of the harassing persecutions of the Minister, Elders and Session Clerk and many others, by some of the Heritors.' This harassment was because the Session had decided to petition both the Lord Advocate and the General Assembly to grant aid to the oppressed people of the parish by maintaining their right to the road. The heritors counter-attacked by having a summons served on the minister, elders and Session Clerk requiring the Session minutes to be made available to them immediately so that they could discover how the poor's fund was administered, failing which there was a threat of imprisonment, at which the Session made a statement to be presented to the Sheriff justifying all that they had done. Neither the result of this dispute nor the fishermen's case are given in the minutes but as the Lord's Supper was celebrated shortly afterwards, it appears that things must have settled down and when the cholera outbreak of 1832 started the following year, everyone had to pull together for the common good which was a well-disguised blessing.[15]

This was a remarkable case of the Kirk Session having to fight opposition and intimidation in order to protect the rights of the people and to enable them to maintain access to worship, but such concern was understandable. In a surprisingly advanced concern for communications, however, the Kirk Session of St. Andrews got involved with a very early postal service with their minutes for 5

April 1645 saying, 'This day, with consent of the whole session was ordained ane post to travell to the north to Aberdeen and pairt yr away when the Magistrates shall be pleased to direct him to bring intelligence here and agreed to contribute thr shilling about for that end to any post whom the Magistrates shall be pleased to direct yr unto.'[16]

As fishing gradually developed, as well as trade with other countries, so harbours became important and in this context too Scotland relied on the kirk to organise collections for their construction and repair. In 1682 the Berwickshire parish of Bonkle and Preston was one of those collecting for the harbour of Roseheartie in Aberdeenshire and the very next year the people there were busy collecting money for repairing the harbour at Aberdeen and raised the sum of 42*s*. Scots although in Banffshire the Moderator of the Presbytery of Fordyce was still telling the brethren that autumn to 'mind' about this collection. As with other public works, some harbours needed more than one collection and so minutes may show that while a collection was, for instance, recommended by Synod for building and repairing the harbour at Eyemouth, Berwickshire, in 1677 'by an Act of His Majesty's Secret Council', yet in 1701 funds were still being sought, even in Orkney, for this Berwickshire port. In 1670 'an inundation of the sea' destroyed Anstruther's harbour and 'chocked' it up and with the bulwarks washed away, many of the nearby houses became unsafe. It appears that it was this disaster which led in 1688 to voluntary contributions being called for at kirks nationwide to repair the damage.[17] In 1647 the parishioners of St. Cuthbert's Church, Edinburgh, collected 525 merks for the people of Orkney who were suffering from a local famine which shows a proper awareness of the sufferings caused by a scarcity. Even during times of national famines, however, public works still went on and collections for them continued so that in 1695, early in the Seven Years' Famine, Parliament ordered a collection for building a harbour at Cullen, Banffshire, and the order was carried out in spite of the fact that Kirk Sessions were sorely pressed to deal with their own hungry people. To some extent, however, this problem could be solved by deducting and keeping back from such a collection what would have been the normal Sunday's giving for the poor. During that famine, Banff's harbour needed money and in 1697 Inverness was a parish which held not one but two collections for it, raising over £44 Scots, and in fact this was a cause which was still having collections made for it in 1701, and yet again in 1728. The Seven Years' Famine was barely over before the Privy Council passed an Act for a contribution for the harbour of Lossiemouth and although the Kirk Session of St. Nicholas Church, Aberdeen, had had to close their poor's roll the previous year owing to shortage of funds, they still contributed to this request. It is very probable that this famine showed how valuable harbours could be when there was a need to distribute food around the country but, that apart, when money was needed for public works, it was always to the kirk that the authorities turned. One 'public work' that was surely not essential but was undoubtedly popular was a seventeenth century collection for the 'bruse' or brewhouse of Alness which was discussed by a highland Presbytery with the result that the brethren, considering the usefulness of the work 'promptly promised' to contribute towards it.[18]

It was not just for desirable public works that collections were called for or donations given but also when disasters occurred which left people in distress and hardship. When there was a severe flood in the town of Hawick in 1767 an appeal brought in generous help from elsewhere and money was also raised throughout Scotland in 1764 for 'John Graham, a great sufferer by the inundation of water in England December last.' The help given directly by Sessions to their own parishioners suffering loss by fire has already been mentioned but Sessions often looked beyond their own boundaries and joined in collections, possibly just among one or two Presbyteries or counties, to help fire victims. Thus Greenlaw Kirk Session in Berwickshire was one of those contributing to people suffering as a result of a fire in Yetholm, Roxburghshire, in 1720; in Duns, Berwickshire, in 1723; and in Kelso, Roxburghshire, in 1730, all of them within a radius of some twenty miles, and St. Boswells raised £1 10s. in 1747 to help after a fire in Ashkirk, in the neighbouring county of Selkirkshire. For greater fire disasters, collections were officially called for on a wider scale, such as one in 1623–24 for Dunfermline, Fife, which was in a 'pitifull stait'; in 1652 the General Assembly recommended charity to be given 'to the distressed people of Glasgow' owing to a fire there. In one part of Ross-shire this was a collection which came in 'bot slowe speide' but was eventually gathered in. Assistance for Glasgow was again called for in 1679, again because of fire, and help was sought for Kelso when the whole town was burnt in 1645 as a result of cleansing a house with fire during an outbreak of plague — 'clenging of ane of the houses thereof whilk was infected with the plague.' The following year the town of Cullen was 'utterlie burnt by the rebels', these rebels being Montrose's men who devastated the town when the people opposed him on his march through the northern counties; and a fire in Cupar, Fife, in 1669 ruined many people and reduced them to begging, with the result that the Privy Council ordered a collection in that and the adjoining counties.[19]

Obviously it took time to arrange for such collections to be held and then to gather the money in and this must have caused great problems to people in need when there was no other form of public relief. When fire broke out in the Canongate in Edinburgh in 1709, some of the money raised in distant parts of Scotland could not be delivered until ministers going to the General Assembly in Edinburgh the following year could take it with them, and in the same way, it was 1670 before a collection was completed for the benefit of 120 families made homeless and living in the fields after a fire in Kilmarnock two years before. Where immediate help was needed it was sensible to advance money already collected for something less urgent; when Kelso was again burnt in 1684 and public assistance was called for, Hawick was one place where there was money available which had been raised for prisoners of the Turks — of which more later — and this was sent at once to relieve Kelso, although a collection was still held for that town, with the intention that what had been taken from the fund intended for the Turks' prisoners should be deducted from the Kelso collection. What was not ethical, of course, was to divert money collected specifically for one cause to another, with no intention of making it good as was done by one Session whose minutes in 1736 say: 'The Session appoints the minister to pay the expenses of the windows and other things done about the school house out of the collection gathered for the harbour of St. Andrews, it being yet in his own hands undelivered up', but even if this smacks of malpractice, they probably felt that the condition of their own parish schoolhouse was of much greater importance than a harbour miles away.[20] An explosion rather than a fire produced a most unusual accident for which a large-scale collection was held in the 1690s. Robert Davidson, a merchant in Ellon, Aberdeenshire, was in the habit of storing gunpowder in his house for a regiment of dragoons but by mischance it was kindled and blew up, the house was demolished, a soldier and several of his servants were killed but he, with his wife and children, were 'wonderfully preserved, being blown up to the top of the house altogether and there saved by the feather bed qrupon they were lying.' Did any of the collection perhaps go to the families of those killed in this accident? That is not known. In another fire tragedy, in Ireland, a man died along with two of his children and all the family goods were lost but 'several papers subscribed by people of credit' were sent to Kirk Sessions, recommending his widow and five surviving children to charity, they 'having been in opulent circumstances previously.'[21]

The need to ransom prisoners of the Turks was at one time a fairly common reason for holding public collections. These ransom demands in the seventeenth and early eighteenth centuries were the equivalent of those of twentieth century hijackers but appear to have been far more successful. Piracy was a flourishing trade at that time, with the seas between Scotland and Ireland a favourite area where the ships of any nationality were pursued, plundered and their crews captured and then tortured or killed or sold into slavery. An island on the south-west of Ireland seems to have been a pirate station and these marauders also haunted the western isles of Scotland. The villains of the piece were probably Algerian but were often referred to as Turks and the only hope of rescue from them or from resultant slavery was through the efforts of the church. In 1626 there was an intimation in Falkirk for money 'for the relief . . . of those tane be the Turks' while in 1674 the Privy Council recommended that a charitable collection should be taken up at every church for the relief of Walter Gibson, a skipper from Inverkeithing, and his mate, John Reid, who were prisoners of the Turks and reported to be 'in a miserable and pitiful condition and who are to be ransomed and relieved for no lesse than 500 or 600 dollars apiece . . .' Collections were ordered in 1679 for people from Pittenweem, Fife, and 1682 saw another public appeal for yet more Scots in the hands of the Turks. One which was widely made 'for some Inverness men in slavery among the Sallymen' in 1720 did not have to be sent on as for some reason the men were freed without ransom. These examples are just the tip of an iceberg; an idea of just how frequently such calls for help might be made comes from the records of just one Session, the coastal parish of Dunbar, when in 1723 alone they contributed five times for victims of the Turks or for their needy families:

1723, January 9. 'To three men barbarously treated by the Algerians, 6s.'
April 6. 'To two poor men taken by the Turks, 8s.'
July 15. 'To a passenger taken by the Turks, 4s.'
Sept. 13. Two separate entries on the same day of help 'To a poor man who had his son taken by the Turks.'[22]

A more casual attitude was taken by another Session in 1735 when they agreed to make a collection for the redemption of a man named William Dowell, a slave in Algiers, 'as soon as convenient' but a fierce reaction was shown by Dumbarton Kirk Session in 1621 to a man who admitted that, in a temper, he had cursed the Turks for 'no deteinning and holding' a particular sailor with the rest of the crew; for saying this, he had to stand barefoot and barelegged, wearing a hair gown, on the following Sunday, firstly outside the kirk door and then inside the church during preaching.[23]

Some donations to victims of the Turks may have been on a purely local basis on their return home and certainly the Dunbar donations sound as if this were the case. Other examples of this include the payment of 2s. 10d. paid by the Kirk Session of Rathven to 'a distressed seaman who had his tongue cut out by the Turks' and another of 2s. paid to a man whose tongue had been cut out 'by the Algerines'. Mutilation of their captives in this way seems to have been a favourite practice of the Turks but they may have done even worse to them than that if the report of a 'poor seaman all mangled by the Turks' is anything to go by. It must have been very heart-warming for a Presbytery to be thanked for their efforts on behalf of victims of the Turks, as happened in Peebles-shire with Duncan Mhor, redeemed from slavery, coming before the Presbytery to express his gratitude for their help, although his companion had died. It has been suggested, however, that sometimes people who found themselves in adverse circumstances would make out that they had been abroad and had suffered at the hands of the Turks as a way of getting charity. It was a good hard-luck tale but one which, though accepted at face value, may on occasions have raised suspicions: when one Session gave money to what they called 'a Vallachian youth' the minutes put the words 'he said' in brackets at the end of his account of being 'plundered by sea pirates and put on shore, stripped of his clothes.' Even the case of a poor stranger who arrived in Abernethy, Perthshire, with a story of his house having been burnt and who was therefore given 12s. on the minister's orders makes one wonder, with hindsight, whether his tale was true or whether he found it a good line to take in seeking help. Giving help to recognised Protestant causes abroad has been mentioned already and it was good, but there must be some suspicion about certain of the foreign 'Christians' who came to Scotland seeking financial assistance. When the Privy Council ordered a collection to be taken at all churches for Mercurias Lascaris, a clergyman in the Greek Church, so that he could pay the ransom of his brother and children held captive in Algiers, the ministers of the Presbytery of Fordyce reported that he had come round their manses himself and they had given their collections to him directly, and there is certainly an impression of over-eagerness on his part.[24]

Could there have been any con-men among the following: Constantine Achilles, a Grecian gentleman persecuted by the Turks for professing Christianity, who was recommended for charity by the Privy Council; Christian Fandi, a converted Turkish Mahometan, for whom the General Assembly asked a contribution in 1733; Mr Paul Shalitti, a converted Jew recommended to its Presbyteries by the Synod of Aberdeen in 1699; 'an Arabian Christian' who appeared in 1723; 'Christian Hussein a native Turk converted to the Christian religion' and put forward by the General Assembly for charity in the early 1730s? There was 'a prince's son in Syria' who appeared in Govan in 1738 seeking money to help him ransom his father from the Turks and in the early eighteenth century a quorum of Hawick Kirk Session gave £3 to a 'Christian Prince from Ciria'. Could it have been the same man? One can well imagine the excitement that the arrival of a foreign prince would cause in a small town but it is worth noting that it was a quorum, not the whole Session, which gave him this generous donation. As late as 1772, 'Solomon, an Arabian Christian, recommended by the Patriarch of Jerusalem' was on the move and receiving money as he went — one writer refers to him as 'the enterprising Solomon'. In 1696 the General Assembly decreed that no minister, Session or elder, Presbytery or Synod should give recommendations for charity to anyone outside their respective bounds and in 1710 ordered no petitions for charity to be sent to or considered by the Assembly unless the petitioners produced ample evidence of their life and conduct and that they were truly objects of charity. Although this was largely meant to cover the swarms of beggars who have already been mentioned as haunting the country, it also shows that there was some concern about the validity of certain claims for help from other people who would not regard themselves as ordinary beggars, and in many of these claims from foreigners it was impossible to check the truth of their statements nor the honesty of any recommendations they might bring from abroad.[25]

Various collections have been referred to in other chapters, such as those for widows and orphans after disasters at sea and for those suffering as a result of war and there is no doubt that the church's generosity was wide-ranging. In 1827 Kirk Sessions were organising help 'for the distressed operatives in the manufacturing districts' and in 1785 there were collections to pay for the translation and printing of an Old Testament in Gaelic. Where there was need, then the kirk was ready to help and an excellent account of charity work done by the church appears in George A. Henderson's *Kirk of St. Ternan, Arbuthnott*.[26]

8

Half horrible, half noble

When people consider the early days of the Reformed church in Scotland, they are apt to think immediately of the cutty stool and public rebukes before the congregation and the sheer horror of these but these were late and, in fact, mild forms of the disciplines and punishments available to the kirk and used by it in earlier days.

By the time of the Reformation, the Roman Catholic church had become very corrupt. The people disregarded religious principles, cared little for the Sabbath as such and were really emerging from a state of near-barbarity. The Reformers' attitude to such a state of things was clear: 'As no commonwealth can flourish or long endure without good laws and sharp execution of the same; so neither can the kirk of God be brought to purity, neither yet be retained in the same, without order of ecclesiastical discipline.' The church interpreted ecclesiastical discipline as including religious living and considered that it had a duty to raise standards nationally in all respects of everyday life. At that time both civil and criminal laws were weak and unless there was a body able to implement them, they were of little effect. Ecclesiastical law was the only one that appeared capable of enforcement and it must have been an awareness of this fact that led Parliament in 1592, the year when Presbyterian government was legally established, to decree that elders in addition to purely ecclesiastical functions should attend to maintenance of discipline. In towns there were burgh councils and magistrates to deal with such matters but Kirk Sessions, to some extent in towns but certainly in rural areas, became under this Act the only body, as opposed to individual heritors, with power to control and direct local affairs. Strictly speaking, heritable jurisdictions gave heritors great powers also until these were abolished in 1747 but these do not seem to have caused any conflict — burghs, heritors and kirk were all united in anxiety to keep order, even if from different motives. So it was that discipline became such a prominent part of the work of Kirk Sessions that their minute books were sometimes known as Discipline Books or the 'Register of Discipline' or 'The Minute Book of Discipline.'[1]

Ministers regarded one of their major duties as 'taking order' with local trans-gressors and Kirk Session records are full of testimony to their and their elders' work in this respect. The result has been described as 'an oligarchic tyranny of the most inquisitorial sort, extending to the minutest details of daily life,' and as 'half horrible, half noble'. It must have affected the minister's relationship with his flock, making him a judge rather than a pastor but many ministers managed to combine the double function very well, although much depended on their and their elders' concept of their powers. The question really is, why did people put up with all the punishments inflicted upon them, often for very minor offences? Were the common people excessively submissive or did what went on have the tacit ap-proval of the masses? Whatever the reason, one long-term benefit of it all is that Session minutes, by listing the sins and frailties of the people, also give their names, occupations, place names and descriptions of what they had done, all of which is meat and drink to the parish historian and family history researcher.[2]

Although required by Act of Parliament to maintain discipline, Kirk Sessions as such were only given the legal power to inflict ecclesiastical punishments, not civil ones. In his transcriptions of the early registers of St. Andrews Kirk Session, David Hay Fleming points out that the Second Book of Discipline distinguished with great precision between civil and church jurisdictions and many statements in these registers show that that Session accepted that civil penalties were for the magistrates to inflict, not for them. Initially the kirk got round this by sending supplications to magistrates, asking them to punish wrong-doers not only for the civil aspect of their offences but also for any disobedience to the kirk, or asking that they should be made to submit to church discipline. They might even go further and suggest what the civil sentence should be: in pronouncing their own sentence on an adulterer in 1560, a crime which three years later warranted death, they asked that the 'good and Godly magistrate' should impose this sentence 'with the civil sworde' and then added the words, 'we will that this sentence prejudge nothing.' Some Sessions went still further and ordered magistrates to impose a sentence of the Session's choosing and some would even threaten them with excommunication if they did not do as the kirk wished. This happened in Perth in 1592 when the Session were having trouble with a man named Thomas Taylor who refused to obey them and so they instructed the bailies to imprison him or risk excommunication. In the 1580s, another Thomas in Perth, Thomas Smith, was in trouble with the church for having fathered several illegitimate children. He had been ordered to be imprisoned with shaven head and to be ducked, according to the appropriate Acts of Parliament, but somehow he had managed to escape. For some reason, the Session believed that the magistrates had connived at his geta-way and instructed the minister to take the first steps towards excommunication of the bailies if they did not ensure that Thomas's sentence, and those of any similar offenders, were properly carried out. This threat worked and Thomas submitted to the Session. This all shows the tyranny that the kirk exercised at that time, not only over individuals but also over the civil authorities, although gradually the relation-ship between kirk and magistrates became less fierce and more-co-operative. This meant, for instance, in Tynninghame, in the first half of the seventeenth century, that the Session felt able to advise their clerk to call on the 'civil officer' should he need help to carry out their orders. In Montrose in 1659 the Session passed an Act desiring the magistrates 'to take order with all scandalous persons, and all those that wants testimonials'; it was confidently expected at Peebles in 1571 that those who disobeyed the kirk would be punished by the bailies; and at Grange in 1706 anyone who did not appear before the Session when called to do so was referred to the magistrates as contumacious while in 1711 the Presbytery of Deer wrote to Justices of the Peace 'to oblige certain persons to compear before the Session.' The minister of St. Boswells asked for, and got, the help of a Melrose bailie to prosecute two women 'in case they continue obstinate and refuse to compeir before the congregation' and the Kirk Session of St. Cuthbert's, Edinburgh, ordered their beadles in 1708 'to mind [remind] the Justices of Peace constables in the paroch to prosecute the several references' about a married couple. The man fled but Bailie Gray was asked to ensure the woman's public appearance for rebuke in church the following Sunday for 'atrocious wickedness', which seems to have been nothing worse than 'cursing and reviling' a couple of families; and that month too, that Session had the Justices' constable bring a man before them for the sin of fornication. In 1709 the Kirk Session of Deskford appointed three elders to attend the Justice of the Peace court 'for giving up an account of idlers and those who disobies [sic] discipline.'[3] Sometimes, however, things worked the other way round and it was the magistrates who made use of the kirk. In Elgin in 1582 the burgh council ordered a woman to be imprisoned for twenty-four hours and then to appear on the stool of repentance in church on Sunday for censure there; and in Dornoch there was also a case of the magistrates sending a woman to the Session with orders that she should be publicly rebuked in church 'to deter others from the like practice in time coming.'[4] The civil-kirk co-operation was undoubtedly close.

Writing in 1646 Principal Baillie said that no church assembly in Scotland assumed the least degree of power to inflict the smallest civil punishment (although they certainly used influence) but this was something which Parliament had realised already to be a gap and in 1645 an Act 'for having magistrates and Justices in every parish' was passed, which was followed up by the General Assembly in 1648 who urged every congregation to make use of this Act of Parliament. Another Act of Parliament 'against Profaneness' was passed in 1672 which again ordered the appointment of such officials and thus it was that the role of Session bailie or 'bailie assistar with the kirk' as it was occasionally called, developed. In theory these men were bailies, sometimes elders and sometimes not, who attended Session meetings so that, when a civil penalty was thought neces-sary, it could be imposed there and then by them, simultaneously with any church penalty. One Session described the office as a 'Civil Magistrate for concurring with the Session to the bearing down on scandal' which explains itself well:

immediate sentencing was the usual procedure although in some places the Session might move in a body to the Burgh Council house so that civil punishment might be imposed or confirmed there.[5]

Some Sessions had already got around to the idea of session bailies before Parliament did: it was agreed in Perth in 1616 that the Provost and bailies of the town should always be members of the Session and it was the same in Glasgow. Sometimes it was the Council which appointed session bailies: in 1749 an intimation from the magistrates and Burgh Council of Kirkwall was read from the pulpit, condemning the many sins and immoral practices of the people, especially on Sundays, and announcing that for the 'more regular procedure in punishing such transgressors as shall be delated to them', they had appointed two bailies who were also elders 'to be Session Bailies for judging and determining all such transgressors as may come before the said Session. For whose procedure in said Session as Judges an extract of these presents shall be a sufficient warrand.' They also appointed four men — a merchant, a shoemaker, a wright and a wigmaker — to be constables and ordered the burgh officers 'to attend the constables whenever called upon to do so by either of the Session bailies.' In this case, the Council chose bailies who were already elders which must always have been the best solution as in that case they could attend and participate in Kirk Session meetings in both capacities but the following minute makes it clear that burghs did not necessarily expect session bailies to be elders: 'It is ordained that the baillies by Course, viz every one his month about, should take order with the delinquents that comes before the Session.' In other cases a burgh council might authorise an elder who was not a magistrate to act as session bailie should no magistrate be available, appointing certain people 'quha ar upon the Sessioun, that they, in the absence of the present Magistratis, have commission to exercise the civille power requirit against heresis and uthers lyable to censure that come before that judicatorie.'[6] An alternative was for the Presbytery or Synod to instruct each minister to 'use his endeavours to have a magistrate in their Paroch' or 'to choose one to be a parochial judge for making the censure of the church against delinquents more effective.' The choice could be made by election of the heritors and elders or by the Session itself 'having deputation from the Sheriff according to law', which meant that the person chosen could be of quite humble station, like the portioner elected by the Barony Kirk Session of Glasgow to be a session bailie in 1703.[7] Unfortunately, when a bailie is referred to in Kirk Session minutes, it can sometimes be difficult to know which kind is meant — session bailie, burgh bailie or bailie of Regality. There are also some references to provosts or bailies taking elders' meetings in the absence of the minister but this could have been done as session bailies or as elders.[8]

A problem with all this was that while magistrates seemed to be perfectly willing to assume the role of session bailie, many other people were none too keen to have it thrust upon them. In many parishes it was difficult enough to get elders and even more so to get session bailies, so much so that in 1700 an Ayrshire minister reported that no one who had been elected would accept the office and the heritors had to undertake the duty in turn. Nevertheless, session bailies were to be found all around the country — in Ayrshire in the seventeenth and early eighteenth centuries but seldom after 1723; in Orkney in the mid-eighteenth century, and also at that time in Argyllshire with one Session paying 10s. 6d. in 1768 for the 'clerk's dues for extending our session bailie's commission.' Even so, there were many parishes where session bailies never functioned and although some heritors might undertake the task, not all were willing. When New Abbey Kirk Session, Kirkcudbrightshire, in accordance with a Synod decree about appointing session bailies, ordered a meeting of heritors to elect one, no heritors appeared and the matter had to be held over. Many parishes had no resident heritors and others were so large and so thinly populated that the Session met only once a year and that was to distribute the poor's money and little else. Discipline was not a problem: people were so scattered that their sins, unless there was something like an illegitimate baby to prove them, did not find them out and elders, who might have delated sinners, were almost as few and far between as were Session meetings. In any case, Sessions in such areas knew that they had the support of the landowning classes, either directly or through their factors, even if they did not wish to be session bailies themselves and, as time went on, many rural ministers became Justices of the Peace.[9]

Not only were kirks expected to find session bailies, they might be encouraged to find people to act as constables: in 1709 the Presbytery of Edinburgh recommended their ministers and Kirk Sessions 'to deal with persons of respect in their respective parishes to accept of the office of constables and to give up to the Justices of the Peace a list of suitable people, in order to punish scandalous persons and get them censured conform to law and the Magistrates' pious proclamations.' St. Cuthbert's Kirk Session was one that followed this up by appointing a committee for nominating suitable people 'for the several districts of the parish that want constables.'[10]

While busy Kirk Sessions found it very convenient to have a session bailie, with or without constables, the lack of them was not really a problem as the Session could always refer a delinquent, as has been said, to a civil court and by the eighteenth century this latter course was often taken. In 1715 a man who admitted that his marriage was irregular was referred by the Session 'to the Magistrate for his pecunial mulct' (fine) and such referrals were common. Whatever is said, however, about kirk and civil discipline being separate, except so far as linked by session bailies or such referrals, there is no getting away from the fact that Kirk Sessions, whether they had session bailies or not, did inflict civil punishments, both corporal and financial. However otherwise does one explain the fact that delinquents in St. Andrews were imprisoned, not in the tolbooth but in the kirk steeple with the beadle, who was not a town official, as jailer and moreover, so satisfied were the Session with his efforts 'in keeping the prison hows' that they ordered every prisoner, man or woman, to pay him 2s. on their release. There are many other instances of the kirk usurping civil functions.[11]

Punishment and threat of it were the only ways of maintaining discipline in the early days of the Reformed church and, terrible though many of those deterrents were, they were the ones of the era and must be seen in that light, just as it must also be remembered that whether church government was Presbyterian or Episcopalian made little difference.

First and foremost, there was the death penalty. This might take the form of burning, in the case of witches, of which more elsewhere, or drowning. Falkirk Kirk Session seemed to take a completely casual view of such a thing, ordering a woman in 1635 to be banished or else scourged through the town 'or drowned as shall be thought most convenient.' In 1551 Parliament had decreed that incorrigible adulterers who disobeyed church censure should be put to the horn — be formally outlawed by three blasts of a horn — but after the Reformation, the offence was viewed more seriously, with Parliament decreeing in 1563 that 'notour and manifest adulterers' should be put to death. This was repeated in 1581, along with a definition of just what the words 'notour and manifest' meant, which was when children were born to the parties in adultery; when they notoriously kept company and bed together; and when being suspected of the sin, they failed to satisfy the church about their position and were excommunicated. In the 1580s a man was put to death for adultery in Perth and as late as 1694 it is said that another one was hanged in Edinburgh, and his partner beheaded, all of these being civil punishments. It is interesting however that in 1647, fifty years before, Elgin Kirk Session ordered Mariorine Layng to appear publicly for adultery the next Sunday but they also gave her permission to remain in the town for a month to see if her conduct improved with the intention that, if it did not, they would send south for a commission 'and caus drown her.' An Act of Parliament of 1644 gave power to the Commissioners of Exchequer to grant remission for adultery 'upon testimonials of repentance and satisfaction to the church' so the church not only had a role to play in punishing offenders but was at that time in a position to help people to avoid the death penalty.[12]

The sentence of banishment from a parish or from Scotland was frequent in earlier days. From a local point of view it was a convenient punishment to impose because it got rid of offenders or undesirables but only at the cost of unloading them on to other communities. It was a very severe sentence. Once someone was banished, that was that; there was nothing they could do to reinstate themselves and their position was worse even than that of modern refugees because in the case of banishment, the order went out that no one should 'set house' to them, in other words, that they should not be given accommodation or employment. Even their families were not allowed to help them: a man in Kilmaurs was censured for taking in his sister after her banishment from Kilmarnock had been intimated in Kilmaurs kirk with the order 'that no one should harbour her' and in some cases a financial penalty of something like £4 Scots was threatened for anyone who took in such a person.[13]

In the early eighteenth century a poor lad who had lived for sixteen years in a parish was banished because he could not produce a certificate of character but it is possible that the real reason may have had to do with an implication that private charity which he had been receiving had ended, with the result that he might have had to come on to the poor's roll. Banishment was a civil penalty which magistrates might impose themselves or as a result of a request or a demand from a Kirk Session. In 1702 the 'unseemly and scandalous deportment' of a vagrant woman caused a Session to apply 'to the Magistrates anent her who did banish her out of the town' and the following year that Session recommended 'that the Magistrates should take up lists of loose and visious persons who haunted the place, that they might be expelled.' In the case of a woman who had not only relapsed in fornication but was also thought to be a witch, another Session sought the advice of the Presbytery who in turn sought that of the Synod with the result that the Session were advised to ask the civil authorities to have her banished, in the circumstances a mild sentence. However, many Sessions managed to banish people without any help from anyone else. When a Dundee woman came to St. Andrews and was cited to the Session there for talking and drinking with a scandalous woman and making trouble with neighbours, she said that from infancy she had had the ability to reveal secrets. This was something which smacked of witchcraft, and it is surprising that in this case also banishment was the result, but this time it was ordered by the Kirk Session. Immoral conduct led to much banishment. George Hutchone, described as having been drunk and being 'ane scandalous liver' and 'ane very wicked liver' was ordered to remove himself out of Montrose in 1647 and, of course, women of bad repute always got short shrift. In the unusually dated year of 156^2/$_3$ Aberdeen Kirk Session ordered the banishment, under the act for 'common bordeleris' of Elspet Murray because it was 'sufficiently proven that she is one of those persons', but worse befell Isabel Colzear, found guilty of 'filthie harlotrie and continuing in the same' in Kinghorn, Fife, in 1623. She was ordered to be put out of the town and 'wt sound of drum convoyed wt all the barnis gewing her ane hoyas to the town end', which meant not only banishment but that the children were encouraged to shout and jeer at her as she was being set on her way. Allegations of witchcraft against a particular woman in 1702 were not considered sufficient to assume guilt but she consented to banishment and went to Ireland. The fact that her consent was apparently sought covers the fact that this was a neat way out of what was really a Not Proven case.[14]

On occasion, offenders were escorted not just to the town end, but right away from a parish. After other punishments, a Kilconquhar man was sent, 'due to the troubles of the time', by sea to either Edinburgh or Berwick, in charge of another man, their joint fares coming to £3 12s. 6d. Scots. In other cases a minister might be prepared to do the removing of undesirables himself. This happened in the parish of Ashkirk and was done in keeping with Acts of Parliament which provided for the removal of certain classes of people, including gypsies. The Session ordered that 'no person shall reset [receive] any Egyptians [gypsies], and that if they take reset against their will, then to come and tell the minister and he, with the assistance of the gentlemen that he shall choose, shall go and put them out of this parochine.' It must have been difficult for a Session when they wanted to remove a burgh employee from the parish. This happened in the case of James Olifer, commonly called Jafra, the town piper in Hawick in the early eighteenth century. In 1717 his conduct had made him objectionable to the kirk and as he had no certificate of character from his former parish, they were able to base a complaint against him on this and ordered him to produce a satisfactory certificate within a given time or be handed over to the magistrates to be removed. Presumably this did not go down well with the Burgh Council because he was still there as town piper in 1720 and still misbehaving himself, including having married irregularly. This gave the Session a powerful lever and they decided to repeat their request for his removal, adding that if the magistrates 'concurred not with the Session, the minister would make address to another judge to extrude him from the town and to devest him of his service through the town.'15

It says a great deal for any Session that tried to put things right if banishment produced disastrous results, even although they had originally felt it to be an appropriate punishment. In October 1696, some time after Inverness Kirk Session had banished Hellen Leith, they intimated that they would proceed against anyone who lived with her or gave her lodging, which was a normal thing for them to do. Barely four weeks later, however, they changed their tune entirely and ordered the Clerk 'to give fourteen shillings Scots weekly for the maintenance of Hellen Leith, who of late has become Demented and withal in a starving condition.' Another problem was that families could be left destitute if a breadwinner was banished and then too a Session might have to step in with help: in 1836 one had to allow 8s. stg. per month for the wife and children of a man who had been banished.16

Imprisonment was, like banishment, a civil punishment which was much used by Kirk Sessions, either indirectly through magistrates, or imposed directly themselves, in the seventeenth and even into the eighteenth centuries. Prison and church could even be linked physically, with a number of churches having prisons added to them, often incorporated into an existing steeple or built in the form of one. It was in one of these that the St. Andrews beadle made such a good job of keeping the 'prison hows'. The General Kirk Session of Glasgow had a 'ward house' built in the steeple of Blackfriars Church with those incarcerated in it known as 'steeplers'; at Ladykirk, Berwickshire, the lowest room of the tower was for some time used as a jail although the top is obviously a later addition; in 1682 it was decided to build a loft in the steeple at Fordyce so that there could be a prison underneath and at Pittenweem the lower part of the church tower was used as the jail. One of the best examples of a prison linked to a church is the one that still exists at Greenlaw, Berwickshire, where an addition was made in 1700, designed to look just like a church tower, with a belfry and clock at the top, but below them five cells, one above the other, with the thieves' hole on the ground floor, where the prisoners were chained to staples in the wall and which still has a formidable and forbidding grilled iron door. Not all prisoners were restrained in this manner however as is clear from a minute of Aberdeen Kirk Session in 1605 which ordered the keeper of the kirk to look after the key of the session-house himself and to see to it that no prisoner should come up to the session house to 'abyd therein'. By no means all churches had prisons but where they did, the kirk must to some extent at least have been involved in their construction, which was the result of an Act of Parliament of 1592 which ordered that prisons, stocks and irons should be provided not only at all head burghs and principal thoroughfares but also at parish kirks.[17]

The type of offences for which Kirk Sessions imposed imprisonment, or had it imposed, varied considerably. In Montrose in 1642 it was decreed that those absent from church and wandering about on Sundays should be put in the tolbooth, and offences such as being absent from the catechism examination or from Communion could also lead to imprisonment. Sabbath-breakers might be put in the 'theifs hoal' and even when it was boys who did this, as happened at Banff in 1702, the result could be not just a rebuke but a Sessional recommendation to the magistrates that the culprits should be imprisoned. These boys' particular offence is not stated, but for the sin of firing a midden on a Sunday night, some other boys were 'all put in the Lymhouse, ordanit to be whipped by their parentis or masters and scourged if ever they were found in the like offence again.' The punishment for a 'wyld ryot' about 1607 was twenty-four hours in the steeple and a man who, along with his wife, had kept in their employment a wet nurse who had not satisfied kirk discipline, was kept in the tolbooth of Edinburgh for eight days 'and could not be liberat before the Sessione were contentit.' It was only when his wife brought £5 Scots as satisfaction, declaring that they could pay no more, that the Session accepted this sum and, considering their poverty, gave a warrant for his release. In 1602 two Aberdeen men were ordered to be put in the kirk 'wolt' or vault until they adhered to their wives, and sexual offenders could also find themselves imprisoned. In 1691 a woman was cited to the Kirk Session of Inverness for misbehaving with a soldier and although she denied this, they considered that there was a 'pregnant presumption' of her conduct and ordered her to prison until they 'were better informed of her deportment'. Presumption of pregnancy could lead to imprisonment but pregnancy could itself be a reason for release. Banff Kirk Session had considerable trouble with Margaret Smith, guilty of a relapse in fornication 'and justly suspected of grosser scandals' as well as being 'a person very ill reported of' and therefore asked the magistrates to have her imprisoned, which was done. A month later, however, the magistrates reported to the Session that they had set her 'at freedom out of prison because of her tender condition in being with child.' The Session were 'pleased therewith' but nevertheless asked the Provost to request Lord Banff, on whose land she was living, either to remove her or make her submit to church discipline. In spite of her brief incarceration and various efforts to have her removed, she managed to 'abscond and lurk' for a further eighteen months, at which point it was decided to refer her case to the Presbytery and have several elders speak to Lord Banff again about her. As a result of this she appeared within six weeks before the Session, giving as her excuse for not having done so earlier that her employers had prevented her, which is understandable if they feared that their employee might be imprisoned again. Imprisonment could be a useful weapon should a man deny paternity of an illegitimate child. When Alexander Baldie stubbornly persisted in such denials, he was prosecuted and imprisoned and it was the Session, not the civil authorities, who decided seven months later that if he agreed to pay the costs of the case and of his imprisonment, plus so much yearly for the child, he could be set free and this was what happened.[18]

Non-payment of penalties could also lead to a spell in prison. In 1609 the General Kirk Session of Glasgow ordered that no time to pay would be allowed to those fined; they must pay any penalties imposed before they left the Session House or else be put in the steeple until they could do so. In many cases, caution or surety was accepted for payment of a fine or submission to punishment and, here too, prison featured: in 1693 Inverness Kirk Session ordered the seizure and imprisonment of John Cuthbert until he found caution that he would satisfy church discipline while in 1701, in Wick, Donald Wright was ordered to pay a fine of £20 Scots for adultery 'otherwise to continue in prison till he find surety to pay the same betwixt [now] and Martinmas'. That same year, also in Wick, Katharine Caird was ordered to remain in prison until she paid her fine or found surety for it. Being put in prison did not make it easy for a prisoner to pay a fine or to find a cautioner and when one man who had been imprisoned for six weeks was asked how he intended to pay up, he replied that he knew no way of clearing the sum unless he was set at liberty 'whereby he might with industry pay the same'. The Session realised that this made sense and gave him a month to clear half of his penalty, which was 10 merks Scots.[19]

Part-time imprisonment could also be used. Several Elgin people who admitted in 1602 that they had indulged in superstitious pilgrimages and practices were ordered to make public repentance from Trinity Sunday, the one after Whitsunday, until the 1st August and during that time to be incarcerated in the church steeple from 7.00 a.m. each Saturday until they emerged on Sundays to make repentance. About the same date some people there who had been found guilty of drinking and swearing on Sundays had to enter the steeple on Saturday evening, spend the night there, make repentance in church on Sunday and return to ward for Sunday night also. This was a practical form of punishment as it left them free to work during the week but restricted their weekend activities. A less common reason for prisoners to leave and re-enter prison was because these places were not as wind- and water-tight as they might have been: in 1580 a woman was released after eight days incarceration for fornication 'in respect of the vehemensie of the storme of wedder', caution being given that she would re-enter for a further eight days.[20]

Imprisonment could be used as a threat to bring an offender to submission, as when the kirk officer at Deskford was 'ordered to go to Jannet Muet and desire her to repentance the next Sabbath, otherwise he will cause her to be put in the Tolbooth of Cullen', a real case of carrot and stick which proved effective even if Jannet did take three months to appear. Sessions sometimes fell back on prison when they simply could not think of anything else to do. In October 1672 when a woman was delated to the Kirk Session of Peebles 'the Session not knowing what to make of it seeing the woman was unknown to them until Whitsunday last and had not produced her testimonial [certificate of character] appointed her to be imprisoned till she should find caution for production thereof and for satisfaction.'[21]

There was more to imprisoning people than just making the order. When Jhone Uewin was ordered by his Session in 1625 to pay a fine of 40s. Scots or go to prison for eight days, it was stated that if he did end up there he should have only 'bread and small drink according to Act of parliament.' The Glasgow 'steeplers' also got nothing more than bread and either water or small drink but the point of interest is not that this was all that they were allowed but that there was a legal requirement that they should have it. As has been said elsewhere, the Town Clerk of Banff had to call for a collection to maintain some sturdy beggars in prison in 1730 and various nearby Kirk Sessions helped with this. The diet of prisoners was always subsidised by friends and relations bringing them food but the coming and going of these visitors had to be controlled: Aberdeen Kirk Session had to order the keeper of the kirk not to allow anyone to have access to prisoners in the kirk vault apart from those bringing them food and drink but, of course, those without such outside help could suffer greatly. In 1640 a Session were so concerned about the 'distress and poverty' of Andro Meldrum who had been in the ward-house for a long time, that they allowed him 32d. daily for a month but said that after that he must 'hang his purse out at the prison window for his better help and support.' In 1582, which was not a time of active witch-hunting, the Kirk Session of Perth ordered their boxmaster to give a witch in the tolbooth eight doits a day and Dunbar Kirk Session's minutes for 1729 and 1730 have entries showing £4 12s. Scots 'for clothes for the child in the Vault' and 18s. for the child itself; while there is no explanation of this, it seems to have been assistance given to a prisoner's child. Whatever a Session as a whole might do about imprisoning offenders, there is an interesting implication behind this entry in the minutes of Banff Kirk Session in 1703: 'It was appointed that when any delinquent was imprisoned for not paying of the penalty incurred by them that none of the members of the Session should intpose for liberating them from prison until the Kirk Treasurer should be satisfied as to their penalty.'[22]

In his *History of the Working Classes in Scotland* Thomas Johnston refers to the intolerance which followed Covenanting times and how Episcopalian curates were, with their wives and children, ruthlessly chased out of their livings into beggary after the Revolution of 1689, saying that it was then the turn of the other side to exhibit a tyrannical intolerance, 'an intolerance perhaps scarcely to be wondered at when one thinks of . . . the men with one ear, the women with the branded cheek and the seared shoulder . . .' What he was referring to was the fact that, in addition to the death penalty, banishment and imprisonment, the church with or without the co-operation of the civil authorities, had been inflicting barbarous punishments for many years. In the Act of Parliament of 1574, designed to help the poor and suppress vagrancy, it was laid down that vagrants should be burnt through the gristle of the right ear with an iron 'the compass of an inch about', and so there was legal provision for it when Perth Kirk Session in 1589 banished a woman for an unspecified offence with the order that if she ever returned, she would be burnt on the cheek with the town mark, which seems to have been a common variation of ear-burning. In 1587 two Elgin men agreed to banishment under pain of having their cheeks burnt as well as other punishments and there, two years later, the Session passed a General Act as a result of the return of a woman who had been banished for adultery and theft. Foreseeing 'the decay of all discipline and good order' should she be allowed to remain, they unanimously decided that she should again be banished but that this time she would go 'with the mark of an iron upon her cheik'. There too, in 1597, burning on the cheek was the punishment threatened for anyone indulging in superstitious Yuletide practices. It has been said that nose-slitting, ear-cutting and cheek-burning were mainly inflicted in Episcopalian days but as Kirk Sessions continued in virtually the same form whether under that or Presbyterian government, they were responsible for such things or co-operated in them. If for instance, offenders were 'nailt be the lug' to a church door, that could not happen without at the very least the concurrence of the kirk, but it cannot be stressed enough that these terrible brutalities, though far from Christian in nature, were normal practice at that time and were meant to do good.[23]

Ducking was another unpleasant punishment, authorised by Act of Parliament in 1567 for a third offence of fornication but which seems to have been really designed, according to Professor Smout, for the prostitution of towns rather than the casual morals of rural areas. The choice of immersion spot might be the deepest and foulest pool in the neighbourhood, which was what the Act of Parliament recommended, or it could be in a river or even in the sea, in which a Dundee man was 'thrice doukit' after spending three hours in the gyves in 1559 for fornication. When a woman who had already been banished from Aberdeen for harlotry, returned and once more got up to her old ways, the Session ordered her to be apprehended, put in the kirk 'wolt' and thereafter to be 'doukit at the cran', which could be some kind of tap, and then re-banished although it was provided that if she paid a fine of 10 merks she could escape the ducking. She was fortunate that no other indignities were added to her punishment because they almost always were. After imprisoning several women for fifteen days in 1587, the General Kirk Session of Glasgow had them taken by cart to the River Clyde for ducking, where a pulley system had been devised and installed on the bridge to facilitate the procedure and after that, the unfortunate women were put in the jougs at the cross on the next market day, a day which ensured that the greatest number of people possible would be there to jeer at their humiliation. Carting sinners through the town on market day to add to the official punishment was common and it was not only humiliation that these people received but also the 'rotten eggis, filth and glar' which 'the haill scolaris and utheris, ane great multitude of pepill . . . being his convoy' were encouraged to throw at an adulterer as he was taken to be 'dowkit ower the heid diveris tymes.' According to the records of St. Andrews, Aberdour Kirk Session took the trouble in 1560 to notify them about Besse

Symsoun, 'notoriously a harlot to French, English and Scots men' who had 'been carted thro' their streets' and banished, and asking that 'all gude people' should 'use and handill the said Besse in lyke sort.' In 1623 Elgin Kirk Session ordered Margrat Scott to obey one of their decrees or be carried through the town, a powerful threat, but dreadful though it seems that people, including children, should be incited to treat others in this way, this also must be seen in the light of the times when even executions were regarded as public entertainment for all ages — and at least this was better than the death penalty. It did not, of course, prevent delinquents having to satisfy the church in the normal way.[24]

Indignity and publicity were specific features of early punishment and the term 'public humiliation' appears as such in some records. Not only was there the unpleasantness of being carted through the streets on market days but the market place or burgh cross were popular spots for the exhibition of offenders during the infliction of sentences. In Perth, immoral women were imprisoned, then exposed at the market cross 'fast locked in the irons' for two hours, with their curchies (head coverings) off their heads and their faces bare, without plaids or anything else to conceal their shame. In Perth too, the penalty for ante-nuptial fornication in the sixteenth century was a fine of £40 Scots or imprisonment for eight days before being taken to the market place and forced to sit in the stocks there for two hours; and a repetition of the offence was punished by the shaving of heads, sufficiently common for that Kirk Session to appoint a barber for the purpose, and head-shaving happened widely. In Dundee in the 1560s immoral women were taken to the cross and had their hair cut off; a wretched woman in Aberdeenshire who could not pay her fine had to sit for six Sundays in the gyves at the cross with her hair clipped while, for 'vyle harlatrie confessit be thame baithe', a Session in 1607 ordered a couple to be imprisoned overnight and the minister, elders and magistrates to see them punished next morning by ducking or confinement in the jougs with shaven heads. For women, whose custom it was to have their heads covered, it must have been a terrible degradation to have them not only uncovered but shaven too.[25]

It was not unusual for an offender who was appearing publicly to have to wear something with their offence written upon it for all to see, although this must have rather missed its point as very few people could read. In 1612 an Aberdeen woman who both blasphemed the name of God and assaulted her husband in church in the presence of the minister, was ordered by the magistrates and the Session to be put in the kirk vault until the next market day when she had to spend two hours in the jougs before being carted through the town, wearing a paper crown on her head with the reason for her punishment inscribed thereon. About fifty years later the Kirk Session of Rothesay warned a very inebriate woman that if she failed to mend her ways she would be put in the jougs and have her 'dittay' — her indictment — written upon her face. A man guilty of ante-nuptial fornication who compounded the sin by lying about it, had to stand for three Sundays at the church door 'with a paper on his breast in Capital Letters declaring his guilt.' Many cases of people appearing in public with paper crowns or 'mitres' on their heads were for such sins as adultery or ante-nuptial fornication but in one case of the latter, the punishment was followed by church repentance and then the marriage was solemnised. In the much more serious case of a woman procuring her sister for harlotry, not only was she carried through the town with a paper crown on her head but the reason for her punishment was to be 'openly declared by the hangman.' In towns the hangman, who was an official who did much more than his job-description implies, was much involved with the infliction of these punishments, but it was an unattractive job which appealed to unpleasant people. It must have been a very wicked one, however, who was reported by the Kirk Session of Perth to the Town Council because of his cruelty to and oppression of poor weak people.[26]

As no one was going to stand still to endure public punishment, various devices were contrived both to keep offenders where they were put and to make them suffer. In 1579 Parliament decreed that if fines for Sabbath profanation were not paid, then offenders should be put in the 'stocks or sik other engine' and in 1592 ordered that such implements should be placed at principal thoroughfares and towns, as well as at churches, for the punishment of idle beggars and vagabonds, and decreed in 1645 that vice should be punished by corporal punishments of this sort. Gyves (geivis) were iron shackles which could be applied to the wrists, the ankles or both and were often used for women who could not pay their fines. Their cost and construction may be gathered from the fact that a man named Malcolm Cruickshank was paid 'xx sh for making the geivis and making ane ledde to them, and fastening them in the earde', (earth) plus 8s. 4d. Scots for two planks which were also used in their making.[27] Stocks held a person by the ankles so that he or she endured their time in them in a sitting position while the cockstool or pillory was a heavy frame supported on uprights, with holes for the head and hands which kept the offender immobilised standing up, with outstretched arms. Other names for this include cuckstool, cockstule, golffis or gokstule. One Session had such a pillory erected at a cost of £3 8s. 6d. Scots with a view to stopping cursing and swearing but it is confusing that the words 'pillory' and 'cockstool' are also used for the platform or stool on which offenders appeared in church for reproof and which were something entirely different, that the gokstule could be the stocks, and that *Chambers Dictionary* refers to the jougs, a neck collar, as 'the old Scots pillory'.[28]

Being put in the stocks was imposed or threatened for all sorts of offences, many of them very trifling ones. It could be for little more than profanity of speech, for slandering someone a second time or scolding on the high road but better reasons include a decision that because a kirk was 'troubled with sturdy beggars every Sabbath, appoint James Wilson, constable, to wait at the style next Sabbath to put them away and if refractorie to put them in the stocks or steeple.' When William Pae spoke disparagingly of the elders as he left church one Sunday, he must soon have regretted doing so as he found himself in the stocks for two hours between the ringing of the first and third bells for Sunday worship the following week. In 1619 a Falkirk man sold alcohol during time of worship and when accused, denied it 'with certain great terrible oaths' and then in 'ane most impudent and shameless manner' got down on his knees before the whole Session and swore that he would complain to higher judges 'for ane mendis [amends] of the minister and elders.' Such rudeness made the Session threaten to put him in the stocks which only made him angrier still and it was a further threat to 'communicate with my Lord of Linlithgow' that made him admit his offence and undergo the appropriate punishment for it. In the parish of Kinghorn in 1623 William Allane admitted breach of the Sabbath and abusing his wife that day — note the order in which the offences come — for which he was ordered to be laid in the stocks for twenty-four hours, then to stand in the jougs on market day and afterwards to find caution not to do such a thing again. A St. Andrews woman who in 1574 severely slandered a neighbour was ordered to 'sit in the gok-stuil during the magistrattis will' while two years later another woman there who had been what was termed 'outrageous' to her husband, as well as not attending church, was told that if she repeated either offence she would sit 'in the gok-stule xxiiij howris', (that is, twenty-four hours). Youngsters too could be put in the stocks. A boy who drew a knife on another was ordered by his Session 'to bee brought heer the nixt day and to bee delivered up to the constable for putting him in the stocks', a salutary deterrent for any violent youth.[29]

Twenty-four hours was a long time to sit in the stocks but people could be in them for longer than that or at least be threatened with longer confinement in them; a Fraserburgh, Aberdeenshire, couple were told that if they continued to cohabit or were found together in any suspicious place, they would be fined 10 merks or lie for ten days in the stocks. A man found guilty of immorality and producing a false certificate of baptism was ordered by Kilconquhar Kirk Session to be put in the stocks and to remain in them 'until some course should be taken with him.' It was a week later that it was decided to send him right away and one must assume that he was in the stocks for all of that time, especially as the Session had to spend 5s. Scots on bread and ale for him while he was so confined. What is not clear is whether or not those in the stocks for long periods were taken out at night and returned to them in the morning. It seems likely that this is what happened because an East Lothian blacksmith, John Crawford, is known to have kindly lent his smiddy in the early seventeenth century for the overnight imprisonment of a thief who was in the stocks — but in this particular case he helped the thief to escape in the morning, thereby earning himself immortality in the Kirk Session records.[30]

Offences which merited the stocks could equally well be punished by the cockstool. Inverness was one place where it was often used but although an illustration in a book on Inverness Kirk Session records shows a cockstool as a four-legged stool with a footrest, this appears to be one of the later confusing versions and not the type used there in the seventeenth century. At one time that cockstool or pillory stood near the burgh cross, at another date it was near the Highland Kirk and at a later date inside that building. Its first mention is in 1693 when the Kirk Session records say, 'The Session finding the town to be pestered with so many lous and debauchit persons erected a Cock-stool to be built near the Highland Church for punishing those who will not be admonished to forsake their uncleanness and scandalous deportment.' In 1694 a young woman of the town spent eight days with a drummer, including most of a Sunday which meant that she did not go to church and for this 'scandalous deportment' the Session ordered her to be brought immediately to the cockstool and to stand there for half an hour and afterwards to be imprisoned until she could find surety that she would appear in sackcloth before the congregation the following Sunday. By 1708 this cockstool had deteriorated or been damaged and the Session records show that an overture was made 'anent erecting of a cockstool for the punishment of delinquents, viz. such as give two fayrs' (name two men as father of an illegitimate child) 'or relapse, unless their repentance be more remarkable, yea and to all whom the Session shall think fit to referr to the Magistrate to be put there for punishment and terrour', and in 1719 the Session decided to apply to the magistrates for a new cockstool to be erected at the cross for the punishment of some women who were unable to pay their fines. This was agreed but, although one might have thought that the burgh would provide such an item, it was the Session who ordered their treasurer to arrange with workmen to have it made as soon as possible. Cullen was another place where the cockstool belonged to the Kirk Session and there must have been many other places where this was so but the Kirk Session of Wick was one which arranged things differently. In 1701 'It was put to the vote whether the town of Wick or the box should pay the charges to put up ane Cockstool. It was carried by vote that the town should do it' which saved the poor's box being depleted for something that did not benefit the needy.[31]

Corporal punishment was common; indeed, in 1647 the General Assembly had advised that use should be made of civil magistrates to impose it and that meant public flogging. In 1690 three 'scandalouse and Debaught' women came before Inverness Kirk Session who referred them to the magistrates who ordered them to be handed over to the hangman, to be taken through the streets and then flogged by him at the cross and afterwards to be banished, 'never to be seen here under pain of being more severely used . . .' Katherine Fraser, described as 'a base and vile person in her life and conversation' was also referred by that Session to the magistrates who ordered her to be imprisoned 'and immediately the Session dissolved, to be brought to the Cross and whipped by the hands of the hangman and banished from the town.' Delaying the whipping until the close of the Session meeting can only have been so that the minister and elders could be present to see that it was thoroughly carried out. In these cases it was the magistrates who imposed the penalty after a referral was made to them by the Kirk Session but in 1730 when a stranger woman was found 'in an indecent posture with soldiers' she was rebuked by the minister, told to produce a certificate of character or 'bale' for her future conduct and in addition was recommended 'to the Justices and magistrates now present for such corporal punishment as he in law may inflict'; corporal punishment was being indirectly ordered by the kirk although the Toleration Act of 1712 had forbidden magistrates to inflict church censures or summonses. In 1726 that Session had decided that the usual church discipline was achieving nothing in the case of a woman with several illegitimate children and therefore sent her to the magistrates, asking that they would deal with her by exemplary punishment, including banishment. In some cases, Sessions themselves ordered corporal punishment to be inflicted. When a Peebles woman named Jean Corsor was found guilty of behaving scandalously with a vagabond, 'the Session appointed her to be imprisoned and scourged out of the town the next market day', the man having managed by then to make good his escape, and the minutes of another Kirk Session for 1649 make their role clear: 'It is appointed be the wholl Sessione that [a couple] sould be scourged be hand of the hangman for their scandalouse conversing together.'[32]

The corporal punishment of women seems to have been particularly common but at least Kirk Sessions showed a certain amount of compassion, and certainly of commonsense, in dealing with nursing mothers; in 1720 one decided 'that women that are with child, or are giving suck, should be let alone until their children either die or be Nurced, and then that they should be corporally punished, if they have not wherewithal to pay their penalty.' All the instances given in which men received corporal punishment at the direction of a Kirk Session, were cases where there was a female partner in sin. It was very unusual for the kirk to inflict this punishment on men on their own although it could happen, with an Inverness man threatened in 1708 that if he did not pay his penalty, he would be referred to the magistrates for corporal punishment. Poverty was obviously a major factor in earning whipping or flogging.[33] In rural areas, landowners might authorise the church to use corporal punishment. John Mackay, minister of Lairg from 1714–49, was greatly helped in his efforts to reform a disorderly and immoral community by the Earl of Sutherland, who was also the Sheriff, giving him permission to inflict it whenever necessary and as he was a man of both physical and moral strength, his use of it had every opportunity to be effective. James Robertson, minister of Lochbroom, Ross-shire, in the mid-eighteenth century was another powerful man who is reputed to have often used his tremendous arm to deal with the delinquencies of his people.[34]

As children could receive some of the severe penalties already mentioned, it is natural that they were also whipped and the kirk was perfectly ready to order this for them as well as their elders. In Dunfermline in 1685 several apprentices were whipped before the Kirk Session for Sabbath-breaking and six Elgin boys were 'belted' in 1650 for 'sporting' during the hours of Sunday worship. It was usually something to do with the Sabbath that brought this particular form of retribution on the heads of children: making a nuisance of themselves that day, running and romping noisily through the streets, swearing or playing rowdy games. Whipping was also regarded as a suitable punishment for children too young to undergo rebuke before the congregation: 'The Session considering that the said John — was but a young boy and not capable of church censure, appointed one of the elders to see him whipped' say the minutes of Cromarty Kirk Session in 1679. When two youthful Sabbath-breakers were brought before a Session, their father was ordered to come with them and was reproved for not having taught them better ways, after which 'The Session considering that by reason of their age their public compearance will not be much to edification, ordered that their father chastises them severely', which chastisement had to be supervised by elders. Various young people in the parish of Orphir were regarded as 'ill kirk keepers' and while one of them was ordered 'to be whept about the kirk by the hand of the officer the first Court day', his mother was told to pay half of his fine 'for not correcting him as she should when she found him going astray' and although no corporal punishment was imposed on two Kircudbright boys for wandering around on a Sunday in 1693, their mother was cited to appear before the Session to answer for their conduct. It is very evident from these instances which come from widely separated parts of the country that the kirk was prepared to take strong steps to see that parents took responsibility for their children and brought them up in the way that they should go. Some Sessions even ordered that every home should have a form of tawse at the ready: 'that ilk mr [master] of family have ane palme in his house for chastessein' anyone who, in this case, blasphemed the name of the Lord.[35] Naturally, there were some offences that resulted in whipping although they did not involve Sabbath profanation. In Canisbay, Caithness, in 1731 some children were found to have been 'kail-plucking superstitiously on Hollow Eve' which they said was just robbing an honest man's kailyard as part of the general mischief that went on on Hallowe'en, but they denied that there was anything superstitious in what they had been doing. While girls certainly had a superstition about plucking kail or cabbage stalks to try to divine their marriage prospects, these boys were just up to pranks, such as making kail-runt torches by hollowing out and filling the stalks with tow, lighting them and using them to blow smoke into keyholes. In this Canisbay case only one boy seems to have been caught in the act and the Session decided that 'in regard he is only a schoolboy appoint his master to chastize him' which the schoolmaster, who was also Session Clerk, accordingly did. This was rather bad luck on the boy as very soon afterwards the Session came to the conclusion that kail-stealing was so common that there was really nothing they could do about it, especially as those caught at it denied any superstitious intent and it was decided not to try to suppress the practice any more, apart from an occasional reproof.[36]

A lesser form of corporal punishment which occurred in Aberdeen in 1603 conjures up the picture of people in the streets being told to hold out their hands to be smacked. The elders there were told to note and challenge anyone blaspheming the name of God in the streets or elsewhere in the town and to take a penalty of 4d. Scots from them at the very least or else to give those who could not pay 'a straik on the hand with a palmer.'[37]

But these were by no means the only instruments of discipline. There were others which were very unpleasant too and the worst of them must have been the branks, a word always used in the plural. Known as the witch's or scold's bridle, branks were chained to somewhere public like the church door and took the form of either a metal neck collar or a frame which went over the head, but always with an inward-facing prong or prongs, sometimes as many as four, to go into the mouth to prevent speech. Illustrations in *An Angus Parish in the 18th Century* by

W.M. Inglis shows opposite p.165 two refinements of the branks: one has a long pointed nose and the other large earpieces like those of a donkey, designs which could only have been meant to increase the humiliation of the wearers as much as possible. Putting these gadgets on to a woman — it was usually a woman — was a job for the beadle and although the whole contraption could be very heavy, it might have to be worn for as much as six hours. Branks were widely owned and used by the kirk. The Kirk Session of Glasgow had an elaborate set for the punishment of flyting women, as did the Canongate parish of Edinburgh. Dumfries Kirk Session is known to have ordered sinners 'to stand at the kirk stile on the Sabbath with branks upon their mouths' and the parish of Auchterhouse was another which had branks. Holy Trinity Church, St. Andrews, has a fine collection of items to do with kirk discipline, including branks, while in 1633 it was the Presbytery of Strathbogie, Aberdeenshire, which ordered some offenders 'to sitt on the stoole of repentance tuo Soondays, or then to redeem thamselffis by standing in the joggs or branks.' When at a later date a Session felt it necessary to give some money to a man 'sairly fashed with a long-tongued wife', how they must have regretted the demise of the branks which, along with ear-cutting, nose-slitting and cheek-burning, seem to have gone out of favour by about the mid-seventeenth century. According to Dr Rogers' *Scotland, Social and Domestic*, the soldiers of the Commonwealth 'beheld with surprise and disgust, the degrading sentences inflicted by the church for offences they deemed particularly trivial' and they may well have been instrumental in creating a climate of dislike for such things as gyves, stocks, branks and the cockstool. The dates already quoted however show that some at any rate of these lasted considerably longer than the time of the Commonwealth, although they are seldom found in surviving Kirk Session minutes. The one that did last much longer was the jougs.[38]

Jougs have been mentioned several times already. They were often used in conjunction with some other form of punishment but were often used on their own too, along with the inevitable public reproof in church. Also used in the plural, the word appears in records in a variety of forms — joggs, jouggs, jouggis, joggis, joges, jaggs, joiggis, juggs, jobs, goggs, zowgis, and also as bregan, breggaine, bradzane, bredyane, but whatever the spelling or the term, jougs normally took the form of a clasped iron collar (which could be combined with the branks) which enclosed the delinquent's neck and was fastened by a chain to some firm object which might be the trone — the public weighing-machine or pillory — or a tree, a pillar or a post outside the church or at the churchyard gate but they were most commonly fixed to the outside wall of the church near the main door. Some jougs seem to have been movable: in 1587 an Elgin woman was ordered to stand in the jougs outside the church and then come inside and stand in the same ones in a particular part of the building during the service. In other cases, jougs were fixed to an inside wall of the church or to the stool of repentance, as at Montrose, where the sinner had not only the neck clasped in this way but the wrists enclosed in fixed bracelets as well.[39]

Making jougs was a job for the local blacksmith and although they were used to punish sin, sin could help to pay for them: in 1676 two women found guilty of swearing and cursing one another, had to pay 3s. stg. between them as a penalty; this was used to pay for a pair of jougs. The total weight of jougs and chain could be as much as 28 lbs. as may be judged from the following entry: 'Alex Hay was paid viii sh for ane quarter of iyrn to be joggis.' Two stones of iron resting upon the shoulders and neck of anyone held fast was very severe and depending on the victim's height, he or she had to bear the weight or risk strangulation. Jougs may still be found hanging on church walls, particularly in southern Scotland, but few if any of the surviving examples weigh anything like that, possibly just a few pounds, plus the chain. At Oxnam, Roxburghshire, for example, the collar only weighs about 1 lb. and the chain is not particularly heavy either, but those at the ruined church of Minto, in the same county, weigh much more.[40] Just as an offender might have to sit in the stocks between the ringing of different church bells, the same thing happened with the jougs, and not just on one Sunday but often for several. The church bell was rung three times on Sunday mornings at hourly intervals. The first ringing was a warning, the second required the people to gather in church and the third indicated that the service was about to start. Depending upon the seriousness of the offence, people were condemned to stand in the jougs from either the first or the second bell until the third, derided and reviled by those arriving at the church. They then usually entered the church — one Elgin man was told to do so at 'the last chop of the hyndmost bell' although some delinquents spent the whole service outside in the jougs. On occasion, however, confinement in the jougs lasted more than that. In 1570 a St. Andrews baker's wife who not only sold 'candil and braed' on Sundays but was absent from church as well as 'mis-saying' and being disobedient to her husband, was ordered to desist under pain of £10 or sitting, not standing in this case, for twenty-four hours in them. The paper crown or mitre worn by those exhibited in the market place or carried through the streets, could also be worn by a delinquent in the jougs and other exemplary refinements could be added too. In Dornoch a man who sold so much alcohol on a Sunday that there was a disturbance in his house, had to stand in the jougs with a pint stoup about his neck while in Fordyce a man who stole a tablecloth had to stand in them throughout Sunday worship with the cloth about his neck.[41]

None of this can have induced any feeling of reverence in those coming to worship but it was mainly because the church was the only public building in many parishes that it was a practical place for the instruments of punishment to be placed and, especially when used for ecclesiastical offences, it was thought suitable that this should be so. The result, ironically, was that a church violently opposed to the profanation of the Sabbath largely used Sundays and its kirk buildings as the day and the place for public punishment. A rare exception to the unpleasant nature of these occasions was when a man was ordered to stand in sackcloth for twelve Sundays at the church door 'desiring the people that comes by to pray for him.' It is not clear whether standing in the jougs automatically required the sinner to wear sackcloth or not but this was certainly specified in some cases, and by Elgin Kirk Session in 1587 when a woman found guilty of adultery and incest was ordered to wear the 'hairy claith' when in the jougs as well as having her head shaved. The same year that Session ordered two women described as 'common harlottis and nycht walkeris' to stand in the jougs with their heads shaven too.[42]

Jougs were often used to punish Sabbath profanation. One Orkney youth who was an 'ill kirk keeper' was put in them and fined 30s., and two men in Elgin who had the nerve to leave church during preaching to go to play at port bowls also found themselves in them. In 1700 it was reported to a Session that a man had struck and cursed his wife on a Sunday but it was also stated that she was a 'very wicked person and frequently curses and rails at her husband'; and so it was decided that both of them should stand before the congregation on two Sundays but that she should, in addition, stand from the first to the third bell in the jougs on the first of these days.[43] But they were used for other offences too. In 1658 a man had to stand in them on two Sundays 'for fearful cursing and swearing' and in an Orkney parish about 1685–86 the jougs were the penalty for 'poor people with no gear' who were guilty of 'swearing abominable oaths'. 'Having no gear' meant that they had nothing with which to pay any fine and confinement in the jougs was imposed as an alternative. The Kirk Session of Galston, Ayrshire, passed an Act in 1628 decreeing that where neither one of a couple could pay the penalty for fornication, they should stand in the bradzane for two Sundays, with a further two standing publicly but unconfined in church, while some five years later the Kirk Session of Montrose ordered that all slanderers should pay £4 Scots to the poor's funds or else stand in the jougs 'during the Session's will'. It was not always a matter of either/or: jougs and a fine could go together, as they did in a case of bait-gathering on a Sunday in 1638. Because the jougs were often used to punish slandering and railing, it was frequently women who appeared in them. Between May and October 1615 a case between two women who were both named Janet Shorthouse, went from bad to worse and resulted, because there were other similar cases, in a Kirk Session minute stating that the minister 'regretted that there were so many railers in the town, especially women, and that they troubled the Session so oft; earnestly desired the civil magistrate would concur in punishing them, and that jougs might be made at the kirk door, wherein the delinquents might be put.' Lesser church measures had obviously been of no avail and jougs had to be called into play. Violence could also lead to a spell in the jougs: in 1679 a man was ordered to stand in them between the second and third bells for the next three Sundays for being so drunk that he 'strak' (struck) all he met with and a late instance of the use of the jougs occurred on the island of Coll in 1782 in a case of attempted rape. What happened was that a man assaulted a woman who was some eight months pregnant 'but before he could accomplish his wicked and hellish intentions' her screams alerted a woman neighbour who came to her rescue. There had been a similar complaint about this man some fifteen months earlier, at which time the Session had ordered him to be put in the jougs for three successive

Sundays and then be banished from the island. The first part of the sentence was carried out but because of what was called his 'penitential appearance' the banishment was deferred but for this second offence the sentence was renewed and the Session, with the agreement of the laird, decided that he should be banished immediately he had completed his penance, adding that if anyone engaged or harboured him for as much as one night they should have to answer for it.[44]

Being an unpleasant punishment, the very threat of having to stand in the jougs could bring a delinquent swiftly to heel or to confession, like the Fordyce woman who, after denying a charge against her, immediately admitted it when threatened in this way, but it is always possible that confessions obtained like this could have been false. The threat of jougs could also be used, rather like a suspended sentence, to ensure good behaviour in future. In 1651 a man who absented himself from Galston church for five weeks was ordered to appear there for rebuke and was told that should he be absent again for two consecutive Sundays, he would find himself in the breggan. Sometimes the threat was more than verbal: in 1600 a Session ordered that some minor offenders should be 'presented to the jougs but shall not be put therein.'[45]

The parish of Kilconquhar used two other forms of punishment which appear to have been unusual — the 'chanzie' or chains and the belt. While these chains may have been similar to jougs, there must have been some difference because in 1641 a woman slanderer had to stand in the chanzie at the east kirk door between the second and third bells while one of two female 'flyters and feighters' was sentenced to the jougs and the other to the belt with the option of a fine of 20*s*. 'if she go not to the belt.' In 1645 the belt was again used for a woman, a man was put in it for 'bauling' and scolding, in 1706 it was used for another woman who was denying an accusation made against her and the Session sometimes ordered the bailies to put offenders in it. Unfortunately it does not seem that anyone knows just what the chanzie and the belt were, apart from being some form of constraint-cum-punishment, with the belt almost certainly going round the waist.[46] A form of standing publicly, though not in the jougs, was 'standing under the bell strings', that is, under the bell rope which came through a hole in the church roof so that it could be pulled. This was considered very ignominious and must have been singularly uncomfortable with the bell-ringer hauling the rope up and down about one's head.[47]

A very common punishment for flyting, slandering and moral offences was to stand publicly 'in sacco' — in sackcloth, something taken over from Roman Catholic penances, sometimes done in the jougs and sometimes unconfined at the church door. As time went on, it was only worn inside the church and continued to be used in this milder form of punishment well into the nineteenth century. Sackcloth, as the name implies, was a coarse material, used for mourning as well as for penitential garments. For this latter use, it represented humiliation, disgrace and, if possible, repentance. Sometimes a material called harn(e) or harden was used, very similar to sackcloth but probably even coarser, or even a 'hair gown'. In 1658 £2 Scots was spent by one Session 'for buying harden for two sackcloths' while about 1729 another appointed the treasurer 'to give £1 6s. Sc. to buy sackcloth and 5s. to a taylour for making coats of the said cloth.' One which is still in existence is fifty inches long, hand-sewn, open down the back (or front) and gussetted at either side to give the fullness that would be required to go over women's skirts. These gowns might be borrowed or lent, which was not a good thing to do with perishable articles and a minute of Ettrick Kirk Session shows that in 1697 they had to buy a 'new sacco' for penitents, 'Yarrow having borrowed the gown and used it to raggs.' As with the women whose fine was put to paying for jougs, so too with sackcloth gowns and in 1667 a man who failed to pay his fine on time was 'poinded in 8 elne of harne' which the Session had made into two 'sackcloathes'. On occasion people might be told to make their own sackcloth garments or at any rate pay for them, which added expense to humiliation and which, in at least one case, had tragic results. William MacMorran, an Edinburgh man, was ordered to buy a sack gown to wear at the church door and then to appear in church in it. Several Sunday appearances in it were required of him but within a month he 'turned distempered' and ultimately became a raving madman. Although standing publicly in sackcloth was nothing like such a punishment as stocks, branks, jougs or prison, people's sensitivities had increased as barbarism receded and it was all too much for this unfortunate man.[48]

In an Ayrshire parish in 1676 two delinquents had to stand in public but while one wore sackcloth, the other wore sheets. Sheets were regarded as a lesser garment of shame and were only permitted for lesser sins. Some Sessions bought these 'whyt sheets' — Kinnell Kirk Session paid 16s. 8d. Scots for some in 1694 — but sometimes they got people to provide them, particularly in return for being allowed to stand in ones of their own. This happened when Margaret Couts, found guilty of charming, agreed to appear in church for reproof provided that she could do so in her own sheets. She seems to have been making her own conditions — perhaps she was regarded as a very powerful charmer — but the Presbytery, to whom her case had gone, took a practical view and agreed to her request as it would free the sackcloth for use by some other sinner and on condition that she left her sheets for the future use of the kirk. Such sheets were probably what was meant by standing in linen or 'standing in her lynnings' which was the punishment imposed on Janet Hunter, a scolding wife, by the Kirk Session of Ayr in 1606. It was regarded as a serious offence for a penitent to appear in any other garb than that specified by the Kirk Session. When a Galston woman came before the congregation 'with ane uther habite than was enjoined to hir be the Session' she was ordered to appear the following Sunday 'in sackcloth or ane window claith'. Repentance could be made in one's own clothing if the sin was not too great but when a Banffshire woman came to church to do so but not 'in a grave habit' she was smartly ordered 'to enter again more gravely' to make her public profession before the congregation. A woman who was accused of 'denuding herself' of the sackcloth said she had done so because her employer forbade her to wear it if it was an old one, with the result that she had to wear it whether he liked it or not the following Sunday, and for a further Sunday as well for contempt.[49]

There was more to all this than just standing at the church door or in the church in a garment of shame. An idea of the procedure comes from the Kirk Session minutes of Craig. A man, guilty of adultery, was ordered to stand at the 'most patent door of the church' the next Lord's Day between the ringing of the second and third bells and continue standing there during the praise and prayers before sermon and lecture, and then be led in by the beadle and put in the place of repentance and there be rebuked before all the congregation when it was expected that he should show 'some signs of his repentance for the said hainous crime and sin.' Offenders might have to appear barefooted, a sentence which might be imposed for the duration of the punishment or only for part of it, as in the case of a woman who was ordered to stand publicly for twenty-six Sundays and for 'the hyndmost thrie Sabbathis to be bairfootit.' A further refinement was the indignity of having to stand barelegged and it does seem extraordinary that a church, so concerned about moral conduct, would wish women to exhibit their legs in this way if, in fact, that is what being barelegged meant in this context. In a case in Cullen in 1624 the punishment of standing barelegged had to be continued 'ay and quhill the minister and elders of Cullen be satisfied wt the signes of her repentance.' This minute, which is from the Kirk Session of Boyndie, shows that they were co-operating with Cullen Kirk Session in punishing this unfortunate woman, yet a man guilty of the same offence in that parish the same year only had to stand barefooted in sackcloth, not barelegged, although he did have to pay a fine of at least 100 merks. An even worse punishment was standing barefooted in a tub of water. In 1661 a man guilty of fornication twice and adultery once was ordered to stand in sackcloth every Sunday 'among water' from the first bell to the third — two hours at a stretch, beginning in March and going on until he gave acceptable evidence of repentance and made satisfaction, which was in June; and that was not an isolated instance of what must, in bitter weather, have caused serious ill-health. Even when the punishment was to stand in sackcloth inside and not outside the church, cold and wet might be added to it if the following story is anything to go by, although it was the result of individual malice and not a Kirk Session decision. During the ministry of Alexander Sage at Kildonan from 1787–1824, one of his elders was an exceedingly rigid disciplinarian and when a woman was found guilty of fornication for the third time, he took it upon himself to add his own bit of vicious cruelty to her punishment. Although it was a cold, frosty day, he dipped the sackcloth in the burn, threw it over her dripping wet and made her wear it like that for the three long hours of the service. The story was told by Mr Sage's son, Donald, in his *Memorabilia Domestica*.[50] It was not unusual for sinners to be called before the Presbytery to give evidence of repentance, be rebuked and have any further punishments decreed and, should the offence be grave enough, then they might have to show their penitence, not only wearing sackcloth but also on their knees. In fact, in cases of slander, they might have to go on their knees to ask God's forgiveness and that of the person slandered and to do this in church in addition to any other repentance. In view of all the unpleasant associations which sackcloth had in the minds of the people, it seems surprising that it could be thought to have any virtues at all, yet the records of South Ronaldshay and Burray in 1664 show that in itself it could be thought to have special healing powers although there is a possibility that this case could be one of belief in the influence of anything stolen by night: Jonet Budge was called before the Session 'for taking forth of the kirk the pennetentiall sackcloth and making us of it to her own body and her (alleged) [sic] distracted daughter' but only ended up having to buy another one for the kirk.[51]

The barefooted and barelegged part of standing in sackcloth died out before the eighteenth century but just when appearing in sackcloth before the congregation ended is not certain. While Rev. Andrew Edgar refers to someone appearing in it in Mauchline Church *as late as* 1781, the sackcloth gown which is still in the possession of Holy Trinity Church, St. Andrews, has sewn into the back of the neck a handwritten label which is now largely illegible but the words 'presented 1836' can still be made out and give a much later date for its use. It really should go without saying that those making repentance were bareheaded but, in fact, this was decreed by the General Assembly in 1570.

Stools of repentance were used all along for the in-church part of censure but perhaps they really came into their own when the outdoor part of it was dropped and the whole punishment of rebuke and confession took place within the church. Stools came into use at different times in different parts of the country. St. Cuthbert's Church, Edinburgh, had one made in 1591; Montrose Kirk Session were having one made in 1649; and one of the first actions of the minister who came to Coldingham in 1694 was to set up 'a seat for scandalous persons'; yet, as late as 1729, there was no such thing in Dornoch although a member of Session considered 'that there was much need of it.' It is said, however, that some churches which in the seventeenth century were in extraordinarily bad repair, with neither pulpit nor desks, might still have a stool of repentance, an instance of this being Lochcarron, Ross-shire. If there was no proper stool, it is thought possible that in earlier days offenders may have had to get up on the 'loupin'-on-stane' or mounting block at the churchyard gate but any formal stool of repentance was always inside the church.[52]

The stool of repentance went by several names such as the 'publict stool of repentance', the 'ordinary place of repentance', 'the penitents' stuill' or the 'penitentiall seate' and was of two main types. An example of one type is shown in David Allan's painting *The Stool of Repentance* in which the offender is standing in a raised wooden gallery opposite the pulpit which, surprisingly, places him fractionally higher than the minister. It is enclosed with planks and has a seat for delinquents to sit on when not actually being rebuked and this type could be locked to keep them in. This particular gallery is shown set on a wooden framework but Captain Burt described some as being like an armchair raised on a pedestal, nearly two feet higher than the other seats in church and directly facing the pulpit. The pedestals were often known as pillars which is the reason that this form of place of repentance was often called the pillar or common pillar as was done in the case of Margaret Broun who in 1640 had to 'sit upon the pillar for the space of twenty-six Sabbaths' or a couple who in 1691 had to appear 'at the pillar'. This pillar could also be called the pillory but it must not be confused with the quite different pillory mentioned earlier. To confuse matters still more, the seat of repentance on an elevated platform could be called the cutty-stool although that term is usually used for stools of the other main type; and the place of repentance could also consist of three small pews, placed one above the other. The raised nature of these stools probably explains a reference in some Kirk Session minutes to a 'faulter's laft' (loft).[53]

Penitents might sit on the pillar, enter to it, continue at it, be admitted to it and, as a lesser punishment, stand at it or at its foot, or there could be a combination punishment like that of the women who had to 'got to the stool two Lord's Days, and to the pillar foot one day.'[54] The place of repentance could often accommodate several people at once, even as many as ten. This was necessary because punishment could mean repeated appearances on the stool for any one delinquent, as the following minute shows:

18th February 1759. Stood this day the third time Archibald Campbell
fourth time Katherine McIntosh
third time Mary Ferguson, delinquent with
John Macpahil and was absolved.[55]

Making this large form of repentance stool required the work of both wright and mason. Two men were paid 200 merks 'to big [build] the laft and a pillar' for St. Cuthbert's Church, Edinburgh, in 1591, the one already mentioned, but with a bit of make-do-and-mend, the construction could be much cheaper, as when the Kirk Session of Aberdour, Aberdeenshire, decided to use an old broken boat to make 'a four-nooked big stool . . . an ell high' so that the whole cost only came to 5s. Scots. Whether an ell in height or as high as the pulpit, access was by a ladder, an extra cost that could come to a shilling Scots or so, or by a stair, but whichever it was it had to be kept in repair, all of which meant added expense. Not only was clambering up a ladder a dangerous and frightening proceeding for the elderly, the infirm and the pregnant but when the pillar was unenclosed on top, as some were, it made the punishment even worse. Kirk Sessions were however prepared to listen to special pleas about this and when a Kirkcudbright woman said that she could not appear in the place of repentance because of her infirmity, she was excused that part of her punishment and ordered simply to appear publicly in church for rebuke the following Sunday. Similarly, when Bailie Laing, a prominent townsman of Hawick, pleaded that though he was willing to make satisfaction to the church for his sin, he had become 'valetudinarie and troubled with an uneasiness in his hough and foot whereby he is not able to go up to the usual place of repentance', his request to make repentance from his own seat was allowed, on his promising to pay a sum of money to the poor.[56]

Some churches had more than one place of repentance, set at different heights, or at different levels, and so there are references to the 'heicher pillar' and the 'laicher pillar', to 'the umest stuil of repentance' or 'the hieest of the penitentis saiet' or 'the highest degree of the penitents' stool'. Just how high a stool could be may be judged from the fact that it was possible to set up a parishioner's seat under one example. 'Standing high' could be used as a threat, just as other forms of punishment could be threatened, which was why a woman found guilty of 'railing on the Ladie Barr, cursing, swearing and divilish passion' was ordered to show signs of repentance from her own seat 'with certification that the first time she sould be fund in the lyk she sould stand heich.'[57]

The proper positioning of the place of repentance was of great importance. David Allan's painting shows the stool opposite the pulpit so that the offender could get the full force of the minister's wrath and admonition and that would seem to have been the sensible place for it. Traditionally, pulpits in Scottish kirks are on the south wall and it seems that a logical place would therefore always be on the north wall but, while this was so in some cases, in others the stool was on the south wall and therefore on the same side as the pulpit. This of course had the advantage of placing the offender where the congregation could have the best view of his or her shame and repentance. Even so, the stool was not always given the prominence one would have thought desirable; in Mauchline in later days it was just a common pew, a little higher than its neighbours and on the left of the pulpit but under the drop of the west gallery, which made it the least public place in the church and it was only its slight elevation that made it stand out at all, while the stool at Falkirk in 1696 was 'at so great a distance from the pulpit, and so darkly situat that he [the minister] judged rebukes given to persons to be exposed to contempt' and in time a form was placed in front of the pulpit instead. One early St. Andrews penitent had to sit beside the precentor. Could all the other places of repentance have been occupied? From this it is obvious that the large raised stool of repentance degenerated in some places into little more than a small pew, specially positioned in front of the pulpit or perhaps against a wall. A stool which appears to be of this type is still in existence, one of the collection already mentioned at Holy Trinity Church, St. Andrews. It measures 43" high, 40" wide and the depth of the seat is 13" with a definite forward tilt of about 10°) and the word 'Repentance' appears at the top of the back of the seat, visible from the front. Apart from the tilt, this seat is not uncomfortable and in the days when there was little fixed seating in churches apart from those which a few people provided for themselves, there was always someone ready to grab any available seating, whether entitled to it or not. That could go for the stool of repentance too and one parish minister had to 'publicly intimate from the pulpit that none could sitt in the pillar except . . . had a right unto . . .' There was, of course, the world of difference between voluntary and compulsory occupation of this seat.[58]

There is a record of a boy having to sit on something called the 'maister stool' for playing golf on a Sunday though what this was is not known, but the other main type of stool of repentance was closer to the modern idea of a stool and this was the one usually known as the çutty stool or sometimes the cockstool. It could be a short three-legged stool or it could be like one still to be seen in the church at Auchterhouse which is four-legged, made of oak and looks just like a backless kitchen chair. A couple of cutty stools at Holy Trinity Church, St. Andrews, are also four-legged, 20" high and with seats measuring 16½" x 17". A book on the Old West Kirk of Greenock shows a photograph of the cutty stool there, a polished wooden bench some five feet long, with four turned legs, altogether an attractive piece of furniture. Some of these stools had a footrest which seems a kindly piece of additional comfort to give to delinquents. This type of stool was not expensive to provide and it may well be that the choice of type depended as much on the state of kirk funds as on the size and style of the church for which it was required. It only needed a wright to make it and virtually no maintenance thereafter and had the added advantage that there was no difficulty of access for those who were unfit. Such a stool could be placed in front of the pulpit when occasion demanded and removed when not needed and it could be specifically for this reason that a Session might decide to get a 'movable stool'.[59] Those ordered to appear on the stool were expected to get to it themselves and to do so punctually which is why, when it was found in Elie in 1642 that people were not there at the third bell precisely, the kirk officer was instructed 'to stay them from going that day at all', which meant coming back the following Sunday to do things properly. The stool of repentance gradually died out of favour across the country but it was certainly still in use in northern Scotland in the early nineteenth century.[60]

A lesser sentence did not require the delinquent to sit or stand on the stool of repentance but just to stand and confess the fault before the pulpit, as happened to a man who played his fiddle on a Sunday night and had to testify his repentance the next Sunday 'before the pulpit in face of the whole congregation.' There is a reference in the Kirk Session minutes of Wick to 'calling a man over the pulpit' but what this involved is not known. People were sometimes allowed to remain in their own seats while making their repentance or 'removing public scandal' as it was called but this privilege usually carried with it a money penalty for the benefit of the poor; in 1728 two people guilty of being drunk and scandalous the previous Sunday were ordered 'to stand up in the breast of their own loft and be rebuked and to pay 1s. to the poor.' In 1741 the Kirk Session of Hownam felt it necessary to regularise this matter, decreeing that 'Any who sit in their own seat for removing any public scandal, shall pay £6 for the benefit of the poor' while in Arbuthnott, a minute of 1769 does not actually say that people might remain in their own seats but gets round it by saying that on payment of 40s. Scots above the usual penalty (for fornication) offenders could make repentance in church 'where they can be seen and spoke to be the minister' which in fact was in their own seats.[61] As time went on, people made repentance wearing their best, if at all possible, but in time too, the whole idea of public rebukes gradually declined, with some parishes more advanced in their thinking than others. It was in 1772 that Arbuthnott Kirk Session decided that delinquents need only appear before the Session, except in serious cases, and the last recorded case of a public appearance in Ordiquhill was for adultery in 1776. In general, however, it was in the early nineteenth century that changes in church discipline were most apparent, although with some variations. Mauchline did not give up public rebukes until 1809, the last case occurred in

Grange in 1816 and Deskford, after a gap of nearly forty years, made five people appear in public in 1831. Mr Alexander Macgregor who came as minister to Balquhidder in 1804 took an unusual attitude to parents of illegitimate children, rebuking the mothers before the Session but the fathers in public. Public rebukes continued in the church of Kilmaurs until 1844, 'in the face of the congregation' if not in the place of repentance, and as late as 1846 the Kirk Session of Kilmacolm, Renfrewshire, had considerable reservations when the minister suggested an end to public rebukes although they finally agreed. Nevertheless, against these dates there must be set the use of the jougs in Coll in 1782 and the presentation of a sackcloth gown to St. Andrews in 1836.[62]

Sessional rebukes had, in fact, always been used where thought appropriate and it was fairly common in such cases, in earlier days, as has been said, for delinquents to have to go on their knees during them; a Coldingham man was ordered in 1699 to be reprimanded before the Session 'and that on his knees' and in Hawick too, a young shepherd who had untruthfully boasted of his intimacy with a young woman was rebuked on his knees before the Session for the sin of lying. This was a much lighter penalty than appearing before the congregation and it was thanks to her age and poverty that a woman, delated for 'dichting some knockit beir' on a Sunday was sharply admonished before the Session rather than in church but, in spite of her years, it was on her knees that she had to crave God's mercy. Some Sessional rebukes were given with a warning that if the offender was found guilty again, he or she would have to appear publicly in church, which must have been a great encouragement to good behaviour. In later years, conditions were sometimes attached to Sessional rebukes; in Yester, for example, it was decided in 1822 that while delinquents should be rebuked before the Session, they should have 'frequent conversing' with the minister or an elder and only be absolved after six months or so, a type of private guidance which was meant to be helpful and acceptable. Oldmachar was more casual and a typical entry from the minutes around 1834 is 'Having paid the penalty of 22s. to the poor . . . was rebuked and dismissed from censure.' The next stage was what was decreed in Arbuthnott in 1905 — that first offenders should come before the minister and others before the Kirk Session, and as conditions changed still further, even these rebukes died out altogether.[63]

Fines — 'pecuniary mulcts' or 'reprobat money' as they were sometimes called — have been mentioned in other chapters but, being punishments, they belong among all the other methods of enforcing discipline. As time went on, the custom of fining increased until it took over from severer penalties, with the benefit that if there was sin, then the kirk might as well turn it to good purpose for the benefit of the poor, in addition to punishing it. Fines were authorised by Parliament for various sins at various times: for profane swearing in 1551, for fornication in 1567, this being the Act which also provided for ducking, imprisonment and banishment for that offence, while in 1639 it was decreed that any Scotsman who lived in Scotland but got married in England should pay a fine for the poor's funds. From 1640 until the Act was repealed in 1690, fines were imposed on anyone who was excommunicated. These fines were intended to be entirely used for pious purposes which largely meant the care of the poor although, to some extent, they had to be used for other expenses too, such as work on churchyard dykes. Fines for immorality which came to the kirk, although imposed by the civil authorities, might be, for ordinary people, 40s. Scots for the first fault, 100 merks for the second and £100 Scots for the third, for the man and the woman, in addition to possible imprisonment, ducking or other extras. Social status was involved in deciding what penalties were payable. For the first fault, a nobleman paid £400, a baron £200, a gentleman or burgess £100 and an 'inferior person' £10, all Scots money and payable by men and women. For succeeding faults, the fines were doubled in theory but in practice they varied considerably and can never have been fully exacted as otherwise, as has already been said, the poor's boxes of the country would have been overflowing.[64]

In 1644 the General Assembly passed an Act to encourage the in-gathering of any fines which were due to the church, advising both Presbyteries and ministers to be diligent in procuring the full execution of any Acts of Parliament which allowed for 'pecunial pains for restraining of vice and advancing piety' and urged them to see to 'uplifting the said penalties contained in the same, and for faithful employment thereof', repeating this recommendation in very similar terms in 1647. Parliament helped in 1661 with an Act against Profaneness which required collectors of fines to be appointed, leaving it to ministers, Kirk Sessions and heritors in landward areas to decide how much these men should be paid 'according to their pains and diligence' and stating that the balance should go to the poor. A further Act of Parliament in 1672 ordered judges to try those delated to them by Kirk Sessions for the sins of drunkenness, profanity and others too, saying that half of any fines should go to the kirk, each Session having to appoint their own collector, who was very possibly their treasurer, to ensure that the money was received for the care of the poor, and much of the fining that brought money into kirk coffers was based on this Act. Royal burghs had to appoint their own collectors. With such a splendid way of raising money available to them, it does seem surprising that as late as 1715 the Presbytery of Dornoch considered

> with grieff the abounding of the horrid sin of uncleanness in the bounds, and that the loss of goods is of more weight to deter the generality from their filthiness than any regard of God or the censures of the Church, and considering that the pecuniary mulcts appointed by the Law of the Land are far from being exacted by those concerned to do so, Doe therefor appoint that the Several Brethren use their utmost endeavours with the Session Bailies to be more diligent in raising such fines . . .[65]

To start with at any rate, magistrates were not always willing to hand over to an offender's parish half of the fines they imposed. They might sound co-operative enough but that was as far as it went and Inverness, for example, was one place where it was not until about 1695 that the Burgh Council agreed to give the Session their proper share. Nevertheless, things improved slowly so that, far from a Kirk Session having to send in their collector, fines were often sent directly to the Kirk

Session from Justice Courts or other quarters or were, on the orders of the magistrates, paid by the offenders directly to the kirk. Thus it was that in 1722 Logie Kirk Session, Stirlingshire, received £1 from the Sheriff of Clackmannan which was half of a fine 'taken from one in this parish for swearing'; in 1762 Cathcart Kirk Session received 'from Mr. James Hill, Writer in Glasgow, a fine taken from a person for selling excisable liquor, exacted by the Justices in Renfrewshire, 2s. 6d.'; and Sprouston Kirk Session, Roxburghshire, found their funds helped to the tune of £2 16s. that year which they were given as Robert Hope's penalty for not taking out an ale licence. In 1765 the Collector of Stamp Duty wrote to parish ministers asking them to warn their parishioners that the Act of Parliament concerning retailing of spirits without a licence would be rigorously executed, something which they doubtless did, even if it was liable to decrease kirk funds because alcohol-related offences were a fruitful source of income for the church, as were certain other non-ecclesiastical sins. In 1819 the minister of Stow received 3 guineas from the Procurator Fiscal for the poor of the parish, being fines imposed on two men guilty of assault on the night of the last Stow Fair while, in Banchory-Devenick in 1756, a fine of £14 was received from the Procurator Fiscal at Stonehaven which had been recovered from a salmon fisher. In 1567 Parliament decreed that fines for offences against the game laws should go half to the king and the other half be shared between the judge and the apprehender, which must have encouraged both arrests and convictions, but that changed and fines for poaching then went entirely to the kirk. Yetholm Kirk Session's minutes in 1835 report that 'It was generally understood in the parish that Andrew Young, Kirk Yetholm, lately convicted of poaching, had paid a fine of 2 gns which by sentence of the Justices was to be sent to, and spent by, the Kirk Session of Yetholm for behoof of the poor of the parish' but in spite of obvious good intentions about it, in this case the fine had not been handed over and the Session had to write to the Justice Clerk asking for it but it had still not been received the following year. The Act anent Burial in Scots linen, passed in 1686, was another which provided for half the fines to go to the poor, but which had a nasty ring about it by allowing the other half to go to the informer.[66]

The Act of Parliament of 1672 made it plain that it was not for Kirk Sessions to impose fines themselves. They were a civil penalty and the kirk was meant to refer offenders to a court which alone had the power to fine delinquents and this, of course, was why Session bailies were so convenient. However, if no bailie or magistrate was present at a Session meeting, it saved trouble all round, particularly in rural districts, if the Kirk Session just stated what the fine was and took it directly from the offender. Furthermore, although Parliament had decreed which offences could be punished by fines, Kirk Sessions began to use fines for all sorts of sins which they did by passing their own Acts of Session and fines imposed by Sessions became a very important source of revenue, especially as the whole of them came to the poor's box and Sessions cheerfully imposed penalties for all sorts of things such as ignorance of the Commandments, not coming to catechising and absence from church without good reason. Even an elder's bad headache was considered no excuse for failing to attend a Session meeting and he was fined 2*s*. and a deacon pleading toothache as a reason for absence had to pay 1*s*. A fine of 2*s*. Scots was decreed in 1634 by one Session for any elder or deacon who failed to attend the Tuesday Session meetings without reasonable excuse and while all of these might be regarded as ecclesiastical offences, in addition Oldmachar Kirk Session imposed a fine of 6*s*. 8*d*. on anyone bringing a dog into church, at Elgin anyone bringing a horse into the kirkyard was also fined and digging up turf in the churchyard at market time was a finable offence too. There were many more sins, especially Sabbath profanation, for which fines were imposed but these are mentioned elsewhere. One writer described the situation thus, 'Having got its hand among the fines, the Kirk Session began to fine right and left.' No wonder that there was such diligence in seeking out sins and so useful were fines to kirk funds that they were often imposed on a well-off delinquent rather than the public appearance and rebuke in church which would be the lot of a poor person.[67]

Although the kirk in general wanted fines paid in cash, it could be difficult for some people to do this when wages were very low and often paid six-monthly. It was easier for them to pay in kind and this was sometimes allowed if it fitted in with what a kirk might need at the time. One Session which had decided to have the church walls lime-washed arranged that two men with penalties owing should pay part of them in the necessary lime, and elsewhere a man promised his Session that he would give 'staines for bigging of the bridge for his penalty.' Some might pay in grain and some in service; one man had his penalty withdrawn altogether because 'of some services done to the Parish at the re-entry of the minister.' Others might pay their fines in household goods; one woman who was quite unable to pay cash offered a blanket worth 40*s*. Scots in lieu which her Session accepted, either for some needy person or for sale. It is said that in the parish of Ewes young offenders used to be sent to pull heather for the kirk thatch, which meant going to the hills for it, a fore-runner of community service.[68] Still other methods were devised to help people pay. Many Session minutes show payment by instalments as when Simon Simpson in Cromarty 'paid in a merk of his penalty', or they might accept security in the form of a pledge, usually some household article or clothing. A man who had wrongly called another a thief was ordered in 1665, in addition to standing in sackcloth, to pay a fine of 4 merks, with his plaid accepted until the money was forthcoming, and the minutes faithfully record the date on which he 'relieved his plaid'. In some cases, delinquents made a formal promise to pay, like a man in Coll who gave in a bill stating that he would pay his fine for ante-nuptial fornication in August, probably hoping to have secured his harvest by then and to be in a position to pay. Even when certain offences carried fixed penalties, a compromise about this might be made, shown in accounts by the words 'Accepted in full' alongside whatever had been paid. A different word for the same thing was 'modification' of a fine, such as appears in the minutes of Kilninian and Kilmore Kirk Session. In 1768 a fine for ante-nuptial fornication was modified to 5*s*. and in 1770 a man paid £1 for relapse in fornication and a modified fine of 10s. for the woman concerned. Although it is not so stated, the reason for these reductions must have been poverty and certainly another Session halved a fine in 1828 because the delinquent was 'just a poor apprentice' while in 1779 yet another waived a girl's penalty entirely 'in regard of her poverty'. This was kind and sensible but in earlier days such merciful mitigation was strongly disapproved of, with Elgin Kirk Session decreeing in 1596 that any elders voting to 'mitigat and deducis' any penalties laid down by the Session, should themselves pay as much as they mitigated.[69] Where there was a possibility that a delinquent, although poor, might ultimately be able to pay a fine, a Session might allow unlimited time; in 1728 a man guilty of immoral conduct paid a crown of his fine 'which considering their poverty the Session accepted of at present he having promised to pay the oyr twentie shillings Scots how soon he can', but a delay in the time allowed to pay could alternatively be turned into a suspended sentence. A man who relapsed in fornication paid £1 for himself and 10s. for the woman involved 'and gave bill for 20s. more for himself with the minister's promise not to exact this unless he relapses again in which case it is to be charged as due for his second offence' and another Session minuted that two men guilty of cursing and swearing had not yet paid their fines but 'they both being poor, the Session delay their exacting of them till they see how they carry in time coming.' A woman guilty of flyting and scolding, something to which she was prone, had to pay 3 merks Scots in case of 'any outbreak hereafter' and also 'to give baill for her behaviour in future.' In spite of efforts to help those who found payment difficult, and using unpaid fines as a deterrent to future bad conduct, arrears of penalties could be a serious problem and a very common way of trying to ensure payment was by requiring a delinquent to find a cautioner both for payment of the fine and for his or her public appearance in church, hence the following minute: 'Donald McKenzie, Fornicator, called, compeared, and acknowledged his guilt, and presented Alexander Cormack who hereby enacts himself surety both for mulct and satisfaction to discipline.' Cautioners had to give evidence of their willingness to undertake this responsibility, hence 'Roderick M'Neil and Neil Paterson gave a bill for Hector Paterson and party's fine' said the minutes of Kilninian and Kilmore Kirk Session in 1770 but so frequently do cautioners appear in Session records that it seems doubtful whether all of them really understood the implications of becoming guarantors, especially when the person for whom they became surety was poor. Such a person had little to lose except the cautioner's friendship if the latter was left to pay but the system of accepting caution must have saved many a Session having to pursue a non-payer as the cautioner would be only too ready to do it for them. There were, of course, cases where caution could not be found and commonsense had to be used. When a stranger to one parish was unable to find anyone to act as surety for his fine, the Session remitted half of it, probably feeling it was better to have a bird in the hand than two in the bush.[70]

Some Sessions tried to deal with the problem of non-payment of fines by imposing a time limit. In Falkirk for instance, in the early seventeenth century, this was just fifteen days. Others charged interest on unpaid fines. The longer fines were unpaid, the more difficult recovery became and in 1680 Fordyce Kirk Session had about £147 Scots of penalties lying out, as well as some which were regarded as 'desperate' and would never be paid. In 1772 an Argyllshire Kirk Session became so concerned about the amount of fines unpaid that they asked the minister to make out a list of those owing money 'in order that some method may be fallen upon to make the payments effectual' and also recommended him 'to be as exact and punctual as possible in uplifting such fines as shall become due, without giving delinquents such long delays as they have been in use of getting, by which they are encouraged to trifle with the Session.' There was considerable variation in the methods 'fallen upon' by Sessions to deal with those who persistently failed to pay. One Session banished a female non-payer in 1673 but one suspects that there must have been more to it than the reason officially given. Cautioners could of course be pursued, while people with goods and chattels might have some articles 'poinded' or impounded. When a couple relapsed in fornication in 1702 their Session empowered the kirk officer to 'sease and apprehend any goods whatsomever that belongs to either party within this parish and to bring the same to the Treasurer.' In 1664 four people appeared before their Session for not being at church, three of whom each paid a fine of half a merk but the fourth, who did not pay on time, was poinded in a plaid; and three years later that Session poinded a man in 8 elne of harne for not paying a fine on time, which harne was made into sackcloth garments, as has been mentioned earlier. In 1640 a Session ordered the poinding of some refractory and contumacious people and it was reported that a pan had been taken from one woman, a coat from each of two others, and 'ane yron pot' from a fourth. Another Session decided to poind any linen webs found on Sundays at the waterside, which was really a fine by confiscation, in the same way that lint which a woman was found winding one Sunday was forfeited to pious uses.[71]

It was very important for the welfare of the poor that Kirk Sessions should insist on payment of penalties and if things got too bad, warnings were given to delinquents from the pulpit 'to get up their penalties' before legal proceedings were taken against them, or else the kirk officer was told to warn them that they were in danger of being summoned to court. This was no idle threat even although no Session wanted to have to resort to court action which was costly and generally unpleasant. But sometimes it was the only way and had to be used. In 1701 the Kirk Session of Kilmaurs got decreet in the Burgh Court for £40 Scots from a man and £20 from the woman in a case of immorality, with the Session Clerk acting as pursuer and in 1686 the minister of Deskford produced to the Session 'a decree purchast before the justices of the peace against delinquents who would not pay the penalties', while in 1701 the Kirk Session of Fearn obtained not only a decree for a fine of £10 but also for 30s. of expenses. When legal proceedings were threatened, however, this could still be done with considerable leniency. The kirk officer of an Argyllshire parish was ordered in 1760 to announce at the church door that all fines must be paid before the following Martinmas or else prosecutions would follow. This was done on 16 November but as Martinmas is on 11 November, it meant that delinquents were being given a year's grace unless there was some local variation in dates. It must have been very galling for a Session when a single man, with no dependents and no poindable goods, solved the problem of a fine by letting it be known that he would not pay 'without the same was evicted by course of process' and then promptly joined the army, knowing that it would be exceedingly difficult for the Session to catch up with him as he moved around the country. None of the legal processes available to Sessions could cope with that. Having said all that, the fact remains that many Sessions allowed fines to lie out year after year. An example was the case of John Smith, a Greenlaw man, who was fined in December 1719 for his irregular marriage and only paid up in May 1729, some 9½ years later. In practice, if money was not urgently needed and those owing it seemed fairly secure financially, fines were often not called in in the knowledge that they could be got when required although it does seem that it might have been better to get them in and invest the money for the poor.[72]

As this money was intended for the poor, it could be practical for a delinquent to pay his fine, not to the Session but directly to a needy person in cash or in kind, so long as the amount of the fine and that person's needs were compatible. A man fined 10s. 6d. in 1776 was ordered by the Session 'to pay the same to Hugh McDonald in Tobermore for behoof of his son Samuel, an object, which he promised to do', and a poor widow in Cromarty must have been delighted when a firlot of victual came her way in the same manner. On the island of Coll in 1733 the Session ordered that two very destitute orphans should receive 4 merks and that they should 'get this money from Catherin —, a Fornicator,' but sometimes it was the bills, the promises to pay at a later date, which were passed on. Kilninian and Kilmore Kirk Session 'gave Magnus Morrison who is now reduced to want, the bill due by William Mackenzie in Torolisk, with directions that in case said Mackenzie refuses or delays to pay 10 shillings stg then to return the bill to the minister who is hereby empowered to give any sum not exceeding 10s out of the Session's other funds.' Magnus was more fortunate than the other people mentioned, as in his case provision was made for possible non-payment, whereas there was no word of that for them. In rather the same way, when the kirk owed money for services rendered, then fines might be assigned to creditors with responsibility for gathering them in assigned also. In 1680 the Kirk Session of Fearn had outstanding fines imposed on thirteen people over the previous six years for fornication, Sabbath breaking and scandalising, and these they assigned to David Forbes 'for certain onorous causes and good deeds done . . . with full power . . . to persue . . . before any judge competent,' a somewhat onerous form of payment.[73]

Obviously fining by the kirk had its faults. One writer considered that a particularly objectionable function of both Episcopalian and Presbyterian church government was fining of delinquents, with the money going into a fund administered at the will of the Session. There came to be sufficient criticism of the practice for Rev. Thomas Easton, writing his report on pauperism in 1825, to feel it necessary to defend it:

> I am aware that the payment of penalties has been misunderstood. There are some who deny the legality of it. The payment of a penalty is due, in whatever manner the culprit is censured. It is provided by Acts of Parliament that pecunial sums be levied from all guilty of fornication. Presbyteries and ministers are ordained by the same authority to be diligent in exacting the same . . . All that is done by the Kirk Session is to see that these fines, which are by most acknowledged to be just, are levied.

In this, however, Mr Easton was defending the legal imposition of fines by civil courts when what was objected to was fines imposed directly by Kirk Sessions which were never legal, although people paid them, and which were wide open to abuses which soon crept in. Although the General Assembly had decreed in 1572 that sackcloth must never be dispensed with in return for money for pious uses and had laid down minimum numbers of days of public appearances for different offences, nevertheless the church began to fine those able to pay rather than to require the making of public satisfaction, or to accept additional sums to reduce the number of appearances, which smacked of Roman Catholic indulgences and was one of the sins laid at the door of the Church of Scotland by the Cameronian sect in 1742. Indeed the word 'indulge' was occasionally used in this context in Kirk Session minutes: in 1777 a Kirkwall bailie was found guilty of immorality and confessed with every mark of sincerity before a Session meeting which, whether by chance or intention was held in a private house, and it was there that he was rebuked 'and indulged (upon paying the extraordinary penalty of one guinea) from appearing before the congregation.' Also in Orkney, 'two delinquents of quality' were allowed at their earnest request to make private satisfaction to church discipline and were absolved from church censure, paying for this privilege £12 12s. Scots as well as their marriage fee of £1 10s. Scots and 1s. stg. each to the clerk and the kirk officer. In the same way, an Argyllshire man 'Alexander M'Niven in Letirmore having paid for himself and party a fine of one pound, offered to give 10s. more if the Session would pass from his public repentance which upon mature deliberation they agreed to accept and absolved him upon a Sessional rebuke which was done', and four years later Colin Campbell paid that Session a fine of 1 guinea for fornication and another one 'in lieu of standing', 10s. for the privilege of being allowed to marry with only one instead of the normal three proclamations and 16s. for 'his party's fine'. This word 'party' is often used in minutes, with the woman's name not given, whether from delicacy or as part of the financial package is not known but it is likely to have been the latter as Sessions were not normally squeamish about naming women. The only valid reason for speeding up public appearances was during a vacancy when every opportunity for administering rebukes had to be taken when a minister was available.[74]

Whatever the rights or wrongs of fining in this way, it was an excellent means of bringing in money — a Banffshire parish received £999 Scots between 1701–4 from fines alone — and when Sessions were hard-pressed financially, why insist on public appearances or the wearing of sackcloth or standing in a particular place in church to be rebuked before the congregation when the empty poor's box could be so easily filled and the needs of the poor provided for? The simple logic of it all appears in many Kirk Session minutes. In Orphir, Orkney, in 1789 a man's punishment of three public appearances was converted into an extraordinary payment of 1 guinea 'considering the low state of the funds'; in 1740 a man in Fordyce asked to be rebuked before the Session rather than in church if he paid an extra sum and this was allowed 'because of the great number of poor and lack of victual'. In the same way, a Galston man was allowed in 1637 to stand before the congregation in his own clothing rather than in sackcloth on payment of an increased fine, for the very good reason that the Session had need of 'present money'. Not everyone could pay enough to get out of appearing before the congregation entirely and some were glad enough to settle for some reduction in public appearances in return for money. The records of Galston, for one, show that while the poor would have to 'stand high' for the appropriate number of Sundays, those who could pay at least something for the privilege would only have to stand for one day in linen and the other two days in their own clothing in return for 40s. Scots which gave the Session 'money in hand' and was a useful sum as it was sufficient to 'pey for a [winding] sheet for a puir deid body.' In 1748 a Rathven man gave a sum above the normal fine in the hope that his satisfaction could be completed the following Sunday which the Session permitted but in another case where a couple admitted fornication, the man asked if he might be absolved after just one appearance if he paid a little more than the usual fine, saying that his health was bad and that his business would take him away before the following Sunday. For this he had to pay half a guinea but, very ungallantly, he did not include the woman; she was left 'to begin appearances after him'. The poor people meanwhile suffered punishments in the traditional way:

> Now Tom maun face the minister
> And she maun mount the pillar
> And that's the way that thae maun gae
> For poor folk hae nae siller.[75]

On occasion a sinner might give an ultimatum of 'take it or leave it' as happened in Ayrshire in 1735 when a man of some standing from Cumnock asked to be absolved if he appeared on just one Sunday, morning and afternoon and paid £16 Scots, otherwise he said he would pay the ordinary penalty and appear for three days. This mixture of threat and bribery worked and the Session accepted his suggestion. It says much for any Kirk Session which resisted this attractive form of fund-raising and the minister of Tynninghame in the first half of the seventeenth century was one who did not agree with fines for the privileged in return for special consideration, believing that it was 'not in his power' to allow them. He did not hesitate to call the highest in the parish before the congregation if he thought this was right; only once did he commute a penalty into money and that was because 'there were so many poore' at a time when the 'collects' were very small but he told the Session and had it minuted that this was not to form a precedent. Yetholm Kirk Session was one which held out against fines for the well-to-do until 1818 and even then, it was only because neighbouring parishes had already accepted the practice that they took, because their funds were low, 5 guineas from a farmer in return for giving him a Sessional rebuke for fornication instead of public appearances, although they took care to minute that they might return to their former stricter penalties if this change was not 'conducive to edification'.[76]

In addition to the money received, the element of favouritism which emerges from all this is understandable in the social climate of the times when ordinary people, and that included elders, were dependent on the goodwill of the gentry and no one wanted to fall out with a landlord; in addition, heritors funded much of the work of the kirk and it would have been foolish to offend them lest doing so indirectly harmed the community. Some might argue that the upper classes were in any event penalised more heavily for moral offences, with a sliding scale of penalties according to rank, although rank itself must have saved many a kirk prosecution or at any rate mitigated its consequences. An example of this was a case of gross Sabbath profanation in Ross-shire in 1722. Some gentlemen, including the laird of Skibo in Sutherland, crossed the Dornoch Firth by ferry into Ross-shire, spent much of the day eating and drinking, fired their pistols in the air and rode their way through three parishes before departing for home. This resulted in a *fama clamosa* which the Presbytery referred to the Commission of the General Assembly which replied saying that the profanation had been very great and deserved censure — but all that happened was a Presbyterial rebuke. 'Reading between the lines it is evident that a good deal of influence, both in Edinburgh and within the Presbytery of Tain, was employed on behalf of these men . . . otherwise they would not have been so submissive nor would they have got off with a Presbyterial rebuke.'[77]

There were other aspects of abuse that could creep into fining by Kirk Sessions. In 1772 one Session had no money at all, yet there was in the parish one particularly needy woman. What could they do but authorise the minister to give her a little something 'out of the first poor's money that shall come to hand' and to give himself credit for the same? How they must have longed for someone to fine and there were other cases where similar feelings must have existed. When a new Session Clerk was appointed by a Session around 1705, he was promised that he would receive £10 out of the fines if there were any but if there were none, then he would get nothing. What an encouragement this must have been to him and to others in a similar position to see that those who could afford it were fined rather than undergoing the public censure given to the poor. When another Session appointed a collector of fines, with power to prosecute where people would not submit to discipline, he was allowed a percentage of what he could extort, again an incentive to have as many cash penalties as possible.[78]

In Queen Anne's reign it was decreed that no civil penalty whatsoever should be incurred by anyone prosecuted by the church courts of Scotland but church fines still continued to be imposed, including a rather odd case which occurred in

Mauchline in 1732. A woman offered to pay half a guinea to the poor if she might stand for just one day in the place of repentance, rather than the full number of appearances. Although she had not confessed her sin, this was perhaps assumed by her offer but, properly speaking, guilt should either have been confessed or proved by evidence before a rebuke was intimated or a fine exacted. Arbuthnott was one parish where financial penalties were given up in the early 1770s, at the same time as public appearances ended, although those in a position to do so might choose to give something for the poor. When Banff Kirk Session decided in 1835 to 'depart from the exaction of a penalty in consequence of such having a tendency to lead to un-Scriptural and papistical views', they were really referring to Roman Catholic indulgences. About that time the General Assembly called for a committee report on the fining of delinquents and concluded that this should be forbidden, leaving it to the curators of the poor's funds of each parish to adopt such measures as they might for the benefit of the poor, and passed an Act to that effect in 1837. However, it did not immediately get through to all parishes that the position had changed. It was only in November 1839 that Presbyteries, in the north anyway, were told about this and passed the information on to their Sessions, which explains how the Kirk Session of Edderton brought an action in July that year before the Sheriff-Substitute against a pensioner for payment of a penalty of £10 Scots (unusual to find Scots money as late as this) alleged to be due from him for violating an Act of 1664. This demand was resisted on the grounds that the kirk treasurer had no right to pursue for it without the Procurator Fiscal's agreement, particularly as only half of it was applicable to pious uses, and the case was dismissed.[79]

One reason why so many people submitted to the many forms of punishment available to the church was because they dreaded the most terrible one of all, excommunication, of which there were two degrees, Greater or Higher, and Lesser. Put into modern English, the sentence of Higher Excommunication ran more or less thus:

> Having God only before our eyes [name of person] be excommunicated, separated and cut off from the congregation and mystical body of Christ Jesus, and all benefits of his true kirk (the hearing of God's word only excepted); delivering him unto Satan for the destruction of the flesh, that the spirit may be saved in the day of the Lord; and that none of the faithful, fearing God, from this hour forth, accompany with him in communing, talking, buying, selling, eating, drinking, or other way whatsoever, except they be appointed of the kirk for his amendment.

Terrible though it sounds to deliver even a sinner to Satan, doing so was based on Scriptural authority. Paul, writing to Timothy said, 'It was through spurning conscience that certain persons made shipwreck of their faith . . . whom I consigned to Satan, in the hope that through this Discipline they might learn not to be blasphemous.' Ironically, there is an instance of a woman being excommunicated and handed over to Satan for consigning someone to the devil herself, saying 'De'il tak ye', or something of the sort. Excommunication was sometimes known as 'cursing,' as when a couple promised not to repeat an offence 'under pain of cursyng'. Greater Excommunication excluded a person from all church privileges such as baptism, marriage and the Lord's Supper and even burial in the kirkyard was forbidden but had to take place apart and possibly at night, like suicides and unbaptised infants. It is said that the dead bell was rung when people were excommunicated but whether that was so or not, the Kirk Session of Elgin was one which ordered in 1596 that the dead bell should be rung through the town and a warning given to all parishioners not to accompany the body of any excommunicated person to burial under pain of £10 Scots and making public repentance. In 1569/70 the General Assembly ruled that excommunicated people, who were not fugitives from law, might stand bare-headed at the church door between services and enter the church for the sermon only, sitting in the place of repentance and being sure to leave before the last prayer. In other words, they were excluded from prayers as being past praying for because, in the preliminaries to the pronouncing of the sentence of Higher Excommunication, the transgressor would have already been prayed for publicly three times, and resisted these prayers, and so could expect no more. In spite of this, excommunicated people must have attempted to attend the whole of services very frequently as in 1587 Parliament felt it necessary to pass an Act decreeing that should any such person enter the church during common prayers or during the Sacraments, he or she was to be ordered out by the minister and in the event of disobeying, to be imprisoned until they found caution to reconcile themselves to the kirk. They were outwith the society of Christian people; civil laws ordered that if they did not reconcile themselves to the church within forty days they would be declared rebels and have their goods forfeited.[80] No excommunicated person was allowed directly or indirectly to hold land, rents or revenues, these being initially uplifted for the monarch's use although in 1641 Parliament decreed that their penalties should pertain to the kirk for pious uses. All in all, the practical effect of these ecclesiastical and civil penalties together was meant to be that an excommunicated person was deprived of income, virtually ruined, rendered unemployable and boycotted by all respectable people. According to Professor Smout, excommunication was used sparingly in the days of royal control through bishops but after 1640 the Covenanters in the General Assembly resorted to it again and again for political as well as moral offences and it was for this reason that, although the civil penalties of excommunication were retained in the Episcopalian days of Charles II, they were finally abandoned in 1690 lest the restored General Assembly should ever again be tempted to misuse its independence. The ending of civil penalties for excommunication is said to have greatly weakened discipline although Kirk Session minutes do not seem to bear that out, but excommunication itself continued as an ecclesiastical punishment with ecclesiastical penalties for some time thereafter, used mainly as a last desperate measure to bring to heel those who, in serious cases, would not submit to discipline. The General Assembly declared in 1707 that 'All processes, in order to Greater Excommunication, are to be founded on manifest contumacy, or scandalous practices, and where these are not, the Lesser Excommunication needs only to have place . . .' The Act in which this was stated referred, although with an implication that such things were in the past, to the church having 'according to Scriptural warrant, summarily excommunicated persons guilty of atrocious, scandalous sins, to show the church's abhorrence of such wickedness' and indeed where civil courts had failed to pronounce the death penalty for murder, there were cases of the church imposing the sentence of Greater Excommunication instead. A slant on the kirk's early attitude to the civil offence of murder and ecclesiastical offences is that in 1598 Elgin Kirk Session ordered that the child of someone excommunicated for murder could be baptised but not the children of those excommunicated for religious reasons.[81]

Examples of initial sins which ultimately brought Greater Excommunication upon the sinners' heads include being 'an infamous strumpet' or a notorious one, continuing to cohabit after being ordered not to do so, especially where there were children of the liaison, bigamy, sodomy and incest, as well as the more usual offence of producing illegitimate children without cohabitation. Persistent offending was dealt with by the kirk through excommunication because it indicated a disregard of discipline already imposed and explains why a woman 'having been pregnant five times in fornication and she being a nuisance in the parish was ordered to be excommunicated forthwith in terms of the appointment of the Presbytery.' In all these cases, excommunication was inflicted not so much for a particular sin as for contumacy about it — refusing to submit to kirk discipline — because if that were allowed to continue, it would undermine the authority of the church.[82]

The basic aim in discipline cases was to make people confess, repent and submit to censure and punishment. Excommunication was something which neither Kirk Session nor Presbytery hastened to inflict. It was only if a delinquent refused to appear before the Kirk Session, having been called upon to do so, and was therefore remitted by them to the Presbytery and also refused to appear before them, that the possibility of excommunication arose. Even then, it was something to be deliberated about in depth as it was only imposed with Presbytery authority. In 1707 the Presbytery of Dornoch discussed the case of a man who had failed to appear when summoned, who did not 'wait upon' several ministers in order 'to converse with them for his further instruction' as he had been told to do, and who was contumacious after three citations to appear and then left the district. The members of the Presbytery could not fail to think about excommunication at this point

> and after prayer to that effect, it being put to the vote, excommunicate or not, it carried excommunicate, wherefore the Presbytery did and hereby do, excommunicate the said Hugh McDonald and deliver him up to Satan . . . and appoint that his sentence be intimate at the most patent church door by the Clerk and the Church Officer and that each minister of the Presbytery intimate the same from their pulpits next Lord's Day,

and in fact such intimations were sometimes made beyond the Presbytery bounds.

After such a decision there were still various formal procedures to be gone through before excommunication was made final. There was a series of public admonitions and prayers for the sinner; the Presbytery of Fordyce ordered a man to receive the first, second and third admonitions in July, August and September and the first, second and third prayers on three Sundays in November which was all so overwhelming that he confessed in December and he was by no means the only one to give in when the prospect of excommunication became a reality. In August 1705 the Presbytery of Selkirk ordered that an Ashkirk man should be 'three several Lords dayes prayed for publickly before the congregation, ere they yett proceed to the sentence of excommunication' but he still did not appear. The Session once again asked the Presbytery for advice and it was only in September 1706, a year later, that he was finally excommunicated although his case might have been regarded as fairly serious as, starting with adultery, he had sent his partner in sin to England so as to be out of the way, forged a letter from her husband and then fled to England too, only returning in August 1705.[83]

The whole process of a case of potential Higher Excommunication which lasted from 1720–23 appears in the minutes of St. Boswells Kirk Session:

> December 1720. The whilk day, the session, considering that the sentence of Lesser Excommunication had been passed against Margaret Currie, spouse to Andrew Smith in Lessudden, according to the appointment of the Presbytery for her contumacy in not appearing before them when cited and called to answer for her sin of uncleannes, viz Adultery . . . and had been lying under the said sentence since the 11th day of May one thousand seven hundred and eighteen years.

Her husband had also been guilty of adultery in Falkirk but neither of them 'had ever signified any Remorse for their sin but on the contrary have turned their Back upon Gospel ordinances and Do Contemn church discipline, therefore the session thought fit that they should be proceeded against with the highest censure of the church and for that, did and hereby do Refer them to the Presbytery.' On 8 January 1721 'Andrew Smith and Margaret Currie got the first admonition in order to the pronouncing of the sentence of Higher Excommunication according to the appointment of the Presbytery.' In February she received the second admonition and in March confessed her adultery and was referred to the Presbytery, as a result of which the minister informed the Session in April that the Presbytery 'had ordered Margaret Currie to wait upon our session . . . she was called and ordered to appear before the congregation in sackcloth the next Lord's Day.' In May her husband got the third admonition and was cited to appear before the Presbytery but it was only in September that the first public prayer was made for him and followed by two more Sundays' prayers that month. In December that year the minister

> informed the session that Margaret Currie came to him and Desired to be absolved, qrupon the session thought fit to call her before ym in order to give some evidence of her sorrow and humiliation for her sin. She was called and compeared, was examined about the nature of true Repentance and God's sorrow for sin; and gave no satisfying answers to the questions propounded to her. She was ordered by the session to continue in her public repentance before the congregation and to wait

upon the minister sometimes at his own house in order to be better instructed in the nature of true repentance and Godly sorrow . . .

Three weeks later, the minister told the Session that Margaret

> had come several times to him and that he had taken some pains upon her to instruct her in the nature of true repentance, qrupon the session thought fit to call her, she being called and having given satisfying answers to some questions proposed to her and the elders being severally Enquired at annent their being satisfied with qt they had heard from her and Discerned in her conversation they all signified their being satisfied with her answers and referred her to the Presbytery in order to her being absolved.

Her husband however had still not got himself sorted out and just over a year later, in January 1723, the minister reported that Andrew, 'against whom the sentence of Excommunication was to have been pronounced upon Sabbath first, had come to him and showed himself ready to acknowledge his sin of Adultery'; he was called before them and confessed 'but having little sense of sin he was long and earnestly dealt with . . . the session thought it most proper to delay the pronouncing of the sentence of Excommunication for this time' and referred him to the Presbytery. As a result of this he appeared before the congregation in sackcloth in March but did not keep up his public repentance and in September that year the Session

> taking into their serious consideration that Andrew Smith has now for a long time absented himself from making public repentance before the congregation in sackcloth and that he had not come down to the minister as he was appointed, therefore they appoint their officer to desire him to come down to the minister some time this week and make his appearance before the congregation in sackcloth as formerly otherwise they will proceed against him, the said Andrew, to the pronouncing of the solemn sentence of Excommunication.

He duly appeared on 15 September but cheated the Kirk Session in the end: on 24 October the minutes report that he 'was making his repentance and not yet absolved' when he was 'carried off by death', and go on to say 'The session considering that none of Andrew Smith's relations is in a condition to defray his funeral charges, therefore they ordain John Jameson, Treasurer, to pay part of them out of the poor money.'[84] This case shows how prolonged the whole business could be and how the delinquent was given every opportunity to avoid excommunication by confession and repentance. Another dramatic conclusion to the long process occurred at Kinghorn in 1646. After Henrie Chrystie had received the third admonition and the minister was moving on to the first prayers as a prelude to excommunication, 'god smote the said henrie chrystie wt sickness that he died.'[85]

Where excommunication was finally carried out, the awful words were spoken from the delinquent's own parish pulpit, either by his or her own minister or one appointed by the Presbytery to do so but, in practice, people under sentence of Higher Excommunication might not be as socially isolated as the kirk would have them be. A Selkirk woman who had been excommunicated for a year, cheerfully went to a 'cummering' feast to celebrate the birth of a baby and although when the

Kirk Session heard of it and summoned the man of the house to explain how he had allowed her to be there, the fact remains that although he denied having invited her, nevertheless he and those present must have been perfectly happy to have her with them. A more surprising instance of people associating with an excommunicated person happened in Kirkwall in 1734. Two men, one an elder, were accused by the Session of voting in favour of Robert Greenfield, under sentence of Higher Excommunication, to become a freeman in what seems to have been a trade guild. This they admitted but said that it had been 'carried by a plurality of votes before their signing the same.' The minister explained to them the evil of what they had done and the Session referred the matter to the Presbytery. The man who was not an elder agreed to have no further dealings with Robert but the elder did not appear before the Presbytery and was suspended, at least temporarily, from the eldership.[86]

The threat of excommunication was very effective in making people submit to church discipline about sins they had committed but it could also be used as a threat as the following minute from the Presbytery of Lewis in April 1776 shows:

> The Presbytery took into their consideration that a great number of the inhabitants of this island, especially in and about the town of Stornoway are by their situation addicted to a seafaring life, whereby the exercise of discipline, more particularly with regard to the fathering and maintenance of bastard children are retarded and sometimes frustrated; it being a common practice when a woman guilty of fornication gives up a seafaring man as the father of her child, even should he be ashore and within the bounds of the parish, he pays little regard to one or more summons, with a view to going to sea before he can be called to appear, and after he goes to sea, it is the common practice to discontinue the process against him till his return, at which time he generally repeats the same conduct or has recourse to some other species of chicanery to put off any decision till he can get to sea . . . while during this time the poor woman and child are probably perishing with cold and hunger . . .

It was decided therefore that whenever a man was named as father of such a child, he should immediately be summoned to the next meeting of Session, and if at sea at the time 'he shall be summoned howsoon his landing is known to the Session', and if he went to sea in these circumstances, without appearing before the Session or getting permission from them to go, then the Session and Presbytery should proceed against him as contumacious, even to the imposition of Higher Excommunication, and this decision was read within all the bounds of the Presbytery.[87]

Serious and greatly dreaded though excommunication was, it was not nearly so bad in practical terms as banishment which drove sinners out of their homes and their parishes, without prospect of help. For the sentence of excommunication to be lifted, all that was needed was submission to the laws of the church, confession, repentance and acceptance of whatever punishment the kirk inflicted and, just as imposition of the sentence was widely notified from pulpits, so was the fact of its lifting. In 1707 the General Assembly laid down how such absolution should be granted and no one could find fault with the very loving and welcoming way in which an excommunicated person was to be received back into the fold. Should such a person show signs of true repentance and a humble desire to recover peace with God, his people and the Presbytery, and ask to be received back once more, the Presbytery if they were satisfied, gave a warrant for absolution. Then the penitent was brought before the congregation to make a free confession of the sin committed, something which might have to be done more than once as the General Assembly decreed that it should 'be as often as shall be found for edification, and trial of the professing penitent's sincerity.' Once this was satisfactorily completed and after praise and prayer in the congregation, the sentence of absolution was to be pronounced in the following or similar words:

> Whereas, thou — , has been for thy sins, shut out from the Communion of the faithful, and has now manifested thy repentance, wherein the church resteth satisfied, I, in the name of the Lord Jesus, before this congregation, pronounce and declare thee absolved from the sentence of Excommunication formerly denounced against thee, and do receive thee to the Communion of the church, and the free Use of all the ordinances of Christ, that thou mayest be Partaker of all his benefits to thy eternal salvation,

which was followed by the minister speaking to the penitent 'as a brother', by embraces from the elders 'and the whole congregation holdeth Communion with him as one of their own.'[88] The wording of this Act referred to male excommunicants but Lorimer's *Early Days of St. Cuthbert's Church* gives an example of a woman being received back after what must have been excommunication. This case comes from St. Andrews and includes Lorimer's comments. In 1586 Cristane Zwill was 'ressavit againe to the unite Kirk in the manner following' — her offence was briefly mentioned which she acknowledged and promised not to repeat, she humiliated herself on her knees and asked God's mercy and the congregation's forgiveness. The minister then took her by the hand where he stood in the pulpit, and appointed her to go to as many of the elders as had been told to sit together for that purpose and who, in the name of the kirk, should receive her and embrace her as their sister, thank God for her conversion and make public prayer for her continuance. 'Although the elders chosen may have been quite willing to do their duty in the way of embracing their erring sisters, there may be doubts,' says Lorimer, 'as to whether it was for the edification of the congregation and it is certain that the elders' wives would have had an objection to it.'[89]

Lesser Excommunication, which was not infrequent, was formal suspension from the Lord's Table but it was not the same thing as being refused a token to partake of the Sacrament, which was what happened to all those who were undergoing church censure and had yet to complete satisfaction or those whose religious knowledge was insufficient for them to be allowed to communicate. Lesser Excommunication was a special sentence added to a rebuke, intended to show that the official censure was very serious and not to be forgotten all at once and that the offender was not fit to be a Communicant until a different spirit came over him or her.[90] The following case from Elie in 1661 is not called Lesser Excommunication but that is what it appears to be. An Act of Session was read by the Session Clerk 'concerning David Nairne his suspension from the Sacrament of the Lords Supper till he evidences his repentance in his afterwalke' which described how he 'by diverse sad provoking scandalous sin has frequentlie before, and now of late (by grosse drunkenness horid cursing and swearing and also railing, and also by casting his ticket in the fire)' had come to be suspended. The Session required the congregation 'to shunn unnecessarie conversation with him . . . and when in necessarie conversation . . . to shunn to sit with him till he be overcome with drinke, And . . . such as sell drinke shunn to sell drinke to him to excess as they would shunn the Sessions censure.' Although Kirk Sessions could impose Lesser Excommunication by Act of Session, this was only done after they brought all the facts before the Presbytery; and the Act of the General Assembly of 1707 concerning both degrees of excommunication, provided for Lesser Excommunication to be increased to Higher in certain circumstances: 'If people continue under Lesser Excommunication for a considerable time, and are frequently found relapsing in those vices they were censured for, it may be considered such a degree of contumacy as to found a process for Higher Excommunication', which was in the course of happening in the St. Boswells case already quoted. It is not always clear in Kirk Session minutes which degree of excommunication was imposed but cases in which it was clearly the lesser include that of a ship's carpenter who went for timber on a Sunday and refused to submit to the Kirk Session's censure for doing so, a woman who was 'disobedient and contumacious' to all orders from the Session and another who was suspected of having been bribed to say that the father of her child was someone she had met on the road and had never seen before. A woman, guilty of ante-nuptial fornication, who declared that she would only make public satisfaction when John Tytler's wife did so too, and persisted in this attitude, was also sentenced to Lesser Excommunication.[91] So was Agnes Scott, an unmarried Hawick woman who, in 1700, discovering that she was pregnant, went to 'physical purging wells' to try to get rid of the baby but did not succeed. After it was born, she persistently denied carnal knowledge of any man but eventually named one, saying that she had not wished to say who he was as he was 'blundered with thift' to which the minister retorted that that was not so bad as being blundered with incest and adultery, as she was, and the following sentence was read out from the pulpit:

> . . . seeing it is written, Give not holy things to Dogs, neither cast pearls before swine, the Session, lest they should be guilty of you, the said Agnes Scott's sin in prophaning the holy Sacrament, have in the name of our Lord Jesus Christ, debarred and suspended and by these presents debarrs you, the said Agnes Scott, from the holy table of the Lord till the truth of what you have said in giving up the said . . . to be the father of your child be made clear in some way or other, liklie and probable, and you by your walk give ground in charge to them that you said the truth and come truly penitent for your weakness and your using means while with child tending to the destruction thereof. And for your dissumulation having at first impudently denied that you had brought forth ane child and then blasphemously offered to swear that you never knew a man, when after it was clearly made out that you had brought forth a daughter. And We do this in the name and authority of our dearest

Lord, Suspend and Debarr you from the holy Communion of his body and blood for the destruction of your flesh, that your spirit may be saved in the day of the Lord, praying that God would according to his word, ratify this our sentence in heaven and make it an effectual means for discovering the truth and bringing you to the hearty and true repentance. And for the terrour of all others, that they commit not the like abomination. Amen. So be it.

As if that were not enough, the Session also recommended that the magistrates might impose civil punishment as well.[92]

Lesser Excommunication was only lifted when the Kirk Session was satisfied about a sinner's repentance but a sad case of this happening too late for absolution to be granted in church occurred in Dornoch in 1721. George Newl who had received the sentence of Lesser Excommunication was 'in all human appearance on his death bed, and labouring under the most loathsome and nauseous disease imaginable, in a most humbling manner' in the presence of the minister and three elders 'earnestly with tears begged pardon of God for his sin and of the congregation of Dornoch for his Stumbling and great Offence to them, & especially of the Modr. for the bad treatment he had met with from him, Likewise beseeching to be relaxed from that heavy sentence under which he was that he might have the benefit of the prayers of all good Christians', and this desperate last request was, after much consideration, granted by the Kirk Session.[93]

A rather odd form of suspension of privileges was thought up, but not actually inflicted, in the parish of Portmoak, Kinross-shire, in 1780, something which did not seem to have any authority higher than that of the Session. They were angry with a man named William Skinner who, after making many difficulties, was discovered to be the father of his maid's pregnancy. They decided that the facts 'in a narrow compass' should be read out to the congregation and also passed the following resolution which, although not so called, was really a form of Lesser Excommunication:

That William Skinner, for the causes above specified, shall be continued and looked upon as no longer a Christian member of this congregation, and consequently shall be denied all Christian privileges in this congregation, not only in regard his present position as a Fornicator and unpurged of the Scandal but Ay and while he shall demean himself in such a way as the Session shall think him unworthy to be admitted to the censures and privileges of the church, and they accordingly appoint a Narrative of this affair to be read from the pulpit next Lord's Day.

This story had an odd twist in the tail but one which is not relevant to this chapter and appears in that on marriage.[94]

But as rules are proved by exceptions, there was always the odd person to whom excommunication did not matter, almost invariably someone of a social class high enough not to be easily intimidated by kirk rules. Thomas Dudgeon of Arboll, in the parish of Tarbat, Ross-shire, was one such. In 1803 he and a woman named Jane Purves were summoned before the Session for fornication and both came to the manse where she cannot have endeared herself to the minister by saying 'if you were not a dirty scoundrel, you would never call me here. I am free before God and man,' adding for good measure to two elders who were present, 'You are a set of black hypocrites.' This was laid before the Sheriff, and after the inevitable baby was born the two of them were ordered to stand publicly before the congregation and pay the usual fine. On being exhorted before the Session in advance, Dudgeon said that not only were the minister's admonitions of no effect but that the parishioners were 'a parcel of Thieves, Liars, Backbiters and Hypocrites', adding various other 'insolent expressions' which made the minister order him to leave, which he did after saying to the minister that he despised his company. The Presbytery's advice was sought and their opinion was, hardly surprisingly, that he was guilty of contempt of the Session as a church court and he was excommunicated until he acknowledged his contempt and submitted to discipline. Jane Purves meanwhile had left the district and was declared a fugitive from discipline and it was not until five years later that Dudgeon applied to the Presbytery to have the sentence of excommunication lifted. He was ordered to submit to the Session for questioning and to stand publicly for three days but after doing so twice, the Session decided that 'his conduct on both these days was very unbecoming' because on one day he had 'read a book during all the time of preaching and when he stood up to be rebuked, the levity of his behaviour was very offensive to many of the congregation.' However, the minister wanted to proceed as the Presbytery had instructed and allowed him to stand publicly the third day. 'He accordingly stood for about two minutes and then stooping down leaned upon the seat, whereupon the Moderator told him that he must stand up and receive the rebuke. He then arose and with much seeming contempt turned his back to the Moderator. Upon this the Moderator intimated that he did now sist procedure in Thomas Dudgeon's case.' The Session thought that he had shown 'symptoms of mental derangement' and decided that it would not be 'for edification' to proceed further, but the Presbytery ordered him to appear before them for rebuke and once more remitted him to the Session to re-start discipline, giving the minister the right to stop proceedings if he did not behave properly. He did appear before the congregation but when his rebuke began, 'with an audible voice [he] denied his having expressed any regret for the offence given and continued to speak until the Moderator ordered him to be silent' and again sisted further procedure. Back the matter went to the Presbytery where Dudgeon admitted that he did 'contradict and interrupt' the Moderator and so they also decided to leave things as they were and the sentence of excommunication remained.[95]

What proved as efficacious as excommunication in bringing a contumacious person to heel was what happened in Kilconquhar in 1734. The beadle's wife refused to submit to a charge of being drunk and disorderly and so the Session decided to attack the matter through her husband. As he was their employee, they thought that she might become more submissive if they debarred him from his work and his wages for a time, saying that it would be a bad precedent if their own dependents did not obey their orders. The beadle said that he did not know if such action was within the power of the Session, adding that his wife would have got more justice in any other court in the land but in spite of his objection, the Session suspended him with the result that his wife appeared when ordered to do so.[96]

Excommunication and withholding of the Sacraments survived to the end of the nineteenth century but these were considerably weakened by the fact that by then people could move to a rival sect if they sought leniency. A note of great satisfaction appears in the following minute of Channelkirk Kirk Session in August 1761: 'Received from James Wilson a contumacious Seceder who was prosecuted for his sin of fornication and fined by the Commissary . . . £10.' Even if the Kirk Session could not themselves prosecute this backslider, how pleased they were that the courts dealt with him and that they got his money.

9
Called, Compeared and Confessed . . .

The words 'Called, compeared and confessed' occur time and time again in Kirk
Session minutes, showing how people came before Sessions when called upon to
do so and confessed their sins as the kirk put parish discipline into practice.

To start with there was the problem of strangers. Although the kirk used to be
only too ready to take certain Biblical instructions very literally, such as not
working on Sundays or the killing of witches, they did not heed all Scriptural
injunctions, such as this one: 'And if a stranger sojourn with thee in your land, ye
shall not vex him. But the stranger that dwelleth with you shall be unto you as one
born among you, and thou shalt love him as thyself; for ye were strangers in the
land of Egypt . . .' Strangers most certainly were vexed at one time in Scotland.
The reasons for this have been made clear in earlier chapters. Not only were there
problems with poverty, there was so much trouble with discipline that no Kirk
Session wished people of bad character — 'a multitude of fugitives and other
louse people' as one Presbytery put it — to come in and settle in the parish
although they had no compunction themselves about banishing undesirables and
driving them into other parishes. As has already been said, parish funds were
usually scanty and it was thought essential to prevent strangers from establishing a
residence and ultimately having a claim on these funds to the detriment of a
parish's own native poor, but obviously strangers could not be prevented from
entering a parish to take up work and so it became customary to demand that they
produce certificates of character from their Kirk Sessions which appear in Session
minutes as testimonials, testificates, testificals or even testimonies. In towns, these
certificates might be given by Burgh Councils. Without one, a person was regarded as scandalous and so it was important to have one. They stated whether the
person was married or single, whether he or she was free from scandal and, if not,
what the offence had been and what had been done about it. An Act of the General
Assembly in 1648 decreed that care should be taken when engaging servants to see
that they had testimonials 'of their honest behaviour' and that those giving testimonials should 'take heed that these to whom they give them, be free of scolding,

swearing, lying or such like more commons sins; as well as fornication, adultery, drunkenness and other gross and heinous evils' and that in ordinary circumstances, testimonials should be given 'in the face of the Session' except for any pressing case when they could be given by the minister, with consent of the elder of the bounds where the person concerned lived. It was further required

> that all persons who flit from one parish to another have sufficient [adequate] testimonials — this is to be extended to all gentlemen and persons of quality and their followers; and that the minister from whom they flit advertize the minister to whom they flit, if they be lying under any scandal . . . and if they have fallen or relapsed into scandals . . . that their testimonial bear both their fall and their repentance.[1]

This Act was implemented, so far as it was possible to do so, for some time after 1648, then fell into disuse but was revived after the Revolution and so it is that a minute like the following one of 1706 could appear in Sessions records:

> The Provincial Synod of Fyfe, considering that there are several families and persons removing from one paroch to anoyr without testimonials bearing of their freedom from scandell and that such families or persons do oftentimes require the benefits of church privileges for themselves or oyrs, notwithstanding of the want of testimonials from the place of their former residence, therefore the Synod appoints that all persons removing from one place to anoyr, be obleidged to bring testimonials of their Christian behaviour, where they have been and that ministers and elders be diligent in inquiries after the samen and that Intimation be made from the pulpit requiring all persons coming from one paroch to anoyr that within six weeks after they have taken up their new residence, doe produce their testimonials either to the Session or to the elder of the quarter to be by him carried to the Session, and that advertisement be given to all who bring in either tennents, cottars or servants, that they allow none of these to reside forty days without their Testificates and that the minister and Clerk of the Session subscribe all the testimonials and that the premises be intimated from the pulpits within the bounds of the Synod twice every year, viz, before Whitsunday and Martinmas, and the intimation be marked in the Session book.[2]

Testimonials might be given to an individual, to a married couple or to whole families and not necessarily to those on the move. Sometimes written on long narrow strips of paper, they went something like this:

> Thes are to certifie that the berar Hereof Robert llow [Low] and Janet haswell llived in this town and parish for the space of eliven years frie from all public scandal or church senser known to us, so that we know no Resen whuy they may not be Reseved into aney Christen Congrition or famuley wher God in His providence may order tther lot.
>
> Given under our hands at Kelso this 21 day of July, 1738, James Ramsey, minister, Robert Davidson, elder, George Selby, Session Clerk.[3]

The granting of a testimonial was regarded as a formal action of the Kirk Session and so each one was copied into the minutes. In the early years of the eighteenth century one Session's records show a certificate given to one woman 'of her behaviour during her abode in this parish'; another woman received one 'of her well behaviour for the space of two years' and a man was given one about 'his deportment during his abode in this parish'. Yet another Session gave one to a man concerning 'his honest cariag' and there are many similar entries. But not all testimonials could speak favourably. The General Assembly's Act required information to be fully and honestly reported and so any wrong-doing was mentioned, even if satisfaction had been made and absolution given. A man who had informed on a neighbour and had a lawburrows — a writ requiring a person to give security against doing violence to someone — taken out on him, received an extract of the relevant Kirk Session minute when he asked for a certificate. When another Session discovered that there were complaints about a couple who wanted a testimonial, in particular about their habit of borrowing money and getting goods under false pretences, it was not a certificate that they got but a request 'to compt with their creditors' and they had to leave the parish with a reputation of being notorious cheats. Mere rumour might be included in a testimonial; when another couple asked their Session for one, that body were unanimous that they were 'not at liberty to grant them any certificate but in the following terms: "These certify that Alexander Fowler and his wife have resided in this parish since Martinmas 1804 — that they have been regular attendants on the public Ordinances of Religion, that although of late rumours have been circulated in the parish against the honesty of Alexander Fowler no evidence of the truth of them has been laid before us, as individuals or as a Session."' Certificates sometimes referred to political activities, such as involvement in the battle of Bothwell Brig in 1679 or having taken 'illegall steps in the late Rebellion' of 1715 but in this latter case, because the man had 'behaved civilly since, attending ordinances punctually, they appoynted ane testimoniall to be drawen to him.' Past moral offences were, as said, always mentioned, so that a testimonial might include such wording as 'with this quality that she fell in fornication, and satisfied discipline.' When 'gross Immoralitys' by a Session Clerk ultimately led to his resignation, he agreed to this 'upon his getting a sufficient Testificate and his fees as Session Clerk and all the money of baptisms and marriages since he was laid aside from being Session Clerk and Precentor.' The Session allowed him to have £6 Scots and the marriage and baptism money which he had earned but 'a Testificate in common form they could not give him.' Special precautions had to be taken should anyone leave a parish owing money to the Kirk Session, so that when Thomas Allan asked for a certificate from the Kirk Session of Lauder while owing 'mortcloth silver', he had first of all to find caution for payment of this debt, which he found in the person of one of the elders.[4]

The following two cases show different attitudes in different circumstances. In 1704 a girl was refused a testimonial as she had not paid her penalty, saying sadly that she had spent all she had upon the child whose birth was obviously the cause of her predicament, yet the previous year when a different girl was asked to pay her penalty and said that she did not have enough to pay the expense of travelling from and back to Edinburgh, the Session forgave her and ordered the clerk to write a 'testimony' showing that she had satisfied discipline.[5] One must assume that this leniency was because by leaving the area she would not be a burden on the funds and it was better to be rid of her rather than insist on her paying her fine. What is clear however, is that once an offence was purged, it was no bar to receiving a certificate of character even although past misdemeanours were included, but this made it very difficult for anyone moving elsewhere to cover up an old sin or to make a fresh start.

While it was one thing to mention past immorality committed by the person named in the certificate, it seems wildly unfair that the slur of illegitimacy, in the days when it was a slur, was also passed on by Sessions, even going to extra effort to ensure that this fact was not omitted. In 1733 the Kirk Session of Kirkwall gave a certificate to a woman which stated that she was the lawful (legitimate) daughter of the couple named in it, only to receive a letter from the Kirk Session of Tingwall, Shetland, in 1740, saying that her parents had never been married. The Kirk Session consulted their records and found that this was so — it seems very surprising that they had not spotted this long before — and it was agreed to write and confirm this to Tingwall Kirk Session who presumably amended her certificate. It is hardly to be wondered at that people were not always satisfied with the testimonials they were given but dissatisfaction achieved little. When an Orkney woman received one, signed by the Session Clerk on behalf of the Session, her husband replied with a 'scurrilous paper' saying that the clerk should have his right hand cut off, that the testimonial was not so full as he would have had it and that it would be a laughing matter in other parishes. The Session were having none of that, however, and decided to pursue him before the Sheriff-depute and he ended up paying a fine of 8s. stg. to the kirk. An unusual case was that of Robert Carson, a barber, who had been forced against his will to shave some men on Sunday. Although no notice had been taken of this offence at the time, it was remembered when he planned to leave the parish and asked for a certificate and he had to make repentance for the sin 'of profaning the Sabbath by taking off beards' before his request was granted.[6]

Just as testimonials were formally granted, so they were formally received and recorded in Kirk Session minutes: '8th July 1802. Robert Young, servant in Hunterstown produced a sufficient testimonial' was one such entry. Not everyone, of course, brought in their certificates so obediently, even if they had them, in which case Sessions had to take steps themselves. One, finding the district 'pestured with stranger servants' gave orders 'to go search all the houses in the town and see if there be any to be found who have not their testificate.' In another case, orders were given to the beadle 'anent the in bringing of testimonials of those lately come into the parish' and in some areas elders were required to visit their quarters monthly to demand testimonials from those who had recently arrived. In still others, the minister joined in the search, calling for the production of testimonials from all new arrivals and ordering those without them to get them within a fortnight or three weeks although certificates from Episcopalian clergy who had continued in their parishes under the Presbyterian regime after the Revolution were not always accepted by Kirk Sessions.[7]

Even with all the efforts that went into ensuring that people took and brought certificates with them when they flitted, it is evident that many managed to move from place to place undetected and it was perhaps only when something like marriage was wanted that this came to light. One of the great benefits of testificates was that they showed whether or not the person named was married and saved a deal of inquiry and sending back and forth for information. An instance of what could happen without one occurred in 1679 when a man in an outlying part of the parish of Melrose asked the minister for a testificate for his future wife, only to find that the Session did not have one from her former parish. She was ordered to get one from there first of all, before they could give her one themselves, something which was probably very difficult for her to do. Another example of the problems that arose when someone moved without a certificate was when a Kinross woman went to Corstorphine, Edinburgh, but was later summoned to appear before her home Session. It was found there that she had no certificate about her conduct in Corstorphine because she had failed to get one when she left Kinross. All she could produce to Kinross was a 'line' from the Corstorphine Session Clerk saying,

> We are being importuned for a testificate to one Mary Graham who hath been here in this parish since Lammas last and she having brought no testificate with her from Kinross, we desire to know, by a line with the first occasion, with respect to her behaviour with you and her circumstances . . . because there were several reports going which we have no certain ground for, and after that we shall not fail to let you know her behaviour here during the time she hath resided among us.

Kinross Kirk Session replied to this, saying that about Lammas last she had deserted her husband for no known reason and that they expected Corstorphine Kirk Session, on receiving this information, to send Mary back again to Kinross with an account of her conduct during her stay there. The unfortunate woman 'was ordered to carry a line to Corstorphine' and all this to-ing and fro-ing was simply due to the lack of a certificate at the right time.[8]

The problem of undesirable incomers could be tackled from another angle, by forbidding parishioners to employ or let accommodation to anyone who did not have a testimonial. In 1642, before the General Assembly's act of 1648 that is, Montrose Kirk Session forbade people to arrive there without testimonials and also decreed that 'if it happen any in our said congregation to resett [receive] any into their houses as servants, or yet sett [let] any house little or meikle unless they first acquaint the Magistrates before they sett any house and next acquaint the ministers for their testimonials, they shall pay two merks precisely', which was yet another reason for a fine. This was repeated in more or less the same form in 1649 and 1657, and in 1659 an Act of Session was specifically directed at employers — 'none are to receive any servant within their house without a sufficient testimonial . . . or pay £4 Sc.' It was the same in many parts of Scotland; no heads of households were meant to 'recave as servants aney strangers from others shairrs or parochs' without certificates and all such people were expected to have them at the ready, but more effective still was making those who took people in without certificates liable for any expenses arising out of their presence in the parish. In 1735 Tweedsmuir Kirk Session were having so much trouble with vagrants coming from elsewhere without testificates that they 'decided that hereafter those who harbour vagrants without sufficient testificates, that the Session would be free of any trouble or expense that may be incurred thereby' and that those who harboured them should 'bear the burden thairof themselves.' This was very similar to a ruling of Hawick Kirk Session in 1773 that landlords letting to strangers who could not produce an obligation from their parish of residence to support them if they should fall into need, would themselves — the landlords — be held responsible.[9]

It was mainly at hiring fairs that rural employers engaged staff and it must have been very annoying for them to engage a good worker, only to find that he or she had no testimonial from a previous parish, with the result that the new employer risked a fine and might also be ordered to send the worker away. Some Sessions reminded people about the importance of testimonials as the time for hiring fairs came round: one minister told all those leaving his parish at the May term, one of the change-over times in the agricultural employment year, to come to get testificates before that, also reminding employers not to engage anyone without one; but in the hurly-burly of a hiring fair remembering to ask about or to produce testimonials was easily overlooked. This could be serious for the workers too: in 1710 Elgin Kirk Session decreed that those who could not produce them when asked, nor appeared when summoned to account for this, would have their wages arrested by a town and kirk officer, on the order of a bailie, and would also have to answer before the Kirk Session. At one point the Baron Court of Lasswade, Midlothian, forbade farmers to employ workers who had not had their testimonials 'vised' by the Kirk Session which meant that a landowners' body used the kirk to check up on people on their behalf, although it was a duty which the Session would gladly have undertaken.[10]

In the second half of the seventeenth century, Falkirk Kirk Session was in the habit of instructing the magistrates to banish from the town anyone lacking a certificate, and this was always done, usually followed by an exhortation from the pulpit to heritors and heads of families not to take in such people. Session minutes, such as those of Hawick, have references to incomers being 'extruded the burgh' for not having testimonials and when the Town Council there expelled a man in 1738 for this offence, it was undoubtedly as a result of a close link between burgh and kirk. When Marjorie Sutherland from Tain was engaged in 1723 by Roderick Mackay in Dornoch, 'having no testificate [she] was ordered forthwith to procure a testificate from the Session of Tain in whose bounds she was last against their next meeting under the pain of being banished the place by the hand of the Hangman.' The Session Clerk added a note to this minute saying 'NB. The said Marjorie Sutherland goes under a very bad character' and the next minute reports that Marjorie 'being denied a Testimonial from the Session of Tain was banished the place.' There is a strong inference here that it was not so much lack of the necessary testificate as her bad reputation which was her undoing and certainly lack of certificates proved a good way of purging a parish of undesirables and also those who were an unfair burden on the funds. One such was Agnes Robinsone to whom in 1702 Dumbarton Kirk Session sent an order 'to remove out of the place with all speed, and that upon the account that she lives separate from her husband, and burdens this place with the maintenance of her children, and never yet produced a testificate, though oft required. As also appoints this order to be intimate to Agnes Watson, her Landlady.' Just as an employer or landlord might be ordered to remove someone with no certificate, so could a family man be forced to get rid of a member of his family should that person be undesirable. When John Robb came before the Kirk Session of Cruden in 1724 to present a testimonial from Peterhead Kirk Session for his wife and himself, it was accepted but only on condition that he 'dismiss his daughter in law out of the parish because of her bad and scandalous conversation.' But things could be quite different and Sessions very co-operative if a newcomer appeared respectable or came with that reputation, even although a testimonial was not forthcoming. Not only would time be allowed for one to be obtained but even greater leniency might appear. One Session did not require a man who had come into the parish and later became engaged to be married, to produce a certificate to show whether or not he was already married, not that there were doubts about this; they were perfectly happy to take his oath about it, just saying that they thought it proper to do so.[11]

Most strangers who managed to enter a parish without testimonials were wise enough to keep a low profile and avoid giving needless offence which could only draw attention to themselves — but it could happen. Jean Collier was a woman who arrived with no certificate in Falkirk and there kept a very disorderly house with others of her sort, drinking and generally behaving badly, and when the elder of the district went to see her about this, she greeted him with such a torrent of abuse that he fled to another house, only to have her follow him there and continue her tirade. She was summoned before the Session but, knowing that all the evidence was against her, she refused to appear a second time and finally left the district. Her conduct had however been such that it was ordered to be 'advised' from all the pulpits of the bounds.[12]

To have a testimonial was so valuable that it was not unknown for them to be forged. A young couple who wanted to get married but were about to be excommunicated by their own Session of Lairg 'caused forge a testificat with the forged subscription of ane elder of Larg and, with the said testificat, were married by Mr. Alexander Gray, present incumbent at Assynt.' Quite apart from the forgery, Mr Gray, who was a former Episcopalian clergyman who had remained in his charge after the Revolution, should not have married people of another parish in this way and the Kirk Session of Lairg complained about this to the Presbytery who were left to deal with the matter. In 1684 a Session were suspicious about a certificate in which the text and the signature were all written in the same hand. They must have expected that the Session Clerk would have written it and the minister signed it, although there seems no reason why a certificate should not have been written and signed by the same person but, in any event, the woman who presented it was ordered to leave the parish, a decision which may have had something to do with the fact that she was presenting a child for baptism on her own, the father being dead according to the testificate and so there was no one to support mother and child apart from kirk funds. Forged certificates were also carried by wandering strangers to support their pleas for temporary relief and one minister reported to his Session that such people with counterfeit testimonials 'carried away much of the poors money' and proposed therefore that it should be enacted that no stranger should in future be given more than 2*d*. Scots and when there were more than one in a group, only 1*d*. Forgery meant that while landlords might check that would-be tenants had testimonials, these could well be forged and for this reason one Session decreed that even if those wanting to rent property were 'clothed with testificates that they were free from scandal' these should not necessarily be accepted and that further inquiries should still be made concerning them. Even a schoolmaster, who should have been above such things, might use his superior skills to forge certificates, like one in Caithness who prepared a testificate for a man who was going to Banffshire, and was presumably paid for his services. Somehow or other the Banffshire Kirk Session spotted that something was wrong and the man had to satisfy discipline although what happened to the schoolmaster is not known.[13]

Testificates were not issued free but were a source of income to the Session Clerk, with varying charges at different times and in different parishes. In 1707 he might be paid something like 3*s*. 4*d*. Scots for each one, not quite 3½*d*. stg, but by 1782 perhaps as much as 6*d*. stg. There could be some reduction in the cost in certain cases and certificates also had to be kept reasonably up to date as otherwise they were of little use. A combination of both these features occurred in 1741 when a lame girl brought back to her Session the certificate she had been given in 1735 as, owing to the recent death of her father, she had to go to Morayshire with her young brother. The testificate was not only updated as she asked but 'she having nothing wherewith to maintain the boy' was given 10*d*. out of the box 'to help to bear her expense' and the certificate was free. In the same way, that Session gave a testificate free to someone in whose family there had been sickness for a long time, along with 4*s*. Scots from kirk funds. Another Session told their Clerk that they would accept his 'honest word' in any case where he gave testimonials free or for less than the usual price out of charity but he was warned that if he gave them for any other reason, they would deduct the cost of them from his usual salary. Testificates from Kirk Sessions or parish ministers could also be specifically required as a reference for work. Parliament ordered in 1649 that sub-collectors of taxes should have such evidence of honesty and fidelity and so far as other employment went, an example is Hugh Munro, a lint manufacturer in Tain, who was being so defrauded by those to whom he gave flax to spin at home, that in 1760 he asked the Presbytery if the ministers of the bounds would help him by giving certificates of character to any of their people applying to him for spinning work, saying that he would not employ anyone without such a certificate, and his request was granted. The use of testimonials went on for a long time, certainly into the 1820s, but as has been said in relation to other matters, times changed and church influence declined, in addition to which policing developed, all of which contributed to the end of testificates from the kirk.[14]

Testimonials were obviously an effective weapon in trying to prevent the settling of undesirables but nevertheless there was still much need of discipline in parishes, so how did Kirk Sessions get to the stage of imposing the wide range of punishments available to them? Much depended on the elders. In 1648 the General Assembly decreed 'that every elder have certain bounds assigned to him that he may visit the same every month at least and report to the Session what scandals and abuses are therein.' There was nothing pastoral in that but the role of parish spy, because that is what it amounted to, had been laid on elders well before that. In Aberdeen in 1568 the Kirk Session swore all the elders to faithfulness in delating all that they heard because, in those days, if minister or elder heard of anything amiss they considered it their duty to report it because not to do so would be tacitly condoning it. Kirk Session minutes often have the phrase, 'Inquiry being made if there were any public scandals known to any of the elders, it was reported . . .' In the late nineteenth century, a parish minister in the Borders described what used to go on in earlier days:

> Elders met, Sunday by Sunday, primed with all the gossip and scandal which they had been able to rake together during the preceding week, that they might have the pleasure of bringing a fresh batch of victims under the notice of the congregation by placing them on the jougs or raising them, clothed in white sheets, upon the stool of repentance in front of the pulpit. On rare occasions the clerk is compelled, with evident grief, to insert that there is nothing to do in the Session this day.

One of the most blistering attacks on kirk discipline was made some two hundred years earlier by Sir Ewen Cameron of Locheil, an Episcopalian, who lived from 1629–1719. Every parish, he said, had a tyrant whose court was the kirk and his throne or tribunal the pulpit, from which he issued terrible decrees to the twelve or fourteen 'sour, ignorant enthusiasts under the name of elders, who composed his court' and should anyone disobey, then the sentence of excommunication was thundered out which meant that his goods and chattels could be seized and he himself doomed to perdition. The word 'Inquisition' has been applied to the methods of the kirk but it is not accurate as the rack and other forms of extreme torture which were used in Roman Catholic days were never employed by it, apart from witch trials in which civil authority was paramount although the kirk was also involved. It is certainly true to say, however, that during the Covenanting reign of terror, there was great severity, tyranny and oppression as well as excessive interference in people's lives. Much of what happened was quite unnecessarily vexatious although in fairness, it must be said that many kirk inquiries and decisions were properly conducted and constructive.[15]

With the very close communities of the times, everyone used to know every-body's business and it cannot have been difficult for elders to discover what was going on but Kirk Session minutes show that informing was only too common, 'a grievously mischievous and poisonous system sustained by spying and informing by petty autocrats and malicious neighbours.' Some of it was well-meaning and some spiteful. People seemed to have an uncanny instinct for scenting vice afar off and thought no trouble too great that gave them a chance to report their neighbours to the Session, even spending all night dogging the footsteps of someone they suspected or perhaps lying in ambush to catch them out. Tale-telling went on, even in families, such as the case of the West Kilbride woman who wrote the minister to say that her brother was living in sin with his servant who was a cousin; to do such a thing was not considered to be the degrading or discreditable thing it really was, but quite the reverse. The relatives of a young woman who took her in when she was 'in trouble' were fined 40s. Scots for not telling the Session about her and they had to make public satisfaction for this. It must be remembered, of course, that at a time when people had few entertainments or opportunities for relaxation, gossip was prevalent. There seems to have been real pleasure in watching what others did and perhaps, by the action of reporting it, people may have hoped to curry favour with the Session as well as having the enjoyment of seeing those they had reported punished.[16]

In the early post-Revolution years, by no means all parishes had enough elders or even any at all, which posed a problem for discipline. One such was Forfar where about 1717 the minister had to ask for delinquents to be called before the Presbytery as he had not yet got any elders, which was agreed. Because Kirk Sessions were police, prosecutor, judge and jury, how kirk discipline was carried out depended greatly on the quality of the people implementing it but whatever various writers or anyone else thought about it, its aim was always meant to be good, 'that the name of God by reason of ungodly and wicked persons living in the church be not blasphemed — and that the godly be not leavened with, but pre-served from contagion — and that sinners who are to be censured may be ashamed to the destruction of the flesh, and saving of the spirit in the day of the Lord Jesus.' That being so, it was logical that Kirk Session reaction to any special circum-stances should be to approach God first of all and then to take action themselves, something which appears in the minutes of one highland Session in 1828: 'The Session taking into their most serious consideration the present state of this parish and finding that vice, more especially the sin and scandal of fornication, has for some time back . . . been unusually prevalent, resolved at this meeting to hold a Diet of Prayer to plead with Almighty God for the outpouring of the spirit in order to check open vice' and they then proceeded to divide the parish into eight districts with an elder in charge of each. This was a late instance of allocating districts to elders and it was perhaps lack of them that had resulted in so much immorality. In 1746 the Kirk Session of Dornoch in efforts to put down immorality and crime appointed what they termed 'observators', no fewer than fifty of them, described as 'men of good repute and fair character', to admonish anyone they found guilty of such sins and to delate those who were obstinate to the Session on the first Monday of every quarter so that they could be prosecuted. In addition they co-opted not only magistrates but also several gentlemen of good standing 'to assist in judging of all matters submitted to them by the observators'. This was a form of the session bailie system although it was not called that and in this case was only used for a few years. Wick Kirk Session appear also to have had something similar, with men called 'surveyors of the town' who worked on a monthly rota to keep an eye on things. In some parishes one or two elders might be ordered to attend fairs and race meetings to see if anything wrong was going on, 'to goe through the faire and take notice of what immorality they hear or see', as one minute put it. This must have made of lot of work for elders, especially where they were few and a parish large, but on the other hand, the minutes of a not-very-big parish such as Sorbie, Wigtownshire, were able to say in 1701, 'Seeing the parish is compact, its convenient that two elders be always joined together in taking the oversight of any part of the parish.' Lauder had an exceptionally vigilant Session which not only supervised the parish but at one point extended this supervision to parishioners who went to Edinburgh and should there be anything amiss in their conduct there, called them to account for it in Lauder: in 1683 John Stelhous was delated for staying in the capital for too long, 'manytimes whole weeks together and sometimes longer spending and debauching as was alleged', but it was not usual to go to such extra-parochial lengths as that. Much of the work of elders involved Sabbath profanation and there is more information on this in the appropriate chapter.[17]

While the Kirk Sessions of very large and thinly populated parishes might meet no more than once a year, and then only to distribute the poor's money, many met regularly to deal with anything needing their attention such as delations, as allegations made to them were called. Many of these turned out to be gross exaggerations of very trifling matters and where injury was done to people as a result, then Sessions tried to undo any harm by publicly intimating the result of their inquiries. On hearing of any alleged scandal, the first step strictly speaking for an elder or minister to take was to speak privately to the person or persons concerned, to try to get them to confess, 'to give glory to God by an ingenuous confession', and if that did not work, to try to discover what facts there might be and then to bring the whole matter to the attention of the Session. Rev. Thomas Boston, minister of Ettrick from 1707–33, was an eloquent preacher who drew great crowds to any Communion services in which he took part but his dealings with a dying elder, only five months after his arrival in the parish, are a terrible instance of what should never have happened and were mercifully not generally copied. Little wonder that although he was esteemed and admired for his preaching abilities, he was also regarded with terror when, as a result of his visit to this man to investigate the truth of his sins, he wrung from him the following confession:

> I, W.L. having fallen into sin, and not having in the time of my health satisfied the discipline of the church, and being now under the afflicting hand of God in such sort

that I have little or no hope that ever I shall be able to satisfy in the usual manner, yet, being sound in mind, I do hereby, for glorifying God and edifying of the congregation, take shame to myself, and with grief and sorrow of heart confess and acknowledge my sin whereby I have provoked the Lord, grieved his Spirit, offended the congregation of his people, made the hearts of the godly sad, and hardened the hearts of the wicked. I confess my sin is attended with aggravating circumstances, for I have returned with the dog to the vomit, and with the sow which was washed to her wallowing in the mire . . . wherefore I am now ashamed. I was honoured of God to bear office in his house as a ruling elder, of which I never was worthy, and I acknowledge God would be just if he should for this and my other sins of heart and life, exclude me for ever from his presence, and give me my portion with unclean spirits in that lake that burns with fire and brimstone. But I desire to flee to the blood . . . Finally I desire these presents may be publicly intimat before the congregation of Ettrick. Signed before Thomas Nasmith in Bowerhope and Walter Welsh, the writer. 17th September 1707.

With this in their hands, the Session, presumably at Mr Boston's instigation, decided to deal further with the poor man's conscience but, fortunately for him, he died before they could do so. Some authorities say that fanatical discipline was found more in elders than in ministers, with the former instructing the latter about what to do but this example shows what a powerful moving force a minister could be and, in fact, parish discipline seems to have resulted more or less equally from the efforts of elders and of ministers, depending on the personalities of each.[18]

Many delations, in fact, were made directly to the Kirk Session, whereupon the Kirk Officer was instructed to cite the person concerned to 'compear' (appear) before the next meeting of Session. This meant that they had to present themselves at the right time and wait patiently outside until they were called in once the Session were ready for that part of their business. If any scandal was thought to be of a very serious or pressing nature, then a special meeting of Session was called to deal with it and, just as Session Clerks might have a personal financial interest in the imposition of fines, so some kirk officers had too in relation to summonses, receiving 2s. Scots for all those called by them who were found guilty. Admittedly, summoning alleged offenders made extra work for them but such payments must have added enthusiasm to the task. It would be interesting to know the outcome of a case where the beadle was sent to summon a barber for shaving a man on a Sunday but who failed to appear. On the beadle's fourth attempt, he insisted on being accompanied, only to be attacked by the barber, an assault which was referred to the Presbytery. Citations to appear *apud acta* were peremptory and when not obeyed without a good excuse implied disobedience but in ordinary cases, it was only when people failed to appear after a third citation that they were regarded as contumacious. The third citation was sometimes made at the church door and if the offender persisted in refusing to obey, the ultimate outcome could be, as has been said earlier. excommunication or, in later days, being declared a fugitive from discipline. An Act of the General Assembly in 1707 decreed that where an alleged offender did not appear after being duly summoned, the Session might go ahead and call whatever witnesses were necessary to discover the truth of the original accusation before censuring for contumacy although a third refusal to appear when cited had, in any case, to be reported to the Presbytery. On occasion, a Session might be specifically ordered by the Presbytery to call witnesses as happened in Dollar in 1706 when that body remitted a case of disputed paternity back to the Session, with instructions 'to summon witnesses and to examine all facts and circumstances which may tend to throw light upon the affair and report . . .' In another instance, two witnesses who were essential to a case were visited by a commission or committee of the Session as they were unable to attend the Session themselves owing to age and infirmity.[19]

The evidence of witnesses was always gone into and recorded in Kirk Session minutes in great detail. Each one's name is given, along with the statement that he or she was 'solemnly sworn and purged of partial counsel', of 'malice and partial counsel', of 'malice, bribe and partial counsel' or even 'sworn and purged of malice, bribe or good deed done or to be done, and of partial counsel.' Each witness's evidence as given in the minutes usually ends with some such wording as 'This is true as I shall answer to God' and is signed by those who could write but those who were unable to do that, had it signed by the minister, with this so stated or 'with their hands held at the pen' which words are written half and half on either side of their 'X' although, if they could not read, it is difficult to know how they could really vouch for the accuracy of what was set down. Although they signed to show that what they said was true, it does not appear that they had to swear at the outset to tell the *truth* which explains why on one occasion the Kirk Session of Kinross 'finding themselves much in the dark' about a case of slander 'through the partiality of the witnesses . . . thought fit the said witnesses should be put on their oath to declare solemnly what they know of the affair.'[20]

Many witnesses relished their role and made the most of it. An instance of this comes from Edinburgh in 1708. A tailor was accused of immoral behaviour but would only admit to having been invited early one summer morning into a house by a woman whom he suspected to be of a somewhat light character. According to him they had had some drink and then went for a walk but that was all. However, Widow Garden whose house it was and who apparently took in lodgers, gave evidence that she had never seen either the man or the woman before but that after drinking there, they 'went in to her yard, and when they were there, the Deponent [Widow Garden] followed them and saw them in the very act of uncleanness and the Deponent ran to them and stroke the woman and took the cloaths off her head, which she produced and laid upon the Session table, and declares she upbraided David, saying Mr. Hutton, you must not think to come here to make my house a baudy house and David did strike the Deponent for abusing the woman who did leap the yard dyke.' Other people there had seen nothing wrong and this may have been a real case of immorality or one where suspicious behaviour led to wrong assumptions but Widow Garden's enthusiasm to report it is undoubted. Some minutes show that it was not witnesses who were called to clarify matters but neighbours. In 1582 a Perth woman complained of her husband's adultery and of his beatings when she spoke to him about it, whereupon the Session ordered him to be imprisoned and 'an inquest made of her neighbours' about what was going on; and in 1607 when an Aberdeen woman was accused of shutting her husband out of the house, she was put in the tolbooth steeple on bread and water while 'an inquest of neighbours' was held to see if she was a 'lawful neighbour or not.'[21]

One impression got from Kirk Session minutes is that cases were carefully considered and so one may imagine the anger of the Kirk Session of Dornoch when a man declared publicly, whether true or not, that when his wife was satisfying discipline, her father had given 'Wedders, Hens and Eggs' to the Session so that they might show her favour. Unfortunately, another impression is that once a delation was made, there was a presumption of guilt and that while witnesses might be called, it was mainly to confirm that guilt. Admittedly, elders knew their people and their circumstances and could probably make an accurate enough guess about guilt, but the possibility that they might be wrong does not seem to have struck them. In one case a man was accused of fathering a child and the Session appointed someone to speak to him 'about the circumstances of the guilt that it may be better fastened on him' which no one could call an impartial attitude, nor could the action of a Session which exhorted a man to confess his sin, 'showing him that they who covers their sin, shall not prosper', which was an attempt to intimidate him. A particularly bad example of this approach happened in Kilmaurs in the late 1690s. A man who had earlier disagreed with the minister's proposal for seating part of the church, was accused of grievous wrongdoing by a woman who had formerly worked for him. This case dragged on for three years, the man insisting all the time that he was innocent, until he was sentenced to Lesser Excommunication. When a child of his marriage had to be baptised, however, he had to come before the Session to have that sentence lifted so that this privilege might be allowed him and the relevant minute went as follows:

> Being seriously intreated again and again by the minister to tell the truth, he said that if he be guilty, he wishes that God may give him a scarlet-coloured sight of his sins . . . whereupon the minister, coming to him and laying his hand on William's breast, said unto him, William I admire that you are so hardened that you do not confess. I perceive by your countenance that you are guilty. I'll wager that there is such horrour and terrour in your conscience from the sins of your guilt that your spirits are spent and there is such a heat within you drawing up your moisture that you cannot at present set over your spittle, to qlk the said William replied [to the observation of the Session standing trembling] Sir, it is so. Thereupon the minister told him he and others were convinced he was guilty.[22]

But was he? It is very seldom that one comes across a church verdict of Not Guilty. Even when a civil court might have brought in one of Not Proven, that did not happen in the kirk, and what happened to a St. Andrews woman in 1663 is therefore most unusual. In January that year she pled old age and weakness as a reason for not coming before the Session when delated for charming and the minutes show that 'therefore is ane six pence allowed for ane Slaid [sledge] to bring her in the next Thursday *to clear herself*' which seems to indicate that although the delation had to be followed up, the elders had some reason to believe her innocence.[23]

The General Assembly laid down guidelines for parish discipline in 1707: nothing should be censured but what had been declared censurable by the Word of God or by some Act or general custom of the kirk. If someone voluntarily confessed fornication but there was no child to prove it, the Session must inquire as to the truth, including why the confession was made, and should it turn out to be false, then the person making it must be censured as defaming himself and slandering the supposed partner in sin — men did sometimes try to make out that they had been involved with girls when it was not true — and application must be made to the magistrates for punishment. In practice, there were many cases where sin was reported immediately, convincingly confessed or easily proved but once any process of church censure had begun, the delinquent was debarred from church privileges — marriage, baptism, Communion — until satisfaction had been made and absolution pronounced. It was for this reason that it was not at all uncommon for those guilty of fornication or ante-nuptial fornication to come voluntarily to confess what they had done so that they might get on with their punishment as quickly as possible so as to be able to have the almost inevitable baby baptised, and this was something with which Sessions seemed willing to help. When a girl told her Session in 1835 (by which date the most severe punishments had fallen into disuse) that she had an illegitimate child, that the father was in another parish but acknowledged it and was making appropriate payments for it, she was rebuked there and then and again in two weeks' time and the Session ordered 'the child to be baptized with all convenient speed.' Similarly in 1803 a Kirk Session were informed 'that Robert Henry wanted to speak with them. He was called in and being asked what he wanted, said he had been guilty of ante-nuptial fornication with Margaret Galbraith, now his wife, and that it was their desire to be taken upon discipline' and this the Session allowed. Some people wisely wished to have everything straight before moving elsewhere and it was for this reason that one couple moving from West Kilbride to Greenock asked to appear for ante-nuptial fornication, which would certainly save later problems about testificates. A Mull man's conscience must have pricked him for a long time as he came one day to the Kirk Session in Tobermory to confess having fathered an illegitimate child which had been born on the mainland ten years before but, because he had by then left Mull, he had never been absolved and he 'craved to be admitted to discipline', which was granted. Kirk Session minutes often refer to the 'privilege of discipline' and it is clear that in a considerable number of cases, people were glad to confess, knowing that once satisfaction was made, absolution would follow and privileges be restored. And more than church privileges could be withheld; secular ones could be too. A woman came to her Session in 1704 in great straits, saying she could get neither lodging nor work until she had made satisfaction. The Session allowed her to start her repentance at once and very compassionately gave her 16*d*. 'for present supply.'[24]

However, cases could not always be cleared up and so, rather than start or continue a protracted process, Sessions would sometimes let matters lie in the hope of the truth ultimately emerging, 'to let the affair ly over till Providence throw more light upon it', as it might be put. A case where this course should have been applied but was not, happened in Thurso in 1808. There were rumours, nothing more, about the conduct of a man who was a Communicant and because of them he was suspended from church privileges until his conduct could be inquired about. If a delation had actually been made, this would have been fair, but on the basis of pure speculation it was not. An alternative to leaving things as they were to see if time would give enlightenment was to apply the oath of purgation. When any serious scandal was alleged and denied, especially in cases of disputed paternity and fornication, the matter could be decided by the accused person taking an oath purging him or herself of the alleged crime. Long before things got to that stage, of course, the supposed sinner would have been urged to confess before the Session, to 'mourn for their sin', been made to confront the person alleging the sin, usually a woman with a child, and only if innocence was still asserted would the taking of the oath be allowed. It is more fully described in the chapter on the morals of the people.[25]

Delinquents were not usually allowed to start making their formal public repentance in church at once but had to 'lie under scandal', as it was called, for some time until it was felt that they were truly penitent or, as one Session minute put it, could show 'mair signis of penitence nor thair is at present.' Many of the sins which brought people to the notice of their Sessions were very little ones and their ignorance, through lack of education, was such that they were often unable to understand in what way they had sinned and as a result they might be required to visit the minister to be taught about sin and of what it consisted. One such was Margaret Birnie who appeared before her Session 'but being found as yet exceeding ignorant notwithstanding the pains that have been taken with her, the Session recommend to the Moderator to speak with the minister of Peterculter who lives near the place where she dwells that he be at pains for some time to instruct her and to bring her to a sense of her sin and report thereafter to the Session.' Six months later she again appeared before them and was still found to be 'verrie ignorant' and was yet again appointed to speak with the Peterculter minister and to come before her own Kirk Session when called. Sometimes it was left to the elders to deal with such people, 'that they may be brought to some kindly sense of their sin' which was the way one Session put it although it seems doubtful that delinquents would have found the process kindly. It was probably a frightening experience: '12th June 1659. This day the Session ordained two of their number . . . to deall with the said Agnes in privat . . . to see if they make her sensible of her sin' is the wording of one minute and when John Ladlaw committed adultery with his woman servant, no fewer than five elders 'by courses conversed with him.' These private methods could give the opportunity to apply a bit of pressure as almost certainly happened to a Roman Catholic woman who appeared for fornication before the Presbytery of Aberdeen where she 'did renounce the erroneous Tenets of the

Popish religion', was interrogated before the Kirk Session about some articles of faith and ordered to attend sermons for a month and to 'speak and converse with the Moderator and Deacons at such time as they should call for her and to speak with the Moderator every Saturday', before being allowed to start her public repentance. Not only ex-Roman Catholics but others too, were required to exhibit religious knowledge in this way: it was not unusual for a delinquent's religious learning to be examined prior to being allowed to make public satisfaction. In 1594 the Kirk Session of St. Andrews ordered that anyone whatsoever who had to make public repentance should come to the kirk at the time of catechising 'to learn the doctrine of true repentance, before they come to the stool of public repentance so that when they come to it, they may answer to the heads of repentance, as the minister shall propone to them, before they are received' and a man there who was not 'fund verie penitent for his sin' was ordered 'to keip the catechising for his better instruction.' In 1703 a woman was called before the Barony Kirk Session, Glasgow, and asked which of the Commands (Commandments) she had broken by the sin of uncleanness and was quite unable to answer. Being found grossly ignorant, she was ordered to confer with two elders and to appear publicly for rebuke but when she still said that she had little sense of her sin, she was ordered to confer further, to appear publicly again before the congregation and also before the Presbytery. Her baby was sick 'and by her thus going forth to Session and Presbytery, it was ready to grow much worse', a problem which her Session appreciated, ordering her to speak with the four elders living nearest to her so as to prepare her to appear before the Presbytery again — and that body had the good sense to grant her absolution. In some cases it was not catechism or Commandments but portions of Scripture that had to be learnt and repeated before the Kirk Session.[26]

Conferring with ministers and elders and gaining religious knowledge could make it a long time before a delinquent ever got to the stage of appearing publicly in church, which could produce its own problems. A woman seven months pregnant and abandoned by the man she had been going to marry, asked her Session if she might be 'received on discipline' as they called public repentance because 'her life was uncertain and . . . her friends would not receive her until she was freed from church scandal' and that is only one example of the difficulties people faced. Protracted preliminaries were the reason why caution often had to be found for payment of fines and for serving discipline, which has already been mentioned. Caution was widely used in the seventeenth century and in at least one parish the Kirk Session decreed that anyone who refused to find it would not be heard unless double penalty was laid down. Caution must have been an effective enforcer as, although Inverness Kirk Session decreed in 1689 that it would no longer be accepted there, they very soon went back to using it again.[27]

It was only when a delinquent was considered suitably penitent, 'a fit subject for that privilege', that the beadle or kirk officer would be ordered to notify him or her to appear in church for 'the course of discipline' or 'course of repentance' to begin which, once completed satisfactorily, led to absolution. 'Chas. McLean,

Calgary, Delinquent, having gone through the usual course of church discipline, was this day absolved of the scandal' is a minute which sums this up. Although discipline was delayed until sinners were considered adequately penitent, it could also be held over in order to help them. Knowing how necessary casual harvest work was to rural people and to the rural economy, Kirkwall Kirk Session allowed Barbara Rousay, who was two or three months pregnant in fornication, to go to this work 'and she was therefore delayed for discipline till it was over.' This was fairly general practice and permission might even be given to a man to go to sea on condition that he reverted to discipline on his return.[28]

While a course of discipline might include some of the severer punishments mentioned already, at its simplest it consisted of a specified number of public appearances in church, in whatever garb and place was decreed, with confession, rebuke and exhortation from the minister. The number of these appearances was laid down by an Act of the General Assembly in 1648 under the general title of 'Remedies': one offence of fornication required repentance on three Sundays, a relapse required six, for trilapse of fornication or one offence of adultery it was twenty-six Sundays; quadrilapse in fornication or relapse in adultery required three-quarters of a year and where incest or murder were not punished capitally by the magistrate, then the punishment of the kirk was fifty-two Sunday appearances where there was not excommunication. These were, in fact, minimum sentences. The following extracts from the minutes of one parish refer to different people but show their progress on the way to absolution:

> 1 October, 1769, a woman delinquent 'compeared pro 1mo and was suitably exhorted.'
> 17 December, 1769, two men 'compeared pro 2o and were exhorted to repentance.'
> 5 November, 1769, 'John M'Lean, Delinquent, compeared pro 3tio and being rebuked and suitably exhorted, was absolved.'[29]

Normally only one appearance was made on any Sunday, at the morning service, but on occasion the length of the course of discipline could be reduced by appearing at both forenoon and afternoon worship. When James Murray sent a letter to Tweedsmuir Kirk Session saying, 'I own I have been guilty of the sin of fornication with Helen Calderwood and am willing to make satisfaction at conveniency' the Kirk Session accepted this as a sufficient confession and allowed him to appear twice on two Sundays, with absolution on the second one whereas Helen had to appear once a day for three Sundays; in this case there does not appear to have been any special payment for the privilege. Church vacancies, with irregular services, made the business of serving discipline even more prolonged and so delinquents might ask the Presbytery if they could appear twice in any day when there was preaching in the parish and it was usual for this to be allowed, even if some Sessions did not approve. In 1697 a man from Cumnock begged the Presbytery of Ayr to allow him to appear twice in one day 'for his more speedy absolution' because services were only being rarely held during a vacancy and to this the

Presbytery agreed so long as it 'was not offensive to the congregation.' Whatever the congregation may have thought about it, the Session were displeased because of it 'not being an ordinary practice' but the Presbytery brusquely reported that they 'disliked their carriage'. A good solution to the problem of serving discipline during a vacancy was found by the elders of Elie in 1692. They asked the minister and Kirk Session of Kilconquhar to 'condescend that the accused should make public satisfaction in their church, there not being a minister settled in Elly and it being uncertain when they should be provided of a minister. It was thought fit that two of the elders of Elly should represent the same to the Presbytery that they might give order thereanent.' The accused man was called before the Presbytery, with some of the elders from Elie, and referred to Kilconquhar 'anent his satisfaction and was appointed to appear on the pillar the next Lord's Day and to deliver his penalty to the Kirk Session of Elly for the poor of that parish.'[30]

The extension of sentences by Kirk Sessions, beyond the basic punishment laid down, was quite common. Unless repentance was considered adequate, Kirk Sessions could require delinquents 'to continue Sabbathlie during their wills', which was how a Cromarty woman, having stood publicly for a given number of Sundays, was still not considered sufficiently penitent and 'was appointed to stand the next Lord's Day that she might be truly humbled' and it was only because she showed suitable signs of remorse on that occasion that she was absolved. A Resolis couple had to stand for nearly three months in 1828 before they 'finally convinced' the Session of their repentance. Elizabeth Melrose stood 'in the habit of an Adulteress' for twelve months at Peebles in 1666 when six months was the basic punishment. Issobell Steinsone appeared for over a year and a quarter before the congregation of Deskford in the 1670s and there are other instances of a year or more of public repentance. Presbyteries could also increase sentences if they wished, which explains how Marion Macdowall was only allowed to finish her Sabbath appearances on the place of repentance for relapse after 'having sitten on said place for ane year, compleat, conform to the order of the Presbytery, and that in sackcloth.' This was a great fault of church sentences as opposed to civil ones; the latter were finite but those of the kirk could go on and on although not necessarily with public appearances. A letter of Robert Burns referred to a man who appeared before Mauchline Kirk Session in 1786 for an offence which was never proved but who thirty-two years later appeared asking for absolution for this unproven scandal. In this case, the Session made a sensible decision which, whether in accordance with the evidence or not, was at least Christian in attitude, saying that he had 'suffered greatly by being kept so many years from enjoying church privileges.' That same Kirk Session absolved a woman with a mere Sessional rebuke, she having stood publicly but without absolution some nine or ten years before, on the grounds that it would not be edifying for her to appear publicly again as she was old and infirm and so the case became a *scandalum sopitum*, a scandal gone to sleep.[31]

The type of rebuke given was based on the degree of sin and how much scandal it had created but it could be long enough to be known as the 'wee sermon' as opposed to the proper one. Sinners were 'exhorted to sincere and hearty repentance' or 'to a sincere repentance and to fall to the blood of Christ who alone cleanseth from sin' or, in a warning manner, to 'lay sin seriously to heart and to guard against it in time coming.'[32] Not only did standing publicly in church embarrass people but there was also the requirement to speak out in public as sin had to be confessed and, in some cases, delinquents might have to answer in church 'to the heads of repentance, as the minister shall propone to them.' To an obstinate sinner none of this was too dreadful an experience and repeated appearances could make them more shameless, so much so that in 1597–98 Elgin Kirk Session ordered that anyone under church discipline who gave way to 'shameful and insolent lauching' (laughing) in church during the service should pay a penalty of 10s. and serve one day's repentance for it. Some delinquents feigned repentance when they did not feel it, such as a man who did 'mack ane moke' of repentance by putting sneishen (snuff) in his eyes to make them shed tears. In any event, elders had a very good idea of who was truly repentant and who was not and those of Hawick must have had real doubts about Margaret Gray who appeared in 1720 on the place of repentance and testified her sorrow for her trespass 'by loud crying and weeping' which cut no ice and she was ordered to appear for a further seven Sundays. To more sensitive people public appearances caused great strain. The case of the man who had to pay for his own sackcloth gown and subsequently went mad with stress has already been mentioned but his was not an isolated case. In the same Edinburgh parish, Walter Rae made one appearance in sackcloth and then the minutes say that his case was being continued 'quhill he be weill quho is distracted for the present.' When it was later reported the he had become 'somewhat solid' which meant that his mental condition had improved, the Session decided to avail themselves of this lucid interval and ordered him to appear again but he did not come. It was the Presbytery which ultimately ordered the Session to close the case but the permanent effect on Walter is not known. For women in particular, public appearances in church were a nerve-racking experience which was not helped by the fact that they were not allowed to hide their faces while they made repentance; the minutes of St. Andrews Kirk Session in 1640 show that intimation was made 'that those in the pillar of repentance suld stand their plaids down from their heidis otherwyas that they should not be counted a day off their public repentance that was enjoined them.' Aberdeen Kirk Session decreed that immediately before any women's 'upganging to the pillar' they should have their plaids removed by the kirk officer or his servant because by concealing their faces, they could hide their identities which encouraged them to 'persevere in their harlotrie' and to disregard the punishment of public appearance. This edict cannot have been properly implemented at the time as some forty years later that Session had to order that everyone making repentance should face the congregation. What seems rather surprising therefore is that some sixteenth century Kirk Session minutes may show that women had to make repentance with 'hair castin doon about hir eene' but perhaps a dishevelled appearance was considered evidence of disgrace, and particular severity to women is said to have arisen because they were believed to be the channel by which sin had entered the world. The stress of public repentance appears in the case of an erring couple from Kilmaurs. The man had to stand in sackcloth on seventeen successive Sundays and the woman for twenty, but when she broke down completely on the seventeenth appearance, the Session considered that 'she mocks God by feigned sounin [swooning] and shaking.' Was this a case of elders knowing their people or hard-heartedness to women? However, when a Tweedsmuir girl, guilty of adultery, appeared before the Kirk Session they 'could have little thing of her but weeping and crying out on herself of her misery' and even the Presbytery found her simple and harmless and recommended that she should be spared any severe censure. This meant that she only had to appear once before the congregation but the exhortation she received on that occasion was such as to make her drop to her knees and show such distress and penitence that the minutes record that it was 'to the affecting of the congregation'.[33]

Kirk Sessions generally showed compassion to delinquents where there was some simple-mindedness or physical handicap. In 1724 when a woman admitted drunkenness but showed an exceptional dread of appearing before the Session, in addition to the fact that she seemed to be a weak and silly creature, utterly incapable anyway of church discipline, the Session simply passed over her case. In late 1716 a woman had an illegitimate child and as soon as possible after its birth went and told as many elders as possible about it. The Session did not think that she was 'Ingenious and free in her confession' and referred her to the Presbytery who remitted her back to the Session who then decided that she was 'a little Hypondriak woman' and that they were 'loth to midle strictly with her' and so she only had to appear on one Sunday. When a deaf and dumb woman was found guilty of fornication but could neither speak to confess her sin nor hear the minister's rebuke, the Session were unanimously of the opinion that calling her before them or making her appear in church 'would not be for edification', but the man in the case had to undergo punishment. Other instances of sympathy for sinners stemmed from the elders' knowledge of their circumstances. In 1770 a girl appeared before her Session once and thereafter they 'in consideration of her submission and seeming penitence and *for other reasons* did agree to absolve her, which was accordingly done.' She was seeking a testimonial and so was almost certainly planning to leave the parish but it would be interesting to know what the 'other reasons' were and the reason for the delicacy that did not specify them. A man was summoned in 1728 before his Session but did not come, writing instead to the minister, admitting the sin and asking that punishment might be delayed because if it came to his grandmother's ears 'it would prove hurtful to him, because that by her he had his living at that time'. The Session accepted this as a good reason for delay. Elsewhere a man told the minister that if he had to make public satisfaction for slander as ordered by the Presbytery it would result in 'bad consequences in his family, and that he would be obliged to go off the countrey and leave his family because of the variance it might put betwixt himself and his wife.' If the Session would agree to alter his sentence, he said, then he would undergo whatever punishment they ordered, promising at the same time never to repeat the offence that was the cause of the trouble; but if they would not alter his sentence, then he would submit to it. The Session must have felt that there was something in what he asked and referred the matter to the Presbytery but unfortunately the outcome of the story is not given.[34]

Just as imminent childbirth could be a reason for being released from prison, so too could it lead to relaxation of censure. In 1749 Cruden Kirk Session considered the position of a woman pregnant in fornication whose circumstances were 'so meane' that she could not pay the full penalty and nor could her father give her any financial help. They remitted £1 of her fine and she agreed to pay the remaining £3 the following Saturday. The Session agreed 'that she, having earnestly requested the same, should be dismissed from discipline next Lord's Day, on consideration that the time of her being brought to bed was at hand.' Her sentence was either speeded up or shortened, not postponed, and in this she was fortunate because many of the sins requiring penitence resulted from childbirth, with post-natal illness common, and should a woman be too ill to make repentance at the right time, that did not usually mean that she was let off; censure was simply delayed until she was fit to undergo it. The minutes of one Session refer to a woman, guilty of fornication for the third time, who was summoned to appear when she recovered from childbed and the repeated entries of 'Grisall Lesly still not recovered' show that the Session had most certainly not forgotten about her. The same thing lay behind a minute concerning a couple due 'to enter at the pillar whenever his wife was recovered from her sickness' or a husband excusing his wife's failure to appear 'by reason of her tenderness.' A group who received consideration was nursing mothers and when a woman was called to confess her sin in church — she had pulled grass on a Sunday — this was delayed until her child was weaned. In cases of post-natal illness or any illness, it can hardly have been an encouragement to recovery to know that a return to health also meant a return to the stool of repentance: when Isobel Paterson 'having by reason of sickness, been but three days in the place of public repentance' was told by the kirk officer, on the instructions of the Kirk Session 'that whenever she recovers health, she return to the foresaid place' it cannot have made her feel any better; and just how sick one had to be to have censure delayed may be judged from the case of Anna Ross, an adulteress, who in 1706 had to stand for twenty-six Sundays along with the man concerned. The minutes say that because she was 'not able to stand, being diseased in her feet, the Session allows her to sit at the foot of the pillar and appoints her to be supported by the beadle when the Minister rebukes her.' What a dreadful picture this conjures up, of a woman hobbling to church for six months on diseased feet to endure public censure.[35]

Where an offence had caused scandal in other parishes, a delinquent might be required by the Presbytery to make what was called 'circular satisfaction'. This meant making a round of the parishes affected, in addition to the home one, and making a public appearance and satisfaction in each. In 1664 the Presbytery of Forfar ordered a woman to begin her repentance before them *in sacco* and then go the following

Sunday to the kirk of Rescobie, on the next to Aberlemno and so on, with reports being made of her progress. That was a lowland area but where parishes were very large and widely separated, circular satisfaction produced great transport difficulties, especially should the delinquent be ordered to go, not just to some, but to all the kirks of the Presbytery. That is what happened to Rachel McCoan in 1760, 'in consideration of the Atrociousness of her Crime' of incest with her sister's husband. This sentence was imposed in December, with the worst of the winter weather to come, in the scattered Presbytery of Lorn, Argyllshire, and must have caused poor Rachel great hardship. Oddly enough there is no mention of her brother-in-law's punishment but that is probably because he lived in another parish which is not named. Circular satisfaction obviously took some time to complete — three months in the case of Mungo Campbell in Mauchline who was called before the Presbytery of Ayr in 1642 for the murder of his cousin but failed to appear. It was only after being found guilty of fornication three years later that he finally appeared in sackcloth before the Presbytery for both offences and was ordered to stand for two Sundays in Mauchline before making a tour of six or so other churches. He seems to have got off very lightly in the circumstances. A reversal of circular satisfaction occurred in 1651 owing to what can only have been regard for the offender's social position; it was the ministers who did the travelling, not the delinquent. Lord Ogilvy appeared in sackcloth before the congregation of Alyth and confessed 'his accession to Major Middleton's rebellion and his sinful miscarriages against the Covenant' and present in the church to hear him, by order of the Presbytery, were the ministers of Newtyle, Eassie and Kinnettles.[36]

People sometimes resorted to various devices to try to evade the worst of Kirk Session discipline, one of which was to pretend that they could only speak Gaelic. In Inverness this meant that they would have to make their repentance at the Gaelic church where there was less publicity than in the High Church and therefore the Session decreed in 1708 that 'none of any rank or degree whatever . . . being found to have English, shall be allowed to stand in order to their giving satisfaction in the new [Gaelic] kirk where Irish [Gaelic] only is taught.' In general, however, people answered summonses when called and served discipline when ordered to do so but some exceptions deserve a mention. There may well have been some truth in one man's complaint to the Session 'that as long as the Minister believed some of his elders he and his people would not be at peace' which the Session regarded as 'immanerly malicious language' for which he had to appear on two Sundays in church. A Kilmaurs man accused of several petty offences, declared openly 'that it all proceeds from ane old pick the minister had at him' while another said that he 'would stand on the crown of his head on the day he appeared on the repentance stool because he was innocent.' When a deputation of elders was sent to see a man who had not appeared when called, he told them roundly that if he chose to keep twenty women and could support them, he would do so and would not thank the Session to interfere, adding 'other expressions he made use of, with which the Officers and witnesses were very much shocked', and he was remitted to the Presbytery, as was a Portsoy man who threatened that if the kirk officer came to lay a summons on him, he would be a dead man. When reproved for Sabbath profanation by lolling about on stacks of heather or turf, a Coldingham man retorted to the elders who had spoken to him that 'it was an ill world since the like of them are reproving folks for sin', and another, challenged by an elder for gathering cabbage on a Sunday retorted, 'What have ye to do with it? . . . Who will nail my lug to the trone?' A man accused of drinking for a whole night with others, 'most contemptibly turned his back and went away saying he would not stay to be flitton with' whereupon several elders were ordered to speak to the magistrates about this 'indignity', so that he might be suitably punished. Sometimes it was blatant impertinence combined with callous indifference that the elders had to deal with. When a Session, trying to establish paternity of a child, asked a man whether he had been in a particular house with the woman, he 'answered that he might be with her or not but he did not mind, he did not keep a Journal to mind things after they were past and desired the Session to make of it what they pleased.' Even when confronted with the woman, who looked him in the face, weeping as she stuck to her story, he still denied it.[37]

While such opposition to discipline might start out bravely enough, it tended to collapse when the full weight of kirk authority was brought to bear. A man who referred to the elders as 'a set of drunken bitches' and then boasted that he 'cared nothing for the minister nor elders' changed his tune when he was threatened with the jougs. When another man who was summoned to appear before the Session, did not do so, the kirk officer reported that he had 'said he did not care a strae for the Session and what they could do to him' but within four months he was expressing his 'regrate and remorse' and saying that he had only spoken in jest when he made 'his contemptuous expressions to the officer.' Sometimes submission took a little longer; yet another man told his Session that 'never minister, Bailie, nor Justice of the Peace should make him stand at the pillar though they should offer to hack off his head or yett pay.' This he said in February 1717 and managed to hold out until July the following year. It seems surprising that excommunication was not threatened in such cases.[38]

Some comments about Kirk Sessions may have been a bit too near the knuckle for their comfort and those making them were treated rather differently from what might have been expected. One man seems to have been very lucky when his plea not to appear publicly was accepted and he was allowed to make his repentance on his knees before the Session as well as helping to mend the 'cheeks of the door of the new church and harl the back wall of the church.' His offence had been saying that some of the elders helped themselves to the collections at the church door. Was such leniency intended to play down what he had said, either because there was some truth in it or, even if untrue, because it was not the sort of rumour that could be allowed to go the rounds? Could something of the same sort have lain behind the fact that when a man came before his Session for scandalising some of the elders, he was allowed off with a mere rebuke after 'declaring his grief'?[39]

The insolence of the excommunicated Thomas Dudgeon has already been mentioned but there were others besides him who, having got as far as appearing in church, then refused to submit, for example, Andrew McHamish who refused 'to stand according to the sessions appointment before the congregation for his opprobrious language and drunkenness, tho' he was in the kirk, and desired by the minister, but slighted and contemned the same.' There are a good many instances of people speaking back when on the stool of repentance, like the man in Ordiquhill who when appearing for adultery gave 'very insolent language to his minister' but only made things worse for himself as he was referred to the Presbytery and ordered to appear in church in sackcloth. Thomas Johnson appeared in the place of repentance in Falkirk in 1692 and not only 'railed offensively' but was alleged to have 'thrown peise among the people.' He said that someone had told him to behave like that, adding that several young men had been set there to mock him. It is recorded that three men stood on the place of repentance in Mauchline in 1675 but far from showing any evidence of repentance 'did strive all the time to break the stools whereon they stood, and which accordingly they did' but such behaviour only brought further retribution.[40]

The General Assembly realised that there could be occasions when people might feel that they had been injured by a Kirk Session and very soon after the Revolution passed an Act saying, 'All persons who judge themselves lesed [injured] by a Kirk Session, may apply to the Presbytery on passing of the sentence . . . If the appeal fails, he shall be held contumacious and proceeded against by the Kirk Session.'[41]

Once a course of repentance was completed, and the bulk of them were straight-forward and lasted no longer than the specified time, the delinquent was absolved — or even 'dissolved' — and this was pronounced from the pulpit by the minister. In the case of the couple who 'finally convinced' their Session of the sincerity of their repentance, it was decreed that after the blessing the following Sunday, the minister 'would declare before the congregation all the steps of the process against them before this and the superior court and the compliance of the parties with all that was required of them'; and then he would call on them 'to declare *in verbis de presente* their contrition and sorrow for the aggravated sin of which they were guilty', after which they would be absolved. In the case of a gross scandal committed elsewhere than in one's home parish and censured in that other parish, the General Assembly laid down the steps that should be followed: 'A person censured and absolved from scandal in another congregation than where he lives, is to bring a testimonial of his absolution, this to be intimated to the congregation where he lives, if the scandal be also flagrant there, otherwise it will be sufficient to intimate the same to the Session, and the same is to be done in the case of profession of repentance, where there has been a sentence of Lesser Excommunication.' Absolution, once pronounced, meant what it said, so that the woman who had to make circular satisfaction in Rescobie and other parishes was allowed to be baptised later that year and a Dingwall woman, found guilty along with her husband, of holding a raffle, went through her course of discipline, was absolved and was soon admitted as a new Communicant. There were cases, of course, where absolution could not be granted even although confession was made. The Barony Kirk Session records show that a woman 'asked for absolution which the Session could not grant, they not knowing whether the man she fell with was married or not and so they agree not to proceed in the matter until their doubts are resolved.' Their problem was that, not knowing whether the offence was fornication or adultery, they could not inflict the appropriate punishment to qualify for repentance, but it was very hard on the woman concerned who had to lie under scandal until the matter could be sorted out.[42]

A constructive approach to discipline was to require delinquents to give an undertaking to behave themselves in future but this was not the same thing as finding caution. If a Session thought it desirable, they would require people to sign 'bands' (bonds) as a pledge of their good conduct in time coming and these were written into the minute book. An example of this occurred in Dumbarton in 1703 when a man, Lauchlane Grant, was found struggling on the highway with a girl and was only stopped by a drummer who chanced along and put an end to whatever was going on. For some reason, the Session did not think that Lauchlane had had any carnal intentions towards the girl and just gave him a private rebuke but made him sign the following undertaking: 'I, Lauchlane Grant, doe by these prents [presents] promise and oblige myself, that I shall carrie and behave myself more regularly for the future, and that I shall abstain from all appearance of evil, particularly from drunkenness, swearing, and light carriage with women, in testimony whereof I have sub[t] thir pnts. at dumbartan the 13 day of May 1703, sic sibtz. L. Grant.' (sic)[43]

Discipline always had to be served in the parish where the sin was committed but as people frequently moved between parishes as they changed jobs, especially in rural areas where farm workers often changed employment every six months, this made for considerable difficulties. Where sin was known about before making a move, it was sensible to have censure speeded up, as has already been said, but very often things did not come to light until those concerned had moved on and so Kirk Sessions not uncommonly had to try to get delinquents back or else co-operate in sending such people to parishes which asked for their return. While it might be sufficient to send a message to an erstwhile parishioner 'to repair forthwith to the parish in order to satisfy discipline for delinquency' it could be necessary to send someone to make inquiries. This happened in Ashkirk from where an elder was sent, at the request of the minister, all the way to Linlithgow to interview a girl with the assistance of the minister there. In a case of incest, a man was ordered to bring the woman in the case back from England to where she had fled but, although he promised to do so, he neither went nor sent, so that the Session in this serious case, decided to employ someone to find her. The offending man said that he would pay for this but as he later fled too, it seems unlikely that he did so. Shotts Kirk Session paid a constable 12s. Scots in 1722 for searching for Agnes Young although, as such expenses had to come out of the poor's money, the poor would probably much rather have had it spent on them than on searching out delinquents; but to the kirk authorities, it was essential to maintain discipline and keep control. It was, of course, cheaper and easier to enlist the help of the Kirk

Session of the parish to which the sinner had gone, if that was known, and one Session might ask another to make some initial investigations or to examine possible witnesses and send extracts of their evidence, and this was always done. The following case is only included as a rule-proving exception: Kirkwall Kirk Session were asked by the minister of Eday to find out about reputed scandalous behaviour by Jane Murray, from Eday, on a Kirkwall market day. It was left to the elders to make inquiries and there is a definite impression in the minutes that not much effort was put into the matter before they reported that they could find no legal proof against her but co-operation between Sessions in this type of case was normally excellent. In 1760 the minister of an Argyllshire parish received a letter from Mr Lambie, minister of Kilmartin in the same county, saying that Ann Fisher, guilty of trilapse in fornication, had fled before finishing her course of censure and was said to be in his parish, asking that his Session would 'use their endeavours to send her back to the parish of Kilmartin.' As a result of this, the kirk officer was sent, along with two elders, to where she was believed to be living with her mother, to summon her to attend the Session of Kilmartin with certification that if she did not obey, both she and her mother would be turned out of the parish, which seems very hard on her mother. In 1702 the minister of Canisbay wrote to his counterpart in Wick asking that a woman should be returned to Canisbay to answer to a charge there. Wick Kirk Session agreed to this and went further, ordering their officer 'to incarcerate her for fear of running away some other way, and to be sent tomorrow to Canisbay parish.' In 1730 a request was made to the Presbytery of Inverness asking that Kirk Sessions would help in the case of Mary McRae, a 'very flagicious person' (guilty of enormous crimes), asking that she might 'from Parioch to Parioch be returned to the bounds of Garloch,' for which extra work kirk officers were to be paid 8d. Scots per day. Sometimes letters or 'refers' were sent after delinquents who had moved, requesting that they should have 'no rest or residens' until they returned to satisfy discipline in their former parishes.[44]

Should someone manage to show a clean pair of heels, however, widespread inquiries were likely to follow. After a Coldingham girl, believed to be pregnant, slipped out of the parish, the Presbytery who were consulted by the Kirk Session, ordered that her father should be asked where she might be found and if he did not know, then the minister should write to the Presbyteries of Edinburgh, Haddington, Dalkeith and Dunbar, 'that they may use all diligence to find her out . . . to forward her to the bounds until the truth of her scandalous report be tried', and all that was just on the basis of suspicion. But even with all the determination to drag people back to undergo censure in the appropriate parish, common-sense still prevailed. In 1705 some people who had sinned in the parish of Nigg had moved to Nairn, on the other side of the Moray Firth. The Kirk Session wrote to the minister there about sending them back but said that 'considering that they are poor servants and . . . the distance of the parishes being such that he cannot attend two Sabbaths on end seeing they seem somewhat repentant the Session appoint them to appear publicly next Sabbath and the second when the term comes', that being when a brief break between jobs would enable them to get to Nigg. Another example of thoughtfulness on the part of a Kirk Session occurred when a man crossed the Moray Firth to appear before the Kirk Session of Auldearn, Nairn-shire, a week earlier than he should have done, and the Session were kind and sensible enough to hold a special meeting for him. Bringing people from a distance should have required, in all humanity, that something should be done about accommodation for them but, if so, it is seldom mentioned. Ashkirk Kirk Session was one which was prepared to arrange for a girl from Galasheils to have somewhere to spend the night but their good intentions were to no avail as she did not turn up.[45]

An odd case occurred in Melrose in 1783. An unmarried mother had gone away to South Leith and although the Kirk Session asked for her return, she did not come. When the minister asked the elders what should be done next, they voted that she should not be summoned again because it was needless. The minister protested at this, saying that it was contrary to the laws of the church, that he would apply to the Presbytery to consider the matter and that he would at the same time lodge a complaint against the elders for their irregular and unlawful conduct, a state of affairs that rumbled on for a couple of years. The elders were probably just facing facts and accepting what the Kirk Session of South Leith said, that it would be impossible for them to find this particular woman among so many, especially as she could have changed not only her lodgings but her name. Something similar must have been in the minds of the Barony Kirk Session, Glasgow, in 1700 when they stated that a man 'was gone out of their bounds, and so the Session had not access to deal further with him.'[46]

Not only did Sessions answer requests for the return of delinquents to the parish where their offences had been committed but they made a point themselves of sending back anyone whose offence they discovered to be attributable elsewhere, rather than deal with it themselves; there was no point in being drawn unnecessarily into what was another parish's problem. The minister of Abernethy, Perthshire, received in 1751 a letter from the minister of Montrose enclosing an extract of a process against Janet Brydie who had an illegitimate child, giving the father as Robert Olyphant from Abernethy. Abernethy Kirk Session briskly retorted 'that the said Janet Brydie resided but a short time in this parish and neither brought us testimonials when she came nor demanded any when she left, and further that she was gone before the scandal was known to us, and also that the said Robert Olyphant is sailed some time ago to the West Indies' and they thought it proper to remit the whole case back to Montrose where the scandal was most flagrant and could be better judged. Similarly, when a couple in the parish of Nigg were found to have committed fornication in Cromarty, the kirk session of Nigg decided to 'refer those Delinquents to the session of Cromarty whose proper province it is to make them appear in publick'. Some years earlier Ashkirk Session, after examining a girl who had become pregnant in the parish of Roberton, made her promise to make satisfaction there when required to do so. Should delinquents flee, every effort was made to locate them through the Presbytery, efforts which have already been mentioned, or by pulpit intimations like the following one: 'This day Agnes Leishman sometimes in the paroch of Ettrick was cited from pulpit as fugitive from church discipline and the people exhorted to use their utmost diligence for discovering apprehending and bringing in the said Agnes Leishman to church discipline.' It was in paternity cases, in particular, that men fled, in order to avoid having to support mother and child and it was easy for them to go to sea or to join the army. Efforts might be made to catch up with them: when an Inverness shoemaker promptly joined up rather than find caution to serve discipline, the Session Clerk was ordered to speak to his captain to oblige him to make satisfaction but it was usually too difficult to get a hold of these men and they were generally left to themselves unless they ultimately returned home.[47]

The matter of letting lodgings without testimonials has already been mentioned. When anyone was asked to give lodgings to someone and there was reason to suspect sin of some sort, they might do so but were expected to let the Kirk Session know about it although this was not always done. Jennet Robin was asked whether she had taken in a pregnant woman 'into the time that the child was born and afterwards did lett her go without appearance before the Session or, at the least, acquainting the minister.' She admitted that she had done so at the request of another woman who had assured her that she would see to it that 'anie danger that might flow from it' would not harm Jennet. However much the kirk might disapprove of such things, people were human and it turned out that this woman had also spent some time in the home of Robert Benny, an elder, although he blamed his wife, saying that she had allowed it against his wishes and 'that all the time he and his wife were at no good agreement because of it.' The fact that this woman had been in an elder's house, with or without his approval, shocked the Kirk Session very much. People with transport were also likely to be in trouble for helping delinquents to escape, although whether they did it knowingly or not does not seem to have been considered. In 1707 a hirer was delated for taking an expectant mother away from Inverness and in 1762 a Borders Kirk Session met specially on hearing that a chaise had been hired to take a young woman with a child to Edinburgh and 'judging it their duty to do all that lies in their power to bring this secret work of darkness to due light' they decided to send information to the appropriate Edinburgh parish.[48]

Certain types of offence always had to be referred to Presbyteries but, in addition, should a Kirk Session have any doubts about the action to take in certain circumstances, they always consulted that body. In some cases, Presbyteries told them what to do and it was left to the Sessions to do it; in others, delinquents were simply remitted back to Kirk Sessions for them to make up their own minds about the steps to take. It has been said of kirk discipline that although it was meant well, it never did the good it was meant to do. It destroyed but it did not build up; it reproved but did not inspire; it condemned but it did not renew and just as nowadays people feel that violence and sex on TV harm young minds, so people began to feel that public confessions of sin at church were harmful rather than helpful to youngsters. Social changes of the late eighteenth and nineteenth centuries, which have already been mentioned, and rising standards of living, education and behaviour made people unwilling to accept church censure of the kind previously imposed. 'Our discipline has no effect to check the evil, and exposes us to witness very disagreeable scenes of equivocation, falsehood and perjury', wrote one parish minister in the late eighteenth century. About the same date, Falkirk Kirk Session was one of these which realised how things were going and if someone chose to repudiate the Session's right to interfere with him, then no further attempt was made to censure him. He was simply understood to have cut his connection with the church and to be responsible for his own conduct. Around that time a custom developed of people writing to the Kirk Session in such terms as 'I acknowledge the guilt and there need be no further settlement.' In the 1830s the Kirk Session minutes of some parishes show that while people might be cited, even three times, if they did not appear than that was an end of it, leaving 'further prosecution of the matter to the parties concerned', the inference in such a case being that there would be a court case for aliment. It was this changed attitude that caused a Session in 1834 'in the meantime [to] make no further appointment in regard to her', in the case of a woman who presented herself for discipline after having had a child to a married man but who failed to appear again before the Session as she was ordered to do. By 1883 the mother of an illegitimate child came before her Kirk Session, 'expressed her penitence for her sin and having been suitably admonished, the Kirk Session agreed to restore her to the privileges of the church' — changed days indeed, but it was not until 1902 that the General Assembly caught up with what was already being practised at local level, by passing an Act which abolished the citations and censures of the 1707 Act which had guided church discipline for so long. In order that these cases might have more privacy, it was decreed that they should be recorded in a special book, separate to the Session minutes and that after five years the names should be deleted, although this was not necessarily done — Dollar Kirk Session's 1909–12 discipline book, for example, has very few entries, but it also has no deletions. Discipline continued to be relaxed to the point where the kirk, though still greatly concerned, no longer punishes sins. When Mr Douglas Hurd, the Home Secretary, said in February 1988 that parents, schools and churches should do more to combat crime, he was saying no more than is true but, while not wishing to go back to the severity of earlier days, there is little that can be done without the back-up of the law.[49]

10
The Sins of the People

Officially, it was the state that dealt with crime and the church with scandal but in fact the kirk, especially in rural parishes where civil authority was lacking, became an unofficial arm of the law and dealt with a whole variety of offences, with or without the help of session bailies. Thus it was that a man was called before his Kirk Session for stealing apples from a garden while another came voluntarily to confess a theft he had committed ten years previously, for which he was duly rebuked. His crime must have weighed heavily on his conscience for him to feel the need to admit it so much later and it was good that there was a body available to receive his confession and relieve his mind. A potentially more complicated case fell to Bonhill Kirk Session, Dunbartonshire, in 1775 when the Presbytery ordered them to investigate suspicions of theft concerning two brothers, William and John Smith. The Session offered to summon anyone the Smiths wanted examined but this they refused and so the man from whom the money had been stolen was called instead. Meanwhile, the brothers asked for certificates of character which were of course refused whereupon they asked the Session to stop all further procedures as they would take the matter themselves to a civil court.[1]

The great day for theft, or at least reported theft, was Sunday. This may have been because people were working rather than stealing on the other days of the week but it seems more likely that it came to the notice of Kirk Sessions because by happening on that day it became Sabbath profanation which was in itself an ecclesiastical sin. By classifying it under this heading, the burden of proving theft was lifted from Kirk Sessions and ensured that the offence, whatever it really was, came easily within their authority. Thus there are records of Sessions rebuking youths for stealing peat on Sundays or ordering a man who stole a sheep that day to stand for one day in public; and there are many other examples of theft which as Sabbath profanation are dealt with in a later chapter.[2]

The kirk records of Elgin show that in 1597 it was minuted that the elders found themselves competent to judge those who made up 'cokalenes' which were lampoons or satires, and to punish anyone who produced these defamatory writings.

That they felt it necessary to minute confidence in their own competence as judges in such cases is interesting and it also shows the sort of thing that could go on at that time. In a largely illiterate population libel was seldom a problem although there were cases of it, such as that of Andrew Goram who fixed a 'scandalous libel' to the market cross concerning two young women, and it was they who brought the matter before the Kirk Session with the result that Andrew was rebuked publicly because he could not prove what he had written. Slander, however, was very common and as civil courts were not really interested and actions in them expensive, it was to the kirk that people looked for redress. For example, a couple were slandered by a woman who said that the wife was pregnant before marriage, which meant that their eldest child was illegitimate. They could produce no certificate of their marriage because there were no marriage records in the relevant parish at that date but they did have a certificate of proclamation of marriage signed by the Session Clerk and that, along with witnesses to the date of the girl's birth, enabled the Session to clear the couple and declare their daughter legitimate. This must have been a great relief to them, but if they wished to take the matter any further, it was up to them to go to a civil court.[3]

People were always ready to accuse others of all sorts of things — drunkenness, witchcraft and the evil eye, doing harm to animals and to people, theft, whoredom and much more. An example of the kind of thing that was said and complained of was a man calling a woman a 'lown Queen and salted whoorie', lown in this context probably meaning a rascal while a salter is one who salts fish, giving a meaning of sharp, sharp-tongued or sarcastic — but that was mild in comparison with some comments. A miner complained in 1747 that Catherine Campbell, wife of a fellow miner, had entered his house uninvited and abused his wife 'with very bad language, calling her a la'ed about limmer [rogue, thief, hussy] and whore, and a common hen stealer, and charged with stealing of clothes and said that she heard that the said Mary Mongomerie called her own husband a hundred horse stealers.' An even more surprising case was when a minister reported to his Session that Duncan McLachlean had come to him complaining that Patrick Maclean and his son had scandalised him and his family by saying that they were all infected with venereal disease. The Session considered 'that such calumny should not be overlooked' and ordered those concerned to appear before them. After this the story becomes a little complicated but the end of it came a month or so later when it was reported that the men had sorted it out themselves. What began as a slander case in an Edinburgh parish had an unusual outcome. One woman accused another of being a witch and proved it but investigations showed that there had been a feud between the two of them for a couple of years and the Kirk Session decided that they should be imprisoned together, perhaps in the hopes that presence would make their hearts grow fonder. However, the husband of one of them broke into the prison and rescued his wife, upon which the bailie was instructed to have her locked up again, only to have her husband release not just her but all the other prisoners too. He then burst in upon a Session meeting. All of this was referred to the Presbytery who seemed none too keen to take him on and the matter was resolved before the Edinburgh bailies, but he at least managed to avoid making repentance on the stool.[4]

In what must have been a rare type of slander case, when rumours were flying round a parish about a man's adultery, he tried to misuse the Kirk Session to prove that he was innocent although he knew perfectly well that he was not. This happened in 1833 and began with James Boyd, a farmer, coming to the Session to tell them of these rumours and saying that they were causing him great uneasiness 'and that he desired the Kirk Session to inquire into the grounds of the report in order that his character might be cleared.' When asked if there were any grounds for the stories, he said he thought that it was all because of ill will towards him. A year previously he had approached three elders about the matter and brought the woman concerned before them, they had questioned her and taken down her answers — an example of elders working on their own — and the Session Clerk had written to the minister of her parish but had received a reply which by no means tallied with all she had said. The Presbytery declined to give any advice 'in the present state of the case' and so the Session summoned the people James Boyd said he thought were responsible for the slander, as well as other witnesses, to come before them. They did not manage to complete their examination of them all in one day but had to adjourn and return the next afternoon and so it is not surprising that the details of this case run to many pages of minutes. The Session found the evidence against James very strong and referred him to the Presbytery who approved all that they had done and remitted him back to the Session, telling them to proceed in accordance with the rules of the church and it was thus that he was in the end found guilty of the adultery he had sought to have the Session deny on his behalf. He had not bargained for the effort that the Session would put into establishing the truth but he still tried to resist their findings and sought liberty to appeal to the Presbytery. As has already been said, in many cases which came before Kirk Sessions, to be accused was almost automatically to be considered guilty but in the case of slander this was not so. Sessions took great trouble to establish the facts when someone brought a complaint to them and, although it was up to the complainer to find his or her own witnesses, the Session would help by granting a warrant for the kirk officer to summon them and the alleged slanderer to appear, as in the following minute: 'This day James Murray appeared and gave in a bill against Isabell —, for calling him a thief and saying that he was found with a stolen sheep on his bark. The said Isabell — is appointed to be called to the next Session as also the said witnesses who are to prove the bill.' Although the wording given in that minute implies guilt, the pages and pages of witnesses' evidence in slander cases are as likely to show that a case was not proved as that it was and in James Murray's case, when the Session 'proceeded to examination of the witnesses, found it not proven.'[5]

In the seventeenth century slander cases became so frequent as to be a thorough nuisance to Kirk Sessions. In 1633 Montrose Kirk Session reported 'complaints of sclanderers daily coming before them' and by 1644 the Kirk Session of Kinghorn found that not only were unprovable slanders increasing all the time but that all they amounted to was 'jangling words to the fashing of the Session', and so they ordered a pledge of 20s. Scots to be laid down that persons alleging slander could prove what they said and if this could not be done, then the pledge was forfeit to kirk funds. Montrose Kirk Session had taken these steps a little earlier, requiring a pledge of 40s. Scots to be given and this practice became common throughout the country, although the sums involved varied. At Hassendean, Roxburghshire, the pledge was 12s. Scots, the same amount as at Orphir, Orkney, but there half was retained even when the case was proved. Orphir Kirk Session decided on this course as a real deterrent to frivolous complainers although it was hard on those whose case was genuine. These pledges were sometimes given in kind, like the plaid given in to Fordyce Kirk Session when a man complained that a woman called him a 'loun carl' (rascally fellow) and cursed both him and his wife.[6] The penalties for slander varied according to time and place. In 1633 Montrose Kirk Session ordained that anyone convicted of it should pay £4 Scots, not to the person slandered but to the poor, which perhaps helps to explain how Sessions allowed themselves to be involved in such cases, or else to stand in the jougs during the Session's' will and also to 'make their repentance either in their own habit or otherwise as the Session thinks fit and greatness of the offence doth merit.' So far as the person slandered was concerned, it must have been more satisfactory to have public repentance made so that the whole parish might know that what had been said was refuted — how satisfying, for instance, it was for the person slandered by a man named Adam Alcinor to see him confess on the stool of repentance and then kneel in the midst of the congregation to beg God's and his forgiveness. Sometimes, of course, there was a double penalty of fine and public appearance. In 1672 an Inverness woman had to make repentance for two Sundays wearing sackcloth for calling a man a murderer while in 1680 at Hassendean rules were laid down as follows: 'All sklanderis, bacbyteris [backbiters] and railyearis [railers] being convicted, shall for the first fault ask God's mercy and that of the party sklanderit in presence of the congregation, and for the second fault, be put in the cukstulis and say 'toung ye leid', and for the third fault, be banished.' Having to say 'Toung ye leid' did not necessarily require the culprit to be in the cuckstool; in Inverness in the latter part of the seventeenth century or early eighteenth, the slanderer was just made to stand at the churchyard gate as the congregation was leaving and say, in Gaelic, 'This is the lying tongue', and there is a record of a St. Andrews man who had miscalled his wife having to go on his knees before the congregation and, holding 'his awin tung in his hand' declare 'Fals tung, thow leid' — and speaking while holding one's tongue is a very difficult thing to do. Some slander cases ended with the Kirk Session exhorting the parties 'to Christian love and peace'.[7] A case that seems unfair was that of two girls found innocent by Nigg Kirk Session about 1706 of a reported offence, but who were nevertheless rebuked for being slandered.

Slander cases were that much more difficult when they involved the minister's household. Although there was a definite element of slander in the following case concerning a former servant in the manse at Kilmaurs who was summoned to answer various questions and complaints, it seems that the whole thing arose out of pique on the part of the minister. The points complained of were:

1) Deserting the minister's service without any just cause or provocation and that in the middle of the term to the laying him desolate of a servant to his great prejudice;
2) for deserting the provoca (sic) as said is, or if she have any, let her mention it here;
3) for lying and raising calumnies and reproaches upon his family and principally upon his spouse;
4) for threatening to leave her death upon his spouse;
5) for offering to give one of his daughters the witch-mark;
6) for defaming the minister.

The young woman pled guilty to all of these charges but qualified numbers 5 and 6 by saying that she 'had no evil design in it' but all in all, it is hardly surprising that this case was dropped.[8]

People used to start fighting and quarrelling very readily but as with many other offences, this was much more likely to be dealt with if it happened on a Sunday and so came under the heading of Sabbath profanation. Two men who fixed up a duel were not found guilty of that but of doing so on a Sunday, and it was because it was on a Sunday that a man struck his wife with a spade and another beat and cursed his spouse, that they had to confess the sin of Sabbath profanation, not the actual offences, and pay a penalty for doing so. In the same way, 'casting clods at Jennet Taylor' on the Sabbath merited a mention more for the day than the deed. An elder was deposed for fighting and brawling on a Sunday and if a man in that position could do that on such a day, there was much excuse for other people to do so too, and on other days of the week also. In 1648 the Presbytery of Fordyce decreed that 'shedars of blood be stricking and wounding, not being on the Lord's Day' should be censured, drawing kirk attention to weekdays as well as Sundays, but in fact where any such problems were serious enough Kirk Sessions always dealt with them. Many fights arose over the animals which every other person seemed to keep in the country and, indeed, in towns too. Grazing, even on the verge of a street, was valuable and any interference with it or beasts on it could quickly lead to blows; a man appeared before his Session for throwing his neighbour's son into the mill dam for putting beasts on his grass and in a case which went on for some time between two men about disputed grazing and beating an animal which belonged to one of them, it was left to the Session, in the absence of any witnesses, to decide the rights and wrongs of it, as a result of which both of them were rebuked in their own seats in church. In another case, when a cow which had been left tied to a door was let loose without permission, there was scolding and beating and even trampling of the offender in the burn.[9]

Flyting or scolding among women was a very common occurrence but not really a very serious one, which merited sensible but not severe handling — for example, two women were rebuked for it by the Session, told to go on their knees to ask the forgiveness of God and each other and were dismissed, reconciled. Cases were sorted out one way or another but possibly one of the most practical solutions appeared in the case of James and Janet Simpson, a difficult couple who were briskly ordered by the Presbytery to whom their behaviour had been reported by the Session, 'to agree within aucht [eight] days with Will Scott there, and also with their neighbours.' It would be interesting to know what the feuds and quarrels were, which involved a man representing the town of Greenlaw, and seven nearby lairds which made the Kirk Session of that parish order them to make repentance and 'not to be removed from the place of repentance till they made redress to the minister and elders and show tokens of repentance.'[10]

Married women frequently suffered rough handling from their husbands, so much so that in 1627 the Presbytery of Fordyce considered the common habit of men 'putting hand to their vyves upon anie licht occasion and striking them unmercifully after admonition . . .' and felt it necessary to 'bear doune this enormity.' The actual 'bearing down' had to be done by Kirk Sessions which, usually so severe on women in other cases, were the only resort for what would nowadays be called battered wives, and some ill treatment of women was so serious that very strong steps had to be taken to deal with it. A complaint from Elspet Dalgarno of her husband's 'debarring her from his company' for six weeks and 'also for dinging and hurting her on the face with a gryt key maist crewellie and unmercifullie' as a result of which he 'almaist dung out ane of hir eyne' resulted in his being put in the steeple and made to find caution to behave properly in future. It might be left to Kirk Sessions to initiate legal action in such cases and an Act of Parliament in 1649 refers to proceedings which were started by the Session of Cathcart regarding the cruel treatment of Agnes Stewart by her husband, James Stevinsone — 'wrangs and violences done be him to hir, And by forcing her to leive his company.' In the end a Parliamentary Committee heard the petition which by then came from the Presbytery of Glasgow and she was granted a money sum but was also ordered to return to him and he was told that he must treat her properly. In most cases, however, Kirk Session action took the form of public rebuke possibly with an attempt at reconciliation, as happened in the parish of Auchterhouse in 1647 when a man who had struck his wife until she bled, had to make public repentance and then come before the Session with her to be reconciled. Great efforts were made to bring squabbling couples together again; in 1737 a couple accused of strife and scurrilous language towards each other were exhorted to forgive each other and live at peace; and elsewhere another couple delated 'for disorderly behaviour in the married state by imprecations and beating one another' came before their Session and as a result of that body's efforts they 'promised to live with more love and harmony thereafter.' Although a Session could find no actual proof of Janet McGorie's accusation that her husband Peter had 'beat and bruised her with his hands and his feet' which he 'confidently denied', they assumed that she would not have made such a complaint without good grounds and 'did sharply rebuke the said Peter' and then 'exhorted them both to their relative duties.' Could Marriage Guidance counsellors have done any better at that time?[11]

Somewhere between 1725–30 Falkirk Kirk Session had to deal with an odd case. A tailor named Hardie was too fond of drink and whenever he was the worse of it, used to offer his wife for sale. This was not as bad as battering her but must have been very humiliating, especially as he never met with any great demand. However, one day a man named Alexander Watson offered him £5, which was accepted. On hearing of this the Kirk Session summoned both men and, while accepting Watson's statement that he had done it purely to cure Hardie of a nasty habit, they gave him a Sessional rebuke. He deserved something better for a well-meant effort but the odd thing is that there is no reference to Hardie being punished. It was very seldom that a man complained about his wife's violence but one who assaulted her husband 'to the shedding of his blood' had to give caution that she would appear before the Session for punishment. When James Yong told his minister that he could have no peace with his spouse, it does not seem that she ill-treated him physically but she was told to appear along with him before the Session. In the event, however, it was reported that he had fallen ill and had wisely made it up with her. By no means every domestic quarrel came to the Kirk Sessions of the country; it only happened in the event of a complaint being brought to them or where things had got to such a pitch that they had become a public scandal. This happened in Dumbarton in 1701 when there were such difficulties and accusations between a man and his wife that the Session found 'that there is a flagrant scandal and that the mouthes of the countrie are mightily opened, and that therefore it will be necessary that it be removed in a public manner.'[12]

As married couples quarrelled between themselves, so did parents and children and their disputes could also come to the Kirk Session for resolution and punishment. A young man who used 'very irreverent language' to his father and also struck him was ordered to make repentance before the congregation for this 'horrid and unnatural sin'. When two young fishermen gave great offence by quarrelling and struggling with their father to prevent him going to sea, even to the extent of taking away the oars of his boat, their conduct was thought 'so notoriously culpable and scandalous' that they had to stand publicly for one Sunday. Some quarrels were much more violent than that and when Patrick Levingstoun struck his son and blinded him, both the kirk and the civil authorities were involved in the case, with the magistrate forbidding him to do such a thing again 'for which he has humblie reservit him self in the Session's will', which was that he should make repentance the following Sunday and pay the penalty they imposed. A combination of punishments befell a young man who in 1594 assaulted his father. The Kirk Session asked the magistrates to put him to a 'condigne' (well-merited) assize according to law, as a result of which he had to appear bareheaded and barefoot in sackcloth on the highest degree of the penitent's stool, holding in each hand the hammer and the stone with which he had attacked his father, and with a paper 'written in great letters' on his head describing his offence. On the following day he had to stand for two hours at the market cross, also in sackcloth and holding the hammer and stone, and was warned that if ever he offended against his father or mother again, that whatever part of the body offended, it would be cut off. Where possible, Sessions encouraged reconciliation in all cases: Petty Kirk Session, for example, summoned a young man who was 'rebuked for his disobedience to his father and mother, and exhorted to crave of God mercy and grace to behave himself towards the said old persons as dutiful children ought.'[13]

Disputes between employers and employees might also require to be settled by the kirk. In 1695 a goodwife in Coldingham accused her maid of beating her with an oxgoad to such effect that she had 'blae marks' which she showed to a number of people. The Kirk Session became involved and called witnesses who had seen these blue marks. After much reasoning with the maid, she explained that the dispute had been because she had refused to take in the washing until she had winnowed the oats. She probably thought that she was planning her work well, but she had gone too far and had to remove the scandal in public. A couple on the island of Coll complained to their Session that Hugh McDonald, who worked for someone other than them, had offered brutal violence to their twelve-year-old daughter. Witnesses were called and Hugh admitted the offence but said that it happened because she was calling him nicknames as he went about his master's work. After much argument on both sides, the Session fined him £5 stg. to be given to the girl, and 20s. for the kirk funds, a decision which meant that the girl did very well out of taunting a servant. Although Kirk Sessions tried to be fair in their decisions, another case where the outcome seems hard on a servant occurred in Dumbarton in 1702. A company of Masons, which included the Provost, were meeting in a house and when a maid went into the room to make up the fire, someone suddenly pushed her forward and she found that a trail of powder had been lit beneath her and some of the men held out her skirts. This was a long case, which went to the Presbytery because of various points of concern which are detailed in the minutes, one of which was that 'The Session doubts whether such riotous actions, not being affected with drunkenness or swearing' — this they had established in investigations — 'be usually animadverted against by the censures of the church.' Such a doubt seems almost unbelievable but the presence of the Provost, and possibly the status of the Masons, seem to have had their effect.[14]

Trouble-making could take many forms and one of these happened in Clackmannan in 1685. A woman complained to the Session that Thomas Russell and his wife had thrown down her husband's gravestone, for which they were duly summoned. Thomas said 'that he only laid his hand on the burial stone and it fell over' but whether that was the truth or not, the Session dealt with it in a way that was both practical and a deterrent to anyone who might have thought that knocking down gravestones was fun: he and his wife had to go the woman who had complained and 'crave her pardon wherein they had injured her, and to be assisting in the upsetting of the said burial stone, and to appear at the next diet of Session to hear what should be imposed on them for throwing down the burial stone.' When St. Andrews Kirk Session found that the church windows were being damaged by boys playing at 'Catt and Dog' in the churchyard and also by stone-throwing, they forbade them and anyone else to play there in future. This was understandable as church property was involved but in many places Sessions passed Acts to control what they considered to be public nuisances, even where these had nothing to do with the church, such as an intimation in 1647 'anent profane boys that sings together bawdy songs through the streets, both evenings and mornings that if any be found in the like again, they shall be severely punished.' Something as harmless as running races in the streets after supper could be called 'troubling the town and perturbing the neighbours, and breeding an evil example to others to do the same' and for doing this five girls had to appear before their Session in 1623 and pay 6s.8d. of a penalty. A Hawick man had to crave the pardon of God and the Session upon his knees in 1702 'for rambling up and down the streets and disturbing people in the silence of the night'. Silly bravado also led to kirk disapproval. As a result of a youth and his teacher talking about eating eggs, the youngster boasted that he could eat three dozen and as many again, as well as a quantity of butter, all for a wager, and for doing so he was called before the Session, the main charge being his boast that he could manage this feat which he then said had been a jest and done in ignorance. Elsewhere a fiddler was persuaded by some jokers to ride through the town on horseback 'with boots, spurs and red clothes, in a military posture, with the town's piper playing before him'. For doing so he found himself before the Session, and he too said it had just been done for sport although it transpired that he was to get a pint of brandy and a gallon of ale for doing so. What he got, 'for the terror of others', was an order from the Session to appear in church to confess the sin and be rebuked; and there were many other cases of the same kind of thing.[15]

Carvings on three feet of a table stone in the churchyard at Legerwood, Berwickshire show a drunkard's progress, starting with him sitting astride a barrel, then drinking deeply, and ending up with his head in his hands. This seems a very unlikely thing for a family to have put on a stone; could the carvings have been put there as a cautionary tale for all to see as they went to and from church? Certainly drunkenness was a great problem but in earlier Kirk Session records it is usually associated with swearing and fighting, seldom appearing on its own. Perhaps there was not so much of it in the days when, apart from water and milk, the drink of the peasantry was ale which was not so potent as the whisky which came into fashion after 1750. Tea, being imported, was subject to duty and therefore expensive, whereas ale was home brewed and whisky largely produced in local stills, both of them made with home-grown grain, and it made economic sense for them to be the staple drinks of the common people. More than that, drinking was regarded as a convivial thing to do and was thought to be sufficiently respectable for ministers, in the early post-Reformation years, to keep ale-houses to augment their incomes, although it does not seem that very many did in fact do this; perhaps more schoolmasters did so. Owing to nobles taking over church lands for themselves following the Reformation, there was virtually no provision for stipends so that clergy often had to subsidise themselves by finding other sources of revenue such as this, although the General Assembly decreed in 1567 that any 'minister or reader that taps ale or beer or wine and keeps an open tavern, should be exhorted to keep decorum', in other words, to run an orderly house; but in fact the practice of ministers running inns, where it occurred, did not last long. Once proper arrangements were made for payment of their stipends, however, it is said that the barley which formed part of them might not be used for food but for 'the ready sale which it generally meets with from distillers.' There was nothing wrong with this; it was a good way of turning kind into cash. There was no stigma attached to normal drinking and the giving of drink was such an acceptable thing that it appears in church accounts. In 1671 a Session paid Patrick Thomson, 'for sklatting [slating] a part and pointing another part of the church 4 lib; to his servant for drink money 3s. 4d. And spent with him in drink 6s. 8d.; for nails 15s.; the sum of all the particular proceedings 5 lib 5s.', and when a man gave in his expenses to Jedburgh Kirk Session for lodging some workmen who were repairing the church in 1703, these included 'meat, drink, coal and candle'. It was normal for drink to be given to workmen in this way, as well as when they gave some special service, which is why in 1830 another Session listed 'whisky for erecting the [Communion] tent, 2s.' among other pre-Communion expenses such as washing the church and schoolhouse.[16]

Unfortunately the Scots will drink both for consolation and for celebration and would happily sit in taverns till all hours, turning what was a perfectly reasonable enjoyment into a very serious vice, the excessive drinking which greatly concerned the kirk. As early as 1436 Parliament had decreed that anyone found drinking in an inn after 9.00 p.m. would be imprisoned but, as with much early legislation, this made little difference and in 1617 control of drinking was committed to sheriffs, bailies and Kirk Sessions by an Act of Parliament which provided for punishment by fine or imprisonment for anyone 'convicted of drunkenness or haunting taverns after 10.00 at night.' The position of Kirk Sessions in this matter was further strengthened in 1645 when Parliament decreed that anyone found guilty by a kirk court of excessive drinking, especially the drinking of healths, should be fined according to their degree. In 1672 a further Act required that of 1617 to be enforced and ordered judges to try those delated before them by Kirk Sessions for drunkenness, as well as other sins such as profanation. It is obvious that Parliament intended Kirk Sessions to refer those guilty of drunkenness to civil courts but, as has already been said, Sessions readily dealt with offenders themselves and passed their own Acts in response to their own local needs: in 1625 the minister of Tynninghame intimated that anyone found drunk should pay £3 *toties quoties* while in 1640 an Act of Session was passed there 'against druckness,' (sic) that if anyone was found the worse of drink they should be fined four merks. Inn-keepers could be liable to censure not just for selling alcohol after hours but if they let people have so much that they became intoxicated; or they might be summoned *en bloc* if too much drink was sold on fair days or other such special occasions and Elie Kirk Session was one that laid down 'the quantitie and measure off drinke to be sold by sellers thereof' on any day of the week whatsoever.[17]

The Kirk Session of Montrose decreed in 1636 'that if any sell aille or wine after ten hours at night which may be an occatione of drunkenness, the seller [shall pay] two merks and the buyer one merk, except by strangers.' Strangers in this sense were what Broughton Kirk Session, Peebles-shire, called 'passengers upon the road' or what, until comparatively recently, were known as *bona fide* travellers, while the term 'hotel residents' would cover the wording used by Hawick Kirk Session in 1702 when they excepted this group from drinking regulations which forbade inn-keepers to entertain and supply alcohol to anyone after 10.00 p.m. 'except strangers and wayfaring men who are comd to lodge with them for the night.' For the first fault such innkeepers were to be rebuked before the Session and for the second, before the congregation 'for as there would be no thieves if there were no resetters, so there would be no night untimeous drinkers if there were not inn-keepers to encourage and entertain them.' In Falkirk the Session were even stricter and imposed Lesser Excommunication for a third offence. Even when not carried to excess, late drinking could lead to censure, with Lauder Kirk Session decreeing that anyone drinking after 10.00 p.m., whether drunk or not, would be liable to church censure, as would the 'entertainers' of such persons and if anyone should commit a second offence of drunkenness, public censure would be made in sackcloth.[18] As neither inn-keepers nor their customers were going to let it be known if 'untimeous drinking' was going on, it was up to Sessions to find out for themselves and so it was that elders were made responsible for supervision of inns in their districts. In 1703 the Kirk Session of Tynninghame decided to prevent late drinking by kindly methods, appointing two elders 'to go to the Innkeepers in the town and tell them from the Session that they must suffer no persons to drink in their house after 8.0 o'clock at night', an earlier hour than usual, with the warning, 'or they will be taken course with', but they realised that more was likely to be needed and ordered 'the rest of the elders to go through the town every night to see who contravenes this Act and delate them.' In Hawick the elders' inspection rota changed monthly about 1712 and they were frequently admonished by the minister to produce due information about any offenders. To 'perlustrate,' meaning to 'traverse and inspect' the streets, was the phrase used for this night-time activity of the elders who, sometimes under the term 'visitors' or inspectors, cleared an inn if they found it still open. This is the origin of the saying that 10.00 p.m., the former closing hour, was 'elders' hours'.[19]

Few people had clocks or watches, which provided a ready-made excuse if they drank overlong and so any form of notifying the time was invaluable. It could be done by the church or by Burgh Councils, through provision of clock towers or possibly by the beating of a drum through the streets at 10.00 p.m. Sunday drinking was so bad in the parish of Fordyce at one point in the seventeenth century that the minister and Session decided that only an hour and a half would be allowed for it after worship, following which the kirk officer had to ring a bell which came to be known as the Drunken Bell. The minister, Mr William Blair, then visited the ale-houses in person and sent home anyone he found still in them. This custom had ceased before 1716 although his two succeeding ministers, from 1716–46 and from

1747–90 had both found it necessary 'to make a step through the village, after dinner, and break up drinking companies.' In the same way, it was found necessary in Monifieth, Angus, 'to send a committee of the Kirk Session to perlustrate the inns of the parish' after worship ended on Sundays.[20]

Over-drinking had all sorts of consequences. One example of this which would nowadays simply be regarded as stupid was considered very offensive in 1702: an intoxicated man went rambling up and down the streets in women's clothing, so serious a scandal that he was rebuked in church 'and then was recommended by prayer to the mercy, grace and protection of God.' When it came to violence that resulted, that was much more serious. When a man drank so much that he 'struck all he met with' the Session punished him by making him 'stand three several Sabbaths betwixt the second and the third bell in the jobs [jougs] and thereafter during the time of divine service to stand in the place appointed for public repentance.' A very bad case occurred in 1678 when Elspeth Allan was charged with allowing sturdy beggars to drink so much that a woman was killed, and another happened in 1705 when four young gentlemen, including Lord Blantyre, drove one Sunday from Edinburgh to Leith, sat drinking during the time of afternoon worship, went for a stroll on the sands and then continued drinking till 8.00 p.m. Returning home, they insisted on the coachman and post-boy driving so furiously that a woman was knocked down and died half an hour later. The civil authorities arrested the drivers but a letter of the time commented that 'it will be a great pity that the gentlemen that were in the coach be not soundly fined for breach of Sabbath', which was the only way of getting at them for the death they had caused.[21]

Sessions were aware of the effects on families if one member drank to excess and one rebuked a young man for wasting his father's substance on drink and 'Ryoting and revelling', warning him that if he went on in this manner he would be 'given up to the Magistrates and [put] in prison to live upon bread and water.' It is not known whether this threat was carried out at that time but three years later, in 1717, he was in trouble again for cursing his father and wasting his money and this time was told by the Session that if he could not refrain from drinking to excess, he would be given up to the bailie of regality to censure him as he deserved, and he was dismissed with certification by the bailie [the Session bailie, it seems] 'that he would cause delate him to the circuit ensuing if he walked not more submissively and obtempering of the laws both of man and God.' The Kirk Session of St. Nicholas Church, Aberdeen, showed very real concern for the welfare of Hugh Ross, a young man given to heavy drinking, cursing and swearing, and asked the minister to speak to his parents about him, which he did. They reported that he was more sober than formerly and was 'now willing to abstain from company-keeping and to take himself to ane employment.' He appeared before the Session and promised 'to amend what has been amiss' and after a rebuke was dismissed with due warnings for the future. Another parish where a helpful effort was made to stop drinkers was Lauder where in 1681 Hugh Dodds of Muircleugh and James Mason were often in trouble, especially Hugh, and so the Session 'considering

Hugh Dodds his excessive drinking, appointed the minister to intimate to the congregation that no person entertain him in drink under pain of censure.' Unfortunately for these good intentions, Hugh had some thoughtless friends and one of those who continued to entertain him was the wife of an elder and he, poor man, was deposed for not reporting his wife's misplaced hospitality. Hugh's drinking became worse and worse and in 1685 the Session fined him £40 Scots as a scandalous person and recommended him to the 'baylif' who imprisoned him until he paid the fine or found caution to answer when called; but at least the Session had done all they could for him. In 1604 an effort was made in Aberdeen to prevent a known drinker being led astray: two men were forbidden to go 'night-walking' themselves or to entice him to go drinking with them, 'nor draw him out for that effect on the nicht in time coming', showing an awareness of what bad company could do. In 1832 West Kilbride Kirk Session suspended three men from church privileges because of habitual drunkenness 'until a reformation in their character shall appear', another instance of trying to improve rather than just reprove.[22]

The customs associated with funerals provided a great opportunity for the consumption of alcohol. It was given to guests at the lykewake when the body was watched overnight until burial; it was served at the kisting when the corpse was coffined and vast sums of money were spent on what were called 'services' of alcohol at the funeral meal, these services being a formal sequence of different drinks interspersed with particular foods. It was considered a point of honour to offer this kind of entertainment and a family would often spend on a funeral what would have kept them for a year; even poor families would part with their last horse or cow rather than be thought mean or lacking in respect to the departed. When there was a long walk to the burial ground, with people carrying the coffin turn and turn about, alcohol was served at the various resting places and yet again in the graveyard after the interment was over, something that often led to fighting there. For many people, funerals were a chance to get food and drink gratis and they took all they could get and the drinking could well continue after the official proceedings were over. One of various instances of this was in Cromarty in 1742 when the Session had to order two men to be rebuked on Sunday because after a funeral they had got so drunk on brandy with which they had been entrusted, that they were incapable of disembarking from the boat they were sailing in, fell into the sea and had to be fished out. Elders were just as concerned with a decent — in other words lavish — funeral as other parishioners and it seems to have been the efforts of particular clergymen, such as Rev. Henry Duncan of Ruthwell, Dumfriess-shire, rather than Kirk Sessions themselves, which ultimately brought the custom of funeral drinking to an end or virtually so. Dr Duncan's method was to persuade members of his congregation to sign a declaration binding themselves neither to give nor to accept more than one glass of wine or spirits at a funeral. This caught on in neighbouring parishes and by 1840 had even spread to islands such as Skye through the efforts of ministers and the example of respectable families.[23]

Another excuse for tippling, as drinking was often called, was drinking at cummerskales, which were mixed gatherings to drink the health of a new baby. The Session minutes of Kinghorn in 1645 show an awareness that not only was this a waste of money and of time but also that it could harm the new mother's health, referring to

> the inconveniences that arise therefrom as the loss and abusing of so much time which may be better employed in attending business at home. The prejudice which persons lying in child bed receives both in health and means being forced not only to bear company to such as come to visit but also to provide for their coming more than either is necessary or their estate may bear, considering also that persons of the better sort carry a secret dislike of it and would be gladly content of an Act of this kind . . .

and so that Session passed an Act forbidding all visits of this nature under threat of a Sessional rebuke for the first fault and public confession for a second. What made these occasions even more drunken was that it was considered dangerous to the health and looks of the baby if the visitor did not empty the horn or glass.[24]

Drinking at wedding festivities does not seem to have worried the kirk overmuch but the 'practice of drinking bridegrooms the second day after the marriage unto beastly drunkenness' — excessive drinking of the young couple's health — caused such concern to St. Andrews Kirk Session that in 1710 they forbade friends of the groom, inn-keepers and anyone else to do it. A worry for at least one Kirk Session in the Borders was the habit people had of giving excessive amounts of liquor to each other in the open streets during Common Ridings; in fact, the Cornet's father had the privilege of selling liquor without a licence from the choosing of the Cornet until the Common Riding. But funerals, births, marriages and so on were not regular events and it was Sunday that was the regular serious drinking day for the masses, including women. It was the only day off work for the ordinary people and because social drinking was a favourite relaxation, that was how they spent much of the day but so far as the church was concerned, drinking offences that day were classed as Sabbath profanation and to drink overmuch on fast days was also profanation.[25]

Drinking, especially on Sundays, has already been briefly mentioned as the single greatest cause of poverty. Drinking parties or 'companies' as they were often called, or 'drinking to a Confluence of people' were a feature of the Sabbath and a prohibition from one Kirk Session about carrying ale from house to house, appears to have been a reference to an early eighteenth century equivalent of a bottle party on a Sunday. The New Statistical Account for Prestonpans, East Lothian, describes vividly the degrading and squalid results of Sabbath drinking:

> An enormous quantity of inebriating liquors were at one time sold on Sundays. At a very early hour in the morning, after a night of drunkenness and riot, mothers of families might be seen hurrying with vessels containing gallons of spirits, but partially, if at all, concealed. Later, withered-looking children might be witnessed passing to and fro, amid the severities of the wintry storm, in fearful ministry to the cruel and remorseless passions of their benighted and ruined parents. From the

closing hours of the preceding evening, until the midnight darkness of the day of God, the peace of the community was ever at stake. Coarse shout of brutal merriment — vicious and vulgar oath — shriek of fear bursting from woman's lips — appalling sounds of injury and violence, all might be heard.

The reference here to Saturday night drinking was relevant because even if it ended there and did not continue on a Sunday, it could still affect worship that day. In the mid-seventeenth century it was recommended to ministers that they should point out to their people, both publicly and privately, the evil of sitting too long in taverns, particularly on Saturday nights, which caused some people to miss Sunday worship altogether and others to attend drowsily — although it was not drowsiness but a straight-forward hangover which caused one Hawick woman to be summoned for unChristian behaviour in church. She admitted having had some alcohol which had 'occasioned her indecent carriage in the house of God, being often troubled with a giddiness in the head' but she promised to live soberly thereafter. Women were much involved in drinking offences which could bring severe retribution upon them: two who were delated for drinking to the point of incapacity on a Sunday were fined and imprisoned and one of them was banished, although such a punishment may indicate that more lay behind it than appears in the minutes.[26]

Normal drinking, as has been said, was acceptable, so much so that in some places 'drinkings' were held to help someone in need, an early form of a charity cocktail party; and even some Sunday drinking was permissible. Because many people walked a long way to church and because services were very long, refreshment of some sort was necessary and an excellent location for an inn was opposite or close to the kirkyard gate, so close sometimes that it might take its name from its position like the 'house [inn] of the Kirk Style' at Canisbay, Caithness, or the Kirk Style Inn which is still in operation at Dunning, Perthshire, or it might be named after the church, like Reay Kirk Inn, also in Caithness. A reviving drink or two, taken in a sensible manner either before worship or between morning and afternoon services, did no harm. A minister said in the mid-nineteenth century, 'As soon as the congregation is dismissed, the inn is their common resort' while another, writing in the late eighteenth century said that 'It must be admitted that several houses [inns] of this kind are necessary for the accommodation of the people who come from a distance to attend public worship on Sundays.' Yet another was so hospitable and aware of the needs of his people that it is said that he used to have a pail of small beer in the manse kitchen for any parishioners who had come a considerable distance to church — but when his son succeeded him, only water was provided, with a remarkable falling-off in the thirst of the people. Even in the mid-seventeenth century, Mr John Lauder, minister of Tynninghame, while saying that no ale should be sold before noon on Sundays, tacitly accepted its sale after that hour by saying that at that time of the day, the inn should be kept as quiet as possible. What was objected to was not the fact of taking a drink on Sunday but when people drank too heavily before and after worship or, having begun tippling before it, simply sat on and did not go to church at all.[27]

After an 'outrageous fray' in a vintner's house one Sunday morning in 1808 Thurso Kirk Session petitioned the Sheriff Depute to investigate it and to deal with such practices 'according to the laws thereanent' because Parliament had been aware of drinking problems back in the sixteenth century and passed an Act in 1579 forbidding 'passing to taverns and alehouses and wilfully remaining away from church' on Sundays. In addition to that Kirk Sessions passed their own Acts to control the sale of alcohol during time of worship; one decreed in 1641 that whoever drank or sold drink at that time should pay a dollar to the poor and make public satisfaction and in 1655 forbade the sale of liquor on Sundays 'to any but at their ordinair in a sober way in their own houses.' Another forbade all sale of alcohol on Sundays except 'as much as serves for refreshment, or to those that send for it to their own houses'. In 1685, yet another Session still threatened a penalty of £4 Scots and standing for three Sundays in sackcloth for anyone who sold alcohol on Sundays, especially during the time of divine service, except where it was needed for anyone who was ill. The words 'in time of divine service' left a loophole. The first hour of church services was in the hands of the reader, not the minister, and the first psalm was only given out just before the latter entered the church to start the main part of the service and this could result in a fine point of argument about drinking times: when two people were summoned for drinking during the time of worship, they said that they had only had three chappins of ale between sermons, the last being finished before the first psalm ended, a point of view which apparently confounded the Session who found it 'a little intricat' and referred it to the Presbytery. Elders who acted as inspectors on Sundays, checking for general Sabbath profanation, are more fully discussed in another chapter, but much of their time was taken up with drink-related offences that day — in addition to supervision of weekday closing hours — and they were specifically directed to watch over inns, 'to go from alehouse to alehouse next Lord's day and report diligence,' as one minute put it. In towns they could call upon civil support so that when people were found to be absent from St. Nicholas Church, Aberdeen, because they were drinking at home, the inspector for the day was advised by the Session to 'take with him one of the touns officers and to go to these houses in the time of afternoon service and see if anyone was drinking there.' An early Kirk Session minute from Montrose shows that there, at that time anyway, not only were the inspectors required to carry out this duty but that they were penalised if they failed to do so: 'The Session ordains that there are collectors to visit the town in time of Divine service, both forenoon and afternoon, and there to search and seek all Tavern houses if there be any drinking in the said time or otherwise working any trade or calling whatsoever. Qlk failing to do they shall pay to the poor every one of them, 12 shs.'[28]

A rather torn minute of Kirkcudbright Kirk Session for April 1693 shows a rather unpleasant type of undercover operation:

> Considered the manyfold [torn] . . . flowing from persons drinking excessively [torn] . . . unseasonable times in this town and parish whereby a [torn] . . . is made

> to the committing of many heinous [torn] . . . of several sorts . . . the Session for preventing the same in time coming . . . has appointed public and clandestine searchers to search for and delate all drinking on Sabbath in time of fore or afternoon sermon or any other time unseasonably that day,

and also all such found drinking any day of the week after 10.00 p.m., especially on 'the mercat day or Sabbath'. Not every parish, of course, had Sabbath inspections by elders and neither were these necessarily regular where they occurred. It might only be now and then that it was felt that a check should be made but the following minute makes it seem as if word had got out ahead of what was planned: when Sorbie Kirk Session heard reports of 'people drinking in alehouses beside the kirk in time of sermon' and appointed two elders 'to inquire thereunto as also to search the alehouses in time of sermon the next Lord's Day and report', all that they could find to say was that the rumours had been groundless.29

Things were not always easy for inn-keepers. Guests who demanded alcohol on Sundays outside the hours of worship and behaved badly, could make life very difficult for them; one had his door broken in late at night because he would not open up and serve drink. Such customers could also make life very hard for inn servants. In 1825 William Thomson along with Alexander Fraser, a maltsman, and two women waited for a boat at Hugh Ferguson's inn so that they could cross a ferry and, while there, called for whisky, had supper and then more whisky, all of which they were given because, presumably, although it was a Sunday they were travelling. However, when Thomson called for still more whisky, the innkeeper felt that they had already had enough and as he did not wish the evening of the Lord's Day to be spent in drinking — that is how he put it to the Kirk Session later on — he sent a maid to say that he refused to supply any more whereupon Thomson 'began to sing and dance upon the floor.' Ferguson had by then gone to bed but got up, planning to turn them out but his wife prevented him from doing so, thinking that their visitors would just fall to quarrelling outside. The four visitors said later in their defence before the Session that they had got completely drunk and had been given all the alcohol they asked for, which turned out to be true as the maid admitted having given them more than she had been instructed to do. However, with a charge like Sabbath profanation available, the Session were able to get round it all by finding William Thomson guilty of profane swearing on a Sunday. It was not an inspecting elder who had complained to the Session about all this, but the innkeeper himself, although he seems to have been, to say the least, negligent in going off to bed leaving a young girl to cope with people he thought had already had enough to drink and who were demanding more.30

Although how an inn was run was, strictly speaking, a matter for civil law and not the church, that did not necessarily prevent a Session from tackling any problems and in 1832 Resolis Kirk Session reprimanded a vintner in Jemimaville for keeping an irregular house, violating the terms of his licence from the Justices of the Peace and for having profaned the Sabbath, but as it was his first offence, he was only warned to watch out for the future. In fact, in the 1760s a royal proclamation was made 'for the encouragement of piety and virtue, and for the preventing and punishing of vice, profaneness and immorality' which was a wide-ranging edict and which is found inserted into some Kirk Session minutes, along with the statement that it was to be read four times a year in every parish church by the minister. Not only did it require people to attend worship on Sundays but it imposed all sorts of restrictions on inn-keepers and keepers of similar establishments, by preventing 'all persons keeping taverns, chocolate houses, coffee houses and other public houses whatsoever, from selling wine, chocolate, coffee, ale, beer or other liquors, or receiving or permitting guests to be or to remain in such their Taverns in the time of Divine Service on the Lord's Day . . .' This was a great extension of the type of refreshments forbidden to be sold during time of worship and cannot have made an inn-keeper's lot any easier. All in all, it says much for some inn-keepers in East Lothian that in the mid-nineteenth century they agreed not to open on Sundays, but this was the exception rather than the rule. As time went on and the temperance movement developed, encouraged by people like Dr Duncan with his anti-drinking moves at funerals, and as standards of living rose, so the desperate need for alcohol to soften the miseries of the working week and life in general — even although it was a contributory cause — gradually diminished.[31]

Many counties called for a certificate of character from the Kirk Sessions before issuing licences to sell alcohol which gave the kirk some control over inn-keepers but this broke down, at least to some extent, with the introduction of turnpike roads. The right to collect tolls was let out and a better rent could be obtained if alcohol was sold at toll-houses; because this benefited road-making it was allowed by many Road Trustees, with or without a proper licence. As with any other aspect of community life, it did not make the work of Sessions any simpler when people in certain positions let the side down, but even so it seems surprising that in 1647 a Presbytery found it necessary to recommend to all the *ministers* within its bounds to have a care to abandon the sin of drinking (and swearing) on the Lord's Day in accordance with an ordinance of the last Provincial Assembly. This injunction members of the Presbytery probably had in mind during a parish visitation four years later when they expressed their satisfaction that the minister 'was not a haunter of ale-houses since his last visitation.' In Cullen a minister who had been drunk had to stand publicly in his own church for six Sundays to be rebuked by six of his clerical brethren and in Hawick in 1701 a drunken Town Clerk was ordered to make repentance and if he refused to do so, to be cited publicly from the pulpit. This unfortunately did not do any good and his intemperance continued. A particularly sad case appears in the Minutes of the Presbytery of Lewis after a meeting at Stornoway when the brethren considered the 'visitation at Stor'. When asked about their minister, the people there said that they had a true regard and love for him but much regretted his low condition in the world and the condition of his family because his wife was an habitual drunkard. Nothing being understood at that time about alcoholism from which she was clearly suffering, the Presbytery recommended 'for his own character and the zeal they have to the interest which they espouse, warmly and brotherly advise the minister to find a distant place from Stornoway for his wife to live where she cannot have access to the excess of spirits'; they also gave the minister advice to avoid certain things which were 'found to do him much hurt' but which were not specified.[32]

It follows from the kirk's attitude to Sabbath drinking that the act of brewing was not considered a suitable occupation for that day either; indeed no unnecessary work was. In the seventeenth century, a large number of people, both men and women, were maltsters and had to be restrained by Acts of Session from doing this work on Sundays. St. Andrews Kirk Session forbade all brewers to 'mask ane broowat of aill on the Sabbath day at night as they used before ordinarily to do, but that hierafter they keipp the Sabbath', and the following year, 1640, the Session of Montrose ordered that whoever 'shall dry malt or toom [empty] or fill Kilne or Coble upon the Sabbath Day shall pay £3 to the poor toties quoties' and in a further two years, raised the penalty for drying malt to £4 Scots plus making public repentance. Along with all Sabbath restrictions, that applied to fast days too and when a man brewed ale on a fast day in 1756, he had to stand before the congregation for one Sunday but his wife, who had tried to stop him from doing so, only received a rebuke before the Session.[33]

Illicit distilling, which was often called smuggling, was widespread at one time, especially in the highlands, but if Kirk Session minutes are anything to go by, it does not seem to have come to the notice of Kirk Sessions or to have earned their disapproval; and the other type of smuggling, which was the running of uncustomed goods, was not thought sinful by the majority of the population. It was the only possible way of obtaining tea or brandy or other special goods at any sort of affordable price, articles or items which would have been as welcome in a manse as in a mansion, and not only was there an element of adventure for those actually involved in it, but it also put money in their pockets. The kirk nevertheless found itself involved, willingly or unwillingly, in condemning smuggling and when the General Assembly passed the following Act in 1719 it was dutifully read from pulpits and the people were suitably exhorted:

> All men are warned of the sin, evil and danger of running uncustomed goods. And all ministers, especially in sea-trading towns and places, are strictly enjoined to represent to their people and hearers, the great Impiety and monstrous Wickedness of such methods, to gain this world to the endangering of their souls; and earnestly to obtest them, to abstain from such crying sins and deadly courses. And this Act is ordained to be read once in all churches, and as oft in particular parishes as the prudence of ministers shall direct.

In spite of this and in spite of some Presbyteries' efforts at times to stamp on smuggling, the impression gained is that it was usually only when smuggling took place on a Sunday that it merited Sessional attention. A minute referring to 'profaning the Sabbath by the running of brandy, even in the time of divine worship' shows concern primarily for the sanctity of the Sabbath; it does not indicate that there was much worry about smuggling itself. Any sensible smugglers, of course, realised that a good day for their deeds was Sunday when people should be in church and not watching what they were up to and in 1740 on the Banffshire coast there was a 'very disorderly practice of the fishers . . . running prohibited goods and many times on Sabbaths, evenings and mornings.' In an effort to stop this Sabbath profanation the Presbytery of Fordyce enlisted the help of the Earl of Findlater and Seafield, on whose land most of the fishermen lived, but though his lordship promised his help and intimations were made from several pulpits the practice still went on. On the other side of the Moray Firth, in 1756, the skippers of two Avoch, Ross-shire, boats had been employed on 'a Lord's Day in smuggling off the point of Wilkhaven' and were referred by the Kirk Session of Tarbat, off whose shores the offence took place, to the Kirk Session of Avoch where they duly appeared before the congregation for Sabbath profanation. Something that greatly affronted Kirk Sessions was when churches or their associated buildings were used by smugglers to conceal their goods. There are various cases of this because these made good hiding places and one instance of this, which happened in 1734, took place at St. Cuthbert's Church, Edinburgh. The Session were horrified to learn that ten casks of smuggled brandy had been discovered in one of the kirk lodges and a few months later, just as the congregation was gathering, Custom officers swooped and in the dim recesses of a loft in the church belonging to the Hammermen and Cordiners of Portsburgh, found four casks of brandy and one of rum. The beadles who kept the keys of the church said that they could give no explanation and to be fair to them, at a time when pews were owned rather than let, pew-owners often had church keys too and so it was decided that for the future, beadles alone should have keys. From later evidence, however, it appeared that it was one of the beadles, George Halden, who was guilty. The Supervisor of the Excise Board appeared before the Session and confirmed the report about the casks in the kirk lodge and said that on the day the find was made in the church loft, a full cask and many empty ones were found in Halden's house, as well as three empty ones hidden under bedclothes there, 'which gives ground for thinking that he had sold the brandy which was in them.' In spite of this remarkably obvious conclusion, he was neither arrested for smuggling nor instantly dismissed because his appointment was one in which the heritors had a joint interest with the Session. The minutes say, 'The Session found themselves unable to act promptly in the matter without the consent of the heritors' and at a meeting to consider all this, the astonishing decision was that, 'The heritors and Session having considered the proof, found no evidence of any of the beddels, their having access of lodging the said Brandy in the church, and therefore assoilzies [acquits] them.' Could all this have had any bearing on the fact that in 1774 an Act in the Court of Session allowed this Kirk Session to appoint beadles themselves?[34]

A smuggler who had a general influence, albeit indirectly, on church life, was Andrew Wilson, whose attempted rescue from execution by an Edinburgh mob in 1736 caused the riots which were named after Captain Porteous of the Town

Guard who ordered his men to fire on the would-be rescuers and some thirty people were killed or wounded. Porteous was sentenced to death but reprieved, only to have a mob drag him out of the tolbooth and hang him. The Government ordered a proclamation to be read in every pulpit before sermon, on the first day of every month for a year, ordering the perpetrators of the crime to give themselves up and threatening anyone who sheltered them with a heavy penalty. Such an intimation was considered a blasphemous desecration of the Lord's Day and every minister who read it was accused of putting the death of a murderer before that of the Saviour. One minister did his best to get round it by telling the people to withdraw from the kirk because although he was obliged to read the proclamation, they were not bound to listen to it but it was hard on the kirk as a whole because there are said to have been eleven secessions from congregations because of it.[35]

Something that was, and still is by some churches, regarded as a vice was the holding of raffles which, from the early eighteenth century onwards, appear now and then in Kirk Session minutes. A favourite item to raffle at one time was a three-cornered hat, a luxury item which cost about £7 Scots and was within the reach of few apart from lairds and ministers. A man with a hat was reckoned to be a man of substance and to have a dignity which no blue bonnet could possibly impart. On the same principle, by the late nineteenth century it had become quite common to raffle a silver watch, and other items as well. Unfortunately raffles led to trouble and although a Kirk Session minute in 1716 refers to a brawl, without giving the reason for it, this is understood to have been a raffle which degenerated into a riot, even although a man who was both an elder and a magistrate was present. The drawing of any raffle must have been a great cause for excitement and it was because holding one in their house caused 'much indecency by collecting idle and disorderly people at unseasonable hours' that it led to a Dingwall couple appearing before the Session in 1806. It seems surprising that intimation of raffles was ever allowed to take place at the parish church after worship but it was, although owing to 'various bad consequences' that followed from them, it was decided by the Kirk Session of Banchory-Devenick in 1805 to forbid the practice. That however did not stop the raffles themselves and their associated problems so that in 1827 that Session forbade the holding of raffles entirely. In all these cases, the kirk was concerned primarily with the disorder caused by raffles but in the following case, it was the gambling element that worried them: it was reported to a Session in 1824 'that a Raffle was to be held at the house of Alexander Munro, vintner in Jemimaville. The Session considering that Raffles being a species of gambling are not only illegal but if tolerated as a practice would be very pernicious to the morals of the people, feel it to be their duty to use their authority and best endeavours to put a stop to it.' This they did by warning Alexander that if he went ahead with his plan they would prosecute him before a magistrate.[36]

Gaming at cards, dice and horse races on any day of the week worried the kirk and the state far more than any gambling involved in raffles and in 1621 it was made illegal for an inn-keeper to allow anyone to play at cards or dice in his house, or for any individual to play in a private house unless the householder was playing.

It was also decreed that any sum over 100 merks won at horse racing, or in less than twenty-four hours at other play, should be forfeit to the poor although it seems most unlikely that the last part of this Act was implemented. Well before this Act, Sessions on their own did what they could to stop particular cases of gambling: Elgin Kirk Session in 1599 forbade a man to 'haunt dicing or playing at cards' and in 1604 Aberdeen Kirk Session accused a man of being a 'common nycht-walker, carter and dicer, and ane intertenar of players at cartis [cards] and dyce' and forbade him to continue doing so under threat of punishment. Even after the 1621 Act was passed, Sessions might still pass their own Acts such as the following: 'It is ordained that whatsoever person or persons shall be found drinking or playing at Keards or Dyce after ten hours at night in any tavern shall pay to the poor ane dollar and make their public satisfaction in the face of the whole congregation.' In 1699 Galashiels Kirk Session ordered heads of families who sat up at night playing cards to be admonished privately and told to desist and felt so strongly about gambling that in 1701 they deposed Robert Wilson, their football-playing elder, for 'having played at the wheel of fortune in the public market.' A couple who lived in Hawick were delated to the Session for entertaining men, both married and youths, 'yea, even boys' with 'Candle and Cards, they cursing, swearing and blaspheming the name of God in the season of the night, which hath caused great grief to their parents' and the beadle was ordered to forbid them to do so in future. Three years later, in 1724, playing cards for stakes was still going on there with a report received 'that many did still haunt the house of Robert — for gamming at cards' and this time the beadle was ordered to go from time to time as the Session should decide 'to summond them to desist' and if they refused, to tell the minister or the appropriate elders. All such activities were regarded as being much worse when indulged in on the Sabbath and the royal proclamation of the 1760s, which has already been mentioned, specifically referred to gambling on Sundays, in public or private houses, and also required efforts to be made to suppress public gaming houses.[37]

Horse racing has always been popular with the people but an idea of the kirk's attitude to gambling on it appears in the Kirk Session records of Ettrick. It was discovered that a race was to be held the day after Communion tokens were due to be handed out and so the Session ordered that the tokens should not be distributed until after the race and also forbade any elder to go racing — but in the event, the race was cancelled. Writing in the mid-nineteenth century, the minister of Dirleton reported that two training stables for race-horses had opened at Gullane because the ground in that area was suitable for them, but he pointed out that whatever advantages these stables might confer on the parish, it was in some respects 'to be feared that they do serious injury to the morals of the neighbourhood.'[38]

Because gravity and self-denial were considered essential to a worthy life, the Presbyterian church would tolerate no amusements in which the devil might be thought to lurk. Although dancing ultimately came to be used for fund-raising, at one time it was thought to be a great temptation to immorality and under the term 'promiscuous dancing', which was men and women dancing together in the same room, it frequently appears in Kirk Session minutes but, as it was a particular feature of weddings, more about it appears in the relevant chapter. Even when things had become less strict, the kirk for a long time did not approve of any sort of fun and perhaps the Kirk Session of Dingwall was glad of the inconveniences mentioned in a letter they sent to the Town Council in July 1879 as these gave them a reason to complain and try to have the cause of them stopped. They protested strongly against 'the obstructions of the thoroughfares leading to the church on the evening of Tuesday the 1st inst of itinerant shows, shooting saloons, and other objects of amusements, much to the discomfort and annoyance of people going to church, and also to those who worshipped within; and they earnestly hope the council will in the future prevent a recurrence of the same, and allow no stands to be erected in such close proximity to the church.' And it never did happen again, at least, not in any way that caused offence to the Session although it must have caused disappointment to local people.[39] Examples of two uncommon offences include a woman delated in 1568 as a usurer, who was ordered by her Session to 'desist and cease' under threat of excommunication, and two women, considered to have given themselves over to evil by being tricked by a gypsy woman and allowing her to go to their kists (chests of belongings) and take money on her promise that she would 'restore the double'. All that she left was 'colles [coals] bound in ane napkin' and, poor gullible things that they were, they lost not only their money and clothing but the church felt that they should be made an example to others and they had to stand in church and to pay 55 bodles each to the poor, which of course they had to borrow. The gypsy woman seems to have got off scot-free.[40]

Poetry was at one time considered a 'profane and unprofitable offence' and play-acting was considered exceptionally dangerous to moral standards. In 1696 the minister of Greenock reported that some people, including a quack doctor, had arrived in the town and erected a stage for dancing and plays and a deputation was told to suppress the performances; but they allowed the doctor to sell his potions which seems to show more concern for morals than the people's health. Less than twenty years after that, it was reported to St. Andrews Kirk Session that a stage had been erected in the town 'where there is a great deal of unChristian and offensive behaviour openly acted, whereby the spirits especially of the young people in this place are debauched and the hearts of the Godly greatly grieved.' The minister, Dean of Guild and two elders were appointed to speak to the magistrates about it 'and crave that they would intersperse their authority for suppressing it.' The Dean of Guild, however, told the minister that what was going on could not legally be forbidden but promised to ask the magistrates to prohibit anything that was immoral or offensive in the plays. In the event, the stage only remained in place for about a month, without any sensational developments during that time. Six years later, however, another stage was set up by a man named as 'D. Allan' where 'several obscene and undecent expressions together with several abominable lyes' were used and the Session asked the magistrates to forbid Allan to appear any more on the stage in the town because he had given such offence and scandal to people of the congregation. A week later the minister and some others met with Allan who 'bigged pardon' and promised that any offence that had been given would not be repeated, which proved to be true. With such an attitude to plays, the horror of the kirk may be imagined when John Home, minister of Athelstaneford, East Lothian, wrote *The Tragedy of Douglas* which was produced with great success in Edinburgh in 1756. He was suspended by the Presbytery as a result and resigned from the ministry in 1757; but opinions were about to change and William Creech, describing the alteration of attitudes in the twenty years from 1763 to 1783 said that at the earlier date, even among those who did go to the theatre, Saturday was the most improper night to be there and any clergy who went would have been open to church censure. By 1783 however the morality of plays was no longer a worry and Saturday was the most popular theatre-going night; so much was this so that by the end of the eighteenth century the charity workhouse in the Canongate parish of Edinburgh was supported by, among other things, a benefit play, granted annually by the manager of the Edinburgh Theatre. Play-going on Sundays was, of course, considered very sinful but it did happen; at one point there were frequent accusations about it in Rutherglen, Lanarkshire.[41]

These however were minor offences compared with some which came before Sessions, some of which have been mentioned already in connection with excommunication. Before 1571 all adulterers, murderers, incestuous persons and others guilty of heinous crimes were required, in theory at any rate, to appear before the General Assembly to receive their first injunction and to return to the following Assembly 'in linen clothes' for a second admonition. That year, however, it was ordained because of the practical difficulties of getting to Assemblies, that for the future such offenders should be called by the Superintendents and Commissioners of Provinces to appear before their Synodall conventions, to be held twice a year. In 1588 a further relaxation was allowed by the General Assembly, that adulterers and those guilty of homicide could give satisfaction to the kirk 'before the Presbytery, in such form as they were accustomed before the Synodalls.' The civil authorities frequently did not trouble themselves overmuch about murder and it was for that reason that the Presbytery of Fordyce in 1624 gave thought to the 'divers murthers and slauchters' committed within their bounds and asked what course the brethren — the parish ministers — should take. In November that year they decided that as 'no ordour is taken by the Magistrates nor kirk' in connection with murders that henceforth every parish minister should delate 'such persons within their congregations as are guilty thereof that at least some ecclesiastical ordour and discipline may be taken thairin . . .' Inevitably this meant involvement of the elders, to make inquiries if nothing else, but in 1707 the General Assembly laid down what the Kirk Session's role should be in a whole range of serious offences — atheism, idolatry, witchcraft, charming, heresy, 'error vented and made public by any of the congregation', schism and separation from the public ordinances as well as 'suchlike gross scandals' which of course included the adultery, murder and incest already referred to. Such cases were to be 'natively begun by the Kirk Session yet the Session does not finally determine them themselves, but having received information of them, they are to weigh the same according to the rules and direction prescribed in other processes . . . and to deal with the accused to confess: which being done, they are to refer the case and send an extract of their procedure thereanent to the Presbytery.'[42] Thus in addition to dealing with what might be called ordinary offences, Sessions found themselves handling parts of more serious ones involving the initial delation and inquiries, the reference to the Presbytery, perhaps summoning a murderer to appear before that body, and then at the end supervising public appearances or ensuring that the terms of excommunication were carried out. For instance, when Thomas Herd, excommunicated for murder, begged to make repentance in 1663, he was absolved by the Presbytery, before whom he appeared barefoot in sackcloth, but this only happened after he had professed his repentance for three months in his own church of Deskford. In 1738 Donald Mackay, a Golspie man, was convicted of murdering the husband of a woman of whom he was over-fond and, while awaiting execution, he tried to implicate her by saying that he and she had committed adultery, that he had been with her 'as surely as her own husband'. Although the Session were not involved in his sentence of death, they felt that this statement was something they should check and visited him in the death cell, in this case the pit at Dunrobin, an examination which continued for several months but which produced no proof of what he said. So far as he was concerned, it made no difference anyway, and hanging was his end. Sessions and sometimes Presbyteries might also be required to see that the bereaved family was all right in the aftermath of a murder case. In earlier times, there was a custom of settling with the family by a 'letter of slaines' which was signed, in the case of murder, by the widow or executors of the person killed, acknowledging that satisfaction had been made; or it could beg the pardon of a person harmed. In 1595 the Presbytery of Glasgow ordered the murderer of John Adams to produce letters of relaxation from the horn (from being outlawed) and letters of slaines from the man's widow and his 'bairns, kin, friends, and alayance' (alliance) and ordered the minister of Campsie, Stirlingshire, to summon the widow and children so that they might declare whether or not appropriate settlement had been made with the murderer. In 1596 Alexander Gadderer begged to be reconciled with the kirk for murder and with his victim's widow, friends and children, all of whom he was willing to satisfy according to the advice of the minister and elders. It was the elders who fixed the assythment (indemnification) and satisfaction for her and the children at 80 merks, with her giving security that he should be 'skaythless' of her or her children, in other words, freed from further harm from them. One of three murderers was ordered in 1625 to be excommunicated unless he could present a sufficient letter of slaines. His brother had already asked that the process might be continued, hoping that an agreement could be reached, after which he, the brother, promised that the murderer would satisfy the discipline of the church. While the bereaved family had to settle for the best arrangement that could be made in the circumstances, under this system murderers could live freely in a parish and this was sufficient of a problem for the ministers in the Presbytery of Fordyce to seek the Synod's advice in 1669. The reply was that 'such persons shall remove the scandal in sackcloth within such parishes wher the slauchter is committed', which meant under Kirk Session supervision. A very sad case of homicide was reported to a Presbytery by a minister in 1652. Three years earlier a boy aged about 12–13 years, had recklessly handled a pistol lying in his father's house and accidentally killed his sister, after which his father 'had began to bring him to a sense of his sin so much that he had been utterly cast down with much shedding of tears and had ultimately fled.' However, he had finally returned and the case was referred to the next Provincial where it was found to be something to be pitied and lamented and any punishment, for the time being anyway, was refused. In 1668 a minister reported that he had been about to celebrate the Lord's Supper but 'by reason of ane scandalous pley and horrid murther that fell out among his people he was necessitate to suspend for the tyme till his people should be better fitted for the samen withal', and he asked the Presbytery's advice about the problem of murderers who fled. It was decided that all the ministers of the diocese, this being in Episcopalian times, should intimate that such men should not be received in any parishes, and the minister who asked the original question was advised 'to keep back from Communion all who are suspected of accessione to the said murder till they be cleared of the scandal.' How much greater must the scandal have been when it was the minister who was guilty or suspected of murder. John Kello, minister of Spott, East Lothian, from 1567–70, found himself in straitened circumstances and decided to solve the problem by killing his wife and remarrying advantageously. He tried poison first of all but when this was unsuccessful strangled her instead, then went to church and 'made sermon as if he had done nae sic thing', and took some neighbours home with him after the service, ostensibly to visit his wife. Finding her dead, he put on an act of sorrow but in the end, presumably plagued by conscience, confessed to one of his 'brether in office', Mr Simson of Dunbar, with the result that he was tried and hanged in Edinburgh.[43]

The Kirk Session minutes of Slains and Forvie, Aberdeenshire, show that there was no sermon on November 13th, 20th or 27th, 1698, 'the minister being valetudinary' and nor was there preaching on the 4th or 11th of December, the reason this time being that he had gone to Aberdeen 'where he was far beyond his expectation detained.' In fact, gossip must have been flying round the parish by then but it only became official so far as the minutes were concerned in January 1699 when the minister of Logie-Buchan preached and intimated that the Presbyteries of Ellon and Deer and Garioch had appointed him a month before to announce that Mr William Fraser, the parish minister, had been suspended from the exercise of his office, 'while the scandal lately raised anent the manner of his consort her death be removed, and until he be fully purged and cleared thereof of civil law.' His wife Jean, who had been sick in both body and mind for some years and was almost certainly a great burden to her family, had been found dead in bed one day and was duly buried but shortly afterwards, suspicions arose against her stepson, William Fraser, a licenciate of the church and a son of her husband by an earlier marriage. It was said that he had poisoned and bled her to death, in spite of the fact that he maintained that he had been in Aberdeen at the relevant time and a warrant was obtained for the body to be exhumed and examined for external marks, as at that time there was no way of detecting internal evidence of poison. As there were no marks, it was decided to try to detect whether or not there had been foul play by a method long accepted by vulgar superstition. The corpse was laid out in open view and Mr William Dunbar, minister of Cruden, prayed that God would show if violence had been done and if so by whom. After this those present, including the stepson, one by one touched the body, although it is not clear what was supposed to happen should there be guilt. If there had been gossip before, the parish must have been humming with the scandal of it all by then but as no particular outcome of this procedure appeared, a precognition reporting all the circumstances but making no charges, was sent to the Lord Advocate. However, the late Mrs Fraser's friends continued to suspect the stepson and had him arrested and imprisoned in Aberdeen where he lay uncharged for three months, to the ruin of himself and his young family, until they at last agreed to have him charged before the Commissioners of Justiciary for the Highlands. He petitioned the Privy Council for trial before the High Court of Justiciary and this was granted but the upshot does not seem to be known. In October of that year, Mr Fraser senior demitted office because of suspicions that he too had had a hand in his wife's death — and all that was because of a few people's suspicions, justified or not.[44]

Infanticide was the form of murder with which Kirk Sessions were most often directly involved. Sudden deaths of babies could become such a source of speculation and gossip that they simply had to investigate any rumours about them. While many illegitimate children were born and survived — 85 out of 211 baptisms in Perth in 1580 were fatherless, about 40% — it is known that the extreme severity of the kirk to immoral conduct was a considerable cause of child murder. Four women who were all condemned to death on one day in Edinburgh for that offence, all declared that it was dread of church censure that caused them to kill their babies: cross-examination by the Session, perhaps a physical examination by midwives, followed by public appearances on the stool of repentance, confession of what they had done and rebuke before the congregation, could bring comparatively innocent people to such a pitch of terror that some fled the country, others committed suicide and some concealed their pregnancy with the implied intention of murdering or abandoning the baby after birth. In time it came to be believed that Scottish women were the worst child-murderers in the known world and so, it is said, the clergy gradually began to change their attitudes but until that change took place, Sessions had much to do with these murders to which their discipline had contributed.[45]

The Kirk Session of Kirkwall were very much upset when it was reported to them that a maidservant, Katharine Harkness, had given birth to a baby and that both she and it had been found dead in bed. Although the magistrates had 'very dutifully taken cognisance of it' the Session still felt it was their duty to inquire further to know whether there had been any suspicion of her pregnancy and if so, whether she had named the father. They felt that they had failed in some way and were anxious 'for stopping the mouths of such as may unjustly blame them for not having taken notice thereof', ordering the girl's employers, Bailie Pottinger and his wife, as well as other witnesses, to attend the next Session meeting. Evidence was given this way and that and later it was recorded that the bailie had been rebuked 'and that public intimation should be made from the pulpit of Kirkwall of the Session's procedure in this affair and the people warned to give timeous advertisement to the elders when any woman was suspected to be with child to prevent all such murderous actions.' This death was called a 'murderous action' because the pregnancy had been concealed, something which was very common; on one occasion there were five women in the tolbooth of Aberdeen at the same time for that offence. So serious was it that Parliament passed the Act anent murder of children in 1690 which stated that murder would be the charge if pregnancy was concealed for its whole duration, of if the mother did not seek help in childbirth, or if the child died or went missing 'tho there be no appearance of wound or bruise upon the body of the child.' This Act was meant to be printed and published at the market crosses of head burghs of counties and read out in all parish churches by the reader — but the crime still went on and as late as 1763 an Act of General Assembly about infant murder was being read yearly from pulpits. A very sad case was that of Christian Adam whose lover, 'a gentleman', was one of those who wished to avoid censure for himself and told her that it would ruin him if she let her pregnancy be known and she was executed for the crime he had persuaded her to commit, but in fact the death penalty, which needed civil authority, was by no means always imposed for child murder. In 1700 a married woman whose husband had been away too long for her baby to be his, admitted to Kirkcudbright Kirk Session that she had had a child by another man 'and had parted with it, admitted that she had not called any women to help her, and said that she had buried it in a corner of her toun yard.' The Session's reaction was to try to find out about her husband's supposed death so as to know whether the moral part of the sin was adultery or fornication but they also told some of the elders to take some women and go to where the child was said to be buried to see what they could find; but there was nothing but a bloody cloth 'which was supposed to have been laid down by her in the meantime'. She was referred to the magistrate, and the minutes later show that 'being continued before the Toun Counsell for Countervening an act of parliament she was sentenced by an act of banishment.' Banishment was also the penalty imposed on Bessie Muckieson who, after two years in the tolbooth in Edinburgh, petitioned the Presbytery in 1706 for release.[46]

The following instances show what Kirk Sessions did in several other cases, at different times and in different parts of the country, to deal with or combat child murder. In May 1708, Katharine Myre, wife of Ro Thomson, told John Brand, who was her employer and an elder, that Elspit Thomson, her mentally retarded stepdaughter, 'a natural fool' as she put it, had given birth to a child by a married man and had thrown it 'upon a dunghill or midding as she termed it, and the said Ro Thomson finding the said child next morning exposed as aforesaid, took and buried the same in the yard dyke.' John Brand 'reckoning himself obliged to get all the information he possibly could in a matter of such weighty moment' made what inquiries he could. Thomson admitted what he had done and gave the reasons why he did not think the baby was full term, adding that he would not mind about what had happened 'were it not that the said John Martine continued in the commission of wickedness with the said Elspit Thomson his daughter, and particularly of late . . . had been guilty of wickedness with her in the said Robert's byr [byre] and between two of his Kine [cattle] which affected him much in regard it was not happy that such things should be done among or betwixt beasts.' Witnesses were present at the digging up of the little corpse which had been buried 'without so much as being wrapt in any cloath or winding sheet' and far from being before its time, it 'was truly so big, and hair on its head, and nails on its fingers that all who were witnesses to the digging up thereof were convinced that it had been born to the full time.' All things considered, the Session decided that this case was 'above their reach' and referred it to the Presbytery; but Presbyteries too might find such things above their reach, like that of Dingwall which inquired into a case of child murder in 1685 but found it above their 'cognizance and decision' and passed it to the civil judge. In 1752 information was laid that David Black and Margaret Lamb, both of whom worked for the miller at Letham Mill in the parish of St. Vigeans, had murdered a baby which she had borne. On the instructions of the Provost of Arbroath, the minister had the couple imprisoned and then read to his Session an extract of the precognitions taken at Arbroath, according to which Margaret had told no one that she was pregnant. The miller's wife had obviously not suspected anything either, until one night when she discovered that Margaret 'was very bad' and went and got Black out of bed about 4.00 a.m. to go for the girl's mother. By the time Black arrived back with Mrs Lamb, they were told that Margaret had given birth to a dead child and the miller's wife asked Black to bury it, which he did in the presence of the two women, at the head of the miller's yard. Two nights later, however, he returned alone and reburied the body in the churchyard near the back gate of the minister's enclosure. By the time all this information was available, it was reported that 'the people of Arbroath had let them slip out of their prison' and Black returned to the mill, only to be summoned by the Session and have the precognition read to him. That was in April. In October it was reported that he had fled to the nearby parish of Tealing, also in Angus, and it was decided to write to the minister there to have him returned to St. Vigeans to answer for fornication with Margaret. Any suggestion of murder had been dropped and nothing was done about concealment of pregnancy either. A few years later a woman in a highland parish told no one she was pregnant until after the child was born prematurely and found dead, hidden in her bed. She said she had had a fever and been insensible of what had happened and that was the reason she had not called for help. Both she and the man concerned had to appear before the congregation for the scandal, according to the rules of the church, and she had to appear for a further six days as punishment for her additional offence. Another case of concealed pregnancy occurred in 1779. The baby was born dead but the mother had prepared no clothing nor anything else for it and had indeed been denying that she was pregnant. As her crime was 'attended with many aggravated circumstances, particularly with an apparent design of secreting her pregnancy, denying her guilt to the last, and providing no cloaths for the child' it was not surprising that the Session were 'of opinion that there is a great ground to suspect that she had a bad design upon the life of the child' and that she should be rebuked not only as fornicator 'but also for the other crimes connected therewith; and the Session reserve a power to themselves to free her from censure when they shall have any satisfying evidence of the sincerity of her repentance, and the Session are willing to wait till she make application for this privilege, but cannot say anything as to the time of her absolution until they are satisfied as above.' When another girl gave birth out of doors and said the child was dead, murder was suspected and she was kept under guard in her mother's house on the orders of the Kirk Session until the Sheriff could be informed.[47] The variety of punishments given indicates a good knowledge of the circumstances.

A form of sudden infant death with which Kirk Sessions also had to deal was 'smooring' or smothering of babies in bed at night. There are many early references to this, usually involving women but sometimes men as well. In 1592 three women parishioners of Cadder, Lanarkshire, were accused of this and called before the Session to be 'tryit thair' and the following year an Elgin woman, Margaret Grieff, who admitted bairn-smooring, was ordered to stand for three Sundays barefoot and bare-legged, wearing hair or sackcloth, starting at the first bell in the porch of the church and then inside it throughout preaching and prayers, with a mitre on her head or breast. A woman accused of smothering her child denied doing so explaining that it had been in bed with her and had died suddenly, having been sick for ten weeks, which fact she offered to prove and the Session ordered her to do so within eight days. Many sentences for smothering were so light, however, that it seems that Sessions realised that no harm had been intended and that the deaths were believed to be due to overlying the babies by carelessness or intemperate habits.[48]

These were cases where there was tangible evidence in the form of a dead baby and the mother's identity was known but there were other cases where pregnancy was suspected but there was no baby to show for it. About 1703 the Kirk Session of Selkirk thought that a woman had had a child but she and her mother both denied this and so the minister, along with two elders, the kirk officer and a midwife, went to her home and compelled her to show them her breasts — this implies that the men were present throughout and took part — which they drew and found full of milk. At this, she admitted birth of a child but said that it was stillborn and had been buried in Lindean churchyard. She and her mother were committed to prison but the civil authorities, for some reason, would not prosecute and so the minister resolved to do what he could with church penalties, and consulted the Lord Register, Murray of Philiphaugh, who was hereditary Sheriff of the county of

Selkirk, and his brother, the Laird of Bowhill. The latter, however, must have felt that evidence of crime was lacking and advised the Kirk Session to limit their accusations. In 1703 Ashkirk Kirk Session were told that a young woman had left the area for a time and then returned and it was rumoured that while she was away she had given birth. It was important to ascertain if this was true and, if so, what had happened to the baby and therefore an elder's wife and a married woman who lived in the same house as the girl were ordered 'to try her, which they did with some difficulty because of her reluctance to suffer it', which indicates the use of force, but although they found milk in her breasts, she would still not confess. The elder of that quarter told those living in the house with her not to allow her to leave the parish without appearing before the Session, but she flatly refused to appear. The Session were beaten by this and saying, 'we cannot force her to confess, us not having a Judge within the paroch, it being surmised that the child she hath brought forth may be quite out of the way', decided to refer the matter to the minister and Session of Jedburgh' where she had been during her absence. As the original sin must have been committed in Ashkirk, this was a clear case of buck-passing but there is no more about the case in the Kirk Session minutes of either Ashkirk or Jedburgh, although the Session were certainly justified in seeking to uncover what might have been abandonment or murder of a child. In the spring of 1834 a Session were concerned about an unmarried woman 'who had lately all the appearances of pregnancy but in the course of this week these appearances had subsided, and that there were strong suspicions that all was not right.' Two married women were appointed as midwives to examine her and reported that she had 'all the appearances that the mother of a child has' which she denied, saying that she had a certain complaint or obstruction but it had got better since the previous Wednesday. Further witnesses were called and the Session remitted the case to the Procurator Fiscal; later that month they were informed that she had been taken into custody on suspicion of child murder.[49]

Now and then 'good families' fell foul of the kirk about such matters. One such was the Gordons of Dalpolly who lived at Uppat House near Golspie. In 1742 the son of the house fled when unable to deny accusations of paternity levelled against him by two girls in the parish and the following year his sister Anna, whose husband, Captain Mackay, had been abroad for some time, gave birth to a child and her mother made every effort to conceal what had happened. But such an event could not go unnoticed and as a result of a report that a baby had been born dead and then buried, the minister of Golspie and a quorum of elders met at Uppat, calling before them those who might know what had happened because there seemed to be an element of doubt about identity, although the fact that they met where they did indicated some very strong suspicions. There, a man told how Lady Dalpolly, Anna's mother, had made provisional arrangements for wet-nursing by his wife, giving him half a crown and the promise of a boll of meal 'of the first and readiest that should be made in the house of Uppat' which was in addition to the usual wet-nurse's wage. In addition, one of the farm men named Anna as the baby's mother. It had died and been buried at night by them. This turned into a long case, with the Session ordering women to examine Anna to see if she had indeed given birth, with the result that both Anna and her mother fled the country, and the midwife who had assisted at the birth absconded as well. This is one of the few examples of midwives being ordered to examine women of the upper classes, albeit unsuccessfully in this case. Such people were well able to stand up for themselves and to protect their families: Coldingham Kirk Session minutes refer in 1702, for example, to one such midwife's visit 'when the Lady would not let her see her daughter.'[50]

There were also cases where a dead child was discovered, with no clues as to whose it was, and here too it fell to the kirk to try to find the mother. It was in 1653 that the Presbytery of Dingwall recommended all the ministers within the bounds 'to search if there has been anyone with child who has absented themselves as fugitives or remains in the country without a child, being formerly with child, whereby the murder of a child in the parish of Urray may be tried.' When Falkirk Kirk Session were informed in 1698 that a murdered infant had been found in the River Carron they ordered 'the elders in landward to get an order from the justices of the peace, and the elders in the town to get an order from the magistrates impowering them to take along with them constables and midwives for making speedy and diligent search both in town and landward, if by the good providence of God directing them, the blood-guilty may be discovered.' They also had their clerk write to the ministers of neighbouring parishes and the outcome of their efforts was that Margaret Mitchell was apprehended and handed over to the civil authorities. Dunghills were found at many a door and were handy places of concealment and in the 1720s the body of a child was found in one in the parish of Selkirk. There must have been a fairly widespread search for the mother as she turned out to be a woman in Jedburgh, who was then brought to Selkirk where she confessed before the Session, begging 'that they would have sympathy with her' and entreating the minister to come frequently to visit her in prison to instruct her and to pray for her. In the late eighteenth century, the minister of Tarbat, Ross-shire, reported 'that a female infant lately born was this morning found dead and naked as when it was born, lying among the rocks betwixt Portmaholmack and the place of Hilton, that he had ordered the body to be carried up to the church and to ly there until the Kirk Session should convene' in order that the elders might inspect the corpse and so that women could be sent for to see whether or not it was full time. The women concluded that it was and the Session decided to apply to the Sheriff Depute for a warrant to make a search throughout the parish for the 'inhuman mother' and to ask him to order the parish constables to help with this. A woman was eventually found who appeared to have given birth but she said that she had had a miscarriage and had disposed of the child under a gravestone in the churchyard and that the baby on the shore was not hers. When asked to point out the gravestone, she was unable to do so but continued to insist that the dead baby was someone else's, understandably enough as, being full term, murder was almost implicit. The man concerned, who had known nothing of her pregnancy, had to serve discipline in the usual manner but she was imprisoned in Tain to await trial before the Circuit Court in Inverness. In June 1790 the minutes show that the trial had taken place the month before and that, on her own petition, she was banished from Scotland for life. One Session carried a search of this sort to extraordinary lengths in 1740 when, after the finding of a dead baby, they ordered every single young woman in the neighbourhood of where it was discovered, to come to the church to be examined by midwives. Offensive as such examinations must have been, it was the kirk's surest way of establishing guilt or innocence before going further and where there was innocence, then gossip could be silenced and speculation ended. Although no body was found in the case of the Kirkcudbright woman who admitted having a baby and burying it 'in a corner of her toun yard', her admission of a birth was sufficient for her to be found guilty but in some cases there was only negative evidence and while child murder might be suspected, it could not be proved although that did not necessarily deter a Kirk Session from pursuing the matter. One such instance occurred when a Session met

> in consequence of a flagrant fama viz. that Mary Latto, wife of William Allan, sailor, who has had an uninterrupted absence of about two years, had lately brought forth a child, of which child having been feloniously put away strong suspicions are entertained. The Session considering all the bearings of the case and the difficulties attending it from the want of a Corpus delicti, unanimously commit it to the Moderator to correspond with the Procinator Fiscal that the necessary steps may be taken for a precognition for him.[51]

All in all, Kirk Sessions tried hard to make sure of their facts as best they might and the following case, when the Session of Kintail failed to do so, must be a rare one. It arose after a couple of handkerchiefs were found in a river, one them with the initials R.B. which belonged to Robert Black, manager of the farm of Killillan for the Lochalsh Trustees. The other, which was noticeably smelly, was wrapped around a stone weighing about 6–7 lbs. About a year before, Kate Fraser, a housemaid with Mrs Black, had been suspected of being pregnant, had been sick for a few days and thereafter there was no appearance of what the minutes describe as 'fullness of body'. There was much calling of witnesses after the handkerchiefs were found, concerning Kate's sickness and second-hand reports of what the supposed father had or had not said. The Session sent a report about it all to the Procurator Fiscal and his reply was written into the minutes, including an extract of the fairly blistering letter he had received from the Sheriff of Ross on the matter:

> As to the case of child murder from Kintail, I cannot suppose that you sent it to me from any difficulty you had in making up your mind regarding it. There are no grounds whatever for such a charge in the depositions taken before the Kirk Session. Mrs. B. in her cookery book begins her receipt for Hare Soup, 'First catch your hare etc.' Now to make a case of child murder, you must have a child. There is no evidence that a child was born. There is no sufficient evidence even that the woman was with child, of if she was, she might have had a miscarriage. To fasten such a charge upon the old handkerchiefs trailed out of the bottom of the river is too absurd. Any old clout lying any time in the bottom of a pool will have a bad smell. In short,

my opinion is that you have in these depositions nothing on which to ground such a charge . . .[52]

Where negligence was thought to have caused a child's death, that too was something with which Kirk Sessions were concerned. Perth Kirk Session called before them a woman with the unusual name of Nicholson Brown and 'after a long inquisition about her negligence and sloth to her young infant bairn' got her to confess that it had died through her careless neglect and she was ordered to make repentance the following Sunday in linen clothes. Even when a child was burnt to death, St. Andrews Kirk Session summoned the parents and 'rigorously examined' them about what had happened which, if it was an accident as seems most likely, must have added greatly to their grief.[53]

How many different agencies would it take nowadays to handle the variety of cases mentioned, all of which Kirk Sessions used readily to undertake?

11
The Morals of the People

Open almost any volume of Kirk Session minutes and the words fornication, ante-nuptial fornication and adultery are almost sure to leap out at one because these sins kept Sessions constantly busy, in the belief that they were doing the Lord's will because the seventh Commandment forbids adultery and the fifth chapter of Paul's Letter to the Ephesians gives very firm guidance on the prevention of immorality. Vigilant elders and willing informers all did their bit and in any case it was impossible to conceal physical evidence in the form of 'being illegitimately pregnant' or 'with a bastard child'. Fortunately, however, the unattractive word bastard is seldom used in Kirk Session minutes to describe fatherless children. As Professor Smout has pointed out, the pity is that the sins of greed, pride, untruthfulness, self-righteousness and hypocrisy were hard to define and could not be dealt with in the same way, so that in the popular mind immorality was considered to be almost exclusively sexual, to the neglect of other forms of sin.[1]

Of these sins the most serious was adultery and the least serious ante-nuptial fornication which was simply anticipating marriage. In between the two came fornication. In rural areas this usually took the form of casual intercourse which merited punishment, but in an Act of Parliament of 1567 it was called 'the fylthie vice of fornication', which really referred to harlotry or prostitution, a problem of large towns such as Edinburgh where brothels abounded in poor streets.[2] Fines, imprisonment, exhibition in the market place and ducking of the women were all authorised punishments but they did not stop the problem. It was usually clear which of these three sins had been committed but sometimes further inquiries might have to be made or particular points considered, as in the case of a man who appeared before his Session in 1767 to speak up for his sister who had had a baby and since died. He brought with him two letters from the father who was by then abroad, in which marriage was promised and he insisted that she be regarded as a married woman, a difficult decision for the Session to make and one which had to be referred to the Presbytery. Another Session took it upon themselves to presume the death of a man who had married seven or eight years previously and soon afterwards disappeared, deciding therefore that his wife's moral offence should not be adultery but the lesser one of fornication.[3]

In straightforward cases of fornication, in addition to serving their punishment, it made good practical sense to get the couple to marry each other, which lent respectability to the whole situation and ensured maintenance for the almost-sure-to-be-born baby and Kirk Sessions very wisely urged this kirk equivalent of a shot-gun wedding. When John Hind, an Assynt man, admitted fathering Flora Mackaskle's child, 'The Session having exhorted him to repentance and amendment of conduct, inquired whether he was willing to marry the said Flora Mackaskle, he answered after some hesitation that he was and Flora Mackaskle having also declared her willingness to join herself in lawful wedlock with the said John Hind, the Session appointed the Moderator to marry them accordingly.' A couple of years later, their attitude was rather different in the case of Alexander Mackenzie. He confessed that he was the father of a girl's pregnancy and said that he wished to marry her the next day and she said that she was willing to do so. However, that did not happen; it is puzzling that the Session did not agree to them marrying forthwith but they must have had their reasons for this and also for calling him to their next meeting to ask if he 'was still minded to marry her'. At this he said he wished to retract his former confession and promise of marriage and offered to undergo church censure and to pay his fine for stopping proclamation of the banns, as well as paying her fine for fornication. To this the Session agreed and he offered to begin standing publicly the next Sunday but within a few days the Session were informed that he had absconded to America. Sometimes the decision of a Session in fornication cases might be delayed 'till it is known whether he will marry her' and an additional inducement was that the normal penalty might be halved if marriage followed, or at any rate reduced, something which seems in the following case to have been regarded as a right: Donald M'Lean, a cooper, paid 5s., only half the usual fine 'which he claimed in virtue of a promise as an abatement of his fine for having married his woman he fell with.' On the same principle, there might be a reduction in formal discipline: when two people appeared before the congregation one Sunday for rebuke, the Session decided that as they declared 'that they are to marry their respective partners with that first conveniency if they give into the minister evidence of their repentance and satisfy the Treasurer as to their penalty, they be absolved upon their next appearance', in other words only two appearances were required of them instead of three. Marriage could even produce complete remission: one man was given the alternative of standing publicly for three days 'or otherwise to marry the woman'; or a fine might be remitted but discipline still have to be served. John Hind and Flora Mackaskle were almost certainly married there and then at the Session meeting when they agreed marriage because it was not at all uncommon, once everything was settled, for this to happen, hence such entries in minutes as 'they were married accordingly coram.' A couple who admitted fornication told their Session that they were willing to serve discipline but that they wished to marry first and begged that their banns might be published and the marriage take place before they made their satisfaction. The Session thought them penitent and genuinely anxious to marry, 'all of which were circumstances that seemed to alleviate their guilt' and therefore dispensed with the usual forms and allowed the banns to be read thrice on the next Sunday and the marriage 'to take place with all convenient speed'; and speedy it certainly was, with wedding and public appearances completed in three weeks.[4]

In the days when breast-feeding was the norm, there was a considerable demand for wet-nurses and as a result women with illegitimate babies could often find comfortable, if temporary, posts. When needed, such women were needed at once but this was something not appreciated by the magistrates and Kirk Session of Aberdeen when they decreed in 1609 that no nurse from a rural area should be received in the burgh unless she had a testimonial from her own minister that she had served discipline for her offence. Montrose Kirk Session tackled the problem in a different way; they ordered that should any such woman who had been delated and who had not completed church discipline be employed as a nurse, then the employer should be liable to censure and a fine such as the Session might think fit. As time went on, however, Sessions became more realistic and would delay proceedings until nursing was finished, as happened in the case of Helen Tush in the parish of Banff who 'becoming a nurse in the country . . . pleaded to be excused for a time.' An employer might contact the Session to tell them about engaging such a woman and would perhaps undertake to present her to them when she had finished the work, which was just making use of her and then handing her over for punishment when finished with her. An example of this happened at St. Cuthbert's Church, Edinburgh, in 1708 when a man gave a bond that he would produce Margaret Fraser, guilty of fornication, when she was free from nursing, and to this the Session agreed. A kinder way of doing things was that of Mr David Polson of Kinmylies who wrote to his Session, also in 1708, to say that a woman was nursing his child and that he would present her and pay her penalties when, please God, she had done with the fostering. An earlier chapter has referred to the frequent need for Sessions to find a wet-nurse for a foundling or for a baby whose mother was ill or had died. This work went where possible to married women but when a wet-nurse was required urgently, it could be that no married woman was available and so a woman guilty of fornication might find the consequences of her sin being made use of by the Session. In Fordyce in 1667 a woman who was undergoing church discipline died, leaving a baby to be cared for, and the Session's decision was that Jannet Thain, herself under discipline, should be asked to nurse the child, for which she was given the mother's plaid, which had perhaps been given in as a pledge, and had her penalty withdrawn, an altogether sensible way of putting a child's needs first. A similar yet different instance occurred in Traquair, Peebles-shire, involving Mr John Carmichael, minister there from 1662–5, a man of singularly broad mind for the times, who baptised gypsies, dealt with offenders himself without recourse to the Kirk Session and, it was thought, admitted people too readily to the Sacraments. Inevitably complaints were made about him to the Presbytery and one of these was that he had taken a very scandalous person from the place of repentance to nurse his child, to the great scandal of the congregation, but a manse could need a wet-nurse just as much as any other home.[5]

In spite of kirk efforts to get couples to marry, marriage could not or did not always take place and illegitimacy was only too common and the only way for an unmarried woman to establish paternity, should a man deny it, was to come before the Session, name the man and leave it to them to establish his guilt, without which she could not claim maintenance from him. Kirks were as anxious as the mothers to do this, knowing that if the father was not found to pay for the child, the cost of keeping it could fall on the poor's funds, perhaps till it was ten to fourteen years old. A procedure for any disputes about paternity was laid down by the General Assembly in 1707 which said that if an unmarried woman was found to be pregnant, she must be asked to name the father and, if she would not do so, she was to be regarded as contumacious. If she did name someone, he must be told and spoken to privately and if he denied the accusation, must be summoned; if he persisted in his denial then he and the woman must be made to confront one another. An unusual instance was when a man would not admit fatherhood until another man would clear himself by oath of the possibility of paternity. The Session decided to have the two men confront each other which worked very well as the man originally accused accepted that the child was his. In general, if the truth of an allegation seemed fairly obvious, there might be no way of removing the scandal but by the man's appearance in church for rebuke but if he refused to submit to this it might be considered 'more for edification that a true narrative of the case be laid before the congregation and intimation given that there can be no further procedure in the matter till God give further light and sist there at the time, than that an oath be pressed, and upon refusal, proceed to Greater Excommunication.'[6]

The oath mentioned here was the oath of purgation. Where a man was wrongly accused of fathering a child, it gave him an opportunity to clear himself but where he was sufficiently hardened to withstand it even when guilty, the wretched woman was left not only with a child to support but additional church censure to endure for wrongful accusation. In one sad case, the man cleared himself in this way and the woman 'being ideot' was banished, either pregnant or with a baby. Little wonder that in another case, as a man was about to take the oath, 'the woman in the most hideous and lamentable manner cryd out in the face of the congregation not to take the oath as he was guilty and the father of her child.' In such cases, of course, the woman would in any event have to make public satisfaction as the evidence of her sin was all too plain to see. Although confrontation and the oath of purgation were put on a formal basis by the General Assembly in 1707, they were already being used before that date with individual ministers composing their own oaths. When two Fordyce men persisted in denials in two separate cases in 1667 the minister drew up 'ane oath in the most terrible termes he could' and told them they were to purge themselves by it, with their hands upon the heads of the children alleged to be theirs. One of them was so terrified that he confessed but the other continued in his denial although the minister felt hopeful that he might ultimately confess, another instance of guilt being assumed.[7]

No wonder that one of these men was terrified if the oath to be sworn was anything like the one quoted by Henry Grey Graham in which the person swearing did so

> before the great God, and Jesus Christ and the Angels, wishing that all the curses of the law and the woes of the Gospel should fall upon him, that he may never thrive in this world, and that his conscience may henceforth never give him rest, and torment him as it did Cain and that he may never hope for mercy, but die in desperation, and in the great day be cast into hell if the oath he hath sworn be not true from the heart.

The wording of a ministerially-composed oath in the late seventeenth century went as follows and is almost word for word that later put forward by the General Assembly in 1707 when it regularised the phraseology of an oath specifically for men named as fathers of illegitimate children:

> I, Donald MacDonald, now under process before the Session of Inverness, for the sin of adultery alleged to have been committed by me with Elizabeth McGregor, Slander being Reputed as one guilty of that sin, I, for ending the said process and giving satisfaction to all the good people, do declare before God and this congregation that I am innocent and free of the said sin, and Hereby call the great God, Judger and Avenger of all falsehood, to be Witness and Judge against me in this matter if I be guilty, and that I do by taking His Blessed Name in my mouth and swearing by Him, the Great Judge, Punisher, and Avenger, as said is, and that in the sincerity of my own heart, according to the truth of the matter and my own conscience, as I shall answer to God in the last and Great Day when I shall stand before Him to answer for all that I do in the flesh, and as I would partake of his glory in Heaven when this life is at an end.

This oath was sworn by Donald with his hand stretched heavenwards and the other on the head of the child which was held in the arms of its mother, who stood beside him throughout. A basically similar but more erudite version, complete with Biblical references, was prepared by the minister of Sorbie in 1701 at the request of the Kirk Session, and with Presbytery approval which always had to be obtained for this oath-taking:

> Whereas I, Andrew McConnell, have been and am accused by the Session of Sorbie (upon the confession of Elizabeth McGoune lately my servant) of the horrid sin of fornication that the said woman alleges I did commit with her, I do hereby solemnly declare myself innocent of the said guilt and in testimony of my innocence I invocate the eternal God, the searcher of all hearts as witness, Judge and Avenger, wishing that in case I be guilty, he himself may appear as witness against me and fix the guilt upon me, he himself may proceed as Judge against me who has [certified?] that whoremongers and Adulterers he will judge Job 13. 4, he himself may avenge his own cause, who has declared he will not hold them guilty that take his name in vain Ex. 20. 7, and that the roll of God's curse which enters the house of the false swearers Zech. 5. 4, may enter my house if I be guilty and remain in the midst thereof till it consume timber and stones, root out the remembrance thereof from the earth and that the righteous Lord may make me an example and terror to all false swearers

before I go of this world and that this paper may stand as witness against me, I have subt. it with my hand the . . . day of one thousand seven hundred and . . . years.[8]

Once it was decided that an oath should be administered, it might be read over to the man by the minister or perhaps a copy would be given to him to be mulled over, assuming that he could read or had someone able to read it to him, and a considerable amount of time was allowed to think about it. The Act of the General Assembly which gave one form of wording for an oath of purgation continued by saying:

In taking this oath, all tenderness and caution is to be used, nor is the Session to press any man thereto. But they are to deal with him and his conscience in the sight of God; and if he offer to give his oath, the Judicatory shall accept it, or not, as they shall see cause . . . but this oath is not to be taken in any case but this, when the presumptions are so great, that they create jealousy in that congregation and session, that nothing will remove the suspicion but the man's Oath of Purgation, and when his oath will probably remove the scandal and suspicion. In all other cases, the Oath is in vain and should not be admitted, and never but by the advice of the Presbytery. This oath is taken before the Kirk Session, Presbytery or congregation as the Presbytery shall determine, if taken before the Session or Presbytery, it is to be intimated to the congregation, and the person may be obliged to be present in the congregation and may be put publicly to own his purging himself by oath, and so be declared free from scandal. Note — These are not standing rules, but recommended to be observed.

A girl could also take her oath that a man *was* the father of her child: one Session held several meetings to consider a paternity case and knowing that there had been 'indecent familiarities that passed between the parties about the 15th of August' and that the man could not give his oath that the child was not his, they decided to put the woman on her oath that she had not 'had carnal knowledge of any man whatever but the said Angus MacInnes for the space of half a year immediately preceding the first of November last.' This she was able to do, permission was given for the child's baptism and the man was declared the father.[9]

This oath could be used by both men and women to counter a variety of allegations. The minutes of Kilninian and Kilmore Kirk Session have several references such as 'The oath of purgation was administered to Mary McLean . . . and she freed herself of the scandal alleged against her by John Morrison' or that a man took the oath 'by which he freed himself of carnal dealing with the said Mary McKellich.' This Session seems to have been readier than most to allow the oath to be taken and in many parishes it might be offered to people or accused persons might ask to take it but, in the event, Sessions were usually very hesitant actually to administer it. This was probably because it was never suggested unless there was a very strong presumption of guilt, although proof of innocence could also be the outcome. What happened in Arbuthnott is a good example of how long it could be before oath-taking was allowed: a woman accused another of immoral conduct in January 1709, a matter which went from Session to Presbytery, as a result of which it was advised that she take the Oath of Purgation. On 10 June she was given a copy of it 'in write' to study and the minister reported that he had spoken to her several times 'to bring her to confession of what Mary Tulloch alleges against her but she still denies the guilt.' By June 1710, almost eighteen months later, she had still not been allowed to take it although she wanted to do so and therefore 'after much dealing with her, the Session could not refuse, and so thereupon a great multitude of people who were at the doors being allowed to come in, after solemn calling upon God, she did upon her knees with hands uplifted swear.' At this, the woman who had accused her was ordered to be censured as a slanderer, was sharply rebuked and made to promise that she would never mention the matter again. This was a satisfactory outcome, but how much better if it had not taken a year to achieve, especially as the whole time from an initial delation until the accused either confessed or was allowed to take the oath, he or she and any alleged partner in sin, lived under church censure and were deprived of church privileges.[10]

Just as Sessions sometimes let things lie in other discipline cases until Providence shed further light, so withholding the taking of the oath of purgation could give time for enlightenment too. In 1698 a couple in New Abbey were accused of fornication but though called several times to appear before the Session, they did not do so, only coming eventually to say that they were prepared to purge their scandal by oath. 'The Session having considered the whole affair thought fit to delay it till further' and ordered an elder to make inquiries, which he and other elders did but 'got no light'. The Session delayed any oath-taking until more inquiries could be made but the elders could still 'find nothing material whatever thereunto' and the Session refused to accept the oath for the meantime. As there is no further mention of this case for at least a year, it seems to have been allowed to lapse. Holding back the taking of the oath of purgation had faults but benefits too. In the case of Andrew McConnell in Sorbie who was offered the Biblically referenced oath already quoted, there was no excessive delay but good was achieved. It all began in June 1701 with a report of McConnell's fornication with a maid in his house, something which she admitted but he denied. Three witnesses said that they had seen no evidence of 'scandalous carriage' but in August the Presbytery decided that he should be given a copy of the oath to consider for a month, after which he should appear before the congregation to hear it read out to him. When the minister asked 'if he would swear himself innocent of the alleged scandal of fornication, he declared his willingness to swear according to the form read immediately but the minister desired him to take it to further consideration and he was delayed for this time.' In October he was again delayed and at the beginning of the following month the minister reported that he had seen him and dealt with him and that while he still denied actual guilt, he admitted offering the young woman what he called 'baseness' but that he now said he wished to marry her and asked that the Session would delay her public appearances until after their marriage. This they agreed to on condition that he came to the Session and told them this officially. This meant that the carefully composed oath was not used after all and instead he confessed fornication, gave a bond of 50 merks and an obligation that he and the girl would make public satisfaction. This was an almost classic case of a Session dragging its feet so as to get a satisfactory outcome, whether fornication had in truth been committed or not.[11]

The prospect of taking the oath was an effective way of wringing confession from an accused person. Just as the Fordyce man already mentioned was terrified into admitting paternity, so did the same thing happen to Donald McLean on the island of Coll who was accused in 1776 of being the father of an expected baby. The minutes say that though the Session used 'all the means in our power by Threatenings and promises temporal and eternal to bring him to confess the truth, he still continued obstinate' and offered to swear that he was innocent. At the end of the year, when the Presbytery advised that his oath should finally be taken, 'God of his goodness, moved him to repentance' and he owned that he was the father. When a couple in another parish offered to take the oath the minister replied that 'he had known persons stand as firmly resolved to purge themselves of what they afterwards were found guilty' and it was decided that they should appear on the pillory one Lord's Day 'to see if their conscience might be awaked.' The fact that fear of the oath's terrible wording made so many people confess in the end, can only have encouraged the kirk to believe that these people were guilty when that was not necessarily so. For many confession, true or not, may have been the only solution to their dilemma.[12]

An interesting case involving two families in Caithness happened in 1716. The minister of Canisbay reported to his Kirk Session that as instructed by them he had spoken to Lady Mey

> and in the Session's name required her to remove Christian Harrow fornicatrix out of her family, because of the open and avowed countenance and encouragement which she continued to give to that Strumpet, after such abuse committed in her family was not only dishonourable to herself and family but also opened the mouths of many to talk to her prejudice, and gave but too great grounds to more Sober and considering people to suspect that there must be some secret reason that made her to shelter and encourage such a naughty, profane person, that he particularly told her that as long as that slut had any encouragement from her, either within or without doors, directly or indirectly, he could not but suspect that there was more in that matter than was alleged or certainly known, and that he did not believe that she was ignorant of what was continually spoken.

If he did indeed say all that, it was strong stuff from the minister to a lady of quality. The man in the case was William Sinclair of Freswick and when the minister had finished this diatribe to Lady Mey she replied, 'Yes, I know what Freswick says but it shall not go that way, say it who wills, for I will get Witnesses to prove Freswick's guilt with her.' Freswick offered to purge himself of the scandal but wanted to exclude Lady Mey's witnesses 'as being all Menzial servants to the Lady Mey, whom he doubts not will promote her to practise upon the said witnesses.' He had written to the Session in the most fulsome terms, speaking much of his honour, but when they referred the matter to the Presbytery, they were instructed to have him purge himself by oath, which succeeded in making him confess that he was indeed guilty. Had it not been for Lady Mey's conviction, courage and determination to see fair play for the girl, as well as the power of the oath of purgation, what would have befallen her? Some minutes refer to people being 'threatened with the Oath of Purgation' but it might be offered and withheld at the same time in rather a strange way. When Ann Buchanan was asked if she could purge herself of guilt alleged against her, she said she could and insisted that her oath should be taken but the minister told her that as she was a married person and had broken her marriage vows, her oath could not be received. She denied ever having been married and when the Session thought this over, they decided that it was possibly so and in the end she was allowed to take the oath which convinced the man in the case that he was the father of her child and he promised to maintain it. Two years later, in 1762, that Session had a long case to do with a woman named Sarah Campbell who was prepared to take the oath. The Session asked the man concerned if he objected to her doing so, which seems a most extraordinary thing to do but they must have had some reason to believe him when he said that he thought she had been involved with other men and that this was something which should be investigated. One young woman in the parish of Melrose in the 1840s was not prepared to submit when a man wrongly denied on oath that he had fathered her child and the Kirk Session, naturally enough, accepted what he said. A couple of years later, by then living in the parish of Legerwood, she was able to send proof to Melrose Kirk Session that a civil court judgment had been obtained against him, as a result of which he was paying maintenance. The Session asked the advice of the Presbytery who instructed them to impose censure according to the rules of the church. This they seemed reluctant to do and instead referred the case to Legerwood, who returned it saying it was outside their jurisdiction and so Melrose rebuked her and restored her to church privileges, but there is no mention of what happened to the man. An unusual oath-taking was a mass one in the parish of Galston in 1635 when the Session summoned all the inhabitants of the parish to purge themselves by oath that none of them took, or knew who took 'ane daill from the kirk'. This seems an extreme measure to take for one deal board even when stolen from a church although it is a comment on the value of wood at that time.[13]

It was because establishing paternity was of such importance to the father as well as the mother, the child and the Session, that the particulars of moral cases appear in such detail in minutes. There may well have been some salacious interest in it all but the facts of just when and where the child was conceived could help to accuse or to clear a man if his presence or absence at the relevant time could be proved and, when more than one man was involved, such information could be a deciding factor in finding the truth. It is thus that minutes may show a man agreeing 'to father a child of which Mary McKinnon in Tobermorrie goes pregnant if it answers the time she has condescended viz one week before St. Patrick's Day next' or evidence that a child 'was begotten when they were in the open field when they were winning the turfes . . .'[14]

A valuable service often performed by Kirk Sessions was helping to enforce maintenance payments from a father. It was in the interests of the poor's funds to do so and might be achieved in several ways, one of which was simply a brisk order to pay up. This happened in 1718 when a Caithness woman lodged a complaint with her Session that the father was refusing to maintain her child, saying it was not his, 'which the Session upon inquiry finding false, did strictly enjoin the said George that further Demurre to perform the duties incumbent on a Christian parent to the child' would not be tolerated. Even when an illegitimate baby died, there were still costs to pay and some parishes laid down a rate for this, 15s. stg. to be paid to the poor's funds for its burial. In the mid-nineteenth century, one Session went further and ordered a man to pay 15s. and also the girl's medical expenses as well as the baby's burial costs. Some Sessions left it to the mother to take civil action for maintenance, 'to apply to the Judges Competent in case he does not do justice conform to use and wont of the parish in paying for nursing and maintaining said child.' What is surprising, however, is that St. Monance Kirk Session ordered their clerk to write to a man concerning lying-in expenses and aliment for a child in June 1845, yet when six months earlier a girl had asked them to prosecute the father of her child to enforce payment of lying-in and funeral charges, they advised her to deal with this herself through the courts. Why the difference? Was one man in the parish and easy to pursue while the other case required civil action which would be expensive? Or could it have been because a dead child did not need continuing care? Or could the imminent Poor Law Amendment Act have made the difference?[15]

To some extent a Session might vary maintenance, even when it had been laid down in court. In 1842 a St. Monance man named Alexander Baldie denied being the father of a child, a matter which apparently went from the Session to a civil court where a decree of £5 yearly aliment and £1 of lying-in money was awarded against him. It appears that he resisted this and was sent to prison and by April 1843, the Session were told that the prosecution had come to a standstill for lack of funds. The following month they decided, although the matter was by then really out of their jurisdiction, that he should pay all the expenses so far incurred in the case, plus £4 yearly for the child. Later in the month, things changed somewhat, with the clerk reporting that with the agreement of the minister and some of the elders, orders had been given to the civil authorities to free Baldie on his agreeing to pay all the expenses plus 15s. per quarter for the child, a further reduction of the original award. He was warned that if he did not do this, the Session would fall back on the provisions of the original sum of £5 per annum plus £1. He must have accepted this as, about eighteen months later, he was rebuked and absolved, along with the child's mother. Obviously it would have been greatly to the mother's and child's benefit if the Session had insisted on the original amount being paid and one can only assume that they thought it too high, that what was to be paid should be sufficient and, in any case, a bird in the hand was better than two in the bush in such a case. A case of lenience to the father of an illegitimate child was that of John Macpherson, a young man in Laggan. He was about to leave the parish and was recommended by the Session to give what allowance he could for the immediate support of the child and in regard they consider him a young man whose finances are probably not very large, he is not able with convenience to himself to pay the ordinary fines for trespasses of this kind, they require of him to give an obligation to the Session that, if ever he returns or is in a way to enable him to satisfy them in a pecuniary fine, that he will do so, and hope that until such satisfaction be made that he will consider this measure as a great indulgence and the fine a debt of honour.

This was eminently reasonable but it cannot have been of much immediate consolation to the unmarried mother left behind.[16]

It was one thing to assign paternity when the father could be found, quite another when he could not and in such cases it was up to the woman to make the necessary inquiries. This was a very difficult thing for a pregnant woman or nursing mother to do when transport was inadequate, postal services lacking and she almost certainly needed to take a job to support herself and the child and could not go off searching for the man. In 1702 a girl called Janet Gill committed fornication with a travelling pedlar when she was working in England and returned pregnant to her home parish in Scotland, only to be ordered by the Session to find him or to remove herself. The baby was born the month after that and two months later she came to the Session and said that she had not been able to search for the pedlar but that a merchant in Hawick was probably the best person to give information, 'being well acquaint with him'. The Session told her to go there, a journey of several miles, to ask where the pedlar might be found and to report back to the Session the following Sunday. She did this and was able to tell the Session that the merchant said that he was in England but that news of him might be had from his father's parish where, although there was a vacancy at the moment, a new minister was about to be appointed. The Session decided that they would write to this minister once he arrived, giving an extract of the process so far. The girl was willing to serve discipline but 'being poor, she behoved to take service' which was a 'nurseship' — as a wet-nurse — and so discipline was delayed. In January 1703 it was learnt that the pedlar's father had not seen his son for some time and there was an unconfirmed report that he had been tried at an assize and hanged. After all that worry and trouble, Janet appeared before her Session in June 1703 and was told that she was not obliged to satisfy discipline as the sin had occurred in England. This must have been extremely galling for her, but the whole exercise had had its point as maintenance might have been obtained. In fact, she wanted to get the whole thing over and done with so as to be restored to church privileges, and that was what was done. In that instance the Session gave practical help by writing to the pedlar's home parish; in other cases they might give a woman a little financial assistance like the 10s. paid to Jean Cowie 'to assist her to find the father to her child.' In 1862, by which time the church was in general no longer required to support the poor, the Kirk Session of Stow granted a woman a certificate to help her establish paternity of her child as the man she named lived some twenty or so miles away. It is not clear from the minutes what kind of certificate this was but it may have been one to enable her to sue *in forma pauperis*. [17]

Rather than find themselves having to pay maintenance for illegitimate children, as well as having to make public repentance, men were quite ready to bribe women not just to conceal the fact of pregnancy, which has already been mentioned, but not to name them once pregnancy was established. In Kintail a man pledged a girl to secrecy while she was still pregnant 'as the child might die and that the laws of the church might possibly be evaded', something which could well have been an incitement to child murder. A Yetholm woman admitted that she had been offered £10 by the father of her child if she would accuse someone else who had by then gone to America and was safely out of the way. Another man accepted the offer of a gallon of whisky to accept paternity of a child but he then increased his demand, asking for half a guinea as well, which was given in the form of a pair of new shoes worth 9s. 6d. and a little cash to make up the difference but it all came to the ears of the Session who had then to sort out the plot. The very next year, that particular Session reacted swiftly when a woman said the father of her child was someone she had met on the road and never seen before; they sentenced her to Lesser Excommunication, intimating to the congregation that this was for the purpose of 'marking out' this 'contumacious, impenitent and aggravated offender' and to act as a warning to others. While she may indeed have been a woman of exceptionally loose morals as this minute indicates, it seems possible that the Session may have suspected some bribery in the background, especially after their experience the previous year. Much about the same date a pregnant girl told the Session that she had been raped and that the man had come to ask if she was pregnant and offered her 20s. if she would name someone else but she had the good sense to refuse to do this as, quite apart from the fact that it would have been untrue, she had never had any such relations with other men. Cheaper for a man than bribery was plain trickery. When a Glasgow girl accused a man of being the father of her child, he was able to produce a paper in which she declared that he was not guilty. It had been prepared by a writer and witnessed by two men, who were possibly friends of his. At later Session meetings, she admitted having signed a paper but said that she could not read and thought it was just an acknowledgement of 5s. which she had been promised for doing so, although in fact she only got 1s. 6d. Witnesses were called but the Kirk Session could not decide the rights of the case and referred it to Presbytery.[18]

The lengths to which some men would go could be surprising. In 1773 Helen Amoss named one man before Tweedsmuir Kirk Session, then changed her story and said that Robert Hope was the father. According to her new account, he and his sister, Mrs Turnbull, who lived in Edinburgh, had told her what to say and he had given her money, assuring her that she and the child would be cared for so long as she did not name him. He had persuaded her to have the child baptised in Edinburgh which was done, with the precentor holding it up, Robert's brother-in-law paying the charges, and his maid and another woman present as witnesses. In spite of all this, he still persisted in denying paternity. As Helen could not afford the expense of bringing two witnesses from Moffat to Tweedsmuir, her Session wrote to the minister there to ask him to examine them before his elders and to send a copy of their evidence to them. Meanwhile, Robert's witnesses, one of them a servant of his, were giving evidence against the girl. There the story ends but it is to be hoped that the Session managed to deal fairly with what seems to have been a clear case of evasion of paternity. When Janet Barbour, servant to James Fleck, told him in 1809 that she was pregnant, he replied that 'she must leave the bounds in order to keep the matter a secret in this part of the country'; and proposed that she should go to Greenock where he would take a room for her, but she refused this offer, saying she would rather go to Kilmarnock, to a widowed cousin of her father's. This she did and he visited her there to insist that 'she should remain until the child was born and it would be put out to nursing and the thing would be kept a secret in Kilbride.' He paid a second visit, again urging her to stay where she was 'or else it would be worse for her' and he also wrote the doctor there, asking him to tell her to send him a letter to 'free him of the child for that the Session of Kilbride was giving him trouble about it.' The child was duly born and the doctor wrote Fleck telling him to pay for the girl's lodging but this he did not do and an officer was sent to demand it from him. The baby was put out to a wet nurse and the mother produced certificates from her father's cousin and the woman in whose house it had been born, but even with so much evidence, it still took almost a year before Fleck was declared the father and that only after witnesses had actually been called. He seems to have been a very determined man and called for extracts of proceedings but seems to have got off scot-free so far as discipline was concerned although Janet had to stand three times before the congregation.[19]

Real problems arose when a Session did not believe that the man named as father of a child was guilty or where a girl refused to name a man, either because of bribery or fear of some sort or because she genuinely did not know which of several men he might be. An instance occurred in the parish of Foveran, Aberdeenshire, in 1748 when a pregnant woman could not say who was the expected baby's father. She said that one dark March night she had met three men on her way to or from Ellon and lay with one of them. All she could say was that he had said his name was James Gordon, that he lived in Torry, was fair-headed with a pock-marked face, wore blue clothing lined with red and rode a black horse. Having particularly mentioned how dark the night was, it seems surprising that her description was so detailed but she was able to describe the colour of the coats and of the horses of the other men as well. The Session solved this tricky case by deciding that the sin was committed in the parish of Ellon and should be passed to them. If what she said was basically true, it was not such an unusual thing to happen as one might expect and the General Assembly in 1707 had felt it necessary to give instructions that censure for adultery was to be imposed in cases where a woman, married or not, confessed pregnancy without being forced but did not know the man.[20]

It is understandable that Kirk Sessions felt that they simply had to know who was the father of any illegitimate child, and in this way they were supported by Presbyteries, such as that of Fordyce which ordered in 1663 'that such women as are found to be with chylde and will not declare the reall and trew fathers of them be processed till they declare the real and trew parents of them.' The attempt to get a confession could pursue a woman even to her deathbed so that when Elizabeth Kemp gave birth and lay dying 'her deposition was taken by the Session who exhorted the poor wretch and set a guard over her till the Sheriff be acquainted.' In that case death spared her further questioning but where death did not intervene, Sessions could behave in a way which seems totally outrageous, questioning the woman during labour. In the very early eighteenth century five Edinburgh mid-wives had to sign a bond requiring them to carry out their professions properly, under a penalty of £20 stg. if they did not do so, the most important condition being that if a woman refused to name the father, they should 'call for the said ministers or elders in time of labour, or in their absence for two habile witnesses in the neighbourhood, and thoroughly examine the mother before childbirth, in order to compel her to give an impartial account of the father.' In that parish some fifty or so years earlier a girl said that the father of her expected baby was a soldier whose regiment had left the district but the Session appear to have thought she was protecting someone nearer home whose name they wished to discover. Four times she appeared before the Session and was also 'dealt with quaetlie be the minister' which was no more successful and so twice more she came before the Session. Still they did not get the result they wanted and so her case was continued so that she might be 'posed' when in the agonies of childbirth, but this too did not alter her story. The Session consulted the Presbytery but got no help from them and so, maliciously it seems, they banished her from the parish without a certificate, thereby branding her for life as a bad character. In 1665 the Presbytery of Fordyce, not believing that the man named was really the father of an expected child, ordered the minister not only to continue trying to find out the truth but also to see if the midwives at the woman's delivery 'could extort anie confession' and if they could not, to send her as soon as possible to the Justice Court 'to see if imprison-ment could do anie thing for that effect.' The Presbytery of Penpont, Dumf-riesshire, directed that a woman should 'be strictly questioned in her pains by the women who shall be present' while in Inverness in 1690 it was not midwives but David Steward, an elder, who along with others was appointed by the Session to attend a woman 'when she was in her pangs, to get a true account of the fayr of her child, in respect the man who she gives to be father to it, is att London.'[21]

It was only a short step from questioning a woman in labour to refusing her help during it until she named the father. When in 1611 two midwives appeared before the Kirk Session of Perth and gave their oaths to be faithful and honest in their calling, they were instructed under the threat of dismissal, that they must give no help to any unmarried woman or one suspected of whoredom unless they first of all got her to name the father on oath and this they promised to do 'with a solemn oath and an extension of the hand, in presence of the whole session.' This was not an isolated case. Wick Kirk Session ordered that when a particular woman 'was in travail, that the midwife would not help her in her pains till she would declare the father'; the same thing had happened in Oldhamstocks; and in Thurso in 1705 when a man flatly denied being the father of a baby which was on the way, the woman was called before the Session more than once and 'being exhorted to glorifie God by making a genuine confession' at length confessed that the father was a west country seaman whose name she did not know and so 'she being found to prevaricate . . . it is enacted that in childbirth she have no assistance from the midwife or any other woman until she make an Ingenuous confession' concerning the child's father. This may have been because they doubted her truthfulness but it sounds suspiciously like a piece of additional punishment. The danger in such cases must have been that a girl would name any man in sheer desperation.22

Kirk Sessions were always on the lookout for any suspicious plumpness of female parishioners which might be the result of fornication or adultery and it was this that caused one Session to summon a woman to ask her if she were pregnant, to which she replied that she was not and that it was only because of disease that she 'had a swelling in her belly'. In this case the matter was delayed 'till the event appear in providence' but in many instances, should guilt be denied in spite of apparent evidence to the contrary, the Session did not wait for providence but ordered midwives to give a physical examination, as happened in the case of suspected mothers of foundlings and dead or abandoned babies. When Mary Smith, a Cruden woman, was thought to be pregnant, an elder was appointed to take a particular woman with him 'and some other discreet women' to where she stayed 'in order to know if she is with child.' The following week she was cited to speak with the minister but as there is no more about the case it seems likely that she was innocent and had suffered this indignity for nothing. In 1725 a servant girl in the Borders was reported to be pregnant and as it was coming up to the November term when workers moved to other jobs, it was feared that 'she might make off with herself and so escape the censures of the church', for which reason the Kirk Session appointed the minister and four elders as a committee to hold Session at the girl's place of employment, taking midwives with them 'for trying her in case she denied herself to be with child' and, thanks to the midwives' help she confessed. Twenty years before, a girl had come to another Borders parish and was very soon suspected to be pregnant but denied it, whereupon the Session ordered two elders to visit her along with 'a midwife and another woman that had skill . . . and to cause the said women to draw her breasts.' The girl would neither confess nor submit to this although she was badly swollen with what she claimed was some disease. Her father had taken her to a gardener to get some herbs to try to cure her and intended to take her home to her own parish and the Session, baffled, decided to send an extract of the proceedings to that parish.23

The women making these inspections had to be paid: it cost £7 4s. Scots to send two midwives from St. Vigeans to Auchmithie to inspect a woman there in 1743, and as Kirk Sessions did not readily waste the poor's money, it seems that in certain cases they felt it essential to know what was what without waiting for time to produce the truth. They might fear that a woman would leave the district before paternity was established and maintenance arranged, or that the man would do so; or that discipline might not be served in the case of departure; or that the child might come to harm. The following is a case in point. In 1756 a woman suspected to be pregnant did not appear before the Session, even after two citations and so some elders and women were sent to see her. Later they reported that 'having obliged her to submit' they were of the opinion that she was indeed expecting a baby. The Session considered that she was 'of bad fame, in regard of her obstinate refusal to compear before the Session or to make any acknowledgement otherwise' and that this gave grounds 'to suspect her having a bad intention with respect to her pregnancy' and decided that 'a proper measure to defeat further bad intention' would be for the Session to ask the Judge ordinary for a warrant to imprison her until she found caution to submit to the Session as the law required. However, before that could be done, the minister was told that she had 'got free of her pregnancy and that it was alleged she made away with the birth' whereupon he got as many of the elders as he could muster to visit her, along with two midwives. These women gave their reasons for thinking that she had indeed given birth but before things could go much further, she fled and was declared by the Presbytery to be a fugitive from discipline. As has already been said, civil help was enlisted for medical inspections when there was a suspicion of evil intent or of crime but sometimes it was sought when there were no apparent wrongful designs. A warrant granted to one Session by a Sheriff appointed 'the women therein named to examine and inspect the body of Kathrine Rintoul in order to discover whether or not she was with child in regard she had positively refused to submit to an examination at their [Session's] instance only' and other cases where legal assistance was called for appear from around the country. Time and again there are references to elders, and sometimes the minister too, going to these examinations, along with suitable women, but to what extent they themselves were directly involved is not clear. Certainly in the case of Kathrine Rintoul, the whole Session, 'constituted by Prayer', adjourned to the house where she was living to see the Sheriff's warrant put into execution.[24]

Child murder has been mentioned in an earlier chapter but in some moral cases what was being guarded against was criminal abortion. In the 1740s Cromarty Kirk Session questioned a woman as to whether she had sought what they termed 'some things' from a doctor and she admitted that she had indeed been 'seeking things for loosening a woman'. She had already told lies, saying she had been raped when she had not, and the Session were by then suspicious that she had tempted the man she now named as father into sexual relations with her so that he would have to take the blame for her pregnancy 'to cover a greater guilt'. Another Session called a man before them and found that he had recommended a woman to procure something for an abortion and had himself got for her a phial of yellow-coloured liquid, telling her that a little of it in water would produce the desired result, adding that if she named him as father he would poison himself. The contents of the phial turned out to be muriatic acid which the Session decided to keep in their own hands for the meantime and to delay any decisions until they brought the couple to a full confession as the man firmly denied any part in it all. Kirk Sessions undoubtedly had a detective role to play.[25]

Ante-nuptial fornication was a very common sin and midwives' evidence was called for when any baby arrived less than nine months after the parents' marriage. In a case where one arrived about five weeks before it should have done, the midwife and other women present at the birth were able to tell the Session that they believed it to be premature because it lacked nails on its toes and so the parents were not censured, whereas after another inquiry the midwife affirmed 'that the child had all the marks of one that was come to full term' which meant that the father and mother did have to make repentance.[26]

Prevention of fornication of either kind was obviously better than cure and it was for this reason that one Session intimated in 1676 that a penalty of £7 Scots would be imposed on heads of households who allowed men and women to sleep in the same room at night. In addition, Sessions were watchful for what they called light and scandalous carriage, carriage in this sense meaning behaviour or conduct, which could lead to trouble. Some so-called bad behaviour was very mild but obvious examples of scandalous carriage were when a married man and an unmarried woman were alone in a room after everyone else had gone to bed and he also 'trysted her to his Kiln in the night time', and when a man and a woman spent a whole night drinking together and in 'other unChristian behaviour'. Couples planning to marry were naturally in each other's company more than normal and 'light and scandalous carriage' between them was sometimes more scandalous than the term was meant to indicate. In the case of one such couple, the Session delayed their censure for that offence in case it turned out that the charge should really be ante-nuptial fornication which, in fact, it was.[27] In that particular case, marriage was planned but when people were guilty of fornication with no intention of getting married, or of adultery when marriage was impossible, or when there was doubt about the freedom of one or other of them to marry even if they wished to do so, then Sessions might forbid them to speak to each other: 'Norman Denoon and Isa. Elice being compeared, and being interrogate anent their too familiar and unseasonable converse, denied the same but withall acknowledged their converse to be frequent having designs of marriage, and the Session considering the whole, discharged [forbade] them under pain of censure to converse together and enjoined them to lay aside all thoughts of marriage till there should be a sure document anent the death of Isa Elice's husband.' A man and woman guilty of fornication were 'inhibited to converse together' and another Session forbade an adulterous couple to meet or talk to each other. One Session suspected that a couple were getting over-friendly, presumably with no prospect of marriage, and forbade any association between them 'except at kirk and mercat'. When people reported to the Session that they had seen a young woman go to a man's room and in the true spirit of informers, had 'followed her in a little time with a candle' and found her in bed 'stript to her shift and an under petticoat', the two sinners were required to appear publicly in church and were also forbidden 'to haunt or frequent each other's company in time coming.'[28]

Should people associate with one another after being forbidden to do so, they were immediately summoned before the Session 'for the scandal of converse' which was followed by public repentance. All this may sound excessively and unnecessarily strict to modern ears but without birth control and social security, there was real need for it. Kells Kirk Session, Kirkcudbright, however, perhaps went too far in their alarmist attitude to the consequences of young people speaking to each other:

> 28th May 1699. The Session of Kells taking to their serious consideration, the unnecessary and unseemly converse of some young women with strangers, through their having company with them unnecessarily on fairs and public mercat days especially, in aill houses, and oyr places more remote, and sometimes too late in the evening, qʳ great offence has arisen, their own credite and reputation has been marred, and much trouble has been given to the said Session, by reason of leading of process against them, upon such flagrant reports, and [?] in the mouth and minds of many concerning them, therefore the said kirk session for the prevention of the like in time coming, do foind it their deutie to inhibit and consent expressly inhibit [sic] and discharge all young women within this congregation to converse or keep company with strangers or other young men unnecessarily . . . or too familiarly at any time qtsomever, whether soon or late, or at any place qtsomever, whether in town at fairs, or in mercat days in aill houses, or other places more remote. They exhort them to keep themselves at a distance from strangers and likewise young men . . . that they labour always to behave themselves modestly, gravely and . . . without any offence. . . that God be not dishonoured by them, nor their good name wronged, nor any further delations and complaints given in to the Session against them, with certification to them that if they do in the contrair, they shall be ipso facto (that is upon the very deed itself) processed against and incur public censure and shame before the congregation, and shall after intimation hereof, be counted inexcusable.

That statement was made in 1699 but even in 1836 the minister of Glenshiel, Ross-shire, stated that a recently-introduced custom of exposing pedlars' wares at their thrice-weekly fairs 'threatens by attracting young females to them, to do injury to their morals.' The minutes of Kirkwall Kirk Session refer to 'a woman of a bad character' named Elizabeth Wallace who was given to hanging about the prison in bad company — 'doth scandalously haunt the tolbooth notwithstanding of admonitions given her and others concerned (and notwithstanding of the injunctions upon our application to the provost given to the jailer)' and as a result they appointed a Mr Baikie to speak to the Provost 'that the said Elizabeth may be kept from haunting the tolbooth and appoints the officer to charge the said Elizabeth Wallace and James Shearer to the next Session day.' The jailer turned up and promised to keep the woman out of the tolbooth and although she did not appear then, she came later and promised never to be found in any scandalous company again and especially not in the tolbooth and promised, in addition, that she would attend church which she had not been doing.[29] To enjoy company at fairs and to look at pedlars' wares was understandable but to want to hang around a prison seems a very undesirable occupation.

Any report of unmarried couples living together brought immediate action. In 1728 when a couple were found in bed together, local knowledge must have indicated that this was a permanent rather than a temporary arrangement and so the minister and an elder 'applied to the Baillie of the parish' to send his officer 'to discharge them to cohabit together.' In another case a Session ordered the man concerned to pay a penalty of £10 Scots and also to promise on oath 'that he would not cohabit with Sarah C — any more and that he would not be seen there unless it were with company' and with this promise and payment of a penalty, he was absolved of the sin. Not everyone gave in so easily, however, and a man named William Cowbrough who continued to live with a woman after being forbidden to do so and failed to appear at a Presbytery meeting when called, was sentenced to Greater Excommunication.[30]

Home brewing, which has been mentioned in an earlier chapter, was an every-day part of domestic economy, mainly for home use but often allowing some for sale as well. It was done by both married and unmarried women but some Sessions thought that it was not something which should be done by the latter, probably because its availability whether offered in hospitality or paid for, would be an attraction to men. The following edict of the Presbytery of Fordyce in 1657 implies knowledge of some irresponsibility or scandal in connection with the practice: 'If there be any women within the Presbytery that be unmarried and scandalous brewars, they be restrained from brewing and if they will not desist, that they be excommunicated excommunication minori for their disobedience', in other words receive the sentence of Lesser Excommunication. In 1640 the Kirk Session of Kinghorn decreed that Isabell Blackadar should be prohibited 'from brewing and keeping ane hows hir selfe alone unmariet longer thane the malt qlk she has p'sentlie in her hows be brewed' — she was not only being forbidden to brew but also to live on her own any longer. This was something quite common, designed to prevent the appearance or the suspicion of sin. The Kirk Session of Perth were told in 1621 that Janet Watson 'holds ane house by herself, where she may give occasion of slander, therefore P. Pitcairne, elder, is ordained to admonish her in the Session's name either to marry or pass to service.' It was intimated from the pulpit of Fenwick church in 1653 that 'no young woman shall live alone without fitting and beseeming company,' something which was enforced the following year when several women were suspended from the Lord's Table for living alone. Some years before that, the Kirk Session of Tynninghame ordered that single women wishing to work in the parish must not only bring certificates of character but that no cothouses should be let to them without the consent and approval of the Session; and St. Andrews Kirk Session made an overture to the magistrates for an Act of the Town Council that whoever let accommodation to women on their own should have the rent confiscated for the use of the poor and so that no one could pretend they did not know about this, 'to cause the drum to be beat for that effect through the city.' At Elie, letting of houses to women on their own 'who ar able to work and will not abyd at service 'was forbidden in 1655, which may have been concern for their moral welfare but equally possibly may have been a labour regulation as the only way of finding alternative accommodation, other than with friends, was by entering service. Similarly in another parish, a girl whose parents were dead, was told not to continue to live on her own but 'to enter service with some honest person' by Whitsunday and as that was some months away 'to keep herself honest in the meantime.' Even when living perfectly virtuous lives, women on their own might be called before the Session to account for themselves. Christon Black appeared before St. Andrews Kirk Session in 1645 'for ane single householder' and though they 'found no scandal of her at this present time' they gave her permission to remain where she was only until the May term, after which she was told 'to go in service or to go and dwell with some of her own friends in ane house with them.' Even when not told to move in with other people, such women were liable to be watched, with elders expected to take notice 'of single women keeping house by themselves'.[31]

These instances of women living alone, with or without brewing, all appear comparatively harmless but there were cases where certain women were definitely not leading blameless lives. In 1649 a St. Andrews woman was delated for masking (brewing) ale at night and it was also alleged 'that she holds ane prophaine bawdrie house' which she denied although it was said that people went to her house at night. Proof must have been difficult to get in this case as she was only admonished with the threat that if she ever did the like again she would be severely punished. It was reported to Dumbarton Kirk Session in 1702 that a woman was entertaining people throughout Saturday nights and other times too. That she did this had already been established in a civil court and as the Session had already forbidden her to sell alcohol or to entertain people, they ordered her to appear publicly in church 'and that her house be declared an ill house and all within the congregation discharged to haunt the samen, under the pain of being prosecuted as scandalous persons.' Two months later she was found to be brewing as before and the Session asked the magistrates to suppress the house and, if that was ineffective, decided that they would seek help from the Presbytery.[32]

Fear of what women might get up to was a constant source of worry to the kirk and one can well understand the disapproval there was when several 'wives and maids' — women and girls — joined in 'unseemly recreations . . . under cloud of night' which consisted of the women running races and the girls putting the cannon stone, ongoings which attracted a large audience although this was not a matter of causing a nightly disturbance. Evening jollity was always considered a potential source of moral troubles, which lay behind Banff Kirk Session's forbidding people 'staying or keeping at public noddings after eight', although just what sort of activity a nodding was has not been discovered. What was feared could come to pass: in 1731 when Jean Knols was returning to her employer's house after a happy evening out, she was followed by a man and thrown to the ground. Her cries brought people to her rescue so swiftly that it was not known whether he had had 'any ill design against her' but so as to guard against any recurrence the Session 'recommended to the minister to advertise from the pulpit, the young persons in the parish to beware of night meetings in their neighbours' houses under pretence of mirth or drawing of valentines, in regard this scandal had happened upon the like occasion.'[33]

In spite of that example of a Kirk Session wishing to avoid girls being raped and in spite of St. Andrews Kirk Session making a man who had 'deflorit hir virginitie' give a dowry to a woman in accordance with her parents' wishes, as well as paying for the resultant child's maintenance, rape victims got fairly inconsiderate treatment from the male-dominated kirk. There seems to have been an idea that girls cried 'Rape' when it was nothing of the sort: the General Assembly decreed in 1707 that if a woman did not name the father of her child, as could happen in rape cases, then great prudence should be used, her former conduct inquired into 'and if she be of entire fame' (of good repute) 'she may be put to declare the truth, as if she were upon oath, but not without the advice of the Presbytery, and no formal oath should be taken.' When Elspeth Scott was raped one Sunday in 1696 she had to appear before her Session. She said that her attacker had been a gentleman and witnesses were called to the fact that on that particular day a gentleman on horseback had indeed been seen in her vicinity when she was out walking and later on she had been seen running after him with her hair hanging down, crying and calling out that he was a 'debauched rascal'. As if all that was not enough, the Presbytery advised the Session that she should appear before the congregation to be cleared of the scandal and in addition that she should be admonished for her 'light wandering on the Lord's Day when she was forced and ravished.' Some six years later another girl in that parish was raped by a trooper who followed her as she took food out to a man working in a barn and she too had to appear before the congregation to be purged and absolved of the scandal of being raped. When Agnes Pringle was raped in Kelso, the culprit was found to be a dragoon visiting the town. She too was summoned to her Session and told 'that since guilt could not be proved against her, the Session would wait until Providence should in time discover if she were so or not, in the meantime she was exhorted to be circumspect' and when it was apparent that she was pregnant, she was rebuked before the congregation. In each of these cases, the men did not live locally and appear to have got off entirely. With censure and public appearances in church for being raped, it is not surprising that some girls concealed what had happened and it was only if pregnancy resulted that they would mention the word rape. Sessions however were always suspicious about any case of alleged rape where the girl had not called for help or at least let someone know as soon as possible what had happened. Although the following case is not one of rape, it shows the extent to which women simply could not win. Anna God, a married woman, was delated for calling a man an adulterer and so as to explain things to the Session, described in graphic language what had happened one day as they were riding home together. He 'lighted off the horse from before her' saying it was to make water and then said, 'Will you let me shake my breaches upon you, it maybe will do more to you than your husband can do and your husband will miss nothing', all of which he began by denying but finally admitted and had to appear publicly — but she was rebuked for not reporting the scandal more timeously.[34]

It is debatable in this next case whether the girl or the man was at fault but all the Session's attention seems to have been focused on her: a servant girl in

Edinburgh, Jane Baptie, said that a man working in the same house had raped her but she had not called out because he forbade her to do so. It happened again, and again she did not call for help 'which gives the Session ground to think that she has been a snare to the youth, for had she cried the family below would easily have heard her. And because the Session suspect the said Jane to be a naughty woman, and are informed that she has been guilty with others' they proceeded against her with the type of questioning thought necessary. A case of assault, though not of rape, happened when Catherin Ross was walking by the highway near Inverness one day in 1723. Along came William MacRobert yst of Oirleachin, in company with an officer and an ensign of Colonel Kirk's regiment, who 'tossed and tumbled' her, dragged her into a cornfield, 'shuffled her clothes' and then MacRobert 'beat her naked body with a drawn broad sword.' He was summoned to appear before the Session but replied that he preferred to speak with the minister and any of the elders that he pleased, which was allowed, a clear case of favouritism due to social position, of which more later. In 1669 the Presbytery of Fordyce found that a number of young women were being surprised and carried off by force, especially in the upland areas, under pretence of marriage, and decreed that 'all such carriers away' should satisfy discipline as adulterers; but in 1732 a case which was treated as Sabbath profanation because of the day on which it happened, was really one of abduction, albeit only for one day. The brother of a laird in the highlands came with some servants by boat, broke into a house and dragged a girl from where she was trying to hide behind her dying mother's bed. Not even allowing her to put on shoes or stockings, they carried her off to the laird's house and kept her there till sunset when they took her home. This disgraceful matter went from Session to Presbytery to Synod and after some investigation, the guilty men were publicly rebuked. What happened to the girl is not known, nor whether for this abduction the men received civil punishment as well.[35]

During the politically troubled years of the seventeenth and first half of the eighteenth centuries, there were many times when troops were stationed around the country and the official kirk attitude to these men was stated by the General Assembly in 1697: ministers and Sessions were recommended to provide any troops quartered in their area with convenient seats for worshipping in church, 'to inspect and notice them, as they do other parishioners' and if necessary to apply to Commanding Officers to see that 'inferior officers and soldiers should attend ordinances and walk inoffensively' and to try to provide preachers and other ministers for regiments. Unfortunately, the men themselves were not very receptive to such concern for their welfare and were in general a great problem to the morals of any area in which they were based. Although several of the rape cases already mentioned involved soldiers, the fact is that to many of the female population the presence of troops was an irresistible attraction. Their smart uniforms compared well with the working clothes of local men and their tales of travel and dashing exploits, true or not, were much more exciting than anything an untravelled civilian could speak of. So far as soldiers were concerned, girls were almost unbelievably gullible and quite unaware of the risks of getting involved with men about whom they knew nothing and Kirk Sessions had to try to save them from themselves. A description of Kelso about 1708 when there was a troop of dragoons in the town sums up the kind of thing that happened. 'Deluded women' went off with them, as did others from the surrounding district, and not only were local women seduced but the presence of troops attracted women of loose morals from Edinburgh. The fact that a local girl was called before the Session for nothing more than speaking to a dragoon shows how serious was the problem at that time. She said she only asked him to deliver a letter for her but she was admonished and told that if she was found speaking to a dragoon again, she would be put out of the town. When Scone Kirk Session heard that a girl from the parish, then in service in Perth, had gone 'after the souldiers to Stirling' they did what they could by writing to the minister there about her, but when the minster of St. Nicholas Church, Aberdeen, wrote to his counterpart in Stirling in 1700 to find out if a soldier in Strathnaver's regiment who was there, was married or not, it was not to prevent trouble happening but to discover whether the girl's offence in Aberdeen was fornication or adultery. To be fair, not only soldiers ran off with girls. Ordinary civilians could do so too as a minute of 1790 shows. Finlay M'Donald was fined 10s. for running off with Catherine McLean but added insult to injury as a note alongside this minute says of the fine, 'Not Paid'.[36]

Bringing a case home to soldiers was very difficult. Although Inverness Kirk Session ordered some of their number to speak to a colonel stationed in the town about 'uncleanness committed by his soldiers' in the late seventeenth century, very few years later they were considering the difficulty of getting both men and officers to appear before the congregation and George Murray, writing about the parish of Falkirk, says that when a regiment was quartered there in 1753, with a great deal of debauchery going on, all Kirk Session references to this are retrospective and he suggests that either the Session could not find out the facts at the time, or lacked the courage to interfere then and there and waited to have it out with the inhabitants after the troops had left. This impression of reluctance to tangle with the army is strengthened by the fact that in Dunbar in 1659 a woman was rebuked and fined £20 Scots for immoral conduct when Cromwell's army had been in the neighbourhood eight years previously, although to be fair, scandals could lie out for a long time. The General Assembly was aware of the problem and in 1710 passed an Act to serve as guidance to the kirk in disciplining soldiers, advising ministers, Kirk Sessions and Presbyteries to apply to the magistrates and commanding officers, as need be, to crave that both officers and soldiers under scandal should be obliged to submit to the discipline of the church. When Sessions did try to deal with troops, however, the military authorities were not always co-operative. When the beadle of St. Cuthbert's Church, Edinburgh, was ordered to summon a soldier he reported that the man was not in a battalion of the Scots Greys as had been thought, but was under the command of a Major Cunninghame and 'therefore the Session did and hereby do refer the sd David to Major Cunninghame to oblige him to answer against next dyet.' A fortnight later the beadle reported that Major Cunninghame had said that David Bell was not in his company and as he himself was only a titular major he could not order his appearance before the Session and the beadle was told to try to find out who the commanding officer was. Certainly none of this was helpful but whether it was deliberately obstructive is not clear.[37]

Another group of men thought to pose a threat to the morals of a community was students and the Kirk Sessions in the four university towns of the time all had this problem to contend with. Examples from St. Andrews alone show the sort of thing that worried them. John Glasgow, a student at New College, had to be admonished by the Session in 1640 for 'nychtwalking and untymous byding out of the college' and was referred to the Magistrates of the College. Students did more than stay out of college at night; they also made up to women servants, hence this entry in 1645; 'The Session considering that the sin of fornication abounds, especially with students in this University, that has fallen in the sin with women that comes into their chambers, therefore Session thought it expedient that in time coming, no women shall be suffered to go within the colleges to do any service in them and this to be communicat to the masters of the three colleges.' As a close eye was being kept on their own morals, it perhaps gave students particular pleasure to be able to delate other people for immorality. In 1641 two who were walking in the fields met a girl gathering pease who told them that if they walked faster they would find two sinners lying together. This they did and found 'ane man and ane woman lying together in the act, whether of adultery, fornication or otherwise we know not.' They asked the couple their names and, although the man gave a false one, the woman gave hers correctly and was reported by the students to the Session. Although not really to do with this chapter, another matter to do with students was non-attendance at church on Sundays and, in St. Andrews again, because of this Sabbath profanation, the Session was instrumental in having the college authorities 'visit the fields in time of sermon upon the Lord's Day to prevent their students vaging there' and it seems very probable that their concern was as much to do with what the students were up to as anything else.[38]

In former days, the degrees of marriage which were forbidden were wider than they are today, which resulted in many charges of incest. In 1646 the kirk begged Parliament to ensure that such laws as there were about such matters should be made effective, 'these odious sins having grown to such a height of abomination as is horrid to express,' but it was not until three years later that Parliament laid down, in a very detailed way, just what relationships constituted incest. Kirk Session minutes, instead of stating simply what any particular relationship in a case was, always gave the tortuous progression from person to person whereby relationship and incest was established, which must have made it very difficult for elders, many of whom had little education, to try to decide the truth of things. Inter-marriage was inevitable in small rural communities when lack of transport made it difficult to find a spouse from outside, which made it possible for everyone to be related to everyone else in a district and many people were ignorant about what relationships were incestuous. In 1643 when a man was charged with incest with his first wife's sister's daughter (a niece by marriage and no blood relation) he said he did not understand about it and the matter had to be referred to the Presbytery. Some thirty years later than that, Margaret Downie who had fled seven years before from the discipline of Inverness Kirk Session for incest with her dead husband's brother's son (nephew by marriage) finally appeared before the Presbytery. Her mistake was also made through lack of knowledge, to the extent that she and her young man then asked if they might get married. Many cases were between women and nephews, men and nieces, and brothers and sisters-in-law. What made it even more difficult was that sexual intercourse with someone who had already had it with a close relation was also regarded as incest. Sometimes, of course, it was suspected where it did not exist. This happened to a poor widow whose son was stricken with fever and, having only one bed, she took him in with her. 'Poor thing,' she pleaded, 'what could I do with him but what I did?' 39

While most people committed incest in all innocence, there were some who knew perfectly well that they were doing wrong and did their best to conceal it. A Ross-shire woman was called before the Presbytery in 1686 because, having been guilty with her sister's husband, she got another man to accept paternity and to serve discipline for this. It was only later that it turned out that he was a relation of the guilty man and had done it 'to clok [cloak] that incest'. Almost thirty years earlier that Presbytery had had a tricky case to cope with — a youth who had 'fallen in incest and not coming to years of discretion.' Some cases were very protracted, such as that of John McTaggart who married a widow whose late husband, whose surname was McHarg, was a brother of McTaggart's grand- mother who was said to be the illegitimate daughter of McHarg's father. An unusual feature of this case was that McTaggart was defended by a solicitor when he came before the Presbytery of Ayr but the affair ultimately went to the General Assembly who left it to be dealt with by a commission, where it hung for six years during which time McTaggart and his wife were either made to live apart or only lived together under the censure of the church. It was only in 1738 that it was sent back, along with the case of John Baxter, an elder in Tealing, who had appealed in 1730 against the Synod's finding that his marriage to his dead wife's brother's daughter's daughter (great-niece by marriage) was incestuous but unfortunately the outcome of neither case is known. In 1701 a man named John Mackenzie petitioned his Presbytery saying that he had for a long time been on terms of marriage with Isobel Hassock, which seems to mean that they hoped to marry but that marriage had so far been refused them by the Session because he had formerly been married to her great-aunt. He seemed to think that it was an extenuating circumstance that his wife had been what he called 'father-children' and not 'mother-children' with Isobel's grandfather or grandmother and begged the Pres- bytery either to appoint one of their number to marry him, seeing that the pro- clamation of banns had passed, or else to write south for advice. The Presbytery decided that as things were, he could not be lawfully married to Isobel but they did appoint Mr Hugh Duff, minister of Fearn, to ask for advice when he went in six months' time to the General Assembly. Unfortunately there is a five-year gap in the Presbytery minutes after this, so there is no word of what happened in this case either. In another case, an old man's wife died. She had been a widow when he married her and he then wished to marry one of her daughters by her first marriage but this the kirk would not allow. Had it been explained to him properly and kindly why he could not do so, all might have been well as he was a reasonable man, but it was done so harshly that the couple simply went and got married in another parish where the circumstances were not known. The Session and the Presbytery did all they could to separate them but they refused to part and so the sentence of Greater Excommunication was pronounced and only lifted after his death at her request. Firm treatment was also meted out to an 'incestuous woman' who came from Skye and settled in Lochalsh, Ross-shire, from where she was ordered to be removed 'and not suffered to abyd in the country' unless she could produce a certificate of character from her minister in Skye.[40]

Depending to a great extent on whether the sin had stopped or not, punishments for incest varied widely — from removal out of the parish in 1649 to Greater Excommunication as late as 1817 to much milder public appearances for six Sundays in 1832 until nowadays when the offence is entirely handled by civil law. To some extent, of course, this also happened formerly and because such cases were difficult, any Session must have been thankful when they could pass them to courts of law. When a man in the parish of Lauder was found guilty of both adultery and incest, involving both civil and kirk punishments, the case was made worse by the woman fleeing and having to be brought back, after which the man took flight too. At this point the Session decided that they would proceed no further as, at that time, adultery was a capital offence. Even when the man returned and admitted his guilt, the Session maintained that it was not safe 'to meddle therein' until they saw whether the courts took the case up or not. However, when nearly a year went by with no civil action taken, they decided that they could no longer allow such a scandal to go unpunished and the minister consulted the bishop, these being Episcopal days, but he did not lift the problem off their shoulders and just empowered them to do as they saw fit. Civil courts do not seem to have been as enthusiastic in pursuing incest cases as Sessions were and in 1808, for example, the Lord Advocate would not take up a case involving a widow and her late husband's nephew and it was returned to their Session. Thorough investigations were always made before anyone guilty of incest was re-admitted to church privileges. When a woman who had gone to look after her dead sister's children and was accused of incest with her brother-in-law, asked to be accepted back into the kirk fold, it was reported that 'his sobriety is owing not to his having from any proper conviction given up his habits of drunkenness to which he was so notoriously addicted but merely from want of the means wherewith to gratify his evil propensity' which had nothing to do with the sin of incest, but at least the woman got a satisfactory report. As with other sins, offenders might have to speak with the minister and elders of the parish but one woman excommunicated for incest and asking to be received by the church once again was required 'to converse with the several brethren' (ministers) of the Presbytery of Dornoch, an onerous requirement as that Presbytery is a large and scattered one. The outcome of a case of incest which, though very long drawn out, must have been very gratifying to the kirk was that of John Grant, Glenmoriston, Inverness-shire, a papist who had some twenty years before been excommunicated for marriage to his late uncle's wife, a marriage performed by a Roman Catholic priest. In 1687, after her death, he returned to the reformed faith and the Presbytery received him back willingly.[41]

With so much official pursuit of sexual sins between men and women, it is not surprising that men turned to men. Professor Smout says, 'There is some indication that homosexuality also increased at the time of the most intense and hysterical puritan inquisitions in the middle of the [17th] century, though whether more was practised or more was found out . . . is an open question.' Burning was the punishment for offences of this 'horrible and unnatural kind' at that time and males of all ages, from boys to old men, were heard of every few months as being burnt on the Castle Hill of Edinburgh, sometimes two together, but while incest and homosexuality were very serious moral offences, they were as nothing compared to bestiality. It is said to have been unknown before the Reformation but to have grown to large proportions afterwards. While early Kirk Session records which are now lost, may refer to this vice, it seldom appears in later minutes but where it does, it shocked the affected communities as much as it did the kirk. Nigg, Ross-shire, was one parish where an instance of this 'dreadful wickedness' occurred in 1707 when 'William Taylor, son to Alexander Taylor, tenant of Shandwick, did commit bestiality with a cow and a mear'(mare). The whole parish was appalled and the Session 'considering the abominations abounding in the place, especially the above named gross wickedness does call aloud for mourning and humiliation, therefore they have set apart Wednesday next for a solemn humiliation within the parroch to be spent in prayer and fasting and the Acts of publick worship.' A similar incident occurred in St. Boswells in 1731. As a man was on his way to church one Sunday he saw 'William Wood, servant on the Templeland, with his clothes loose and his body appear, attempting the horrid abomination of bestiality with a brown horse beast, one of those he was keeping. When he called to him, he desisted from following the beast and clapsed down upon the ground.' He then got up and fled and although the Session, who were quickly informed, sent men in search of him he appears to have made good his escape.[42]

So far as the upper classes went, the official attitude to their discipline is apparent from the fact that an Act of Parliament laid down that they should be penalised for moral sins according to their quality — the higher the rank, the heavier the penalty. But this did not happen although some efforts were made to enforce it: in Dornoch the Episcopalian Bishop Wood was instrumental in having regulations laid down by Synod in 1687, enacting that delinquents of both sexes of 'of what qualities soever' should be 'equallie processed' because 'the passing by of noblemen and gentlemen makes people suppose the church doe them free from censure, and that they are not lyable to discipline as inferior persons are . . . the greater they are, the greater need there is that they be brought off their evil wayes, that they may be good examples to the meaner people.' That of course was more easily said than done, although a few members of the aristocracy did serve discipline such as the Earl of Lauderdale, forced by John Knox in 1563 to appear before the congregation at Largo, and the Countess of Argyll who appeared in sackcloth in church at Stirling in 1567. So did members of some landed families. William Lennox of Milnhouse, Kirkcudbright, made frequent appearances in 1704 which proved 'very satisfying' to the congregation; John Sinclair jr. also served discipline when named by a chambermaid in Lochalin House, Morvern, Argyllshire, as father of her child; but Session minutes in general show that, just as the gentry and the better off were allowed to pay fines rather than undergo public censure for ordinary sins so was much more lenient treatment given to their moral offences than would have been allowed to the common people. Sessions might go through the motions of citing them, perhaps asking Presbytery advice, but they did not follow up and pursue them as they might have done. Private conversation with the minister could be allowed in place of coming before the Session, conversation which could be delayed and delayed, presumably in the hopes that the whole business would ultimately die a natural death. These differing attitudes to different social classes appeared in a case in Elgin in the 1580s. James Douglas, the Provost, confessed fornication and said that he would obey church censure but pointed out that repentance did not consist in the external gesture of the body or public place of repentance but in the inner conscience and said that he wished to remain in his own seat during preaching and sermon and not in the place of repentance, and he confessed before the minister alone. Upon this the elders 'hearing his good meaning' agreed but, with a practical streak, ordered him to repair the north window with glass, which was a form of fine. Yet, the very next year a woman, also guilty of fornication, was treated quite differently, having to make repentance on Sunday barefoot and barelegged and she was threatened that if she ever did the same again, she would be banished. Contrasting treatment for comparable offences also occurred when a minister's nephew, guilty of fornication, excused himself from coming to give satisfaction and the Session just said that they 'know not how farder to proceed in the matter for the time.' To be fair, the youth was by then at Oxford; but the following year the minutes show that 'This day Agnes Leishman sometime in the paroch of Ettrick was cited from the pulpit as fugitive from church discipline and the people exhorted to use their utmost diligence for discovering apprehending and bringing in the said Agnes Leishman to church discipline.'[43]

The following cases are all examples of favouritism. In 1710 John Don of Attonburn was cited to Kelso Kirk Session for immorality but 'signified his inclination to see the minister at his [the minister's] house' and as the minister wished to discuss several other aspects of his conduct with him and also 'fearing lest the citing of him might have deprived the minister of an opportunity of discoursing with him on these things' the Session delayed calling him for the time being. At a later meeting, his case was again delayed, 'the minister having had no seasonable opportunity of speaking with him, and now the Sacrament approaches' and after that was over, the case was again delayed 'till the minister have an opportunity to meet with him.' There is no record of what happened in the end but the Session seems to have been trying hard to justify the delay being allowed. Similarly, in 1736 Alexander Ross of Ankerville was accused of fathering the child of one of his maids. He was in London at the time and could not attend the Session meeting but on his return it was the minister who 'conversed with him privately' and it was agreed that, although he could not be present at the ensuing meeting of Session, he would come to the following one. But this he did not do and just continued to make excuses for non-appearance although he had admitted his guilt to the minister. The minute book closes, perhaps conveniently, at this point and there is no way of knowing what happened in the end. Another case which was allowed to drag on began in Edinburgh in February 1708. Elspeth Clerk said she was guilty of fornication with Colonel John Hamilton whereupon 'The Moderator asked the said Elspeth what documents she could give to prove that Colonel Hamilton was guilty with her', an unusual step to take. She replied that he had paid for her midwife and when her baby died, paid for its burial and since then he had sent money to her via a gardener. 'Session recommend to their Revd. ministers to write to the Colonel anent the said affair and refer the said Elspeth to the Baillie for her fine.' (There were two ministers in this Edinburgh parish and this is not a reference to the Presbytery.) In March the minutes say, 'Session considering that the times are somewhat perplexed at this juncture because of a threatening invasion by the French who were seen upon 13 of this instant about the may upon the [ink blot] of the ffirth. Delay Col. Hamilton and Elspeth Clerk till the perplexity be over.' Again one cannot help feeling that the 'perplexity' was almost a welcome justification for more delay but it was over by June and the Session ordered a written summons to be sent to the gallant soldier. He did not, however, appear and so in July they recommended a baillie to 'converse' with him. In April 1709 this affair was still going on, without Colonel Hamilton appearing and although an entry on 7 April says 'Col. Hamilton still continued', it is noticeable that the margin annotations, which give the names of those referred to in the minutes, never include his, so he must have been part of the anonymous 'etc' attached to some names in the margin, which seems a way of avoiding drawing attention to him. There was obviously no difficulty about locating him so one can only infer that the Session were not anxious to press the matter.[44]

In January 1703 an Ashkirk girl became pregnant by Robert Scott, a local laird and, although he suggested to her that she should leave the district until after the birth, she preferred to stay where she was, to confess and to satisfy discipline, all of which she did. The Session instructed the minister to speak with Scott but when he went to his house, he found him absent and ordered him to come to the manse instead, which he refused to do. The kirk officer then 'affixed and left a written summonds upon the Lock-hole of his Door according to appointment, Whereupon he was ordered to call him three times at the church door which he did but he compeared not, whereupon he was declared Contumaciouse.' It was reported that Scott had said that he would speak or write to the minster and he did indeed write, saying he was willing to serve discipline and asking at the same time if the minister would write a couple of lines to his counterpart at Wilton, Hawick, so that the child could be baptised. Before this could be done, of course, Scott had to appear before the Session and admit paternity which he did and so the Session allowed a letter to be written about the baptism, with the laird of Woll, who was an elder, becoming cautioner that Scott would satisfy discipline. That was in May 1703 but Scott did not do what he had promised and in October, Woll wrote to him telling him that he must do so. He appeared once before the congregation in November and was ordered to continue his public repentance but as he had not appeared again by June the following year the Session sent extracts of the girl's confession to the Hawick minister asking him to summon him before that congregation. That was simply passing the buck rather than grasping a nettle; and while the Session had attempted to discipline him, the matter should in the end at the very least have been referred to the Presbytery, even possibly to the point of excommunication for contumacy as would have happened to other people at that date. Furthermore, nothing seems to have happened about the laird of Woll who was cautioner but failed to enforce Scott's repentance. A case which leaves an unpleasant impression, although the elders may have known more than the minutes say, was that of a girl in Banff who named the son of the laird of Meldrums as the father of her child. It did not help that she was a Roman Catholic, of course, but the minutes say that she appeared and proved contumacious in spite of the fact that there does not seem to be any evidence of particular resistance to the Session, and that she 'continued to frequent company, both here and elsewhere'. They therefore passed her to the magistrates 'to punish her according to the law in regard this is a proper mean to dispose obstinate sinners subject to the discipline of the church . . .' Was she an immoral girl, as the remark about frequenting company implies, or was she being slapped down for her assertion about her child's father? Favouritism to a laird's family also appeared in the parish of Sorbie in 1702. Katharine Baird confessed to the minister that she had had a child in adultery to the Laird of Barnbarroch yr. 'The session considering this woman is but lately come to this parish and that the sin was committed and the scandal given in the parish of Kirkinner, they do not think fit to meddle with her, only they desire the minster to carry this her confession and put it to the next Presbytery.' That was a perfectly proper action on their part in the circumstances but when the minister offered to table her confession at the Presbytery meeting 'they would not receive it, being it was extra judiciall' and he was told to cite her to his own Session who then referred her to the Presbytery. There is no more in the minute book at this point and not a word of any censure going the way of the man concerned nor any information being sent to his Session.[45]

In 1775 Colonel Mackay of Balnakeil admitted to Durness Kirk Session that he was the father of the child of a maid in his household. He accompanied the girl to the Session meeting and told them roundly that he would not order her out of the house as they wanted him to do; she would remain until Whitsunday or until the child was weaned and while she would satisfy the church, the Kirk Session would not force him to turn off a servant so long as he had a mind to keep her. He insisted on them accepting from him a fine for the girl's offence, saying this was the custom elsewhere, which they took although they pointed out that they 'could not and would not sell any Indulgences.' The Session in this case continued to try to cite both of them and to make the girl leave Balnakeil but a reason for delay was still allowed to slip in: 'The design of summoning them was to persuade them to separate. There was a copy of the summons extended and ready to be sent to the Colonel but because of the paucity of members, it was agreed to defer proceedings.' Faced with the Colonel's strong will the Session comforted themselves with the belief that the girl would leave in the end but realised that they could not achieve her departure at that moment and that giving him more citations would be of little use, and so they simply referred it to the Presbytery. When Mary Smith came to the minister of Foveran in 1748 to say that she was pregnant and named Benjamin Forbes yr. of Edinglassie, her employer's son, as the father, she was able to support her statement with a letter the young man had written her:

> I received a note concerning you being with child which I am sorry for, however your best is to leave the town and go up the country among your acquaintance, for my Mother will be unsupportable if she find you out to be with child in her service. Since you lay the blame on me, I can't help it, but since you did, if you have a boy, you'll call his name Findlay. I'm just going to sail, so you'll best take my advice and leave the town. I am, your Friend, Benjm Forbes.
>
> PS. If the child be mine, it's been gotten when asleep, however, when I return to the country, shall find the certainty of that, and take care of it, if it be mine. Adieu.'

Mary asked to be allowed to make repentance and appeared three times but, yet again, there is no mention in the minutes about the young man and what happened to him. A doctor told Dollar Kirk Session that a woman had called him in to ascertain whether her daughter, Betty, was pregnant, which she was. He suggested that she should name the father but when she said Taylor the Engineer, her mother and sisters fell upon her and the doctor had to intervene to protect her. 'After their beating and abuse she at length gave William Henderson as the father of her child, on which the mother was much pleased' but three days later the Session found — decided, would perhaps be a better word — that there was no evidence for the girl's assertion 'and therefore dismiss the case, Apologize William Henderson and relieve him from the scandal.' Although it is not so stated, there is a clear impression that Henderson was a man of standing whose position was such that the Kirk Session were kowtowing to him. Even when a Session did successfully pursue a sprig of the gentry, the sentence imposed might be ludicrously light according to the standards of the times. Inverness Kirk Session harried young Alexander Fraser of Culduthel for four years for keeping a woman in his house but it appears that it was only when a baby was on the way that he appeared before them and the congregation, whereupon the Session, feeling that his outward appearance was sufficiently repentant, 'voted that his rebuke yesterday and exhortation should serve for his absolvitor', a mild sentence indeed after four years of contumacy and persistent co-habitation.[46] Even when a landowner submitted to church censure special consideration might be shown. Some members of Chirnside Kirk Session pointed out in December 1699 that Alexander Home of Blackburn had appeared many times before the congregation and had expected to be absolved on a particular day and that his 'humour is eagerly capable of Irritation'; as a result it was agreed to absolve him the following Sunday.

Having said all that, it needs to be said yet again that the kirk depended on heritors for much of their finance and individual elders could not afford to offend landlords and it is therefore all the more surprising to read the minutes of Latheron Kirk Session, Caithness, for November, 1762. A petition, signed by two elders, was presented to the Session saying that they were 'not a little surprised' that no step had been taken by the minister to have removed from the house of James Sinclair of Dunbeath a woman named Janet Robertson who, about three years previously, had had his child. She was married, there was no legal evidence of her husband's death and she had already had three illegitimate children, something well known to the Session, and for the third of these she should have made public satisfaction in sackcloth according to the rules of the church. In fact, a fine had been accepted but the minister had failed to report the case to the Presbytery as he should have done, nor was Janet ever ordered to come to any Session meeting; furthermore, without the knowledge of the Session, her child had been baptised the day after its birth. The two elders said that they were alarmed that 'giving sanction to vice in this manner might endanger the cause of virtue and religion' and referred to the countenance given to what they called this 'Worthless Woman', making it clear that they would not name those who were failing in their duty at that point but could and would do so when properly called upon. They moved that the woman should be made to leave his house and the parish too and asked the Session to consider whether or not she should stand in sackcloth. This resulted in the minister and some of the elders going to see Sinclair who said he was an infirm old man but that he would do all he could to oblige them, but only as soon as he could get another servant. The Session then decided that it should all be laid before the Presbytery who returned an answer which more or less let Sinclair off but reprimanded the two elders who had been brave enough to bring the matter up, an almost classic case of favouritism.[47]

Although it is not clear just what the outrage was which four men and a woman inflicted on a poor cottar woman in the parish of Falkirk in 1699, it was certainly done without reason or provocation and although not apparently a moral offence, it may be mentioned here as showing the different treatment meted out to different people. The case does not appear in Falkirk Kirk Session's minutes, which it should have done as it happened within their bounds. It was the Presbytery who heard about it with horror and wanted the principal offender to appear before them but as he lived outside their jurisdiction they had to write to the minister of Larbert, Stirlingshire, about him. This minister, apparently to shield one of his most important parishioners, himself appeared at the next Presbytery meeting and reported that he had spoken, not with the man concerned but with his wife who said that they had thought nothing of the incident and that it was not worth the

Presbytery's time to trouble with it. The Presbytery ordered the minister to summon him, but he did not come and a deputation was sent to see him, to whom he confessed and offered to give the woman something 'in charity'. The Presbytery stood up to him and made him appear and plead forgiveness; it was Falkirk Kirk Session who were lax.[48]

If one goes by Kirk Session minutes, famines seem to have had either a beneficial or a detrimental effect on moral standards. In some, such as Fordyce, the Seven Years' Famine put an end to adultery and fornication for some time, where these had previously been common, whereas in Nigg, Ross-shire, there was said to have been a startling decline in morals after it. It seems probable, however, that the presence or absence of recorded immorality had something to do with the ability of a Kirk Session in post-famine years to seek it out. But the various changes which overtook the church over the years, which have already been mentioned, ultimately resulted in moral matters leaving their care too at local level.[49]

12
Witchcraft and Superstition

Witchcraft in itself was not a crime in Scotland prior to the Reformation but could, if necessary, be dealt with under other laws. After the Reformation, however, things changed and Professor Smout, who is considerably quoted in the first few pages of this chapter, says that from 1560 until after the Union of the Parliaments in 1707 more than 3,000 people, perhaps even as many as 4,500, were executed in Scotland as witches whereas in England, with a population five times greater, only about 1,000 were put to death. He suggests, however, that what caused such persecution was not the Reformation itself but an influence which came from the Continent, where publication in the late fifteenth century of the *Malleus Maleficarum*, a compendium of witchcraft compiled by two priests, Jacob Sprenger and Heinrich Krämer, gave the impression that all the rural superstitions of Europe were a vast conspiracy organised by the devil and his witches against man and the church. Little wonder that in 1484 the Pope published a bill enjoining the extirpation of sorcerers and that for 150 years thereafter many parts of Europe were swept by wave after wave of persecution. In addition to the *Malleus Maleficarum*, sixteenth century European writing and thinking about the threat of witchcraft influenced those Scots who travelled to the Continent or who read the works of European writers. Both the church and the law accepted the literal interpretation of the text from Exodus, 'Thou shalt not suffer a witch to live' but it was only in 1563 that witchcraft became an offence in Scotland, with death the penalty for both witches and their clients. In the next thirty years, however, while there were some trials, they did not necessarily end in conviction and even if they did, the witch might not be executed. In 1580, for instance, Perth Kirk Session merely banished a witch from the town and although two years later one was immured in the tolbooth, the Session ordered the boxmaster to give her eight doits per day, while in 1589 the minutes actually record a false accusation of witchcraft. The first witchcraft trial in St. Andrews was in the mid 1570s but when the accused woman and her husband fled no attempt was made, so far as can be seen, to find them, and in 1581 when another woman failed to appear before the Session to answer a charge of witch-craft, no further action seems to have been taken in that case either.[1] None of that indicates any great enthusiasm for witch-hunting but things changed in the 1590s, beginning with a notorious case in North Berwick when some witches confessed under torture to trying to kill the king by conjuring up a storm to sink the ship in which he was returning from Denmark with his bride. This was soon followed by great efforts to seek out witches, something which began to die down towards the end of the decade, only to be revived by publication of James VI's treatise on witchcraft, *Daemonologie*, and by an order from the General Assembly that Presbyteries must in future take action against any magistrates who set free anyone convicted of witchcraft. Thereafter persecution of witches went in waves. It was very bad in the 1620s and, thanks to several Acts of the General Assembly, in the 1640s too. One of the Acts, in 1640, was designed 'to take notice of witches and witchcraft' while another in 1643 began by saying that it was gross ignorance, infidelity, want of love of the truth and profaneness of life that were the causes of a great increase in witchcraft and went on to recom-mend the establishment of a legal standing commission of 'understanding' gen-tlemen and magistrates in areas where Presbyteries might ask for them, with power to arrest, try and carry out justice against witches. Parliament backed this up in 1644, providing that a number of lawyers and doctors should consult with certain divines and ministers concerning the punishment of witches. It was in 1649 that the General Assembly appointed a Commission of ministers, lawyers and physicians to see to the trial and punishment of witchcraft, charming and consulting, and as a result, Kirk Session minutes of that date show how ministers asked their elders 'to make search everywhere in their own quarters if they knew of any witches or charmers in the parish and to delate them to the next Session.' Quite clearly, therefore, the church from top to bottom became involved in witch-hunting although even the most diligent searching might result in reports that 'they had not yet found any clear ground against anyone for sorcery or witchcraft.'[2]

At this time life was already very difficult for the common people of Scot-land. In their enthusiasm to rid the country of everything popish, the Reformers had destroyed many of the tangible ecclesiastical items, such as holy relics, in which people had formerly placed their trust — destruction of 'superstitious monuments' in churches was still going on in the mid-seventeenth century — and so there were no relics to touch when seeking cures, no effigies to pray before, and to go on pilgrimage to special places to seek help or forgiveness was forbidden. All this was at a time when there were insufficient Reformed clergy to fill the places of the Roman Catholic priests who were removed at the Refor-mation and a climate was created in which simple people, with no one to help or guide them, turned to witchcraft and superstition even more than before, as the only alternative they could see. Many of the practices to which they turned were ancient ones: in *Druidism Exhumed* James Rust says that some of the supersti-tions still current in the seventeenth century went back to druidical days. The help of the devil or 'Old Goodman' as he was sometimes called, could be sought either by leaving a little grain in the ground for him or by having in the parish some patch of land known variously as the Goodman's Croft, Halie Man's Rig, Cloutie's Croft or the Black Faulie (fold, sheepfold), regarded as his and left untilled as an offering to avert his malice from the crops. This happened in many places; in the parish of Elgin, for one, some men were called before the Kirk Session in 1602 to explain why they had 'reserved a peise land to the devill callit the Gudeman's' and gave as their reason that it was in the hope that he would not harm their stock or crops. A Presbyterial visitation of the parish of Boyndie in 1649 elicited the information that 'there was some piece of land in this parochin unlaboured (called the halie man's ley) dedicated to superstitious uses'. When the minister of Slains asked his elders that year whether they knew of any land in the parish 'that was calit the goodmanes or fauld or dedicatit to Satane or lattine unlabourit', he was told that there was such a place on one man's land; a month later a further goodman's fauld was reported, which the occupier promised to till, which was the kirk's immediate solution to this practice. Slains also had druidical fields where people went to work charms and spells, as well as three places dedicated to the fairies. Such superstitious practices continued for a long time; as late as 1861 Sir James Simpson, the discoverer of chloroform, told how a relative of his had bought a farm near Edinburgh only a few years previously and that one of the first things he did was to enclose a small triangular corner with a stone wall to be such a 'croft'. 1649 also saw a case of alleged idolatry. A man was said to have set up a stone and 'used superstitious ceremonies to it', such as doffing his bonnet before it. According to him, he had erected it as nothing more than a march stone and he denied any worship or ceremonies in connection with it offering to give his oath about this but the outcome was that two elders and two 'honest men' were appointed to go and see him break it up.[3]

The English government which ruled the country in the 1650s more or less prohibited witchcraft trials but after the Restoration of 1661, says Professor Smout, the 'flood-gates of restraint burst, and cases that had been festering in local communities for a decade were brought to justice.' This made the 1660s, especially the early years of the decade, a time of terrible persecution but successful witch trials became increasingly unusual from 1680 onwards and although the General Assembly revised some of their former Acts against witchcraft in 1700, active persecution seems thereafter to have depended very largely on the zeal of particular ministers.[4]

Although there are a few instances of the nobility and gentry being involved in witchcraft, it was something almost entirely associated with the common people and what does seem extraordinary is that the peasantry who already suffered so much repression themselves, were ready to see terrible indignities and torture inflicted on helpless people of their own class. Unfortunately, it was only too easy to attribute anything and everything, be it disaster, epidemic or just a sick cow, to the machinations of witchcraft and equally easy for mass hysteria to grab a community so that the finger of suspicion, and then of direct accusation, was pointed at some old woman — it almost always was an old woman — who seemed to fit the bill by being ugly, withered, morose, possibly a bit of a virago, living aloof from others. Many of these were completely innocent but many so-called witches practised their craft at a simple level, allowing people to think that they could put a spell on anyone who annoyed them and, should something out of the ordinary happen, they let it be thought that it was the result of their skills. Thus they were held in a kind of fearful respect which made them feel important and gave them a reputation which discouraged people from offending them and persuaded them to do little favours instead. They were glad to be able to make a living from people prepared to pay cash or to offer food for services rendered, be it a simple herbal cure or something more potent. However, Professor Smout says that it seems likely that aspects of the Reformed religion affected the character of witchcraft, 'so that in addition to witches who were no more than herbalists there arose a class of deluded Satanists who really believed that they had sold themselves to the devil. The power of preachers on a simple rural population should not be underestimated — Sunday by Sunday they poured out dreadful warnings and vivid descriptions of hellfire and the personal devil, a piercing insistence on predestination, and on the hopelessness of a man ever attempting to earn redemption by his own efforts and spiritual strivings' and so it is not surprising that some came to 'believe that they were irretrievably damned, and being damned were the devil's own servants, and as servants should become witches and learn to imitate the rites which were so widely publicised by confessions at witchcraft trials.'[5]

Witchcraft as defined in the king's *Daemonologie* consisted of holding meetings and making conventions with Satan, renouncing baptism and injuring people who had caused displeasure but when those accused of witchcraft were asked questions about renouncing baptism or convening with the Evil One, what sort of replies could they be expected to give? Simple minds had no idea of what the questions meant, let alone how to answer them and it seems likely that many just agreed with what was put to them through sheer lack of understanding and as it was believed that witchcraft was practised in covens of thirteen, when one witch was induced to confess, it followed that there should be twelve associates and these she was expected to name. Torture made many a woman admit to witchcraft of which she was innocent and involve other equally innocent people, who were put to death as a result.[6]

A case which came before Kirkcudbright Kirk Session early in 1702 is a good example of how readily witchcraft could be imputed to someone and how, that having been done, other people tried to dredge their memories for anything they could think of to fuel the fires of accusation. A woman named Janet McRobert had kindly helped another woman thresh grain and then had asked for some chaff for her cow. She was given a little in her apron and the implication is that she did not consider it enough as the woman who gave it to her, a nursing mother, found afterwards that her left breast was badly swollen and also that her own cow began to give milk with a bad taste and colour. Witchcraft was immediately suspected and witnesses were called by the Session, one of whom came out with the allegation that at his son's lykewake, the watch over a corpse before burial, three years previously, one of Janet's poultry had made a great deal of noise — one's mind boggles at the idea that such a thing could support an accusation of witchcraft. What would have happened to Janet in earlier years may be imagined but this being 1702, and more rational thought prevailing, the commission to which this information was passed, regarded it as a trumped-up case — Janet had said that the noisy hen was just a clocken one — and so the Kirk Session minutes of 10 April that year say, 'As to Janet McRobert, an extract of the delations against her being sent to Edinburgh and a Commission written for to pursue her legally, it was denied in regard they judged the delations not to be sufficient presumphons of guilt so as to found a process of that nature . . .' but notwithstanding that, Janet agreed to banishment and went to Ireland. Just a year later, Twynholm Kirk Session, also in the county of Kirkcudbright, proved a case of witchcraft but the witch claimed the right of banishment and was sent away under threat of the death penalty if she returned; and excommunication could also be imposed for witchcraft.[7]

In a case in 1666, as that decade's persecution was beginning to die down, it was a minister who insisted on sensible investigations before allowing allegations of witchcraft to develop into a major matter. Four widows, whose husbands had all died suddenly at sea while fishing, were all required to appear before the minister and elders before sermon one day

> because several people in the island had declared that they had been troubled with dreams and apparitions by them, as if they had spoken to them, saying that they had perished by wicked persons, servants of Satan, having cursed them, whereby the hearts of the said spouses were much troubled and earnestly desired the minister to intimate that inspection might be made of their graves to see if any wickedness might be brought to light concerning them. After the sermon and prayer, the minister did intimate this and the next day, the parish convened, and thereafter the minister went to the pulpit and prayed, and then accompanied by the bailzie and the Session, and several other honest persons, went and inspected the opened graves of two of the men.

Several people who had seen the bodies when they were first found and 'did handle them and wynd them when they were buried, were now caused to handle their naked bodies, and no suspicion of evil was found. The minister then publicly exhorted the people to lay aside all sinistrous and evil thoughts towards any people and if any should reproach any of them afterwards, they should be punished.'[8]

Ministers were often called upon to assist in obtaining confessions from witches. In 1661 Sir John Veitch of Dawyck and Alexander Baillie of Flemington Mill, both Commissioners for the trial of witches, asked the Presbytery of Peebles to send some of their number to Traquair to bring two witches to admission of their guilt and to prepare them for death and, as a result, three ministers were ordered to go to the execution which took place at Traquair. In the same way, Mr David Munro, minister of Kilconquhar, was appointed by the Presbytery to go to Anstruther-Easter and Crail to speak to some people arrested as witches. Strictly speaking, Kirk Sessions were only involved in deciding whether or not delations of witchcraft made to them should be sent to higher courts for trial, but in practice they could have a great deal to do with the whole process, sometimes in conjunction with burgh authorities and sometimes not. At Kinghorn, after Katharine Walenge and Jonnet Smythe had been imprisoned as alleged witches, the Session appointed eleven men to accompany the minister to examine those accusing them and also to go with him 'when he goes to examine the persons empressed and to do their best endeavours to bring them to confession.' By February of the following year, the process against one of them was sufficiently advanced for the Session to instruct two men to go to Edinburgh about her, 'to put her to assize', with the result that she was condemned and burnt to death in March 1644. In cases of witchcraft, as with other lesser crimes, there was always anxiety to establish guilt, which is apparent in the case of Isabel Malcolm who was convicted of charming by the Presbytery of Strathbogie but had her case continued 'in the hope that she should be found yet more guilty'. At that date, even when a particular charge of witchcraft could not be made, Sessions were reluctant to leave things at that, so that in 1644 the Kirk Session of St. Cuthbert's Church, Edinburgh, having in vain asked for evidence against Marion Fisher, ordered her to make repentance, not for being a witch but for being suspected of it.[9]

In 1606 the Kirk Session of Deer were ordered by the Presbytery 'to proceed in taking ane inquest and tryell of witches' and as one way of discovering a witch was by witch-pricking, this was something which Sessions used to have to arrange. The physical examinations by midwives to which various women submitted were as nothing to what happened to a suspected witch. So that pricking could be done, a woman was stripped and a man 'skilled in the art' would prick all over her body until he claimed to have found a so-called 'witch-mark,' often a mole or birthmark, that was insensitive to pain or that would not bleed, which was thought to indicate that she had been marked by the devil for his own purposes; this alone was enough to prove guilt. Witch-prickers were specialists and often had to be sent for from a distance: in 1633 the Kirk Session of Kirkcaldy had to pay someone to go to fetch 'the man that tries the witches' and another year the Presbytery of Lanark 'sent for George Cuthie the pricker who hath skill to find out their mark.' John Kincaid, a witch-pricker whose reputation rested on his use of 6-inch and 8-inch needles, which were 3–5 inches longer than usual, had a considerable reputation with the clergy until he made the mistake of accusing a noble lady and found himself in prison at Kinross. One witch-pricker whose name was Paterson travelled all over Scotland in pursuit of this unpleasant art and became rich enough to employ a couple of servants. His method was to run the palms of his hands over the women's bodies, then stick a long brass pin into their flesh, up to its head, and ask them to find it. In one case at least, he began by cutting off the witches' hair, piling it all together and hiding it behind a nearby stone dyke, before proceeding to the pricking. Some did more than prick their victims, favouring vaginal examinations, 'knowing by certain pro-truberances or a sustained issue' that suspects had had commerce with the devil.[10]

This awful procedure sometimes, and perhaps often, took place within church buildings for the very good reason that in many parishes they were the only public places. A woodcut by Douglas Percy Bliss in 'The Devil in Scotland' shows it taking place in a church in the presence of a number of men. One confession, with or without pricking, even took place on a Sunday 'between sermon'. When fourteen women and one man were pricked by Paterson in War-dlaw Church, Inverness-shire, there must have been real sadism as well as sal-acious enjoyment for the pricker in handling a woman's body in this way and also for those watching what was going on. It was pornography in practice, something not altered by the fact that Paterson was later discovered to be a woman in disguise.[11]

While Kirk Sessions do not seem to have been involved in the shocking forms of torture which were applied to accused witches by the civil authorities, they might put a witch's bridle upon them, something similar to the branks but with four inward-facing prongs which lacerated the mouth, and they certainly de-prived suspected persons of sleep in attempts to extract confessions. Skilful 'wakers' took turns of this, although in some parishes such as Dunfermline, every householder had in the mid-seventeenth century to take his turn of keeping them awake. In 1643 a woman complained to the Privy Council that she was kept awake for twenty days, naked except for a sackcloth, but it is not clear if that was the doing of the kirk or not. It seems to have been witch-waking that caused an East Lothian Session to 'set down orders anent the watching of those that are apprehended for witchcraft nichtlie, sex to watch every nicht and twa every day . . . and ane elder every nicht with them.' The only other possible reason for this additional night watch may have been that those guarding an alleged witch required extra people to hold their hands — after all, what super-natural and nocturnal assistance might not a witch be able to call up? All this, of course, could cost the kirk money; the elders of that parish reported 'that it was hard to get people to watch all the day (albeit the witch was precisely observed all the nicht) and therefore it behoved to take something from the box, or rather to borrow . . .' and as watching could not be done in the dark, there might be such extra expenses as 'a candle to watch the witch.'[12]

Should the result of these procedures indicate guilt, as it virtually always did, then Sessions were required to pass all the information to the Presbytery and the Commission but, even so, the final trial of any witch could still be held locally by that Commission. In 1662 the trial of some witches in Forfar took place in the Session House, with admissions made to the minister and gentlemen of the Commission, and another example of this was at Tynninghame where in 1650 the minister informed his elders that the Commission to try David Steward and

Agnes Kirkland had 'come east' and the following Tuesday had been fixed for their assize, when all the elders and honest men were instructed to be present. Their fate was soon sealed and 'upon the nynt of April, Being Tysday, 1650, David Steward and Agnes Kirkland were execut' but in the time between assize and execution, the minister constantly prayed and read with them. Condemned witches were often, though not invariably, burnt locally. Records from East Lothian during the first half of the seventeenth century include such entries as 'Upon Tysday January 22nd ane man in Whittinghame brunt for witchcraft' or 'Upon Wednesday six people at Stentoun parish brunt', while on one occasion ten alleged witches were burnt at Dunbar and on another, two at Tynninghame. Ministers were expected to attend executions in nearby parishes and were appointed by Presbyteries to do so, like Mr John Lauder, minister of Tynninghame, who attended the burning of the ten witches at Dunbar, 'being ordanit thereto'. One writer, describing the county of Angus said that ministers and elders even 'found it expedient in several instances to postpone church services in order that they and their fellow Christians might be present at such shocking displays of inhumanity', and there is no reason to think that such things were confined to Angus.[13]

Although witchcraft was a civil offence, Kirk Sessions might contribute to the expense of executing witches. 'The kirk's part' of the cost of burning William Coke and Alison Dick on the sands at Kirkcaldy was made up as follows:

To Mr. John Miller, when he went to Preston for a man [probably a witch-pricker]	£ 2	7	—
To the man of Culross, when he went away the first time [also probably a pricker]	—	12	—
For coals for the witches	1	4	—
In purchasing the commission [permission for trial and execution]	9	3	—
For one to go to Finmouth for the laird to sit upon their assize as judge	—	6	—
For harden to be jumps to them	3	10	—
For making of them	—	8	—
Total [Scots]	£17	10	—

The town's contribution included more coal, a barrel of tar, tows, a man to fetch the executioner and his payment and expenses.[14]

As has been said, witch-hunting ebbed and flowed but when the climate was right for it as it was in the 1620s, 1640s and the earlier part of the 1660s, a fanatical minister could contribute very greatly to its virulence. James Guthrie, incumbent of Lauder from 1642–50, is said to have been so active, in conjunction with the magistrates, that sometimes the tolbooth could not hold all who had been delated and some witches had to be put to death before others could be cited and arrested. Some of the worst cases occurred in Mr Guthrie's last year there, the year in which he was made a member of the newly established Commission for trial and punishment of witches, and in the early twentieth century, digging at a knoll known as the Witches' Knowe near Lauder is said to have produced the remains of thirty bodies, with evidence of burning on some stones, and all the victims' heads turned in the opposite way to what is usual, to indicate that as witches, there was no hope for them after death. Another anti-witch enthusiast was Mr John Dysart at Coldingham from 1694 until about 1725 who, particularly in 1698, was very much involved with witchcraft cases there. Although witch-hunting died down in the early 1700s, it broke out again in Sutherland in the 1720s, largely thanks to two newly appointed ministers, Robert Robertson who came to Loth in 1721 and Francis Robertson who arrived in Clyne in 1719. By 1727 Mr Robert Robertson was in active pursuit of witches, almost certainly because he regarded himself as a victim of their attentions, in particular Janet Horne and her daughter, who lived in the parish of Loth. There are differing stories and dates about this case and Janet's execution is put at either 1722 or 1727 but, whichever is right, hers was the last witch-burning in Scotland. Caithness also suffered from some late witch-hunting. In 1719 several suspected witches were imprisoned in Thurso and the Presbytery was anxious that they should be kept separate from other prisoners 'in respect, it was suggested, that they hardened one another by their mutual conversation', a sentiment which would appeal to modern prison reformers but did not apparently have much effect in Thurso at that time.[15]

Throughout all this, Kirk Sessions truly believed that they were doing the Lord's work and will, by not suffering witches to live and, unfortunately, they could be unwittingly used by various vested interests. Some landowners such as Chisholm of Comar managed to get rid of undesirable or wealthy tenants in the early 1660s by accusing them of witchcraft. The medical profession also was not keen on herbalists who could undermine their interests and were only too keen for the kirk to weed out as witches those who would now be called practioners of alternative medicine, and would therefore initiate actions against them: for instance, Thomas Grieve, an Edinburgh man, was executed in 1623 as a result of a process instigated by the Surgeon's Guild. His crime was curing William Cousin's wife by having her husband heat the coulter of his plough, then cool it in water from a holy well which she was given to drink. Perth's Kirk Session records also show that medical men informed against herbalists purely to protect their own financial interests.[16]

To be accused of being a witch was a very serious matter but should people think that the word had been unjustly applied to them, or if relationship to a witch was implied, it was to the Kirk Session that the injured person had to go for redress, just as happened in other slander cases. A woman complained in 1655 that a man had said that she could take away a cow's milk and a quarter of the udder too which, he said, proved that she was a witch. The Kirk Session agreed that this was slander but referred it to the Presbytery — perhaps they suspected that he might be right after all — although the outcome was that he was punished for what he had said. William Wilson, a tailor in Galashiels, had to make satisfaction for calling

Jonet Wylie 'an ill-favoured thief, and loun, that rade in the devil's saddle, manifesting her to be such in the audience of many witnesses', and phrases like 'witch-faced carlin' or 'brazen-faced quean' were taken to imply a witch-like quality, as did the term 'lang-legged'. If unfounded, such allegations could not go unchallenged but as with other slander cases, pledges were taken and in one case a man who had called a woman a witch had to appear in church and repair her good name by begging the pardon of God, of the congregation and of her and, in addition, had to pay a fine of one merk.[17]

During the years when witchcraft was still a crime, not everyone delated supposed witches to the kirk or to the magistrates but dealt with them themselves by 'scoring them above the breath', drawing blood on the forehead in the belief that if a witch was cut there with the sign of the cross, then the power of Satan would be broken. To do this, of course, was to fall into the trap of counter-charming, in itself a form of witchcraft, and Kirk Session records have fairly frequent entries concerning it. About 1695 a Coldingham man appeared before the Kirk Session, accused of scratching a woman he suspected was a witch above the breath but his explanation was that he was 'fashed or vexed with her, oft at his door, scolding.' Five years later, also in Coldingham, there was another case of a man bleeding a woman above the breath. When he was asked if he thought that doing this would save him from witchcraft, he replied that he had heard many people say so, and when asked whether he had been given any advice about doing it, he said he did it to be revenged against her for threats she had made against him. Both these cases show how little it took to make someone seek the protection that scoring above the breath was thought to give but, in this latter case, the woman assured the Session that she had not threatened him. They must have had reason for believing her rather than him and asked what she wanted done with him, to which she replied that she wished him to make satisfaction to the church for what he had done to her. The Presbytery of Penpont held meetings from January to March 1706 about a man who complained of being slandered by a woman who maintained that he had called her a witch, accused her of taking away his health and then bled her on the forehead and in this case too, it was he who was rebuked, not her.[18]

By 1736 the wind of change had blown sufficiently for Parliament to decree that witchcraft was no longer a criminal offence but Kirk Sessions might still rebuke those they regarded as witches, and excommunication imposed for witchcraft prior to that date, could still be in force after it. People's minds, of course, did not change overnight about witchcraft whatever Parliament decreed and so Sessions still found themselves dealing with people who continued to score supposed witches. In 1737 the ministers of Ross-shire and Sutherland were told by the Presbytery to instruct their flocks about this superstitious matter of cutting fore-heads and as late as 1845 a court trial resulted in three months' imprisonment for a fisherman from Portmahomack, Ross-shire, who had made a knife wound on the forehead of an old woman, thinking that she had bewitched him and his nets so that his crew were unwilling to go to sea with him while he was under her curse.

Another intriguing effort to counteract the power of witches still appears in the graveyard at Trostan, Caithness. Although the date when it happened is not known, a woman who had the reputation of a witch was buried there but the local men decided that they would take no chances with her and carried up from the river two large, long smooth stones which they placed on her grave, to be sure that she stayed underground where she had been put. To pretend to exercise magical rites remained a civil crime after 1736, punishable to start with by the pillory and a year's imprisonment but when a woman was tried at Dingwall in 1843 on a charge of fraud by pretended witchcraft, she was sentenced by the court to three months' imprisonment. She was a confidence trickster: she tied up and charmed parcels in exchange for a pound or two and told those who asked for them to put them under their pillows but when two such parcels were opened, one was found to contain sand and rags, the other breadcrumbs.[19]

There would have been less witchcraft, genuine and pretended, good or bad, had there been fewer clients for it, which was the reason that when Parliament made witchcraft a criminal offence in 1563, those who consulted witches were included, with the death penalty laid down for both. In 1573 an Act of the General Assembly specifically referred to those consulting witches and in 1649 Parliament repeated the decree of death for such people. But, forbidden or not, people constantly went to witches and charmers for spells and cures, and not just herbal ones. They also sought the help of those thought to have occult powers because if bodily or mental ills were ascribed to the devil, it was felt that it was his assistance that must be invoked to put things right. One man had to appear in church to confess 'his sin in consulting Donald Ferguson the charmer, for the relieff of his children, whereby he cast off much of the fear of God and yielded to Satan' and a woman charmer hedged her bets and when called to a sickbed pronounced the words, 'If God hath taken away health, let him restore it, and if the devil hath taken it, let him restore it', upon which the patient recovered. On the other hand, many cures were performed by wise women whose natural knowledge of herbal remedies could be very successful but Kirk Sessions had to pass all charmers on to Presbyteries or civil courts for trial, because officially no difference was made between black and white witchcraft; but the death penalty seems rarely if ever to have been imposed on them or on those who sought their help. Charming was never regarded as seriously, so far as punishment went, as outright witchcraft, almost certainly due to the fact that most charms were used to try to achieve a good result and who knew when they might not need such help themselves, when no other assistance was available. Elie Kirk has a 'witch's stone' inserted in the east gable near the north-east corner, put there by the masons building the church in the seventeenth century, to keep witches away from their work and from them while doing it. What was that if not a charm, right in the fabric of the church? With such an attitude, no wonder a Presbytery found in 1669 that requests for charms and spells were 'abounding in all parts of this country.' From time to time, pulpit intimations were made requiring all who had charms to report themselves to be dealt with and when they admitted having perhaps something like a little southernwood or a verse of some sort to cure the sick, they would be told not to use such things again, and punishment would be imposed, but there was no mention of anything like the death penalty and, in fact, a charmer who wished to be admitted to Communion in 1620 was only required to make repentance in sackcloth and the woman who consulted her, in linen, and to promise never to do the like again.[20]

As to charms themselves, two men were charged before Dornoch Kirk Session with 'practising Charms and that lately they did cast the pattern of a Child's heart in lead, and they gave that heart of lead . . . to . . . that he might give water of it to some tender Children he had.' One of the men admitted the offence and when asked 'if he had used any words at the Casting of it, Confessed that he invocated the Name of the Ever Blessed trinity Father Son & Holy Ghost.' This case went as far as the Synod who found that many people who were guilty of charming did it out of ignorance rather than any compact with the devil and that therefore the minister should preach on the sin of charming and rebuke the man who had cast the heart and the man who had made use of the water 'taken in such a manner of the said heart', from which it seems that the lead heart was dipped in water which was then given to the patients to drink or to wash with. Many charms invoked not the devil's help but that of holy powers, as these men had done, and some Kirk Session records, such as St. Andrews in 1664, give the wording of verses used as charms. Another case of this was when Marion Fisher appeared for charming in 1643 before the Kirk Session of St. Cuthbert's Church in Edinburgh. She said that in her youth she had learnt a spell, had used it on a child and broken a spindle over it, and also that a man asked her help for a sick child 'and she desired him to put a clean sark [shirt] on it.' The words of her charm were:

> Our Lord forth raide
> His foal's foot slade
> Our Lorde down lighted
> His foal's foot righted,
> Saying, flesh to flesh, blood to blood,
> Bane to bane
> In our Lorde's name.

The Kirk Session thought that this was 'horrible and awful' and continued the case, ordering the woman to be put in prison for the time being and inquiries made to see if anyone knew anything against her. When no further allegations were made, she had to appear in sackcloth, confess and promise not to do the same thing again under pain of death as a witch, although she was using her powers for good and surely advising the wearing of clean clothing was advanced thinking rather than anything else.[21] About the same date Alexander Moore appeared before St. Andrews Kirk Session for 'charming and giving of drinks' which seem to have been curative ones, and was sent for further trial. Two years later a woman came before them for charming and particularly for trying to cure 'the disease of wildefyre in bairns' and servants' faces by saying the Lord's Prayer over, as some said, with a mumbling quyet voice and a light candle held to their face all the while', either in the morning before sunrise or else after sunset. She said that she only did it for good and asked nothing in return, adding that she had learnt how to do it from Mr Robert Cornwall, minister at Linlithgow (1626–46) by seeing him cure a child there. Although witnesses gave evidence that she had indeed managed to make people better, she was nevertheless ordered to go for trial but was dismissed in the meantime. In the early 1660s Kathareen Mansone was called before the Session of South Ronaldshay and Burray 'to answer to the scandalous reportes which ar of hir in curing of sick persones and beasts by charming or witchcraft', which implies that she was having success and giving a useful service; nevertheless, the witnesses who were called mainly reported deaths following her treatments and, one way or another, the Session decided that it was beyond them and decided to seek advice from the civil authorities while a man who had used her services had to make repentance before the congregation before being allowed to get married. In yet another case where a woman appears to have been an effective herbalist, the Session summoned her and because 'the said Janet goes under the name of a witch or a deceiver by undertaking to heal desperate disease by herbs and suchlike, the Session do discharge the said Janet in time coming, to use the giving of any physick or herbs to any body under the certification that she shall be esteemed a witch if she do so.' That was in 1661, a time of persecution, and so the Session's threat would have been a frightening one for the woman, but what a loss it must have been to those who needed her help. Some twenty years later, a woman named Margaret Coutts was ordered by her Session to appear before the Sheriff for charming. The minutes say that she cured men, children and cattle thought to be bewitched, something which was often thought to be the cause of illness, and this she admitted doing, having learnt the skill from her late husband and practised it in another parish while he was still alive. She strongly denied, however, an accusation that she claimed connection with three distinct fairy courts, described as Black, Green and White. She was skilful enough for her services to have been sought in several parishes which was why, when she appeared before the Presbytery two years later, she was made to promise never 'to practise upon sick persons thereafter, under hazard of excommunication' and in addition every minister in the Presbytery was told to inform their congregations that anyone employing her in future would be in trouble. The records of Elgin give details of some of the mixtures prepared by a much sought-after sixteenth century woman charmer: one was a plaster of 'swynis sawine' (which could be its bedding), 'rossat, walx, blak peppir, honey and cannel' to be mixed and applied to a child which was also washed with a 'clak clout'. Another of her cures included honey, vinegar and butter. From the patient's point of view, it was far better to have help from a skilful woman, along with the psychological boost of knowing that something was being done, than to depend on the airy kind of advice which neighbours gave to the mother of one weakly child. They bade her use foxglove leaves as a treatment 'so he would either end or mend.' One way or other, they were bound to be right — and he ended.[22]

In addition to the type of charms already mentioned, one west highland minister wrote in the 1790s that there were still no common calamities or distressful accidents to man or beast but had their own particular charm or incantation, generally made up of a group of unconnected words, and an irregular address to the deity or some saint. The people's desperate need for health when there was no welfare state and the power of superstition encouraged the use of such charms, particularly among the lower classes. Some fifty years later, in the mid-nineteenth century, the New Statistical Account for a parish in Skye said that while the people were ignorant of true religion, yet they all had a sense of the religion of nature and that while charms or incantations were occasionally used to treat humans, it was still a regular practice at that time to use such methods for animals. Silvered water, fairy arrows and charmed stones were believed to have great power and those able to use them were held in high esteem. Some of the cures for stock have a very unpleasant ring to them. A man admitted before the Presbytery of Deer that he had beheaded a beast and put the head in one heritor's land and the body in that of another, as he had seen done 'for curing of sudden disease among cattle'. In the same way, another man beheaded a living calf with an axe and buried it on the march between two estates to prevent the disease called sturdy occurring among his beasts, and was duly called before the Session. There seems to have been an idea that there was virtue in beheading the sacrifice — another man did the same thing in Coldingham, at much the same date, taking a lamb from his flock, cutting off its head and putting it into his own chimney head, to cure some illness among his flock. This practice was sufficiently common for the Synod of Aberdeen to recommend all ministers to speak against it in 1659. A cure for what was called the routin evil, a cattle sickness, involved digging a grave and burying a beast in it and although it is not so stated in a reference to this, it seems probable that the animal was buried alive. Both beasts and poultry were sacrificed to cure disease in the animal world and occasionally in the human world too which, in some cases, disturbed the kirk greatly. In the middle of the seventeenth century, the parish of Applecross in Wester Ross became a centre of bull sacrifices. Basically these were offerings made to 'St. Mourie' (St. Maolrubha) on his feast day of 25 August, after which the meat, and other gifts as well, were given to various unfortunates, mainly the mentally ill, who were as a consequence known as St. Mourie's afflicted ones. In 1650 the Presbytery asked the Justices of the Peace of the area to suppress these sacrifices. This does not seem to have been very effective, as six years later they had spread to Lochcarron, Lochalsh, Kintail, Gairloch, Lochbroom and to two inland parishes — Contin and Fodderty — and a landowner in the west was asked to compel certain people to appear before the Synod to answer for making sacrifices. Applecross was obviously thought to be the real source of this trouble and so the Synod ordered the Presbytery of Dingwall to meet in that parish and search out and censure all such superstitious customs. Not only did they find that the 'abominable and heathenish practice' of sacrificing bulls was going on but that people were circling round chapels and adoring at wells — of which more later — and they declared that anyone found doing this should be rebuked in sackcloth for six

Lord's Days in six different churches, ending up in Gairloch. Here the minister was required to order any offenders to appear before the Presbytery, who also ordered that Justices of the Peace should be informed so that they might see to these matters too. In addition, the minister of Gairloch was instructed to go to Applecross every five to six weeks and to stay there for three days at a time, catechising some part of the people each day to try to convince them of their sin. Perhaps this did not bear fruit, or perhaps folk memory lingered on because in 1678 the same Gairloch minister found that Hector Mackenzie and his three sons, John, Murdoch and Duncan, had sacrificed a bull 'in a heathenish manner' on an island in Loch Maree in a bid to help Hector's wife, Cirstane, to recover from illness. Both loch and island were closely involved with superstitions to do with health and the four men were summoned to appear before the Presbytery for their action.[23]

Another instance of sacrificing a living creature to cure a human being happened just over fifty years later. Golspie Kirk Session regarded it as gross piece of superstition when they learned that Elspeth Buie had tried to cure her child's convulsion by digging a hole in the ground and burying a live cock in it, which she said she had seen done by other people to cure convulsions. She was ordered to confess before the congregation but refused to do so, only to be remitted to the Presbytery who insisted that she should do so and, moreover, in sackcloth. Another instance occurred in 1804 when a school child collapsed while standing at his lessons and was believed to be having an epileptic fit. On hearing of this, his aunt 'came to the school and dug a hole in the floor where her nephew fell, in which she buried a live cock together with some hair from the boy's head.' When asked by the Session to explain why she had done such a thing, she said that she 'had no bad design but had been advised to do this as a thing which was practised by others in similar cases, and she did it in the expectation that her nephew would not again be seized with epilepsy.' The Session expressed their abhorrence of such unscriptural customs and she had to stand before the congregation the next Sunday. Burial of living cocks continued for much longer than that; about 1870 one was buried under the hearth stone of a cottage in an Easter Ross village while a psalm was read and a prayer offered up for the cure of a mentally-ill girl but this case did not apparently come to the attention of the church.[24]

A nasty form of charming was the making of effigies. There was an instance of this near Inverness in 1691 when a clay image of a living child was brought to the Kirk Session who ordered everyone living in the area to come to their next meeting to clear themselves by oath 'of this base and unChristian work'. All of them denied any hand in it and, not knowing any other way of discovering the truth, the Session decided to 'receive it for a time till God of his infinite power was pleased to find it out.'[25] Effigy-making was something widely done, even into the 1930s.

In the case of the schoolboy's aunt, she did what she did without the aid of any charmer, just doing something she had heard would cure the child. In the same way, a woman urged her husband, immediately his father died, to strike the couple-tree of the house with an axe as she had heard that doing this three times when there was a death would prevent disease spreading, and when a St. Andrews woman was alleged to have broken a spindle over a sick person with the intention of hastening death, she admitted doing the breaking but said that she had not known what was meant by doing it. Folk memory kept a great deal of superstition going and indeed still does. There used to be a belief that something taken at night, such as stealing a few potatoes out of a field, could be used as a charm and so could even the kirk sackcloth, as has been said in an earlier chapter.[26]

Should people think that a bit of charming, as opposed to outright witchcraft, had been used on them or theirs, they might also use native instinct to counteract it. When Christian Roy thought that Christian Wallas had dried up her cows she retaliated by milking her sheep, which caused both women to fall out and 'scandalously scold and imprecate'. This of course came to the ears of the Session, who rebuked one of them forthwith and the other in church. Theirs was a much less drastic action than cutting the forehead of a witch.[27]

Divination used to be very common: using magical means to tell the future or to find hidden objects or to identify a thief. One method of divining the whereabouts of stolen articles was by use of the sieve (riddle) and shears, sometimes with a comb as well. 'The points of the shears were stuck into the rim of the sieve about an inch apart, the whole being balanced on two fingers by the person performing the magic, who kept repeating an incantation until the sieve oscillated to one side or the other, the significance of a turn in either direction having been previously agreed' or alternatively, should the sieve tremble or move around when a suspected person's name was spoken, then that person was held to be guilty. An account of this being done comes from the minutes of Kilmory Kirk Session in 1709, which describe how a woman turned the riddle to discover the name of a thief. She admitted doing so and having said, 'By Peter by Paul, it was such a person', and when asked if the riddle turned when she named a certain person, she said that it did. Two other women had been present and also had to appear before the Session and their answers to questions show how blindly they accepted the whole thing. One was asked if either of them had turned the riddle, the point being made to her that if none of them had done so, then it 'behoved to be God or the devil that turned it.' Her very practical reply was that she did not think that it was God and hoped it was not the devil. So common had this practice become within the bounds of the Presbytery of Dornoch by 1717 that they handed down an exemplary sentence of excommunication to try to stop people from doing it. 'Turning the key' was another way of discovering the identity of a thief. In a case in Edinburgh, the practioner opened a Bible at Psalm 50, placed a key on the eighteenth verse and then mentioned the names of various people. The Bible remained still until one particular name was said, when it moved and 'the boull of the key fell from her finger.' This was tried twice and the same thing happened each time that particular name was spoken. Many of those who practised so-called divination needed no such implements to help them but just kept an eye on what was going on, then used their common sense and their knowledge of people and events to make a good guess at the truth. Their clients genuinely believed that consulting in this way was sensible, not sinful, as with no police force to make investigations for them, how else could they recover lost or stolen property or discover who had wronged them. When one woman found money missing from her pocket and consulted a particular man about who might have taken it, it came to the ears of the Session who summoned her to explain herself because 'consulting with such persons anent lost things was a very unChristian practice', only to have her say that she did not think it wrong to have done so and, in fact, she was only rebuked and admonished.[28]

The parish of Cromarty had what they called 'a most grievous scandal' in 1740 when two men and four women who had had articles stolen were accused of consulting a woman in nearby Munlochy about them. Although witchcraft had recently ceased to be a civil crime, this woman was still under earlier excommunication for it and was referred to as a witch on this occasion in the Kirk Session minutes, which give a full account of what had happened. One man denied consulting the woman, saying that if he lost anything, he would not go to the devil to seek it. Esther Hood, one of the women, said that she had sent one of the accused men, who worked for her, to ask about stolen goods and he had brought a beggar woman to her who, it was suggested, would be able to tell her who had them. She admitted that she had asked this woman about them and that she had said that they were in the third town to the west, not a very helpful answer. The man's account was that his mistress had sent him to Munlochy to a particular woman who was not at home but he was told of another equally skilled woman to go to and she — it was the beggar woman — went to the home of one of the women making inquiries and told her that the missing articles were with a black-haired man who lived to the west, again not a very helpful answer. The other accused woman said that although she had gone to Munlochy, it had not been to consult the witch but to challenge her for having told Esther Hood that she had stolen salt from Esther's house while she was out hearing a minister from the south. How the Kirk Session made sense of these muddled and conflicting stories is puzzling but they found some of the accused innocent and ordered the rest to appear at the next Session meeting which they did not do. However, they came to the following one but not apparently feeling that they had committed any great offence and as a result were ordered to appear again before the Session and in the meantime 'to wait frequently on the minister in private that he might deal with their consciences.' This worked, and when they next appeared they said that they had now 'got a sight of the evil and danger of their sin.' The Session were very understanding about it all, saying that they had fallen into a sin which was only 'too commonly practised in the country' and punishing them with a rebuke the following Sunday, when the minister took the opportunity to 'set forth the heinousness of their crime to the congregation with certification that, after the evil of it is set before them, any that shall be found guilty shall be proceeded against to the sentence of excommunication which the sin deserves.' A final warning and exhortation was given by the Session to those who had done the consulting and then they were dismissed. It does seem that Kirk Sessions had considerable sympathy for those who consulted witches, charmers and diviners and nowhere is this more clear than in Fordyce in 1631. Although this was at a time when a spell of witch-hunting was coming to an end, a man named Johnne Philp had recently been burnt for witchcraft at Banff. At a subsequent meeting of the Presbytery the brethren asked why all those people known to have consulted him had not been ordered to appear before them, only to be told by the ministers to whose parishioners this applied, that some of the consulters were both poor and ignorant. Kirk Sessions had obviously taken this into account when they did not send these people to Presbytery; however, ministers were told to have these people make repentance in their own churches and to report to the Presbytery that this had been done.[29]

Imprecation is a word which appears fairly often in Kirk Session minutes. It means invoking evil upon someone by prayer or the sheer power of ill-wishing, perhaps calling on the name of God, of the devil or of 'our dear Lady' to help in something which was malevolent. There was a very wide belief in the power of ill-wishing which meant that there were people prepared to do it, like witchcraft and charming, for money. An obscure minute of one Kirk Session refers to 'giving alms to a poor person as hire for imprecation for their vindication for theft alleged against them' which meant that someone had been paid to ill-wish someone who had accused them of theft. A Cromarty pauper boasted of the success of her imprecations, declaring that she had got her prayers answered against the *deceased* Thomas Hood and that she hoped to achieve the same against his successor. She may have been one of those who sought power by pretending success and certainly it was for her boasting in this way that she was delated. When imprecations were as evil as she claimed hers were, it is little wonder that the kirk was very concerned about them. One woman prayed that another 'might gett a cold armsfull of her husband' which was possibly a favourite curse there as some year later another woman in that parish wished that the devil might take a seaman out of his boat, away from the rest of the crew, and 'that his mother might get a cold arms full of him.' A mother was delated for cursing her son, with her face to the sun, wishing him sudden death, as in fact happened, but she denied having done so and was dismissed. A man wished that another 'might wither by a wall'; a woman wished a man an ill end, saying that she would pray on her knees every day for an ill meeting to him; an Edinburgh woman called a shoe maker 'a blackened knave and hoped to see the hangman draw down his feet', adding for good measure that as his wife was 'a vile adulterous murdering Limmer and a thief', she therefore imprecated the curse of God upon their family. Jean Patison was delated to the Kirk Session of Cathcart, Lanarkshire, for having 'uttered very prophane expressions such as wishing her brother were hanged at the Howgate Head and the Devil Hangman: that she would find in her heart to wring her hands in the heart blood of them that slandered her name, and that she would give them a hot awakening: that she made profane application of some threatenings in the Psalms to them that slandered her, such as Strong Bulls of Bashan me surround etc.' She was a woman much given to lying and was also reported to have stolen a small cheese off the Trone of Glasgow which its owner had managed to get back from her. She denied imprecating her brother and stealing the cheese but confessed to everything else and was rebuked for what she had admitted.[30]

The variety of fates ill-wishers could think up for their would-be victims was really quite impressive. One was that some people might 'fall and tumble nineteen times in the falling ill' for which a fine of 20*s*. Scots was imposed. A Shetland woman prayed that the devil might burn another woman and her peats and another woman, who obviously felt that she had been unfairly ousted from her home, begged that 'God reward them that was the cause of her flitting, asking that God might cause them to be turned seven years on a tedder', which earned her a penalty of £4 Scots and several public appearances. A father, angry at accusations that his children had pulled up neighbours' corn, imprecated them, 'wishing that neither iron nor timber might bear them up' and a woman wished that a man might have as 'many bairns as hairs in his head and that he might carry them to the kirk in a riddle.' In 1658 another woman prayed 'to God and our dear Lady' that someone's next child might 'be like a wedder' (castrated male sheep), adding that she never asked anything from God without obtaining it, presumably to increase the terror of her imprecation. Going down on her knees, a Speymouth woman ill-wished her neighbour in these words: 'Let never himself, wife, bairns, or family thrive or otherwise go and let never horse, oxen, kye or anything that belongs to him luck or stand.' After such examples of imprecation, it seems positively mild for a woman to have prayed to God that he would send certain fishermen a scarcity of fish and positively extraordinary that a seaman wished that the whole crew of his boat might sink in the depths. When he had to answer to the Session for this, it turned out that not only he but all the crew had wished in this way, not being satisfied with the fish Providence had allotted to them.[31] In a number of the cases mentioned, the punishments given seem to have been very mild and it seems possible that Kirk Sessions were playing the whole thing down. To have done so would have made sense, as the less people were allowed to think about such things and the less publicity about them the better and the obscure phraseology used in the case of the hired imprecator may have been chosen for that very reason.

It is a small step from imprecation to cursing, something which in Kirk Session minutes often goes hand in hand with swearing. It was considered sufficient of an offence for Parliament to pass various Acts against it, including one of 1581 which ordered swearers convicted for a third time to be imprisoned for a year and a day or else to be banished, and Kirk Sessions also took a serious view of it. The type of cursing could be so obscene that it was 'not proper to insert in the minute book' which is saying something as Kirk Session minutes are not usually squeamish, but the punishments imposed reflected the degree of swearing which had occurred. In 1658 two Fordyce men had to stand in the jougs and be rebuked on two Sabbaths for 'fearful cursing' but though jougs were also used elsewhere for this sin about that date, many Sessions relied on fines to control it. About 1635 one ordered that anyone guilty of 'hard sweiring' should pay 2*s*. Scots and an Act of Montrose Kirk Session decreed that any master or mistress found swearing should pay 4*s*. Scots and any servant 12d. Scots, with any who failed to do so having to pay double, and anyone relapsing making public repentance. It was essential that punishment should be effective if anything was to be achieved and one Session bailie was 'entreated to fyn more severely such as ar guilty of the prevailing sins of cursing and swearing, thereby if possible to put a stop to its increase.' In some cases public repentance had to be made which gave a good opportunity to issue a warning to everyone else: 'and the congregation were warned to avoid this abominable sin, that so universally prevails the commons, as they would escape the fearful judgmts of God, denounced agst this Sin in his Word.'[32]

The 1581 Act of Parliament about swearing said that householders should inform on those they found swearing and that 'censors' or inspectors should be present in market places to watch out for it and if necessary, to imprison profane swearers. Sooner or later, Sessions got round to this part of the Act by appointing elders to be present in ordinary markets and also in fish markets. Such places were an obvious source of trouble — even ministers were known both to drink and swear when at them. St. Andrews Kirk Session ordered elders and deacons in 1640 to take turns in seeing 'that no misorder, banning [cursing] or swearing be heard amongst any bargainers' on market days and nine years later Montrose Kirk Session decreed that there should be 'every week four visitors by Course to take notice of those who swears and to give in their diligence every Session day.' These inspectors, who might be accompanied by church officers, sometimes had summary powers to fine those they heard swearing so that in Elgin they were each required to have a purse with a 'brazyn mouthe' to collect these fines on the spot for the benefit of the poor. It seems that they had to buy these purses themselves as it was stated that as any elder removed from office, his successor should buy the purse at the price it cost, 'and so continually'. In the early seventeenth century, elders in Aberdeen were told to note and challenge anyone indulging in profane swearing in the streets and anywhere else in the town and to take a penalty of at least 4d. Scots from those who had this sum on them and those 'that hes nocht silver to pay to gett a straik on the hand with a palmer', which meant a stroke on the hand with a tawse. In a century or so, civil help was enlisted and Kirk Session minutes of Aberdeen have reports of elders attending markets to watch out for swearers, along with statements that 'such as were found transgressing were delated to the Magistrates and were punished.' Such methods either proved a real deterrent or else the elders were not paying proper attention on one occasion as they reported that they had 'attended the mercate but found no ground for delation.'[33]

Profane swearing was the sin of taking the name of God in vain or using the name of the devil. Prior to the Act of Parliament of 1581 there had been one in 1551 which decreed fines according to rank and provided that poor people who swore but could not pay fines, should be put in the stocks or jougs for four hours. Kirk Sessions made their own Acts as they found necessary, one decreeing that anyone taking the name of God in vain should be punished as Parliament decreed, and to be sure that 'none could pretend ignorance' a general announcement was made about it 'with tuck and drum'. The sin was so common in another parish that the people were exhorted from the pulpit and told that for the first fault there would be a rebuke before the Session, for the second, before the congregation, and any further offences would merit the censure of the church. One Session spent twelve days considering the case of a woman who had said 'Devil tak' you' and finally sentenced her to the pillory while another woman who said 'Deil tak' the skin off you and mak a winnock [window] in hell with it' suffered Higher Excommunication. A fisherman in Craig was found guilty in 1720 'of horrid curses and execrations in swearing and profaning the name of God and wishing frequently that God might damn him and some others there present'; his wife 'did curse and swear by using and uttering horrid imprecations and curses' and both of them were known to be given to 'the hellish sin of swearing and cursing' in spite of private admonitions from the minister. The last straw in their catalogue of swearing was when the woman wished that the devil might put a slit in the forehead of one of the elders. In 1732 John Urie of Holm appeared before his Session for using 'most unaccountable and blasphemous expressions which are very stumbling to others, such as God damn me, and speaking to others, God damn you, such as Devil confound me and, speaking to others, Devil confound you for a Bugger or Bitch' and when told that action would be taken about this he answered, 'What Devil do I care for a reproof from either minister, elders or bedrell?' Although he often used such phrases, this was the first occasion on which it had been brought to the attention of the Session and it was agreed that the minister should speak to him privately — as happened in the case of the fisherman in Craig — 'to see if he was sensible of the ill of his behaviour' but that there need be no further proceedings unless the Session heard that he was persisting in this conduct. Comparing his choice of words with those of others, and his insolent attitude to the prospect of reproof, this was a mild attitude for the Session to take but it was almost certainly due to his social position.[34]

From the time of Moses, the cursing of parents by children was regarded as so sinful that death was the punishment, something repeated in the New Testament. It was sufficiently common in Scotland for Parliament to feel the need to pass an Act about it in 1639 and another in 1649 which decreed that any children who were mentally normal — 'not distracted', as the Act put it — and over the age of sixteen, who cursed or beat their parents would be put to death. Those under sixteen were to be punished at the discretion of the judge. This was ratified in 1661, along with specified penalties according to rank and status for both cursing and swearing, although it does not seem that the death penalty was often, if ever, imposed; certainly about a hundred years later a man guilty of 'uttering profane oaths and for cursing and otherwise maltreating his father', and on a Sunday too, was merely rebuked publicly.[35]

Although Kirk Sessions would administer an oath of purgation, even calling it a 'holy ordinance of ane oath', they regarded what they called 'abominable oaths' as quite another matter. People suspected of doing harm to anyone or to their property by witchcraft, charming or the like were often required by the injured person to give such oaths — give them privately, fasting, on the Bible or on iron, stating that they had not done nor intended to do any harm. Parliament disapproved of these oaths and passed an Act in the reign of James VI laying down penalties and, as so often happened, Parliament's rulings were re-framed into Acts of Session or of Presbytery. In 1709, for instance, the Presbytery of Dornoch passed its own Act on this subject but four years later the Presbytery minutes show that the Synod of Ross and Sutherland were still worrying about the matter of people obliging those 'they suspect to bear malice, envie, or ill will against them to meet and swear' an oath about it. They concluded that it was a horrid profanation of the Lord's most holy name 'as also acknowledging of the Devil in afflictions which should be taken from the Lord's hand, and further a cherishing of a most abominable heathenish superstition' and therefore the guilty must be exhorted to repentance and amendment. In addition, people might also be delated for swearing by their souls. What is more surprising is that what were called 'minced oaths', that is ones of 'affected nicety' such as losh, gosh, teth, heth, fegs, lovenenty or saying 'begad' for 'by God' could be thought most unsuitable and when Rev. J. Wightman was minister of Kirkmahoe, Dumfries-shire, he so disapproved of them that he debarred anyone using them from Communion.[36]

There used to be a great deal of folklore and superstition associated with springs and wells. According to F. Marion McNeill, 'The custom of visiting certain wells on Quarter Days or on the days of the saints to whom they were dedicated may be traced to a pagan water-cult of pre-Druidic origin . . . [and] both hope and dread urged the adoption of ceremonial visiting rites.' At one time there were said to be six hundred holy wells in Scotland. Wherever there was rising water, as in a spring or a well, there must be a life-force, a spirit, and each had its own deity with the well as its shrine. Such wells were in due course Christianised and 'denominat of sancts' and were thought to be particularly powerful on Quarter Days but, owing to the cold weather, were seldom visited at Candlemas which falls in February or at Hallowmas in November. The time when they were most visited was on the first of May or the first Sunday or Monday of that month, in other words on or near the ancient Celtic festival of Beltane. Visits to these wells were nothing less than pilgrimages and the custom of venerating saints, combined with certain rites which had to be performed on these occasions, found no favour with the Reformed church which believed that it was Satan who gave people such beliefs. The fact that those taking part often arrived at night, with various resulting abuses, only confirmed them in this idea. 'Adoring at holy wells, was something that was exercising the minds of the members of Dingwall Presbytery in the 1650s, while in 1674 another Presbytery 'ordered that all those persons who go to wells upon superstitious design shall be censured by the minister of the parishes where they live' but orders of this sort were unable to stop such an inbred custom. In 1707 the minutes of Nigg Kirk Session show that, 'In regard many out of the paroch of Fearn and several other parishes within the Sheriffdom profanes the Sabbath by coming to the well of Rarichie, John and William Gallie, elders, are appointed to take inspection every Saturday evening and Sunday morning of such as come to the well, and to report the same accordingly.' Among the superstitious practices which bothered the church in this connection, was that of 'silvering' the water of wells, if possible with money, a form of votive offering. In 1618 two Perth women went to a well at Huntingtower, drank some water and each left a pin, which the Session regarded as a form of idolatry but, knowing that others had been with them, punishment was delayed in the hope that they would name these people; and when Margaret Davidson from Aberdeen washed her child in St. Fiache's Well in the hope of recovering her health, and left an offering in the well, she was fined and everyone else was forbidden to go to it. Those who went to wells tried to leave behind them some small personal item, a symbolic identification of themselves and a leaving-behind of ills and troubles, something which can still be seen at the Clootie Well in the Black Isle, Ross-shire, where it is a recognised and popular thing to wish at the well and to hang a piece of cloth or rag in the trees around it although, of course, those who do so nowadays have different motives from those of their forebears.[37]

The reason why certain wells gained and retained a special reputation for their powers while others did not was often thought to be magical but it was really because they were genuine healing wells, containing minerals with curative properties so that those who drank their waters as part of the process of seeking health or good fortune really felt the better of it. Chalybeate (iron-bearing) wells were the most common of these and when the diet of the common people was very poor and anaemia almost inevitable, such water cannot but have improved their health which, of course, increased public regard for the well. Certain wells were regarded as specially efficacious for particular complaints and although making pilgrimages to them at special times of the year was considered desirable, many wells were visited as and when necessary. Rathven, for instance, had one where whooping cough patients were taken but as spells or incantations were often recited during any washing or drinking at the well, this made the sin of going there in the first place even worse and explains why a healing well in Dumfries-shire, famous for curing diseases of women and children, was referred to as 'the idolatrous well at Cargen'. In 1652 a Mrs Robertson was summoned before her Session for trying to cure her daughter's eye complaint at a well by washing the girl's eyes with its water and saying,

> Fish beare fins and fulle beare gall,
> All yer ill and my bairn's eyen in ye wall fall.

The minister referred her to the Presbytery and she, along with the woman who had taught her the charm, were both ordered to sit on the stool of repentance until they showed their remorse. In the event, the mother died before her repentance was completed. The well at Rarichie, which has already been mentioned, was visited not only out of superstition but because of its health-giving properties, so beneficial that people would walk a considerable distance to get its water to carry home. In 1707 a man fetched some of it and carried it thirteen miles or so to his home parish, which speaks highly of his opinion of its properties. This he did on a

Sunday, so that his offence was recorded not as a superstitious action but as Sabbath profanation. Rathven had, in addition to the well where whooping cough patients went, one which was called the Nyne Maiden Well, which women in particular visited whether or not it did them good, but the minutes show that in 1648 the Session 'regretted' its existence and ordered it to be blocked up with stones.[38]

The minister who wrote the New Statistical Account for Gairloch told of a practice only beginning to die out in the mid-nineteenth century, whereby the insane of that parish and neighbouring ones were taken to a well on Island Maree — the island where the Mackenzie family sacrificed a bull in 1678 — and were made to drink some of its water. It was considered a good sign if the well was full when the patient was brought to it and the treatment might have been acceptable if it had stopped there, but it went further: they were then towed round the island behind a boat. At an earlier date this would have brought horrified reaction from the kirk but at that date, 1836, the minister seemed happy enough to comment upon the custom but makes no mention of attempts to stop it. As a treatment for insanity, this seems more likely to aggravate the condition than to cure it. Another cure of a horrible sort was at one time used in the parish of Logierait, Perthshire. Mad patients were taken forty miles to Strathfillan, bathed in a pool and then left bound overnight in a chapel; if found loose in the morning, recovery was expected. It is safe to assume, though it is not so stated, that anyone found still bound in the morning would have lost any reason they had. Although this was still going on in the late eighteenth century, the minister who wrote of it in the Old Statistical Account thought it worthy of comment rather than censure, so clearly ideas were changing.[39]

The water of certain lochs was also thought to have curative properties. In October 1830 a correspondent of the *Inverness Courier* gave an account of the scenes in 1826 at Loch-mo-Naire, five miles from the mouth of the River Naver in Sutherland. On the first Monday of every quarter many people gathered at the loch which was thought to have the virtue of curing both physical illnesses and lunacy. On the occasion described, a crowd of about a hundred gathered on the Sunday night, keeping warm round a large peat fire, until the arrival of Monday morning was announced when, with loud shouts, they stripped off their clothing without any fuss and, each throwing a piece of money into the loch, all plunged in. 'They dive thrice, during each of three rounds, after which they dress and away in procession to the further end of the loch, where they gather some weed which alone gives effect to the operation just performed. When a sufficient quantity of the weed had been collected, we again moved slowly in procession round the enchanted loch three times.' Unfortunately the Kirk Session records for 1826 are missing; it would be interesting to know what they would have had to say about such goings-on although perhaps as at Logierait some time before, and at Gairloch only ten years later, they would have been regarded as worthy of comment only.[40] The fact is that as witchcraft ceased to be a crime, as the fear of papacy receded and less rigid views prevailed, the church began to appreciate the medicinal value of certain waters and began, as has been said in an earlier chapter, to pay for people to seek cures at particularly well-regarded places. That one Session paid for a girl to be taken to a 'seventh son to be cured of the cruels' shows the extent to which they had become reconciled to the idea of using the skill of someone who at an earlier date would have been regarded as evil, and by the late eighteenth century the church generally did not concern itself with superstitious practices.[41]

Going back again in time, when the Presbytery of Dingwall had expressed concern in the 1650s about 'adoring at holy wells' in what was a superstitious as opposed to a health-seeking process, they linked with it the custom of circulating chapels. Parliament's Act of 1581 had referred to a whole range of superstitious practices: going in pilgrimage to chapels, wells and crosses, superstitious observance of several papistical rites and saints' days, making bonfires and singing carols in and around churches at certain times of the year, with a fine ordered for a first offence and death for the second. This shows how seriously such conduct was regarded at the highest level, mainly because much of it was thought to smack of Roman Catholicism, although in practice penalties do not seem to have been as severe as was laid down. To circulate chapels was to process around them, perhaps kneeling about them; but in addition many people liked to visit old ones to pray and, as there was often a well nearby, to drink its water. In 1602 an Elgin man admitted going to the chapel of Speyside in pilgrimage, barefoot and barelegged, and having got there had gone about the chapel barefoot and drunk from the well. Twenty-five years later people were still going there to kneel and to pray to Our Lady and to drink the water. In 1653 an Elgin woman confessed having been at the Chapel of Grace while another admitted going to the 'idolatrous chapel' and drinking from a well there. At one time in that area, the Chanonry kirk was a particular attraction. In 1596 Elgin Kirk Session forbade any kind of 'pastime' or meetings in the kirk or kirkyard and certain people who had already offended were told not 'to make their public or private prayer at the Chanonry kirk.' On Christmas Eve 1597 intimation was made with ringing of the handbell, forbidding visits to that kirk or to any other superstitious places in the parish on Christmas day, under threat of the penalties already laid down and of burning on the cheek, and to enforce this, half of the elders were appointed to visit the Chanonry kirk, the rest to be at the Cross to see that no disorder should happen there. Two years later, as Christmas was approaching, there was another order about the Chanonry kirk: 'Women and lassies forbidden to haunt or resort there, during this time which is superstitiously kept fra xxv December to the last of January.' While most visits were certainly made in order to pray or for superstitious ritual, what this 'haunting and resorting' could degenerate into is evident in an Act of that Kirk Session passed in 1600, referring to dancing, guysing, singing of songs and of carols through the town and at Chanonry kirk on holy days, for which it was decreed that offenders would be put in the jougs, barefoot and with their heads shaven.[42]

In 1631 some people were found kneeling superstitiously about the church of Ordiquhill. Although certain of the women said that they had only come for water from Our Ladie Well for a friend who had been ill for a long time, they admitted that they had also knelt and for that they were each fined 40*s.* Scots and had to stand in sackcloth, but one of them who was 'destitute of means' had to make satisfaction in the jougs. The minister was among those who caught the offenders in the act and he took their plaids from two women who were 'disaguysed' as they knelt, in order to discover who they were because many of them came from other parishes. Although he made it plain that he intended to return the plaids once he knew the owner's names, his action caused great anger to those concerned and the husband of one woman and the brother of the other came, with accomplices, to the manse that night and attacked him so that 'for shortness of breath and disfigurement of his face' he was unable to attend a Presbytery meeting and sought the advice of the Synod. The practice still went on, however, around that area, and elsewhere too, so that in 1648 the Presbytery of Fordyce, when visiting Boyndie, admonished the minister and elders to punish several superstitious offences and to censure severely those 'that goes to wells or chapells in superstitious manner.' Another superstitious and obviously related custom appeared in 1641 when the Kirk Session of Kilconquhar, acting on instructions from the Presbytery, ordered that, among other things, 'all those who superstitiously carried the dead about the kirk before burial be censured by the Session.' Not just ecclesiastical buildings and wells but also other places, it was believed, had certain virtues. People used to go secretly to the cave of St. Gerardine in Lossiemouth to seek the blessing of the saint, sometimes going there barefoot and barelegged. There was a hole there which was thought to have beneficial properties if a limb was inserted into it. On one occasion one man put his arm, another his leg, into it in the hopes of a cure: one recovered, the other did not.[43]

As has already been said, after the Reformation everything Popish was forbidden. According to F. Marion McNeill, every religious rite or custom, however harmless in itself, if ordained by Rome and not expressly decreed by holy Scripture, was condemned, in order to try to make the gap between the old church and the new as wide as possible. The Reformers waged war, with the help of the Act of Parliament of 1581, on saints' feast days and customs associated with them and a collection of Acts of St. Andrews Kirk Session, re-adopted in 1595, actually provided that those who kept Christmas or any other holy days should be deemed Papists. The people, however, clung to what they knew and enjoyed any festival commemorating a particular saint which was already traditional in a parish and such days continued to be the great days of the year for the parishioners. This might be technically superstitious but so far as those who took part in them were concerned, it was wonderful fun in otherwise drab lives, although it often tipped over into abuse of one sort or another. When these occasions were turned into fairs, they became acceptable to the kirk but otherwise they were not, and so efforts were made to cover such days with a cloak of respectability in this way. All things considered, it is surprising how long the Roman Catholic termination 'mas' has survived, for example Martinmas and Candlemas; and until very recently the name Mary-Ann was a common one in the highlands.[44]

Yule, the whole season or feast of Christmas which included Hogmanay, was recognised in times of Episcopalian church government, as shown in such Kirk Session entries as, 'Being Christmas day, there was a sermon.' This was in keeping with an Act of Parliament of 1621 which said that every minister should observe the birth of Christ but that he should rebuke superstitious observances and licentious profanity of the day. In practice, Reformed doctrine required that only Sundays should be holy days; Christmas Day was meant to be a normal working day. In Aberdeen in the mid-seventeenth century a man had to appear publicly for refusing to 'grindle flower' on Christmas Day, picturesque spelling for grinding flour; a St. Andrews mason had to promise that if he had no work to do that day, he would find something to occupy himself with, 'work sum riggin and stanis of his awin', and in 1640 someone in that town was cited for not working on Christmas Day and 'promised not to do the like again.' Not to be working implied superstitious observance of the day and in 1645 the General Assembly decreed that whoever after that date was found guilty of keeping Yule day, or indeed any other superstitious days, would be proceeded against and if masters of schools or colleges should be 'accessory' to this by giving holidays, they should be summoned to account for it. Aberdeen Kirk Session extended this by forbidding the deacons of certain crafts to allow the keeping of holy days or festivals as well as ordering the master of the Song School not to 'give any play to scholars on days dedicated to superstition.' Salters were a group who used to move to new jobs on Christmas Day and in 1647 Parliament supported the General Assembly's ideas by forbidding them to do so as it occasioned observance of the day and ordered them to make any moves they wished to, on 1 December. But people continued to take Christmas Day off, such as those in St. Andrews in both 1649 and 1650 who were found guilty of 'playing idly at the goufe [golf] on Yule day.'[45] Nevertheless, Christmas Day continued to be a working day well into this century, into and after the 1939–45 War. A carpet factory at Kilmarnock worked that day in the 1960s but, as everyone knows, it is now a holiday and the kirk pays great attention to the season and celebration of Christmas.

In former days a particular feature of Yuletide merrymaking was guising or 'guizarding', mainly during the closing nights of the year and especially on Hogmanay. Youths and boys, masked and disguised, might act a simple play in the kitchens and halls of better-class homes while in rural areas, it was just youngsters, dressed up, who went from house to house, singing a verse or two or giving some little performance, just as is still done to some extent at Hallowe'en today. Sometimes men dressed up in women's clothing and danced through the streets, although for either sex to put on the others' garb was regarded as an ungodly abomination. A minute of Aberdeen Kirk Session in 1606 shows that women took part in dressing up too and when an Edinburgh girl, Jonet Cadye, was reported as 'disaguysing hir in welvot breikis, and dansing in menis clething' the horror felt by the Kirk Session almost jumps off the page at the reader; it is little wonder that people might have to declare on oath that they had not gone guysing at Yule. Disguise was fun and could help people to evade church censure: one year the minister of Traquair had been unable to discover the identity of guysers because they were masked but in 1749 the Kirk Session of Cromarty were more successful and managed to discover the names of seven guysers with the result that 'the persons that went in disguise were called and the sin of it opened up to them and were rebuked and promised not to be guilty in time to come.'[46] Going about in disguise at any time of the year, even when not associated with superstitious days, was sure to lead to reprimand. For dancing in a close and in the kirkyard at Elgin 'with maskis and wissors [visors] on ther faces' some men were each fined 40s. Scots in 1623 and a woman in Aberdeenshire who dressed up and 'personated a ghost and displayed surprising . . . impudence and obstinacy' was fined the large sum of £12 12s. Scots and had to appear in sackcloth for four Sundays. Such activities gave lots of scope for pranks and other abuses: there might be 'singing of idolatrous songs through the burgh' or 'plaing, dancin and singin off fylthe carrolles on Yeul day.' Dancing through the streets with bells and wearing masks resulted in some young men being delated as 'fosteraris of Superstitioun' and although it is not stated whether or not the following man was masked or disguised in any way, he was in trouble with the Session for 'going about on the last night of December out of a superstitious popish Custom repeating a Rhapsody of nonsense', while James Scarty was stupid enough to have 'upon new zier even, under night, come to the minister his house and thair sung wantone and prophane songs in contempt of the minister' for which he was punished by standing in sackcloth and paying a fine.[47]

F. Marion McNeill describes how every festival had its special cakes or dishes which are lineal descendants of those used sacramentally or sacrificially in pagan times. Scottish Yule-bread belongs in this class: baked on Yule E'en between sunset and sunrise, it was made in honour of the Virgin's delivery, with the usual large round bannock cut twice cross-ways to symbolise the Cross. With such a background, is it any wonder that the baking of Yule bread was regarded by the Reformers as an offence? In December 1583 the Glasgow bakers were required to tell the Kirk Session the names of those for whom they had baked this bread so that they could be dealt with, and when William Williamson, a Perth baker, was accused of baking and selling great loaves at Yule, his offence was described as 'cherishing superstition in the hearts of the ignorant'. Special Christmas pies were also considered superstitious and a baker in Aberdeen was sharply rebuked for carrying pies one Yule Day — it sounds as if he carried or hawked them through the streets for sale — and as a result he promised never to bake them again nor carry them through the town. It is said that Rev. Murdo M'Kenzie (1645–77) searched the town of Elgin at Christmas time to prevent the popish observance of eating geese — so the people who had looked forward to a bit of feasting were denied their Yule bread, their pies and, in Elgin anyway, their geese too.[48]

Fire has long been regarded as a powerful purifying force and in 1670 some fishermen appeared before Drainie Kirk Session, Morayshire, accused of 'the idolatrous custom of carrying lighted torches round their boats on New Year's Eve.' This was meant to bring luck to their boats or at any rate, to ward off evil, and in spite of kirk disapproval, the custom continued and the minutes show that in 1699 William Edward was found guilty of 'kindling a blazing torch of fire and carrying it round his boat.' Indeed, the practice continues there to this day with the burning of the Clavie at Burghead on 11 January, the old-style New Year's Eve. The lighting of bonfires, referred to in the Act of Parliament of 1581, was originally a pagan custom which continued into Christian times and persisted after the Reformation, particularly at Beltane which was at the beginning of May, and on Midsummer Eve. Early in the seventeenth century a number of people in Aberdeen were accused of having bonfires on Midsummer evening and Peter-even, right outside their doors on the street, but although they could hardly pretend to be ignorant about them, they blamed it on children or servants. Some forty years later 'users of bonfyres' were being censured in other places but it still went on; in 1776 a Banffshire minister warned the people of the superstitious and heathenish practices he had observed 'of burning fires and other idolatrous customs which the more ignorant and weak part of the parish were addicted to on the [blank] day and evening.' As late as the 1790s the custom was still being carried on in some places, with shepherds and young people kindling fires in high ground in honour of Beltane, although by then the kirk, as with other superstitions, disregarded it. Interestingly enough, Sorbie Kirk Session have a minute of 1701 which refers to something happening 'about Beltane', which shows that even in the days when the kirk tried to suppress such superstitious festivals, they might still use them to identify a date.[49]

Fastern's E'en, the night before Lent begins, was widely celebrated with football matches which, for some reason, were also thought to be a profane and superstitious custom. The minutes of Galashiels Kirk Session show that in 1697 one of the elders played football that day — this has already been mentioned — in spite of the fact that a visiting minister had just preached in the town 'and spoke particularly against that profane superstitious custom', and he was duly punished for what he had done. What seems strange is that playing football on Fastern's E'en was unacceptable in 1697 and yet within five or so years, cock-fighting in schools the same day, with the schoolmaster benefiting from it, was being permitted. The only reason for this seems to be that one was thought to be based on superstition, the other was not and was of financial benefit indirectly to the kirk by helping the parish schoolmaster. Nevertheless, playing football and then eating pancakes in houses which were thrown open to the public managed, somehow, to continue in Kirk Yetholm till a much later date, and the game itself is still played in a few places on that day.[50]

Certain times of the year had their associated plays or 'unruly dramatic games' as one writer described them: *Robin Hood*, the *Abbot of Unreason* and the *Queen of May* were enacted every May which was one of the months when most celebrations were held, probably owing to the long bright days, and the Reformers had a hard task to stop people enjoying their May games. (When the Assembly of Divines at Westminster appointed the second and third Sundays of May as fasts, as preparation for the forthcoming meeting of the estates of the realm, they took care to state specifically that these fasts had nothing to do with superstition.) 6 June was when people took part in *Corpus Christi Play*, it being his festival, with resultant appearances before Sessions, and 10 December was the day when *St. Obert's Play* took place, in Perth at any rate. He was the tutelary saint of the Bakers' Incorporation of Perth in whose honour a procession took place through the town with people disguised and carrying torches, a fantastically dressed horse, on which one of them was mounted, and the accompaniment of drum and pipes. This was happening in the 1570s and greatly angered the Kirk Session and promises were extracted in 1577 that it would not happen again. There were, of course, other plays than these. In this context, the Kirk Session of St. Andrews has an intriguing minute. In 1574 the daughter of Thomas Balfour, who was both an elder and a bailie, was married and the Session gave permission 'to play the comede mentionat in Sanct Lucas Evangel of the Forlorn Sone' although it was decreed that it must not be done in a way which could cause people to stay away from church in the afternoon or the morning; yet in the following March, 1575, everyone and especially young men, were warned from the pulpit that they must not profane the Sabbath by 'using of playis and gemmis publiclie as they war wont to do, contrasting the playis of Robin Huid.'[51]

Not a play as such, but amusement of some sort, which also happened in Perth in the month of May, was when young men and women went, with piping and drums, to a rather inaccessible cave. This was said to be done superstitiously and caused the Session, with the agreement of the magistrates, to forbid it in future under threat of a fine of 20s. Scots for each offender, plus making repentance one Sunday, but this may have had something to do with the suspicion that those who went to the cave did so with the intention of getting up to 'filthiness'. If 'filthiness' was the intention of these young people, the choice of such a cave is understandable and the same idea probably lay behind a 'most pernicious custom' which went on in a remote part of the parish of St. Andrews every Trinity Sunday, the one after Whitsunday, and took the form of piping, dancing, drinking and disorder. In 1599 it was said that this had gone on since the Reformation and if so, it is amazing that it had escaped the attention of the Session for so long as the remote spot is only about six miles from the town of St. Andrews. At that point, however, the kirk officer was ordered to go and forbid the tenants to allow it to happen — but it still continued. Such things, and others too, went on elsewhere: it would be interesting, for example, to know what nineteen men and eleven women were doing in the wood of Spynie, near Elgin, from 11.00 p.m. one Saturday in May until 4.00 a.m. next day. All that the records say is that they had to make repentance for whatever it was from their own seats the next Sunday.[52]

Penalties for various superstitious activities have already been mentioned but an easy way of dealing with a case which might be difficult to prove was simply to bring it in as Sabbath profanation if it had conveniently happened on a Sunday, and many of these occurrences did fall on that day. An alternative was to look for a Sunday activity which could be punished in lieu of the superstitious one, which had the advantage of punishing the person concerned but at the same playing down undesirable elements, one of the best ways of counteracting superstition. In 1695 a Session was concerned about a man named Robert Shortwood who was suspected of charming and recommended the minister to make inquiries about him as he went through the parish. Early the following year, he reported that he had spoken with Robert 'anent his charming but that he denied it and found upon enquiry though there were some grounds of suspicion yet it could not be proved against him, the Session taking this to consideration and Likewyas having a new complaint of his breaking the Sabbath Day by binding of corn thought fit to summon him to appear before them next Lord's Day.' Although he denied both charges the Session used the opportunity to give him a public reproof and an 'admonition to carry more circumspectly afterwards.' In 1708 some girls admitted that they had 'treated and handled' a man 'in a profane manner'. What they had done was to persuade another girl to put a straw ring upon him and the Session 'considering the heinousness and obscenity of this Crime' ordered them to be rebuked for two Sundays. This sounds like using a sledge-hammer to crack a nut but a straw ring could be regarded as a form of magic circle and it seems very probable that the charge of Sabbath profanation, which was the one made, was being used as a cover for charming, albeit what sounds a mild and playful sort.[53]

It must have pleased the kirk when magic back-fired on the practioner: this happened to a man who had put hot stones above his door to cure a child's illness 'wherethrough the judgment of God, the house and plenishing were burnt to ashes, the hot stones taking fire in the thack', and seldom can blasphemy, cursing and lack of repentance have produced such dramatic results as in the following case, nor such good advantage been taken of it. A man complained to Mr John Mill, minister of Dunrossness, that a neighbour had taken the name of God in vain and imprecated damnation upon him. Though this was unproved, the minister rebuked the man concerned, who promised to amend his ways and asked for his first child to be baptised, saying that he truly repented of his sin. On the following Saturday, the minister called upon him and asked about the sincerity of his repentance and being reassured about it, he baptised the child the following day. After that was over, the father went home and prepared to take a dram without asking any blessing on it and the minister, who was present, checked him 'whereon he trembled and was in great confusion', so much so that the minister suspected the genuineness of his attitude, and was right to do so because after he left, the man gave 'loose reins to daft mirth', only to drop dead when he went out to the peat stack. This cautionary tale was well used by Mr Mill: 'I laid the whole matter, as it stood, before the congregation, warning all thereby to guard against that heinous sin, as they would wish to escape God's righteous judgment.'[54]

In spite of kirk disapproval of superstitions, there were some little ways in which individual kirks fell in with them, although this only happened once a milder approach was taken towards such things. In the days when the kirk bell at St. Monance hung from a tree, it used to be removed every year during the herring fishing because the fishermen had a superstitious idea that the fish were scared away by its noise. At some early point, it is said that the right hands of baby boys in the Border counties were left unbaptised so that they might be free to deal more deadly blows against enemies; some ministers fell in with marriage superstitions; and the two heavy river stones placed on the witch's grave at Trostan were certainly not allowed to remain there without the knowledge and tacit agreement of the Kirk Session.[55]

13
Holy Matrimony

Marriage is always topical. At the moment, so is living together but that is not so modern an idea as may be thought: there used to be a type of 'marriage' known as hand-fasting which developed before the Reformation and continued for some time thereafter. In its original form, however, hand-fasting was simply betrothal or engagement to marry, an undertaking made by joining hands (hands-on-fist), and the term continued to be used in this sense for some considerable time. The records of an Orkney parish in 1705, for instance, refer to Magnus Ame being 'handfasted with Margaret', the context making it plain that this was an ordinary marriage contract, and an entry in the minutes of a highland Presbytery in 1707 shows that its ministers were required to observe the General Assembly's Acts concerning the proclamation of banns, specifying that there should be no hand-fasting without either the knowledge of the minister or, in his absence, two or three elders, and this clearly also refers to ordinary betrothal.[1]

However, hand-fasting could also be trial marriage for a year and a day, a frequent condition being that the woman should bear a son within that time. When it was up, the couple could decide whether they wished to marry or to part and if they parted, it was understood that they were free to enter into other relationships. In the event of parting, any child of the union was the responsibility of the partner objecting to marriage and if they did get married, any child was automatically legitimated. A place particularly associated with this custom was at one time shown on OS maps as the 'Handfasting Haugh' in Dumfries-shire, a flat area at the junction of two rivers, the Black Esk and the White Esk, where an annual fair saw the beginnings, and possibly endings too, of many handfasting ceremonies.[2]

Naturally enough, the kirk disapproved of hand-fasting, especially when the period of co-habitation stretched out for year after year with the couple perfectly content to leave matters as they were and regard themselves as married. Should there have been witnesses at their espousal, before whom they declared their intention of becoming man and wife, it was not surprising that many felt that they really were married but the fact was that they were not. It was probably this custom that was meant when the Kirk Session of Govan referred in 1659 to highlandmen in the parish who 'tak unto themselves wives not according to order practised in the church.' The kirk records of Aberdeen refer in 1562 to many people being hand-fasted 'as thai call it' for as long as six or seven years; and their failure to complete 'that honourable band' with marriage, continuing instead to live 'in manifest fornicatioun' caused the kirk great concern. All that could be done at that date, when there was so much else to see to so soon after the Reformation, was to try to compel such couples to marry properly, and in Aberdeen they were given a time limit: 'to complete the same between this date and Fastern's E'en next.' Other early Kirk Session records have similar entries but what is interesting is that at that time, should any partner in hand-fasting commit fornication with anyone else, then the sin was classed as adultery and punished accordingly, showing not so much that the kirk recognised hand-fasting as marriage but that they wished those involved to do so and to complete the contract and not get entangled with other people. Within five years of the Reformation, the General Assembly decreed that 'such as lye in sin under promise of marriage, deferring the solemnisation, should satisfy publicly in the place of repentance upon the Lord's Day before their marriage', and an Act of Parliament was passed in 1579 referring to 'The wrath and displeasure of God caused by the wicked and ungodly form of living among the poor by neglect of marriage'. In neither of these decrees is the term hand-fasting used although it is obviously what is meant. As late as 1772 Thomas Pennant referred to it when describing his tour through Scotland, although for all practical purposes it had died out well before that date. Even so, a relic of it lasted until 1855, up to which date the rights of parties to a marriage differed according to whether or not the marriage had lasted for a year and a day and a child had or had not been born of it. Hand-fasting was not, of course, the same thing as ante-nuptial fornication.[3]

What contributed to the end of hand-fasting was the decision of the kirk to put marriage on a proper footing by replacing the erstwhile betrothals with formal contracts of marriage and proclamation of banns, which became a feature of the seventeenth and eighteenth centuries. As with other aspects of life, a certain amount of knowledge often had to be exhibited by those wishing to marry, which was thought to be a good way of raising standards. One Kirk Session decided in 1598 that neither marriage nor baptism would be allowed for 'any parishioners that wants understanding' and some fifty years later a Presbytery ordained 'that ignorants be catechised before baptism or marriage'. What this entailed appears in the minutes of a Session which decreed that no marriage would be 'maid or parties proclaimit until baith the parties also recite the Lord's Prayer, the Belief [Creed] and the Commands or ells pay five libs. That [they] sall have them before the accomplishment of the marriage qlk of it be not dune, they sall forfeit.' Another Session tackled the problem in a slightly different way, saying in 1594 that people presenting themselves to be contracted in marriage would be refused if they could not repeat the Lord's Prayer, Creed and Commandments and would be fined 40s. Scots for their ignorance, which seems to have been a punishment rather than the taking of a pledge. In the eighteenth century, a Caithness Kirk Session required any candidate for marriage to repeat the Shorter Catechism or else find two cautioners to the extend of £12 Scots that it would be learnt within six months of marriage or forfeit that sum. This meant that a good memory was an important asset for anyone wanting to marry, without any emphasis being put on understanding, but at least there was the let-out of time to learn.[4]

When a prospective spouse lived in another parish, a Session might well demand a certificate to show that he or she attended church regularly because they certainly did not always do so. In 1700 Galston Kirk Session decided that parishioners who neither came to worship nor submitted to discipline, yet expected the privilege of marriage, would not be granted it until they undertook to behave in an orderly way in future. In 1599 Elgin Kirk Session required any people being married to give caution that they would attend Sunday worship both morning and afternoon and when in 1643 a couple were threatened with the jougs if they were absent from church again, it seems likely that they had given an undertaking to attend but were not adhering to it. As has already been said, marriage was the most satisfactory follow-on of any immoral conduct and Sessions were wise enough to allow weddings to go ahead, so long as an undertaking to serve discipline was given, rather than 'marr the design of the marriage', hence such an entry as the following:

> 1701. Mary Lyell in Latheron parish, now in process of marriage to John Sutherland in Berriedale, formerly guilty of fornication with David B — in Thrumster, for which she had not as yet given public satisfaction, the Session not willing to Impede her present design of Marriage, require surety for her satisfaction whereupon she presently presented James Doull, Weaver in Wick, who hereby made himself to present her to the Session on Sabbath next, being fourteen of this instant and that under the paine of 10 pounds Scots in case of failure, whereupon the Session ordered a lyne to be given her for marriage.[5]

In this context, an odd case cropped up in Portmoak, Kinross-shire, in 1780. Kathrine Rintoul, mentioned already in relation to midwives' inspections, was a servant in William Skinner's house and when suspected of being pregnant and 'planning to withdraw secretly from the place to conceal her guilt' the Session ordered such an inspection which she refused to undergo; they then obtained a Sheriff's warrant to enforce it, only to be refused admittance to the house. Skinner, who was the father of the expected child, was most obstructive throughout, gave up attending worship and continued to keep Kathrine in his house, where she was the only woman. Normally a Session was anxious for a couple to marry when a baby was on the way, so long as satisfaction was made or promised, but when Skinner and Kathrine let it be known that they intended to marry, several of his friends objected, saying that some time before they had advised him not to marry her and he had promised that he would not do so. 'We therefore hope,' they said, 'the Session will find it inexpedient to grant him liberty to contradict and perjure himself by allowing him to break his faith.' By this they meant breaking faith with what he had promised them, not with what he had promised her. Skinner was called before the Session, agreed that he had told his friends that he would not marry Kathrine and said that he wanted to be relieved of his promise to marry her. The Session supported this extraordinary position and in what must have been an endeavour to prevent her ensnaring him again, decided that if he should at any time in the future want to marry her, it would not be allowed 'until he be convicted before the Session of violating his promise to his friends.' It all sounds so extraordinary that the Session must have known more than appears in the minutes.[6] Anxious though Sessions were for marriage to take place in such cases, they were just as anxious to ensure that satisfaction was made and in 1716 one Session told a couple that their marriage proclamation would be 'stopt and all church benefit denyed' if they failed to give caution. Indeed, they did stop the proclamation of another couple six years later until they gave their bond for public satisfaction.[7]

Contracts of marriage — sometimes called 'bands' or 'bonds' of marriage — were formal agreements to marry, made with the approval of the church and often entered in Kirk Session records, signed by the Session Clerk and also by the couple if they could write and, if not, by their mark. To ensure that all was proper and above board, one Session passed in 1708 an 'Act anent parties contracting in order to marriage' which required them not just to appear on their own before the Session Clerk but to do so along with two elders, whereas in 1702 another Session required couples to come with the elder of their particular quarter and present themselves before the minister. It is said, although it seems surprising that it should be so, that at one time it was the custom in Perthshire for the parties to meet at an inn and to send for an elder to come to draw up the marriage lines. Pre-contract was an obvious stumbling block to any new engagement and everything in such a case had to be sorted out before a new one was allowed to proceed. After an Elgin girl promised to marry an English soldier who then moved away, she decided to marry someone else and her father came to the Session, asking permission for this and bringing witnesses who said that at their parting the soldier had set her free by ceremonies such as the cutting of a glove and the breaking of a shilling and, on the strength of this, she was allowed to marry whom she pleased.[8] In Stornoway where people married young, it came to be accepted by the late eighteenth century that if a husband or wife died, and the survivor wished to remarry quickly, then they could do so. A wife whose husband accidentally shot himself had her next marriage contract settled before his burial and re-married the day after it. This swift action must have had church approval, most probably because it solved maintenance problems and saved the poor's money but it was very different from a regulation entered in the records of St. Cuthbert's Kirk Session, Edinburgh, in 1645 which said that, 'In respect sundrie women desires the benefit of marriage a little space after their husband's death, that none have the benefit of marriage quhill neir three quarters pass after their husband's death.' This meant that they could not marry again for nine months after the first husband's death and was obviously designed to prevent a cover-up of any ensuing immorality. Stornoway's attitude was much more practical.[9]

The settling of contracts of marriage was a cause of great celebration which meant heavy drinking which could in turn lead to all sorts of trouble and, in one case, to a 'throng [crowded] meeting' on the shore at Buckie, with fighting and 'blooding one another'. If contracts were made on a Saturday, hangovers and continued drinking could cause all kinds of Sabbath profanation and so from all around the country there are references to them being forbidden on that day 'to prevent untimeous drinking on the Lord's Day approaching', as one Session put it. Some Sessions specified that contracts should be drawn up on Fridays, others that they should be on a weekday, while 'because of abuses through crowds, and through banquets at the time of contracts and banns' Perth Kirk Session ordered at one time that they should not be made on Mondays.[10]

Once the contract was made and signed, it was expected to be followed soon, if not at once, by proclamation of banns and then by marriage within about six weeks. Should a contract not be carried out, it was of course to the Session that any complaints came and it was they who sorted matters out. They felt that having been involved in the making of it they were involved in any breach of it, which was why one ordered that the 'partie-breaker' of any promise of marriage should make public repentance 'for deluding the kirk'. A man who broke his contract with one woman, later asked his Session for a testificate because he was 'in process of marriage elsewhere' but he had to find surety first of all for making satisfaction for his breach of contract. In 1789 Alexander Bain, a ground officer in Tongue, Sutherland, complained to the Session that Ann Mackay who was contracted to him did not wish to marry him after all. She appeared before them and said that since agreeing to marry Alexander, another man by whom she had previously had a child, had come back into her life and that her uncle, who was her cautioner for £40 Scots in her contract with Alexander, was willing to pay her fine for breach of promise if the Session would allow her to marry the father of her child. That man also appeared and insisted that he had the best title to her hand in marriage 'in consequence of prior engagements and connection.' Alexander declared that 'he did not mean to insist that she should marry him but he would object to her marrying any other, until he should be reimbursed in the expense incurred in the contract.' The girl's uncle agreed to this and on paying a guinea, which was the reduced fine the Session asked, she was allowed to marry the man she preferred on the following Friday. When another girl refused to carry out her contract, her Session pointed out the sinfulness of her conduct towards the man she was engaged to but by then she had decided to marry someone else and, as there was no way of changing her mind, the Session settled for her paying a penalty of £2 Scots to the poor's fund. The reasons why an Elgin man decided not to marry a girl to whom he was contracted, make one wonder why he ever got engaged to her in the first place: he said he could not get the consent of his parents nor of his employer and added that she was 'lous fingered'; the Session agreed that he should be freed of the contract but that he should pay £8 Scots and stand at the pillar foot the next Sunday. In another case, it also seems odd that the couple ever thought of marriage as the Session, seeing the 'great inanimicity and mutual contention' that was likely to arise between them, decided with their consent that they should be 'absolved and made free the one of the other', but they still had each to pay a fine for breach of contract. This was sensible and, in fact, in 1570 the General Assembly had declared that should people wish to resile from a contract of marriage, they should be allowed to do so, so long as nothing had followed on the contract (by which they meant pregnancy). Rev. Andrew Edgar tells of how when one Kirk Session tried to be brutally strict, it was the General Assembly which showed consideration: for several years in the late 1560s a man had craved permission from his own church to get married but was told that, even although she had given him a discharge, the only woman they would allow him to marry was a former servant whom he had wronged. Not accepting this, he 'suted liberty' for marriage from the Assembly and this was granted, with the comment, 'yea, and there is injury done to him already.'[11]

There were occasions when Sessions tried to get damages if a man reneged on his promise to marry although not always successfully. One man refused to marry a girl, saying he had been more or less tricked into his promise to do so but when he offered to pay the penalty of £40 Scots laid down in the contract, the Session suggested that he should also offer her £7 as a solatium. Her friends replied that they would accept no less than £15 stg., a large sum in 1830. The man asked for time to pay £10 but this they refused and so 'the Session after labouring a long time to adjust the matter betwixt the parties were obliged to desist and to leave them to settle it as best as they could' — but at least they tried.[12]

At the time of making a contract of marriage it was common to give caution that the wedding would go ahead — Ann Mackay's uncle in Tongue had done so — but many people were unable to pay this should the need arise. 'The penalty usually exacted for breach of contract has in many instances been incurred but very seldom recovered, by reason of the poverty of the parties', said one Kirk Session and so it came to be usual to insist on a cash pledge being laid down at the time of the contract or of proclamation of the couples' banns. When a Clackmannan girl, Margaret Anderson, reneged on her marriage in 1698 after proclamation, the Session acted swiftly to stop such a thing happening again and 'made an Act that from this time forth, there should be no persons proclaimed without laying down two dollars in pawn for performing their purpose of marriage, which is to be intimat the next Lord's Day.' As another Kirk Session put it, there was no longer to be 'caution fundin anent proclamations of marriage, bot onlie consignation money, to wit £5 for ilk partie.' Often called a 'pawn' or 'pawnds', the giving of consignation money was known as 'laying down the pawns', when a sum of money was deposited with a Session as a guarantee of intention to marry within forty days. This resulted in entries in Kirk Session records showing that couples or perhaps just the man would appear before the Session and give 'in £6 of their pledges' or whatever sum a particular Session might decree. Those who did not have money were allowed to deposit instead some article of value, as happened with other things than marriage. John Shepheard deposited a sword estimated to be worth 36s. Scots which was confiscated on 'non-performance of his intended marriage' and the Session decided that it should be 'sold to any who will buy it.' In 1630 a couple came to the Kirk Session of the Canongate Kirk in Edinburgh and 'gave up their names to be proclaimed, and consigned ane gold signet ring' while another handed in 'ane gold ring with ane quhite stone'. That being in Episcopalian times, this choice of pledge may have been because in most Episcopalian churches, rings are regarded as symbols of pledges or contracts.[13] Spoons or clothing were also pledged. A particularly severe, if understandable, form of caution which would not be tolerated now, was sometimes applied to the poor — that they should 'before their marriage give sufficient caution not to be burdensome to the Session, or else remove themselves out of the congregation.' An Act was passed in Elgin in 1636 stating that no one, 'especially of the poorer sort', should be allowed to marry 'except they first set caution that they be diligent and careful in the vocation God has called them to, whereby they nor their posterity be burdensome to the town, through their sleuth [sloth] and negligence but that they endeavour by all means lawful to acquire their own living', but an exception was provided for where 'poverty comes through long sickness or some visitation.' It seems that this particular Act was introduced to stop the intended marriage of David Gray, a man of ninety, to a young woman.[14]

The benefit of pledges was that the Kirk Session had the money in hand instead of having to pursue for it later and couples knew that it would be returned so long as the marriage went ahead as planned. Evidence of this had to be provided, such as 'producing to the clerk a certificate of their being married, under the hand of the minister who married them within six weeks of the date of entry of their names for proclamation failing which the pawns shall be forfeit for the poor of the parish.' In some cases the pawn was returned by special warrant of the Session as well as that of the minister. Should one of a couple refuse to get married although the other was willing, then his or her pledge was forfeit, possibly with a fine as well, but the pledge of the innocent party was returned. In the case of illness delaying a marriage, then the pawn was either returned or left in abeyance for a time but an explanation was expected: a Galston man who was summoned in 1640 because he had not got married as expected was excused when he explained that his bride-to-be was sick, but he undertook to complete the bond in eight days' time. However, a woman who appeared before that Session the same day to say that her prospective husband had 'with ane fall, brack some ribbes and his collar bone' found that her elder was told to find out whether or not this was true because the frequency with which Galston people broke ribs or fell soon after being 'cried' in church was making the Session suspicious. The giving of consignation money in this way gradually fell out of use and probably ended about the late eighteenth century although it is impossible to be exact about this.[15]

Public proclamation of banns was the announcement in church on three successive Sundays of a couple's intention to marry, the expectation being, as said, that the marriage would take place within forty days although in some cases the forty-day rule applied to contracts rather than to proclamations. The kirk strongly encouraged proclamation of banns but it was something which had to be ordered by the General Assembly more than once. In 1638 an Act of Assembly forbade marriage without proclamation stating that this was 'according to the former Acts' and the same thing was repeated yet again in 1690. The right to be proclaimed was not lightly given. Evidence had to be produced that the couple were free to marry and this was where testificates were very useful, proving the status of people already in the parish. Where necessary, they could be sought from other parishes: 'Received a testificate in favour of Margaret Landels from the parish of Bunkle, declaring her to be a single person free of public scandal and that she may be proclaimed in order to marriage with William Renton of this parish' is an entry in the records of Coldingham Kirk Session in 1699. In the same way, death of a previous marriage partner had to be established and Banff's Session records for 2 April 1705 give a detailed testificate given by the Sheriff of Ross declaring that a particular man had died and that his wife was therefore free to marry again, while in other cases a witness to a death might be called for rather than a certificate. Furthermore, according to an Act of the General Assembly in 1699, before any proclamation could be made, not only the names and designations of the couple wishing to marry, but those of their parents, tutors or curators if they had any, had to be given into the hands of the minister of the parish so that it could be discovered 'if their parents and friends give consent.' The requirement for parental consent was not something new: in 1605 James Watson, apprenticed to a shoemaker, was not allowed to marry because his father, for reasons which he gave to the Session but which are not minuted, refused agreement and, as a minor, James could not make a legal promise without his father's permission. Even so, it was not unknown for someone to forge a testimonial saying that banns had been proclaimed in another parish; and there does seem to be a remarkable overlap in the requirements for contracts and for proclamations.[16]

In the late sixteenth century entries about proclamations of marriage were very formal: 'Appeared Robert Walker wright in Elgin and Beatrix Vobster, Dochter to John Vobster, tailor there, and has ratified a promise of marriage . . . with consent of their parents and friends, neither of them compelled thereto against their wills, and has promised to perform the same how soon their banns can be proclaimed and to abstain from utheris and therefore by these presents give consent that their banns be proclaimed on Sunday.' Should there be any objections, then it was to the Kirk Session that they were made and it was up to them to check their validity: in 1727 two brothers Waugh complained that their sister was about to marry the master of the Grammar School in Selkirk without their advice or consent and asked the minister not to proclaim the banns. In this case, however, their objections were not such as to prevent the marriage taking place.[17]

Proclamations had to be paid for and were an important source of money for the poor and a useful supplement to the income of the Session Clerk and the kirk officer and sometimes to other kirk functionaries such as the bell-man. This was one reason why pulpit intimations were made saying that anyone marrying without proclamation would not only be prosecuted before the civil magistrates but would also receive the severest rigour of church discipline. It was necessary for the kirk to ensure that its staff and the poor received everything to which they were entitled and to take action if they did not get it which was why the Synod of Orkney had to decree in 1753 just what Session Clerks and officers should receive because they were 'being wronged with respect to their dues for marriage and baptism.' Sometimes the whole proclamation fee went to the kirk staff: in 1706 proclamation of marriage in Langholm cost 5 groats (20d. stg.) of which 12d. went to the precentor and 8d. to the kirk officer, leaving nothing for the poor. An idea of how proclamation money was often shared out appears in the minutes of Earlston Kirk Session, Berwickshire, in 1782 when it was decided that 4s. stg. should be paid for each proclamation, divided as follows: 18d. to the poor;18d. to the clerk; 12d. to the kirk officer.[18]

So important were these dues towards maintaining the living of kirk staff and helping the poor that legal action might be used to get them. In 1748 when Abernethy Kirk Session, Perthshire, were 'informed by Mr. Smyth that he had raised a process before the Sheriff Court against several persons for non-payment of Baptism and marriage dues, owing to him as precentor and Session Clerk' they approved of his action and themselves resolved 'to pursue for the dues payable to the poor and beadle on such occasions, [and] did agree and hereby do agree unanimously to authorise and commission him to insist in their name for the recovery of said dues, and also agree to defray the charges of said process out of the public funds.' That they paid £9 18s. as the expense of the process and £3 4s. to the Sheriff officer for executing summonses in a case which lasted some eight months, shows how worthwhile the income was. Proclamation on three Sundays cost 14s. Scots in Hawick in the early years of the eighteenth century, in 1755 Torpichen Kirk Session exacted 2s. 6d. stg. and in 1830 Kilbride Kirk Session levied 10s. stg. for proclamation, in all of which the Session Clerk and kirk officer shared.[19]

It could be difficult to have banns read on three Sundays during a vacancy or if the minister was ill, during an epidemic or if something exceptional occurred like a hurricane lifting off the roof of the church, as once happened at Elie; or if the minister was away at other parishes' Communion services which, in summer, was a considerable reason for absence. In 1688 the Presbytery of Irvine, Ayrshire, dealt with this problem by declaring that in vacant parishes proclamation should be 'once of [sic] thryce' on a day when there was a service, or else at the meeting house of the nearest parish where there was a settled minister. It does not seem that there was any extra charge for this privilege when the need for it was not of the couple's making but when proclamation was completed at their request on fewer than three Sundays, then an extra charge was made, either by way of a fine or as a donation for some charitable purpose:

> Session taking the proclamation dues under their consideration, and finding that severals upon giving up their names to be proclaimed insist upon being proclaimed out in two Sabbath days, contrary to the established rule and yet were unwilling to pay any more than the dues formerly stated for three Sabbaths, viz 1s and 8d, therefore the Session did and hereby do enact that all persons upon giving up their

names to be proclaimed in order to marriage shall pay in all time coming 2s to the poor of the parish, allowing the Session Clerk a liberty to proclaim them any three or two Sabbaths as they judge most convenient.

So said the Kirk Session of Tweedsmuir in 1773 while in Hawick in the early eighteenth century, reading of banns twice in one day was charged at £1 10s. Scots, and thrice at £5 12s. Scots. In 1823 the Kirk Session of Kilmaurs laid down the charges for proclamations when completed on one, two or three days and the proportions to go to the poor and the kirk staff:

		poor	clerk	officer	
3 days	4s	—	3s 3d	9d.	
2 days	10s	4s	5s —	1s —	all stg.
1 day	20s	14s	5s —	1s -	

"For the privilege of marriage on two proclamations' a man gave 2s. stg to the poor of his parish but it is not clear if that was a kindly donation or a charge. Sometimes such sums are entered in accounts as money 'mortified' for the poor, with the word in one instance underlined for some reason.[20]

Because Kirk Sessions fixed proclamation charges themselves, they could adjust them as they saw fit. When the Kirk Session of Falkirk ceded the management of the poor to the heritors in the very early nineteenth century, the latter claimed part of the marriage and baptism dues as well as part of the collections to enable them to carry out this work and when they found themselves in great straits for money, the Session obligingly helped by increasing proclamation dues from 1 guinea to 1½ guineas, a 50% increase, for three proclamations on the one day, which was later raised to 2 guineas. Fees were always fixed on the assumption that both man and woman lived in the same parish but where one did not, there was a reduction which in the first half of the nineteenth century might produce a charge of 3s. for one person as against 5s. for both, and should the marriage not go ahead for any valid reason, then proclamation fees as well as consignation money were returned.[21]

In 1880, in view of changing circumstances, the General Assembly passed an Act on Proclamation of Banns which rescinded all their previous Acts and provided that an applicant for proclamation should be resident in the parish for the space of fifteen clear days immediately before, that applications should be made to the Session Clerk of the parish; that the proclamation, where it could be conveniently done, be made from the pulpit or reading desk by the minister or his officiating substitute acting on his authority, at some time before the end of the service of the first diet of public worship, and where this could not be done, that it be made in such manner as the minister and Kirk Session agreed, but always in the presence of the congregation. When through unavoidable circumstances, there was no service, a proclamation by the Session Clerk made at the church door, in presence of at least two witnesses, together with a written proclamation signed by him and posted on the church door, should be equivalent to normal proclamation;

the minister was given the power to complete proclamation of banns in a single Sabbath and, while it was his duty to celebrate marriages on production of the Session Clerk's certificate of proclamation of banns within three months immediately preceding, there was provision for him to receive as a valid notice of marriage a Registrar's certificate granted under the Act of Parliament entitled Marriage Notice (Scotland) Act, 1878. Since the Marriage (Scotland) Act 1977 banns are no longer read in church except where a minister obliges by reading the banns of a Scottish person who is to marry in an English church where banns are still required.[22]

Going back in time again, things did not always go smoothly. For one thing, people who were already contracted to one person might ask for proclamation of marriage with someone else and in such cases the aggrieved person would probably refuse to set them free and would try to stop the proclamation going ahead. These could be tricky cases. In 1760 George Chrystie was proclaimed in order to marry Janet Storrer, widow of a brewer, whereupon Ann Robertson who came from another parish and had had a child by him six years before, alleged that he had promised to marry her, both before and after the child's birth. She said that he had given her £4 stg. in order to be 'loosed from the said promise and allowing him to go on with the proclamation and binding herself under a penalty of £40 stg to give him no more trouble' but in giving this discharge, she still insisted that she had had this promise of marriage. The Session met her to discuss the whole thing, making it plain that they thought it right for them to do so and managing thereby to imply that there was some doubt about it — and the outcome was that they appeared to agree to what amounted to buying the woman off. It has been said that this was a case of a Session encouraging a man who was an elder to do this but there is no *George* Chrystie in the list of elders although the name Chrystie appears in it. The Presbytery of Selkirk forbade the ministers of Ashkirk and Selkirk to proceed with a proclamation because a woman named Janet Scott alleged that the man had already promised to marry *her* and he was ordered to appear before the Presbytery to answer her complaint. He denied her claim and Janet was told to pursue it before a civil judge without delay 'with certification that if she fail to prove her case the said minister shall proceed with the publication of the said Walter's banns', and as she could not support what she alleged, his banns were duly read. The prospect of having to prove allegations was a considerable factor in sorting out such cases: 'This Sabbath Marion Dykes who had last Sabbath caused staye William . . . his proclamation of marriage with Jean Cuthbertson for aledging promise of marriage came to the elders, and desired that his proclamation might go on and declared that she would not meddle any further in the matter, nor offer to stop his marriage any manner of way after this day, marry whom he would and accordingly his proclamation went on.' It is no wonder that a Session wanted to know the background to the case before dealing with James Waldie who had been proclaimed with one woman one Sunday and wanted to be proclaimed with another the following Sunday. The minutes say that this was 'denyed unto him until we know what the woman he hath been proclaimed with hath to object and James Turnbull, one of the elders, is to speak to her for that report.' An unusual case came up in 1821. Donald Mackay stopped proclamation of a couple's banns because, he said, his sister Barbara, 'a decent well-behaved girl, very useful in the family' had been seduced by the man and was now pregnant and had not only lost her character but was 'disabled from being useful for some time.' The Session, however, did not believe that the girl had been forced and allowed the proclamation to proceed but told the brother that he should raise an action for any damages he wanted in a civil court; loss of her working ability seems to have been his main concern. A Session's knowledge of the people concerned and their circumstances seems to have come into play when David Brown alleged that Maisie Bower refused to marry him in spite of their banns having been called three times. She denied refusing and the Session gave her a month to think about it 'and to give a resolute answer whether she will marry him or not.'[23]

When a woman after being proclaimed with one man, went off with another, the Session's opinion was that she ought to be prosecuted 'for scorning the kirk' — this was a common term for resiling on a marriage contract — and they asked the Kirk Session of a neighbouring parish, from which presumably one or other of the couple came, to join with them in an action before the Sheriff. A Dornoch woman who broke her agreement to marry with no reasonable excuse for doing so was remitted to the civil authorities, yet that Session appear to have accepted it when another woman, on being asked why she had broken her banns, said that 'she had not affection for said McGrigor & will not Marry him, & said She was not able to pay the penalty.' A man in that parish gave poverty as his reason for not marrying but evidence was given which showed that 'it was his Moyr [mother] that Disswaded him and threatened to bestow her means upon others if he should Marry that woman.' The Kirk Session however ordered him to pay £40 Scots of a penalty in terms of his contract 'and charged him to be more Cautious in Time coming.' What was unusual was for the kirk to allow proclamation and then refuse marriage, what might be called the kirk's reneging on a promise that someone might get married. This happened to William Ross, a tacksman in the parish of Tarbat, Ross-shire, who asked and received permission to speak to the Presbytery, telling them that he had been regularly proclaimed but that the minister held back from marrying him and he asked the Presbytery to appoint one of their number to perform the ceremony. Their answer was to order the Presbytery Clerk to write to the minister in their name, instructing him to marry the couple unless there were good reasons for not doing so.[24]

Adultery or fornication by one of the parties committed after a marriage contract was made and detected before the marriage took place was a legal reason for an innocent person to have the contract dissolved and when one Session inquired why a couple were delaying their marriage, the man explained that he suspected that the woman was guilty with someone and he would only marry her if and when she cleared herself. As it turned out he was right in his suspicions and she and her partner in sin had to stand publicly for three Sundays and pay £10 Scots and, although the minutes do not say so, the marriage plans presumably fell by the wayside. It would be interesting to know what lay behind another case in that parish in 1739. John Munro, a boatman, had been proclaimed long before with a young woman who is not named in the minutes, and was summoned by the Session to explain why they had not got married. He replied that 'he had not freedom to go on in it for reasons known to some of the elders but that he did not think it proper to bring them forth judicially' and 'put himself in the Session's will for the failzie and the Session, understanding the case, did exact of him only 10*s* stg.' In this case, social position cannot have been the reason for this special consideration and delicacy, so what can it have been?[25]

Misconduct by couples intending marriage was fairly common in former days. If it occurred before the contract was made, then it was regarded as fornication and they were punished as single delinquents but if it happened after the contract was made, then it became the lesser sin of ante-nuptial fornication. Knowing how easy it was for contracted couples to slip up, Kirk Sessions took their own measures, with that of Perth decreeing in 1585 that 'all persons to be married give their oath the night before' in the presence of the reader and two elders, that is, an oath declaring that there had been no misbehaviour; but an extension of consignation money rules was more effective. Although in many cases consignation money was demanded only to ensure that the marriage went ahead as intended and was returned once it did, nevertheless in other cases it was expanded into a double or even a treble pledge, one of the extra conditions being that the couple should not commit ante-nuptial fornication between contract and marriage. So as to be sure that this was so, the money was retained for nine months after the wedding by which time visible proof of misconduct was likely to be evident. This might appear formally in Kirk Session records:

'Mauchline, 23rd November 1771.
Gentlemen, Conly [conjointly] and seally [severally], and nine months after date, pay to Robert Miller, Kirk Treasurer in Mauchline, the sum of ten pounds Scots in case of ante-nuptial fornication or non-performance of marriage betwixt you, John Steward, in the parish of Sorn, and Jean Black, in this parish — this for the use of the poor of this parish.

Accept — [sgd] John Stewart.
Accept — [sgd] Jean Black.[26]

Kirk Session minutes do not mince matters about such things: in one a man became cautioner that 'if his daughter was brought to bed before the ordinary time, he should pay the penalty and cause her to satisfy the church' but pawn money was returned when nine months were safely up and usually returned in full although when one man asked for his money back, he found that there was 'retained for the use of the poor 12*s* Scots according to a late act anent bridegrooms.' This was a local Act of Session allowing a proportion of the pawn to be kept back for the poor even when all the conditions of the pledge had been fulfilled, something which a number of Sessions did, but the same result could be achieved with what might be regarded as an involuntary donation: when a Kelso man came to his Session 'desiring up his dollars' the Session allowed this but 'referred it to his discretion what he will give to the poor.' This was different from the donations to the poor sometimes given on the occasion of proclamation and was little better than nicely-phrased extortion.[27]

If all the preliminaries of contract, consignation and proclamation were safely got through, the wedding took place on a Sunday or at a weekday service, with the couple or couples — there were often more than one — occupying the special marriage pew or 'bride-stool' where they sat in full view of the congregation during the preliminary sermon. A minute of the Kirk Session of Aberdeen in 1577 stating that no one would be married 'bot upon the stool before the desk, conform to the use of Edinburgh and other kirks' implies a desire to keep up with elsewhere rather than any special merit in the position of the marriage seat. The minutes of Dunfermline Kirk Session in 1641 show that a new form was to be set before the pulpit for 'the brides and bridegrooms the day they are to be married' and where possible, special marriage seating came to be provided in churches around the country. The final church formality was the 'kirking' when the newly-weds attended the church the Sunday after their wedding, something which was considered essential. Unfortunately, all sorts of misbehaviour used to occur at marriages. When two couples were married in 1750 there were very disorderly scenes because people ran out of the church as soon as the last prayer had begun, not even waiting for the blessing. This was due to a superstition that the first bride to go out would carry the blessing and so the brother of one bride got her out of her seat to leave first, while another man called on the day's two brides to go out of the door hand in hand. All this caused great disturbance in the church, with the result that not only were those concerned rebuked before the congregation but also had to forfeit their pledges. In the mid-nineteenth century one minister dealt with this superstition and prevented church-door struggles when more than one couple were married on the same day, by marrying them in the order in which they were contracted. Two men guilty of 'fyring pistols in time of worship' during a marriage in 1732 were rebuked by their Session but this form of *feu de joie* continued and was sufficiently common for that Session to decree in 1839 that shooting at marriages was forbidden. Firearms were especially dangerous when combined with alcohol and in 1724 a man died of wounds received at a wedding. This was by no means the sole incident of its kind as the Presbytery Book of Aberdeen referred to abuses at weddings, 'especially drunkenness and murder' and, to add to the heinousness of the offences, 'that upon the Lord's Day'.[28]

Nevertheless, the kirk accepted, at one time anyway, that people liked to have some wedding festivities and Sessions were sometimes asked to, and did, pass protective acts securing to particular people the exclusive right of supplying marriage banquets within a parish. In 1635 Galston Kirk Session were asked by the 'hostelers and changers of meit and drink within the claghan of Galstoune' about the problem of bridal and baptismal dinners being in 'in landwart with other hostelers, to the hurt and prejudice of them within the said claghan'. In other words people were going from the village of Galston into country areas and bypassing the village inn-keepers and suppliers who added, for good measure, that what was happening was also to the 'great detriment of the poore quha gate [got] help and supply in their necessitie at sic lyke meetings' because going farther afield made it more difficult for the local poor to get to them. The poor always tried to latch on to weddings and to share in the provisions available which helped to give them a square meal now and then and, for one reason or another, the Session agreed with the Galston inn-keepers and decreed that all such wedding dinners must be held within the village except where people held them in their own houses. But things changed and in 1756 the minutes of another Kirk Session show that 'those that shall go with their weddings to any public house where ale is sold or money taken on that account, shall forfeit £3 Sc to be kept off their pledge', because as time went on, it was realised that the large numbers of people which wedding festivities attracted, led to trouble and so a third condition might be required when laying down the pawns — that there should be no crowds, no disorderly behaviour and no promiscuous dancing. An example of the security required and minuted by one Session went as follows:

> I, William Olifer, merchant in Hawick, in testimonie of my detestation and abhorrence of the manifold abuses and disorders which do accompany and attend marriage feasts and especially penny bryddalls, and that I may the more effectually restrain myself from inviting and conveening by myself or others in my name to be with me, or Christian Hart, my affidate spouse, att our marriage, infare, or any meeting on occasion thereof a greater number of persons than is allowed by the laws of the kingdom, do solemnly promise to give in the sum of forty pounds Sc to the Kirk Session of Hawick, or any of them they shall appoint to evade, cist and receive the samen for the use of the poor within the said parish, in case we shall exceed the number of persons allowed by the laws of the kingdom at our marriage, infare or any meeting on occasion therefor. Or if there shall be any insobriety, untimeous drinking, or revelling among those who be attending any of the above-written meetings. In witness thereof I have signed these presents written by Mr. John Purdome, Clerk to the Kirk Session of the parish of Hawick, December the first 1702.

To this there were six witnesses but when he signed this before them, William Olifer was reckoning without his prospective father-in-law, as appears later on.[29]

In 1621 Parliament forbade banquets at marriages (and burials) but in 1681 found it necessary to put a limit of not more than four extra guests who might be present, in addition to the bride and groom, their parents, any children, brothers and sisters and 'the family where they live'. In spite of official decrees on the subject, there was considerable variation in practice around the country about permitted numbers of wedding guests: St. Andrews Kirk Session limited them to ten a side in 1642, in 1624 Dumbarton Kirk Session stated that thirty-two was the maximum while in 1710 within the bounds of the Presbytery of Fordyce it was down to three a side, along with a requirement that the couple appear before the Kirk Session on a Sunday to give their pledge to this effect.[30] But these rulings were not very effective.

The only way that poor people could have a wedding celebration of any sort was if those who came to it contributed towards it. These festivities came to be known as penny weddings, silver or siller bridals or pay weddings and were open-house affairs which anyone could attend , whether friends of the families or not, so long as they made a small cash contribution, often only a penny Scots, or else gave something in kind, which resulted not only in everyone having a tremendous time but usually left a little over to form a nest egg for the newly married couple. Penny weddings were sufficiently accepted in 1617 for Parliament to pass an Act that year requiring Justices of the Peace to fix the price of ordinaries (food and drink) at them which explains how, because of concern about overcharging, the Justices of the Peace of the shire of Edinburgh stated in an assessment of wages in 1656 that 'The Makers of Penny Bridals are not to exceed Ten Shillings Sc of a Man, and Eight shillings Scots, for a Woman, whether at Dinner or Supper.' This they said in spite of the Act of Parliament of 1621 which limited numbers at wedding feasts but perhaps they had not caught up with the Act or did not consider that it applied to penny weddings. These weddings attracted enormous crowds and resulted in drunkenness and fighting but they were very popular with the people and when a Presbytery tried to suppress them in 1627, they got no co-operation from other Presbyteries. One Synod did not forbid them in 1640 but just said that they should not take place on Sundays to avoid profanation of that day. As the kirk gradually had more opportunity to turn its mind to such matters, its opinion of penny weddings became less and less favourable, with one Presbytery saying that as a result of going to them many people 'fell a sacrifice to lust and luxury and some loose persons usually frequenting these occasions, do by the influence of their bad example embolden others to sin', but even when the General Assembly passed an Act against Penny Bridals in 1645, describing them as 'fruitful seminaries of all lasciviousness and debaucherie' it still did not seek to stop them but just to restrain abuses at them. A practical result of this Act appears in the minutes of a Presbytery which decreed in 1646 that such social groups as craftsmen, cottagers, grasmen and others of that rank might have penny weddings but that they were forbidden for anyone higher up the social scale. However, it was laid down by this Presbytery for one, that those to be married must consign money, and only money, as a guarantee that there would be no piping, dancing, drinking, fighting, swearing, scolding or other abuses at the wedding, which was a considerable extension of the undertaking required of William Olifer in Hawick, and they also tackled the problem from the other end by decreeing that any householder in whose home a wedding feast was held should consign two dollars as a guarantee that he would not admit more than six guests a side, in addition to the married couple, nor for the space of forty-eight hours, allow in any non-invited guests or 'country vagers'.[31]

As time went on, the Kirk at various levels passed acts as necessary against penny weddings. When one couple gave in their names for marriage in 1703 the minister told them that 'it was the Session's mind that they should go soberly about their marriage, and beware of having penny bridals, there being an Act of

Synod against the same', and in 1706 the General Assembly recommended Presbyteries to apply to the judges ordinary to put laws about penny weddings into
force and passed a similar Act in 1719. Nevertheless, the records of just one
Presbytery show that in the year 1724 great numbers of people were going to
penny weddings and ministers were asked to take more note of them; but in spite
of any efforts they may have made, three years later the advice of the Synod had to
be sought about the problem. Seventy years on, in 1798, that Presbytery was still
finding the effects of these weddings so harmful that they decided to apply to the
judge ordinary to suppress them as the General Assembly had said to do but they
still continued and, while deprecated, seem ultimately to have become accepted,
there and elsewhere. Rev. James Smith, writing the Old Statistical Account for the
parish of Avoch, in the 1790s, said that most marriages at that date there took the
form of penny weddings with bread, ale and whisky provided in the house and
dancing going on in a barn to the music of a fiddler or two, all of which was kept up
for two or three days until the Saturday night. The couple then went to church on
Sunday and on their return gave a dinner or similar form of entertainment, all of
which was done with little loss or gain to them. Although much about penny
weddings was said to be 'lamented, deprecated and amended' they were common
in the nineteenth century and lasted into the twentieth; Bob Morrow described in
The Scots Magazine the 'pay weddings' of his youth during the Hungry Thirties.
The wedding ceremony was attended only by the families concerned but there
after friends could come to the reception, paying a shilling each, which covered
the charge for the hall, a simple meal and music for dancing. It was a very practical
idea.[32]

The kirk was always concerned about 'promiscuous dancing' which was men
and women dancing in the same room. Dancing was a feature of weddings but
there is no evidence that Kirk Sessions ever fined lairds or their guests when
members of the opposite sex danced at weddings in mansion houses. In itself
dancing was an innocent enough form of enjoyment but it was one which could
lead to considerable immorality when coupled with drinking and Kirk Sessions
greatly deplored it going on in lower social circles. One referred to 'great dansing
and vanitie' which occurred at the public cross at a wedding and another described
dancing at wedding dinners as

> most abominable, not to be practised in a land of light, and condemned in former
> time by Presbytery as not only unnecessary, but sensual, being only an inlet of lust
> and provocation to uncleanness through the corruption of men and women in this
> loose and degenerate age, wherein the devil seems to be raging by a spirit of
> uncleanness and profanity, making such practices an occasion to the flesh, and
> thereby drawing men and women to dishonour God, ruine their own souls, and cast
> reproach upon the holy ways of religion.

In 1649 the General Assembly passed the Act forbidding promiscuous dancing
and the following year Presbyteries were telling their ministers to inform their
congregations about it. The General Assembly revived this Act in 1701 and this

particular aspect of wedding entertainment became specifically added to consignation undertakings: 'Robert Halliewell being proclaimed with Jeannie Halliewell signed two bills that the marriage would be consumat and that there will be no promiscuous dancing and lascivious piping', the last part because the best way to prevent dancing was to forbid or control the music-making. The Presbytery of Glasgow decreed in 1647 what whoever had a piper playing at their wedding would lose their consignation money and individual Kirk Sessions passed their own Acts, such as at Kinross where an 'Act anent piping at weddings' ordered 'that there be noy^r pyper nor violer at any wedding w^t in the paroch unless they be invited by the bridegrooms or some commissioned from him.'[33] The custom of 'pipers playing to persons when they are going to church to be married, and when they are coming from church to their homes' may well have had the effect of the Pied Piper of Hamelin and encouraged all and sundry to join in, which was probably why pipers at weddings were a particular target of Kirk Sessions. In 1638 Adam Moffat was found guilty of piping at weddings and had to stand in sheets at the church door, barefoot and barelegged, and then come in to the place of repentance 'and so to continue Sabbathlie' during the Session's will. Dancing, of course, did not only take place at weddings but at other times too and when the piper who was employed by many towns, played through the streets this was an immediate encouragement to the light of foot. It was for a combination of these reasons that in 1649 St. Andrews Kirk Session summoned 'a viler and a pyper' before them for 'pyping and fiddling unseasonablie in taverns or ale houses' and as a result forbade all music at weddings and limited the piper's playing in the town in morning and evening to only four hours. Anyone found in possession of a fiddle was liable to be summoned before his Session and by the eighteenth century, to have played at a gathering where dancing took place could result, not necessarily in the kind of punishment Adam Moffat received but in a fine of £20 Scots for each offence while those dancing might be refused the sealing ordinances of baptism or Communion.[34]

Highlanders especially loved dancing, at weddings or anywhere else, hence the following entry from the minutes of the Presbytery of Lewis in 1759 which has a marginal note saying, 'Merry People at Shawbost':

> The Presbytery being informed that a house . . . has been built in North Shabost for fiddling, dancing and other sports suitable to the dispositions of those who frequent it, and that a vast number of people of both sexes, and a fiddler resort to the same on Saturday nights, where thereon music, dancing, drinking of spirituous liquors, loose carriage, cursing and swearing are practised, and where these persons continue so long, that the Presbytery may have reason to be persuaded they encroach on the Sabbath . . . Mr. Murdoch Morison' [minister of Barvas] by the advice of the Presbytery, having dealt with the bulk of those who are principally concerned in the said house to pull down the same, which they unanimously promised to do without loss of time. Nevertheless, it has as of late been repaired and continues to be used as formerly. Therefore Presbytery appoint the Kirk Session of Barvas to prosecute the fiddler and the other persons concerned in the irregularity in the diversions and

appoints the kirk officer of Barvas to cite the said people before the Kirk Session as they shall see cause.

However, when a dancing school for adults was opened in another northern parish in 1888 and proved an 'irresistible attraction' to the school children of the area as well, the Kirk Session minutes do not mention it, showing that by that date things had greatly changed.[35]

To go back to weddings, it was one thing for elders to implement decisions of Parliament and of the General Assembly and Presbyteries about wedding festivities, and to pass their own Acts of Session too, but it was quite another matter when an elder was himself involved, perhaps as father of the bride. It was a matter of pride to put on a good show and to have a large number of guests present, and John Hart, an elder in Hawick and father of Christian Hart who was to marry William Olifer, whose bond has already been quoted, was obviously anxious to give his daughter a good send-off. In spite of the assurances that William gave the Kirk Session, when the 'kirk censer' perlustrated the streets on the night of the wedding, he found John Hart 'and his company with him dancing and making such a noise that they were heard in the very streets.' Hart craved pardon for this sin but was deposed as an elder until the Session could see what his 'after-carriage' might be and presumably the unfortunate William forfeited the £40 Scots he had pledged. Another instance, also from Hawick, happened in 1706 when 'the sound of revelry by night' was heard from the inn kept by William Atkine in the Kirk Wynd where a large number of people were drinking. The occasion was the marriage of a daughter of the house to John Hardie, a respected and well-known merchant in the town, and in this merry company were two magistrates, the town clerk, two ex-bailies, a neighbouring laird and the local doctor. It says much for the Session that they had the courage to stand up to such important local personages, with the result that the magistrates sat in judgment on their host and his son-in-law and ordered them each to pay a fine of £10 for breach of the law limiting the number of guests allowed to attend weddings, an offence in which they had shared. The bailies resented the church's attitude in this case and tried to browbeat the minister and those elders who challenged their conduct, asserting that they were being summoned in their capacity as magistrates and when ordered to appear before the Session responded by calling a special meeting of the Town Council which agreed to 'owne and defend' the two bailies, but to no avail. The Session stood up successfully to the whole Town Council and the offenders had to give in, with the result that on the following Sunday a remarkable scene was witnessed at a Session meeting with the magistrates of the town, who were elders of the kirk, appearing before the minister and the other elders.[36]

On the subject once more of consignation money and disorderly marriages, some Kirk Sessions tempered justice with mercy and as pawn money which was forfeited went to the poor, it was sensible to take pity on a bridegroom who was also poor. When James Hardie asked for 'his dollar which was consigned at his marriage', although the Session found that he 'had a great abuse and public promiscuous dancing at his marriage, whereby the dollar is forfeit' they realised that he was poor and allowed him have it back apart from 20*d*.; and these were by no means isolated instances of compassion. The best thing to do, of course, was to set a reasonable figure for consignation money in the first place and then stick to it. In Orphir, for example, pawn money was initially set at £3 but it was found that in the case of forfeiture a reduction almost always had to be granted and so in 1747 the Session passed an Act anent Pawn money, putting the figure at £2 'without diminution in case of forfeiture', although the figure had to go back to £3 in 1794 owing to a decrease in the value of money. It was said in 1872 that in Orkney until 'very recently', should pawn money be returned, it was given not to the husband but to the wife to buy a new dress. Payment of pawn money made marriage expensive and abuses could creep in to make it more costly still: in 1658 the Kirk Session of St. Andrews learnt that those who held the pawns of couples 'had been in practice of getting some money at the delivering again of these pands' and had to forbid this to happen again.[37]

The Reformers decreed that marriages should be solemnised in church on Sundays in face of the congregation but at the General Assembly of 1579 questions were put about the possibility of marrying on other days of the week and it was agreed that this could be done so long as there were sufficient witnesses, the banns had been published for three Sundays and that there was preaching as well. Perth Kirk Session decreed in 1585–86, however, that marriages should not take place on Sunday mornings and although their reason for this Act is not given, it may have been similar to one made by the Kirk Session of Elgin where in 1626 Sunday marriages were forbidden because people had gone to a wedding elsewhere and were not at worship in their own parish church. Nevertheless, Sunday was for a time the favoured day for weddings. In 1645 the Westminster Directory, accepted by the General Assembly and ratified by the Scottish Parliament, emphasised what had been said in 1579, saying that marriages could be solemnised by a minister in the place appointed for public worship before a sufficient number of credible witnesses at some convenient hour of the day, at any time in the year except on a day of public humiliation. This allowed marriages to take place at the weekday services which were regularly held, such as at Largo, Fife, where the mid-week service in the seventeenth century was held at 9.00 a.m. and anyone wishing to be married was required to attend at that hour. In spite of what the Westminster Directory said about 'any time of the year', some parishes did not allow Monday marriage lest Sunday should be desecrated but people could be very demanding. In Kilmarnock, Ayrshire, they expected to be married more or less whenever they pleased with the result that the Session, considering how 'dystractite' it was for the minister to be expected to attend 'every several time of dyat that parties to be married will probably incline to, ordained that all marriages shall be on Thursday only' although if they had a good reason they could be married on a Tuesday if they paid 30*s*. Scots for the poor. That order was made in 1658 but by 1706 it had fallen into such disuse that the people were coming to the minister at all hours, often 'desiring to be married early, sometimes about 5.0–6.0

o'clock in the morning', with the result that another ruling had to be made, that no townspeople might be married before 10.00 a.m. unless they paid 20s. Scots for the poor, while those in the landward part of the parish were told that if they wanted to be married on Thursday, the preaching day, then they must attend for the sermon or else not be married that day. In some places in the earlier part of the seventeenth century, marriages took place on market days which were days of greater freedom for ordinary people but for that very reason they tended to licence and riotous behaviour anyway and at least one Presbytery forbade market day weddings in 1635.[38]

Until 1811 celebration of a marriage anywhere other than in a church made it technically irregular and clandestine and about the late sixteenth century ministers could be, and were, deposed for marrying people in private houses but it is not surprising that people were not always keen on being married in a church. Distance, bad roads or none at all, bad weather and other factors made marriage at home a much more attractive prospect whatever the rules might be and so private marriages began to take place — and in 1690 an early Act of the church after the Revolution was to forbid them. But money always talked and if private marriages could help to raise funds for the poor, then private marriages there would be and a mere six years later Drymen Kirk Session, Stirlingshire, was permitting them, not specifically but by implication, saying that if a wedding did not take place in church, then there must be a payment of 20s. Scots. A similar attitude was taken that year in Stirling where the Session enacted 'that none be married privately in tyme coming except they first pay a dollar to the poor.' This phrasing implies a compulsory donation, as does the 2s. stg. given in 1732 to Mauchline Kirk Session 'for being allowed to marry out of the kirk in a private house' but the term 'fine' was also used in connection with payments to do with private marriages, which had been becoming steadily more fashionable. From 1700, in fact, private or 'chamber' marriages as they were sometimes called, were seldom if ever considered irregular and the ministers performing them were neither censured by church courts nor fined by civil ones. Should it be found that private marriages were not benefiting the poor, then a Session would take steps to put things right. In 1731 that of St. Michael's, Linlithgow, found that while it had become customary for people being married to give £3 Scots to the poor for the privilege of doing so privately, the poor's funds had recently been 'greatly disappointed' by people marrying in other parishes and avoiding contributing to their own poor's funds. It was therefore decided that any parishioner or anyone from another parish, who got married anywhere other than in the local church should pay £3 Scots for each couple, and anyone wanting a testificate to be married outside the parish should also pay £3 Scots per couple, except in cases when one of them lived in another parish or when the minister was absent or ill or in special cases which were left to the Kirk Session's discretion. As with poor people who suffered if the consignation money was forfeit, so with those wishing to marry privately: the kirk was compassionate and might take no more than 6d. stg. in such a case although, in general, the poor continued to marry in church long after those able to pay were being married in private.[39]

Kirk officers were sometimes allowed to make a collection for their own benefit at marriages in church; in the later nineteenth century it became the custom, in one area of Ayrshire at any rate, for there to be a contribution for the bell-man at weddings, and while private marriages did not involve kirk staff in any work on the day itself, nevertheless they meant a loss to them of rightful dues and so it became normal for the beadle or kirk officer to receive a small fee for every private marriage. For the same reason the parish of Morebattle laid down a fee and a penalty of 18s. Scots for private marriages, of which 12s. was for the poor and 6s. for the kirk officer. The penalty element of this was due to what was called 'the needless inconvenience of marrying persons out of the church.'[40]

So popular and accepted did private marriages become in time that they even took place in the manse but this too incurred an extra charge, hence a minute of 1723 which said, 'None to be married privately in the minister's house unless they pay 2s stg to the poor' — and this was in spite of the fact that private marriage was contrary to the law, whether it took place in the manse or any other house. By the very end of the eighteenth century the custom of marrying in church went out of general use in Scotland and to such an extent was this so that when Dr Borland performed a marriage ceremony in Yarrow Kirk, Selkirkshire, where he was minister from 1883–1912, he was waylaid by an old parishioner the next day who asked him what John Knox would have thought of the ongoings in the church the day before, quite unaware of the fact that marriage in church was exactly what Knox and the other Reformers had specified. At the end of the nineteenth century the common custom was still for marriages to take place in private houses and any in church were rare enough to cause a special paragraph in the press but nowadays a religious wedding ceremony is virtually always held in a church although if the minister is agreeable, it may be held elsewhere, such as in a garden.[41]

Something which only happened infrequently was night-time marriage but it was frowned upon as it could very well be a cover-up for something wrong: one Session found that such a marriage had been celebrated by a clergyman who had been both deposed and excommunicated and the couple came from another parish. Another fault of night-time marriage was that even should it be properly conducted by the parish minister, it was such an exciting spectacle that it could lead to a 'tumult of idle gazers who run so disorderly together at such times', as the minutes of St. Andrews Kirk Session put it at the same time as they forbade it — but there was still the usual let-out and if money was forthcoming people could be married after the setting of the sun if they paid 40 merks to the poor.[42]

In 1587 Parliament ordained the death penalty for any Scotsman who married an English woman living in England, without having a licence from the king to do so and in 1639, on the petition of the General Assembly, passed another Act forbidding Scottish couples from going to England to marry. This was followed up by yet another Act in 1641 decreeing that no Scottish people were to marry in England or Ireland without proclamation of banns in Scotland, which was ratified in 1649 and 1661. These Acts were designed to prevent people from eluding the vigilance of the kirk by slipping over the border or the sea for marriage but a more effective deterrent was something like refusal of baptism for a child, which was the punishment of one man 'for running over the march with Agnes Turnbull'. In 1641 Parliament also decreed that anyone married by a Jesuit priest or anyone else not authorised by the kirk should be imprisoned and fined and the celebrator banished and in 1661 yet another Act ordered that anyone married by an un-authorised person should be imprisoned for three months, with the celebrator to suffer the same fate as before. 1641 was a time of Presbyterian church government while 1661 saw the return of Episcopacy and the purpose of both these Acts was to force people to worship in whichever was the official manner for the time being, as was an Act of 1695, passed after the Revolution, which specifically forbade 'outed' ministers to solemnise marriages. The Act of Toleration of 1712 gave people freedom to worship in their own manner but intolerance still continued in connection with being married by a clergyman not of one's own church: in 1715 an Edinburgh man admitted being married by an Episcopalian incumbent and was sharply rebuked by the Kirk Session and referred to the magistrates for fining, while in 1723 a Banffshire Kirk Session 'thought fit that Mary Sutherland, being a professed Protestant should be rebuked for taking marriage from a popish priest.' Roman Catholic marriages in that area of Banffshire were fairly common at that time and several non-Catholics married by priests were duly referred by the Session for civil punishment.[43]

Any clergyman, deposed because of a change in church government or for any other reason, was only too willing to put his professional skills to the service of those wanting marriage and to be paid for doing so. Mr David Strange was one of these; he was deposed from the church of Cabrach in the Presbytery of Alford in 1730 for neglecting his duties and came to Edinburgh where he married people without banns. As a result he was cited to appear before the Kirk Session of St. Cuthbert's Church and ultimately Lesser Excommunication was pronounced — but he still carried on marrying. Higher Excommunication was then imposed but still he married people and continued to do so even after he was arrested in 1738 and imprisoned. Also in Edinburgh there was David Paterson, a probationer for the ministry who was unfrocked and excommunicated for adultery, who married people thereafter and was imprisoned for eighteen months for doing so.[44]

Some people regarded marriage anywhere but in the parish church of one or other of the couple as irregular but that was overlooking the fact that during a vacancy there might be no minister to marry them in the parish church; and where a parish was very large or had many unbridged rivers, it could be virtually impossible for a couple to wed in their own parish church and so they might be permitted to go to another which, although in another parish, was more accessible. The problem of very large parishes was recognised by officialdom with the appointment in the eighteenth century of missionaries and itinerant preachers for certain scattered areas. When one such man was offered to a Presbytery in 1727 he was accepted with a particular mention of how useful he would be for marrying people (and for baptisms) and there was every anxiety to ordain him and annexe him as a member of the Presbytery. This was a practical way of helping people over the difficulties of marrying in their own church.[45]

However, the irregular marriages which feature so largely in Kirk Session records are those where an unmarried couple, without proclamation of banns, declared themselves married before two witnesses who signed to that effect. This type of marriage had developed in Scotland when clergy were scarce during the religious to-ing and fro-ing of the seventeenth century and it was realised that if there was no minister to perform the marriage, it was better to regularise a union which would occur anyway, by accepting it as a fact, even if there were laws against it. In 1685 Parliament ordered Justices of the Peace to enforce laws against disorderly marriage, which included irregular marriage, but the reason that there were so many irregular weddings was that the kirk more or less forced people into them by placing so many obstacles and expenses on the bridal path to regular marriage, to which was added that of stamp duty, introduced by the government in 1783. One can imagine the affront, to put it mildly, that was caused by one couple who managed to be irregularly married in church during the weddings of several other people. This happened in Peterhead, Aberdeenshire, in 1681: as the minister was marrying the others, these two joined hands and proclaimed themselves married persons, thereby achieving irregular marriage before witnesses although of course no 'lines' were given to them by the minister. The Kirk Session were very displeased about it all but after summoning them, referring them to the Presbytery and having them returned, they were married publicly before the congregation in the proper way. It was mainly poorer people who married irregularly but sometimes professional people and even lairds' families did so too. There was a lawyer in Linlithgow who married the daughter of a late bailie of the town irregularly in 1731, the Town Clerk of Falkirk who married the daughter of a bailie in 1743 and a Hawick doctor who wed the sister of a local laird in 1724.[46]

Any mention of irregular marriage immediately makes people think of Gretna Green in the parish of Graitney, Dumfries-shire, where the much publicised runaway marriages of English couples began after 1754 when an English Act of Parliament made fourteen years' transportation the penalty for solemnising marriage in England without banns or other licence in any other place than a church or chapel. It was only in 1856 that the position changed for English people when the Marriage Act required one of the contracting parties to have lived in Scotland for at least twenty-one days before the marriage. But Scots were marrying in Gretna well before the English discovered it and at other places along the border too, such as Coldstream and Lamberton Toll and although generally more common in southern Scotland, irregular marriages took place further north too, for instance in Angus, in Aberdeen and in Sutherland. The odd thing is that so well known did Gretna Green become for these marriages that Scottish people were known to go there even from the far north of the country, when they could just as well have been married at home with a few lines witnessed by two people.[47]

In spite of just two witnesses and their signatures being all that was required to authenticate such a marriage, it became usual for there to be a celebrant who was often termed a 'priest', who was in fact anyone who did not let the disapproval of the church prevent him earning money by giving a sought-after service which many people regarded as legal. These priests were seldom, as is sometimes thought, unfrocked clergy although there were a few. One was Rev. Thomas Blair, known as the 'curate of Cornwall', who was ejected in 1689 from the parish of Lennel, Berwickshire, for not praying for King William and Queen Mary and who thereafter not only performed irregular marriages but compounded his offence in several cases by back-dating the marriage lines to conceal ante-nuptial fornication. All sorts of people became 'priests' — blacksmiths, shoemakers, bakers, anyone at all could, if they wished, put a couple through a ceremony in the presence of the required two witnesses and then provide a short certificate, the marriage lines, which set forth the particulars of the event. One man who tried to make the ceremony as near to the real thing as he could was William Dickson, a shoemaker in Coldstream, who would ask the bride and groom their names and require them to repeat after him, 'I — take thee — to be my wedded husband/wife, to have and to hold from this day forward, for better, for worse, for richer, for poorer, in sickness and in health, to love and to cherish till death do us part,' and for the bride the word 'obey' was inserted, after which he concluded with the words: 'Thus I pronounce you man and wife, All the days of your life.' His register was then signed — unfortunately his registers have now disappeared — a marriage certificate written out and a fee of half a guinea was handed over. Another Coldstream celebrant was John Rutherford, a blacksmith, whose door was always open and whose wife was always ready to act as a witness. While these irregular marriages could take place anywhere in the town, Coldstream became famous for what is now called the Marriage House, a toll-house still standing on the north side of the bridge over the River Tweed. In the very early years of the eighteenth century, the name of John Barclay occurs frequently as a celebrant in Edinburgh and some twenty years later, Patrick Middleton was also operating there. Some of those who performed marriages regularly put the words 'as minister' after their signatures on the marriages lines and Patrick Middleton went further and styled himself 'Min^r of the Gospel' which he most certainly was not entitled to do; it was presumption of this sort which made a Lanarkshire Session Clerk refer disparagingly to a 'man who designes himself minister.'[48]

An example of marriage lines from Coldstream which seems to have been intended for an English couple, was as large as a handbill, 13" by 8¼", headed with the royal arms and with the words, 'Kingdom of Scotland. Coldstream Bridge. Parish of Coldstream', written in large letters. In bold writing, the celebrant gave his assurance that the couple had been married 'agreeable to the laws of Scotland after the manner of the laws of the Church of England.' Invaluable though marriage lines were, they were not usually so splendid as this and were usually just a sheet of paper giving the essential information as in the following examples: 'These are to certfie that William MacLean and Margaret Watt do acknowledge themselves to be lawfully marryed as man and wife before these witnesses and so acknowledge the seam this 22 day of July 1747 at Stirling as we do hear attest the seam by [names of three witnesses]' or 'I, John Brown, do hereby acknowledge and take you Jannet Allen to be my lawful married wife and do in presence of God promise and Covenant to be a faithful and loving husband to you until God shall separate us by death. Signed — John Brown.'[49]

The wording of irregular marriage certificates often appears in Kirk Session records because couples married in this way were expected, when called upon to do so, to give the Session the names and status of the celebrant and witnesses and most couples, once they were safely if irregularly married, wasted no time in going before their Sessions voluntarily to declare themselves man and wife. The minutes of Cambuslang Kirk Session, to take only one parish, have various entries in the late eighteenth century of couples appearing *sûa sponte*, professing their sorrow for what they had done, which must have been pure hypocrisy, and asking to be taken on discipline. Their readiness, indeed eagerness, to do so was largely because the sooner they started discipline, the sooner it would be over and baptism would not be allowed for any child of the union until everything was settled. Thus it is that the minutes of a Berwickshire Kirk Session in 1809 show that John Anderson, a carrier, and Isabel Aitchison came before the Session of their own accord and 'having been married irregularly in June last produced a certificate of their marriage, the tenor whereof follows: 'Lamberton Tollbar. 30th June 1809. This certifies to whom it may concern that according to the form of marriage observed in the Church of Scotland, John Anderson and Isabel Aitchison, were solemnly united by me in the holy bonds of Wedlock and so far as can be known they were free of all church censure, which is attested by these witnesses, Signed George Lamb, minister' — another self-styled one — 'William Ker, George Tod, witnesses.' This marriage was then confirmed by the parish minister, an elder and the Session Clerk because Kirk Sessions realised that it could do nothing but good to recognise irregular marriages once they were a *fait accompli* and to make sure that there were properly recorded which was a great safeguard to the woman and ensured that if there were children, paternity was established and maintenance would not fall on the kirk. That gives the impression that it was all quite easy but in fact couples were soundly rebuked and exhorted to repentance. They might be urged 'to be humble in the sight of God and to fly to the blood of Jesus Christ for washing and cleansing and to live together in all time coming as becometh true penitents and married persons' or 'encouraged to adhere to each other as husband and wife, during life, and exhorted to live in love and peace together'; they could be 'exhorted to their marriage dutys' or be more simply enjoined 'to live regularly', and only thereafter were they absolved and declared to be married persons. In some cases there were penalties but a general tenor of acceptance of what they had done is evident. Sometimes Kirk Sessions were sufficiently co-operatively to give duplicates of what was put in the kirk records: when one couple's certificate was presented to the Session, the Clerk was ordered to insert it in the Session register 'and a double thereof to be given to them' and this was common there although it made extra work for the Session Clerk.[50]

It was essential for marriage lines to be produced before any Kirk Session would accept that an irregular union had taken place and when a young woman, Ann Ruxton, was reported to be pregnant and called before her Session, she had to give her bond with caution that she would produce documents on or before a certain date to show that she had been married in London and that she would accept the kirk's discipline if it was found that there had been any scandal and, with this agreement, when her child was born it was baptised and she was in the end able to prove her marriage. Lines also had to be satisfactory. Any doubt about them had to be cleared up and when Marie Bruce produced a marriage certificate only to have it 'much jealoused' (suspected) by the Session, she was told to get another one which, even if the original had been genuine, would not have been an easy thing for her to do. A couple produced a certificate to Tillycoultry Kirk Session which was considered totally insufficient to prove marriage as it contained nothing more than their own declaration that they were married and as the man had nothing to prove that he was free to marry at the time, he was told to procure a certificate with all possible despatch and in the meantime the Session forbade them to live as man and wife until further notice. This case went to the Presbytery who reported that the man had produced a certificate that he was single and their advice was to declare them married and rebuke them for ante-nuptial fornication. In 1800 a woman who was pregnant produced marriage lines of a sort and her husband, working at the time in another parish, returned to support her statement that they were married, bringing with him a certificate from Muirkirk, dated 1796, which stated that he was then unmarried and free from scandal, but that was not enough for the Session. They demanded a more up-to-date certificate from that parish which three months later he was able to produce and after 'long reasoning' by the Kirk Session and the minister's statement that several members of the Presbytery had advised him that 'in order to encourage marriage, the best way would be to rebuke them before the Session for their irregularity and declare them married persons', the couple paid a fine of 10s. stg. and the usual dues were exhorted and the minister 'admonished them to a regular, decent and circumspect behaviour for the future and after asking their mutual consent, declared them married persons.'[51]

There was considerable variation in the penalties for irregular marriage. No fines, punishments, dues or even undue reprimand are mentioned in some Kirk Session minutes such as those of Yetholm and Swinton and Simprim in the first quarter of the nineteenth century, although it is always possible that they existed but were unrecorded, whereas in 1697 Kirkcudbright Kirk Session tried to bear down on the practice by ordering a guilty couple to 'arise out of their sates' the next Sabbath for public rebuke, with an intimation made to the congregation that if anyone else followed their example, further censure would be inflicted. In spite of this, irregular marriages increased there and around the country and in 1720 one Session felt it necessary to have a proclamation read to the congregation 'to terrifie anie in this parish to follow such irregular way of marriage' and they decided to implement all earlier Acts of Parliament on the subject. Only four years later, however, the doctor and the laird's sister, whose irregular marriage there has already been mentioned, were rebuked not before the Session but in the manse, after which the certificate of their marriage was entered in the kirk records, a procedure which can hardly have terrified them.[52]

It seems fair enough that the kirk should not lose financially on these marriages and so one finds Kirk Sessions such as Dunbar requiring offending couples in 1733 to pay the church dues for irregular marriage — what would normally be paid for proclamation, the Session Clerk's and kirk officer's fees, and a shilling to the poor in addition; at Sprouston one couple had to pay the church dues and a shilling to the poor but another couple were fined £3 stg. At Bonhill a man irregularly married eight years previously had to pay £1 stg. on the understanding that the Session would 'prosecute the matter no further' but the following year other offenders were paying the same sum, which included the Clerk's and officer's dues. By 1780, however, that Session found that there were still so many irregular marriages that they decided to fine all offenders £5 stg. per couple for the poor's funds, plus a guinea to the clerk and the officer, although some twenty years later Falkirk Kirk Session was imposing only a fine of two guineas. In Banffshire, in 1728, a principal heritor who was therefore interested in raising as much money for the poor as possible so as to reduce the burden on himself and his fellow-heritors, ordered the Bailie of the Regality to issue extracts of decreets against six couples who had all married irregularly, requiring each of them to pay to the Kirk Session for various uses £9 Scots each, a total of £54. It says much for the Session that they overrode this and reduced the penalties to a total of £24, being either more compassionate than the heritor or realising that there was no point in asking for the impossible. From this it is apparent that some Kirk Sessions were primarily anxious to see the marriage recorded, others were thankful to receive the marriage dues and would settle for them along with a rebuke; still others required the dues and a little something for the poor, and some fined heavily. Income from irregular marriages undoubtedly helped kirk funds but for ordinary people, irregular marriage was cheaper than paying the costs contingent upon a regular marriage and avoided the inquisitorial interference of the kirk prior to it. Although most people wished to get an irregular marriage accepted by the Kirk Session and to pay whatever charges might be imposed, when Hawick Kirk Session, as a deterrent to increasing numbers of these marriages, ordered one offender to pay 100 merks, he thought this was far too much and declared 'that he was att great enough expense anent his marriage and would not allow anything for his trespass' and simply refused to pay and nothing could be done about it. In the latter half of the eighteenth century it became possible to apply to the Procurator Fiscal for a Justice of the Peace to perform a marriage ceremony. Although this made the marriage technically irregular, it avoided paying a fine, which affected the poor's funds and it was for that reason that one Session made a representation to the

Justices asking them to ensure that what the poor would normally receive from fines should be allowed to them.[53]

While most couples lived more or less happily after an irregular marriage, there could be problems as it was easy for a man to deny that there had ever been a marriage unless it had been confirmed by the Kirk Session and for one reason or another, there were always some people who neither came nor were summoned to their Session to have their marriage investigated and established; but when such problems arose the kirk was prepared to try to deal with them. Jannet Gorely told her Session that one night when she and her husband were in bed, he asked her for their marriage lines in order to show them to the Session. Trustingly, she gave them to him but when she asked for them back, he said that they were lost and denied being married to her although he had already told someone that they were husband and wife. The matter was referred by the Kirk Session to the Presbytery and the next mention of the matter in the minutes was two months later when the man 'having been obliged by the order of the Justices of the Peace to acknowledge Jannet Gorely for his wife and so to cohabit with her, or allow her a separate maintenance', appeared with her before the Session where they were declared married, were rebuked and paid a fine for the poor. In the late eighteenth century a woman discovered that the man she had married irregularly some years before was planning to marry someone else. She and the man had not had their marriage recorded by their Session and so she could produce no written proof of what she said but she managed to bring forward several witnesses who could state that they had been introduced to her by him as his wife; this was accepted as proof of marriage and was sufficient to stop proclamation of his banns with anyone else. In an unusual case a man's banns were stopped when evidence was given to the Kirk Session by a witness that he was already married. This witness was an inn-keeper who had thought there was something up when a couple arrived at his inn along with 'a stranger man', and he was sufficiently suspicious after they had had some refreshments, to follow them when they went out to a quiet place 'behind Sir Lawrence's dog-house'. In this unromantic-sounding spot he heard the stranger go through a form of marriage service and pronounce them man and wife. This the Session accepted as marriage even although there had been no witnesses, and he was not allowed to proceed with marriage to someone else.[54]

Because of the nature of irregular marriage, not only might it be denied where it existed but claimed where it did not. There was a further twist in the case of the Tillycoultry couple who were forbidden to live together as man and wife until the man produced satisfactory evidence that he was free to marry. The Kirk Session could not declare them married persons, as the Presbytery said they should, because a woman came home from harvest work in the lowlands with a child and said that she was married to him. He admitted that the child was his but denied the marriage, a tricky problem which the Kirk Session solved by ordering him either to bring her before them so that they might take her judicial confession or else to produce witnesses to prove matters one way or the other. This brought the woman to her senses and a week later she brought a declaration, signed by four witnesses, that she was not married to him, but she left her child with him. The outcome was that the man and the woman he had married irregularly were declared to be man and wife. A claim of apparently false marriage came before the Kirk Session of Stranraer, Wigtonshire, in 1744 when they were informed that John Main, skipper of the sloop *Pelican*, and Janet Campbell had gone to bed together in the house of Alexander McWhinnie, a ship's carpenter, and lay together as man and wife 'in consequence it is said, of a pretended marriage, or if there is no marriage, the above two persons lay together . . . in uncleanness.' When summoned, Janet said that they were married in McWhinnie's house but that Main, in presence of others, had asked her to deny the fact of marriage to the minister and Session so that they 'could make nothing of it'. She had refused to do this, saying that there had been witnesses to the marriage 'and that he should not advise her to make a lie, for that she would not.' His version of events was that he had got very drunk and remembered nothing but had been told by other people who were there that Janet had joined the company 'upon which as he imagines, his comrades wanting to divert themselves with him, carried him upstairs and threw him into bed along with the said Janet Campbell but that he knew not whether she was man or woman for he had no commerce with her as a woman, and that he knows nothing of a marriage and that he had no intention to be married that day to any woman, much less to her whom he had never seen before.' He declared that he had not asked her to deny marriage but admitted offering her a dram if she could tell him who had helped her to carry off two of his barrels of herring from the shore, behaviour which hardly seems a likely basis for marriage. He apologised for his drunkenness and agreed to submit to censure but when the Session decided that he should be rebuked for 'his confessed drunkenness and any indecencies that may have followed' he begged that they would accept a fine for the use of the poor instead of having to stand publicly and, on payment of 10s. he was allowed off with nothing more than a Sessional rebuke. All in all, it is not surprising that sometimes a Kirk Session might take it upon itself to dissolve an irregular marriage if circumstances seemed to warrant this step. It is recorded in one case that although a properly signed certificate had been produced, the woman claimed that 'advantage had been taken of her simplicity and that she refused to be bound to him in contract' as a result of which the Session refused to confirm the marriage and allowed her to be proclaimed with another man.[55] Irregular marriage was ended by the Marriage Act of 1857.

An abuse that could arise from irregular marriage was bigamy which explains Kirk Sessions' anxiety to ensure that both parties who had contracted such a marriage were free to do so. Some 'priests' who performed these ceremonies inquired if the man and woman were single but even where they did, they certainly did not check to see if what was said was true and many of them were completely slap-happy about it, as appears from the evidence of a man and woman married by Edinburgh's John Barclay. He married them, they said, 'upon their simple desire without inquiring if they were free persons or not' and for one reason or another, very shortly after hearing this statement the Kirk Session referred him to one of the magistrates. Vigilance by the kirk as regards bigamy was essential because until 1855 when registration of births, deaths and marriages became a legal requirement, there was no other body to authenticate marriages and to clear the way for some or to prevent others. Bigamy could occur or be suspected without any initial report of an irregular marriage, of course; when a man who had been absent from his parish for some time, returned to it with a different wife to the one he had left with, his Session charged him 'to report Testimonials of his first wife's death and of his being thereafter married' which he was able to do. Just over twenty years later that Session required a man to produce witnesses to his first wife's death and burial and when he did so, they accepted what these people said and the Session 'found it not necessary to put it to any further probation.' In 1793 a Chelsea outpensioner came to a highland parish and was married there, saying that he was single. In this case, the Kirk Session cannot have made proper inquiries and after the marriage, he changed his story and said that in fact he was a widower. This also turned out to be untrue when he 'was claimed by another woman from Inverness as her husband, who produced a certificate of their marriage.' He was imprisoned in Tain 'to take his trial for polygamy' which made it sound worse than it was, and also for perjury, as a result of which he was sentenced by the Sheriff 'to stand in the pillory with a Label on his breast specifying his crimes and thereafter banished from the county of Ross and Cromarty for life.' It was a letter from Mr Pearson, a Fellow of St. John's College, Cambridge, in 1714 to the Kirk Session of Craig that started inquiries there about John Lindsey who came from the parish and had a wife, Margaret Prophet, living there. It appeared that John had gone south to Cambridge and married a woman in England before returning home to his first wife. He told the Kirk Session that when he was in the south he was somehow given to believe that Margaret had died and so he had remarried but when he later learnt that she was alive, he had come back and they were living together happily. He was told that he was guilty of 'perjury, bigamy, and of several other atrocious aggravations' and with the advice of the Presbytery what was called a 'singular censure' was imposed but which was only standing between the second and third bells at the church door and remaining there during the service until he was called in to be rebuked. Kirk Sessions undoubtedly seemed to be more concerned with punishing bigamists than with the plight of their wives.[56]

When a strong rumour arose in Cambuslang in 1784 that David Dewar had married his servant, Margaret Hay, although he was already married, the Kirk Session drew up a list of questions to be put to him and they give a good idea of how such investigations went:

1. Are you married to Margaret Hay?
2. When and where were you married?
3. By whom were you married and what persons were present?
4. Have you any written evidence of the marriage?
5. Were not you formerly married to Mary Simcae?
6. What has become of her?
7. How long is it since she went away from you?

8. Has she not offered more than once, since that time to return to live with you, if you would agree to it?
9. Do you know whether she be still alive?
10. Have you any intimation of her death?
11. Have you obtained a divorce from her?
12. Is it true that you carried on your marriage with Margaret Hay in a public manner, telling openly before you set out for Edinburgh that you were going thither to be married and accordingly went away from your own house in a carriage with her, and another woman of her acquaintance?
13. Did you not on your return from Edinburgh openly declare that you were married to Margaret Hay and introduce her as your wife at a dancing meeting in your neighbourhood?
14. Did you not say that you had the direction of God, that he approved . . .?
15. Did you persuade people that a man may have as many wives as he pleases, without being guilty of sin, provided he can support them, and that you regard not the laws in this matter?
16. Is it true that you have endeavoured to persuade people in your neighbourhood that a man might innocently have carnal knowledge of a woman, provided she consents?

The tenor of these questions showed that the Kirk Session already knew a great deal about the whole matter but David Dewar refused to answer them and the case was referred to the Presbytery which ordered his excommunication. At much the same date, a woman came to that Session on her own initiative to admit that she had been present at a marriage although she knew that the man's lawful wife was alive. For doing so, she was rebuked and admonished — but why did she go to the wedding and then tell tales?[57]

Not only did soldiers father illegitimate children when their regiments were quartered in any particular area, as has been mentioned in an earlier chapter, they also married girls who seemed so blinded by their glamour that they never thought to check on their marital status. It was here that the vigilance of a Kirk Session could be invaluable and prevent much later heartbreak. When, for example, a trooper courted a Kilconquhar girl and their conduct brought them to the notice of the church, he insisted that his wife was dead, only to have her reappear. This so enraged him that he beat her so savagely 'that she was not like to live', but live she did and the prospective bride was saved from worse trouble by the Session's intervention which brought on this result. In 1716 Scone Kirk Session called a young woman before them to ask if she had married a soldier. Yes, she replied, but when asked who had married them, she could not say. Had she got a line stating that she was married? Again she answered no. What was the name of his regiment? That she did not know either. In fact, all she knew was that his name was Thomas Duffus. The minister told her to inquire most narrowly after him and to find out whether or not he was already married, which she said she would do, adding with happy confidence that he had said he would come back to her. She was unable to get written evidence of her marriage or any other information and in the end the minister asked her whether she wished to follow him or not. By then she seemed to have thought better of the whole business and decided that after all she was not really married and would seek him no more. It transpired that he had obtained 10s. stg. from her, a lot of money. She was exhorted to repentance for her conduct and made three public appearances which re-established her former position; a good example of a Session saving a credulous girl from the results of her stupidity. Another problem with soldiers or sailors, whether their service started before or after marriage, was that they might be away from home for years without keeping in touch with their wives in any way and as a result many women did not know whether they were married or widowed; and until this was established no Session would sanction a second marriage. When a woman petitioned the Presbytery of Irvine in 1734 'to be allowed the privilege of marriage, in regard her husband had gone off to England ten years ago and though summoned at the pier of Leith, he had not returned', the Presbytery answered 'that there being neither a Divorce nor any document of her husband's death, they could not allow the petitioner to marry.' This petition had resulted from the Kirk Session's initial refusal of marriage.[58]

Summoning or proclaiming at the Pier of Leith, from where many regiments sailed for foreign service, and where they returned from abroad, was about the only way anyone could try to make contact with a soldier or seaman abroad, or discover where he might be or whether anyone knew if he were alive or dead. But it cost money. In 1723 a Hawick man was told by the Kirk Session to prove the death of the husband of the woman he wished to marry. His employer had offered 40s. stg. for this to be done but the person who would actually do it insisted on getting no less than £5 stg. This made it virtually hopeless for him to get the desired information for not only was proclamation at Leith by no means certain to produce the necessary information but for a man earning something like 6d. a day, it was an impossible sum to find and so the couple had to make public satisfaction for adultery. After being left on her own for fourteen years a soldier's wife in Falkirk decided to remarry but, once again, the Session would not allow this unless she could prove that she was a widow. This was perfectly fair but in fact that particular Session could have found out the position themselves from the officers of various army companies which had been in Falkirk. They did not however feel that it was up to them to do so, with the result that the couple got married irregularly in Edinburgh, then submitted themselves for rebuke. The woman said that she had been told that her husband had married no fewer than three times since leaving her but that she was unable to get any more information about him and while she would have asked for a divorce, she did not have the money to pay for it. The Presbytery, when consulted, said that she should continue to try to find her husband and that until she did so, both she and her new husband must remain under scandal but they were not apparently required to live apart. When a Greenock woman remarried irregularly, believing her seaman husband to be dead, all might have been well but unfortunately for her he returned. In this case, because the woman appeared to have been sincere in thinking she was a widow, the Presbytery, to whom the matter was referred by the Session, decided that she and her second husband should be found guilty of adultery rather than of bigamy but as the couple did not appreciate this lenience and refused to submit to church discipline, the final outcome was Lesser Excommunication. In the case of a woman whose husband had been in the army and away for nine years and then came home to find her remarried, it appeared that he had written to her during that time and she had no excuses for saying he was dead. She tried to get out of it by saying that the returned man was not the one she had married but as this was obviously untrue, she too was sentenced to Lesser Excommunication. Some people, in the event of wishing to remarry, were fortunate enough to be able to prove the death of a former partner, such as a woman whose husband joined the army two years after their wedding and had been away for ten years thereafter. She was able to find witnesses to his having died in hospital in Brussels and this information was enough to satisfy the Kirk Session and the Presbytery and to allow her next marriage to go ahead.[59]

Although the church put the onus of proving the death or otherwise of a husband long absent from Scotland onto his wife, whenever Sessions heard of more or less local desertions by husbands or wives, they were themselves instantly on the deserter's track, threatening penalties which at one time could include imprisonment, for failure to return to live with their spouses. On the same day in 1602 in Aberdeen, John Mitchell was ordered to be put in the kirk 'wolt' until he found caution that he would live with his wife and 'intertaine her as becomes him' and John Davidsoun, warned for the second time to appear before the Session, was ordered to be arrested and 'put in the steeple until he agrees to adhere to his wife and to behave thereafter.' A man appeared before Selkirk Presbytery in 1610 to answer to the charge of 'having put away his wife' and after being earnestly dealt with by the Moderator promised 'to take her hame, if by the grace of God she would amend her manners.' Another gave as his reason for not living with his wife that they were so poor that they could not live together, while yet another said that he 'dishauntit' his wife 'because she was a waister'. It was to her Session that Mary M'Lean, wife of a labourer, came to say that her husband had twice turned her out of the house because a soldier in the 78th Regiment of Foot, lodging with them, had said in his presence 'that she had been greater with him than any in the house.' For her husband's satisfaction and her own good name, she asked the Session to cite the soldier, by then living elsewhere, to appear before them so that the matter could be investigated. This they agreed to do and told her husband of the steps they were taking and although neither he nor the soldier appeared when called, the fact that the woman had taken the matter to the Session resulted in her and her husband soon living together in peace. When Janet Kyd complained that her husband, William Cryste, had put her away and taken in her place a woman she described as 'ane hwyr' (whore) he flatly refused to return to his wife and the Session punished them both as adulterers. A man in the island of Coll who was accused by his Session of 'wilful desertion in refusing to cohabit with his wife' was exhorted to return to her but he too refused to do so and was suspended under censure until the Presbytery could be consulted.[60]

Women could also be at fault and one was put into the tolbooth of Aberdeen on bread and water until inquiries could be made among her neighbours about her after she had shut her husband out of the house and said that he would never be a husband to her 'and a blankatt should never cover thame.' A woman who repeatedly refused to live with her husband was referred by her Session to the magistrate with a request that he keep her in 'firm ward' until she agreed either to 'discharge her dewtie' by living with him or else left the parish. Another woman, one who developed a violent physical aversion to her husband, saying that his feelings towards her were those of an animal and that she had developed a disgust of him and for that reason had left him, was ordered to return under pain of excommunication which, as she did not go back, was imposed. After eighteen months she asked the Session for absolution and was told to go back to her husband first of all and then six months later she was told to bring a testimonial from him that she had adhered to him in bed and board and mutual cohabitation. After a further two months, excommunication was lifted on her finding caution of £40 Scots that she would undergo whatever further censure was ordered.[61]

Cruelty to wives which did not cause separation has been mentioned in an earlier chapter but when women left their husbands it was usually because of maltreatment of some sort. William Meldrum, a tailor in the parish of Kinross, and his wife, Euphan, were delated to their Kirk Session for not living together and although he said that she had left for no reason he could think of, apart from his having reproved her because some things had gone missing from their house, she countered by saying that she could not stay with him as she was afraid that he would murder her. When asked what made her think such a thing, she replied that he had said to her one night that he would put her head beneath the pot that was boiling on the fire. The Kirk Session's response to this was to rebuke them both then and there and exhort them to live more peaceably and Christianly together. Some two and half months later it was reported that she had again gone back to her father's house, whereupon she was summoned once more and again asked why she had broken her promise to the Session to return to her husband and also broken her marriage vows. Again she said that she was frightened of being murdered but the Session, believing that there were no grounds for thinking such a thing, rebuked her sharply and urged her to return to her husband and to 'dwell with him in the fear of the Lord which she promised to do', and which seems to have worked out quite satisfactorily. When it was believed that cruelty did exist, however, Kirk Sessions showed sympathy to wives forced into desertion. One such was Margaret Fraser, an Edinburgh woman, who had felt obliged to leave her wheelwright husband, Thomas Watsone. He had since gone to Fettercairn, in Kincardineshire, where he began living with another woman, denying that Margaret was his wife and saying that she was just 'one suborned to raise a bad report upon him.' The Presbytery of Kincardine felt that it would be best if she would come north so that things could be straightened out but, as she was poor, the minister of Fettercairn asked her own Kirk Session to advance her the money for the journey — they gave her £4 Scots — promising that it would be repaid, which was a most helpful attitude.[62]

Kirk Sessions might well find that trouble with in-laws was a source of friction. A Dornoch man was charged by the Kirk Session with 'abusing and maltreating his wife, and both parties being present being interrogate as to the above the said Margaret asserted that it was fact that she had been used in a very unchristian manner by her said husband, being continually loaded with reproaches, wrongously charged with mismanagements, and so pinched as to the necessaries of life that she was obliged to separate from him.' In his defence her husband alleged

> that his wife was much to blame in several respects. But that it was mostly owing to his Mother who assumed that part in his house which belonged to his wife, that he was heartily sorry for any mistakes that had hapned 'twixt them, to prevent which in time comeing he promised to remove his Mother to another house, and allow his wife to enjoy all the freedom that became her in her own house. Upon the whole, the Session having rebuked said Angus for the treatment he had given his Wife, dismissed him with this certification that if he should give any further cause of complaint, he might expect more severe usage.

The couple were still disagreeing six months later and the Session interrogated Angus as to

> whether or not he had obeyed the former Sentence of this Session & what was the cause of his Wife's separation from him. To which he answered that he had actually, in obedience to the Session & to remove all Cause of Complaint from his Spouse, built a house for his Mother at a Distance from his own where she has lived ever since, that his Wife not only squandered away his Effects as he was ready to prove in severall instances if judged necessary, But likewise treated him wt. very Opprobious Language particularly told him one night when alone that the Divel's picture was in his face, & that she could never love him . . . And further that the main cause of their Separation was owing to her Mother who in the throng of Bear harvest sent Kathrine Ross express for his Wife & brought her along, since which time his Wife never returned to him.

All in all a sad case, at the end of which the Session had to conclude that the wife's conduct justified her husband's behaviour to her.[63]

When it was reported to a Session that a man was 'lying up in Adultery with a woman, he having a wife in Kirkaldy' he was called and admitted it but said that he and his wife had separated by mutual consent, she being a bad woman with whom he could not live. He was 'most severely and suitably rebuked by the Moderator for his most niquitious conduct' and ordered to leave the town and parish without delay, which he promised to do but that did not necessarily mean that he returned to his wife and nor is any provision for her mentioned. But many Kirk Sessions' attempts at reconciliation were obviously successful and the minutes of St. Andrews Kirk Session go so far as to record that one formerly jealous husband 'kissed and embraced' his wife and 'drank to hyr'. In the following case of desertion, however, there was little that the Session could do but try to ensure that the man and his new friend did not have the benefit of each other's company. In the autumn of 1699 James Souter, an Aberdeen man who was married to a woman named Elspeth Walker, deserted her and went to Newcastle with a woman appropriately named Anna Swap. In the following May information came to the Kirk Session in Aberdeen that James and Anna were in prison there and the Session decided to write, through the minister and magistrates, to anyone there who knew them to let them know that James was already married 'and recommending to separate them from one another and to punish them according to law.'[64]

While Kirk Sessions endeavoured to get couples who had parted to make it up and live together again, separation could meet with a degree of acceptance. A valid reason for it was expected and so were arrangements for maintenance. When James Small said that the reason he did not 'adhere to his wife was because she had wasted all that he had', the Session ordered him to be imprisoned, not until he agreed to return to her but until he could find surety that he would produce a testimonial that he had 'given contentment to the Session and her'; and a Glasgow couple agreed to live apart from each other 'until God put more love into their hearts' to which the Session agreed, it being clear that the man would give her a small yearly allowance. In Perth in 1587 James Walker was ordered either to live with his wife or to keep two of the children of the marriage and 'sustain them in bed and board' and to allow his wife and the other child a weekly sum of 40d. Scots and 40s. Scots yearly for house rent but an Elgin couple's 'variance' was such that the Session 'desired [them] to live separate for a time till it please God to move their hearts to live more quietly with each other' and in this case 'each one of them is ordered to live upon their own means severally', in other words, to support themselves. Awareness for the need for separation of husband and wife in some cases is very evident from the fact that the elders of Deskford allowed a woman who was apart from her husband have a token for Communion, even over-ruling the minister about this.[65]

Well-meant though the efforts of the kirk were to reconcile couples, they could lead to divorce because if a man and wife were living apart and there was insistence that they should give reasons for doing so, this reinforced and confirmed the differences they already had. In 1611 Adam Chisholm appeared before the Presbytery of Selkirk asking, for some reason which is not given, for an order granting him a separation from his wife but this was refused with the order 'to adhere to her except he convict her of adultery and get divorcement from her.' Although cases of divorce started with the Kirk Session they had to go to the Presbytery for proof and to the Commissioners of the county or the Sheriff for decree. This happened in the case of a man who was summoned to the Session for not living with his wife only to have it transpire that he was impotent and the Presbytery, to whom he was referred, advised the woman to apply to the Commissioners for divorce; and when John McConnel reported to his Session that his wife had run off with another man, his case ultimately came before the Presbytery whom he begged to give him a recommendation to the Commissioners of the county to sue for divorce. As what he said was supported by a letter from his minister, the Presbytery gave him such a letter as he asked for.[66]

Marriages which would have been incestuous have been mentioned in an earlier chapter but a variety of other problems to do with marriage used to come before Kirk Sessions. One was clandestine weddings when, for reasons of their own, the couple kept the fact of their marriage secret. This seems extraordinary to modern ears but seems to have been quite common at one time, particularly among people of some standing and so may have been to do with inheritance prospects, parental disapproval and the like. Clandestine marriages were private ones, although normally conducted by a clergyman. In 1770 George Balfour, minister of Tarbat, Ross-shire, was married secretly by another minister to the daughter of the late minister of Loth. The only people who knew of it at the time were the Macleods of Geanies, heritors of the parish, but when it ultimately came to light it caused a great deal of talk, as may be imagined, but because he made a full confession to the Presbytery he only received an admonition. The clandestine marriage of Anne Taylor was to cause much concern to the Kirk Session of Nigg, Ross-shire, until they learnt the truth of it. She lived alone in a house in the parish and then went away for some time, returning with a fairly well-grown infant. The Session immediately summoned her to explain the child's birth but she ignored this, also refusing to attend the Presbytery to whom the matter was reported and instead sending a letter to say that she was an Episcopalian, that the child was already baptised and that she did not consider herself under the jurisdiction of the Church of Scotland. The Presbytery gave her several opportunities to change her mind but when she did not accept these, they excommunicated her and announced the fact from all the pulpits of the bounds. Some years later, Colonel Ross of Nigg, one of the heritors, died and who stepped forward as the widow but Anne Taylor who had been married to him all the time but said that she had promised to keep the fact a secret. She asked the Presbytery for removal of her excommunication which was granted, along with an exhortation. She must have been a forgiving and kindly woman as she bequeathed £100 for the poor of Nigg and the same amount for those of Tain, and her brother-in-law, Colonel Walter Ross, presented the church of Nigg with 1,200 'beautiful tokens' when the Kirk Session decided that these were necessary.[67]

Complicated phraseology in a minute of Kinloss Kirk Session, Morayshire, does not make clear what form of illegal marriage had taken place but it shows that an elder, or at any rate a man of some authority, had spent £1 stg. in legal expenses 'to frustrate the evil designs of some persons in Findhorn who threatened bodily injury, in consequence of the information which he gave respecting an illegal marriage which had been newly celebrated in that place.' The Session thought it right that he should be reimbursed by them 'as it may serve to convince the Public that they are determined to support the Eldership, or any person acting as an Elder for the time, in the regular discharge of his duty.'[68]

On the island of Coll the Kirk Session had at one point to deal with a man's unusual way of trying to persuade a girl to marry him. Catherin McLean came to them, complaining that her character had been aspersed by Donald McNiven, a tailor, who threatened to ruin her by saying that they had lived together. 'In the course of examination, it having appeared that he had been courting her for a considerable time with a view to marriage and not finding her at last so compliable as he would choose, took a foolish Fit of jealousy that she had another suitor whom she preferred to him, that he left her in a passion and threatened revenge, for the accomplishment of which he alleged as above.' Bringing all of this into the open before the Session was the only way in which Catherin could retain her reputation and it also did good as the couple later made it up, he confessed that he had accused her falsely and they were contracted to marry.[69]

The Falkirk tailor who used to offer his wife for sale has already been mentioned but there used to be an idea on the Continent that a man in Great Britain could sell his wife by putting a halter round her neck and leading her to the public market for sale by auction, something which gained credence among the lower classes, and was at one time common in Smithfield Market in London. That must have been what lay behind a most unusual marriage case which came before Kilsyth Kirk Session, Stirlingshire, in 1696. It started with information being given against William Thomson and James Waller of scandalous carriage at the New Year's Day fair when the two men indulged in wife-swapping. William apparently exchanged his wife for James's Janet, with a black mare thrown in to even up the bargain which cannot have been very flattering for Janet but possibly it was the mare he really coveted. This was shocking behaviour even allowing for the licence of the New Year and the Session were probably only too glad to be able to pass the buck to the parish of Wester Lenzie to which they both belonged.[70]

Much to do with marriage has now greatly changed, with the role of the kirk drastically reduced but, in former days, Kirk Sessions did remarkable work, not least as unofficial matrimonial courts and women in particular must have had real cause to be grateful to them.

14

The Sacrament of Baptism

Not only marriages, but baptisms too, gave a lot of work to Kirk Sessions. The Book of Common Order (Knox's Liturgy) of 1562 which was meant, says Professor Smout, to be a guide to ministers in the performance of their functions, required children to be baptised in church, but an Act of the General Assembly which met at Perth in 1618 during the first Episcopacy, allowed what were called the Five Articles, one of which said 'that baptism might be administered at home, when the infant could not be conveniently brought to church'. This was given indirect backing by an Act of Parliament in 1621 which declared that, unless baptism was urgent, it should not take place at home. However, the whole idea of home baptism was thought to introduce a new and false doctrine, allowing people to have church privileges without submitting to the conditions of Christian duty and that those baptised at home would be accepted and declared to be members of the church by the minister alone, instead of by the whole congregation. According to Rev. Andrew Edgar, 'There was no point on which the genuine Presbyterian church was more firm than on the necessity of baptism being administered in church from 1618 down to . . . 1718.' The Five Articles were rescinded in 1638 and in 1643 the Directory of Public Worship decreed that baptism should always be administered in public in church and, taking a swipe at popery, declared that it should not take place where fonts, in Roman Catholic days, were 'unfitly and superstitiously' placed, which was near the church door and behind the backs of the congregation. This became a law of the church in 1645 with the General Assembly stating 'That the Sacrament of Baptism be administered in the face of the congregation that what is spoken and done may be heard and seen by all, and that it be after the sermon and before the blessing.' This was in accord with Presbyterian views and in 1690 the General Assembly once more decreed that private baptism was forbidden although, like private marriages, it ultimately became very common.[1]

Baptism in church did not necessarily mean that it took place on a Sunday nor, at an early post-Reformation stage, that it was administered by the minister. Both marriages and baptisms at that time could be celebrated by the reader, something which the minister at Elgin had to forbid in 1599. The mid-week services which it was customary to hold for many years have been mentioned earlier and they were considered by many Kirk Sessions to be the appropriate occasion for baptisms, which may have been because baptisms, like marriages, were usually followed by a celebration of some sort at home which could lead to profanation if they happened on a Sunday. Certainly Aberdeen Kirk Session in 1568 and St. Cuthbert's Kirk Session, Edinburgh, in 1592, both decreed that no child should be baptised except on mid-week preaching days, with Aberdeen stating that it was to take place after preaching. Such a regulation could be so firmly adhered to that sad results could ensue. According to Spalding, an Aberdeen burgess brought his very weak new-born child to church and asked the minister to come to baptise it but this was refused until after the lecture, as a type of preaching was called, was over. The poor father rang the church bell himself to try to make people come to church sooner but they waited till the right time and the baby died in the arms of a woman friend: 'befoir the lecture was done, the sillie infant deceissis' as it was put. At that date at St. Cuthbert's, Edinburgh, baptisms took place at 8.30 a.m. before preaching. At Kilmarnock where parents persisted in bringing their children on Sundays, the Kirk Session stressed that although baptism was permitted that day, there must be no ensuing feasts, while in 1611 Aberdeen parents were reported to be feeling 'grieff' at not being allowed to have their children baptised whenever they wanted, a matter some elders brought before the Kirk Session. The answer given however was that the decision of 1568 was still in force and the only exception could be if a midwife gave evidence that the child was so weakly that it should be baptised at once. A long discussion followed at which it was agreed that all legitimate children should be baptised as and when their parents wanted, a privilege which was unfortunately so abused that in 1640, with the magistrates' agreement, it had to be rescinded because ministers were so often 'withdrawn from their studies by the importunities of neighbours wanting their children baptised.'[2]

A different slant on the timing of baptismal and marriage ceremonies occurred in the parish of Tynninghame in the seventeenth century when the minister persuaded the Kirk Session to decree that these should be held on Sunday afternoons, simply to ensure attendance at worship then, 'seeing that the people did not resort so much to the kirk at efertnoon as need were.' Attendance at the morning service would, of course, have been expected too and one can well see how no one would have wanted to keep a very young, possibly ailing and almost certainly fretful baby hanging around for most of the day. The preference for morning baptism could however, be put to good use, the kirk being ever mindful of the needs of the poor, and the records of Auchterhouse in 1656 show that because people were 'importuning' for their children to be baptised at the first service and then did not come to church in the afternoon, it was decreed that in such cases they must pay 30s. Scots for the privilege.[3]

The Confession of Faith of 1560 decreed that baptism should not be unnecessarily delayed, something that was taken so literally in some cases that baptism took place the day after birth and although Parliament ordered in 1621 that it should be administered on the Sunday following birth, either way it must have been a high-risk thing to carry a baby possibly a long distance over roads or tracks or open country which were difficult to negotiate in good weather and almost impossible in bad, with mud and water to get through, not to speak of crossing flooded unbridged burns. The story is told of a man carrying his baby through the snow to church, thinking it was safely wrapped in his plaid, only to discover when he got to his destination that it had slipped out and a search found it lying where it had fallen in the snow. To follow a long, difficult journey to church with a long wait in what was most probably a cold, damp, draughty, dirty building was asking for trouble. By 1648 the General Assembly realised these problems and how difficult it was for parents in many districts to bring babies to church, and decreed that ministers should catechise one day a week 'wherein they may also baptise and lecture.' This turned catechising into a proper service and so the basic requirement that baptism should take place in public, even if not in church, was obeyed. An alternative was to let baptism take place at a later age and a more convenient time or to allow babies to be taken to a more accessible church. In bad weather parishioners in one part of the parish of Tynninghame, for instance, were permitted to go for baptism and marriage to Whitekirk, a route which had smaller burns on the way, while those who lived south of the River Tyne went to Prestonkirk when the river was in flood. The same thing was happening in the late eighteenth century in Tongue, where people in some parts of the parish were much closer to the churches of Farr and Durness and so baptisms were allowed to be administered by the ministers there, but their details were supposed to be entered in the records of Tongue.[4]

So far as legitimate children were concerned, the Book of Common Order said that they should be brought to church by the father and godfather, the latter word being interpreted by the Confession of Faith as 'a Christian friend' and by one Kirk Session as 'a faithful neighbour'. The godparent, often called a 'gossop', was not merely a witness but a joint sponsor. A custom of bidding between twelve to sixteen gossops instead of the original two or so became so common in Aberdeen in the 1620s, even among what the Kirk Session termed base, servile people, that should there be several children to be baptised on the one day, there simply were not enough places for all of them to sit and so in 1622 it was decreed that there should be two to four at the most and the kirk officer was instructed not to accept more than two or three names. Where there were a large number of gossops, the father, with just two or three, stood for the baptism and the rest remained seated, assuming that there was sufficient seating for them. In old baptismal registers of the Church of Scotland it was customary to write in besides the name of the child and its parents, the names of two other people who were described as witnesses. This happened regularly in the parish of Galston, for instance, from 1569 until after 1626 and occasionally between 1637–51 and it seems that these witnesses were the same as gossops. Although godfathers soon ceased to be required, it was from this that the custom developed of friends accompanying the parents to the baptism and also from it that in some churches the baptismal pew was called the 'gossops' seat'. In time many churches came to have a little complex of seating in the vicinity of the pulpit, including this particular pew. At Dalmellington, Ayrshire, for example, a minister's seat, pulpit, reader's seat and baptismal seat were all provided in 1776 at a total cost of £12 stg., while the provision at Carnbee, Fife, in 1793 was described as 'a Pulpit and Lettron of fir, bound work, with a Passage to ascend by one side, and a place of Baptism on the other.'[5]

It was because of their fear of all things popish that the Reformers regarded the Roman Catholic use of oil, salt, wax or saliva in baptismal ceremonial as superstitious. Only water must be used, but fonts themselves were considered superstitious and so they were disposed of but it is nice that, in spite of this, some very old ones do still survive to this day and may be seen in a number of graveyards or churches, albeit having had some adventures along the way. A Norman font is now back once more in Linton Church, Roxburghshire, having been used for some time by a blacksmith for holding small coal. There is a particularly interesting one at Dalarossie, Inverness-shire: it is a large flat round stone, two feet by three feet across with the centre hollowed out into the shape of a bowl, used in previous centuries for river baptism and possibly with a pre-Christian use. It has now been removed from the river and set on a cairn of stones inside the church where it is used as the baptismal font. There is a similar stone at a burn in the linked parish of Dunlichity which Nigel Tranter suggests was at one time used by Episcopalians for baptisms. Although fonts were discarded after the Reformation, it was not until 1617 that Parliament decreed that basins and ewers for the administration of baptism should be provided at every parish church, to be in charge of the minister whose duty it should be to make parishioners provide them, under threat of losing a year's stipend. This did not of course produce them immediately and what happened in one East Lothian parish gives just one reason for such delays: in 1625 an assessment was made on the heritors for a baptismal basin, as well as Communion cups and cloths, but it was diverted to pay for hanging the church bell which explains why that church just had what they called an 'iron' for holding water for baptisms. This may well have been the type of basin fastened to the side of the pulpit which was all that many parishes had until they were able to provide themselves with something better. That parish also had a 'water cloth' for use at baptisms, and elsewhere christening cloths of various sorts were in use too, so that accounts may show such expenses as 'To sop and blew to washing christening cloth 2d'. On rare occasions, where the utensils for baptism were not available or circumstances prevented their use, necessity had to be the mother of invention and a story is told of a highland minister going to administer private baptism to a child whose home was on the far side of a burn. Unfortunately, the burn was so badly swollen by a spate that he could not get across and called over to the father, who was waiting on the other side, to fetch the baby which was duly baptised by naming it and aiming water at its head with the aid of a wooden scoop, from one side of the burn to the other.[6]

Rulings about the baptism of legitimate children did not mean that those who were illegitimate went unbaptised, just that their very existence proved that a moral sin had been committed and therefore church privileges, which included baptism, were withheld until satisfaction was made because until that was done, the parents were regarded as unfit to transact a solemn covenant with God. In the 1580s one Kirk Session required the person presenting the child to see the reader and two elders the night before the proposed baptism and to give them the details of the baby, so as to prevent any illegitimate ones from slipping through the net, but baptism of such a child was allowed to go ahead if caution was given that both mother and father would satisfy discipline. Aberdeen was one place where this caution was extended to include not only satisfying the church but giving an undertaking that the couple would not repeat the offence or would get married. Sometimes of course, it fell to the mother alone to take responsible steps:

> Margaret Burnside daughter to Ritchard Burnside and Jean Duddingstone was baptized presented by the said Jean the child being begotten in fornication and born about two years ago and the baptizing of the child still delayed until now because of their obstinance and presented by the mother because she had given satisfaction and the father is yet obdurate and fugitive from church discipline, the said child was baptized before the whole congregation that was met at the ordinair weeklie sermon.

Should an illegitimate child's health be such that the need for baptism was urgent, caution was readily accepted. A Hawick couple asked that their baby might be christened 'in regard to the weakness thereof' and on their giving an undertaking to serve discipline, they were told to bring it to the minister either that night or the next day. In 1712 the General Assembly passed an Act which declared that every child had a right to baptism but that no sponsor should be accepted other than the parents, or at least the mother, unless they were dead, absent, grossly ignorant, under scandal or had refused to serve discipline. Should parents urgently needing baptism for a sick child be unable to find caution, then someone else had to be found to act as sponsor in their place and to undertake to see to the Christian upbringing of the child. So desperate was one girl that she threatened to run off and 'leave the child upon the session' unless it was baptised. The Session however were not prepared to be blackmailed in this way and sought the advice of the Presbytery which was that she should start her public repentance at once and that the child could be baptised immediately if she could get a sponsor for it, which was what happened.[7]

Extracts from a Baptismal Register in the late nineteenth century show that at that date the sponsor of an illegitimate child was not always named but in one case in 1875 the records do give it in an entry showing the baptism of 'the illegitimate child of Effie Halliday and James McLean, residing in the neighbourhood of Forres, the grandfather, William Halliday, acting sponsor. The child's name is Alexander, born 4th March 1872.' Baptismal registers never used to pull any punches about illegitimacy: '1873, Baptised at Auchindrean, the 14th May, a boy begotten in fornication by Hugh McGregor and Kate McRae, at Inverinate, named

Donald', says one, or where there was some doubt about paternity the wording might go as follows, '1873, Baptised at Dundalloch, 24 March, a boy of eight years, born in fornication, named Alexander, the alleged father being John McRae, gamekeeper, "Iron House", Killillan.' The same Register has an entry in 1878 which may seem unkind, saying as it does, 'The child's mother, Mary McRae, taking the vows, her husband being affected in mind', but without the reason being given for her having done so, a less respectable one might have been imagined.[8]

Evidence of sponsorship could be used in a case of disputed paternity. In one such case in 1736 a Session asked the mother what presumptions she could give about the alleged father and she was able to tell them that the father of the man she named stood sponsor at the baptism and his mother helped to buy and prepare the christening feast, strong evidence of a close involvement, which the Session accepted. As attitudes to moral offences changed, so baptism for these children became easier but as late as 1908 a minister who was begged to baptise an illegitimate child which was desperately ill and indeed died shortly afterwards, did so but even in these distressing circumstances he still felt it necessary to speak seriously to the mother and to report all that he had done to his Session who fully endorsed his actions.[9]

Although the Confession of Faith made it clear that while it was a great sin to neglect baptism, it was nevertheless not essential to salvation — 'yet grace and salvation are not so inseparably annexed unto it, as that no person can be regenerated or saved without it', but in spite of that many people believed that without baptism a soul was damned. How, after all, could it be identified at the Resurrection if it did not have a name? — and there was also a superstitious belief that until it was safely baptised, a child might be carried off by the fairies and a changeling left in its place. The following lines sum up the general feeling:

> I wat aweel it's an uncanny thing
> > To keep about a house
> > > A body wanting a name.[10]

So uncanny were dead unbaptised children thought to be that they were refused burial in the kirk yard, putting them into the same category as suicides, excommunicants and murderers, even though this was a contravention of Protestant practice. In 1641 the Synod of Fife had to order that 'those who buries unbaptized bairnes apart, be censured by the Session', but the custom of burying unbaptised infants separately from other people went on for long after that and special areas were designated for them although records of such places are not common. In the 1690s on the island of Iona such children were interred along with murderers in a piece of empty ground between St. Mary's Church and the gardens; at Watten in Caithness, they ended up along with poor strangers — beggars — on the site of a ruined chapel at Scouthal; while in the parish of Nigg, Ross-shire, tradition says that they were buried until 1790, along with suicides, around an ancient Pictish Stone at Shandwick, although recent excavation there seems to disprove this.

What is interesting, however, is that even if these burials were outside the parish graveyard, each of the sites mentioned was special in some way. There used to be in the Torridon area of Wester Ross at least three such burial areas, two of which are marked on the 1881 6-inch OS maps of the district as 'Infant burial ground, disused' but there is nothing on the sites now to show any special significance for the choice of these spots. Into the 1880s an open grassy space surrounded by blackthorn at North Ballachulish, Inverness-shire, had a very eerie reputation, long after the fact that it was an old burying-ground for the unbaptised and suicides had been forgotten. Writing in 1884 Rev. Charles Rogers said that the custom of separate burial continued 'till a recent period', which means that at some point in the nineteenth century the burial of the unbaptised in churchyards began, but usually only in a special part of them or else beside rather than within them. Nowadays these children are buried in a regular manner. Even occasionally as late as the twentieth century, stillborn babies used to be buried between sunset and sunrise but by that date it was more usual for these little unbaptised corpses to be buried in a graveyard. In places such as Berwickshire, they were buried on the verge of the graveyard footpath, with no memorials. Nowadays they are usually dealt with by hospitals but the Very Rev. Dr John Gray recommended in *Life and Work* in 1982 that they should be buried by the minister and that their births should be recorded.[11]

Is it any wonder that, in the days when the kirk treated the unbaptised in the way that they did, an Inverkeithing woman who was accused of deserting and casting away her child, explained that she did so because it had not been baptised, the implication being that baptism was being withheld pending church censure? Is it surprising that the father of a child which died unbaptised buried it, with the help of a couple of friends, on the shore near his home rather than where it might have been interred? Can one blame the man who sprinkled water on the head of his dying child and gave it a name himself? Unfortunately, that being in 1653, the Kirk Session called him to account for doing so and although he said he 'did it in drunkenness' this may very well have been said to cover up the fact that he was doing what he thought best for the child by giving it unofficial baptism but, whatever his intentions, they earned him excommunication. It says a good deal for Mr John Oswald, minister of the East charge of St. Nicholas, Aberdeen, in the 1640s, that when the 'silly infant' died before the end of his lecture and before it could be baptised, he declared that having died in the church it should be buried there.[12]

Most people were desperately anxious to have their children christened and it was concern for them that brought unmarried couples, or girls on their own, voluntarily to their Sessions to confess the sin that had led to a birth and made them thankful to accept rebuke and public censure, or to give caution that they would do so, so as to be able to have the child baptised. This was also something which could help to establish paternity as sometimes it was only refusal of baptism that could shame a man into confessing being the father although where a paternity case was disputed in court, a Session would not grant baptism until it was settled. At the crux of a dispute in Drymen, Stirlingshire about 1815 was a child born to Margaret Buchanan in 1813 when she alleged the father was James King, a weaver. He resisted this claim although he admitted fathering a child she had had in 1810. The Sheriff-depute of the county heard the case in mid-1815 but it was still unsettled three years later when King petitioned the Kirk Session, complaining that he and his wife could not get their children baptised as he was excluded from church privileges owing to Margaret's 'vexatious allegations'. Ultimately the matter was submitted to the Presbytery of Dumbarton who in 1819 'appointed the parties to be left under scandal' which was very right and proper but which left several children as unbaptised victims. While a Session would allow an unmarried woman to have her child baptised after repentance was made or promised, re-peated requests from the same woman for more baptisms were naturally much frowned upon and when a woman who had twice had illegitimate children chris-tened became pregnant again 'in very aggravating circumstances and open proof of impenitency' she found that censure was refused and Lesser Excommunication imposed, 'aye and until scriptural evidence of true repentance be manifested by her.'[13]

Married couples innocent of any ante-nuptial fornication were terrified that their first child might be born prematurely as this immediately brought them to the attention of their Kirk Sessions with resultant delay in the child's baptism. An example of this occurred in 1705 when a minister, knowing that a baby he was asked to baptise was the parents' first one, checked up in the marriage register and calculated that it had been born twenty days before it should have been. Baptism was refused until the Session could consider the matter, with the midwife and the other women who had been present at the birth, attending the meeting to give their opinions. They thought the child could have been premature but said that it was hard to be positive about such a short difference in time and as nothing could be proved one way or the other, the Session gave permission for the baptism. Had things gone the other way, the parents would have had to make satisfaction for their sin or give caution for it first of all. A man who asked for baptism for his five-month baby said that there had been no ante-nuptial fornication but that the birth had been deliberately brought on by the midwife after the mother had been upset in a cart. The Session asked the doctor for his opinion and the couple were told that they should bring proof of what they said but that if they could not do so, nor tried to obtain it, then they would remain under scandal and the child would remain unbaptised. The following year they were still denying any guilt and were cited to the Presbytery who found it 'peculiar and unusual that persons in their circum-stances should persist so in denying their guilt' and recommended the Kirk Ses-sion to act prudently in the case. Where someone moved to a new parish and was discovered to have left uncompleted repentance behind, this too was a reason for delayed baptism. When Norval the Wigman, as he was styled, was refused bap-tism for his child in Hawick this was because he had not finished censure at Greyfriars Church, Edinburgh, and in spite of being a decent man and good at his work, he had to make the journey to Edinburgh, fifty or so miles each way, so as to be able to purge his scandal there and bring back a testimonial to that effect before being allowed to present his child for christening.[14]

Refusal or postponement of baptism was obviously a powerful weapon in the hands of the kirk, not only for trying to control immorality but also for bringing recalcitrants to submission for a variety of offences. When one man asked for his child to be baptised the Session remembered that he had been guilty of drinking since his last one was christened and ordered him to be publicly rebuked before the second baptism could go ahead. David Hamilton, a vintner in Glasgow, was refused baptism for a child on the grounds that he had kept his house open for the sale of alcohol on Sundays or at any rate had sold spirits that day to be consumed off the premises; and the same thing happened to a man who took a load to another parish on his employer's orders on the day of Harvest Thanksgiving, although his employer declared that there was no law, English or Scottish, that prevented him ordering his servants to work any day except Sunday. Yet another man, clerk of the burgh of Kilmaurs, was unwise enough to slander the minister 'in a hasty though harmless expression descriptive of his preaching' and had to expiate his sin before baptism was permitted.[15]

Even when there was no scandal, that did not mean that baptism was automatic because it was also refused to parents considered to be grossly ignorant. This was not an indictment of their ignorance but so that they might 'better train their Family and train up their Children.' In the same way that people under censure might be required to learn the Commandments or portions of Scripture, so it was for such people who were illiterate: in 1615 the Kirk Session of Lasswade ordered that no child of ignorant parents would be baptised unless the father laid down a pledge of 10s. Scots that he would learn the Lord's Prayer, Belief and the Commandments within a month and would have some knowledge of the Sacraments and Catechism, failing which the pledge would be forfeited although at least the child would be baptised. In what seems to have been another baptismal case in 1660, Dougal Macandrew was found ignorant in the grounds of religion, was sharply rebuked and undertook that through the Lord's strength he would be well grounded within a month, failing which he would forfeit what he had laid down, and this became fairly general practice, sometimes with added strictures. When John Ker, a poor man in Lauder, was allowed to have his child baptised on condition that he 'learned to be a better scholar', there was the added requirement that he should live more soberly than formerly. A Mauchline man was subjected to a theological examination which was beyond him but he undertook to read up on it and on the strength of that, and also a promise of good behaviour, both of which were written into the Kirk Session minute book, he was allowed to have his child christened, but another man who had not attended church for a long time was told that baptism for his child would only be allowed when he began coming to worship regularly. Not only were theological questions asked of the father beforehand but possibly during the baptismal service too. The Ecclesiastical Records of Aberdeen for the sixteenth and seventeenth centuries describe how baptism was conducted. The minister spoke on the institution, necessity and benefits of it, prayed for a blessing on what was being done, put some questions on the Creed to the father as he held the child and also asked about its education. After replies were given, there was another prayer before the child was named with the sprinkling of water, and then everyone was dismissed. Just as a witch-hunting minister could make life terrifying for his parishioners, so a minister with very strict views on baptism could make life difficult for them, which was why an appeal was made to a Presbytery in 1824 when Mr Roderick Macleod, inducted to the parish of Bracadale, Skye, the year before, refused baptism to one child. The Presbytery ordered him to baptise the child, which the General Assembly confirmed, but he disobeyed these instructions and for this was suspended from May to July 1826, although he was reinstated and remained in the parish until 1838. That is what *Fasti* says about him but Ronald Blakey, in *The Man in the Manse* says that he refused baptism so often during his time there that the number of unbaptised children in the parish soared.[16]

Where parents found difficulties in having their children baptised, they often tried to get round them by various means. In Govan in the mid-seventeenth century, it was found that people from within and outside the parish cheerfully brought children for baptism with neither certificate nor elder to prove that they were married, hoping that this would be overlooked, but they were forbidden to 'gett their bairnes bookit' before marriage was proved and also told not to take them to other parishes in the expectation of evading proof. Sometimes a bit of private influence was sought, by resorting 'to courses implying some sort of friendly negotiation between them and one or more members of the Kirk Session', something which happened often enough in Inverness in the 1690s for the Kirk Session as a body to decree that no child should be baptised without a sessional order and, failing that, that at least five elders must be present at the writing of any order. It would be interesting to know just how a Glasgow man named Charles Stewart 'procured a line' which resulted in his child being baptised when it should not have been — the records do not say why — and what was in the line, but the result was that he was admonished and had to 'converse' with two elders. Some people fell back on plain trickery. About the same time that the 'friendly negotiations' were being used in Inverness, a man there admitted holding up another man's child for baptism as his own, an offence which was at once referred to the Presbytery. The fact that a Session had to order a penalty of £10 for anyone who having fathered an illegitimate child did not 'hold up the child to be baptised himself' may imply that what happened in Inverness was not an isolated incident although it could just mean failure of a father to shoulder his responsibilities. The story is told of a coal carter in Gilmerton, on the outskirts of Edinburgh, who used an entirely different way to get his child baptised. Knowing that the gate to the manse was in a precarious condition, he tethered his horse to it and the minister did not take over long to agree to his request.[17]

The easiest solution, of course, for people liable to be refused baptism by their own minister, was to find another clergyman willing to administer it without asking awkward questions and these irregular baptisms became a great worry to the kirk. During the times of Episcopalian rule, Parliament passed several Acts on the subject of disorderly, irregular baptism, one of which in 1670 forbade it to be administered by any but clergy of the established church and then, because many Presbyterians were unwilling to submit to this, tried to force them into it by decreeing in 1672 that parents must have children baptised within thirty days of birth or else produce a testimonial of baptism from their parish minister. The Synod of Galloway had been ahead in this matter and in 1668 had ordered all ministers to summon to their Presbyteries any parents who had not had children baptised within forty days of birth by their own ministers. The 1670 Act was repeated in 1681, ordered to be enforced in 1685 but rescinded in 1690 after the Revolution when Presbyterian church government returned once more, and thereafter it was 'outed' Episcopalian clergy who were forbidden to baptise under threat of imprisonment. This emphasis on baptism arose not so much out of concern for the children's spiritual welfare as from a desire on the part of church and Parliament to force people to accept whichever form of church government held power at any particular time; it was politically motivated rather than anything else. It was difficult for people to switch from one form of worship and custom to another at the pleasure of governments, politicians and intellectuals and therefore many of them had their children baptised in an irregular manner. It must have been a blessed relief when the General Assembly recommended in 1711 to all ministers in whose parishes there were members of other Protestant denominations that they should show 'all tenderness to them in regard to sealing ordinances' and so long as parents were free of scandal and professed faith in Christ, then ministers should 'chearfully comply with their desire, in administering the Sacrament of baptism to their children.' The Act of Toleration of 1712 provided for freedom of worship and so these particular problems were solved but prior to that, one can understand how a clergyman of the wrong persuasion at any particular time must have been perfectly ready to baptise, or marry, even though it was illegal for him to do so. It enabled him to use the rites of his own church, it made him feel useful and it almost certainly brought him in a little money. It was by no means uncommon for people who had Presbyterian parish ministers to apply instead to outed Episcopalian clergymen for baptism for their children, usually so as to avoid censure from their own church as such baptisms took place 'without testimonials being asked for or granted by their own ministers.' What is difficult to understand is why any Presbyterian minister, during Presbyterian church government, should have encroached on the rights of a neighbouring minister, but an instance of this happened when Dr Foord, minister of Lauder, baptised in the adjoining parish of Channelkirk without permission from its minister, which led to a rebuke from the Moderator of the Presbytery. The sensible provision, which has already been mentioned, which enabled children to be baptised in certain circumstances in a more accessible parish with the approval of their own minister and Kirk Session did not, of course, rank as irregular baptism.[18]

Irregular baptisms were technically private ones. One result of changing from a particular form of church government to another was that during Episcopalian days Presbyterians got used to worshipping and baptising secretly as and where they could, and vice versa. Both groups therefore got used to the idea of private baptism and came to think it was desirable even when it was not necessary and much as the kirk disapproved, there were purely practical and domestic reasons why it was much in demand, reasons which have already been given in relation to the problems of getting babies to church. The Act of General Assembly of 1648 which allowed for baptism to take place at a service in conjunction with catechising has also already been mentioned and this prevented many a baptism being labelled private. When the parishioners of Maybole, Ayrshire, complained in 1718 that, among other faults, their minister baptised privately, his answer was that he tried to comply with church law and that except for cases of great necessity, he baptised at church or else at diets of catechism and visitation in remote parts of the parish when there would be sure to be a considerable number of people present and, he added, 'I always preached before I baptised.' It became common for ministers to announce in church that public worship would be held at some place where there was a child or children needing baptism so that everyone was given the opportunity to be present if they wished and so that all might know that there was nothing private about it. These ministers were trying to be helpful to their flocks and to obey church law but there is an exception to be found in everything: Dean Alexander Pitcairne, minister of South Ronaldshay and Burray parish in the late seventeenth century, was a man who tried to make things difficult. 'Out of private pike [pique] towards parents, even though some were his own elders, he sometimes refused to baptise in kirk or house' and would only do so in the churchyard; at least this was stated in a libel brought against him in 1698.[19]

With the kirk's usual eye to any potential source of fund-raising, it was not long before private baptisms were being permitted in return for money for the poor's box and although the General Assembly had re-stated in 1690 that baptism should only take place in church, a mere six years after that the Kirk Session of Drymen stated that anyone wishing to have baptism out of the church should pay 20s. for the privilege — they allowed the same thing for weddings too. The Kirk Session records of Dunbar in 1727 and again in 1728 show that there were three private baptisms, each of them yielding £1 10s. Scots to the poor's funds, while in 1771 Greenock Kirk Session decreed the charge of half a guinea Scots for private baptism, with discretion to the minister to dispense with this charge if he thought fit. Traquair Kirk Session carried the idea of privacy even further when they decided in 1763 that no child which could be brought to church should receive private baptism unless the parents paid the minister 1s. stg. 'to be bestowed in *private* charity.' In some places, such as Kirkoswald, Ayrshire, at the end of the eighteenth century collections were being made at private baptisms and about 1700 some ministers in the bounds of the Presbytery of Fordyce allowed the tolling of the church bell for baptisms, whatever day of the week it was, in spite of this being forbidden by the Synod, and it seems likely that money must have been forthcoming for this privilege.[20] There seems to have been considerable variation around the country about private or public baptism for many years. In 1838 a public christening in the High Church, Inverness, was sufficiently unusual there as to attract press comment although the report admitted that public ceremonies were common in many parts of the country; yet just three years later, in 1841, it was said of Banff that 'public baptism has been discontinued for upwards of fifty years.' In 1849 the minutes of a Fife Kirk Session clearly state that a man's request for home baptism was only granted because the child was sickly while by the end of the nineteenth century, Rev. Andrew Edgar said that there were ten private baptisms for every public one, and this was in spite of the fact that there was never any Act of General Assembly permitting this, apart from the short-lived one of 1618. Although private baptisms were certainly taking place into the 1950s and 1960s, nowadays most or all parish churches insist on them taking place in church in the old way.[21]

In spite of what the General Assembly said about every child having a right to baptism, refusal by a Kirk Session could mean that children grew up unbaptised and had to seek it for themselves in later life. In 1601 a nineteen-year-old man was required to make his confession of the Articles of Faith publicly, which was followed by baptism, but as time went on Kirk Sessions became stricter. In 1752 a committee of one Session was appointed to examine a young woman asking for baptism and was able to report that she had 'such a degree of knolidge as she might receive the Sacrament of Baptism.' Where sufficient knowledge was not apparent, however, the preliminary to adult baptism could be the tedious one of making the rounds of a number of elders for instruction and then appearing before a Kirk Session meeting to give evidence of adequate understanding; but in the case of one young Kilmarnock girl, even that was not enough and she was told that she needed more instruction and prayer and must visit the minister with some of the elders for it. A request for baptism which was very surprising at the time was when a black woman servant in the Eglinton family asked to be christened, something which was referred to the Presbytery who considered that this should not be gone about hastily but in the end she was granted what she asked.[22] Some children went unbaptised through their parents' negligence, surprising as this seems in view of the superstitious dread concerning lack of baptism. It could happen where a disregard for religion overcame superstition and where dissenters would do almost anything rather than have a child baptised by the parish minister. This happened in Glasgow in the early seventeenth century when Robert Stewart defied the church over a child's baptism and ended up a prisoner in the castle of Glasgow with two ministers appointed to confer with him to see 'gif he be penitent'. In 1588 Elgin Kirk Session said that should anyone fail to have children baptised they would, 'when the elders so ordain', be put in the jougs and then banished. In the early 1660s a man became a Quaker and refused to ask for his child to be baptised in the parish church, only to have his wife and brothers ask the Presbytery for it, offering to take the vows themselves. When John Gray refused to present his child for baptism in 1734, a Justice of the Peace ordered soldiers to be hired to arrest him but he escaped by joining the army although a warrant was issued by the Justices to arrest and imprison him until the child was baptised. Such determined resistence to baptism was not common, of course, although it was understandable in particular social groups, something which was recognised by the General Assembly in 1647 when Presbyteries were recommended to consider the best means of getting the children of ordinary beggars baptised. Gypsies were an unfortunate group as at that date they risked death just for being gypsies, unless they were prepared to renounce their gypsy way of life and it says much for John Carmichael, minister of Traquair from 1662–65, that he baptised gypsy children although, as has been said earlier, doing so became just one in a list of complaints made against him. One cannot help but feel that the intentions of the General Assembly were being rightly interpreted by him.[23]

In spite of people's normal anxiety for baptism for their children, in later years ministers often had to baptise several children of a family simultaneously as they went catechising: 'Baptized at Dornie on the 9th December 1871 to William McMillan, Shepherd at Dornie, a daughter named Mary, then six years of age, a son named Thomas three and a half years and Angus, two years of age,' says the Baptismal Register of Kintail, and similar entries are by no means uncommon. A most unusual baptism was a mass one of over 160 children which took place at Kiltearn, Ross-shire, during a visit by Dr Macdonald, Ferintosh, a notable preacher, and Dr Kidd of Gilcomston Chapel. The children were divided into two rows, according to whether they came from English or Gaelic speaking families; Dr Macdonald baptised the Gaelic ones and Dr Kidd the others. Many of the children were old enough to talk and let it be known that they did not enjoy having water sprinkled upon them.[24]

The superstitious attitude to lack of baptism could be carried to lengths as ignorant as they were unkind. In 1700 an Aberdeen woman who had been given the care almost a year before of a little foundling girl, told the Kirk Session 'that several persons would not suffer her or the child to enter their houses upon account of the want of baptism' which it was assumed she had never received as she had been found when she was only about eight days old. Her foster mother asked if she might be baptised and the Session asked the minister to inquire of the Presbytery how this might be done. There must have been other similar cases around the country as in 1712 the General Assembly ruled that in the case of foundlings 'whose baptism after inquiry cannot be known, the Kirk Session is to order the presenting of the child for baptism and to see to the education of the child.' Although the following case is not that of a foundling but of an abandoned, motherless and apparently illegitimate child, it shows how the Act of Assembly of 1712 was carried out in such circumstances: 'The Session finding that William Campbell late of Auchindoun had fled off the country and left his child unbaptised, and that the mother of the child is dead, doe think it fitt that if the minister can find a proper sponsor for the child, he should baptize her.' One can see the reasoning behind an interesting decision of Elgin Kirk Session in 1598 that the child of someone excommunicated for murder should be baptised but not that of anyone excommunicated on religious grounds; and in 1573, long before the Act of

1712, the Kirk Session of St. Andrews had itself ordered the baptism of a particular child. The requirement that Kirk Sessions should baptise and then see to the education of foundlings seems also to have been something expected of baptismal sponsors of illegitimate children, a neat way of providing for them and keeping the cost of at least their education off the poor's funds but it cannot, and if the following case is anything to go by, did not encourage people to assume that role. In 1682 Elspeth Boddy, a widow, had an illegitimate child 'and the minister, being desirous of having the poor child baptised, called her father-in-law and two of her brethren, offered baptism to the child providing any would Ingadge for its education which they all refusing, the minister is to speak to the woman and to show her that they are refusing to present her child and also to require her to speak the truth.' In fact, the child died the following month and although there was some suspicion of murder, no further proceedings are mentioned in the minutes. A happier case occurred in 1838 when a Kirk Session agreed to a man's request to sponsor his illegitimate grandson, undertaking to bring him up and educate him as best as he could. The father was emigrating to America and, having paid his passage, could not wait to serve discipline and the mother, who was known to be a bad character, had been refused baptism.[25]

The fact that there were special charges for private baptism did not mean that baptism in church was free. There were fees for it and what church staff received of them was a valued supplement to their salaries. Although Parliament decreed in 1701 that half the fees for baptism (and burial) should be devoted to the poor it appears, both before and after that date, that these dues might still go entirely to kirk staff. In Kilmarnock in 1670 the charge was 6s. 8d. Scots, of which 4s. went to the Session Clerk and 2s. 8d. to the beadle; in Langholm in 1706 the fee was 9d. with 6d. of this going to the precentor and 3d. to the kirk officer; and in Earlston in 1782 out of a fee of 1s. stg., 8d. went to the Clerk for registration, which involved the work of record-keeping, and 4d. to the kirk officer. Some Sessions allowed equal shares to the Session Clerk and Kirk officer, perhaps 3d. to each, and others shared out the different categories of income, with one member of staff receiving 'the baptizing silver' and another the marriage money. One beadle augmented his fees off his own bat by taking a groat, (an English coin worth 4d. stg.) instead of his 2s. 8d. Scots, just over 2½d. stg., saying that he took no more than people were pleased to give, but for his greed he found himself confessing before the pulpit. Baptismal fees varied to some degree around the country but rose very little over many years, before finally dying out altogether. These fees were not always paid promptly and could lie out for a considerable time and it was to prevent this happening that Dumbarton Kirk Session appointed their kirk officer in 1702 'to set no water for baptising children' until he could report to the minister that the dues had been paid, with the threat that if he did otherwise he would lose his post. In the days when they were charged, baptismal fees must have been a stumbling block to even the best-intentioned poor people.[26]

By the very early eighteenth century, the General Assembly passed an Act requiring every Kirk Session to have registers for children's births and baptisms (and marriages too) but although a Session might pay attention to this and tell their Clerk to obtain the necessary books and 'carefully fill them up from time to time', there were many that did little or nothing and even where they did something, there could be many flaws. One of these was that in the case of private baptism registration could be omitted — this was why Bonhill Kirk Session imposed a charge of 3 merks Scots in 1773 for private baptisms in an effort to overcome the problem by dissuading people from having them, but it was the upper classes who were the worst offenders in this connection. Some registers do not give the mother's name, something which was common in the parish of Greenlaw until 1721 and sometimes happened even after that date, which was a serious omission. Furthermore, a register of baptisms meant what it said and children who were stillborn or who died unbaptised, as many did, or even grew up unbaptised as some did, were never mentioned in these registers. Even at a much later date, carelessness or oversight might mean that registration was omitted: in 1832 a Mrs Shaw came to the Kirk Session of St. John's Church, Glasgow, craving permission for the Clerk to register the births (not baptisms in this case) of her five children, which had not been done at the proper time, something which was fairly common then for that Session — perhaps the creditable thing is that it got done at all, at a time when Glasgow had an ever-increasing influx of people due to the Industrial Revolution. By the late eighteenth century, registration of baptisms, as well as marriages and deaths, became the subject of stamp duty which required Kirk Sessions to take out a licence in terms of an Act of Parliament, and transgressors were liable to a fine of £5 stg. How well this was implemented is open to question but Falkirk Kirk Session was one of those which took it seriously, ordering their Clerk to acquire the necessary licence and telling those requiring baptism to apply to him to register the child and then to call on the minister with signed confirmation from the Clerk that a regular entry had been made and dues paid. The Session Clerk, who was almost certainly overworked already, was from then on required to be at home every Saturday 'for the accommodation of those who may require entry in the register . . . of children's names.' 3d. was levied under this Act of Parliament on each baptism, marriage and death registered but it appears that there was no compulsory clause and one minister suggested that as the sums brought in could be of little importance to the Government, how much better it would be to allow them to the Session Clerk for his trouble which 'would unite his interest with his duty and would make registers complete.' Some parents did not appreciate the value that such registers could have in the future. They could be a means of establishing a right to heritable property, for instance, or a qualification to hold certain offices for which proof of age was required. Whatever one thinks about private baptism being allowed in return for payment, it did have the great advantage that so long as payment was made it was recorded, even if there was no registration and, in time, wise Kirk Sessions insisted that the minister should not baptise any child privately without a line from the Session Clerk certifying that the child's name had been recorded. There are now no fees for registration of baptisms, the function having been taken over by registration of births which became a legal requirement in 1855 and which has since then been enforced.[27]

As to baptismal feasts, it is said that one minister, Mr Thomas Young of Kirkmaiden in Rhinns, Wigtonshire, lived in a very miserable manner himself but was very fond of eating and drinking in other people's houses and his custom was to baptise on Sunday evenings after preaching which meant that he was properly dressed, his normal attire being very homely, and then he expected to attend the baptismal feast which he looked for from even the poorest people. That apart, the kirk's anxiety to avoid celebrations on a Sunday, which has already been mentioned, was not dislike of a feast in itself but of any disorderly behaviour arising from it. Parliament forbade banquets at baptisms (and marriages) in 1621 but had to try again, in 1681, to restrain exorbitant expense at such occasions by limiting the number of witnesses at baptisms to just four; but undoubtedly many more people attended the ensuing festivities. There was a serious riot at one of these in 1762, with the result that the Kirk Session considered it a matter for the civil courts, recommending those who had been injured to insist on such proceedings, and also using the opportunity to remind people to be more careful in their conduct in the future and to avoid inviting an 'unnecessary concourse of people and preparing banquets in their families' which could give rise to such occurrences. That was not really forbidding a simple baptismal feast for, after all, the members of the Kirk Session were men of the people who understood the desire for celebration of such events and might well wish to hold them in their own families. Moreover, entertainment was accepted practice in good households: at the baptism in August 1679 of a future Earl of Haddington the accounts in the family household book show that for dinner there were 6 pieces of fresh beef; 16 pieces of mutton and 4 of veal; 3 legs of venison; 6 geese; 4 pigs; 2 old and 8 young turkeys; 4 salmon; 12 tongues and udders; 14 ducks; 6 roasted and 9 boiled fowls; 50 chickens, of which 30 were roasted, 12 stewed and 8 fricasséed as well as 10 'in pottage'. There were 2 sides of lamb; 22 wild fowl; 182 baked, roasted and stewed pigeons; 16 hares of which 10 were roasted and 6 fricasséed; as well as 3 hams. For supper there were 2 pieces of roast mutton and 2 pieces of mutton in collops; 26 roast pigeons; 6 hares; 16 gallons of ale; 100 rolls; and 124 loaves.[28]

In highland parishes, it was not baptismal feasts that were the problem so much as a particular feature of hospitality there. Examples of this are recorded in one very large parish, thirty-five miles long and varying between five and twenty miles broad, with the church badly situated at one end of it. This made it very difficult for many parishioners to attend worship but 'marriages and baptisms however obliged many to go to church on which occasions a great expense was incurred for the convivial highlanders would not pass a public house without entertaining those who accompanied him, to the number of perhaps two thirds of a village.' Perhaps it was something of this sort which contributed to the baby's fall from a plaid into the snow.[29]

One cannot leave the subject of baptisms without mentioning some modern outdoor ones. In 1983 Rev. George Thomson of Yarrow baptised two children from different families in the kirkyard of the now-disappeared Kirk of St. Mary's of the Lowes on the hillside above St. Mary's Loch, Selkirkshire, at the annual Blanket Preaching in July. Since then two more infants have been baptised there, while at Crawfordjohn in Lanarkshire there is a baptismal stone by a roadside which is still used by descendants of the Borthwicks, a parish family.[30]

In addition, an article by Muriel Armstrong on a modern view of baptism in *Life and Work* for May 1990 gives views which are understanding, compassionate and well worth reading.

15

Burial of the Dead

Important although they knew proper disposal of the dead to be, the early Presbyterian Church took a stark attitude to the matter of burial, making it entirely secular for reasons which are implicit in the instructions 'Concerning burial of the Dead' decreed in the Directory of Public Worship which was drawn up in the mid-1640s:

> When any person departeth this life, let the body, upon the day of burial, be decently attended from the house to the place appointed for publick burial, and there immediately be interred without any ceremony. And because the custom of kneeling down and praying by or towards the dead corpse and other such usages, in the place where it lies before it be carried to burial, are superstitious; and for praying, reading and singing, both in going to and at the grave, have been grossly abused, are no way beneficial to the dead, and have proved many ways hurtful to the living; therefore, let all such things be laid aside.
>
> Howbeit, we judge it very convenient, that the Christian friends, which accompany the dead body to the place appointed for publick burial, do apply themselves to meditations and conferences suitable to the occasion; and that the minister, as upon other occasions, so at this time, if he be present, may put them in remembrance of their duty. That this shall not extend to deny any civil respects or deferences at the burial, suitable to the rank or condition of the party deceased, while he was living.

This meant that for many years there were no burial services at all, except during times of Episcopalian church government. The Book of Common Order (Knox's Liturgy) made plain what the minister's role was: *if he should be present* he could, if asked to do so, go 'to the church and make some comfortable exhortation' while the corpse went straight to the grave. Comfortable exhortations were not burial services but they and the graces said at 'kistings', of which more later, were the thin edge of the wedge which, with Scripture readings added, became the modern burial service for the dead. In answer to a query on the introduction of burial services a Church of Scotland spokesman said in 1982 that they 'just slid in', initially with official disapproval – when a minister held a funeral service in the graveyard of a parish in the south of Scotland about 1850, it caused a great to-do in the district, with all his elders leaving him because they said he was going post-haste to Rome – but ultimately the custom met with the approval which it now enjoys. Nevertheless, with or without burial services, the kirk had many respon-sibilities and functions to do with burial of the dead and the many special require-ments for funerals which the kirk provided became a valuable source of income for the poor.[1]

A visit to any large church nowadays makes it abundantly clear that burials used to take place within the building. There are memorials on the walls or stones in the floor to show that this was so but what is often not realised is that intra-mural burial, as it was called, also took place in virtually every parish church. It was complete unawareness of this on the part of most of the parishioners of one parish that caused great surprise when twenty-four skeletons were found in 1978 under the floor of the boiler room, which was originally part of the body of the church, but local surprise could have been avoided by a look at the Kirk Session minutes which show that burials inside the church only ceased in 1729.[2] Heritors whose ancestors had very probably given gifts of land to religious houses and who were themselves responsible for much of the funding of parish needs, undoubtedly felt that the least they were entitled to was a burial place within the church, which also gave them the exclusiveness after death that they had enjoyed during life. This explains the minute of Banchory-Devenick Kirk Session in 1780 which shows that a meeting of heritors decided that although there should be no further burials inside the church, this should not apply to resident heritors and the minister – ministers also liked to be laid to rest inside the churches they had served. In large burgh churches certain craft guilds used to buy burial places, presumably for leaders of the guild, and these special places were normally under or adjacent to the person's or guilds' seats.

Continued burials inside a church, especially if it was small and had an earthen floor, posed obvious problems. It was said of the highland parish of Boleskine where all classes were buried inside the church, not just the gentry, that 'the floor was oppressive with dead bodies, and unripe [undecomposed] bodies had of late been raised out of their graves to give place to others for want of room, which frequently occasions an unwholesome smell in the congregation, and may have very bade effects on the people while attending divine service.' Where graves were shallow, as they undoubtedly were inside a church, and as more interments were added, it was not unknown for bones to stick out of the earth among the feet of the congregation so that the dogs that accompanied their owners to church enjoyed a bonus meal. 'Nauseating and unhealthful' was the description given by Mr Bethune when he arrived to be minister of Dornoch in 1778 and found church burials still taking place there. Not to put too fine a point upon it, many churches smelt foully of putrefying flesh and were considered to be a considerable health risk, and all this was going on in spite of the fact that burials inside church had been condemned in the First Book of Discipline in 1560 and forbidden by the General Assembly in 1576 under threat of excommunication. This Assembly prohibition was repeated in 1588 when it was ordered that transgressors should make public repentance in addition to being suspended from benefits of the church and any minister who allowed such a burial should be 'suspended fra his functioun of the ministerie'. In yet another attempt to stop intra-mural burials, the General Assembly decided in 1597 to send a supplication to the next Parliament asking that every nobleman should be required to build what they called 'sepultures' — special aisles or vaults — for themselves and their families. In 1638 the Assembly repeated the Act of 1588 and in 1643 ratified all former Acts concerning burial inside churches, decreeing that no one 'of whatever quality' should bury anyone within the body of any church where people met 'for hearing the Word'. During the seventeenth and eighteenth centuries in a large church such as St. Michael's, Linlithgow, the Word was sometimes heard in the chancel and sometimes in the nave and so long as burials were not taking place in the part being used for services at any particular time, then the Act of General Assembly was observed, even although ultimately the whole church was filled with the bones of the dead. It was this kind of thing which made it possible in some churches for graves to be found under the pulpit, but the Assembly's Acts gradually bore fruit, as for instance, when the lairds of Barr and Galston, in Ayrshire, begged permission from the Kirk Session of Galston 'to bigg an ylle to the body of the Kirk for their burial places' but burial inside churches had been customary for so long and was so much accepted that in spite of anything that might be said officially about it, there was little concerted effort to stop it.[3]

As with so many other church prohibitions, the payment of money could overcome those on burial within churches. In 1624 the charge for burial inside the church of Fordyce was 10 merks but by 1711 had risen to £4 Scots, heritors excluded. In 1707 the cost of 'breaking of the ground for interment in the church' at Montrose was £20 Scots and when John Fairweather's 'corpose' was buried within the church about 1728 'his friends having referred to the discretion of the Session what they would take for that privilege the Session agreed to take only twenty merks.' Burgh records show that Burgh Councils accepted intra-mural burial in churches where they had some control and welcomed the money it could bring in. When Linlithgow Burgh Council fixed burial fees in 1694, the charge inside the church was 24s. Scots as against 12s. Scots 'within the six quarters of the Kirk wall' and 6s. Scots in the rest of the churchyard. The records of the Burgh of Stirling show in 1731 that the Council was frequently asked for permission to bury inside the West Church 'without any gratification being made'; and decided thenceforth that no such privilege would be granted without first of all 'satisfying the Council', but as payment was not always made as it should have been it was not unknown for a Kirk Session to forbid the kirk officer to dig any grave without payment first of all being handed over. What was given for intra-mural burial might take the form of a fine but acceptance at local level is clear from the slightness of any penalties and even where a minister, Kirk Session or Presbytery was averse to the practice, they were still more concerned with the wishes and authority of their own landlords than they were with those of a distant General

Assembly. As an example of this, when the laird of Ancistoun appeared before the Presbytery of Lanark in 1625 to confess taking the key of Symington Church, Ayrshire, from the minister so as to bury his father within it, he was simply dismissed with an admonition to 'abstain from all kirk burial in time coming.' It was probably due both to the Act of Assembly of 1638 and the form his offence took that made that Presbytery more severe in 1639 with the laird of Shieldhill for 'forcibly entering the structure' of the Kirk of Quothquan in order to bury his wife: he was punished by having to confess his sin before the congregation. Thirty years earlier, John Schaw of Sornbeg in Ayrshire also used force when he decided to bury his wife's corpse in the kirk of Galston although the minister and Kirk Session had refused permission for him to do so. Accompanied by his brother and a considerable number of men, he broke in the church door with fore-hammers, dug a grave and buried her but was obliged to make repentance and to pay £20 Scots to the poor of the parish; in addition, the Privy Council, to whom the matter was referred, ordered him to appear as a penitent and to promise solemnly that never again would he attempt to bury the body within a church.[4] But it was not just lairds who used devious means to try to bury their dead inside churches; elders could do so too. It would be interesting to know the outcome of yet another case which came before the Presbytery of Lanark when an elder 'wyled' the church key from the kirk officer by pretending that he had lost something in the church but once inside, he quickly dug a grave and 'would no ways be stopped.' An elder in Lochbroom who 'presumptuously avowed his resolution to bury in church' certainly did not get off lightly. He had to appear before the Presbytery during their Visitation of the parish, was deposed from his office and ordered to appear again before the Presbytery in Dingwall, a distance of some forty-five miles each way over very difficult country, a journey which in 1650 must have been a punishment in itself.[5]

It appears that what really stopped burials within churches was not Acts of Assembly but flooring of these buildings which made such burials generally impractical. In some cases at least, however, those who were thus obliged to give up their church burial places received compensation, and even after churches were seated, a Kirk Session might co-operate with the wishes of people to bury in what they regarded as their proper place. In 1695 the Kirk Session of Kilmarnock made special efforts to help the families of Rowallan, Craufordland and Grange by agreeing that when any member of these families required burial, the pews which by then filled the north aisle would be lifted and put back again at the Session's expense. This was at a time of food shortage and so such generosity on the part of the Session may seem strange but the reason may have been because it was the heritors who would have to be called upon for extra help should things get worse and it made sense to humour them.[6]

Although burials of the gentry, and in some cases the non-gentry as well, took place within church buildings, that did not mean that there were no graveyards. Ordinary people had to be buried somewhere and it was into the graveyard surrounding the church that they were put, into 'God's acre' as it was sometimes called. These kirkyards were originally gifted to the church by land-owners, possibly as early as the twelfth century, but as they filled up, they were extended and sometimes Kirk Sessions bought land themselves for burials. Owing to the poverty of those buried outside in the kirkyard, they seldom had gravestones to commemorate them and so these areas remained open space for many years. Parliament passed Acts to do with graveyards in 1503, 1563, 1597 and 1640, that of 1640 requiring Presbyteries to appoint stent masters to tax the people for repair of kirkyards, which meant repair of their walls, although decisions to 'stent the parochin' for such work might already have been made by some Kirk Sessions before that. An early method of getting walls built was found by the Kirk Session of Elgin in 1596 when both town and country parishioners were ordered to build their share of the kirkyard dyke and certain of the townsfolk agreed, 'under pain of 40s' to build sections of it within fourteen days. One was to do six feet in length, another seven feet while yet another promised to build eight feet 'anent his awin house', all of these to be of the required height. In general, however, owing to the turbulence of the seventeenth and first half of the eighteenth centuries, graveyards of that time were in a deplorable condition which is hardly to be wondered at as churches and manses were frequently in the same state. However, once the Revolution was past and things gradually began to settle down throughout the country, Kirk Sessions found that much of their time was spent on the matter of graveyards, trying to find money for their maintenance and working out what could be managed and what could not. One parish planned improvements for the churchyard dyke in 1741 only to discover that they could not afford their initial ideas and decided instead just to use stones and, being a coastal parish, were able to arrange to have a certain number of boat loads of these brought in, and they then harled the wall on both sides. As that sounds perfectly adequate, one wonders what their original plans can have been. A good solution, similar to that of Elgin, but more appealing to participants, was that of a Kirk Session which allowed people to have ten feet of the kirkyard for their burial places if they would build ten feet of churchyard wall. Sometimes money which would otherwise have gone to the poor had to be diverted for graveyard care: in 1764 Inverness Kirk Session decided to use some mortification money and also income from ringing bells at burials for this, another used delinquents' penalties for graveyard dykes and yet another used money from hire of the mortcloth for churchyard repairs. What seems surprising is that as late as 1722 the minutes of Langholm Kirk Session say that the Earl of Dalkeith promised a warrant for £12 stg. towards building, not rebuilding, a dyke about Langholm Church and in this case the Kirk Session, feeling that more would be needed for the work, decided that there should be a public collection around the time of the Winter Fair when 'money would be in the people's hands'. Even more surprisingly, Kelso's graveyard lay unwalled until 1807 when a public subscription was raised to enclose it.[7]

The Act of Parliament of 1597 required parishioners to build graveyard walls of stone and mortar to a height of 6½ feet with sufficient stiles and entries to give easy access to churchgoers. One writer described these dykes as being 'partly for ornament, partly as a preservative to the dead bodies from being digged up and devoured by beasts.' Pigs were a particular problem in graveyards, probably because a pig was the one animal that a great many people kept whether they had any other livestock or not, and they were none too fussy about where they wandered in their search for food. One Session 'finding that the kirkyard is frequented by swine and considering how unsuitable and dangerous this is, do unanimouslie enact that no swine go therein' while another has a minute of 1762 saying that 'The Session having met a representation from some of the parish on an indecency occasioned by the kirkyard dyke being fallen down and swines getting in and rutting the graves, it was agreed that they should be rebuilt at the inspection of the minister and that the parish, together with the session, would contribute according to their holdings, to defray the charge thereof and to put doors thereon', which was indeed done. While these parishioners had been sufficiently concerned to seek the help of the Session to deal with the problem of pigs in the kirkyards there were many people in both country and town who did not mind inadequate dykes in the least because it meant that their beasts, whether pigs or anything else, had easy access to the graveyard, and what owner was going to miss the chance of free grazing? No wonder that one Session spoke of 'ane common loaning and pasturing in the kirkyard' because all sorts of stock grazed there. In 1634 one Kirk Session had to order that 'if anie hors or ky beis fund in the kirkyaird in tymes cuming (the kirk dyke being at the present sufficientlie bigit and made fenceable) they sall be keipit untill the awners thereof pay 20s toties quoties', in other words, as often as the offence occurred. One Session's problem was that the graveyard walls were 'compassed with middens wherethrow beasts have free entries to the kirkyard.' These were the middens of houses just outside the churchyard wall which enabled animals to clamber over and get in. Another Kirk Session in a nearby parish found this same thing sufficient of a problem for them to decide to fine the owners of such middens 40s. Scots but in that particular case it seems likely that the middens were not the whole source of the trouble as only two years later a Presbytery Visitation reported that the kirkyard dyke was so ruinous that 'hors and kye enter thereby.' In some parishes the kirkyard grass was available, according to use and wont, to the minister. In 1750 the grass at Mauchline was rouped for the coming year for 18d. stg. which the minister kindly gave to the poor but when a minister used the grass himself, his beasts could prove just as much of a nuisance as other people's. In 1733, for instance, after the magistrates and Council of Peebles had gone to considerable expense to build a stone and lime dyke round the old churchyard, they were not amused when the minister put his horses in and several monuments were 'wronged'.[8] Some people even built stables in kirkyards, something forbidden in Perth in 1587 under threat of a fine of £10 Scots. Time and again kirkyard grazing was forbidden with the result that people might try to put animals in under cover of night but as one man who was detected doing this was pardoned, simply on his promising never to do so again, this cannot have been a forceful deterrent. As late as 1822 sheep were not just being grazed in the kirkyard of Lauder, but fed on turnips there, something which was only stopped when Lord Maitland made his disapproval known.[9]

A custom which caused dreadful damage to graveyards was holding markets in them, many of which at one time took place on Sundays and which are therefore discussed in the next chapter. A manuscript of 1777 showed that the heritors and parishioners of Kincardine O'Neil, Aberdeenshire, wanted to have a market in the churchyard stopped but its custom dues belonged to Lord Forbes who naturally opposed this idea. Another pro-marketeer was a Mr Clark who leased houses in the village from Lord Forbes and sub-let them. Many of them were built against the churchyard fence — some had back-doors into the churchyard — which made it easy for the tenants to join in the market money-making by selling refreshments and Mr Clark felt that if the market were stopped, his rents would fall; presumably Lord Forbes also feared a knock-on effect from this. The answer which the heritors and Kirk Session gave to these objections included a good description of the effects of a market in a churchyard. As bad weather had usually begun before it was held, the ground was not only poached by horses' hooves but vendors of all sorts had no compunction about digging up turf and sward for their stalls. This last was not an isolated instance as in 1638 another Session had to decree that whoever 'delves or breaks the sward of the laigh kirkyard and common mercat place' would have to pay £5 Scots plus whatever additional punishment might be ordered.[10]

Because people found it difficult to get space for bleachfields they might well bleach linen in graveyards although, by the sound of things, great care must have been needed to keep it clean. Craft guilds sometimes met in them and some even carried out certain of their operations in them too, such as the Skinners and Glovers of Kelso who were debarred from using one area and found the churchyard a good place for drying hides. A prohibition on secular activities in the graveyard of St. Andrews in 1595 gives a good idea of the secular activities that were going on there: people were ordered not to 'flaik dicht dry nor pak woll nor lint, dicht malte corn, pak or dry skins'; none of these things indicated disrespect for graveyards but were a comment on the lack of provision made for the work of ordinary craftsmen and tradespeople. Parish schools were initially so closely associated with the church, as has been mentioned in the chapter on education, that they were sometimes held in the church or in a building adjacent to it and therefore within the churchyard and this meant that the donkeys of those children lucky enough to ride to school, let their beasts graze there during school hours. Between 1557 and 1571 the great gate east of the Kirk of St. Giles in Edinburgh had to be closed to prevent boys breaking the church windows and turning the churchyard into what was referred to as a 'symmer field' or summer play area. Even as late as 1845 Dumbarton Kirk Session minuted their opinion 'that the churchyard should not be made into a play-ground and otherwise desecrated', but at some stages, in some parishes, play in the graveyard was accepted. At Kincardine O'Neil a space behind the church but still within the churchyard was the football field and known as the ball green and certain special-occasion ball games, such as the Hobkirk Ba' in Roxburghshire, on Fastern's E'en, were allowed to take place in part in the churchyard. This resulted in associated activities there, with table gravestones, which were an ideal shape, being used as stalls for the sale of sweets and other small articles while tents for the sale of alcohol were set up in the churchyard too, usually by people from the nearby towns of Jedburgh and Hawick. Before this exciting day began, it was the custom for some of the youngsters to climb onto the church roof and to ring the bell until they were exhausted. For this reason, in 1803, the heritors, minister and elders forbade the schoolmaster to allow any children to do so, or indeed to produce balls to be played for, and the heritors and what they called their 'doers' agreed to stop employees playing at the Ba' that day. Notices to this effect were put on the church door and at the doors of smiddies in the parish but more important things cropped up and this effort to stop the Ba' failed; and ball games of this sort, though not in churchyards, still take place in parts of the Borders on Fastern's E'en.[11]

Many of the problems of graveyard care were summed up in the minutes of Mauchline Kirk Session in 1779:

> By reason of the school kept in the church, by reason of many doors, opening upon the churchyard and ready access to it from all quarters, it is altogether a thoroughfare and a place of rendezvous for all sorts of idle and disorderly persons, who break the windows of the church, break the tomb and grave stones, and deface the engravings thereon, and the complainers are sorry to add the churchyard is now become a sort of dunghill and common office house [a public lavatory] for the whole town, a receptacle of all filthiness, so that one can scarce walk to church with clean feet.

In the 1680s, almost a hundred years before these comments were made about Mauchline, the grave-diggers of Greyfriars Kirk, Edinburgh, were forbidden by the Burgh Council to allow people 'to abuse the said kirkyard by filth and excrements' as they were in the habit of doing. It is easy to see how graveyards came to be used for sanitation purposes, especially in towns and particularly by women and children, before proper facilities were introduced, but that did not lessen the problems this caused and made attendance at public worship, especially in bad weather and at times of markets, a muddy, messy business and, should the church also reek of decomposing bodies, a revolting one too, and it was not just the church that might smell. Fairly shortly before 1885 the minister of Duthil declared in the Court of Session that within the previous twelve months he had seen in his parish graveyard 'piles of coffins and heaps of human bones, sometimes with flesh on them, and that he had witnessed dogs bounding over the fence with some of these flesh-covered bones in their mouths.' With coffins so accessible it is little wonder that the people of one Aberdeenshire parish were in the way of collecting bits of decayed ones for firewood.[12] The Session minutes of a Banffshire parish in 1740 refer to something else unpleasant which was that the churchyard was much infested with earth rats which dug holes in vaults and graves and broke into houses next the wall, doing great damage, so that the Session decided to buy poison to destroy them. These earth rats were almost certainly what were also known as 'yird swine', which had nothing to do with pigs, although just what the creature was is uncertain. Some said it was half rat and half mole; others maintained that it was the grey rat which replaced the black rat in spite of the fact that the yird swine was present in Scotland before the grey rat arrived. Whatever it was or was not, it was mysterious and a source of dread because it was believed that shortly after any burial it would gnaw its way through the coffin to feed on the corpse and that this gnawing could be heard above ground. For some reason, this fear was particularly prevalent in north-east Scotland.[13]

In large burghs churchyards came under the authority of Burgh Councils and when townspeople wished to have their own particular burial place they had to petition for an Act of Council to that effect. Country parishioners were entitled to be buried in their parish graveyard although an order from Elie Kirk Session in 1639 that burials must be in the kirkyard rather than in other places, indicates that a variety of locations were used, probably when people were poor and when distance made carriage to the kirkyard difficult. Graveyard burials may have been slightly haphazard to begin with but in time things came to be done in a more organised manner, with those requiring a family plot receiving it by Act of Session and one Kirk Session minute book for the years 1810–49 consists almost entirely of matters to do with this. Written into it are certificates showing grants of burial lairs from the Session to individuals and thereafter from person to person, and also transfers of such plots because anyone owning one could, in that parish anyway, sell or bequeath them to someone else. The certificates of ownership give details of the size, the exact location and any markings on stones already there; all transactions are signed by those involved and witnessed by the Session Clerk and sometimes by the kirk officer as well. Burial places for non-resident people had, of course, to be paid for at the outset. The right to burial in a kirkyard was jealously guarded and was a source of many arguments which Sessions had to try to sort out, not that this was always possible. Some time prior to 1784 a Session had made a decision in a dispute about a burial plot but that year the matter came up again. Two groups of people disputed its ownership, with one of them having cut out a capital letter on the gravestone inscription so that the letter 'I' appeared instead of a 'K' to fit a different woman's name. Having already dealt once with this affair, the Session seemed to think that was enough and 'finding that [it] . . . now came before them [it] turns upon some points of law of which they do not sustain themselves competent to judge, they therefore decline judging it, leaving it to the parties concerned to terminate the difference among themselves', which was one way out of the problem.[14]

'No one to bring through-stones into the churchyard until the Session are acquainted and liberty given by them' declared a Kirk Session in 1694, because permission to erect gravestones, of which through-stones were one type, had to be obtained from Kirk Sessions or, in some places the heritors, and in some towns, from the Burgh Council. The giving of permission was entered in the minutes and payment required, with the charge proportional to the size and elaboration of the stone. For instance, in 1675 the Kirk Session of Bonkle and Preston, Berwickshire, decreed that the right to put up a through-stone would cost £1 4s. Scots and every headstone 12s. Scots while by the 1830s the dues for a headstone at Kirkliston, West Lothian, were 5s. 7^1/$_2$d. each, which in the five years from 1833–37 brought in a total of £2 5s. stg. to the kirk funds. This was in addition to the cost of the stone itself, of course, with the result that although charges might be laid down, they were not always paid. When one Session found that the poor's funds were suffering because of this, they enacted that in future 'none shall have a burial place marked and registered till they pay the dues imposed upon throughs and headstones' but St. Cuthbert's Kirk Session, Edinburgh, showed compassion to a woman who asked for the privilege of putting a through-stone on her husband's grave and 'considering the poverty of her state' reduced the charge. Unauthorised erection of gravestones could lead to presumption of ownership of burial plots and this was something which had to be guarded against. In Stirling, for example, it was reported in 1640 that people were beginning to put little stones at the head and feet of graves 'whereby in process of time they apprehend to have a property' and so all unauthorised stones had to be removed. Once permission was given for a gravestone to be erected, that was that and no unofficial meddling with it was tolerated. When in 1875 a Session learnt from the grave-digger that someone proposed to replace an existing stone with a new one, that was stopped; a new one might certainly be put up but removal of the original one was not allowed.[15]

It would be interesting to know why the Kirk Session of Kirkliston paid £3 Scots for a headstone for a man named John Hill. Gravestones were not regarded by the kirk as funeral necessities so he must have been a special man to deserve this extra consideration after death. Could he perhaps have been a long-serving Session Clerk or beadle? It would also be interesting to know whether the kirk had any influence on the types of carvings which appear on gravestones.[16] There can be carvings illustrating the stories of Adam and Eve and of Abraham and Isaac which gave simple people who never saw picture books an illustration of these Bible stories. Skulls, bones, hour-glasses, coffins, sexton's tools and weapons of death appear on stones to remind the living of mortality while emblems of immortality cheered them with the prospect of life after death — angels, crowns, trumpets, plants and evergreens, as well as the Winged Soul, so often thought to be a cherub but actually representing the human soul arising after death.

The digging of graves came under church or burgh supervision. In 1576 the General Assembly ordered every parish to have a grave-digger before which, one must assume, people dug graves themselves for their own deceased. This decree meant that, in addition to paying a wage, suitable tools had to be provided: two new shovels with their irons cost £1 10s. Scots in 1695 while 'laying the spade and mattock' — a mattock was a turf cutter — cost 8s. Scots, and 'a shaft for the kirk pick' cost 6d. Scots in 1722. Large burghs and burgh churches could employ full-time grave-diggers whereas in rural parishes the work fell to the beadle or kirk officer. In town parishes a special dress was in time expected of the grave-digger which was why in 1841 the Recorder of St. Cuthbert's Church, Edinburgh, sought estimates from various suppliers for four or five 'suits of black clothes for the men belonging to the burying-ground.' The trousers had to be lined with strong cotton cloth and, along with the waistcoat and topcoat, to be made of a specified material and strong stout gaiters had to be provided too. There was no such uniform for the rural grave-digger: for Sundays he would be soberly dressed in his best but his working clothes were his own affair although, as has already been said, shoes were possibly provided for him in his role as kirk officer and occasionally a cloak also. The work might be hard, but it could be sweetened by something like 'a dram to the kirk officer at Lady Aldie's funeral', something which would have been repeated at many other burials — and the grave-digger received a proportion of the charge for each grave dug. In 1641 Montrose Kirk Session ordered that 'the kirk officer should have of every one of us able to pay it, 13s. 4d., and others that is of meaner sort, 6s. 4d., old use and wont, for breaking of the eard [earth].' Various other church officials might also be entitled to a share of funeral fees: in 1687 an Act of the Privy Council stated that it was the king's pleasure that Session Clerks, staff such as readers, precentors and beadles, and others who served the clergy, should not lose their accustomed dues for burials, as well as for baptisms and marriages, which were their ordinary means of subsistence, although only one or two of these would be likely to receive anything at any one time.[17] In 1583–84 the Burgh Council of Edinburgh allowed grave-diggers a quarter of the total charge for any grave and other charges at different dates might be 6d. for each grave in 1687 but only a groat — 4d. stg. — for a pauper's grave, at much the same date, the reason for the lesser charge being that the grave would be shallower than an ordinary one. By the early nineteenth century the payment for big graves was about 1s. 6d. stg. and 9d. for small ones while in the 1920s a rural grave-digger and keeper of a cemetery received a wage of something like £25 per annum from the Parish Council.[18]

In 1709 the keeper of the mortcloths, of which more later, at St. Cuthbert's, Edinburgh, produced his accounts 'for mortcloths, great bells and Turfs' which came to £471 7s. Scots or nearly £40 stg. and indicates that the Kirk Session provided turf for graves. Many however did not and owing to the many secular uses to which graveyards were formerly put, there was a demand for it, and so providing it seems to have developed into a kind of racket in some places, something which Mauchline Kirk Session tried to end in 1796 by suggesting to the heritors that when they appointed a new grave-digger he should be told, among other things, to keep any turf and replace it after graves were filled in without any extra charge. Grave-diggers might also levy their own charges for such things as providing staves and it is hardly surprising that people sometimes tried to escape from the expense of official grave-making. In the 1730s the Kirk Session of Drainie were told that people had dug graves in the churchyard themselves so as to avoid the grave-digger's fee and in the process had disturbed other graves; it was therefore intimated that should this happen again those concerned would be sent to the Sheriff and accused of 'disorderly walking'. In spite of the General Assembly's Act in 1576 about having grave-diggers in every parish and in spite of the fact that eventually most parishes had someone whose job this was, there were always some places where there might be no grave-digger. This might be a temporary state of affairs because of illness or because no one had been found to fill a vacant post or it might be because some large rural parishes had several graveyards and no beadle could be expected to dig graves in them all. All that could be done in such cases was for the mourners who had carried or accompanied the corpse to the burial place to lay it down and get on with the digging. In Bute in 1660 this custom of leaving the corpse on the ground during the grave-digging was considered most unseemly and the Kirk Session of Rothesay ordered that 'in time coming the grave be hocked before the corpse comes to the kirkyard, under pain of 40s. Sc to be paid by him whose duty the Session shall think it is to look after the deceased's burial.' Nevertheless, there are still living memories of burials, well into the 1930s and even later, carried out without any assistance from a grave-digger.[19]

There was at one time a superstition that it was a good thing to dig graves on the Sabbath, something which cannot have met with church approval as it not only profaned that day but must have been very distracting to worshippers. Burials also took place on Sundays and they too met with disapproval. In the mid-seventeenth century the clergy themselves sometimes showed a lax attitude to the Sabbath (taking part in marriage festivities that day), and to burial regulations too, which was why the Synod of Moray felt it necessary in 1640 to order 'that ministers exhort from burieing on the Sabbothe and that hereafter no minister leave his awne flock to goe to burialls on the Sabbothe unless the necessitie be approven be the Presbiterie.' Funerals to which Presbyteries might allow a minister to go were those of important people which it would have been as tempting as it would have been advisable to attend. The Presbytery of St. Andrews forbade Sunday burials in 1643 unless there was some special reason, in which case it was sufficient for permission to be given by the minister and Session, but even so some restrictions were necessary, with one Presbytery decreeing in 1650 'that in time coming, when the people shall burie their deid upon the Lord's day, they doe it timouslie; in the winter season before sermon, and in the simmer tyme after the afternoon sermon.' In spite of these various limits on Sunday burials they went on all round the country and at St. Cuthbert's Church, Edinburgh, it was only in June 1840 that they were finally forbidden, although with a proviso that they could be permitted in special cases, such as when a person died on a Friday or a Saturday and the disease or state of the body was such as to be dangerous to the family if burial were delayed, and also where a family lived in one room and would have to share it with the corpse; but no Sunday funerals were allowed on these or on any other grounds where death took place before a Friday. Coffin-making could sometimes be necessary on a Sunday but it was always condemned unless it was considered to be absolutely essential.[20]

Private burial was something which in earlier days was clearly open to abuse and as early as 1586 the Kirk Session of Perth forbade its happening without the knowledge of the bell-man. Just as there used to be marriages at night, so there might be burials at night also and where this occurred, or at any rate where it led to trouble of any sort, then Sessions endeavoured to stop it as minutes such as the following show: '26th February 1654. The Session being informed of disorders and reports of scandalous miscarriages caused by night burials here, do discharge any night burials, and that none of the kirk servants be accessory thereto by tolling of bells or making graves.'21 However, after doing great work for some three hundred years, Kirk Sessions bowed out of graveyard care, provision of grave-digging and burial regulations with the passing of the Burial Grounds (Scotland) Act 1855. There were amending Acts from 1857 onwards, with major changes in 1929 and 1947 and now, although parish churches belong to the General Trustees of the Church of Scotland, graveyards are in the care of District Councils.

Going back to pre-Reformation days, the ringing of bells played a prominent part in funeral proceedings. Firstly, there was the passing bell, tolled when anyone was dying so that people knew to pray for the departing soul as the priest went to perform his last duties. After death the 'soul bell' was rung to remind people to give thanks for the deceased's deliverance and the tolling of bells at funerals called people to pray for the departed soul. Superstition also came into funeral bell ringing, however, as it was believed that the sound of bells could frighten away evil spirits as well as disconcerting the devil who had a natural dislike of bells because of their connections with prayer. The Reformers, as has already been said, forbade funeral services and prayers for the dead, believing them to smack of superstition and so, naturally enough, the ringing of church and steeple bells in connection with deaths was forbidden too. But established practice could not be killed off as easily as all that and in some places it went on to a limited extent, as in the parish of Mauchline where the tolling of bells at funerals in the seventeenth century was described as 'not uncommon', and in 1666 the kirk officer of Aberdeen received £8 Scots, a considerable fee, for tolling the kirk bells at the funeral of Sir Robert Farquhar of Mouny, a former Provost. In parishes where funeral bell-ringing was permitted in this way the bell-ringer was paid but the Kirk Sessions did not at first make any charge; it was the desperate poverty of the famine of the late 1690s that made some kirks decide that the ringing of bells at burials should be allowed and used to raise money for the poor. It was in 1696 that Mauchline Kirk Session decided that there were so many desperately needy people, that anyone wanting use of the Big Bell, as the church bell was called, should be allowed to have it rung in return for a donation for the poor's funds; the needs of people dying of hunger had to over-ride official regulations. Similar provisions were made by other Kirk Sessions about the same time, such as that of Broughton who decided in 1699 that 'due to the poverty of the box' and the need for a fund to repair and maintain the kirk bell, it might be rung for funerals if 6s. Scots was given for these purposes as well as 2s. Scots to the officer who rang it. One Session wisely stipulated that the kirk bell should not be rung at burials on Sundays; there would have been inevitable confusion with the bell rung to call people to worship.22

In the Aberdeenshire parish of Tough, forty-two of the principal parishioners paid for a new church bell in 1734 with the proviso that when any member of their own families died, it should be rung as soon as the kirk officer was informed of the death, and then again on the day of the burial from morning until the coffin was laid in the ground, stipulating that this should be done by no one other than the kirk officer, thereby preventing him from delegating this wearisome task to anyone else. As time went on, ringing of the Big Bell came generally to be used only for the funerals of the better-off classes and generous donations were expected in return for its use: in the Burial Register of Inverness the words 'Big Bells' appear after the names of such people, to indicate a sum given or expected. Bell-ringing at funerals contributed considerably to the income of kirks and kirk staff and so far as one Ayrshire parish was concerned 'bell-penny' appeared in accounts from 1696 to the latter part of the nineteenth century. The ringing of the church bell for funerals died out in general about the time of the 1914–18 War but it is occasionally to be heard at Roman Catholic churches, with varying numbers of peals, according to who has died and whether they were male or female.[23]

Another type of bell which featured in kirk fund-raising was a hand-bell. Although sometimes used for public intimations such as when someone was excommunicated, for warning people not to accompany the corpse of any excommunicated person to burial, for ordering stranger beggars out of the parish or for calling people to worship before a church bell was obtained, it came into its own as a mort-bell. For obvious reasons it was also known as the little bell or the deid bell, the hand deid bell, the corpse bell or lych bell. These bells belonged to kirks (and also to burghs) and were needed because, before the introduction of hearses, the coffin was carried to the graveyard, however long the way might be, by relays of bearers. It was essential to have sufficient people bidden to the funeral by the bell to undertake this task, and some to spare, because some of the mourners, funeral hospitality being what it was, were unlikely to be able to walk, let alone carry a coffin, by the time the cortège set out. Bereaved families, therefore, paid for the use of the mort-bell, sending a message to the beadle (or a town officer) as soon as a death occurred so that he could notify everyone, which he did just like a town crier, walking slowly through the streets, ringing the mort-bell as he went and stopping at intervals to make the announcement. This was usually taken as a blanket invitation to all and sundry to come to the burial although sometimes announcement and invitation involved two trips. In addition the bell-ringer rang the bell at the head of the cortège.[24] The basic wording used on these occasions appears on a gravestone in Jedburgh Abbey graveyard, that of Adam Wilson who was the last person to ring the mort-bell there and who died in either 1812 or 1816 — the final figure is difficult to read. His announcements went as follows: 'A our brethren and sisters, we let ye to wit that we hae a brother departed at the pleasure of Almighty God yestreen at ten o'clock and ye are invited to attend the funeral at eleven o'clock.' So solemn was such an announcement that the beadle or bell-man might go bare-headed all the way but in some areas he just doffed his hat when he came to the words 'at the pleasure of Almighty God'. With only slight variations this happened around much of the country. The name and address of the dead person were always given and everyone regarded this as an invitation not only to attend the burial but to come to the lykewake as well and, in fact, although the news of a death was doleful the implicit promise of food and drink contained in the bidding to the burial, and even the prospect of merriment at these proceedings, had a great appeal. The charge for use of the mort-bell outside a parish was something like 1 merk at the end of the seventeenth century and half a merk within it, of which the bell-ringer received half. In the late eighteenth century one beadle was given permission to charge '3d a mile going in ringing the small bell' which was followed rather surprisingly by an order not to ring it for less than 2d. per mile. Income from the mort-bell, after the ringer received his share, went to the poor's box to be used as needed although on occasion some of it might be given out immediately if there was any specially needy parishioner: '10d of Little Bell and 10d of the ordinary collection given to Lillias McCulloch, a poor indigent person' is an example of this being done.[25]

Because announcing a death was always urgent, use of the mort-bell was often allowed before payment was made which made account-keeping difficult for the man who rang it, particularly if he had had no education at all. In addition, when large numbers of people died during times of famine, there were great demands for the bell, and enforcing payment for it when there was already destitution was difficult for any Session. Some of these problems appear in the minutes of Nigg Kirk Session, Ross-shire: in 1698, during the Seven Years' Famine, charges were laid down for the mort-bell but ten years later, in 1708, it was discovered that no account could be found of any income from it during all that time, the kirk officer firmly denying that he had received any payments at all. The long delay in discovering the position was probably due to the fact that the Episcopalian curate who remained in the parish after the Revolution died in 1701, following which there was a four-year vacancy; but once the position was realised, the Session revived their order of 1698 and told the clerk to make a list of everyone who had the bell, both inside and outside the parish, and forbade the kirk officer to ring it unless he was first of all paid for it.

The use of mort-bells declined as roads improved and hearses came into use, doing away with the need for large numbers of funeral bearers, and so the former general invitation to come to the burial which had been given by bell-ringing was no longer necessary. This fitted in well with efforts which gradually began to be made to limit drinking at lykewakes and funeral feasts. All this was an excellent thing — unless one was the bell-ringer. In 1741 William Stivenson, beadle at Stirling, found that it had become the fashion to have burials without intimation by the bell and he applied to the Council for a ruling on the matter. The Council knew that until very recently he had always rung the bell both to announce deaths and to lead the funeral procession, for each of which services he had received 1s. stg., and they decided that he should be paid these fees whether he rang the bell or not. There was normally no compulsion to pay for the bell if it was not used and Stirling Burgh Council must therefore have been working closely with the Kirk Session in an effort to ensure that this member of the church staff, who relied so much on these payments for a decent living, should receive them. Use of the Big

Bell and the mort-bell for funerals were both relics of Roman Catholic usage but while ringing of the former for funerals had been forbidden by the Reformers, although it still went on, use of the mort-bell was allowed. This can only have been because the mort-bell was essential whereas the Big Bell was not. That is understandable; but it is difficult to see why the mort-bell was allowed to lead the cortège to the graveyard and was sometimes placed at the head of the grave to ward off evil spirits. It is said that at Hawick and some other places the bell was taken to the house where the corpse lay awaiting burial and was put into the bed beside it, a purely superstitious action although it was considered sacriligious to remove it until the body was lifted for the journey to the graveyard. As parishes normally had only one mort-bell and as mortality was high, the puzzling thing about this story is what happened if someone else died while the bell was still abed with a corpse. So far as there was a superstitious element in the use of the mort-bell, could it be that people who were denied any burial service for their dead clung to this little piece of remembered ritual? (The carrying of corpses around the church at Kilconquhar, mentioned in an earlier chapter, which was forbidden in 1641, was almost certainly something of the same sort.) Did the Reformed church take so little notice of burials that they saw no need to interfere with burial superstitions, not that that was something they normally hesitated to do? Was superstition so ingrained that even Kirk Sessions failed to stop something which perhaps they really believed could frighten away demons? Whatever the reason, the kirk which tried in every way to suppress popish practices, happily made money from the continuance of an old Roman Catholic custom.[26]

Some parishes had no mort-bell and in that case notification of a death had to be made by a 'burial warning' passed from house to house by word of mouth. In 1715 a man was summoned before the Kirk Session of Orphir because he had 'put down' a burial warning, wording which sounds as if it was something in writing although it appears to have been verbal. The result was that very few people came to the funeral 'for carrying the corpose of the deceased Jennet Gune to her burial place' and of those who did, most were just 'weak boys', not really able to carry a coffin, 'which occasioned great disorder and gave offence.' In his defence, the man accused of failing to pass on the message, said that he was not told the time of the burial and could not therefore let anyone else know. Not wanting such a thing to happen again, the Session within a month passed an Act anent Burials which decreed that the relations of anyone who died should let the elder of the bounds know the time of the burial and it would be up to him to 'raise the said warning and put it to the next house giving them notice of the day and time when they shall convene.' In 1732 that Session found it necessary to make a Burial Regulation which repeated what had been laid down in 1715 but with the addition 'that a corp should not be lifted' (to start the final journey) 'before the 11th hour in winter and one o'clock in summer.'[27]

A funerary item which came to be very important was the mortcloth or funeral pall. Its use originated with people who could not afford coffins and instead covered the shrouded corpse in a sheet, a plaid, a piece of blue homespun or 'a black cloath', such as the Kirk Session of Glasgow ordered in 1598 'to be laid on the corpses of the poor' for the journey to the kirkyard. Once there, the body was unwrapped from this additional covering and lowered into the grave. Although originating in poverty, mortcloths in time became very handsome and were regarded as indispensible features of funerals of whatever class. They came into use certainly by the fifteenth century but there is no doubt that a Proclamation in Council in 1684 greatly increased their popularity. Although the proclamation was meant to reduce extravagance at funerals and other special occasions, forbidding among other things, the decoration of coffins with metal work and fringes, in practice those who wanted funeral finery found that a lavishly fringed mortcloth made of a rich fabric was a very good alternative and ultimately no one would see a member of their family buried without one of better or lesser quality. It did not take long for it to be realised that providing mortcloths for hire could be a profitable business but although a few were privately owned, the capital outlay was such that they generally belonged to bodies such as burgh councils, craft guilds, trade incorporations, some privately-run charities and funeral societies and, of course, Kirk Sessions. The church found that buying a mortcloth was a good investment of any spare poor's money and lack of a mortcloth was always keenly felt. One Session minuted in 1693 'the great loss the [poor's] box was at for want of a sufficient mortcloth' and when another Session decided in 1756 that a new cloth was necessary, this was because 'it would be a loss to the parish to want [lack] one.' In fact, one cloth was seldom enough and most parishes found it worthwhile to have at least two, a best and a second best, so that people could choose which they could afford, and there could be a child's size too and sometimes a middle one as well.[28]

Mortcloths were always black and the best ones were made of velvet or plush. The quality of the material was of importance and when a merchant in London sent Hawick Kirk Session a gift of one for behoof of the poor he made sure that they knew just how good it was, stating that it was of 'a right Genoa Vellivet, the former was only Dutch.' Mortcloths were lined with a variety of materials — blink, buckram, even white satin — and bordered, sometimes with lace but more usually with fringing which could be of silk or of hair but of whatever it was made, it added greatly to the appearance of the cloth. When the Kirk Session of Logie, Stirlingshire, bought 9 ells of finest black velvet along with 7 ells of blink for lining, they also got 3 lbs 5¹/₂ oz. of 'great and small' fringing to adorn it although some cloths had to make do with just small fringes. The value of a mortcloth was largely decided by the weight of the fringing and this of course allowed for considerable variety. At the time that mortcloths were in greatest use, ready-made goods were not easily found and so material usually had to be bought to be made up by a local tailor. When, however, the Kirk Session of Fowlis Easter and Lundie, Angus, asked the beadle's brother who was planning to go to Edinburgh 'to do his uttermost to get one there' and the Kirk Session of Tynninghame asked the minister to do the same thing when he went to the capital, it is not clear if cloths could be bought made-up there or whether they would have to have this done.

Mortcloths were a major investment and not one to be entered into without due care and if a Session which needed one knew of another Session which had recently got one, careful inquiries would be made of them on all aspects of the purchase.[29]

Kirk Session accounts and minutes give full detail of these expensive items. In 1695 the minister of Coldingham and another man were appointed to go to Berwick to get materials for a mortcloth. What they bought was

14 yards of hair fringe at 10s per yard	£ 7	—	—
4 yards of fine cloth at £7 10s per yard	30	—	—
10 drop of silk	—	15	—
8 ells sarking for lining	3	4	—
dying of the forsaid lining	1	12	—
threed, workmanship and the tailor's pains, in going to Bk. to bring out the cloth —	1	10	—
[all in Scots money]			
Total £42	41	—	[sic]

In 1737 Old Rayne Kirk Session, Aberdeenshire, obtained materials for a new mortcloth from Aberdeen and the minister later produced the accounts of the merchant and tailor:

To Alexander Christy

7½ yards black plush at £3. 10s per yard	£29	—	5 [sic]
3 yards white mantua at £2. 4s per yard	6	12	—
3 drops white silk	—	4	6
½ yard white buckram	—	6	—
¾ yard white Sattin	2	—	6
8 yards of Loupon [cord or braid made of loops, used to trim or fasten]	—	12	—
4 yards more of Loupon	—	6	—

Also to Robert Joyner, tailor

For making the mortcloth	£6	—	—
6 ells of [cl]aze at 12 s per ell for lining	3	12	—
1 ell Sarge (serge) for a Pocke [bag, poke, wallet for carrying]	—	12	—
Dying the Sarge	2	4	—
Lettering the Belt	1	4	—

The total came to £52 10s Scots.

By 1765 Old Rayne needed another mortcloth which was made from:

5 yards fine Genoa velvet at 21s per yard	£5	5	—
6 yards glazed linnen at 16d per yard	—	8	—
6 yards Shalloon at 22d per yard	1	11	—
2 ozs of Thread	—	—	6
5¹/₈ yards of white mantua at 15s per yard	1	6	10¹/₂
24 yards of waling at 1d per yard	—	2	—
11 drop Black Silk at 2d per drop	—	1	10
7 drop white at 2d per drop	—	1	2
³/₄ yard white Buckram at 16d per yard	—	1	—
2 yards Shalloon at 18d per yard [woollen lining]	—	3	—
2 yards of Tep [patterned material]	—	—	2
¹/₂ oz of Threeds	—	—	1¹/₂
	£8	—	8
To making the mortcloth	—	12	6
	£8	13	2 stg.

Although this itemised account given by the minister to the Kirk Session is in sterling, the cost of the mortcloth appears in the accounts as £103 18s Scots, a system of book-keeping which cannot have helped accounting. A grander cloth made for the parish of Arbuthnott in 1752 included silver lace, silver cord and thread and best quality velvet so that the total cost came to £12 19s. 10d. stg. but at Fordyce in 1769 £11 stg. was sufficient to produce an 'extremely genteel' cloth.[30]

British-bought materials, like Genoa velvet, might well be imported but as trade with Europe developed, so mortcloths or the wherewithal for making them could be obtained directly from the continent. A Selkirkshire parish got one 'bought at Holland' and the Kirk Session of Dunbar, a coastal parish well placed for foreign trade, decided in 1734 'that the Moderator should desire Captain Hall to commission by some of their shipmasters now at Genoa as much velvet as may serve for a mortcloth.' Mortcloths were subjected to very considerable wear and tear. Not only was there a custom of 'busking' or decorating them by pinning, stitching or even nailing family honours or verses on to them but any cloth, let alone a velvet one, was bound to suffer from bad weather, flapping in the wind or being soaked with rain during the long walk to the burial ground. Damage was also caused by contact with the rough wooden hand-spokes on which the coffin was borne; in 1694 one cloth was 'worn to rags' and the following year the Session which owned it bought 6 fathoms of 'small towes' — 36 feet of hemp or flax — to bind round the spokes to prevent such damage occurring in future. Because a shabby mortcloth could not bring in as much money as a decent one, Kirk Session records are full of the efforts made to repair and refurbish them by mending, relining and even dyeing them — many a cloth had its useful life lengthened by 'dyeing the lining and sewing of it' or some such repair work. Andrew Martin was employed in 1746 by Melrose Kirk Session to do 'tailor work about the mort-cloths' while in Tarbat, Ross-shire, where the cloths 'had suffered in the linning [lining] and otherwise' the kirk officer was ordered 'to get them mended by a proper hand', something which cost £3 9s. Scots. Any part of an old cloth that could be re-used was kept and the minutes of one Session show that the fringes of one cloth were in good enough condition to be put on to a new one.[31]

When a second-best cloth was specifically provided as a cheaper alternative to the velvet cloth or for use by the poor, it was not made of velvet but of something like English cloth or of shag (a long coarse nap) and very occasionally of sack-cloth. One cloth made of this last material must have been a poor thing indeed, costing only 1s. Scots (1d. stg.) to make up and it cannot have failed to be associated with shame and penitence in the minds of those who saw or used it. Often, however, the second cloth was of shabby velvet or plush because a policy of waste-not, want-not, operated and when the best cloth was too worn to bring in the hire charge it used to, a new one was bought and the worn one was handed down to be the less good cloth and, in the same way, an adult-sized cloth could be cut down to make a child's size. Another instance of making the most of things happened in Dornoch in 1718. Two mortcloths, one of velvet and the other of a lesser material, were bequeathed by a merchant in London to the Kirk Session for the benefit of the poor. They were of such a good size that the Session decided that 'each of them will be two' and had them 'made up in four for the better improve-ment of the same' and so the gift provided not two but four mortcloths which must have reduced wear on each of them, whether or not it increased income because with the best will in the world the number of funerals could not be increased.[32]

Gradually the increasing populations of large cities justified Kirk Sessions in having a considerable number of mortcloths. An inventory in the records of St. Cuthbert's Church, Edinburgh, shows that in 1839 there was a total of 24, of first, second and third size, graded in quality from A to F, the best ones kept in a wardrobe, those for the poor kept less grandly in a press, and all of them in the mortcloth room at the church. In lesser towns and in rural parishes, mortcloths were usually kept at the church, often in a box, a wallet or a bag, the latter sometimes called a pock. Morebattle Kirk Session bought a 'chest to hold the mortcloth' in 1733 and the merchant who sent the Genoa 'Vellivet' cloth to Hawick wrote that he had sent it 'in a fine milled serge Bagg, with Silk and Strings, and altogether in a Dale [deal] box.' Bags or wallets were practical as they could be used both for storage and as carrier bags when a cloth was called for, 'for keeping and the more safe carrieing of them', as one Session put it. Serge was often used for them, and so was tartan which must have given a brighter look to things. Some of the items for making these bags have been mentioned in Old

Rayne's accounts but what went to the making of a pock in 1728 was:

For the tartan	£1	13	—
Sarking and cording	—	10	—
For silk	—	6	—
For thread	—	1	—
For work	—	6	—
Total	£2	16	—

'Ane wallet for the mortcloth' cost Shotts Kirk Session £2 5s. 6d. Scots from a Glasgow merchant in 1727 while the one got by Old Rayne in 1765 cost £1 12s. Scots. What were called towels were sometimes used to tie up the mortcloth, possibly inside the wallet or perhaps in lieu of it: 'the towels that tie the mortcloth being now worn and ragged' caused a Session to order sufficient cloth to make two new ones in 1701, and fifty years on they again needed towels and spent £1 10s. on two yards of linen to make them. It was probably only too easy to return the mortcloth to its carrier bag immediately after use, even if damp, and one Session specifically required its keeper 'to frequently brush it and expose it to the air.'[33]

Mortcloths were always put in charge of specific people. At churches like St. Cuthbert's, Edinburgh, there were special mortcloth keepers but in smaller places it was usually the beadle or kirk officer who looked after them in return for a fee of something like 3s. 4d. for keeping the best one, 2s. for the children's one, Scots money. In Kiltearn, Ross-shire, however, in 1723 the kirk officer only had charge of the 'course' mortcloth while another man was 'collector of the velvet mortcloth dues'. In Cambuslang in 1788 it was the schoolmaster who kept the mortcloth and received a fee of 10s. stg. per annum but that was perhaps just a temporary arrangement as it only started because the former mortcloth keeper had died. In view of all his other work he could hardly have been expected to fall in with the normal practice of a mortcloth keeper, which was to deliver it to any house of mourning himself. This was something which brought further income to whoever did the work and, fairly enough, there was always more money if the cloth had to be taken outwith the parish. Some examples of this come from Melrose in 1763:

	Hire charge	Kirk officer received
Best mortcloth used inside the parish	5s.	6d.
Best mortcloth used outside the parish	10s.	6d.
Best little mortcloth	1s.	2d.
Second-best little mortcloth	— 8d.	2d, all stg.

Examples from Channelkirk in 1804 show:

	Hire charge	Beadle received
Best mortcloth used inside the parish	6s.	1s.
Best mortcloth used outside the parish	7s.	1s.

Second mortcloth in/outside parish	3s. 2d.	— 8d.	
Small cloth in/outside parish	1s. 4d.	— 10d. stg.	

In the earlier part of the nineteenth century a kirk officer was allowed to charge 4d. per mile for taking the mortcloth outside the parish — and there could always be nice extras such as 'drink silver to be given to the caryer of the mortcloths'.[34]

There was obviously variation in mortcloth hire charges around the country at different times (and only very occasionally is the charge given in victual, as at Kiltearn in the early eighteenth century):

	Best	Second	Child	Outside Parish.
1693 Fowlis Easter and Lundie Kirk Session	14s. Sc.			£2 Sc.
1730 Nigg Kirk Session, Ross-shire	2 merks Sc.	1s. stg.		
1736 Corstorphine Kirk Session	£4 Sc.		£1 10s. Sc.	
1740 St. John's Clachan Dalry, Kirkcudbright	£1 10s. Sc.			
1752 Channelkirk Kirk Session	£2 2s. Sc.	16s. Sc.	6s. Sc.	
1756 Cromarty Kirk Session	1s. stg.		6d. stg.	18d., 9d.
1765 Old Rayne Kirk Session	£1. 4s. Sc.	12s. Sc.		
1773 Ordiquhill Kirk Session	1s. 5d. stg. (incl bell)			
1775 Channelkirk Kirk Session	5s. stg.	2s. 9d. stg.		

(In 1804 Channelkirk Kirk Session's charges became a little more complicated. The hire of the best cloth was 6s. stg. + 1s. for dykes (churchyard walls) for the second 3s. 2d. + 6d. for the dykes; for the child's size 16d. stg. with no extras; while the charges for use outside the parish were 7s. stg. for the best, 3s. 2d. for the second best and 16d. stg. for the small cloth with no additions.)

1821 Edderton Kirk Session	5s. stg.	3s. 6d. stg.
1826 Nigg Kirk Session, Ross-shire	5s. stg.	3s. 6d. stg.

Mortcloth charges were quite often combined with bell-ringing, as at Tarbat, Ross-shire, in 1764.

Interest rates during the relevant times varied from 2–4% and as an average best quality mortcloth cost £10–12 stg., the following figures show what a good investment it was to use some of the poor's funds for a mortcloth. Taking just one parish as an example, the % income in the mid-nineteenth century produces the following figures:

Income		Original cost £ 10 stg	Original cost £ 12 stg.
1824	£2 9s. 6d.	24.75%	20.5%
1831	— 17s. 6d.	8.75%	7.3%
1833	— 3s. 6d.	1.74%	1.45%
1842	£1 3s. 6d.	11.75%	9.75%

In fact a mortcloth bought by that Session in 1781 cost £11 8s. stg. and at 5s. stg. per hire in 1785 brought in £1 15s. or 14.8%[35]

Good though this income was, nevertheless a mortcloth's life, given good care, was only about forty years and when its days were finished, it meant that the capital it represented was gone too. On occasion Sessions were over-ambitious in the charges they asked for their best mortcloths which simply redounded to the detriment of the poor's box but if that happened, it seldom took them long to appreciate the problem. One stated quite simply in 1733 that 'the two big mort-cloths are too dear' and when another realised in 1805 that their 'high quality mortcloth' was so costly to hire that people simply got one from elsewhere, they dealt with the difficulty by providing an 'inferior mortcloth' for their use. Because of the outlay needed to buy a mortcloth and the healthy income that it could bring in, Kirk Sessions wanted to have a monopoly of them. In 1724 Auchterhouse Kirk Session forbade the use of plaids on corpses specifically so that the parish cloth would have to be hired and they also decreed that 'none without [outside] bury here without our mortcloth.' This was directed at non-parishioners wishing to bury their dead in Auchterhouse and meant that the Auchterhouse mortcloth had to be paid for, whether used or not. Similar conditions became general around the country and to enforce them Sessions might forbid their grave-diggers to open any grave unless the parish cloth was to be used. Yet Kirk Sessions wanted to have it both ways and when that of St. Cuthbert's, Edinburgh, learned that its parishioners were burying their dead in Greyfriars kirkyard and therefore not using St. Cuth-bert's mortcloths 'to the great prejudice of the poor thereof', they and the heritors decided to refuse use of their mort-bell unless people either buried their dead in St. Cuthbert's graveyard and used that Session's cloth, or at least paid the mortcloth dues for it.[36]

In the latter part of the nineteenth century the colliers and carters of Newton, Edinburgh, had what was called a 'box' or fund which supported any of their members who were sick and provided free use of mortcloths for those who died. As the parish population consisted largely of these two groups and their families, the Session soon realised that there would be no income for the kirk's mortcloth if this practice was allowed to continue and they and the heritors decided to have the matter settled in court. The neighbouring parish of Liberton, which was in the same position, joined them in the action and a decree of the Court of Session was obtained in 1792 prohibiting the use of any but parish mortcloths. However, the Kirk Session were aware of the help which the 'boxes' gave to the needy of the parish who would otherwise have had to seek help from the kirk poor's funds and so, with the heritors' agreement, they decided to grant these two groups the right to continue to use their mortcloths for the next twenty years, by which time it was reasonable to suppose that they might have worn out, on condition that every time they were used, they should pay the kirk treasurer the small sum of 4s. stg. for the benefit of the parish poor, which was in fact quite a lot to pay. It was expressly stated, however, that this provision would last only so long as aid from the 'boxes' continued to be given to the colliers' and carters' own poor. Paying something for the parish poor was normal practice when non-kirk bodies had their own mortcloths. In 1721 the minister of Hawick decreed that a mortcloth belonging to the Tradesmen must not be used by any but their own members but in this case there was no need to go to law as the Chamberlain to the Duchess of Buccleuch, who was Bailie of the Regality of Hawick and the senior elder, said that he would ensure that this was done. In Falkirk too, there was trouble about a privately-owned mortcloth and there the Kirk Session got authority from the heritors to raise an action, with the minister and treasurer to act in their name to prosecute the 'havers and users' of the 'private mortcloth which has lately set up in opposition to the parish mortcloth, and to the great prejudice of the poor's fund before the Court of Session.' No outcome of this case is reported so it may be that the threat of legal proceedings was sufficient to stamp on the opposition cloth. The nobility and some of the gentry owned mortcloths but while Kirk Sessions could do nothing about them, they could stop lesser people from keeping cloths for private gain by insisting on what can only be called compulsory purchase of any in private hands. The minutes of a Kirk Session say in 1729 '. . . there are some private persons who keep mortcloths which are commonly made use of in the parish and these persons apply the money which is collected for the said mortcloths to their own private use' and so they forbade this to continue and ordered 'such as have these mortcloths to bring them to the next dyet of session to be purchased by the session for the benefit of the poor.' They paid £12 Scots for one of these cloths and accepted another one free but allowed its owner life rent of it. When the Kirk Session of St. Cuthbert's, Edinburgh, decided to buy the mortcloths of the Incorporated Trades of Portsburgh, the Trades at first refused to sell them but a threat to take the whole matter to the Privy Council was sufficient, as happened in Falkirk, to make the Trades agree to the sale. They tried, however, to make some conditions but these the Session thought excessive and said that unless they were more reasonable, they would simply buy mortcloths themselves and as they controlled burials in their own graveyards, would prevent use there of any mortcloths but their own. This changed things and the Cordiners gave their one to the Session free on the understanding that their poor would be looked after and that their members could have use of a coffin and velvet cloth gratis. The other Trades' cloths were bought for a total of over £922 Scots, more than £86 stg., and proved a good investment. At Castleton, Roxburghshire, the mortcloth was still, surprisingly, in private hands in the 1790s. On the subject of going to law over use of mortcloths, such action might have to be threatened to obtain a promised one. In 1670 John King left

Drainie Kirk a legacy of 40 merks which the Session decided to use for a mortcloth and asked his son William, who was a partner in a ship trading with Holland, to get one from there. He generously gave an extra £10 Scots for it and the Session brought the total up to £150 Scots but he did not produce the cloth and thirty years later it was only threats of being taken to law that finally produced it. Why did the Kirk Session wait so long, especially as they had advanced some of their own funds?[37]

Once collected, mortcloth money normally went straight to the poor's box but, as with bell money, it might on occasions be paid out directly to anyone in special need — one Session received £1 10s. for mortcloth hire and paid it out forthwith to ten people at 3s. each. Sometimes it was used for churchyard maintenance, as has been said, or repair of the church, while about 1712 income from a mortcloth which had been donated to a Kirk Session paid some of a schoolmaster's salary. Charges might be fixed and monopolies enforced but that did not prevent irregularities to do with mortcloth money. The best way, obviously, of preventing it lying out was to order the kirk officer to hand it in to the treasurer immediately after any funeral but that did not happen by any means. In Lauder in 1681 it was necessary for one of the elders to become cautioner for payment of this money due from the man who had been collecting it but who had not handed it over, while in 1683 a mortcloth bequeathed by John Turner to the Kirk of Birse was sent there in charge of his cousin, William, who unfortunately held on to it and its income for sixteen years, a long time for a Session to be out of pocket. At that point he finally agreed to hand it over along with details of those who had hired it and a note of any money still owing so that the Session might gather it in. One way, although not a common one, of overcoming the problem of undelivered mortcloth money was for the Session to rent out the cloth, just as toll-houses were let, giving an assured income without the trouble of collection. This happened in Dornoch in 1733 when the Session's cloths were let to Hugh McCulloch for seven years at a yearly rent of £3 stg.[38]

As the standard of coffins was allowed to improve enough to give adequate dignity to burials on their own, and as hearses came into use, so mortcloths gradually ceased to be used but a major factor in their demise was the Poor Law of 1845 which took the burden of the poor off the kirk and it was no longer necessary for Sessions to raise money for their care. As with many other customs, however, the use of mortcloths did not die out overnight. In a Borders parish use of the mortcloth was described as '*almost* wholly discarded' in 1900 while about 1905 one was still being used in an Easter Ross parish although by that date it was simply laid over the coffin at the churchyard gate.[39] The use of mortcloths outlasted that of mortbells but the bells themselves have outlasted the mortcloths. A good number of bells may still be seen in churches and museums but there are very few mortcloths in existence. Although George Hay was able to list several still to be found in 1952 in his book *Architecture of Scottish Post-Reformation Churches*, most of these have since been lost. Midcalder's has not been seen for a number of years; those at Monzievaird and Strowan seem to have disappeared when the church was demolished in the 1960s and that of Rosemarkie disappeared some time after 1978. Fortunately, there are at least two in existence, that of Old Rayne, which is of fine velvet but lacks almost all its lining and fringing, and that of Glasserton, Wigtownshire, which is in almost perfect condition; and there may be a third one at Kilmany, Fife.

Until the Registration of Births, Deaths and Marriages (Scotland) Act of 1855, death registration was largely a hit-or-miss affair although very soon after the Reformation the General Assembly had realised that registration was desirable and tried to achieve it at various times and by various agencies such as ministers, readers, grave-diggers, Kirk Sessions and Presbyteries. In 1574 two Senators of the College of Justice requested the General Assembly, in the name of the College, to ask every parish reader to give in to their Superintendents annual lists of deaths in their parishes, to be passed on to the General Assembly, but because 'manie understood not of it' this was not effective and one of the main reasons why the General Assembly ordered every parish to have a grave-digger, as has been mentioned already, was so that he could notify deaths to parish readers who would inform the Commissioners to the General Assembly who would report to that body. In spite of this, between 1575–1600 only six parishes began to keep burial registers. In 1616 as a result of royal pressure, the Assembly then ordered all ministers to keep a 'perfyte and formall Register' failing which they were threatened with suspension but this was not effective either and in the quarter-century from 1600–25 the number of parishes keeping registers only rose to eighteen. But things gradually improved and between 1725–50 the number of registers being kept was 336, which may have been attributable as much as anything to the development of parish schools and the appointment of schoolmasters as Session Clerks. The Session Clerk was keen to register deaths as he received something like 4s. Scots for each one by the early eighteenth century and so far as Kirk Sessions were concerned, this meant another addition to the income of a key member of their staff. In 1783 registration of deaths, along with baptisms and marriages, was made the subject of stamp duty and Kirk Sessions found that they were expected to see that this was paid when the mortcloth was asked for, but people resented having to pay a fee to register deaths so that this was always a difficulty and Old Statistical Accounts of the 1790s frequently refer to the lack of proper registers. Counting burials was not an accurate way of reckoning the number of deaths in a parish because people who died in one parish were often buried in another; some parishes had several burying grounds — Glassary in Argyllshire had six — and even where mortcloth records were kept and gave the names of the deceased, they could show duplication in cases where one cloth had to be hired but another was used. They also omitted very young children for whom a cloth was not normally considered necessary; and in addition people of different religious denominations did not have their deaths recorded by the kirk. In 1816 the General Assembly enjoined Presbyteries to see that every parish kept three registers, one each for births — not baptisms as formerly — marriages and deaths but it took the Act of 1855 to put registration on a proper basis, after which Kirk Sessions only had an indirect role. Some parishes kept death registers before these were legally required. This was more likely to happen in burghs, such as Dumbarton where in 1694 the Kirk Session were told that several people were buried without their names being recorded in the register of the dead and ordered that thenceforth the friends of the deceased must give in that person's name to the Session Clerk; so as to make this more effective, they forbade the grave-digger to make any grave unless the relevant entry had been recorded. At a later date, in the mid-nineteenth century, the parish of Kinnell kept a list of births, marriages and deaths in the one book, identifying them by the letters, B, M or D, which must have been very confusing. On the subject of abbreviations, Montrose Mortality Register's first page, in 1767, gave the following:

BT	Bells tolled	CBM	Chapel's best Mortcloath (Episcopal
BM	Best mortcloath		Chapel under the Bishop of
SM	Second Mortcloath		Carlisle St. Peter's, licensed 1722.)
BR	Bells Rung	BCM	Best Children's Mortcloath
BG	For breaking Ground	PM	Poors Mortcloath
BC	Buried in Church	SPM	Poors Second Mortcloath.[40]

Although death registration was regarded by the people as an unnecessary funeral expense, they never grudged the money spent on the giving of lavish hospitality on the occasion of a death, and that began with the lykewake. It was possibly because the Reformed kirk did not initially allow any burial service for the dead that the lykewake came to have the prominence in funeral proceedings that it did. A lyke is an unburied corpse and the lykewake or late watch (sometimes but more unusually called a lacke walk, with other spellings too) was basically a constant vigil kept over it until burial although there was more emphasis on watching at night rather than in the daytime, possibly because evil was thought more likely to be abroad after dark but even more possibly because people were freer to attend then. The duration of the lykewake depended on social and financial circumstances. In a great household, it might last for several weeks while arrangements were made for the funeral and the entertainment and accommodation of important guests, and perhaps to allow for summoning members of the family home from abroad; but for ordinary people, lykewakes lasted for just two or three nights prior to the burial while for the poor they lasted no longer than the time it took to have a coffin made. At ordinary lykewakes the body was placed in bed in the best room or in the kitchen, and there everyone gathered, although use of a box bed made the corpse less conspicuous than it might otherwise have been. As well as a vigil the lykewake was intended to be an opportunity for people to pay their respects to the dead but its real appeal for most of those who attended was the hospitality provided. Their normal fare was so frugal that they thankfully grasped the chance of free food and drink and there is no doubt that, abuses apart, the chance of a square meal or two at funerals must have done the living nothing but good. In former days abundant entertainment was an essential part of a decent burial. It was a terrible disgrace to the departed and to his or her family if it was not provided as generously as possible, indeed in many cases in a way they could not really afford. Unfortunately, what was considered suitable provision at lykewakes caused such an atmosphere of conviviality that what was meant to be a solemn occasion 'for Christian converse about death and eternity' had a way of turning into a very jolly party. Story-telling sounds a reasonable enough occupation but there could also be 'playing at cards and dice, and other riotous gaming, to the disturbing not only of the family where the dead lies but also to the neighbourhood by their unaccountable practices in night time without doors.' Some might go 'to the hot cockles and other frolics' or join in other abuses 'committed at late watches by Several Games and Diversions in which young people exercise themselves' or get involved in 'most unsuitable pastimes'. One of these would certainly have been the dressing-up in men's clothing done by Mage Morison in Aberdeen in the 1570s, which was something regarded as superstitious and very wrong at the best of times, let alone at a lykewake. Psalms and dirges were a feature of lykewakes but music for entertainment slipped in too and became so common that in 1728 when John McEdward 'confessed that he had a fiddler in the house at a leickwake of a dead person . . . [he] said he did not think it a sin, it being so long the custom in this country.'[41]

In many parts of the world dancing is or was a part of worship and it also occurred at funerals, where it was thought to drive away evil and to free the living from fear. So far as Scotland was concerned, it was in the highlands particularly that the lykewake often included a solemn dance around the corpse, always opened by the next of kin who frequently wept as they moved. In 1748, on the death of his mother, a man called his neighbours together to testify his and their sorrow by a dance which continued throughout the night until morning but the kirk did not agree with the idea of dancing on such occasions and the fiddler who had provided the music for that night of dancing had to appear before the congregation for six Sundays, although the severity of this punishment was partly because the offence had taken place on a Sunday night. In theory such dancing as might take place at a lykewake was meant to be grave and dignified but as the evening wore on and drink flowed, both the music and the dancing got merrier until lykewakes became 'more boisterous than weddings, the chamber of the dead being filled night after night with jest, song and story, music of the fiddle and the pipe, and the shout and clatter of the Highland reel.' In just one parish several men and one woman were charged by their Kirk Session in 1723 with 'dancing at lykewakes' and in 1724 a man had to satisfy discipline 'for his unChristian Behaviour in dancing' at them and promised 'thro' the Lord's Strength never to be guilty of the Like again.' The very next year three more women were found 'guilty of scandalous behaviour by Dancing, Singing and Playing at a Lykewake.' They denied the charge and the Session decided to summon witnesses but it seems to have come to nothing as no further reference to the case appears in the records. During a Presbyterial Visitation to the parish of Moy, Inverness-shire, in 1675, one of the questions put to the minister was whether he laid any 'restraint upon pypeing, violeing and dancing at Lickwacks' to which he replied, 'Not as yet', an answer which was not considered satisfactory and he was ordered to do so at once and to punish any offenders with church censure. In that year also the Synod of Moray considered the 'superstitious and heathenish practices' which went on at lykewakes 'during which tym sin and scandell does greatlie abound' and so they forbade all 'light and Lascivious exercises, sports, Lyksongs, fidling and dancing' and ordered that the ordinary 'crowding multitude' should be kept out and that only near relatives should be present or those who might give suitable comfort to the bereaved, and they also recommended that during lykewakes the time should be spent as it was meant to be, in such occupations as reading the Scriptures.[42]

Limiting the numbers attending lykewakes during an outbreak of plague in Aberdeen in 1606 has been mentioned as a health measure in an earlier chapter but the relevant minute also says that it was because 'of the abuses that fall out at lykewakes' which shows that a Session could turn misfortune to good account and kill two birds with one stone if they considered that to be in the public interest. There is an idea that it was in the highlands that lykewakes were the most riotous but although old ways lingered there longer than farther south, it is clear from the steps that had to be taken all around Scotland to control behaviour at them that neither dancing nor unruly conduct was confined to the north. In an Act of 1621 Parliament forbade all eating and drinking at lykewakes under threat of a fine of 1,000 merks but this did little good and the General Assembly forbade lykewakes entirely in 1645 and urged Presbyteries to censure transgressors. In 1646 Parliament backed this up with an Act discharging them under a penalty of £20 Scots to the Kirk Session and gradually some Sessions tried to implement this, for instance St. Andrews Kirk Session which forbade sitting up at lykewakes and drinking dirigies — drinking healths to the dead — but even so in 1701 the General Assembly had to revive their Act of 1645. Lykewakes however were part of the way of death and public feeling was so strongly in favour of them that Sessions did not usually try to stop them, only to stop abuses at them, as happened in other matters also. In fact, there was some active approval of this long-established custom because in 1676 on the death of two Mauchline paupers, the Session allowed 3s. Scots for 'tobacco and pipes that night they were waked' and in an East Lothian parish an entry in the records 'for a candle and other necessaries at a child's death' can only have been for a night watch. These night watches are remembered into this century, mainly up to the 1914–18 War but some even later, although in much reduced and more sober forms.[43]

The next stage of burial preliminaries was the kisting, the laying of the corpse in the kist or coffin. Kirk Sessions as such had nothing directly to do with this but individual elders and deacons came to be involved through later ratification of the Act anent Burial in Scots Linen, initially passed by Parliament in 1686. About that date the Scottish linen trade required support and to give it a boost this Act required all corpses to be shrouded in plain linen or cloth of hards (a coarse material of flax or hemp) without decoration of any sort. This linen had to be prepared and spun in Scotland and to enforce the Act every parish minister was ordered to keep a record of everyone who was buried in the parish, and one or more relations of the deceased or some other 'credible persons' were required to bring him within eight days of the burial a written certificate sworn by 'tuo famous persons' — two well-known people of good repute — confirming that the body had indeed been wrapped as required. It this were not done, it fell to the minister to seek from the deceased's estate a penalty of £300 Scots for each offence by a nobleman and £200 for anyone else, half of which went to the poor and half to the informer, failing which the minister himself became liable for the fine.[44] At that date, enforcement of any law was difficult and this one had to be ratified in 1695, with the difference that instead of relying on relatives of the departed to produce a certificate, it should be the nearest elder or deacon of the parish, along with a neighbour or two, who must be asked to attend the kisting to see that Scots linen was used and to sign the certificate to that effect. By this Act the penalties were wholly assigned to the poor and any elder or deacon was empowered to pursue for them. Neither of these Acts required the presence of the minister at the kisting although it has been said that this was so; his involvement was purely administrative. However, as the years went by it became common for the minister to attend kistings and, if so, he (or an elder if the minister was not present) would be asked to say grace before any refreshment was offered, and this developed into prayers and ultimately into a kisting service. This was a great comfort to people when the kirk still denied any burial service for their loved ones and became so well liked that kisting ceremonies continued long after burial services became accepted and normal. Kistings were common in Caithness until the 1920s and took place occasionally in areas such as Ross-shire and Dumfries-shire until around 1940.

The day of a funeral was an occasion for yet more hospitality to be given, something that was accepted practice and opposed only by certain determined ministers rather than by Kirk Sessions but should a parish have such a minister, then the Session had to take action. This happened at Mauchline where Mr Auld, minister from 1742–91, made great efforts to reduce funeral drinking, hence the following minute:

> 19th December 1771. The Session considering that the manner in which the Burying of the Dead is conducted consumes a great deal of time unnecessarily in regard the invitation fixes ordinarily ten o'clock in the forenoon as the time of attendance notwithstanding the corpse is not lifted until about 3 or 4 in the afternoon being at the distance of 5 or 6 hours from the time appointed for Neighbours to attend, it is therefor the unanimous opinion of the Session that the Regulations in respect to Burials agreed upon by the Session of Galston be adopted for this parish which regulations are as follows.

The Galston regulations do not, in fact, follow but this minute goes on to say that the Session 'also agree that a copy of these Regulations be extracted for each Elder in order to his getting the Heads of Familys in every several Quarter to declare their Approbation and Assent to the same by their Subscription.' It was not so much the waste of time as the amount of time available for drinking that lay behind this decision. By tradition those menfolk who went to the burial preliminaries and were entertained at them, were expected to help with carrying the corpse to the grave but in Orphir in 1722 there was what was called a 'burial scandal' in this connection. Robert Inkster complained to the Kirk Session that people in the east end of the parish who carried his brother's coffin to the kirkyard had tried, even as he was putting it into the grave, to get him to pay for their service, pulling his coat off 'in an inhumane manner . . . until he should pay them for their pains in going to the burial, and that he was forced to give each of them 18 pennies Sc.' To make matters worse, one of two elders who were present co-operated in this extortion by collecting the money for distribution to the others. As a Bailie Court was to be held next day at the church the Session adjourned until then and cited those concerned to attend. The two elders admitted what had happened but said that 'it was the wish of the dead that each of them should have a pint of ale.' The Session condemned the whole affair, in which twenty-two people were implicated, as scandalous, barbarous and unChristian, suspended the elders for a time, ordered everyone involved to make public satisfaction and also ordered 'for keeping better order in time coming that the elders of each quarter shall attend the interment of the corpse within their district that there be no discord or indecency thereafter.' What happened in this case shows that people were not really willing to carry a coffin unless there was some benefit to themselves, which probably explains the lavishness of funeral hospitality, quite apart from the feeling that it was the done thing. Just about twenty years after that burial scandal, Orphir had another one when a man complained to the Session that no one would help him with his father's burial. They came to the house all right but because he 'would bestow nothing upon them, not so much as a mutchkin of ale or a piece of bread . . . they declined to accompany his corpse to the church and returned to their houses, whereon the man took his father's corpse, being now coffined, and held them on the back of a horse to the grave.' The son's extreme meanness seemed inexcusable because an elder, who had been owed a considerable sum by the dead man, who had only one cow with which to pay the debt, had 'quit the cow to the son to bury his father with.' Far from considering that the son had cause for complaint, the Session found him 'very censurable and punishable' and referred him to the bailie who fined him £6 Scots.[45] The records of St. Andrews Kirk Session in 1595 show how strongly they felt about the necessity of public attendance at funerals, as an accompanying party if not necessarily as bearers, stating that everyone, including elders and deacons with their wives, 'should convoy the dead to burial' under threat of a small fine for failure to do so. This Act of Session included the statement that no one should be buried except between sunrise and sunset, nor in time of sermon or 'dennar'.[46]

For years the corpses of the common people, coffined or uncoffined, got to the grave on people's backs or on sledges until the introduction of the bier made this a lot easier, even if not totally so. The bier had two forms: it could be the common coffin, of which more later, or it could be nothing more than a frame made of a couple of poles with two or three cross bars on which the body lay covered with the mortcloth. Such a frame was often referred to as carriage spokes, handspokes or just spokes or spakes, and as with other funeral equipment, these spokes came to be provided for hire by the kirk and, as time went on, were used to carry a coffin, as now, from hearse to grave or other short distances, rather than for the whole journey to burial. In rural parishes spokes were usually stored somewhere along with the mortcloth but in a large town the number and variety of sizes, as with mortcloths, often justified having a special storage place for them, such as an 'under-apartment' at St. Cuthbert's Church, Edinburgh, where there were 25 sets in 1839 — 11 large, 7 small, 4 of strong hardwood and a further 3 of the same. There was also a burial conveyance known as a litter but the exact form it took is not clear. One Kirk Session had a horse litter in the first half of the seventeenth century and as roads had not developed much at that date, it does not seem to have been wheeled. Another had 'nine carriage spokes and the litter' in 1759 and it may be that a litter could be either handspokes or a rudimentary form of horse-drawn hearse on the lines of the earliest development of draught transport in rural areas which, under various names, was just two parallel poles, the front part of which acted as shafts for a single beast, while the rear part, suitably shaped, slid along on the ground behind but had cross bars upon it to form a frame to hold whatever was to be carried. Just as Kirk Sessions bought materials to be made up into mort-cloths, so it was with litters: in 1706 one paid £1 6s. Scots to have one made and about 1723 another 'depursed' £2 13s. Scots 'for a tree to be a litter' although in 1763 they paid 8s. stg. for a new one. As with mortcloths, litters needed to be refurbished now and then: St. Vigean's Kirk Session spent 10s. Scots in 1732 for 'dighting [adorning, equipping] and blackning the litter'; and as with joint charges for mortcloths and bells, so there could be a joint charge for mortcloth and litter which in the mid-eighteenth century might be something like 2s. 9d. stg. for the smaller cloth and litter or just over 8s. stg. when the litter was used along with the best cloth.[47]

Where road conditions made it practical, horse-drawn hearses were introduced before the turn of the eighteenth century and any Kirk Session which thought that it would profit the poor's box to have a hearse for hire, obtained one — 'ane mourning hearse which would bring in some money to the box' as one Kirk Session put it, but the average type of hearse provided by the church or 'under the management of the Kirk Session' was generally plain and clumsy, with little more than some black plumes at the corners. Some Sessions paid outright for a hearse and operated it themselves while others joined with a local hearse committee, using a subscription system which allowed subscribers' families to have free use of it but making a charge to others. One such was the Ruthwell, Dumfries-shire, hearse committee, the minutes of which were found in a Kirk Session minute book of 1849–63. In 1849 the minister intimated that owing to the 'frail and disabled state of the hearse' which they had at the time, it was planned to get a new one and in December 1853 the rules for its use were laid down and included the following:

> That the hearse remains as heretofore under the care of the church officer who must attend that it be properly cleaned, both before and after it has been used, and that he shall be empowered to demand the sum of 1s 6d from the person requiring it. That each subscriber shall be entitled to the use of it, to the family burying ground. When

two or more ask for it, priority of application shall decide, and any disputes to be decided by the minister . . .

That as the Poor Board of the parish has contributed nothing for the hearse, that the charge for a pauper's funeral shall be 2s. 6d.[48]

The Kirk Session of Bolton, East Lothian, acquired a hearse in 1723. What it cost is not known but harness to go with it cost the Kirk Session £19 10s. Scots in 1744, plus a payment of £1 4s. Scots to the man who went to fetch it. The income from the hearse varied from year to year depending on how many deaths there were in families able to afford its hire but in 1744 church collections brought in about £60 Scots, the mortcloth and bells raised £20 while the hearse brought in £14 6s. Scots. The following year must have seen more deaths as the mortcloth and bells realised about £46 and the hearse income rose sharply to £42 Scots but the position changed the following year when the mortcloth and bells raised £49 Scots but the hearse income slumped to £15 Scots. Nearly forty years later, in 1783, the heritors considered that a 'new fashionable hearse' should be bought although it is not known whether the old one was worn out or not smart enough to attract custom, or whether the improvements then being made to roads in the area justified something much better than the old one. Whatever the reason, the old one was sold and the heritors decided to call in poor's money which was out on loan to a firm of Edinburgh merchants to pay for the new one. Its cost came to £37 14s. stg. but with alterations to the hearse house and other expenses the total came 'upon the whole' to £39 13s. 2d. a rather airy form of accounting. Even allowing for the change in the value of money, it seems surprising that this astonishing vehicle, now preserved in the Royal Museum of Scotland, should not have cost more. Fashionable it certainly is and somewhat un-Scottish in its elegance while its elaborate top looks positively eastern. Its sides are black and painted on them in soft colours are two of the emblems of mortality commonly found on gravestones — skulls and hour-glasses — along with the words '*Memento Mori*' (Remember you must die) and '*Hora fugit*' (Time flies). In addition there is 'tearing', a representation of tears which look rather like fat tadpoles, a funeral decoration much used in great Scottish households but which goes unremarked in the written description alongside the hearse. Uprights around the sides of the hearse are painted yellow which may seem an odd choice of colour but which probably had something to do with the belief that yellow is obnoxious to evil spirits. It is difficult to see how this hearse fitted into the existing hearse-house at Bolton, even with the alterations made to that building at the time it was bought, unless its superstructure could be removed. One of the most surprising things about the Bolton hearse is that something so ornate and splendid was acquired in 1783, a time of severe famine in Scotland as a whole but perhaps, as with mortcloths, it was felt that the only way to ensure a good income was to keep up standards. This hearse was hired at a charge of 10s. stg. per mile when two horses were used or 12s. per mile with four horses, plus 1s. for the hearse-keeper and a further 2d. per mile if he went out with it. This must have put its hire right outside the reach of most people and although income did increase with it in 1784, bringing in £8 stg. as against £4+ stg. from church collections and £1+ for mortcloths, at 10s. or 12s. per mile that does not indicate much distance covered nor many hirings. It must have been realised that these charges were too high as in December that year (1784) the Session reduced them by 2s. on the first mile to 8s. or 10s. respectively. It may be that the reason this hearse has survived in such good condition is because it was too expensive to be much used, but it was nevertheless well cared-for. It was good that this hearse brought in an adequate return but it must have been hard on the ordinary parishioners who could not afford it and would have been glad of the old, plainer hearse.[49]

Because hearses were expensive things to buy, it must have seemed like manna from Heaven to Kirkliston Kirk Session when the Earl of Hopetoun gave them one. Made in Edinburgh, it was fairly high and had a fine appearance but unlike the Bolton one, it was not black with yellow touches but completely yellow. Unfortunately it has not survived. Apart from the colour yellow, the black trappings of woe essential to eighteenth and nineteenth century funerals also applied to any horse drawing a hearse, over and above the black plumes on their heads, and in the same year that they dighted and blackened their litter, St. Vigeans Kirk Session paid a man £2 4s. Scots for buying, dyeing and making up 'horses cloaths' and by December that year spent a further 6s. Scots 'for a pock for carrying the horses cloaths' so that, just like the mortcloth, they could be easily carried to wherever they were needed, because people often provided their own horse for the hearse. Thus Kirk Session accounts may show items such as:

> Received from Singlie for the horscloath, £1. 16s Sc
> Mrs. Scott for the bestcloath wt the hors clos [cloths] £4. 10s Sc.'

There was never any compulsion to use the parish hearse but doing so caught on fairly quickly in the south although more slowly in the highlands. Although Rev. Andrew Edgar complained in the 1880s that hearses introduced a 'new element of expense' to funerals, one of their great benefits was that they did away with the need for large numbers of funeral guests to provide bearers and so avoided the resultant abuses. The Poor Law of 1845 which ended the need for much of the kirk's fund-raising ended the reason for Kirk Sessions to provide hearses although they still did so, as did other bodies and individuals. Relics of these days are the hearse-houses which still survive near to or inside the grounds of many church-yards, particularly in southern Scotland. What started out as a basic hearse-house might have been enlarged to fulfil more purposes, like the one at Lauder which in 1812 had an upper storey added to provide a vestry-Session house, and since others ceased to fulfil their original function, they have to some extent been put to good use. *Life and Work* reported in March 1987 that the Church of St. Athernase at Leuchars, Fife, planned to celebrate its eighth centenary in a variety of ways, one of which was converting the hearse house, built in 1798, into a club-room, kitchen, day-centre and hall, and there are other useful conversions to be seen elsewhere although many hearse-houses are now grave-diggers' sheds.[50]

As a general desire for funeral panoply developed over the years, so Kirk Sessions pandered to it in pursuit of income for the poor and, especially in large towns, put considerable investment into provision of this sort, in addition to what has already been mentioned. The inventory of St. Cuthbert's Church, Edinburgh, in 1839 has already been quoted in connection with funeral equipment but smart funerals came to require a variety of functionaries such as baton men, mutes (a type of professional mourner) or just 'extra men', all of whom required special dress in which to perform their duties. At St. Cuthbert's, these clothes and other items were kept in the room of the Recorder for graveyards, who was in charge of everything to do with burials, and included 2 cloaks, 2 cocked and 2 flat hats, 12 velvet caps, a band box containing 12 white linen bands for hats, 2 white silk rosettes, 4 white silk knots, 4 crape knots and 2 linen cravats. There was also a box containing 7 sets of black silk ribbons, 9 in each set, as well as 3 old sets; there were 5 sets of white silk ribbons, again with 9 in each set; one set of 9 narrow ribbons, one of 8 narrow ribbons and 2 odd sets. There was a 'large press for holding Batonmen's Hats and Mutes' Mountings and Batons' and a clothes brush. In addition, there were 16 Batons with green baize covers, and 2 poles with black silk mountings for mutes. All of these were available for hire and for the two years from November 1843–October 1845, while the mortcloth brought in £36 15s. 6d. stg., weepers (which some of these items were) raised £4 9s. and ribbons made £3 16s., which proved a worthwhile investment. Some lesser parishes held a limited amount of similar equipment for hire under the general term of 'mournings' and so Kirk Session accounts may show entries such as 'For the litter and mournings to James Watson's funeral, £5.'[51]

There were still other ways in which the kirk could make money out of death. One Session ordered a small box to be made for the churchyard for receiving charity at burials and should a corpse be laid in the church or Session House before burial it was normal for a donation to be given to the relevant Kirk Session: the records of Melrose for 1748 have this entry — 'William Douglas of Cavers his corpse from Edinburgh was lodged in our kirk all tuesday's night last, and there were given in for the use of the poor 2 gns.' There is a voluntary sound to that particular payment but some Sessions, such as Montrose, laid down a charge for each night any body lay in the church prior to burial which, in 1707, was £6 6s. Scots. About 1703 it was decreed in Inverness that the kirk officers should receive 'half a dollar out of every corpse that shall be laid in the Session House, for their attendance upon the said corpse and friends therein concerned' so kirk staff benefited too. In addition to the organised funeral money-raising of Kirk Sessions, when a bereaved family was in a financial position to do so, they often gave money to the Session to distribute to the poor, a gift which might appear in rather charming phraseology: 'Received from Lady Blantyre as a compliment to the poor on the burial of her daughter, £6 6s' Money donated like this was often given out immediately after the burial and any funeral where such largesse was expected acted as a magnet to beggars from far and near who had nothing to do with the parish poor for whom the gift was intended and this could cause problems. The minutes of Ashkirk Kirk Session for August 1700 show that the Session arranged 'to meet Monday next to distribute £33 pounds six shillings, and that as the just and equal half of the sum of Sixtie six pund thirteen shillings scots given into the box by the Laird of Wooll which was intended to be distributed at his lady's burial but because there was a number of stranger poor gathered at the time and every paroch being obliged to maintain their own poor . . . it was given in to the box as said is.'[52]

While much of the money raised by Kirk Sessions because of death went to the box to support the living poor, a good deal of it had to be spent on those of them who died. If possible, paupers' families paid for their burial or it could be provided by burgh councils or craft guilds but in rural areas it was the Session who provided this final service, particularly as in 1692 a Proclamation of Privy Council, strengthened by an Act of that Council the following year, made every parish responsible for its own poor and this included seeing them into their graves. Everyone hoped for a 'decent funeral' with all the men of the parish present and hospitality shown to them before they set out to carry the coffin to the grave and, however miserable their lives on earth had been, the poor hoped for a decent burial too. A problem when they died, was, of course, that their friends were unlikely to be numerous and very possibly not fit enough to carry a coffin any distance and so Kirk Sessions realised that it was essential to encourage sufficient people to be present to perform this vital task. Unless they did so, how was the coffin in pre-hearse days to get to the graveyard and what would a Session have done if it did not get there? One way was to order people to help at such burials, as the General Assembly did in 1563, decreeing that when any poor person died their immediate neighbours should carry them to the grave; but there could be refusals, although refusal to bury a pauper was not the same thing as the instances of unwillingness to bury non-paupers already mentioned. In 1695 an Orkney man was cited 'for not giving assistance to the burial of a poor person that died in the bounds of Suart-quoy and giving indiscreet language to Jerom Alme, elder qn he offered to reprove him for his fault', and as a result he had to appear publicly in church and pay a penalty of 14s. Shortly after this it was 'complained by the whole elders that there is many within the parish that are very refractory in giving assistance to the burying of the dead, especially qr the partie deceased is of the meaner sort, wherefore it is ordained by the Session that whosoever shall be found guilty of the forsaid fault in time coming, having no lawful excuse for their absence, shall make satisfaction before the congregation and pay 6s of penalty' and this local 'Act anent absenters from burieles' was intimated from the pulpit on two Sundays. A more unusual attitude was over-enthusiasm to get someone to burial. In September 1699 the Kirk Session of Falkirk called George and Elspeth Gardiner before them to ask about 'their dragging a dying man out of their house to the churchyard door on the Lord's day in time of divine Worship.' It is not clear whether the Session were more concerned with the Sabbath profanation involved or the cruelty to a dying man. In the report made to the Presbytery, prominence was given to violation of the Sunday although it was for their 'inhuman conduct' that they were rebuked.[53]

A far better way to get people to attend paupers' funerals and then shoulder the coffin to the grave was by the normal inducement of food and drink and although there was no way a Kirk Session could spend much on this type of entertainment, something was often paid for it out of the poor's box for the reason given and almost certainly also out of sympathy for the desire of even the humblest person not to be disgraced in death. In addition a small amount might be allowed for a lykewake, something which has already been mentioned as an indication of tacit kirk approval of sitting up with the dead although it could always be justified as protecting the corpse from the overnight attention of rats. Tobacco and pipes seem to have been regarded as an essential to while away the hours of a lykewake and appear quite frequently in Kirk Session accounts of paupers' burial expenses. An instance of this from Mauchline has been referred to earlier and another example was 'for cloath, knitting, pips and tobacco for the Irishman's burial' which was paid by Yetholm Kirk Session in 1693. Whether or not alcohol was provided for the lykewake is not clear but some was certainly made available on the day of burial; in 1696, for example, in addition to basic funeral necessities, a Session paid 2s. 4d. Scots for a pint of ale for those who buried a pauper woman. As this was a Scots pint, it was more than it sounds, equal to nearly 3 English pints or nearly 4¹/₂ of the common pint bottles and in 1775 Ashkirk Kirk Session included a bottle of whisky in their funeral provisions for a poor man while Arbuthnott Kirk Session paid £2 12s. Scots in 1771 'for some spirits and ale needed att the burial' of a pauper, making a particular note in this case that it was necessary. Perhaps it was a long way to the graveyard. Even at the funeral of Choppin's poor little boy, whose sad death and that of his parents has been mentioned in an earlier chapter, there was still something allowed for entertainment and payment was made 'for drink and bread to the folks that came to the burial of the bairn.' When a poor woman named Jean Hall died in Morebattle in February 1732 the Session paid £3 14s. 3d. 'to James Robson in Kirk Yetholm for cheese, tobacco and pipes for her funeral' and £3 'to James White in Morebattle for brandy and more tobacco upon the foresaid occasion.' A further 12s. was spent on bread and £ 1 1s. on oatmeal, all this in addition to a coffin and grave. This generous provision seems to have been due to the fact that she had bequeathed her effects in order to be admitted to the poor's roll and they must have been sufficiently plentiful to entitle her to what seems to have been an extra good funeral. Because of kirk provision of food and drink at funerals of the poor, an extraordinary situation arose at Borgue. People there took to going to paupers' burials which they turned into 'occasions of bibulous mirth' and cheerfully charged the expenses to the Session. This made these funerals so costly that the living poor were liable to suffer and that particular Session had to put a limit of 12s. stg. on any pauper's funeral to cover everything — coffin, grave, grave-digger's fee and ale, but even so ale continued to account for more than half the total costs. Once roads improved and funeral transport of some sort became available, such entertainment costs were unnecessary and so a Session might instead pay something like 1s. stg. or so for 'carriage to the grave'.[54]

There was, however, much more to do for paupers' funerals than just providing food and drink. 'To a woman for handing the corpse, 13¼d' say the accounts of Dunbar Kirk Session about 1720 because laying out the body was one of the varied expenses which fell on the kirk when a pauper died. Sufficient linen for a winding sheet might come to something like £1 7s. Scots but, as with mortcloths, there could be a bit of make-do-and-mend so far as they were concerned and that was how in 1773, 5 ells of an old Communion cloth at Fordyce were given to James Sandison to make a shroud for his wife as the Kirk Session had just bought 21 yards of linen @ 1s. 5d. per yard for new communion cloths and were putting the old linen to good use. The nearby Kirk Session of Deskford went even further in re-use of Communion equipment for the burial of the poor: when a stranger woman had to be buried in 1728, part of the old Communion table cloth made her grave clothes and the old Communion table her coffin. Grave-digging for paupers had to be paid for too, which cost something like 6d. for an adult at the end of the eighteenth century and possibly 2s. stg. by the mid-nineteenth century. The second mortcloth was always provided free for the poor but the following entry reads badly, although it is puzzling why there was any charge for the boy's cloth:

> 1738. To the best mortcloth and bell to John Salmond, £3. 3. 4d
> To the worst mortcloth to a poor boy, 12s.

In a fairly large parish it was a thoughtful idea to keep a mortcloth in an outlying area so as to be readily available for the poor there, something that happened in Melrose where in 1759 'a plush mortcloth was deposited at Blainslie for the use of the poor of that quarter.'[55]

Shortly after the Reformation, in 1563, the General Assembly ordered that a bier should be provided in every country parish to carry the dead poor to burial. The bier in its simple form of handspokes has already been mentioned but the General Assembly's use of the word also meant a common or re-usable coffin, sometimes called the 'parish burying box' or dead kist. It was usually a closed wooden or iron box or chest, attached to a frame for lifting; sometimes it had four feet on which to stand and in some cases it was painted, especially during times of epidemics when it was blackened. It was designed for re-use and so a part of it was always hinged for easy opening. When it was the base that opened, the coffin was lowered part of the way into the grave, a bolt was drawn and the body dropped into the grave; when it was the top or side that was hinged, the corpse, wrapped in its winding sheet, was lifted out and lowered into the grave and then the coffin was borne away for a future occasion. In some parts of the highlands there was a different type of common coffin — in Sutherland it was a long basket of twisted rushes with a strengthened rim to keep its shape. Called the *sgulan ruhairbh* or dead hamper, it was carried by short crowbars put through three side-handles or loops and lowered into the grave by ropes attached in such a way that it could be tipped over, the body deposited and the hamper recovered. Technically, therefore, all bodies taken to the grave in a common coffin were buried uncoffined.[56]

By no means all parishes had common coffins, supplying the poor, if they possibly could, with individual coffins but where it was found necessary to have them, then common coffins were used. Their initial cost was about four times that of an ordinary coffin — in the mid-seventeenth century from £4–£6 Scots, whereas an individual pauper's coffin cost 30s Scots — so that it did not take many paupers' funerals to make it worthwhile and as it was sometimes hired by those a little above poverty level for about 1s. Scots per time, it could bring in a little income which, if nothing else, could pay for its maintenance. It was in times of scarcity or epidemics that the common coffin really came into its own. During the Seven Years' Famine, by which time coffin prices had risen, one Kirk Session found that paying £3 Scots for an adult's and £2 for a child's was too great a drain on the poor's funds when the prime need was for food for people to eat and in July 1699 the records say, 'Considered the poor's box is now burdened with paying coffins for the poor, at a time when there is such difficulty to provide them with bread, by reason of the present dearth, therefore the Kirk Session thought fit to order the mending of the Common coffin for burying the poor.' The repair cost £3 14s. 0½d. Scots, little more than the price of one adult's coffin. It was during this famine that the Kirk Session of Chirnside, Berwickshire, could not even rise to a common coffin: an entry of 1701 says 'for a dale [board] on which Alison Tait was buryed 5s Scots,' showing that all they could do for this poor woman was to carry her to the grave on a plank of wood.[57]

Famines tended to make people move around the country seeking better conditions but not necessarily finding them and it was because so many strangers came to one parish and died in it during that particular famine, that its Kirk Session decided in 1698 'to cause ane bier to be made for carrying all such strangers to the grave.' Just how useful a common coffin could be is apparent from the fact that in a national epidemic in 1645, thought to have been typhus, the 'dead kist' of Anstruther made no fewer than fifteen trips to the churchyard in one day. No Session could have paid for fifteen individual coffins in twenty-four hours. 1641 was a time of famine and because of the great cost of 'kists for the decrepit poor' another Kirk Session decided that the 'Beare should be prepared and made ready for them and ane winding sheet given them and a cloth of black furnished to cover the Bear at all times hereafter.' In spite of that decision, only three years later individual coffins were somehow still being supplied for the poor and as much money was being spent on them 'as would supply many poor indigent persons' and it was decreed that the bier must be used but, only seven years on, the Session still found the same thing going on and had to forbid the giving of individual coffins for the poor and ordered a common bier to be made for them. What can have befallen the one prepared only ten years earlier? Discrimination could enter into who should or should not go to burial in the common coffin: 'The coffin commonly called the common-coffin should be made use of unless they [the poor] be persons of character' was the decision of a Borders Kirk Session in 1723. That was in fact a late date for use of that type of coffin which generally ceased to be used after the Seven Years' Famine was over. For that reason very few common coffins survived although until fairly recently there were three at Abercorn and one at Linlithgow. Linlithgow's one was wooden and was kept latterly in the triforium but sadly it was thrown out about the late 1960s when improvements were being made.[58]

In later years, when there were many deaths combined with a shortage of funds, Kirk Sessions might solve the problem of burying the poor by 'a general collection for the purpose of defraying such extraordinary expense' as happened at Tongue in 1796. Coffins for the poor were locally made, sometimes at a contract price. One Kirk Session appointed a wright to make all paupers' coffins for the future 'so long as he makes them for 40s Scots each', another agreed that a particular man should be paid '7s stg for each of the coffins made for such as are on the Poors roll' and it was only if a coffin had to be extra big that a Session would allow more than the agreed sum. An agreement which was made between a wright and his Session implies that some unauthorised coffin-making on his part had been going on: 'A final contract has been entered into with Alexander Mackenzie, wright, Migdal, for making the coffins for the poor @ 7s 6d each. He is not to charge the Session for any Coffins without having previously had the order from the Session for making of such Coffins.' A decision to provide coffins was a matter for the whole Kirk Session but it seems that elders or others sometimes instructed coffins to be given to the poor on their own and because of this a Session had to state that none should 'take upon themselves to buy a coffin for any poor without consent of the Kirk Session.' Just as the wherewithal for mortcloths could be bought by Sessions, so might wood be got to make into coffins. In 1695 one Session spent £6 Scots 'for twentie dales that were bought to be coffins for the poor' or alternatively money might be advanced to a wright so that he could have wood available to make coffins whenever necessary, and in the same way that the Kirk Session of Melrose kept a mortcloth in an outlying area so as to be readily accessible to people there, so too there could be a supply of coffins arranged for such districts: 'Given to Allan Milner who engages to furnish for nails and workmanship to coffins for poor objects who die in that part of the country, at 5s each . . .' say the minutes of Kilninian and Kilmore Kirk Session in 1768, just as winter was drawing on in that scattered parish. An intriguing Act of Session was passed in Montrose in 1641 to clarify some confusion which appears to have arisen about coffin-making but not, apparently, coffins for the poor: 'It is ordained that the haill wrights should have free liberty to make to any man who pleases to employ them, kists of oak or otherwise firre kists to ane frind as was in old use and wont.'[59]

When it came to burying the poor of a parish, it was of great help if they had previously bequeathed their effects to the Kirk Session. The liberal provisions for

Jean Hall's funeral in Morebattle have already been mentioned but that was not always what happened. A cross entry from about 1836 says:

> Paid for Widow Munro's funeral and grave 19s stg.
> Received from the effects of Widow Munro 19s stg.

showing that her effects just paid for her burial and no more, although had there been a deficit the Kirk Session would have made up the difference, and had there been a surplus then it would have gone to the poor. What seems invidious is that even when a pauper's effects paid for his or her funeral, often with something to spare for the box, there might still be restrictions put on their burial entitlement from the Session although this seems to have been the exception rather than the rule. Rev. Roderick Mackenzie, minister of Knockbain (Kilmuir Wester), Ross-shire, a man who was considered to be very good to the poor and who was affectionately known as 'Parson Rory', stated in the early nineteenth century that in his parish, even when paupers had signed over their effects, the Kirk Session would provide a coffin and sometimes linen for a shroud 'provided that no whisky is drunk at the burial'. Perhaps ale was permitted to be drunk but that may not have been allowed either, if provision of a shroud was doubtful. Furthermore, being buried as a pauper meant a grave in that part of the churchyard where free ground was set aside for the poor, usually on the north side, sunless and ill-favoured, where they were buried along with wandering gypsies and beggars. Although the General Assembly had decreed in 1563 that the graves of the poor should be six feet deep, they were often only four feet or so, which made a pauper's grave an easier proposition for body-snatchers than an ordinary one and in addition, as the ground available for burial of the poor filled up, other problems arose: in 1845 the Kirk Session of St. Mary's, Dumfries, considered the conduct of Michael Short-house, the officer of the Old Church, who had 'carelessly left part of the remains of a human body, exposed in the churchyard . . . not having covered it with a sufficient quantity of earth. On investigating this matter, it was quite evident that the Beadles had great difficulty in getting the bodies of paupers decently interred from the excessive crowded state of the ground adopted for this purpose.' This was causing 'some unseemly scenes . . . very harassing to the feelings of the community' and so the Kirk Session resolved to ask the heritors and magistrates to provide additional burying ground for paupers and strangers; and elsewhere too Kirk Sessions had to see to the provision of additional burying space.[60]

There were, of course, always some people who although not actually on the poor's roll were nevertheless very poor and the kirk would often contribute something towards burials in their families. One Session gave £4 Scots to a man in that position so that he could pay for his mother's burial, and also paid a woman's funeral costs when her very needy husband begged for help because people who were owed money for it, were daily pressing him to pay. Another gave a poor man 3 merks to buy a coffin for his wife. Appropriate help of this sort in times of particular need was not only kind but kept people from becoming paupers and a regular drain on the parish, not only saving kirk funds but also maintaining their self-respect.[61]

The stranger poor who were such a plague to Kirk Sessions in life were equally so in death, one of the great problems being that any parish in which one of them died or was found dead, had to pay for their interments although if the parish of origin could be discovered, then it could be charged with the costs. But that seldom happened and very many kirk records have references to the provision of coffins and/or winding sheets for these unfortunate people. Some would be found dead by roadsides or in fields: 'To a coffin and grave digging for Janet McCormack a child dyed upon the road, 2 shs and seven pence' is an entry of 1774, while another of 1830 says '10s stg for a coffin for a body found at Daan.' Some strangers lodged briefly in parishes while journeying elsewhere but did not live to move on. In 1721 'a stranger woman who happened to lodge at . . . surprisingly dieing there and immediately after her decease being brought to the kirk on a cart was by the Session provided of a chest and a hood £2 Sc' while another Session 'paid for a poor woman who came from Aberdeen and died here 4 ell linen to be her winding sheet.' Pregnant vagrant women had to pause in their travels when childbirth was imminent and mother and/or child might well die: 'To William Williamson for a coffin and a winding sheet to a child brought forth in his house by a travelling woman' appears in the accounts of one Kirk Session in 1758. When many people travelled even short distances by sea rather than overland and accidents at sea were very common, coastal parishes had the extra problem of drowned bodies washed up on their shores, men, women and children, people who had never set foot in the parish in life. Thus accounts may show expenses such as '4s stg for a coffin made by order of the Moderator for a dead body thrown in upon the shore' or the cost of a coffin 'for a corpse washed ashore near Mains of Usan' or the burial costs of 'two children found at sea'. All these bodies were properly buried but in the following case things were different and caused great concern to the Kirk Session. In March 1748 the Session of Foveran

> being informed that a stranger beggar had died in the fields of Old Miln and that she had not been buried, they could not miss to bemoan the carelessness of any of the congregation in suffering a mendicant to die so near a door, and therefore agreed that the minister should next Lord's Day intimate a caution and exhortation suitable to the purpose, and further appointed that wherever any stranger beggars fall sick or die in the parish, immediate notice be given to the Elder of the Quarter, that he may know what belonged to them and take care of the funeral, which the minister is also to intimate.

A fortnight later he did so, 'that so care may be taken of them and not suffered to die in the fields as of late.'62

Burials of strangers were a considerable drain on the poor's funds and Kirk Sessions were obliged to sell anything found on them to pay for their funerals, hence the reference at Foveran to the elder 'knowing what belonged to them'. In 1775 the Kirk Session of Kilmarnock decided that coffins could not be provided unless there were clothes or other articles which could be rouped to pay for them and it became customary to do this, the heirs after all being unknown. An instance of this occurs in the burial records of Ancrum. A totally exhausted woman arrived there one evening and although given shelter, died that night. It was never discovered who she was but 11*s*. stg. was found in a purse in her pocket and that exactly covered the cost of her burial. When a poor sick vagrant woman came one day to the manse of Rathven and died there two days later, the minister advanced 7*s*. 2*d*. for her funeral needs and her belongings, which included a dress and a Book of Common Prayer, were later rouped to repay him.[63]

Although these strangers and the parish's own poor were buried in an unfavoured part of the kirkyard, they were at least buried within it, which was more than was allowed to the unbaptised of the parish, as has already been said in the appropriate chapter. Not surprisingly, stillborn babies were also discriminated against, as has also been mentioned. There was an idea that they should be buried between sunset and sunrise, something thought to be based on Psalm 58 : 8 which says, 'As a snail which melteth, let every one of them pass away; like the untimely birth of a woman, that they might not see the sun.' For some reason it was thought that if buried when the sun was up, these babies would have difficulty in getting into heaven and, according to Alasdair Alpin Macgregor, writing in 1965, burying such a baby after the sun was down was seen 'quite recently' in Ross-shire and in Sutherland. It was nice to read in *Scotland on Sunday* that on 23 April 1989 memorials in two Edinburgh graveyards were unveiled, specially to comfort the parents of stillborn babies, and that the inscription, 'For all our Babies — Briefly Known — Forever Loved', is designed to include those of all religious faiths or of none; in addition, for the past few years Aberdeen's Trinity Cemetery has held an annual memorial service in that part of it set aside for the burial of stillborn babies.[64]

As has been indicated, suicides and excommunicants were also buried apart under cloud of night. Suicide was considered very shocking, with the civil authorities sometimes hanging the corpse in the gallows as a self-murderer, and the church also heaped indignity upon these unfortunates, little understanding the circumstances or conditions that had led to their doing away with themselves. After William Fary had drowned himself in the River Tay in 1582 some of his friends asked the Kirk Session for permission to bury him in the Greyfriars churchyard in Perth, 'the burial place for the faithful departed', only to be told 'with one voice that they would not suffer him to be brought through the town in daylight nor buried among the faithful, but ordered him to be buried in the Little Inch [an islet] within the water, and this to apply to all such persons, and if anyone contravenes this, the dead shall be taken up again and the people concerned shall make repentance on the seat and pay £10 for the poor.' Burial of suicides at night and in special burying areas, such as one still remembered in the parish of Tannadice, Angus, or at cross-roads or in outlying spots was not done without the knowledge of the church although such things seem mild in comparison with William Fary's last resting place. Well into the eighteenth century a particularly unpleasant attitude to suicide, as well as a shocking example of religious intolerance, appeared when a dissenter committed suicide and the Session Clerk of the parish wrote in the Register of Deaths in exultant capitals, 'HUGH CAMPBELL, A SECEDER, CUT HIS OWN THROAT 3rd JANUARY.'[65]

There are many superstitions to do with burial and graveyards but to mention just one, it was reported in 1741 to an Orkney Kirk Session that as a woman was being coffined, her husband took some grain and put it between her fingers and toes, put some barley in her mouth, laid some more in the coffin and then threw the rest in around her. He explained that he had done this in the belief that it would prevent her coming back to trouble his daughter, her step-daughter, as the two of them had not got on together. The Session considered that this idea was the result of gross ignorance and required him to make public satisfaction and pay a penalty of £2 Scots.[66]

In time, it became not enough to see the dead safely buried; their corpses had to be protected for a while thereafter because of the attacks of body-snatchers. Body-snatching is a classic case of the end justifying the means: until 1832 there was no legal provision for a supply of fresh human corpses for dissection without which medical students could not study anatomy. Edinburgh, which is rightly famed as a centre of medical teaching, appointed its first Professor of Anatomy in 1707 at a time when the only bodies available were those who died in the Correction House and foundlings dying in infancy. These were however insufficient and an illegal supply was the only solution, and so body-snatching began there in a limited way not very long afterwards. It was in 1722 that a widow reported to St. Cuthbert's Kirk Session, Edinburgh, that the body of her seven-year-old son had been lifted, whereupon they decided to petition the Lord Provost and magistrates about the matter, who decided that graves were not deep enough and must in future be five feet for adults and three feet for children and later, in 1738, after more bodies had been taken, they raised the churchyard wall to eight feet. They also introduced a system of grave-watching but it transpired in at least one case that the watchers had connived at the lifting of a body. Such desecration of graves was viewed very seriously but for practical reasons rather than ethical ones: the Session were 'apprehensive of a loss to the Poor if the sale of ground in the churchyard is interfered with' and therefore appointed a committee to try to bring the offenders to justice, a successful effort as two months later Colin Rhind was brought before a civil court, found guilty and sentenced to be whipped. When the Session learnt that the whipping had not been carried out they sent a deputation to the Lord Provost who told them that this failure was not due to clemency on his part but because he had been advised that it would have been illegal and so Rhind remained in prison until he agreed to be banished from the town. A year after this, not only was a Recorder of graveyards appointed but it was decided that at any burial there should always be a measured gauge handy beside the grave and if it had not been dug to the proper depth, then no payment would be made for it. Just as watchers might connive at body-snatching, so those working about a graveyard were in a good position to do so and in 1742 George Halden, the beadle who some years earlier managed to avoid dismissal for keeping smuggled brandy in the church, was found to be involved with the stealing of bodies. Half-burned coffins were found in his house, which an angry mob burned down, and this time the Session did not hesitate but immediately dismissed both him and his fellow-beadle.[67]

The rules of demand and supply meant that there was a great increase in body-snatching during the first three decades of the nineteenth century when there was a burst of medical education in Scotland and Kirk Sessions had to double and re-double their efforts to guard their kirkyards. When Kirkliston Kirk Session dis-covered in 1818 that two bodies had been snatched, not only did the minister write to the Lord Advocate, who gave orders to the Sheriff-Substitute to make the necessary inquiries, but in addition the Session formed a committee to try to discover the perpetrator themselves and advertised in three newspapers offering a reward of £20 stg. for information leading to an arrest. Although the offer does not appear to have borne fruit, there was an immediate local response of £14 towards the reward and a subscription paper was sent round the parish to raise the balance needed, although no one was asked to hand over any money unless and until the body-snatchers were found and, in any event, a decision was also made to watch the graveyard at night after any funeral. Grave-watching might be arranged by a Kirk Session to bring in some money for the funds: the records of St. Cuthbert's, Edinburgh, show an income from this of £28 stg. for the two years 1843–45 although by then it should not have been necessary, as the Anatomy Act of 1832 regularised the provision of corpses for dissection. In general, however, grave-watching was arranged by watching societies, which were communal co-oper-atives with which Kirk Sessions must have been closely involved. People paid a small sum to join these societies but had to take their turn on guard, in return for which their and their families' corpses would be guarded after death. Occasionally societies employed regular watchman but this was not satisfactory as they were open to bribery to make them turn a blind eye to the nefarious works of the grave-robbers. Those on watch had to be armed. Some had helmets and truncheons and the inventory of equipment of St. Cuthbert's in 1839 listed, in addition to lanterns, '1 gun, 1 blunderbuss, 2 powder flasks' and these were used. To give just one instance, in 1827 three body-snatchers visited that churchyard but were driven off by the watchers' gunfire and fled over the wall and although they tried again the next night, they were foiled then too. Watchers required shelter and so a variety of little watch-houses were built in churchyards, many of which still exist; they must have been erected with the permission of the Kirk Session and heritors although it seems that they were usually put up by watching societies or by public subscrip-tion but one at Oldhamstocks was built at the expense of Mrs Agnes Moore, wife of the minister. Each Session laid down rules for the conduct of watchers in the churchyard, forbidding visitors and drinking although Kirkliston's grave-watch-ing committee decided that those on duty in cold winter weather should be allowed a glass of spirits and some bread, to be paid out of money in hand. But whether permitted or not, watchers often felt the need of a little alcoholic boost to their morale which may be what lay behind a report in 1820 that the watchers had broken several of the church windows one night at Kirkliston.[68]

Another form of protection was the use of mortsafes, iron cages placed over the coffin in the grave, which was then filled in for six to eight weeks, the time it took for a body to decompose sufficiently to be of no use for dissection, and after that time they were removed for re-use. Mortsafes required block and tackle to lower and raise them, and a good alternative was to erect morthouses, very secure buildings with the lower part perhaps half underground, in which coffined bodies could lie, usually on shelves, for the required six weeks without the need for watchers. Like watch-houses they were usually provided by public subscription but Kirk Session co-operation was needed for their erection. There is a good example at Culsalmond, Aberdeenshire; and a one-off design, known as the Round House, at Udny, also in Aberdeenshire, where coffins were placed on a turntable which was given a push round to await the next one and each was buried once it had got right round. That at Marnoch, in Banffshire, is said to have housed the parish school in an upper storey above its vaulted underground chamber but a plaque on it says that, though built by subscription in 1832, additions were made in 1877 and it may well be that it was then that its use and appearance changed completely to its present aspect of an L-shaped house, albeit with an unusual arrangement of windows. Certainly the Culsalmond morthouse has an upper storey which may have served as a Session house or something of the sort while the watcher's shelter at Duddingston was built to serve a dual role, with the vestry and Session house in the lower storey. Like hearse-houses, watch-houses and morthouses now tend to have become grave-diggers' sheds.[69]

Even after the passing of the Anatomy Act in 1832, precautions still continued to be taken in churchyards for a number of years but, all in all, the maximum length of life of most anti-snatching methods, watching apart, was probably not more than thirty years as many parishes did not start taking steps until the late 1820s or early 1830s when the Burke and Hare case alerted them to what had been going on unknown to many of them, because a good body-snatcher was the one who could conceal the fact that a grave had been robbed so that the graveyard would remain unwatched. Kirk Sessions in cities with medical schools still had a role to play in that connection however; the Anatomy Act required proper burial for dissected corpses after they had been through the hands of medical students and returns for this had to be made officially. That of 'The Inspector and Manager for the Edinburgh Schools of Anatomy to the Kirk Session of St. Cuthbert's for coffins furnished and interments in the Burying-Ground of St. Cuthbert's, of bodies which had undergone anatomical examination in the Edinburgh Schools of Anatomy', which starts in 1836, is divided into columns, giving the name of the corpse, which medical classroom it came from, its age, the price of the coffin, the grave-digger's charges and a column for the total. Coffin prices range from 3s. 4d. to 4s. 10d. to 6s., totals coming for each burial to no more than shillings although in 1841 they became more expensive as it was then that the column for the grave-digger began to be used, with entries in it of 2s. to 3s. to 5s. and totals of anything up to just over 11s. [70]

Perhaps the modern equivalent of the depredations of body-snatchers is vandalism which requires many city churchyards to be kept locked for much of the time but where they, or any others, are open, the morbid fascination or fear of graveyards that existed formerly has given way to enjoyment of their peace, to study of gravestones and awareness of their value in social history.

16
Remember the Sabbath Day . . .

So associated with the kirk is the word Sabbath that it can be forgotten that for several years after the Reformation, the Lord's Day was called Sunday, not the Sabbath, but this soon changed, even to the extent that in the highlands the word Sunday came to be distrusted.[1]

Nicholas Dickson, writing in 1912, described the old Scottish Sabbath as the delight of the people, saying that while pure religion possibly lay at the root of this, there was the pleasure of meeting friends at church and the intellectual stimulus of a good sermon, while heads of households rather liked lording it over their families as they conducted worship in the home that day, although they would never have admitted that this was a pleasure. It was the great day of the week for the minister and one which gave elders added authority; the precentor had an opportunity to air his talents and the beadle basked in the minister's reflected glory, but the truth was that for many other people the Sabbath gave no pleasure at all.[2]

In the later days of pre-Reformation Roman Catholicism, abuses and corruption of all kinds had crept into the church. Priests had little moral influence over the people and public worship was something to be hurried through as quickly as possible with the result that, to a large extent, the people had given up attending church and Sunday was often regarded as a public holiday. The only way to rectify this was to reverse it totally and the strictness which ultimately pervaded the Scottish Sabbath was the opposite swing of the pendulum, a very tyrannical consequence of what had gone before, with incarceration in the thieves' hole or in the stocks an early punishment for Sabbath-breakers. There were both morning and afternoon services on the Sabbath and, in the seventeenth century anyway, town parishes might well have a daily service throughout the week, at two of which the minister would preach while at the others the reader would read prayers and passages of Scripture. It is puzzling to know who attended these services but certainly some did, and it was reported from one Angus parish that at one time people went to church in considerable numbers on market days when there was a weekday sermon, although conversely it was not uncommon for ecclesiastical activities to stop to enable people to go to special markets: 'No sermon nor Session and that by reason the most part of the inhabitants went to Chanry mercat' say the minutes of Inverness Kirk Session in 1690 and in the same way, a market at Pittenweem was a reason for no sermon being preached at Elie. At St. John's, Perth, Thursday sermons began in 1560 with a Tuesday morning lecture instituted somewhere about the end of the century and it was similar in parishes where the population justified this but these weekday services gradually became less frequent: in Mauchline by 1680 they were held only every second Tuesday but at Elie they were held once a week, on a Monday, changing in the eighteenth century to a Tuesday, although the two a week continued at Perth until 1755. Whatever the day of the weekday services, it was at them that many marriages and baptisms took place although during busy seasons of the year, such as harvest or herring fishing, weekday services might be intermittent or temporarily suspended.[3]

The timing of Sunday services varied in different parts of the country, at different seasons of the year and at different dates. In the seventeenth century the forenoon service might be as early as 6.00 a.m. in summer but later on it became more usual for it to start at 10.00 a.m. The further north one went, the later services seem to have been. In 1794 the Kirk Session of Orphir, Orkney, decreed that in the lighter months from Candlemas to Martinmas – February to November – morning service should be at 1.00 p.m. and in the darkest winter months at midday and in some parts of the highlands a midday service continued until the 1960s, if not longer. Afternoon services were gradually replaced by evening ones, perhaps held elsewhere in the parish so that people of particular areas, especially the aged and infirm, could manage to attend. Evening services have now largely died out but linked charges, with one minister taking two or even three services in a morning, have resulted in considerable variety in the hours of morning worship.[4]

For those without a beast on which to ride, getting to worship could mean a long walk, possibly with bad conditions underfoot as well as wind and rain, so that many carried their bonnets and footwear until they got near to the church and only donned them in time to make a tidy entrance. Some of the better-off had their footwear carried by servants but in one parish there was disapproval of this carrying of clog-bags 'which no servant ought to do only to please his master.' Those who had Bibles took them to church in napkins – napkins seem to have been used for all sorts of purposes – and although working men always shaved on the Saturday night a masculine desire to look one's best for the Sabbath led to surgeons and barbers having to be forbidden to shave gentlemen on Sundays in places such as St. Andrews in 1678 and in Portsoy in 1742. Periwig-makers might try to get round possible prohibitions by dressing wigs in their booths and only delivering them to their owners on Sundays but that too had to be stopped with, in Montrose in 1738, a penalty of £10 Scots. A minister too might have similar little vanities and wish to look good on Sundays and on one occasion the incumbent of New Machar was libelled before his Presbytery for powdering his wig on the Sabbath.[5]

On Sunday mornings the church bell was rung three times, at hourly intervals. The first bell told those who could hear it that it was time to set out for church, the second that they should enter to listen for an hour to the reader reading passages of Scripture in what was called 'the reader's service', and the third heralded the minister's arrival to start the service proper. One of the reasons for the hour-long reader's service was stated quite baldly by Dornoch Kirk Session as being 'to prevent the Commons from running to Alehouses and the like.' The role of the reader was a valuable one in any parish at a time when people had few opportunities for education. It arose after the Reformation when Roman Catholic priests were forbidden to conduct worship and there simply were not enough Protestant clergymen to replace them. The First Book of Discipline said that 'to the church where no ministers can be had presentlie, must be appointed the most apt men that distinctly can read the common prayers and the Scriptures, to exercise both themselves and the church till they grow to greater perfection.' One thinks of ministers taking charge of several parishes as a modern phenomenon but in the early years after the Reformation, a minister could well have the care of two or three parishes and it was the assistance of the reader, who could conduct a limited form of service, that made it possible. Apart from an ability to read and having a suitable standard of conduct, readers were unqualified but as schools were gradually established it became common, as has already been said, for the schoolmaster to be appointed as reader although in important parishes, the post might be a specific one, a form of assistant to the minister. The intention of the First Book of Discipline was that readers should be encouraged to learn more, perhaps to become exhorters in time, which was the next step up, and possibly to qualify as fully fledged ministers, but while they were readers, they were only permitted to add a few explanations to what they read and were forbidden to slip into what was regarded as preaching. It was for this reason that when Alexander Watt was appointed schoolmaster of Cullen in 1694, it was on condition that he should not apply himself to the study of preaching, under threat of immediate loss of his post, in spite of the fact that many schoolmasters were aiming for the ministry. When a seventeenth century schoolmaster in East Lothian, reading in church during the minister's absence, helpfully sought to explain what he had read, this became a matter for the Presbytery. Poor man, he was doing his best although he was by then ill, but the result was that he gave up his school and went home to Fife, with the help of a collection organised for his benefit in the parish. Thereafter the minister took care to see that whoever became schoolmaster in future was licensed to preach so that if he should 'raise notes' as it was called, it would be legal. An over-zealous catechist who was in trouble for the same sin is mentioned in the next chapter.[6]

To start with, readers were not allowed to marry or baptise but after 1572 they were permitted to do so, although they never celebrated Holy Communion. In 1581, however, the General Assembly declared that the office of reader was without warrant and decreed that no more should be appointed, perhaps feeling that they were too easy a means of supplying pulpits. They were so useful however that, in fact, they were employed for long after that date, both during the Episcopacy of 1606–37 and during the ascendancy of Presbytery from 1637–45; their office was sanctioned by the ultra-Presbyterian Assembly of 1638 and it was from this that the reader's service, prior to the minister's, developed. In the early post-Reformation years, the reader read printed prayers from Knox's Liturgy but by the 1660s, during Episcopalian days, what a reader might do was set down clearly by one Synod: he should begin with a set form of prayer, especially the Lord's Prayer, then some psalms, with some chapter of the Old Testament; he must then 're-hearse' the Apostles' Creed, standing up to do so, then read from the New Testament as the minister decided, and lastly he was to rehearse the Ten Commandments.[7] Readers were expected in some parishes to go straight through any book of the Bible they began from start to finish but as the Bible and the Shorter Catechism were the two books mainly used in parish schools, a few Kirk Sessions such as those of Inverary, Dunfermline and of Lochwinnoch in Renfrewshire, arranged with the schoolmaster for schoolboys, two at a time, to repeat the Catechism in church between the second and third bells 'for the edification of their seniors'. Later on, readers were debarred from praying, 'discharged to pray in the kirk', as one Kirk Session put it in 1800; only four years previously, that Session had required the reader during his service to be 'constantly employed . . . in singing psalms with those who shall have come up, or reading from the Scriptures.' Many parishes continued to have readers long after that but more surprisingly, at some point in the late nineteenth century, Lord Polwarth installed a woman as Bible reader in the parish of Mertoun, Berwickshire, a woman lacking much education but making up for this by her character and worth. The modern reader is a lay preacher who largely provides pulpit supply but cannot administer the Sacraments.[8] The office of exhorter, a layman appointed to give religious exhortation, was common in the late sixteenth century but seems to have fallen out of use fairly soon, presumably as more clergymen became qualified. To a large extent, the functions of reader, exhorter and catechist overlapped, all of them being instructors of one degree or another.

People were sometimes reluctant to come to church for the reader's service between the second and third bells and Montrose Kirk Session was one that passed an Act in 1642 to deal with the problem: 'It is ordained that whatsoever person or persons shall be found talking or discoursing in the churchyard and not being in the church a little after the second bell, shall pay precisely 4s. Sc.' It was not enough, of course, to make such a decree; it had to be enforced and Kirk Sessions often appointed elders to 'attend in the churchyard in the forenoon and the afternoon in order to deal with the people, and make them punctually attend, and delate such as refuse to obey to the next Session.' The truth is that the men often went to church a little ahead of the women and children to have the opportunity of a good crack with their friends although worldly converse was forbidden. It is said, however, that everyday topics could be introduced indirectly by saying something like, 'If it wasn't the Sabbath, what would you be asking for your old mare?'[9]

When the minister's arrival was imminent, the precentor would start a psalm, the church bell would be rung for a third time to indicate that he was about to enter the pulpit and then, with a sign from him to the precentor to stop singing, the service proper began. The usual order of a forenoon service was a prayer, a lecture, then another prayer, followed by the sermon, another prayer, a psalm and then the blessing, after which the rebuke and admonition or 'wee sermon' when delinquents made their appearances, was fitted in too. On Sunday mornings congregations got a double dose of instruction from the minister on top of what they had already received from the reader because the lecture was a passage of Scripture read by the minister and commented upon by him, verse by verse. If well done, the lecture could be of real interest to the listeners but because it was less formal than the sermon, it is said that it could sometimes become too casual with secular remarks thrown in which did not improve it.[10]

Because preaching had largely fallen into disuse in later Roman Catholic days, the Presbyterian Church in an effort to change everything that smacked of those times, laid great stress on regular sermons and upon the exhorting and admonition of the people. It used to be common for a minister to select a text and preach on it for some time, perhaps six to eight weeks, this repeated text coming to be known as his 'ordinary' or 'ordinar'. Sometimes it was the Kirk Session who decided what his ordinary should be: the Canongate Kirk Session asked their minister at one point to take up the Book of Acts; St. Andrews prescribed II Samuel; in 1620 in Aberdeen it was Romans; and it was not long before Session minutes began to record each Sunday's text. The Presbytery of Fordyce introduced the practice in 1665 and when a new text was introduced some minutes state that 'the minister changed his ordinar'. Although generally liked, too-long continuation of the ordinary could cause complaint and one of the faults found on a Presbytery Visitation in 1651 was that the minister had preached on the same text too often – ten Sundays on the Fourth Commandment, nine on the Fifth and ten times on one part of Psalm 94. Some ministers however preached far longer than that on the one text, even up to a year and one is reputed to have preached on the first two verses of Psalm 9 for eighteen months. It is said that it was a difficult thing to preach week after week on the same text and that would indeed have been so if original thoughts and illustrations were produced each time, but they were not. Old-style sermons were doctrinal in character and according to Rev. J. Y. Scott the backbone of nearly every one was the three cardinal doctrines of justification (that man is justified – vindicated – by faith in Christ), adoption (that Christ as Man is the adopted Son of God) and sanctification (setting apart for holy use, to free from sin or evil, to consecrate). To modern ears, the type of sermon preached to our forefathers sounds quite unendurable but when there were few books or opportunities for stimulating talk or exchange of any but the simplest ideas, many people, as has already been said, looked forward to Sunday preaching with real anticipation and critical attention. There was general disapproval if a sermon was read which was all very well for men who were skilled and eloquent preachers and blessed with good memories: they could divide and sub-divide their sermons into sections, even as many as eighty on occasion, but for those not so gifted things were different. Objection to use of the 'paper', as written sermons were called, made them fall back on repetition and endless quotations so that, as Ronald Blakey put it, their texts were a starting point for rambling rather than an anchor.[11] As a wider range of psalms began to be used, some ministers 'prefaced the psalm', in other words, gave a fairly elaborate talk on authorship, date and teaching and all this made for very long services although there seems to be some difference of opinion as to just how long they lasted. The morning one might be about $2^3/_4$ hours, with a $^3/_4$ hour break between it and the afternoon one, which was a repetition of the earlier one but without the lecture. The hourglass was the minister's aid to timing. Sometimes it was the duty of the precentor, whose desk was immediately below the pulpit, to keep an eye on the hourglass and turn it when necessary. One is said to have reminded the minister how long he had gone on by holding the empty glass up above the pulpit Bible and although what happened in that case is not recorded, in another case, the minister is said to have turned the glass over himself when the sand had run through saying calmly, 'We will have another glass.' Mr John Brand, minister of Bo'ness in the 1690s, used to allow 'two turns of the glass' for his afternoon sermon on Sundays and it was this kind of thing which explained how Presbyteries might find it necessary to order a minister to 'keip his hour preciselie' and 'not to exceid his glasse' or to 'keep the glass and no farder', in other words to time his sermon properly. Little wonder that a Session once referred to 'the inconvenience the parish have in want of a sand-glass'.[12]

Many people sat so long in taverns on Saturday nights that they were drowsy on Sundays but it was women in particular who were given to falling asleep during church services. Having slaved at home throughout the week, worked extra hard on Saturday to get ready for Sunday and then walked possibly a long way to church, they were exceedingly tired, if not exhausted, once they got there. How glad they must have been to sit down for a while and how natural that they should just doze off. Mr Archibald Bowie, minister of Dornoch, complained to the Presbytery in 1707 that the church was 'such a confused place' that a third of those present could not see him, nor he them, and that some of them slept the whole time. The introduction of seating did not necessarily help this problem as flat book-boards encouraged people to lay their heads upon them and fall asleep; but sleeping in church was often intentional. People would go into corners if they could, specifically to have a good rest. A late sixteenth century minute from Glasgow decreed that women must not 'lie down in the church on their faces in time of prayer, sleeping that way' and that the beadle was either to 'raise' them or pull their plaids off their heads. Plaids over heads contributed to sleeping and concealed identity and Kirk Sessions had to make various injunctions about them. At Elie in 1656, the Session considered the fact that men and women 'does frequentlie sleip in the kirk but especiallie women and that . . . thair sleiping may not be knowne does wear their plaids over thair heads and faces' and appointed the minister to 'give warning anent sleiping' in church in future and forbade women to have their plaids about their heads in church 'under paine of such censure as the session sall think fitte to inflict.' The minutes of another Kirk Session have the following entry: 'Considering the indecency of plaids about women's heads in church on the Sabbath and that it is a meane to provock sleeping, appoints it to be discharged and 6 fs [sic] exacted from contraveners.' In 1640 Dumbarton women were frequently ordered by the minister from the pulpit not to keep their plaids about their heads in church and the Provost and Council co-operated by decreeing a fine of 20s. for the first offence, 40s. for the second and confiscation of the plaid and imprisonment during the magistrates' will for the third, half of which penalties were to go to the poor's funds, the other half to the magistrates. 'Febill women of three score years and over and servand women' were allowed a little leniency in that they only had to pay half the penalty for first and second faults, but those in St. Andrews were exempted altogether when a prohibition about plaids was decreed for young women there in 1645.13

An effective method of preventing sleeping in church was to order known offenders to sit on their stools right in front of the pulpit but in some parishes the beadle used a stick with a cleek [hook] on the end to twitch the plaid off any woman who came to church with it over her head or about her face and she then had either to put it on correctly or leave it with him. As he made rounds of the church to waken sleepers, he might do more than that. In 1643 Monifieth Kirk Session gave their beadle, Robert Scott, 5s. with which to buy a pint of tar so that he might slap it with a brush on to the face of anyone asleep or with a plaid about their heads. The county of Angus seems to have been one where the tar brush was particularly favoured for the prevention of slumber during worship. The Kirk Session records of Perth show that there the kirk officer used to 'have his red staff in the Kirk on Sabbath days wherewith to waken sleepers and remove greeting bairns' although in the Laigh Kirk in the Trongait in Glasgow it was a white staff that the beadle carried as he walked through the church during worship for the 'crubbing [curbing] of bairns' and anyone else who caused any disturbance. A far kinder way was that of a minister who once stopped abruptly during his sermon and addressed the congregation thus: 'Try and sit up! Sit up and A'll tell ye an awn-ecdote' but another minister is reputed to have been so exasperated by a snoring member of the congregation that he flung his Bible at him with the words, 'If ye'll no' hear the word of God, I'll mak ye feel it.' Arousing a sleeper could produce unexpected reasons: a man 'gave great offence by his behaviour in the Church . . . by presuming to answer the Minister who had occasion to reprove him for sleeping in time of divine service', saying 'publickly and in an insolent manner that he was not asleep' and when he was immediately reproved for this 'he laid down his head again upon the Desk where he sat in a sleeping posture.' He excused his conduct by saying that it was the effect of surprise but nevertheless he had to stand before the congregation for one Sunday. Naturally enough the favouritism so often shown by the church to certain people in other matters also applied to sleeping during worship. There was neither reprimand nor tar-brush for a laird whose loud snoring 'waukened us a'' as a farmer said when the preacher later complained to him about it; and another minister is said to have stopped during his sermon and called out to a bailie, 'Ye mauna snore sae loud for ye'll waken the Provost.'[14]

At first sight, one would imagine that the beadle or kirk officer walking about the church to detect sleepers and using a staff to waken them or to evict crying children, or slapping tar onto people's faces, would have been most disruptive to worship. People think of church services in former days as being decorous and quiet but that was far from the case and the disturbances already mentioned were only a few of the many that interrupted old time church-going. At one time taking snuff in church was regarded as Sabbath profanation – selling it on Sundays certainly was – but it continued and Rev. W. M. Inglis, minister of Auchterhouse in the early years of this century, was told by an old precentor that in his youth the minister used to have a 'snuff-rest' during his discourse, when he took out his own snuff mull and so did everyone else, which saved much clattering of them and sneezing during the service. Until churches were seated, people were expected to stand throughout church services, long though these were, or to 'sit laigh' which meant to 'sit low', probably on the floor, which was earthen, damp, draughty and could have weeds or even toadstools growing in it and there was always the chance of rain coming through a leaky roof to make matters worse. Even when people brought boards or plaited straw for their feet, these were only a very minor comfort and they often fought over the creepies [stools] which others brought to sit on. Even after churches were floored and seating was provided, there was still insufficient for everyone and poor people who could not afford to rent any for themselves had to do without and it is no wonder that they became restive and bad-tempered. Those who had no right to seats viewed those who had with envy and tried to operate a system of first come, first served, with fighting over seating only too common; in 1735 a Kirk Session ordered a man to be fined and rebuked before the pulpit for pushing another man out of a seat, wringing his nose and thumping him on the back while in 1724 there was trouble with some miners in the parish of Falkirk. They attended church regularly but caused a riot one Sunday when they refused to sit on the 'common forms' because their houses were on the lands of Callendar and they felt entitled to seating in the north loft which was already occupied by that estate's farm tenants, who naturally enough objected to being ousted by people they regarded as coal howkers. On this particular Sunday, the miners decided to go to church very sharp, before the ringing of the second bell, only to find that word of their plan had somehow got out and the tenants had got there before them, with the result that there was a free fight in the church. Some twenty or so years later a Dornoch doctor had to answer to the Kirk Session for forcibly removing an unruly child out of a seat which he regarded as his pupils' property. The child made a great deal of noise during its forced removal which offended the congregation and resulted in a public rebuke and a fine of one guinea for the doctor. People would even push themselves into the grandest of pews: a Coldingham man was rebuked for his undecorous behaviour in thrusting himself into the Duke of Douglas's seat and the Session 'discharged him to commit the said . . . again, nor making any disturbance in the church on the Lord's Day', and family harmony cannot have been helped by a man who 'maliciously and unreverently rackt and ruggit' his mother-in-law from her seat one day in 1639.[15]

Women were as belligerent as men when anyone took a seat to which they felt entitled and the minutes of one Kirk Session describe how 'Marjory Young and Janet Gowans were cited before Session for contesting and striving together in church for a seat.' In 1769 a Session chose some people to have seats in a particular loft in the church to stop 'the frequent disorders which happened in the fore breast of the common loft by disorderly young people pressing to get in.' It would be nice to think that this showed the anxiety of these youngsters to attend worship but it seems more likely that it was a desire not to have to stand throughout it. There may also have been some feature about this loft that attracted trouble-makers. At another time the minister had to admonish those in it 'for their great disturbance almost every Lord's Day' and later on it was described as 'so crowded by disorderly persons who make disturbances in the services' that some of the seats were allocated to different people. Disturbance in church was not a post-Reformation feature: Parliament had had to pass an Act in 1551 ordering those who 'commonly make perturbation' in church to be fined.[16]

Fighting could break out in church for other reasons than seating, such as two men who had to be warned about 'struggling together in the kirk' over taking a bridegroom's gloves, which appears to have been to decide which of them should be best man and it was due to that sort of thing that Montrose Kirk Session passed the following Act in 1639: 'If it happens that any person or persons whatsoever misbehave themselves in falling out one with another in the kirk, that they shall be severely punished, and make their repentance before the whole congregations and also pay sick ane pecunial soume as the Session shall enjoin.' People who should have known better unfortunately also fell to fighting. At one point, the minister of Glenholm, Peebles-shire, had to complain to the Presbytery that one of the elders, Robert Crichton, along with some others, caused a brawl before the service ended, by striking a gentleman with a cudgel which he had concealed below his cloak and also drawing his sword. Crichton was deposed from the eldership and the Presbytery ordered everyone involved to appear before the Privy Council.[17] Disturbance was also caused by noisy and ill-mannered conduct. One Kirk Session found a young man 'guilty of unseemly behaviour in the church by laughing and jeering in time of worship' although he tried to mitigate his offence by saying he had been encouraged to it by another youth. Another Session passed an Act ordering those who 'laugh in the kirk or use any unseemly behaviour' to be censured and some forty years before that they had a woman put in the steeple until she paid a fine of 6s. 8d. Scots and made public repentance one Sunday for talking during the psalm or 'using conference' as it was put. Mr Bowie of Dornoch, who complained of people sleeping in church, also deplored the fact that some of those who were out of his sight, and obviously not sleeping, talked during the service as if they were in a tavern. St. Andrews Kirk Session made a public intimation in 1639 that 'all sik servand women lassies and idling vaging boyis that maid any noyse or din in the kirk after sermon wt kirk chairis or wt their lousse behaviour on the Sabbathis at nycht at Catechising or other week dayis at sik exercises or prayers, suld be taken notice of by the elders, deacons and kirk officers and their names given in to the Session to be punishet.' That such conduct could come from example higher up the social scale is clear from an Act of General Assembly in 1709 which recommended to people of all ranks that among other civil respects paid to their acquaintances in church, they should refrain from 'entertaining one another with discourse while divine worship is performing and holy ordinances are dispensing'. Intimations from the pulpit about disturbances might not make much difference but withering comment from the same source could be very effective. Fishermen in the parish of Petty used to arrive at church more or less when they pleased and go into a gallery in a group where they sat and shuffled their feet in a very noisy way until one day the minister declared in church; 'The fishers of Pettie come to and go from the church like a parcel of goats, when they choose themselves, but God will sweep them down the hill when he chooses', which swiftly cured their late arrival and their shuffling feet.[18]

It is said that the 1650s saw a particular form of disturbance in churches, with Cromwell's soldiers showing their opinion of Presbyterian discipline by pulling down or facetiously entering stools of repentance during services, as a result of which many a stool was maimed, mutilated, thrown down and trampled on, both in mirth and in wrath. Seating particular people in a particular loft has already been mentioned as one Session's solution to troubles in it and this practice became quite common elsewhere. At Elgin in 1599 a man was ordered to sit at the entry to a new loft, partly to reserve the front seat for particular people but also 'to stay the tumult', and in 1648 Montrose Kirk Session instructed some of those taking up the collection to sit in the north loft in the quire during both morning and afternoon service and to take notice of any bad behaviour 'and delate it to the Session that order may be taken therewith.' In 1670 that Session enlisted the help of the town officers, ordering one of them to sit in the Mariners' loft during worship and the rest in the quire loft 'that no disorder be in time of sermon', adding the threat that 'otherwise their weekly allowance off the Session is to be taken from them.' Some years after that St. Andrews Kirk Session 'appointed two men to go through and about the Church on Sabbath Day to hinder abuse in time of sermon', patrolling it, in fact, in the way that beadles had earlier done to seek out sleepers. Yet another distracting habit was leaving the church before the blessing, which is said to have been because the sermon was all that some people came to hear and once they had done so they saw no point in waiting for anything else and one Presbytery had to decree in 1663 that 'none go from church before the pronouncing of the blessing'. Yet an East Lothian Kirk Session ordered that 'none go out of the kirk in time of divine service, *before the sermon*, prayers and blessing, except in case of sickness' which indicated that there were people who did *not* want to hear sermons.[19]

Being overcome by sickness in church was obviously a valid reason for departure, as was the medical need of others which could cause a midwife to get up and leave, and when a woman left church 'to give her barne the pape and was not weill herself' this also was accepted as a sound reason for going home. Even as late as

1872 leaving church before the end of worship still went on although in the following case it is difficult to see why the 'certain people' mentioned had gone to worship in the first place: 'The attention of the Session was called to the practice of certain people of rising and leaving the church at the commencement of divine service' and although the minister went to see them at the request of the Session, he had to report that they 'had not consented to desist' and it was decided to wait for a while to see whether further reflection might make them see things differently. On the other hand, another minister complained that although the Sheriff came regularly to church he 'did not fail . . . by his restlessness of manner to indicate when he was not being edified', something which was not helpful in a public figure and it might have been more peaceful for all concerned if he had not attended if that was how he behaved.[20]

The removal from church of 'greeting bairns' has already been mentioned but other children appear to have been frequently out of control during services. In Aberdeen the kirk authorities realised the problem of pre-school age children 'not of such an age or disposition' to sit still, who wandered about during worship causing 'perturbation and disorder', and so the Kirk Session ordered them to be kept at home 'for eschewing of clamour and disorder in the kirk', although it was different once children were considered to be of a suitable age to attend. Then parents might be ordered to 'bring their children to the church, especially that be any way considerable in age for hearing of the Word' but they were expected to behave themselves. In 1696 parents in Kirkcudbright were told 'to have a care of their children on the Sabbath day from making abuse in or about the church' and an idea of such abuses appears from the fact that in Elgin a man had to watch for children coming into the church to break stonework of a tomb on preaching and Session days. If these children had nowhere to sit, they could hardly be blamed if they ran about the church – one Session referred to 'bairns and utheris vagabondis' – and the best way to stop 'their tumults and running through the kirk, and likewise . . . their clattering and fighting' was to provide seating for them where they could be made to stay still. There was rather an odd case of older young people making a nuisance of themselves in church. This was in 1694, when several students made a practice of interrupting the minister of Old Aberdeen by striking up the doxology in different corners of the church at the very moment he was pronouncing the blessing. They found themselves charged before the Privy Council where it was alleged that they must have done this to vex the minister and disturb the congregation. Three of them appeared, submitted and were absolved but another three failed to show up and were put to the horn and had their goods confiscated.[21]

As if all that was not sufficiently distracting, worshippers also had to contend with problems caused by animals. Dogs frequently came to church with their owners and chased and fought each other during the service, especially when a new one appeared, and people had constantly to lift their feet to avoid getting them entangled with snapping teeth. Rev. Thomas Dyce, minister of Teviothead, Roxburghshire, in the very early eighteenth century, is said to have once clapped his Bible shut when a dog fight began and leant eagerly over the pulpit, offering a bet on the one he thought would win, but he was an exception, a very eccentric man who ultimately went insane. The dogs joined in the singing too and it was said that at a service in the highlands not only did the dogs begin to bark when the precentor started a psalm, but the babies began to cry too, to such an extent that the minister could stand it no longer and stopped the precentor singing and at once all was peace again. The dogs of one parish got wise to the fact that the end was in sight when the elders went round with the ladles for the collection and reacted accordingly but the congregation were more intelligent than the dogs and remained sitting for the blessing 'to cheat the dogs' because if they stood up for it there was invariably a storm of barking. Although the practice of taking dogs to church is often thought to have been a rural custom, with shepherds automatically taking them with them so as to 'look the hill' on the way home, town dogs also went to church. The records of the Kirk Session Presbytery of Aberdeen show that 'whereas against the decency observit within all well-reformit churches, many of the inhabitants of the burgh, both men and women, brings with them their dogges to the paroch kirk in time of sermons and divine service, whairthrow and be the barking and perturbation of these dogges the people are aftin withdrawn from the hearing of God's word and often divine service is interrupted, ane thing that is not comelie to be seen in the house of God.' To overcome this problem it was decreed that no one should allow dogs to follow them to church on Sundays or on weekdays and if they did, a penalty of 40s. Scots would be imposed for the use of the poor. In 1641 Oldmachar Kirk Session ordered a fine of 6s. 8d. to be imposed on anyone bringing a dog to church and at Banchory-Devenick in June 1732 the Kirk Session considering the great trouble 'occasioned by the multitude of dogs in time of worship, did agree to employ Alexander Coutts to keep them out, and allow him three pence every Lord's Day out of the collection for the same.' There must have been some difficulty in removing such dogs as managed to get in as six months later he was given 14s. Scots to get 'an iron instrument wherewith to keep out the dogs' which was probably a long-handled instrument called a 'slip', a form of tongs, with which they could be dragged out from under the seats. Alexander must either have been very good at this job or else needed the authority given by some sort of uniform as three years later, in 1735, the records show that 4 merks Scots were 'given to Alexander Coutts who holds out the dogs, to buy a new coat to him.' Even so, thirty years later, the minister there was still having to warn people not to bring their dogs to church. Preventing dogs getting into church or throwing out those that did, merely moved them into the churchyard and dogfights there must have continued to be a great distraction to worshippers inside. What contributed most to the end of rural 'collie shangies' was when churches were floored and box seats with doors installed, so that each shepherd could keep his dogs beside him, although they still ran about outside on Communion Sundays when they could be a considerable nuisance. According to William Aiton who wrote one of the General Views of Agriculture, church doors which were left open during services allowed cats and poultry to come in too to add to the confusion already caused by dogs.[22]

Anyone who had a suitable beast rode to church which meant that their horses or donkeys had to wait outside until worship was over. These animals might be tied up in the open or put into the stables which were often provided close to churches. There used to be a considerable range of stabling at Edrom Church, Berwickshire, for instance, but it has now gone; and at Castleton there is a building close to the church which provided stabling beneath and the schoolroom above, while Yarrow still has a stable with its fitments intact. There must have been many more stables at churches which have disappeared as the need for them lapsed or else they have been converted to some modern use, such as one at Cleish, Kinross-shire, which is now a most attractive house. As animals were often put into these stables loose, the fuller they were the better for safety but 'the neighbourhood of the many horses in the stable, among which there was no more harmony than among the dogs, the noise proceeding from their kicking and neighing by turns, often put the minister fairly hors de combat.'23

Churchyards also saw Sabbath disturbances and murder on Sundays was sufficiently common for Parliament to pass an Act in 1592 decreeing, among other things, that if anyone committed 'slauchter in kirks or kirkyards during service, their single and liferent escheat shall fall to the king on denunciation.' One can also imagine the sensation there must have been in Lairg when, one Sunday in 1711, on the orders of a Justice of the Peace, a deserter was arrested by some local people in the churchyard after worship. There was obviously no thought of sanctuary and a general mêlée ensued which caused great confusion before the mob could be sent home. The minister reported this Sabbath profanation to the Presbytery but unfortunately their advice is not recorded. Fighting of course could break out in the churchyard as well as inside the church, even over such small things as crossing the kirk style.24

Whether the kirk approved or not, the churchyard was a recognised place for recreation but, even so, it is astonishing what went on there at the same time as services were being conducted. In 1696 Ashkirk people had to be forbidden to leave worship to occupy themselves in an unspecified manner in the churchyard and a few years later two lads were summoned for walking about there during the sermon and were admonished on promising not to do so again. About the same time, some Hawick children who were found playing in the churchyard during service, had their names taken and their parents were ordered 'to refrain them from such practices' but in Auchterhouse it was not children but adults who were found amusing themselves playing at Pennie-stone there when they should have been in the church.25

Because the church was the one regular weekly gathering point in any parish, it was the churchyard that was the best place to give out public notices but an Act of Parliament in 1644 made it clear that even the most official of these should be read after the service and not during it: 'Warnings, inhibitions, requisitions and other letters not to be read before the conclusion of divine service.' This meant in practice that such notices were normally given out in the churchyard so that worship was not interrupted but a captive audience was still present. Official notices might concern the 'calling out of fencible men and for seising horses and arms' of disaffected people, they might be to do with forthcoming statute labour on roads which always had to be notified at parish churches on the Sunday immediately prior to when the work was required, or they could be lists of people claiming the right to vote under the Reform Bill of 1832. Included in 'official' notices might be those to do with roups and fairs which Burgh Councils regularly intimated at church doors and kirk roups of paupers' bequeathed effects were also notified in this way. A very important public health notification was made at the church of Cullen in 1792 when there was a panic about mad dogs thought to be in the district; the magistrates ordered all dogs to be shut up for three weeks and offered 1s. stg. reward for every dog found at large which was killed but there cannot have been many of these as a total of only 9s. was paid out.[26] Many churchyard notices, however, were neither ecclesiastical nor official. It was common, apparently, for the precentor or some other church official, acting as a general advertiser, to announce such things as Mrs So-and-so's spectacles being lost. Sometimes it was the crier who made these churchyard announcements but in the following case it was the Commissary Clerk's officer who did it. Landlords and others used to advertise sales at church and in 1762 the factor for the estate of Inverbreakie, in Ross-shire, wrote to the Commissary Clerk saying, 'Cause one of your officers to read the enclosed notification at your church next Sabbath: "If you want any horses, oxen and cows young and old you cannot be better served than at Newhall, and if you know any of your friends that want such, acquaint them of the Roup."' In 1729 a highland Synod passed an Act forbidding the proclamation of sales of merchants' goods, horse races and the like in the churchyard after worship, making it clear that only notices enjoined by law or to do with works of necessity would be permitted. In the days when landlords were entitled to services from their tenants such as carrying of goods or work at hay and harvest time, notification was often made at church doors as to when this was required but this was also considered unsuitable. Indeed, when the Presbytery of Dornoch were told 'that some officers in their bounds make intimation at Kirk doors on the Lord's day to their masters' tenants of the carriage they are to do on the ensuing week' they declared that this was Sabbath profanation and forbade it under threat of church censure. The beadle of Ordiquhill notified people in the churchyard one Sunday about 'a shooting for a wheelbarrow and a pistol' the following Thursday, a competition which was doubtless keenly contested but the announcement earned him a Sessional rebuke and instructions never to do such a thing again. But secular notification in churchyards went on for some time, so that in 1804 Dingwall Kirk Session considered 'that much indecency and confusion arises from the present mode of making proclamations or publishing advertisements on the Lord's Days in the Churchyard' which they regarded as 'no General Theatre for Criers' and decided that for the future only announcements approved by the Session and paid for, might be made and then only by the kirk officer.[27] During this time, some secular intimations were made not outside but inside churches, something which was sufficient of a problem for the Presbytery of Fordyce to ask the Commissioners going to the General Assembly in 1728 'to get advice from the Assembly how the profanation of the Lord's Day by reading intimations concerning secular affairs from the Latrons [precentor's or reader's desks] may be prevented.' About 1784 the reading of advertisements from the precentor's desk was said elsewhere to be giving offence to some people and it was suggested that these should be written out and displayed on the main door of the church and announced by drum through the town on market day. The Session Clerk however did not think that this was necessary, saying that the only advertisements given out were read from his desk and were those he felt bound to read as part of his office but he suggested that in future he would submit them to the Kirk Session for approval first of all, which was agreed and which was very much the same as Dingwall Kirk Session later on decided for kirkyard intimations. However, as late as 1900 the door of a mausoleum in Strathdon, Aberdeenshire, was used as a noticeboard to advertise, silently, such things as local turnip sales.[28]

All in all, therefore, it is inaccurate to think that Sabbath worship in former times was as sombre and well-behaved as is often thought. Another misconception is that 'everyone' went to church but the size of many parish kirks shows that they could not possibly have accommodated anything like the population there used to be in the area. While many people were perfectly prepared to walk ten or so miles each way to church, there were many others for whom such distances were impossible and although the kirk did what it could to enable people to get to church by providing water crossings of one sort or another, quite clearly there were still a large number who could not possibly attend worship. Old age made it difficult for some: a person delated for 'frequent dishaunting of the church' in 1660 was let off with a private rebuke because of 'being old and weak' and illness at home also hindered church-going; several women explained their absence from Communion 'because their bairns were all lying in the pocks.' Poverty was also a cause of absence: a woman blamed her seven to eight months' non-appearance at church on the cold winter, not being able 'to afford the necessary defences against it' and her children's consequent illness. While church collections were not a great burden, other items of expenditure could make attendance difficult. Seat rents were high and as standards of dress improved and a better show was expected, many who might have wished to attend felt that they could not do so, not that that was the fault of the kirk. In 1735 the Kirk Session of Coll minuted 'the great aversion of the people to come to worship.' What lay behind their aversion is not stated but certainly there were always some people who might just be uninterested or lazy, like the man who 'did not keep the church but alwise did lye at home on the Sabbath days' and when reprimanded by the elders about this he 'was very obstinat and gave them very little condescendence.'[29]

Parliament tried to enforce church attendance in 1663, 1670 and 1672 by imposing penalties for failure to do so but this happened during the return to Episcopalian church government after the Restoration of Charles II and was not intended so much for religious reasons as to compel Presbyterians to attend Episcopal services and to prevent conventicles. The church itself, of course, was always genuinely concerned that people should, for the good of their souls, attend worship and Kirk Sessions did what they could to enforce this. About 1679 it was intimated in the parish of Roberton that a fine of 6s. would be imposed on everyone absent from church *when the roll was called* but this was something quite impractical and does not seem to have been effective. Certainly, on one stormy day, the collection came to only 2¹/₂d. which does not indicate a full house. In 1684 the Kirk Session of Holm ordered a similar fine but it was for heads of families who were absent from church, with a lesser fine of 2s. for servants 'unless their rexive [respective] excuses be found relephand [relevant].' Both these examples were of course during Episcopalian days but prior to them, and later too, fines were also being imposed. Heads of households might have to pay 3s. 4d. for every member of the family who, having been in good health the night before, failed to appear in church on Sunday and in Coll, at the time when people were proving averse to church-going, it was decided that anyone absent 'without a very sufficient reason' should pay 1s. stg., and a further 1s. if they failed to appear before the Session to have this fine ascertained. There, at that time, a censor – of whom more later – was required to help the collector gather fines, if necessary calling on an elder to assist him and the more people fined, the better for those doing the collecting as the censor and the collector each received a quarter of what came in, with the other half going to the poor.[30]

Plainly such fines could not always have been imposed because people simply could not have managed to pay them and it would be nice to think that Kirk Sessions sometimes tried to find solutions to difficulties which prevented attendance. This certainly happened once at Elgin in 1599: a man was told to get a lock for his house 'whereby his daughter may come to the kirk on Sundays' from which it appears that she was being left at home to mind the house. Unfortunately there were many punishments other than fines which could be imposed for absence from church. As mentioned in an earlier chapter, in 1709 the Kirk Session of Orphir decreed that of two youngsters who were 'ill kirk keepers', one was to be fined or put in the 'goggs' and the other whipped round the church by the kirk officer. The jougs were a fairly common threat in this connection: just two examples are an Elgin couple threatened with them in the 1640s and a Galston man who was absent from church for five weeks and was ordered to be rebuked publicly with certification that if he was ever absent again for two weeks together, he too would be put in the jougs. At Montrose in 1642 anyone found 'vaging' on a Sunday was ordered to be put in the tolbooth and although in 1680 Lauder Kirk Session merely admonished a couple who stayed at home during the time of worship, they took much stronger steps three years later by instructing the landlord of a blacksmith to order him to attend church or else put him out of his smithy. Cambuslang Kirk Session were worried in the mid-seventeenth century about the non-attendance of an important heritor but in this case, the Session thought that the best thing would be for the minister to speak to the Presbytery about his 'constant absenting himself from church' although when some people of standing in the

parish of Channelkirk did not go to church for about two years, they were firmly
told that they would not be admitted to Communion.[31] In slightly later times, in
Glasgow at any rate, anyone found outside during the time of worship without
good reason, or in an alehouse could, if they wished, return home rather than be
sent to church; if they refused both these options, they were taken into custody.
This only came to an end there in the mid-eighteenth century when the Kirk
Session had a young man named Peter Blackburn apprehended for walking on the
Green and he raised and won an action against the magistrates over the matter. As
it was desirable to catch offenders in the act, the elders who have been mentioned
in an earlier chapter as watching over weekday and Sabbath drinking, were also
required to see to it that people attended worship. By the early seventeenth century
it was not unusual for Kirk Sessions to appoint inspectors, sometimes termed
censors, visitors, searchers, collectors, observators, surveyors or informers to see
that everyone went to church and behaved properly on Sundays as well as during
the week. In Aberdeen in 1603 a bailie and two elders were required to go through
the town every Sunday to see who was absent from church, to search houses as
they saw fit and to discover if anyone was using a ferry boat so that any offenders
could be punished as Sabbath breakers. Having finished their searching, these men
were then expected to come to church and in Elgin it was for this reason that
someone was appointed not only to keep order in the new loft but also to keep its
front seat free for the searchers when they finally arrived. Elders could save
themselves a lot of effort by waiting until they saw who was absent and only then
going in search of them. Should a minister have a colleague preaching for him, he
would often take the opportunity of going himself on one of these tours of
inspection, which was how the minister of Forfar found people in an alehouse, two
drinking, another sitting with his coat off and a fourth eating, when they should
have been at church. Anyone found absent without good cause was delated to the
Kirk Session: 'This day Alexander Davidson seairchit the towne and delatit some
persons absent frae the kirk in tyme of preiching', as one Session minute put it.[32]

A series of Acts passed by the Kirk Session of Montrose gives a good picture of
inspections in that parish, which included both a burgh and a landward area. The
elders had to take turns and to do the job thoroughly:

> 1649. It is ordained that two elders by course should go through the town when there
> is preaching and divine service and make search in every corner of the town whom
> they can find absent from the preaching, not being under suspition, and give in their
> diligence every Session day that order may be taken therewith.

This was one place where the inspecting elders were called 'visitors.' They were
entitled to the support of the town officers who might be armed with halberts and
who were expected to carry out their duties faithfully and 'under pain of depriving

them of losing of their place, to wait precisely every one by course upon the visitors.' The visitors, through use of these town officers, had considerable powers:

> 1642. It is ordained that the town's officers shall carrie along with them the keys of the tolbooth upon every Sabbath Day with those that shall happen to be visiting, so that if it shall happen any of the said visitors to find any vaging upon the streets or elsewhere out of the church that they be ready with the keys to put them into the said tolbooth any that they shall find out of the church on the Lord's Day.

Sixteen years later the following Act of Session, worded to express concern for the magistrates, in fact neatly by-passed them:

> 1658. The Session take to consideration that it would be tedious and troublesome to the Magistrates at every occatione to give order to their Officers to put in ward any vager on the Lord's Day in the tolbooth gives full power to all those who shall happen to [be] visitors as it were done by their authority.

Just as Kirkcudbright had clandestine inspectors to try to catch people drinking on Sundays, so Montrose Kirk Session warned those who were 'neglective in family worship morning and evening' that there would be 'secrett visitors appointed for every quarter of the town that the neglectors of it may be noticed and their faults corrected by admonition and public rebuke as necessary.' Although this Act of Session referred to weekday worship and not to Sundays, it shows once again that the kirk was not above using undercover agents.[33]

Church attendance meant going to one's own parish church and at one time anyway, going to worship in another parish, other than at Communion seasons, was a breach of Sabbath observance. In 1647 a Montrose man 'went to Morphie, and afterwards went to the church of Inglisgrieg [Ecclesgreig] and heard the preaching', and for this offence had to humble himself before his own Session, promise never to do such a thing again and pay 20s. Scots to the poor's box. The parish records of Kirk-andrews-on-Esk, Dumfries-shire, contain a note written by the incumbent describing a boating disaster on 1 November 1696 when twenty-eight people were drowned. Six of these he described as parishioners of his, people of years of discretion, who had gone from the parish to attend the church in Canonbie. They had with them two boys, aged nine and eleven, who were the only ones saved. 'Surely God almighty showed his displeasure to those persons who being of age, past by their own Church to Canonbie but showed his mercy to the boys, who knew not what they did but went for company's sake. This is so distinguishing a evidence that every one should ought to take notice of it and take heed how they run from their own parish church.' So strongly did he feel about this, that he signed his note with his name and designation. It is said that one of the fortunate casualties of the 1914–18 War was the taboo on entering any church but one's own, whether it be a parish church or one of a different denomination. Yet as has been said in an earlier chapter, certain worshippers might not be welcome in their own parish kirk. The congregation of St. John's, Glasgow, were finding it difficult in the late 1820s to get sittings in the church because of the number of charity children occupying the seats and as these children's presence was inconvenient to the congregation in other ways, a couple of the elders were asked to bring this matter to the notice of the proper authorities so that the youngsters could be transferred to some other less crowded city church. And it was not only children but adults too who could find their presence unwelcome in churches. It is said that, especially in large towns, ministers shrank from going into poor homes and feared to lose their wealthier 'gathered' congregation by encouraging into the church those considered socially undesirable.[34]

So far as weekday services went, no work was meant to be done while the service was in progress, the idea being that people should be free to attend and when numbers were falling off in one parish in 1645, the Session ordered that those working in their booths, or who kept shops open or who supplied or loaded ships, during the hours of worship, should be fined at least 6s. Scots for the poor. A somewhat blotted minute of Dumbarton Kirk Session for November 1694 says that the Session 'considering that several persons go about their [blot] affairs in the time of weekday sermon, therefore appoint, according to some old and [blot] Acts of the Session for the due observation of weekday sermons, that at the ringing of the third bell to sermon on any weekday, all merchants' shop doors shall be shut, and all tradesmen and labourers leave their work to attend divine service, except in case of necessity.' Domestic shopping was also an offence and a woman who bought fish during preaching on a Wednesday found herself before the Session but in fact Kirk Sessions might well arrange with cadgers, as fish salesmen were called, neither to bring in fish before weekday sermons nor sell it till afterwards. Once weekday services were over, normal life resumed for the rest of the day which was quite different from what was meant to happen on Sundays. Worship apart, Sundays were expected to be spent indoors, quietly and reverently, but while that was the intention of the kirk, the repeated Kirk Session injunctions against Sabbath profanation, and the constant cases of it, show that that day, or part of it, was frequently differently spent. Even doing nothing for the remainder of Sunday was regarded as reprehensible. 'Standing in the streets' or 'idly gazing out of windows' are both mentioned in Kirk Session records of Edinburgh and about 1695 several Coldingham men were found guilty of profaning the Sabbath by idleness, standing by a cart upon which they said they were keeping an eye, while another man there was rebuked by the elders for idling away his time lolling about on heather or turf stacks. A story of ludicrous strictness on the Sabbath tells of an elder in Perth who had a starling with a singular ability to sing but one Sunday the minister passed by and chanced to hear it performing 'Over the Water to Charlie' and was so shocked at this profanation of the day that he ordered the elder to strangle it or demit office – and he chose the latter course.[35]

Further Acts of the Kirk Session of Montrose indicate the kirk attitude to the Sabbath: '1652. It is to be remembered to intimate to the people that all masters and mistresses should keep their servants within doors on the Lord's Day' but four years later the Session found that women and servants were gathering 'in their convocations under Staires' and because 'family duties were not so performed by masters and parents in that day as became, therefore ordered this to be amended and masters and parents to be exhorted after public meeting to be employed in reading, catechising, praying and taking accompt of those that are under their charge . . .' In a further three years' time, not only the Kirk Session but the Town Council too, ordained 'in one voice that every person in whatsoever degree or quality, shall repair after sermon on the Lord's Day to their own houses and there to exercise their families Catechising them . . .' Another Session decreed that parents and heads of households should restrain their children and servants and 'keep them within doors at their books and other religious exercises, as they will be answerable for it themselves.' The books which were approved for Sabbath reading included the Bible, of course, and also such titles as Boston's *Fourfold State*, *The Pilgrim's Progress*, *Holy Living and Holy Dying*, *The Holy War*, *The Letters of Samuel Rutherford*, *A Cloud of Witnesses*, *Ambrose on Angels* and *Commentaries on the Lesser Prophets*. It seems almost unbelievable that in 1703 the minister of Peterculter was rebuked for profaning the Sabbath by having the schoolmaster come to read 'Cartesius his philosophical writings' to him on a Sunday afternoon when he was ill in bed, although it is not clear whether the book was considered light-hearted or that the schoolmaster's reading could be described as working. Every activity other than a work of necessity was regarded as Sabbath profanation, something which was a great burden to the people who suffered it but which is a great joy to social historians, giving a wonderful record of the ordinary things that people did, both as work and for pleasure, which would never have been mentioned had they not been done on a Sunday. An offence which was sinful on a weekday was that much worse if done on a Sunday: a woman who not only stole meal on the Lord's Day but took it into church with her, had therefore to stand in the jougs between the second and third bells and a Nigg woman who threw clods of earth at another one Sunday was also in trouble for the day rather than the deed. What was called 'the great duty of sanctifying the Sabbath' was very hard on people who worked from dawn to dusk on six days of the week, leaving Sunday as their only chance to get on with their own affairs, as exemplified by a man who went to another parish one Sunday to fetch a horse and was duly summoned to his Session, to whom he explained that as he was employed all week as a herd he could neither go for it himself nor find anyone else to do so any day but Sunday.[36]

Strictures about Sundays referred to the whole of the day but there was considerable confusion over when the day began and ended. In some places, such as Glasgow for a time, it was regarded as from sun to sun in summer and from light to light in winter although in time the Presbytery declared that it lasted from midnight on Saturday to midnight on Sunday which was how Parliament defined it in 1648. Nevertheless, many people continued to equate the day with the light. In 1699 a man felt he had done no wrong in taking a horse and a cow to Rutherglen fair after the sun had set on a Sunday but nonetheless found himself up before the Session. Similarly, a woman named Euphan More carried in water after sunset, thinking she was doing no wrong, and she too was called before her Session and rebuked for her sin. In the north of Scotland, where midsummer nights are hardly dark at all, it was difficult to judge the time, especially without a clock or where people possibly could not tell the time even if they had one. One unfortunate woman went to gather ware on the shore between 9.00 and 11.00 p.m. one Sunday but was spotted by two righteous parishioners who 'went to check the miserable creature' and delated her to the Session. She said that she had misread the time and thought that it was 3.00 a.m. but even so she had to appear in church for reproof and admonition. In 1755 one Session extended the length of Sunday to Monday morning by passing an Act 'discharging persons to go to the shore to gather seaweed on Monday before day light' but there was reason behind this somewhat surprising decree. There had been a 'scuffle' when some 'very offensive and abusive things happened such as their throwing stones and beating one another, uttering oaths and imprecations, giving approbrious names and scurrilous language', which happened because two women had gone to gather seaweed very early on a Monday morning and had finished just as others were on their way there – 'in their returning they were met long before day light appeared by the fishers of Arbol going to sea.' One of the late-comers reproved the early ones for Sabbath profanation, malicious stories were put about and so the trouble developed, which explained the Kirk Session's decree. They had got wise to the fact that some people were trying to steal a march on their neighbours to get the pick of the seaweed while others observed the Sabbath strictly. This must have been a widespread practice in coastal parishes and some Sessions passed their own Ware Acts to try to control it. In 1826 some farmers in the parish of Drainie felt that the law about gathering seaware should be more fairly operated and asked the two lairds to renew an old Act in the Kirk Session records and to set a stated time on Monday mornings for gathering it to begin – sunrise was suggested and agreed and this was written into the kirk minutes. Nevertheless, in spite of the threat of prosecution in the Sheriff Court for violating this ruling, in 1843 enforcement was needed and once again the help of the heritors was enlisted as appears in a Kirk Session minute that year:

> We the heritable proprietors of those parts of the Baronies of Gordonstoun and Kinneddar lying within the parish of Drainie . . . knowing that much profanation of the Sabbath is occasioned by tenants and servants going on Sabbath evening to the shore with rakes, horses and carts in order to collect and carry off seaware, and that the profanation of the Lord's Day takes place from the avaricious desire of one to anticipate and over-reach another, by marking and collecting seaware before his more conscientious and religious neighbour could dare to trespass on the Sabbath – and knowing from the records of the Session of Drainie that in former times there was a wise and salutary regulation on the Baronies of Gordonstoun and Kinneddar which established a set hour on Monday morning before which it was permitted to none to make, collect or carry off seaware, and being petitioned by the most worthy and respectable portion of our tenantry to renew the old Regulation . . . we therefore do appoint sunrise on Monday morning to be the time . . . at which it shall be permitted . . . and hereby declare that all seaware collected and gathered on Monday morning before sunrise is justly forfeited . . .'

On Monday morning their tenants could carry off without hindrance or molestation as much seaware as their strength, industry and activity enabled them to do. This Act anent gathering of seaware on Monday mornings was ordered to be engrossed in the Session records for ready inspection and to be read from the pulpit or precentor's desk on three consecutive Sundays 'that none may pretend ignorance.' Elsewhere too, Sunday might be somewhat extended by Kirk Sessions, such as that of Falkirk, where going fishing about 1.00 a.m. on Monday was regarded as profaning the Sabbath.[37] Not only did the varying hours of daylight throughout the year confuse people about the start and finish of the Sabbath but when many of them lived in isolated or very self-contained communities with no newspapers or radio or TV to remind them what day of the week it was, it was very easy, if they were self-employed, to forget altogether that Sunday had come round again. Such cases as the following were by no means unusual: a man who cut grain on crofts about his house until a neighbour reminded him what day it was, declared that it was forgetfulness and mistaking the day that caused him to do such a thing but he still had to stand before the congregation for one Sunday, and another who went shearing said quite straightly that he 'forgot it was the Sabbath.' However, even when people knew perfectly well what day of the week it was, there were things which they considered essential to do although the kirk did not share their views.[38]

The most basic domestic requirements are water and fuel. Fuel was scarce and had to be gathered as best might be and was often only found at a distance; and peat was particularly time-consuming to secure. Anyone working from 6.00 a.m. to 6.00 p.m. on week days, especially in the darker months when fuel was most needed, could hardly get it any other day than Sunday but the kirk thought this very sinful and as with many prohibitions, had good authority for saying so: when the children of Israel were in the wilderness, they found a man gathering sticks on the Sabbath and brought him to Moses and Aaron and all the congregation and he was put in ward until it was decided what should be done with him. When the Lord said to Moses 'The man shall surely be put to death and the congregation shall stone him with stones without the camp' that is what they did, but fortunately for a man caught pulling and gathering sticks and heather one Sunday in Coll and a person found cutting broom in Ross-shire and many more like them, such drastic Biblical punishment did not come their way – they just had to appear before their respective Sessions. Wood was very difficult for ordinary people to obtain, with landlords jealously guarding their timber, and when anyone was able to gather 'pieces of timber from the waterside brought down by spate' or join in 'the breaking and cutting down of a ship boat that came in by sea' they did it, Sunday or no Sunday, and must have regarded it as a gift from Heaven, to be gladly accepted and used.[39]

Kirk Session minutes are full of references to profaning the Sabbath by carrying of water. The worthy members of the Session, who probably never had to carry it themselves seem to have forgotten the great difficulties involved: if one lived far from a well, a spring or a burn it was very heavy work to carry sufficient on a Saturday to last until Monday and, in any case, many people did not have suffi- cient containers to hold what was needed for that length of time. In a drought water could be scarce and if a lot of people were using the same well at the one time, it could fill only slowly which made getting enough almost impossible. Was it truly a mistake when Andrew McLennan 'confessed that a little child of his brought in water on the Lord's Day, but that he was not in knowledge of it when she did it'? A certain lenience was allowed when there was illness in the home but in such cases, the container in which water was fetched had to be of a size equal to the medical needs as otherwise nothing would convince a Session that it was not meant for some other purpose.[40]

Just as some modern working wives do their washing on Sundays, so did the much more hard-worked working women of earlier days. Any change of clothing was always made on a Saturday night so as to be clean for Sunday and how tempting it must have been, if the weather was right, to get on with the washing and get everything dry that day, rather than wait till Monday and risk having garments out on the line for days or hanging damply inside a small cottage in front of an inadequate fire. One Kirk Session ordered their officer 'to go through the yards of Kirktown to see if there was any clothes drying' and to report back if he found any but a real deterrent must have been the decision made by another Session in 1649 that any clothes found drying on dykes would be confiscated and used for behoof of the poor and that their owners would have to make satisfaction. But threaten as Sessions might, the sheer practicalities of domestic life meant that they were constantly having to give warnings about drying clothes, carrying fuel and bringing in water.[41]

Before milk was cooled at source and before the days of refrigeration, it did not keep well in summer and it was tempting both to sell and buy it daily, which meant on Sundays too, something which got three women who went 'landward for milk in tyme of sermon' into trouble one summer, and even selling it after 10.00 p.m. on a Saturday night could be regarded as an offence. Making butter and cheese on Sundays was probably done for the same reason but that was never accepted as an excuse although when a woman was summoned before her Session for weighing butter on the Lord's Day, she explained that some soldiers had arrived and threatened her with bodily harm if she did not give it to them. The Session were not entirely satisfied about this explanation but knowing her to be a 'timorous person' they just gave her a private rebuke. Kail was an important part of the old Scottish diet and 'watering kail' appears as Sabbath profanation, in fact a double offence as it involved not only the care of the kail but the carrying of water. In 1597 in Elgin a general ban was placed on the pulling, transporting or selling of kail plants or onions on Sundays and 'gathering gooseberries in time of sermon' also brought trouble on the head of the person who did it. Any food to be eaten on Sunday was meant to be prepared the day before which was why a Dunfermline man was fined 'for putting a roast to his fire' on a Sabbath. To many families meat was a rare treat and not one to be missed and when a man found one of his calves accidentally strangled on a Sunday, he skinned, dressed and prepared it – and was summoned for doing so. He probably did not help himself by saying that he had thought that no one would have known what he was doing and the result was that he had to stand publicly for one Lord's Day. It was also considered sinful to use any implement of weekday work on a Sunday. A woman might therefore scrape up a few potatoes for supper with her bare hands or a lad might carry turnip for cattle in his arms, but nothing like a spade, graip or barrow could be used to make things easier.[42]

The kirk's attitude to the care of livestock on Sundays was the same as to household matters. Absolutely nothing that was not essential must be done. In July 1703 a Session ordered all who had 'bestial', a collective name for cattle, to keep them out in the fields on Sundays, which can only have been to avoid feeding and watering them but that was in summer time, whereas in winter they were housed. 'It is ordained that if any be found carrying water to their horses on the Sabbath day, they shall pay 6s 8d for every fault', said one Kirk Session in 1649, which meant of course that they either had to be taken to water or that sufficient had to be carried on Saturday to supply them over Sunday, in addition to what had to be carried for domestic needs. Where a beast had to be kept inside because of illness, it was meant to be cared for, yet when a woman pulled grass one Sunday for a sick animal that could not go outside, thinking it a work of mercy, she had to confess the scandal before the pulpit. Cleaning a byre could not possibly have been regarded as urgent, but with time to do it, it happened and in any case, dung was a valuable commodity, to be gathered and carefully husbanded wherever possible. That was what led to an Ashkirk woman gathering sheep muck on the Sabbath and her consequent delation to the Session; and on that subject, the elders of Auchter-house were told in 1649 'to mak search for any that did spread muck on Sunday after sermon.'[43] When beasts grazed on common land it was only too easy for them to stray or to be taken away and so Kirk Session minutes often refer to people searching for missing stock on Sundays. A Dornoch man who went looking for an ox, aggravated his offence by taking the bed-clothes off a dying woman 'upon suspicion of the ox being taken away by her husband' but the sin was still classed as Sabbath profanation. In the context of livestock, the word 'carrying' is often used when the modern word would be 'driving' – in 1706 a man had to stand in church for one Sunday to confess that he had 'carried bestial to the parish on the Sabbath' which was bringing back eleven cows which had run off. To show how seriously such offences were regarded, in another case witnesses were called to give evidence that a particular sheep belonged to a man and other details too, when he was accused of using a dog to catch it one Sunday. The shielings where people took animals to graze in the summer months were somewhat out of the way but it never took long for news to find its way back to Kirk Sessions about any disagree-ments between those herding there. One year there was a delation that two men were guilty of profaning the Sabbath by beating and swearing at others who were herding with them; and in another case a herd refused to share some pease with a man who 'did upon that, throw a Dog with violence at his head which irritated him so that he gave him a blow with his clenched fist and that thereafter David Ross did in return strike him repeated times on the head and face to the effusion of his blood.' A report about this filtered back to the Session and standing in public one Sunday was the punishment. A different case which also featured a dog was dealt with by the Presbytery of Alford some time in the seventeenth century when a man was found guilty of Sabbath profanation 'by wronging his neighbour in killing his dog.'[44]

The growing and processing of flax was an important part of rural economy in former times. It involved a lot of work, which was often done on Sundays with many delations as a result. Flax was steeped in water and then beaten to separate the fibres, a process which appears in minutes as 'swinging' or 'sweenging' of lint or as 'battering of cloth' but in one case a couple did not just batter their linen on Sunday, they sang while they did it! Linen also had to be bleached, something which may appear as 'bletching'. Leaving it outside steeping or bleaching on Saturday night and on Sunday was of course a sin, regardless of what stage the process had got to, and in the spring of 1693 the Kirk Session of Kirkcudbright ordered 'keepers of yr Linnings wt out on the Saturday and Sabbath . . . to be proceeded against' with the result that the following month several men were delated for this offence. As with washing left outside, a dire threat was made by one Session, ordering their kirk officer 'to poind [confiscate] all linnen webs that are found at the water on the Sabbath' and a woman found winding lint one Sunday had it forfeited for the use of the kirk, a very harsh punishment as it may have represented her livelihood. In 1723 a man, wanting to dry a quantity of wool, put up a tent and put the wool inside it to dry on Friday and then on Saturday night he wrapped it together and left it to lie that way until Monday morning, obviously thinking that he was doing everything properly – but no, even for that the Session found him guilty of Sabbath profanation, although religious discrimination may have come into this case as 'being papist he was sharply rebuked for his sin and ordered to pay 40s Sc.'[45]

Country people knew how vital it was to secure their crops when conditions were right. Making a little hay to feed such animals as were over-wintered was a job for good weather and 'mawing and shearing of grass' when a Sunday was fine must have seemed worth the censure of the kirk so long as the work was safely done. Food for beasts was one thing; grain for the people themselves was another and when they lived at or near subsistence level, they were desperate to make sure of their own winter food. Nevertheless, to do harvest work on a Sunday was asking for trouble: a woman who cut just four sheaves was 'warded' until she could find caution to appear before the Kirk Session the following Friday which, even although this happened in 1603, seems an excessive punishment. Weather conditions had to be exceptional for the kirk to overlook Sabbath harvesting and it was probably with the memory of the recent very bad years of 1634–35 when the price of meal rose to £10–12 Scots per boll that the Kirk Session of Kilconquhar, while decreeing that there should be 'no masking or leading of corn on Sundays' added the proviso 'except in case of great necessity.' When grain is ripe a very strong wind can snap off the heads and when the Kirk Session of Banchory-Devenick were told that 'upon the windy Sabbath night' a very large number of people had yoked their horses and gone to see to their crops, the Session realised that there had been a real need to get the work done and decided that the best thing to do in the circumstances was for the minister to give a general rebuke from the pulpit on Sunday and leave it at that. This was a sensible reaction to what was obviously very necessary harvesting but when in 1795 a Tongue man took in his grain on a Sunday, saying he feared wind and rain were coming, it was found that no one else in the parish had thought it necessary to do so and he was publicly rebuked before the congregation. Preparing grain for consumption on a Sunday also fell foul of the kirk and so 'dighting' (winnowing or preparing) bear, 'knocking' (pounding) grain or 'dressing and grinding Corn with a Quern' all appear as Sabbath profanation.[46]

Parishioners were expected to make long journeys to church on Sundays and such moving about was acceptable; should they use an animal to carry them there, then its harnessing, unharnessing and stabling during services was allowed too, but other forms of transport were in general forbidden. No one was meant to operate or use a ferry boat on a Sunday except for church-going – a payment to a boatman 'for his waiting on the boat the tyme of the Sacrament' is an example of this – but sometimes people might take a ferry boat themselves in the absence of the ferry man, leaving him to be the person to get into trouble. This happened to Andro Cochrane, a Govan man, and as a result he was forbidden to ferry anyone on a Sunday unless 'some of the elders were there and desired the same.' This was because Kirk Sessions realised that a river of any size lying between the church and centres of population was an impediment to attendance and, as has been said earlier, they sometimes provided boats themselves or contributed towards the boats of others; but where a boat was provided, it was meant to be used in a respectable and decorous manner. What could the inhabitants on the north side of the River Dee, 'especially the younger sort' have been up to, that caused the minister to admonish them 'to behave more gravely and decently in going in and out of the boat?' Gradually the prohibition on the use of ferry boats came to apply only to the hours of worship and in 1641 a Session ordained that if any fisherman – a group who were always keen to do a little ferrying – 'should go over the watter during time of pretching upon the Sabbath' then he should pay 30*s*. Scots or be put in ward during the pleasure of the Session if he could not pay. In 1709 a boatman explained to the minister of Kelso that it was not his fault that some people had been taken over the River Tweed during a church service but, in order to prevent a recurrence, the Session ruled that no one should be ferried over the river after the third bell for church had rung, apart from cases of necessity. In the same way, when needless Sunday crossings of a ferry in the parish of Holm in Orkney were causing complaints, all such crossings were forbidden although, once again, there was provision for them in exceptional circumstances. An idea of what could constitute necessity came from there in 1684: with a marginal note in the minutes

saying 'Toleration for the ferrie' the record says, 'This day upon a humble supplication, the Session did grant a licence to the ferryman to transport some catteil
upon Sunday at night, upon this consideration that the multitude of them was so
great that there could be no accommodation for them without intolerable skaith
[damage] to cornes.' Animals travelled in those days in the same small boats as
humans did and if there really was a multitude of cattle, the ferryman probably had
to make several trips to get them all across.[47] Ferryman were jealous of their rights
which was what led to a 'gross Sabbath profanation, riotous conduct' one Sunday
in 1788 in the parish of Edderton. Some people who were described as being frail
had nevertheless come across the Dornoch Firth to attend a Communion service in
Edderton and afterwards they were taken back in Dr Scobie's boat. The regular
ferrymen were furious about this and committed a 'most gross profanation of that
holy day by attacking, beating and bruising' Dr Scobie's men and even thought of
carrying off his boat 'as their interest was much hurt by his boat ferrying so many
across the firth.' The ferrymen were exhorted to repent for the 'horrid sin they
were guilty of' and ordered to confess it next Sunday in Edderton, and the Presbytery, to whom the matter was referred, reported it to the Sheriff-Depute asking him
to impose any further punishment he thought fit. By the 1790s, however, 'modern
times allowing a slacker rein', many a ferry became busier on Sundays than on any
other day of the week. Travel restrictions on Sundays could bring other problems.
Because no vessels were allowed to pass through the Forth-Clyde Canal on
Sundays the town of Grangemouth was one which generally found itself with a
larger number of idle seamen that day than any other and the New Statistical
Account for Falkirk suggested that, as in other seaports, a part of the church should
be allocated to these men as a 'means of preserving them from spending the day in
idleness and drunkenness.'[48]

What happened in the parish of Holm in 1684 was permitted carrying of
livestock by boat on a Sunday but plenty of it was done without any authority,
which therefore fell into the category of Sabbath profanation. This could be the
taking of a foal by sea from Dunskaithness in Nigg to Chanonry in the Black Isle in
1708 or the 'selling and delivering two cows . . . carried from Dornoch mercat to
the crew of ane English ship lying in Cromarty road . . . [on] the Lord's Day
Evening.' The owner of the cows defended himself by saying that he had refused
to sell them on a Sunday but the master of the ship had declared that he would
simply come and take them anyway. As a result of this, owner and master went to
where the cows were and then to a nearby inn and 'while they were Drinking and
Chappen ale there, the ship men had carried off two of the cows and put them
aboard their boat.' A put-up job, one would think, but the owner said 'that he knew
nothing of it till he came out and saw the cows in the boat.' His story might have
carried more weight had he not accepted 46s. for the cows which the master sent to
his house that night although it is arguable that by that stage there was nothing else
that he could reasonably do and that he might as well have the money for them —
but he was publicly rebuked for it all.[49]

Unnecessary sailings on Sundays were forbidden too: 'All skippers and sailors inhibited to begin any voyage on the Lord's Day or to louse any ships etc that day' decreed the General Assembly in 1646 and so it was that the crew of a boat which left Inverness about 7.00 a.m. one Sunday and arrived at its destination that afternoon were found guilty and had to appear publicly in church. When some Portmahomack men sailed home across the Dornoch Firth on a Sunday with some furniture which they had bought on the other side, they blamed their trip on a shifting wind which had initially delayed them and then, when it changed on the Sunday, they took advantage of it and sailed home. The Session knew that there was an inn on the north side where they could have stayed until Monday and therefore considered that their conduct was 'very reprehensible' and ordered them to make public repentance. Quite apart from the cost of staying at an inn and a desire to get home, the Session did not allow for the fact that the wind might have changed again and prevented these men's return for even longer. Great offence was caused in that parish at much the same time when the skipper and crew of a boat from Morayshire which had been lying there, 'loosed from the harbour of Portmahomack on the morning of the Lord's Day and carried burdens of victuals and other necessaries.' A couple of local men were in trouble over this too as one had gone on board to see to his employer's grain which had been put on the boat and the other had taken a firlot of grain to it from the storehouse. They were all ordered to be rebuked, with one who refused to submit being remitted to the Presbytery. Some West Kilbride people were called before their Kirk Session in 1802 when it was pointed out to them 'that their going out in boats [to a ship] upon the Lord's Day without any necessity, any of their relations aboard the ship being in good health, and especially carrying goods aboard from boats is a breach of the Sabbath.' On admitting this offence, they were let off very lightly, with nothing more than a rebuke and admonition before the Session as that body wished 'to have this scandal removed by as mild a censure as is in their power, considering an instance of this kind has not happened in this place for many years' but even so this decision was intimated from the pulpit.[50]

Unnecessary travelling overland on Sundays was just as bad as going by boat: 'It is ordained that whatsoever person or persons happen to be found travelling on the Sabbath, either by land or ships to go to sea, shall pay accordingly to their quality a pecunial sum as the Session shall think fit and expedient for the first fault and for the second fault both pecunial and satisfaction according as they transgress' said Montrose Kirk Session in 1649 and in 1663 a Presbytery ordered 'Notice to be taken of those that travel on the Lord's Day' while in 1705 the General Assembly decreed that 'All the brethren of the ministry and other officers of the church are to try to suppress profanation of the Lord's Day by idle vagueing, unnecessary travelling.' It was realised, of course, that there were occasions when people had to be away travelling on Sundays and in 1648 the General Assembly decided that an eye should be kept on them during their absence from home: 'It will be a good remedy against Sabbath breaking by carriers and travellers that the ministers where they dwell cause them to bring testimonials from the place where they reside on Lord's Days wherein they are from home.'[51]

As has already been said, for many people Sunday was the only day that they were free to do certain things but Kirk Sessions paid no regard to their needs. A man who went some fifteen miles one Sunday to see some cattle – not stray beasts – did it because he was unlikely to have time to do so on any weekday, but he had to stand for two Sabbaths as a punishment. A breach of the Sabbath which had aggravated circumstances occurred in St. Andrews in 1643. A man rode to Abdie Kirk, thirteen miles away, on the pretence that he was going to Communion there although the real reason for his journey was because he wanted 'to supplicate at some noble man's handis there for Margaret Balfour being in ward as a witch.' He was probably very lucky to get off with only paying £5 to the poor and acknowledging his fault before the pulpit. Things of course worked both ways and the people were just as stern when a minister transgressed and so Mr Thomas Porteous, incumbent of Nenthorn, Berwickshire, found himself before the Presbytery because he 'had ridden to Ingland' on a Sunday, something which was 'lamented by the brethren', who ordered him to confess publicly on his knees before his parishioners the following Sunday.[52]

Carrying goods or articles, even for a short distance on a Sunday, was a kind of double or even treble Sabbath profanation, combining travel with a form of work and possibly with a view to gain of some sort. In this connection, too, the question of when Sunday ended and Monday began, reared its head with one Kirk Session ordering all burden bearers to carry nothing before 4.00 a.m. on Monday morning, under threat of a penalty of 30s. Scots. Examples of carrying offences include taking plaiding from one place to another, which involved a journey through a different parish; a man who carried kail and barrel hoops on his back from one parish to another in time of service; another who went 'through the parish to the highlands with horse and creels etc'; there was 'caring of timber and packes frae touns and mercates' and carrying a millstone through three parishes, this last offence resulting in a fine of £10 Scots and making repentance in sackcloth. Lesser carrying journeys might just be carrying a cauldron through the streets or taking a peck of bere for ale a couple of miles or so within a parish.[53] An unusual case of carrying happened at Cromarty in 1743: 'carrying away of the corps of Alexander Nicholl on the Lord's Day in time of divine service to another parish where no sermon was that day whereby the people was altogether diverted from hearing sermon, whereby the Lord's Day was prophaned.' Some of these journeys must have involved use of an animal which made the offence worse. When Gilbert Stirling was reported in 1723 to have driven a loaded horse through the parish of Cruden one Sunday, his offence was thought serious enough for witnesses to be called to prove that he had indeed done so. Roads were just beginning to be made in the mid-eighteenth century which may explain why in 1752 the Presbytery of Fordyce and the Synod of Aberdeen ordered steps to be taken to suppress the scandalous custom of carriers travelling on Sundays with loaded carts, wagons and other conveyances to and from places such as Aberdeen and Banff. It seems that sometimes all sense of charity was lost in the kirk's passion for Sabbath observance so that a man in Stow who went on Sunday to visit his sick mother had to appear before the Session for doing so and a man from Lumphanan, Aberdeenshire, was excommunicated in 1785 for 'going to see his mother on a Sabbath day and taking a stone of meal to her.' Fortunately severity over such trips could be tempered with common sense so that when in 1708 John Roy was asked whether he had carried a letter one Sunday, he admitted doing so but said that he had been sent with it by a farmer who told him that it was a matter of life and death, upon which John was absolved. Not so very long before this, in August 1697, the Kirk Session of Ashkirk discovered that some parishioners had been going to Newcastle at the weekends for food and it was intimated from the pulpit that no one should set off for Newcastle on a Saturday and thus fall into the temptation to return on a Sunday. 1697 was during the disastrous Seven Years' Famine and August was the time of year when food supplies were most critical as food ran out and harvest was awaited and it seems surprising that going for food in such a situation was not also regarded as a matter of life and death.[54]

Sunday trading is nothing new, nor is opposition to it. In the 1690s Marion Moore offered sweetmeats for sale on a Sunday. One can well understand how a woman might seek to augment the family income by making a few sweets and trying to sell them on the day when people would be about and seeking little treats – but it is for that offence that her name is recorded forever in the minutes. Other people made all-out efforts to sell far larger goods on Sundays, as when people from Cullen went in 1624 to Fordyce to sell harrows, barrows, ladders and similar articles. Not only that, but people came to Fordyce on Sundays from Inverboyndie bringing cloth to be worked and taking back cloth which had been treated, 'thereby carrying on their trade and market on the Sabbath', and it was left to the ministers of the respective parishes to decide their punishment. In the mid-seventeenth century the problem of Sunday trading was tackled in the parish of Alyth by the Kirk Session summoning the merchants and getting them to promise to sell no goods at all on Sundays between or after sermons, except where something was required for the sick or the burial of the dead, which usually meant bread and tobacco, the staple requirements for lykewakes and funeral meals. An Aberdeen cordiner (shoemaker) was publicly admonished in 1606 for sewing shoes in his booth on a Sunday, because that was trading by use of a craft, and 'niffering' [haggling] or any sort of bargaining also came under the heading of Sabbath profanation. Trading of more professional skills was just as sinful and so it was that in 1649 the Kirk Session of St. Cuthbert's Church, Edinburgh, rebuked and fined several people 20s. each for writing out, subscribing and witnessing bonds that day.[55]

Markets caused a variety of problems so far as the Sabbath went. Well before the Reformation, Parliament passed an Act stating that there should be no markets or fairs in kirkyards or in kirks but even at the beginning of the seventeenth century, the Presbytery of Ellon was trying to stop Sunday markets inside *churches.* The fact was that for some time after the Reformation, the kirk continued to tolerate markets in churchyards, as has been said, partly because there might well be no alternative public open space for them. These markets were a survival of the days when crowds gathered at churches for Roman Catholic religious festivals and food and drink were needed by those attending which was sold to them under the protection of the church, right there in the churchyard which, at that time, would have been little encumbered with gravestones. Gradually the range of what was sold increased until full-scale trading developed. An unusual churchyard market must have been an ancient one held on the green around Christ's Kirk, later annexed to the parish of Kennethmont, Aberdeenshire, unusual in that at one time it was held during the night and became known as the Sleepy Market. There is still evidence in some graveyards of these old trading times such as market crosses within those of St. Peter's, Duffus, and Kinneddar, Michaelkirk and Dallas, all in Morayshire. Dornoch Cathedral's kirkyard has the market cross immediately outside the wall, but that is only because there formerly was no wall and, in addition, it still has in the churchyard the 'plaiden ell', which looks remarkably like a flat gravestone but was something used for measuring plaiden and other materials during markets there. Not only were many markets held in graveyards but, in a good many cases, held there on Sundays and the Old Statistical Account for Fordyce, written in the 1790s, particularly mentions how old people could still at that date remember churchyard markets there on Sundays although Sabbath trading in that particular churchyard had been ended by Rev. Alexander Gallie whose method was simple: he saw a bag of snuff offered for sale and just tossed it out of the churchyard but was fair enough to pay the would-be vendor its value. As he was minister from 1684–1715, this says much for the long memories of the 1790s. Whether in the churchyard or not, to the population at large, Sunday seemed an ideal day for fairs and markets but Parliament thought differently and passed various Acts against markets and trading that day, one of them in 1579 'discharging of mercats and Labouring on sondayis' which ratified an earlier one of 1503.[56] In 1593 Parliament ordered magistrates and Presbyteries to enforce earlier Acts against Sunday markets and ratified this the following year by an Act forbidding profanation of the Sabbath by the selling of goods and increasing the penalties for the offence. In addition, Sunday markets in specific towns were either forbidden or altered by different Acts of Parliament: for instance, in 1587 Crail's market was ordered to be changed from Sunday to Saturday and Forfar's weekly one was changed from Sunday to Friday in 1593 while in 1592, in a very democratic manner, Parliament ordered those living in country towns where markets were held on Sundays to choose another day for them, but not the day of the nearest burgh's market, although it is noteworthy that this Act had to be repeated a hundred years later. Having altered or tried to alter markets from Sundays to other days, Parliament realised that Mondays were not suitable either as people did preparatory work such as setting up stalls and bringing in stock and wares on the Sunday – 'driving a cow towards Kilmarnock fair' on the Sabbath landed one man in trouble for doing just that – and just as goods and stock might be brought in the day before, so they might be removed the day after the market which made Saturday an unsuitable day too. To solve this problem Parliament passed Acts in both 1644 and 1663 ordering no markets to be held in burghs on Saturdays or on Mondays, and in pursuit of the same objective also forbade anyone, in 1656, to travel to or from Sunday markets under threat of a penalty of 10s.[57]

During this time, Presbyteries and Kirk Sessions themselves did what they could to stop these markets. In 1591 the minister and elders in Elgin ordered that St. James Fair, which fell on a Sunday that year, and indeed any other markets which might in future fall on Sundays, should be held on the following Monday but five years later, presumably realising as Parliament was also to realise in time, the problems associated with Monday markets, they decided that markets falling on Sundays should be held over until Tuesdays and additionally they asked all gentlemen and merchants to let them know of any proposed Sunday markets so that something might be done to prevent or postpone them. In 1638 the General Assembly suggested that burgh councils should see to the prevention of Saturday and Monday markets but these efforts, in common with much early legislation, were ineffective and in 1695 Parliament again prohibited markets on Saturdays and Mondays but excluded fleshers. (This was the Act already mentioned as repeating one of 1592.) But such an exemption could itself cause trouble and as late as 1829 the Kirk Session of St. John's, Glasgow, considered that Sundays were being greatly profaned by beasts being brought in to the cattle market that day and asked the minister to draw this to the attention of the Council. As he also wrote to the Lord Provost about it, the Session agreed to wait for a few weeks but if there was no satisfactory result, to present a petition to the Presbytery. A local exemption was made in Elgin in 1649 when the Session and Council ordered Saturday markets to be changed to Fridays but allowed the fish market to continue all week as before and it is to be hoped that the same applied in any community where fishing was important to the economy. In fact, in burghs where trade was of the greatest importance, there was little that the church could do to control it; when the Synod demanded the end of Saturday and Monday fairs in Selkirk about 1720, the Town Council co-operated to a large extent but insisted on keeping one Saturday Fair and that was that. The best that the kirk could do was to try to influence Parliamentary legislation which was why in 1703 the Synod of Aberdeen expressed the hope that Parliament would remedy one particular form of Sabbath profanation which was worrying them, the carrying of timber on Sundays for 'Munday's Markets'. Throughout all these rulings about markets and fairs, it must be remembered that ministers themselves depended greatly on the produce of their glebes to augment their incomes and to supply their tables and a number were remarkably advanced in their farming ideas and they too needed to buy and sell at markets. It was because of this that one Synod felt it necessary in 1702 to 'prohibit ministers resorting to public markets and fairs unless absolutely necessary, and even, to take care to be seen as little as possible.'[58]

As the cattle droving trade developed in the highlands, it too could cause serious Sabbath profanation. Before the Presbyterian church got a firm hold on the people of the northern areas of Scotland, drovers from these parts cared little for any offence they might give as they passed through southern parishes. In Falkirk, which was a main arrival point for the drove trade, they cheerfully took cattle through the town on any day of the week, including Sundays, and the Kirk Session ordered a Justice of the Peace 'to give an order to a constable to challenge and secure such persons until they find caution to answer as law will for the scandal.' No further complaints were made for several years which may mean that these steps were effective but it could also mean that it was found totally impractical to 'secure such persons' because who then would look after their beasts? Another influx from the highlands of Scotland to the lowlands was in summer when people came south to seek harvest work as 'shearers', which was cutting grain and binding it into sheaves. This meant that not only they but those wanting to employ them, travelled to the various feeing markets or hiring fairs around the country where the terms of any engagement would be settled and plenty of alcohol drunk to seal the bargain. These often fell on a Sunday and Mr John Lauder, minister of Tynninghame, attempted in 1620 to stop anyone planning to engage shearers on that day by ordering them to come to hear preaching but it was 1640 before Parliament ordered both Justices and Kirk Sessions to remedy the abuses caused by hiring shearers on the Sabbath. There were, of course, regular feeing markets, an early form of labour exchange, twice a year for all categories of rural workers and many of these also fell on Sundays – a particularly disgraceful case came before Fenwick Kirk Session when someone went to Mearns market to be feed not just on a Sunday but on a Communion one. A case which seems to have arisen either out of feeing markets or the result of hiring casual workers occurred in Banff in the summer of 1701:

> The Session considering that there has been much scandall given by entertaining Hiremen in alehouses on the Sabbath Day, when they meet in companies to drink, do hereby appoint and order with consent of the Magistrates that no change-keeper [inn-keeper] shall entertain hired servants on the Lord's Day in companies for drinking under the strictest penalties and the same to be intimated from the Latern which was done accordingly.[59]

People living on the coasts depended greatly on the sea for fish both to eat and to sell, while the shores provided bait, shellfish and a working area for drying fish and nets. In addition, it provided the seaware which has already been mentioned in relation to the time of night when Sunday was considered to have ended. Some of this seaweed was gathered to eat, some was burnt to make kelp but mostly it was collected to manure the land which fisher folk commonly rented from nearby farms, as they came increasingly to rely on potatoes. Tides and weather are no respecters of days of the week and so those who lived by the sea were constantly in trouble for Sabbath profanation; seaware had to be gathered when the tide was low, at whatever hour that was and, for those working elsewhere all week, it was natural to use Sunday as a ware-gathering day. It was always more plentiful after a storm at sea had driven it ashore and in that case, Sunday or not, the people tried to make the most of what Nature had given them and endeavoured to be the ones to get what was most accessible and best. It was because of this that the Kirk Session of Rathven passed an Act in 1723 forbidding gathering of seaweed or of dulse, an edible variety, on Sundays and it seems surprising that when some people were accused of profaning a Sunday by collecting partens, which were edible crabs, in 1730 that they should have said that they were in fact getting 'dilse', but that did not help their case at all and they had to appear before the congregation for their sin. Even to be 'in the wair on the Sabbath' was sufficiently suspicious to warrant being called before the Session to explain what was what.[60]

White fish were caught with baited hooks on long lines but suitable bait might only be found at a distance of several miles and if every one on a line of 800–1000 hooks was to be baited ready for Monday morning's fishing, it was almost essential to get the bait on Sundays or possibly so late on Saturday nights that it encroached on to Sunday, and tides played a part in this too. In 1625 two women in Fife were each ordered to pay 32*d*. Scots 'for gaddering sand eills upon the Sabbath in the morning' to use as bait but not so many years later the penalties laid down in another east coast port were very much stiffer: 'that if there be found any of the fishers gathering beat on the Sabbath day, the masters shall pay for the servants fault as well as for their own, the first fault is 20 shs, the second 40 shs and the third 4 lib and also shall stand in the jougs at the Kirk door and thereafter shall come before the pulpit and make their repentance before the whole congregation, this done with their consent.' It was imperative that fish, once caught, should be prepared quickly so as not to go bad. One way of preserving white fish was to clean, split and salt it and then dry it by laying it on some stony part of the shore or fixing it to boards on a cottage wall to cure in the sun and wind. Obviously this needed good weather and not to take advantage of a fine Sunday was too much for most fisherfolk. After a Session found a man guilty of doing just this, intimation was made 'that fishers should not set forth fish to dry on the Lord's Day.' Many people liked to get in a supply of herring to salt for winter use but to do anything about them on a Sunday was a sin too and a Hawick man who had got such herring and gutted them on a Sunday was duly hauled over the coals even although he pointed out 'that they would spile if lying ungutted till Monday' which would be only too true.[61]

Herring fishing was seasonal, starting off with shoals which appeared off Shetland about May and gradually worked their way south until they were off the English ports of Lowestoft and Yarmouth by the autumn. Not unnaturally, when they appeared offshore there was great anxiety to catch as many as possible while the going was good and people did this every day of the week, something based it seems, on long-standing custom. A Papal Bull of 1451 had stated that by both canon and common law the right of fishing for herring on Sundays was conceded to all the faithful but this was not something with which the Reformers agreed. Their attitude to fishing is evident from the case of a Tynninghame man who tried to excuse himself from a charge of Sabbath-breaking by drying nets; he said that he was only speaking about spreading them to dry as he was walking along the shore but the minister retorted that that in itself was a sin as he should have been thinking about heavenly things. At the same time as this, this minister was making tremendous efforts to stop abuses at the 'draife' as the herring fishing was called, and was so 'heavily grievit' at what was going on that one year he took the kirk officer and some of the elders and set forth for the shore to try to 'preserve the day'. Another year he appealed to Lord Haddington and the Laird of Scoughall to see what they could do about the problem but he found that no authority in the parish was as effective as that of the church and so, in yet another year, after complaining to the Session 'that the civil magistrates were not careful herein as need were', he had a team of churchmen march to the shore after morning service and there they patrolled up and down among the fishermen until midnight. When it was reported to Sorbie Kirk Session in 1700 that some people were going to the herring fishing on Saturdays and Sundays at night 'through which the Lord's Day was broken', similar steps were taken, with four elders appointed 'to use their endeavours to obstruct the same.' Considering the effort which must have been involved in 'obstructing the same' the Session were wise to dismiss the fishermen on their profession of sorrow and on 'engagement never to do the like again' and to leave it at that.[62] As time went on and herring fishing took on a more international character, more impressive steps had to be taken. In the summer of 1851 the Kirk Session of St. Monance were concerned about the approaching fishing season which in previous years had caused 'a grievous amount of Sabbath Desecration, both by foreign ships lying off the coast and by fishermen in this and the neighbouring parishes.' The minister had interviews about it with the French and Belgian Consuls and with the Secretary of the Board of Herring Fisheries 'who entered warmly into his views and asked him to state at length the nature of the desecration, and the mode in which he proposed to put a stop to it.' He prepared a statement of facts and it was agreed that each of the St. Monance elders should sign it and that the ministers and Kirk Sessions of neighbouring parishes should be asked to attest the truth of what he said. Whether this was effective or not is not reported but it certainly showed real effort.[63]

Salmon fishing was particularly prevalent on Sundays and it too was something which, in certain parts of the country anyway, was of long standing. The Papal Bull of 1451 which permitted herring fishing, also expressly allowed salmon fishing in the River Dee on Sundays although this privilege was limited to the five months of the year in which salmon were most common and it was a condition that the first one caught each Sunday must be donated to the parish church. But the Reformers would not accept that either and in the same way that the minister of Tynninghame and his team patrolled the shore to stop herring fishing, so similar watching went on in regard to salmon. It can only have been salmon fishing that was referred to in the minutes of the Kirk Session of St. Nicholas Church, Aberdeen, in 1702. Marginal notes for July that year say 'Burnet and Moorison for the water' which referred to two elders being appointed to 'attend the water of Dee next Sabbath.' The following month, with a margin note of 'Water attended', two other elders 'reported that they attended the water of Dee but found none fishing.' Some people must have been caught and referred to the magistrates, however, as shortly after this the minutes state that 'The Magistrates reported that they fined all such as were given up to them as guilty of fishing on the Lord's Day and that several have already paid their fine.' When it was reported in the Falkirk area that several people 'in Kerse do goe into the water with their netts to take fish upon the Sabbath Day', elders were told to take note of this and a man was found with a 'staff nett upon his shoulder' making his way to the River Carron at 10.00 p.m. one Sunday. The minister of Banchory-Devenick tackled salmon fishing by letting it be known that, according to an earlier Act he, together with some of the elders, was going to watch the water until midnight on Sundays 'to see if any would be so wicked as to fish before that time.' That was in March 1738 and early the next month nine members of the Session watched at several fishing stations; and two weeks later elders and deacons were again instructed to be on watch, with the minister taking two particular beats himself. Some men were caught and ordered to appear on the stool of repentance but failed to do so and were referred to the Presbytery who resolved to excommunicate them. This Kirk Session was one that took a practical and helpful decision in 1750 when they ordered their officer to ring the church bell every Sunday at midnight to let the salmon fishers know when they might begin their work. In 1773 there was some trouble with the bell and the minister ordered its repair. The heritors however refused to pay for it but the minister was able to report to the Session that as a result of an application made during the vacancy and renewed by him, the Presbytery had ordered that the bell should indeed be rung to warn the fishers, whether the heritors liked it or not, and some of them were displeased by this. However, the Session agreed with the steps the minister had taken and decided to pay for the repair themselves. Much earlier, in 1695, the Kirk Session of Tulliallan, Perthshire, paid for a clock to be put into the church steeple because Sabbath-breaking fishermen had sometimes alleged ignorance of the time although there were those who thought that the ringing of the bells could scare herring away from the coasts.[64]

Whenever there might be difficulty about proving certain offences, punishment could always be imposed under the heading of Sabbath profanation so long as the person concerned had done *something* wrong on a Sunday. Catching salmon in rivers was of course poaching although so far as the kirk was concerned, if done on the Lord's Day it was profanation, but as fines for poaching came to the church, no Kirk Session wanted to smother a poaching charge unduly. When three men appeared before Stow Kirk Session for taking fish one Sunday 'on the Gala Water, or some of the streams therewith connected' the matter was treated very seriously, with more than one minister involved, one of whom read extracts from Acts of Parliament 'showing that such things were an open violation of the laws of God and of man and could not be passed unnoticed.' One of the alleged poachers said that all he had done was to catch a fish in the mill run using only his hands when the water was low and he denied that he had used a leister (salmon spear) 'which alone is called fishing in the sense in which he was accused of it', in other words, poaching, but in the end this case seems simply to have fizzled out. The reaction of the Kirk Session of Banchory-Devenick when a delation was made in 1740 that one of the deacons had his mill working before 10.00 o'clock on a Sunday night is interesting in the context of fishing. Although he put the blame on his boy, saying he had set it going too soon and that he would ensure that this did not happen again, the Session nevertheless found that it had caused scandal 'and specially that it had given occasion to the salmon fishers to make a handle of it to justify their wicked practice of fishing on the Sabbath Day' but they delayed any further procedure against him until they might be 'ripely advised thereanent', the outcome of this delay being a deposition from him.[65]

A less common form of fishing was for edible eels, not the sand eels which were used for bait. Although Scottish people did not particularly like eels, they sold well in such countries as Holland and an 'Act anent Eel-fishing' passed by Kinross Kirk Session in July 1701 shows that it must have been a profitable exercise whatever day of the week it was done:

> Taking Eel-fishing to their consideration, the Session finds that it is a manifest breach of Sabbath because they travel miles to it on Saturday nights and fish till Sunday morning when the sun is risen, and go miles back, carry the eels either on their own or on horses' backs or otherwise . . . to such persons as has them taken at a set price and . . . immediately returns to the same Eel-fishing travelling miles, sets their nets on the Sunday afternoon towards night . . .[66]

November 1608 saw a great earthquake which some people attributed to 'the extraordinar drouth in the summer and winter before' but in Aberdeen the Kirk Session accepted it as a 'document that God is angry against the land, and against this city in particular, for the manifold sins of the people' and appointed a solemn fast to be held the next day. One sin that was thought to have particularly contributed to the earthquake was the salmon-fishing that went on on the Dee on Sundays and so the owners of the fishings were rebuked before the Session. 'Some promist absolutely to forebear both by himselfs and their servands in time coming; others promised to forbear upon the condition subscryvant, and some plainly refusit anyway to forbear.' Whether it was superstition or a fear of profaning the Lord's Day, it is said that to rescue a drowning fisherman on a Sunday was considered a sin in some parts of the country. But fishermen must not be thought of as particular profaners of the Sabbath, whether they sought to catch white fish, herrings, salmon, eels or anything else – far from it. They are a deeply religious section of the community and a touching example of this is that when an additional church was built at Cockenzie, East Lothian, in 1838 by private subscription and with financial assistance from several outside sources, the fishermen who were desperately anxious to have this church near to their homes but were totally unable to contribute to its building or the support of its minister, felt that the only way in which they could show how much it mattered to them was by making sure that they were present for its opening although this meant delaying their departures to the northern herring fishing for several days, even although the wind was favourable and in spite of the great importance of this fishing to them.[67]

Millers and salters also attracted the attention of the General Assembly and of Parliament because they so frequently worked on Sundays. In 1638 the Assembly recommended to Presbyteries to use some of its old Acts concerning Sabbath breaking by going to mills, salt pans and such places, and thereafter Parliament joined in efforts to stop such work. In 1639 Sunday working in salt-pans and mills was forbidden by law while in 1648 Parliament decreed that anyone working in mills, kilns or salt-pans (or fishing) between midnight and midnight was to be regarded as profaning the Sabbath and yet another Act of Parliament in 1661 referred to a penalty of £20 Scots for going to mills. Parliament passed these laws but left it to the kirk to hand them down the line until they got to parish level where pulpit intimations were duly made, such as one in 1644 which informed the congregation 'that no mills grind on the Sabbath, under pain of censure, penalty and repentance.'[68]

The forms of Sabbath profanation so far mentioned have had to do with domestic life and everyday work, but although Scotland became well known for strict Sabbatarianism, this did not start immediately after the Reformation. For some forty or more years after it, Sunday recreation was permitted and even as late as 1618 the king made a declaration that no lawful recreation should be barred to the people on Sundays or other holy days. In fact, it seems to have been at the very end of the sixteenth and during the very early years of the seventeenth centuries that the church developed a forbidding attitude which made any form of relaxation a matter for censure. There is a distinct note of injury in the words of David Wemyss, in trouble with the Kirk Session of St. Andrews in 1599 for dancing on Trinity Sunday when he said that 'he never saw that dancing was stayed before.' 'Riding a race on the common haugh' was one such recreation and games that rate a mention in Kirk Session minutes because they were denounced as Sabbath profanation include pennystane or pennie-stone, which was quoits; putting the stone; bowls; and also football which in 1659 led to the public rebuke of some young people who played it one Sunday afternoon but only to a reproof for some young men who played it on the links about the same date, 'seeing they were very penitent.' There was also knottie or shinty and nine holes, the game of nine-men's morris, in which a ball has to be bowled into nine holes in the ground or on a board; kyles were skittles or ninepins or games played with them. 'Gameing by the Bob and penny stave' went on and golf was a popular game. In addition, a game called cheaw or chew also appears in the records of Elgin but it has been impossible to discover what it was; and many of these games were not just played on Sundays but during worship too. A great scandal was caused in Buckie when youngsters were caught skating one Sunday, and playing with kites in St. Andrews resulted in the Kirk Session recommending the offender to be punished by the magistrates. Two Hawick men who walked about on stilts 'thereby causing crowds of bairns to follow them' had to make repentance on their knees and 'playing at carts' and 'playing at the coppiehoal at the kirk door on Saboth' brought those who had played before their Session. What fun children must have had 'playing bogill about the stacks' on a Sunday, but the kirk was not amused.[69]

'Killing and hounting hairs on Sabboth,' catching laverocks (larks) and fishing for trout were all sports which got people into trouble on Sundays. The case of a man who killed a fish one Sunday by throwing a stone at it from a bridge and then went into the water to get it, throws an interesting light either on the number of fish there must have been in the water at the time or on the astonishing accuracy of his stone-throwing. A touching case of Sabbath profanation occurred in an Orkney parish in the summer of 1717. John Weilie was delated for being 'guilty of Sabbath breach in sporting himself with a little play ship, or some such childish fancy, and his taking down a boat near the time that divine worship was beginning, in order to recover his play ship.' He admitted taking a boat to recover it because it was his son's, 'alleging he did it out of pity for the weeping child', but his kindly action resulted in him having to make satisfaction before the congregation.[70]

Music, which was thought to lead to many abuses at the best of times, was a particular sin on the Sabbath. A man confessed that he had played his 'pyp' one Sunday night and a woman admitted having a piper playing in her house but not, she said, 'upon the gait' – outside in the street – obviously thinking that what she did in her own house was her own affair. 'Young women and lasses' found singing and dancing after supper on Sundays in Perth were forbidden to do so in future and at the same date the records of Elgin show that a man gave caution that a girl would not dance on Sundays while employed by him, and the same condition was laid down for six other girls at the same time. In 1826 'a subject of very great importance . . . the martial music with which the public are entertained on the evenings of the Lord's Day' caused the minster of St. John's Church, Glasgow, to write to the army commander, Colonel Duffy, saying that although he knew the band was confined within the barrack yard, yet 'I need not tell you that it has a much wider influence.' The Colonel, however, was having none of that and replied saying that on his arrival he had been told that so long as regimental music was not played as the soldiers returned from worship, then it would be acceptable to the people. He pointed out that it was played softly and added, 'Surely no inhabitant who has ever witnessed the thousands of stragglers on the green of the town at the same hour, doing as much mischief as possible, need think of going into the barrack yard to find fault with a few quiet people listening to the band.'[71]

One of the great pleasures of Sunday church-going, especially for those from outlying areas, was the opportunity it gave to enjoy a bit of gossip and chat, what one Kirk Session referred to as 'worldly and vagging converse', but the freedom from work that day also encouraged 'meeting and talking together in the streets both in time of public worship and after the samen is over' and 'needless confluences of people on the Sabbath'. It could be Sabbath profanation when people 'frequent each others houses unnecessarily, and by walking abroad in the fields; and particularly in the evening of the Lord's Day severals going into their neighbours houses and there sinfully diverting one another' as one Kirk Session put it, while another complained of people 'walking in the fields in cabals, and sitting in cabals without [outside] doors' and going to visit one another when there was no need for such visits unless there was sickness. Parliament passed an Act in 1656 forbidding unnecessary walking about in churches, churchyards or elsewhere during the time of worship, and the afternoon walk, which came to be a particular feature of Scottish family life on Sundays, was for many years regarded as something wrong. 'Resorting in crowds to the shore or gathering together in Knots on the streets, at their doors or Closeheads and also by going a vaging through the fields in simmer tyme in fair weather' sounds harmless but was forbidden, although when Hawick people were told in 1713 that they must not walk about in groups after church as they were in the habit of doing, they not only continued to do so but also went in crowds for country walks, what the minutes called 'betaking themselves to the fields on the Lord's Day after divine worship in crowds for discoursing anent their secular affairs.'[72] Banff Kirk Session decided that people 'should avoid wandering on the Sabbath days after noon (this being reported by some of the members as very unbecoming.)' Vaging or extravaging was idle wandering, something concerning which the General Assembly passed an Act in 1705, requiring all ministers and other officers of the church to try to suppress it. An unusual term was applied to a man in the island of Coll found 'straggling' on a Sunday: 'It's remarkable that Charles – straggles from place to place on the Lord's Day,' say the minutes in 1735. The appointment of inspectors to discover those absent from worship has already been mentioned but because how the rest of Sunday was spent mattered too, the General Assembly ordered in 1648 that elders should not only pay heed to how people attended church but also 'how the time is spent before, betwixt and after public worship.' Because of the varied ways in which people liked to enjoy themselves on Sundays, the inspectors' duties extended over much of the day so that in addition to the usual tour during the time of services there might 'also be the like method observed in the afternoon when worship is over, for visiting the streets, the shore and other places of resort, where idle people are wont to resort on the Lord's Day.' So zealous were the inspectors that one may well wonder whether their activities were not sometimes Sabbath profanation too.[73]

An outward appearance of good behaviour on a Sunday could give rise to suspicions that all was not well within doors and to satisfy themselves about this, elders visited houses not just during but also after services. The visiting of houses implied a right of entry: in 1709 a minister and some of his elders went on a tour of inspection during the time of worship and found a house door shut but could hear people inside and knocked, but could get no answer. The man of the house said later that he had not been well but he was rebuked before the Session and 'ordered to give access to the elders when they knock at his door and exhorted to wait upon public worship.' On that same tour of inspection, a woman was seen at the door of her house but she hurried inside when she saw who was coming and would not let the minister and his companions in although they knocked several times and she, too, was later told to give access in future. About the same date it was announced from the pulpit in Falkirk that on Sundays elders would 'visit families as they shall think fit . . . and in caice they shall be refused access, the civil magistrate's concurrence will be given to make patent doors', meaning that they had to be patent or open, and where they were not, the elders would enlist civil powers to gain entry. People could hardly be blamed for keeping doors closed against these intrusions which, while well intended, were positively offensive. Janet Yett, wife of John McNeil, was delated for keeping her door fast against the visitors during the time of a Sunday afternoon service. It was only with difficulty that they finally got access to the house and 'saw a man smoking tobacco through the keyhole of the door of a chamber which she would by no means open to them.' At the next Session meeting, she admitted that people had been in that room drinking and smoking but promised that it would never happen again. She was rebuked before the Session and warned that any repetition would result in a public rebuke – but what a picture it conjures up, of elders with their eyes to a keyhole in their pursuit of sin. St. Andrews Kirk Session went so far as to propose that no husband should kiss his wife, nor mother her child on the Sabbath, interference in private life which was as excessive as it was ludicrous and it is hardly surprising that people sometimes rebelled against the inspections associated with it. One was Andrew Tennent, a vintner in Edinburgh, who was found by the inspectors to have several people eating and drinking in a room with him and was delated for 'upbraiding the visitors when searching on Sunday the 15th instant in time of afternoon's sermon by saying to them, "I know not what you are seeking, ye are nothing but impertinent idle fools"', but his outburst availed him nothing and he was referred to one of the magistrates as a result.[74]

Unpleasant although all this was, there could on occasions be good secular reasons for knowing what was going on while the majority of the population was at church and it was because of 'many crying sins' carried out during the time of worship, including breaking into a poor widow's home and stealing most of her possessions, that the Kirk Session of Fordyce decided that inspections should take place to see what anyone not in church was up to. Children's Sabbath conduct has already been mentioned once or twice in this chapter but their behaviour also led to a particular need for watching. In Cromarty in 1681 it was reported that children were going through the streets on Sundays swearing and generally being a nuisance and, in addition to speaking to their parents about this, the Session decided that an elder should go through the streets to stop it happening in future. Kirkcudbright Kirk Session gave 'power also to the searchers to take notice of all children . . . that shall be found unnecessarily vaging on the streets or keeping at home on the [Sabbath day] . . . declaring hereby that the parents of the children thereof guilty shall be proceeded against for their children as said is, and ordains publication hereof to be made before the congregation . . . that none pretend ignorance.' In 1709 the elders of Kinross who visited the town before, during and after worship, found all sorts of abuses going on and also 'children not being refrained from playing on the streets' and the heads of the offending households and the parents of the children were warned that in any future cases they would be summoned and censured. In Govan two men, both from Partick, were exhorted 'to educat and instruct their bairnes better and nowayes suffer them to abuise the Sabbath Day' by playing, swearing and staying away from church. A remarkable example of supervision of children by a Kirk Session was partly, though not entirely, 'so as to prevent any disorders or abuse by them, especially on the Lord's Day.' In May 1703 the Dean of Guild and Convener members of the Session were appointed by the Kirk Session of Banff to make up lists of all poor idle children in the town that they could 'be disposed upon by their parents and the Kirk Session to apply some lawful calling.' The following month the minutes show that 'the Session being constituted, the lists of the above mentioned boys were brought in and the Magistrates did undertake to dispose of them so as to prevent any disorders . . .'[75]

The immediate reaction of the kirk in Aberdeen to the earthquake of 1608, which has already been mentioned, was to accept it as a judgment on the people for their sins and, in that particular case, especially the sin of salmon fishing on Sundays. Any disaster was attributed to God's anger with the people and as has been said in relation to famines, the only way of expiation was a fast to show repentance, to pray for forgiveness and to ask that whatever trouble had befallen the people might be lifted. That was why Aberdeen followed up its immediate reaction with the holding of a fast, but such fasts, which made weekdays equivalent to Sundays, were totally separate from the pre-Communion fasts which began to be held from about the late seventeenth to the early eighteenth centuries. Any expected or actual agricultural or other calamity held great potential for disaster and many fasts were held to try to avert such things – a fast day was held in Yetholm in 1866 to try to ward off cattle plague, for instance, and some two hundred years earlier, Innerwick Kirk Session, East Lothian, ordered one because of the anticipated destruction by bad weather of the crops, something they associated with an apparent lack of piety among the people. In 1694 the Burgh Council of Lauder ordered a fast, obviously with the active co-operation of the Kirk Session, because of the 'great contempt of the Gospel, abuse of peace and plenty, profanity, error and other sins . . . which did provoke God to kill many of the beasts by the long storm and most sharp frost of the last winter and to threaten the loss almost of plowing and seed time by the great coldness of the spring.' Almost inevitably a service of thanksgiving was held once the trouble had passed, the origin of modern Harvest Thanksgivings, and thanksgiving days were treated as fast days.[76]

Many fasts and thanksgivings were ordered by higher church courts, by Parliament or by royal command when there was felt to be national need for them. In 1645 a public thanksgiving was ordered 'to be keepit and maid for the great victorie at Philiphauche' – Philiphaugh near Selkirk, where a bloody battle had been fought – and one Kirk Session recorded the event thus: '19th October 1645. This day the publick thanksgiving weill keepit, praised be God for the notable and great victories never to be forgot at Philiphauche, quherin James Graham and his forces were utterlie defaitt and overthrawin, we thank the Lord God of our Salvation through Jesus Chryst therefor forevir.' The Kirk Session records of Petty in

1648 show an official fast held to ask God to move the king's heart to peace and unity with his subjects, to which was added a request that God would remove the extraordinary rain which threatened universal famine. Fasts were held during all sorts of national emergencies, including one in June 1651 when Scotland was about to send men into England to fight 'for kirk and kingdom'. When the Dutch war of Charles II broke out in 1665 a national fast was held for the king's naval forces and to ask for success to the venture, followed, a month later, by thanksgiving for success. In 1715, at the start of the Stuart risings, the General Assembly ordered a fast and solemn day of prayer and humiliation that God might be pleased to disappoint the designs of those intending to invade the kingdom, and the following year Kirk Session minutes from non-Jacobite parts of the country record services of thanksgiving 'for the gracious deliverance wrought by God in this land and church by suppressing the late Godless and unnatural rebellion raised in favour of the popish pretender.' May 1661 saw a national thanksgiving for the restoration of the king but one minister cautioned the congregation in this instance against observing it as 'a sacred festival or anniversary holyday' and therefore on a level with the Sabbath, although the fact that he did not conform to Episcopacy which was reintroduced then and in consequence left the parish the following year, perhaps coloured his attitude to this particular day of thanksgiving. National epidemics were another reason for fasts; one was enjoined in 1587 to start on a Saturday and last for eight days in the hopes of averting plague then in and around Edinburgh and Leith. In September 1665 a public fast was held in Scotland because of the Great Plague in England in hopes of preventing it coming to Scotland and similar concern was shown in 1720 with a fast ordered by the church for the plague, then raging in France, along with the thanksgiving in 1723 at the end of that outbreak. In 1691 the king and queen ordered a summer fast to be held on the last Wednesday of every month from June to November, something which cannot have been popular with rural people in particular as these were especially busy months in the country. At a more local level, the Presbytery of Glasgow ordered a fast in 1598 'for eschewing of the Pest within this cuntrey' and the Kirk Session minutes of Bo'ness, West Lothian, for 30 July 1696 give detailed reasons for a local fast there. After the minister had consulted some of the Presbytery, he and the elders gave consideration to the state and condition of the parish and decided that they should have a fast for the following reasons: to 'offer to engage their hearts to the Lord and walk before him in the narrow way of holiness and newness of life'; because they realised that some people 'pretend to be professors and yet now fear' and they also wished to show their gratitude for the many mercies, both spiritual and temporal conferred upon them, especially being saved from dangers such as the 'sea and cruel enemies' when people could have been 'swallowed up by the raging sea'. They realised that they were not 'so tender and humble' as they should be and admitted that there were 'great animosities' between some families and individuals 'which doe give great advantage to an ensnaring Devil.' Although God had not only called them by his Word and visited some with his rod in the form of sickness and pain, deaths of children and poverty, 'yet many still do not turn to the Lord.' In addition, 'scandalous and debauched persons' were being passed over without appropriate punishment, several cases of immorality had not been taken note of by those whose duty it was to stop and punish them and there was little worry about the many horrid sins which abounded in the land and while people cared plenty for their own concerns, there was no thought for the things of Christ. This was a comprehensive list and for all these reasons, a day of fasting was considered the appropriate way to approach God and to try to turn the people back to righteous ways. That was a sincere and repentant fast as most fasts were, but there is always an exception to prove every rule and occasionally a fast could be held, at local level, for trifling reasons. A story is told of one old minister who was displeased with his son who had been appointed as his assistant and successor and who intimated a 'day of solemn fasting, my frien's, for yere ain sins, for my sins, and for our Jock's sins.'[77]

Fasting and humiliation meant what it said. Apart from breakfast, no food was eaten unless it was necessary for health reasons, no work was done other than such essentials as milking cows and feeding stock, there was meant to be no conversation and, as on Sundays, all thoughts were meant to be of holy things. Both Aberdeen and Perth have records of prohibition of marriages during times of fasts but people could slip through this net, even though they might be caught in the end. Thus it was that in the early 1580s two Perth women had to make repentance because during a time of fasting 'they passed up at once to their feasting and solemnising of marriage, contrary to good order.' During a time of fasting there was always at least one service each day in church, perhaps more, and profanation of a fast day or a thanksgiving day was regarded as profaning the Lord's Day. It seems rather surprising that on just one fast day in the parish of Tarbat, Ross-shire, not only had a local man yoked his horse and brought in his grain and a fisherman had gathered bait on the shore, but square wrights from another parish had been 'employed in making up the wright work of a storehouse' and spent the evening 'in binding and putting up the couples of the roof of the said storehouse.' What a day of profanation it was and the outcome was reproof by the Kirk Session for the local men while the wrights were referred to their home Session.[78]

Although the General Assembly had ordered in 1710 that all ministers and members of the kirk must religiously observe all fasts and thanksgivings appointed by the church or the civil authorities, for one reason or another these were not necessarily welcomed by those expected to keep them. Three prominent Dornoch men, for example, ignored the national fast ordered in 1715 – two of them had 'their tennents lead home their fewel on the said day' and the other, Sir John Gordon of Embo, moved house, all which was referred to the Presbytery before whom they expressed regret and it was left at that. Thanksgivings could be made to serve a double purpose, such as discovering who had secretly supported what was considered to be a wrongful cause. Orphir Kirk Session has the following entry in the minutes for 7 June 1716, the day appointed for a thanksgiving for the defeat of the Jacobite rebels: '. . . and the minister having from the pulpit, after sermon, called on the names of the heads of families to see who were absent, did give up a list of such to the session who appointed them to be cited' and three days later these people were rebuked and exhorted to keep better order while the magistrate fined each of them 20s Scots.[79]

After two days of continuous rain in October 1621 the River Tay rose and flooded much of the town of Perth and not only did the minister have the church bell rung and exhorted the people to repent but afterwards the Town Council and the Kirk Session, in a very practical piece of thanksgiving, ordered a voluntary collection to show their gratitude to God for their deliverance, the money going to the poor except for some which was given to Charles Rollock, a boatman, 'for his dangers, pains and efforts in saving many people's lives'. At a later stage it was not unusual for thanksgiving to be combined with a good cause; one held in 1828 for 'the late abundant harvest' was linked with a collection for the Scottish Missionary Society.[80]

But things changed in regard to Sundays, fast days and thanksgivings. By the end of the eighteenth century it became as fashionable for the tenantry to stay away from worship as it had formerly been to attend. By then the sin of Sabbath profanation was also somewhat modified with the General Assembly in 1794 repeating the various Acts of Parliament concerning it but nevertheless advising Presbyteries to deal with it in 'such a prudent manner as shall seem best calculated for checking the further profanation of the Holy Sabbath' and forbade Kirk Sessions to try such cases themselves. According to H. G. Graham, the factors which contributed to this general wind of change began between 1707–50: there was the union of the Scottish and English Parliaments in 1707 which began to break up the austere religious character of Scotland; linen and woollen trades took up people's attention; other industries gave work at home and foreign trade gave outlets for energy and travel while agricultural improvements gave new interests. So long as there had been social stagnation, people's thoughts remained in old grooves but as they changed their ideas of work, and indeed dress, so they changed their ways of thinking. The various secessions which occurred weakened the authority of the established church and as the Industrial Revolution developed and grew, it drew people into the anonymity of large towns. In the latter half of the nineteenth century, railways offered people the chance to go for expeditions on Sundays, which also contributed to a fall in church attendance. The kirk was of course very averse to Sunday train services and did all it could to prevent them starting, working on a policy of giving encouragement to those companies which avoided profaning the Sabbath in this way. In 1847 a memorial addressed to the Board of the Edinburgh and Glasgow Railway, which came before Kirk Sessions, approved the Board's resolution to put an end to the running of Sunday trains and expressed the hope that the Board would adhere to this. In the same way, in 1840 the Kirk Session of Kilmarnock High Church was one of those that had approved an address to the Directors of the Glasgow and Greenock Railway Company and the Glasgow, Paisley, Kilmarnock and Ayr Railways, congratulating them on not operating on Sundays and they also sent a memorial, prepared by Sir Andrew Agnew, to the Post Master General asking him to avoid anything that would involve Sunday work. Excursion steamers also posed great problems on Sundays. Aberdour in Fife was one place 'where during the summer the village is crowded with visitors who desecrate the day by pleasure-seeking' but in spite of all of this, by 1830 Sabbath observance again increased, partly through lay influence and various revivals. Later it died down once more so that by the end of 1931 the total membership of the Church of Scotland was 1,280,620 while at the end of 1989 the total membership was 804,468, with 458,421 attending Communion at least once a year.[81]

17

The Lord's Supper

Some time in the early part of the seventeenth century a Falkirk man was accused of 'misbehaviour and trublance to the kirk upone Pasche Day by louping in at a windo after the dores were clossit and the sermoun begun.' He explained that he had done this because he earnestly desired 'to hear the word of God preached and to communicat of the Sacrament' and this the Session accepted on his promise that he would never do such a thing again. To leap into church through a window in order to receive Communion shows the tremendous importance which the Sacrament held in this man's life and so indeed it did in the lives of many people. Because of the Reformed church's suppression of saints' days and festivals, the only great occasion of the church year that was left was the Lord's Supper. So far as social life went, the ordinary people had few regular events to look forward to, apart from the New Year and an odd fair or two, and Communion came to be such a high spot of the calendar that farm workers often made the number of Communions that they could attend a part of their bargain with an employer.[1]

Holy Communion went under a variety of names, many of which expressed the great importance, indeed awe, felt about it. The Lord's Supper, possibly with qualifying adjectives, is the commonest term, but it might also be called The Occasion, The Solemnity, the Great Work, the Sacred Solemnity or the Sacramental Solemnity. More rarely the term Eucharist or the Holy Eucharist was used and at Peebles, in 1673, the wording was 'the blessed memorial of our Saviour's death and passions'.[2]

As soon as it was decided that the Lord's supper should be celebrated in any parish, this was intimated from the pulpit so that everyone could get into a state of readiness. One minister not only told his elders that they should prepare themselves 'for partaking of that solemn ordinance' but that they should take particular inspection of the morals of the people that no one who was scandalous in their lives or careless in attending the ordinances of the Gospel might be admitted to that solemn, sealing ordinance. It came to be expected that elders should try to get people to make up quarrels before taking Communion: because 'the giveing of

Communion Approacheth' one minister begged the elders to be 'careful in their several quarters to search who are at variance and discord with their neighbours and either reconcile them or els delait them to the session to the end that those who are contumacious and will not be reconciled may be debard from coming to the table of the Lord.' Where it was well known that certain people were at odds with one another, elders might be given specific instructions to speak to them about it and give an account of how they had got on. Some elders who found themselves in this position in 1709 were able to report 'that Margaret Young and Agnes Burt were fully reconciled to each other' and a few days later were also able to say that 'for aught they could learn' they had successfully brought two couples 'to a good understanding'. So strongly was the need for harmony felt to be at the time of Communion that a woman who gave 'ill wordis' to another and then took Communion 'unreconceillit' had to make repentance the next Sunday. Had Communion achieved nothing else – although it did – this alone would have been valuable.[3]

Just as religious knowledge was expected of those seeking marriage for themselves or baptism for their children, so it was considered even more necessary for those hoping to partake of the Lord's Supper and so special catechising was carried out in parishes prior to it. Catechising is defined as instruction by question and answer, questioning as to belief, or systematic examination by questioning. It was meant, of course, to be a regular feature of parish life and was never intended to be only a pre-Communion exercise although in some parishes that is what it obviously was, with the result that in 1639 the General Assembly 'appointed that every minister besides his paines on the Lord's Day, shall have weekly catechism of some part of the paroch and not altogether cast over the examination of the people till a little before Communion.' Leaving catechising too late could mean that there might be insufficient time to fit it all in before the Lord's Supper, something which happened in the parish of Ellon in 1670 where it was complained that the time the minister had allowed for it was 'too scrimpe and short for such ane numberous and vaste congregation in catechising of some of which, it is given out he is too superfitiall.' Where for one reason or another it proved impossible to catechise would-be Communicants prior to Communion, ways had to be found round the problem. This could be done by asking only those who actually wished to communicate to come to be tested by the minister and elders, at the same time requesting those who were ignorant or under scandal 'to forbear to offer themselves for trial', although those guilty of some offence but who were truly repentant and qualified in knowledge could be accepted. Alternatively would-be Communicants were sometimes allowed to come 'with their elders to testify for them' in order to qualify for admission to the Lord's Table.[4]

All this meant that the people had to learn the Catechism, the Commandments and the Creed and in 1649, in furtherance of this, the General Assembly not only sought to enforce diets of catechism but decreed that every minister, with the help of his elders, should see that in every house where there was anyone who could read – an important condition – there should be at least one copy of the Shorter and

Larger Catechisms, the Confession of Faith and the Directory of Family Worship. One of the earliest books of catechism was prepared by John Calvin, 'The Catechisme or maner to teach children the Christian religion, wherein the minister demandeth the question, and the child maketh answere', but there were others as well. A book containing several catechisms lists that one and also a 'Little Catechism' of Calvin's; the Palatine Catechism; Davidson's Catechism'; one by John Craig, and a shorter one by him described as 'ane forme of examination before Communion, approved by the General Assembly of the Kirk of Scotland, appointed to be used in families and schooles . . . 1590.' Also included are two metrical Latin catechisms of Pont and of Adamson, and an English metrical one which seems to have been a very early product of the Reformation and may have been the work of the Wedderburns. While not a true catechism in the way the word is usually understood, nevertheless as a piece of rhythmic instruction, it is one. Such books were not necessarily easy to obtain but some Kirk Sessions, at any rate, did what they could to help. In 1650 in Ceres elders went round distributing copies of the Shorter Catechism in their districts while in 1648 the minister of Tynninghame went through the parish himself selling 'buiks of private worship and mutual edification' and managed to dispose of thirty copies at 2s. Scots each, but with the best will in the world, there must still have been many cottages with neither books nor anyone able to read.[5]

In spite of the Act of General Assembly of 1639, the Assembly found it necessary in 1648 to order once again that ministers should catechise one day each week, 'wherein they may also baptise and lecture', which had the advantage of providing the already-mentioned form of service which provided a suitable occasion for christenings. Even so, ministers at that date were not very keen about catechising and the very next year the General Assembly stated that diets of it were 'much slighted and neglected by many ministers throughout the kingdom' and all the clergy were directed so to order 'their catechetick questions as thereby the people . . . may at every dyett heere the chief heads of saving knowledge, in short view presented to them.' To ensure that this was done, Presbyteries were required 'to take trial of the ministers within their bounds at least every half year and if they find any who are neglectful, that they admonish them for the first fault, rebuke them sharply for the second, and if that does not make them amend, they shall be suspended.' The truth was that it was not easy for ministers to get round their flocks, nor for people to come to a central point as regularly as the General Assembly wished, for the reasons given in earlier chapters in relation to churchgoing, baptism and marriage. 'Visitation of families not observed because the water could not be crossed,' say the minutes of one Kirk Session in 1717 and, such travelling difficulties apart, at certain times of the year the people were too busy on the land which at best, could only provide them with a subsistence living, and so the same minutes some five years later stated that 'this being the seed time there is an intermission of examination', as catechising was often called, and it was the same at harvest time and during the fishing season.[6]

Although children did not partake of Communion, they were not exempt from catechising, which in time became a great feature of Scottish life. In 1570, only ten years after the Reformation, an Act of General Assembly laid down how this should be done:

> Anent the tryall of young children, and how they are brought up by thair parents in the trew religion of Jesus Christ, it is ordainit, that ministers and elders of the kirks shall, universallie within this realm take tryall, and examine all young children within thair presbyteries that are come to nyne years, and that for the first time; thereafter when they are come to twelve years for the second time; the third time to be examined when they are of fourteen years, where through it may be knawne what they have profited in the schoole of Christ from time to time; and that thair names may be written up by the ministers and elders of thair parishes.

After the General Assembly's Act of 1639, it became understood that the parish minister could claim a right of entry to every house in the parish at least once a year to see to the catechising of children and servants – this of course was different to the right of entry demanded for Sabbath inspections. In 1579 Parliament had tried to encourage the dissemination of religious knowledge by decreeing that all householders worth 300 merks of yearly rent in land or goods should have a Bible and a psalm book, under a penalty of £10 Scots, and every parish was ordered to advance £5 towards a copy of the Bible 'weel and sufficientlie bund in paste and timmer.'[7] So far as the household Bibles were concerned, by 1580 the minutes of one Kirk Session show that they were assiduously following up the Act of Parliament by appointing someone to search every house in the parish and not only see the books but also see that they were marked with their 'ain name'. Could they have feared that the books might be passed from house to house in advance of the official's visits? The General Assembly Act of 1639, already quoted, also ordered that the head of every household should catechise the children and servants and that the minister and the elders who assisted him in visiting families, should take note of whether or not this was done. At a time when few people could read the only way in which most of them could learn was by verbal instruction and the best place for that, if done adequately, was in the home; but compulsory family worship must have been very difficult for householders who themselves could not read and even when younger members of the family could do so, it was not thought proper that they should presume to conduct family worship. Only the head of the family was meant to do so but prayers at least should have been within their scope as they were meant to be spontaneous. The ceremony of 'taking the Books' for family worship, particularly on Sunday evenings, which occurred well within living memory, was a product of the Act of General Assembly of 1639.[8]

The people's inability to read was a problem for so long that ways around it had to be found, something which has been referred to in the preceding chapter. In Aberdeen in 1578 the reader, whose real job was to read for an hour prior to the minister's arrival in church, was ordered to read a portion of catechism too 'and the bairns shall answer him.' In 1604 the reader there was instructed to repeat at the end of prayers on Sundays and on weekdays the Ten Commandments and the

Creed so that the people might get to know them by constant repetition. In Kinnell two boys were instructed to stand up during the interval between services on Sundays and answer questions from the Shorter and Larger Catechisms 'in a distinct voice' while in the island of Coll it was the bellman who had to repeat the questions of the Shorter Catechism every Sunday before worship. Even now, in a few churches, for instance Edrom, the Commandments and the Lord's Prayer may be found written up on large boards on either side of the pulpit, prominently displayed for all to see and learn, and many churches formerly had these and/or Scripture texts on boards or on the wall itself.[9]

It was soon found, however, that it was far better to give instruction at regular 'diets' of catechising in the church or some other suitable place and fairly soon after the General Assembly Act of 1570 'anent the tryall of young children', some parishes began to hold these in church on Sundays between morning and afternoon worship, something primarily designed for youngsters. Around 1656 it was the practice of the minister of Ceres to order different groups of people, on a district rather than an age basis, to remain behind each Sunday after morning service for catechising – the rest of the congregation could stay for it if they wished – and this became fairly general. This instruction was not in fact usually given by the minister but by catechists who began to be employed by Kirk Sessions and who were often the parish readers as well. Their duties were to read the Scriptures to young and old, to teach the people the catechism and to hear them repeat it. It was not for catechists to explain things, useful though this might have been; that was regarded as something for the ministry and no one else but it must have been hard for a catechist of any intelligence to have to refuse to clarify something when people asked about it. During a vacancy when there was no minister to guide the congregation, Murdo Macleod, catechist at Tarbat, Ross-shire, was summoned before the newly-formed Presbytery of Tain because of his zeal in trying to answer questions people asked about the Scriptures. He had unfortunately also offended by singing a different tune from the precentor's, which must have been very distracting, and as a result of both sins was discharged from his office of catechist and ordered to appear before the congregation in sackcloth. Although most parishes had just one catechist, a very large one might require two. This happened in Dornoch in 1739 because of 'the spaciousness of the parish and the number of catechisable persons which are such that any one person is not able to instruct them sufficiently.' The two were expected to work 'one in each end of the parish', receiving £4 10s. Scots per half year each for their efforts. The parish of Kilninian and Kilmore found a similar solution but used a different title for what was just a catechist. In 1767 the minister and one catechist found themselves 'unable to overtake the instructing of all the people in the principles of Religion in their course of Catechising' and decided to have 'some other persons going about from house to house whose only business it shall be to teach the Questions of the Shorter Catechism to all that shall be willing, and especially to the young children through the parish.' A suitable man was suggested for the post and appointed 'Question-man' with the task of going round the parish as the minister directed, 'to stay one night in each gentleman's and tenant's house and be at pains to teach the questions of the Assembly's Shorter Catechism to such as shall attend him overnight and in the daytime to the children in that quarter where he shall happen to be, and the Session promises him one Guinea in the twelve-month for wages out of the box and that he shall be maintained by the people.' This designation of question-man seems to be unusual if not unique although that of catechist was very common, but apart from lodging with parishioners, their work and treatment by the Session was for all practical purposes the same. The following July the question-man complained about his low wage and 'considering how useful he is in the parish' the Session gave him 'by way of encouragement' an additional 5s stg., at the same time 'declaring themselves satisfied with his diligence.' When he died a replacement was appointed but in December 1772 the poor's funds were low and the Session decided that they could not 'afford the high wages which has been promised to the present Question man, and that through the summer season he cannot be of any good service to the people because of the shortness of the nights' – which meant that the people would be working outside – 'and therefore they appoint that for the future he officiate only through the winter half-year and have for his wages 15 shillings each season.' In less than a year it was decided that he should 'every day he can attend . . . begin repeating the questions aloud in the kirk whenever the bulk of the congregation are convened and before the minister comes in' in just the way that readers and others did elsewhere and it seems that this particular question-man took over the role of catechist in the end as by 1784 there had been no mention of the catechist for some time.[10]

For reading the catechism in church this second question-man received 30s. stg. per year but, as with other church staff, there were little additions and even although funds had been so low in 1772 that his months of service were reduced, money was still given to him to help him buy shoes, and when the minster paid him the arrears of his wages in 1776 they included '5d heretofore given him for snuff'. All catechists were paid, of course, and such extras as shoes were not unusual. Inverness Kirk Session made special arrangements in 1703 for the man who taught the Gaelic-speakers of the congregation, 'that he that catechises the Irish people shall have 2s Sc out of every burial, also [as] much out of every baptism and 4s Sc out of every marriage', which would have been in addition to any fees going to kirk officers or bellman; and one Session went further and recommended 'to each head of family and tenant to give him a peck of victual for his pains.' Such extras sound generous but the question-man must have suffered by having his summer work cut out and by having wages outstanding and there was always the possibility, as happened to other church staff, that if money was short then the wage itself could be reduced: in July 1784 in the aftermath of the Black Year when the Kirk Session could not even pay for coffins for the poor unless the case was particularly clamant, the question-man's Session 'reserved to themselves the power to pay the Question-man wages in proportion to the smallness of their funds after this date.'[11]

After receiving instruction, from whoever it came, everyone had according to their age to undergo a verbal examination of their knowledge of the catechism. Parishes might be divided into districts for this – the parish of Rothesay, on the island of Bute, was broken up into four quarters in 1658 and the people of each quarter were expected to present themselves when told to do so at the church or some other specific place. If the examinations were held in church, extra lighting might well be required: the bellman in Elgin was instructed in October 1646 to light four plak candles for four nights every week for as long as the examinations went on, and when the examination venue was a farm, barn or anywhere else that was suitable, then it was up to the people living there to see that facilities were provided. In fact, much catechising was done household by household and when and where such examinations were to be held was always intimated from the pulpit or by the kirk officer informing families directly. The Kirk Session records of Coldingham for March and April 1752 describe the progress of examinations that year. There was one 'dyet of examination' in the first week of March and three during the following week, on Monday, Wednesday and Thursday, the last of these with a baptism as well which appears to have been additional. The following week there were three days of examination, two more during the next week and four the week after that. In mid-April there were four more days. All these were held in different places in the landward area but on 19 April it was intimated that the people of the town of Coldingham would be examined on two days and, lest any escape the net, it was announced on the 26th that there would be a day of examination 'for the absents in Coldingham'. The General Assembly Act of 1639, already quoted, made it clear that elders were expected to assist with this and by 1641 at least some elders 'joined with the pastor in catechising the people'. In 1649 the Presbytery of Dunfermline ordered that elders should 'go with the people of their division to catechising and examination' and in 1656 not only the elder of a district but an additional one too should be present with the minister at examinations. Where catechising was conscientiously done, it must have been a considerable burden on elders who had their own livelihoods to see to and in 1699 Kilmartin Kirk Session found it necessary to state that they should be 'circumspect and watchful to be present at the circular examinations in their respective precincts.' In spite of the fact, however, that catechising became of such major importance in Scottish church life, Kirk Session minutes show that it was not necessarily inevitable – the parish of Thurso had none during the forty years up to 1797 and other parishes managed to do without it also.[12]

Thomas Henderson in his book, *Lockerbie, A Narrative of Village Life in Bygone Days*, says that catechising was regarded as a sacred event and when done in people's homes, any conversation on the ordinary things of life was considered to be out of place. When the minister arrived, he shook hands with all present and then engaged in prayer in which the salvation of the souls of everyone present was particularly sought. The children over eight years old were taken first – the age had gone down from the nine years given in the Act of General Assembly of 1570 – and had to go through the Shorter Catechism even although they might not understand it. In some cases certain psalms and passages of Scripture had to be memorised and children had to be able to repeat a text or passage which had been prescribed for them on the minister's last visit. The young unmarried people were then taken through the Catechism, Commandments, Lord's Prayer and Creed, after which it was the turn of the adults, men and women taken separately, with the women usually being much better at anything that had to be memorised. This was followed by examination of the workers – it was always expected that they would be allowed off work to be catechised – and satisfactory answers were expected to all questions. In 1609 a Kinghorn man was charged with not knowing the Commandments and was ordered to 'get them' under a threat of being fined 40s. Scots while in Culross several people were debarred from Communion in 1642 and threatened with other penalties too 'if they were not able by Martinmas next to rehearse the Lord's Prayer, Belief and Ten Commandments and to answer the ordinary Catechism.' As catechising was an essential preliminary to partaking of the Lord's Supper, the General Assembly sought to clarify the position in 1648, making it clear that grossly ignorant people should be debarred and saying that the first and second times they were found ignorant, their names should not be made public but that the third time they should be announced, while for the fourth time it was stated that they should be brought to public repentance. It seems very unlikely that such stern measures were ever fully carried out but debarring was frequent; 'much people was debarred' for one reason or another when the first Communion was held in Edinburgh in 1655 after a gap of six years, owing to the various troubles of those times, and Kirk Session minutes from elsewhere confirm that this was not uncommon.[13]

At examinations, quick thinking on the part of those questioned and tact on the part of the minister if he was of a kindly disposition, could save much trouble. The story is told of a man who was asked 'What is the chief end of man?' and replied, 'Indeed, Sir, it is no' for me to presume to answer sicna' a question as that and we would rather a' hear it frae yoursel,' and the minster gave the answer. But that was an exception; young people dreaded these awful occasions and their parents must have done so too, if lectures by Alexander Gerard of Aberdeen University, which were published in 1799, are anything to go by. These lectures formed the course of instruction for northern Divinity students – and things would have been similar elsewhere – and gave guidance as to how ministers should conduct catechising visits. Not only were questions about religious knowledge asked but the minister might inquire how husband and wife behaved to one another, he might give them instruction about their several duties and point out to them their faults of conduct and ask how masters and servants treated each other and so on. Such severe and intrusive catechising was in general very unpopular and when people were required to go to diets of it away from home, with no one left behind to look after their houses, stock, grain or other property it caused them a lot of worry. In fact, a Presbytery Visitation in Aberdeen in 1642 declared that it was 'noysum' [harmful, troublesome] to country people to have to do this and it must have been to overcome such problems or at least prevent them being put forward as an excuse for absence that in 1630 the Presbytery of Fordyce had decreed that families should attend by halves, but this was coupled with a threat that if servants were absent on both days their employers would have to pay 6s. Scots for each of them. Fining those who were not present at examinations was fairly common: 'It is ordained that the master or mistress of every family shall come to the examinations with their family and hear them examined, with certification if they fail they shall pay 3s 4d to the poor whether they be master or servants', say the minutes of one Kirk Session in 1637. Impounding goods was another way by which several Kirk Sessions tried to enforce attendance at examinations. The records of Aberdeen show that the inhabitants of Futtie were poinded in 1608 and in the parish of Holm two families who were several times cited for absence from diets of examinations in 1686, and added to the offence by not appearing before the Session when called, had their goods poinded to the value of 20s. Scots for each family. Even after being called a further five times, these people still failed to appear and were ordered to make satisfaction and relieve their poinds which were valued by an elder 'and another honest man' at 8s. Scots in excess of the penalty imposed; this surplus was given to the officers for their pains, with the rest being put into the box for the poor. Probably as effective a punishment as any was that which befell a tenant farmer in the parish of Falkirk who refused to attend an examination, only to find that he was ordered to appear before the congregation on the following Sunday to answer publicly the questions the minister put to him. Holding examinations on a Sunday had the benefit from the kirk's point of view that non-attendance could be easily brought in as Sabbath profanation. In 1697, for example, also in the parish of Holm, it was intimated 'that those who willingly absent themselves from the examination on the Sabbath day afternoon shall be punished as Sabbath breakers' but just as Sabbath profanation was a charge which could be used to ensure conviction for all sorts of offences, so the following case which was officially to do with catechising, seems to have been a way of punishing other sins. In the summer of 1646 an elder interrupted a minister during catechising and was warned to appear before the next meeting of Session and was forbidden to come to the Lord's Table. When he was called in church a third time and stood up in his place for reproof, he spoke up for himself and said to the minster, 'Ye called me a beast, sir, ye sall prove me a beast first.' Such an outrageous remark was referred to the Presbytery and he ultimately appeared in church in sackcloth and made satisfaction, only to be accused a week later of being 'drunk to womiting'.[14]

Very strict catechising lasted into the 1860s but then, particularly in the lowlands, a more homely approach developed although there was still prayer and an address. In the highlands the severe type of examination continued for rather longer and it is even said that in time people prided themselves in having the minister visit them for catechising and in being able to give the right answers, but it may well be that this was mainly in the case of those who wished to take Communion and really did want to prove that they had acquired the basic religious knowledge which would entitle them to receive a token as a passport to the Lord's Table. For most adults, this was what made catechising worthwhile but, however much knowledge an individual might have, the kirk could always use the right to withhold Communion as a weapon to ensure that adults brought their children and employees to examinations. This was made very plain by one Session which ordered 'that every master and mistress of every family shall come precisely themselves with their children and servants to the examinations with Certification to those who doeth refuse they shall not have the benefit of the Communion whatsoever they be, either master or mistress or servant, without exception to any.' Little wonder, all in all, that the belief in the need for thorough catechising before Communion was one, but only one, reason for infrequent administration of the Lord's Supper. Catechising, however, had a spin-off benefit for historians because it was what provided ministers with their lists of 'catechisable persons' – all those over eight years old – which give population numbers in Old Statistical Accounts and other works. Undoubtedly there was laxity in some parishes about the educational and personal standards required of Communicants and it might well take the arrival of a new minister, sweeping clean, to enforce stricter rules. Rev. Donald Sage arrived in Resolis in 1822 and the following year examined all those already on the Communicants' roll privately, people who in theory had already acquired a proper degree of knowledge and conduct, but he found that some of them were unfit to receive the Sacrament 'on account of their gross ignorance not only of the ordinance of the Supper but of the doctrines of the Christian religion in general.' In view of the great concern that those taking Communion should be adequately instructed and examined beforehand, it says much for Rev. John Morrison, minister of Petty (1759–75), that he allowed the parish idiot, known as Jamie Petty, to come to the Lord's Table. This poor harmless innocent man was perhaps nearer to God than many who could recite the Catechism faultlessly because afterwards he described how, as he took the bread and the wine, he had seen a beautiful man in a white robe who told him to be good till he would come for him in exactly a year and, sure enough, Jamie did die just a year later.[15]

Character references could also be required of would-be Communicants. In 1837 there were some unfavourable reports of a man who wished to communicate who had to get people to come to the Kirk Session to speak up for him and whose employer gave a reference saying that he was a sober, honest and upright man but, even so, his name did not appear on the Communicants' roll for a further four years. As has already been said in an earlier chapter, use of such 'minced oaths' as losh, gosh, teth, lovenenty and others were thought very wrong and so affronted a minister of Kirkmahoe that he debarred all who used them from Communion, and several women in other parishes who committed the sin of living alone were suspended from the Lord's Table for doing so. A particularly unfair case occurred in Mauchline, beginning in 1777. There appears in the list of those debarred from the Lord's Supper that year the name of Jean Mitchell 'for stealing a hen as alleged'. Although it was never proved that she had stolen the bird, yet for five years her name was on this black list, each year with the alleged offence written beside it. The scandal was never removed and when she died in 1782 her name and the allegation were both struck out and the word 'dead' was written in the margin of the book.[16]

New Communicants were admitted on the Thursday fast day preceding Communion or else at the preparatory service on the preceding Saturday or on the previous Wednesday, should there be a service that day, but before that there was usually special additional instruction for them at the manse or the church. Although ages are not given in Kirk Session records, it appears that new Communicants might be fairly youthful. In 1649 for instance, in Ceres, several young people were summoned to meet the minister in the church on a Wednesday prior to Communion 'that he might speak to them' and explain the duties and privileges of Communicants. One young man's age is recorded only because by mistake he gave a 6*d.* instead of the Communion token to the elder collecting these, as they were more or less the same size, but as it was realised that it was an error – and he was only sixteen – he got nothing worse than a Sessional rebuke. In spite of these youthful Communicants, the minister of a highland parish from 1954–66, tried hard to persuade people who were suitable in every way to become Communicants but found that what he called a 'strange highland hesitation' held them back – and yet the oldest member on the Communicants' Roll, still attending services in 1967, had become a Communicant in 1904 when she could not have been more than twenty years old.[17] Once catechising of all Communicants was completed, the list of those entitled to come to the Lord's Table was checked, something which frequently appears in Kirk Session records. One minute puts it thus, 'The Session met at the manse for prayer and to read over the examine roll as usual before the Sacrament.' Names were added or deleted as necessary but, should there be deletion, there could be some objections. While some of those whom Mr Donald Sage found ignorant 'declared their resolution not to come forward . . . until they were further instructed' there were others who 'notwithstanding their ignorance declared their resolution of holding their privilege', in other words, they maintained their right to remain on the roll. Perhaps the fact that by then it was 1823, with church secessions having already taken place elsewhere in Scotland, that had something to do with this because, in earlier years, to take Communion after being debarred for lack of knowledge or for any other reason was a great sin. A woman who was delated in 1674 for 'coming to the Lord's Table notwithstanding she was debarred because of her ignorance was sternly rebuked by the minister and ordered to confess her fault publicly.' Important though the keeping of the Communion Roll was, it was only from 1835 onwards that it became a duty of Kirk Sessions to keep one but this was mainly so as to provide a list of people with church voting rights; and in 1896 the General Assembly passed an Act which provided that at the annual revision of the Roll, those who had been absent from Communion for three consecutive years without an adequate reason should have their names removed and that these could only be restored by resolution of Kirk Sessions.[18] The General Assembly of 1991, however, ended the keeping of a record of attendance at Communion.

There are many references in Kirk Session records to Communion tokens which were, for all practical purposes, admission tickets to the Lord's Table. The earliest reference to the use of these tokens in the reformed Church in Scotland appears to be from St. Andrews in May 1590 when Patrik Gutherie was instructed by the Session to make the irons for 'streking of the takynnis to the Communion' and was later paid 10 merks for 2,000 tokens. Their general use may only have begun, however, after the Revolution: certainly 1707 is the first reference to them in, for example, Inverness. Tokens were usually referred to as tickets in old writings but were made of lead or tin, a mixture of the two, or of bronze. 'Making the tickets' could be done by casting them in moulds or having them made by a local metal worker. One minister reported in 1745 that, in accordance with an order of the Session, he had had the blacksmith 'make Tokens for the use of This Parish and Shewed by the workman's discharge produced this Day that the Expence of Cutting the Stamp and making the Tokens with the Lead amounted to two pounds fourteen shillings Scots.' As there were at least 400 tokens needed, besides the cost of cutting the stamp, this particular craftsman did not ask much for his labour. The minutes of another Session show that in 1731 it was Hugh Simson, a gunsmith, who was given the job of making 200 tokens for the parish, but even a slater might be given the work to do. In 1851 Tobermory Kirk Session, on the island of Mull, were buying two Communion cups from a Glasgow jeweller and so they got 300 tin tokens from him as well but they cannot have intended to continue buying them because they also bought a die stamp so that they could make any more that were needed themselves. A number of churches still have the die-stamps with which their tokens used to be stamped: Holy Trinity Church, St. Andrews, is one. The earliest tokens usually bore only the initial letter of the parish, and later the letter 'K' for kirk might be put on the other side. This could cause confusion when there were several parishes with the same initial letters in the same neighbourhood – Hawick, Hobkirk and Hassendean, for instance, are all close together in Roxburghshire – and so in such cases the letters were made in different sizes or forms so that they could be distinguished. Later still, a date might be added and, for a while, some tokens were given the minister's initials; sometimes there were ornamental lines, Scripture texts, views of the kirk, ecclesiastical emblems and other decorative features and occasionally the crest or coat of arms of the principal landowner. A gift of Communion tokens was always very acceptable to any congregation that needed them.[19] Because they were made of metal, tokens lasted well and there are still many examples of them to be found although considering the large number of them originally – one small highland parish was given 1,200 in 1812 – it is surprising that there are not far more. What happened to them, apparently, is that many were given out but not handed in. In 1606 one church issued 123 but not a single one was returned and the elders were ordered to search for those with tokens who had been absent from Communion. Some were put aside by people who had been issued with them but who in the event did not feel worthy to take Communion and did not like to make this obvious by returning them later. Some may have been melted down for the lead and some may have been hidden lest they fell into profane or unworthy hands; this latter may have been the reason why in 1889 a considerable number were found among the roof couples of a manse. As it became common for the people of surrounding parishes to come in large numbers to other Communions, so it became common to see that they were supplied with tokens by the parish celebrating Communion, without which they could not partake. This was done by the minister sending some tokens to neighbouring ministers for distribution to their parishioners on the preceding Sunday; and when any minister from farther afield was to assist at a Sacrament, he was always given some tokens to hand out to his own Communicants who would come to hear him and whom he would meet among the crowds of people present. Such generous issue of tokens to people outwith the parish also helps to explain why so many went missing.[20]

At an early stage in the use of tokens, Sessions had been very particular in seeing that only their own parishioners received them for their own Communions, because it was initially thought wrong to partake of it in any parish but one's own. In Elgin at the very beginning of the seventeenth century, it was decreed that 'such as go to any other parish to communicate shall be censured as those who do not communicate' although later on it became perfectly proper to do so with permission from one's home parish, although not without it. In 1746 an Orkney minister reported 'that a woman had gone to Kirkwall and partaken of the Sacrament without any warrant from this place to receive a token to that end, and as there is a surmise that others in this parish have done the same without warrant from the minister' he recommended that the elders should find out within their bounds who had done so and report back so that such 'audacious and unChristian presumption may be suitably censured.' With such an attitude to sharing in the Lord's Supper in a Presbyterian church, no wonder that the kirk disapproved when Episcopalian clergy who offended by baptising and marrying, offended even more by administering Holy Communion without any evidence that those receiving it were fit to do so.[21]

There were different ways in which tokens were issued. Once pre-Communion fast days were introduced, they might be handed out immediately after them or be distributed just after the service of preparation. If a visiting minister was preaching, the parish minister would step forward from the manse pew, place himself in front of the precentor's desk, constitute the Session by prayer and hand each person on the Communicants' Roll a token. In some areas intimation was made that tokens would be distributed at the church on certain days for specific districts. In Hawick, for instance, it was announced about 1717 that the Communicants of the landward parts should come on either the Tuesday or Thursday of the week before to get their tokens and those in the town should come on the Wednesday or Friday. When he visited Cawdor, Nairnshire, on his Scottish tour in 1773 Dr Johnson found the minister very busy distributing tokens as he went on his rounds, which was a practical way of giving them out, especially if he was catechising at the same time. Sometimes it was the elders who delivered them and they may have been subjected to pressure on occasions because one was deposed for giving a token to a woman who had been debarred. It has been said in an earlier chapter how, about 1727–28, on the very Sunday when tokens were to have been handed out in the parish of Ettrick for Communion the following Sunday, it became known that a horse race was to be held the next day, Monday, which meant that it would take place the day after a Session meeting and only a day or two before the fast day. This was considered very shocking and the Session forbade any of the elders to go to the race under pain of censure. Distribution of the tokens was ordered to be delayed until after the race but, in the event it was cancelled.[22]

There was a gradual change from tokens to cards in the nineteenth century and it is said that by 1840 most parishes used the latter, although in fact some parishes used tokens for at least a hundred years longer: Nigg, Ross-shire, was one, which only gave tokens up following a union in 1966, after which they were handed out to Communicants as keepsakes. It was only by producing a token or a card that anyone could partake of Communion, something which could at one time be used as a weapon for behoof of the poor. It was intimated to the people of St. Andrews in the late 1590s that no one would receive tickets for Communion but 'sic as hes payit thair bigane contribution', in other words, no contribution for the poor meant no ticket. So great was the desire of many people to partake of the Lord's Supper that some unorthodox methods were used to get hold of tickets. One man produced 'ane fangyeit [forged] tikket' and another came 'with his maisteris tikket' while in 1826 the minister of Kinloss reported to the Session that he had received a note enclosing a £1 note and signed, 'Your dependent subject, Elsy, continually'. He had discovered that the writer was a Findhorn woman known as 'Blind Eppie' and said that when he went to see her about it 'she stated that it was a pledge from his handmaid for a token from the Lord, from which expression the Moderator concluded that she intended it as a bribe for getting a token on the occasion of dispensing the Sacrament of the Lord's Supper.' The Session were very sympathetic about this case and required Eppie to appear before them only in order to receive her money back although, as she did not come when expected, it was put into the poor's box temporarily and, in fact, she claimed it in a fortnight's time. It must be remembered, of course, that to be refused a token because of ignorance was not the same thing as Lesser Excommunication which involved suspension from the Lord's Table for other reasons.[23]

Communion tokens, however, were only one of various tangible items required for the dispensation of Holy Communion. Although Communion became the most important single feature of kirk life, it did not become a regular event overnight following the Reformation. It took time for it to be established and it certainly also took time for Kirk Sessions to acquire the equipment considered necessary for celebrating it, in spite of an Act of Parliament of 1617 which decreed that every parish should provide cups, tables and cloths of which the minister was to take charge, decreeing also that he should 'cause the parishioners to provide the same under pain of loss of a year's stipend.' Even so, in 1682 the Inverness-shire parishes of Petty and of Croy still had nothing more than a Communion table each while Daviot had nothing at all. When the minister of Sorbie told his Session in

1702 that he intended to celebrate the Lord's Supper some time during the coming summer he also asked 'what course to take to provide tables and tokens and it was agreed that a meeting of the heads of families to meet at the kirk this day eight days should be intimated Sabbath next, that they may lay on some what on every plough-stilt [plough handle] for the end foresaid and also for repairing the roof of the kirk and furnishing doors there.' This meeting was duly held and a stent or tax of 12s. Scots was laid on as suggested, with the elders appointed to collect it. In this case the intention to use some of the money gathered for purposes other than Communion necessaries was made clear at the outset but in another parish in 1625 a church bell was hung with money raised by stenting the heritors, under the Act of 1617, for provision of Communion and baptismal requirements. Any parish wishing to celebrate Communion but lacking equipment had no alternative but to borrow what was needed from one which was better supplied, and even when a parish had cups of its own, more were often needed to provide for the huge crowds which ultimately began to flock from one parish Communion to another. Although the Kirk Session of Inverness decided in 1712 that their Communion cups should be given to a goldsmith to be 'reformed and made more fashionable' – after which no more appears about them in the minutes – yet in 1722, with Communion about to be celebrated, they decided to borrow more and wrote to the Kirk Session of Calder [Cawdor] 'desiring the use of two Communion cups, which are necessary besides the two that belong to the Session.' Their request was granted and the kirk officer was paid £3 Scots for fetching and returning them. With four tin cups made by a pewterer in 1763 and eight pewter plates in 1778 Inverness then found that they were the ones doing the lending; but lending is seldom satisfactory and the Session which had itself borrowed in earlier days, minuted in 1794: 'Session considering that by lending out of the Communion cups and cloths they have greatly suffered particularly the cups lately lent out to the minsters of Moy, which was returned much injured' and they decided to lend no more in future.[24]

With the kirk's constant need to raise money, it is not surprising that hiring out Communion utensils overtook lending of them. In 1661, and after that date too, an East Lothian parish hired cups from a neighbouring one, so that entries like 'Given out for the cups £1 10 Sc' appear in the records until 1688 when the Session seem to have obtained some of their own. In the mid-eighteenth century at Dornoch, where Communion was then celebrated twice a year, cups had to be hired from Golspie, perhaps because Dornoch had none but more probably because they did not have sufficient, and an entry in 1764 in the accounts of Kilmaurs Kirk Session 'for Kilmarnock cups at the Sacrament' shows that that Session needed to hire them then. The four tin cups made for Inverness in 1763 cost £1 10s.; 'two hard metal flaggons' cost Kilninian and Kilmore Kirk Session 6s. stg. in 1767; and in 1851 two Communion cups plated with silver, along with the tokens and die stamp already mentioned, cost Tobermory £5 7s. stg. from a Glasgow jeweller. Lauder Kirk Session were fortunate to be 'sent in guift' by the Duchess of Lauderdale a service of two 'Cuppes' and two flagons in 1677 and by purchase and gift churches gradually built up their own equipment, with the result that in 1797 the inventory of Sacramental utensils in a rural Borders parish showed that there were 4 pewter cups, 2 pewter flagons, 2 pewter plates, 1 pewter basin and a parcel of tokens, as well as Communion linen. It was after the 1939–45 War that there was a move towards using individual cups, something hastened by an outbreak of typhoid in Aberdeen, and many churches have now adopted this practice although, even where they have, the communal cup may still be passed round at special Communion services.[25]

While the Communion elements of bread and wine were placed on a small table, the Communicants used to be served sitting at long tables, which were not fixtures in the church but were movable and installed as required. This meant that any parishioners' seats which had been placed in the church might have to be removed for the occasion and as people quarrelled only too readily over seating anyway, Sessions had to walk warily about the 'removing and planting of seats' as one minute put it. Tables could be rough and ready, perhaps just boards supported on barrels, which is all they were at one point in Orphir, or they could be trestles, carried from parish to parish as they were needed. The accounts of Kilninver and Kilmelford Kirk Session in 1758 show that 5s. was paid for 'carrying Communion tables from Cuan and back' while in the 1730s, 1s. was the cost of bringing tables from Kilmuir Easter to Nigg. Should a Session have tables made, then this was work for a local wright, whose costs included the wood and the nails also. Where adaptation could be used it was; should a church have a form for the Session's use on Sundays, it might well be suitable just as it was for a Communion table, and another alternative was to instal some pews to be used as seats for the congregation throughout the year but which could convert into tables when required. In the nineteenth century some churches installed these seats, with hinged backs and movable benches to every second row so that they could turn into tables with seats. In 1821 three such pews were placed on either side of the aisle immediately in front of the pulpit in one church and were used for some time but as their use declined, with decreasing Communion numbers, their ability to convert, which was well concealed, was entirely forgotten. It was only when a joiner who was working in the church in the 1960s, sat in one of these pews to eat his lunch, that he noticed some features which led to his re-discovery of their original purpose.[26]

There seems to be some difference of opinion as to when large crowds from other parishes began to come to Communions. Some sources say it began in Episcopal times in the form of conventicles and certainly a tract of 1657, 'A True Representation, Rise, Progress and State of the Divisions of the Church of Scotland' said that by then a 'new and irregular way' of celebrating Communion had started, with great crowds present and six to seven ministers, sometimes double that number or even more, preaching on the Saturday, Sunday and Monday. Other writers say that crowds started after the Revolution, but dates probably varied with places. In time the numbers attending could be quite out of proportion to the normal population of a parish. Ronald Blakey in *The Man in the Manse* says that 5,000 people were present at one Communion in Grandtully, Perthshire, in 1841, an estimated 9,000 at another in Uig, Lewis, and yet another crowd of 10,000 attended in a parish whose normal population was only 1,000. Because these 'gathered Communions' as they were called, brought so many people from other places, the Sacrament was dispensed in many parishes both inside the church and outside it. Tables were therefore needed in the graveyard as well, which involved additional work and expense such as 'levelling a part of the chapel yard for the Communion tables' in Inverness in 1771 which took two men five days to do and cost 5s. stg., and gravestones might have to be temporarily moved to make way for tables and replaced later. In 1810 a Session had two tables, each 45' long and with seats, made specifically for outdoor use and the following year a different Session decided to have a 60' long table made for outside; it was made in six ten' lengths @ 16s. stg. each, and the forms which were made in similar lengths cost 11s. each. The old graveyard at Tulliebole, Kinross-shire, is one with an unusual feature, in this case a Communion table formed by digging a ditch around a 9' × 18' area of grass so that people could sit around it. This is not so clear as it once was as workmen cutting the grass have been in the habit of throwing cuttings into the excavation which has therefore built up considerably. It is said in some quarters that it was made for Covenanting Communions but it seems surprising that they would advertise their activities in such a manner and it seems possible that this was simply a permanent piece of outdoor Communion furniture. Not far away, the graveyard at Cleish, also in Kinross-shire, has something which may be another out-of-doors fitting for the Lord's Supper. Along the inner edge of one side of the graveyard wall is what can only be called seating, reminiscent of the *sediliae* seen in ancient church buildings and, although there is nothing to say so, it seems reasonable to suppose that this was to provide seating in the graveyard on Sacrament occasions. When the fashion for large gathered Communions died out, graveyard services ended, outside tables ceased to be needed and the importance of the Communion table which held the elements, increased.[27]

White cloths with which to spread the tables were another essential feature of Communion Sundays and were yet another expense to be met although, as with other items, linen was also borrowed if necessary. For example, in the summer of 1720 Langholm Kirk Session borrowed linen from Ewes, because although a collection to buy linen had been made in Langholm, none had been obtainable at the fair where it had been hoped to get it. In 1775 the minister of an Argyllshire parish bought out of kirk funds 'a piece of cloth for the Communion table . . . long enough to afford a piece for the spare table, being in all 17 market yards in length at 1s 6d per yard £1 5s. 6d.' Once a parish had got these cloths, every imminent Communion saw them being washed ready for the great day, or else washed after it: 6s. Scots was paid in 1704 to one woman 'for washing the cloths that were made use of at the Communion' and in 1750 'washing the kirk cloths' cost another Session 12s. As Communion crowds declined, it became general practice in the first quarter of the nineteenth century to take Communion sitting in ordinary pews, in spite of the fact that this was condemned by the General Assembly in 1825; but although there was this change of practice, the old custom of using white linen continued with pew book-boards covered with cloths. The cloths were numbered according to the pews they fitted and latterly were laundered by elders' wives or other women of the congregation; and while this custom has partly died out, it still is common to find white-covered book-boards in some churches and very pleasing it looks too. There were other down-to-earth pre-Communion preparations to be made and paid for such as 'washing the schoolhouse and church' which cost Kilbride Kirk Session 3s. stg. in 1830, or 2s. 7d. 'given to the people who red [cleaned, put to rights] the kirk and placed the tables etc' by another Session. In addition to paying for such services the kirk fell in with custom and often gave a dram to anyone who had done a job for them and so the following type of entry may appear in accounts in the run-up to Communion, '. . . for a dram given to the people who put the kirk in order before the Sacrament, 8d.' or 'By paying for drink to those that red the church.'[28]

Not only was Communion dispensed on Sacrament Sundays both inside and outside churches but in the days leading up to this climax various ministers preached both in and outside too. People liked outdoor services – sometimes they were held in a wood near to the church – as they were reminiscent of the Covenant-ing tradition of out-of-doors worship. If they wanted to hear any particular minis-ter who was preaching in the open air, they had to make the best of the weather, whatever it was, but he was always protected by what was called the tent. This seems a slightly misleading term for what was a portable wooden covered pulpit which has been described as a cross between a sentry box and a bathing hut or a Punch and Judy theatre, but whichever of these descriptions best fitted it, a tent provided shelter in wet weather and shade on hot days and acted to some extent as a sounding board to project the preacher's voice. Entries in the minutes of Cathcart Kirk Session showing payment for bread and drink 'to them that lifted the tent from place to place' do not make it clear whether it was being moved from parish to parish or just from its place of storage to the graveyard and back again, although the latter seems the more likely; certainly at Assynt in 1837, 10s. stg. was paid 'To Angus Mackay to defray the expense of carrying the preaching box from and to store in time of the Sacrament.' Either way, tents regularly suffered damage and whenever a parish was about to hold Communion, the accounts show ex-penses such as 'To John Watson, wright, for taking care of the tent and table 4s' or 'For fitting up and taking down the tent £1, To nails and pins for the tent 16s' and possibly 'Whisky for erecting the tent 2s stg.'[29]

Tents were fairly costly to provide. A 'timber tent and desk for the ministers at Communion time' cost one Kirk Session £2 5s. 1d. in 1793 from a local wright, but only two years later a nearby parish was hard-pushed to pay for a 'Box for preaching in' which they had already got. They managed to find £4 stg. in part payment but it was not until three years later that the balance of £2 12s. was handed over. It was because of such financial considerations that another Session decided when their tent had become 'old and unfit' that they would have a collection for a new one but although that brought in £3 17s. stg. it was not enough to cover the cost. In 1808 Boleskine Kirk Session decided to get a wooden tent and to pay for it through a collection, in the belief that the cost would be 'cheerfully defrayed by the parishioners' voluntary contributions', only to discover that no more than a 'pretty trifling sum' could be raised in this way and so they decided instead to levy the expense on the land. They notified a Mr Fraser, a tacksman who was also a factor to Lord Lovat, about this and asked him to collect the money along with the rents but he replied that as one of Lord Lovat's tenants himself, he would resist this and would prevent other tenants paying such a levy either. The Session had decided, unwillingly, to use their legal right to apply half of their income otherwise than to the poor, although they had never done this before, and so it was from the poor's box that the £6 4s. stg. for the tent came, leaving £15 17s. $^{1}/_{2}d$. for the needy of the parish. As has already been said, Kirk Sessions did not have sufficient funds to be squeamish about disposing of equipment which was no longer fit for church use, and in 1770 Mauchline Kirk Session decided that the 'remains' of their tent which had fallen to pieces with age should be rouped as soon as possible. This was the same practical spirit which would allow an old Communion table to be made into a coffin or worn Communion linen into a shroud. Before leaving the subject of Communion tents, an *ad hoc* version of a preaching shelter, of canvas stretched on metal poles, is used every July at the annual Blanket Preaching at St. Mary's of the Lowes on the hillside above St. Mary's Loch, Selkirkshire.[30]

The most essential requirement for Communion is of course the elements of bread and wine. In 1572 Parliament decreed that the parson of the parish should provide these but there were difficulties about this in many places. A burgh might pay for them – Ayr did so in 1644 – but at St. Cuthbert's, Edinburgh, the cost of the elements was borne by the Bishop of Edinburgh until the end of Episcopacy after which it was paid out of the poor's money, which was wrong. In 1695 a petition was sent to the Lord High Chancellor of Scotland pointing out that the Bishop's revenues were not coming to the Crown and were administered by the Court of Exchequer and asking that payment should come from them but there is nothing to show that this petition was ever acknowledged. When the Court of Exchequer was approached directly, the result was an offer of the vacant stipend of a Morayshire parish which that area refused. In 1724 the Kirk Session of St. Cuthbert's again consulted the Barons of the Exchequer and were told that they had a good claim against some of the heritors for Communion elements and an action was raised with the result that four years later it was announced that the heritors were liable for the estimated amount of £18, which was similar to what had been formerly paid to the Bishop of Edinburgh in the name of victual stipend. Heritors did become legally required to provide a certain sum for Communion elements but this could mean that parishes had to claim their allocation from a fund. In 1772, when the ministers of the Presbytery of Tain were asked their intentions concerning the Sacrament, Mr John Urquhart of Fearn said that 'he was willing to have that solemn work set about in Fearn some time in the harvest season on the condition that he has access to the funds discerned for Communion elements', whereupon a factor who was present, declared that he would supply them. In some cases a sum was added to the minister's stipend and paid directly to him, like the

£40 Scots allowed to the minister of Stichell and Hume, Berwickshire, in the 1790s and provided equally by the Earl of Marchmont and Sir James Pringle of Stichell. By the late nineteenth century the elements were an expense which fell on the minister but for which he received a fixed allowance appointed by the Court of Teinds, to be paid to him by the heritors. This provided for only one Communion a year; Kirk Sessions could and did pay extra where there was more than one: it was 'better to pay the costs out of the day's collection than that the people should want [lack] the more frequent use of the Sacrament', said the General Assembly in 1638. Unfortunately, in the days of gathered Communions, what was allowed certainly did not cover expenses and should there be something like a revival, then costs were even higher so that during the 'Cambuslang Wark' of 1742 over £6 Scots was spent on bread and over £96 Scots on 112 bottles of wine for two Communions although the 'legal fund for the elements' only came to £33 6s. 8d. Scots.[31] Nowadays Kirk Sessions pay for the elements unless they are gifted, which they often are.

In 1758 the minister of Kilninver and Kilmelford, Argyll, presented an account of what he had spent on Communion. This included three dozen bottles of wine which cost £2 14s., and 5 pecks of 'flower bak'd into bread' which came to 8s. 4d., with the cost of going to Inverary to get the bread adding on a further 4s. 6d. There were other expenses too, all of which came to £3 11s. 10d. stg. but Lord Breadalbane's allowance was only £2 15s. 6²/₃d. which left a debit balance of 16s. 3¹/₃d. which was repaid to the minister out of kirk funds. In practice it was often the poor's funds which had to subsidise Communion costs: 'Taken out of the box 4 lb for buying Communion wyne' say the minutes of Holm Kirk Session in 1679 and this was not uncommon; indeed the Synod of Aberdeen expressed great disapproval of ministers using the poor's money for Communion elements.[32] The wine, of which a surprisingly large amount was used, was generally light claret or burgundy which, in the early days, was mixed with water to produce 'mixed cup' which was almost universal in the north, in spite of which in some places it was felt necessary to prove that it was not mixed by decanting it from the bottles at the Communion table in full view of the congregation. It has been suggested that ale may have been used as well because the records of St. Cuthbert's, Edinburgh, refer in 1687 to '9 pints wyne and 2 pints ale' which were 'to the kirk' and therefore not part of the additional supplies provided for the refreshment of ministers and elders. So far as wine was concerned, it was always stored with great care and every effort made to avoid leaks. 3d. was paid by Auchterhouse Kirk Session to 'Davit Syddie for girding the barrel that holds the Communion wine' which must have been done for just such a reason. When the old pulpit there was removed some years before 1888 the Session were surprised to find beneath it a recess which held a well-constructed case, with sub-divisions capable of holding a considerable number of bottles and although it had long since been forgotten, in spite of the fact that there was a small door into it, albeit somewhat concealed by the precentor's desk, it is said that this must have been the Communion wine cellar which succeeded the decayed barrel.[33] Cockburn's Port Wine is used by some Kirk Sessions now for Communion.

There was some variation in the type of bread used. In general, it was ordinary barley bread but in 1752 Kildonan Kirk Session in Sutherland sent an elder all the way to Greenock to get 4 pecks of wheaten flour to make the bread, and in Galloway shortbread was used which in some districts was flavoured with caraway seeds and orange peel. Sometimes the bread was made by a baker but very often the services of a local woman who was known to be good at the job were enlisted. In 1698 the Kirk Session of an Orkney mainland parish paid a local woman 8s. Scots for doing the baking but at the same time paid Nicoll Craigie 16s. 'for his expense in going to Kirkwall and buying the elements, the weather being bad that occasioned him to stay a whole day and night in Kirkwall.' The implication is that it was the wine that he bought which was in this case regarded as the essential element although the word 'elements' should refer to both the bread and the wine. In fact, Nicoll Craigie did not bring back these elements himself although he did the buying; it was the kirk officer who had to go for them and who was paid 4s. Scots 'for carrying the elements from Kirkwall'.[34]

Where Communion was celebrated only once a year, it usually fell between June and August when the weather was expected to be at its best and the light longest and, so far as rural parishes were concerned, work on the land left some free time. In any given area, during those months the various parishes held their various Communions, normally at fortnightly intervals and it became the custom for all the ministers of neighbouring parishes to be asked to go to wherever Communion was being dispensed and for all the people of a wide area to go too. There were several days of services during the Communion week, with the actual dispensation of the Sacrament on the Sunday. In districts where there were considerable numbers of parishes within a reasonable distance of each other, there must have been some sort of fixture list but in the large highland parish of Tongue by 1786 the decision about when to hold Communion appears to have been a purely local one. That year the minister proposed 23 July as a suitable date 'if the Session thought that day convenient for the parish – after some deliberation, they were unanimously of opinion that said day would suit the circumstances of the parishioners as it would not interfere with any public fair or Tryste.' This sounds as if Communion was not to interfere with secular activities but it seems likely that the real meaning was that Communion should be given full attention. As to the frequency of Communion, the First Book of Discipline recommended that it should be celebrated four times a year, the Book of Common Order suggested that it should be monthly, the Directory of Public Worship said 'frequently', yet the final decision of the Assembly of Divines at Westminster was in very general terms which meant that it was really left to the decision of individual kirks. There were three Communion services a year in Edinburgh for at least four years after the Reformation; at the beginning of the seventeenth century Aberdeen decided that it should be celebrated at the beginning of every quarter; while in Glasgow from 1583–1645 it was held annually, except for six years when it was celebrated twice. During Episcopalian times churches were also encouraged to hold an Easter Communion which was an unwitting return to the canon passed in 1215 by the 4th Council of Lateron requiring Communion to be celebrated once a year at Easter. The Synod of Aberdeen recommended an Easter Communion to clergy in the seventeenth century, 'if they can possiblie doe it', and that of Moray made a similar recommendation in October 1677. The brethren of the Presbytery of Fordyce were able to report in April 1686 that they had celebrated it that day 'conform to Act of Synod'. The Falkirk man who affronted the Session 'by loupin in at a windo' of the church did so during an Easter Day Communion service, while at the other end of the country, up in Orkney, the records of a Kirk Session show that in 1686 they celebrated 'the Holy Sacrament of the Lord's Supper, it being Easter.'[35]

In both Episcopalian and Presbyterian times, some parishes celebrated Communion on two successive Sundays: in 1617 it was held both on Easter Sunday and the preceding Sunday in Aberdeen; the parish of Arbuthnott held Communion on 6 April 1651, and on the 13th the minutes state that 'The ilk day some who had not come to the first day communicated this day.' In Forfar where Communion was regularly dispensed on two successive Sundays until 1720, the records show that one Sunday in July 1697 was 'the first Communion Sunday' and the following one 'the second Communion Sunday'. In 1708 St. Cuthbert's, Edinburgh, celebrated Communion on two successive Sundays and in 1742 a reference in the minutes of Cambuslang Kirk Session to 'bread for the two Communions' implies that the same thing was happening there too. A second Communion, not necessarily on the following Sunday, was sometimes held for the benefit of those unable for good reasons to be present at the first. This happened, for instance, in May 1604 in Aberdeen when Communion was administered to merchants, skippers and mariners who had been 'at the saill' at the time of the previous one and to such of the people who had been absent through sickness. At one time it was customary in parishes with both a town and a landward population for the town and country people to communicate on different days, but the country inhabitants might have to make a special request for this.[36]

In spite of that, throughout much of the seventeenth century, in Presbyterian and in Episcopalian days, Communion was celebrated only rarely in many parishes. In Glasgow between 1645–61 it was only celebrated six times in all and only twice in the next twenty-odd years, and that seems surprising. What is less surprising is that in 1650 it had not been celebrated in Lochbroom for seven years, in 1665 not for twelve years in Fodderty, also in Ross-shire, and during the whole incumbency of Mr Duncan MacCulloch from 1647–71 in Urquhart, Inverness-shire, it was not dispensed once. In 1698 a Presbyterian Committee produced a libel concerning Dean Alexander Pitcairne, one point of which declared that he had only administered Communion three times in twenty-six years although a witness stated in his defence that it had been five times. In 1678 the Synod of Moray ordered the members of Inverness Presbytery to administer Communion but in October of that year found that they had not done so 'because of the frequent charges that there people gott to be in armes against the Macdonalds obstructed their friedom to that great work.' The seventeenth century was certainly a very troubled time in Scotland but one writer says that although several of Inverness Presbytery dispensed the Sacrament in 1684, the rest blamed bad weather and various other impediments and 'in short, any and every excuse was seized upon to put off the sacred rite.' The parish of Greenlaw held Communion yearly in the three years from 1720–23 but failed to hold it in fifteen of the following sixty-five years, in other words, a failure rate of about one in four, whereas in Falkirk, Communion was held only rarely between 1688 and 1723 but annually thereafter, and in general that last example seems to have been the norm, that Communion began to be held yearly in most places after 1720.[37]

Celebrating the Sacrament only once a year was thought by many to be based on the annual Jewish feast of the Passover and many also thought that it was observed with greater solemnity than if held more frequently, but the following cry from the heart from the large parish of Tongue goes back to the matter of costs and explains why, even in 1790, Communion was not being celebrated there every year. The Moderator reported to his Session that the Synod insisted on the Sacrament being administered annually in each parish within the bounds

> although an Act of Synod past in favour of this Presbytery about 32 years ago, appointing that Holy Ordinance to be administered only once in every second year, on account of the peculiarly detached situation of the county and the want of pecuniary subsidies to defray the expense of Communion elements. The Moderator further reported that he mentioned to the Synod . . . the difficulty in administering the said Sacrament yearly, arising from the smallness of their benefices, though they wished very much to have it done, and believed the frequent administration of it might be of essential service to the interest of religion in the bounds. To remedy this grievance, till redress can be obtained for it by an application to some public fund to that effect, the Synod proposed that the money collected upon these public occasions should be given to defray the expense incurred thereby; that the surplus of such collections shall be given to the public for the use of the poor; that the people concerned should know this Overture, that their charity might be liberal, in that event the poor shall be gainers instead of losers, by this mode of temporary redress of a grievance which has hitherto retarded the frequency of the administration of the Sacrament of the Supper.

And from being annual events, Communion services then became more frequent again. At Cambuslang, in connection with the revival of 1742, the Session decided to celebrate the Lord's Supper in two successive months. Before his death in 1859, Rev. Robert Storey of Rosneath, Dunbartonshire, managed to introduce a second Communion service in the year, then a third, and his son who succeeded him, celebrated Communion four times a year before he left the parish to become Professor of Ecclesiastical History at Glasgow in 1886. Highland parishes lagged behind but there too half-yearly Communions became the norm because, as one Kirk Session put it, 'doing so might be instrumental in advancing the cause of religion and of drawing the affections of the people to God.'[38] In many parishes Communion is still celebrated twice a year but perhaps with special Communion services at, for example, Easter and where it is desirable they may be held at more frequent intervals.

One would think that drawing people towards God was the prime purpose of Communion but to at least some heritors it used to be the large Communion collections that were the attraction. While they were obliged to contribute a certain sum for Communion elements, this was more than offset by these collections which went to the poor's funds and as the heritors were in the last resort responsible for the maintenance of the poor, a good income at the Sacraments was very welcome as it could save or at least reduce unpleasant things like assessments. It was for this reason that holding a second Communion in winter could lead to problems, as happened in the 1820s in West Kilbride. Although many of the parishioners asked for a second Sacrament in the winter months, the heritors objected that the collections at it, which would normally go the poor's funds, would be entirely used up on the expenses of the occasion. The minister was determined to get around this objection and in December 1825 decided that the normal amount collected on a winter Sunday for the poor should be set aside from the Communion takings and the balance used to pay for expenses and should that be insufficient, then he would pay what extra was needed himself. As a result the parish was able to have a winter Communion in January 1826 without interfering with the poor's funds. In Baldernock the accounts were passed in the summer of 1844 but there was a protest about £5 spent for a winter Sacrament with two elders reserving 'their rights to claim repetition of the payment'. This was not objecting to the extra Communion service but to the poor's funds being used for it which, though officially condemned, often had to happen.[39]

So much for the practical arrangements that a parish had to make so that the Lord's Supper might be celebrated but, as has already been said, several ministers were required to cope with the large amount of preaching which went on, both indoors and outside, once Communions developed into the great gatherings that they did. This meant that if a minister was assisting at Communion in another parish his own church was closed. An idea of the number of Sundays that a clergyman might be helping at other parishes' Sacraments comes from St. Boswells in 1747 when the minister was absent for eight Sundays one year, equivalent to two months of 'Silent Sundays' as these were called when, with no services in his own parish, there were no collections for the poor. In March this minister went one Sunday to Melrose; in May to 'Annick' and to Selkirk; in July to Ednam and Lilliesleaf; in August to Ettrick, in October to Bowden and in December he was at Maxton. The problems that this could cause had made the General Assembly advise that only one, or at the most two visiting ministers should assist at Communions and that they should have a special care of their own parishes while giving comfort to others, but that did not make much difference and in 1701 the Assembly advised Presbyteries to see that the number of ministers helping at Communions should 'be restricted so that neighbouring churches be not thereby cast desolate on the Lord's Day.' Nevertheless there often were as many as ten or twelve ministers assisting with the various services of any particular Communion.

It was, of course, not only ministers who left their parishioners desolate when they went to participate in Communions elsewhere; their flocks were perfectly happy to leave their own ministers desolate, should they not be assisting, as they deserted their churches to attend other Communions and as a result churches often had to be closed on the day of a nearby parish's Sacrament, even if the minister was not taking part. Every parish liked to have some famous preacher at Communion, such as 'Roaring Willie' – William Campbell, minister of Lilliesleaf from 1760–84 – who was particularly celebrated and every church in his part of the Borders was left empty when it was known that he was to 'mount the tent' at a Communion service. In his *Reminiscences of Yarrow* Dr Russell says that the usual observation of the people about his preaching was, 'Eh, how he roared, and eh, how he swat', but unfortunately such a preacher only served to make large crowds larger and also showed up the deficiencies of less talented clergy.[40]

While visiting ministers might return home at night if their parishes were near enough, many had to be given hospitality for the duration of the Communion 'season' which was the better part of the week, either at the manse or some other suitable house. Their travelling expenses do not normally appear in Kirk Session records, probably because they often came on horseback and so long as the horse was accommodated there were no other costs. Such costs as there may have been were probably offset by return visits and in any case ministers enjoyed going to other Communions; it is only occasionally that an entry like 'for a boat to bring the minister' is shown in accounts. Normally it was nearby ministers or at least those within a limited area who were asked to assist at other Communions but Thomas Henderson tells how when a Mrs Macdonald in Lockerbie suggested that Dr Erskine of Greyfriars Kirk, Edinburgh, (1767–1803) who had been a friend of both her father and her late husband, should assist at Communion there, it caused considerable comment and interest, firstly because for a minister to come so far was unusual and secondly because when he arrived the white curls which showed under his hat made people suspect him of vanity and, in addition, there were some who suspected his orthodoxy because he accepted Mrs. Macdonald's invitation to stay with her, a widow, something she had kindly offered in addition to paying all his expenses. Still others thought that he must be a sound man seeing that it was she who had suggested having him. One way and another, great things were expected of him but in the end no one was pleased with his preaching, a story which perhaps tells one as much about some of the people's approach to Communion as anything else.[41]

As to the various services in which these ministers took part, it was enjoined in 1645 by the General Assembly that there should be a sermon of preparation delivered in the usual place of worship on the day immediately before Communion, which meant on a Saturday. This was not apparently popular as is evident from the fact that when it was intimated to one congregation that the service of preparation would be held at 2.00 p.m. the following Saturday, an Act of Session was passed the same day decreeing that anyone failing to attend it would be fined 6s. Scots. In the 1680s a similar fine was being imposed elsewhere for the same offence, sometimes with the additional punishment of making repentance as a Sabbath breaker unless a suitable excuse for absence was produced, and a Forfar man had his token taken from him because he observed neither the preparation day nor fast day. In parishes where Communion was held on two successive Sundays, then preparatory services were held on each of the preceding Saturdays and Saturday continued for some time to be the day for these services, with shops closed and worship not just in the afternoon, but in the morning as well although in time, the Saturday preparation became overshadowed by the Communion fast day.[42]

Pre-Communion fasts were never enjoined by the General Assembly but Rev. Andrew Edgar says that in the mid-1650s the Protesters, who were strict Covenanters, held them in Dalgety and Dunfermline, both in Fife, something which was opposed by the more moderate sections of the kirk who considered that they were not in keeping with established practice of the church. In fact, according to Woodrow, Glasgow Session records show an injunction to keep a fast on the Communion Sundays of 1596 and just a couple of years later a Communion fast was held in St. Andrews, where it is said that such a thing was 'not a novelty' because they had sometimes been observed during Robert Hamilton's ministry from 1566–79. Communion fasts were not generally held during times of Episcopacy but Covenanting ways soon prevailed so that methods of celebrating Communion changed and during the late seventeenth and early eighteenth centuries, fasts became more general until by about the 1720s, they were widespread all over the country. Sometimes they evolved more or less naturally, such as a Weekly Exercise begun in the parish of Arbuthnott in December 1700 which soon afterwards became a fast day. Thursday became the usual day to hold a Communion fast but that did not preclude them being held on other days instead: the Barony Church, Glasgow, held fasts on Thursdays in both 1701 and 1703 but on a Friday in 1702, while in the 1780s and 1790s Wednesday was the fast day in Banchory-Devenick and a tract of 1800 spoke of the fast being held a month before the celebration of Communion. Obviously there were variations at different times and in different parishes but as fast days developed, it was usually the parish minister who took the first part of the forenoon fast day service because, being a day of fasting and humiliation, he was thought more fitted than a stranger to try to bring his flock to repentance for sins. Three ministers usually preached on a fast day, two in the morning and one in the afternoon and in the evening the parish minister was expected to 'pirlequey' or summarise the addresses of the day, although in some places this was not done until the end of all the various Communion services, in order to impress what had been said on the minds of the people. This must have been an exceptionally difficult thing to do, requiring great concentration to select the essentials without giving offence by omitting other parts but it was undoubtedly helpful to the people to be given a summing-up, especially if it explained anything they had not understood.[43]

Although Communion proceedings began, by the eighteenth century, with a fast day, usually on a Thursday, many parishes began their own preparations before that. This could take the form of a meeting of elders for private prayer and privy censures, similar to those held at other times of the year; or it could be a meeting which allowed public censure, with the laity permitted to point out what they considered was amiss in the lives of the minister, elders, deacons or readers. Robert Chambers wrote of the idea behind this, saying of Edinburgh in 1619:

> If anything was amiss in the lives, doctrines, or any part of the office of their pastors, every man had liberty to show wherein they were offended and if anything was found amiss, the pastors promised to amend it. If they had anything likewise to object against the congregation it was likewise heard, and amendment was promised. If there was any variance among neighbours, pains were taken to make reconciliation, that so both pastors and people might communicate in love at the banquet of love.

This meeting might take place upon the Tuesday prior to Communion. In some parishes, proceedings started with a service on the Wednesday, which it was usual for the youngest of the visiting ministers to conduct. After his address, some of the elders engaged in short earnest prayers, asking God's blessing on the services to come in the next few days and thereafter the minister and elders met privately, as a Session, for privy censures, ending the meeting by making any final arrangements for Sunday. When any form of pre-Communion service was held before Thursday, in spite of privy censures if these took place, there was still a certain freedom about them which entirely disappeared as soon as Thursday, the fast day, dawned. It became a very important day, and then came Saturday, the Preparation Day. That left Friday – and while some parishes held an evening service on a Friday, most did not and that was when great numbers of visitors began arriving, as well as all the pedlars, hawkers, travelling merchants and beggars who appeared wherever there was a crowd with whom to do business, and that included crowds at Sacraments. There were country women who never came to any village except at Communion time, and the Friday prior to it was their great shopping day of the year. There were meetings of friends who rarely saw each other, great bustle and activity, along with what has been called the fearful excitement about the prospect of participating in the Sacrament.[44]

In the highlands, but not in the lowlands, Friday was quite different as it became noted for 'the Men's meetings'. While there seem to be some different opinions about the character of the Men in general – the word always has a capital letter – a synopsis of various accounts of them including John Macinnes's *Evangelical Movement in the Highlands*, produces the following picture. They were notable laymen of undoubted character who were designated Men to distinguish them from mere ministers. The Men would certainly have denied that they subscribed to anything so secular as fashion, yet they maintained a distinctive appearance, wearing their hair long to show that they despised the vanity of combing it and, although there was variation around the country, dressing in a distinctive manner. A long cloak often formed part of their garb and had special significance because a cloak was part of what St. Paul left behind at Troas. It was often blue and in

Caithness and Sutherland was of woollen or hair material. A spotted cotton handkerchief might be bound about their heads and, according to an article in the *Inverness Courier* of 23 October 1851, the Men in Skye wore, even in church and at the administration of the Sacrament, red striped or blue woollen night caps, the colours said to indicate different degrees of godliness. 'We have not,' the article said, 'learnt the authority for their particular head gear; whether with spots or stripes, it culminates in white as the *ne plus ultra* of evangelism. Alexander Gair, a catechist of very eminent sanctity, never appeared in church or meeting without a pure white napkin over his head, with the ends hanging down.' (In fact, many who did not belong to the Men wore handkerchiefs on their heads on this way, regarding it as unbecoming to wear a hat or bonnet in church as many others did.) A week after that article appeared in the *Inverness Courier*, 'A Highland Minister' replied, refuting some of the statements made, including the assertion that varying colours indicated degrees of holiness. Many of the Men were thought to have the power of telling the future as if by spiritual second sight and although the kirk denied such a power, prophecies were their forte and they were listened to with superstitious reverence; their utterances became memorable and their Gaelic prayers, described by some as unctuous, were nevertheless thought to be miraculously effective. They usually belonged to the working class and were generally elders or at least regarded themselves as self-constituted ones. They all had a particular natural ability as men of prayer and also had some gift for public speaking. Some had a little education while others were illiterate but somehow or other, they all knew the Scriptures and catechism thoroughly and possibly some Puritan writings as well. Many were deeply reverent with an abiding sense of the nearness of the unseen world and lived good and devout lives and were accordingly regarded as especially holy and guided by divine grace. They were grave in mien, stern in teaching, prominent by their piety and austere mode of living and, as they went from parish to parish for the Sacraments, they were welcomed everywhere and given suitable hospitality. In some country parishes the Men, by virtue of their claim to spiritual superiority, were allowed to exercise a general superintendence over both minister and kirk and unfortunately seem often to have assumed a role which was far from Christian. It is said that every Sunday some of them took up position near the reader's or precentor's desk and while the service went on, those of the most extreme leanings, kept up a muttering nasal whisper, either of comment or of spiritual communion, sometimes nodding approbation or groaning disapproval of the utterances from the pulpit, all this because their reputation in the parish required them to present a peculiarly devout and critical air before the congregation. While many were deeply sincere and worthy men, there was undoubtedly some truth in the statement that others were spiritually proud, self-sufficient, fanatical, ignorant and hypocritical. Rev. Archibald Clerk, minister of Duirinish, Skye, from March 1840 to November 1841, wrote in that parish's New Statistical Account of a group of men in it, as there were, he said, in almost every other parish in Skye, who were obviously 'Men' although he did not use that term for them. Surprising though it seems, they did not regard sealing ordinances such as Communion or baptism as of great importance, seeming to think that their efficacy depended to a large extent on the man administering them and they would only accept them from the hands of a minister of whom they approved in every respect but would on no account receive them from someone to whom they had any objection, however trivial. They believed that the benefit of the Lord's Supper was completely taken away by the presence at the same table with them of even one person they regarded as unworthy and, being very uncharitable about those whose opinions differed in any way from their own, were very particular about those with whom they would partake of Holy Communion.

> Through the influence of these men (among whom there are some lay-preachers), aided by others who ought to have known better, the majority of the people have been brought to regard the sacraments, especially that of the Lord's Supper, with a degree of horror which causes almost all of them to avoid partaking of it. Thus there are nearly two hundred children in the parish unbaptized, and the table of the Lord is unfrequented. It has, to a certain extent, become a proof of piety to avoid partaking of the sacraments; and it is much to be feared that, when Christ's commands in regard to one subject have come to be set aside for the opinions of men, His commands in regard to others will, in process of time, be treated with equal disregard.

In fact, Communion was not celebrated in that parish for the eleven years up to 1840, the year before Mr Clerk wrote what he did. The reason for this is said to have been because the parishioners were unworthy to partake of it but is it not possible that the real reason was the formidable effect that these men were having upon the people? Certainly there seems to be some quiet desperation in Mr Clerk's description of those who through their 'religious' behaviour were having such a drastic and unChristian effect on the lives of other parishioners. In connection with these men in Duirinish, it is worth noting that after one ministry which lasted from 1814–c.1836, the next lasted for only two years, 1836–38 and, after a vacancy, there was Mr Clerk's brief incumbency, followed by another short one from 1842–44 and thereafter, perhaps because the Men in general joined the Free Church in 1843, there was a long ministry from 1844–88. It is easy to see how the Men became so powerful in the church that in some areas they dominated the clergy and gained great influence over the people and even popularity with them and how in some parishes no one was permitted to partake of the Lord's Supper without their approval.

But how did ordinary men enter the ranks of the Men? The earliest of them seems to have been John Munro, from Kiltearn in Ross-shire, in the 1650s; natural ability, piety and eloquence were almost a prerequisite for the Men and although these were qualities which would bring anyone to the fore, it was very often parish ministers themselves who brought men with these attributes forward. According to Dr Kennedy of Dingwall, should a highland minister discern special qualities in a man of his congregation, he might encourage him by asking him to take part in congregational meetings, the fellowship meetings which were held monthly or weekly in evangelical kirks, firstly by leading prayer and then by speaking, and if he acquitted himself well on such occasions, he might be asked to be one of the 'Friday speakers' at Communions. The scarcity of ministers at certain times has already been mentioned and this made it necessary to use laymen to hold scattered congregations together so this was another way in which Men developed, and they also came into particular prominence when a weak ministry was forced on to a parish by patronage or otherwise at a time when there was a strong lay eldership, and even an excellent ministry could be a breeding ground for Men. During the time of Rev. John Balfour, whose remarkable ministry produced a revival in Nigg between 1730–45, with no fewer than ten praying societies developing, there grew up in the parish a group of four men, described as a 'chosen generation', which included Donald Roy, a noted seer. While Mr Balfour was there all was well but after his death a minister who was regarded as unsuitable was forced on to the parish and it was Donald Roy and one other of the four who led a secession from the church and split the parish. This attitude was not an uncommon one for the Men; if ministers were not gospel and orthodox in their eyes, they were perfectly prepared to quit the kirk and hold meetings for prayer and discourse elsewhere. While they were not hostile to the church or to ministers as such, the Men formed too high a standard for the ministry and some ministers who disapproved of them had to turn a blind eye because of a fear of unpopularity if they suppressed their activities.

It was some time before 1737 that what had begun as fellowship meetings on pre-Communion Fridays became public meetings although when this change took place is not known. It was the Men who took the prominent part in these Men's meetings, Question meetings or Day of Questions, as they were called. Normally conducted in Gaelic, their object was to help intending Communicants in self-examination, something which is said to have been so greatly relished that they were well attended. Although it is sometimes said that no minister was present at these meetings, it was in fact usual in many parishes for the minster to attend and the great moment was when he asked if anyone had a portion of Scripture on which he would like the opinion of his fellows. Ultimately, someone would raise a point upon which they sought clarification and a noted Christian from another parish would be asked to give his opinion. It was normal for him to demur to start with but he would soon agree to give what were called his 'marks' upon it, generally from his own experience. Sometimes it was a senior elder who gave out a particular text and Man after Man rose in his place to speak when invited to do so – it was only Men who were asked to hold forth upon the subject. None of them normally spoke for more than a quarter of an hour each but even although the meeting might last from three to five hours, it is said that their contributions always seemed fresh and to the point, probably because they spoke from their own practical knowledge. Naturally enough, all this gave the Men a a great opportunity to become prominent both locally and farther afield for their knowledge and zeal.

The Men had the courage or the audacity, depending on one's point of view, to denounce anything they thought wrong with the ministers of the kirk at these Friday meetings, which must have made life very difficult for the clergy and sown doubts and caused trouble in the minds of the people in the run-up to Communion. The parish of Latheron was one which had a considerable quota of such forceful characters. At one time, the Friday meetings there heard furious denunciations of the 'big parish ministers . . . who feed themselves and not the flock – those idle shepherds into whose flock the true sheep do not enter – those carnal worldlings, who unlike the apostles, wear boots' (this brought deep groans from the old women) and who 'travelled in gigs', a statement which brought more expressions of disapproval from every part of the meeting. Little wonder that it was said to be 'quite impossible to avoid feelings of deepest pity for the poor clergy on a Sacrament Friday, so high was the superiority of the Men in native talent, and still higher in the degree to which these talents were exercised by divine truth', and in self-defence the clergy of Sutherland tried in 1750 to put an end to the cavilling Friday meetings at which the fast day preachers were hauled over the coals and they decided that the fast day should be moved from Thursday to Friday so as to put an end to these meetings. But the people complained bitterly that their 'time of preparation for the solemnity was shortened' and, although the Synod had agreed to the proposed change, it was referred to the General Assembly who were not prepared to come down on one side or the other without further investigation and the Friday meetings remained as they were for the time being. A few years later, however, the Synod forbade Friday fellowship meetings on the grounds that it was usual for the minister to attend them and that his time, 'it was imagined, might be better employed', but this produced such a strong reaction from the people of Dornoch that the Friday meetings were allowed to continue. However, as has been said regarding Duirinish, the Disruption of 1843 took most of the Men away from the Church of Scotland and into the Free Church with an obvious result on pre-Communion Men's meetings in the established church.[45]

And so Saturday came around, the day of preparation services but also a day when still more people arrived for the next day's Communion and so Saturday nights tended to be noisy with many strangers patronising the inns.

And at last it was Sunday, and in the very early days after the Reformation the day's activities began exceedingly early. The old Roman Catholic idea that Communion should be taken fasting lasted for about fifty years after the Reformation and although there was no requirement that this should be so, in all probability people had had nothing to eat in any case owing to the earliness of the hour. Elgin's first bell was rung at 2.30 a.m., services began at 3.30 a.m. in Stirling, at 4.00 a.m. in Glasgow and 5.00 a.m. in Edinburgh, Perth and St. Andrews. The first hour was taken up with preaching, followed by dispensation of the Sacrament and, lest any should expect the one without the other, it was decreed in Elgin that no one might receive the Sacrament unless they had been present at the preaching immediately before it and that no one should come to that either unless it was their intention to communicate and therefore at the end of the last bell-ringing the kirk doors were closed and remained so throughout the service. The same thing was happening in St. Andrews although there the doors were not locked until the end of the first psalm. This may explain why Communion was sometimes dispensed on two successive Sundays but this was in the last years of the sixteenth century, before the days of 'gathered Communions', when Communion was still something for each parish alone, and these very early services were mainly for servants, with a second service beginning about 8.00 or 8.30 a.m. or even a little later, for other people.[46]

Once Communions began to be thronged with people from outwith the parish, services were not especially early and Sunday saw more people arriving in the morning. In island or coastal parishes they might come by boat, in landward areas they came on foot, on horses or ponies, in gigs or carts, and as their animals and their vehicles had to be tethered or parked somewhere, the scenes of crowding confusion may be imagined. There was much for the elders to do that day and kirk records show that their instructions were very clear and, in earlier times, repeated yearly and minuted so that there could be no doubt about what had to be done and who was to do it. Some of the instructions given may seem surprising but wherever there are large crowds, precautions must be taken. In Falkirk at one time elders were appointed to guard each of the six entrances to the church with instructions 'to keep the entries as easy as possible'; three more were told to 'take care that there be no disorder in the isle and that none climb over the ravel' (railing); others were to see that there was 'no contention in the minister's seat nor baptism room' and yet another had to see that the 'dead door at the west end of the church' was barricaded. In the late 1590s among other tasks at Communion, three of the elders were allocated the duty of 'avaiting on the calsaye [street] and keiping comelie ordour outwith the kirk' while in 1640 one of Dundonald's elders was appointed to receive the tickets [tokens] and to 'tak good heid . . . that he receave not the tickets of other parishes instead of our own or turners [small copper coins] instead of tickets.'[47] There were also detailed minuted instructions about the dispensation of Communion in which, where a parish had deacons, these men were required to help, at least to a limited extent. At St. Andrews in 1598 it was decreed that half of the elders and deacons were 'to serve the table' on each occasion but in Elgin in 1603 distinction was made between their duties, with the elders appointed 'to wait on the ministration' or service of Communion while the deacons were to 'wait on the materials', in other words, to have them in readiness and to replenish them as necessary. In Glasgow in 1603 it was the town officers who were to 'bring the stoups with the wine' but there was a clear statement that none but elders and deacons might serve at the tables. In 1696 two elders of the parish of Arbuthnott were ordered to take up the tokens, another two had the task of 'conveying the wine at the tables', while an elder and three deacons were to 'fill the wine into the cups' and were also responsible for 'waiting upon and drawing the wine'. It is apparent that, as at Elgin in 1603, the deacons' role was seeing to supplies, under the eye of an elder, but not distribution of the elements to Communicants. Yet in 1730 the instructions given by Kirkwall Kirk Session were that both elders and deacons should 'carrie the elements to the table and serve the same.' When such people as town officers were needed to help, they had to be paid for doing so but even in a more rural parish like Abernethy, Perthshire, it could be necessary to pay for assistance, such as the 6s. Scots given 'to Robert Myler for cutting the Communion bread and drawing the wine' in 1700. Nowadays it is the Session Clerk who makes all the necessary arrangements.[48]

In some parishes, the Sacrament itself was always dispensed inside the church, the occupants of the table leaving the church by one door after taking Communion to make way for those waiting outside another door to come in to take their places at the vacated seats – a request to one Session in 1807 for tables without doors seems to have been so that the change-over could be made as quickly as possible – and at Greenock's Old West Kirk a temporary shelter, rather like a workman's shed, was erected over and on either side of the south door, to serve as a form of waiting-room for the people standing in readiness to enter the church. This running system meant that if families lived near enough, husbands who had communicated could go home and wives and others who could not leave their homes and children unattended, were then able to go to church themselves. Preaching would, of course, be going on outside in the churchyard while the 'table service' went on inside the church although Communion was also dispensed outside; in the south of Scotland, this may have been mainly when the weather was favourable or crowds especially large but in the highlands it was common practice, sometimes with English services in the church and Gaelic in the churchyard, with the English congregation joining the Gaelic one outside for the actual dispensation, where the tables were then served using the appropriate language. An outdoor Gaelic service was considered to be even more impressive than an indoor one, partly just because of its being in the open air but also because of the singing, with the precentor intoning the first line which was then sung by the congregation, so that it could take twenty minutes to sing four stanzas. Although this was very sombre it appealed greatly to highlanders and even after it had stopped for ordinary services, intoning was still retained in some places for Communion: Rev. J. H. Brydon said that in 1936 he had heard a precentor intoning the lines of Psalm 103 as Communicants were leaving the table.[49]

But that is moving ahead. Although the tables were spread with white linen and the benches alongside waited emptily to be filled with Communicants, nothing could go ahead until the 'fencing of the tables' was completed. In early post-Reformation days, this was real physical fencing: Edinburgh Dean of Guild accounts for 1561–62 show a payment for 'ane traviss [fence] for holding forth of the non-Communicants' while some records refer to the fence as 'flakettis' or flakes such as those used on farms to keep animals separate. Just how necessary it was to enclose tables in this way appears from a decision by Stirling Kirk Session in 1597 that the people should be given an admonition before the next celebration of Communion because they had behaved so badly the last time, with 'rash and suddan cuming to the tabill, in spilling of the wyne, and in thrusting and shouting in thair passage out at the dur after the ministratione.' These early fences had two doors, with an elder at each and it was these doors that were locked at St. Andrews to ensure that those who attended preaching should also communicate although, as said, at Elgin it was the church doors that were shut. One such early fence is shown in an old print illustrating an article in *Life and Work* of December 1924 (which may be a picture of the original Lady Glenorchy's Chapel in Edinburgh which was taken down about 1907). Although this was the origin of the practice, fencing the tables soon changed totally in character, becoming entirely verbal and addressed to those who had qualified themselves and been granted tokens, requiring them nevertheless to think very seriously about what they were about to do, so as to debar the unworthy from partaking, and it was based on Biblical authority:

> It follows that anyone who eats the bread or drinks the cup of the Lord unworthily will be guilty of desecrating the body and blood of the Lord. A man must test himself before eating his share of the bread and drinking from the cup. For he who eats and drinks eats and drinks judgment on himself if he does not discern the Body. That is why many of you are feeble and sick, and a number have died. But if we examined ourselves, we should not fall under judgment.

An idea of the thinking behind the tables comes from a minister of Morebattle who declared that as the Lord's Supper is a

> sacrament and feast of the covenant of grace – a feast for the friends of Christ and not for his enemies – it is proper and necessary doctrinally to set a rail about this holy table of the Lord. The distribution of tokens doth not make the doctrinal debarring unnecessary; for the distribution of tokens excludes only the ignorant and scandalous, whom the church cannot admit, but all that have not a right to the Lord's Supper in *foro Dei*, or before God; all unbelievers, all unregenerate persons, and the enemies of Christ, yea, the principal design of the doctrinal debarring is to show who they are that have a right to the Lord's Supper before God, that so persons may be excited to a due care in exercising themselves before they come. We intend not first to debar all and then to invite all; the first to debar and exclude the enemies of Christ, and then to invite his friends.

A ferocious attitude to fencing the tables is made very clear in a collection of sermons preached at several Communions by Rev. J. Spalding, minister at Dundee and printed in Edinburgh in 1702 under the title *Syntaxis Sacra* which was especially recommended by the General Assembly and which included the following terrifying statement:

> To partake of the Supper unworthily is to break the command 'Thou shalt not murder.' It is a body-murdering sin; for this cause many are sick and weak among you, and many sleep. It is a church-murdering sin; for it threatens to give us a bill of divorcement. It is a soul-murdering sin; many drink and eat their own damnation. It is a relation-murdering sin; for your wives and your children bear marks of your unworthy communicating. O dreadful! How many are the worse of Communion, and their salvation more difficult and seven times worse a child of the devil than before. O, how so, I tell you that Satan goes out of you as out of the madman for eight or ten days before the Communion, and that he returns with seven worse devils than before.

Could anyone really describe such a sermon as being in keeping with the instruction of the Confession of Faith which told ministers to warn the ignorant, profane and scandalous that they must not presume to come to the Lord's Table, making it clear to them that this would be to eat and drink judgement to themselves but which also instructed them to invite to the Table and encourage in a special way all who laboured under the burden of their sins and wished to reach out to a greater progress in grace?[50] Is it any wonder that Rev. Archibald Allan, writing in 1900 of the Lord's Supper of earlier days, said that it had been an affair of almost superstitious regard, with all its simplicity and brotherly love buried and that the same feeling of Boo-man with which children used to be terrified into obedience, was called up whenever the season of its observance came round? 'The awe and trembling with which savages regard eclipses of the sun and the moon had its counterpart in the most holy yet most natural of all the observances of the Christian religion . . . the simple majesty of the act . . . was overwhelmed by whirlwinds of words and a feverish atmosphere.' Another example of terrifying fencing is given by Thomas Henderson, describing Mr Patrick Nisbet, minister of Hutton on Dryfe and Corrie, Dumfries-shire, from 1767–99, who was an old-style minister whose denunciation of those who unworthily dared to eat and drink the body and blood of Christ was savage. 'Oh my brothers, wull ye seal damnation tae yoursel's an' mak it sure ye shall be damned and so drive the last nail in your damnation? Rather pit a knife tae yer throat than approach. What, man, wull ye kill an' be guilty o' His body and blood? The worst morsel that ever ye tasted is tae eat and drink eternal vengeance.' One writer said that the success of a minister 'was judged not by the number he brought to the Holy Table but by the number whose consciences were so touched that they had not the heart to come forward.' About the 1930s Lord Alness wrote that he had 'known men and women who had intended to communicate but who, after such an address, were restrained from doing so by a feeling of unworthiness. Men and women feared lest they should "eat and drink damnation" to themselves, and so abstained.' The practical effect of fencing the tables was that many who had studied their catechism and tried to qualify themselves to share in this great occasion were frightened off at the last moment and, along with the ignorant and those otherwise debarred, did not partake of it as the number of tokens put in the plate on Mondays showed, in addition to those never returned. In the highlands, of course, the Men saw to it that the fence was rigidly applied. Mr Nisbet's words would have put off all but the hardiest but he then threw everyone into greater confusion. Having told everyone of the risks they ran if they partook unworthily of Communion, he went on to inform them that they would be guilty if they withdrew from the table: 'Dare ye bide awa' an' tak his anger upon ye, an' gie that affront tae dae whit in ye lies tae spite His Supper and frustrate the wull of God?' This was because it was an offence not to be at Communion if one was eligible, which was why Abyl Jamison was delated to the Kirk Session of Arbuthnott in 1640 'for absenting himself from the Lorde's Table when he had occasione for it' and he had to confess this fault in church because the reason he gave for absence was not thought adequate.[51] In 1651 in the parish of Petty, many people described as ignorant and of the baser sort, were individually asked why they did not communicate but the excuses they gave were considered insufficient and they had to make public repentance next Lord's

Day for their high contempt. In an earlier instance, a man who failed to communicate as he had promised, was ordered to do so on the next occasion but no punishment was threatened. In time the rigid fencing which so terrified people was overcome as they grew better informed and more self-confident and the church became less severe and one reads of five or six tables in use, sometimes ten or twelve, although it is not always clear whether these figures refer to the number of tables or to the number of times Communion was served each day. There was also variation in the numbers of people these tables could accommodate at one sitting – it could be forty or as many as seventy to eighty at once, which is in keeping with the length of the tables already mentioned. As each successive group of Communicants came forward and took their places at the tables there was an 'action sermon' – a sermon at the action of Communion – which resulted in Communion services usually lasting anything from three to five hours, with the record perhaps being held by an Ayrshire parish where there were seventeen services of the Sacrament over twelve hours. It was usual for the parish minister to fence the tables and to serve the first table but thereafter visiting ministers helped to serve the others. Thomas Pennant was none too flattering about how this was being done when he toured Scotland in the late 1760s: as many Communicants as possible, he said, 'crowd each side of a long table, and the elements are rudely shoven from one to another.' Was he accurate, did he see an unfortunate example or was he biased?[52]

Protracted services meant that refreshment was needed for those involved with running them and an account paid by St. Cuthbert's Kirk Session, Edinburgh, in 1687 for alcohol supplied by the beadle who was also a publican, shows that the kirk realised the need to provide not only for the minister and visiting preachers but also for the precentor and his helpers, the elders, deacons, officers and attendants. 9 pints of wine and two of ale, mentioned earlier as being 'to the kirk' at a cost of £8 6s. Scots, may have been for the Sacrament itself, but in addition there was listed:

To Mr. Hepburn, minister 4 pynts wine	£3 12 – Scots
To John Wishart, precentor, 2 pynts wine	1 16 – Scots
To the elders and Deacons, 4 pynts wine	3 12 – Scots
To William Byers, beadle, 2 pynts wine	– 18 – Scots
To the officers, 3 pynts	2 14 – Scots
To the Baxter, 1 chopin wyne, 2 pynts ale	– 13 – Scots
To ane pynt of ale to the man that drew the wine [all sic]	– 2 – Scots

In fact, the treasurer when settling this account apparently considered that the minister's 4 pints of wine were too many and noted in the margin '2 pynts allowed' and the precentor's two pints were also reduced, to one. At a meeting of the Kirk Session prior to Communion, twenty-three members were present and consumed about half a bottle of wine each, but it must be remembered that this was the only sort of liquid refreshment available to them and that drinking was a normal, acceptable practice.[53]

During the Sunday services there was a break of about 1¼ hours halfway through when the ministers were entertained in the manse or in a suitable nearby house. When Mr John Urquhart, minister of Fearn in the 1770s, reported to the Presbytery about his plans for celebrating Communion, he made a point of saying that Mrs Sutherland, widow of the minister of Tain, who by then was living with her father in Fearn 'would have a drink of ale and some spirits, and other entertainments ordinary on such times, for accommodating the ministers and others who might attend.' Those permitted to entertain visiting clergy almost certainly regarded doing so as an honour and generous provision was always made for them and Thomas Henderson, in his book on Lockerbie, gives a good description of the lowlier entertaining that also went on. Where numbers permitted, bread, cheese and milk might be provided in the manse kitchen for the congregation, with a bowl placed at the water pump or well so that the thirsty could help themselves, with nearby publicans supplying the needs of those wanting something stronger. Long open-air services meant that in bad weather people got thoroughly cold and chilled, with the prospect of ill health to follow. It was easier for ministers who at least had the tent to shelter them or, if things got too bad, they could do as one minister did. Writing of a Communion in 1756 he said that 'rain drove us in to the kirk, where I preached at the kirk door' which clearly means that he preached there while the people listening were outside getting soaked. In hot weather, everyone became exhausted, irritable and sometimes faint and needed food and drink to offset conditions but while much food and drink was sold, there was always a great deal of free hospitality also. It was accepted custom at the Sacrament season that any visitors who asked ordinary people for food and shelter would be given it. For days beforehand women were making preparations so far as they could for the arrival of both friends and strangers, with everything planned so that as many as possible of the household could get to the services. Many visitors showed their appreciation by bringing a little something with them and when their offering was tea, which at one time cost 6s. per lb. and was a great luxury, it and they were more than welcome; and houses, cottages, barns and haysheds were filled with people.[54]

From the kirk's point of view there were both good and bad results from this generous hospitality shown to strangers by parishioners. It certainly encouraged many people to attend Communions and hear preaching even if they did not actually communicate but the burden which it imposed on the parishioners was something which had to be taken into active consideration when deciding how often to celebrate Communion. Not only might a Kirk Session have barely enough to pay for the elements but in poor, scattered parishes, where neither food nor shelter were readily available, how to feed and accommodate all those who might come became a real worry, because many arrived on Thursday and stayed until Sunday. One reason for Communion being celebrated in some places only every second year was due to the problem of feeding all who came. Some visitors of course brought their own baskets of food and ate them in the intervals between services or, indeed, during them because something like a windy day, for instance, could prevent people hearing and so they just hung around, occupying themselves by eating and drinking; and an indifferent preacher also encouraged people to slip away to the ale barrels, something which could result in such clergy becoming known as 'yuill [ale] ministers'. Kirk Sessions accepted alcohol as a part of everyday life, though condemning excessive consumption of it, and so the ale barrels were not hard to find on Communion Sundays. For example, a way of supplying refreshments at Communions in the parish of Kilmaurs, one which lasted until about 1870, was for both food and drink to be provided in the beadle's house which backed on to the graveyard. No charge was made but the visitors left the value of what they consumed on a table and all was done with decorum and propriety. At Auchterhouse the usual practice was to have a tent pitched in the kirkyard for the sale of ale and other supplies and at Westruther, Berwickshire, there was also a refreshment tent and this was a common, though not universal, practice. At Lockerbie, stalls were arranged alongside the kirkyard dyke, selling baps and bread, scones and farles, cheese and light ale and inn-keepers brought barrels of spirits and stronger ale which sat on the carts in which they had been brought to the kirkyard. Because the source of refreshments was so close to where services were being conducted, it was only too easy for there to be constant movement between one and the other. In addition, many of those at Communions were inevitably 'idle spectators', as Pennant called them, rather than participants and the lure of conviviality was all too strong. Many of the men resorted to ale-houses rather than refreshment tents and there was a lot of indiscriminate drinking and mutual treating so that to some extent the Sacrament Sunday degenerated at one time into a day of excessive indulgence and unseemly behaviour, with the real purpose of the day forgotten or obscured.[55] Noisy rabbles usually kept away from the preaching so that the services were not unduly interrupted although this could happen. In 1709 a group of gentlemen were found 'guilty of scandalous profanation of the Lord's Day, who being convened about the tent in the churchyard, when the minister was preaching in the evening, did curse, swear and mock the ordinances, and committed several rude insolencies and did greatly disturb the people in hearing of the Word of God preached.' One of this 'profligate company', Robert Hunter of Polmood yr., was caught and taken into burgh custody and later, after a long examination of witnesses, the sentence of Lesser Excommunication was pronounced against all the offenders, whose names Robert had given. Even into the first quarter of the nineteenth century Kirk Session records have references to rioting and drunken behaviour at the Communion season. When this happened at Stow in 1824 a mason, a carter and a shoemaker, who had all been involved, were ordered to undergo church discipline before they were allowed further church privileges; and it must have been very offensive when in the mid-nineteenth century a band of Kilmarnock youths left a public house and passed through the churchyard during the Sacrament in the parish of Craigie and drunkenly pitched the remains of their food at the preacher in the tent. An early instance of a Communion disturbance had nothing to do with drinking, however. The mourners burying Sir William Hamilton of Sanquhar in 1573 broke into Mauchline Church on the day of the Sacrament, overthrew the 'table boords' and buried him beneath. The Kirk Session were so angry that they complained to the General Assembly which ordered those concerned to submit to the Session's discipline. A mild case of trouble was that of Isobel Petrie who appeared in 1650 before her Session for breaking 'a glassin window' on the day of Communion. She had been asleep in the churchyard, which says something about either the refreshment tent or the preaching, and her head fell against the window and broke the glass. That, at any rate, was her explanation but there is a possibility that some brawling or fooling-about may have been the real cause of the incident.[56]

According to H. G. Graham, it was unquestioned that it was Satan who 'raged in parishes as Communion drew near, causing drunkenness and immorality' and when a 'storm' came down on some people as they returned home from the Sacrament, their minister and elders saw this as the devil beginning a broadside. Be that as it may, a large part of the problem of bad conduct at Communions was that, although many people returned home immediately after the Sacrament services, which could include an evening service too, there were many others who hung about afterwards so that the village or street was thronged at night with people, all more or less worked up with excitement and in an elated holiday mood which could even end in dancing. It was for this reason that Pennant, while admiring the conduct of Scots on ordinary Sundays, said that 'their conduct at the Sacrament in certain places is to be censured', adding that 'in some places before the day is at an end, fighting and other indecencies ensue. It is often a day for debauchery . . .' It was certainly not unusual for immorality to result, just one example of this being when a Tillycoultry woman named a man as the father of her child and when asked 'when he had ado with her' replied that it was 'in the month of July last, coming from the Sacrament at Alloa', even though he maintained that there had been nothing more than a certain amount of horseplay. But it was not only the common people who overdid things at Communion time. Ministers, who were well entertained, could fall into the same trap and the very forthright journal of Rev. George Ridpath records how in May 1755 he went to Abbey St. Bathans to assist at Communion there. There was, he said, 'a considerable congregation, and the sermon without [outside] agreed ill with my toothache. Sat till near six. Drank rather too long and were too noisy.' Hard drinking was fashionable and regarded as manly as the following description from Argyllshire in the second decade of the nineteenth century shows, in describing a dinner given on the Communion Monday for the officiating clergy: 'We drank, roared and sang, fired our grapeshot (nothing less than royal port) and bumpered every young lady in the country. About eight in the evening, some were sick and others groaning.' Similarly, it is said that at a dinner for ministers and other special guests after Communion at Abbotrule, Roxburghshire, wine bought for sacred use was consumed in large quantities, the amount which had been bought being quite out of proportion to the number of Communicants – and this conduct did nothing to encourage temperance on the part of ordinary people.[57]

The first effective protest against licence at Communions came in Robert Burns' poem 'Holy Fair'. Written in 1785, it is said to have depicted pretty accurately, if somewhat freely, the celebration of Communion in the parish of Mauchline that year. W. H. Davies, commenting on the poem, points out that in spite of the daring levity of some of the allusions and incidents in it, not once is the sacred rite itself mentioned which may be why, although the poem met with a storm of abuse from pulpits all around the country, both clergy and people took what it said to heart and there was a move towards a general improvement in the conduct of all concerned although as late as 1889 Banff Kirk Session had to stop Thursday fast days 'in view of the abuses committed with fast days in recent years in this parish.'[58]

Monday morning must have been a considerable anticlimax after all the religious fervour which had culminated on the Sunday. People cleared up the litter in front of their houses and everyday work began again but stopped in time for the thanksgiving service (which had been held on Sunday evening in Episcopalian times) whether it be in the morning, afternoon or evening. At thanksgiving services the white linen used on Sunday was left on the tables in the church to emphasise that they were a further part of the Sacramental observances but the services themselves were like those of a Sunday, shortened sufficiently to allow people to get home before it was too late. Monday was the day when the aforementioned dinners were given, usually by the parish minister, to the elders and any heritors who were present and, of course, for any ministers who had stayed overnight and this came to be regarded as the closing event in the Communion proceedings. Some ministers of highland country parishes were sufficiently under the thumb of the Men to allow these dinners to be used as an opportunity to criticise the efforts of those who had assisted at the Sacrament and, that apart, many of the dinners were serious affairs with 'the books' fetched when the meal was over and the clergy and guests perhaps singing Psalm 122, 'Pray that Jerusalem may have peace and felicity', after which everyone went home and another Communion season was over. Unfortunately lavish entertainment could turn these occasions into less than seemly affairs and some Presbyteries began to look unfavourably upon them and passed resolutions forbidding any minister to entertain to dinner anyone who had not been assisting at the Sacrament.[59]

While the Monday after Communion meant a good dinner for the minister and his guests, convivial or not, what mattered to the poor of the parish was that that was the day when the money collected during the various Communion services of the previous week was distributed. What was raised then often came to half the total collected during the year in spite of the fact that it has been estimated that many people gave no more than $1/2d.$ each and that for every $3d.$ of good copper, $2d.$ of bad was put into the plate. Another of the many tasks allotted to specific elders in pre-Communion instructions was taking up these collections. Some might have 'to collect att the diets of the Solemnity and to begin upon the Humiliation Day' although in other cases collections were only taken up on the Sunday and Monday. As with ordinary Sabbaths, what was given was always recorded: 'This day the Sacrament of the Lord's Supper was Celebrate in good order, there was collected at the Styles £8 6s.' Distribution of this money to the poor usually took place after the manse dinner, on Monday afternoon. While a minister's absence at other parishes' Communions gravely affected collections for his own poor on days when he was away, as has already been said, this was probably evened up by the increased collections when it was his parish's turn to celebrate Communion. Extracts from the records of Nigg Kirk Session, Ross-shire, about 1729 show how these givings were shared out there. £86 14s. 8d. Scots (about £7 5s. stg.) had been raised at the various Communion services, of which £6 8s. Scots was given out on Monday to beggars who appear to have been strangers, and £5 4s. 8d. Scots went 'to sundry godly poor people', who were the deserving poor of the parish. These may have been the parish's licensed beggars; certainly in 1792 Inverness Kirk Session allowed some of those who had been given beggars' badges, to share in the charity distributed at the Sacrament. At Nigg, £7 4s. Scots was put into the poor's box, which was the equivalent of the normal weekly collection and thereafter the large sum of £36 Scots was given to the godly poor of the several parishes within the Presbytery bounds who were present and the surplus was distributed further among the parish's own godly poor. Nearly half, therefore, went outside the parish and considering that visitors were also given hospitality, that was very generous but this too would even out as Nigg people went to other Communions. What Sacrament charity was not meant for was the hordes of vagrants who gathered at these occasions, as they did at burials, because it was known that money would be distributed. Poor they might be but deserving they were not, although even so, some of them at any rate received a share of what was going. Sometimes an allocation to stranger poor was made on the Monday before they moved away, possibly to encourage them to do so, and then the parish poor received their share later. In Ashkirk over £50 Scots was gathered on the Communion Sunday of 1698 and £12 at the thanksgiving, of which £9 6s. was distributed that day to stranger poor and beggars and it was not until four days later that £40 Scots was shared out among the parish poor. In the same way, in 1704, that parish collected £35 12s. Scots in all but 'there being a great number of stranger poor gathered together', just £6 6s. was distributed to them then and there and £20 was held back for a few days and then given out to the local poor 'according as they judged their necessity.' An intriguing announcement was made by the minister of Hawick in 1719. Four Dutch companies of Colonel Amerongon's regiment had been quartered in the town for several weeks and only after they left did the minister inform the congregation that he would distribute the Sacrament collections. Had these men been causing trouble of some kind? Or had they hoped to share in the Sacrament charity to supplement their pay?[60]

The problem of vagrants at Communions was sufficiently bad for the Synod of Aberdeen to decree in 1762 that no public charity at all would be distributed to them, but as changes in Communion practice developed the custom of the begging poor coming in large numbers seeking alms, died out and in time, even into the 1840s, when the size of collections indicates that there were still large crowds in some places, parishes began to retain these collections for themselves. Sometimes the money might be distributed privately and discreetly by the minister. In 1825 the heritors of Stow, always anxious to know about finances, asked for a statement of weekly takings and also of the annual Sacrament collection. The Session readily gave the information about weekly collections, and were perfectly prepared to give the amount of Communion collections and disbursements but they refused to give the names of recipients, pointing out that for years it had been the practice of the minister to distribute it among the industrious poor who through temporary trouble needed a little help, 'given in the most private way possible in order to spare their feelings of independence', the idea being to maintain their self-respect and hard-working habits which might have been lost in the humiliation of receiving public charity.[61]

Some changes in Communion practice have already been mentioned but obviously many more took place before regular Communion services became what they are today. The custom of thronging to other parishes' Sacraments with outdoor services was slowly abandoned about the first quarter of the nineteenth century. For example, at Inchinnan outdoor preaching was given up about the 1820s although at the same date Communion was still being celebrated in the open air at Keir, Dumfries-shire, with large numbers of people coming from elsewhere, and at Penpont in the same county, Communion was dispensed outside, not inside the church, until 1834. A crowd of 5,000 at Grandtully in 1841 has already been mentioned and in some highland parishes such as Criech, outdoor Communions with large numbers attending were still common in the later nineteenth century. As late as 1879 the Black Isle Farmers' Society, Ross-shire, asked that Communion should be celebrated on the same day in all parishes in the Presbytery for the convenience of employers but as crowding to Communions was still popular there, the suggestion was not well received. While Burns' 'Holy Fair' may have started the end of abuses, the development of transport and education widened people's physical and mental horizons and the lengthy Sacramental proceedings which had once seemed so attractive, no longer appealed in the same way. Agricultural progress also interfered with gathered Communions as enclosures prevented space for enormous crowds and it was realised that a vast amount of time and money was being wasted in a non-constructive way while farm work was being interrupted when its produce was most needed with a rising population – it was estimated that in the eighteenth century the loss to the country, not through Communions themselves but through their protracted nature, was £230,000 per annum, an enormous sum at that time.[62]

In spite of having had a considerable appeal, it is said that services on fast days never had large attendances and they died out gradually from about the 1880s, lingering longest in the highlands. Writing in 1896, William Mackay said that the north of Scotland had been slower to accept the southern fast days and the 'preaching week' but, once begun, these became a prominent feature of religious life there even although, at the date when he was writing, they had all but disappeared in southern Scotland. The fast day service was abandoned in 1932 in one Easter Ross parish owing to poor attendance and in general an evening preparatory service on a Friday became a substitute for both fast day and the Saturday service of preparation, with a service of thanksgiving on Sunday evening instead of on Monday. Well after that, however, the fast day Thursday remained a non-working day and became a holiday, until that too died out in the north about the 1960s; although an article in *Life and Work* in January 1992 describes a Communion 'season' from Thursday to Monday still persisting in northern Skye, the present position generally appears to be that there is neither preparatory service nor thanksgiving, and the Communion service is conducted on Communion Sundays by the parish minister for his parishioners, although any visitors are made welcome. But special demands or occasions require special Communions and a particularly special one must have been that celebrated by Rev. Roderick Fraser of Dingwall, at the request of a prisoner of war camp commandant, for some forty Protestant prisoners on Christmas Day 1947. The language used had to be English, but the singing was in the men's native tongue; the camp provided bread and wine and the local Kirk Session was happy to lend its cups.[63] Another special one took place in 1990. To celebrate the bicentenary of Ashkirk Parish Church, the first of several events during the summer was a traditional open-air gathered Communion service, open to visitors from elsewhere and with six neighbouring ministers officiating. A table to seat about eighteen people was spread with a white cloth and people went forward in groups, with each minister giving a very short address and serving Communion. An electric keyboard was used to play over the tunes of the psalms sung although the singing was unaccompanied as it would have been in the days this service movingly recreated.

For all that the great Communions of former days are said to have been such a drain on the economy of the nation, nevertheless, religion apart, they were a valuable source of income at local level. There was work for wrights making and repairing tables, forms and tents and perhaps repairing barrels; for metal workers making tokens; for women baking bread and washing cloths; there were odd jobs such as carrying tables, cutting bread, fetching Communion cups and elements and cleaning buildings to be used for services. There could be payments for things such as 'service and running errands about the Sacrament', for removing seating in the church and putting it back after Communion was over and there was extra work for boatmen in parishes which had water crossings. Sales of food and drink increased and even where there was no regular market for butcher meat, the Sacrament season was one time of the year when those keeping stock could be sure of a good sale. Not only did town officers get extra pay when they served in any way at Communions but so did 'servants and doorkeepers' and the kirk's own staff were assured of additional income too. An extra precentor singing at the tent at Kilmaurs in 1744 received 18*s*. Scots while the regular one was paid £4 Scots, and charity could even come into this: the man precenting in the tent at Falkirk in 1723 was paid £7 not just for his services but 'upon consideration of his poor young family.' The kirk officer could expect extra money 'as usual on this occasion' as the minutes of Coldingham Kirk Session put it in 1755 when recording a payment of £4 Scots made to him.[64] In addition to what was given to the parish poor, stranger poor and beggars must have longed for Communions to come round so that they might have just a little more money to ease their conditions. Quite apart, therefore, from the true significance of The Occasion it provided great social benefits also.

18
Candie for the Foundling

It is a sad fact that so much of Kirk Sessions' time was taken up with discipline cases, usually moral ones, that their minutes soon sicken the casual reader so that it is easy to miss the nuggets of gold that they contain. Certainly Kirk Sessions did do things which appal the modern reader, especially in connection with witchcraft cases and by imposing extreme punishments, but these were in keeping with the times and were meant well, as was the prohibition of help in childbirth for unmarried mothers until they named the fathers of their children, because without a taxpayer-supported social security system, it was essential to try to establish paternity so as to ensure maintenance. That apart, Kirk Sessions' care of the sick, foundlings and orphans and the often imaginative help given to the poor, the varied shifts made to raise funds, their involvement in education, marriage, baptism, burial, public works, famine relief, health matters and epidemic-control, were all responsibilities readily shouldered by men who were usually unqualified to undertake them but who nevertheless made a remarkable job of what they did. They achieved things in spite of a constant fight against lack of money and still managed to be compassionate, and the gift of a book and an ounce of candie for a foundling, given in a true spirit of loving kindness by Greenlaw Kirk Session to a sick little boy in their care is, in itself, a revealing comment on the nature of Kirk Sessions in Scotland.

Abbreviations used in Notes

Aberdeen Eccl. Recs: Aberdeen Ecclesiastical Records, Spalding Club.
AGA: Abridgment of the Acts of the General Assembly of the Church of Scotland.
Allan: Allan, *History of Channelkirk Church*.
Allardyce: Allardyce, *Bygone Days in Aberdeenshire*.
APS: Acts of the Parliament of Scotland.

Baird: Baird, *Muirkirk in Bygone Days*.
Barron: Barron, *Northern Highlands in the 19th Century*.
Beaton: Beaton, *Ecclesiastical History of Caithness*.
Bentinck: Bentinck, *Dornoch Cathedral and Parish*.
Blakey: Blakey, *The Man in the Manse*.
Brotchie: Brotchie, *History of Govan*.
Brydon: Brydon, *Some old Parish Customs*.
Buchan Field Club: Buchan Field Club, III, Ecclesiastical Punishments, by Milne.
Burleigh: Burleigh, *A Church History of Scotland*.

Cormack: Cormack, *Susan Carnegie, 1744–1821*.
Craig-Brown: Craig-Brown, *History of Selkirkshire*.
Cramond, *Syn. Aberdeen*: Cramond, *Synod of Aberdeen relative to the Presbytery of Fordyce*.
Cramond, *Boyndie*: Cramond, *Church and Churchyard of Boyndie*.
Cramond, *Cullen*: Cramond, *Annals of Cullen*.
Cramond, *Deskford*: Cramond, *Church and Churchyard of Deskford*.
Cramond, *Elgin*: Cramond, *Records of Elgin*.
Cramond, *Fordyce*: Cramond, *Church and Churchyard of Fordyce*.
Cramond, *Ordiquhill*: Cramond, *Church and Churchyard of Ordiquhill*.
Cramond, *Rathven*: Cramond, *Church and Churchyard of Rathven*.
Craven: Craven, *Church Life in South Ronaldshay and Burray*.

Dick: Dick, *Annals of Colinsburgh.*
Dickson: Dickson, *The Kirk and its Worthies.*
Dobson and Sanderson: Dobson and Sanderson, *Scottish Life and Character.*

Easton: Easton, *Statements relative to the Pauperism of Kirriemuir.*
Edgar: Edgar, *Old Church Life in Scotland.*
Edwards: Edwards, *Glimpses of Men and Manners about the Muirside.*
Extracts Kinghorn KS: Crawford, *Extracts from the Minutes of the Kirk Session of Kinghorn.*
Fasti: Fasti Ecclesiae Scoticanae.
Fyfe: Fyfe, *Scottish Diaries and Memoirs.*

Gibson: Gibson, *An Old Berwickshire Town.*
Gordon: Gordon, *Death is for the Living.*
Graham: Graham, *Social Life in Scotland in the 18th Century.*
Grant: Grant, *Golspie's Story.*
Gunn, *Drumelzier*: Gunn, *Book of the Church and Parish of Drumelzier.*
Gunn, *Traquair*: Gunn, *Book of the Church of Traquair.*
GVA: General View of the Agriculture of . . .

Hay: Hay, *Architecture of Scottish Post-Reformation Churches.*
Henderson, *Arbuthnott*: Henderson, *The Kirk of St. Ternan's, Arbuthnott.*
Henderson, *Banchory-Devenick*: Henderson, *History of the Parish of Banchory-Devenick.*
Henderson, Lockerbie: Henderson, *Lockerbie, A Narrative of Village Life in Bygone Days.*
Henderson, *Religious Life*: Henderson, *Religious Life in 17th Century Scotland.*
Hill: Hill, *Story of the Old West Kirk of Greenock.*
Hyslop: Hyslop, *Langholm as it was.*

Inglis, *Angus Parish*: Inglis, *Annals of an Angus Parish.*
Irving: Irving, *History of Dunbartonshire.*

Jeffrey: Jeffrey, *History and Antiquities of Roxburghshire.*
Johnston, *Orkney*: Johnston, *Church of Orkney.*
Johnston, *Working Classes*: Johnston, *History of the Working Classes in Scotland.*
Johnstone and Hunter: Johnstone and Hunter, Confession of Faith.

Keith: Keith, *Parish of Drainie and Lossiemouth.*
KS: Kirk Session/Kirk Session minutes.
KS Reg. Perth: Extracts from the Kirk Session Register of Perth.

Lorimer, *Early Days*: Lorimer, *Early Days of St. Cuthbert's Church.*
Lorimer, *Neil M'Vicar*: Lorimer, *Days of Neil M'Vicar.*
Lorimer, *West Kirke*: Lorimer, *Leaves from the Buik of the West Kirke.*
Love: Love, *Scottish Kirkyards.*
Low: Low, *Church of Montrose.*

MacGeorge: MacGeorge, *Old Glasgow*.
MacGill: MacGill, *Old Ross-shire and Scotland, I*.
Macinnes: Macinnes, *Evangelical Movement in the Highlands*.
Mackay, *Pres. Recs*: Mackay, *Records of the Presbyteries of Inverness and Dingwall*.
Mackay, *Sidelights*: Mackay, *Sidelights of Highland History*.
MacNaughton: MacNaughton, *Old Church Life in Ross and Sutherland*.
Martin: Martin, *Church Chronicles of Nigg*.
Mathieson: Mathieson, *Politics and Religion . . . to the Revolution*.
McNeill: McNeill, *The Silver Bough*.
Mitchell: Mitchell, *Inverness Kirk Session Records*.
M'Michael: M'Michael, *Notes by the Way*.
M'Naught: M'Naught, *Kilmaurs Parish and Burgh*.
Murray, *Falkirk*: Murray, *Records of Falkirk Parish*.
Murray, *St. Andrews*: Murray, transcription of St. Andrews Kirk Session minutes.

NSA: New Statistical Account.

OSA: Old Statistical Account.

Perth KS Reg: Extracts from the Kirk Session Register of Perth, Spottiswoode Misc. III.
PSAS: Proceedings of the Society of Antiquaries of Scotland.

Reid: Reid, *Royal Burgh of Forfar*.
Russell: Russell, *Reminiscences of Yarrow*.

St. Andrews KS Reg: St. Andrews Kirk Session Register, Scottish History Society.
Sharpe: Sharpe, *Selkirk, its Church, its School and its Presbytery*.
SHS: Scottish History Society.
Smout: Smout, *History of the Scottish People, 1560–1830*.
SN & Q: Scottish Notes and Queries.
Sprott and Leishman: Sprott and Leishman, *Book of Common Order and Directory of Public Worship*.
SRE: Henderson, *The Scottish Ruling Elder*.

Tait: Tait, *Two Centuries of Border Church Life*.
THAS: Transactions of Hawick Archaeological Society.
THAS 1876, Poor Law: THAS May 1876, Notes on Laws and Customs relating to the Poor, by Frank Hogg and others, pp. 13–21.
THAS 1879, Hassendean: THAS 1879, Hassendean and its Kirk, by J. J. Vernon.
THAS 1900, Vernon: THAS 1900, Hawick Parish and Kirk, pp. 93–146, by J. J. Vernon.
THAS 1902, Lauder: THAS 1902, Church and Social Life in Lauder, pp. 60–65, by Rev. T. Martin.

THAS 1904, Coldingham: THAS 1904, Kirk Session Records of Coldingham, by A. Thomson.

Thomson, *Lauder: Thomson, Lauder and Lauderdale.*

Tranter: Tranter, *The Queen's Scotland, the North-east.*

Turnbull: Turnbull, *A South Ayrshire Parish.*

Waddell, *East Lothian*: Waddell, *Parish Records in East Lothian.*

Waddell, *Kirk Chronicle*: Waddell, *An Old Kirk Chronicle.*

Notes

1

Kirk Sessions

1   Early Kirk Sessions: St. Andrews KS Reg, SHS 4, lvii. According to this
    Register, p.xxiii, in the years immediately after the Reformation, the elders
    of St. Andrews were known as the 'assembly' but after 1568 the terms 'seat'
    or 'session' were used and sometimes the word 'kirk' appears, with the same
    meaning.
2   Knox's account of early days: SRE pp.36–37. According to Rev. Andrew
    Edgar in *Old Church Life in Scotland*, I, pp.182–183, from the time of the
    Reformation most parishes had ecclesiastical boards. First and Second
    Books of Discipline *re* elders: Burleigh, pp.171, 199;   yearly elections: *St.
    Andrews KS Reg*, SHS 7, xcvi;   Fenwick Kirk Session: Edgar, I, pp.190–
    191.
3   Elders put off: Mitchell, p.31;   KSs proposing elders, etc.: Kilconquhar KS,
    1690;   objection: Ancrum KS, 1850;   unmarried elders rejected: Barron,
    III, p.19;   21 years of age: Kilninian and Kilmore KS, 1776 *quo* Acts of
    General Assembly 20 May 1776;   ordination by fasting etc.: Smout,
    p.199;   uplifted hands: Waddell, *Kirk Chronicle*;   Confession of Faith and
    Formula: Edgar, I, p.193.
4   Ruling elders: Edgar, I, pp.190–191;   eldership defined: APS 1592. III.
    542a.
5   Elders of standing: Mackay, *Pres. Recs.* xxv;   Kinross elders: Kinross KS,
    1699;   Book of Common Order: Sprott and Leishman, pp.13–14;   'as
    grund could produce': Waddell, *East Lothian*, p.32;   making further in-
    quiry: Sorbie KS, 1700;   ignorant people to be put off: AGA p.227,
    1648;   elders catechised: Cramond, *Presbytery of Fordyce*, p.22, 1650.
6   Episcopal rule: Mackay, *Pres. Recs.* xiii;   Kirk Sessions forbidden, permit-
    ted: Henderson, *Religious Life*, p.141;   KSs needed during Episcopacy:
    Mitchell, p.30–31, and p.15 *re* Inverness minute book.
7   Deacons as Inspectors of Poor: Edgar, II, p.39;   deacons' qualities: Sprott
    and Leishman, p.14;   advancing deacons: Barony KS, Glasgow,

1700; deacons not required to appear: Cathcart KS, 1702; deacons/elders in Montrose: Montrose KS, 1634, 1642, 1658; Arbuthnott deacons: Henderson, *Arbuthnott*, pp. 95–96. The modern Diaconate began with deaconesses — Lady Grizell Baillie was the first, *c*. late 19th century, and about the mid–1980s men joined too and the term Diaconate began. The members are trained and paid by the church.

8 Elders and 'ordinaries': SRE, p. 137.

9 Supervision of minister etc.: Burleigh, p. 172; Falkirk Visitation: Murray, *Falkirk*, I, p. 161; privy censures: Sorbie KS, 1702–03.

10 General Sessions: *Maitland Misc.* I, p. 97; Glasgow General Session: Denholm, *Historical Account of the City of Glasgow*, pp. 186–187.

11 Mr Dysart's meetings: Chambers, *Domestic Annals of Scotland*; East Lothian (Whitekirk) KS's meetings: Waddell, *East Lothian*; 'diets': St. Michael's KS, Linlithgow, 1730s; fortnightly fellowship meetings: Kinross KS, 1702; local versions of official Acts: *St. Andrews KS Reg*, SHS 7, lxvii, p. 159.

12 'Not keip session': Murray, *Falkirk*, I, p. 161; no one coming: *Extracts Kinghorn KS*, 1631; Aberdeen fine, 1568: *St. Andrews KS Reg*, SHS 4, xxvii; fine raised: *Aberdeen Eccl. Recs*, p. 93; 'haill sessioun' warned: *St. Andrews KS Reg*, SHS 4, xxvii.

13 Land-setting etc.: *THAS 1900, Vernon*; noblemen/General Assembly: *SRE*, p. 160; Earl of Lauderdale: Lauder KS, 1801; Archibald Hamilton: St. Mary's KS, Dumfries, 1843; Banff, 1838: *SRE*, pp. 258–259; governors, charities: College Church KS, Glasgow, 1805.

14 Secrecy sworn, Aberdeen: Edgar, I, p. 201; visitors: Cambuslang KS, *c*. 1752.

15 Elders' 'quarters': AGA, p. 227, 1648; elders/family worship: *THAS, November 1906, Hawick KS Records, Vernon*, pp. 93–94.

16 Treasurer, collecting etc.: Martin, p. 19, *c*. 1729.

17 Arbuthnott, 1691: Henderson, *Arbuthnott*, pp. 97–98; 'comotoe': Ashkirk KS 1691, and Mr Charles Gordon: 1695.

18 Collecting excise: APS 1645. VI. 301 b; man's Will in minutes: Daviot and Dunlichity KS, 1845; widow's trustees, and Francis Ruecastle, 1751: *THAS 1900*, pp. 147–148, *Excerpts from the KS of Hawick*, 1751; Roger Bennet: Murray, *Falkirk*, II, p. 177, 1754; loss at Balvraid, etc.: Edderton KS, 1841, 1830.

19 Harvest work: *THAS Sept. 1871*, pp. 90–97, *Ashkirk Records*; labour rules in Elgin, 1647: Cramond, *Elgin*, II, p. 256; fugitive servant, 1664: Craven, p. 45; daughters to take work: *THAS 1871*, pp. 90–97, *Ashkirk Records*; unemployed woman imprisoned: Cramond, *Elgin*, II, p. 120, 1604; tailor: *Aberdeen Eccl. Recs*, p. 75.

20 Elders liable for legal costs: Cambuslang KS, 1749.

21 'Ydill men', 1627: *Extracts Kinghorn KS*, p. 31; fencible men: APS 1650. VI. 625 b; 373 men raised: Bentinck, p. 282; Lord Dudhope's Regiment: Inglis, *Angus Parish*, p. 98; recruiting fears: Kiltearn KS, 1711.

22 Press gang in Dunrossness: Fyfe, p. 51, and Sir John Sinclair: pp. 58–59.

23 Caithness caterans: Chambers, Abridged Domestic Annals, pp. 280–281; elders slain, more widows, etc.: Extracts Kinghorn KS, pp. 61–62; elders/plague: Lorimer, Early Days, p. 115; recruiting fears: Kiltearn KS, 1711.

24 Highland Host: Baird, p. 24; military activity at Whitekirk, Inveresk, Leith: Love, pp. 133–135; horses in church: Cramond, *Elgin*, II, p. 283; St. Ninian's Church, Stirling: Love, p. 133. It is said that after the Battle of Bothwell Brig in 1679 Covenanters were imprisoned in Greyfriars Churchyard, Edinburgh, but according to *Ruins and Remains* by Anne Boyle, Colin Dickson, Alasdair McEwan and Colin Maclean, the ground now said to be the Covenanters' prison has been wrongly identified; that area was not incorporated into the graveyard until 1703 and the stone archway with iron gates, which gives credence to the prison story, was not built until 1704. The place where they were imprisoned was land to the south and east of the graveyard, now occupied by the Drill Hall, Forrest Road and Bristo Place.

25 Meeting of Committee of Estates: NSA Alyth, X, Perthshire, p. 1115. This Committee was also in existence 1660–61, 1688–89. Speymouth: Tranter, p. 250; Hendrie Cargill: NSA Alyth, X, Perthshire, pp. 1114–1115, and trooper preaching: p. 1115; theft by troops: Allan, p. 161, and box 'plunderit' at Dunfermline: p. 89; thefts by rebels: Bentinck, p. 282, 1746.

26 Auchterhouse rebels, 1650: Inglis, *Angus Parish*, p. 109, and going on knees: pp. 102–103, 1646; signing Covenant: Murray, *St. Andrews*, 1650; delivering up arms, etc.: Edwards, p. 111, and appearing on stool of repentance: p. 109, 1745.

27 John Brown: Edwards, pp. 108–109 and note to p. 109; Petty elders, 1649: NSA Petty, XIV, Inverness-shire, p. 389; Session interrogated: Scone KS, 1716.

28 Charles Air: Edwards, pp. 111–113; schoolmaster: Craig KS, 1716; Thomas Young: Presbytery of Forfar, 1717.

29 Help for 'captive sojors': Cramond, *Presbytery of Fordyce*, p. 24; money, cheese, etc.: Murray, *St. Andrews*, 1650; kirk attitude to troops: AGA p. 12, 1697; Trafalgar collection: Swinton and Simprim KS, 1806; Waterloo collection: Auldearn KS, 1815. A small book, *Notes on the History of the Parish of Lairg*, by Rev. Donald Macrae, pp. 36–63, gives a good account of local attitudes during the risings of 1715 and 1745.

30 Inventory: Cruden KS, 1720.

31 Fearn Abbey roof: NSA Fearn, XIV, Ross-shire, p. 361; Rosskeen Church: Barron, I, p. 63, and Kintail church: III, p. 339; Deskford Church, 1698: Cramond, *Deskford*, p. 18; Rathven church, 1722: Cramond, *Rathven*, p. 59; Strath church: NSA Strath, XIV, Inverness-shire, p. 312; Simprim

barn: Dawson, *Abridged Statistical History of Scotland*, note to p. 208; Mr Bowie: Bentinck, p. 250; South Uist: NSA XIV, Inverness-shire, p. 195, and Eigg: p. 153, and Strath: p. 312.

32 Heritors' duties: *SRE*, p. 110; tax, 1597: Cramond, *Elgin*, II, p. 46; magistrates' order: M'Naught, p. 119; collections for school: Craig KS, 1849.

33 Re-thatching: Ashkirk KS, 1650, 1661; church rebuilt at Tain: MacGill, I, pp. 54–55; parish to carry heath, etc.: Nigg KS, 1706–07; 'deficients' fine': Kiltearn KS, 1707; Tynninghame pulpit: Waddell, *East Lothian*, p. 23; Sunday offerings for windows: M'Naught, p. 119; special collections for windows, etc.: Tarbat KS, 1722, 1776; pane of glass: Swinton and Simprim KS, 1806; lime stolen: *THAS 1900, Hawick Town Council Records*, pp. 149–152.

34 Hand-bell rung: Waddell, *Kirk Chronicle*, p. 78; Bell Knowe: M'Naught, p. 115; Nigg bell-house: Nigg KS, 1730; 'hinging' bell: Waddell, *East Lothian*, p. 21; new bell, 1694: *THAS 1900, Hawick Town Council Records*, pp. 149–152; funeral tolling: Denholm, *Historical Account of the City of Glasgow*, pp. 186–187. A few churches such as Ardclach near Nairn, Clyne in Sutherland, and Latheron in Caithness have detached bell-towers situated some way above these low-lying buildings so that the bell could be heard. Glasgow Tron had a detached tower in 1595, and Daviot, Inverness-shire, had one until 1865.

35 Strangers in bell-houses: Waddell, *East Lothian*, p. 21; pigeons: Waddell, *Kirk Chronicle*, p. 32; bell rung evening, morning: NSA Kirkliston, I, Edinburghshire, p. 145; 4.00 a.m. bell: Montrose KS, 1659, and William Low: 1655; mending bell: Ashkirk KS, 1786, and new tow: 1736; butter, soap: Thomson, Elie Kirk, p. 19; candles for ringer: Mitchell, p. 4.

36 Collecting for clock, 1718: *THAS 1900, Hawick Town Council Records*, pp. 149–152; Arbroath bell: St. Vigeans KS, 1831; shared costs: Kirkwall KS, 1764.

37 James Young: Shotts KS, 1724; stile near sea: St. Monance KS, 1856.

38 Fairs, etc. in churches: Edgar, I, p. 13; Seamen's loft, etc.: Hill, pp. 32–33; James Vaus: Mitchell, p. 6; trees cut, sitting laigh, etc.: MacGeorge, p. 202; women sitting together, Glasgow: *THAS April 1879, Hassendean*.

39 Elgin, 1598: Cramond, *Elgin*, II, p. 63; John Low: Montrose KS, 1634; kirk officer's mother: Edgar, I, p. 13, Fenwick KS; compulsory stools: *Aberdeen Eccl. Recs*, p. 40; Elspet Cuthbert: Mitchell, pp. 3–4, 1695; incoming/outgoing tenants: NSA Kirkmichael and Cullicudden, XIV, Ross-shire, p. 51.

40 Seat for goodmother: Montrose KS, 1634; payment for seats: Craig KS, 1719 and Edwards, pp. 131–132; rent charged: Johnston, *Orkney*, p. 129, Orphir KS; charge for space: *Life and Work*, December 1924, article by Rev. Thomas Burns DD; 'sundries built seats': Montrose KS, 1658; complaints: Johnston, *Orkney*, p. 56, Holm KS; trades' seats: *THAS 1900, Vernon*; 'tumult' over seating: Irving, p. 566.

41 Buying wood: Cromarty KS, 1738; seats as property: Banchory-Devenick KS, 1773; auctioning seats: Low, p.140; seating gifted: Tongue KS, 1802; James Bailie's gift: Bara and Garvald KS, 1747.

42 Manse seat: Edgar, I, p.15, Stirling, 1627; manse seat: Montrose KS, 1634; elders' seats: Dick, p.91; schoolmaster's seat: NSA Dollar, VIII, Clackmannanshire, p.161; midwife's seat: Henderson, *Banchory-Devenick*, p.262, 1773; elders ousted: SRE, p.182. George Hay's *Architecture of Scottish Post-Reformation Churches*, p.33, shows the plan of early 19th century arrangements in Burntisland Church.

43 Heritors let seats: Nigg KS, 1729; Beatrix Sinclair: Kirkwall KS, 1731; heritors', Town Councils' seating obligations: Hay, p.195; Eccles seating: M'Naught, p.121 and note to p.121.

44 Communion/paupers' seating: Hill, p.11; Communion seats let: NSA Dollar, VIII, Clackmannanshire, p.116; unlettable seats for paupers: NSA Gladsmuir, II, East Lothian, p.195. In the mid–19th century the rent of seating at Communion tables during the year was about 1*s*. stg. Free sittings: NSA Tranent, II, East Lothian, p.300; poors' sittings: NSA Dunbar, II, East Lothian, p.89; all seats free: NSA Kilmalie, XIV, Inverness-shire, p.125; common loft: Martin, p.18 and Nigg KS, 1729.

45 Charity children: St. John's KS, Glasgow, 1829; seat rents ended: M'Naught, p.181. *Old Church Life in Scotland* by Andrew Edgar has very good information on church seating.

46 Friction: NSA Dunbar, II, East Lothian, notes to pp.89–90; controversy in Inverness: Barron, III, p.25.

47 'Gryt hears': Cramond, *Elgin*, II, p.248, *c.* 1643; it was there in 1618: p.158; candles provided: Craig KS, 1851; gas lighting, electricity: Macdonald, *St. Clements Looks Back*, p.27; heating church: NSA Clackmannan, VIII, Clackmannanshire, p.134; special collections for coal: Craig KS, 1847; 1*s*. for cleaning: St. Boswells KS, 1849; 'scattering nuisance': St. Monance KS, 1844; Properties and Endowments Bill: Burleigh, p.403; fabric fund: Martin, p.63.

48 Need for Session Clerk: Kilninver and Kilmelford KS, 1758; new Clerk owing to bad writing: Nigg KS, 1707.

49 Clerk at college: Tongue KS *c.* 1781; blank record: Ashkirk KS, 1705; Town Council appoints Clerk: Sharpe, pp.14–15; precentor's appointment: St. Michael's KS, Linlithgow, 1736.

50 Clerk's salary: Montrose KS, 1707; salary raised: Johnston, *Orkney*, p.123, Orphir KS; income from registration: OSA Borthwick, II (1975) p.74; fines for Clerk: Cramond, *Rathven*, p.49.

51 Clerk's salary: Tongue KS, 1786, 1795; town officers' payment: Kirkwall KS, 1749; Kilconquhar beadle: Kilconquhar KS, 1690; sharing perquisites: Montrose KS, 1634; dues either side of river: Wick KS, 1701; kirk officer's fixed salary: Edderton KS, 1863.

52 Depriving Clerk: OSA Borthwick, II (1975) note to p. 75. Payment to Session Clerks etablishes legal liability.

53 Sub-contracting precenting: Ashkirk KS, *c.* 1764; Falkirk precentor: Murray, *Falkirk*, II, p. 220; Clerk/precentor — separate posts: Johnston, *Orkney*, p. 124–125; £2 salary: Cramond, *Rathven*, p. 76, 1806; £15 salary: St. Boswells KS, 1874; 1889 salary: Martin, p. 56. The old Scots word for precentor is 'lettergae', one who lets go, in words or tune. The editor of *Life and Work*, March 1928, asked for information about use of this word and about phrases such as to 'take up the line' or 'uptakar of the psalm'.

54 Cleaning, 'vagabondis', church steeple as prison: *St. Andrews KS Reg*, SHS 7, xciii/lv; keeping order: Montrose KS, 1635; bell- ringing, grave-digging, cripples, sackcloth, etc.: Inglis, *Angus Parish*, p. 18; warning people to pay: Montrose KS, 1642.

55 'Kirkstile': Gibson, p. 113; shoes: *THAS 1900, Vernon*, and Kilbride KS, 1831; cloak: Dick, p. 119, Kilconquhar KS; 'clok or juip': Waddell, *Kirk Chronicle*, p. 78, Tynninghame KS; coats, white plaid: Mitchell, 1697, 1703.

56 1645 salary: Dick, p. 119, Kilconquhar KS; Borgue salary: Gordon, p. 167; £12 salary: *THAS 1900, Vernon*; £20 salary: Montrose KS, 1707.

57 'Common gift': Boleskine KS, 1802; corn for kirk officer: Inglis, *Angus Parish*, p. 150, Auchterhouse KS; cheese, etc.: Coll KS, 1733.

58 Dornoch beadles: Bentinck, pp. 455–56.

59 Waddell, *Kirk Chronicle*, p. 78.

60 Drunken beadle: Dick, pp. 118–119; Mauchline beadle: Gordon, pp. 97–98; concern over beadle's conduct: Craig KS, 1716; John Scott: Hawick KS, 1720, and *THAS 1900, Vernon*; bad beadle: Thurso KS, 1804.

61 Beadles join police, etc.: Dickson, p. 249.

62 Unpaid bell-man: Kilninian and Kilmore KS, 1772; bad copper for bellman: Coll KS, 1795; peck of oatmeal: Kilninver and Kilmelford KS, 1758.

63 Donald Robson: Cromarty KS, 1748; playing football, 1697: Craig-Brown, I, pp. 498–499; Robert Hall: Chambers, *Domestic Annals of Scotland*; St. Andrews deacon, 1580s: *St. Andrews KS Reg*, SHS 7, xciv.

64 Free mortcloths were allowed at, for example, Arbuthnott, Inverness. Free bell-ringing: Kirkwall KS, 1738; James Todd: Banff KS, 1775; Mr Davidson's horse: *THAS 1900, Vernon*; Kilconquhar elder's horse: Dick, p. 101; coffin-making: Craig-Brown, II, p. 104.

65 Robert Hogg: Russell, II, pp. 17–18; elder's intemperance: St. Monance KS, 1851; 'bad conversation': Allardyce, p. 99, 1650, Culsalmond; John Ross: MacNaughton, p. 45, 1757; elders 'not edified': Portmoak KS, 1788.

66 Changes for KSs: *SRE*, pp. 229–230. *The Book of the Church of Traquair* by Dr Gunn is very informative about the 20th century.

2
The Poor's Money

1 APS 1424. II. 8;   APS 1503. II. 251.
2 APS 1574. III. 88 ab.
3 APS 1579. III. 39;   APS 1592. III. 576;   APS 1597. IV. 140;   APS 1600. IV. 232.
4 APS 1649. VI. i. 39;   APS 1672. VII. 90 b;   APS 1698. X. 177.
5 SRE, pp. 239–240.
6 OSA Garvald and Bara, XIII (1794), note to p. 360.
7 NSA Balfron, VIII, Stirlingshire, p. 301.
8 Kilninian and Kilmore KS, 1768.
9 Kinnell KS, 1828. Henderson, *The Kirk of St. Ternan, Arbuthnott*, gives a good description of the donations given by that one church.
10 OSA Rerrick, V (1983) p. 309;   OSA Edzell, XIII (1976) p. 227.
11 NSA Prestonpans, II, East Lothian, p. 315.
12 OSA Straiton, VI (1982) p. 631.
13 Stow KS, 1844.
14 Easton, pp. 31–43.
15 OSA Grange, XVI (1982) note to pp. 211–213.
16 Poor woman: Resolis KS, *c.* 1826;   St. Andrews 1597: *St. Andrews KS Reg*, SHS 7, p. 835.
17 Act of Justices of the Peace, 1775: OSA Cargill, XI (1976) p. 68.
18 OSA Cargill, XI (1976) p. 69;   OSA East Kilbride, III (1790s) p. 428;   Headrick, *GVA Angus*, p. 244. *You the Jury*, Radio 4, discussed on 23 September 1987 whether the able-bodied should be obliged to work for benefit money.
19 Craig-Brown, I, p. 499.
20 Nigg KS, Ross-shire, 1830.
21 'All these can work': Hawick KS, 1725;   Susan Wilson: St. Monance KS, 1844.
22 Tongue KS, 1781.
23 Montrose KS, 1650.
24 Currie KS, 1745.
25 Loose letter from Edinburgh Charity Workhouse, 8 June 1843, among Dingwall KS minutes.
26 Henderson, *Arbuthnott*, p. 194.
27 Poor attending worship, 1570: *St. Andrews KS Reg*, SHS 7, note 1 to p. lxxxvi;   Elgin, 1596–97: Cramond, *Elgin*, II, p. 44, 58;   Perth, 1599: *Perth KS Reg*, p. 281;   Aberdeen, 1620: *Aberdeen Eccl. Recs*, pp. 94, 97.
28 Contumacious couple: Barry KS, 1734.
29 Scott, *Lauder — a free burgh for ever*, p. 30.
30 St. Boswells KS, 1770.

31 Keeping strangers out, 1640: Murray, *St. Andrews*; parishioners not to help strangers: Murray, *Falkirk*, I, p.65; poor strangers to leave or find surety: Montrose KS, 1649.

32 Decrepit Irish woman: M'Naught, pp.169–170; poor's landlords: *THAS 1876, Poor Law*, quo. Wilton Heritors' Book; Greenlaw: Gibson, p.105.

33 West Kilbride KS, 1827.

34 Baldernock KS, 1845.

35 Stow KS, 1789.

36 West Kilbride KS, 1826.

37 Ibid, 1832–33.

38 Grissel Orock: Coldingham KS, 1752; Stow KS, 1772.

39 Tillycoultry KS, 1838; Craig KS, 1851; 'going to Fala', 1784: Allan, p.226.

40 Conveying paupers: Craig KS, 1845, 1842, 1843, and 1842 *re* constable conveying pauper; taking a woman to the Mairns: Cathcart KS, 1780; shared travel costs: Craig KS, 1843.

41 Tarbat KS, Ross-shire, 1781.

42 Henderson, *Arbuthnott*, p.220.

43 OSA Melrose, III (1979) note to p.570.

44 St. John's Clachan KS, Dalry, Kirkcudbright.

45 Arbuthnott KS, 1717.

46 Mackenzie, *GVA Ross and Cromarty*, p.287 — written by the minister of Resolis.

47 Resolis KS, 1840.

48 Redeeming effects: OSA Grange, XVI (1982) note to p.227; families repay KSs: Kilconquhar KS, 1724; families' sharing: Mackenzie, *GVA Ross and Cromarty*, p.287, written by the minister of Resolis; position in Kirriemuir: Easton, p.86; Bina Fial: St. Monance KS, 1843; position in Knockbain: Mackenzie, *GVA Ross and Cromarty*, p.285, written by minister of Knockbain.

49 1737 County Act (Morebattle KS): Tait, pp.71–72; procedure legalised: St. Monance KS, 1832.

50 Arbuthnott KS, 1717.

51 Resolis KS, 1840.

52 Crying roup: Tait, pp.62–63; Session Clerk's roup fee: *THAS 1900, Vernon*; judge of roup (Rathven KS): Gordon, p.127; costs of roup: Kirkliston KS 1833–37.

53 Kinnell KS, 1837.

54 Payment of deficiency: St. Monance KS, 1843; re-rouping unsold effects: Banff KS, 1783.

55 St. Monance KS, 1836.

56 Henderson, *Arbuthnott*, pp.222–223.

57 James Birnie: Baldernock KS, 1844, and 1843–44 *re* reclaiming money given.

58 OSA Melrose, III (1979) note to p.570;   OSA Dingwall, III (1790s) p.12.

59 Roup of effects, 1851: Henderson, *Arbuthnott*, p.223.

60 Ibid, p.222.

61 Thomson, *Elie Kirk*, p.74, 1841.

62 Bonhill KS, 1774.

63 Poor's money undistributed: Nigg KS, Ross-shire, 1705;   distribution by 'well-affected': Kilconquhar KS, 1689.

64 OSA XIII (1794) shows: weekly payments – St. Andrews, p.213.
monthly payments – Borthwick, p.629, Carnbee, p.30.
quarterly payments – Rathven, p.415.

65 NSA XIV, Inverness-shire, shows: distribution every two years, Kilmuir, p.282;   money kept to bury paupers, Harris, p.158;   no distribution owing to no collections, South Uist, p.196.

66 Urr KS, *c.* 1808.

67 Hawick KS, 1712.

68 First and second class: Kirkcudbright KS, 1690s;   highest, middle, lowest: Banchory-Devenick KS *c.* 1805;   ordinary, extraordinary and widows: Dunrossness KS, 1786;   blind, bedridden, widows, strolling beggars: Mackenzie, *GVA Ross and Cromarty*, p.288;   Rosskeen parish, and benefit of classification: pp.286–287.

69 'Scanty pittance': OSA Nigg, XIII (1794) p.19.

70 OSA Alvie, XIII (1794) p.381, Glassary, p.662, and Borthwick, p.629.

71 19th century allowances: *Headrick, GVA Angus*, p.244;   widows: OSA Garvald and Bara, XIII (1794) note to p.360.

72 NSA Kilmuir Easter, XIV, Ross-shire, p.310.

73 OSA Garvald and Bara, XIII (1794) p.360.

74 Visit by elder: *SRE* pp.236–237;   visit by minister, catechist, beadle: Kilninian and Kilmore KS, 1768;   visit by bailie: Hawick KS, 1712.

75 Kilninian and Kilmore KS, 1768, 1769, 1771, 1774.

76 Minister's, treasurer's expenses: St. Vigean's KS, 1732, and visiting poor's house with tradesmen: 1773;   buying mortcloth, 1804: Allan, p.268.

77 Ashkirk KS.

78 Cloth, mending: Nigg KS, Ross-shire, 1782;   blanket: Kilninian and Kilmore KS, 1780.

79 Elders get clothing, blankets: West Kilbride KS, 1832.

80 Thomson, *Elie Kirk*, pp.70–72, 1639.

81 NSA Ormiston, II, East Lothian, p.151.

82 Casting peats: *THAS 1900, Vernon*;   load of coal, 1732: Tait, pp.62–63;   bad weather fuel: Hyslop, p.472.

83 Coal for old people: OSA Inchinnan, III (1790s) p.535;   Inverness Poor's Coal Fund: Barron, I, p.4;   subscription: NSA Dollar, VIII, Clackmannanshire, p.119;   Coal Fund managers: Aberdeen St. Nicholas KS, 1827;   collections for coal supplemented: NSA Gladsmuir, II, East

Lothian, p. 200;   coal given after heritors assume control: Murray, *Falkirk*, II, p. 223.

84   House rents paid: Craig KS, 1841–42;   non-paupers' rents paid: OSA Garvald and Bara, XIII (1794) note to p. 360;   James Glasgow: *THAS 1900, Vernon.*

85   David Wyllie's lodging: Kinnell KS, 1841;   poor man's lodging: West Kilbride KS, 1825.

86   Repairs: Resolis KS, 1829;   thatching: North Berwick KS, 1694–95.

87   Turnbull, p. 99.

88   Ashkirk KS, 1738;   Nigg KS, Ross-shire, 1730.

89   Thomson, *Elie Kirk*, p. 69. The parish of Elie raised the sum given.

90   Cramond, *Rathven*, p. 83.

91   *Perth KS Reg*, pp. 274–275.

92   NSA Tynninghame, II, East Lothian, pp. 40–41.

93   Slide 44, *The Road to the Isles — the Hebrides in Lantern Slides*, ed L.M.H. Smith.

94   APS 1661. VII. 311 b.

95   APS 1672. VIII. 90 b.

96   St. Monance KS, 1843–44.

97   King James Hospital: South Leith KS.

98   Dalkeith workhouse: NSA Dalkeith, I, Midlothian, p. 530;   KSs etc. on workhouse committees: Brown, *History of Paisley*, II, p. 66;   pulpit intimations *re* management committee: Inveresk KS, 1752;   Canongate parish: OSA Edinburgh, II (1975) p. 9;   'tender child': Inveresk KS, 1752.

99   NSA Tynninghame, II, East Lothian, p. 41.

100   OSA East Kilbride, VII (1973) p. 415.

101   Lending to poor able to repay: OSA Cleish, III (1790s) p. 558;   giving to prevent debt: OSA Carnbee, XIII (1794) p. 30;   James Kennedy: Turnbull, p. 99, 1750.

102   Mary M'Lean: Kilninian and Kilmore KS, 1790;   19 years' desertion: Aberdeen St. Nicholas KS, 1827;   Jean Ellice: Banff KS, 1782.

103   3rd Veterans pensioner: Aberdeen St. Nicholas KS, 1828;   man in need: Forgandenny KS, 1764;   Thomas Clark: Craig KS, 1843.

104   John Scott: Ashkirk KS, 1699;   John Wilson: *THAS 1900, Vernon*;   tobacco: Craig-Brown, II, pp. 76–77;   widows' shops: St. Monance KS, 1849;   widow's wool: Turnbull, p. 99, *c.* 1740s.

105   Isa Helm, Old Dand: *THAS 1900, Vernon*;   Colin Bayne: Thomson, *Elie Kirk*, p. 73, 1791;   David Wales: Craig KS, 1841;   boy's comb: Ashkirk KS, 1703;   Robert Hyslop, Matthew Thornton: Gibson, p. 100.

106   James Hardie: *THAS 1900, Vernon*;   John Low: Cramond, *Fordyce*, p. 64, 1773;   horse died 'by misfortune': Gibson, p. 100, 1727;   horse stolen: Henderson, *Banchory-Devenick*, p. 238, 1804;   coal cadger: Turnbull, p. 99;   two men's money for horses: SRE p. 96, Ceres KS, 1661;   horse for motherless child: *THAS 1900, Vernon*;   dying man's horse: *THAS 1900,*

Excerpts from the KS of Hawick, pp.147–148. There are further references to the buying of beasts in Robert Gibson's *An Old Berwickshire Town*, 1742, 1764, also Cambuslang KS, 1743 and Abernethy KS, 1759, etc.

107 George Coupar's cow: Inglis, *Angus Parish*, p.143; Andrew Donald's cow: Henderson, *Banchory-Devenick*, p.232, 1712; collection for cow: Craig KS, 1731.

108 Johnston, *Orkney*, p.108, Holm parish.

109 William Bell, 1651: *THAS Sept 1871, Ashkirk KS Records*, pp.90–97, by a minister of the parish; robbed widow, 1734: Cramond, *Fordyce*, p.62; man robbed near causey moss, 1755: Henderson, *Banchory-Devenick*, p.236; house robbed: Kilninian and Kilmore KS, 1767; flood: Cramond, *Fordyce*, p.58, 1732.

110 Apprentice's indentures: Murray, *Falkirk*, II, pp.197–198; David Craig: *Perth KS Reg*, p.277; foundling: Gibson, pp.97–98, 1725, 1727; James Edie, 1704: Henderson, *Arbuthnott*, p.195; repayment of apprentice fees: Aberdeen St. Nicholas KS, 1705; Morebattle KS: Tait, p.62.

111 Kilconquhar KS, 1741.

112 Inglis, *Angus Parish*, p.115, 1741.

113 Child maintained for a year: Nigg KS, Ross-shire, 1706; motherless children: Kilninian and Kilmore KS, 1771; five poor children: Coldingham KS, 1744; various needy people helped by unspecified KSs: Edwards, p.133; tobacco for two women: Gibson, p.100, 1826; Excise Officer: Cambuslang KS, 1742; temporary casual help: OSA St. Andrews, XIII (1794) p.213.

114 Euphen Rutherford: Yetholm KS, 1831; James Findlay: St. Vigeans KS, 1832; Alexander McKenzie: Creich KS, 1838; Mrs Bank: St. Monance KS, 1842; Donald Mackenzie of Newhall: Resolis KS, 1831.

115 'Compliments': Urr KS, 1800; anonymous help: Stow KS, 1825; money given by minister's order: Shotts KS, *c.* 1721, and Port Glasgow KS, 1699; donations only known to minister, heritors: Dick, p.98; 'to a private family': *THAS 1900*, Vernon; recommendation 'by a person of honour': North Berwick KS, 1696; money given 'by order of the committee': Torphichen KS, 1755; 'right to conceal': Thomson, *Elie Kirk*, p.72; private donations: Traquair KS, 1763.

116 War widows: *Extracts Kinghorn KS*, pp.56–57 and 61–62; man 'herried': *THAS Sept. 1871, Ashkirk KS Records*, pp.90–97, by a minister of the parish; press gang: Cramond, *Rathven*, p.22, 1757; highlanders: Channelkirk KS, 1745–47; highland women lurking: Melrose KS, *c.* 1715, 1745; Spaniards: *Perth KS Reg*, p.264.

117 Irish travellers: *Session Book of Bunkle and Preston*, 1689; horse hurt: *THAS 1900, Vernon*; Shotts KS, 1725.

118 Sailor's pass: Nigg KS, Ross-shire, 1822–23; passengers: Coldingham KS, 1744; testimonials: Port Glasgow KS, 1699; sufficient testificate: Shotts KS, 1721; John Anderson: *Session Book of Bunkle and Preston*,

1688; Oxford recommendation: Portmoak KS, 1703; Jean Guthrie: *Session Book of Bunkle and Preston*, 1686, and 'an honest gentleman': 1689; gentle beggar: Nigg KS, Ross-shire, 1818–20.

119 Stranger with dropsy: Abernethy KS, 1757; woman in Newstead, coffin and attendance: Melrose KS, 1758.

120 Coldingham KS, 1751, 1752.

121 Cramond, *Presbytery of Fordyce*, p. 56, 1719.

122 Craven, p. 28, 1659.

123 Episcopalian minister: NSA Morham, II, East Lothian, p. 266; Roman Catholic poor: Laggan KS, 1805.

124 Headrick, *GVA Angus*, pp. 244–245.

125 Remaining in established church for relief: OSA East Kilbride, III (1790s) p. 429; dissenters maintain poor, contribute to poor's funds: NSA Alloa, VIII, Clackmannanshire, p. 64; seceders begging: OSA Nigg, XIII (1794) p. 19; seceders admitted to poor's roll: Nigg KS, Ross-shire, 1830.

126 Types of beggars: Somerville, *My Own Life and Times*, pp. 369–370; beggars outside churches: Inglis, *Angus Parish*, p. 93; Elgin beggars, 1587: Cramond, *Elgin*, II, p. 47; Robert Guthrie: Edwards, p. 134; John Anderson: Montrose KS, 1645; Aberdeen, 1608: Johnston, *Working Classes*, p. 104; stocks and steeple, 1665: NSA St. Ninians, VIII, Stirlingshire, p. 319; Patrick Crombie: *Perth KS Reg*, p. 288, 1616.

127 Beggars at Session house, 1687: Low, p. 156; irons, stocks at kirks: APS 1592. III. 576; collection for imprisoned beggars, Banff 1730: Cramond, *Rathven*, p. 65; maintaining beggars in prison: APS 1655. VI. ii. 893 a.

128 APS 1424. II. 8; APS 1535. II. 347; Elgin: Cramond, *Elgin* II, p. 163 *re* 1620, and 1601 reference is general around that date.

129 King's missive: APS 1625. V. 178 b; APS 1649. VI. ii. 220; APS 1672. VIII. 89–91.

130 Beggars' 'meddals': Mitchell, p. 148, 1722; Synod Act *re* beggars' badges: Tarbat KS, 1757; Montrose beggars, 1775: Low, p. 156.

131 Cost of beggars' badges: Low, p. 157; attestations on parchment: Kilconquhar KS, 1724; minister signing certificates: Mackenzie, *GVA Ross and Cromarty*, p. 280, parish of Avoch; minister and others signing: Craig-Brown, I, p. 228.

132 Prosecution for giving to non-parish beggars: Craig-Brown, I, p. 228; tenants to be stented: Cramond, *Fordyce*, p. 60, 1742; beggars given clothing, etc.: Robertson, *GVA Perthshire*, p. 384; beggars badly off: NSA Duirinish, XIV, Inverness-shire, p. 356; strolling beggars: Mackenzie, *GVA Ross and Cromarty*, pp. 280, 281–282, 285, 289.

133 Advertising issue of badges: Kilninian and Kilmore KS, 1775; names read: *THAS 1876, Poor Law*; beggars given share of poor's money: OSA Dalry, XIII (1794) p. 62; beggars disqualified as witnesses: Graham, quo. Presbytery of Penpont, 1715.

134 Mackenzie, *GVA Ross and Cromarty*, p. 280, parish of Avoch.

135 Oldhamstocks beggars, licensing of beggars during famines, etc.: *SRE*, pp. 238–239; beggars in Ross-shire, 1812: Mackenzie, *GVA Ross and Cromarty*, pp. 229, 281–282.

136 Generosity: Robertson, *GVA Perthshire*, pp. 384–385; bags at mills: Kilninian and Kilmore KS, 1783.

137 Dunbar KS, 1725.

138 Bedridden, travelling poor: Cramond, *Fordyce*, p. 60, 1742; blind woman led: Henderson, *Banchory-Devenick*, p. 233; blind disabled, 1751/53/54: Henderson, *Arbuthnott*, pp. 225–226.

139 Jean Guthry, 1756, and Margaret Steinson: Cramond, *Fordyce*, p. 63; orphan in barrow: Ashkirk KS, 1702; Wallace: Cramond, *Rathven*, p. 60, 1724.

140 Barrows in Lauder: Thomson, *Lauder*, pp. 247–248; woman in creel: Cramond, *Fordyce*, p. 46; man carried on ass: Cramond, *Rathven*, p. 68; object on crutches: Thomson, *Elie Kirk*, p. 72; stilts: Edwards, p. 134; clogs: Cramond, *Fordyce*, p. 67, 1726.

141 Horses for cripples: *THAS 1900, Vernon*; taking turns to remove cripples: Waddell, *Kirk Chronicle*, pp. 64–66, Tynninghame; women take cripples in barrow: *THAS 1900, Vernon*.

142 High-handed beggars: *THAS 1876, Poor Law*.

143 Conditions for King's Bedesmen: *St. Andrews KS Reg*, SHS 7, lxxxvi, 1583; beadmen, 1727: Cramond, *Rathven*, p. 62; blewgown, 1734: Cramond, *Fordyce*, p. 62.

3

The Fatherless, the Foundlings and the Famished

1 Coll KS, 1734, 1733.

2 Kilninian and Kilmore KS, 1772.

3 Orphans being heritors' responsibility: Resolis KS, 1842; relief for orphans, foundlings till 14 years old: Edgar, II, p. 47.

4 OSA Stornoway, XX (1983) pp. 38–39.

5 West Kilbride KS, 1832.

6 Approaching orphan's uncle: Scone KS, 1720–22; friends carried away family: Forgandenny KS, 1773; sending children to half-sister: Edwards *re* Kinnell KS.

7 Sending collection to Presbytery for Edinburgh Orphan Hospital: Bara and Garvald KS, 1735; payment for child in Orphan Hospital: Currie KS, 1743.

8 Elders 'make sale' of effects: Ashkirk KS, 1702; apprysing goods and gear: Henderson, *Arbuthnott*, p.224, 1690; roup of orphans' parents' goods: Scone KS, 1716.

9 Payment to Katharin: Coldingham KS, 1744; payment to James Scott: Ashkirk KS, 1694, 1701, 1703.

10 James — , orphan: Ashkirk KS, 1703; Margaret Paterson: Tweedsmuir KS, 1763; James Alme: Johnstone, *Orkney*, p.53, Holm KS, 1698.

11 Costs of boarding orphans: Ashkirk KS, 1702, 1703, and Adam Scott: 1697–98; promise of blanket: Mitchell, p.154, 1782.

12 Resolis KS, 1842, 1844.

13 Teaching orphan to beg: Johnston, *Working Classes*, p.104, Gask, Perthshire, 1679; seven-year-old to beg: Henderson, *Arbuthnott*, 1750; nine-year-old to shift for himself: Edgar, II, p.47; orphan to beg during famine: Ashkirk KS, 1699.

14 Surgeon's costs for orphan: Cathcart KS, 1782; 'cureing' orphan's face: *SRE*, p.96, Oldhamstocks area; harn for 3 shirts for orphan: Cathcart KS, 1782; 'coarse suit' etc.: Mitchell, p.155; William Scott: Ashkirk KS, 1702–03.

15 William Scott sent to school: Ashkirk KS, 1702; employment at Draning: West Kilbride KS, 1832, and fifteen-year-old leaving job: 1827.

16 John Botch: Ashkirk KS, 1702; Chopins' baby: Waddell, *East Lothian*, pp.30–31.

17 Collection for orphan children: Banchory-Devenick KS, 1811; collection for widows, orphans: Edderton KS, 1839.

18 Stotfield disaster: Drainie KS, 1780, 1784; 1807 collection: Henderson, *Banchory-Devenick*, p.238.

19 Kirkwall KS, 1738.

20 'Child Dalbeattie': Urr KS, 1808, 1810; Shotts KS, 1721, 1724, 1726; Alexander Greenlaw: Gibson, pp.97–98.

21 1712: AGA p.18; Nicholas: Reg. of Births and Baptisms of Logie Easter, 1788; Janet Smith: Perth KS Reg, p.309, 1627.

22 Child in ditch: St. Cuthbert's KS, Edinburgh, 1708; elders make inquiries: Cruden KS, 1742; examination of 248 women: *SRE*, p.109.

23 Search for mother: Mitchell, pp.151–153, 1764.

24 Child concealed in hay: *THAS 1876, Poor Law* (1811); abandoned baby dying shortly: Kinross KS, 1703.

25 Nursing child in mother's illness: Abernethy KS, 1748; 'nurse for one of his bairns': Coll KS, 1801; Thomas Denoon's child: Tarbat KS; John Garland's wife: Craig KS, 1717; keeping foundling till inquiries made: Murray, *Falkirk*, II, pp.60–61.

26 Resolis KS, 1832. Payments were sometimes made in kind to a wet nurse, such as a plaid or clothing — Mitchell, pp.151–153.

27 Foundling girl: Edwards, p.136–137; Alexander Greenlaw, 1723, and foundlings better off than if kept by parents: Gibson, pp.97–98.

28 Andrew Shotts: Shotts KS, 1721, 1724, 1726; 'hanging down coat', etc.: Cathcart KS, 1778, 1780; 2¹/₂ years' unpaid board: Mitchell, p. 151.

29 St. John's KS, Glasgow, 1833.

30 Foundling from Elgin: Banff KS, 1700; Sheriff to apprehend foundling's mother: Cramond, *Boyndie*, p. 23.

31 Resolis KS, 1832, 1833, 1845; soliciting charity by collection: Mitchell, p. 153, 1779.

32 Foundling dismissed to beg: Fordyce KS, 1741, 1746; 'travel for her bread': Mitchell, p. 154; ten-year-old to work: Edwards, pp. 136–137.

33 Alexander Greenlaw, 1725: Gibson, p. 97–98; catechising: St. John's KS, Glasgow, 1831, and charity children occupying seating: 1829.

34 St. Cuthbert's KS, Edinburgh, 1709.

35 Banchory-Devenick KS, 1802.

36 Craig KS, 1735.

37 Bellie KS, 1829.

38 1563 famine and Queen Mary: Chambers, *Abridged Domestic Annals*, pp. 23–24.

39 Smout, pp. 148, 270; J. A. Symon, *Scottish Farming*, pp. 90, 157, 158, 373; 1595 famine: Chambers, *Abridged Domestic Annals*, p. 143, and people dying in Edinburgh streets, 1623: p. 223; NSA Kirkintilloch, VIII, Dunbartonshire, notes to pp. 170–172; Henderson, *Arbuthnott*, p. 189; Easton, p. vii.

40 NSA Kirkintilloch, VIII, Dunbartonshire, notes to pp. 170–172.

41 OSA Duthil, XVI (1982) p. 519.

42 Collection for Orkney: Lorimer, *West Kirke*, p. 38; limit on bridal meals, 1620: Irving, p. 567; thunderstorm after fast: Chambers, *Abridged Domestic Annals*, p. 223.

43 Impact of famine: NSA Nigg, XIV, Ross-shire, p. 27; moral cases outstanding: Mitchell, p. 66.

44 Crossing River Esk, 1697: Hyslop, p. 469; people forbidden to go to Newcastle: Ashkirk KS, 1697.

45 Ashkirk KS, 1696–99; Holm distribution: Johnston, *Orkney*, p. 54; Arbuthnott relief, 1700: Henderson, *Arbuthnott*, p. 167.

46 Common coffin: Ashkirk KS, 1699.

47 Currie KS, 1740. Buckhaven Parish Church Agency (Rev. Dane Sherrard) is a modern example of job creation.

48 Gunn, *Traquair*, pp. 90–91.

49 Murray, *Falkirk*, II, pp. 145–146.

50 Ibid, II, pp. 180–181.

51 Cromarty KS, 1757.

52 Tweedsmuir KS, 1773.

53 Kilninian and Kilmore KS, 1773.

54 Reasons for Black Year: NSA Kirkintilloch, VIII, Dunbartonshire, notes to pp. 170–172; elders soliciting aid, generosity of the rich: Tongue KS, 1782–83.

55 Knockando KS, 1783.

56 Henderson, *Arbuthnott*, p. 168, 1783.

57 Banff KS, 1783.

58 Money lent for bread: Tarbat KS, 1782; lending £18+ stg.: Nigg KS, Ross-shire, 1783.

59 Search for coal: Dr John Gilbert, Melrose; buying coal: Banff KS, 1783.

60 Banff KS, 1783.

61 Banff KS, June 1783, gives in full a letter from the Deputy King's Remembrancer to the minister.

62 Pease-meal year: NSA Kilmuir, Skye, XIV, Inverness-shire, p. 271.

63 Details from Deputy King's Remembrancer's letter: Banff KS, 1783.

64 Ibid.

65 Comments on government supplies: Nigg KS, Ross-shire, 1783.

66 Meal distributions: Tarbat KS; continuing number of needy people: Cromarty KS.

67 Calling in money to pay for meal: Nigg KS, Ross-shire, 1783; paying 1*s.* arrears for delivery of meal: Kilninian and Kilmore KS, 1784.

68 Minister/unmilled grain: Cromarty KS, 1783.

69 £30 raised for poor: Cromarty KS, 1782; people buy peasemeal for poor: Banff KS, 1783; cockles: OSA Tain, III (1790s), note to p. 396.

70 Payment to treasurer: Banff KS, 1783; Question-man's payment: Kilninian and Kilmore KS, 1784.

71 KSs borrowing to buy meal, 1796: Cramond, *Ordiquhill*, p. 37; subscription papers: Henderson, *Arbuthnott*, p. 169, and difficulties owing to price fall, 1800: p. 172.

72 Lauder KS, 1800–01.

73 Reasons for 1836–37 famine: NSA Kilmuir, Skye, XIV, Inverness-shire, p. 271; not celebrating Lord's Supper: Edderton KS, 1836.

74 Ashkirk KS, 1699.

4
Poor Bodies and Sick Folk

1 1574 and 1587 pestilences: Chambers, *Abridged Domestic Annals*, pp. 63–64, 108; 1587 pestilence: *Perth KS Reg*, p. 261.

2 1606 plague and 'wettis': *Aberdeen Eccl. Recs*, p. 53, and 'plague of the pocks', 1610: p. 74, and plague in Torrie and salmon fishers, 1608: pp. 64–65.

3 Notifying minister of sickness: *St. Andrews KS Reg*, SHS 7, pp. 817–818.

4 Craig-Brown, I, p. 499.

5 Nursing burned woman: Kilninian and Kilmore KS, 1779; Helen Glendinning: Melrose KS, 1741; dying pauper: St. Monance KS, 1845; waiting on Margaret Kerr: Ashkirk KS, 1766; boarding costs for wholly helpless people: OSA Edzell, XIII (1976) p.227; James Strachan: Craig KS, 1736.

6 *THAS 1900, Excerpts from the KS of Hawick*, pp.147–148.

7 Washing: Craig KS, 1842–43, and cleaning house: 1841, and washing clothing after death: 1849.

8 Keith, p.102.

9 Mad dog bite: Henderson, *Banchory-Devenick*, p.237, 1777; man without arms, 1736: Cramond, *Fordyce*, p.62; boy with rupture: Edwards, p.134; 'support in her illness': Resolis KS, 1838; 'sickness and straits': Coldingham KS, 1752; John Fairfoul's child: Abernethy KS, 1757; woman, children confined by sickness: Banchory-Devenick KS, 1809; Alex Robson: Bentinck, p.457.

10 'Charitable supply' for boy with King's Evil, 1685: Cramond, *Presbytery of Fordyce*, p.47; girl with cruels in her leg: Kilninian and Kilmore KS, 1775; man 'newly cutt of the gravel': Mackay, *Pres. Recs*, xlv; 'paralytick schoolmaster': Henderson, *Banchory-Devenick*, p.232, 1708; bloody flux: Kirkwall KS, 1763; sundry persons confined to bed: Tarbat KS, 1791.

11 Henderson, *Banchory-Devenick*, p.233, 1716.

12 Alisone skugall: Waddell, *Kirk Chronicle*, p.65; Janet Morrice: Keith, p.96, 1741; seat for woman unable to stand: Craig-Brown, I, p.499; Bible with large characters (early 1700s): Dr John Gilbert, Melrose.

13 Ale infused with herbs: Craig-Brown, II, 1718, Selkirk parish; Janet Greig: Gunn, *Drumelzier*, p.54; mutchkin of sack: Hyslop, p.470; bills at Sandie Davidson's: Waddell, *East Lothian*, pp.28–29; Alexander Spinks: North Berwick KS, 1695; wine for widow: Craig KS, 1850; Andrew Bruce: Shotts KS, 1725; ale etc. for Thomas Crawford: Cathcart KS, 1798.

14 Margret Lochhead: Brotchie, p.65; cataract operation: Gunn, *Drumelzier*, p.54; 'couching' eyes: Cramond, *Fordyce*, p.58, 1731; purging and blooding: Craig-Brown, II, pp.76–77; William Wood, 1722: Gibson, p.99; calling in Mr Constable: St. Monance KS, 1844; calling in Mr Fordyce: Henderson, *Arbuthnott*, p.196, 1795; operation on child, 1682: Gunn, *Traquair*, p.52; David Laird: Craig KS, 1725; George Minty's operation, 1728: Cramond, *Fordyce*, p.58.

15 Merrilies' foot: Cambuslang KS, 1743; woman with broken leg: Kilninian and Kilmore KS, 1768; Isobel Denning: Gibson, p.99, 1719; leg cut by Act of Presbytery: Edwards, p.134; leg hurt by mill-stone: M'Naught, p.181; Coldingham payments: *THAS 1904, Coldingham*; Robert Weir's leg: Cathcart KS, 1782; cost of long illness and amputation: Tarbat KS, 1782.

16 Auchterhouse KS, 1713: Inglis, *Angus Parish*, p.151.

17 Jean Lobban's leg, 1785: Cramond, *Fordyce*, p. 65; rupture bandage: Craig KS, 1851; 'drogis and cures': Edwards, p. 134; 'batter': Brotchie, p. 68, 1704; collection for medicines: Johnston, *Orkney*, pp. 112, 79.

18 Janet's herbal cures: Edgar, I, note to p. 269, Rothesay KS, 1661; reports of herbal cures, etc.: Craven, pp. 29–30; seventh son: Edwards, p. 134; drink to cure convulsions: Ashkirk KS, 1701, 1702; boy 'likely to be a cripple': Waddell, *Kirk Chronicle*, Tynninghame KS, 1647; payment when leg is 'heall': Cramond, *Elgin*, II, p. 193, 1626.

19 Elspeth Inglis: *THAS 1900, Vernon*; minister's sanction for taking medicine: NSA Moy and Dalarossie, XIV, Inverness, p. 108; ministers' medical supplies: Blakey, p. 78.

20 Rev. Patrick Grant: OSA Nigg, XIII (1790s) p. 17; Rev. James Gordon: OSA North Yell and Fetlar, XIII (1790s) note to p. 283. Mr David Robertson, Tain, has made inquiries about the condition anafarca. J. Gilbride of the Information Department of the National Pharmaceutical Association could find no reference to it, nor could the Pharmaceutical Society library trace it, but it is suggested that it was akin to glanders which involves lymph glands, skin thickening with skin lesions and abcess-forming nodules which is called an infarction. The prefix 'ana' can mean severe: 90% of victims formerly died of glanders. Minister's sister's cure: OSA Kinnellar, XIV (1982) p. 564.

21 John Wilson's blood-letting: Murray, *Falkirk*, II, pp. 70–71.

22 Minister at Peterhead well: Macrae, *The Parish of Lairg*, p. 24; mineral water from Aboyne and going to Pitkethly wells: Henderson, *Arbuthnott*, p. 156; Margaret Turnbull and John Ekron: *THAS 1876, Poor Law*; London trip to recover sight, 1708: Mitchell, p. 50; Isobel Millar: Tarbat KS, 1776, 1780; sea trip to Edinburgh Infirmary: Craig KS, 1737; horse hire to Edinburgh, 1731: Tait, p. 62, Morebattle KS.

23 Blind boy taught music: Inglis, *Angus Parish*, p. 143, 1792; educating cripple to become teacher: Cramond, *Fordyce*, p. 64, 1761; cripple put to tailoring: Waddell, *Kirk Chronicle*, p. 56, 1647.

24 Woman travailing in childbirth: Ashkirk KS, 1707; John Ferrier's wife, Will Smith's wife: Abernethy KS, 1757, 1758, and twins: 1751, and absent father of twins: 1775; collection for triplets: Henderson, *Banchory-Devenick*, p. 236; fisher's triplets: Mitchell, p. 39, 1700.

25 *Report on the Sanitary Condition and General Economy of Tain and Easter Ross* by James Cameron, Surgeon in Tain, 1841; midwifery training: Forgandenny KS, 1773.

26 Keith, pp. 95–96.

27 Woman in jougs, 1592: Cramond, *Elgin*, II, p. 26, Elgin KS; Margaret Alexander: *Perth KS Reg*, p. 296.

28 Mary McNeil: Kilninian and Kilmore KS, 1767; Janet Hay: Gibson, p. 99, 1720s; 'clamorous wife': Cramond, *Fordyce*, p. 58, 1732; young damsel: Cathcart KS, 1782; Alexander Gairdn: Cramond, *Fordyce*, p. 62, 1731; Ann McCulloch and William Macleod: Cromarty KS, 1842.

29 St. Boswells KS, 1765.

30 Clackmannan KS, 1702.

31 Idiot girl banished, 1667: Cramond, *Fordyce*, p. 47; idiot banished: Banff KS, 1702, and Jean Carr: 1784. *The Scots Magazine*, November 1988, pp. 206–208, has an article, 'Jean Carr's Stone' by Walter Jack.

32 Henderson, *Arbuthnott*, pp. 227–230.

33 John Spark: Henderson, *Arbuthnott*, p. 230, 1805–12.

34 Boarding out: *Nigg Parish Council minutes*, 1925.

35 Angus Hutton: Cromarty KS, 1841, and Christy Smith: 1832.

36 Presbyterial Lunatic Fund: Banchory-Devenick KS, 1808; Montrose Communion collection: Cormack, p. 280; collection for Montrose Lunatic Hospital: Henderson, *Arbuthnott*, p. 251; Royal Asylum, right of presentation 'for ever': loose papers in Dingwall KS minutes, HM Register House, CH2/711/8; bedding and clothing required: Cormack, p. 289; £60 contribution to Royal Asylum: Cromary KS, 1842.

37 Thomas Allan: St. Monance KS, 1832, 1841/42/43, and John Irvine's son: 1832.

38 Mrs Duncan: Ibid, 1841/42/43.

39 Helen Currie: Ibid, 1845.

40 Number of lunatics: Easton, pp. 18–19; 'fetters and shakles', 1693: *SRE*, p. 96, Grange KS; Catherine Chisholm: Letter from Treasurer Office of Charity Workhouse, Edinburgh, 1839, to minister of Dingwall, among loose papers in Dingwall KS minutes, HM Register House, CH2/711/8.

41 Presbytery of Elgin, IX, 12 August 1829.

42 Collection for Infirmary for 'diseased poor': Craig KS, 1729; collection for 'curable disease': Bara and Garvald KS, 1729; collections for Infirmary: Headrick, *GVA Angus*, p. 247.

43 No collection for Aberdeen Infirmary: Mitchell, p. 159.

44 Kelso Dispensary Records shown in HM Register House exhibition, August 1986.

45 Security taken from employer: Banff KS, 1783; funds for patients running out: Minutes of General Session of Perth, 1811; patients' burials: Banchory-Devenick KS, 1796 — the Mistress of the Infirmary wrote to that Session demanding 14s. 2d. stg. for a burial.

46 St. John's KS, Glasgow, 1825.

47 Ibid, 1832.

48 Destitute Sick Society accounts, 1834–40: South Leith KS.

49 'Skathly dog': *THAS 1876, Poor Law*; pigs: Bentinck, pp. 289–290, and prison conditions: p. 361; water supply: Murray, *Falkirk*, II, p. 130.

50 Innoculation, vaccination: Smout, pp. 222, 271; smallpox deaths in highland parish: OSA Tarbat, XVII (1981) p. 645; 50 die in 1792: Gordon, *A Changing Parish*, Health and Sickness, p. 10; prejudice due to cost: OSA Rogart, XVIII (1979) p. 469; free innoculation: OSA Eccles, III (1979)

p.155; Rev. Patrick Forbes: Blakey, p.78; Rev. James Nichol: Gunn, *Traquair*, p.102.

51 Removing lepers, 1583: *Perth KS Reg*, p.245; master of leper hospital, 1578: *Aberdeen Eccl. Recs*, p.23, and hospital 'betwixt towns', 1604: p.34, and woman put in 'lipper house,' 1610: pp.73–74; Burgh Councils supervise leper hospitals: Chambers, *Abridged Domestic Annals*, p.127; OSA North Yell and Fetlar, XIII (1794) p.282 and note to p.282.

52 Wapinshaws, 1604: Cramond, *Elgin*, II, pp.123–124; wedding banquets, 1585: Chambers, *Abridged Domestic Annals*, p.97; lykewakes: *Aberdeen Eccl. Recs*, pp.53–54; 1645 epidemic: Lorimer, *Early Days*, p.112, and 1648 epidemic: pp.115–116; Dundee cleansers: *Aberdeen Eccl. Recs*, pp.53–54.

53 Black Death: Smout, p.163; anthrax: The *Scotsman*, 25 July 1989, 'Dangers of raking over the past', by Maria MacDonell; landward area: Montrose KS, 1649; 1645 Edinburgh epidemic: Lorimer, *Early Days*, p.112 and Chambers, *Abridged Domestic Annals*, p.272.

54 Churchyard preaching: *THAS Sept. 1871, Ashkirk Records*, by a minister of the parish, pp.90–97; cancelled worship: Melrose KS, 1645 and Lorimer, *Early Days*, p.115.

55 Bier/re-usable coffin: Edwards, pp.182–183; reverting to common coffin: Gordon, p.119.

56 No coffins in common graves: *Edinburgh Burgh Council Records*, 1597; individual coffins: Easton, p.40, 1819; houking up foul graves, 1648: Lorimer, *Early Days*, p.115.

57 Cholera burials: St. Vigeans KS, 1832; cholera victims buried north and south: Gordon, p.120; burial and self-burial, 1690s: NSA Kirkmichael and Cullicudden, XIV, Ross-shire, p.44 and note to p.44; resumption of worship, 1646: Lorimer, *Early Days*, p.115; petitioning JPs *re* burials: Nigg KS, Ross-shire, 1832.

58 Burial in Graham's Muir: NSA Falkirk, VIII, Stirlingshire, p.7, and control in 1645 epidemic: p.6; typhus burials: Montrose KS, 1649; kirk officer buries cholera: Gordon, p.120.

59 Mortcloth: Nigg KS, Ross-shire, 1832.

60 Resolis KS, 1832.

61 Kilconquhar KS, 1832.

62 St. Vigeans KS, 1832. Balnagown Estates Rent Book for Mr Ross, tenant, Pitmaduthy, Ross-shire, shows a share of cholera assessment in addition to rent.

63 1849 epidemic: Craig KS.

64 Prayer meetings recommended, 1832: Fraser and Munro, *Tarbat: Easter Ross*, p.184; people going to church, etc., 1832: Macrae, *Life of Augustus Aird*; Day of Thanksgiving: Resolis KS, 1832. The *Ross-shire Journal*, 22 September, 1989 has an article on the Lochbroom Yair Riot of 1832 which refers to cholera, although not in relation to Kirk Sessions.

5
The Poor's Box

1 John Knox's expectations: Edgar, II, p.2; teinds: Donaldson and Morpeth, *Dictionary of Scottish History*, p.213; early Christian collections: Barclay, *Daily Study Bible — Acts of the Apostles*, p.51.

2 APS 1574. III. 88 ab; collections to be at church doors: *SRE*, p.75; collections during services: Montrose KS, 1635; collections forbidden during services: Johnston, *Orkney*, p.13; collections in most convenient place: Cramond, *Elgin*, II, p.20, 1591; Banff 'boxes': SRE p.79; Pencaitland, Torphichen: Hay, pp.232–233.

3 Three-monthly rota: Sorbie KS, 1701; elders relieved from collecting: Tongue KS, 1788; collectors refusing or untimeous: Montrose KS, 1642, 1655; collectors to give normal collection if absent: Cramond, *Elgin*, II, p.20, 1591.

4 Bred, brod: *SRE*, p.75; collection plates on ground: Dobson and Sanderson, pp.11–12; 'basons on Casles': Murray, St. Andrews, 1642. George Hay, *Architecture of Scottish Post-Reformation Churches*, has an illustration of an offertory stool of 1709 at Dalmeny which is there still but no longer used; and Nigg Old Church, Ross-shire, has a felt-lined and fringed wooden bowl fixed by a bracket just inside the church door.

5 'Raming past': *SRE*, p.75, Markinch, Fife; bailies etc. at church doors: *Aberdeen Eccl. Recs*, pp.93–94; only one entry to kirkyard: Edgar, II, p.17, Mauchline KS, 1783; Communion tickets refused to non-contributors: *St. Andrews KS Reg*, SHS 7, p.845.

6 Landward and burgh poor: Reid, p.138; collections at quire door: Montrose KS, 1650; Kilrenny: SRE, p.79.

7 APS 1701. X. App 99b; OSA Melrose, III (1979) note to p.571; heritors' bag: Ashkirk KS, 1751; recording collections: Sorbie KS, 1701; collectors to deliver collections at Session House: Montrose KS, 1670; new timber box: Abernethy KS, 1749; big box: Craig KS, 1737; larger and little boxes: Bara and Garvald KS, 1737, and repository for Communion cups: 1732; poor's bag: Ashkirk KS, 1751, and Bara and Garvald KS, 1737; mid-box, sea- box: SRE, p.79.

8 Mean collections (Lilliesleaf) and 'verie small' ones (Melrose): Sharpe, p.139; amount of collections 1578, by 1651, 1678, 1790s: OSA Monifieth, XIII (1794) note to p.495; intrusion of Episcopalian clergyman: Cramond, *Elgin*, II, p.326, 1702; very small collections given to beadle: Dickson, p.200; no collection: NSA South Uist, XIV, Inverness-shire, p.196; heritors and collections: OSA Borthwick, XIII (1794) note to p.630.

9 Speaker of House of Commons: Gibson, p.91; Lord Sutherland: Golspie KS, 1756; Portuguese coins etc.: *SN & Q* — 'Barry in the 18th Century'; coins returned if overmuch given: Edwards, p.134.

10　Marriage collections for beadle: Inglis, *Angus Parish*, p.124, Auchterhouse parish, 1652;　Ceres, 1657, and laird's wedding, 1679: *SRE,* pp. 87–88;　regular collections at marriages: Kilbride KS, 1830;　collection or fine at private marriages: Johnston, *Orkney*, p.130, Orphir KS;　collections at baptisms, private Communions: *SRE*, pp.87–88, Aberdeen, 1630–31.

11　Lack of pulpit supply, 1836: Martin, p.46, and lawsuits: p.14, Rev. George Munro, Nigg, 1715–24;　minister at Synod: Kilninian and Kilmore KS, 1772;　exercises in minister's family: Craven, p.26, 1658;　storm prayers: Edwards, p.131;　'raire meeting': Craven, p.25, 1658.

12　Minister exhorts people *re* bad coin: *THAS 1876, Poor Law*;　base money from abroad: Chambers, *Abridged Domestic Annals*, p.56, 1574;　Edinburgh and Inverness halfpennies: Cramond, *Rathven*, p.75;　Irish halfpennies: *THAS 1900, Vernon*;　Woods halfpennies and Maggie Robs: Barry KS, 1734;　raps: Bentinck, p.291;　sanded halfpennies: Gibson, p.59, 1759, and Tait, p.64, 1732;　clipped coins: Johnston, *Orkney*, p.49, 1697, Holm KS;　bad brass: Swinton and Simprim KS, 1803;　bad copper: Cramond, *Rathven*, p.75, 1800;　bad silver: Gibson, pp.92–94.

13　Aberdonians remove good coin: Allardyce, p.107. Agnes Keith in *The Parish of Drainie and Lossiemouth* says that in 1714 the minister had to rebuke the congregation for wasting time by taking change out of the collections, possibly putting in a halfpenny and taking out a farthing. Buying doits for church collections: Gibson, p.95;　thief stakes doits etc.: Allardyce, p.107.

14　Two shot bags: Swinton and Simprim KS, 1800;　1152 doits: Nigg KS, Ross-shire, 1708;　vast amount of bad copper: St. Vigeans KS, 1754;　bad copper made into collecting cups: Allardyce;　melting of bad coin: Cramond, *Syn. Aberdeen*, p.51, 1752.

15　Elders to watch for raps: Bentinck, p.291;　Peterculter KS, 1771: Cormack, p.13;　advancing £3 for farthings: Cramond, *Fordyce*, p.62;　£50 stg. worth of farthings: Cramond, *Syn. Aberdeen*, p.71, and £100 stg. worth: p.72, and no more farthings available: 1764, and request to Customs *re* bad coin: 1755;　doits cease: Cramond, *Fordyce*, p.63;　doits cease 1760s, bad silver: Gibson, pp.92–94.

16　General KS of Glasgow, 1595: MacGeorge, p.199;　JPs to raise poor's rate, 1623: Smout, p.92, and assessments in England: p.93;　effects of English poor's rates: Headrick, *GVA Angus*, pp.242–243;　debauchery following poor's rates: Robertson, *GVA Perth*, note to p.80;　'fertile source of corruption': OSA East Kilbride, VII (1973) p.415.

17　Poor's rates south of Tweed: Robertson, *GVA Perth*, p.80;　obsolete laws: Headrick, *GVA Angus*, p.243, and poor not to rely on assessment: p.246, and heritors' and KSs' emergency meetings, meeting called by minister: p.245;　JPs call emergency meeting, intimation for two Sundays: OSA Cargill, XI (1976) p.68;　householders etc. vote *re* poor's money: OSA Bowden, III (1979) p.376;　heritors, tenants deficient in paying: Bara and Garvald KS, 1732.

18 Heritors not at meetings: Resolis KS, 1829; assessments 'absolutely needful', amounts kept from poor: Headrick, *GVA Angus*, p.246; tradesmen paying, 1699: M'Naught, p.179; approach to non-resident heritors: Resolis KS, 1840.

19 Occasional assessments: NSA Ormiston, II, East Lothian, p.151; assessments in England: Headrick, *GVA Angus*, p.245; kirk officer collects assessment: Kilconquhar KS, 1692; Session Clerk paid £36 Sc.: *THAS 1900, Vernon*; special collectors' payments: OSA Langholm, IV (1978) p.365.

20 Assessments cause withholding of givings: NSA Aberlady, II, East Lothian, p.259; collections 'almost annihilated': NSA North Berwick, II, East Lothian, p.343; seating: NSA Denny, VIII, Stirlingshire, p.136; giving up assessment, Dirleton, 1823: NSA Dirleton, II, East Lothian, p.220.

21 Law case: NSA Dunbar, II, East Lothian, pp.91–93.

22 Minister's right to enforce payment: Headrick, *GVA Angus*, p.245; pursuing for rates unheard of: Robertson, *GVA Perth*, p.81; asking Sheriff's advice: Kilconquhar KS, 1692; Kilconquhar assessments, 1697 etc.: Dick, p.100.

23 Overseers of the poor: OSA Eckford, III (1979) p.431; heritors taking over poor: Headrick, *GVA Angus*, p.245; Balfron heritors: NSA Balfron, VIII, Stirlingshire, pp.299–301; heritors and poor: Baldernock KS, 1843/44/45.

24 Minister defends poor's funds: Murray, *Falkirk*, II, pp.185–186; improper use of bequest: Martin, pp.49–50.

25 Riding committee: *Fasti* I, p.231, Torphichen; difficulties of getting records etc.: Torphichen KS, 1751, 1758.

26 Assessments becoming routine: OSA Langholm, XIII (1794) p.602; assessments favoured in towns and after Disruption: Blakey, p.92.

27 Penalties for excommunication: APS 1641. V. 351, APS 1690. IX. 199; fines for Sunday salmon fishing: MacGill, I, p.53.

28 Lists of belongings and seats: Banchory-Devenick KS, 1773; Tarbat KS, 1767, 1771, 1782, 1787; Golspie seating: Grant; Ile of the church: Cromarty KS, 1755.

29 Half baptism and burial fees to go to poor: APS 1701. X. 294 b. App. 99 b. These had been the subject of Proclamations of Council 1692/93/94. Burial in church: Edwards, p.171; mortuary: Gordon, p.153; bread stored in kirk officer's house: Mitchell, p.162.

30 Andrew Gibson: Brotchie, p.66, *c.* 1706–07; asking for donations: St. Monance KS, 1832 and Kirkwall KS, 1729; Macleod of Geanies's gift: Tarbat KS, 1806; Major Munro of Poyntzfield, Thomas Urquhart of Kinbeachy: Resolis KS, 1833.

31 Parliamentary candidate's donation, 1820s: Fyfe, p.471, Resolis parish; Col. Grant's donation, 1832: Keith, pp.90, 93.

32 Kirkmahoe's benefaction board: Hay, p.221; St. Cuthbert's benefaction board: Lorimer, *West Kirke*, p.35; legacy of £120 debt: Keith, p.99; Dr Oswald's legacy: Thurso KS, 1809; kirk officer sent to Caithness:

Johnston, *Orkney*, p.44; Umphery Menloch's bequest: Stirling (Holy Rude) KS, 1701.

33 Lord Cromartie's mortification: Tarbat KS, Ross-shire, mid–18th century; John Forrester's bequest: Nigg KS, Ross-shire, early 18th century; mortification money in minister's hands: St. Vigeans KS, 1682; Gabriel Hamilton: Cambuslang KS, 1700.

34 Innes's mortification: NSA Yester, II, East Lothian, p.171; John Watson's mortification: Banff KS, 1721; Alexander Hogg's legacy: OSA Durris, III (1790s) p.601 App.

35 Mortified croft: OSA Tain, III (1790s) p.395; lands mortified mid–17th century: Cromarty KS, 1755; feu duty: NSA Ormiston, II, East Lothian, p.151.

36 Vacant stipend, 1733: Cramond, *Rathven*, pp.56–57.

37 Chest for meal: Nigg KS, Ross-shire, 1731, 1730; bonds, bills in big box: Craig KS, 1737; bonds, bills in larger poor's box: Bara and Garvald KS, 1737; ordinary box: NSA Morham, II, East Lothian, note to p.265; money lent to soldier: Cramond, *Fordyce*, p.60, 1743; 'good hands': St. Boswells KS, 1724; Inverness Town Council borrowing: Mitchell, p.161; Banff Town Council borrowing: Banff KS, 1775; £400 loan to town treasurer: Aberdeen St. Nicholas KS, 1828; Arbroath Town Council borrowing: Craig KS, 1719 and St. Vigeans KS, 1754, 1755; public bodies pay cash, others perhaps victual: Henderson, *Arbuthnott*, pp.224–225.

38 Lord Seafield's borrowing: *SRE*, p.93, Alves KS; Sheriff's borrowing: Scone KS, 1716, 1724; Ankerville's tenants: Nigg KS, Ross-shire, 1729; Patrick Nisbet's borrowing: Yester KS, 1728.

39 Capital lying out: OSA St. Madois, III (1790s) p.573; old bills renewed: Abernethy KS, 1748.

40 James Boynd: Kirkwall KS, 1735.

41 Money called in for church improvements: Nigg KS, Ross-shire, 1729; Issobell Clark: *Maitland Misc.* i, p.112, 1574, Edinburgh; young people lending money: OSA Kincardine, Ross-shire, III (1790s) p.515.

42 Buying 13 acres: NSA Yester, II, East Lothian, p.171; kirklands: Abernethy KS, 1748; poor's tenants: Scone KS, 1720; Inverness KS's properties: Mitchell, p.161; 12 poultry: Thomson, *Elie Kirk*, p.68.

43 Kilconquhar KS, 1740, refers to a man given a loan of 40*s.* for which he had to give heritable security on his house. House, repairs and sale: St. Monance KS, 1836, 1837, 1840.

44 Andrew Wallace: St. Monance KS, 1834, 1836.

45 Repairs etc. to Session house: *THAS 1900, Vernon*; road along field, unauthorised draining: St. Monance KS, 1834.

46 Evicting Andrew Buist: Abernethy KS, 1748; evicting non-paying tenants: Kirkwall KS, 1749; rents per acre: St. Monance KS, 1844.

47 'Falling upon' ways of fund-raising: Mitchell, pp. 38–39; KSs' or heritors' right to kirkyard trees: Headrick, *GVA Angus*, p. 243; beadle intimates sale: Edwards, p. 143; conditions of sale: Inglis, *Angus Parish*, pp. 150–151; barter of trees: Love, p. 141.

48 Churchyard announcements: Macdonald, *St. Clements Looks Back*, pp. 15–16; stray beasts sold: *SRE*, p. 92, post–1646, and Johnston, *Orkney*, pp. 121, 129, Holm KS and Orphir KS; pointed beasts: Nigg KS, Ross-shire, 1818–20.

49 Useless Communion cup sold: Tarbat KS, 1774; Communion tent rouped: Edgar, I, p. 117; Aberdeen organ: *Aberdeen Eccl. Recs*, p. 19; hiring Communion tables for stalls: Edwards, p. 180; kirk ladders, 1736: Henderson, *Banchory-Devenick*, p. 262; hiring cows: Edwards, p. 180.

50 Minister's limestone: Kilninian and Kilmore KS, 1776; lime viewed: Kirkwall KS, 1744, and slate: 1764.

51 Letting mission station land: Eday and Harray KS, 1856.

52 Servant's 5 gns: West Kilbride KS, 1826; man's £54: Lorimer, *Neil M'Vicar*, p. 78.

53 Gambling winnings: APS 1621. IV. 613; Sir Andrew Ramsay: Chambers, *Domestic Annals of Scotland*; boxing match, 'Inkle and Yarico': *THAS 1876, Poor Law*; charity workhouse: OSA Edinburgh (1975) pp. 9, 57.

54 Treasurer: Dickson, p. 198; Session Clerk as treasurer: Kilbride KS, 1755; minister takes over from treasurer: Kilninver and Kilmelford KS, 1758; minister as treasurer: Kilninian and Kilmore KS, 1776, 1780; minister as treasurer till he requests relief: Fetlar KS, 1815; box under pulpit, etc.: Tongue KS, 1781; minister to keep distant collections: Kilninian and Kilmore KS, 1768.

55 'Charge and discharge': NSA Morham, II, East Lothian, note to p. 266; 'box being sighted': Johnston, *Orkney*, p. 24, 1680, Holm KS; John Jameson's accounts: St. Boswells KS, 1720; minister, elders counted the box: Ashkirk KS, 1738.

56 Unrecorded money given out: Tongue KS, 1790; Alexander Brodie: Mitchell, p. 161; faulty arithmetic: Creich KS, 1838, 1839; 12*d*. in wrong column: Melrose KS, 1745.

57 Session box stolen, 1734: Gibson, p. 95; box stolen from school: Henderson, *Banchory-Devenick*, p. 262, 1760; box stolen from Session House: Kilconquhar KS, 1706; Kilconquhar theft, 1710, and Presbyterial Visitation, 1716: Dick, pp. 99–100.

58 William Dickson, bankrupt (1745) and James Watson's Elopement: Gibson, p. 95; elder, beadle questioned: Edwards, p. 155; elder-catechist embezzled: Macdonald, *St. Clements Looks Back*, p. 16; Alexander Sutherland: Bentinck, p. 283; treasurer's Elopement: Tongue KS, 1797.

59 Mr Livingston: Gunn, *Traquair*, p. 84, 1730. (*Fasti* lists the reasons for his debts.) Rev. Henry Home: Allan, pp. 213–214; Mr Patrick Nicholson: Thurso KS, 1808; Mr Hugh Duff: MacNaughton, p. 144.

60 Minister advanced money for pauper and Communion table: Kilninian and Kilmore KS, 1767, and minister's widow: 1768, and new minister advanced money: 1775.

61 Church funds became inadequate: *SRE*, pp.235–236; Dr Chalmers: Burleigh, p.316. Lack of funds probably explains why the heritors and KS of Comrie, Perthshire, prepared schedules of questions for all paupers to answer by 1 April 1842 but the minutes unfortunately do not list the questions.

62 Reduced collections owing to Disruption: Nigg KS, Ross-shire, 1843–44; Parochial Boards and Parish Councils: *SRE*, pp.233–234. Because collections were reduced after the Disruption, but before the passing of the Poor Law, some special collections had to be made for the 'occasional poor', e.g. at St. Mary's, Dumfries, 1844.

63 New system of care: Edgar, II, p.43; unyielding conditions: St. Michael's KS, Linlithgow, 1851.

64 Collections reserved to KS, 1845: *SRE*, pp.233–234; intimation *re* collections not for poor: Edderton KS, 1847; collections at Keith, distributions at Daviot: *SRE*, p.234.

65 KS representation on Parochial Boards: St. Mary's KS, Dumfries, 1849, and Dumbarton KS, 1858; John Maim: Baldernock KS, 1845.

66 Parochial Board defers assessment: Baldernock KS, 1845; Session Clerk paid for checking: St. Michael's KS, Linlithgow, 1852; £12 paid to Inspector of Poor: St. Mary's KS, Dumfries, 1849; meeting at Jemimaville Inn: Resolis KS, 1846; providing abstracts: St. Mary's KS, Dumfries, 1849; poor's money, stock etc.: St. Michael's KS, Linlithgow, 1851.

67 Property case: St. Michael's KS, Linlithgow, 1851, 1852, 1863.

68 Poor House: St. Michael's KS, Linlithgow, 1853.

69 Room in house: St. Monance KS, 1857.

70 Mortcloths, spokes retained: Dumbarton KS, 1857.

71 KSs helping poor dependent on voluntary assistance: SRE p.235.

6
A School in every Parish

1 Sending sons to school: APS 1496. II. 238.

2 Music in education: Allardyce, p.126; sang schools: APS 1579. III. 174; instruction in psalms, Old Aberdeen: *SRE*, pp.155–156; Town Council, KS gave holidays, 1613: Cramond, *Elgin* II, p.136; song schools become parish/grammar schools: Smout, p.87.

3 Kirk exercises superintendence prior to petitioning Queen: Edgar, II, pp.65–66; teachers to be approved by kirk: APS 1567. III. 24, 38 a.

4 Schoolchildren to beg: Edwards, pp.194–195; kirk superintendence of schools: APS 1662. VII. 379 b.

5 Ratification of 1616 APS, providing for tax for schools: APS 1633. V. 21; overture for schools in parishes, and readers: APS 1641. V. 646 b. George Hay's *Architecture of Scottish Post-Reformation Churches*, pp. 219–220, gives a good description of painted texts, etc.

6 Kirk wishes 1633 APS extended: APS 1646. VI. i. 552; decree for schools, etc: APS 1646. VI. i. 554.

7 Education 'not needful': Smout, p. 471; Rev. Nathaniel Paterson: NSA Galashiels, III, Selkirkshire, p. 23.

8 Family prayers etc. encouraged, Channelkirk: *Berwickshire Naturalists' Club*, 1977; ministers, elders 'take course': AGA, p. 35, 1649; Lauder people engage teacher: Thomson, *Lauder*, p. 88; minister visits all families, Channelkirk, 1653: *Berwickshire Naturalists' Club*, 1977; school in Channelkirk, 1661: Allan, p. 173.

9 Synod of Fife's instructions: Edwards, pp. 194–195; Presbytery declaration, school in Dunino: NSA Dunino, IX, Fife, note to p. 373; Abernethy school: Abernethy KS, 1695.

10 Act for Settling of Schools: APS 1696. X. 63; ministers to ensure schools are established: AGA, p. 238, 1705.

11 Schools in barns, byres, stables: Edwards, p. 195; school in church, 1624: Cramond, *Fordyce*, p. 14; school at Whitekirk: Waddell, *East Lothian*, pp. 35–36; Auchterderran, 1688, Laigh Kirk, Kilmarnock, 1695: *SRE*, p. 149; Hawick school, 1718: *THAS 1900, Vernon*; Blackford Church, 1738: Love, p. 138; Mauchline school and prosecution for damage, 1782: Edgar, I, pp. 33–34; Kilchoman school in church: OSA Kilchoman, XI (1982) p. 283.

12 Ashkirk school in aisle: Sharpe, p. 69; Moneydie school adjacent to church: Love, p. 159; Gladsmuir school: NSA Gladsmuir, II, East Lothian, p. 196; Marnoch school in morthouse: Tranter, p. 55; school in manse: OSA Forbes and Kearn, XV (1982) p. 142; school at manse: OSA Farr, III (1790s) p. 542.

13 Paying rent of school: *THAS 1900, Vernon*; rented school, proposal to have it in church: Murray, *Falkirk*, II. pp. 188–189.

14 Rev. Thomas Boston: Sharpe, pp. 68–69; Mr John Sutherland and horning: Grant; Ayshire parishes take action against heritors: Johnston, *Working Classes*, p. 108; case taken to Lords: Tweedsmuir KS, 1766; Mr Alexander Pope: Macinnes, p. 233.

15 Building school: Kilninian and Kilmore KS, 1774; lending money for school house: St. Boswells KS, 1727; 'friendly borrowing': Kiltearn KS, 1728.

16 Argyllshire parish school: Kilninver and Kilmelford KS, 1758, 1759, and KS makes up stent if insufficient: 1760; lending workman 17s.: Kilninian and Kilmore KS, 1769.

17 Dr Cameron Lees' description: Edwards, p. 203; £1 4s. for windows: St. Boswells KS, 1728; 18s. stg. for mending windows: Ashkirk KS,

1774; providing straw etc.: Johnston, *Orkney*, p.120; Golspie heritors, 1743: Grant; JPs petitioned: Kiltearn KS, 1727.

18 Children bring straw: Edwards, p.195; Archibald Tweedie: Gunn, *Drumelzier*, p.54, 1726; repairs of school house, paying Alexander Corbett: Ashkirk KS, 1788, 1790; thatching, rethatching: St. Vigeans KS, 1742–43; thack divots, etc. for school house etc.: Cathcart KS, 1734.

19 Table for school: Kinnell KS, 1694; seats like pews: Craig KS, 1724; bed and table, 1713: Cramond, *Ordiquhill*, p.29.

20 Inverkeithing schoolmaster's widow: *SRE*, p.156, and readers as teachers: p.148; William Gray's curriculum: Smout, p.88; Mr James Carmichael: *Fasti*, I; minister's school: OSA Forbes and Kearn, XI (1790s) p.196.

21 Thomas Whyt: Ashkirk KS, 1653; urging Presbyteries to find schoolmasters, 1701: Cramond, *Syn. Aberdeen*, p.68; teachers from Elgin, 1707: MacNaughton p.45; placard set up: Kiltearn KS, 1710; Mr Walter Anderson: Clackmannan KS, 1685; Alexander Falconer: MacNaughton, pp.62–64; KS approves Town Council appointment of schoolmasters: Dumbarton KS, 1695.

22 Adam Gibson: Nigg KS, 1821; schoolmaster elected yearly, etc.: College Church KS, Glasgow, 1828–29; heritors, feuars elect schoolmaster: Tillycoultry KS, 1745; Zaccheus Laurie: St. Boswells KS, 1720; recording heritors' meeting in KS minutes: Resolis KS, 1829; KSs appoint schoolmasters: *SRE*, p.152; Mr John Row: Kinross KS, 1700; Patrick Mclaus's demission: Cathcart KS, 1734; heritors' consent and concurrence: Ashkirk KS, 1697.

23 Schoolmaster on trial for reading, Ballingry KS, 1677: *SRE*, p.155; James Murray: Ashkirk KS, 1697.

24 Licensed preachers teaching while awaiting a charge: Grant; licenciates teaching in Turriff: *SRE*, p.157; stickit ministers: Mackay, *Sidelights*, p.130.

25 'Reader's Bear': OSA Duffus, XVI (1982) p.495; heritors, tenants pay school salary: APS 1696. X. 63; 'school meal', 1718: Cramond, *Rathven*, p.46; salary in Petty: OSA Petty, III (1790s) p.33.

26 Heritors' proportions: Nigg KS, 1827; Speyside schoolmaster: *SRE*, pp.152–153; schoolmaster collects minister's meal: Cramond, *Fordyce*, p.23, 1684.

27 Payment to schoolmaster because of few pupils: Edwards, p.154; shoes for schoolmaster/Session Clerk: Kinnell KS, 1664, 1695, 1698; £20 for Jedburgh Grammar School master: Jeffrey, II, p.188; Crail salary: *SRE*, pp.152–153; David Ross: Nigg KS, Ross-shire, 1822–23; Mr John Mackay: Edderton KS, 1850–53.

28 Delinquents' penalties for schoolmaster: Edwards, p.153; writing beggars' badges: Kilconquhar KS, 1734; Session Clerk keeps mortcloth: Cambuslang KS, 1788; collecting special stent: *THAS 1900, Vernon*; Session Clerk collects statute road money: OSA Bonkle and Preston, III (1790s)

p. 159, and OSA Borthwick, XIII (1794) p. 628; schoolmaster collects for kirk boat: Henderson, *Banchory-Devenick*, pp. 261–263; schoolmaster as postmaster: Smout, p. 460; schoolmaster's Saturday afternoons: Murray, *Falkirk*, II, p. 196; schoolmaster preaching, etc., 1684: Cramond, *Fordyce*, p. 23; schoolmaster reading in church: Cramond, *Cullen*, p. 68.

29   Schoolmasters and land-surveying: Smout, p. 46.

30   Cockfighting: McNeill, II, p. 42; schoolmaster's entry money, fugies etc.: Edwards, p. 200; cockfighting in Dingwall: Macdonald, *St. Clements Looks Back*, p. 18; cock-money at St. Cuthbert's, Edinburgh: Lorimer, *Neil M'Vicar*, p. 60; cockfight dues in schoolmaster's perquisites: OSA Applecross, III (1790s) p. 378; Mauchline KS forbids cockfighting, 1782: Edgar, I, p. 317; Cromarty school cockfighting: Miller, *My Schools and Schoolmasters*; last fight in Dingwall: Macdonald, *St. Clement's Looks Back*, p. 18.

31   Candlemas King etc.: OSA St. Andrews, X (1978) p. 726; comments on schoolmaster's income, 1790s: OSA Borthwick, XIII (1794) p. 628; 'a paltry consideration': OSA Nigg, XIII (1794) p. 18; meal-dealing, 1732, 1734: Cramond, *Rathven*, p. 56, and public house, 1736: p. 57; running errands: *SRE*, pp. 156–157.

32   Schoolmaster illegally deposed: Cramond, *Fordyce*, p. 19; school 'totally dissolvit': Waddell, *East Lothian*, pp. 35–36; Mr James Williamson: Bentinck, pp. 264–265; Mr Georg Redpath: Ashkirk KS, 1695, and torn minute book: 1697.

33   Elders urged to encourage education: Craig KS, 1715; Presbyterial queries *re* chastisement: Cramond, *Presbytery of Fordyce*, p. 41; complaints disregarded, 1806: Cramond, *Ordiquhill*, p. 25; Kirkcaldy schoolmaster, 1638: *SRE*, pp. 156–157; Moffat boy killed: Chambers, *Abridged Domestic Annals*, pp. 370–371.

34   Seven years' negligence: Grant; charity schoolmaster's conduct: Edderton KS, 1836.

35   Sleeping, drunken schoolmaster: M'Naught, p. 163; graceless, prayerless schoolmaster: *THAS 1904, Coldingham*; stealing wig: M'Naught, p. 163.

36   List of schoolmaster's duties, Tynninghame KS: *SRE*, pp. 155–156; giving days off: Dumbarton KS, 1701.

37   Compulsion attempted at Aberdour, Torryburn, Yester, Inverary: *SRE*, p. 154.

38   Trees for a bridge: Huntly, *Fala and Soutra*, p. 112; children ferried 'over water': Henderson, *Banchory-Devenick*, p. 234; schools on either side of River Ythan: Allardyce, p. 132; additional schoolmaster: Tynninghame KS, 1703; four salaries divided: Barony KS, Glasgow, 1703.

39 Inverchaolin School, 1755: Smout, p. 462; school at Portsoy: Cramond, *Fordyce*, p. 34, 1751; timber for school: Kilmory KS, 1714; glass for windows: Edderton KS, 1823, and repairs to desks: 1839–40; feu duty, chalkboard: Craig KS, 1846, 1845; KS pays salaries: OSA St. Andrews, XIII (1794) p. 213; school at Davidstoun: Cromarty KS, 1758.

40 Help for private teaching: Michie, *Church of Scotland Social Development, 1780–1870*, pp. 139–140; none to teach without Presbytery approval: Cramond, *Presbytery of Fordyce*, p. 7; none to teach without church approval: APS 1662. VII. 379 b; teacher from Lairg: Edderton KS, 1833.

41 KSs close schools: Smout, pp. 454–455; use of magistrates to close schools, 'encouragement' of schoolmaster: Murray, *Falkirk*, II, p. 86; rules in Hawick, and Greenock School, 1697: *THAS, 1900, Vernon*; closures in spite of over-crowding: Murray, *Falkirk*, II, p. 86. In September 1672 the Kirk Session of Kelso were informed of a baron court decision that all boys of seven years old should attend the 'common school . . . and to be put to no uther school, nether within the town nor without the samin' and any who did not attend were obliged to pay 13s. 4d. Sc. to the schoolmaster quarterly. (Moffat, *Kelsae*, pp. 117–118.)

42 KSs take no action *re* private schools in Aberdeenshire, Stirlingshire, Ayrshire: Smout, p. 455; most children in private schools: Michie, *Church of Scotland Social Development, 1780–1870*, p. 138.

43 Poor children's fees: APS 1641. V. 646 b; KSs pay poor children's fees: *SRE*, p. 151, and Edwards, pp. 194–195; 'wages': Ashkirk KS, 1703; 'school-maile' and 'quarters': North Berwick KS, 1690s; 'schoolage' and 'college fee': Cramond, *Ordiquhill*, p. 35, 1767.

44 English school, and Woman's School: Bentinck, p. 284, 1738; payment according to progress: Edwards, pp. 194–195; paying for children not at parish school: NSA Denny, VIII, Stirlingshire, note to p. 121.

45 Buying Bible, Psalm book: Ashkirk KS, 1698, 1700; buying books for sale: Kilninian and Kilmore KS, 1781.

46 Less school progress in highlands: Smout, p. 461; 17th century schools closed: Mackay, *Sidelights*, pp. 120–121; location of SPCK schools, spinning schools, promoting Hanoverian sympathies, Gaelic forbidden: Smout, p. 463; Gaelic: OSA Moulin, quo. APS 1616; Gaelic New Testament: Mackay, *Sidelights*, p. 134; English in highland schools: Smout, p. 463.

47 Early examinations of SPCK teachers: Macrae, *The Parish of Lairg*, p. 33; later examinations and duties: Mackay, *Sidelights*, pp. 130–132; books at Hall-Morton: Hyslop, p. 471. An Association of Elders' Wives and Daughters, founded in 1849, was mainly concerned with female industrial schools. (Scotland, *History of Scottish Education*, I. p. 237.)

48 Free Schools: Macrae, *The Parish of Lairg*, p. 33; missionaries: Macinnes, p. 238; ex-officio catechists: Mackay, *Sidelights*, p. 132.

49 SPCK funding: Smout, p. 463; collecting for books, building, etc.: Scone KS, 1716; minister collecting for SPCK: Thomson, *Elie Kirk*, p. 70; grass for cow: Tarbat KS, 1781; carriage of books: Coll KS, 1800.

50 Lairg SPCK school: Macrae, *The Parish of Lairg*, p. 45.

51 Orphir SPCK school: Johnston, *Orkney*, pp. 108–109.

52 Building SPCK school at Orphir: Johnston, *Orkney*, p. 106, and refusal to build a school house, 1744: pp. 114–115.

53 Drumcudden school: Resolis KS, 1823–26.

54 Forfeited Estate Schools: Macinnes, pp. 252–253, and Royal Bounty Schools, co-operation with SPCK and closure of Kildonan school: pp. 249–250; Gaelic Societies, 1811–92: Mackay, *Sidelights*, p. 124; Ladies' Auxiliary: Scotland, *History of Scottish Education*, I, p. 247; Kelso Friendly School Society: Haig, *Topographical and Historical Account of Kelso*, pp. 118, 125.

55 General Assembly Education Committee and Assembly Schools: Scotland, *History of Scottish Education*, I, pp. 242–244.

56 'Church school' at Lairg: Macrae, *The Parish of Lairg*, p. 45; Principal Baird's School: NSA Kilmuir Wester and Suddy, XIV, Ross-shire, p. 62.

57 Assembly schools in lowlands: Scotland, *History of Scottish Education*, I, p. 243; Assembly School log book, Yetholm, 1864–73.

58 John Baird: Gordon, *Hearts upon the Highway*, pp. 43–52.

59 Burgh schools/parish schools: Macinnes, p. 226; school in South Leith: NSA Edinburgh, I, pp. 779–786. The Valuation Roll for Brechin, 1851, shows the schoolmaster's house as the property of the KS. Ringing of bell in Kelso: Moffat, *Kelsae*, pp. 117–118; payment of schoolmaster's salary: Reid, p. 147; paying for school upkeep: Murray, *Falkirk*, II, p. 86.

60 Sessional schools in Edinburgh: Scotland, *History of Scottish Education*, I, p. 245; Linlithgow school: St. Michael's KS, Linlithgow, 1863, referring back *c.* 20 years, and 1873.

61 First Sabbath School: OSA Banchory-Devenick, XIV (1982) p. 20; spread of Sunday Schools: Macinnes, p. 257; Sunday Schools under patronage of KSs: *SRE*, p. 258; kindling fire: Craig KS, 1853; willingness to teach Sunday Schools a recommendation: College Church KS, Glasgow, 1829; minister teaches Sunday School: NSA Bolton, II, East Lothian, p. 280; people 'bred up' to teach: NSA Balfron, VIII, Stirlingshire, p. 298.

62 Soirées etc.: Cambuslang KS Sabbath School minutes, 1878.

63 Viscount Stormont's donation: Abernethy KS, 1753; Dollar Academy: NSA Dollar, VIII, Clackmannanshire, pp. 117–118; Salton legacy: NSA Salton, II, East Lothian, pp. 112–113 and notes to these pages.

64 Presbytery bursar: AGA, p. 26, 1641, and money to come from kirk penalties: p. 26, 1644–45; £11 returned: North Berwick KS, 1695; bursary system for Highlands and Islands: AGA, p. 109, 1648, and gentlemen's sons, Gaelic-speaking ministry to be planted: p. 109, 1646; educating Gaelic-speaking youths: APS 1644. VI. i. 195; extension to Argyllshire: APS 1661. VII.

130;   10*d*. for Psalm book: Nigg KS, Ross-shire, 1731. *Life and Work*, July 1991, carried an advertisement from the Presbytery of Perth offering bursaries to students of Divinity.

65   Synods vary bursary use: Bara and Garvald KS, 1730.

66   Libraries in highlands: AGA, p.134, 1704;   donation to Kirkwall library: Johnston, *Orkney*, pp.78–79, Holm KS;   libraries of Tain and Dingwall Presbyteries: MacNaughton, p.95.

67   Lairg's box of books: Macrae, *The Parish of Lairg*, pp.24–25.

68   Donations to library: Kinnell KS, 1839;   parish library: St. Monance KS, 1849.

69   Library costs paid: Evie and Rendall KS, 1843;   College Church KS, Glasgow, 1828–29.

70   Coll minister: Mackay, *Sidelights*, pp.120–123.

71   Eviction of Contin schoolmaster: Barron, III, 18 September 1844.

72   Petition against proposed Education Bill: Tobermory KS, 1851;   petitions against Bill: Dumbarton KS, 1855;   Parochial and Burgh Schoolmasters' Act: M'Naught, p.199.

73   School Board: Cromarty KS, 1873.

74   Effect of Education Act, 1872, on kirk: Smout, p.250;   teacher training colleges: *SRE*, pp.249–250.

7
Such Good and Christian Works

1   'So good a work': PSAS 47, p.212, *Fords, ferries and bridges near Lanark*, Thomas Reid;   lack of bridge: Coldingham KS, 1701;   people wet through: NSA Applecross, XIV, Ross-shire, p.104;   minister barred by waters, Langholm KS: Hyslop, p.470;   delinquent couple: *THAS 1909 Vernon*, Hawick KS Records, pp.25–45.

2   Magnus Clark's boat: Waddell, *Kirk Chronicle*, pp.48–49;   kirk boat: Henderson, *Banchory-Devenick*, p.261;   Arthur Gibbon's repairs: Banchory-Devenick KS, 1730;   boat pierced: Henderson, *Banchory-Devenick*, pp.261–263;   new boat: Banchory-Devenick KS, 1806;   boats carried off in spates: Henderson, *Banchory-Devenick*, pp.232, 234.

3   Laying steps: Ashkirk KS, 1704;   Greenlaw's steps: Gordon, *To Move with the Times*, pp.83–84;   Roberton's steps: *THAS 1924, Roberton Parish in older times*, Thomas Wilson, pp.47–51;   request for trees, Morebattle: Tait, pp.59–60;   OSA Edenkillie, XVI (1982) note to pp.575–576.

4   Hire of wain: Tait, pp.59–60;   cutting decaying tree: Kinnell KS, 1694;   bridge repairs: Ashkirk KS, 1697, 1698, 1701, 1704.

5   Putting money aside: St. Vigeans KS, 1732;   £6 collected: Fettercairn KS, 1722;   money 'gotten in other ways': Melrose KS, 1704;   'earnest desire'

for collection: Coldingham KS, 1701; house to house collection: Cramond, *Rathven*, p. 49, 1717; church door collection: Hownam KS, 1738.

6   Keith bridge: Tranter, pp. 49–50.

7   Rack Miln bridge: Dollar KS, 1794.

8   Alexander Christie's bridge: OSA Grange, XVI (1982) pp. 220–221; James Black's bridge: OSA Fettercairn, XIV (1982) pp. 105–106.

9   Bridge at sawmill: Fettercairn KS, 1733; bridge at mill dam: Cramond, *Rathven*, p. 63; bridge at ford: Fettercairn KS, 1735.

10   General Assembly orders collection: Craig KS, 1723; collections 'south of the Forth': PSAS 47, p. 212, *Fords, ferries and bridges near Lanark*, Thomas Reid; General Assembly edict *re* Bridge of Strong: APS 1661. VII. 54; collection for Berriedale bridge: Kirkwall KS, 1724; repair of Leith bridge: Banff KS, 1717.

11   Kelso Bridge Trustees: Macdonald, *Bowden Kirk*, p. 24.

12   Collection for Queensberry: Ashkirk KS, 1697; St. Ninian's: Scone KS, 1717; Livingstone: NSA Morham, II, East Lothian, p. 266; Lairg: Scone KS, 1723; Durness: Hawick KS, 1722; Slammanan: St. Michael's KS, Linlithgow, 1730.

13   Meeting-houses in England: St. Boswells KS, 1724, and NSA Morham, II, East Lothian, p. 266, 1742; meeting-houses in Ireland: Gibson, p. 90, 1723; Konisberg: Johnston, *Orkney*, p. 51, Holm KS, 1697. Killearn KS minutes, 1697, contain loose papers referring to Konisberg church. Lavonia: Scone KS, 1718; Breslau, 1750: Henderson, *Banchory-Devenick*, p. 236.

14   Protestants in Lithuania: Craig KS, 1718; brethren in Franconia, 1719: NSA Morham, II, East Lothian, p. 266; French Protestants in Saxony: St. Boswells KS, 1721; French refugees: Craig KS, 1725; church in Copenhagen, 1729: Cramond, *Rathven*, p. 63, and Bara and Garvald KS, 1730; brethren in New York: NSA Morham, II, East Lothian, p. 266; Presbyterians in New York, 1725: Gibson, p. 90; plantations in North America: Ashkirk KS, 1752; Anastasius Camnenus: *THAS Sept 1871, Ashkirk Records*, pp. 90–97, by a minister of the parish.

15   Lochar moss: *Session Book of Bonkle and Preston*, 1685, and Lauder KS, 1685; Kirk Street, Dingwall: Mackay, *Pres. Recs*, xlv; court cases *re* church access: Lorimer, *Neil M'Vicar*, pp. 3–4; Nigg right of way, 1831: Martin, pp. 38–40.

16   Post to Aberdeen: Murray, *St. Andrews*, 1645.

17   Roseheartie harbour, 1682, Aberdeen harbour, 1683: *Session Book of Bonkle and Preston*; Eyemouth harbour: Cramond, *Presbytery of Fordyce*, 1683, 1677; Eyemouth, 1701: Johnston, *Orkney*, p. 66, Holm KS; Anstruther harbour: OSA Anstruther Wester, III (1790s), p. 86; Anstruther repairs: Cramond, *Presbytery of Fordyce*, 1688.

18   Collection for Cullen harbour, keeping back some money: Ashkirk KS, 1695; two collections for Banff harbour: Inverness KS, 1697; collections for Banff harbour: Ashkirk KS, 1701, and Johnston, *Orkney*, p. 65, Holm

KS; Banff harbour: Cramond, *Presbytery of Fordyce*, 1728; Lossiemouth harbour: Aberdeen St. Nicholas KS, 1702; 'bruse': Mackay, *Pres. Records*, xlv.

19 Hawick flood: *THAS 1900, Vernon*; John Graham: Cathcart KS, 1764; Greenlaw's help for fire victims: Gibson, p.89; help for Ashkirk: St. Boswells KS, 1747; collection for Dunfermline: *Extracts Kinghorn KS*, pp.26–27; collection for Glasgow: Murray, *St. Andrews*, 1652, and Mackay, *Pres. Recs*, xlv; Kelso fire, 1645: Chambers, *Abridged Domestic Annals*, p.272; Cullen burnt: Cramond, *Presbytery of Fordyce*, p.15; Cupar fire: Chambers, *Abridged Domestic Annals*, p.316.

20 Ministers take collections when going to General Assembly: MacNaughton, pp.54–55; Kilmarnock fire: Cramond, *Presbytery of Fordyce*, p.37, 1670, and Chambers, *Abridged Domestic Annals*, p.316, 1668; schools windows etc. paid out of collection for St. Andrews harbour: Fettercairn KS, 1736.

21 Explosion: *THAS 1904, Coldingham*; Irish fire tragedy: Kilmory KS, 1714.

22 Piracy: Chambers, *Abridged Domestic Annals*, pp.189–190; Algerians/ Turks: Mackay, *Pres. Recs*, xlv; 1626 collection: Murray, *Falkirk*, I, p.63; Walter Gibson and mate: Cramond, *Presbytery of Fordyce*, p.41, 1675, and Pittenweem people, 1679: p.44; collection for Turks' prisoners: Cromarty KS, 1682; Inverness men freed: Cramond, *Deskford*, pp.19–20.

23 Collection 'as soon as convenient': NSA Morham, II, East Lothian, p.266; man punished, barefoot etc., 1621: Irving, p.569.

24 Tongues cut out: Cramond, *Rathven*, pp.59, 66, 1723–24; man 'all mangled':Cramond, *Fordyce*, p.58, 1732; Presbytery thanked: Gunn, *Traquair*, p.81, 1727; Vallachian youth: *THAS 1904, Coldingham*, c. 1694; man with house burnt: Abernethy KS, 1749; Mercurias Lascaris: Cramond, *Presbytery of Fordyce*, p.44, 1679.

25 Christian Fandi, 1733: Cramond, *Rathven*, p.66; Paul Shalitti: Cramond, *Presbytery of Fordyce*, p.36; 'Arabian Christian': Dunbar KS, 1723; Christian Hussein, 1730s: Martin, p.18; prince's son, 1738: Brotchie, p.66; quorum *re* prince's son: *THAS 1900, Vernon*; Solomon, 1772: Johnston, *Working Classes*, p.105; no recommendations for charity to be given: AGA pp.37, 38, 39 (1696, 1710).

26 Operatives in manufacturing districts: Cramond, *Fordyce*, p.68; Gaelic Old Testament: Gunn, *Traquair*, p.98.

The Savings Bank movement, though not kirk-originated, was kirk-supported, for instance, when Mrs Susan Carnegie, with the help of two parish ministers, set one up in 1815 in Montrose, it was held in the Session House. (Cormack, *Susan Carnegie*, p.315.)

8
Half horrible, half noble

1 Need for ecclesiastical discipline: Henderson, *Arbuthnott*, p.105, quo. First Book of Discipline; ecclesiastical law: *SRE*, p.104; elders to maintain discipline: APS 1592. III. 542 a; Discipline Books: Lorimer, *West Kirke*, p.41; Register of Discipline: Banchory-Devenick KS; Minute Book of Discipline: Barony KS, Glasgow, 1727.

2 'Oligarchic tyranny': M'Naught, p.161; 'half horrible . . .': *SRE*, p.101, quo. Lorimer; minister's double function: Waddell, *Kirk Chronicle*.

3 Civil penalties: *St. Andrews KS Reg*, SHS 4, liv, lv; KSs order sentences: *Extracts Kinghorn KS*, note to p.1; magistrates threatened with excommunication, 1592: *Perth KS Reg*, p.268, and Thomas Smith: pp.249–250 and note to p.250; calling on civil officer: Waddell, *Kirk Chronicle*, p.35; Peebles bailies to punish offenders, 1571, and Grange 1706, and Presbytery of Deer, 1711: *SRE*, pp.111–112; minister calls on Melrose bailie: St. Boswells KS, 1720; beadles 'to mynd' constables etc.: St. Cuthbert's KS, Edinburgh, 1708; elders attend court: Cramond, Deskford, p.19.

4 Magistrates use KSs: *SRE*, p.113.

5 Principal Baillie: *St. Andrews KS Reg*, SHS 4, liv, lv, note 7 to lv; magistrates in every parish: AGA, p.224, 1648, and referring to APS 1645; Act against Profaneness: APS 1672. VIII. 99; 'bailie assistar': *THAS 1900, Vernon*; civil magistrate for bearing down on scandal, Fenwick KS: Edgar, I, p.309; Session moving to Burgh Council house: Low, p.151.

6 Provost, bailies on KSs, Perth, Glasgow etc.: *SRE*, p.114; appointment of session bailies: Kirkwall KS, 1749; bailies taking month about: Montrose KS, 1649; elder to be session bailie if necessary: Edgar, I, p.307, Glasgow, 1649.

7 Alternative ways of appointment: Edgar, I, pp.305–309 *re* Presbytery of Ayr, 1698, and Cramond, *Syn. Aberdeen*, p.67; portioner elected: Barony KS, Glasgow, 1703.

8 Types of bailie: *THAS 1900, Vernon*; provosts etc. taking elders' meetings: Thomson, *Lauder*, p.87, and *SRE*, p.113.

9 Heritors take turns as session bailies, refusal to accept, session bailies in Ayrshire: Edgar, I, p.309; Orkney session bailies: Kirkwall KS, 1749; extending commission: Kilninian and Kilmore KS, 1768; no heritors attend meeting: New Abbey KS, 1703; rural ministers became Justices of the Peace: *SRE*, pp.52, 114.

10 Appointing constables: St. Cuthbert's KS, Edinburgh, 1709.

11 Referral for pecunial mulct: St. Cuthbert's KS, Edinburgh, 1715; prisoners in kirk steeple: *St. Andrews KS Reg*, SHS 4, lvi, liii.

12 Falkirk KS, 1635: *SRE*, pp. 112–113; 'notour and manifest' adultery: APS 1581. III. 213; death for adultery, 1580s: *Perth KS Reg*, note to p. 242; man hanged, Edinburgh, 1694: Edgar, I, note to p. 330; drowning if conduct not improved: Cramond, *Elgin*, II, p. 258; remission for adultery: APS 1644. VI. i. 235 b.

13 Brother censured *re* banished sister: M'Naught, pp. 169–170, *c.* 1700; penalty for taking in a banished person: Montrose KS, 1647.

14 Boy banished: M'Naught, pp. 169–170, *c.* 1700; requests to magistrates for banishment: Banff KS, 1702, 1703; witch banished: Beaton, p. 143; Dundee woman banished: Murray, *St. Andrews*, 1676; George Hutchone: Montrose KS, 1647; Elspet Murray: *Aberdeen Eccl. Recs*, p. 12; Isabel Colzear: *Extracts Kinghorn KS*, 1623; woman consented to banishment: Kirkcudbright KS, 1702.

15 Man escorted by sea: Dick, p. 115; removing gypsies etc.: APS 1609. IV. 440 and APS 1617. IV. 563; minister removes gypsies: 3rd SA, Peebles and Selkirk, p. 286, parish of Ashkirk; James Oliver: *THAS 1900, Vernon*.

16 Hellen Leith: Mitchell, p. 35; help for banished man's family: St. Monance KS, 1836.

17 Blackfriars Church ward house: MacGeorge, p. 201; prison in steeple: Cramond, *Fordyce*, p. 52; Pittenweem jail: Love, p. 136; prisoners 'abyding' in session-house: *Aberdeen Eccl. Recs.* p. 46; prisons etc. at kirks: APS 1592. III. 576. An unusual prison was a 12' square cell built in the 1680s into the solid part of an arch of a bridge over the River Ness, a bridge paid for from voluntary collections made by Kirk Sessions on the order of the Privy Council. It was later used as a mad-house and was only closed around the 1820s. (NSA Inverness, XIV, Inverness-shire, p. 34.)

18 Imprisonment for church absence: Montrose KS, 1642; absence from catechism etc.: MacGeorge, p. 201; 'thefis hoal': Edgar, I, note to p. 311; prison recommended for boys: Banff KS, 1702; boys in 'lymhouse': Murray, *St. Andrews*, 1644; 'wyld ryot': *Extracts Kinghorn KS*, pp. 14–15; wet nurse: Lorimer, *Early Days*, p. 157, 1641; men in 'wolt': *Aberdeen Eccl. Recs*, p. 23; woman and soldier: Mitchell, p. 64; Margaret Smith: Banff KS, 1701, 1703; Alexander Baldie: St. Monance KS, 1842–43.

19 General KS of Glasgow: MacGeorge, p. 201; John Cuthbert: Mitchell, p. 69; Donald Wright and Katharine Caird: Wick KS, 1701; prisoner freed for a month: Mitchell, p. 56.

20 Part-time imprisonment, Elgin: Cramond, *Elgin*, II, pp. 97, 104; temporary release due to weather: *St. Andrews KS Reg*, SHS 4, p. 466.

21 Jannet Muet: Cramond, *Deskford*, p. 19, 1713; imprisonment for lack of alternative: Peebles KS, 1672.

22 Jhone Uewin: *Extracts Kinghorn KS*, p. 28; bread and small drink: APS 1567. III. 25–26; steeplers' diet: MacGeorge, p. 201; Banff prisoners, 1730: Cramond, *Rathven*, p. 65; access to prisoners: *Aberdeen Eccl. Recs*,

p. 46, 1605, and Andro Meldrum: p. 113, 1640; witch in tolbooth: *Perth KS Reg*, p. 242.

23　Episcopal curates: Johnston, *Working Classes*, p. 36;　ear burning: APS 1574. III. 88 ab;　woman's cheek to be burnt: *Perth KS Reg*, p. 264;　cheek burning, 1587, 1589: Cramond, *Elgin*, II, pp. 9, 12, and cheek burning for superstitious practices: p. 61;　'nailt be the lug': Reid, p. 141.

24　Ducking: APS 1567. III. 25;　'thrice doukit' in sea: Johnston, *Working Classes*, p. 101;　ducking at cran: *Aberdeen Eccl. Recs*, p. 23, 1602;　ducking in Clyde, etc.: MacGeorge, pp. 202–203;　'rottin eggis' etc.: *St. Andrews KS Reg*, SHS 7, lxvii, lxviii, 1593;　Besse Symsoun: *St. Andrews KS Reg*, SHS 4, p. 55;　Margrat Scott: Cramond, *Elgin*, II, p. 177.

25　Public humiliation: *St. Andrews KS Reg*, SHS 7, pp. 817–818;　women at market cross: Mathieson, II, p. 186 quo. Perth KS Reg;　barber appointed: Johnston, *Working Classes*, p. 100 and note to p. 100;　gyves and hair clipped: Allardyce, p. 98;　minister etc. to see couple punished: *Extracts Kinghorn KS*, p. 10.

26　Crown on woman's head: *Aberdeen Eccl. Recs*, p. 78;　'dittay' on face: Edgar, I, pp. 310–311, Rothesay KS, 1661;　paper with capital letters: Mitchell, p. 65, 1690;　mitres etc, marriage solemnised: *Aberdeen Eccl. Recs*, p. 22, 1566–67, and punishment to be declared by hangman: pp. 23–24, 1602;　cruel hangman: *Perth KS Reg*, pp. 288–289.

27　Stocks or other engine: APS 1579. III. 138;　punishment for idle beggars etc.: APS 1592. III. 576;　punishment of vice: APS 1645. VI. i. 458;　gyves: *Buchan Field Club*, III, p. 174.

28　Cuckstool, pillory: Allardyce, p. 99;　cuckstool: *THAS April 1879, Hassendean KS*, 1680;　golffis, gokstule etc.: Cramond, *Elgin*, II, p. 52, 1597;　cost of pillory: *Buchan Field Club*, III, pp. 174–175;　gokstule/stocks: *St. Andrews KS Reg*, SHS 4, liv, 1574.

29　Stocks for profanity: Allardyce, p. 99;　stocks for slander: *THAS April 1879, Hassendean KS*, 1680;　scolding on high road: Waddell, *Kirk Chronicle*;　sturdy beggars, 1655: NSA St. Ninians, VIII, Stirlingshire, p. 319;　William Pae: Waddell, *Kirk Chronicle*;　man sold alcohol: Murray, *Falkirk*, I, p. 9;　William Allane, 1623: *Extracts Kinghorn KS*, p. 24;　St. Andrews women: *St. Andrews KS Reg*, SHS 4, 1574, 1576;　youth in stocks: Brotchie, p. 61, 1651.

30　Fraserburgh couple: *Buchan Field Club*, III, p. 174;　Kilconquhar KS: Dick, p. 115;　thief in smiddy: Waddell, *East Lothian*, p. 28.

31　Illustration of later cockstool: Mitchell, p. 177, cockstool, 1693: p. 61, girl and drummer: pp. 61–62, overture *re* cockstool, 1708: p. 62, cockstool, 1719: pp. 61–62;　vote *re* cockstool Wick KS, 1701.

32　Corporal punishment, 1647: AGA, pp. 206–207;　flogging three women, 1690: Mitchell, p. 62, and Katherine Fraser: pp. 62–63, and woman in indecent posture, 1730: p. 184;　Act of Toleration: *SRE*, p. 112;　exemplary punishment, 1726: Mitchell, p.182;   Jean Corsor: Peebles KS, 1672;   couple scourged: Dick, p.116, Kilconquhar KS, 1649.

33   Nursing mothers, 1720: Mitchell, p.179, and man threatened with corporal punishment, 1708: p.63.

34   Mr John Mackay: *Fasti*, VII, p.93;   Mr James Robertson: NSA Lochbroom, XIV, Ross-shire, p.79.

35   Apprentices whipped: Johnston, *Working Classes*, p.104;   boys belted: Cramond, *Elgin*, II, p.270;   noisy children in streets, St. Andrews: Johnston, *Working Classes*, p.104;   children swearing: Cromarty KS, 1681;   father to chastise children: Beaton, p.142, Canisbay KS;   mother pays half fine: Johnston, *Orkney*, p.99;   man to answer for sons: Kirkcudbright KS, 1693;   tawse: Cramond, *Fordyce*, p.13, 1624.

36   Kail runts etc.: McNeill, III, pp.36, 25;   Canisbay kail-plucking: Beaton, p.147.

37   'Straik on the hand': *Aberdeen Eccl. Recs*, p.26.

38   Beadle applied branks: Inglis, *Angus Parish*, p.83;   branks worn six hours: Johnston, *Working Classes*, p.100, and Glasgow KS's branks: p.104, and Canongate KS's branks: p.100. Information on Dumfries's branks comes from notes on instruments of punishment shown in Queen Street Museum, Edinburgh, and the *Dictionary of the Older Scottish Tongue* gives information on the Presbytery of Strathbogie and branks. 'Long-tongued wife': Edwards, p.133.

39   Jougs combined with branks: *Buchan Field Club*, III, p.173;   jougs and trone: *Extracts Kinghorn KS*, p.14;   jougs at churchyard gate: Edgar, I, pp.310–311;   movable jougs: Cramond, *Elgin*, II, p.8;   indoor jougs, bracelets: Low, pp.114–115, 156. An illustration of bracelets appears opposite p.177 in Mitchell's *Inverness Kirk Session Records*. The jougs at Yester are said to have been made of wood and sited in the middle of the village (NSA Yester, II, East Lothian, note to p.166) but in this case the word 'jougs' may have applied to something other than a neck collar.

40   Penalty pays for jougs: Cramond, *Fordyce*, p.49;   weight of jougs: *Buchan Field Club*, III, p.173, and Allardyce, p.98.

41   'Hyndmost bell': Cramond, *Elgin*, II, p.79, 1600;   person in jougs throughout service: Craven, p.45, 1664;   24 hours in jougs threatened: *St. Andrews KS Reg*, SHS 4, xlvi;   crown, mitre worn in jougs: Cramond, *Elgin*, II, p.8, 1587;   pint stoup about neck: Bentinck, p.289, 1729;   tablecloth about neck: Cramond, *Fordyce*, p.43, 1661.

42   Man desiring prayers: Cramond, *Elgin*, II, pp.30–31, 1593;   sackcloth worn in jougs: Beaton, p.145, Olrig KS, 1700;   'hairy claith' and shaven heads: Cramond, *Elgin*, II, p.8.

43   'Ill kirk keepers': Johnston, *Orkney*, p.99;   playing port bowls: Cramond, *Elgin*, II, p.53, 1597;   husband struck wife: Beaton, p.45, Olrig KS, 1700.

44   Jougs for cursing etc.: Cramond, *Fordyce*, p.41;   poor with no gear: Johnston, Orkney, p.36, Holm KS;   couple guilty of fornication: Edgar, I,

p. 322; slanderers, bait-gathering: Montrose KS, 1633, 1638; Janet Short-house(s): Waddell, *East Lothian*, p. 38; man 'strak' people: Cromarty KS, 1679; rape case: Coll KS, 1782.

45 Woman confesses when jougs threatened: Cramond, *Fordyce*, p. 46, 1666; threat of breggan: Edgar, I, p. 312; offenders 'presented' to jougs, 1600: Cramond, *Elgin*, II, p. 77.

46 Chanzie and belt: Dick, pp. 114–115.

47 Standing under bell-strings: *SRE*, p. 127, Perth, 1623.

48 Sackcloth as a RC penance: Keith, p. 108; hair gown: Murray, *Falkirk*, II, p. 37. The sackcloth gown described is at Holy Trinity Church, St. Andrews. Gown 'worn to raggs': Craig-Brown, I, p. 269; poinded harne: Cramond, *Fordyce*, pp. 46–47; making own sackcloth gowns: Edwards, p. 157; William MacMorran: Lorimer, *West Kirke*, p. 51, 1693.

49 Standing in sackcloth or sheets: Henderson, *Religious Life*, p. 147, Galston parish; Margaret Coutts: Cramond, *Presbytery of Fordyce*, pp. 47–48, 1686; Janet Hunter: Johnston, *Working Classes*, p. 102; Galston woman: Edgar, I, p. 293; 'grave habit': Cramond, *Fordyce*, p. 44, 1663; woman 'denuding herself': Cramond, *Elgin*, II, p. 48, 1597.

50 Procedure for repentance: Craig KS, 1716; barefoot during punishment: Cramond, *Fordyce*, p. 41, 1659; barefoot for last three Sundays: *Extracts Kinghorn KS*, 1640; barelegged women: Lorimer, *Early Days*, p. 129; barelegged woman at Cullen: Cramond, *Boyndie*, p. 7; standing 'among water', 1661: Cramond, *Fordyce*, pp. 42–43.

51 Sinners on knees before Presbytery: Cramond, *Presbytery of Fordyce*, p. 16, 1647; asking forgiveness on knees in church: *Buchan Field Club*, III, pp. 170–171, 1612; Jonet Budge, 1664: Craven, p. 45.

52 St. Cuthbert's stool of repentance: Edgar, I, note to p. 292; stool of repentance: Montrose KS, 1649; Coldingham seat for scandalous persons: Chambers, *Domestic Annals of Scotland*; need of stool: Bentinck, p. 288; Lochcarron stool of repentance: Mackay, *Pres. Recs*, xvi; loupin'-on stane: *Buchan Field Club*, III, p. 172.

53 'Publict' stool of repentance (1624) and 'penitentiall seate' (1629): Cramond, *Boyndie*, p. 21; 'ordinar place of repentance': Kinnell KS, late 17th century; 'penitents' stuill': *THAS 1900, Vernon*; lockable stool: Lorimer, *Neil M'Vicar*, p. 40, 1742; common pillar: Cramond, *Elgin*, II, p. 117, 1603; Margaret Broun: *Extracts Kinghorn KS*, 1640; 'at the pillar': Ashkirk KS, 1691; pillar called pillory: Lorimer, *Neil M'Vicar*, p. 40; cutty-stool: Hay, p. 195; three pews above each other: Lorimer, *Neil M'Vicar*, p. 40; 'faulters laft': Cramond, *Boyndie*, p. 21, late 1700s.

54 Sit on pillar, enter to it (1653), continue at it (1665), be admitted to it (1729): Cramond, *Boyndie*, p. 21; stand at pillar (1628): Cramond, *Elgin*, II, p. 205, and stand at its foot (1646–47): p. 455, and combination punishment (1648): p. 262.

55 Several people together on stool: Cramond, *Fordyce*, p.40, 1658, and Graham, p.322; Archibald Campbell and others: Kilninver and Kilmelford KS, 1759.

56 St. Cuthbert's stool of repentance: Edgar, I, note to p.292; four-nooked stool: SRE, p.95; cost of ladder: Henderson, *Arbuthnott*, 1724; stair, unenclosed stools: Edgar, I, note to p.292; infirm woman: Kirkcudbright KS, 1700; Bailie Laing: *THAS 1900, Vernon*.

57 Heicher, laicher pillars: Lorimer, *Early Days*, pp.118–119; 'umest', 'hieest' seats: *St. Andrews KS Reg*, SHS 4, li; 'highest degree of stool': *St. Andrews KS Reg*, SHS 7, lxxvii; parishioner's seat under stool (1635) and 'standing high' (Galston KS, 1650): Edgar, I, pp.290–291.

58 Raised pew under gallery: Edgar, I, p.291; stool 'darkly situat': Murray, *Falkirk*, II, p.52; penitent beside precentor: *St. Andrews KS Reg*, SHS 7, civ. Bentinck's *Dornoch Cathedral and Parish*, p.298, says that it was not unusual to have the words 'This is the place of publick repentance' inscribed on stools. Sitting in place of repentance by non-penitents forbidden: Kinnell KS, 1671.

59 'Maister sear': *Buchan Field Club*, III, p.172; picture of cutty stool: Hill, opp. p.78; picture of cutty stool with footrest: Mitchell, opp. p.177; movable stool: Dick, pp.113–114, Kilconquhar KS, 1731. In *Architecture of Scottish Post-Reformation Churches*, George Hay suggests that the simple type of stool could be placed upon the elevated type.

60 Unpunctuality on stool: Thomson, *Elie Kirk*, p.53; stool used till early 19th century: SRE, p.244.

61 Standing before pulpit: Kinnell KS, 1660; 'calling over pulpit': Wick KS, 1702; paying 1s. and staying in own seats/loft, 1728: Cramond, *Fordyce*, pp.57–58; paying £6 for poor: Hownam KS, 1741; paying 40s. Sc.: Henderson, *Arbuthnott*, pp.127–128.

62 Wearing one's best: Edgar, I, p.293; appearance before Session, 1772: Henderson, *Arbuthnott*, p.128; last public appearance: Cramond, *Ordiquhill*, p.36; discipline changes in early 19th century: SRE, p.241; Mauchline, 1809: Edgar, I, p.301; Grange, 1816: *SRE*, p.242; Deskford, 1831: Cramond, *Deskford*, p.24; Mr Alexander Macgregor: Beauchamp, *Braes o' Balquhidder*, pp.231–232; Kilmaurs, 1844: M'Naught, pp.170–171; Kilmacolm, 1846: *SRE*, p.244.

63 Going on knees: Coldingham KS, 1699; young shepherd: *THAS 1900, Vernon*; old woman on knees: Murray, *St. Andrews*, 1638; threat of public appearance if offence repeated: Barony KS, Glasgow, 1700, 1703; Yester, 1822 and Oldmachar *c*. 1834: *SRE*, pp.242–243; Arbuthnott, 1905: Henderson, *Arbuthnott*, p.128.

64 Pecuniary mulcts: Bentinck, p.259; 'reprobat money': *THAS 1900, Vernon*; profane swearing: APS 1551. II. 485; fornication: APS 1567. III. 25; Scotsmen marrying in England: APS 1639. V. 596 a; imposition/abolition of fines for excommunication: APS 1641. V. 351, APS 1690. IX.

199;   fines used for dykes: Cramond, *Deskford*, p.11, 1676;   nobles, barons etc.: APS 1649. VI. ii. 152.

65 Ingathering fines, 1644, 1647: AGA, p.185;   Act against Profaneness: APS 1661. VIII. 99–100;   drunkenness etc.: APS 1672. VIII. 99;   Dornoch Presbytery, 1715: Bentinck, p.259.

66 Inverness Burgh Council, 1695: Mitchell, p.46;   fines sent by courts: Easton, p.87;   offenders pay to kirk: Melrose KS, 1760;   Logie KS: *SRE*, p.92;   fine: Cathcart KS, 1762;   Collector of Stamp Duty: Cramond, *Presbytery of Fordyce*, p.72;   assault at fair: Stow KS, 1819;   game law fines: APS 1567. III. 26;   Andrew Young: Yetholm KS, 1835–36;   Act anent Burial in Scots linen: APS 1686. VIII. 398.

67 Headache, toothache: Dickson, p.204;   Tuesday Session meetings: Montrose KS, 1634;   Oldmachar dogs (1641), Elgin horses (1646): *SRE*, p.92;   fining right and left: Dickson, p.204.

68 Lime washing: Johnston, *Orkney*, p.40, Holm KS, 1698;   stones for bridge: Edgar, I, p.316, Galston KS, 1640;   paying in grain: Tarbat KS, 1759, 1762;   services done to parish: Edgar I, p.316, Mauchline KS, 1671;   blanket in lieu: Cramond, *Rathven*, p.67, 1748;   Ewes thatch: Hyslop, p.474.

69 Simon Simpson: Cromarty KS, 1688;   plaid as security: Cramond, *Fordyce*, p.45, 1665;   fine to be paid in August: Coll KS, 1776;   poor apprentice: Forres KS, 1828;   girl's penalty waived: Tarbat KS, 1779;   elders' mitigation: Cramond, *Elgin*, II, p.43.

70 Man's promise to pay: Kirkwall KS, 1728;   suspended fine: Kilninian and Kilmore KS, 1779;   fines delayed for two men: Sorbie KS, 1701;   woman gives bail for the future: Kilmory KS, 1714;   Donald Mackenzie's cautioner: Wick KS, 1701;   half stranger's fine remitted: Nigg KS, Ross-shire, 1729.

71 15–day time limit: Murray, *Falkirk*, I, p.9;   charging interest: Tarbat KS, c. 1770s and Yester KS, 1728;   £147 lying out: Cramond, *Fordyce*, p.51, 1680;   minister to list non-payers: Kilninian and Kilmore KS, 1772;   woman banished, 1673: Cramond, *Fordyce*, p.48;   officer to 'sease' property: Wick KS, 1702;   poinded plaid, 1664, and 8 elnes of harne, 1667: Cramond, *Fordyce*, pp.44, 46;   pans, coats poinded: Johnston, *Working Classes*, p.105;   webs at waterside: Cramond, *Fordyce*, p.50, 1667;   lint forfeited: Dick, p.108.

72 Getting up penalties: M'Naught, pp.168–169;   officer gives warning: Scone KS, 1722;   decreet in Burgh Court: M'Naught, pp.168–169;   decree purchased, 1686: Cramond, *Deskford*, p.17;   Fearn KS: MacGill, I, pp.41–42;   payment by Martinmas: Kilninver and Kilmelford KS, 1760;   man joins army: Tarbat KS, 1760;   John Smith: Gibson, p.86.

73 Paying fine to Hugh McDonald: Kilninian and Kilmore KS, 1776;   widow's firlot: Cromarty KS, 1686;   two orphans: Coll KS, 1733;   Magnus Morrison: Kilninian and Kilmore KS, 1774;   David Forbes: MacGill, I, pp. 41–42, 1680.

74 Objectionable practice of fining: Mitchell, p. 38;   defence of fining: Easton, pp. 88–89;   General Assembly decree, 1572: *St. Andrews KS Reg*, SHS 4, lii;   indulgences and Cameronians: Edgar, I, p. 314;   Kirkwall bailie: Johnston, *Orkney*, pp. 121–122, and 'delinquents of quality' (Orphir KS): p. 114;   Alexander M'Niven, Colin Campbell: Kilninian and Kilmore KS, 1770, 1774.

75 £999 in fines: Graham, note 1 to p. 322;   three appearances converted to money payment, Orphir KS: Johnston, *Orkney*, p. 125;   Fordyce man, 1740: Cramond, *Fordyce*, p. 60;   'present money': Edgar, I, p. 317;   Galston: Gardner, *History of Galston Parish Church*;   Rathven man, 1748: Cramond, *Rathven*, p. 67;   woman left to appear: Cruden KS, 1753. 'Now Tom maun face the minister' is a verse from a song beginning, 'O, mither dear, I gin to fear . . .' (*THAS 1900, Vernon.*)

76 Cumnock man: Edgar, I, p. 316;   Tynninghame minister: Waddell, *East Lothian*, p. 42;   fining farmer: Yetholm KS, 1818.

77 Laird of Skibo: MacNaughton, 1722.

78 Needy woman: Kilninian and Kilmore KS, 1772;   Session Clerk's fines, Nigg KS: Martin, p. 13;   collector to have percentage: *SRE*, p. 245.

79 Mauchline case: Edgar, I, p. 316;   Arbuthnott ends fines: Henderson, *Arbuthnott*, p. 128;   Banff KS, 1835: *SRE*, p. 243;   General Assembly Act of 1837: *SRE*, p. 243;   information given *re* General Assembly Act, 1837: Creich KS, 1839;   case against pensioner: Edderton KS, 1839.

80 Higher Excommunication wording: Johnston, *Working Classes*, p. 106, and Gunn, *Traquair*, p. 77, also gives wording;   *The Bible*, 1 Timothy 1: 19, 20;   woman excommunicated for consigning someone to devil: Graham, pp. 325–326;   cursing: *St. Andrews KS Reg*, SHS 4, xlvii;   dead bell rung: *Border Magazine*, IX, p. 72;   attendance at burials forbidden, 1596: Cramond, *Elgin*, II, p. 40;   General Assembly 1569–70: Edgar, I, pp. 302–304;   public prayers: *Buchan Field Club*, III, p. 168;   excommunicated persons to be ordered out of services: APS 1587. III. 430;   reconciliation in 40 days: Johnston, *Working Classes*, p. 106.

81 Excommunication penalties for pious uses: APS 1641. V. 351;   increase of excommunication 1640–90: Smout, pp. 79–80;   civil penalties for excommunication ended: APS 1690. IX. 199;   Greater Excommunication: AGA, p. 93, 1707;   excommunication for 'airt and pairt' of murder: *SRE*, p. 65, 1598, also MacGeorge, p. 212, 1600, and Beaton, p. 148, 1709, Thurso;   murderer's child baptised: *SRE*, p. 65.

82 Infamous strumpet: Cramond, *Presbytery of Fordyce*, pp. 47–48, 1686;   notorious strumpet: St. Cuthbert's KS, Edinburgh, 1709;   co-habitation: Presbytery of Glasgow, 1755;   children of co-habitation: Presbytery of

Dornoch, 1709; bigamy: Henderson, *Arbuthnott*, p.117, 1716; incest: Presbytery of Dornoch, 1719; woman pregnant five times: Nigg KS, Ross-shire, 1833.

83 Hugh McDonald: Presbytery of Dornoch, 1707; admonitions and prayers: Cramond, *Presbytery of Fordyce*, pp.48–49, 1673; man prayed for, etc.: Ashkirk KS, 1705, 1706.

84 Margaret Currie and Andrew Smith: St. Boswells KS, 1720, 1721, 1723.

85 Henrie Chrystie: *Extracts Kinghorn KS*, p.64.

86 Excommunicated Selkirk woman: Craig-Brown, II, p.79; Robert Greenfield: Kirkwall KS, 1734.

87 Presbytery of Lewis, 1776.

88 Absolution, 1707: AGA, p.4.

89 Cristane Zwill: Lorimer, *Early Days*, p.153.

90 Lesser Excommunication: Edgar, I, p.305.

91 David Nairne, 1661: Thomson, *Elie Kirk*, p.60; Lesser Excommunication increased to Higher: AGA, p.93; ship's carpenter: Coll KS, 1784; 'disobedient and contumacious woman': Aberdeen St. Nicholas KS, 1702; woman denied knowing child's father: Resolis KS, 1829; woman and John Tytler's wife: Aberdeen St. Nicholas KS, 1702.

92 Agnes Scott: *THAS 1909, Hawick KS Records*, pp.25–45, Vernon.

93 George Newl: Bentinck, p.295.

94 William Skinner: Portmoak KS, 1780.

95 Tarbat KS, 1803–04.

96 Beadle's wife: Dick, p.118.

9
Called, Compeared and Confessed

1 Strangers: *Bible*, Leviticus 19: 33, 34; 'multitude of fugitives': Cramond, *Presbytery of Fordyce*, p.35, 1667; Burgh Councils give certificates: Jeffrey, II, p.106; giving testimonials, flitting: AGA, pp.225–227, 1648.

2 Return to testimonials after Revolution: Inglis, *Angus Parish*, p.148; Synod of Fife's order, 1706: Portmoak KS, 1706.

3 Robert Low's testimonial: Gibson, pp.105–106.

4 Testimonials for women: Nigg KS, Ross-shire, 1706, 1709; man's 'honest cariag': Johnston, *Orkney*, p.20, Holm KS, 1676; lawburrows case: Edderton KS, 1829; notorious cheats: Cramond, *Ordiquhill*, p.30, 1721; Alexander Fowler: Banchory-Devenick KS, 1808; Battle of Bothwell Brig: *THAS 1902, Lauder*; 1715 Rebellion: Arbuthnott KS, 1716; 'she fell in fornication': Nigg KS, Ross-shire, *c.* 1708; dismissed Session Clerk: Edwards, p.135, 1731; Thomas Allan: *THAS 1902, Lauder*.

5 Girls' penalties: Ashkirk KS, 1704, 1703.

6 Tingwall KS: Kirkwall KS, 1740; dissatisfaction with certificate: Johnston, *Orkney*, pp. 106–107, Orphir KS; Robert Carson: Turnbull, pp. 90–91.

7 Robert Young: West Kilbride KS, 1802; orders to seek out any without certificates: Mitchell, p. 36, 1691; orders given to beadle: *THAS 1900, Vernon*, 1711; elders demand testimonials: Cramond, *Presbytery of Fordyce*, p. 35, 1667; minister joins search: *THAS 1909, Hawick KS Records*, Vernon, pp. 25–45, 1702; certificates from Episcopal clergy: Murray, *Falkirk*, I, p. 37.

8 Melrose KS, 1679: *THAS 1902, Lauder*; Mary Graham: Kinross KS, 1709.

9 Letting houses, etc.: Montrose KS, 1642, 1649, 1657, and employers: 1659. Elgin KS, 1647, ordered all servants to have testimonials, which was also prior to the General Assembly Act of 1648. Heads of households not to take staff without testimonials: Tweedsmuir KS, 1691, and bearing the burden: 1735; landlords letting: *THAS 1876, Poor Law*.

10 Minister's reminder *re* testimonials: *THAS 1900, Vernon*; wages arrested: Cramond, *Elgin*, II, p. 328; Lasswade Baron Court: Johnston, *Working Classes*, pp. 106–107, almost verbatim.

11 Falkirk KS: Murray, *Falkirk*, I. pp. 64–65; man expelled, 1738: *THAS 1902, Hawick Town Council Records*, pp. 149–152; Marjorie Sutherland: Bentinck, p. 293; Agnes Robinsone: Dumbarton KS, 1702; dismissal of daughter in law: Cruden KS, 1724; taking man's oath: Cromarty KS, 1748.

12 Jean Collier: Murray, *Falkirk*, II, pp. 135–136.

13 Forged certificate, Lairg: Macrae, *The Parish of Lairg*, p. 50, *c.* 1716; certificate suspected, 1684: *THAS 1902, Lauder*; strangers 'carrying away' poor's money: Hyslop, p. 470, Langholm KS, 1721; 'clothed with testificates': Murray, *Falkirk*, II, p. 135, *c.* 1725–30; schoolmaster's forgery: Cramond, *Rathven*, p. 25.

14 Cost of testificates: Nigg KS, Ross-shire, 1707, and Earlston KS, 1782; lame girl: Cromarty KS, 1741, and 4*s.* Sc. given: 1739; Session Clerk's honest word: Dumbarton KS, 1702; Sub-Collectors of tax: APS 1649. VI. ii. 466; Henry Munro: MacNaughton, p. 246; testimonials still in use: Nigg KS, Ross-shire, 1820–21, and also Edderton KS, 1829.

15 Elders to report abuses: AGA, p. 227, 1648; Aberdeen, 1568: Edgar, I, p. 201; elders met Sunday by Sunday: *THAS Sept. 1871, Ashkirk Records*, written by a minister of the parish; Sir Ewen Cameron: Edgar, I, pp. 197–198, and Inquisition: p. 200; Covenanting days: *Spottiswoode Misc.* II, 1845, p. 229; interference etc.: Henderson, *Arbuthnott*, p. 107.

16 Informing: Henderson, *Arbuthnott*, p. 107 quo. Dr W. D. Maxwell in Baird Lectures, *History of Worship in the Church of Scotland*, pp. 147–148; dogging footsteps etc.: Murray, *Falkirk*, II, pp. 191–192; woman and brother: West Kilbride KS, 1808; relatives and young woman: Johnston, *Working Classes*, p. 100.

17 Delinquents to go to Presbytery: Presbytery of Forfar, 1717; aims of discipline: Henderson, *Arbuthnott*, p. 106, quoting Form of Process of General

Assembly, 1707; Session's reaction to fornication etc.: Resolis KS, 1828; observators etc.: Bentinck, pp. 289–290; surveyors of the town: Wick KS, 1702; elders visit fairs, etc.: Edgar, I, p. 209, Mauchline KS, 1702; Lauder supervision: *THAS 1902, Lauder*.

18   AGA, p. 227, 1648, said that the minister should deal in private with those professing public repentance, before the elder of the bounds, to try the evidence of their repentance. 'Ingenuous confession': M'Naught, p. 167; Rev. Thomas Boston: Craig-Brown, I, p. 274.

19   Payments to kirk officers: M'Naught, p. 167; barber attacks beadle: Lorimer, *Neil M' Vicar*, pp. 48–50; third citation at kirk door: *Buchan Field Club*, III, p. 168; calling witnesses: AGA, pp. 66–67, 1707; third refusal reported to Presbytery: Johnston, *Orkney*, p. 17; witnesses in paternity case: Dollar KS, 1706; commission visits witnesses: *THAS 1902, Kirk Session Records of Hawick*, pp. 147–148, 1752.

20   Partial counsel: Aberdeen St. Nicholas KS, 1700; 'malice, bribe . . .': Kirkpatrick-Fleeming KS, 1785; '. . . bribe or good deed': Portpatrick KS, 1833; evidence signed by minister: Kirkpatrick-Fleeming KS, 1784; witnesses on oath: Kinross KS, 1708.

21   Widow Garden: St. Cuthbert's KS, Edinburgh, 1708; Perth woman, 1582: *Perth KS Reg*, p. 242; Aberdeen woman, 1607: *Aberdeen Eccl. Recs*, p. 58.

22   Wedders, hens, etc.: Bentinck, p. 291, *c.* 1740; 'fastening guilt': Sorbie KS, 1701; 'shall not prosper': Barony KS, Glasgow, 1701; Kilmaurs man, 1690s: M'Naught, p. 165.

23   Woman to clear herself: Murray, *St. Andrews*, 1663.

24   Discipline guidelines, 1707: AGA, pp. 37, 65; KS orders baptism: St. Monance KS, 1835; Robert Henry: West Kilbride KS, 1803, and couple going to Greenock: 1802; Mull man: Tobermory KS, 1846; privilege of discipline: Edderton KS, 1823, and others; lodging difficulties etc.: Melrose KS, 1704.

25   Letting affair 'ly over': Portmoak KS, 1791; Communicant suspended: Thurso KS, 1808; 'mourn for sin': Barony KS, Glasgow, 1700.

26   'Mair signis of penitence': *Buchan Field Club*, III, p. 167; Margaret Birnie: Aberdeen St. Nicholas KS, 1702; 'kindly sense of sin': Barony KS, Glasgow, 1701; dealing with Agnes 'in privat': Cambuslang KS, 1659; John Ladlaw: Tweedsmuir KS, 1773; RC woman: Aberdeen St. Nicholas KS, 1700; learning doctrine, 1594: *St. Andrews KS Reg*, SHS 7, p. 778, and man 'not verie penitent', 1598: p. 876; woman and Commands: Barony KS, Glasgow, 1703; learning Scripture, 1838: Cramond, *Ordiquhill*, p. 38.

27   Pregnant woman: Edderton KS, 1843; double penalty if caution not found: Edgar, I, p. 293, Galston KS, 1633; return to taking caution: Mitchell, p. 59.

28   'Fit subject for privilege': Edderton KS, 1829; Chas. McLean: Kilninian and Kilmore KS, 1776; Barbara Rousay: Kirkwall KS, 1735; harvest work, going to sea, (1585, 1589): *St. Andrews KS Reg*, SHS 7, lxxxiii.

29 Remedies, 1648: AGA, p. 227; delinquents' progress: Kilninian and Kilmore KS, 1769.

30 James Murray: Tweedsmuir KS, 1765; Cumnock man's request, 1697: Edgar, I, note to p. 294; Elie man's satisfaction: Kilconquhar KS, 1692.

31 'Continue Sabbathlie': *THAS 1900, Vernon*; couple stand three months: Resolis KS, 1828; Elizabeth Melrose: Henderson, *Religious Life*, p. 146; Issobell Steinsone: Cramond, *Deskford*, p. 11, 1671; Marion Macdowall: Gibson, p. 84; man appears after 32 years and woman unabsolved 9–10 years before: Edgar, I, pp. 217–218.

32 'Wee sermon': *THAS 1900, Vernon*, 1718, 1721; sincere, hearty repentance: Dunrossness KS, *c.* 1778; '. . . fall to blood of Christ': Ashkirk KS, 1772; guard against sin: Barony KS, Glasgow, 1703.

33 'Lauching' in church: Cramond, *Elgin*, II, p. 62; snuff in eyes: *Aberdeen Eccl. Recs*, p. 136, 1655; Margaret Gray: *THAS 1900, Vernon*; Walter Rae: Lorimer, *Early Days*, p. 140; women's plaids: Murray, *St. Andrews*, 1640; kirk officer removes plaids: *Aberdeen Eccl. Recs*, pp. 62–63, 1608, and facing congregation: p. 116, 1651; hair 'castin doon': Cramond, *Elgin*, II, p. 52, 1597, 1599; severity to women: Johnston, *Working Classes*, p. 102; woman's 17th appearance: M'Naught, p. 169; 'weeping and crying': Tweedsmuir KS, 1773.

34 Weak, silly woman, 1724: *THAS 1900, Vernon*; 'hypondriak' woman: Banff KS, 1716–17; deaf and dumb woman: Tarbat KS, 1803; absolution for other reasons, etc.: Kilninian and Kilmore KS, 1770; man and grandmother, 1728: Mitchell, p. 184; request for altered sentence: Portmoak KS, 1706.

35 Pregnant woman: Cruden KS, 1749; Grisall Lesly: Nigg KS, Ross-shire, 1705; couple due to enter at pillar: Ashkirk KS, 1691; wife's 'tenderness': Kirkwall KS, 1736; waiting till child weaned: Cramond, *Fordyce*, p. 56, 1713; Isobel Paterson: Craig-Brown, I, p. 499; Anna Ross: Nigg KS, Ross-shire, 1706.

36 Woman's circular satisfaction: Presbytery of Forfar, 1664; Rachel McCoan: Kilninver and Kilmelford KS, 1760; Mungo Campbell: Edgar, I, pp. 249–250; Lord Ogilvy: NSA Alyth, X, p. 1120.

37 Gaelic church: Mitchell, p. 68; 'immanerly, malicious language': Nigg KS, Ross-shire, 1708; 'ane old pick', (*c.* 1698) and standing on the crown of the head: M'Naught, pp. 165–166; 'keeping 20 women': Tarbat KS, 1803; Portsoy man: Cramond, *Fordyce*, p. 65, 1785; Coldingham man: *THAS 1904, Coldingham*, *c.* 1695; 'nailing lug to the trone': Chambers, *Domestic Annals of Scotland*, 1690s; 'not stay to be flitton with': Melrose KS, 1703; man 'did not mind . . .': Culross KS, 1741.

38 Man threatened with jougs: M'Naught, p. 168; 'not care a strae': Nigg KS, Ross-shire, 1730; 'hack off his head': Cramond, *Deskford*, p. 19, 1717–18.

39 Elders accused over collections: *SRE*, p. 118, Banff KS, 1691; scandalising elders: Henderson, *Banchory-Devenick*, p. 248, 1738.

40 Andrew McHamish: Nigg KS, Ross-shire, 1706. Edgar, I, p. 325 gives examples of delinquents speaking back. 'Insolent language': Cramond, *Ordiquhill*, p. 21, 1738;   Thomas Johnston: Murray, *Falkirk*, II, p. 37;   breaking stools: Edgar, I, p. 325.

41 AGA, p. 11, 1695.

42 Delinquents 'dissolved', (Nigg KS, Ross-shire, 1706): Martin, p. 12;   couple's absolution: Resolis KS, 1828;   censure in another congregation: AGA, p. 3, 1707;   woman baptised: Presbytery of Forfar, 1664;   woman admitted as Communicant: Macdonald, *St. Clements Looks Back*, p. 15, 1806;   absolution denied: Barony KS, Glasgow, 1729.

43 Lauchlane Grant: Dumbarton KS, 1703.

44 Delinquent to 'repair forthwith . . .': Tarbat KS, 1776;   elder goes to Linlithgow: Ashkirk KS, 1701;   sending to England for woman: *THAS 1902, Lauder*, c. 1680;   Agnes Young: Shotts KS, 1722;   KSs assist with inquiries etc.: Tweedsmuir KS, 1772;   Jane Murray: Kirkwall KS, 1744;   Ann Fisher: Kilninver and Kilmelford KS, 1760;   Canisbay woman: Wick KS, 1702;   Mary McRae: Mitchell, p. 185;   'refers': *Buchan Field Club*, III, p. 170.

45 Writing to other Presbyteries: Coldingham KS, 1702;   delinquents in Nairn: Nigg KS, Ross-shire, 1705;   special meeting in Auldearn: Auldearn KS, 1816;   accommodation for Galashiels girl: Ashkirk KS, 1701.

46 South Leith: Melrose KS, 1783;   man left bounds: Barony KS, Glasgow, 1700.

47 Janet Brydie: Abernethy KS, 1751;   couple guilty in Cromarty: Nigg KS, Ross-shire, 1706;   Roberton case: Ashkirk KS, 1698, and Agnes Leishman: 1701;   shoemaker joined army: Mitchell, p. 69, 1693.

48 Jennet Robin: St. Ninian's KS, 1666;   hired chaise: Sprouston KS, 1762.

49 Comments on kirk discipline: Waddell, *East Lothian*, pp. 37–38;   unwillingness to accept censure: *SRE*, p. 241;   ineffective discipline: OSA Banchory-Devenick, XIV (1982) p. 15, written by Rev. George Morison;   Falkirk KS, and acknowledging guilt: Murray, *Falkirk*, II, p. 190;   position in 1830s: *SRE*, p. 245;   'no further appointment' for woman: St. Monance KS, 1834;   woman restored to privileges: St. Boswells KS, 1883;   General Assembly's 1912 Act: *SRE*, p. 247.

10
The Sins of the People

1 Stealing apples: Nigg KS, Ross-shire, 1729;   voluntary confession of theft: St. Michael's KS, Linlithgow, 1851;   Smith brothers: Bonhill KS, 1775.

2 Peat stealing: Ashkirk KS, 1697;   sheep stealing: Coll KS, 1734.

3 Cokalenes: Cramond, *Elgin*, II, p.47; libel on market cross: Scone KS, 1724; slander concerning marriage: Edderton KS, 1829.

4 'Lown Queen': Cambuslang KS, 1658; miner's wife: Tillycoultry KS, 1747; venereal disease: Kilninver and Kilmelford KS, 1759; woman released by husband: Lorimer, *Early Days*, p.135, mid–17th century.

5 James Boyd: Portpatrick KS, 1833; KS gives warrant to call witnesses: Cromarty KS, 1741; Isabell — : Sprouston KS, 1693–94.

6 Daily slander reports: Montrose KS, 1633, and pledge of 40s. Sc.: 1644; jangling words, and pledge, 1644: *Extracts Kinghorn KS*, pp.55–56; 'loun carl': Cramond, *Fordyce*, p.4, 1664.

7 Slander punishment: Montrose KS, 1633; Adam Alcinor: *Buchan Field Club*, III, pp.170–171; fine + repentance: Cramond, *Fordyce*, p.45, 1665; Hassendean's rules, 1680: *THAS April 1879, Hassendean*, Vernon; lying tongue, Inverness: Mackay, *Pres. Records*, xlii; 'fals tung': *St. Andrews KS Reg*, SHS 4, li, 1579; exhortation to Christian love: Craven, p.21.

8 Minister's servant: M'Naught, p.164.

9 Duel: Cramond, *Fordyce*, p.40, 1664, and wife struck with spade: p.44, 1664, and wife beaten, cursed: p.54, 1702; Jennet Taylor: Nigg KS, Ross-shire, 1729, and elder fighting: 1706; 'shedars of blood', 1648: Cramond, *Presbytery of Fordyce*, p.17; throwing boy in dam: Cramond, *Rathven*, p.66, 1732; cow let loose: *THAS 1904, Coldingham*.

10 Flyting women reconciled: *Buchan Field Club*, III, p.168; Simpsons: Sharpe, p.141, Lilliesleaf parish; feud with lairds: Gibson, pp.81–82.

11 'Putting hand' to wives: Cramond, *Presbytery of Fordyce*, pp.10–11; Elspet Dalgarno: *Aberdeen Eccl. Recs*, pp.44–45, 1605; Agnes Stewart: APS 1649. VI. ii. 742 b; Auchterhouse reconciliation: Inglis, *Angus Parish*, p.93, 1647; couple exhorted to forgive, 1737: Henderson, *Banchory-Devenick*, p.247; couple to live in peace: Tarbat KS, 1761; Janet McGorie: Cawdor KS, 1721.

12 Wife-selling: Murray, *Falkirk*, II, pp.128–129; violent wife: *Perth KS Reg*, p.237, 1570s; James Yong: Waddell, *Kirk Chronicle*; flagrant scandal: Dumbarton KS, 1701.

13 Very irreverent language: Barony KS, Glasgow, 1701; young fisherman: Tarbat KS, 1756; Patrick Levingstoun: Murray, *Falkirk*, I, p.47; hammer and stone: *St. Andrews KS Reg*, SHS 7, lxxvii, 1594; young Petty man: NSA Petty, XIV, Inverness-shire, p.407, 1647.

14 'Blae marks': *THAS 1904, Coldingham*; Hugh McDonald: Coll KS, 1790; meeting of masons: Dumbarton KS, 1702.

15 Thomas Russell: Clackmannan KS, 1685; playing 'Catt and Dog': Murray, *St. Andrews*, 1654, and profane boys: 1647; girls running races: Cramond, *Elgin*, II, p.178; rambling at night: *THAS 1909, Hawick KS Records*, Vernon, pp.25–45; Robert Wilson: Craig- Brown, I, pp.498–499; egg-eating: *THAS 1904, Coldingham*; fiddler, 1718: *THAS 1900, Vernon*.

16 Barley for distillers: *GVA, Ross and Cromarty*, Mackenzie, p. 166; Patrick Thomson: NSA Dirleton, II, East Lothian, p. 223; workmen's expenses: Jedburgh KS, 1703; whisky for erecting tent: Kilbride KS, 1830.

17 Drinking after 9.00 p.m.: APS 1436. II. 24; drinking after 10.00 p.m.: APS 1617. IV. 548; excessive drinking: APS 1645. VI. i. 458; enforcing 1617 Act: APS 1672. VIII. 99; Tynninghame Acts of Session 1625, 1640: Waddell, *Kirk Chronicle*; inn-keepers liable for censure: Cramond, *Boyndie*, p. 22, 1705, and Thomson, *Elie Kirk*, p. 60, 1647; inn-keepers summoned *en bloc*: M'Naught, p. 167; quantity of drink specified: Thomson, *Elie Kirk*, p. 60.

18 'Except by strangers': Montrose KS, 1636; Broughton KS: Baird, *Annals of a Tweeddale Parish*, pp. 268–269; 'hotel residents': *THAS 1909, Hawick KS Records*, Vernon, pp. 25–45; Lesser Excommunication for third offence: Murray, *Falkirk*, I, p. 9; Lauder KS: Thomson, *Lauder*, p. 87, 1677.

19 Tynninghame regulations: Tynninghame KS, 1703; Hawick elders: *THAS 1900, Vernon*; 'visitors': Cramond, *Fordyce*, p. 31, 1663; 'elders' hours': Inglis, *Angus Parish*, p. 95.

20 Drum beaten in streets: M'Naught, p. 167, 1690s; Drunken Bell etc.: OSA Fordyce, XVI (1982) p. 164; perlustrating inns: OSA Monifieth, XIII (1794) p. 498, 1676–1710.

21 Man dressed as woman: *THAS 1909, Hawick KS Records*, Vernon, pp. 25–45; man struck people: Cromarty KS, 1679; Elspeth Allan: Thomson, *Lauder*, p. 87; Lord Blantyre etc.: Chambers, *Abridged Domestic Annals*, p. 382.

22 Wasting father's substance, 1714, 1717: *THAS 1900, Vernon*; Hugh Ross: Aberdeen St. Nicholas KS, 1701; Hugh Dodds: *THAS 1902, Lauder*; night-walking etc., 1604: *Aberdeen Eccl. Recs*, p. 29; suspension of church privileges: West Kilbride KS, 1832.

23 Men fell in sea: Cromarty KS, 1742; funeral drinking, Skye etc.: Gordon, pp. 24–31, 36–45.

24 Cummerskales, 1645: *Extracts Kinghorn KS*, pp. 57–58.

25 Drinking 'bridegrooms': Murray, *St. Andrews*, 1710; Common Ridings: *THAS 1900, Vernon*; Cornet's father: *THAS June 1872, Marriage Customs*, Watson, pp. 142–145.

26 'Confluence of people', carrying ale from house to house: Nigg KS, Ross-shire, 1706; Sunday drinking: NSA Prestonpans, II, East Lothian, pp. 315–316; ministers and evils of Saturday night drinking: Inglis, *Angus Parish*, pp. 85–86, 1646; woman drunk in church: *THAS 1900, Vernon*, 1721; women drunk to incapacity: Aberdeen St. Nicholas KS, 1700.

27 'Drinkings': *THAS June 1872, Marriage Customs*, Watson, pp. 142–145; Canisbay inn, Reay Kirk Inn: *Duncan's Itinerary of Scotland*, 1823; inn as common resort: NSA Barray, XIV, Inverness-shire, p. 216; inns being necessary: OSA Carnock, X (1978) p. 131; beer in

kitchen: Allardyce, p.111 — Dr George Skene Keith of Keith-hall, 1778–1822.

28 'Passing to taverns': APS 1579. III. 138; penalty of 1 dollar: Montrose KS, 1641, and 'in a sober way . . .': 1655; alcohol for refreshment etc.: Dick, p.107, 1647; £4 Sc. and standing in sackcloth etc., and elders going to alehouses (1691): NSA Petty, XIV, Inverness-shire, note to p.408; calling on town officers: Aberdeen St. Nicholas KS, 1700; penalties for inspectors: Montrose KS, 1634.

29 Groundless rumours: Sorbie KS, 1700.

30 Inn door broken in: Cramond, *Deskford*, p.16, 1685; William Thomson: Resolis KS, 1825, and vintner's irregular house: 1832.

31 Royal proclamation, 1760: Scone KS, 1763; East Lothian inn-keepers: NSA Tranent, II, East Lothian, note to p.303.

32 Ministers not to drink: Cramond, *Presbytery of Fordyce*, p.16; minister not haunting ale-houses, 1651: Cramond, *Fordyce*, pp.17–18; Cullen minister: Cramond, *Cullen*, p.139; Town Clerk: Hawick KS, 1701; minister's wife: Presbytery of Lewis, 1743.

33 Brewing on Sundays: Murray, *St. Andrews*, 1639; drying malt: Montrose KS, 1640, 1642; brewing on fast day: Tarbat KS, 1756.

34 Act of General Assembly *re* smuggling, 1719: AGA, p.231; running brandy on Sunday: Dick, p.108; Earl of Findlater's help requested: Cramond, *Fordyce*, p.33; Avoch smugglers: Tarbat KS, 1756; George Halden, 1734, and appointment of beadles, 1774: Lorimer, *Neil M'Vicar*, pp.53–54.

35 Porteous Riots: Graham, pp.368–369.

36 Raffling hat, watch, and brawl, 1716: *THAS 1900, Vernon*; indecency due to raffle: MacDonald, *St. Clement's Looks Back*, p.15; forbidding raffle intimations, 1705, and raffles, 1827: Henderson, *Banchory-Devenick*, p.241; raffle at Jemimaville: Resolis KS, 1824.

37 Gaming: APS 1621. IV. 613; Elgin KS, 1599: Cramond, *Elgin*, II, p.72; Aberdeen KS, 1604: *Aberdeen Eccl. Recs*, p.29; post–1621 Act of Session: Montrose KS, 1649; Galashiels KS, 1699, and Robert Wilson: Craig-Brown, I, pp.498–499; Hawick couple: *THAS 1900, Vernon*, 1721; continued gaming: Hawick KS, 1724.

38 Ettrick horse race: Craig-Brown, I, p.271; Gullane stables: NSA Dirleton, II, East Lothian, p.214.

39 Itinerant shows etc.: MacDonald, *St. Clement's Looks Back*, p.24.

40 Usurer: *St. Andrews KS Reg*, SHS 4, p.309; women and gypsy: Lorimer, *Early Days*, p.147.

41 Poetry: Johnston, *Working Classes*, p.104; quack doctor etc.: Hill, pp.74–75; stage, plays etc.: Murray, *St. Andrews*, 1713, and D. Allan: 1719; Canongate parish charity workhouse: OSA Edinburgh, II (1975) p.9; plays in Rutherglen: MacGeorge, p.213.

42 Heinous offenders to go to Assembly, Synods, etc.: Edgar, I, note to p.304; 'murthers', etc, 1624: Cramond, *Presbytery of Fordyce*, p.8; KS's role *re* crime, 1707: AGA, p.106.

43 Thomas Herd, 1663–64: Cramond, *Deskford*, pp.9–10; Donald Mackay: Grant; murder of John Adams: MacGeorge, p.212; Alexander Gadderer: Cramond, *Elgin*, II, p.42; murderer's brother, 1624–25: Cramond, *Fordyce*, p.14; advice from Synod, 1669: Cramond, *Presbytery of Fordyce*, p.35; homicide by boy: Cramond, *Ordiquhill*, p.13; Lord's Supper withheld, 1668: Cramond, *Deskford*, p.10; Mr John Kello: Chambers, *Abridged Domestic Annals*, pp.50–51.

44 Mr William Fraser: Chambers, *Abridged Domestic Annals*, pp.369, 370, 698, and Slains and Forvie KS, 1698–99.

45 Illegitimacy in Perth: Johnston, *Working Classes*, pp.101–102; 4 women's reason for murder: Graham, note 2 to p.323, and fleeing, suicide: p.323, and worst child murderers: note 3 to p.323.

46 Katharine Harkness: Kirkwall KS, 1738; women in Aberdeen tolbooth: Chambers, *Domestic Annals of Scotland*, III, pp.26–27; Act anent Concealment of Pregnancy: APS 1690. IX. 195; Act of General Assembly read in churches: Grange KS, 1762, and Gunn, *Traquair*, p.97, 1763; Christian Adam: Chambers, *Domestic Annals of Scotland*, III, pp.26–27; married woman in Kirkcudbright: Kirkcudbright KS, 1700; Bessie Muckieson: Chambers, *Domestic Annals of Scotland*, III, pp.26–27.

47 Elspit Thomson: Arbuthnott KS, 1708; Dingwall child murder, 1685: Mackay, *Pres. Recs*, xxxv; Margaret Lamb: St. Vigeans KS, 1752; six days extra punishment: Tarbat KS, 1759; no clothing prepared: Portmoak KS, 1779; baby born out of doors: Banchory-Devenick KS, 1742.

48 3 Cadder women: MacGeorge, p.208; Margaret Grieff: Cramond, *Elgin*, II, p.32; proving child's sickness: *St. Andrews KS Reg*, SHS 7, p.558; light sentences: MacGeorge, p.208.

49 Selkirk woman: Craig-Brown, II, p.79; Ashkirk girl: Ashkirk KS, 1703; signs of pregnancy disappeared: Edderton KS, 1834.

50 Anna Mackay: Golspie KS, 1743 and Grant; midwife's visit: Coldingham KS, 1702.

51 Search for murdered baby's mother: Mackay, *Pres. Recs*, p.254, 1653; Margaret Mitchell: Murray, *Falkirk*, II, pp.60–61; body in dunghill: Craig-Brown, II, p.104; dead baby on shore: Tarbat KS, 1789–90; examination of single women: Cramond, *Fordyce*, pp.59–60; Mary Latto: St. Monance KS, 1832.

52 Letter from Sheriff of Ross: Kintail KS, 1834.

53 Neglected child: Perth KS Reg, p.263, 1588–89; child burnt: *St. Andrews KS Reg*, SHS 4, p.424, 1577.

11
The Morals of the People

1 Sins of greed etc.: Smout, pp. 82–83.

2 Prostitution etc.: Smout, p. 81. Acts of Parliament and of General Assembly to do with fornication and adultery include:
APS 1563. II. 539–adulterers to be put to death.
APS 1581. III. 213 repeats this and defines adultery.
APS 1567. III. 25–26 — fine of £40 for both parties, imprisonment for 8 days, appearance in the market place; for a second offence, 100 merks, prison and appearance; for a third offence, £100, then ducking and banishment.
APS 1649. VI. ii. 152–153 — laid down penalties for fornication according to rank. Act of General Assembly, 1648, enforced penalties already laid down — AGA, p. 224.

3 Man and sister, 1767: Kilninian and Kilmore KS, 1767; presumption of death: Tarbat KS, 1770–80s.

4 John Hind: Assynt KS, 1818, and Alexander Mackenzie: 1820; decision delayed to see if marriage would follow: Dunbar KS, 1728; penalty halved if marriage followed: Tarbat KS, 1757; Donald M'Lean: Kilninian and Kilmore KS, 1769; two appearances instead of three: Kirkwall KS, 1732; complete remission: *THAS April 1879, Hassendean*, Vernon, 1686; fine remitted but discipline continued: Edderton KS, 1823; marriage permitted before satisfaction made: Cruden KS, 1749.

5 No nurses without testimonials, 1609: *Aberdeen Eccl. Recs*, p. 69; nurse's employer liable: Montrose KS, 1649; Helen Tush: Banff KS, 1706; Margaret Fraser: St. Cuthbert's KS, Edinburgh, 1708; Mr David Polson: Mitchell, p. 68; Jannet Thain: Cramond, *Fordyce*, p. 47, 1667; Mr John Carmichael: Gunn , *Traquair*, p. 42.

6 Maintaining child till 10–14 years old: Bellie KS, *c.* 1829; procedure for disputed paternity: AGA, pp. 217–218, 1707; two men confronted: Ashkirk KS, 1696; 'true narrative': AGA, p. 101, 1707.

7 Woman 'being ideot': Cramond, *Fordyce*, p. 47, 1667; woman 'cryd out': Cramond, *Ordiquhill*, pp. 21–22, 1743; minister's oath, 1667: Cramond, *Fordyce*, p. 21.

8 Wording of oath: Graham, pp. 323–324 and note to p. 324. AGA, p. 217–218 gives wording of Oath of Purgation. Donald MacDonald's oath: Mitchell, pp. 60–61, late 1680s; Andrew McConnell's oath: Sorbie KS, 1701.

9 Oath read over: Cramond, *Fordyce*, p. 21, 1667; copy given to read: Clackmannan KS, 1680; advice about taking oath: AGA, pp. 217–218; girl takes oath: Kilninian and Kilmore KS, 1783.

10   Mary McLean, Mary McKellich: Kilninian and Kilmore KS, 1782, 1790;   18–month delay for oath-taking: Henderson, *Arbuthnott*, pp.121–125.

11   Oath delayed for inquiries: New Abbey KS, 1698;   Andrew McConnell: Sorbie KS, 1701.

12   Donald McLean: Coll KS, 1776;   couple to go to pillory: Henderson, *Banchory-Devenick*, pp.242–243, 1714.

13   Lady Mey: Canisbay KS, 1716;   'threatened' with Oath of Purgation: Nigg KS, Ross-shire, 1708;   Ann Buchanan: Kilninver and Kilmelford KS, 1760, and Sarah Campbell: 1762;   Melrose/Legerwood case, 1842, 1845: Oliver, *History of Blainslie*, pp.44–45;   mass oath-taking: Edgar, I, p.218.

14   Mary McKinnon's pregnancy: Kilninian and Kilmore KS, 1778;   'winning the turfes': Ashkirk KS, 1701.

15   Caithness woman's complaint: Canisbay KS, 1718;   father to pay medical expenses etc.: Resolis KS, 1842;   applying to Judges Competent: Kilninian and Kilmore KS, 1783;   two St. Monance cases: St. Monance KS, 1845.

16   Alexander Baldie: St. Monance KS, 1842–44;   John Macpherson: Laggan KS, 1782.

17   Janet Gill: Ashkirk KS, 1702–03;   Jean Cowie: Edwards, p.134;   certificate given to woman: Stow KS, 1862.

18   Girl pledged to secrecy: Kintail KS, 1828;   £10 offered: Yetholm KS, 1818;   whisky offered: Resolis KS, 1828, and woman met man on road: 1829;   girl raped: Tongue KS, 1824;   girl tricked: College KS, Glasgow, 1807.

19   Helen Amoss: Tweedsmuir KS, 1773;   James Fleck: West Kilbride KS, 1809.

20   Woman and three men: Foveran KS, 1728;   censure for adultery if man not known: AGA, p.8, 1707.

21   Women not naming fathers, 1663: Cramond, *Presbytery of Fordyce*, p.32;   Elizabeth Kemp: Henderson, *Banchory-Devenick*, p.249, 1742;   midwives: Lorimer, *Neil M'Vicar*, pp.40–41;   girl gives soldier as father: Lorimer, *Early Days*, pp.138–139, 1647;   doubts about man named, 1665: Cramond, *Presbytery of Fordyce*, pp.33–34;   Presbytery of Penpont: Graham, note to p.324;   David Stewart: Mitchell, p.36.

22   Midwives and unmarried mothers, 1611: *Perth KS Reg*, p.286;   no help in childbirth: Wick KS, 1702;   Oldhamstocks KS: *SRE*, p.108;   'ingenuous confession': Thurso KS, 1705.

23   'Swelling in belly': Cromarty KS, 1741;   Mary Smith: Cruden KS, 1741;   Borders servant girl, 1725: St. Boswells KS, 1725;   girl refused examination: Ashkirk KS, 1705.

24   Midwives paid: St. Vigeans KS, 1743;   woman 'got free' of pregnancy: Tarbat KS, 1756;   Kathrine Rintoul: Portmoak KS, 1780;   civil help enlisted for examinations: Kirkwall KS, 1765.

25 Woman seeking 'some things': Cromarty KS, 1740s; muriatic acid: Resolis KS, 1828.

26 Baby's toe nails: Ashkirk KS, 1707; full term baby: Aberdeen St. Nicholas KS, 1707.

27 Men and women not to share room, 1676: Cramond, *Fordyce*, p.50; man trysted woman to kiln: Nigg KS, Ross-shire, 1706; couple drinking all night, etc.: Cromarty KS, 1681; possibility of ante-nuptial fornication: Ashkirk KS, 1705.

28 Norman Denoon: Banff KS, 1702; 'inhibited to converse': Nigg KS, Ross-shire, 1729; adulterous couple: Tarbat KS, 1786; no association except at kirk etc.: Edgar I, p.300, Fenwick KS, 1674; informers followed girl: Tarbat KS, 1776.

29 'Scandal of converse': Banff KS, 1702; minister and pedlars: NSA Glenshiel, XIV, Ross-shire, p.209; Elizabeth Wallace: Kirkwall KS, 1731.

30 Cohabiting couple: Kirkwall KS, 1728; cohabiting with Sarah C — : Cromarty KS, 1679; Greater Excommunication for cohabitation: Presbytery of Glasgow, 1755 *re* Campsie and Antermony KS.

31 Unmarried 'scandalous brewars': Cramond, *Presbytery of Fordyce*, p.27; Isobell Blackadar: *Extracts Kinghorn KS*, 1640; Janet Wilson: Edgar, II, note to p.161, and woman suspended from Lord's Table: p.293; no cothouse to be let: Waddell, *Kirk Chronicle*; Act of Town Council: Murray, *St. Andrews*, 1649; Elie regulation, 1655: Thomson, *Elie Kirk*, p.60; girl to enter service by Whitsunday: *Maitland Misc.* i, p.128, Stirling KS, 1597; Christon Black: Murray, *St. Andrews*, 1645; elders to watch single women: Tait, p.16, Kelso KS.

32 'Bawdrie house': Murray, *St. Andrews*, 1649; woman entertaining at night: Dumbarton KS, 1702, 1703.

33 Wives and maids: Craig-Brown, I, p.497, Galashiels KS, 1673; 'noddings': Banff KS, 1703; Jean Knols: Banchory-Devenick KS, 1731.

34 Dowry for raped girl: *St. Andrews KS Reg*, SHS 4, lii, 1571; oath *re* rape: AGA, pp.101–102, 1707; Elspeth Scott: Ashkirk KS, 1696, and girl raped by trooper: 1702; Agnes Pringle: Moffat, *Kelsae*, p.136, 1723; Anna God: Colinton KS, 1696.

35 Jane Baptie: St. Cuthbert's KS, Edinburgh, 1715; Catherin Ross: Mitchell, p.182; women carried off, 1669: Cramond, *Presbytery of Fordyce*, p.36; abduction, 1732: MacNaughton, pp.137–139, parish of Kincardine, Ross-shire.

36 Kirk and troops: AGA, p.12, 1707; girl and dragoon: Tait, pp.8–9; girl 'gone after souldiers': Scone KS, 1716; soldier in Strathnaver's regiment: Aberdeen St. Nicholas KS, 1700; Finlay M'Donald: Kilninian and Kilmore KS, 1790.

37 Elders speak to colonel: Mitchell, pp.35–36, and difficulty in getting soldiers to appear: p.66, 1703; troops in Falkirk, 1753: Murray, *Falkirk*, II,

p.182; Dunbar woman, 1659: Edwards, p.127; discipline of soldiers: AGA, p.247, 1710; David Bell: St. Cuthbert's KS, Edinburgh, 1708.

38 'Nychtwalking': Murray, *St. Andrews*, 1640, and women in colleges: 1645, and students report couple: 1641, and students and Sabbath profanation: 1703.

39 Kirk and incest: APS 1646. VI. i. 552; man ignorant about incest: Murray, *St. Andrews*, 1643; Margaret Downie: Mackay, *Pres. Recs*, p.41, 1673; widow's son: M'Naught, p.170.

40 Ross-shire woman, 1686: Mackay, *Pres. Recs*, p.361, and youth 'fallen in incest', (1658): p.299; John McTaggart and John Baxter: Chambers, *Domestic Annals of Scotland*; John Mackenzie: MacNaughton, pp.37–38; marrying wife's daughter: Murray, *Falkirk*, II, p.128; incestuous woman: Mackay, *Pres. Recs*, p.149, 1649.

41 Greater Excommunication for incest, 1817: Tarbat KS, 1817; standing six days for incest: Kintail KS, 1832; case in Lauder: *THAS 1902, Lauder*; Lord Advocate refuses incest case: Tarbat KS, 1808; woman and brother-in-law: Resolis KS, 1827; woman to speak with the brethren: Presbytery of Dornoch, 1710; John Grant: Mackay, *Pres. Recs*, p.125.

42 Homosexuality: Smout, p.82; burning for homosexuality: Chambers, *Domestic Annals of Scotland*, II, p.243; sodomy after Reformation: Johnston, *Working Classes*, p.102; 'gross wickedness': Nigg KS, Ross-shire, 1707; William Wood: St. Boswells KS, 1731.

43 Bishop Wood: Bentinck, p.244; aristocrats making repentance: Johnston, *Working Classes*, p.87; John Sinclair jr.: Tobermory KS, 1846; James Douglas: Cramond, *Elgin*, II, p.4, and woman's treatment: p.5, 1585–86; minister's nephew: Ashkirk KS, 1700, and Agnes Leishman: 1701.

44 John Don: Tait, pp.9–10, Kelso Parish; Alexander Ross: Nigg KS, Ross-shire, 1736; Col. Hamilton: St. Cuthbert's KS, Edinburgh, 1708–09.

45 Robert Scott: Ashkirk KS, 1703–04; Banff girl: Banff KS, 1703; Katharine Baird: Sorbie KS, 1702.

46 Col. Mackay: Durness KS, 1775; Mary Smith: Foveran KS, 1748; girl and William Henderson: Dollar KS, 1831; Alexander Fraser: Mitchell, pp.65–66.

47 James Sinclair: Latheron KS, 1762.

48 Assault on cottar woman: Murray, *Falkirk*, II, p.62.

49 Improved morals: OSA Fordyce, III (1790s) p.62–63; decline in morals: NSA Nigg, XIV, Ross-shire, p.27.

12
Witchcraft and Superstition

1 Professor Smout's information: Smout, pp.198–207; not suffering a witch to live: *Bible*, Exodus 22:18; witchcraft a crime: APS 1563. II. 539; witch

banished, 1580: *Perth KS Reg*, p. 240, and witch given 8 doits, 1582: p. 242, and false accusation, 1589: pp. 266–267; two St. Andrews cases: *St. Andrews KS Reg*, SHS 4, xlix.

2 Professor's Smout's information: Smout, pp. 202–203; Act *re* witches and witchcraft, 1640, and legal standing Commission 1643: AGA, p. 277; lawyers, doctors, etc.: APS 1644. VI. i. 197; Commission appointed: AGA, p. 278, 1649; elders to search for witches: Inglis, *Angus Parish*, 1650; witchcraft not yet found: Cramond, *Presbytery of Fordyce*, p. 22, 1650.

3 Destruction of superstitious monuments: Cramond, *Presbytery of Fordyce*, p. 20, 1648; Gudeman's Croft etc. and Elgin, 1602: McNeill, I, p. 62; Boyndie's unlaboured land, 1649: Cramond, *Boyndie*, p. 12; Slains minister's query: Rust, *Druidism Exhumed*, pp. 38–42, 1649; Slains druidical fields: McNeill, I, p. 28, and Sir James Simpson: p. 62; idolatry of stone, 1649: Cramond, *Elgin*, II, p. 268. McNeill, *The Silver Bough*, I, p. 52ff. is very informative on magic and witchcraft.

4 Witchcraft trials prohibited till Restoration: Smout, pp. 203–204, and few successful trials after 1680: p. 204; General Assembly witchcraft Acts 1700: Murray, *Falkirk*, II, p. 69–70.

5 Common people and witchcraft: Tait, p. 3; mass hysteria: Smout, p. 205, and deluded satanists: p. 202.

6 Definition of witchcraft and questioning: Reid, p. 117.

7 Janet McRobert: Sorbie KS, 1702; Twynholm KS: Graham, p. 329. Cromarty KS, 1740, refers to a witch who had been excommunicated prior to that date.

8 Four widows: Craven, p. 54.

9 Ministers at execution, 1661: Gunn, *Traquair*, p. 39; minister sent to Anstruther-Easter: Dick, note to p. 112; Katharine Walenge etc.: *Extracts Kinghorn KS*, p. 50, 1643–44; Isabel Malcolm: Johnston, *Working Classes*, p. 118; Marion Fisher: Mathieson, ii, p. 160.

10 Deer KS: *SRE*, p. 127; witch mark, mole, birthmark: Smout, p. 205; mark not bleeding: *Border Magazine*, XIX, 1914, Witch-burning in Lauder; Kirkcaldy KS, 1633: *SRE*, p. 127; George Cuthie: Hillaby, *Journey Home*, p. 78; John Kincaid: Johnston, *Working Classes*, p. 115; Paterson: Carruthers, *Highland Notebook*, pp. 221–222; vaginal examinations: Hillaby, *Journey Home*, p. 78.

11 McNeill, *The Silver Bough*, I, opp. p. 128, shows illustration of a witch by Douglas Percy Bliss. Wardlaw Church, Paterson being a woman: Carruthers, *Highland Notebook*, pp. 221–222.

12 Witch's bridle: Mathieson, ii, p. 196; skilful wakers: Johnston, *Working Classes*, p. 110; woman awake twenty days: Mathieson, ii, p. 160; East Lothian KS's watching: Waddell, *Kirk Chronicle*, 1649–50, and candle for watching: 1661.

13 Trial in Session House: Reid, p.115; David Steward etc.: Waddell, *Kirk Chronicle*, 1649–50; witches burnt in East Lothian, Mr John Lauder at Dunbar burning: Waddell, *East Lothian*, p.42; worship postponed for executions: Inglis, *Angus Parish*, pp.103–104, *c*. 1650.

14 Costs of witch-burning: Chambers, *Abridged Domestic Annals*, p.247.

15 Mr James Guthrie: *THAS 1902, Lauder*; Witches' Knowe: *Border Magazine*, XIX, 1914, Witch-burning at Lauder; Janet Horne: Bentinck, pp.461–5; Thurso witches: Beaton, p.143. Johnston, *History of the Working Classes in Scotland*, pp.109–121, gives a brief but excellent description of witchcraft trials.

16 Chisholm of Comar: Johnston, *Working Classes*, note to p.113, and medical interests and Thomas Grieve: pp.113, 117; Perth medical men: *Spottiswoode Misc.* ii. p.232.

17 Taking away cow's milk, 1655: Cramond, *Fordyce*, p.19; William Wilson: Craig-Brown, I, p.497, 1673; 'lang-legged' etc.: *THAS 1904, Coldingham*; repairing woman's good name: Cramond, *Rathven*, p.69, 1751.

18 'Scoring above breath': Graham, p.330; Coldingham man: *THAS 1904, Coldingham*; bleeding woman above breath: Coldingham KS, 1700; Presbytery of Penpont: Graham, note 1 to p.330.

19 Excommunication after 1736: Cromarty KS, 1740; 'superstitious matter' of cutting foreheads: MacNaughton, pp.145–146; Portmahomack fisherman, 1845: Barron, III, p.85, and fraud by pretended witchcraft, 1843: p.35.

20 Consulting witches: APS 1563. II. 539; 1573 Act of General Assembly: *SRE*, p.127; death for consulting: APS 1649. VI. ii. 152; Donald Ferguson, woman hedging bets: Graham, note 2 to p.328; witch's stone: Thomson, *Elie Kirk*, p.37; charms etc. abounding: Cramond, *Presbytery of Fordyce*, p.36; southernwood etc.: *Border Magazine*, XIX, 1914, 'Witch-burning in Lauder'; charmer admitted to Communion: Irving, p.566. The former school at Covington, Lanarkshire, now a private house, still has upon a gable wall a small anti-witchcraft figure and, in what was the schoolroom, there is another such figure inside.

21 Lead heart: Bentinck, p.459. Murray, *Extracts of St. Andrews Kirk Session*, p.31, gives verses of charms, 1664. Marion Fisher's charm: Lorimer, *Early Days*, p.146. The words of this charm occur elsewhere, e.g. Markinch, Fife in 1642, and Shetland in 1845.

22 Alexander Moore: Murray, *St. Andrews*, 1642, and curing 'wyldefyre': 1644; Kathareen Mansone: Craven, pp.29–30; Janet: Edgar, I, note to p.269, Rothesay KS, 1661; Margaret Coutts: Cramond, *Fordyce*, pp.22–23 and Cramond, *Presbytery of Fordyce*, pp.47–48, 1684; details of mixtures: Cramond, *Elgin*, II, pp.44–45, 1596; 'end or mend': Waddell, *East Lothian*, p.24–25, *c*. 1625.

23 Charms etc. in 1790s: OSA Applecross, III (1790s) pp.379–380; charms in a Skye parish: NSA Duirinish, XIV, Inverness-shire, p.345; Presbytery of Deer: *SRE*, p.129; beheaded calf: Baird, p.32, 1670; lamb in chimney:

THAS 1904, Coldingham, c. 1695; Synod of Aberdeen recommends ministers: *Aberdeen Eccl. Recs,* xxxv; routin evil, Tynninghame KS: Waddell, *East Lothian,* p. 25; St. Mourie: Mackay, *Pres. Recs,* xxxiii, and sacrifices spread to other parishes: xxx, and Presbyterial visit to Applecross etc.: pp. 280–281, and Hector Mackenzie: p. 338.

24 Elspeth Buie: Golspie KS, 1732; boy's aunt: Tarbat KS, 1804; cock buried, *c.* 1870: Macdonald and Gordon, *Down to the Sea,* p. 122.

25 Clay image of child, 1691: Mitchell, p. 44. According to the late Miss Joan Ross, Millbank, Evanton, Ross-shire, Rev. Donald Sage, minister of Resolis from 1822–34, found a clay effigy of himself on the shore, lying among seaweed to waste away by the action of the sea. He took it home, wrapped it up with care but broke one of its fingers and was never able to use his own comparable finger again; and in the 1930s a Col. Cuthbert, who had been or was ill, also found an image of himself in a river.

26 Striking couple-tree: MacNaughton, pp. 77–78, 1714; breaking spindle: Murray, *St. Andrews,* 1659; stealing potatoes at night: Martin, p. 55, 1865.

27 Christian Roy etc.: Nigg KS, Ross-shire, 1731.

28 Use of sieve and shears: Bentinck, p. 460 and MacGeorge, pp. 208–209; women turning riddle: Kilmory KS, 1709. Cases of turning the riddle occur in Perth in 1589, Deer in 1654, Aberdour in 1669, Minnigaff in 1702, Croy in the early 18th century. Turning key: Lorimer, *Early Days,* p. 150; woman's missing money: Tait, pp. 64–65.

29 Consulting about stolen goods: Cromarty KS, 1740; consulters of Johnne Philp: Cramond, *Ordiquhill,* p. 7.

30 Hiring person to imprecate: Nigg KS, Ross-shire, *c.* 1729; imprecating Thomas Hood: Cromarty KS, 1741; 'cold armsful': Cramond, *Rathven,* p. 60, 1725, and p. 67, 1748, and mother cursing son: p. 62, 1727; 'wither by wall': Nigg KS, Ross-shire, 1706, and wishing an ill end: 1709; woman's curse on shoemaker: St. Cuthbert's KS, Edinburgh, 1708; Jean Patison: Cathcart KS, 1732.

31 Tumbling nineteen times: Cramond, *Fordyce,* p. 58, 1729; wishing woman might burn: Dunrossness KS, 1770; woman ousted: Cramond, *Fordyce,* p. 53, 1689; father's imprecation on neighbours: Johnston, *Orkney,* p. 51, Holm KS, 1697, and carrying bairns in riddle: p. 99, Orphir KS, 1710; child 'like a wedder': *SRE,* p. 129, and Speymouth woman: p. 128, 1651; scarcity of fish: Nigg KS, Ross-shire, *c.* 1731; boat to sink in depths: Cramond, *Rathven,* p. 69, 1750.

32 Swearers: APS 1581. III. 212; 'not proper to insert': Nigg KS, Ross-shire, 1730; men in jougs, 1658: Cramond, *Fordyce,* p. 41; hard 'sweiring': Waddell, *Kirk Chronicle,* 1635; fines for masters etc.: Montrose KS, 1643; fining more severely, and warning congregation: Beaton, p. 146, Canisbay KS, 1708.

33 Elders at markets: Cramond, *Elgin,* II, p. 184, 1624; ministers at markets: Cramond, *Presbytery of Fordyce,* p. 16, 1647; elders, deacons to take turns:

Murray, *St. Andrews*, 1640; four visitors: Montrose KS, 1649; summary fines: Johnston, *Working Classes*, p.103; elders' purses: Cramond, *Elgin*, II, p.63, 1598; fine or stroke with tawse: *Aberdeen Eccl. Recs*, p.26, 1603; swearers delated to magistrates, elders found no swearers: Aberdeen St. Nicholas KS, 1702.

34 'Tuck and drum': Montrose KS, 1659; punishments for profane swearing: *THAS 1909, Hawick KS Records*, Vernon, pp.25–45, 1703; 12 days' consideration: Graham, note 1 to p.285, Fowlis Easter KS, and Higher Excommunication for woman: pp.325–326; fisherman and wife: Craig KS, 1720; John Urie: Cathcart KS, 1732.

35 Cursing of parents: *Bible*, Exodus 21: 17, and Matthew 15: 4; APS 1639. V. 615 a; APS 1649. VI. ii. 231; APS 1661. VII. 202; cursing father etc. on Sunday: Tarbat KS, 1752.

36 Holy ordinance of oath: Presbytery of Dornoch, 1709; giving oaths, Presbytery of Dornoch, Synod of Ross and Sutherland: Bentinck, p.262; Mr. J. Wightman: *SRE*, p.56.

37 Information on wells: McNeill, I, pp.65–67; adoring at wells: Mackay, *Pres. Recs*, xxxix; going to wells 'on superstitious design': Cramond, *Presbytery of Fordyce*, p.40, 1674; Rarichie well: Nigg KS, Ross-shire, 1707; Huntingtower well, 1618: *Perth KS Reg*, p.289; St. Fiache's well: *Aberdeen Eccl. Recs*, p.110, 1630; leaving something at wells: McNeill, I, p.67.

38 'Idolatrous well': Macleod, *Discovering Galloway*, p.125; Mrs Robertson: Inglis, *Angus Parish*, p.123; carrying water thirteen miles: Nigg KS, Ross-shire, 1707; Nyne Maiden well: Cramond, *Fordyce*, p.27.

39 Island Maree: NSA Gairloch, XIV, Ross-shire, note to p.92; Logierait cure: OSA Logierait, XII (1977) p.714.

40 Loch-mo-naire: Barron, II, p.87.

41 Changing attitudes: Edwards, p.134.

42 Presbytery of Dingwall, 1650s: Mackay, *Pres. Recs*, pp.280–281; superstitious practices: APS 1581. III. 212; man at Speyside chapel, 1602: Cramond, *Elgin*, II, p.97, and going there 25 years later: pp.201–203, and Chapel of Grace etc., 1653: p.282, and Chanonry Kirk, 1596: p.46, and Christmas 1597: p.61, and Christmas 1599: p.76, and Act of Session, 1600: p.77.

43 Minister takes plaids: Cramond, *Ordiquhill*, p.8; Presbytery orders superstitious practices punished, 1648: Cramond, *Boyndie*, p.12; carrying corpses round church, 1641: Dick, p.119; St. Gerardine's Cave: Keith, p.110; hole in cave, (called St. Geretynes and assumed to be the same one): Cramond, *Elgin*, II, p.97.

44 Roman Catholic customs etc.: McNeill, III, p.58; Acts of Session, 1595: *St. Andrews KS Reg*, SHS 7, lxii.

45 Christmas sermon: Johnston, *Orkney*, p.33, Holm KS, 1685; Christmas Day: APS 1621. IV. 597; Christmas Day a working day: *St. Andrews KS Reg*, SHS 4, xlvii; 'grindling flower': *Aberdeen Eccl. Recs*, pp.138–

139;   St. Andrews mason: *St. Andrews KS Reg*, SHS 4, xlvii, 1573;   keeping Yule Day, masters of schools, etc.: AGA, p.286, 1645;   Song School: *Aberdeen Eccl. Recs*, p.16, 1573–74;   salters: APS 1647. VI. i. 761;   'goufe': Murray, *St. Andrews*, 1650.

46   Men, women dressed in others' garb: *Bible*, Deuteronomy 22: 5, and *Aberdeen Eccl. Recs*, pp.21–22, 1575–76;   Jonet Cadye: *Maitland Misc*. i, pp.104–105, *c*. 1570s;   oaths *re* not guysing: Cramond, *Elgin*, II, p.213, 1630;   masks hide identity: Gunn, *Traquair*, p.40, 1663;   guysers identified: Cromarty KS, 1749.

47   'Maskis and wissors': Cramond, *Elgin*, II, pp.176–177;   'personating a ghost': Allardyce, p.96, Chapel of Garioch parish;   'idolatrous songs': *Aberdeen Eccl. Recs*, p.77, 1612, and 'plaing, dancin': pp.18–19, 1574, and 'fosteraris' of superstition: p.49, 1605;   rhapsody of nonsense: Nigg KS, Ross-shire, 1708;   James Scarty: Craven, p.29, 1659.

48   Yule bread: McNeill, III, p.62, and bakers: p.59;   William Williamson: *Perth KS Reg*, p.275, 1596–97;   Aberdeen baker: *Aberdeen Eccl. Recs*, p.121, 1654;   eating geese: Johnston, *Working Classes*, p.104 (Rev. Murdo Mackenzie, Elgin, 1645–77).

49   Torches and boats, burning of the Clavie: Keith, pp.110–111. OSA Logierait, XII (1977) p.714 describes Hallowe'en and Beltane fire ceremonies. Bonfires in streets: *Aberdeen Eccl. Recs*, p.61, 1608;   'users of bonfyres': Cramond, *Boyndie*, p.12, 1648;   bonfires in 1776: Cramond, *Deskford*, p.23;   shepherds etc. had fires: OSA Louden, III (1790s) p.105;   'about Beltane': Sorbie KS, 1701.

50   Elder plays football: Galashiels KS, 1697;   Kirk Yetholm: Jeffrey, III, pp.238–239.

51   Robin Hood etc.: Chambers, *Abridged Domestic Annals*, pp.13–14;   Assembly of Divines: Sprott and Leishman, p.151;   Corpus Christi play, 1577: *Perth KS Reg*, p.233, 1577, and St. Obert's Play: p.234, 1577;   Thomas Balfour's daughter: *St. Andrews KS Reg*, SHS 4, xlvi.

52   Filthiness at cave: *Perth KS Reg*, pp.238–240, 1580–81;   St. Andrews 'remote spot', 1599: *St. Andrews KS Reg*, SHS 7, lxiv/lxv;   men, women in wood: Cramond, *Elgin*, II, p.170, 1622.

53   Robert Shortwood: Ashkirk KS, 1695–96;   straw ring: Nigg KS, Ross-shire, 1708.

54   House caught fire: Graham, note 3 to p.328, Aberlour KS, 1702;   Mr John Mill: Fyfe, p.41.

55   St. Monance bell: Dawson, *Abridged Statistical History*, note to p.400;   unbaptised right hand: Brydon.

13
Holy Matrimony

1 Hand-fasting/betrothal: *THAS 1905*, Hand-fasting, Dr C. B. Routledge, pp. 8–9; Magnus Ame: Johnston, *Orkney*, pp. 68–69, Holm KS; Presbytery ruling, 1707: MacNaughton, p. 48.

2 Hand-fasting conditions: Donaldson and Morpeth, *Dictionary of Scottish History*, p. 94 and Johnston, *Orkney*, p. 69.

3 Continued co-habitation: *St. Andrews KS Reg*, SHS 4, xliii; Govan KS, 1659: Brotchie, p. 61; people hand-fasted 6–7 years: *Scottish National Dictionary* quo. *Aberdeen Eccl. Recs*; time limit for hand-fasting, 1562: *Aberdeen Eccl. Recs*, p. 11; fornication punished as adultery: *St. Andrews KS Reg*, SHS 4, xl–xli; General Assembly *re* lying in sin: Edgar, II, note to p. 160, 1565; neglect of marriage: APS 1579. III. 139 b; hand-fasting relic, 1855: *Scottish National Dictionary* quo. Sc. 1896. W. K. Morton, Law Scot. 32. Under the heading 'Handfast Marriage', The *Scotsman* of 12 February 1989 reported a woman visiting her husband in prison on St. Valentine's Day and smuggling in super glue with which she joined his right and her left hand so that they were literally handfast and the prison authorities had to send for special solvent to separate them.

4 Contracts, proclamation of banns: Edgar, II, p. 136; parishioners 'that wants understanding': Gunn, *Traquair*, p. 4; 'ignorants catechised': Cramond, *Presbytery of Fordyce*, p. 21, 1649; reciting Lord's Prayer etc.: Edwards, p. 127, Kinnell KS; fine of 40s. Sc, 1594: *St. Andrews KS Reg*, SHS 7, lxxxv; a Caithness KS: *THAS June 1872, Marriage Customs*, Watson, pp. 142–145.

5 Galston KS, 1700: Edgar, II, p. 163; caution *re* attending worship, 1599: Cramond, *Elgin*, II, p. 73, and jougs threatened for absence, 1643: p. 246; 'marriage design' marred: Murray, *Falkirk*, II, p. 125; Mary Lyell: Wick KS, 1701.

6 Kathrine Rintoul: Portmoak KS, 1780.

7 Church benefit stopped for lack of caution: Scone KS, 1716, 1722.

8 Contracts of marriage: Bentinck, p. 293; 'Act anent parties . . .':Portmoak KS, 1708; couples + elder to come to minister: Clackmannan KS, 1702; Perthshire custom: *THAS June 1872, Marriage Customs*, Watson, pp. 142–145; girl freed by soldier: Cramond, *Elgin*, II, p. 283, 1653.

9 Stornoway marriages: OSA Stornoway, XX (1983) pp. 38–39; St. Cuthbert's KS regulation, 1645: *THAS June 1872, Marriage Customs*, Watson, pp. 142–145.

10 Saturday contracts forbidden: Scone KS, 1716; Friday contracts forbidden: Cramond, *Deskford*, p. 22, 1756; weekday contracts: Bentinck, p. 293, 1739; Monday contracts: *Perth KS Reg*, p. 247, 1583.

11 'Deluding kirk'.: Cramond, *Elgin*, II, p.122, 1604; process of marriage elsewhere: Wick KS, 1702; Alexander Bain: Tongue KS, 1789; girl's £2 for poor: Tarbat KS, 1754; 'lous fingered' girl: Cramond, *Elgin*, II, p.255, 1646–47; couple's inanimicity: *Perth KS Reg*, p.254, 1586; 'suting liberty': Edgar, II, note to p.164.

12 Damages for reneging: Sharpe, p.99; £7 solatium: Edderton KS, 1830.

13 Penalties not recovered: Aberdeen St. Nicholas KS, 1827; Margaret Anderson: Clackmannan KS, 1698; money, not caution: Edgar, II, p.147, Mauchline KS, 1629; laying down pawns: *THAS 1900, Vernon*, 1711; £6 of pledges: Banff KS, 1711; John Shepheard: Allardyce, p.108; rings consigned: Edgar, II, note to p.143. Inglis, *An Angus Parish Parish in the 18th Century*, p.116, takes the word 'pawn' to mean that Kirk Sessions became pawn-brokers but that was not so. An example of a marriage contract, dated 1899, now in Tain Museum, Ross-shire, comes from the nearby village of Shandwick. The penalty for failure to carry out the contract is given as 100 merks Scots, coinage which had long gone out of use, showing that at that late date this aspect of the contract was purely a formality.

14 Spoons, clothing: Graham, p.327; poor not to be burdensome: Edgar, II, note to p.145, Kilmarnock KS, 1674; David Gray: Cramond, *Elgin*, II, p.232, 1636.

15 Evidence of marriage: Aberdeen, St. Nicholas KS, 1827; pawn returned by warrant of Session: Sorbie KS, 1701; innocent person's pawn returned: Cramond, *Cullen*, p.64, 1730; sick bride-to-be, man's broken ribs: Edgar, II, pp.145–146, and end of consignation money: p.248.

16 Marriage within 40 days of proclamation: *Perth KS Reg*. p.247, 1583; marriage within 40 days of contract: Nigg KS, 1729; Assembly Acts *re* proclamation, 1638, 1690: AGA, p.199, 144; witnesses to death: Nigg KS, 1729; parents', friends' consent: AGA, p.199, 1699; James Watson: *Aberdeen Eccl. Recs*, pp.45–46; forged testimonials: *Perth KS Reg*, p.259, 1587.

17 Robert Wright etc.: Cramond, *Elgin*, II, pp.24–25, 1592; Waugh brothers: Sharpe, p.95.

18 Prosecution, discipline, for marriage without banns: Cramond, *Rathven*, p.63, 1728; Session Clerks etc. 'wronged': Johnston, *Orkney*, Holm KS; proclamation fee, 1706: Hyslop, p.469; division of proclamation fees: Earlston KS, 1782.

19 Legal action for dues: Abernethy KS, 1748; Hawick proclamation charge: *THAS 1900, Vernon*.

20 Hurricane etc. = Thomson, *Elie Kirk*, p.45; Presbytery of Irvine: Edgar, II, p.141; proclamation on two Sundays: Tweedsmuir KS, 1773; Hawick proclamation: *THAS 1900, Vernon*; Kilmaurs proclamation charges: M'Naught, p.173; privilege of proclamation on two Sundays: Kilninian and Kilmore KS, 1768; money 'mortified': Abernethy KS, 1749.

21 Falkirk proclamation dues: Murray, *Falkirk*, II, p.223; reduced fees for non-parishioners: Nigg KS, 1810, 1821; fees returned: Edgar, II, note to p.145.

22 Act on Proclamation of Banns: Compendium of Acts of General Assembly, 1883.

23 Stopping proclamation: Edgar, II, pp.164–165; George Chrystie: Kinglassie KS, 1760; Janet Scott: Sharpe, pp.94–95; Marion Dykes: Ashkirk KS, 1690; James Waldie: Sprouston KS, 1691; Donald Mackay: Tongue KS, 1821; David Brown: Allardyce, p.101, 1627.

24 'Scorning the kirk': Stow KS, 1792; Dornoch woman, mother dissuaded son: Bentinck, p.294; William Ross: MacNaughton, pp.245–246.

25 Fornication suspected: Cromarty KS, 1681, and John Munro: 1739.

26 Oath required, 1585: *Perth KS Reg*, p.251; consignation *re* ante-nuptial fornication: *THAS 1900, Vernon*; John Stewart's pledge: Edgar, II, note to p.148, 1771.

27 Daughter brought to bed: Allan, p.171, 1655; 12*s*. Sc. retained: Coldingham KS, 1699; Kelso man: Tait, pp.10–11.

28 Stool before desk, 1577: *Aberdeen Eccl. Recs*, p.22; Dunfermline KS, 1641: Edgar, II, p.173; one bride left first: Cramond, *Rathven*, p.69; marrying in order of contract: NSA Avoch, XIV, Ross-shire, p.393; 'fyring pistols', shooting forbidden: Henderson, *Banchory-Devenick*, pp.246–247; man died of wounds: *Cramond, Deskford*, p.2.

29 Galston inn-keepers: Edgar, II, p.155; going to ale-houses forbidden, 1756: Cramond, *Deskford*, p.22; William Olifer: *THAS 1902, Penny Bridals and Infares*, Vernon.

30 Banquets forbidden: APS 1621. IV. 426; only four guests: APS 1681. VIII. 350; three guests, 1710: Cramond, Presbytery of Fordyce, p.54.

31 Although not a feature of penny weddings, there used to be a custom in different parts of the country for the bride to sell ale on the wedding day, for which she received a handsome price from the guests. This was called bride ale, bride-bush, bride-wain — *THAS 1872, Marriage Customs*, Watson, pp.142–145. Price of 'ordinaries': APS 1617. IV. 538; Edinburgh JPs: Kelsall, *Scottish Lifestyle 300 Years ago*, p.84; efforts to suppress penny weddings, 1627: Cramond, *Presbytery of Fordyce*, p.11; Synod of Moray, 1640 *re* no penny weddings on Sundays: Mackay, *Pres. Recs*, xxiv; sacrifice to lust etc.: Cramond, *Presbytery of Fordyce*, p.54, 1710; Act against Penny Bridals, 1645: AGA, p.184; penny weddings for social groups, 1646, householders' consignation: Cramond, *Presbytery of Fordyce*, pp.15–16.

32 'Going soberly' about marriage: Barony KS, Glasgow, 1702; putting laws into force: AGA, pp.154–155, 1706, and a similar Act: p.185, 1719; penny weddings 1724, 1727: Cramond, *Presbytery of Fordyce*, pp.56–57; Rev. James Smith: OSA Avoch, XVII (1981) p.324; 20th century penny weddings: *The Scots Magazine*, June 1989, p.256, 'Customs and Excess', Bob Morrow.

33 Dancing in mansions: Graham, pp. 327–328; 'dancing and vanitie', Stirling KS: *Maitland Misc*, i, pp. 135–136; dancing 'most abominable,' Morton KS, 1715: Graham, pp. 327–328; Act *re* promiscuous dancing, 1649: AGA p. 70; Presbytery's and General Assembly's Acts, 1650: Cramond, *Presbytery of Fordyce*, p. 22; Robert Halliewell: Allan, p. 171, 1655; Presbytery of Glasgow, 1647: *THAS June 1872, Marriage Customs*, Watson, pp. 142–145; Act anent piping: Kinross KS, 1701.

34 Pipers to and from church: Murray, *Falkirk*, II, p. 44; Adam Moffat: *THAS 1900, Vernon re* Ashkirk KS; 'vyler and pyper': Murray, *St. Andrews*, 1649; fine for owning fiddle: Graham, p. 327.

35 Dancing house: Presbytery of Lewis, 1759; dancing school: Nigg Public School log book, 1888.

36 John Hart: *THAS 1902, Penny Bridals and Infares*, Vernon; John Hardie's wedding: *THAS 1902, Supernumerarie and Exorbitant Marriage*, Vernon.

37 James Hardie etc.: Tait, pp. 10–11; Orphir KS's Act anent pawn money etc.: Johnston, *Orkney*, pp. 117, 123; pawn given to wife: *THAS June 1872, Marriage Customs*, Watson, pp. 142–145; abuses *re* pawns: Murray, *St. Andrews*, 1658.

38 General Assembly, 1579: *St. Andrews KS Reg*, SHS 4, xliv; no marriages on Sundays: *Perth KS Reg*, p. 253; no Sunday marriages in Elgin: Cramond, *Elgin*, II, p. 194, 1626; Westminster Directory: *Westminster Directory*, Leishman's edition, p. 57; no Monday marriages: *THAS June 1872, Marriage Customs*, Watson, pp. 142–145; Kilmarnock: Edgar, II, pp. 171–172; no market day marriages: M'Michael.

39 Drymen KS: Graham, p. 298 and note 3 to p. 298; private marriages: Stirling KS (Holy Rude), 1696; 2*s*. stg. donation, 'fine': Edgar, II, note to p. 173, and acceptance of private marriage: note to p. 172; marrying elsewhere: St. Michael's KS, Linlithgow, 1731; 6*d*. for poor people: Edgar, II, note to p. 173; poor still married in church: Graham, pp. 229–230.

40 Collections for kirk officer etc. (Mauchline area) and beadle's fee for private marriage (Kilmarnock KS, 1709): Edgar, II, p. 175; Morebattle: Tait, pp. 66–67.

41 Marriages in manse, 1723: *Cramond*, Rathven, p. 58; Dr Borland: *THAS 1910, Church of Scotland as depicted in the Waverley Novels*, pp. 40–47.

42 Excommunicated clergyman, night marriage: Cramond, *Ordiquhill*, p. 14, 1655; tumult of 'idle gazers': Murray, *St. Andrews*, 1688.

43 Marrying Englishwomen: APS 1587. III. 464; marrying in England: APS 1639. V. 569 a; Scots not to marry in England, etc.: APS 1641. V. 348; 'running over march': *THAS 1909, Hawick KS Records*, Vernon, pp. 25–45, 1702; marriage by Jesuits etc: APS 1641. ch. 12; three months' prison for marriage by unauthorised person: APS 1661. VII. 231; 'outed ministers': APS 1695. IX. 387; man married by Episcopalian: St. Cuthbert's KS, Edinburgh, 1715; Mary Sutherland, 1723: Cramond, *Rathven*, p. 59, and Roman Catholic marriages common: p. 60.

44 David Strange, David Paterson: Lorimer, *Neil M'Vicar*, pp. 43–45.

45 Missionary, 1727: Cramond, Presbytery of Fordyce, p. 57.

46 Disorderly/irregular marriage: APS 1685. VIII. 472. AGA, p. 120, 1690, refers to taking notice of ministers performing irregular and clandestine marriages without proclamation of banns. Couple irregularly married in church: Peterhead KS, 1681; lawyer's marriage: St. Michael's KS, Linlithgow, 1731; Town Clerk's marriage: Murray, *Falkirk*, II, pp. 149–150; Hawick doctor's marriage: *THAS 1900, Vernon*.

47 Irregular marriages took place in Angus, 1729 (Craig KS), in Aberdeen, 1705 (St. Nicholas KS) and in Sutherland in 1710 (Presbytery of Dornoch.) People from northern Scotland: NSA Graitney, IV, Dumfries-shire, p. 273.

48 Unfrocked priests: Lochinvar, *Romance of Gretna Green*; Rev. Thomas Blair: Tait, p. 11; William Dickson: *Border Magazine*, X, 1905, Coldstream Marriage House; John Rutherford: Burleigh, *Ednam and its Indwellers*, pp. 98–99; John Barclay: St. Cuthbert's KS, Edinburgh, 1708; Patrick Middleton: St. Michael's KS, Linlithgow, 1729; 'designs himself minister': Cambuslang KS, 1754.

49 Coldstream marriage lines: Burleigh, *Ednam and its Indwellers*, pp. 98–99; William Maclean's lines: Tillycoultry KS, 1747; John Brown's lines: Dollar KS, 1700.

50 John Anderson's marriage: Swinton and Simprim KS, 1809; 'to be humble': Cambuslang KS, 1752; 'encouraged to adhere': St. Michael's KS, Linlithgow, 1729, and 'marriage dutys': 1729, 1733; 'live regularly': Sprouston KS, 1762; couples absolved: Stow KS, 1773 and Yetholm KS, 1826; copy given to couple: Hawick KS, 1718.

51 Ann Ruxton: Craig KS, 1716; Marie Bruce: Stirling KS (Holy Rude), 1701; 'insufficient' certificate: Tillycoultry KS, 1747; up-to-date certificate: Dollar KS, 1800.

52 Censure for irregular marriage: Kirkcudbright KS, 1697; proclamation 'to terrifie', 1720, and doctor's marriage: *THAS 1900, Vernon*.

53 Marriage dues paid: Dunbar KS, 1733; dues and fine: Sprouston KS, 1762; marriage dues: Bonhill KS, 1773, 1780; £2 fine: Murray, *Falkirk*, II, p. 223, 1803–06; principal heritor's demand, 1728: Cramond, *Rathven*, pp. 62–63; refusal to pay: *THAS 1900, Vernon*; marriage by JPS: OSA Aberdeen (town), XIV (1982) p. 294; KS request to JPs: Murray, *Falkirk*, II, p. 179.

54 Jannet Gorely: Kirkpatrick-Fleeming KS, 1784; woman introduced as wife, inn-keeper's evidence: Murray, *Falkirk*, II, p. 195.

55 Tillycoultry couple: Tillcoultry KS, 1747; John Main: Stranraer KS, 1744; dissolving irregular marriage: Murray, *Falkirk* II, pp. 193–194.

56 John Barclay: St. Cuthbert's KS, Edinburgh, 1708; proving wives' deaths: Nigg KS, Ross-shire, 1706, 1729; Chelsea out-pensioner: Tarbat KS, 1793; John Lindsey: Craig KS, 1714.

57 David Dewar: Cambuslang KS, 1784, and woman at bigamous marriage: 1786.

58 Kilconquhar girl: Dick, pp.117–118, 1708;   Scone girl: Scone KS, 1716;   woman petitions Presbytery of Irvine: *THAS 1900, Vernon.*

59 Proving man's death, 1723: *THAS 1900, Vernon;*   soldier's wife in Falkirk: Murray, *Falkirk,* II, pp.126–127;   Greenock woman: Greenock KS, 1763;   husband absent nine years: Murray, *Falkirk,* II, p.127;   husband died in Brussels: Presbytery of Dornoch, 1707.

60 John Mitchell, John Davidsoun: *Aberdeen Eccl. Recs,* p.23;   three reasons given for leaving wives: Sharpe, p.100, 1610;   Mary M'Lean: College KS, Glasgow, 1804;   Janet Kyd: *Aberdeen Eccl. Recs,* p.13, 1568;   Coll man: Coll KS, 1734.

61 Woman in Aberdeen tolbooth: Stuart, *Records of the Kirk Session of Aberdeen,* Spalding, Club, pp.58–59, 1607;   woman in 'firm ward': *Buchan Field Club,* III;   woman excommunicated: Lorimer, *Early Days,* pp.123–124, quo. *St. Andrews KS Reg,* 1568.

62 Woman feared murdered: Kinross KS, 1708–09. Bentinck, *Dornoch Cathedral and Parish,* p.449 ff. gives good examples of domestic discord which came before the Kirk Session. Margaret Fraser: St. Cuthbert's KS, Edinburgh, 1708.

63 Dornoch couple: Bentinck, pp.451–452.

64 Man 'lying in Adultery': Lauder KS, 1800;   man kissed wife: *St. Andrews KS Reg.* SHS 4, 1562;   James Souter: St. Nicholas KS, Aberdeen, 1669, 1770.

65 James Small: Extracts Kinghorn KS, pp.28–29, 1626;   wife given yearly allowance: MacGeorge, p.203, 17th century;   James Walker: Perth KS Reg, p.256;   Elgin couple: Cramond, Elgin, II, p.219, 1631;   woman's Communion token: Cramond, Deskford, p.21, 1744.

66 Adam Chisholm: Sharpe, p.98;   divorce proof and decree: Mackay, *Pres. Recs,* p.338 and MacGill, I, p.40;   impatient man: Mackay, *Pres. Recs,* p.361, and John McConnel: p.338.

67 Rev. George Balfour: MacNaughton, pp.268–269;   Anne Taylor, 1801–02, and tokens, 1812: Martin, pp.31–32.

68 Illegal marriage: Kinloss KS, 1826.

69 Catherin McLean: Coll KS, 1777.

70 Wife-selling: Craig-Brown, II, pp.105–106;   wife-swapping: Kilsyth KS, 1696.

14
The Sacrament of Baptism

1 Urgent baptism: APS 1621. V. 597;   Act of Assembly, 1645: AGA, p.18.

2 Reader forbidden to baptise etc.: Cramond, *Elgin*, II, pp. 74–75; baptism after preaching, 1568: *Aberdeen Eccl. Recs*, p. 14; burgess's baby: Edgar, II, p. 212, quo. Spalding; baptisms 8.30 a.m.: Lorimer, *Early Days*, p. 93, 1592; Kilmarnock: Edgar, II, pp. 228–229; grief felt, 1611: *Aberdeen Eccl. Recs*, pp. 75–76, and privilege rescinded, 1640: p. 114.

3 Sunday afternoon baptisms: Waddell, *East Lothian*, p. 22; morning baptism: Inglis, *Angus Parish*, p. 128.

4 Baptism day after birth: Waddell, *East Lothian*; baptism on Sunday after birth: APS 1621. IV. 597; baby in snow: Edwards, p. 171; catechising and baptising, 1648: AGA, p. 226; baptism later, going to Prestonkirk etc.: Waddell, *Kirk Chronicle*, p. 48; baptism in Farr etc.: OSA Tongue, III (1790s) p. 523.

5 Father and godfather: Sprott and Leishman, p. 135; 'Christian friend': Johnstone and Hunter, p. 382; 'faithful neighbour': *St. Andrews KS Reg*, SHS 7, lxxxviii; joint sponsor: Edgar, II, pp. 214–215; 2–4 gossops: *Aberdeen Eccls. Recs*, pp. 109–110; gossops sitting: *St. Andrews KS Reg*, SHS 7, lxxxviii; Galston witnesses: Edgar, II, pp. 214–215; gossops' seat: Thomson, *Lauder*, p. 78; Dalmellington baptismal seat, 1776: Edgar, I, p. 60; Carnbee baptismal seat: Hay.

6 Linton font: Jeffrey, III, p. 228; Dalarossie, Dunlichity stones: Rev. Lillian Bruce; baptismal basins etc.: APS 1617. IV. 534; baptismal basin, 'iron': Waddell, *East Lothian*, pp. 21, 23; basin fastened to pulpit: Henderson, *Religious Life*, p. 156; water cloth: Waddell, *Kirk Chronicle*; washing cloths: Dunbar KS, 1721; baptism across burn: Edwards, pp. 169–170.

7 Church privileges withheld: *THAS 1900, Vernon*; seeing reader and elders: *St. Andrews KS Reg*, SHS 7, lxxxviii, 1583–84; Margaret Burnside: Thomson, *Elie Kirk*, p. 58, 1704; weakly child baptised: *THAS 1900, Vernon*, 1714; child's right to baptism: AGA, p. 18, 1712; alternative sponsor to be found: *THAS 1900, Vernon*, 1713; threat to leave child 'upon the session': St. Boswells KS, 1726.

8 Effie Halliday and other baptisms: Kintail KS, Register of Baptisms, 1875, 1873, 1878. The Record of Baptisms etc. of Tarbat KS, beginning 1823, uses the term lawful son or daughter, sometimes abbreviated to 'ls' or 'ld' to indicate legitimacy.

9 Sponsorship/disputed paternity: Edgar, II, p. 229; baptism in 1908: Edderton KS, 1908.

10 Baptism not essential to salvation: Johnstone and Hunter, p. 116; superstition etc. and 'I wat aweel . . .' by Dougal Graham: Edwards, p. 167.

11 Synod of Fife, 1641: Dick, p. 119; unbaptised, stillborn children: Gordon, pp. 144–145.

12 Inverkeithing woman: *Perth KS Reg*, p. 309, 1627; baby buried on shore: Mitchell, p. 45, 1690; man baptised child, 1653: Cramond, *Ordiquhill*, pp. 13–14; Mr John Oswald: Edgar, II, p. 212.

13 Man shamed into admitting paternity: Coll KS, 1792; James King: Drymen KS, 1815 ff.

14 Premature baby: Ashkirk KS, 1705; five-month baby: Resolis KS, 1840–41; Norval the Wigman: *THAS 1906, Hawick KS Records, Vernon*, pp. 93–94.

15 Rebuke for drinking: Comrie KS, 1839; Glasgow vintner: St. John's KS, Glasgow, 1831; carrying load: Edderton KS, 1828; Kilmaurs town clerk: M'Naught, p. 166, 1699.

16 Ignorant people to 'train their Family': AGA, p. 225, 1648; Lasswade KS: Edgar, II, p. 218; Dougal Macandrew: NSA Petty, XIV, Inverness-shire, note to p. 407; John Ker: Thomson, *Lauder*, p. 88 and *THAS 1902, Lauder*, 1680; Mauchline man: Edgar, II, p. 223, 1799; church attendance required: West Kilbride KS, 1833; baptismal service: *Aberdeen Eccl. Recs*, lxvii; Mr Roderick Macleod: Blakey, p. 26.

17 No marriage certificates: Brotchie, pp. 59–60, 1651; 'friendly negotiation': Mitchell, pp. 45–46; Charles Stewart: College Church KS, Glasgow, 1806; holding up another man's child: Mitchell, p. 46, 1695; £10 penalty for not presenting illegitimate child: Montrose KS, 1641; coal carter: *The Scots Magazine*, March 1987, 'Getting to know Gilmerton', p. 624, Marjorie Wilson.

18 Baptism to be administered by established clergy: APS 1670. VIII. 10; APS 1672 and Synod of Galloway: Edgar, II, pp. 220–221; General Assembly recommendation, 1711: AGA, p. 60; testimonials not asked or granted: Cramond, *Syn. Aberdeen*, p. 67, 1700; Dr Foord: Allan, *Channelkirk*, p. 229.

19 Maybole minister: Edgar, II, p. 211; announcements *re* worship and baptism: Edwards, p. 167 and Russell, p. 19; Dean Alexander Pitcairne: Craven, p. 70.

20 Drymen KS: Graham, p. 298 and note to p. 298; private baptism charges: Dunbar KS, 1727–28 and Greenock KS, 1771; private charity: Gunn, *Traquair*, p. 97; bell tolling, 1700: Cramond, *Syn. Aberdeen*, p. 67.

21 Press comment: Barron, II, p. 220; Banff baptisms: *SRE*, p. 254; home baptism for sickly child: St. Monance KS, 1849; 10 private baptisms to 1 public: Edgar, II, pp. 207–209.

22 Nineteen-year-old man, 1601: Cramond, *Elgin*, II, p. 86; woman's 'degree of knolidge': *THAS 1900, Excerpts from KS of Hawick*, pp. 147–148; Kilmarnock girl (1705) and black woman (Kilwinning, 1721): Edgar, II, pp. 224–225.

23 Robert Stewart: MacGeorge, p. 211; jougs and banishment: Cramond, *Elgin*, II, p. 10; Quaker: Burleigh, *Ednam and its Indwellers*, pp. 81–82; soldiers hired, 1734: Cramond, *Fordyce*, p. 58; beggars' children: AGA, p. 19, 1647; Mr John Carmichael: Gunn, *Traquair*, p. 42.

24 160 children: Macrae, *Life of Gustavus Aird*. It does not appear that this was a Free Church baptism.

25 Foundling girl: Aberdeen St. Nicholas KS, 1700; baptism of foundlings: AGA, p.18, 1712; William Campbell's child: Cawdor KS, 1720; Elgin KS, 1598 and St. Andrews KS, 1573: *SRE* p.65; Elspeth Boddy: St. Vigeans KS, 1682; grandfather's sponsorship: Edderton KS, 1838.

26 Half baptism fees for poor: APS 1701. X. App. 99 b; Kilmarnock charges: Edgar, II, pp.227–228; Langholm's charges: Hyslop, p.469; Earlston's charges: Earlston KS, 1782; equal shares for staff: Johnston, *Orkney*, p.123, Orphir KS, 1794; sharing different categories of money: Montrose KS, 1634; greedy beadle: Edgar, II, pp.227–228; kirk officer to 'set no water': Dumbarton KS, 1702; fees a stumbling block to poor: OSA Liff and Bervie, XIII (1794) pp.407–408.

27 Carefully filling up books: Nigg KS, Ross-shire, 1706; 3 merks Sc. for private baptism: Bonhill KS, 1773; upper classes: OSA Borthwick, II (1975) note to p.75; mother's name omitted: Gibson, p.79; Mrs Shaw: St. John's KS, Glasgow, 1832; Falkirk baptismal register: Murray, *Falkirk*, II, p.196; minister's suggestion *re* 3d. levy: OSA Borthwick, II (1975) note to p.75; value of registrations: Edgar, II, p.226; 'line' from Session Clerk: Bonhill KS, 1773.

28 Mr Thomas Young: Todd, *Clerical History of Kirkmaiden*, p.32; banquets forbidden: APS 1621. IV. 426; numbers limited: APS 1681. VIII, 350; riot: Tarbat KS, 1762; Earl of Haddington's feast: NSA Whitekirk and Tynninghame, II, East Lothian, note to pp.37–38.

29 Highlanders' hospitality: OSA Kincardine, Ross-shire, III (1790s) p.513.

30 The Crawfordjohn baptismal stone lies to the north of the Glentaggart road about one mile from the Douglas to Crawfordjohn road — Information from exhibition in Crawfordjohn Church.

15
Burial of the Dead

1 'Concerning burial of the dead': Johnstone and Hunter; minister's role: Sprott and Leishman, p.78; development of burial services: Gordon, pp.49–50.

2 The 24 skeletons were found at Nigg Old Church, Ross-shire, when the boiler-room was being prepared to receive the Nigg Pictish Stone. They were reverently reburied in the graveyard. Church burials ceased, 1729: Martin, p.16, Nigg Old Church, Ross-shire.

3 Boleskine church: Mackay, *Pres. Recs*, xvii; Mr Bethune: Bentinck, p.311; 1638 and 1643 Acts *re* burial in churches: AGA, p.25; burials in St. Michael's Church, Linlithgow: *Emblems of Mortality*, Linlithgow Academy History Society; graves under pulpit: Gordon, p.92; laird of Barr etc.: Edgar, I, p.43, 1633.

4   1624, 1711 charges: Cramond, Fordyce, pp.13, 56;   Montrose charges: Montrose KS, 1707;   John Fairweather: Edwards, p.171;   Linlithgow charges: *Emblems of Mortality*, Linlithgow Academy History Society;   fine for church burial: Craven, p.28, 1659;   lairds of Ancistoun, Shieldhill: Gordon, p.93;   John Schaw: Chambers, *Abridged Domestic Annals*, p.188, 1609.
5   Elder 'wyled' key, Lochbroom elder: Gordon, p.93.
6   Compensation paid: Martin, p.18, Nigg KS, Ross-shire, 1729;   Kilmarnock KS, 1695: Gordon, p.93.
7   St. Cuthbert's KS, Edinburgh, acquired additional land for burials in 1819, on the corner of Dalkeith Road and East Preston Street, when the Buccleuch Cemetery was considered to be full — *Ruins and Remains*, p.49;   stent masters: APS 1640. V. 278 a;   stenting the parochin: Cramond, *Fordyce*, p.24, 1634;   wall-building, 1596: Cramond, *Elgin*, II, p.42;   boatloads of stones: Cromarty KS, 1741;   building 10 feet of wall: Cranna, *Fraserburgh Past and Present*, p.197;   mortification, bell money for graveyards: Mitchell, p.104;   penalties for graveyard care: Cramond, *Deskford*, p.11;   using mortcloth money: Channelkirk KS, 1804;   Langholm dyke: Hyslop, p.470;   Kelso graveyard: Haig, *Topographical and Historical Account of Kelso*, p.120.
8   Dykes being ornamental, preservative: OSA Bedrule, III (1979) note to p.352;   kirkyard frequented by swine: Yetholm KS, 1703;   'rutting' graves: Johnston, *Orkney*, p.81, Holm parish, 1762;   'common loaning': St. Boswells KS Benefice Book, 1617;   'hors, ky': Edgar, I, p.48, Galston parish, 1634;   'compassed with middens' Cramond, *Fordyce*, p.23, 1684;   fining midden-owners (1628) and Presbytery Visitation (1630): Cramond, *Rathven*, p.12;   minister's grass rouped: Edgar, I, p.49;   monuments 'wronged': Chambers, *History of Peebles-shire*, 1733.
9   Stables forbidden: *Perth KS Reg*, p.256;   man pardoned for night grazing: Murray, *Falkirk*, I, pp.29–30;   sheep fed on turnips: Gordon, p.85.
10   Kincardine O'Neill market, delving sward, etc. at Galston, 1638: Gordon, p.84.
11   Bleaching, Kelso Skinners: Gordon, pp.84–85;   St. Andrews graveyard prohibitions: *St. Andrews KS Reg*, SHS 7, lxxxviii;   donkeys (Ashkirk parish) and Kincardine O'Neill ball green: Gordon, p.86;   Hobkirk Ba': Tancred, *Rulewater and its People*, p.352.
12   Mauchline churchyard, 1779: Edgar, I, p.50, and minister of Duthil: II, note to pp.251–252;   coffins for firewood: Love, p.141.
13   Poison for earth rats: Cramond, *Fordyce*, p.57;   yird swine: Gordon, p.87.
14   Non-kirkyard burials, 1639: Thomson, *Elie Kirk*, p.35;   burial lairs: Nigg KS, Ross-shire, 1810–49;   non-residents' lairs paid for: OSA Banchory-Devenick, XIV (1982) p.15;   disputed lair: Tarbat KS, 1784.
15   Through-stones: Dumbarton KS, 1694;   cost of erecting stones: *Session Book of Bonkle and Preston*, p.49;   headstone costs: NSA Kirkliston, I,

Edinburgh, p.148; payment before burial place registered etc.: Clackmannan KS, 1702; reduced charge: St. Cuthbert's KS, Edinburgh, 1708; little stones: Gordon, p.102, Stirling parish; non-removal of original stone: Nigg KS, Ross-shire, 1875.

16 John Hill's stone: Kirkliston KS, 1734.

17 Shovel and mattock, 1695: North Berwick KS, 1695; kirk pick: Tweedsmuir KS, 1722; grave-diggers' clothes: St. Cuthbert's KS, Edinburgh, 1841; Lady Aldie's funeral, 1757: MacGill, I, p.154; grave-diggers' payment: Montrose KS, 1641.

18 Edinburgh grave-diggers' fees: Gordon, p.167; 6d. per grave: Borgue KS, 1687; groat for pauper's grave (Galston KS, 1676) and early 19th century charges at Channelkirk: Gordon, p.170; 1920s payments: Nigg Parish Council, Ross-shire, 1922.

19 Accounts for mortcloths etc.: St. Cuthbert's KS, Edinburgh, 1709; turf at Mauchline: Edgar, II, p.256; digging own graves: Keith, p.115; Rothesay KS and 1930s: Gordon, p.98.

20 Synod of Moray, 1640: Mackay, *Pres. Recs*, xxiv; Presbytery of St. Andrews, 1643: Gordon, p.86; Presbytery order *re* hours for Sunday burials: NSA Alyth, X, Perthshire, p.1120; Sunday burials: St. Cuthbert's KS, Edinburgh, 1840; Sunday coffin-making: Low, p.158. There is still a limited provision for Sunday burials but this does not now affect Kirk Sessions.

21 Private burial forbidden: *Perth KS Reg*, p.255; night burial forbidden: Murray, *St. Andrews*, 1654.

22 Bell-ringing 'not uncommon': Edgar, II, p.256; Sir Robert Farquhar: Gordon, p.85; Mauchline Big Bell: Edgar, II, p.258; Broughton KS: Baird, *Annals of a Tweeddale Parish*, p.268; no bells for Sunday burials: Scone KS, 1722.

23 Tough bell: Gordon, p.16; 'bell-penny': Edgar, II, p.258.

24 Hand-bell for excommunication: *Border Magazine*, IX, p.72; ordering beggars out: Cramond, *Elgin*, II, pp.40, 47, 1596–97; handbell for worship: Waddell, *Kirk Chronicle*, p.78, Tynninghame parish, pre-1625; 'little bell': Nigg KS, Ross-shire, 1729 and Tarbat KS, 1764; 'deid bell': Love; hand deid bell: *THAS 1900, Hawick Town Council Records*, pp.149–152, 1694; corpse/lych bell: Inglis, *Angus Parish*, p.112, 1741; two trips for bell-man: Gordon, p.17.

25 Mort-bell charge, 17th century: Nigg KS, Ross-shire, 1698; 3d/2d per mile: Gordon, p.18, Galston KS; Lillias McCulloch: Nigg KS, Ross-shire, 1729.

26 William Stivenson: Gordon, p.19; bell in bed, etc.: *Border Magazine*, IX, p.72.

27 Burial warnings: Johnston, *Orkney*, p.130, and 'putting one down' (1715): p.101, and Burial Regulation, 1732: p.110.

28 Glasgow's 'black cloath': Edgar, II, note to p.259; lack of mortcloths felt: Dalgetty, *History of Fowlis Easter*, Lundie KS, 1693; lack of mortcloth a loss to the parish: Cromarty KS, 1756; middle size: Tweedsmuir KS, 1763.

29 Gennoa Vellivit cloth (1720): *THAS 1900, Vernon*; silk fringing: Tynninghame KS, 1703; hair fringing: Shotts KS, 1734; Logie KS's cloth: Gordon, p.52; small fringes used: Dalgetty, *History of Church of Fowlis Easter*, Lundie KS, 1693; value of fringing: Lorimer, *Neil M'Vicar*, p.73; beadle's brother to get cloth: Fowlis Easter and Lundie, 1693 Gordon, p.53; minister to get cloth: Tynninghame KS, 1703; inquiring of Sorn KS: Mauchline KS, 1771.

30 Coldingham mortcloth: Coldingham KS, 1695; Old Rayne mortcloth: Old Rayne KS, 1737, 1765; Arbuthnott cloth: Gordon, p.160, and 'extremely genteel' cloth: p.52.

31 Mortcloth bought 'at Holland': Craig-Brown, I, p.499; Captain Hall: Dunbar KS, 1734; towes for spokes, dyeing, etc.: Thomson, *Coldingham Parish and Priory*, p.145; mending by a proper hand: Tarbat KS, 1756.

32 Sackcloth cloth: Channelkirk KS, 1705; cutting cloth down: Craig-Brown, I, p.499; two cloths to be four: Bentinck, pp.291–292.

33 24 cloths: St. Cuthbert's KS, Edinburgh, 1839; Morebattle's chest: Tait, pp.60–61; 'fine serge Bagg' (1720): *THAS 1900, Vernon*; 'more safe carrieing': Craig KS, 1715; costs of pock: St. Boswells KS, 1728; cost of wallet: Shotts KS, 1727; towels: Coldingham KS, 1701, 1752; airing, etc.: Kiltearn KS, 1711.

34 Payment to keeper of cloth: Montrose KS, 1707; schoolmaster as mortcloth keeper: Cambuslang KS, 1788; Melrose charges: Melrose KS, 1763; Channelkirk charges: Channelkirk KS, 1804; 4*d.* per mile: Nigg KS, Ross-shire, 1826; drink silver: Waddell, *Kirk Chronicle*, 17th century.

35 Mortcloth charges and % interest: Edderton KS, and Gordon, p.161.

36 Cloths were too dear: Coldingham KS, 1733; inferior mortcloth: MacDonald, *St. Clement's Looks Back*, p.17; Auchterhouse KS: Gordon, p.56; orders to grave-digger: Allardyce, p.109, Cruden KS; burial in Greyfriars kirkyard: St. Cuthbert's KS, Edinburgh, 1708.

37 Newton colliers, etc.: OSA Newton, Edinburgh, II (1975) p.365; Duchess's Chamberlain: *THAS 1900, Vernon*; 'opposition cloth': Murray, *Falkirk*, II, p.186; compulsory purchase of cloths: Nigg KS, Ross-shire, 1729; Galston merchant: Gordon, p.57; St. Cuthbert's/Trades' cloths: Lorimer, *Neil M'Vicar*, pp.71–72, 1700; Castleton mortcloth: OSA Castleton, III (1979) note to p.388; John King's legacy: Keith, pp.97–98.

38 £1 10*s.* given out: Nigg KS, Ross-shire, 1833; mortcloth money for church repair: Thomson, *Lauder*, p.98; schoolmaster's salary: Gordon, p.57; cautioner for mortcloth money: Thomson, *Lauder*, p.83; John Turner's cloth: Gordon, p.58; rented cloths: Bentinck, p.292.

39 Borders parish, 1900: Gordon, p.59. A mortcloth was used till *c.* 1905 in Nigg, Ross-shire.

40 General Assembly/burial regulations: Gordon, p.109; 4*s* Sc. for registration: Montrose KS, 1707; stamp duty when mortcloth obtained: Murray, *Falkirk*, II, p.196; death registers, 1694: Dumbarton KS, 1694; B, M, D

registrations: Kinnell KS, 1838–41; Montrose abbreviations: Cormack, pp. 4–5.

41 'Lacke walk': Kirkcudbright KS, 1702; 'Christian converse' at lykewakes, cards, etc.: Murray, *Falkirk*, II, p. 121; 'hot cockles': Gordon, p. 25; games and diversions: Nigg KS, Ross-shire, 1731; unsuitable pastimes: Presbytery of Dornoch, 1707; Mage Morison: *Aberdeen Eccl. Recs*, p. 21, 1575–76; John McEdward: Inverness KS, 1728.

42 Dance for mother's death, 1748: NSA Croy and Dalcross, XIV, Inverness-shire, p. 451; boisterous lykewakes: Gordon, p. 26; dancing, etc. 1723–24; Bentinck, pp. 454–455; Visitation at Moy: Mackay, *Pres. Recs*, xxiv; Synod of Moray's rulings: Gordon, p. 27.

43 Lykewakes and plague: *Aberdeen Eccl. Recs*, pp. 53–54; no food etc. at lykewakes: APS 1621. IV. 626; sitting up at lykewakes, etc.: Murray, *St. Andrews*, 1658; reviving 1645 Act: AGA, p. 143, 1701; Mauchline paupers: Gordon, p. 27; candle/child's death: Waddell, *Kirk Chronicle*.

44 Act anent Burial in Scots linen: APS 1686. VIII. 398.

45 Mauchline, 1771: Gordon, p. 42; burial scandal: Johnston, *Orkney*, pp. 105–106, and mean son: p. 113, 1741.

46 Everyone to attend burials: *St. Andrews KS Reg*, lxxxvii.

47 Carriage spokes: Melrose KS, 1759; spokes: St. Cuthbert's KS, Edinburgh, 1839; litter: Waddell, *Kirk Chronicle*, p. 67, early 17th century; nine spokes and litter: Melrose KS, 1759; cost of litter, 1706: Channelkirk KS, 1706; tree for litter, etc.: Tweedsmuir KS, *c.* 1723; charges for cloth and litter: Channelkirk KS, 1755 and Melrose KS, 1757.

48 'Ane mourning hearse': Waddell, *Kirk Chronicle*, p. 67; 'management of Kirk Session': NSA Athelstaneford, II, p. 53.

49 Hearse income, costs and hire of new hearse: Bolton KS, 1744–46, 1783–84.

50 Kirkliston hearse: Hay, p. 238; buying horse cloths: St. Vigeans KS, 1732; accounts for 'hors cloths': *THAS 1900, Vernon*; Lauder hearse-house: Lauder KS, 1812, loose note in hearse accounts.

51 Baton men, etc.: St. Cuthbert's KS, Edinburgh, 1856; mourning clothing, and hire: St. Cuthbert's KS, Edinburgh, Abstract of Accounts for New Ground, 1843–45; James Watson's funeral: St. Vigeans KS, 1732.

52 Box for charity: Inveresk KS, 1752; William Douglas: Melrose KS, 1748; charge for corpse in church: Montrose KS, 1707; Inverness kirk officer's share: Gordon, p. 96; Lady Blantyre's donation: Bolton KS, 1745.

53 Proclamation of Privy Council, 1692: Gordon, p. 124, and General Assembly order, 1563: p. 95; unwilling Orkney man and people: Johnston, *Orkney*, p. 47, Holm KS, 1695; George Gardiner etc.: Murray, *Falkirk*, II, pp. 61–62.

54 Pint of ale: Gordon, p. 124, Galston parish, 1696; spirits, ale needed: Henderson, *Arbuthnott*, 1771; Choppins' child: Waddell, *Kirk Chronicle*; Jean Hall: Tait, pp. 62–63; Borgue funerals: Henderson, *Borgue, its Church, Pastors and People*, pp. 70–71; carriage to grave: Keith, p. 101.

55 Old Communion cloth used: Cramond, *Fordyce*, p.64; Communion cloth, table used: Cramond, *Deskford*, pp.20–21; 6*d*. for grave: Johnston, *Orkney*, p.123, Orphir KS, 1794; 2*s*. for grave: Tillycoultry KS, 1838; worst cloth for boy: St. Vigeans KS, 1738; Blainslie mortcloth: Melrose KS, 1759.

56 Parish burying box: Inglis, *Angus Parish*, p.80; hinged coffin: Edwards, pp.182–183; hinged common coffin: Gordon, p.32, and *sgulan ruhairbh*: pp.32–33.

57 Costs, hire of common coffin: Gordon, p.32, Galston, 1641, 1675; repair of common coffin: Ashkirk KS, 1699; Chirnside 'dale': Gordon, p.33.

58 Bier made, 1698: Henderson, *Arbuthnott*, p.166; Anstruther's coffin: Gordon, p.119; 'beare' for poor etc.: Murray, *St. Andrews*, 1641, 1644; 'persons of character': *THAS 1900, Vernon*; Abercorn, Linlithgow coffins: Gordon, p.33.

59 Collection at Tongue: KS, 1796; coffins @ 40*s*.: Henderson, *Arbuthnott*; coffins @ 7*s*. stg.: St. John's Clachan Dalry KS, 1781; extra big coffins: Murray, *Falkirk*, II, p.73; Alexander Mackenzie: Creich KS, 1838; none to order coffins themselves: Gordon, p.125, Mauchline, 1675; 20 dales: Henderson, *Arbuthnott*, 1695; money advanced: Kilninian and Kilmore KS, 1771, and Allan Milner: 1768.

60 Widow Munro: Nigg KS, Ross-shire, *c*. 1836; Rev. Roderick Mackenzie: *GVA Ross and Cromarty*, Mackenzie, p.285, 1813; burial in free ground: Inglis, *Angus Parish*, p.79; graves 6 feet deep etc.: Gordon, pp.128–129; Michael Shorthouse etc.: Dumfries (St. Mary's) KS, 1845.

61 Help for the very poor: Melrose KS, 1712, 1745.

62 Janet McCormack: Tweedsmuir KS, 1774; body at Daan: Edderton KS, 1830; stranger woman died, 1721: Henderson, *Arbuthnott*, p.236; woman from Aberdeen: Mitchell, 1688; William Williamson: Melrose KS, 1758; body thrown on shore: Tarbat KS, 1770; body near Usan: Craig KS, 1845; two children: Keith, p.101; unburied beggar: Foveran KS, 1748.

63 Kilmarnock decision, burials at Ancrum and Rathven: Gordon, p.127.

64 Edinburgh, Aberdeen graveyards: *Scotland on Sunday*, 23 April 1989.

65 Suicides in gallows: Gordon, p.146; William Fary: *Perth KS Reg*, p.243; Hugh Campbell: Gordon, p.146, Mauchline, 1769.

66 Grain in coffin: Johnston, *Orkney*, p.112, Orphir, 1741.

67 Body-snatching in Edinburgh: Gordon, p.136; Colin Rhind, George Halden: Lorimer, *Neil M'Vicar*, pp.56–59.

68 Reward etc.: Kirkliston KS, 1818; watchers' arms: St. Cuthbert's KS, Edinburgh, 1827; alcohol, broken windows: Kirkliston KS, 1818, 1820.

69 Until shortly before 1957, Inverurie had a complete set of block and tackle, which was described by J. Ritchie, PSAS, 1920–21. School at Marnoch: Tranter, p.55; Duddingston watch-house: Hay, p.236.

70 School of Anatomy returns: St. Cuthbert's KS, Edinburgh, 1836–43.

16
Remember the Sabbath Day

1 Sunday, not Sabbath: *St. Andrews KS Reg*, SHS 4, xlvii; 'Sunday' distrusted: Munro, *Looking Back*.
2 Old-time Sabbath: Dickson, pp. 4–5.
3 Later RC days: Dick, pp. 109–110 and Edwards, p. 162; thieves' hole, 1604: Edgar, I, note to p. 311; stocks: APS 1579. III. 138; sermon on market days: Edwards, p. 145; Chanry mercat: Mitchell, p. 47; Pittenweem market: Thomson, *Elie Kirk*, p. 45; weekday services: *Perth KS Reg*, note to p. 258; Monday/Tuesday services and temporary suspension: Thomson, *Elie Kirk*, p. 45; services until 1755: *Perth KS Reg*, note to p. 258.
4 6.00 a.m. service: Waddell, *East Lothian*; services at Orphir, 1794: Johnston, *Orkney*, p. 123. The morning service at Nigg, Ross-shire, was at midday until the 1960s.
5 Clog-bags: Gunn, *Traquair*, p. 90, 1740; barbers shaving: Murray, *St. Andrews*, 1678 and Cramond, *Fordyce*, p. 60, 1742; wig-makers: Low, p. 176; minister powdering wig: Dickson, p. 9.
6 Letters to *The Scots Magazine*, December 1990, showed that an early 9.00 a.m. bell is still rung at Symington and at Kirkton of Maryculter; that a 9.00 a.m. bell at Ardrishaig only stopped because of the 1939–45 War; that Crail's bell used to be rung at 10.00 a.m. for the 11.00 a.m. service; that there are living memories of Hopeman's bell rung at 9.00 a.m. for the 11.00 a.m. service and of Greenock's rung every few minutes from 9.00 a.m. until the 11.00 a.m. service. Running to ale-houses: Bentinck, p. 288; First Book of Discipline/readers: Edgar, I, p. 55; ministers with 2/3 parishes: Dick, p. 89 and Allan, *Channelkirk*, p. 135; reader as minister's assistant: Murray, *Falkirk*, I, p. 75, 1630s; readers becoming exhorters, etc.: Burleigh, p. 169; Alexander Watt: Cramond, *Cullen*, p. 68; East Lothian schoolmaster: Waddell, *East Lothian*, p. 26.
7 Readers not to marry, etc.: Allan, *Channelkirk*, p. 138; readers permitted to marry etc. 1572, and no more to be appointed, 1581: Smout, p. 64; continued employment of readers: Edgar, I, pp. 58–59; prayers from Knox's Liturgy: Dick, p. 89; Synod's instructions for readers: Cramond, *Presbytery of Fordyce*, p. 29, 1663.
8 Boys repeat Catechism: *SRE*, pp. 155–156, (Inverary 1654, Dunfermline 1653, Lochwinnoch 1691); readers debarred from praying, 1800: Johnston, *Orkney*, pp. 124–125, and 'constantly employed' (1794): p. 123, Orphir KS. Resolis KS had a reader in 1841. Mertoun woman reader: *Border Magazine* VII, 1902, 'The Border Bible Woman'.
9 Talking etc. in kirkyard: Montrose KS, 1642; elders in churchyard: Nigg KS, Ross-shire, 1707; secular topics: Henderson, *Lockerbie*.

10   Order of service: Edwards, p.145; 'wee sermon': *THAS 1900, Vernon,*
(1721); lecture: Brydon.
11   KSs prescribed texts: *SRE*, p.137; texts minuted, 1665: Cramond, *Presbytery of Fordyce*, p.34; complaint/Presbytery Visitation, 1651: Cramond,
Fordyce, pp.17–18; 18-month ordinary: Henderson, *Lockerbie*; doctrinal
sermons: *THAS 1872, Clerical Life in Scotland*, pp.146–151, by Rev. J. Y.
Scott; subdivided and written sermons: Dobson and Sanderson, pp.18, 19,
11, 12; rambling sermons: Blakey, p.60.
12   Prefacing the psalm: Hyslop, pp.786–787; length of services: *THAS 1900,
Vernon,* and Edwards, p.145. George Hay's *Architecture of Scottish Post-
Reformation Churches*, p.53, says that those in the laird's loft would adjourn
between services to a retiring room adjoining the loft for refreshment. At
Abercorn their return could be timed since a squint in one of the rooms gave a
good view of the pulpit. Minister turned glass, etc.: Dobson and Sanderson,
p.112; Mr John Brand: Cadell, *A Sense of Place*; 'keip his hour', etc.:
Henderson, *Religious Life*, p.195, Presbytery of Aberdeen; '. . . glass and
no farder': Cramond, *Elgin*, II, p.122, 1604; inconvenience through lack of
sand-glass: Kiltearn KS, 1725.
13   Mr Bowie, 1707: Bentinck, p.250; flat book boards: Edgar, I,
p.109; Glasgow, 16th century: MacGeorge, p.203; Elie sleepers, 1656:
Thomson, *Elie Kirk*, p.46; a 'meane to provock' sleep: Extracts Kinghorn
KS, 1642, 1645; Dumbarton plaids: Irving; elderly exempted *re* plaids:
Murray, *St. Andrews*, 1645.
14   Sitting before pulpit: Inglis, *Angus Parish*, p.92; Monifieth tar: Edgar, I,
p.113 and Allardyce, pp.95–96; kirk officer's red staff: *Perth KS Reg*,
p.288, 1616; Laigh Kirk, Glasgow: MacGeorge, p.203; 'awn-ecdote':
Hyslop, (Dumfries KS); Bible flung: Brydon; arousing sleepers: Tarbat
KS, 1753; snoring laird, bailie: Edwards, p.165.
15   Snuff a profanation: Johnston, *Working Classes*, p.103; snuff-rest: Inglis,
Angus Parish, p.46; 'sit laigh': MacGeorge, p.202; plaited straw etc.:
Hyslop, p.770; fights over seating: Edwards, p.132, and wringing nose
etc.: pp.131–132; Falkirk miners: Murray, *Falkirk*, II, pp.122–123; Dornoch doctor: Bentinck, p.447, 1747; man in Duke's seat: Coldingham KS,
1750; 'rackt and ruggit': *THAS 1871, Ashkirk Kirk Records*, pp.90–97, by a
minister of the parish.
16   Marjory Young, etc.: Edwards, p.132, Kinnell KS; disturbances in loft:
Cramond, *Deskford*, p.23, and disturbances, seats allocated: pp.20,
23; pre-Reformation Act of Parliament: APS 1551. II. 485.
17   Bridegroom's gloves: Waddell, *Kirk Chronicle*; Glenholm brawl: Baird,
Annals of a Tweeddale Parish, p.218.
18   Laughing, jeering: Bentinck, p.446; laughing, etc.: Cramond, *Elgin*, II,
p.240, 1641, and woman in steeple: p.58, 1597; talking at Dornoch: Bentinck, p.250; 'servand women' etc.: Murray, *St. Andrews*, 1639; civil

NOTES

respects in church: AGA, p. 285, 1709;   Petty fisherman: Bain, *Lordship of Petty*, p. 43.

19   Cromwell's soldiers: Edgar, I, p. 325;   man 'to stay the tumult': Cramond, *Elgin*, II, p. 73;   sitting in quire loft: Montrose KS, 1648, and town officers enlisted: 1670;   patrolling church: Murray, *St. Andrews*, 1703;   leaving before blessing: Henderson, *Religious Life*, p. 153;   Presbytery order *re* blessing, 1663: Cramond, *Presbytery of Fordyce*, p. 31;   leaving before sermon: Waddell, *Kirk Chronicle*.

20   Leaving to feed baby: *Extracts Kinghorn KS*, 1623;   'certain people': Dumfries (St. Mary's) KS, 1872;   unedified Sheriff: Bentinck, p. 480 — the minister preaching was Rev. Donald Sage.

21   Children to stay at home: *Aberdeen Eccl. Recs*, p. 84, 1616;   children to attend: Montrose KS, 1650;   children to behave: Kirkcudbright KS, 1696;   children broke tomb: Cramond, *Elgin*, II, p. 198, 1626;   'utheris vagabondis': *St. Andrews KS Reg*, SHS 7, xciii/lv;   providing children's seating: *Perth KS Reg*, p. 270, 1593–94;   students interrupting: Chambers, *Domestic Annals of Scotland*, 1694.

22   Snapping dogs: Hyslop;   Rev. Thomas Dyce: *Border Magazine*, III, p. 160;   dogs singing: Russell, pp. 145–146;   dogs and babies: Fyfe, p. 492, 1809;   cheating the dogs: Russell, pp. 145–146;   Aberdeen dogs: Allardyce, p. 104, 1640;   Oldmachar dogs: *SRE*, p. 92;   Alexander Coutts: Henderson, *Banchory-Devenick*, p. 235, and 30 years on: p. 251;   dogs/box seats: Russell, pp. 145–146.

23   Stabled horses: Fyfe, p. 559.

24   Murder in kirks etc: APS 1592. III. 544;   deserter arrested: Macrae, *The Parish of Lairg*, pp. 32–33.

25   People left worship: Ashkirk KS, 1696, and two lads: 1700;   Hawick children: *THAS 1909, Hawick KS Records*, Vernon, pp. 25–45;   pennie-stone: Inglis, *Angus Parish*, p. 133, 1677.

26   Church notices: APS 1644. VI. i. 194;   official notices: *THAS 1904, Coldingham*;   Burgh Council roups etc.: MacDonald, *St. Clement's Looks Back*, pp. 15–16;   mad dogs: Cramond, *Cullen*, p. 109.

27   Lost spectacles: Brydon;   criers made announcements: NSA Edinkillie, XIII, Morayshire, p. 183 (but this had been discontinued by the date of the NSA);   Inverbreakie roup: MacGill, I, pp. 55–56;   Highland Synod, 1729: MacNaughton, p. 131;   tenants' carriage duties: Bentinck, p. 269, *c*. 1717;   shooting for barrow: Cramond, *Ordiquhill*, p. 31;   'theatre for criers': MacDonald, *St. Clement's Looks Back*, pp. 15–16.

28   Advice from Assembly Commissioners: Cramond, *Presbytery of Fordyce*, p. 57;   advertisements giving offence, *c*. 1784: Murray, *Falkirk*, II, p. 197;   Strathdon mausoleum: Love, p. 139.

29   'Dishaunting' church, 1660: Cramond, *Fordyce*, p. 42;   children 'in pocks': *THAS 1871, Ashkirk KS Records*, pp. 90-97, by a minister of the parish;   7–8 months' absence: Bentinck, p. 454;   lack of suitable clothing: Blakey,

701

p. 32; people's aversion: Coll KS, 1735; man 'did not keep church': Thomson, *Lauder*, p. 87, 1679.

30 Parliament enforced church attendance, etc.: Johnston, *Orkney*, note to p. 30, Holm KS; calling roll: *THAS 1924, Roberton in olden times*, Wilson, pp. 47–51; fine for heads of families, servants: Johnston, *Orkney*, p. 29, Holm KS, 1684; fine if in good health: Johnston, *Working Classes*, p. 105, Aberdeen; censor, collector: Coll KS, 1735.

31 Lock for house: Cramond, *Elgin*, II, p. 73; 'ill kirk keepers': Johnston, *Orkney*, p. 99; jougs threatened: Cramond, *Elgin*, II, p. 246, 1643; Galston man: Edgar, I, p. 312; vaging/tolbooth: Montrose KS, 1642; couple admonished, blacksmith: Thomson, *Lauder*, p. 88; heritors' 'constant absenting': Cambuslang KS, 1659; Communion refused for church absence: Allan, *Channelkirk*, pp. 230–231.

32 Peter Blackburn: MacGeorge, p. 197; bailies', elders' inspection: *Aberdeen Eccl. Recs*, p. 26, 1603; loft seat kept: Cramond, *Elgin*, II, p. 73, 1599; Forfar minister: Edwards, p. 164, 1720, and Alexander Davidson: p. 127.

33 Officers/halberts: Johnston, *Working Classes*, p. 103; secret visitors: Montrose KS, 1649.

34 Man at Inglisgreig: Low, pp. 157–158; 28 people drowned: Hyslop; 1914–18 War: Martin, p. 63; charity children: St. John's KS, Glasgow, 1829; social undesirables: Blakey, p. 33.

35 Weekday services, 1645: Low, p. 157; Dumbarton weekday services: Dumbarton KS, 1694; woman bought fish: Cramond, *Elgin*, II, p. 44, 1596, and fish cadgers: p. 122, 1604; gazing from windows etc.: Dickson, p. 9; idling, lolling: *THAS 1904, Coldingham*; starling: Blakey, p. 122, quo. Macleod, *Reminiscences of a Highland Parish*.

36 KS Acts: Montrose KS, 1652/56/59; keeping at books, etc.: Dunbar KS, 1719; Sabbath reading matter: Henderson, *Lockerbie*; minister of Peterculter: Cramond, *Syn. Aberdeen*, p. 69; stolen meal: Baird, p. 17, *c*. 1679; clods thrown: Nigg KS, Ross-shire, early 18th century; sanctifying Sabbath: Cramond, *Presbytery of Fordyce*, p. 35, 1667; man went for horse: Tarbat KS, 1781.

37 Duration of Sunday, Glasgow: MacGeorge, p. 205; Parliament's definition of Sunday: APS 1648. VI. ii. 185 (referring to salt pans etc); Rutherglen fair: Edgar, I, note to p. 251; Euphan More: Nigg KS, Ross-shire, 1706; 'miserable creature': Resolis KS, 1842; ware-gathering: Keith, pp. 113–115 and Drainie KS, 1843; Falkirk fishing: Murray, Falkirk, II, p. 120.

38 Cutting grain: Tarbat KS, 1753; going shearing: Edderton KS, 1823.

39 Children of Israel: *Bible*, Num. 15: 32–36; gathering sticks, broom: Coll KS, 1735 and Edderton KS, *c*. 1828; timber at waterside: Dumbarton KS, 1695; cutting up ship boat: Dick, p. 108.

40 Andrew McLennan: Nigg KS, Ross-shire, 1729; water/medical needs: Murray, *Falkirk*, II, pp. 97–98.

41 Search for drying clothes: Inglis, *Angus Parish*, p. 100; clothes confiscated: Montrose KS, 1649.

42 Women bought milk: *Extracts Kinghorn KS*, 1644; selling milk, Saturday night, making butter (1647), making cheese (1645): Edgar, I, note to p. 251, Fenwick parish; weighing butter: Dick, p. 109; watering kail: Johnston, *Working Classes*, p. 103; pulling kail etc.: Cramond, *Elgin*, II, pp. 51, 52, 53; gooseberries: Chambers, *Abridged Domestic Annals*, p. 270, 1645; putting roast to fire: Johnston, *Working Classes*, p. 104, 1641; calf skinned: Tarbat KS, 1770; weekday implements forbidden: Edwards, p. 159.

43 Bestial in fields: Murray, *St. Andrews*, 1703; carrying water to horses: Montrose KS, 1649; pulling grass: Cramond, *Fordyce*, p. 56, 1713; cleaning byre: Edgar, I, note to p. 251, 1658, Fenwick parish; sheep muck: *THAS 1871, Ashkirk KS*, by a minister of the parish, pp. 90–97, 1640s; spreading muck, 1649: Inglis, *Angus Parish*, p. 102.

44 Man seeks ox: Bentinck, p. 445; 'carrying bestial': Nigg KS, Ross-shire, 1706; catching sheep: Edgar, I, note to p. 252, Galston, 1705; herds beating, swearing: Nigg KS, Ross-shire, 1730; throwing dog: Tarbat KS, 1755; killing dog: Henderson, *Religious Life*, p. 146, quo. Records of the Exercise of Alford, p. 201.

45 Battering cloth: Cramond, *Fordyce*, p. 42, 1660; couple singing: Cramond, *Rathven*, p. 61, 1726; 'bletching': Cramond, *Fordyce*, p. 44, 1664; linen outside: Kirkcudbright KS, 1693; poinding webs: Cramond, *Fordyce*, p. 50, 1667; winding lint: Dick, p. 108; drying wool: Cramond, *Rathven*, p. 59.

46 'Mawing grass': Edgar, I, note to p. 251, 1645, Fenwick; 4 sheaves cut: Cramond, *Elgin*, II, p. 117; Kilconquhar KS: Dick, p. 106, 1637; windy Sabbath: Henderson, *Banchory-Devenick*, p. 246; harvesting: Tongue KS, 1795; dighting: Ashkirk KS, 1659, and knocking grain: 1640s; quern: Tarbat KS, 1751.

47 'Waiting on the boat': Tynninghame KS, 1703; Andro Cochrane: Brotchie, pp. 61–62, 1652; misbehaviour in getting out of boat: Henderson, *Banchory-Devenick*, p. 247, 1734; fishermen: Montrose KS, 1641 and Low, p. 151; Kelso boatman: Tait, p. 13; Holm ferry: Johnston, *Orkney*, pp. 50–51, 1697, and transporting cattle, 1684: p. 30.

48 Edderton ferrymen, 1788: MacNaughton, 1788; busy Sunday ferries: OSA Craig, II (1790s) p. 499; idle sailors: NSA Falkirk, VIII, Stirlingshire, p. 30.

49 Foal: Nigg KS, Ross-shire, 1708, and two cows taken: 1731.

50 Sailings forbidden: AGA, p. 139, 1646; leaving Inverness 7.00 a.m.: Nigg KS, Ross-shire, 1731; Portmahomack men: Tarbat KS, *c.* 1750 and Morayshire ship: 1754; going in boats: West Kilbride KS, 1802.

51 No travelling: Montrose KS, 1649; 'notice to be taken', 1663: Cramond, *Presbytery of Fordyce*, p.32; idle vagueing etc.: AGA, p.139, 1705 and carriers etc.: p.227, 1648.

52 Seeing cattle: Nigg KS, Ross-shire, 1708; going to Abdie: Murray, *St. Andrews*, 1643; Mr Porteous: Burleigh, *Ednam and its Indwellers*.

53 Burden bearers: Montrose KS, 1659; plaiding carried: Nigg KS, Ross-shire, 1707; barrel hoops, etc.: Johnston, *Orkney*, p.55, Holm KS, 1700; horse, creels: Arbuthnott KS, 1716; timber etc.: Cramond, *Presbytery of Fordyce*, p.38, 1671; millstone: Cramond, *Fordyce*, p.14, 1625; cauldron: *Aberdeen Eccl. Recs*, p.137, 1656; peck of bere: Nigg KS, Ross-shire, 1708.

54 Carrying corpse: Cromarty KS, 1743; Gilbert Stirling: Cruden KS, 1723; carriers: Cramond, *Syn. Aberdeen*, p.71; Stow man (1653) and Lumphanan man: Johnston, *Working Classes*, p.104; John Roy: Nigg KS, Ross-shire, 1708; going to Newcastle: Ashkirk KS, 1697.

55 Marion Moore: Hill, p.73; selling harrows, bringing cloth: Cramond, *Fordyce*, p.13; Alyth merchants: NSA Alyth, X, Perth, note to pp.1120–1121; 'niffering': Dick, p.108; writing bonds: Edgar, I, p.256.

56 Presbytery of Ellon: NSA Logie-Buchan, XII, Aberdeenshire, p.812; Sleepy Market: Dawson, *Abridged Statistical History of Scotland*, note to p.36; discharging mercats, etc.: APS 1579. III. 138.

57 Enforcing Acts: APS 1593. IV. 16; Crail's market: APS 1587. III. 507; Forfar's market: APS 1593. IV. 39; choosing different market day: APS 1592. III. 548; 1592 Act repeated: APS 1695. IX. 388; Kilmarnock fair: Edgar, I, note to p.251, Fenwick, 1647; Saturday/Monday markets: APS 1644. VI. i. 194 and APS 1663. VII. 481; travelling: APS 1656. VI. ii. 866a.

58 St. James Fair, 1591: Cramond, *Elgin*, II, p.18, and markets on Tuesdays: p.41, 1596; Burgh Councils/Saturday/Monday markets: AGA, p.146, 1638; markets, but fleshers excepted: APS 1695. IX. 388; cattle market: St. John's KS, Glasgow, 1829; fish market: Cramond, *Elgin*, II, p.264; Selkirk fairs: Craig-Brown, II, p.99; carrying timber, 1703: Cramond, *Syn. Aberdeen*, p.69, and ministers at markets: p.63.

59 Drovers: Murray, *Falkirk*, II, p.57; Mr Lauder, 1620: Waddell, *Kirk Chronicle*; hiring shearers: APS 1640. V. 297; feeing on Communion Sunday: Edgar, I, note to p.251; entertaining hiremen: Banff KS, 1701.

60 Gathering dulse etc.: Cramond, *Rathven*, p.59, and partens: p.64; 'in the wair': Nigg KS, Ross-shire, 1708.

61 'Gaddering' sandeels: *Extracts Kinghorn KS*, p.28; fine, jougs: Montrose KS, 1638; drying fish: Cramond, *Rathven*, p.59, 1723; Hawick man, 1721: *THAS 1900, Vernon*.

62 Papal Bull: Chambers, *Abridged Domestic Annals*, note to p.187; Tynninghame man and patrolling shore: Waddell, *East Lothian*, pp.40–41, mid-17th century; obstructing fishing: Sorbie KS, 1700. The word 'draife'

is similar to 'drove,' used for the annual herring fishing, which appears in OSA Eyemouth, III (1790s) p. 116, as the Ground Drove, which lasted only a few days, and the Float Drove, lasting several months.

63 Interviewing Consuls etc.: St. Monance KS, 1851.

64 Papal Bull: Chambers, *Abridged Domestic Annals*, note to p. 187; attending water: Aberdeen St. Nicholas KS, 1702; Kerse, River Carron: Murray, *Falkirk*, II, p. 58, 1697; watching water: Henderson, *Banchory-Devenick*, p. 248, and bell rung: p. 250; bell repair: Banchory-Devenick KS, 1773; Tulliallan bell: *SRE*, p. 95; bell frightening herring: Dawson, *Abridged Statistical History of Scotland*, note to p. 400, St. Monance.

65 Three poachers: Stow KS, 1808; deacon's mill: Henderson, *Banchory-Devenick*, p. 249.

66 Eels: *The Scots Magazine*, February 1989, p. 488; eel-fishing: Kinross KS, 1701.

67 Earthquake/salmon fishing: Chambers, *Abridged Domestic Annals*, p. 187; drowning fishermen: Johnston, *Working-Classes*, p. 104, quo. *Letters from a Gentleman in the North of Scotland*, i, p. 173; Cockenzie fishermen: NSA Tranent, II, East Lothian, pp. 300–301.

68 Mills etc.: AGA, p. 232, 1638; Sunday work forbidden: APS 1639. V. 269; midnight to midnight: APS 1648. VI. ii. 185; £20 fine: APS 1661. VII. 262; intimation *re* mills: NSA Petty, XIV, Inverness-shire, note to p. 406.

69 King's declaration, 1618: Chambers, *Abridged Domestic Annals*, p. 209; David Wemyss: Mathieson, II, p. 193; riding race: THAS 1900, Vernon, (1718); penny-stane: Johnston, *Orkney*, p. 128; putting the stone: Cramond, *Fordyce*, p. 44, 1644; bowls: *THAS 1900, Vernon*, and Cramond, *Elgin*, II, p. 46, 1597; football, 1659: Cramond, *Fordyce*, p. 41; 'very penitent': Waddell, *Kirk Chronicle*; knottie: Beaton, p. 141; kyles: Cramond, *Elgin*, II, p. 285, 1654; Bob and penny staves: *THAS 1904, Coldingham, c.* 1695; 'cheaw': Cramond, *Elgin*, II, p. 71, 1599; skating: Cramond, *Rathven*, p. 57, 1735; kites: Murray, *St. Andrews*, 1702; stilts: *THAS 1900, Vernon*, 1713; playing at carts, coppiehoal: Edgar, I, note to p. 252, 1604–05, Ayr KS; 'playing bogill': Johnston, *Working Classes*, p. 103.

70 'Hounting hairs': Cramond, *Deskford*, p. 17, 1686; laverocks, trout: *THAS 1900, Vernon*; throwing stone: Henderson, *Religious Life*, p. 146; play ship: Johnston, *Orkney*, p. 76–77, Holm KS.

71 Lasses etc. singing, dancing: *Perth KS Reg*, pp. 282–283, 1604; caution for dancing: Cramond, *Elgin*, II, p. 112; Col. Duffy: St. John's KS, Glasgow, 1826.

72 Worldly converse: Nigg KS, Ross-shire, early 18th century; talking in streets: Murray, *Falkirk*, II, p. 45; 'needless confluences': Kirkcudbright KS, 1693; frequenting neighbours' houses: Kinross KS, 1709; walking in cabals etc.: Thomson, *Elie Kirk*, p. 46; walking: APS 1656. VI. ii. 865 b;

resorting to shore etc.: Dunbar KS, 1719;   walking in crowds, after church, in fields: *THAS 1900, Vernon.*

73   Wandering in afternoons: Banff KS, 1708;   extravaging: AGA, p.139, 1705, and how Sunday to be spent: p.228, 1648;   'the like method': Dunbar KS, 1719.

74   Inspection/access required: Kinross KS, 1709;   patent doors: Murray, *Falkirk*, II, p.98, 1710–18;   Janet Yett: St. Cuthbert's KS, Edinburgh, 1708;   kissing: Johnston, *Working Classes*, p.104;   Andrew Tennent: St. Cuthbert's KS, Edinburgh, 1708.

75   'Crying sins': Cramond, *Fordyce*, p.59, 1738;   children swearing in streets: Cromarty KS, 1681;   Kirkcudbright children: Kirkcudbright KS, 1693;   Kinross children: Kinross KS, 1709;   Partick men: Brotchie, pp.60–61;   supervision of children: Banff KS, 1703.

76   Cattle plague: Yetholm KS, 1866;   Innerwick fast (1659): NSA Innerwick, II, East Lothian, p.240;   fast, 1684: *THAS 1902, Lauder.* AGA, p.100 lists specific fasts ordered between 1642–1710.

77   Philihaugh: NSA Whitekirk and Tynninghame, II, East Lothian, p.32, Tynninghame KS;   Petty fast: NSA Petty, XIV, Inverness-shire, note to p.407;   fast, June 1651, and Dutch war: Mackay, *Pres. Recs*, xxiii;   Stuart rising: Craig KS, 1715–16;   1661 thanksgiving: NSA Innerwick, II, East Lothian, p.240;   eight-day fast: *Perth KS Reg*, p.261;   fast for English plague: Mackay, *Pres. Recs*, xxiii;   plague in France: Cruden KS, 1720, 1723;   summer fast, 1691: Johnston, *Orkney*, p.43;   Glasgow fast, 1598: *Maitland Misc.* i, p.91;   reasons for fast: Bo'ness KS, 1696;   Jock's sins: *THAS 1900, Vernon* (but this does not refer to a Hawick minister).

78   Marriage during fasts: *Aberdeen Eccl. Recs*, p.17, 1574 and *Perth KS Reg*, p.240, 1580–81;   profanation of fast day: Tarbat KS, 1751.

79   Three Dornoch men: Bentinck, pp.260–261;   1716 thanksgiving: Johnston, *Orkney*, p.102.

80   Tay flood: *Perth KS Reg*, pp.298–299;   Scottish Missionary Society: Forres KS, 1828.

81   Fashionable to avoid worship: Graham, p.365;   General Assembly, 1794: *SRE*, p.112;   reasons for change: Graham, p.348–350 and Geekie, *Scottish Reminiscences*, p.78;   Edinburgh and Glasgow Railway: Daviot and Dunlichity KS, 1847;   address approved, etc.: Kilmarnock High Church KS, 1840;   Aberdour: *A Sense of Place*, p.185, article 'Aberdour, the Evolution of a seaside port', by Eric Simpson;   increase and decrease of Sabbath observance: Blakey, pp.121, 50.

17
The Lord's Supper

1   Leaping in window: Murray, *Falkirk*, I, p.30.
2   The Occasion: Henderson, *Lockerbie*; The Solemnity: Kirkwall KS, 1730; Great Work, Sacred Solemnity: Graham, p.302; Sacramental Solemnity; West Kilbride KS, 1823; Peebles wording: Henderson, *Religious Life*, pp.155–156.
3   Elders to prepare themselves, etc.: Craig KS, 1718; elders/reconciliation: Henderson, *Religious Life*, 1677, Auchterhouse KS; reconciling Margaret Young etc.: Kinross KS, 1709; 'ill wordis': *Maitland misc.* i, p.132, 1599, Stirling KS.
4   Weekly catechism: AGA, p.35, 1639; Ellon parish, 1670: Henderson, *Religious Life*, p.155; examining only would-be Communicants: *Aberdeen Eccl. Recs*, p.119, 1653; elders testify: Henderson, *Religious Life*, p.155.
5   Catechisms in households: AGA, p.35, 1649. *Catechisms of the Scottish Reformation*, ed. Bonar, includes the Catechisms mentioned. Shorter Catechism/Ceres: *SRE*. pp.46–47; Tynninghame minister: Waddell, *East Lothian*, p.34.
6   Catechising, baptising etc: AGA, p.226, 1648; General Assembly/catechism slighted (1649): *Catechisms of the Scottish Reformation*, ed. Bonar; family visiting not observed, 1717, and seed time: Henderson, *Banchory-Devenick*, p.255.
7   Catechising of children: *Catechisms of the Scottish Reformation*, ed. Bonar, quo. *Book of Universal Kirk*, p.121, Peterkin's edition, and also Calderwood, iii, pp.2,3; right of entry: Blakey, pp.20–21; householders worth 300 merks: APS 1579. III. 139; £5 for Bible: Inglis, *Angus Parish*, p.71.
8   Searching for Bibles: Inglis, *Angus Parish*, p.72, Auchterhouse KS; catechising children, servants: AGA, p.35, 1639; family worship: *Borders Magazine*, XIX, 1914.
9   Aberdeen reader, 1578, 1604: Edgar, I, p.58; two boys/catechism: Edwards, p.145; bellman/catechism: Coll KS, 1782; texts on walls: Hay, p.220.
10 Catechising between services: Edgar, I, p.91; Ceres minister, 1656: *SRE*, p.47; Murdo Macleod: MacNaughton, p.40, 1706; two catechists: Bentinck, pp.295–296; Question-man: Kilninian and Kilmore KS, 1767–68, 1772–73, 1784.
11 Shoes, snuff: Kilninian and Kilmore KS, 1772, 1776; Gaelic-speaking catechist: Mitchell, p.177; 'victual for his pains': Nigg KS, Ross-shire, 1706; Question-man's wages: Kilninian and Kilmore KS, 1784.
12 Parish of Rothesay: Edgar, I, pp.93–94; lighting candles: Cramond, *Elgin*, II, p.255; kirk officer informing families: Banchory-Devenick KS,

1773; diets of examination: Coldingham KS, 1752; elders at examinations, and Kilmartin KS, 1699: SRE, pp.48–49; Thurso catechising: Blakey, p.18.

13 Examination at home: Henderson, *Lockerbie*; workers catechised: Blakey, p.68; Kinghorn, Culross men: *SRE*, p.46; ignorant people: AGA, p.226, 1648; 'much people debarred': Chambers, *Abridged Domestic Annals*, pp.296–297.

14 Minister's answer: Henderson, *Lockerbie*; Alexander Gerard's lectures: Blakey, p.68; 'noysum' to leave stock etc.: Edgar, I, pp.93–94; coming in halves, 1630: Cramond, *Fordyce*, p.16; 3*s*. 4*d*. fine: Montrose KS, 1637; poinding at Futtie: *Aberdeen Eccl. Recs*, p.60; poinding, Holm KS: Johnston, *Orkney*, pp.34–35; tenant farmer: Murray, *Falkirk*, I, p.15; absenters as Sabbath breakers: Johnston, *Orkney*, pp.50–51; elder interrupting: *Extracts Kinghorn KS*, pp.62–64. The term 'slighters of the examination' appears in Johnston, *Orkney*, p.30.

15 Pride in catechism visits: Blakey, p.69; withholding Communion: Montrose KS, 1649; Rev. Donald Sage: Resolis KS, 1823; Jamie Petty: Bain, *Lordship of Petty*, pp.41–42.

16 Man's references: Nigg KS, Ross-shire, 1837–41; minced oaths: *SRE*, p.56; Jean Mitchell: Edgar, I, p.248.

17 New Communicants: Dobson and Sanderson, p.13; young Ceres people, 1649: *SRE*, p.47; sixteen-year-old boy: Edgar, I, p.202, 1771, Mauchline KS; highland hesitation: Martin, p.75.

18 'Examine roll': *SRE*, p.28, 1769, Yester KS; ignorant people: Resolis KS, 1823; debarred woman, 1674: Henderson, *Arbuthnott*, p.102; Communion roll required, 1835: SRE, p.251; Act of General Assembly, 1896: *Compendium of Acts of General Assembly*, 1883 (sic).

19 Patrick Gutherie: *St. Andrews KS Reg*, SHS 7, xc; tokens, 1707: Mitchell, p.4; tokens/tickets: Edgar, I, p.139; 'making tickets': Dick, p.95; casting in moulds: *THAS 1900, Communion Tokens*, Heatlie, p.160; cost of tokens, 1745: Edwards, p.103; gunsmith: Bentinck, p.292; slater ('sclater' in original): Edwards, p.134; tokens etc. from Glasgow: Tobermory KS, 1851; decoration etc. on tokens: *THAS 1900, Communion Tokens*, Heatlie, p.160.

20 1,200 tokens given: Nigg KS, Ross-shire, 1812; tokens issued, melted, hidden in manse, and neighbouring parishes: *THAS 1900, Communion Tokens*, Heatlie, p.160; issue to neighbouring parishes: *THAS 1900, Vernon*.

21 Communicating elsewhere: Cramond, *Elgin*, II, p.99, 1602–03; Communion taken in Kirkwall: Johnston, *Orkney*, p.79, Holm KS; Episcopalian clergy: Cramond, *Syn. Aberdeen*, p.67, 1700.

22 Communion tokens were handed out after the preparatory service in Nigg, Ross-shire, until at least 1966, which was done as people left, without constituting the Kirk Session by prayer. Parish minister gives out tokens:

Borders Magazine, 1902;   landward town tokens, *c.* 1717: *THAS 1900, Vernon;*   Cawdor minister: *SRE*, pp. 50–51, and token for debarred woman: p. 52, Alvah KS, 1657;   Ettrick race: Craig-Brown, I, p. 271 and SRE, p. 51.

23   Cards, 1840: *SRE*, p. 50;   'bigane contribution': *St. Andrews KS Reg*, SHS 7, p. 845, 1597–99, and forged and master's tickets: p. xc, 1583;   Blind Eppie: Kinloss KS, 1826.

24   Providing cups etc.: APS 1617. IV. 534;   Petty, Croy, Daviot: Mackay, *Pres. Recs*, xxi/xxii;   stent for tables etc.: Sorbie KS, 1702;   church bell hung: Waddell, *East Lothian*;   borrowing, lending cups: Mitchell, pp. 90–91.

25   Hiring cups: Waddell, *Kirk Chronicle*;   Dornoch hiring cups: Bentinck, p. 292;   Kilmarnock cups: M'Naught, pp. 122–123;   cost of cups: Mitchell, pp. 90-91;   'flaggons': Kilninian and Kilmore KS, 1767;   cups etc.: Tobermory KS, 1851;   inventory of equipment: Ashkirk KS, 1797.

26   Removing, planting seats: Murray, *Falkirk*, II, p. 130, 1723;   boards, barrels: Johnston, *Orkney*, p. 129;   convertible pews: Hay, pp. 182–183. The rediscovered Communion pews are in Nigg Old Church, Ross-shire. Some outlying churches, such as Canna, still have a long Communion table down the centre of the building.

27   Conventicles: Henderson, *Lockerbie*. Sprott and Leishman's edition of the *Book of Common Order and Directory of Public Worship of God*, pp. 348–349, refers to p. 35 of the tract of 1657. Crowds beginning after Revolution: *THAS 1900, Communion Tokens*, Heatlie, p. 160;   Grandtully, Uig etc.: Blakey, pp. 24–25;   'gathered Communions': Henderson, *Arbuthnott*, pp. 101–102;   levelling yard: Mitchell, p. 92;   grave-stones removed: MacDonald, *St. Clement's Looks Back*, p. 16;   45-foot tables: Martin, p. 32;   60-foot table: Tarbat KS, 1811;   Tulliebole 'table': Love, p. 142.

28   Borrowing linen: Hyslop, p. 470;   minister bought cloth: Kilninian and Kilmore KS, 1775;   washing cloths: Ashkirk KS, 1704 and Coldingham KS, 1750;   3*s*. stg and 2*s*. 7*d*. for cleaning, redding: Kilbride KS, 1830 and Kilninian and Kilmore KS, 1767;   drink given: Kilninian and Kilmore KS, 1771, 1780.

29   Services in woods: Munro, *Looking Back*, pp. 166–167;   sentry-box/bathing hut: Blakey, p. 26;   Punch and Judy theatre: Hill, p. 80;   lifting tent from place to place: Cathcart KS, 1764, 1780;   carrying to/from store: Assynt KS, 1837;   John Watson: Cathcart KS, 1761;   fitting up tent, etc.: Coldingham KS, 1755;   whisky/tent: Kilbride KS, 1830. An elegant 18th century white-painted pine tent, with an enriched door and a window-like opening, survived in Kirkmichael, Ayrshire, until after 1957, and a simpler one from Carnock, Fife, is in the Royal Museum of Scotland. A tent appears in Alexander Carse's picture 'Holy Fair' — Hay, p. 188.

30   Cost of tent: Tarbat KS, 1793;   part payment for tent: Nigg KS, Ross-shire, 1795;   collection for tent: Resolis KS, 1828;   difficulties over tent:

Boleskine KS, 1808–09; tent rouped: Edgar, I, p.117. Rev. George Thomson, formerly minister of Yarrow, revived the custom which had lapsed for well over fifty years of a shelter for the minister at the Blanket Preaching in the kirkyard of St. Mary's of the Lowes. To start with he used the old arrangement of three gates covered with a stack hap but after the gates were accidentally burned by District Council workmen clearing the kirkyard another covering on four wooden stakes was introduced. A movable (folding) Communion table also exists for the Blanket Preaching (originally a Communion service) but it has not been used for many years.

31   Parson to provide bread, wine: APS 1572. III. 77; Burgh of Ayr: Edgar, I, note to p.144; elements: Lorimer, *Neil M'Vicar*, pp.74, 76, St. Cuthbert's KS, Edinburgh; Mr John Urquhart: MacNaughton, pp.267–268; £40 for elements: OSA Stichell and Hume, III (1979) p.657; KSs pay for extra Communions: Edgar, I, pp.142–143; payment from collections: AGA, p.140, 1638; Communion expenses: Cambuslang KS, 1742.

32   Minister's account, 1758: Kilninver and Kilmelford KS, 1758; costs from poor's box, 1679: Johnston, *Orkney*, p.23; Synod disapproval: Cramond, *Presbytery of Fordyce*, p.56, 1722.

33   'Mixed cup': McMillan, *Worship of the Scottish Reformed Church*, pp.203–204, and ale: p.206; Dauit Syddie and Communion wine cellar: Inglis, *Angus Parish*, pp.142–143.

34   Kildonan KS: McMillan, *Worship of the Scottish Reformed Church*, pp.203–204; Galloway shortbread: *THAS 1900, Vernon*; Nicoll Craigie etc., 1698: Johnston, *Orkney*, p.53.

35   Date of Communion: Tongue KS, 1786; Westminster Assembly of Divines: Henderson, *Arbuthnott*, p.100; Edinburgh's, Glasgow's Communions: Sprott and Leishman, p.346, and Easter Communion: pp.346–347; quarterly Communions: *Aberdeen Eccl. Recs*, p.52, 1606; Synods of Aberdeen, Moray *re* Communions, and Presbytery of Fordyce, 1686: Henderson, *Religious Life*, p.150; Easter Communion, 1686: Johnston, *Orkney*, p.35, Holm KS.

36   Successive Communions, 1617: *Aberdeen Eccl. Recs*, p.86; successive Communions, 1651: Henderson, *Arbuthnott*, p.102; successive Communions, 1697: Reid, p.139; Communion for merchants etc.: *Aberdeen Eccl. Recs*, p.34; town/landward Communions: McMillan, *Worship of the Scottish Reformed Church*, p.193; country people asking for Communion: *St. Andrews KS Reg*, SHS 7, xcii, 1597.

37   Number of Glasgow Communions: Sprott and Leishman, p.346; Lochbroom, Fodderty, Urquhart: Mackay, *Pres. Recs*, xxi; Dean Alexander Pitcairne: Craven, p.70; excuses for no Communions: Mackay, *Pres. Recs*, p.xxi/xxii; Greenlaw Communions: Gibson, pp.108–109; Falkirk Communions: Murray, *Falkirk*, II, p.124.

38   Tongue Communions: Tongue KS, 1790; Communion advances cause of religion: Tobermory KS, 1849.

39 Winter Communion: West Kilbride KS, 1825–26; £5 for winter Communion: Baldernock KS, 1844.

40 Minister away eight Sundays: St. Boswells KS, 1747; 1–2 ministers at Communions: AGA, p.141, 1645, and churches not 'cast desolate': p.142, 1701; 10–12 ministers, and people abandoning own churches: Henderson, *Lockerbie*; 'Roaring Willie': *Borders Magazine*, VIII, 1903, and Sym, *Parish of Lilliesleaf*, p.90, quo. Dr. Russell.

41 Boat for minister: Port Glasgow KS, 1689; Dr Erskine: Henderson, *Lockerbie*.

42 Service of preparation/fine: Inglis, *Angus Parish*, pp.82–83, 1646, Auchterhouse KS; similar fine, 1680s: *THAS April 1879, Hassendean*, Vernon; token taken away: Reid, p.141, *c.* 1724, and successive Sundays/Saturdays, 1697: p.139.

43 Protesters' fast days: Henderson, *Arbuthnott*, p.101, and Gibson, p.112; Glasgow Session, 1596: Sprott and Leishman, pp.348–349; St. Andrews fasts (1598) and during Mr Hamilton's ministry (1574): *St. Andrews KS Reg*, SHS 7, xciii; no fasts in Episcopacy: Cramond, *Deskford*, p.16; fasts, 1720s: Gibson, p.112; Weekly Exercise: Henderson, *Arbuthnott*, p.101; Barony Church fasts: Barony KS, Glasgow, 1701-02-03; Banchory-Devenick fasts: Banchory-Devenick KS, 1782, 1793; 1800 tract: Sprott and Leishman, pp.349–350; 'pirlequey': Henderson, *Lockerbie*.

44 Elders' private prayers: Coldingham KS, 1752; censures, 1619: Chambers, *Abridged Domestic Annals*, pp.211–212; Wednesday service, Friday crowds, 'fearful excitement': Henderson, *Lockerbie*.

45 Information on the Men comes from the following: Macinnes, *Evangelical Movement in the Highlands*, p.213 ff; Graham, *Social Life in Scotland in the 18th Century*, pp.370–371; *Inverness Courier*, 23, 30 October 1851; Kennedy, *Days of the Fathers in Ross-shire*, pp.84, 100, 104; Brown, *Annals of the Disruption*, IV, p.57; Macdonald, *Chronicles of Stratheden*, pp.57–58; Munro, *Looking Back*, pp.167–168; Edwards, *Glimpses of Men and Manners about the Muirside*, p.244; NSA Duirinish, XIV, Inverness, pp.254–255; MacNaughton, *Old Church Life in Ross and Sutherland*, 1725; Blakey, *The Man in the Manse*, p.27; Henderson, *The Scottish Ruling Elder*, p.55.

46 Communion taken fasting: Hill, p.71; times of services: McMillan, *Worship of Scottish Reformed Church*, p.190; attending preaching, etc.: Cramond, *Elgin*, II, pp.48–49, 1597; doors locked: *St. Andrews KS Reg*, SHS 7, xcii, 1598; early services for servants: McMillan, *Worship of Scottish Reformed Church*, p.190; second service 8.00 a.m. etc.: *Perth KS Reg*, p.239.

47 Crowds arriving: Brown, *Annals of the Disruption*, IV, p.63; elders' duties: Murray, *Falkirk*, II, p.124, and Cramond, *Elgin*, II, pp.63–71; receiving tickets: *Life and Work*, December 1924, article by Rev. Thomas Burns, DD.

48　St. Andrews and Elgin elders and deacons, and Glasgow's town officers: *SRE*, p. 61;　duties in Arbuthnott, 1696: Henderson, *Arbuthnott*, p. 98;　duties in Kirkwall: Kirkwall KS, 1730;　Robert Myler: Abernethy KS, 1700.

49　Table without doors: Martin, p. 32;　shelter erected: Hill, p. 79;　preaching outside:　Gibson,　p. 111;　Communion　outside:　Henderson,　*Lockerbie*;　outdoor highland Communions: Brown, *Annals of the Disruption*, IV, p. 63;　Gaelic singing: Munro, *Looking Back*, pp. 167–170;　intoning, 1936: Brydon.

50　Travis etc.: *Life and Work*, December 1924, article by Rev. Thomas Burns, DD;　Stirling KS, 1597: *Maitland misc*, i, pp. 129–130;　St. Andrews doors: *Life and Work*, December 1924, article by Rev. Thomas Burns, DD;　Biblical authority: *Bible*, 1 Cor. 11:27: Morebattle minister: Tait, p. 109;　Rev. J. Spalding: Graham, p. 309, note 4;　Confession of Faith: Johnstone and Hunter, p. 384.

51　Rev. A. Allan's comments: Allan, *Channelkirk*, pp. 174–175;　Patrick Nisbet *re* damnation: Henderson, *Lockerbie*;　success of a minister: Blakey, p. 26, quo. Norman Macleod;　Lord Alness: Munro, *Looking Back*, pp. 168–169;　Patrick Nisbet *re* withdrawing from table: Henderson, *Lockerbie*;　Abyl Jamison: Henderson, *Arbuthnott*, p. 102.

52　Ignorant people: NSA Petty, XIV, Inverness-shire, note to p. 407;　man ordered to communicate: *Aberdeen Eccl. Recs*, p. 18, 1574;　twelve hour Communion service: Brydon;　minister served first table, visiting ministers subsequent ones: Banchory-Devenick KS, 1782;　Thomas Pennant: Pennant, *A Tour in Scotland*, pp. 86–87.

53　St. Cuthbert's KS costs: Edgar, I, note to p. 146;　treasurer's reductions: Lorimer, *West Kirke*, p. 29. The minutes of the Secession church in Kilmarnock, later reunited with the Church of Scotland, contain the following: '1781. The Committee being met . . . agreed to provide (for the refreshment of the ministers and elders on the Communion Sabbath) one bottle red and one bottle white wine, one leg of lamb, pretty heavy, four pounds beef for broth, one bottle of spirits (brandy) — George Smith's wife to provide bread, tea, sugar, pepper, vinegar;　and to be paid for the same — only the Committee to provide six bottles of porter.' — *History of Henderson U.F. Church*, Kilmarnock, 1773–1923, by Robert Tulloch.

54　Mrs Sutherland, Fearn: MacNaughton, pp. 267–268;　preaching at kirk door: *Borders Magazine* 22, Journal of the minister of Stichell and Hume, 1755–58 (Mr George Ridpath);　tea etc.: Henderson, *Lockerbie*.

55　Feeding problems: Graham, note 1 to p. 304;　'yuill ministers' etc.: Henderson, *Lockerbie*;　beadle's　house　refreshments:　M'Naught,　pp. 132–134;　Auchterhouse refreshment tent: Inglis, *Angus Parish*, p. 149;　Westruther refreshment tent: Gibson, p. 111;　stalls, drinking, indulgence, etc.: Henderson, *Lockerbie*.

56　Robert Hunter etc.: St. Cuthbert's KS, Edinburgh, 1709;　mason etc., 1824: Stow KS, 1826;　Kilmarnock youths: Edgar, I, p. 176;　Sir William

Hamilton's burial: Gordon, p.166;   Isobel Petrie: Inglis, *Angus Parish*, p.123, Auchterhouse KS.

57   Satan raging: Graham, p.341;   dancing at night: Cramond, *Elgin*, II, p.112, 1603;   bad conduct: Pennant, *A Tour in Scotland*, pp.86–87;   immorality: Tillycoultry KS, 1764;   Rev. George Ridpath: *Borders Magazine* 22, p.114, Journal of the Minister of Stichill and Hume, 1755–58;   ministers' Monday dinner: Blakey, p.28;   Abbotrule dinner: Tancred, *Rulewater and its People*.

58   Banff KS, 1889: SRE, p.258.

59   Thanksgiving: *Borders Magazine*, 1902, Recollections of an old parish church;   thanksgiving   services   shortened: Henderson, *Lockerbie*;   Monday dinners and the Men: Edwards, p.244;   serious dinners: Munro, *Looking Back*, pp.172–173.

60   Collections/half annual total: M'Naught, pp.122–123;   little given, bad copper, etc.: Henderson, *Lockerbie*;   collecting at diets: Kirkwall KS, 1730;   Sunday/Monday collections: Ashkirk KS, 1698, and collection 'at Styles': 1740s;   distribution: Nigg KS, Ross-shire, *c.*1729;   licensed beggars received charity, 1792: Mitchell, 1792;   distributions: Ashkirk KS, 1698, 1704;   Col. Amerongon's men: *THAS 1900, Vernon*.

61   Vagrants, 1762: Cramond, *Syn. Aberdeen*, p.72;   retaining collections: Martin, p.47;   private charity: Stow KS, 1825.

62   Communion changes, numbers: *SRE* pp.251–252;   Black Isle Farmers' Society: Resolis KS, 1879;   £230,000 lost: Graham, p.313. The farm diary of John Smith, Maison Dieu, near Brechin, shows that in February 1800 the farm staff all went to church for the Thursday fast day, on Saturday for the preparatory service and on Monday morning for the thanksgiving service;   obviously they went on Sunday but that was not recorded, not being a working day.

63   Fast days etc. in north: Mackay, *Pres Recs*, xxi;   POW Communion: MacDonald, *St. Clement's Looks Back*, p.31.

64   Running errands: Murray, *Falkirk* II, p.130, 1723;   removing seating: Banchory-Devenick KS, 1782;   butcher meat: OSA Swinton and Simprim, VI (1790s) p.333;   servants etc.: Murray, *Falkirk*, II, p.130, 1723;   precentors: M'Naught, pp.122–123;   poor precentor, 1723: Murray, *Falkirk*, II, p.130.

Bibliography

Allan, Rev. Archibald, *A History of Channelkirk Church* (Edinburgh, 1900)
Allardyce, John, *Bygone Days in Aberdeenshire* (Aberdeen, 1913)
Anderson, Rev. Robert, *A History of Kilsyth* (Edinburgh and London, 1901)

Bain, George, *The Lordship of Petty* (Nairn, 1925)
Baird, Rev. Andrew, *Annals of a Tweeddale Parish* (Glasgow, 1924)
Baird, J. G. A., *Muirkirk in Bygone Days* (Muirkirk, 1910)
Barron, James, *The Northern Highlands in the 19th Century*, 3 vols (Inverness, 1901–13)
Beaton, Rev. D., *Ecclesiastical History of Caithness and Annals of Caithness Parishes* (Wick, 1909)
Beauchamp, Elizabeth, *The Braes o' Balquhidder* (Milngavie, 1978)
Bentinck, Rev. Charles D, *Dornoch Cathedral and Parish* (Inverness, 1926)
Blakey, Ronald S., *The Man in the Manse* (Edinburgh, 1978)
Bonar, Horatius (ed), *Catechisms of the Scottish Reformation* (London, 1866)
Boyle, Anne, Dickson, Colin, McEwan, Alasdair, Maclean, Colin, *Ruins and Remains* (Edinburgh, 1985)
Brotchie, T. C. F., *History of Govan* (Govan, 1905).
Brown, Andrew, *History of Glasgow, and of Paisley, Greenock and Port Glasgow* (Glasgow n.d.)
Brown, Robert, *History of Paisley* (Paisley, 1886).
Brown, Rev. Thomas, *Annals of the Disruption* (Edinburgh, 1884)
Burleigh, J. H. S., *A Church History of Scotland* (London, 1960)
Burleigh, John, *Ednam and its Indwellers* (Glasgow and Dalbeattie, 1912)
Burns, Robert, *Poetical Works*, introduction by W. H. Davies (London and Glasgow n.d.)

Cadell, Patrick, *A Sense of Place* (Edinburgh, 1988)
Carruthers, Robert, *Highland Notebook* (Inverness, 1887)

Chambers, Robert, *Domestic Annals of Scotland* (Edinburgh and London, 1858)
Chambers, Robert, *Abridged Domestic Annals of Scotland* (Edinburgh, 1885)
Cormack, Alexander Allan, *Susan Carnegie, 1744–1821* (Aberdeen, 1966)
Craig-Brown, T., *History of Selkirkshire or Chronicles of Ettrick Forest,* 2 vols. (Edinburgh, 1886)
Cramond, William, *Synod of Aberdeen relative to the Presbytery of Fordyce* (Banff, 1885)
Cramond, William, *Church and Churchyard of Boyndie* (Banff, 1886)
Cramond, William, *Annals of Cullen* (Buckie, 1888)
Cramond, William, *Church and Churchyard of Cullen* (Aberdeen, 1883)
Cramond, William, *Church and Churchyard of Deskford* (Banff, 1885)
Cramond, William, *Records of Elgin,* 2 vols (Aberdeen, 1903)
Cramond, William, *Church and Churchyard of Fordyce* (Banff, 1886)
Cramond, William, *Presbytery of Fordyce* (Banff, 1886)
Cramond, William, *Church and Churchyard of Ordiquhill* (Banff, 1886)
Cramond, William, *Church and Churchyard of Rathven* (Banff, 1885)
Craven, Rev. J. B., *Church Life in South Ronaldshay and Burray* (Kirkwall, 1911)
Crawford, John, *Extracts from the Minutes of the Kirk Session of Kinghorn* (Kirkcaldy, 1863)

Dalgetty, A. B., *History of the Church of Fowlis Easter* (Dundee 1933)
Dawson, James H., *Abridged Statistical History of Scotland* (Edinburgh and London, 1853)
Denholm, James, *An Historical Account . . of the City of the Glasgow* (Glasgow, 1797)
Dick, Rev. Robert, *Annals of Colinsburgh* (Edinburgh, 1896)
Dickson, Nicholas, *The Kirk and its Worthies* (London and Edinburgh, 1912)
Dinnie, Robert, *History of Kincardine O'Neil* (Aberdeen 1885)
Dobson, H. J. and Sanderson, William, *Scottish Life and Character* (London, 1904)
Donaldson, Gordon and Morpeth, Robert S., *A Dictionary of Scottish History* (Edinburgh, 1977)

Easton, Rev., Thomas, *Statements relative to the Pauperism of Kirriemuir, 1814–25* (Forfar, 1825)
Edgar, Rev. Andrew, *Old Church Life in Scotland,* 2 vols (Paisley and London, 1885–86)
Edwards, D. H., *Glimpses of Men and Manners about the Muirside* (Brechin, 1920)

Firth, John, *Reminiscences of an Orkney Parish* (Kirkwall, 1974)
Fraser, Alexander and Munro, Finlay, *Tarbat — Easter Ross* (Inverness, 1988)
Fyfe, J. G., (ed) *Scottish Diaries and Memoirs* (Stirling, 1942)

Galt, John, *Annals of the Parish* (London and Edinburgh, 1821)
Gardner, Alexander, *History of Galston Church* (Paisley, 1909)
Geekie, Sir Archibald, *Scottish Reminiscences* (Glasgow, 1906)
Gibson, Robert, *An Old Berwickshire Town* (Edinburgh and London, 1905)
Gordon, Anne, *Hearts upon the Highway* (Galashiels, 1978)
Gordon, Anne, *Death is for the Living* (Edinburgh, 1984)
Graham, H. G., *Social Life in Scotland in the 18th Century* (London, 1937)
Grant, Margaret Wilson, *Golspie's Story* (Golspie, 1977)
Gunn, Dr, *Church and Parish of Drumelzier* (Peebles, 1931)
Gunn, Dr, *The Book of the Church of Traquair* (Edinburgh and Glasgow, 1931)

Haig, James, *Topographical and Historical Account of Kelso* (Edinburgh, 1825)
Hay, George, *Architecture of Scottish Post-Reformation Churches* (Oxford, 1957)
Henderson, G. D., *The Scottish Ruling Elder* (London, 1935)
Henderson, G. D., *Religious Life in 17th Century Scotland* (Cambridge, 1937)
Henderson, George A., *Kirk of St. Ternan's, Arbuthnott* (Aberdeen, 1962)
Henderson, J. B., *Borgue, its Church, Pastors and People* (Castle Douglas, 1898)
Henderson, John A., *History of the Parish of Banchory-Devenick* (Aberdeen, 1890)
Henderson, Thomas H., *Lockerbie, A Narrative of Village Life in Bygone Days* (Lockerbie, 1937)
Hill, Ninian, *Story of the Old West Kirk of Greenock* (Greenock, 1911)
Hillaby, John, *Journey Home* (London, 1983)
Hunter, James, *Fala and Soutra* (Edinburgh, 1892)
Hyslop, John and Robert, *Langholm as it was* (Sunderland, London, Edinburgh, Glasgow, 1912)

Inglis, Rev. W. Mason, *Annals of an Angus Parish* (Dundee, 1888)
Inglis, Rev. W. Mason, *An Angus Parish in the 18th Century* (Dundee, 1904)
Irving, Joseph, *History of Dunbartonshire* (Dumbarton, 1960)

Jeffrey, Alexander, *History and Antiquities of Roxburghshire*, 2 vols. (Jedburgh 1855)
Johnston, Alfred W., *Church of Orkney* (Kirkwall, 1889–92)
Johnston, Thomas, *History of the Working Classes in Scotland* (Wakefield, 1946)
Johnstone, C. L., *Historical Families of Dumfries-shire and the Border Wars* (Dumfries, Edinburgh, Glasgow, London, 1889)
Johnstone and Hunter, Confession of Faith, 1855.

Keith, Agnes, *Parish of Drainie and Lossiemouth* (1975)
Kelsall, Helen and Keith, *Scottish Lifestyle 300 Years Ago* (Edinburgh, 1986)
Kennedy, Rev. John, *Days of the Fathers in Ross-shire* (Inverness, 1897)

Lang, John Marshall, *Glasgow and the Barony thereof* (Glasgow, 1895)

Lochinvar, *Romances of Gretna Green and its Runaway Marriages* (Carlisle, 1909)

Lorimer, George, *Leaves from the Buik of the West Kirke* (Edinburgh, 1885)

Lorimer, George, *Early Days of St. Cuthbert's Church* (Edinburgh and London, 1915)

Lorimer, George, *Days of Neil M'Vicar* (Edinburgh and London, 1926)

Love, Dane, Scottish Kirkyards (London, 1989)

Low, James G., *The Church of Montrose* (Montrose, 1891)

MacDonald, Dr Colin, *Chronicles of Stratheden, a Highland Parish of today* (Edinburgh, London, 1881)

MacDonald, David, *St. Clement's Looks Back, The Story of Dingwall Parish Church* (Dingwall, 1976)

MacDonald, J. and Gordon A., *Down to the Sea* (Fort William, 1989)

MacDonald, J. S. M., *Bowden Kirk, 1128–1978* (Kelso, 1978)

MacGeorge, A., *Old Glasgow* (Glasgow, 1880)

MacGill, W., *Old Ross-shire and Scotland*, 2 vols (Inverness, 1909)

Macinnes, John, *Evangelical Movement in the Highlands, 1688–1800* (Aberdeen, 1951)

Mackay, William, (ed.) *Records of the Presbyteries of Inverness and Dingwall, 1643–88* (Inverness, 1896)

Mackay, William, *Sidelights of Highland History* (Inverness, 1925)

Macleod, Norman, *Reminiscences of a Highland Parish* (London, 1867)

Macleod, Innes, *Discovering Galloway* (Edinburgh, 1986)

MacNaughton, Colin, *Old Church Life in Ross and Sutherland* (Inverness, 1915)

MacRae, Alexander, *Revivals in the Highlands and Islands in the 19th Century* (Stirling, 1907)

MacRae, Alexander, *Life of Gustavus Aird* (Stirling, 1908)

Macrae, Rev. Donald, *Notes on the History of the Parish of Lairg* (Wick, 1898)

Martin, Rev. J. R., *Church Chronicles of Nigg* (London, n.d.)

Mathieson, William Law, *Politics and Religion, A Study in Scottish History from the Reformation to the Revolution* (Glasgow, 1902)

McMillan, William, *Worship of the Scottish Reformed Church, 1550–1638* (London, 1931)

McNeill, F. Marian, *The Silver Bough*, 4 vols (Glasgow, 1957)

Michie, Stewart, *The Church of Scotland Social Development* (London, Glasgow, 1960)

Miller, Hugh, *My Schools and Schoolmasters* (Edinburgh, 1869)

Mitchell, Alexander, *Inverness Kirk Session Records, 1661–1800* (Inverness, 1902)

M'Naught, D., *Kilmaurs Parish and Burgh* (Paisley, 1912)

Moffat, Alastair, *Kelsae* (Edinburgh, 1985)

Munro, Robert (Lord Alness), *Looking Back, Fugitive Writings and Sayings* (London, Edinburgh, n.d.)

Murray, George I., *Records of Falkirk Parish*, 2 vols (Falkirk, 1888)

Oliver, W. H., *History of Blainslie* (— 1981)

Pennant, Thomas, *Tour in Scotland in 1769* (London, 1772)

Reid, Alan, *Royal Burgh of Forfar* (Paisley, Forfar, Edinburgh, Glasgow, 1902)
Russell, Rev. James, *Reminiscences of Yarrow* (Selkirk, 1894)
Rust, Rev. James, *Druidism Exhumed* (Edinburgh and London, 1871)

Scotland, James, *History of Scottish Education*, 2 vols (London, 1969)
Scott, James A. B., *Lauder — 'a free Burgh for Ever'* (Selkirk, 1989)
Sharpe, Rev. J., *Selkirk, its Church, its School and its Presbytery* (Selkirk, 1914)
Smout, T. C., *History of the Scottish People, 1560–1830* (London, 1969)
Sprott, G. W. and Leishman, Rev. Thomas, *Book of Common Order and Directory of Public Worship* (Edinburgh and London, 1868)
Sym, A. P., *Parish of Lilliesleaf* (Selkirk, 1913)

Tait, James, *Two Centuries of Border Church Life* (Kelso, 1889)
Tancred, George, *Rulewater and its People* (Edinburgh, 1907)
Thomson, A. *Lauder and Lauderdale* (Galashiels, 1903)
Thomson, A. *Coldingham Parish and Priory* (Galashiels, 1908)
Thomson, David, *Elie Kirk* (Kirkcaldy, 1989)
Todd, William, *Clerical History of Kirkmaiden* (Glasgow, 1860)
Tranter, Nigel, *The Queen's Scotland — the North-east* (London, 1974)
Tulloch, Robert, *History of Henderson U. F. Church, Kilmarnock* (Kilmarnock, 1923)
Turnbull, George, *A South Ayrshire Parish* (Ayr, 1908)

Waddell, Rev. P. H., *Parish Records in East Lothian* (Edinburgh, 1884)
Waddell, Rev. P. H., *An Old Kirk Chronicle* (Edinburgh, 1893)

Also consulted:
Abridgement of the Acts of the General Assembly; Acts of the Parliament of Scotland; Berwickshire Naturalists' Club Records 1899–90 and 1977; *Border Magazine*; Buchan Field Club; Edinburgh Burgh Records, extracts 1589–1603; *Fasti Ecclesiae Scoticanae; General Views of the Agriculture of . . .; Inverness Courier; Life and Work*; Linlithgow Academy History Society's *Emblems of Mortality*; Maitland Miscellany I; Nigg Public School, Ross-shire, log-book, 1888; papers *re* Kelso Dispensary in HM Register House exhibition, 1986; Proceedings of the Society of Antiquaries of Scotland; Report approved by Advisory

Committee on Artistic Questions, 1967 *re* Reay Church; *Scottish Notes and Queries*; Scottish Records Association, Conference Report No. 7, March 1987; Session Book of Bonkle and Preston; Spottiswoode Miscellany II; *Statistical Accounts; Transactions of Hawick Archaeological Society.*

The following church records have been consulted:

Shetland — Fetlar Kirk Session; Dunrossness Kirk Session.

Orkney — Eday and Harray Kirk Session; Evie and Rendall Kirk Session; Kirkwall (St. Magnus Cathedral) Kirk Session.

Western Isles — Coll Kirk Session; Kilbride Kirk Session; Kilmory Kirk Session; Lismore and Appin Kirk Session; Presbytery of Lewis; Tobermory Kirk Session.

Caithness — Canisbay Kirk Session; Latheron Kirk Session; Thurso Kirk Session; Wick Kirk Session.

Sutherland — Assynt Kirk Session; Creich Kirk Session; Durness Kirk Session; Golspie Kirk Session; Presbytery of Dornoch; Tongue Kirk Session.

Ross-shire — Cromarty Kirk Session; Dingwall Kirk Session; Edderton Kirk Session; Kiltearn Kirk Session (transcription by William Munro); Nigg Kirk Session; Resolis Kirk Session.

Inverness-shire — Boleskine and Abertarff Kirk Session; Daviot and Dunlichity Kirk Session; Kintail Kirk Session; Laggan Kirk Session; Moy Kirk Session.

Nairn — Auldearn Kirk Session; Cawdor Kirk Session.

Moray — Bellie Kirk Session; Drainie Kirk Session; Forres Kirk Session; Kinloss Kirk Session; Knockando Kirk Session; Presbytery of Elgin.

Banff — Banff Kirk Session.

Aberdeenshire — Aberdeen (St. Nicholas) Kirk Session; (also Aberdeen Ecclesiastical Records, Spalding Club, 1846 and Records of the Kirk Session of Aberdeen, Stuart, Spalding, Club); Cruden Kirk Session; Foveran Kirk Session; Peterhead Kirk Session; Presbytery of Strathbogie; Slains and Forvie Kirk Session.

Perthshire — Abernethy Kirk Session; Comrie Kirk Session; Forgandenny Kirk Session; Perth General Session Register; (also Extracts from the Kirk Session Register of Perth, Spottiswoode Miscellany, II, ed. James Maidment); Scone Kirk Session.

Kincardine — Arbuthnott Kirk Session; Banchory-Devenick Kirk Session; Fettercairn Kirk Session.

Angus — Barry Kirk Session; Craig Kirk Session; Kinnell Kirk Session; Montrose Kirk Session; Presbytery of Forfar; St. Vigeans Kirk Session.

Fife — Culross Kirk Session; Kilconquhar Kirk Session; Kinglassie Kirk Session; St. Andrews Kirk Session (transcription by Sylvia Murray); (also St. Andrews Kirk Session Register, 1559–82 and 1582– . . ., Scottish History Society IV, VII, transcribed by David Hay Fleming); St. Monance Kirk Session.

Kinross — Kinross Kirk Session; Portmoak Kirk Session.

Clackmannanshire — Clackmannan Kirk Session; Dollar Kirk Session; Tillycoultry Kirk Session.

Stirlingshire — Baldernock Kirk Session; Killearn Kirk Session; Kilsyth Kirk Session; Stirling Kirk Session (Holy Rude); St. Ninian's Kirk Session.

Argyllshire — Kilninian and Kilmore Kirk Session; Kilninver and Kilmelford Kirk Session.

Dunbartonshire — Bonhill Kirk Session; Dumbarton Kirk Session.

Renfrewshire — Greenock Kirk Session; Port Glasgow Kirk Session.

Lanarkshire — Barony Kirk Session, Glasgow; Cambuslang Kirk Session; Cathcart Kirk Session; College (Blackfriars) Kirk Session, Glasgow; Presbytery of Glasgow; St. John's Kirk Session, Glasgow; Shotts Kirk Session; Tron Kirk Session, Glasgow.

Ayrshire — Kilmarnock Kirk Session; West Kilbride Kirk Session.

Stewartry of Kirkcudbright — Kells Kirk Session; Kirkcudbright Kirk Session; New Abbey Kirk Session; Tongland Kirk Session; Twynholm Kirk Session.

Wigtownshire — Portpatrick Kirk Session; Sorbie Kirk Session; Stranraer Kirk Session.

Dumfries-shire — Dumfries Kirk Session (St. Mary's); Kirkpatrick-Fleeming Kirk Session; Ruthwell Kirk Session (Hearse committee); Urr Kirk Session.

Peeblesshire — Peebles Kirk Session; Tweedsmuir Kirk Session.

Selkirkshire — Ashkirk Kirk Session; Galashiels Kirk Session.

Roxburghshire — Ancrum Kirk Session; Hawick Kirk Session; Hownam Kirk Session; Jedburgh Kirk Session; Melrose Kirk Session; St. Boswells Kirk Session; Sprouston Kirk Session; Yetholm Kirk Session.

Berwickshire — Channelkirk Kirk Session; Chirnside Kirk Session; Coldingham Kirk Session; Earlston Kirk Session; Lauder Kirk Session; Swinton and Simprim Kirk Session.

East Lothian — Bara and Garvald Kirk Session; Dunbar Kirk Session; North Berwick Kirk Session; Tynninghame Kirk Session; Yester Kirk Session.

Midlothian — Colinton Kirk Session; Currie Kirk Session; Inveresk Kirk Session; St. Cuthbert's Kirk Session, Edinburgh; South Leith Kirk Session; Stow Kirk Session.

West Lothian — Bo'ness Kirk Session; Kirkliston Kirk Session; Linlithgow (St. Michael's) Kirk Session; Torphichen Kirk Session.